A History of the World

AKIRA IRIYE AND JÜRGEN OSTERHAMMEL, GENERAL EDITORS

Empires and Encounters

1350–1750

Edited by

Wolfgang Reinhard

The Belknap Press of Harvard University Press

CAMBRIDGE, MASSACHUSETTS

LONDON, ENGLAND

2015

This volume is a joint publication of Harvard University Press and C. H. Beck Verlag.

German language edition © 2014 by C. H. Beck Verlag.

Maps by Peter Palm

Book design by Dean Bornstein

Library of Congress Cataloging-in-Publication Data

Empires and encounters : 1350–1750 / edited by Wolfgang Reinhard.
      pages cm — (A history of the world)
  Co-published in German as Weltreiche und Weltmeere : 1350–1750, by C.H. Beck
Verlag, 2014.
  Includes bibliographical references and index.
  ISBN 978-0-674-04719-8 (alkaline paper) 1. World history. 2. Middle Ages.
3. History, Modern—16th century. 4. History, Modern—17th century. 5. History,
Modern—18th century. 6. Imperialism—History. 7. International relations—History.
8. Regionalism—History. 9. Acculturation—History. 10. Commerce—History.
I. Reinhard, Wolfgang. II. Weltreiche und Weltmeere.
  D21.3.E525 2015
  909.08—dc23   2014040716

Contents

CONTENTS

CONTENTS

Introduction

Wolfgang Reinhard

ALL historical cultures have invariably written the history of "their" world, be it China or classical antiquity or European Christendom. And yet contemporary historical cultures still remain those of older or newer nation-states and consequently generate national "worldviews"; currently, for example, the vogue is to produce national "places of remembrance." Although in contrast to this, there has long been an urge to present an overview of the wider world in historiography, it is only now that this urge has at its disposal a solid, real historical substrate—that is, a widespread economic, political, and cultural uniformity among humankind across the entire globe. As a result, world history nowadays is keen to style itself as "global history."[1] The historical "worlds" with their various histories can therefore have an extremely diverse scope—ranging in extreme cases from the microcosm of a prehistoric village and its environs on the one hand and, on the other, the entire surface of the Earth in the present day.

For this reason, the obvious approach would be to treat older world history merely as a path to modern global history. Despite the fact that it is still far too early to speak of a uniformity of humankind from 1350 to 1750, nevertheless certain important decisions were taken in that period that paved the way for such a phenomenon. The Old World discovered for itself a hitherto isolated New World in the West and established an albeit highly risky but still regular maritime trade that ran from its far western extent in Europe to its far eastern in South and East Asia. Admittedly, the five different "worlds" that are the subjects of the chapters in this volume remained totally separate; an "Atlantic world" first came into being only during this period. But they did begin to interact, and their interaction intensified, pointing the way forward to the "one world" that exists today. So, in fact, the histories of our five separate worlds may also be regarded as the "prehistory" of the global here and now and, like any form of history, are defined by the interest of the present-day society in questioning its own past. And yet history as prehistory can only ever be half the story, for past worlds existed in their own right and conformed to their own set of rules; they had no inkling that, among other things, they would have to fulfill the role of prehistory for our own contemporary world. Accordingly, it is incumbent on historians to forgo any such kind of one-sided reductionism from the perspective of the present and instead to try and reconstruct the various pasts under consideration according to their own circumstances. For if we retrospectively regard their histories as converging on our present, we are in fact falling victim to a perspectival illusion. It is, after all, a matter not of teleology but rather of an accumulation of contingencies, which at some stage become irreversible. Yet this accumulation takes place not in a linear fashion but in sporadic bursts in which it is perfectly possible for reversals to occur. Thus, the foundation and expansion of empires is followed by phases of decline and decay, while contraction ensues after an expansion of global interaction. Globe-trotting journeys like those undertaken by Marco Polo or Ibn Battuta, who is said to have covered a distance of 120,000 kilometers between Morocco and the Far East,[2] were evidently no longer possible after the second half of the fourteenth century, because crises were multiplying around the world.

Yet whenever the talk is of expansion, we naturally think of European expansion and so run up against a problem at the heart of all modern world histories, namely, an inescapably Eurocentric bias, which manifests itself in many ways. (In making this assumption, for simplicity's sake, we tend to identify the "Western world" with Europe, summarily lumping "new Europes" like the United States or Australia into this concept in historiographic terms.) For one thing, we seem incapable of completely dispensing with the aforementioned perspective of the prehistory of a unified world. Because it is incontestable that the decisive impulses of this prehistory came from Europe, the question is predisposed to be Eurocentric in and of itself regardless of the stance of individual historians.[3] But the very disclosure of this fact sets in train a process whereby Eurocentrism begins to self-critically deconstruct itself. In a second step, then, this "enlightened Eurocentrism" demonstrates how much European development owes to the Jewish and the Islamic world above all, and that later other cultures also made their independent contribution to the modern world. For instead of simply expecting Western modernism to spread around the whole globe nowadays, we pay homage to the concept of a "diverse modernity."[4] Ultimately, in a third step, enlightened Eurocentrism even attempts to transcend itself, by switching from the historical navel-gazing of the West to self-referential histories of other cultures, despite being well aware that even the formulation "other cultures" is an intrinsic feature of an ineluctably Eurocentric mode of discourse.[5]

In taking this step, it might at first sight appear possible to overcome the abiding problem of Eurocentrism by requiring that the histories of the still extremely diverse areas of the world existing in the period treated in this volume be written exclusively by citizens of the cultures in question. At present, this state of affairs is still impossible to effect without further ado; nevertheless, we have succeeded in finding contributors who, thanks to an intensive engagement with the respective cultures over many long years of study and a command of the languages involved, may almost be regarded as "natives." However, no amount of self-criticism and no shift in perspective can disguise the basic Eurocentrism ingrained in our language and our thought patterns. Many phenomena in global history are simply incapable of being discussed from anything other than a Eurocentric perspective. This was already true of the aforementioned concept of other cultures or non-Europeans and is also the case for concepts like "discovery," the "New World," the "West Indies," "Indians," and, first and foremost, the whole notion of "America," which immortalizes the name of Amerigo Vespucci, the first person to market the New World in literary terms. However, older terms, too, such as "India," "Asia," and "Africa," are traceable to a European broadening of what were originally more narrowly defined ancient geographical designations, whereas "Indonesia," "Australia," "Philippines," and "New Zealand" were new European coinages. Place names from the Old World recur in the New; they did not by any means invariably just have markers like "Nieuw" Amsterdam or "New" York. Often, European political circumstances were preserved in language; for example, names of royal personages such as Victoria and ministers like Wellington were quite deliberately given to locations in Australia and New Zealand. Although Ceylon was changed to Sri Lanka and Madras to Chennai in the postcolonial period, for all practical purposes politically cosmetic alterations of this kind are possible only to a limited degree.

Furthermore, beyond the linguistic sphere, the academic discipline of history is of Western provenance, not only in its methods but also in its central points of reference, and, as a result of the adoption of the Western educational system by former colonies throughout the world, has been and continues to be superimposed on the thinking of non-Europeans. Although political decolonization has to some extent now been concluded and economic decolonization is well under way, many postcolonial theoreticians contend that mental or cultural decolonization has not even yet begun. A European or an American might be able, or at least could until very recently, write a history of his or her own region without even taking the rest of the world into account, whereas non-Western historians would, regardless of what they were writing about, inevitably end up having to take the modern nation-state of European origin as their point of reference, a yardstick that has also imposed itself on the postcolonial world and that constantly legitimizes itself anew through the educational system and the writing of history.[6] But above all, the non-European historian is almost always shackled to the Western Gregorian calendar, the convention of designating years as either BC or AD, albeit in a secular variant, and also not infrequently even to Western history's arrangement of the epochs.

Therefore, the temporal demarcation of this volume, which for practical academic reasons spans the period 1350–1750, also initially adheres to a standard periodization template of European historical scholarship. In the process, it adopts a somewhat narrow variation of the "Old Europe" concept, which in its most extreme form regards the period from the genesis of villages and the founding of cities during the high Middle Ages to the beginnings of industrialization as the "Old European" epoch of history. The alternative to this would have been the so-called early modern period (1500–1800), but this demarcation is less well suited to grasping long-term processes that emanate from far back in the history of Europe and the Atlantic world. Of course, like most periodization templates, the two end dates are there really only for the purposes of orientation and in the various chapters are freely transgressed in one or the other direction. In the process, it transpires that events of an epoch-making character can be observed taking place in other parts of the world. We may note just the following: the advance of the Ottomans into Europe; Moscow's split from the Mongols; the rise of Tamerlane in Central Asia; the supplanting of the Yuan dynasty in China by the Ming; and the founding of the Ayutthaya Kingdom in Southeast Asia in the fourteenth century. At the far end of the time frame we find the incipient decline of the Ottoman Empire; the fall of the Safavids in Persia; the beginning of the crisis of the Mughal Empire in India; the high-water mark of Chinese expansion under the Qing; and the founding of an expanding empire in Burma in the eighteenth century.

Even if we wanted to, it is impossible to step outside our language and our calculation of time. Furthermore, there is no need to do so. Enlightenment on the question of their Eurocentric provenance turns out to be a precondition for the possibility of their adoption and their correspondingly impartial use by other cultures. Without in any way ignoring their European origins, this process of assimilation renders the accusation of Eurocentrism obsolete for us. English was a European language, which owes its spread to British and American economic, political, and technological hegemony. In the interim, though, it has become the property of many peoples in Africa and Asia and as a global lingua franca even to some extent of the whole of humanity as well.

By contrast, the modern nation-state did not even exist within Europe itself between 1350 and 1750. Even though the concept of the state does appear in several chapters in its broadly defined Anglo-Saxon sense, on closer inspection the entities thus described are in fact prestate polities, which might more accurately be designated as larger or smaller "empires." Although, because of the omnipresence of empire formation, these represent one of the principal reference points of this volume, their sheer multiplicity would have been only confusing had they been used as a basis for its organization. Instead, the volume has been configured on the basis of five cultural–geographical macroregions, whose circumscription is admittedly determined by a certain degree of pragmatic arbitrariness. In other words, we have good cause for regarding this arrangement of ours as especially plausible in the light of the latest research, yet we would not wish or seek to contest the fact that arguments can be advanced for alternative approaches. We are dealing here with a virtual organization of space devised by us, but one that is underpinned by a spatial structure that was predetermined by its sheer plausibility.[7]

This spatial structure is based on the combination of an interactional–historical approach with a dynamic conception of culture. On the one hand, we regard cultures not as factually, spatially, and temporally windowless entities that at root are inaccessible to any outsiders' attempts to understand them but rather as open structures that are in a state of constant transformation, not least as a result of constant interaction with other cultures. In this, migration plays a central role. Consequently, this phenomenon is construed no longer as a historical exception but rather as a quite regular occurrence. And in accordance with this, phenomena traditionally disqualified as "invasions" or "foreign domination," such as the Muslim incursion into India or the role played by the steppe nomads in the history of China—in other words, the Mughal Empire and the Manchu dynasty— have to be reevaluated. Therefore, India and even China, where such a view was positively encouraged, were by no means windowless cultural monads.

On the other hand, notwithstanding all dynamism and differentiation, there is no denying that between 1350 and 1750, such things as a Chinese culture, a culture of the Christian West, an East African Swahili culture, and others did exist as common denominators of a variety of phenomena and as the embodiment of group identities. Human behavior, which is expected to follow a definable canon of rules, forms one side of this relative uniformity. The other consists of objective cultural entities that can be unequivocally attributed, such as the writings of Confucius and pagodas or the New Testament and cathedrals.

If we assume that there was a gradual increase in the frequency of various interactions within and between cultural areas—a highly plausible thesis though not definitely provable—then the contradiction between the simultaneous openness and insularity of cultures can be neatly encapsulated. In this way, we may distinguish between a cultural core area, in which internal communication predominates and cultural identity is established through demarcation from outsiders, and zones, in which external communication plays a greater role and, as a consequence, intercultural hybrids arise. The process of linguistic and cultural "creolization" through hybridization has long since been reevaluated by scholarship. But alongside zones of intensive communication, there are also particularly communication-friendly groups or periods in which such behavior was promoted. Thus, on the one hand, the Jesuits and, on the other, certain Chinese intellectuals were favored at the Chinese imperial court and were particularly predisposed toward communication during the dynastic and intellectual crisis that gripped China in the seventeenth century—a describable interaction that can be related to particular groups, places, and times. The decisive factor was that there was no longer an anticipation of sharply demarcated cultural binomials but rather one of all manners of contacts, interminglings, and transformations.

This corresponds with the finding cited at the start of this introduction that people are capable of feeling that they belong to different worlds at the same time, yet without always expressly articulating these affinities. In all probability, the basic guiding principle for most of the people living during the period under consideration was "my village = my world." Even so, many others were already operating in a more expansive realm, with the result that, in the spirit of our hypothesis, we must reckon on a hierarchy of compartmentalized "worlds," each with a relatively more intensive degree of internal communication and relatively weak external communication. A preglobal world history would therefore comprise the history of such worlds and their interaction. The potential upper limit of global coherence at that time may have been reached with cultural–geographical major regions such as those we have proposed.

We have also defined these hypothetically as areas within which internal communication clearly outweighed external and that as a result manifested if not necessarily a common culture, then at least certain unequivocal common characteristics. So, for example, Chinese ships were hardly ever encountered in the Pacific, and absolutely none were encountered in the Atlantic, while the presence of both European and Chinese shipping in the Indian Ocean remained marginal. Conversely, on each of these major oceans, there was an "indigenous" common seafaring culture with rules long hallowed by experience regarding how to deal with water and wind conditions. Major oceans as historical realms of interaction have, following the example laid down for the Mediterranean,[8] long since become the subject of academic research and consequently form the second reference parameter of this volume.

We commence in Chapter 1 with "Empires and Frontiers in Continental Eurasia." As the largest landmass on Earth, Eurasia also may fairly lay claim to the greatest significance. We ought to get accustomed to regarding not just Cis- and Trans-India but also Europe itself as peninsulas or subcontinents of Asia. In historical terms, the unity of this immense region in our period resides in the direct engagement with the legacy of Mongol rule, the greatest political expansion that has ever occurred in world history, and the resulting global communication system that existed in the thirteenth century. Over time China, which rid itself of its Mongol dynasty, and Russia, which liberated itself from its Mongol overlords and later subjugated them, were to assert themselves as the Mongol Empire's principal heirs. Admittedly, the nomadic horse cultures of Central Asia finally succumbed to competing Chinese and Russian empire-building ambitions only in the eighteenth century. At least temporarily, there arose under Timur the Lame

(Tamerlane) in the fourteenth and fifteenth centuries the last great empire to emerge from Central Asia, though this was far from being the final attempt at creating such a polity. China experienced its greatest expansion under the Central Asian Manchu, whose dynasty had assumed control there in the seventeenth century. It was surrounded by a fringe of smaller countries, beginning with Vietnam and later Korea and Japan, whose more or less independent empire formation took place clearly under Chinese influence, as happened also in Manchuria before it was annexed by China.

The tactics used by Mongol mounted warriors played a decisive role in the formation of empires, particularly those of the Ottomans, the Safavids, and the Mughals, in Southern and Western Asia. They converged in these regions with the integrating role of the Islamic religion, which, notwithstanding the occasionally violent clash between Sunnis and Shi'ites, imposed a much stronger cultural uniformity than elsewhere, constituting a "world" in its own right. Chapter 2, "The Ottoman Empire and the Islamic World," focuses primarily on the empires of the Ottomans and the Safavids and their predecessors. Almost more so than in continental Eurasia, this region was characterized by the geographical contrast between deserts and steppes on the one hand, and oases, irrigated farmland, and cities on the other, and a historical contrast among nomadic peoples, settled nomads, farmers, and city dwellers.

The Islamic world, however, was by no means confined to this heartland. Muslims are found likewise in all the other four "worlds." They play comparatively the most significant role in Chapter 3, "South Asia and the Indian Ocean." In the period from 1350 to 1750, ever larger parts of India, starting in the north, fell under the sway of Muslim princes, before the Mughal Empire then brought almost the entire subcontinent under its control around 1700. Up to the sixteenth century, powerful non-Muslim empires had ruled over parts of central and southern India. Nevertheless, under the Mughals, the non-Muslim majority of the populace was generally not oppressed; their religions, despite being regarded as "idolatry" by Islam, were semi-tolerated. It was only in the nineteenth century that most of these separate religions were yoked together under the artificial umbrella term of "Hinduism." Nor was it just in the matter of religion that the Indian subcontinent presented a scarcely less diverse and colorful picture than Europe. The obvious linguistic, religious, and cultural contrast between northern and southern

India already represents a crass oversimplification. The cohabitation of "Hindus" and Muslims turned out to be extremely creative in cultural terms.[9] And yet barely any of the Indian empires, not even that of the Mughals, became engaged in maritime affairs. Trade in the Indian Ocean lay predominantly in the hands of Muslim merchants. In addition, this state of affairs was intimately bound up with the matter of transporting hajj pilgrims to Mecca. On the coast of East Africa, facing the Indian Ocean, this Muslim seaborne mercantile world also gave rise to the Afro-Asian hybrid culture of the Swahili.

In Chapter 4, "Southeast Asia and Oceania," we also find Muslims engaged in further expansion on the Malay Peninsula, Sumatra and Java, the Moluccas and the Philippines. Also present in this realm are adherents of "Hindu religions," Buddhism, so-called animistic religions, and finally Christianity, too. At first sight, throughout this region, disparate unrelated elements appear to have been artificially forced together. There are four different macroregions: mainland Southeast Asia, which consists of countries under the cultural influence, respectively, of India (Burma, Thailand, Cambodia) and China (Vietnam); the Southeast Asian island world between Sumatra and the Philippines; the maritime side of the Eurasian empires of China, Japan, and Korea; and the endless expanses of Oceania between Australia, Hawaii, and Easter Island. But on closer examination, certain structural similarities become apparent: on the one hand, mountain-dwelling peoples inhabiting small communities, still partly following a hunter-gatherer lifestyle; and on the other, farmers practicing dry- and wet-rice cultivation, who lived in larger or smaller empires. Admittedly, the numerous cities that existed during this period could also be the location of small, independent principalities. But they were predominantly centers of trade and commerce, as Southeast Asia was the site of the most intensive economic and hence also cultural communication. Islam is said to have been spread to this region by merchants, and for Christians, too, trade and the dissemination of faith went hand in hand. Yet if it is true to claim that this macroregion was at that time characterized primarily by maritime communication, then we should qualify this by stating that the realms of communication were only two in number, as Oceania was largely self-contained, while in the absence of shipping, Australia remained unknown.

Originally, people inhabiting the three continents that are treated together in Chapter 5, "Europe and the Atlantic World," lived lives that were as unconnected as their homelands. Until the middle or rather the end of the fifteenth century, people living in Africa, the Americas, and Europe knew practically nothing about the existence of the two other "worlds" and their inhabitants. At most, a few black slaves and vague reports were brought by Jews and North African Muslims to the Mediterranean from the empires of the Sudan. Then, however, chains of contingent activities and developments set in motion the centuries-long expansion of Europe. The five western countries of the Old World brought the New World under their sway and locked western Africa into a trading system that was geared primarily toward supplying the New World with African slaves. Until the nineteenth century, more Africans emigrated to America than Europeans, albeit not of their own free will. Significantly, Angola was at times politically more heavily dependent on its slave client Brazil than on the actual colonial power, Portugal. The Atlantic was transformed into a kind of internal sea between Old Europe and New Europe, along with their common trading partner, West Africa.

Empires and World Empires

On closer inspection, the current, politically driven boom in publications about empires has engendered, both in German and English, a confusion in historiographic terminology. "Empire"[10] is defined as "a political unit of large extent controlling a number of territories and peoples under a single sovereign authority," where the "extent" is relative and depends on how far advanced transport conditions and news dissemination are.[11] The opposing concept is that of the "nation-state":

> Empires are large political units, expansionist or with a memory of power extended over space, polities that maintain distinction and hierarchy as they incorporate new people. The nation-state, in contrast, is based on the idea of a single people in a single territory constituting itself as a unique political community.[12]

The nation-state may be regarded as an important alternative model and sometimes even as the product of a separate line of development. Critical studies on empires emphasize the brutality of their creation through conquest and of the discriminatory nature of their rule.[13] By contrast, those who are nostalgic for empires eulogize their benevolent aspects,[14] while others employ a differentiating method of investigation in order to try and find out how empires set about solving their fundamental problem of exercising dominion over diverse peoples.[15] Approaches such as this are informed by an urge to find a more humane model of a polity than that of the nation-state. In reality, the latter is only in very rare cases an ethnically and linguistically self-contained unit, yet tends by virtue of its self-understanding as a nation to impose such a state of uniformity, if necessary through "ethnic cleansing." A people that identifies itself with its state, such as the post-revolutionary French, strives toward total integration of minorities, who are required to relinquish their separate languages and identities, whereas an "imperial people," like the Castilians of the sixteenth century, contents itself with simple hegemony, which guarantees it all positions of power and other privileges, with minorities being bilingual; in such a polity, multiple identities are just as possible as individual advancement into the ranks of the imperial people.

But "state" also serves as a general term for any "polity" that has exceeded some loosely defined size. Beneath the state and above primordial acephalous minor groupings are tribes, chiefdoms, principalities, and what are usually called city-states but should more accurately be designated urban republics. In this conception of things, though, empires would be nothing but a special form of state. Admittedly, there have been states that have created empires for themselves as well. The historically most significant cases of this are the nation-states of the nineteenth and twentieth centuries with their colonial empires. This high point of Western "imperialism" was made possible only by the fact that the rest of the world at that time had nothing comparable with which to counteract the modern European nation-state, the most powerful political entity that humans have ever created, only its own indigenous "empires."

Yet the same situation had already arisen in Europe during the early modern period, when the Castilian proto-state similarly proved itself more powerful than the empires of the Incas and the Aztecs, with their Stone Age technology, and so was able to fashion an additional colonial empire for itself. By contrast, in Asia, European proto-states like Portugal and even England were for a long time incapable even of dealing on an equal footing with the long-established empires in China, India, and Japan. In terms of their historical development, England, France, Portugal, and Spain were at that time "empires" only in the sense outlined above, yet they were empires that had already gone a long way toward becoming a modern state. The prevailing situation was clearly outlined by Philip IV's favorite, the Spanish prime minister Gaspar de Guzmán, Count of Olivares, in an address to the king in 1625:

> The most important thing in Your Majesty's monarchy is for you to become the king of Spain: by this I mean, Sire, that Your Majesty should not be content with being king of Portugal, of Aragon, of Valencia, and count of Barcelona, but should secretly plan and work to reduce these kingdoms of which Spain is composed to the style and laws of Castile, with no difference whatsoever.[16]

Decisive steps in this direction took place in both Spain and England in the eighteenth century. Incidentally, it was only then that people began to refer to "colonies." Up until then, within the framework of the concept of empire, where colonial rule was concerned, too, the fiction of semiautonomous subsidiary territories analogous to Naples or Ireland was maintained. By contrast, Germany remained an "empire" in name until 1945 and, up to 1918—just like Austria-Hungary, in its structure also—as the "German Empire" was a heterogeneous alliance of principalities, whereas Austria-Hungary was a complex arrangement of countries with unequal status.

This means, though, that the terms "empire" and "state" may be regarded only as synchronous alternatives, grouped under the overarching concept of the "state," from the perspective of nation-states in the nineteenth and twentieth centuries. Yet viewed from the diachronic historical profundity of European or even world history, this binary typology turns out to be inadequate and must be replaced by a more complex developmental history. In this conception of things, then, the "empire" appears globally as the standard model of a larger polity of diverse composition, whereas the "state" shows itself to be a special form of concerted uniformity, which first emerged from the "empire" in Europe. This proven temporal sequence of development renders the concept of the "state" unsuitable as an overarching umbrella term.

In addition, there is the fact that even the proto-forms of the modern state in Europe between 1350 and 1750 began to set themselves apart from the "empire"—and the longer this process went on, the more pronounced the distinction. However, the modern state reached full maturity only in the French Revolution and the nineteenth century.[17] This circumstance saves us from having to take issue with the factually accurate but, precisely for that reason, irritating observation that Europe invented the state.[18] In the period 1350–1750, there are only "empires" throughout the world. This is why, paradoxically, the use of the term "states" as a synonym for "empires" in this volume has no damaging historiographical implications—but only, it must be stressed, so long as we remain within this time frame.

Even so, there were both large and small empires, and the actual term itself is reserved for the former category, notwithstanding the fact that there were no structural differences between the two. The English Act of Parliament of 1533, which stated "that this realm of England is an empire,"[19] merely signifies that the king was thereby endowed with emperor-like authority—an early step toward state formation but far from being a prophetic prefiguration of the British Empire. Yet it does point us in the direction of an English umbrella term for large and small empires: "realm," or the even better (more widespread) term "kingdom," or, best of all, thanks to its abstract nature, "monarchy." For, at least where the period 1350–1750 is concerned, all empires around the world were monarchies.

But what does the term "world empires" mean? Because no one has ever ruled over the entire globe, the only empires one could apply this term to are those that at any one time were the largest and that exerted more or less worldwide influence. Where our volume is concerned, the application and justification of this term can be more precisely defined in two regards. First, in the period 1350–1750, or at least for part of this four-hundred-year span, when viewed from an external perspective, there were empires that ruled over an entire civilization, or at least over significant parts of one: for example, the empires of China and Japan; the Safavid Empire in the central Persian cultural area, which increasingly also became the heartland of Shi'ism; the Ottoman Empire in the core region of Sunni Islam; the Russian Empire as the successful polity that gathered together the Russian lands and Orthodox Christianity; and the Inca as the rulers of the entire South American realm of high culture except for the highland region of present-day Colombia.

Second, viewed from within the respective cultures, more or less every ancient empire that was formed seems to have been inclined toward more or less full-blown claims to universal hegemony or similar pretensions, not infrequently in the context of religious or mythical legitimation discourses on the part of the rulers. It may possibly even be the case that this is a universal phenomenon of political anthropology, for in the twentieth and twenty-first centuries political ideologies such as racism, Marxism, or the "freedom" of the market economy, democracy, and human rights have taken over this same task of universalizing.

As the epicenter of the Middle Kingdom, the Chinese emperor was the ceremonial point of contact between heaven and Earth. In the empires of Southeast Asia, which were influenced by Indian culture, including Buddhism, the king was a *devaraja* ("deity-ruler") or at least a *chakravartin,* who kept the wheel of the law or of religious doctrine in motion and ruled benevolently over the world. Under the Mughals, the names of the rulers Jahangir (1605–1628) and Shah Jahan (1628–1658) meant, respectively, "world conqueror" and "ruler of the world"; the cultural output of their environment is replete with the symbolism of universal rule.[20] The genealogical legitimation took its cue from Tamerlane and Genghis Khan and their quite explicit claims to world domination. Likewise, the Ottoman sultans first legitimized themselves through their successes as champions of Islam until, following their conquest of Egypt in 1517 together with its Arabian territories, they became the guardians of Islam's sacred sites (Mecca, Medina, and Jerusalem) and the successors of the first caliphs and so took center stage in Islam's claim to universal hegemony. Other Muslim empire builders, such as the Safavids, cited their mission to revitalize the faith, invoking the image of an eschatologically righteous leader, the Mahdi, and setting in motion a jihad with the aim of establishing a religiously "pure" polity.

After they had conquered Constantinople in 1453, though, the Ottomans also assimilated the Byzantine imperial tradition,[21] which in its turn harked back to the factually inaccurate but psychologically quite understandable claim of the Imperium Romanum to rule over all the known inhabited and civilized world. In Russia at the same time, the idea was also being nurtured of Moscow as a third Rome, which after Rome itself and Constantinople would rule until the world came to an end. Similarly, the renewed Western Roman Empire was originally motivated by its eschatological role, according to which the Roman Empire, as the last of the four biblical global empires, would last until the end of time. Yet after one last, failed attempt by Charles V to stake a claim to universal rule, the position of Holy Roman emperor degenerated into being merely an honorary title of the German king. In an inversion that was emblematic of European circumstances at the time, the urge toward a universal monarchy was turned around into a commonplace political reproach, generally leveled at whoever was the most powerful ruler in Europe at the time in order to discredit him.[22] Conversely, the Inca Empire was able to present itself unchallenged as the "Tawantinsuyu"—the realm of the Four Quarters. Whether and to what extent universal claims were advanced by the specifically African sacred kingships south of the Sahara, it is impossible for us to say. Nevertheless, it would only be a mild exaggeration to assert that, in the period 1350–1750, the world was host to not only empirically diverse major empires but also to countless emic "world empires."

Empire Building

This discussion of terminology is essential because empire building throughout the world was one of the decisive processes of the period we are dealing with. Of course, earlier ages might also be characterized by this development. In our period, however, empire building also encompassed the "rest of the world" in Africa and the Americas, whereas in Eurasia, crisis-riven interregna grew ever shorter in most empires, as the empires became increasingly larger.[23] In abstract terms, the empire as a political entity now reached the high point of its development, whereupon it promptly ceded its role as a political leitmotif of world history to the modern state, which at that time was just emerging from European empires.

In concrete terms, though, of course this does not mean that what we are faced with here are parallel linear and uniform courses of history. In fact, the converse is true: in our treatment, the apparent simultaneity of things that in actuality were not contemporaneous is taken as read. What we are dealing with here is, as already stated, an uneven accumulation of contingencies across various crises and regressions. Some empires may well have reached the zenith of their development long before 1750 and by the eighteenth century already found themselves in decline. Yet modern historical research is far more reticent to judge the decline of the Ottoman and Mughal Empires lamented, say, from a Turkish or Indian nationalistic standpoint, preferring to regard it instead as a form of political morphogenesis.

In an extended sense, as a process of political shaping, the reorganization of an empire also constitutes a kind of "empire building." Not for nothing does there exist in the otherwise completely linear Chinese image of history the notion of the cyclical reallocation of the "Mandate of Heaven" to every new dynasty. Likewise, the "wrath of heaven" made itself apparent in both temporary deterioration of the climate and the extreme phases of the so-called Little Ice Age, or in the widespread reduction of sunshine that ensued after volcanic eruptions. Periods of cold or drought but also floods, failed harvests, and famines were the result. Often these went hand in hand with epidemics. The populace's response to all this was to stage unrest, which could often culminate in momentous civil wars. The crises that China experienced in the fourteenth and seventeenth centuries had their parallels in other parts of the world, especially in Europe, which was affected by the Black Death in the fourteenth century and then was faced with a series of crises barely three hundred years later.

And yet these crises only briefly weakened the process of empire building, both in China and in Europe, while in the long term actually clearly strengthening it—in China through two successful fresh starts and in Europe through the self-assertion of the powers that be, so that the wars of the seventeenth century might even be designated as "wars of state formation."[24] Similarly, France and Japan were able to successfully take the step up to a modern state only thanks to crises in their political systems which at first sight were catastrophic events. Yet one wonders how it is that in some cases such events led to a strengthening of the system of rule, while in others they led to decline and collapse.

Even if any general conclusions we draw must be hedged with caveats, nevertheless it is clearly apparent that the aggregated total stability of the supporters and beneficiaries of any given system of rule was the decisive factor. In this the family played a key role, as it does throughout early modern society, though in very diverse ways in each individual case. The foundation of an empire could turn into a successful piece of empire building only if some founding hero, who might well have been a usurper, managed to pass down the will to power to a dynasty of competent successors. The reigns of Nadir Shah in Iran (r. 1736–1747), Cesare Borgia in central Italy (r. 1498–1503), and at root even the Central Asian "Earth shaker" Tamerlane (r. 1360–1405) remained just episodes, because they failed to achieve this feat. The royal route to success was in a dual sense an uninterrupted or at least only briefly interrupted succession of capable monarchs, such as the Mughal line in India (1556–1707), stretching from Akbar to Aurangzeb, or the series of Prussian monarchs (1640–1786) from Frederick William, elector of Brandenburg, to Frederick the Great. The opposite scenario also bears out the point: a series of short-lived, weak, or underage rulers reigning through a regent occasioned political crises, such as those that arose in China toward the end of the Ming and the Qing dynasties, in the Mughal Empire after the death of Aurangzeb, or in France under the last rulers of the Valois line (1559–1589).

Dynastic empire building could also greatly benefit a ruling family as an instrument of power. The itinerant Habsburg emperor Charles V appointed family members as regents in his various realms during his frequent absences. In Thailand and several African kingdoms, too, princes were installed as provincial governors, no doubt partially also in order to give them roles that befitted their status. Conversely, dynastic marriages could be used not only to set the seal on peace treaties but also to secure the loyalty of powerful subjects or dependent vassal princes. Everywhere, princesses were obliged to acquiesce in this process. As against Christian monarchs, who at least on paper observed monogamy, polygynous rulers in the rest of the world had the distinct advantage that additional wives could be added at any time for political expediency. For instance, subjugated princes in the Kingdom of Kongo were required to dispatch without delay a new spouse to the royal court.

It is probably correct to regard these women as hostages, as numerous royal courts either expressly or under a veil of discretion practiced a form of hostage taking. Japanese *daimyo,* for example, were obliged to supply hostages to the court of the *shōgun* if they themselves were not resident there. Similarly, it was expected of Thai princes and provincial governors that they would spend the overwhelming majority of their time living at the royal court;[25] their ruling function did not therefore primarily consist of carrying out local administrative duties. It was also once said of Louis XIV of France that he gathered together the most influential members of the French nobility at his court in order to keep them under control and occupy their time with elaborate courtly rituals. In the meantime, though, it has long since been demonstrated that the French court of the *Roi Soleil* was far from being merely a place of ritual but was first and foremost—in common with other royal courts—a marketplace of power brokerage and patronage seething with constant clashes between rival factions.

The same was true to an even greater extent of polygynous courts, because the intrigues surrounding the succession to the throne there were wont to take on quite different proportions to those in Europe, where, the number of legitimate successors who might be considered for the role was mostly very limited, because the principle of primogeniture had become firmly established in most heritable realms since the late Middle Ages. In other parts of the world, such rules were the exception. In West African Dahomey, a form of natural primogeniture operated, while in the seventeenth century the Ottoman Empire switched over to the principle of succession of the eldest male member of the dynasty, who was no longer required to be a son of the preceding sultan. Elsewhere, as was the case at least theoretically in Russia since Peter I, the tsar was entitled to designate his successor and, like the Chinese emperor, choose in the process the most supposedly capable of his sons. Yet this by no means ensured that such an arrangement was universally respected.

To the contrary, one might even contend that in principle the usual method of succession to the throne throughout the world was through civil war, conflicts that were only avoided or quickly ended if the intended or the most competent heir acted with sufficient dispatch and secured himself enough support in time. Nor was it just in England after 1485 or in Russia after 1605 that such clashes were further complicated by pretenders of dubious provenance, who were championed by parties with a vested interest in the outcome. Up until the seventeenth century, the Ottomans regularly solved the problem by legalized fratricide, while the Mughals occasionally improvised the same expedient. Especially impressive orgies of slaughter took place among the Safavids, where Shah Abbas I the Great not only had a whole series of his sons butchered and as a precaution his grandsons, too, but also any women from his harem whom he suspected of potential involvement. There was something to be said for the thesis that the principle of fratricide brought politically more capable rulers to the helm than dubious paternal grace and favor or the genetic lottery of primogeniture.

Despite being isolated in the harem, the wives of the Mughals, the Rajputs, the Safavids, and the Ottomans still exerted considerable indirect political influence. Occasionally, and not just in Europe, women would even succeed to the throne, though the series of four Russian empresses between 1725 and 1796 (with three brief interludes of male rule) remains the most significant instance of this.

Even so, on a global scale these cases still represent only exceptions to the general rule of male domination. Although there is the odd female ruler, there are no instances of women judges, governors, or soldiers—except for the feared corps of Amazon warriors retained by the king of Dahomey. In addition, here we encounter—as in the Kingdom of Kongo and Benin—the curious office of the "king's mother," a kind of co-regent, who was appointed and who was by no means identical with the biological mother of the king.²⁶ Even so, here too the same watchword pertained: the routine business of exercising power and authority remained a male affair.

Nevertheless, one dynasty alone, however capable, is not enough to constitute a successful empire formation. When the male line of four extremely successful Burgundian dukes, established in 1363, was extinguished with the death of Charles the Bold in 1477, Burgundy, which then was just on the verge of attaining the status of a kingdom, instantly collapsed and fell prey to the ambitions of its neighbors. The Austro-Hungarian Empire of the Habsburgs, by contrast, managed to pull through when it found itself in the same position in 1740, although its Prussian neighbor had already seized some territory in Silesia by that stage. In India, the fall of the Mughal dynasty led to the dissolution of the empire into various independent regional empires. In China, despite civil wars, the unity of the empire survived the breakup of the Yuan and the Ming dynasties.

This cannot have been the result of institutional failure, for the Burgundian dukes and the Mughals alike had thoroughly effective central bureaucracies at their disposal. Rather, the decisive factor was the existence or absence of a sufficiently broad echelon of socially influential people, who out of self-interest espoused the cause of the dynasty and in this way came over time to identify themselves with the empire as a whole. In all premodern empires, despite all their individual differences, there were always three social strata: an upper class, which if they were sufficiently socially exclusive can be categorized as an aristocracy; the great mass of free subjects; and last, those who had no freedom—these could be tied bondsmen, slaves who could be sold at will, or both. Successful empire building amounted, in a kind of spiraling-down process, on the one hand to winning over the already existing upper class, while on the other the monarchy created in addition its own upper class of loyal collaborators and at the same time sought to transform, as far as possible, the existing nobility along these lines. In this process, the interest of individual families in raising their social status or increasing their profits was a key variable.

On the basis of a pronounced ethno-cultural consciousness, the class of scholar-administrators was revived in China by means of the reinvigorated imperial examination system; right up to its final demise in 1911, the Chinese Empire based its whole existence on a symbiosis between this class and local dignitaries, from whose ranks they overwhelmingly recruited. On the one hand, this development prevented the formation of a hereditary nobility and enabled some measure of social mobility while, on the other, allowing a high degree of social coherence to be maintained. In India, the Mughals organized the military aristocratic caste of the *mansabdaran*, assigned them rankings with numbers running from ten to five thousand, and either paid them or furnished them with fiefdoms; in return, the mansabdaran were required to provide larger or smaller troops of horsemen for the army. Alongside them there was also the existing resident local caste of dignitaries known as the *zamindaran*, who were co-opted into the empire as tax collectors. When the empire was no longer able to pay the mansabdaran, they withdrew their loyalty to it; at the same time, the empire had never managed to fully bring powerful local interests to heel anyway. Among the European aristocracy, ancient noble families had already begun to coalesce with those who had gained advancement in military, judicial, or courtly service. One feature peculiar to Europe was the scholarly lawyers from an urban background, who were to raise themselves to the status of a real power elite in the development of a modern state. Even when they were ennobled, they remained a separate class in their own right. The distinction between military, courtly, and administrative nobility was especially pronounced in France. But in the African kingdom of Benin, also another environment where lawyers were unknown, we find a corresponding classification of chiefs' families into rural, courtly, and town (that is, administrative) aristocracy.[27]

In Muslim empires and in China, in conjunction with the practice of polygyny among the rulers, there were countless eunuchs, who in China above all played a political role on occasion. From time to time, they were significant officeholders, the most famous example being the admiral of the Western Fleet in the early fifteenth century, Zheng He. Yet under the late Ming dynasty, eunuchs developed into a closed caste, who to a greater extent than ever vied with the men of letters for influence at court; as a consequence, the scribes, who were important opinion formers, portrayed the eunuchs as being implicated in the decline of the dynasty.

Eunuchs had no precursors and no successors; in other words, their offices and income could not become family property at the expense of the crown. Accordingly, in political terms, their employment was thoroughly sensible. The Roman Catholic Church tried to create a similar effect from the Middle Ages on by imposing a ban on its priesthood marrying (enforced celibacy). We may view the Roman church as being the empire of the pope—an empire that, thanks to the head start it acquired in empire building (a process that even displayed early signs of statehood), served as a model for Latin Europe. However, the servants of the church had plenty of relatives, often of aristocratic stock, and so became well versed in circumventing the consequences of enforced celibacy by exercising a kind of informal law of inheritance of church property for their nephews (nepotism).

In addition, as a result of the Roman church's position of power, there developed in Latin Europe—in contrast to all other political cultures, including those of Orthodox Christianity—a pronounced dualism of religion and politics. Of course, there was no neat separation of the two, with popes and other ecclesiastical officeholders claiming political authority, while secular rulers arrogated to themselves a sense of sacrality or religious legitimation "through God's grace" that was independent of the church. However, a decisive factor lay in the fact that for a long time there existed different centers of power with different interests and institutions as well as different personnel with different identities. The upshot was that politics and law and politicians and lawyers, further empowered by the readoption of the Roman legal tradition, slowly began to free themselves from all religious ties. The logical end result would be the secular nature of the modern state, albeit far later than the centuries under scrutiny in this volume.

Elsewhere, there was a much closer connection between religion and politics, especially on a personal level. Cases where religion was dominant, however, such as the development of the Tibetan theocracy, were the exception. Buddhist monasteries in Japan were brutally eradicated by the "great unifier of the empire" Hideyoshi, who knew precisely what he was doing. In the normal course of events, religion had to submit, in one way or another, to being appropriated by politics. Rulers were surrounded with a divine aura, as in Angkor; had special connections to the worlds of the gods and spirits, as in Africa, where distinguished Muslim empire founders partly owed their success to their reputation as sorcerers; or were at least able to gain legitimacy through their claim to be carrying out a divine mission, like the "son of Heaven" in China and many Muslim sultans, who styled themselves as champions of the dissemination of the True Faith *(Ghazi)*.

The autonomy of religious and cultural elites was noticeably more restricted elsewhere in the world than in Latin Europe. Mostly, a form of symbiosis with the political authorities took place. Everywhere, the law remained interwoven with religious and moral strictures, with the possible exception of China, but even there, no lawyers existed as a separate class, as in the West. China's political class continued to be a literary, educated echelon with a moral mandate. And although Islam has no formal church, it does have a well-codified body of religious law with universal validity (shariʿa); the numerous experts in this field (ulama) had a mutual interest in collaborating with the political powers that be. Unlike a caliph, a sultan did not possess religious legitimacy for his authority; accordingly, the laws he passed were automatically subordinated to the dictates of shariʿa. Alongside the religious legal scholars, however, there were also representatives of a more personal devotion, the Sufis, who are deemed to have been highly significant in the spread of Islam, especially in India. Individual Sufis could gain influence over rulers, while their organized Dervish orders played a major role in political life. The Safavid rulers of Iran were fundamentally nothing more than the hereditary heads of the Ardabil Dervish order. Likewise, in India, members of the Brahmin caste were also the guardians of a legal religious tradition (dharma) but were also specialists in ritual, whose services were much sought after. Only the traditional law of Buddhist monastic communities *(sangha)* seems to have embodied a contrast to the political world, teamed with a claim to autonomy, which then, as already noted, culminated in a theocracy.

Before the rise of the jurists, the medieval rulers of Europe occasionally took unfree men into their military or judicial service, who were then elevated to the nobility *(ministerials)*. In a similar but more drastic way, monarchs in various countries sought to create a professional body of men at their disposal and exclusively dependent on them, to act as a countervailing force to the existing aristocracy. In effect, they recruited a slave guard. Even before our period, such forces were found in the Near East, mostly consisting of Turks. In Egypt, these Mamluks took over the reins of power in 1250, holding it in various guises until 1517. In Iran, the Ghulam, recruited chiefly from among Christian Georgians, served the shah and acted as a counterweight to the mounted tribal forces of the Qizilbash. The Sudanese empires of Songhay and Kanem-Bornu also created slave infantry forces alongside their mounted armies.

The most famous instance of this phenomenon, though, is the Janissary force of the Ottomans, an elite unit formed from slaves in the 1400s, which reached the high point of its power in the following century. In the Ottoman Empire, the professional military and the bureaucracy were basically considered as slaves of the sultan and could be killed summarily at any time. Even so, these positions were highly sought after, because they offered opportunities for advancement, and unlike free subjects, members of the Janissary force were exempt from taxation. Among the Mughals and farther east, comparable arrangements do not appear to have existed. By contrast, in 1565 Tsar Ivan IV—otherwise known as Ivan "the Terrible"—created such a force when he founded the *oprichnina,* albeit not from slaves; he used this army to try to consolidate control over his realm by means of terror.

Another major motivation driving this process was the exploitation of resources, as resources to wage war and, conversely, the war to secure resources epitomize every empire's formation. In this, sub-Saharan Africa may serve as an exemplar, because the processes of empire formation set in late compared with Eurasia. What had taken place in Eurasia back in the mists of early medieval history is still very much in evidence in Africa during our period. This was because the continent was poorly endowed with resources. The average crop yield was small, and animal husbandry was out of the question across large tracts of the continent because of the presence of the tsetse fly. Plagues and famine regularly took their toll. As a consequence, population increase was particularly slow, and therefore it was far harder to generate large surpluses in order to sustain an unproductive and economically parasitic system of rule than had formerly been the case in the Nile Valley or in the fertile plains of the great rivers of Eurasia. Yet population and surpluses that can be tapped into are the most important resources promoting empire formation. It is significant in this regard that empire formation in the sparsely populated savannas south of the Congo basin took a particularly long time, while the exploitation of additional abundant resources in the forest belt of the Guinea region through long-distance trade enabled particularly impressive empires to blossom and flourish there. The key resources in question here were the gold of the Asante and the slave trade in Dahomey.

Unfortunately, we have only very general information about the exact way in which these resources were exploited. First, neighbors' resources could be seized through swift, successful military campaigns. Waging war in order to snatch booty not only helped the Ottoman Empire survive and flourish; a significant element of the booty was often prisoners of war, who could be sold as slaves or put to work directly on royal estates and thereby generate additional resources for the ruler. If these prisoners were from a noble background, moreover, enormous sums could be extorted for their release. Admittedly, booty could benefit the ruler of an empire only in part, given that his continuing authority relied on him assigning a goodly portion of the spoils to his commanders.

Second, there were the tribute payments that were due on a regular basis from dependent polities and that sometimes had to be exacted through military coercion. Third were the duties accruing from the ruler's own subjects, generated by their production, distribution, and consumption. For a long time, tributes and levies were paid in kind, most commonly in the form of grain, which could then be stored for lean periods or for taking on a campaign. However, monetary payments were more effective, not least because of the ease with which money could be reutilized. The influx of Western silver from the sixteenth century onward promoted the raising of taxes in cash in the Ottoman Empire, India, and China.[28]

Yet all this did not solve the problem of raising revenue. The basic principle was that all those who could not manage to exempt themselves were taxed. Universally, this tended to be farmers, given the goods they produced and their obvious possessions in the form of land. In contrast, commerce and trade but above all wealth in the form of cash were much harder to pin down. Seizure was at its simplest when taxable goods unavoidably had to pass through an artificially constructed bottleneck. Hence the predilection for customs posts. Excise duty on everyday foodstuffs, the hated money-spinner for many premodern polities in Europe, presupposed that a state was furnished with sufficient potential for supervision. It was no coincidence that in Prussia such duties were levied only by the cities, which had the otherwise useless walls around them maintained precisely for this purpose, whereas the flat, open countryside was subject to a form of land tax.

Tax farming, which was common practice in several European countries and the Ottoman Empire, was a way of simplifying and streamlining tax collection. The prerequisite for this was the presence of a capitalist class. Inasmuch as this process involved advance payments to the monarch, this amounted to a precursor of state credit. Certainly, across large parts of the rest of Eurasia, there were just as highly developed forms of monetary and capital transfer as in Europe. However, we do not know whether there, too, this formed the basis for regular extension of credit to rulers. It has generally been assumed that the greater insecurity of private property precluded such an arrangement. Yet for a long while, extending credit to a ruler in Europe, too, was a highly risky business, primarily because successors did not hold themselves liable for the debts of their predecessors. Even so, toward the end of our period there developed a publicly guaranteed liability of almost unlimited capacity, no longer of the ruler but of the entire polity. It was on this virtually inexhaustible resource that the superior power of the future modern state would be founded.

The purpose of taxation was not so much to finance royal courts and the mania for building commonly displayed by rulers throughout the world but rather to finance wars, be these small wars aimed at gradually expanding the empire, major wars designed as a frontal assault on coequal rivals with an eye to eradicating or subjugating them, or civil wars to stabilize the system of rule (stability would also be the focus of wars of succession). Empires were forged by war, whereas peaceful expansion such as that achieved through, say, marriage politics—like that which commentators, somewhat unfairly, have claimed the Habsburgs practiced—was the exception rather than the rule. In the notoriously pluralistic Europe, though, it was no longer possible for any all-embracing empire to prevail. Consequently, there developed up to the eighteenth century a kind of stable instability, in which monarchs regularly negotiated with one another to contain wars. This business gave rise to distinct institutions such as permanent diplomatic representatives, "international" congresses, and the embryonic beginnings of modern international law. Similar conditions cannot really be identified elsewhere, at most possibly in India in the fifteenth and sixteenth centuries, and then only fleetingly before the Mughal Empire gained the upper hand. Suzerainty was the historic norm.

Firearms

Marshall G. S. Hodgson has called the third part of his history of the Islamic world *The Gunpowder Empires and Modern Times,* while correspondingly the first part was entitled *Second Flowering: The Empires of Gunpowder Times.* And yet firearms are scarcely mentioned in his text; they come to the fore only when he treats the Ottoman Empire. In addition, he merely remarks in passing of the Safavid Empire that it "was able to establish a full-fledged bureaucracy based upon gunpowder military forces."[29] Hodgson is referring here to the aforementioned Ghulam. This neatly formulated offhand classification of one development within the anything-but-linear global historical process of the spread of firearms has become a prevalent doctrine.[30] According to this thesis, then, when the Ottomans, Safavids, and Mughals established their hegemony over the greater part of the Islamic world in the fifteenth to sixteenth centuries, their success was down to the use of firearms. Accordingly, their states came to be designated as "gunpowder empires." A science fiction novel of that name, published in 2003, further helped to popularize and consolidate the term.[31]

However, the term is historically inaccurate, and the actual state of affairs is considerably more complicated. The success of these three empires rested in the first instance on mounted armies in the Turkic-Mongolian tradition, armored or unarmored but always supplied with outstanding horses. These contingents consisted originally of the holders of various types of military fiefdoms (known in the Ottoman Empire as "Timar," among the Safavids as "Tiyul," and in the Mughal Empire as "Jagir") and their retinues. Moreover, the empires of the Sudan also owed their existence to superior mounted forces, after the Muslims had introduced the bit, saddle, and stirrups to that region. Their weapons comprised a lance and sword, though in the Eurasian kingdoms it was primarily the bow and arrow—to be precise, the composite recurved bow, which had great piercing force. Using one of these, a mounted marksman could loose several arrows in a very short space of time but did require extensive training to do so. Although the handheld firearms then just coming into use, first the heavy arquebus followed by the somewhat lighter and more accurate musket, could be fired by anyone, a bowman could have fired fifteen arrows in the time it took a musketeer to reload. In addition, the half-ounce (15-gram) balls fired by the arquebus inflicted little damage; only with the advent of the 2-ounce (60-gram) musket ball did firearms become truly threatening. Furthermore, for a long time firearms could be used only by the infantry. Accordingly, in contrast to the "fiefdom contingents," the so-called household troops, who as mentioned consisted of slaves among the Safavids and Ottomans, increasingly came to be equipped with firearms. Among the Ottomans in the sixteenth century, this trend reached such an extent that this empire—but only this one—could henceforth reasonably be dubbed a "gunpowder empire."[32] But in 1591 the Moroccans, fielding a force of musketeers, triumphed over the lancers and bowmen of the Sudanese Songhay Empire; likewise, mercenaries from the Ottoman Empire were highly regarded as firearms experts in India.

The term "gunpowder empire" also refers to the artillery, an area in which the Ottomans had already attained parity with the West by the fifteenth century, at least initially in the particular realm of heavy siege guns. The victories of Sultan Selim I over the Safavids and the Egyptian Mamelukes can be attributed not just to the deployment of handheld firearms but to field artillery as well. In China and the West, cannons were originally forged from iron, before being cast in bronze. Though bronze was expensive as a material, the casting process was simpler and cheaper than forging. Bronze cannons also were more reliable; forged iron cannons had a tendency to explode. Yet after English forge masters succeeded in the mid-sixteenth century in casting iron cannons, it was possible to equip the land artillery and the navy at reasonable cost, whereas the mid-seventeenth century saw the introduction of light field guns, weighing just over 220 pounds (100 kilograms)— an advance that only the Ottomans were able to match. The secret of Europe's military prowess thereafter was a highly disciplined infantry of pikemen and an increasing number of musketeers, supported by field artillery, until finally the invention of the bayonet in the seventeenth century combined the pike and the firearm and turned every foot soldier into his own pikeman. Russia's subjugation of the steppe peoples of Central Asia also relied on this development.[33]

Like Europe, China and India knew about firearms from as early as the fourteenth century. In the following century, several Indian rulers, including those of Vijayanagara, amassed considerable stockpiles of firearms with the help of Turks and "Franks" for use in sieges and battles. In 1526, Babur first deployed artillery, and his successors were also in the habit of placing artillery and infantry in the center of their battle formations. Yet cavalry charges continued, as they always had done, to be the decisive maneuver in a battle. As a result, the supply of horses from Inner Asia played a disproportionately important role. It is said that the siege artillery of the Mughals was only seldom called upon; for besieging mountain strongholds, it could not even be hauled up to altitude. Yet despite an ongoing series of improvements, their lack of technological know-how meant that the Mughals were unable to keep up with the Europeans in the mass production of cast-iron field guns.[34]

China, meanwhile, had long since relinquished its early role as a technological pioneer. In the sixteenth century, the direction of influence in the matter of weapons technology was reversed. It is possible that muskets were introduced there not just by the Portuguese but by the Turks as well. In the seventeenth century, the Chinese called on the Jesuits who were resident at the imperial court to lend their expertise in casting hundreds of modern cannons of the European pattern.[35]

In Japan, a remarkable—and, for the problem of so-called gunpowder empires, instructive—development unfolded roughly in the period following the unification of the country in the sixteenth to seventeenth centuries. The country's warring *daimyos* had immediately recognized the military potential of the Portuguese firearms and cannons and, thanks to their highly developed metallurgical skills and technology, were straightaway able to make improved copies of their own. Among other advances, they invented a mechanism enabling matchlock guns to be fired even in the rain. In 1575, the first of the unifiers of the Japanese empire, Oda Nobunaga, won a decisive victory by deploying his arquebus troops. In 1593, the second great unifier, Toyotomi Hideyoshi, dispatched an army consisting of a good quarter of musketeers to conquer Korea. All the Koreans could field in opposition were some antiquated Chinese cannons. Significantly, Japanese commanders responded to massive Chinese counterattacks by demanding even more firearms. But Hideyoshi had already begun controlling their spread. Between 1607 and 1625, the third empire unifier, Tokugawa Ieyasu, and his successor made firearms manufacture a monopoly of the shogunate, a position that they used to gradually abolish them altogether. The final use of firearms in Japan in our period was during the Christian rebellion at Shimabara in 1637. Thereafter, samurai swords were the weapon of choice, basically right up to the nineteenth century.

Because of the policy of isolation that it was pursuing at the time, the Tokugawa shogunate could afford to forgo this technology, which was viewed with suspicion from the outset because of its foreign provenance. However, the real reason for dispensing with firearms was a sociocultural one: the country's elite consisted of samurai, warriors who took a highly ritualized approach to waging war and fostered a veritable cult of the sword. The idea that any marksman with a firearm, however lowly, might be able to dispatch them without following any of the knightly and ritualistic code was utterly abhorrent to them. Their strength in numbers allowed them, under the new isolationist foreign policy, to find their "way back to the sword."[36] Others, such as the Mamelukes or the early Safavids, who shared this aristocratic disdain for vulgar firearms, did not have any opportunity to dispense with them.[37] Finally, even European noblemen in the sixteenth century shared this aversion, something that Shakespeare drew attention to.[38] Even as late as the eighteenth century, the well-drilled European infantry was not taken seriously by Indian rulers, as it contradicted the "independent mindset of the Mughal horse-trooper"[39]—what a fatal miscalculation that turned out to be.

Seas and Oceans

"At sea, however, neither the Chinese nor any other people could put up anything to match the European ships. . . . The Chinese, Turks and Indians only recognized the major possibilities of cannons on board of vessels, and the new tactics of naval warfare that perforce resulted from this development, when it was already too late."[40] The so-called turtle boats, the first armored vessels in history, which the Koreans successfully deployed to fight off a Japanese invasion in 1592–1593, may have been the only exception to this generally valid observation. Yet their armor consisted only of wood, not iron.

This is not to say, though, that other modes of shipping were inferior to those of the Europeans in every respect. Rather, on all seas of the world, highly advanced vessels appropriate to the particular prevailing conditions were to be found; when necessary, such designs were readily adopted by the Europeans. Thus, for example, the Dutch East India Company (Vereenigde Oost-Indische Compagnie, or VOC) used a kind of merchant ship from the Moluccas known as the kora-kora to carry out punitive raids against rivals in the clove-growing business. The kora-kora was a relatively flat-bottomed vessel, which, like the European galley, could be propelled by either a square sail or oars.[41]

One renowned form of craft was the large Chinese oceangoing junk of the thirteenth to fifteenth centuries, which is mentioned even in the writings of Marco Polo and Ibn Battuta. On his expeditions to the West, Admiral Zheng He used sixty-two such ships, some of which were said to be as large as 500 feet (150 meters) from stem to stern and 200 feet (60 meters) in the beam. Yet the natural limits of wood technology in shipbuilding make an overall length of 200 feet (60 meters) more likely.[42] With their flat keels, they did not cut through the water so much as glide over the surface. Oceangoing junks were clinker-built and, in contrast to European ships, were already equipped with watertight bulkheads, which made them very difficult to sink. Five masts carried square sails made from woven bamboo, which were divided into segments and were secured to the mast at every crossbeam with a movable ring. This meant that instead of being reefed, they could easily be hoisted or lowered like a curtain, with the pressure distributed evenly across the whole length of the mast and the segmenting preventing the sail from flapping. Movable bow and stern rudders made junks highly maneuverable. It has been shown that the Chinese navigated by means of the magnetic compass from the thirteenth century on. Moreover, the Chinese were known to have, as well as the square sail, the lugger sail, though no information has come down to us about precisely what combinations of sails were used. However, by the sixteenth century, the days of the great junks were over; unlike comparable European vessels, they were never fitted with cannons.[43]

The same was also true of the ships used by Muslim traders on the Indian Ocean, which were largely constructed without using metal. With their lateen sails, they were perfect for the steady crosswind that blew during the monsoon season, though otherwise not very maneuverable. In contrast, thanks to the demands of various different wind systems, Europeans had a combination of square sails on the first two masts and a lateen sail (or later a lugsail) on the stern mast, an arrangement that allowed sails to be positioned into the wind or to tack against the wind when need be. Allied with this great maneuverability was the use of onboard artillery, especially since the invention of the gun port shortly after 1500. For siting too many heavy guns on deck or even on the forecastle or sterncastle threatened to make a ship top-heavy. Now, though, cannons could be placed as close to the waterline as possible along the flanks of the vessel. On the broadsides of ships, the guns could now number in the hundreds. Throughout the world, no other ships could match well-skippered European vessels of this type; over time, tall galleons gave way to low-slung frigates.⁴⁴ Accordingly, European ships came to rule the world's oceans from the seventeenth to eighteenth centuries onward. However, they took much longer to open up the continental landmasses, where for a long time their dominance was by no means as clear-cut.

The Mediterranean was so named because it was located between three continents and thus, according to the worldview of classical antiquity and the early Middle Ages, lay at the very center of the Earth. The people of these three continents had since time immemorial believed themselves to be surrounded on all sides by the *okeanos,* the unknown world ocean that was thought to cover the remainder of the surface of the globe. Despite the fact that other continents had been discovered in the meantime, it remained the case that they covered just 29.2 percent of the Earth's surface, lying like islands in the 70.8 percent of the planet covered by the world's oceans. Today this water surface has become almost as familiar as the land, with the result that it is perfectly usual for us nowadays to distinguish in purely topographical terms between three major oceans: the Atlantic, the Indian, and the Pacific. However, these geographical terms are only of relatively recent origin. As long as people were familiar with only certain parts of these vast expanses of water, correspondingly partial terms were commonly employed. For example, the romantically charged term the South Seas, which was used from the eighteenth century on, derives its name, quite prosaically, from the designation given to the unknown sea south of the isthmus of Panama, discovered by Vasco Núñez de Balboa in 1513.

Long before the "spatial turn," historian Fernand Braudel in 1949 had already considered the Mediterranean as a historical region and in doing so pointed up in epoch-making fashion enduring geohistorical structures and waves of socio-economic cycles spreading across long time spans.⁴⁵ His approach was so seminal that in the interim pretty much every significant sea around the world now has its own historians. Several volumes of a new series, *Seas in History,* have also been published.⁴⁶ We have also in the interim come to identify the reason for the success of this maritime perspective. For if it is true to say that the spatial turn has taught us to look at space as a communications medium, then oceans are particularly amenable to this kind of treatment. In the absence of settled human inhabitants and thanks to the concomitant remoteness of any authority, they are lacking in that excess of qualitative obstinacy that regions and countries some-times exert in order to resist being reduced to having to communicate. In this sense, in Chapter 3, the subject of discussion is not solely the Indian subcontinent but also the world of the Indian Ocean, embracing in addition East Africa, the Red Sea, and the Persian Gulf with their adjoining lands; similarly, to the east, the Gulf of Bengal at the very least also comes within our purview.[47] And in Chapter 5 we go on to discuss the Atlantic World as the characteristic and distinguishing communications realm for the inhabitants of three continents.[48] Even so, in both cases, Braudel's socioeconomic perspective is supplemented by a cultural–historical one, while the human capacity for decision making, which he held in low regard, is once again taken seriously.

It is perfectly possible that a "Pacific World" in the same sense exists today, but it certainly did not in the period 1350–1750.[49] Then, no communication took place between the countries that bordered this immense ocean, or if it did it was only marginal, as in the Manila galleon trade (notwithstanding all the silver bul-lion carried). The huge maritime world of Polynesia remained, despite its dynamic seafarers, a self-sufficient sector of this ocean. Accordingly, we treat it and Aus-tralia alongside Southeast Asia in Chapter 4 of this volume.

Conversely, the diverse maritime communication and interaction within Southeast Asia in the narrower sense and in the maritime Far East may well, from time to time, have been even more intense than what took place across the At-lantic or the Indian Oceans. This begs the unorthodox question whether, from a historical perspective, we might not be justified in regarding (and treating accord-ingly in this volume) the seas of Southeast Asia and the Far East from the Gulf of Siam and the Java Sea in the west to the Yellow Sea and the Sea of Japan in the east, which together made up one large realm of communication, as a de facto fourth global ocean.

Communication and Interaction
Frontiers

The transformation of the Atlantic from a marginal zone between three conti-nents that had what amounted to a totally separating effect on them to a dynami-cally expanding communications realm is merely the most remarkable instance of that growth in worldwide communication and interaction that is alluded to in our mention of "world empires" and especially the transformation of the oceans. Seen from the perspective of the globalized present, it is nothing less than the single most important global historical process that occurred in the period between 1350 and 1750. Yet we are talking here not about individual events but rather about an accumulation of events in a process of boundary transgression that Walter Benjamin once dubbed "Passage."[50]

For rather than being about unique transgression of frontiers, this was about the longer-term alteration of border zones. Although the premodern period did, in contrast to earlier conceptions, recognize thoroughly linear borders, these frequently shaded off into border zones.[51] The cause of this was the aforementioned loose structure of the empire as the dominant political organizational form of the age, as against the modern state. As an exaggerated textbook case, empires ruled over people, states over territories. In historical terms, of course, the two types of frontier cannot be neatly separated, but the fact remains that only modern states rise and fall with linear territorial borders. Empires, in contrast, display a decline in cohesion from the center to the periphery, a concept that fundamentally contradicts the nature of states. Empires, though, are characterized by a hierarchy of allegiances and relationships with indistinct borders, which in addition can rapidly change. As a result, the insufficient clarity of political borders was occasionally compensated for by religious ones, say in Europe following the Reformation. Moreover, empires sometimes show evidence of inner peripheries, which, for instance, in some German territories and in the Mughal Empire were opened up or brought under central control only in the eighteenth century. States have no other choice than to recognize the neighboring state on the far side of their frontiers as an equal, at least in formal terms, whereas empires frequently acknowledge absolutely no neighbors with equal rights.

Two quite distinct lines of research have resulted from this clear contrast. The interdisciplinary Association for Borderlands Studies, formed in 1976, with its *Journal of Borderlands Studies,* began by considering the well-known problems concerning the US–Mexico border but in the interim has gone on to treat the problems of borders worldwide, for example, those of the state of Israel.[52] Also from America comes the contrasting historical research concept of the frontier, which goes back to the essay *The Significance of the Frontier in American History*

(1893), in which Frederick Jackson Turner sought to trace the extraordinary character of the United States and its democratic system back to the experience of the opening up of the West (Manifest Destiny) and the ensuing conflicts with the Native American peoples.[53] In this sense, although the thesis now has only political significance, it did lend impetus to worldwide comparative studies into such frontier regions, including their importance and their exploitation.[54]

Thus, on the margins of colonial America, different types of frontier were identified, which as a rule lay beyond the region occupied by closed settlements of farmers: for instance, the cattle frontiers in North America and northern Mexico, in the *llanos* of Venezuela, in the *sertão* of Brazil and in southern Argentina, which were to attain their greatest significance only in the nineteenth century;[55] the Jesuit missions frontiers in northern Mexico, Paraguay, and the eastern slope of the South American cordillera, as well as in the interior of Brazil (all of which tended to be peaceful); and by contrast the generally hostile Indian frontier in Canada west of British North America, in the south of Chile, and finally, the maroons' frontier of slaves who had run away in the interior of Spanish and Portuguese America.[56] Similar phenomena arose at an early stage on the fringes of the Cape Colony in South Africa, too.[57] But above all, we encounter it in the empires of Eurasia, on the borderline between cultivated land and mountain forest in Southeast Asia, and in the north, northwest, and southeast of China,[58] as well as in southern and eastern Russia.[59] In Europe, England and Castile, in their respective expansions into Ireland and the south of Spain, underwent an "apprenticeship" in frontier politics, which they then applied without more ado in North America.[60]

From the perspective of the modern state, frontier regions such as these can be understood as zones of underdeveloped statehood, which gradually came to be integrated into an empire, and then later into a nation-state. As regards the indigenous population, the prevailing conditions were those of colonial rule, which benefited from a difference in development between the colonial masters and the colonized peoples, if only in the matter of weaponry. According to this, the native peoples were viewed at root as inferior barbarians. Alternatively, the starting point was in the convenient fiction of a *terra nullius,* which posited taking possession of an allegedly empty tract of land. However, unclear or competing conditions of colonial rule sometimes presented the natives with the option of a change of ruler or of ally, as happened with North American Indians between England and France,[61] as well as with Mongols between China and Russia.

Yet the lack of control enticed a particular kind of immigrant, fugitive slaves and bondsmen, dubious wheeler-dealers such as liquor salesmen in Canada and Siberia, escaped criminals, and adventurers of all kinds. Life there was correspondingly violent and uncertain. The not infrequent outcome of such a situation was a very peculiar kind of frontiersman population, whose activities then led to a further expansion of the border. The rangers and later the cowboys of North America, along with the gauchos and llaneros of South America, may be mentioned in this context, and first and foremost the Cossacks of Russia, who went on to develop as a distinct ethnicity. A counterweight to this wild adventurism was the intervention of missionaries, who above all in Latin America did great service in pacifying and developing frontier regions.

Contact Zones

Where external borders are concerned, according to the individual circumstances of power, the one-sided, imbalanced frontier on the verge of boundless barbarian territory can be distinguished from mutual and balanced borders, which were at the same time a contact zone to a neighboring empire or formed a transitional region into such a zone. Within our five major regions, this latter instance was especially true of the frontier between China and the Central Asian empires, on the one hand, and Russia and these same empires, on the other, until the two empires then began to liaise directly with each other. The region around the Great Lakes is nowadays for that very reason, rather than being termed a "frontier," more accurately designated as "middle ground," a place where in the seventeenth and eighteenth centuries the resident Indian groups, or those who had emigrated there as refugees, were exposed to contact not only with the French and British but also with other Native American groups who were by no means like-minded, including the Iroquois and the Sioux.[62]

The world was to a large extent already so densely populated and politically organized that such "contact zones" were encountered more often than "frontiers" in the narrower sense. One particularly momentous case in world history was the border zone between Russia and Latin Europe, which was additionally bound up with the history of the Baltic Sea and Sweden's encroachment upon Finland, into the Baltic, and eventually into Russia. But above all, in the fifteenth century, Lithuania (by the late sixteenth and early seventeenth centuries the dual monarchy of Poland–Lithuania) was on the point of winning control over the Russian realm and thereby claiming Orthodox Christians for the Roman Catholic Church. It was only in the mid-seventeenth century that a backlash set in, which ultimately led to Poland being wiped off the map and left Russia standing on the Central European border of Latin Europe. Admittedly, this was not the same Russia, for running counter to the political movement westward there was a cultural shift east, which made Russia into part of Europe regardless of its clear desire to demarcate itself through its adherence to Orthodox Christianity.

The definition of the fringes of the Ottoman Empire as a clear religious border is disputed. Despite the real historical significance of the academically disputed Ottoman self-image as warriors of the Islamic faith *(ghazi),* there were several ambiguous contact zones with spectacular battles but also with unequivocal frontier phenomena in both southern Russia and Southeastern Europe.[63] First and foremost, the Mediterranean as the paradigmatic maritime contact zone bar none had for a long time been both the scene and the medium of friendly and warlike exchanges between Islam and Christianity, in other words, in our period between the Ottoman Empire and its corsair vassals in North Africa, on the one hand, and the West and the pirate vassals of the Spanish king—namely, the Catholic Knights Hospitallers on Malta—on the other.[64] Furthermore, since the late sixteenth century, northwest Europeans had been making contact with both parties in the Mediterranean.

Even the "sand sea" of the Sahara was more a kind of contact zone than some insuperable frontier, as one might indeed assume from its history, albeit primarily from within the Islamic world. Alongside trans-Saharan trade, there was also warlike contact among Muslims, such as the defeat of the empire of Songhay in 1591 by a Moroccan army, which had ventured across the Sahara with great loss of life and that for a while established Moroccan rule over Timbuktu. European non-Muslims, though, were seldom involved, while Africans took part only as slaves.

Although the coexistence of Muslims with "heathen" Africans on the East African coast, which produced the Swahili culture, may also be treated as a contact zone, the Muslims' contact with others in South and Southeast Asia cannot be organized into clear zones. There it was a question either of closed Muslim regimes in conjunction with others, as on the islands of Southeast Asia, or of cohabitation with people of other faiths within the same polity, as on the Indian subcontinent. Yet in such circumstances limited spatial cohesion was as much a given consequence as social cohesion. But although religion was the decisive factor in demarcation here, and Islam in theory is at least as intolerant as Christianity, what actually unfolded in practice on the ground as a rule was not theoretical tolerance but certainly a form of peaceful coexistence.

Indeed, the very concept of a contact zone should express the idea that initially interactions took place only between immediately neighboring empires, religions, and cultures. The same was true of the economy, of the exchange of goods via trade, for since ancient times it was the case not that goods were transported from one end of Eurasia to the other by one and the same merchant but rather that they were transferred from hand to hand in separate stages. This was also true of the maritime route,[65] although given favorable conditions there, single vessels could cover long stretches, for instance, in the transport of spices from the west coast of India to Egypt. This situation underwent a revolutionary change with the advent from the fourteenth and fifteenth centuries onward of overseas trading by Western Europeans, who knew how to exploit the oceans in a radically new way as realms of communication and who were the first to create completely new contact zones far from their homelands.

Italians, Portuguese, and Spaniards ventured to the islands of the Atlantic and off the African coast and, using these as a springboard, went on to open up the sea route to a world hitherto unknown to them and to gain access to the fabled empires of the East. Their advanced political and technological state of development was sufficient to allow them to subjugate the highly cultivated but technically inferior peoples in the Americas, to make the Atlantic into their exclusive internal contact zone (notwithstanding the individual differences between each of these seafaring nations), and to appropriate the resources of the New World. By contrast, in Asia, it was only their superiority at sea that in the long term ensured them access to the Indian Ocean and to the seas of Southeast Asia and the Far East as new contact zones. Although the Portuguese and Spanish were displaced or supplanted over time by the unequivocally stronger Dutch, French, and English, up until well into the eighteenth century it was the Asiatic peoples themselves who determined what form such contacts should take. Even so, the

Europeans were still able to secure for themselves a portion of Asia's exports for direct transportation by sea and, on the basis of the precious metal resources they had extracted from the Americas, to establish the first global system of trade and monetary exchange.[66] As such, then, by 1750 the terms "world empires" and "oceans of the world" had taken on a fundamentally new and, as it would transpire, highly momentous meaning. At least in spatial terms, this heralded the "time–space compression" of the age of globalism,[67] though in terms of time, these voyages by sea still took months or even years.

Contact Groups

Europeans' contact with Africans, Americans, and Asians took place almost exclusively in the countries of the latter peoples; only in individual cases did people of Indian, Chinese, or African origin come to Europe. As a rule, it was Europeans who sought contact in the first place, while their counterparts frequently had simply to passively endure this contact or, alternatively, to shun it. Admittedly, the contact groups who took part in early European expansion in the West and the East differed greatly from one another, both in their number and their composition.

Although all "Americans," one people after another, were affected at one time or another by contact with whites, on the European side only a minority of either transient or permanent settlers had anything to do with the indigenous people. The number of voluntary migrants to the Americas may well have run into the hundreds of thousands, but it was only up to 1580 that they constituted a clear majority (69 percent) of all immigrants. Even as early as the period 1580–1640, this demographic composition had altered radically, with 67 percent of migrants now being African slaves. For the period 1640–1700, this changed again, with 65 percent of slaves now being supplemented by a further 18 percent of indentured servants, white people who had funded their passage through a form of temporary servitude. Thereafter, the proportion of slaves rose again, constituting fully 85 percent of all incomers in 1760–1820; only in the period 1820–1880 did the share of free immigrants climb to 82 percent.[68] A small but significant proportion of immigrants was made up of convicts, which Great Britain deported to its colonies, in contrast to the other colonial powers, which at least in theory made every effort to recruit only the most upstanding of migrants to people their settlements. Alongside administrators and soldiers, the English and French tended to send farmers as settlers, whereas the Spanish and Portuguese pattern was to have landlords live in towns and benefit from farming activities carried out by Indians or slaves.

Because, in the main, Europeans established only isolated trading bases in Africa and Asia—only exceptionally taking control of a limited territory—the number of immigrants here was far lower. Yet even here we may assume a significant proportion of slaves, as the slave trade flourished there, whether for personal use or as a commodity for selling. The whites were merchants and administrators—a group whose members wanted to stay in Asia or Africa only for a limited period. In addition, there were people from the lower classes in their service, chiefly soldiers, whereas in contrast to America, other settlers were by no means thick on the ground. This class of people often included the husbands of native women or in the second generation were themselves the offspring of such "mixed marriages." The troops employed by the Dutch came in large part from Germany. Alongside the indigenous inhabitants of the European bases, the African and Asian contact groups comprised individual trading partners and local potentates. Here and there, Europeans played an important role beyond their settlements as employers meeting the demands of home markets, in textile manufacture in India, and in tea and porcelain in China. Even so, direct contacts in this context would have been very limited.

Everywhere, there were Catholic or Protestant congregations with their respective officeholders. Latin America boasted an extensive Catholic hierarchy that was linked with the ruling class. Missionaries who were there for the sole purpose of converting the indigenous peoples were a rarity among the Protestants, whereas the Iberian monarchies dispatched Catholic missionaries in large numbers and in part financed them also. In contrast to the normal clergy, the missionaries were exclusively members of religious orders: Franciscans, Dominicans, Augustinians, and Jesuits. Where activities were conducted in areas controlled by the colonial powers, they were highly successful: notably in Latin America, the Philippines, on Sri Lanka, and in the hinterland of Portuguese settlements. Yet whenever they encroached on native empires, the number of converts either remained extremely limited, as in large parts of India and China, or the church experienced a brief period of success and growth before being persecuted, as in Japan.

Conversion was tantamount to renouncing one's own civilization and adopting European culture. This form of transculturation seemed sensible only when the soft power of the Christian Gospel went hand in hand with the hard power of colonial rule. Yet it was deeply problematic when the hard power in a society was wielded by indigenous authorities, which frequently took a dim view of Christianity. In this context, mention must be made of the attempts of the Jesuits to narrow the cultural gap in Japan, China, and India, through their assimilation of native customs and ideas. Never before had Europeans had such an intensive involvement with alien cultures. In addition, they also instigated an indirect, though thoroughly intensive, cultural contact between the European elite and China, as by way of justifying their cultural concessions, which went particularly far in China, they flooded Europe with more or less idealized information on this country.[69]

What was enacted with meticulous planning and on a limited scale in the case of the Jesuits was also repeated elsewhere, either on a grand, organized scale or through individual initiative and either spontaneously or geared to specific opportunities, namely, the transition from one culture and religion to another. The slave troops of the Ottomans and the Safavids were recruited from among Christian communities, and many of the great dignitaries of the Ottoman Empires were so-called renegades, to use the disparaging term employed by Christians. According to the trajectory of their own life story, even returning to their original faith was not out of the question, a fluid switching of sides that also occurred between Catholicism and Protestantism in post-Reformation Europe.

Granted, we now know that such a change of culture and religion rarely turned out to be absolutely thoroughgoing, because a person's preexisting beliefs and attitudes can never be completely eradicated. Therefore, a change of identity may come about not just once and in diachronic fashion but also repeatedly and synchronously. Several identities, which can be selected at will, were and are much more self-evident than was once thought to be the case. Even adherence to several religions at the same time is not unheard of, for instance to Catholicism on the one hand and to Indian or African American religions on the other. We repeatedly encounter the figure of the "cultural broker" on the middle ground between empires and cultures with less than rigid claims on a person's allegiance, a figure who either voluntarily or through compulsion is equally at home in both cultures or who at least is conversant with both. The appropriate backgrounds for such a role are highly varied, though mixed-race people are often positively cut out for it.[70] To some extent, the Jesuits in China attempted to assume this role themselves but also took to using more or less prominent converts from among the scholarly echelons for such tasks.[71]

Islam was spread in Africa and Southeast Asia less through deliberate missions or (certainly prior to the eighteenth century) through jihad than through cultural middlemen of this kind, especially itinerant merchants—in other words, through a "diaspora" in two senses. On the one hand, this term still denotes a religious minority in an environment dominated by another faith, but on the other it means another group of people who have left their original home or had to flee from it and have ended up living in alien cultural surroundings. Characteristic of such a group, and also a prerequisite of its success, are good contacts in the location where they are living, but these contacts are also linked to a worldwide network of solidarity with their group. The most well-known diaspora of this kind are the Jews, who in the period treated in this volume were banished from several European countries but who nevertheless, working from the Netherlands, were able to play a major role in trading with the New World. Greek and Armenian traders in the European countries bordering on the Ottoman Empire are a comparable group, as are, above all, the Chinese merchants resident throughout Southeast Asia.

Communication

When "discoverers" first made contact with other cultures, it tended to occur by means of symbolic gestures and actions. But in the long term, the language barrier had to be surmounted. Peoples from the empire-building nations imposed their language, at least as the second language of the elites they had conquered: thus, Han Chinese and Russian became dominant in Asia; Castilian Spanish and Portuguese in America; Arabic and Ottoman Turkish in the Near East and North Africa. As the inviolable language of the Quran, Arabic also had a distinct advantage when competing with others. The Mughals had no single imperial people and hence no one language of empire. Persian served as the language of the court and of culture, which later merged with the dialect of northern India to form Urdu, the tongue of India's Muslims. The language of power is always attractive, even when it does not—as with the Chinese and the ancient Greeks—maintain that the barbarians cannot even speak properly.

However, language as an instrument of power was often undermined by an understandable avoidance of the colonial tongue in everyday communication or even through a deliberate policy of resistance. In America, missionaries insisted on proclaiming the Gospel in the language of the indigenous peoples, even though they then encountered enormous difficulties in the translation of certain key tenets of the Christian faith (as they had done in Chinese, Japanese, and other Asiatic languages)—misunderstandings were almost preprogrammed in such situations. And the Spanish crown, having initially tried to force people to learn the imperial language, Castilian, ended up tolerating Amerindian languages. Their missionaries in the sixteenth and seventeenth centuries compiled almost five hundred dictionaries and grammars of these languages and in the process saved a good number of them from extinction, not least by making many into written languages for the first time. At the same time, missionaries in Asia likewise became pioneers of Japanology, Sinology, and Indology. First and foremost, it was the well-educated Jesuits who found themselves ideally suited to this role. After all, for over a thousand years, people in Western Europe had been obliged to translate not only the basic tenets of their faith but also its literary culture from foreign languages, namely, Latin and Greek. In this way, some Europeans had developed into excellent philologists and so were well equipped to "understand" totally alien languages and cultures. The only other place where such a constellation in the history of ideas can be identified is Japan.[72]

Members of a diaspora such as the Europeans in Asia and Africa were thus dependent on learning the indigenous languages, while the Asians and Africans conversely had little incentive to gain any knowledge of foreign languages. Merchants were scarcely prepared or in the position to expend so much effort on learning languages as missionaries, with the result that any natives who wanted to do business with them had to somehow meet them halfway where language was concerned. Moreover, the sheer plethora of languages that existed in Southeast Asia especially, but also in the Caribbean region, meant that the problem could not be overcome by learning just one language. Accordingly, some easier solutions were put in place for everyday intercourse, in the form of a lingua franca or of languages with simplified grammar and vocabulary, such as creole or pidgin.

A lingua franca is a language that is left unchanged and used as a widespread second language of trade and commerce, such as English in the contemporary world. Creole and pidgin languages, in contrast, came into being through a hybridization of existing languages and extensive simplification. The principal difference between creoles and pidgins is that the former have become mother tongues, whereas the latter only ever occur as second languages. Even so, the boundaries are indistinct, and changes can be instituted at any time. The former widespread disdain for creole and pidgin languages has long since disappeared. After all, English itself came into existence through creolization, whereas the "lingua franca" from which the term itself derives—a Mediterranean trading tongue of the Middle Ages and early modern period—was actually a pidgin based on Latin but enriched with a vocabulary culled largely from Arabic.

Of course, there are also many creole and pidgin languages that are based on African and Asian languages. But the role of Europeans as the instigators of worldwide trade contacts has spawned a particular creativity on the basis of their languages. Accordingly, creoles and pidgins from Portuguese developed in South and Southeast Asia, which were then picked up by later waves of Europeans to the region and traces of which still survive today. In America, by contrast, slaves developed their creole tongues from the languages of their masters and a mixture of African dialects.[73]

In many cases, even before they made the effort to speak to the natives, foreign interlopers had often had sex with indigenous women. The converse situation was extremely rare, because the first contact groups almost always consisted exclusively of men. Yet sexuality is communication with cultural consequences, namely, the tacit adoption of everyday customs of another culture and the production of offspring that by its very origin is inclined to have an intercultural outlook.

Interaction

Naturally, not just sexuality but also every mode of communication is an interaction. Yet interaction consists primarily of the more exaggerated forms of human activity, namely, the use of force, especially in war, but also the transfer of all manner of cultural goods, principally of material goods by means of trade. Warlike empire building of the kind we have discussed and global, mainly mercantile maritime interaction conducted by Western Europeans were the abiding themes of our period.

As far as the goods that were traded are concerned, the European demand in America may be said to have been innovative, whereas in Asia it merely followed supply, at least initially. Silver, gold, and diamonds were sourced from Latin America, while for a short while, but with far-reaching consequences for the region, beaver pelts were exported from North America, and plantation America centered around Caribbean-supplied, high-value agricultural produce like sugar and tobacco. Africa, too, was a source of gold at the beginning, until around 1700, when the demand for slaves for export to the Americas took precedence. In Asia, however, the first concern of traders was to grab as large a share as possible of the traditional supply of spices (pepper, cinnamon, nutmeg, and cloves), and thereafter interest turned to the silks available, particularly from the Far East and the cotton textiles of India. Alongside these commodities, luxury items like Indian precious stones, Chinese porcelain, and Japanese lacquerware played a minor role, until coffee and tea also became fashionable in Europe and generated a correspondingly massive demand. For its part, Europe supplied metal goods, textiles, and other finished goods as well as wine and spirits to America and Africa, muskets to Africa, and Indian textiles to the plantations of America. By contrast, the quantity of European goods sold in Asia left a lot to be desired, and, as a consequence, American silver kept flowing there by various routes in a one-way stream. However, Europeans became heavily involved additionally in trading within Asia (country trade) with a diversity of goods and in so doing earned part of the money that was needed to pay for the imports to Europe.

But from early on, beneath the surface of this system of global trade, a massive biological transfer was also taking place in various directions, involving commercial crops and livestock, which were the products of particular cultures. Yet the biological exchange between Asia, Africa, and Europe seems largely to have come to an end in the thirteenth century.[74] By contrast, America was only just about to become the recipient of hitherto unknown microbes—such as the germ cells of diseases like smallpox, flu, measles, whooping cough, and other ailments from Europe and malaria and yellow fever from Africa—with devastating results. In addition, all manner of weeds were introduced to the New World from or via Europe, but also wheat, barley, oats, rye, citrus fruits, bananas, and sugarcane, while from Africa there came millet, yams, okra (ladies' fingers), and watermelons. Yet with its one hundred or so cultivated crops, America had far more to offer in return, including some plants that would presently take on global significance: potatoes, corn (maize), manioc, sweet potatoes, tomatoes, and various kinds of beans and squashes, pineapple, groundnuts, cocoa, and tobacco. Manioc (cassava) and maize play a key role in providing staple nutrition for Africa, as do potatoes for Europe and Russia. However, livestock were virtually unknown in the Americas; accordingly, it was soon to receive, imported from Europe, the whole gamut of domestic livestock, along with several species of wild animals.[75]

Whereas elsewhere the increasing global cultural contacts produced rather limited and subtle outcomes, such as the fashion for chinoiserie inspired by the Jesuits, European culture in its entirety was foisted on the New World. Regardless of the development that has taken place since, the languages that are spoken there and all the older buildings there point to the English, French, Portuguese, and Spanish origins of the modern Americas. Yet it should not be forgotten, first, that indigenous cultures are still alive alongside and among settler civilization and, second, that Afro-Americans have developed their own cultures, albeit in both cases with uneven regional distribution.

Underworlds and Worlds of the Divine
Underworlds

The "worlds" outlined in this volume also include "underworlds," which are seldom spoken about. For empire building and maritime interaction are based on the misery of untold numbers of ordinary people. Yet as is often the case in history, victims can become perpetrators in the twinkling of an eye, offer individual or collective resistance, or metamorphose into criminals, even if they do not already hail from such a background. Information on this aspect of history is only patchy, however. For instance, we know a great deal about the persecution of the Jews in Europe and the so-called outcasts of early modern Europe and probably also about the Indian untouchables but hardly anything about the *Burakumin* of Japan or the Chinese *Jiamin*. The Atlantic slave trade and African slavery in the plantations of America have been the subject of excellent research, but far less is known about slavery within Africa and Asia and the part Europeans played in it or about slavery in the Islamic world. Furthermore, it is easier to find out information about male victims than about female victims.

The wars of empire building involved not only mass rapes, torture, and plundering but also massacres on a grand scale. Tamerlane was notorious for the bloodbaths accompanying his wars of conquest, which he perpetrated in the Mongol tradition, and the pyramids of skulls of his victims that he ordered piled up. There was reputed to have been a pile of seventy thousand skulls after the rebellious city of Isfahan fell.[76] But the great Mughal emperor Akbar, to whom history has been kinder, also had thirty thousand people butchered after the city of Chitor was overrun.[77] Under the Dutch "empire builder" Jan Pieterszoon Coen, fifteen thousand rebellious Banda Islanders were massacred, whereas Oliver Cromwell managed to dispatch only some two to three thousand citizens of the town of Drogheda—Irish cities were smaller than those in Asia.[78]

Aristocratic cavalry units and princely regular soldiers in Asia and Africa probably had few grounds for complaint, but not so the mercenaries and common sailors exploited by the European powers. Recruited from the ranks of the lower classes through the press-gang or by underhand trickery, they were given to deserting and to excesses of every kind. Accordingly, they were subjected to a merciless regime of harsh discipline. The Dutch East India Company recruited its troops in part from the orphanages of the Netherlands. Insofar as the children whom these soldiers had with female slaves or other women in Asia were not aborted and survived their childhood in the Company's poorhouses and orphanages, the boys in turn could be recruited themselves for the military, whereas the girls had to become brides, to make up for the notorious lack of women in the colonies.[79] As well as allowing informal relationships with indigenous women, several of the European powers were keen to make up this shortfall by transporting orphaned girls from the mother country—it is open to question how many of these came to the colonies voluntarily to try their luck there.

The cramped conditions on board the ship made the common sailor's existence even more unappealing than that of the soldier. It was said of slave ships that "In the presence of sailors, [even] the Negro feels himself a human being."[80] Early on, the galley rowers of the Mediterranean, whether slaves or convicts, conscripted men or volunteers, were not only subjected to harsh discipline but also scarcely had any freedom to move. Among other things, they were expected to relieve themselves at their posts, with the feces and urine cleared away only occasionally.[81] Diseases plagued the men constantly on the long voyages to Asia, which could last months. In 1640, of the three hundred sailors on board a Dutch vessel, eighty died on the voyage, with scurvy causing their teeth to fall out and their gums to decay;

others suffered so grievously that they had to be lashed to their bunks. Although the VOC at least paid some attention to proper nourishment and accommodation and humane treatment on board its vessels, corrupt shipowners and unfavorable circumstances often combined to negate this. Ultimately, because of a lack of experienced European sailors, crews had to be supplemented with slaves and with Indians, Chinese, Balinese, and Javanese recruits. But the upshot of this was that the dangers of mutiny increased. In 1783, twenty Indonesian slaves were thrown overboard from a Dutch ship sailing between Batavia and the Cape of Good Hope because they were suspected of plotting a mutiny. On another ship, five Europeans were killed when the crew mutinied, whereupon the fifteen Chinese out of a crew of 143 were found guilty and made to walk the plank.[82] For European seamen, a mutiny in Asian waters was too risky; generally they were prepared to undertake such an act only as the ship was nearing home. Tellingly, for instance, in 1701, the cook of a Dutch ship was severely beaten up by the crew while they were still on board, whereas they waited until the ship had landed to dish out the same treatment to the skipper.[83]

Occasionally a mutinous crew would even take over the ship. The next step was to throw their lot in with pirates; piracy made the Caribbean and the Indian Ocean unsafe places in the seventeenth century especially. Once again, victims turned into perpetrators; in stark contrast to the romanticism of many pirate films, this maritime underworld was not only renowned for practiced elementary democracy but also for countless brutal crimes perpetrated by the corsairs.[84]

On land, a comparable transgression was when discharged or deserting soldiers took to a life of banditry; here, too, the fictional portrayal of these men veers between being characterized as rebels against society or as evil criminals. This problem was by no means confined to border zones, even though such regions provided favorable conditions. In any event, though, the leaders of such bands of brigands could become ruling lords; the difference between their career and the rise of Tamerlane and the Timurid Babur appears to be one only of magnitude.

Even the African slaves dispatched to the Americas not only reacted to their fate with frequent uprisings, but also, in cases where slaves managed to escape, as so-called cimarrones or maroons they repeatedly founded more or less well-organized polities (*quilombos*) in the wild. On occasion, they would make common cause against the whites with Amerindians. The maroon city of Palmares in northern Brazil existed from 1600 to 1695 and at its height had up to thirty thousand inhabitants.[85] As well as skirmishes with the colonial masters, there were also peace agreements, albeit sometimes at the cost of having to return newly escaped slaves and even agree to provide paramilitary aid in the event of any new rebellions breaking out among them.

Peasants, too, the world over from China to France repeatedly reacted to various hardships by staging rebellions. As the heavily exploited source of the most crucial economic resources, they formed the most significant underworld in all empires and were by no means content to always behave as a compliant silent majority. This role, rather, was fulfilled by women; they can be said to have been the exploited underworld that is common to most other underworlds.

Worlds of the Divine

Modern secular historiography is prone to overlooking the fact that the histories of premodern people, such as we are dealing with in this volume, are invariably the histories "of gods and men." Each of the worlds under discussion here also had its "world of the divine"—one or several, often competing with one another, as in the West between Catholicism and various forms of Protestantism, in the Muslim world between various strains of Sunni and Shiʿite Islam, in India between the devotees of Shiva and Vishnu (to name but two of the Hindu gods), in China among Confucians, Buddhists, Taoists, and adherents of animistic religions, and so forth.

Above all, our history must also be recounted as the dual history of the "conquering God."[86] For over these four hundred years between 1350 and 1750, Allah and Deus (as the Christian God was called by his missionaries in Japan and elsewhere) saw an exponential increase in the numbers of their followers and came considerably closer to spiritual dominion over the world. Christianity took control of the whole of the New World, as well as isolated regions of Africa and Asia, such as Siberia, the Philippines, and the Kingdom of Kongo, together with scattered minorities of believers in other parts of these continents. Islam brought Southeastern Europe and the Sudan under its sway, gained the upper hand in India, and gradually converted the majority of Indonesia. In the process, force was used by the adherents of both conquering religions, probably more so in the case of the Christians than by Muslims. But it was in the course of Ottoman expansion that violence became, on a scale unheard of since the Crusades, a mode of communication between Christianity and Islam, with consequences that resonate to the present day.

Of course, the devotees of other gods were not necessarily politically any more peaceable. Certainly, massive persecutions of Christians took place in the Far East, and Japan also witnessed the violent suppression of certain Buddhist sects. However, the difference was that, both there and in the non-Islamic parts of India and Africa, there was no concept of the "conquering God" but instead some religious conceptions of a quite different nature, which also filtered through to Europe as a result of its infatuation with all things Indian and Chinese in the eighteenth century and made their influence felt there.

First, there was the "atheistic religion" of Asia—a contradiction in terms only for Western conceptions of religion—which was expressly formulated above all by certain forms of Buddhism. According to this, the world follows its own impersonal forces and laws, with whose effects the enlightened person consciously falls into line, for unlike in Christianity, he or she can claim no privileged position in the universe.

Second (and not without strong intellectual affinities to the foregoing), there was the strain of religious inclusiveness, characteristic first and foremost of India, which interpreted the incarnation of God in Jesus Christ—the central tenet of Christianity—simply as yet one further incarnation of its own principal deities and hence had no problem in incorporating Christians into Hinduism. In contrast to this, Christianity and Islam had always conceived of themselves as exclusive denominations, which originally condemned the adherents of all other faiths to hell.

But in addition, and apparently through its own efforts—thanks to the combination of ancient and Christian impulses—the West found its way to the enlightened ideas of religious freedom of expression and tolerance. This stance was justified in four ways. Either atheism maintains all religions are equally untrue, or, following Indian inclusiveness, they are all equally true, or humans are incapable of determining the truth, or the commandment to love one's neighbor takes precedence over the compulsion to ascertain the truth.

Alongside this comes an empirical experience that horrified many missionaries from this period, but which in the interim has been explained and legitimized as perfectly normal, namely, the survival of old religions in new ones, as observed particularly (though not exclusively) in the syncretic Christian practices of Latin America or in some varieties of Sudanese Islam. The ultimate expressions of this are the interchangeable practices of various religions and the adoption by a person of multiple religious identities. It was from such sources, which gradually appeared in the period from 1350 to 1750, that the worldview of our current global age ultimately took on its modern pluralistic complexion.

Translated from the German by Peter Lewis

·[ONE]·

Empires and Frontiers in Continental Eurasia

Peter C. Perdue

Introduction

THE VAST and diverse region covered by this chapter, which we may call Central and Eastern Eurasia, extended from European Russia in the west to China and Japan in the east, from the forests of Siberia in the north to the subtropical agriculture of South China and Vietnam in the south. It included 27 percent of the Earth's inhabitable surface and 30 to 40 percent of the global population from 1500 to 1800. The two great empires of China, the Ming (1368–1644) and Qing (1636–1911), dominated by virtue of their huge populations, but the geopolitical impact and world historical significance of Russia and Japan were especially important. Central Eurasians, led by Mongols and Turkic Muslims, attempted to carve out autonomous areas in the wake of the collapse of the empires of Chinggis Khan and Timur, but ultimately they all succumbed to encroachment and conquest by Russia and China. Korea and Vietnam, two polities highly influenced by the Chinese bureaucratic tradition, tenaciously asserted their independence against invasions from Japan and China, while also declaring themselves loyal tributaries of the Chinese dynastic regimes.

Certain processes that affected the entire region justify treating it as a single unit. These include common climatic conditions, linked geographies and modes of agrarian and commercial production, and shared practices of social interaction and family life. Two of the most prominent general trends were the expansion of empires and the consolidation of independent states, accompanied by the elimination of borderland zones where people fled or resisted the state, and the concomitant extension of commercial networks into both core and frontier regions, linking the entire region to global trade fueled by the flows of silver originating in the New World.

The period 1350–1750 fits roughly with the essential turning points in the region. No division of time, of course, ever exactly corresponds to the crucial junctures of historical change, and historians constantly debate the significance of critical dates and events. Furthermore, long-term social and economic processes do not change radically in a single year. These limitations apply to states and empires but even more to the scale of world history, where different regions and societies often develop at very different paces. Nevertheless, the time period encompasses a significant period of change.

Historians have generally not discussed this region as a whole. Instead, they have focused on units determined by the boundaries of modern nation-states of the nineteenth and twentieth centuries. We have many separate histories of China, Russia, and Japan, several histories of Korea and Vietnam, and almost none of Central Eurasia in this period, but few of them try to tell a connected history of the region.[1] Several recent studies, however, do provide important conceptual tools for describing changes on this broader scale. Victor Lieberman's powerful synthesis, *Strange Parallels,* in two volumes, argues for common trends toward commercial, political, and cultural integration across many states of Eurasia from 1000 to 1800, driven by administrative centralization of states in Southeast Asia, Western Europe, Japan, Russia, and China. John Richards has described the elimination of the frontier by the combined forces of agrarian settlement, state control, and commercial penetration in his global history entitled *The Unending Frontier.* In *After Tamerlane,* John Darwin has examined the formation and competition of imperial structures from 1400 to 2000, focusing on imperial geopolitics of Eurasia as the fundamental shaping force of the modern world. My study of Qing expansion on a somewhat smaller scale examines how the expansion of the Qing dynasty interacted with the expansion of Russia and the rise and fall of Mongolian state builders. This chapter draws on these works to sketch general themes that characterize much of the important political and social change of the period.[2]

We begin with China, today still the dominant society of the region because of its size, its large population, and the highly centralized bureaucratic regimes created by the Ming and Qing rulers. We then turn to Russia, examining the formation of the Muscovite state in the wake of the Mongol Empire and its expansion into Siberia from the sixteenth to eighteenth centuries. Russian expansion to the east added a new power to the Asian environment, at the same time as Russia also became a great power playing the European political game. Russia's dual personality, Asian and European, heavily defined the course of its history during this period, until Peter the Great radically reoriented the state toward Western Europe. Central Eurasia, lying in between China and Russia, was a much more fragmented region, heavily influenced by Chinese policy and by Islamic movements, but an autonomous and distinct society in its own right. Japan, a group of islands lying one hundred miles off the eastern shore of China, for a long period struggled with its own internal divisions but by the sixteenth century had entered a period of intensive engagement both with the maritime European powers and on the continent through intervention in Korea, repulsed by China. Even under the Tokugawa regime (1603–1867), Japan was not a truly isolated country: it responded to Chinese developments and kept close track of Asian trading and political worlds, while enforcing limited external trade. Korea and Vietnam shared intermediate positions between the Chinese and non-Chinese worlds, showing interesting parallels between their attitudes toward their great neighbor and other engagements with the world beyond China. Unlike the peoples of Central Eurasia, the Koreans and Vietnamese were not squeezed out by the expanding imperial powers around them. They survived in part because they rapidly adapted Chinese bureaucratic forms to local circumstances. The chapter concludes with reflections on common trends and linked developments among these societies.

1. China

CHINGGIS Khan's Mongol empire (1206–1294) had briefly united almost the entire Eurasian continent under a single regime, but it soon broke apart into four giant khanates: the Yuan dynasty of China (1279–1368); the Kipchak khanate, or "Golden Horde," including Russia, Ukraine, and Kazakhstan (1227–1502); the Chaghatai khanate of Central Asia (1227–1370); and the Il-Khanate of Persia (1256–1335). Timur, or Tamerlane (r. 1370–1405), a conqueror from the Chaghatai khanate, repeated some of the amazing conquests of the Mongol warriors in an attempt to restore the empire. He conquered Transoxania, Iraq, and Iran and campaigned against the Golden Horde and the Ottoman Empire. He defeated the Ottoman sultan in 1402, plundered Delhi, and assembled two hundred thousand men for an invasion of China before his death, but his empire fell apart immediately. After Timur, Eurasia remained partitioned into separate empires and states, but these states continued linkages that the Mongols had fostered. We can even recognize the origins of many of the features of our modern globalized world in the relations between empires across Eurasia from the fifteenth century forward.[3] Slowly, with many ups and downs, global markets, geopolitical interactions, migrations, and cultural transmissions among these regions strengthened, laying the foundations for much more intensive interactions on a wider scale in the later centuries.

But the immediate aftermath of Timur's failure was a reversion to closure, especially in China. The Ming dynasty, founded in 1368 by peasant rebels led by Zhu Yuanzhang, a former Buddhist monk, had driven out the last Mongol ruler and established a dynasty ruled by Han Chinese military men from agrarian regions of the south. They had no connections with Central Eurasia, and they were deeply suspicious of mobile merchants, mobile peasantries, and foreign ideologies. During the fifteenth century, Ming rulers, after sporadic attempts at expansion, withdrew from intervention in the steppe and consolidated control over the Han core. Yet the Yuan ideal of a universal empire encompassing many different peoples over a vast Eurasian space never entirely disappeared. In the guise of "tribute,"

Ming rulers attempted to influence polities beyond their own control by using trade and cultural links to draw in other peoples to the emperor's presence. On the northwest frontier, the Ming embraced a defensive policy against the Mongols, but on its southwest frontier, it advanced aggressively against confederations of peoples in the jungles and hills of Guizhou. Although the Ming did not practice the ambitious conquests and pretentious cosmopolitanism of its predecessor the Yuan and its successor the Qing, it was not a completely isolated regime, and its inhabitants were well aware of selected developments in the world beyond China.

The Ming Dynasty (1368–1644)

By 1350, the administration of the Yuan dynasty, the Chinese branch of Chinggis Khan's empire, had decayed into economic ruin, corruption, and natural disaster. Repeated flooding of the Yellow River, yearly famines, and economic disruption stimulated rebellions by peasants all over the country. Millenarian Buddhist teachings inspired them to believe that a new Buddha of the Future would arrive to begin a new age of light. Zhu Yuanzhang (1328–1398), the founder of the Ming dynasty, came from a poor family in south China and spent some time at a Buddhist monastery. As a mendicant monk, he learned about the new doctrines that preached the reincarnation of the Maitreya Buddha and the imminent arrival of a Radiant Prince (Mingwang) who would rescue the people.[4] In 1352, he joined a military uprising, which grew to be the largest army in the country. In 1359, he occupied the city now known as Nanjing, which he made his main capital, and in 1368 he drove the last Yuan emperor out of Beijing, proclaiming himself emperor of a new dynasty, the Ming. Because "ming" means "bright," and because, like Yuan, it is a dynastic name with a symbolic meaning, many historians suspect that this invocation of light refers to Zhu Yuanzhang's early origins as a Buddhist monk who had been influenced by imagery of light and darkness derived from Central Asian Manichaeanism. But Zhu, who renamed himself Ming Taizu, made strenuous efforts to erase evidence of his humble origins, so there are few available sources to prove this hypothesis.

The Ming was the first dynasty in thirteen hundred years, since the second Han dynasty (AD 25–220), to conquer the entire core of China with purely Han Chinese peasant armies. Other dynasties, like the Tang and Yuan, relied heavily on Central Asian military forces, and the Song dynasties, whose armies were primarily Han soldiers, failed to conquer all of the core of modern China, including Beijing. The ruling class of the Ming was less diverse in both ethnic and class composition than the preceding dynasties. The Yuan rulers had welcomed merchants, foreigners, and practitioners of many religions into the ruling elite, while reducing the power of the Confucian literati. Ming rulers, by contrast, elevated the literati and excluded foreigners and Buddhists. Even though the Ming founder was quite suspicious of scholars, he and his successors had to recognize that they were a necessary element for civil administration.

Zhu Yuanzhang, like other dynastic founders, focused on the restoration of the agrarian economy as his primary task, but he went much farther than other rulers.[5] He made huge investments in dikes, canals, and new land clearance, creating thousands of reservoirs and planting millions of trees across the empire. He conducted a very intensive survey of lands and population, revealing a registered population of sixty million. Even if much of the population in frontier areas was still unregistered, this was a substantial drop from the maximum Song dynasty population of about a hundred million people. Most of the losses came among the rural population, devastated by plagues, famines, warfare, and excess taxes. The Yuan rulers had put much greater stress on commerce, favoring Central Eurasian merchants engaged in long-distance trade, but they greatly neglected agriculture. The new emperor was determined to create a healthy agrarian structure and to reduce as much as possible what he considered to be the damaging effects of commerce and rich landlord power. He aimed to set up rural schools all over the country, while he tried to break the power of the wealthy landlords of the lower Yangzi valley with heavy taxes. At the same time, he invested enormous resources in his capital at Nanjing, surrounding it with a wall twenty-four miles long, the longest in the empire.

Yet his attempt to force China back to a self-sufficient agrarian economy ultimately failed. Even the powerful bureaucracy and military that he ruled could not dictate the decisions of millions of producers, consumers, and merchants. He tried to impose a paper currency based solely on government command, but this policy did not make his currency into a valid means of exchange. In addition, he never totally drove out Mongol influence. Mongols who surrendered to his armies were left in peace to settle along the northwest borders.[6] The structure of the Ming military in fact followed many Yuan models.

Yongle's Expansion

The reign of the weak emperor who succeeded Ming Taizu lasted only three years. His vigorous uncle, the prince of Yan, staged a coup against him and established himself as the Yongle emperor, ruling from 1403 to 1424.[7] Yongle revived the Yuan ambition of establishing a universal empire that would exert influence throughout all Eurasia. He promoted rapid expansion in both continental and maritime directions. As a prince who had accumulated extensive landholdings in north China, he knew well the threats from the frontier, and unlike the southern rebels who founded the Ming, he enjoyed traveling in the northwest. He wrote a travel account describing in detail the rugged landscape he had seen. He personally led five campaigns against the Mongols and died in the middle of the last one. With his aggressive frontier policy, he aimed to restore Chinese control over Mongolia, but his successors took a more defensive stance.

Yongle's most famous expeditions, however, were those that he sent into Southeast Asia. A great fleet, led by the Muslim admiral Zheng He (1371–1435),[8] entered the Indian Ocean seven times from 1405 to 1433. Leaving from Nanjing and stopping at the southeastern coastal port of Quanzhou, the ships visited the Malay Archipelago, Java, and Siam, stopping at the ports of Surabaya, Malacca, and Palembang. They then proceeded to India, including the Bengal delta and the southern port of Calicut, from which they went up the Gulf of Hormuz, around the Arabian Peninsula to Medina and Mecca, and down the east African coast to Mogadishu. There were no technological limits to prevent the fleets from rounding Africa and proceeding across the Atlantic Ocean, but they stopped on the African coast when there was no evidence of profitable trade. Zheng He exchanged gifts of gold, silver, porcelain, and silk for exotic tropical products like ostriches, zebras, camels, ivory, and giraffes. One voyage brought sixty-two colossal ships, carrying 2,500 tons of cargo and 37,000 men.[9] These fleets, with their thousands of soldiers, valuable trade goods, and official representatives, showed that China could dominate the southern seas, by suppressing pirates, waging war, deposing local rulers, and confirming important alliances.

What were the goals of these great expeditions? The great historian of Chinese science, Joseph Needham, described them as "peaceful maritime expeditions" for scientific discovery.[10] Although they did bring back valuable information and products from the tropical regions, they also aimed at profits from trade, disguised as "gifts." But the first goal was geopolitical: to stake out a sphere of influence in the South Seas using both "hard" and "soft" power. Unlike the Mongols, who had failed in direct attempts at conquest of Vietnam and Java, Yongle aimed to extend power over the region by demonstrating China's military, economic, and cultural dominance.

Yongle had attempted unprecedented campaigns of expansion by a Han emperor in both the northwest and southern seas, but he was well aware of the primary importance of the northwestern border. He moved the capital of the dynasty to Beijing in 1421, leaving Nanjing as a secondary capital, in order to place the central officials and military forces closer to the threatening Mongols of the frontier.[11] Shortly after the emperor's death, further reaction against activities in the maritime region set in. The voyages were canceled, the ships destroyed or allowed to rot, and much of the valuable information gathered by them was lost. Rational strategic decisions, not simple prejudice against trade, supported the termination of commercial expeditions. Court officials argued that the Mongols were much more dangerous than the small states of Southeast Asia. Disappointing profits from Southeast Asian trade and the uncertain loyalties of local rulers supported a shift of limited imperial resources toward the land frontier. Critics of the overseas expeditions also displayed a strain of nativist agrarianism. The critics argued that the welfare of the local Chinese peasantry deserved primary attention and that the emperor should not waste the people's wealth in distant campaigns in remote territories. But even after the imperial naval forces withdrew, private Chinese traders continued to pursue profitable opportunities in the waters of Southeast Asia and the Indian Ocean.

Yongle also sponsored a great invasion of the state of Dai Viet, in northern Vietnam. In 1407, he sent an army to occupy Hanoi, supporting a usurper of the Vietnamese throne.[12] The occupation forces suppressed Vietnamese resistance and attempted to impose Chinese customs, returning Vietnam to the period five hundred years earlier when it was a part of the Chinese empire. But the guerrilla commander Le Loi (1385–1433), a frontier hill chieftain of non-Vietnamese origin, led a mass uprising that threw off Chinese rule in 1428, ultimately establishing a new dynasty that lasted until the nineteenth century. Chinese forces did not cross the Vietnamese border again until 1788.

Although maritime expansion ceased after Yongle's death, the dream of repelling the Mongols never faded. In 1449, a new young emperor rashly marched out at the head of his troops into the steppe. His eunuch advisers deluded him into thinking that he could win a great victory. Ignoring reports of danger, he headed straight into an ambush and was captured by the Mongol Khan. Court life, however, went on as usual back in Beijing. The emperor's brother replaced him on the throne. When the khan finally sent the useless emperor back, he was placed under house arrest.[13]

Scholars repeatedly advanced ambitious proposals for extended military campaigns to drive the Mongols out of the Chinese heartland, but others noted that the expense would be too great and the goals unattainable. Ming expansion, however, did not end with the debacle in the northwest. In Southwest China, military forces first conquered Yunnan, stationing ninety thousand soldiers in nine major guard posts.[14] They pushed relentlessly into the mountainous, poor region of Guizhou, where travelers said there were never three days without rain, three feet of flat land, or three coins in anyone's hand.[15] The Yuan had established a superficial civil administration in the thirteenth century, designating the powerful local rulers as autonomous "native chieftains," but Ming rulers were determined to make it an integral part of the empire. They moved 250,000 soldiers and one million civilian Han settlers to the southwest, extending military garrisons, postal relay stations, and state farms. They named Guizhou a province in 1413 and relied on Guizhou troops to support their invasion of Vietnam. Even so, the early Ming rulers controlled only the eastern third of the province, leaving the rest as a patchwork quilt of different political structures. The Nasu Yi, a warlike group of Tibeto-Burman people, constantly fought the Ming to preserve their autonomy.

Expansion continued without interruption after 1449, as generals put down native revolts, bringing more troops, more Han immigrants, and clearing more land. The promise of riches from minerals like cinnabar attracted miners, merchants, and grasping officials, as the Nasu Yi now controlled some of the wealthiest regions of the province. But the native officials remained separate from Ming administration. The Ming had no civilizing mission here. It built few schools and prohibited non-Han from taking civil exams. Modernizing leaders of the Nasu Yi adopted Han agricultural craft techniques to develop their local economy, shifting from swidden to settled agriculture and using cattle as farm animals instead of as symbols of wealth. In 1592, they built a major bridge and erected a stela affirming the proud history of the Nasu Yi. These self-strengthening efforts strikingly paralleled efforts of Mongol state builders in the northwest. But the relentless push for profit by Ming officials drove the Nasu Yi into rebellion repeatedly, leading to further military intervention and slaughter. Ming China had, for a time, stabilized its northwestern frontier with a large defensive barrier, but it continued to push outward in the southwest during its entire existence.

Structures of the Ming State

The territory of the Ming dynasty, nearly four million square kilometers, corresponded closely to what we now call China proper, or the "Inner Territories" *(neidi)*, occupied almost exclusively by ethnically Han Chinese.[16] Unlike the Yuan or Qing dynasties, the Ming never controlled the nomadic pastoral regions, but it was by far the largest political unit on the planet in 1500. Its huge population grew from more than sixty million in the early fifteenth century up to at least 150 million people at its peak in the sixteenth century.

Eight large macroregions, defined by mountains and the watersheds of major rivers, formed the economic geography of the empire.[17] Two of these, the core regions of Jiangnan (the lower Yangzi River valley) and North China, each contained an imperial capital. These two capital regions accumulated the most wealth and political power. The first emperor founded his new capital in Nanjing (meaning "Southern Capital") in Jiangnan, near his hometown, while the Yongle emperor founded the dynasty's second capital in Beijing (meaning "Northern Capital"). Although the dynasty continued to have two capitals, Beijing rose to become the primary political center.

In Jiangnan, Nanjing and other nearby large cities, like Suzhou, Yangzhou, and Hangzhou, with their hinterlands, provided most of the agrarian and commercial wealth of the empire. The surplus production of rice paddy fields could support farming households, urban populations, officials, and soldiers at a reasonably comfortable standard of living. North China, an area lacking irrigation, grew mainly millet, wheat, and sorghum. These crops were strong enough to grow in dry soils that received rainfall only for a few months of the year, and they were productive enough to support a large agricultural population. The farmers of north China, however, also had to pay taxes and provide labor services for the imperial administration, and they suffered from frequent droughts and floods.

Other macroregions were more sparsely populated and less central. Northwest China relied on the same crops as North China, but it was even poorer and more arid. The middle and upper basins of the Yangzi River held much sparser populations living along banks of the tributaries, while non-Han populations occupied the hills. Further south, around the delta of the Pearl River, the subtropical climate allowed a dense lowland population to produce several crops per year, but malaria and uninhabitable marshlands limited their development. Chinese farmers occupied small pieces of land along the southeast coast and cleared small fields in the remote hill country, but many others headed out to sea to settle Southeast Asia, while keeping contact with their homelands. The eighth region, the plateau of Guizhou and Yunnan, mainly a non-Han hill population, did not come under complete Ming control until the late sixteenth century, and only after a series of bloody campaigns.

The Ming rulers, following the Yuan model, divided the empire into fifteen provinces, each ruled by a provincial governor. Below the provinces were about 150 prefectures, and under the prefectures were about fifteen hundred counties or districts, each under a district magistrate. China had the oldest bureaucracy in the world, but the entire salaried officialdom numbered at its maximum only twenty-four thousand, including capital and military officials. It was a very small number for such a large population. The rulers limited the size of the bureaucracy in order to avoid the need to increase tax burdens and to limit its independence from the center.

The military was initially rather small, numbering only about one million, rising to four million in the late Ming. The military had a separate structure from the civil administration, but the provincial governors controlled both military and civil officials. A small percentage of the population belonged to hereditary military households. Their male members owed lifetime military service, and they spent their lives in far-flung garrisons on defensive duty or in military campaigns on the edges of the empire. They also acted as local police, putting down uprisings and pursuing bandits.

At the center, the emperors surrounded themselves with a dependent class of servitors, many of whom were eunuchs. In addition, members of the imperial clan grew to become a large group dependent on stipends from the state. The tension between this "inner court" of imperial dependents and the "outer court" of bureaucratic officials marked much of the politics of the Ming and Qing empires. The Censorate, a special institution of the Chinese bureaucracy, provided one means of checking abuses by other ministers and court favorites, but censors themselves could instigate factional disputes driven by personal interests.[18]

Achieving a position in the bureaucracy required candidates to gain top marks in a grueling series of examinations. These examinations enforced the principle of meritocratic selection of the elite.[19] There were three basic levels of examinations, from the district to provincial to metropolitan. Every year, hundreds of thousands of aspiring students took the lowest-level examinations to qualify for the provincial examinations. One could also purchase the lowest-level degree. About four thousand scholars in each province then competed for twenty-five to fifty degrees every three years. Attaining this rank gave one considerable local status but did not qualify the degree holder for a post. Only the several hundred top degree holders, who passed the metropolitan examination in Beijing, had any chance of getting an official position. The vast majority of degree holders never held any official posts, but they could keep taking examinations for decades in the hopes of attaining higher degrees. In principle, the examinations were open to any male adult regardless of family connections or wealth. In practice, because there was no national education system, only wealthy families could afford to hire the tutors who taught the basic learning of the Chinese classics. Yet some promising young men received fellowships from their lineages and wealthy patrons to support their studies. The examination system did not completely remove the advantages of wealth for social mobility, but it did undermine the local power of hereditary aristocratic families.

The examination system had been the predominant method of selecting officials since the tenth century; the Yuan abolished it but later restored it. Although wealthy families still had some advantages, the Ming had removed the hereditary privileges that dominated the Song system, making it more meritocratic. By late Ming times, attaining an official post was no guarantee of passing it on to the next generation. The combination of high competition, the potential to rise from poverty to a high official post, partial subsidies from relatives, and the prestige of scholarship made the imperial examination system an extremely effective tool of imperial integration.

Even those degree holders without official posts retained considerable prestige in their local communities. The district magistrate, who stayed in one post for about three to five years, was the only salaried official in charge of over three hundred thousand people. He could not rule effectively without the assistance of these local notables. The duties of these notables, acting as local gentry, resembled that of local elites in England, although they did not formally judge legal cases or ride horses around their estates. Some of the gentry were scholars studying for higher-level degrees; some were merchants who had purchased lower-level degrees; some were retired officials returning home or officials on leave to conduct mourning rituals for their families. All of them shared a common interest with the state in maintaining a social order that preserved their positions. They would help the official track down thieves, bandits, or peasants who resisted tax and rent payments; they might help prosecute heterodox religious believers or drive out foreign intruders; they would also contribute to charities and famine relief campaigns. Conversely, they also had private interests to protect. They concealed much of their landholding from the state, dodged tax payments and corvée labor services wherever possible, and pursued the interests of their families by currying favor with anyone they knew. The wise local official knew that he should not prosecute members of prominent families of the locality. If he tried to crack down on tax evasion or local abuses of power, the elites could use their contacts with relatives in the capital to have the official impeached. Even the most upright official could do little about the miseries inflicted on commoners by abusive gentry.

Some parts of the empire lay beyond the civil administration. In the southwest, for convenience, the Ming delegated authority to local chieftains of the hill tribes. Most of this poor and remote region had few Han settlers. The local people could settle their disputes according to customary law, and they needed only to provide stipulated amounts of tax and corvée service. On the northwest borders, military garrisons created military farms under their own administrative structure to support themselves while conducting static defense.

Fiscal Structures and Reforms

The first Ming emperor, a peasant warrior from a poor background, distrusted and detested the wealthy elites of Jiangnan. He confiscated much of their property, deported them to Nanjing to build his capital, and imposed extra burdens on the rich production of the lower Yangzi. The fiscal system also reflected his vision of an idealized agrarian economy based on self-sufficient villages.[20] The emperor believed that his static vision echoed the ideals of classical texts. In 1385 he pronounced in his Grand Declaration that his reign had brought back the golden age of the past. The imperial administration relied primarily on a land tax, paid in kind in grain or cloth by peasant farmers. Farmers also owed corvée labor services to build public works or support the military. In principle, every peasant household should hold sufficient land to support itself and pay the exactions required by the state. Tenant farmers and the landless paid no taxes. No one should need to leave his home village; trade was discouraged, and stability had the highest value.

But even the autocratic emperor could not prevent social change. Song and Yuan China had already developed a high degree of commercial activity, encouraging a mobile population to move to large cities. The turmoil of the dynastic transition disrupted trade, but by the sixteenth century many parts of China had once again become a dynamic, mobile, cash-rich society based as much on the pursuit of monetary profit as on stable agriculture.

The fiscal system was not designed for this kind of society. Tax revenues did not go to one central place, and there was no central budget. Instead, particular tax items collected in one locality, paid in small amounts throughout the year, were allocated to individual expenses in other parts of the empire. This fiscal system was a complex structure designed to support at low cost a small bureaucracy ruling a large, static, agrarian population. But as society changed, the structure required drastic reform. From the sixteenth through eighteenth centuries, local officials enacted a series of reforms to meet the demands of a newly commercialized society. They consolidated the local levies, turned grain and corvée levies into cash equivalents, collected them twice a year, and attempted, with mixed success, to uncover concealed landholdings and tax inequalities. The initiative for reform came from the local level, while the central government later approved the changes. From a decentralized, unmonetized, tangled, and unsystematized assortment of separate levies, the tax system gradually turned into a mainly monetized set of regular payments under local official control. This transformation, known as the Single Whip Reform, was one of the few reform efforts in China conducted almost entirely from the bottom up. The Qing dynasty built on the achievements of these Ming officials and systematized collection even further. This undramatic fiscal reform formed the keystone that ensured the survival of the imperial regime until the twentieth century.

Imperial Autocracy?

Since the Song dynasty, civil officials had run the administration based on legal codes and precedent and on philosophical principles derived from Confucian texts. Emperors in principle had complete power over the bureaucracy, but the exercise of power varied greatly depending on the personality of the emperor and his supporters among the officials. In the Song they consulted with a council chaired by a prime minister and often ruled by consensus or passivity. Some powerful prime ministers became the de facto rulers, vigorously pushing through their policies with imperial consent. The first Ming emperor, who rejected this balanced structure, resolved to give commands directly to all of his subordinates. He abolished the prime minister's post and replaced him with a weaker grand secretary.

Some scholars have described the Ming as the most "despotic" dynasty because of this act.[21] But even without a prime minister, the bureaucracy operated much as it did before. Later emperors did not have nearly as much personal dynamism. Most of their actions were controlled by the demands of ritual observance. In the mid-fifteenth century, as we have seen, when Mongols captured the emperor after a bungled expedition, the officials in the capital put a replacement on the throne and carried on business as usual until his return four years later. By the mid-sixteenth century, when the Wanli emperor (r. 1573–1620) had retired to his palace, refusing to appoint officials or put his seal on documents, the grand secretary in effect ran the government.[22] The Ming dynasty lasted for nearly three hundred years not because of autocratic rulership but because of the routine activities of thousands of dedicated civil servants.

Local Government

At the local level, one district magistrate ruled each county, with a small non-official salaried staff.[23] The magistrate had very few coercive resources at his command. He had no regular police force, and he was the sole judicial official. Military forces under the control of provincial officials had only garrisons in some counties in strategic regions. The crucial element in ensuring stability was the local literati, or gentry. Every magistrate relied heavily on them to facilitate his administration. They had some fiscal and legal privileges, such as immunity from corporal punishment and corvée, but in principle they paid taxes like everyone else. They were not a hereditary nobility in the European sense, as they could not formally transmit their elite status to their sons and their descendants had to obtain degrees in order to keep their privileges. And yet the local elites did maintain their power over many generations, and they expanded their authority beyond their formal privileges. Lineages—families sharing a common surname and claiming common descent in genealogies—linked together many elite families in large corporate units.[24] Even if one family's sons did not get high degrees, other members of the lineage would take care of them. Lineages also provided scholarship support for promising young men to study with tutors to train them in the classic texts. China appeared to have a high amount of upward and downward social mobility if we look only at nuclear family units, as many high-degree holders did not have sons with equal status. But if we include lineages, mobility seemed much less because the same families dominated many localities for generations.

The tenacious hold of lineages on local society limited the authority of officials from the top down. Again, in practice, Ming and Qing China were much less autocratic than they appeared. Elite lineages had extensive landholdings, invested in trade, and cultivated patronage networks with other lineages and influential power holders in the capital. They kept their taxes low by concealing land from the state, by bribing local clerks, and by manipulating exchanges of grain for silver. They could also offer tax shelters to other landholders, protecting their lands from confiscation in return for personal services. Many smallholding farmers, conversely, had little independence socially or economically from the dominant lineages. In lawsuits, they could not get equal justice, because the magistrate would generally follow the preferences of the dominant elites. In this sense, the local elites did resemble British gentry, as they enjoyed relatively permanent judicial and economic privileges and controlled local justice and local society in collaboration with the local official.[25]

Buddhist institutions also had significant local power in some parts of the empire. The Chinese mixed together many religious beliefs and practices in daily life. Buddhists in monasteries were only a small part of the population, but monasteries had extensive landholdings, especially in Southeast China. Monasteries had to register with the state, but they kept much of their administration beyond local control. Still, they never controlled large landed properties on the scale of the clergy in Europe.[26]

Intellectual Change

The first Ming emperor was illiterate, but the Yongle emperor received a classical education, and he realized that restoring the prestige of the Confucian classics was an essential element of preserving his rule. He not only increased the frequency of examinations, but he sponsored a project designed to preserve the entire known canon of literary writings from ancient times to his day. This collection, published in 1408 in 22,877 volumes, defined the boundaries of classical learning for all candidates for the examinations. The most important texts were the four books defined by the Song philosopher Zhu Xi as the fundamental elements of Confucian philosophy: the Confucian Analects, Mencius, the Great Learning, and the Doctrine of the Mean, plus the writings of Zhu Xi, his followers, and all the subsequent commentaries on these texts. Although this tradition of Neo-Confucianism, or Song learning, contained many variants, the Ming imposed the most orthodox version as the only possible route to official power and intellectual acclaim. Students, aided by mass publication of commentaries and tests, studied intensively for examination questions that demanded rote memorization and fixed answers. By the fifteenth century, however, in response to growing tensions produced by social change, scholars trained in this tradition began to search for ways to modify and radically reform it. Two of the most prominent reformers were Wang Yangming (or Wang Shouren) and Li Zhi.

Wang Yangming (1472–1528) is much less well known to Western readers than his contemporary Martin Luther (1483–1546), but Wang's intellectual impact was almost as great.[27] Wang, however, was not just a philosopher but a general and a local government official. He served in many posts in the empire, conducted famine relief campaigns, put down rebellions, reformed taxes, and earned immense gratitude from the populations he ruled. But he reacted strongly against the prevailing structures of the Ming administration, which he regarded as stultifying and backward.

He thought that the examinations produced timid, self-serving officials who lacked any sense of obligation toward the people they ruled. Wang, deeply concerned about his own spiritual development, asked himself, "How does one become a sincere and truthful person in the midst of dehumanizing forces such as the irrationality of despotic rule, the rigidity of the exam system, and the hypocrisy of conventional mores?"[28]

When he retreated to a bamboo grove to meditate intensively, he only fell ill from exhaustion. He went to a grotto in an attempt to withdraw from the world but concluded that, unlike Daoists and Buddhists, he could not neglect the world of ordinary life. Finally, he concluded that all the knowledge necessary to lead a moral life could be found in the individual's own sense of right and wrong, not in the dry memorization of ancient texts. Furthermore, the person conscious of his moral sense had to put his ideal into practice, uniting knowledge and action. And he followed his own principles by acting as an official in a remote part of the empire, when he fought wars and endeavored to improve the life of the local people. Wang Yangming as official and philosopher inspired generations of scholars in China as well as Japan with his vision of individual reformation and social change. He added new life to the cultural world by showing that "sageliness," the true goal of any educated man, was found within the self, regardless of one's success in the material world. He opened up an alternative path for intellectuals who were not content with conformity, and in later decades even more radical critics of conventional Confucianism found inspiration in his writings.

Commercialization and Its Discontents, 1550–1650

In the mid-sixteenth century, Ming China joined the global economy. It became the linchpin of a linked network of trade flows leading from Latin America through Europe to India, to Southeast and East Asia. The discovery of silver in the mines of Potosí in Bolivia made these trade links possible, but what drove the system was the voracious demand of Chinese consumers for marketed goods and the productive power of Chinese farmers producing silk, tea, porcelain, and other luxury products. The effects on China itself were as far-reaching as they were in the rest of the world. From an inward-looking society dedicated to protecting agrarian self-sufficiency, the Ming state and society became highly commercialized, mobile, and outward oriented, heavily focused on consumption and exchange. These changes caused great strain on all the major institutions of the empire. During the century of the great silver influx, Ming statesmen and scholars constantly debated how to change inherited ways so as to preserve the strength of the state and the welfare of the people.

Since the end of Zheng He's voyages, the Ming state had prohibited nearly all foreign trade, but along the coast, maritime networks began to develop, pulling together diverse peoples for profitable exchange relations. From Japan to Taiwan to the Southeast Asian islands, sailors and traders carried products that appealed to coastal Chinese. Many Chinese participated in the illegal smuggling of goods to coastal ports, and they soon developed bases on land for distribution of goods to the interior. They also needed military defenses and sources of cash to either resist or bribe local officials into looking the other way. Illegal trade along the coast was a natural product of a growing maritime commercial network confronting a state intent on seclusion.[29]

Ming officials called these traders "dwarf [Japanese] pirates" and launched military campaigns against them. But the traders, reinforced by samurai from southern Japan and other military adventurers, formed large defense forces, occupying and raiding coastal towns. From the 1520s to the 1560s, the confrontation between traders and officials spread all along China's south and southeastern coast, including the cities of Canton, Quanzhou, Zhangzhou, and Ningbo.

At almost the same time, trade conflicts occurred in the northwest. Mongolian pastoralists on this frontier also wanted trade with the Ming, exchanging animal products for Chinese exports of silk and tea, but Ming officials generally refused offers from these "barbarians." Mongols then raided merchant caravans and frontier cities to obtain the goods they wanted, forcing the officials to grudgingly allow limited trade. This cycle of request, refusal, and raiding continued for forty years along the frontier of Northwest China.[30] Some officials argued for aggressive military campaigns to drive out the Mongolian armies. They cried, "We must exterminate the rebel bandits to avenge our shame."[31] Others cited the high cost of military campaigns and promoted trade as a time-honored means of softening up savage nomads. Fierce debates raged at court, stimulating factional alliances, impeachments, and purges. Finally, an emperor favoring the soft line came to power and initiated controlled trading relations with Altan Khan (1507–1582), the leader of the Mongolian confederation. In 1571, in return for nominal surrender to the Ming, Altan Khan gained the title of "Submissive King," the right to trade along the border, and the opportunity to expand a city he had founded where Mongols and Chinese traders could meet regularly for exchange. Named Guihua ("return to civilization") in Chinese or Hohhot ("blue settlement") in Mongolian, it is now the capital of modern Inner Mongolia.

Along the southeast coast, likewise, proponents of trade won out in the end, but only after carrying out a combined strategy of military and commercial mobilization. Qi Jiguang (1528–1588), one of China's greatest generals, had fought against Mongols on the northwest frontier, and when he was transferred to the south, he adopted new tactics to handle the smugglers, pirates, and coastal raiders.[32] He recruited local militia, paid them in silver, and inspired them to fight for their home villages, while also inducing many local raiding groups to surrender in return for amnesties and cash payments. He and others promoted the opening of limited trade relations along the coast. At the same time, the Portuguese appeared, asking for a lease on the peninsula of Macau in return for offering aid in fighting the pirates. The Portuguese had arrived in Macau after founding a series of trading bases in Africa and across the Indian Ocean. Again, furious debate roiled the court, but ultimately it agreed to lease Macau in 1557. This was the first port opened for trade to Western Europeans. The Spanish arrived in Asia across the Pacific, taking the Philippines and founding Manila in 1571. Soon substantial Chinese communities grew in both cities. Macau soon grew into the primary point of access for Europeans to China, a position it held until the rise of Hong Kong in the mid-nineteenth century. Even during the eighteenth century, Europeans had to visit Macau first before obtaining rights of temporary residence in Canton.

The third important economic development of the mid-sixteenth century was the emigration of Chinese from the southeast coast into Southeast Asia.[33] Chinese merchants with connections to the mainland made possible the flow of silver from the New World via Manila and Macau into Ming territory. Japan also sent large amounts of silver to China during the late sixteenth century, exporting from

40,000 to 100,000 kilograms per year over the last half of the century in return for Chinese raw silk, porcelain, and textiles. Japanese supplies, however, ran out in the early seventeenth century when the Tokugawa regime imposed a ban on currency exports.

But the silver needed a demand to attract it. The remonetization of the Chinese economy in the sixteenth century generated a great demand for media of exchange. As agrarian producers and urban consumers contacted each other, they needed more convenient means of exchange than the bulk low-value bronze coins that were imperial China's only approved source of value. The first Ming emperor's disastrous effort to impose paper money had driven many economic transactions back to the level of barter. Japan, after it recovered from civil war, then began to provide significant silver supplies, as the Japanese also demanded the prestigious Chinese products of silk, lacquer, and books. Silver provided a convenient means for long-distance trade. At about the same time, as noted earlier, fiscal reforms changed tax collection from a confusing process based on grain, labor, and cloth into a smaller number of payments calculated in silver. The Single Whip procedure not only made tax collection more reliable for officials, it also forced farmers into market exchange. They now had to sell a portion of their crops to meet tax obligations. Other farmers discovered the benefits of specialization, as they turned to growing nongrain crops that suited local conditions. New World contact brought in new seeds as well, stimulating clearance of fields on mountainous hillsides of South China unsuited to grain. Maize, tobacco, sweet potatoes, peanuts, and chili peppers provided new employment for hillside farmers and substantially transformed the Chinese diet. Fujian Province, in particular, relied on these crops in its hill country to fuel the rapid development of market towns and large coastal cities.[34] The new crops and the intensified production of cash crops on old fields supported a slow but inexorable rise in the aggregate Chinese population, from something over sixty million in 1400 to perhaps 150 million by the end of the sixteenth century. These settlers pushed relentlessly into previously uncultivated regions, including forested hillsides, the borders of lakes, jungles used for slash-and-burn cultivation, and coastal fisheries.

Urban consumers, for their part, enjoyed much greater choices in the marketplace as commercial networks spread.[35] A craze for luxury products drove local elites in search of prestige to search out the rarest carved rocks, inkstones, paper, and special foods to impress their peers.[36] Pious Confucians frowned at the rampant drive for these "superfluous things," but they recognized that the drive to consume and the drive to profit were almost like a natural force. As one disgusted scholarly writer put it, "Since profit is what all people covet, they rush after it like torrents pouring into a valley: coming and going without end, never resting day or night, never reaching the point at which the raging floods within them subside."[37]

Women also benefited from the rise of commercialism. Most of them had to remain in their family compounds under the stern eyes of their husbands' relatives, but they were encouraged to contribute to the household's income by practicing spinning and weaving. The practice of foot binding had spread quite far, even into rural areas, and this crippling social norm sharply limited their mobility. But because they produced surplus textiles with a market value, they could sell their clothing outside the household, raising their social and economic status.[38] The rise of commercial travel businesses to support pilgrimages also helped expand women's geographic horizons. Many route books described how to travel to sacred sites and famous historical relics, giving details on the best places to stay, the best restaurants, and the available souvenirs and local products.[39] Traveling in groups to pilgrimage sites was one of the few ways for women to leave the shelter of their husbands' households and meet with other like-minded believers. Letter-writing services also supported communication over long distances, even between illiterate people. Among the higher literati classes, long-distance communication also created a sense of a larger community, a republic of letters that transcended local governmental positions and state-imposed status.

The Grand Canal and the Great Wall

Higher mobility, greater wealth, and new social opportunities strained the capacities of the Ming administration, which was based on the ideal of an agrarian order in which rural people knew their place, and urban commercial classes accepted their limited political role. But the Ming responded to these tensions creatively to support greater integration of the empire over a vast scale. Its two greatest engineering achievements were the construction of the Great Wall and the Grand Canal. Both of these large projects, built to enhance military security and stabilize the food supply, tied together North and South China more closely than they ever had been in the past, ensuring that the new wealth generated in the south supported the military and administrative institutions of the north.

The Grand Canal had been a vital source of grain for the northern regions ever since the seventh century AD, and the Mongol Kublai Khan had extended it to his capital in Beijing. The Ming developed it further into a large-scale military operation, with thousands of barges, each carrying up to 30,000 kilograms of grain escorted by soldiers from Yangzhou to Beijing.[40] Because merchants also used the canal for private business, the traffic in letters, travelers, luxury goods, and private boats grew so numerous that it crowded out the official barges. The Ming decided to contract much of the grain shipping business to the merchants as well, cutting down the expense of supporting the military and avoiding interference with the private economy. The canal persisted as the major artery linking North and South China, but it evolved from a state project to a commercially profitable enterprise.

The Great Wall in its current form is also a result of Ming dynasty defense policy and commercialization. Although Chinese dynasties had often built sections of "long walls" to ensure military control of the northwest, the Ming was the first to connect the sections together and base its defense policy on a single defensive barrier. But this choice was forced on the Ming by circumstances; it was not their preferred way of handling pastoral nomads. Altan Khan's bold large-scale raids against Ming garrisons stimulated furious debate, but the solution to frontier defense relied on limited trade and wall building. Frontier horse markets opened, and the trade ban was repealed. Chinese merchants sold silk, fur, grain, and metal pots to the Mongols in exchange for horses and sheep. The Ming levied taxes on the trade and restocked its military with the nomads' horses.

The Ming then used these commercial levies to rebuild the Great Wall. The wall itself required enormous amounts of manpower and materials, and all of this had to be paid for in silver. Drawing this line across the steppe also required supporting static military garrisons for long periods of time. Specially designated merchants acted as defense contractors to deliver grain, salt, clothing, and weaponry to them over long distances. The Ming state shipped purchases worth over four million taels of silver annually to the northwest frontier after 1570. The primary source of this silver was the new wealth coming from the New World. The Great Wall policy, then, far from cutting China off from the world, in fact depended

The Great Wall of China, as we know it today, was completed toward the end of the sixteenth century, under the Ming dynasty. It extended for almost 9,000 kilometers along the frontier between the settled and farmed areas of China and the steppe regions and was equipped with watchtowers and signal stations to warn of Mongol attacks. Its massive dimensions have continued to impress Chinese officials and foreign visitors alike right up to the present day, but generally speaking it was an ineffectual and costly defensive rampart, which failed to prevent the conquest of the Ming Empire by the Manchu (Qing) in the seventeenth century. (© Bettmann)

on Ming China's direct linkage to the global flow of silver promoted by its export trade.

Intellectual and Cultural Change in the Late Ming

Early in the sixteenth century, Wang Yangming had advocated disciplined moral scrutiny of the self, as part of a search for spiritual stability and practical action in a time of conformity and moral decay. Followers of Wang Yangming took his message to more extreme ends, arousing considerable controversy. Some argued that because the possibility of spiritual advancement, or "sagehood," was present in every human being, Confucian doctrines should be directly accessible by the common people. They conducted public lectures for men and women together in towns and local schools. Conservatives denounced this immoral mixing of the sexes, and state officials found any kind of public assembly suspicious, unless strictly under state control. The Ming state had promoted small-scale assemblies of village elders who met at banquets in local schools to reinforce their commitment to traditional norms, but random preaching in the streets was a very different matter. Yet the move to the masses, supported by much broader circulation of texts in the marketplace, was a natural outcome of the increasingly mobile and commercialized society, especially in the lower Yangzi valley.

The most notorious representative of this struggle against prevailing norms was the brilliant, iconoclastic scholar Li Zhi (1527–1602).[41] A cantankerous man, he launched scathing criticism against everything hypocritical in his society, sparing no one, including government officials, conventional scholars, and even his closest friends. His two books with the telling titles of *A Book to Be Burned* and *A Book to Be Hidden* and the many letters he wrote had enormous impact on intellectual circles of his time.

Li Zhi was born in Quanzhou, a thriving commercial city on the southeast coast, which had a long-resident Muslim community. Li's family engaged in commerce and may have had Muslim connections. The Ming repression of trade on the coast, which generated pirate raids, inflicted economic damage on the city, but it recovered when the trade ban was lifted in 1567. Li Zhi himself did not go into trade but obtained a classical education. He hated, however, the sterility of preparing for examinations, although he passed the provincial exam and for a time became an official. As he wandered from post to post, he discovered that his true commitment was to moral improvement, what Chinese called "seeking the Way." He found inspiration in Wang Yangming's teachings, but he rejected Wang's synthesis of personal cultivation and practical action. Instead, he resigned his offices, abandoned his wife and children, and took the Buddhist tonsure, moving to a local temple but without entering a monastery. In his eyes, he was the only true Confucian, whereas others were only hypocrites. He denounced his fellow scholars, saying,

> Other people's minds are stuck in received opinions; no matter how clever they are, they have nothing to say to me. There is nothing but phony men speaking

phony words, doing phony things, writing phony writings. . . . If one speaks phony talk to the phonies, they are happy; if you do phony things as the phonies do, they are happy, if you talk to the phonies through phony writings, the phonies are happy. Everything is phony, and everyone is pleased.[42]

His writings and letters became so notorious that local officials incited a mob to burn down his residence; then a powerful court official denounced him, had Li sent to prison, and had many copies of his books burned. In prison he committed suicide by slashing his throat.

Although Li Zhi considered himself a Confucian, he launched the most radical attack on orthodox Neo-Confucianism ever seen until the late nineteenth century. He endorsed the goal of becoming a sage but insisted that moral improvement required open, honest pursuit of one's self-interest. The individual self came before all else, and no one should sacrifice his own beliefs for the benefit of others. In his view, the sage advocates "the desire for goods, for sexual satisfaction, for study, for personal advancement, for the accumulation of wealth." These doctrines completely contradicted the Neo-Confucian ideals of submission, overcoming self-interest, and seeking harmony with existing cosmic and social trends.

Communist critics have praised Li Zhi as an antifeudal revolutionary, but one could just as easily describe him as a proto-capitalist theorist, a radical individualist supporting selfishness and the money economy. He linked himself to Buddhism and commercialization and expressed the undying spirit of liberty that lurked beneath the smooth exterior of Confucian values. In this way, he epitomized the spirit of late Ming China.

Zhang Dai (1597–1689) represents another aspect of Ming culture, more moderate and cosmopolitan, if also decadent.[43] He also grew up in a commercial city, Shaoxing, and his family gained its wealth in trade. He claimed to follow Wang Yangming, but no one would call Zhang a serious philosopher. He is best known for his collections of essays, which describe himself and his friends indulging in parties and excursions, filled with wine, women, and song. As he described himself:

When I was young, I was a fop in white silk breeches, mad about everything that was fancy and stylish: country retreats, beautiful courtesans, seductive boys, new clothes, gourmet foods, fine horses, decorated lanterns, tobacco, theatre, music, antiques, and paintings. And I was crazy about tea, addicted to oranges, consumed by calligraphy, and a demon for poetry.[44]

This is a typical picture of a Ming dandy. Yet Zhang was also attracted to Buddhism. He went on pilgrimages to the sacred Taishan Mountain in Shandong, the island monasteries of Putuo off the coast of Jiangnan, and the King Asoka monastery in Ningbo.[45] He bought fish at the marketplace and released them into ponds, to demonstrate acts of compassion for living creatures. He once led a group of friends into a monastery late at night to stage an amateur production of local opera for the mystified but tolerant monks. It is hard to tell whether this was mere spiritual tourism or a genuine quest. Yet Zhang Dai wrote very sensitively about many different people in the circles he knew, from impoverished prostitutes to local shopkeepers, antique collectors, monks, scholars, and merchants. No one would accuse him of moral sternness, and he demonstrated real empathy for people who enjoyed the ordinary pleasures of life as well as enthusiasm for expanding one's personal world through travel and investigation.

The printing and book publishing industries also flourished in this period, dramatically changing intellectual life. Chinese had pioneered the technology of woodblock printing since the eighth century AD, and there had always been an active market for printed literature to serve the needs of the literati class. Sixteenth-century publishers expanded their markets significantly to meet the demands of newly literate urban populations. They sold not only manuals to prepare for examinations but almanacs, encyclopedias, travel guides, erotica, popular religious literature, and stories written in the vernacular language. They created elaborate distribution networks to bring cheap editions to the major cities of the empire, and they kept testing the market to find new ways to sell both classical and vernacular texts.[46]

In response to new trends of popularization of culture, moral account books, or "ledgers of merit and demerit," spread widely in the seventeenth century in Jiangnan.[47] These books encouraged ordinary people to list their good and bad deeds every day, totaling up a point score every month in order to estimate the rewards they would gain in the next life. They combined aspects of Confucian moral training with Buddhist beliefs in reward and retribution for sins committed in this life, which affected one's reincarnation in the next. Many groups sponsored these publications for different purposes. Government officials promoted them to increase imperial control over the population's daily life. Lower-level scholars used them to promote their own methods of moral cultivation, boasting that performing three thousand good deeds had gained them success in the examination system. Conservative elites reacting against the critiques of Li Zhi and his school sponsored them in order to reinforce the existing social order. Local societies formed to accumulate ledgers testifying to good deeds of one hundred thousand points, which would be distributed among artisans and peasant farmers. The distribution of these texts indicated conflicts among different elite groups for leadership of popular morality. The fluid society of Jiangnan had fostered a public arena in which officials and moral authorities debated and broadcast their programs to a larger public.

In these troubled times, some Ming literati, inspired by Buddhist ideals of compassion and by Confucian goals of harmonious social relations, tried to improve society by practicing philanthropy.[48] They might purchase and release birds and fishes, feed rice gruel to the starving, or sponsor orphanages, old age homes, and homeless shelters. Qi Biaojia (d. 1645), a scholar trained as a doctor, wrote a two-hundred-page diary describing his efforts to relieve a famine in his home town.

In the late Ming, the popular Chinese novel also came into its own. Ever since Song times, fast-talking storytellers on the streets had turned sages, warriors, and statesmen into lovers, gods, and heroes. Elitists looked down on these storytellers, but several eccentric scholars used them to write novels and short stories filled with details of families and daily life. Three of the six most famous novels of ancient China were published in the sixteenth century: *The Romance of the Three Kingdoms; Jin Ping Mei* (or *The Golden Lotus*); and *Journey to the West* (or *Monkey*).[49]

The Romance of the Three Kingdoms tells the story of the battles and intrigues following the fall of the Han dynasty, when good king Liu Bei, a descendant of the Han royal house devoted to justice, and his blood brothers, Guan Yu and Zhang Fei, courageous, honorable strongmen, lose to the arch-villain Cao Cao. Popular tradition deified the heroic warrior Guan Yu and admired the clever schemes of Liu Bei's master strategist, Zhuge Liang. As recommended in the famous ancient military text by Sunzi, *The Art of War,* Zhuge Liang defeated a superior foe while minimizing the use of force. Like Odysseus and his patroness Athena in the Western tradition, Zhuge represents the ultimate master of cunning wisdom. Mao Zedong in fact studied the stratagems of the *Three Kingdoms* as a guide to guerrilla warfare.

In *The Golden Lotus,* the upright Wu Song leaves home, and his wife, Lotus, is seduced by the unscrupulous Ximen Qing. Its one hundred chapters describe life in a wealthy merchant household, including sex scenes so graphic that until recently they could be translated only into Latin. The innocent Lotus turns into a nymphomaniac whose passion literally arouses Ximen Qing to death. Then Wu Song returns, like Odysseus, to his endangered household and sets things right by slaughter. This strange mixture of businesslike description of merchant affairs with equally clinical pornography indicates the wide-ranging tastes of Ming readers, who formed a genuine middle-class, but far from Victorian, audience.

Journey to the West unites a deep spiritual quest with magic, violence, adventure, comedy, and picaresque travel. Nominally, it portrays the historical journey of the monk Tripitaka to India to obtain sacred scriptures, but Tripitaka's two animal companions steal the story. Greedy Pigsy, a fat hog with a vicious rake for a weapon, constantly gets Tripitaka into trouble but fights valiantly to rescue him. Greedy Pigsy represents human lust.

Mischievous Monkey, the most brilliant creation of the Chinese novel tradition, originates in popular stories told by Indian Buddhists and may have a connection to the Hindu monkey god Hanuman and the Indian Buddhist concept of *upaya,* or "skillful means." When Monkey stole the sacred peaches from heaven, he was banished to Earth to help mortals find salvation. Defying demons and seductive women, Monkey's enormous magical powers, controlled by Guanyin, the Buddhist manifestation of compassion, guide the pilgrims to their goal. This fantastic and humorous novel is much more entertaining than *Pilgrim's Progress* and almost as rambunctious as Rabelais. Monkey's clever tricks, like those of Zhuge Liang, exalt the role of cunning. Monkey's sharp eyes, like "glinting-eyed Athena," perceive the demonic traps missed by the obtuse, blind Tripitaka. Guanyin, however, also uses deception and coercion over Monkey to convert him to a saint. Monkey is really an allegory for the "monkey-Mind": the novel exalts the creativity of human intelligence.

Challenges to the Ming State

Under the long reign of the Wanli emperor (1573–1620), many of the deep tensions of the imperial regime grew to crisis proportions.[50] The emperor took the throne at the age of nine, and during his first decade of rule, under the supervision of powerful officials, the country was peaceful and prosperous. The forceful prime minister Zhang Juzheng supported the establishment of horse markets to foster trade with Altan Khan. He made strenuous efforts to crack down on tax evasion and bribery, carrying out the most accurate land survey done in imperial China for several hundred years as a means of raising land revenue.[51] He gave the emperor sermons about the need to be strict in evaluating officials and austere in controlling his personal expenses. Zhang's intolerance of criticism gained him many enemies and, eventually, undermined by opposition and lacking the emperor's support, his efforts petered out. At his death, his critics discovered that he had taken large bribes to build himself a luxurious mansion and collect valuable paintings and expensive clothes.

The emperor, released from Zhang's hypocritical lectures and frustrated at his lack of real power, nearly abdicated his role in ruling, secluding himself in his palace and refusing to make major appointments. His inaction left major official posts unfilled for years, paralyzing the bureaucracy, as factions fought for his attention. Corruption spread widely through the bureaucracy, but no single group could take charge. His main concern was the building of his own tomb, which cost millions of dollars and diverted large amounts of labor and supplies from the defense of the state.

The twelve thousand eunuchs in the imperial palace formed a powerful faction of their own. They were close to the emperor and his harem, so they had intimate access to policy discussions, but because they did not obtain examination degrees, the literati detested them. Official sources written by the scholars blame the eunuchs for the fall of the Ming, but they contain their own biases. Eunuchs did impose extra burdens on parts of the empire, for example, when they demanded precious jewels for the emperor's household, and many of them were corrupt. But officials, including grand secretaries, also demanded bribes. Deficiencies in structure rather than in personalities brought about the end of the empire.

Hall of Supreme Harmony (Taihe Dian), Forbidden City, Beijing. This enormous audience hall, which was built in 1406, is the largest preserved wooden building in China. Situated in the center of the closed imperial district of Beijing, it represented the ceremonial heart of the Ming and Qing dynasties. Here, Chinese emperors would celebrate such grand state occasions as coronation ceremonies, accessions to the throne, and imperial weddings. The Forbidden City in Beijing, which was laid down in the Ming period and expanded under the Qing, symbolized celestial legitimation of the emperor's autocratic rule, which radiated virtue and power throughout the realm from this supposedly central location in the cosmos. (Getty Images)

Conflict among top officials and eunuchs in the inner court brought about near paralysis of the Ming government in the early seventeenth century. After Zhang Juzheng's death, officials prevented any other grand secretaries from exercising discipline over them, and the emperor himself did not intervene in partisan conflicts. A group of scholars called the Eastern Forest Faction (Donglin) organized themselves to criticize the declining moral character of the government and call for significant reforms, but eunuch leaders brutally repressed their protest. A second, even more activist group of scholars, the Restoration Society (Fushe), also tried to exert influence on government policy, but they too were repressed. The late emperors of the Ming, caught between powerful interests on different sides, could not exert much influence and vacillated over critical decisions on military and fiscal policies.

The End of the Ming

The disarray of the central government and the increasing pressure on local people stimulated uprisings in both urban and rural areas. In 1601 in Suzhou, hired silk weavers formed military formations, wielding wooden sticks, and marched on the government offices to demand abolition of new taxes. They beat to death the tax collectors, while some sympathetic lower-gentry groups in the city supported their movement.[52] In Hangzhou, rich landowners blocked a tax reform that would shift burdens from the common people by levying a tax on rich home owners instead of using corvée labor. Local merchants, migrant laborers, and soldiers staged demonstrations and burned down houses of the local elite.[53] In rural areas, certain tenant farmers fell into the status of "bond servants," who had no liberty to move away from their landlord's family estate. They also rebelled against their servitude in the rural areas surrounding Suzhou in 1644 and 1645.

As court disputes escalated, famine, drought, and epidemics struck North and Northwest China, rebel groups contested imperial control, and a new, powerful state formed in the northeast.[54] The poor farmers of the northwest had faced heavy tax levies and poor harvests for many decades, and the unpaid soldiers nearby at the Great Wall deserted their posts. One of these former soldiers, Li Zicheng (c. 1605–1645), organized the discontented peasantry of the region, raising a major rebellion that soon took over the provinces of the northwest. In 1644, Li captured the capital in Beijing and proclaimed a new dynasty, while the last Ming emperor hung himself in the palace compound. In Sichuan, also, another peasant leader organized bands of paramilitary groups to attack local government offices, leading to a collapse of government control.

Famines and epidemics across North China indicated the deep ineffectiveness of local government responses to major calamities. Disruptions in the global flow of silver in the early seventeenth century, both from Latin America and Japan, altered the balance of copper and silver currency in China, inflicting heavier burdens on peasants, merchants, and urban residents. The Ming intervened in Korea in 1592 with a large military force to drive out the Japanese invader Hideyoshi.

They earned the gratitude of the Koreans, but the expedition greatly strained the Ming military budget. The court levied surtaxes on the agrarian population to pay for its increased military costs, stimulating tax revolts. Most ominous of all, northeast of the Great Wall, in Manchuria, a series of tribal leaders created a powerful military challenge to the Ming armies.

The Qing Dynasty (1636–1911)

The Manchus, who founded the Qing dynasty, did not have a name for themselves until 1635. They were merely a group of tribes in Northeast China and eastern Siberia speaking related languages and sharing traditions and ways of life. The Manchu language is one branch of the larger Altaic family, which includes Mongolian and, arguably, Korean and Japanese. Their ancestors, called Jurcheds, who lived in the same area, had created a dynasty called the Jin that controlled Manchuria and much of North China in the twelfth and early thirteenth centuries. The Jin was then eliminated by the Mongols. After the fall of the Mongol Empire, the Jurcheds reverted to a tribal society. Ming officials saw them as a primitive people, living by hunting, fishing, some agriculture, and some pastoralism. They were not true nomads, as they lived off multiple resources from forests, rivers, and fields, but they were mobile and skilled horsemen.

Modern Manchuria has three ecological zones. In the west are grasslands, usually dominated by Mongols, pastoral nomads living mainly off sheep and horses. In the north are forests, an extension of Siberia. In this region lived hunters, gatherers of forest products (ginseng, mushrooms, some gold) and a variety of tribal groups. Southern Manchuria, or Liaoning, contained fertile fields supporting farmers, some Manchu, mainly Han Chinese migrants from the south. One of the secrets of Manchu power was their ability to draw on special skills from all three zones: Mongolian cavalry, Manchu soldiers on horseback and on foot, and Chinese farmers for supplies of food and clothing.

The Ming relationship to these people was shaped by a traditional policy called "loose reign," under which the officials left them alone but offered them trading licenses and titles as local headmen to deal with the state. Because it was profitable for tribes to exchange products across the Great Wall, and more convenient for the Ming than trying to conquer them, relations were relatively stable until

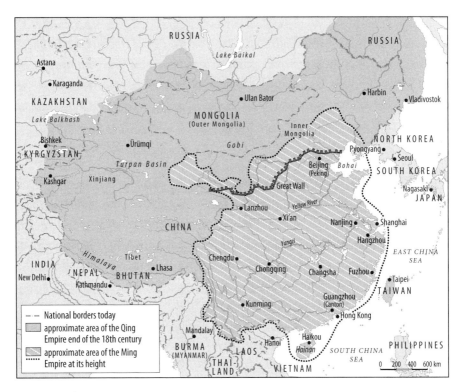

Expansion of the Qing Empire

the late sixteenth century. But as the global economy developed, dynamic leaders in Manchuria used the new sources of wealth to create a centralized state.

Nurhaci (1559–1626) was only one of the many tribal chieftains to whom the Ming had granted titles and trading licenses, but he used his wealth from trade to conquer other tribes, including his kinsmen.[55] Beginning in the 1580s he expanded his military power, and other tribes joined to share the fruits of his success. In 1616, Nurhaci named himself a Han (khan in Mongolian), meaning "supreme ruler," and named his new dynasty the Latter Jin, echoing his Jurched ancestors. He created a written Manchu language by borrowing the Mongolian alphabetic script, but he continued trade relations with the Ming. The Ming granted him military titles, recognizing his authority, but in 1618 he then turned to attacking Ming positions, announcing his grievances against the Ming court. He imposed military discipline on the Chinese settlers whom he conquered in southern

Manchuria, and he forced them all to shave the front of their foreheads and braid their hair into a long pigtail, or "queue." He suffered a major defeat by a Ming general in 1626 and died shortly after this battle.

After Nurhaci's death, his successor Hung Taiji (1592–1643) continued this combined policy of military attacks and state building.[56] Most important was the expansion of a new institution founded by Nurhaci combining civil, military, and social administration: the banners. The banners cut across kinship lines, putting tribal groups under a strict military hierarchy. The banners included not only Manchus but also Mongols and Han Chinese. Certain Han Chinese soldiers, farmers, traders, and scholars, transfrontiersmen who left the Ming area and moved into southern Manchuria, played a crucial role in building the Manchu state. Hung Taiji made good use of their skills in farming, administration, and trade.

But building the Manchu state created severe tensions. Although the Manchu official history of the founding of the dynasty concealed a great deal, we are fortunate to have original Manchu archival documents that reveal a much more crisis-ridden process.[57] Hung Taiji put heavy burdens on the Chinese farmers of Liaoning to build up his army and administration. They paid heavy taxes, and he tried to force every Chinese household to give room and board to a Manchu solider. When stories spread of poisonings of Manchus by Chinese, he abandoned this policy. In 1629 a severe famine struck Liaoning. While soldiers and farmers starved, the banner armies lost battles against Ming, and the state almost collapsed. Hung Taiji then created new provisioning policies, ordering state intervention to allocate grain to both civilian and military populations. Meanwhile, the Ming looked incompetent and helpless to relieve famine in North China. A flood of refugees fled Ming territory for Liaoning. At first, this influx put even more pressure on Manchu relief policies, but it also attracted skilled Chinese officials concerned with public welfare. Now the Manchu leaders took an interest in the vast body of Chinese writings on history, technology, and administration. They translated military manuals first, then practical handbooks of administration: how to judge cases or how to collect taxes. The Confucian classics came last. They were not particularly interested in Chinese philosophy.[58]

Finally, Hung Taiji named the Manchus as a people in 1635. Their identity was first of all given to them from above, by the state.[59] The origin of the name "Manchu" is obscure, but it indicated a new consciousness of ethnic solidarity among the

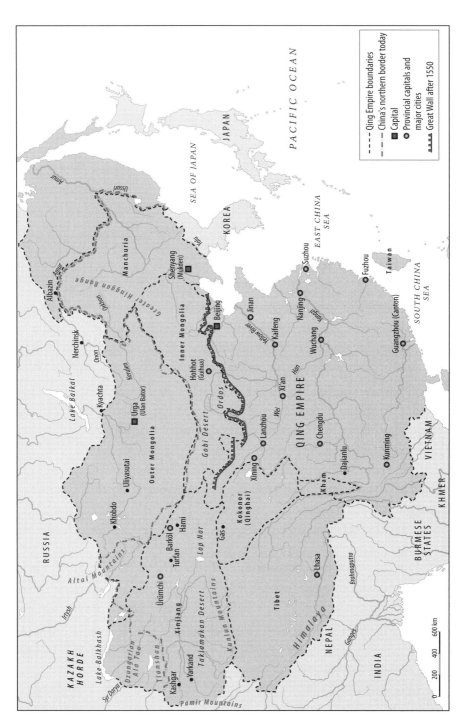

China under the Qing dynasty

military rulers of the state, marking a sharp distinction from their neighbors, the Mongols and Chinese. Then in 1636, Hung Taiji declared the beginning of the Qing dynasty, replacing the Latter Jin. Like "Ming," "Qing" was a symbolic name, meaning "clear." Hung Taiji had openly signaled his intention of conquering all of China instead of recreating the Jurcheds' northern regional state.

Still, without Li Zicheng's revolt, his capture of the capital, the suicide of the emperor, and the chaotic withdrawal, the conquest might well not have succeeded. The Manchu conquest was by no means inevitable; it depended on a multitude of contingent interactions among the contending parties, on the wider geopolitical and climatic environment, and on individual decisions.

One key person decided to let the Manchus into Beijing. Wu Sangui (1612–1678) was a Ming general guarding the Juyong pass north of Beijing, part of the Great Wall.[60] Dorgon, the leader of the Qing troops, persuaded Wu Sangui that they shared the same ideal of "loyalty," a key Confucian virtue. Loyalty meant not the duty to obey a single emperor but the duty to preserve the imperial order of the empire. The Manchus claimed that heaven had transferred the mandate to them, and only they could "wipe out the shame" created by the anarchy of the peasant rebel Li Zicheng.[61] Wu Sangui chose to let the Manchus in, so they swept down on Beijing in 1644, driving out Li Zicheng, and over the next thirty years, they conquered the rest of the former Ming Empire. Wu Sangui has been denounced in modern Chinese history books as a "traitor to the Han people," but this is an anachronistic attitude reflecting the values of a nation-state. No empire in the past ever worked this way. Many non-Chinese had ruled China before; what mattered most was who was capable of restoring peace. The Manchus seemed to most of the elite to promise more security than the dying Ming.

New Men of the Qing and Leftover Men of the Ming

Still, after the conquest everyone had to make individual decisions, whether to resist the Manchus out of loyalty to the failed Ming, surrender and join the new order, or try to escape. Qi Biaojia, for his part, committed suicide, while Zhang Dai ran away and went into hiding. Three other "leftover men," each loyal to the Ming in his own way, refused to serve the Qing and expressed their loyalty in writings. Each had a particular perspective, which contributed to the formation of modern China. They were Huang Zongxi the liberal; Gu Yanwu the scientist; and Wang Fuzhi the philosopher of racialism.[62]

Huang Zongxi (1610–1695) came from a family that participated actively in the failed reform movements of the Eastern Forest Faction and the Restoration Society.[63] As a follower of Wang Yangming, Huang rejected the orthodox school of Confucianism and wrote an intellectual history of the Ming dynasty outlining the differences between various schools of thought. With the collapse of the Ming, he briefly considered joining the military resistance, but instead he retreated to his study to analyze the causes of Ming defeat. In his major philosophical text, *Waiting for an Enlightened Prince* (1662), he fervently criticized the autocratic state order, attacking the emperor for thinking that the entire realm was his personal property. Anticipating the French liberal philosopher Montesquieu, Huang argued for local freedoms based on the security of a hereditary elite, one closer to the "feudal" nobility of ancient China. His ideal was still an elite-led polity, but one where local elites who were closer to the people had more authority than distant officials obedient to the center. Although he did not argue for the complete supremacy of the nobility, only for a balance between local and central interests, his stress on elite property holding as the basis of authority anticipated John Locke by several decades. By singling out excessive centralization as a key weakness of the imperial order, he set the tone for a line of analysis that still persists in China: how to preserve social order while still recognizing the diversity of local situations.

Gu Yanwu (1613–1682) looked to resist autocratic power more actively first by investigating regions suitable for guerrilla warfare.[64] But as he turned away from resistance toward analysis, he concluded that defective philosophy had brought down the empire. A former member of the Restoration Society and a dedicated Ming loyalist, he was punished heavily by the conquerors. His brother was killed and his house ransacked. Soldiers cut off the right arm of his biological mother, and his foster mother committed suicide by fasting. He refused to serve the Manchus and bitterly criticized those who did, as he thought that the main cause of Ming collapse was the irresponsibility of its intellectuals. The orthodox Zhu Xi school taught only posturing, empty words, and useless knowledge, but the opposing schools of the Ming, like Li Zhi's followers, led only to irresponsible and self-indulgent individualism. Gu Yanwu argued that the way out of this intellectual trap led through empirical research. By studying the classical sources carefully, comparing them with each other, the true scholar could discover the authentic text on which to base sound knowledge. He could use new analytical techniques, like phonology, and he should follow the studies of Han dynasty scholars, who lived closest to the time of Confucius, avoiding the elaborate metaphysics of the Zhu Xi school.

Gu Yanwu also wrote a long series of essays on technical subjects like water control, taxation, currency, land reclamation, famine relief, trade, regional military defense, and local customs, providing a comprehensive geographical outline of the empire, sensitive to local variation. In his diary, like a modern blog, he gave his daily thoughts on how to resolve concrete moral questions. Scholars who followed him extended his techniques of empirical research to the entire Chinese classical canon, creating monumental studies that drastically reshaped the study of ancient texts.

The most eccentric of all, Wang Fuzhi (1619–1692), laid the foundation for racial nationalism, by arguing that environmental circumstances had formed an unbridgeable divide between barbarian Manchus and civilized Han.[65] Ignoring the multiethnic character of the Qing banners, he argued that because the Manchus came from the primitive northeast, they could not coexist with the sophisticated Chinese of the south. Only when the barbarians were expelled could the empire be put back in order. In his defiant, openly racialist categorizations, he rejected multicultural integration espoused by the Qing emperors. Wang Fuzhi's texts were suppressed, only to be rediscovered at the end of the nineteenth century as the inspiration for virulent anti-Manchu nationalism.

Ming–Qing China and the Question of a Seventeenth-Century Crisis

Scholars have argued that a general global seventeenth-century crisis displayed common elements across major states in Eurasia.[66] Victor Lieberman describes this period as a time of breakdown striking the continental Southeast Asian states, France, Russia, and Japan. The Ming–Qing transition also coincides with this period, characterized by the fall of states, lower population growth, the outbreak of harvest failures and rebellions, and interruption of currency flows. The underlying causes of the transition are still not clear, but climatic change seems to have played an important role. Volcanic eruptions increased in frequency, causing cooler temperatures.[67] The Little Ice Age of lower global temperatures reached its low point around 1640. The interruption of silver flows from the New World and from Japan reduced prices and market activity in China, and the rulers suffered from revenue shortfalls, political factional strife, along with military uprisings and epidemic disease. Although we cannot be certain of the relative importance of each of these factors, it seems plausible that the fall of the Ming and rise of the Qing was part of a general world crisis with common causes, modulated by local conditions in each region. The crisis was followed by a period of consolidation and recovery across Eurasia, as new regimes took power, agricultural production improved, military expansion resumed, and commerce once again flourished.

Qing Expansion

Just as the transition from Ming to Qing shared features with the general crisis of the seventeenth century found in much of Eurasia, so the period of expansion and consolidation of the Qing Empire proceeded in line with global trends. In the seventeenth century, three young monarchs—Peter the Great (r. 1689–1725), Louis XIV (r. 1643–1715), and the Kangxi emperor (r. 1662–1722)—personally led campaigns of military expansion and centralization, defining absolutist rule in continental Eurasia. All these men loved war and expanded their states, but they also encouraged luxurious court life, built cities around themselves, and claimed to be scholars and state builders as well as military men. In the end, Louis gained little or nothing for France with his wars, but he still centralized the state. Peter expanded his empire by savagely enforcing radical reform to extract military resources from a backward agrarian economy. Of all these rulers, the Qing emperors had the greatest success in defeating nomadic warriors. A French biography of Kangxi written in the seventeenth century compared him favorably with Louis XIV. The wealthy, populous Chinese could afford imperial aims. Kangxi dominated the steppe partly because, as a Manchu, he knew how to manipulate Central Asians with marriages, alliances, and force.

The vigorous young man who became the Kangxi emperor first took the throne under the supervision of his uncles as regents.[68] His first task was to assert his own personal authority against the constraints of the conservative Manchu clans. Rejecting their cautious policy toward military campaigns and their narrow-minded hostility to Chinese learning, Kangxi actively embraced wider horizons of intel-

The Kangxi emperor presented himself in a variety of different guises, in accordance with the many roles he fulfilled; he was a military conqueror, the legitimate ruler of the vast Chinese Empire, and a patron of scholarship. In this portrait, he appears as a simple scholar, dressed in plain clothing and surrounded by books. In other pictures, he is shown leading troops into battle on horseback or reigning in great splendor, seated on a lavish throne. Unlike the later Qing emperors, Kangxi led the active life of a horseman and warrior and the contemplative, quiet existence of an intellectual. He felt at home in these two roles, both as a Manchu conqueror and as an active proponent of Chinese culture. (From *Yuanming Yuan: Le jardin de la Clarté parfaite,* by Che Bing Chiu, Paris 2000)

lectual and military prowess. After the completion of the conquest of the main-land, driving the last Ming emperor to his death beyond the southern border, he pushed farther, attacking the Chinese merchant-pirate regime that occupied Taiwan. Enacting a ruthless policy of evacuating the southeast coast to deprive the regime on Taiwan of resources, he starved out his rivals and conquered Taiwan in 1683. With the conquest of Taiwan, he incorporated a new, previously unknown island into imperial territory.[69] But Kangxi showed his true merits when he moved against the large independent territories of the southwest controlled by Chinese generals who had supported the Manchu conquest. These "feudatories" were semi-independent states, forming a powerful rival base of power to the autocratic monarch. Kangxi induced them to rebel and defeated them in brutal and protracted military campaigns from 1673 to 1681. But the largest challenge, as always, came from the Mongols of the northwest. Galdan, a dynamic Mongolian leader, emerged from a Tibetan seminary to construct a powerful state centered in western Mongolia and Xinjiang.[70] The Zunghars, or western Mongols, who controlled this state exerted considerable influence over eastern Mongolia and Tibet. When disputes over succession to the khanship in eastern Mongolia drew in Galdan's forces, Kangxi intervened on the opposing side. He personally led four campaigns against Galdan, leading large numbers of forces over extremely difficult terrain far into Mongolia. He finally defeated the Zunghars in a major battle in 1696. Galdan died the next year, but the Zunghar state persisted. In 1720, Kangxi sent troops into Tibet to determine the succession of the next Panchen Lama, in another effort to undermine links between the Zunghars and Tibet.

Kangxi's successor, the Yongzheng emperor (r. 1723–1735), gave more emphasis to fiscal austerity than to glorious campaigns. He called back many of the distant garrisons in an effort to stabilize the frontier at lower cost. For a short time, Qing–Mongol relations were peaceful, but Yongzheng seized opportunities to cut relations between Tibet and Mongolia by invading Qinghai and razing to the ground thousands of buildings of the major monastery there. He also sent troops to fight in faraway western Mongolia against what he thought was a weak Mongol force. His unfortunate general, however, walked into an ambush, and Qing forces suffered one of their most embarrassing defeats. In despair, the emperor thought that heaven had deserted him. By the end of his reign, the Zunghars seemed at the peak of their power, a serious long-term contender for control of Central Eurasia.

The Qianlong emperor (r. 1736–1796) observed a truce with the Zunghars for twenty years, while attempting to undermine their economic power. He restricted trade missions from Mongolia to Tibet, which passed through Qing territory. When one of the contending parties in a succession dispute in Zungharia asked for Qing support, the emperor seized the opportunity to intervene. The Qing troops made their ally a khan but soon undermined his sole authority; when he resisted, Qing armies suppressed him and his followers. Massacres in the wake of military defeat effectively exterminated the Zunghars as a people when the state collapsed. They either fled into oblivion, died of disease and wounds, or submitted as bond servants and slaves to be distributed among Qing banner garrisons.

The final stage of Qing expansion culminated in the complete conquest of Xinjiang, a vast region of deserts, oases, grasslands, and commercial caravan routes. It was the economic base of the Zunghar state, connected to Tibet's religious state to the south and the oases of Central Asia to the West. Once the Zunghar state had fallen, Qing armies had little difficulty in taking control of the region, but there were outbursts of resistance by the Turkic oasis peoples who resented abusive authority exerted by military commanders. The Qing promoted substantial migration by Han farmers into the north of Xinjiang, both to relieve demographic pressure in interior China and to tie the "New Borderland," as Xinjiang was called, more closely to the center. These Han migrants stirred up more hostility from the local Muslim population that would simmer beneath the surface for over one hundred years.[71]

By 1760, the three most dynamic emperors of the Qing had achieved spectacular results. They had almost tripled the size of imperial territory to nearly twelve million square kilometers; they had completely subjugated the perennial rivals of China-centered dynasties, the pastoral nomads of Central Eurasia; and they had added new peoples with new languages, religions, and ways of life to their realm. The Qing ruling elite was far more diverse in its composition and in its cultural outlook than the Ming. The Qing sponsored large projects of translation, mapping, and ethnographic research to survey the new peoples of their dynasty, which culminated in huge encyclopedic literary projects of the late eighteenth century. The essential dynamic of expansion had stopped by midcentury, however, along with many of the institutional reforms that it stimulated. In this sense, the mid-eighteenth century was the high point of Qing dynamism.

Institutional Changes under the Qing

The expansionist period of Qing rule produced substantial institutional innovation. Unlike the Ming, which rejected many prominent features of Yuan rule, the Qing took over most of the Ming institutions with modifications. They maintained the same structure of provincial administration but added a new position, that of governor-general, usually spanning two provinces. This official, who was often Manchu, coordinated military and civil policy at a macroregional level. Most of the macroregions of the Qing corresponded fairly closely to the governor-generalships. The rest of the civil bureaucracy remained intact, as did the examination system and the education focused on Neo-Confucian orthodoxy. Part of the bargain the Manchus made with local elites was to assure them that their status would remain unthreatened by the new rulers and that the Manchus endorsed classical Confucian values. The outer court, beyond the small ruling circle, looked much like it did under the Ming. That ruling circle of the inner court, however, worked by the very different principles of Manchu society, stressing personal relationships between the ruler and his officials. Bond servants, who were personal slaves of Manchu military men, could become very powerful advisers and officials with close connections to the court. Some prominent Han families, like that of the famous Qing novelist Cao Xueqin (d. 1763), profited greatly from becoming bond servants.[72] With these close personal loyalties, the Manchus had no need for eunuchs except as menial servants, so their numbers and status were drastically reduced.

The most important institutional change at the top of the bureaucracy was the formation of the Grand Council, created specifically to manage military campaigns. This small coordinating body began as a group of personal advisers to the Kangxi emperor during his Central Eurasian campaigns. Under Yongzheng it expanded to become a regular bureaucratic structure, with carefully outlined procedures for reporting and recording information.[73] It relied on secret memorials sent directly from provincial officials to the emperor, bypassing the routine operations of the regular bureaucracy. The emperor personally read and wrote comments on them and returned them to the sender, while copies were made for the archives. The subjects ranged from inquiries about the officials' health, birthday greetings, and special foods to reports on the weather, famines, military policy, tax issues, and immediate questions of social order. The small group of mainly Manchu grand councilors could meet and quickly decide on major policy questions without waiting for the grinding of the bureaucratic wheels of precedent. The Grand Council and secret memorial system reduced the impact of factional loyalty, which the Yongzheng emperor denounced as treasonous, and increased the autocratic decision making power of the emperor. The archives left by this system have given historians of the Qing the most detailed insight into the internal workings of any Chinese bureaucracy in Chinese history.

Qing officials continued the tax reforms that had begun in the late Ming, but abolished the surtaxes imposed by the late Ming. They aimed to keep taxes low and simple. They merged the land tax and poll tax and converted all payments into silver, payable twice yearly by the taxpayer in person. The Kangxi emperor also promised never to raise taxes once the initial rates were set. In theory, farmers could keep the surplus, giving them strong incentives to raise agricultural production. No new land surveys would expose and tax newly cleared land. In fact, local officials had to impose additional informal taxes simply to run their administration, so actual levies could be double or more the formal amount. The Yongzheng emperor attempted to fix this problem by giving officials large bonuses, called "nourishing virtue silver," and using copper–silver conversion charges to stabilize local administrative costs.[74] For a while, this solution was effective, but the underlying structural weakness of underfunded local government and ineffective constraints on informal levies persisted. The collection system was vulnerable to exploitation by corrupt local officials who could disguise extra levies and divert official moneys into their private household accounts. Periodic crackdowns exposed the most egregious offenders, but many escaped.

The expansion of the ever-normal granary system for price stabilization and famine relief was a major achievement of the high Qing.[75] Other dynasties had promoted large-scale granaries, but only the Qing made them function on an empire-wide scale for an extended period of time. Government purchases in the early eighteenth century filled the granaries, at least one to a county, with enough stores to affect local markets. After that, the granary officers could sell in the spring when prices were high and replenish the granaries during the fall harvest, making the system self-financing while also stabilizing prices. In times of major regional famine, granaries could ship large amounts of grain to stricken areas or contract with merchants to deliver supplies. The granary stores grew from 2.5 to over 4.0 million metric tons of grain during the eighteenth century, and they had a positive effect on the relief of agrarian distress. In 1744, when a major drought struck the region around Beijing and Tianjin, the state granaries and Grand Canal shipped 120,000 tons to provide relief to 1.6 million people.[76] Constant discussion by practical officials about the best methods of famine relief and price stabilization showed that officials paid attention to market conditions, using government stores to supplement the private market.[77] Only in the late eighteenth century, when the granaries grew too large and unwieldy, and the rigorous inspection of stores lapsed, did the granary system decline. The greatly expanded population of the high Qing is due in part to the effectiveness of the granary and relief systems.

The Qing also had much wider contacts with the outside world than the Ming and developed new institutions to handle foreign trade and foreign relations. The Lifanyuan, or Court of Colonial Affairs, established in 1638, demonstrated the special concern of Qing rulers with Central Eurasia. Its role was specifically to handle diplomatic and economic relations with the northwest, while the Board of Rites, inherited from the Ming, dealt with all other tributary relations. During the wars of conquest and after, the Lifanyuan rose in status and power, as relations with Central Eurasia became the key strategic focus of the state.[78] The Lifanyuan received emissaries from many Mongol tribes who allied themselves with the Qing, and it later expanded to include Russians, Turkic peoples, and Kazakhs. The creation of this institution shows that the Qing had a special geographic awareness of its status as a Central Eurasian regime and that it did not treat all foreign peoples as equally subordinate to classical precedents. On the northwest frontier, officials often displayed unusual flexibility, allowing foreigners to violate rules of protocol in the interests of making mutual beneficial arrangements.

Foreign Relations and Trade

Relations with the Russians in particular required great flexibility and cross-cultural bridging.[79] As the Russians moved east across Siberia in search of furs, they came into contact first with the "small peoples of the North," who offered no resistance to imposition of fur tribute, then with a series of Mongol tribes, and finally with the Manchus themselves. The Russian tsars claimed autocratic powers over other peoples and forced them to swear oaths of unconditional submission or else face attacks by Cossacks. But they realized that the Mongols were too strong to be subdued, so they had to develop diplomatic skills, drawing on their experience in dealing with Tatars west of the Ural mountains. As they placed their fortresses across Siberia, they inevitably moved into Manchu territory, building the fortress of Albazin in 1651. The Manchus, for their part, were mainly concerned with driving out the Ming forces in the mid-seventeenth century, but they turned their attention back to Central Eurasia, destroying the fortress in 1685. The Russians promptly rebuilt it, and Qing forces destroyed it again. The stage was set for a confrontation between two autocratic regimes of contrasting religious faiths, each intolerant of a rival. Yet both sides had reasons to compromise. The Russians wanted to sell furs in Beijing, and the Qing wanted Russian neutrality in the forthcoming battle with the Zunghar Mongols. Russians, Manchus, Mongols, and Jesuit missionaries on both sides met to hammer out a peace treaty in Nerchinsk in 1689. The Jesuits on the Qing side, speaking in Latin with a Polish translator working for the Russians, played the key intermediary role. Although negotiations repeatedly threatened to break down, each side eventually backed down from its extreme demands, leading to the first treaty signed on an equal basis by China with a European power, the Nerchinsk Treaty of 1689. It was followed by the Kiakhta Treaty of 1727, which delineated much of the border between the two empires and established regulated trade at the border. The Russians were able to establish an ecclesiastical mission in Beijing, and they kept their agreement to withhold support from Galdan, the Zunghar leader.[80] The Jesuits gained influence in both countries as a result of their diplomatic contributions.

Just as the Ming had offered the Portuguese a small leasehold in Macau, in order to revive the economy of the south and reduce piracy, the Qing created regulated trade on the northwest frontier for economic and political goals. Both experiences turned out to be mutually beneficial, and they set a pattern to be followed when the British arrived seeking trade at Canton in the late eighteenth century.

In handling frontier trade, the Qing turned to private merchant contractors with considerable success. Unlike the Ming, it did not grant monopoly licenses to support the frontier campaigns but simply bought merchant services to supply the troops. After the conquests were finished, merchants continued to provision markets along the borders, with the help of frontier officials. Conflicts arose when canny Central Eurasian traders brought goods to the frontier market that exceeded the amounts allowed by regulations. Officials faced the unappetizing choice of either leaving rejected excessive herds of sheep and cattle dead on the steppe or attempting to dispose of surplus goods to private merchants, and they often chose to rely on these merchants to resolve the conflict, bending regulations so as to provide for the local people. This pattern of official–merchant cooperation, and conflicts with foreign traders pressing for more open markets, would repeat itself in Canton in the late eighteenth century.

Economic and Environmental Transformations

The broadest effects of this unprecedented Qing expansion were the opportunities it offered for economic growth, both in agriculture and commerce. The population at least doubled during the eighteenth century, from 150 to 300 million, while the total land area under the Qing nearly tripled. Not all of this new land was arable, but enterprising farmers pushed out in every direction to exploit all available resources.[81] They moved into Mongolia and Xinjiang to convert grasslands into fields, encouraged by government subsidies. In Southwest China and Taiwan, they drove out swidden cultivators and replaced their low-intensity cultivation with rice paddy terraces and hillside crops. In central China, thousands of small lakes disappeared, while the great lakes of Dongting in Hunan and Boyang in Jiangxi shrank substantially as rice paddies grew. One large lake in Zhejiang Province, renowned for its aesthetic beauty and celebrated by landscape painters and poets for centuries, nearly disappeared because commercial interests dug up its bottom soil to make bricks and exhausted its fish.[82] In Guangdong, farmers intensified cultivation so much that they could produce three crops a year and carefully coordinated production of fish from ponds with mulberry cultivation and silkworm raising.[83] Officials often exulted in the clearance of new lands and the new populations they would support, like the conquistador of Guizhou, Peng Ermi, who boasted proudly:

> We have chiseled through hills, and flattened highways, drums rumbling to
> trumpets' music,

Helmeted on our chargers' backs, parched grain wrapped for travel food,
Ox carts carrying those of importance, while the lesser bear loads on their
  backs,
Every day, for our Imperial Court, we've developed new arable lands.[84]

But some prescient observers warned that excessive clearance, deforestation, siltation of lakes, and neglect of water conservancy could lead to disastrous floods. Yang Xifu, a provincial governor serving in Hunan in 1744, for example, thought that "private" (that is, illegal) dike building had taken over from the common interest in preserving the watershed, and officials needed to intervene to ensure sustainable production.[85] But in general Qing officials were far more effective in promoting rapid land clearance than they were in protecting forests, species, lakes, and vulnerable people from extinction.

Did Qing China face a growing environmental crisis in the mid-eighteenth century? Certain foreign and local observers noted growing strains and signs of increasing poverty and disaster, but in comparative perspective, Qing China was not more overpopulated or resource constrained than the densely settled parts of Western Europe.[86] But much depended on how well the state maintained the agrarian infrastructure. As long as the granaries functioned well, dikes were maintained, and enough reasonably honest and perceptive officials dedicated themselves to the popular welfare, under the close supervision of their superiors, most people prospered. Once the effectiveness of the bureaucracy declined, as it began to do after midcentury, China headed toward more frequent and severe natural and political crises.

Intellectual and Cultural Life in the Qing

The Manchus had come to power promising to restore political and social order, and most of the Han elite besides the die-hard Ming loyalists supported their project. The Kangxi emperor held a special high-level exam to lure back the leading scholars, and he promoted the restoration of Zhu Xi's orthodox version of Confucian learning. Scholars and rulers alike rejected the freethinkers of the late Ming and turned away from open political dispute. They regarded factionalism, or the horizontal organization of like-minded thinkers, as threatening to the hierarchical relationship of rulers and subjects. Yet the Manchus knew that under the obedient

surface many Chinese scholars still regarded them as barbarians. In 1728, an obscure schoolteacher named Zeng Jing appealed to a leading general to overthrow
the Manchus and restore a genuinely Han dynasty. Even though the plot never
went beyond Zeng's imagination, the Yongzheng emperor reacted furiously, inter-
rogating Zeng intensively and then writing his own lengthy refutation of the idea
that the Manchus were a separate race.[87] Yet he pardoned Zeng Jing himself. The
Qianlong emperor, however, when he came to the throne, had Zeng executed and
attempted to search out and destroy all copies of his father Yongzheng's treatise.
Qianlong, more than Yongzheng, endorsed Manchu separatism, as he feared that
distinctive Manchu practices, including their hunting, language, and knowledge
of history, would disappear in the sea of Han culture. Later, Qianlong sponsored
two huge literary projects: one designed to collect and carefully evaluate thousands
of classical Chinese texts with the highest-quality scholarly analysis, the other designed to purge from the canon any texts that hinted at disparagement of the
Manchus or their ancestors.[88] Qianlong epitomized the contradictory tendencies
of celebration and defensiveness embedded in Manchu rule.

At the same time, Han scholars were reevaluating their own tradition, subtly
challenging the prevailing orthodoxy. The "empirical research" school arising out
of Gu Yanwu's critique of Ming thought focused on precise, technical, philological methods to reconstruct the exact sense and sound of the classical texts.[89] One
result of this research was to prove that some of the most admired ancient texts
were in fact forgeries of a later era. These discoveries implicitly shook the foundations of an unquestioned tradition just as much as nineteenth-century biblical criticism undermined Christianity. The scholars could not form political groups to
spread their views, but they could protect themselves within their lineages. Many
of them came from wealthy lineages in the lower Yangzi valley, who had high degrees and official positions. Their patrons could insulate them from political winds
and provide a certain degree of intellectual freedom.

Others decided to work with the state, focusing on practical methods of administration. Chen Hongmou (1696–1771), an official who served in many posts
around the empire, is a good example of a Chinese official who did his best to carry
out the moral injunctions of the classical past under the Manchu regime.[90] He
encouraged land reclamation, famine relief, primary schooling for minority populations, control of water, and active engagement in charitable and fiscal reforms

that benefited the local population. He also encouraged teaching women to read and write, as the best-educated mothers produced the best-educated sons. He found a positive role for merchants and the market principle, arguing that the state should try not to suppress the incentive for profit but to direct it toward useful social ends: for example, by using granaries to adjust prices so that merchants would deliver supplies where they were needed.

The Story of the Stone (also known as the *Dream of the Red Chamber*), written from 1744 to 1763 by the unsuccessful scholar Cao Xueqin, is the crowning glory of vernacular Chinese literature. Cao wrote the novel based on the experiences of his own family, a wealthy Chinese family who were bond servants of the Manchus in Nanjing. They lived a prosperous, leisurely life in a large courtyard house in Nanjing, with over one hundred servants and relatives, until the Yongzheng emperor suddenly confiscated all their property, throwing Cao into poverty. Living in obscurity in Beijing, Cao reconstructed a nostalgic picture of his past in a novel of 120 leisurely, elegantly written chapters. It describes the maturation of Jia Baoyu, a son of a wealthy family with close connections to the imperial court, and the path of his family members from self-indulgence to ruin. Most memorable are the women, like the sober Bao Chai, and the excitable, fascinating Dai Yu, who are rivals for Baoyu's attentions, and the tough matriarch of the household, Wang Xifeng. The delicate interplay of poetic romance, bawdy humor, literary allusion, and rugged dialogue gives us an invaluably vivid picture drawn from Cao's own life of the complex interpersonal relations within one wealthy household. The novel ends in tragedy, with the confiscation of the family fortune, Dai Yu's death, and Baoyu's escape from the world into a monastery.

By the mid-eighteenth century, the emperor and his officials and many ordinary Chinese could look upon the ruling regime with considerable pride and complacency. The Manchus had restored order, encouraged agricultural and commercial growth, and greatly expanded the territory of the empire. They had destroyed the biggest military threats, both internal and external, and warded off the new Western power, the Russians. Nearly all Chinese accepted the Manchus as legitimate rulers, the treasury held a surplus, and famine relief institutions relieved poverty, while farmers could move to clear new lands for themselves. Internal markets provided many new commercial products, but most families worked the land to produce grain and textiles for themselves. Elite women could attain literacy and

The chapbook known as *The Bandits of Liangshan Moor* recounts the noble exploits of bands of rebels who protect the common populace from oppression by corrupt local officials. These bands of brigands were formed of former officers, bandits, outlaws, and frustrated intellectuals, who attempted to combat the injustices of their time through violent insurrection. While stories of such groups were banned under the Qing dynasty, they still gained circulation in printed form, as well as in the form of pictures or as tales recounted by professional storytellers in the cities. These stories expressed the Chinese people's demand for collective action to curtail the immoral excesses of the ruling class. (From *The Cambridge Illustrated History of China,* by Patricia Buckley Ebrey, © Cambridge University Press, 1996)

participate in poetry circles, while commoners supported a prosperous peasant economy with textile production.[91]

Yet there were also underlying fears of social change reflected in official discourse and changes in legal codes. As the rising population put pressure on landholdings, the new mobility provided by marketing systems and transport businesses created increasing numbers of vagrant men, who wandered in search of new jobs away from limited supplies of land. The patriarchal family system, which favored the birth of males and limited the numbers of women, created a demographic imbalance that deprived poor men of partners. These "bare sticks" *(guanggun)* and "wandering hoodlums" *(liumang),* roving rogue males without a settled home, were perceived as major threats to established villages and households. Qing law codes on sexual crimes changed their emphasis, focusing on the protection of women against attacks by these rogue males and protecting men against homosexual rape. Commercial prostitution was outlawed and female chastity by widows given great stress through rewards and legal provisions.[92] In 1768, the Qianlong emperor panicked when he heard that wandering men who embraced anti-Manchu ideas were cutting off the queues Manchus had imposed on the population, and sorcerers were spreading tales of the imminent decline of the dynasty. Qianlong's witch hunt against these elusive rebels produced no results, but it indicated uneasiness about the stability of Qing rule in the face of mobile, freer, and heterodox marginal elements.[93] In the late eighteenth and early nineteenth centuries, these subdued tensions would break out in a catastrophic series of rebellions induced by environmental pressure, official corruption, and cultural conflict. But in the middle of the century, only mild premonitions of the ensuing crises were apparent.

2. Russia

AFTER the breakup of the Mongol Empire, Central and Northern Eurasia fragmented into multiple khanates. Timur's brief rise and fall caused further upheaval, and until the mid-fifteenth century no dominant ruler arose, as the remnants of the Mongolian khans steadily lost influence. Beginning around 1450, however, the grand princes of Muscovy slowly and steadily accumulated territories and military forces, building a large state spanning all of northern Eurasia and contending with European powers to the west. By 1750, the territory of the Russian state had reached about three-quarters of its maximum size. At its peak in 1820, it spanned eighteen million square kilometers, with a population of over forty-two million. Russia had become an empire of vast size and diversity, stretching from the Ukraine and Poland in the west across Siberia to the borders of Manchuria. It was a powerful actor in both European and Asian geopolitics and trade.[94]

Most of the Russian lands lie within the forest zone of northern Eurasia. From early times, peasant settlers had hacked their way through the dense forests, establishing an extensive but thinly populated cultural region. But the Russian settlements closely bordered steppelands, and Russians frequently interacted with steppe nomads through trade, diplomatic exchange, and warfare. Urban settlements arose at the conjunction of rivers and forest trade routes, and princes created states at Kiev, Novgorod, Smolensk, Tver, and other towns. Russian rulers faced four ways: north to the Baltic Sea, west to Poland and Lithuania, south to the Byzantine Empire, and east toward steppe pastoralists. No natural barriers protected the Russian states, so they constantly faced threats on all fronts. The incessant focus on wealth and warfare of Russian state builders was a consequence of their vulnerable position in the flatlands of northern Eurasia and their determination to carve out territorial domination against their rivals.

The Kievan state, ruled by Varangian or Viking warriors, linked the peasant and urban settlements through river networks to the wealthy empire of Byzantium to the south and the Baltic to the north. In 1240 the Mongols destroyed the

The Russian Empire
- Russia 1533
- Russia 1598
- Russia 1721
- Russia 1796

BRITISH NORTH AMERICA
(CANADA)

Novo Arkhangelsk
(Sitka)

RUSSIAN
AMERICA
(ALASKA)

ALEUT

INUIT

INUIT

Bering Strait

INUIT

BERING SEA

CHUKCHI

KORYAK

Kamchatka
Peninsula
Petropavlovsk

ARCTIC OCEAN

Greenland

North Pole

SEA OF
OKHOTSK

Zashiversk

Okhotsk

Severnaya Zemlya

Zhigansk

Lena

Yakutsk

Sakhalin

EVENKI

YAKUT

LAMUT

Amur

Nerchinsk

NORTH SEA

Novaya Zemlya

BARENTS
SEA

KARA
SEA

S i b e r i a

EVENKI

MANCHURIA

SWEDEN

Archangelsk

Ural Mts.

SAMOYED

Obdorsk

Surgut

Ob

Yenisei

TUNGUS

OSTYAK

Bratsk

Lake Baikal

FINLAND

St. Petersburg

Novgorod

Krasnoyarsk

Irkutsk

Riga

TARTARS

Verkhoturye

PRUSSIA

Smolensk

Moscow

Nizhnii
Novgorod

Omsk

Biysk

MONGOLIA

POLAND

Kiev

UKRAINE

Saratov

Samara

COSSACKS

KAZAKHS

QING EMPIRE

AUSTRIA

COSSACKS

Volga

Lake Balkhash

BLACK
SEA

Aral Sea

TIBET

Constantinople

GEORGIA

CASPIAN
SEA

BHUTAN

OTTOMAN
EMPIRE

NEPAL

BURMA

Alexandria

Baghdad

AFGHANISTAN

Indus

INDIA

PERSIA

Russia, 1533–1796

Kievan state and razed the city. Other Russian states, like Novgorod and Smolensk, also fell under Mongol domination. They all owed tribute to the Kipchak khanate, later called the Golden Horde, whose capital was at Sarai on the Volga River near the Caspian Sea. Other khanates, at Astrakhan, Kazan, Sibir, and Crimea, also owed tribute to the khanate at Sarai. Moscow, like the other Russian states, participated actively in the steppe politics of the time. The Muscovite rulers created their vast domain by adroit negotiation with the remaining Mongol and Tatar powers of Central Eurasia.

Russia and the Kipchak Khanate ("Golden Horde")

Although the Mongols destroyed Kiev in 1240, the Russian lands in general, because of their sparse population, were only sporadically damaged by Mongol conquests. The princes ruling the vast steppes and forests all were forced to submit to the khan. In the khans' eyes, Russia itself was a distant, poor periphery, useful only in providing tax revenues and slaves.

Only about four thousand Mongols lived in the khanate, and most of their army was Turkish. Turkish soon became the dominant official language, and the khans converted to Islam. The Russians called them by the insulting term "Tatars." Even so, the Tatars tolerated Christianity, allowing the Orthodox Metropolitan to control his church as long as he paid tribute. The Metropolitan shifted the center of Russian spiritual life to Moscow in 1300. Like the Muscovite princes, he secured his authority by obeying the khans in Sarai. As in Yuan China, the princes beat their heads on the ground, kowtowing before the khans to obtain licenses to rule, helping the khans to suppress other princes, and loyally delivering tribute. Ivan Kalita ("Moneybags"), who married a Tatar princess, was named the first grand prince in 1328.

Centrally located on the classic Eurasian silk routes, Sarai thrived from commerce between Russia, the Middle East, and the Mediterranean. As Italian traders competed for privileges with the khans, the Genoese established dominance there and in the Crimea, driving out their rivals, the Venetians. Sarai also borrowed culture and technology from Egypt. The khans even built dams to provide hydraulic power for extensive ceramic factories.

Until about 1350, Russia and the khanate flourished because of these contacts with the wealthy south. Soon after, however, internecine warfare disrupted trade at Sarai, and Russian princes began to break away. In 1371, the first Russian prince refused to pay tribute to Sarai, and in 1380, at Kulikovo on the Don, Dimitri Donskoi led the Muscovite army to its first major victory over the Mongols. It had little effect, however. The Horde seemed to be breaking apart until eastern nomads injected new energy into it. Tokhtamysh, a follower of Timur, took over the Horde, sacked Moscow in 1382, and forced the Muscovites to resume tribute. Until the late fifteenth century, Russian princes remained firmly dependent on the Mongol khans.

Muscovite Tsars and Expansion

The protracted disintegration of the Mongol Empire, followed by Timur's devastation, created a power vacuum in Central Eurasia. The plagues of the Black Death struck the major cities of the Kipchak khanate in the late fourteenth century, while Timur's attacks delivered the final blow to their trade. Upheaval and fragmentation offered new opportunities. In the Kipchak khanate, regional rulers broke away from the control of the khan at Sarai: Crimea in 1430, Kazan in 1436, and Astrakhan in 1466. Muscovy, which formally cut tribute ties with the khan in 1480, was at first only another of these regional powers, but by 1500, the grand princes of Muscovy had come to dominate western Eurasia. Cooperating eagerly with the khans, they steadily increased their possessions through purchase, inheritance, colonization, diplomacy, and conquest.

Although many Russian historians have described Muscovy's rise as the "gathering of Russian lands," creating a uniform Slavic culture that threw off the barbarian "Tatar yoke," the real story is quite different. Muscovy was no outsider but an experienced player in Mongol–Tatar affairs. Moscow, its capital, controlled the headwaters of four major rivers: the Oka, Volga, Don, and Dnieper, where furs from the north met the major water routes leading south to the wealth of Byzantium and the Ottoman Empire. It had strong commercial and diplomatic ties with Kazan, on the lower Volga, and later with the Crimean khanate on the Black Sea. The Russian princes, who traveled frequently to Sarai, adopted many institutions from the Mongols, whom they knew well.[95] They implemented the Mongols' efficient postal system, used Mongol-style tax collectors, and practiced similar kinds of clan rule. They adopted methods of warfare from the steppe, including the use of cavalry, Tatar-style bows, helmets, saddles, and military maneuvers. Some historians accuse the Mongols of bringing "Oriental despotism" to Russia, replacing the more egalitarian confederation of Kiev. But Muscovy was in fact no more despotic than its neighboring rival states. It was not despotism that Russians learned from the Mongols but how to use family connections to control vast, poor lands.

Other princes in Eurasia aimed at similar goals of territorial expansion, enhanced wealth, and a more rationally integrated administration. Muscovy was a rather poor, remote frontier kingdom, but it practiced steppe politics better than its rivals. The Tatar khans gave their rulers the title of grand prince and protected them against their enemies. Until the mid-fifteenth century, the princes acted mainly as passive dependents, but they were able to expand their territory from a small principality to a significant state of 400,000 square kilometers by 1462. They still faced other states, like Novgorod, Tver, and Smolensk, of equal or greater size and wealth, and the large state of Poland-Lithuania pressed on all of them from the west.[96]

Grand Prince Ivan III (the Great) of Moscow (r. 1462–1505) built his kingdom by engaging in ceaseless military and commercial competition. Over the previous century, his predecessors had expanded the principality enormously, but Ivan aimed for undisputed domination of all the Russian lands. Muscovy's size tripled during his reign. His first goal was to break the power of Novgorod, where Baltic Germans and Scandinavians dominated the fur trade. The city was commercially powerful but militarily weak, with its own *veche* (assembly) of leading boyars and merchants. It rose to its peak of influence in the fifteenth century, but when Ivan besieged the city in 1478, it surrendered without a fight. Ivan abolished the veche, carried away the city bell, executed many top leaders, deported the leading boyars to Moscow, and exiled much of the population to the far north. After eliminating Tver, another serious rival, Muscovy faced no serious princely opposition. Ivan then took the title of *gosudar,* or sovereign, calling himself grand prince of Muscovy and all the Russias.

Ivan also actively pursued ties to the wealthy Middle East. His marriage to Sophia Paleologos of Byzantium brought in Greek and Italian architectural influences. Skilled builders turned Moscow's Kremlin from a crude wooden fort

The Kremlin, a self-contained fortress in Moscow, formed the political and spiritual center of the expanding polity of Muscovy. Tsar Ivan III commissioned Italian architects to build the citadel's walls, towers, and cathedrals in the Renaissance style but to adhere to Russian traditions in the process. The Cathedral of the Dormition, the center of the Russian Orthodox Church, played host to the coronations and burials of all the Orthodox patriarchs. Under Peter the Great, Moscow declined in importance, as the tsar established his new capital of St. Petersburg on the shores of the Baltic, yet Catherine II (the Great) was to strengthen Moscow's role once more through her investment in a series of new churches and palaces. (© Diego Lezama Orezzoli)

into a striking example of Italian Renaissance architecture. The thick brick walls, the Cathedrals of the Dormition and Annunciation, the Palace of Facets, and the bell tower formed the colorful core of the Kremlin compound.

By 1500, Moscow had about a hundred thousand people. It was still a fortress town, whose walls indicated the need to defend against the new gunpowder artillery, but the growing power of the prince created a flourishing urban economy. After recurrent plagues ended in the mid-fifteenth century the Muscovite state's population grew steadily, reaching about 6.5 million in the mid-sixteenth century. The climate of northern Eurasia entered a modest warming phase as well, and newer, more intensive agricultural techniques increased the agrarian surplus.

Commerce also expanded, supported by state initiatives. The rulers required rents and taxes to be paid in cash, forcing farmers to trade their crops in marketplaces. Moscow was able to accumulate silver bullion from Central Europe by exporting furs and forest products. At the same time, the state exacted much higher taxes from peasants and townsmen to fulfill its insatiable military demands, and it created monopolies on alcohol and salt to further increase its profits.

Ivan made a crucial alliance with the khan of the Crimea, Mengli Girei, who prospered from his position on the Black Sea between the Golden Horde, Byzantium, and the Ottomans. Mengli Girei had split off from the Horde in 1430 and become a vassal of the Ottomans in 1475. In the century after its conquest by the Turks in 1453, Istanbul dominated the trade north of the Black Sea, and the Crimeans prospered by supplying the city with grain. This alliance allowed Ivan to reject tribute demands from the khan of the Golden Horde and to resist pressures from the Lithuanian and Polish state to his west. The Lithuanians, in turn, allied with the khan of the Horde against Ivan and the Crimea. In 1480, the year of the final throwing off of the "Tatar yoke," the khan's attack on Ivan failed because his Lithuanian allies never arrived. In sum, the creation of Muscovy did not involve a clear-cut struggle between Christian and infidel but many powers vying for the wealth of the remnants of the Mongol Empire.

As a new state growing on a fluid frontier, Muscovy, like the Manchus, did not have to face established internal rivals, like bourgeois and noble estates, autonomous religious establishments, military brotherhoods, or independent villages. Its primary focus was military expansion and accumulation of wealth. Muscovy imported European firearms and copied the new, expensive military technologies of fortresses and artillery. But like the other gunpowder empires of the sixteenth century, Ivan needed large revenues, and he greedily sought resources for his state. He confiscated 2.7 million acres of church lands. State-promoted colonization of the northeast developed forest industries, salt extraction, fishing, and, most important, the fur trade. To ensure that peasants paid their levies, Ivan began restricting the right of peasants to leave the land. Serfdom grew hand in hand with military demands. New money taxes supported the postal courier system.

In return for service, Ivan gave his boyars land *(pomestie)*, very much like the Ottoman *timar* or the earlier Islamic *iqta'*. Unlike the boyar's hereditary patrimony, the pomestie was subject to revocation at the ruler's whim. Pomestie provided income for cavalrymen under the prince's direct control, freeing him from dependence on the boyars. In return for their service obligations, the state began to restrict the mobility of the peasantry to ensure noble revenues, setting Muscovy on the path to full serfdom.

Nobles in search of rewards competed vigorously for status at court, striving to occupy a "place" *(mesto)* as close to the ruler as possible. An elaborate system of ranks and titles *(mestnichestvo),* carefully recorded in registers, regulated their status. Except for the church, there was no alternative to court service and no choice of princes to serve. The autocracy of Muscovy was a product of the pomestie land system and the lack of independent bases of power and legitimacy for the local elites.

The growing state also needed an ideology, but unlike China, Persia, or France, for example, Muscovy had no indigenous imperial traditions. The Russians did borrow Turkish and Mongolian words like *den'gi* (money), *bumaga* (paper), and *yam* (postal courier), and Muscovite rulers first relied on Mongolian political institutions, but these were not broad enough. Central Eurasians and Chinese called the Russian ruler the "White [Western] khan," but he needed a different, more universal basis of legitimation for his Russian Orthodox subjects. He surrounded Tatar administrative practices with Byzantine and Orthodox theories and symbols.

To legitimate the new state, Orthodox churchmen began to develop the theory of the "Third Rome." According to this theory, Rome had nurtured the early Christian church, but Byzantium inherited the true faith after the Great Schism of 1054. The conquest of Constantinople by the Turks in 1453 demonstrated that Byzantium had lost the grace of God, transferring the Christian mission to Moscow. In 1492, the year 7000 from the date of creation, millenarian thinking flourished, but afterward, the dream of an all-powerful Orthodox leader held on. As one monk wrote, "The Russian Tsar will be elevated by God above other nations, and under his sway will be many heathen kings."[97] As the church stamped out heretics, its leaders exalted the unlimited power of the prince of Muscovy with more ambitious titles. Ivan III had occasionally used the title "Tsar," which combined the Roman-Byzantine legacy of "caesar" with the "khan" of Central Eurasia, making the Russian ruler the "autocrat" *(Samoderzhavets)* and Defender of the Faith in one. Ivan IV assumed the formal title of tsar in 1547. Only a few clergymen genuinely endorsed the Third Rome theory at this time, but supporters of seventeenth-century tsars found it useful for justifying autocratic rule based on religion and power.

The chroniclers also reminded the ruler of his responsibilities to his Christian subjects, and these duties, like the Chinese Mandate of Heaven, could imply limits to autocratic authority. One clergyman wrote, "If the Tsar who rules men is himself ruled by evil passions and sins . . . such a Tsar is not God's servant but the Devil's, and he should not be considered a Tsar, but a tormentor." The Confucian philosopher Mencius had invoked the same right to disobey an evil ruler. Later in the seventeenth century, Orthodox Old Believers attacked the tsar as Antichrist, as did rioters in Moscow in 1648.[98]

Despite conflicts in practice, early modern Russians did create a consciousness of a unified national community. The ideal tsar ensured a harmonious relationship between rulers and subjects by consulting with his boyars, practicing benevolent rule, and supporting the church.[99] The penetration of Orthodox Christianity into the countryside tied rulers and subjects more closely together and came to define a key cultural feature of Russia. Even though most of the boyar noble class were not of Russian origins but were instead a diverse group of Tatars and other Slavic and Central Asian people, they were just as illiterate as their subjects, and they became Orthodox Christians, united by their hostility to enemies in the east, west, and south. The ideology of the liberation of the Slavic lands from the "Tatar yoke," suppressing Muscovy's close ties to the khans, became stronger in the sixteenth century, especially after the conquest of Astrakhan and Kazan.[100] Russians defined themselves as the land of Orthodoxy and the tsar as God's chosen instrument for the victory of Orthodox Christianity over both paganism and Catholicism. The tsar's victories inspired anti-Muslim folk songs, reinforced by official and popular histories. Monasteries spread through the countryside to promote this message among the rural majority, while at rural markets and fairs traveling peddlers communicated with each other in a limited but growing information network. By 1550 monasteries owned one-third of the cultivated land and had enormous influence in the countryside.[101]

The Muscovite bureaucracy was rudimentary. Only about one thousand to fifteen hundred administrators governed the vast lands. Provincial governors literally fed themselves by extracting their provisions from the local population.

Muscovy needed literate clerks to draw up state documents, but the nobility itself was illiterate. Sons of priests provided the first scribes, who became the nucleus of a bureaucracy, but structures of salaries, incentives, and promotions developed slowly. For quite a while, Kipchak Turkish remained the standard lingua franca for internal and external relations, but official Russian documentary language developed in the sixteenth century, while Old Church Slavonic remained with the religious hierarchy. Specialized ministries for finance, foreign relations, and other spheres worked out a technical language in voluminous documents, but Muscovy remained a nearly illiterate society. Church ritual relied on the brilliant imagery of icons, not on the word. Muscovy's many merchants had nothing like Ming China's vernacular printed culture.

By 1500, religious backing, commercial links, and military superiority had made Muscovy the predominant power of the Slavic lands, but its rulers had even more grandiose aims: cautious but continuous expansion across Eurasia.

Collapse and Revival

The strange, paradoxical figure of Ivan IV ("the Terrible" or "Threatening"; r. 1533–1584) nearly wrecked the Muscovite state established in the wake of the Mongol Empire. Historians have never agreed on his character: was he artistic, sensitive, and farsighted or psychopathic, savage, and deranged? He was the first ruler to call himself "tsar and autocrat," but he destroyed much of the elite and the economy. He, or his advisers, reformed the administration and conquered Kazan and Astrakhan but ruined the country with the useless Livonian War.

Ivan grew up under the regency of his mother and leading boyar families like the Shuiskiis, whose intrigues threatened his life. Muscovy's centralization was precarious. Without a strong central leader, the state apparatus dissolved into turbulent factionalism, much like during the late Ming. Ivan's first official act, at age thirteen, was to have Prince Shuiskii thrown to the dogs. His reign began ominously. A fire during his majestic coronation ceremony caused terrified mobs to storm the Kremlin.

At first, capable administrators enacted reforms, and Ivan brought more boyars into the noble assembly *(duma).* The first *zemskii sobor* (Assembly of the Land), convened in 1549 and 1566, brought together people from different estates to consult on public affairs. But at the same time, the new law code of 1550 almost completely eliminated the peasants' freedom to move. New special army units, supported by rationalized service obligations, learned to use firearms. Ivan established the first truly professional soldiers with fixed salaries, the sharpshooters, or *streltsy*.

After 1560, when his young wife died, Ivan struck out on his own. Threatening to abdicate the throne, he returned only when promised absolute power. His notorious *oprichnina,* established in 1565, could prosecute anyone for disloyalty. For seven years, wearing bizarre dark robes, with dogs' heads on their saddles, these young men terrorized princely families, local gentry, townspeople, foreigners, and villagers indiscriminately. Over four thousand people lost their lives. The oprichnina sacked and burned Novgorod because of its merchants' foreign contacts. Some Russian historians have praised the oprichnina for eliminating corrupt boyars, while others have called it a merchant and lower-gentry-class alliance against the nobles, but the devastation showed little economic or administrative rationality. We cannot ignore Ivan's paranoid personality, exacerbated by a painful bone disease. Great (or terrible) men do change history.

Meanwhile, Ivan's foreign minister, Aleksej Adashev, carefully moved against Kazan. He cleverly cultivated supporters within the city, but in the end Ivan had to besiege the city in 1552. The fall of Astrakhan in 1556 consolidated Moscow's position on the Volga but risked causing conflict with the Ottoman Empire. Both sides avoided major conflict in order to keep their profitable commerce.

Muscovy then expanded further south and east with the help of Cossacks. The Cossacks had gathered in the southern borderlands of Russia (the modern Ukraine) from the mid-fifteenth century. These freebooters included Tatars fleeing Moscow's service, peasants fleeing landlords, roving tribesmen, and unemployed soldiers. By the sixteenth century, they had created fortified self-governing communities, electing their own headmen, and were living from fishing and agriculture in the Don and Dnieper valleys. Like Siberia, the Ukraine, far from the landlord, military recruiter, or tax collector, offered freedom to the common Russian. Both Polish and Russian rulers realized that the Cossacks would serve them loyally if given rewards, and so did wealthy merchants. The Stroganovs, who since the 1550s had actively promoted Siberian expansion so as to increase their profits from furs and salt, hired the Cossack Ermak to open up Siberia for them. By 1645 nearly seventy thousand Russians had crossed the Ural Mountains, heading east into new lands.[102]

Muscovy's catastrophic western expansion, by contrast, squandered the profits of its eastern gains. In the Livonian War (1558–1583), Ivan fought the powerful, efficiently armed states of Poland, Lithuania, Sweden, and Denmark. Taxes per acre on the peasant rose by more than ten times in monetary terms from 1530 to 1584, and 84 percent of the state budget went to the military. In sum, Ivan's oprichnina and his wars left the country economically ruined, filled with desolate villages and abandoned land.

The English found their way to Russia via Archangelsk during Ivan's reign, while looking for a northeast passage to China's fabled markets. In 1553 the tsar welcomed Richard Chancellor to Moscow and offered the English commercial privileges, hoping to break a blockade by the Poles, Germans, and Swedes. The English found no river passage to China but expected to reach Persia down the Volga River. They established their first chartered company, the Muscovy Company, to promote overseas trade.

English visitors provided valuable, though biased, accounts of this new "rude and barbarous kingdom." Giles Fletcher depicted "a true and strange face of a tyrannical state . . . without true knowledge of God, without written Law, without common justice," the exact opposite, in his view, of the balanced constitution of Tudor England.[103] Ever since, Russia has often served as the Oriental Other for observers warning Westerners to guard their constitutional liberties. Indirectly, Fletcher's account protested royal absolutism in England. Like Chinese critics of the Manchus and the political theorist Montesquieu, who criticized the arbitrary rule of French kings, Fletcher believed that only a hereditary nobility could prevent despotism. This, he thought, was what Muscovy lacked.

The Time of Troubles (1598–1613)

Ivan the Terrible's overextension of Russia left the country vulnerable to a new crisis in the seventeenth century, known as the Time of Troubles, during which Russians suffered social upheaval and foreign invasion. As in the Ming–Qing transition, one dynasty fell, but in the end, a new native dynasty, the Romanovs, restored the autocracy.[104]

Ivan had murdered his eldest son in a fit of rage, leaving his second son, Fyodor, a much weaker man, to rule. During Fyodor's life and after his death in 1582, the capable minister Boris Godunov took charge. (Godunov is better known as the legendary usurper in Mussorgsky's opera than for his real achievements.) Godunov was elected tsar by the *zemskii sobor* with fervent prayers of support from the clergy and people of Moscow. But he was unlucky. From 1601 to 1603, a catastrophic famine struck the devastated country. One hundred thousand people died in Moscow alone. Soon, rumors spread that because Boris had murdered nine-year-old Dmitri of Uglich, Ivan's youngest son, heaven was punishing the people for his sins. There is no evidence that Boris murdered the young heir, but the myth is as ineradicable as Shakespeare's tale of Richard III and the boys in the tower. A refugee monk, the "false Dmitri," invaded Russia in 1604 with an army of Cossacks and Poles. Boris Godunov died the next year. When the false Dmitri and his Polish entourage alienated the Russians, Prince Basil Shuiskii led a coup and proclaimed himself tsar. On the southern frontier, the Cossack Bolotnikov led a diverse group of people, including runaway peasants and non-Russian minorities, in a major revolt. Slave rebellions, a second false Dmitri, and a Swedish invasion prolonged the chaos until an army led by Kusma Minin, by profession a butcher, and the warrior Dimitri Pozharsky, supported by Cossacks, responded to desperate appeals from the church and freed Moscow from foreign occupation. A zemskii sobor elected as tsar thirteen-year-old Michael Romanov in 1613. The Romanovs finally restored order, preserving the positions of the aristocracy and the Orthodox Church.

The Romanov Autocracy

The Romanovs' autocracy (1613–1917) lasted for three hundred years. They created a durable, though oppressive, political system. The elites followed secret but predictable patterns of conduct. Three cultural spheres held Russia together: the peasant village at the local level, the state and the bureaucracy at the center and provincial level, and small groups who stood outside the system. Let us briefly examine the logic of each.[105]

The State and Agrarian Society

The Russian state had expanded over a vast, thinly populated territory, mostly located in northern lands with low agricultural yields. To hold these lands together, the rulers focused on limited goals. They extracted enough from the population to support a basic military and bureaucratic apparatus. Centralization was the key: all resources had to be funneled to Moscow. Regional autonomy threatened to destroy the entire structure. Rulers exploited all possible sources of revenue, in agriculture, trade, and industry. Foreigners marveled at the "greed," or business sense, of the tsars. The Chinese emperors, equally autocratic and expansive, could afford to leave a greater surplus among the people and ignore mercantile wealth, because they could draw on rich lands in the south. Muscovy had fewer options.

Russian peasants also faced a precarious, hostile environment with relatively few tools. The village community, or *mir* (which also means "world"), insured them against disaster. By periodically redistributing landholdings, no one could get too poor or too rich. Land redistribution protected the most unfortunate and restrained the most aggressive. The village was hardly a collective paradise: it brutally enforced confiscation, marriages, and justice. But Russian, like Japanese, villages most effectively disciplined their members into serving the community. Because the state and landlords in both societies levied taxes and labor on the village as a whole, the community became tighter as state power grew. The law code of 1649 defined all cultivators of the land as serfs, eliminating all legal options for escape from the landlord. Townspeople also fell under state control. The local elites fused into a gentry class that could control its labor, reduce its payments to the tsar, and secure control of land. Conversely, the village of settled peasants ensured a secure, hierarchical community centered on the soil and the church. Villagers themselves enforced discipline that violated local customs or threatened the rural order. Conservatism, informal customary decision making, and isolation protected the village from hazards and blocked change.

The peak of the political structure worked the same way. Russian "autocrats" did not have total power. Historically, the grand princes had mainly refereed disputes among boyar clans. Ivan IV's failure to destroy the boyars with his oprichnina brought only devastation. The turmoil of the Time of Troubles inspired caution. After electing Michael Romanov tsar, most of the nobles went home to their estates, leaving a small, cohesive group of boyar families to control Moscow. Official ceremonies in Russia and Ming China deceived foreign observers into thinking that these rulers wielded autocratic power, but many of the tsars and Chinese emperors were weak, bound by ritual activities, and often excluded from real decisions. Courtiers jockeyed for positions close to the tsar through marriage alliances. They brought suits against each other for insults to their honor and to preserve their status in the ranking system.[106] Without a single person at the center, the boyars' intrigues would tear the system apart, but within this closed world, the political elite had to subordinate family interest to the needs of the whole.

Merchants, Bureaucrats, and Churchmen

"Before reaching the audience hall we passed through a vaulted chamber in which were seated, or standing at the sides, imposing old men with long gray beards, gilded clothes, and tall sable hats. They are called His Tsarist Majesty's *gosti,* or distinguished merchants. Their clothing belongs to His Tsarist majesty's treasury; it is distributed for occasions such as this and then returned."[107]

Russia's twenty or thirty wealthiest merchants, the *gosti,* dominated the trade of Moscow, Archangelsk in the far north, and much of the interior and passed on their wealth for generations.[108] Although the English and Dutch called them poor and backward, Russian merchants were relatively prosperous by continental standards. The Archangelsk trade, opened by the British but soon dominated by the Dutch, brought Russian goods like hemp, linen, leather, and wax to northern Europe in exchange for cloth, gold, and silver. Twenty to sixty ships arrived per year at Amsterdam. This very difficult trade route, frozen in the winter and dangerous at all times of year, which took at least four weeks to navigate, increased dramatically during the seventeenth century. Another trade route, centered at Astrakhan on the Volga, connected Muscovy to the south; a significant Indian merchant settlement in Astrakhan linked Russia to the East.

Russia, like Asia, was a net bullion importer but more closely tied to European markets. Russian prices followed the "revolution" of sharp rises in sixteenth-century Europe and the same stagnation and decline in the seventeenth century. Russian merchants seldom traveled abroad, and protectionist tariffs kept out foreign competition. Merchants profited from collecting taxes for the state. The Russian state did not suck the merchants dry; just as often the merchants squeezed the state out of its revenues. The "subservience" of the gosti reflected their profitable use of ties to the tsar for their own benefit.

State administration developed alongside commerce. A hereditary class of literate clerks produced documents and routine procedures, but nobles resisted by petitioning the merciful tsar for aid in controlling runaway peasants. Petitions stressed not only the tsar's unlimited power but also collective decision making among the boyars. The apparently subservient language implied limits to the tsar's arbitrary power, much like Chinese literati memorials. The phrase "The tsar decreed and the boyars affirmed" indicated that a benevolent tsar should take advice from worthy advisers and "the land," meaning the general population whom he ruled. Some petitions even implied that unresponsive tsars served the Antichrist. In 1648, when the tsar ignored numerous noble petitions, a mob stormed the Kremlin.[109] In the 1649 law code, the nobility got their wish, at a cost. The state's officials would enforce serfdom, but personal appeals to the tsar ended. This bureaucratic growth prepared the way for Peter the Great's radical reforms.

The religious culture of Muscovy also changed dramatically. Monks lost power to church bishops, who supported the centralizing state. As the decline of monastic influence left a spiritual vacuum, believers prayed to icons, like the Virgin of Kazan, for health, while a mostly illiterate class of village priests carried on the traditional rituals. In the mid-seventeenth century, the Orthodox Church split, in a dispute over the power of the religious hierarchy over popular liturgy and the power of the state over the church. Patriarch Nikon tried to create a uniform liturgy based on new interpretations of Orthodox texts. When he ordered that parishioners must not kneel but should bow from the waist and cross themselves with three fingers instead of two, the monk Avakkum attacked him as the Antichrist and led his followers, who came to be known as Old Believers, in reasserting the time-honored rituals. Nikon expelled his critics, but he himself was defrocked in 1667 for resisting the tsar. Avakkum, exiled north of the Arctic Circle, continually defied the authority of both church and state. Old Believers, besieged in monasteries, committed mass suicide by fire rather than surrender. Despite repression, the Old Believers persisted for centuries as stalwart, enterprising dissenters.

Despite the schism, the church did not prevent all change. Reforming clergymen, adopting ideas from the Ukraine and Poland, began to preach sermons about moral self-improvement. In this way, Orthodox religious practice began to converge with that of Western Europe of the Reformation and Counter-Reformation. Before Peter's dramatic intervention, Russia had moved toward greater focus on individual spiritual improvement and a more legal and bureaucratically organized state. Peter accelerated reform, but he did not start from nothing.

In order to fight the Poles, Russian military officers had begun to import new weapons from the West and to learn new infantry tactics from Dutch, Swedish, and other foreigners. When Muscovy's main enemies were the Tatars to the east, it had adopted cavalry tactics from the mobile nomads. But in the sixteenth century, the army also built a large defensive wall, over one thousand kilometers long, to defend the southern frontier.[110] As the gunpowder revolution swept through Western Europe, Muscovy also needed military reforms. By the mid-seventeenth century, extensive use of artillery and defensive fortifications meant the supremacy of infantry and artillery regiments over cavalry and the demise of the old noble service class. Muscovy's army of two hundred thousand was the largest in Europe, consuming half the state budget, and the state, as it had been for two hundred years, primarily focused on military expansion. In military matters, his specialty, Peter could build on the foundations created by the Muscovite period.

Peter the Great (r. 1689–1725)

Few rulers in history have so drastically transformed their societies as Peter I. He built up the country's military forces on a European model, initiated large-scale building projects, including a new city, and transformed radically the visual and textual content of Russian culture. Why did he dedicate himself so single-mindedly to the reform of Russia, and why did he have such an impact? Personal, political, military, and social influences all played a part.[111]

Peter's turbulent path to the throne formed his attitudes at a young age. Military and foreign education set him off from the traditional elites of Moscow. He had formed his own regiment of play soldiers when he was seventeen, with the aid of a Scottish general. The sharpshooter regiments (streltsy), who controlled succession to the monarchy, and his half sister Sofia nearly had him killed. He feared and hated the insular culture of intrigue in Moscow, while he was insatiably curious about the world beyond. After educating himself about the outside world, he reached out to connect with Europe and the Middle East. As always with Peter, war came first. First he turned south, where the Ottomans and the Crimean khan blocked Russian access to the Black Sea. In 1695, he besieged the important fortress of Azov at the mouth of the Don. A failure on the first try, the siege succeeded the next year under Peter's unrelenting supervision. In the Black Sea campaigns, Peter built a new fleet and a new city, and he learned new methods of warfare to prepare for his campaigns in the north.

Peter the Great. In this portrait, which was painted around 1700, Peter is shown in Western military attire and standing in front of a fleet of ships—the new Russian navy—and the buildings of his new capital, St. Petersburg. Tsar Peter gave Russia a new direction, turning it away from Central Eurasia and toward Western Europe, as well as enlarging the empire on both land and sea through military conquest. He erected his new capital on the shores of the Baltic with the express intention of opening "a window on Europe." (The Granger Collection/Ullstein Bild, Berlin)

In 1697 he traveled to Western Europe to study military technology and artisanship. He ignored stultifying ceremonies, art masterpieces, and splendid baroque churches. Instead, he worked as a carpenter in a Dutch dockyard, studied blacksmithing, and observed dissections. Foreigners and Russians admired his simple ways, his curiosity, his openness to people of all classes, while puzzling over his outbursts of rage, his drunken orgies, and his crude practical jokes. But no one missed the force of his will.

Peter observed open debates in the English Parliament, but after a year he rushed home to squelch more revolts by the sharpshooters. Now he took power in earnest. Two years later, in 1700, he launched the Great Northern War against Sweden, the dominant military power of the Baltic, led by the equally young and vigorous King Charles XII.

Peter took on a formidable foe. Like Muscovy, the Swedes had built a powerful military state, despite the low yields of northern lands, but the Swedish peasant and soldier, unlike the Russian serf, was a freeholder, and the Swedes controlled important iron mines and the lucrative Baltic trade. Ivan IV had failed, but Peter tried again to break through to the Baltic. Following a disastrous Russian defeat at the siege of Narva in 1700, the victorious Swedes invaded Russia through the Ukraine. The passive, disorganized Russian army needed a complete overhaul.

In a few years, Peter created a disciplined army by supplementing the unwilling service nobility with four hundred thousand peasant recruits, nearly 10 percent of the male population. These men, literally branded as permanent soldiers, trained constantly for a lifetime of war. Villagers mourned their sons' departure as if they had died. New artillery and cavalry units joined the peasant infantry. Tactical training stressed meeting the enemy in the field instead of waiting for him behind fortified walls. A comprehensive code of military law influenced by the West taught the officers discipline, initiative, and responsibility. Nearly 90 percent of the officers were Russian, but they followed Western European models of uniforms, tactics, drill, and weaponry. Peter's army stressed unquestioning obedience and efficient action in the service of the state. It was a model of a new society.

Peter, however, placed even more emphasis on the navy. His new fleet rose on the shores of the Baltic, as the tsar himself carved timbers with his axe and designed the keels of his ships. By the end of his reign, the Russians had built over eleven hundred ships, along with a huge infrastructure: nails, sawmills, rope yards, sailcloth factories, and harbors. In 1714, at the Battle of Hangö, Russia gained its first naval victory against the Swedes.

Military needs drove the industrialization of the country. All European states of this time endorsed the principles of mercantilism: countries must accumulate wealth through trade at the expense of others, and the state must direct the economy. Peter drove these principles to extremes by directing the entire economy toward military needs. His crash industrialization programs eerily resembled Stalin's Five Year Plans. Russia first cast iron in 1702 from ore deposits in the Urals. Stalin built the huge steel town of Magnitogorsk in the same place two centuries later. Foreign specialists supervised new technologies, while the state requisitioned peasant labor and raw materials, controlling exports and distribution. The salt and tobacco monopolies sold basic necessities to the people at profits of 100 to 800 percent for the state.

The dark side was the destruction of Russia's merchant class, the gosti. Peter forcibly redirected foreign trade from Archangelsk to his new city of St. Petersburg, driving the old merchant lineages out of business. Only a few, like the Stroganovs, escaped by gaining lucrative imperial contracts for the exploitation of Siberia.

A famous edict of Peter stated, "Collect as much money as possible inasmuch as money is the artery of war."[112] The military demanded three-quarters of the state budget. Taxes hit the peasantry hardest. Peasants, legally bound to the land, now owed money, crops, labor, horses, and the quartering of soldiers to the state, in addition to their landlords' levies. They also paid taxes to the state monopolies on salt and vodka. Not surprisingly, large numbers fled to the frontier or became brigands. Once again, the Cossacks rebelled. They occupied large sections of the Don region in the midst of the grinding Northern War.

But Peter did not give up his personal campaign. Despite the fearsome reputation of Charles XII's army, Peter gained an amazing victory at Poltava, on the lower Dnieper River, in 1709, in which the Swedes lost 10,000 of 19,000 men and the Russians lost only 1,300 out of 42,000. This victory put Russia on the map. Peace finally came twelve years later, destroying the Swedish Empire and bringing new respect for Russia as the rising power in Europe. For twenty years Peter had given Russians schooling in the harsh ways of the modern world.

Unlike the tyrant Ivan IV, Peter did not destroy the regime he hated; instead, he remade it into a thoroughly rationalized bureaucratic state. For the first time, Russia's state demanded a separate loyalty from the personal household of the tsar. The Muscovite rulers and officials saw state service as a way of supporting or, as they put it, "feeding" themselves and their families. In Peter's conception, state service meant dedication to the welfare of the entire country, not merely the imperial and noble families. Peter replaced the corrupt provincial governors with new regional units ruled by men loyal only to himself. Because the tsar left the country so often on campaigns, he needed a central executive institution. The Senate, the supreme coordinator of military and fiscal affairs, replaced the boyar duma, which had been made ineffective by autocratic tsars. The Colleges, specialized bureaus for military affairs, foreign policy, tax collection, and documentary coordination, regulated bureaucrats, copying the Swedish model. Peter's reforms seemed like a whirlwind, but they were piecemeal rather than comprehensive. He took Muscovy's bureaucratization to unprecedented lengths but kept many of the old institutions alongside the new.

Cultural change likewise came suddenly. The nobles of Muscovy looked eastward to the steppe for much of their styles of warfare, dress, and customs. But the new tsar needed allies from the established courts of Europe, and to win them he needed to reshape Russia's image. He forced the boyars to cut their beards and abandon Orthodox ritual to avoid embarrassment abroad. He sent the officer corps for training in science and engineering at Europe's universities. The new elite would be literate, educated, secular, scientific, and dedicated to pushing forward the state's program of increasing its wealth and power. Printing came to Russia along with the new state, which demanded that officials be able to read and write.

Like Kangxi, Peter commissioned detailed maps of his realm from foreign experts. Hardly an aesthete, Peter nevertheless purchased classical paintings and statuary from Italy and Germany that became the nucleus of the Hermitage collection, and he hired the most expensive architect in Europe to design the palaces at his new city. The Pavilion at Peterhof featured views of the sea, spectacular fountains, and large gardens. Peter also respected theoretical science. After long correspondence with the German philosophers Gottfried Wilhelm Leibniz and

This painting, depicting a view of St. Petersburg in the eighteenth century, clearly shows the expansion of Peter the Great's capital that was undertaken by Catherine the Great in the late 1700s. She took as her model the French style, including long boulevards and administrative buildings with classical facades. The tsarina entrusted to Italian architects the construction of the imposing Winter Palace, which eventually became home to the renowned Hermitage art gallery, one of the largest collections of paintings in the world. (Private Collection/The Stapleton Collection)

Christian Wolff, he planned Russia's Academy of Sciences, founded after his death in 1725.[113]

Finally, and most significantly, Peter built his new city, St. Petersburg, at the mouth of the Neva in order to "open a window to Europe." Its cost was immense. As one historian said, "It would be difficult to find in military history a massacre which accounted for more men than St. Petersburg."[114] Peter compelled peasants to dig, nobles to build houses, and merchants to trade in empty forests and swamps. "Peter built his own city like a ship," carefully planning streets, palaces, and canals on regular, military lines.[115] Except for his palaces, it looked like a crude camp, but half a century later St. Petersburg had become one of the most beautiful cities in the world.

Peter's reign highlighted the fundamental issues of Russia and of many other developing countries. Modernizers idolized him, but Slavophiles attacked him for wrenching Russia away from her native harmony. Liberals focused on the contradictions between autocracy and democracy: how can you beat people to make them free? Peter responded that English institutions were irrelevant to Russia, where the peasants were uneducated, the clergy illiterate, and the nobles stagnant. So what if the pursuit of military power came at murderous cost? Wealth and power for the state came first; the people benefited later. Under Peter, in a very short time, Russia turned from a continental, Orthodox, inward, and Eastern-oriented autocracy into a secular, modernizing bureaucratic empire. It followed Eurasian trends toward integration and consolidation in the most extreme form.

Eighteenth-Century Expansion

Peter the Great had decisively oriented Russia westward at the beginning of the eighteenth century. None of his successors could turn the clock back. Russia was now an active participant in European politics, economics, and culture, but it was still an autocratic agrarian empire based on bonded labor and a highly privileged minority. Over the next century and a half, the tensions between Russia's nobility and the tsar, and between the elite and the peasantry, continued to cause Russian rulers to seesaw between reform and reaction. At the same time, the empire expanded to an enormous scale, fought many successful wars, and incorporated a huge variety of peoples.

The empire participated in the three-way division of Poland, took the Crimea on the Black Sea, invaded the Caucasus, and secured Siberia and parts of Central Asia. By 1825, it covered eighteen million square kilometers, the largest contiguous empire in the world.

Economic growth after the Time of Troubles had continued at a modest pace in the seventeenth century, supported by settlement of the southern frontier, which encouraged population growth. Frontier expansion supported further population growth and mobility. Cultivated acreage in the steppe expanded by 250 percent in the eighteenth century, and the population grew from sixteen million in 1725 to fifty million people by 1825. The fertile soils of the south supported populations in the north, as trading fairs grew, the money supply increased, and serfs engaged in commercial crafts and industries. Even though its agrarian yields remained very low, the extensive cultivation supported a growing urban economy. Russia came close to creating a national economy in the eighteenth century.[116] It also expanded foreign trade, especially with Western Europe, exporting agricultural products, timber, and iron in exchange for arms, luxuries, and silver. The silver influx, as in China, supported monetization of the domestic economy. The Russian state, however, tapped commerce much more successfully, relying heavily on salt and vodka monopolies and trade taxes, raising its income from 8.5 million rubles in 1724 to nearly 400 million in 1825.

Between Peter's death in 1725 and Catherine the Great's accession in 1762, intrigues by lovers, palace guards, and insider families decided succession to the throne, leading to a series of weak rulers. But the civil administration grew rapidly and kept routine operations going. By 1800 Russia had about one official per 1,100 subjects, more than ten times the density of China's bureaucracy, which ruled 300 million people with about 20,000 salaried officials (or one per 15,000). The detached, routine operations of an impersonal machine began to replace the personal and arbitrary decisions of individual boyars, although it did not eliminate the influence of bribery and corruption. Resistance to the expanding and increasingly penetrating state broke out in the southern borderlands repeatedly, in the Volga and Don basins in 1670–1671 and 1707–1708, and most spectacularly under the Don Cossack Pugachev in 1774. But none of these revolts threatened the central regions or exhausted the treasury. Serfs who chose to remain in the core regions of old Muscovy led a secure if impoverished life, and they found no attraction in the roving peasants and Cossacks of the south.

Although Russia was increasingly tied together by its growing economy and state power, it faced a yawning cultural gap between its elite and its people. As the nobility turned with greater enthusiasm toward the West, it left behind the uncritical faith in the Orthodox religious practices that dominated among the ordinary people. Even before Peter the Great, influences from the Ukraine and from Jesuit schools had begun to disseminate broader, more skeptical views of faith and behavior. Nikon's purification of the Orthodox liturgy, modeled on Greek practices, had caused the Old Believers to denounce foreign influences and assert their autonomy. After Peter's reforms, the religious and social rebels rejected his radical Westernizing policies and reasserted the traditional values of old Muscovy. Meanwhile, the nobility embraced European culture, especially French language and houses, moving to live in Moscow when they could. They hired French cooks and governesses and eagerly followed Parisian fashions.[117]

Even so, the reassertion of Orthodoxy supported by the state and villagers still kept the elite and its subjects bound together. Economic change also allowed more mobility and trade between peasants and merchants of different regions. Some peasants learned to read, especially in Old Believer communities.

The Diversity of Empire

Like Qing China, the Russian Empire had expanded quickly over a territory that included a huge variety of peoples. Its main challenge was to secure control and gain acceptance from the non-Orthodox peoples, who shared little with their rulers. The Baltic and German peoples of the north, the Jews, Lithuanians, and Poles, and peoples of the Crimea, Caucasus, and Central Asia all practiced different religions and lived differently from the core of the Russian population. By 1782, Great Russians were less than 49 percent of the total population. The key to controlling them, in the Russian view, was military and administrative centralization. The state's basis of legitimacy was contradictory: could it boast of its multiethnic composition, encouraging all peoples to embrace the tsar, or should it assert its central doctrine of religious Orthodoxy as the fundamental basis of rule? In Siberia, Russian settlers did see themselves as Christianizing crusaders bringing enlightenment to backward natives.

Orthodoxy did succeed in spreading into the Ukrainian and former Polish lands in the form of Uniates, who returned from Rome to the Orthodox hierarchy. But in general Orthodox missionaries had few successes elsewhere. The Russian language spread as the only permissible language of administration and education in Ukraine, Lithuania, and Belarus, and in part in the Caucasus. But the major spread of Russia was a result of outward migration by Russian peasant pioneers. They pushed out into Siberia, the north Caucasus, and the Baltic regions, turning steppelands into fertile fields.[118] They brought with them the Orthodox churches, village settlements, and agricultural techniques that excluded the looser, more mobile forms of pastoralism. In Siberia, the great explorers and cartographers portrayed a marvelous land, filled with natural wonders and abundant resources, but also fearfully vacant, awaiting the prospect of development from Christian settlers driven to bring God's light to an empty land.[119]

On the Volga, however, where the Torghut Mongols had settled in the seventeenth century, this kind of aggressive missionary activity backfired. The pressure to abandon their Buddhist connection to Tibet and the push of Russian settlers led the Torghuts to forsake their new territories and march thousands of miles eastward across the steppe to seek refuge in the Qing Empire. After they arrived on the border in 1771, the Qianlong emperor, after vigorous debate, decided to let them in. This was the first major violation of the treaties signed with Russia, but the cultural alienation between Russian Orthodoxy and Mongolian Buddhism was far greater that it was with the Manchu Empire.[120]

When Catherine II, a well-educated German princess, overthrew and killed her boorish husband in 1762, Russia once again lurched toward Western Enlightenment. Catherine the Great's legacy was just as contradictory as Peter's: she corresponded with Voltaire and Diderot but extended serfdom and brutally repressed revolt. She continued Peter's program of importing Western European culture, while preserving a modernized autocracy and strengthening the state. Russia in the mid-eighteenth century was a major participant in global politics and international trade, yet its social institutions, based on serfdom, military autocracy, and primitive financial and economic structures, highlighted the gap between the huge empire and its neighbors both in Western Europe and in China.

3. Central Eurasia

UNLIKE Russia, Japan, and China, the lands of Central Eurasia never came under the control of a single ruler after the collapse of Chinggis Khan's empire. They sprawled across a huge expanse of ecologies, climates, settlement patterns, and cultural life, and their political units became increasingly fragmented. Ultimately, nearly all of the region would fall under the control of either Russia or China, but the final stage of this incorporation did not occur until the mid-nineteenth century. The overarching story of the period from 1350 to 1750 was the fragmentation of the region, interrupted by repeated efforts to consolidate parts of it into stable political structures.[121]

Timur, the great Turkish military leader, briefly conquered an expansive territory, but it did not last long after his death in 1405. In Transoxania, the core of Timur's empire, Shaybanid khans established the Uzbek Empire, which lasted for most of the sixteenth century. In the east, in Mongolia, a series of khans attempted to unite the Mongols in regional confederations that drew on resources from China, but they never created anything nearly as expansive as Chinggis or Kublai Khan's empires. Farther west, several khanates that were successors to the Mongol Empire struggled against increasing pressure from the expanding Muscovite state. By the mid-eighteenth century, Central Eurasia was permanently divided in two. All of Mongolia and Xinjiang came under Qing control in the eighteenth century, while the western khanates faced increasing pressure from the expanding Russian Empire.

Economically, the ancient silk routes continued, but they faced new challenges from rising volumes of trade on the maritime routes from the East Asian seas to Europe. Culturally, the region divided sharply between the Turkic and Islamic regions in the west and the Mongolian and Buddhist regions in the east. But these divisions took a long time to take shape, and they overlapped the political divisions imperfectly.

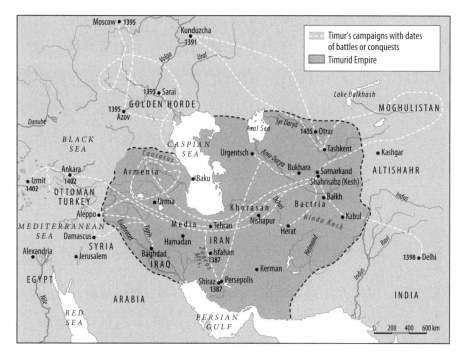

The Timurid Empire

It is difficult to define the boundaries of Central Eurasia with any precision, and different authors use different criteria for different purposes. The narrowest and least appropriate way to view this region is to look back from the present configuration after the fall of the Soviet Union. "Central Asia," by this definition, includes only the five modern Central Asian nations of Turkmenistan, Kyrgyzstan, Kazakhstan, Uzbekistan, and Tajikistan. These states inherited their boundaries from the Soviet Union's classification of their peoples and territory according to Stalinist criteria of nationality in the 1920s. These categories, however, have no direct connection to the actual relations of peoples in the fourteenth to eighteenth centuries. The term "Inner Asia," referring to modern Manchuria, Mongolia, Xinjiang, and Tibet, is also problematic. These regions also were defined as unified entities by the Qing dynasty only in the eighteenth century, so their boundaries are also distant from the realities of the preceding period.

Both narrower and broader definitions are also possible. Many scholars omit Manchuria and Tibet entirely from histories of "Inner Asia" or "Central Asia," while others would add more distant regions like Afghanistan, Siberia, or parts of modern Iran. Because the peoples of these regions constantly mixed and interacted with other, and because there was no stable political structure encompassing the entire region, no completely satisfactory designation of borders and peoples is possible. For convenience, in this chapter, I will discuss primarily the regions of Mongolia, Xinjiang, and the oases of the modern Central Asian states (Bukhara, Samarkand, and so on), with brief reference to Tibet and Manchuria. (Manchuria is discussed in more detail under the story of the Qing dynasty.)

The Ecology of Central Eurasia

Ecological definitions of this region are generally more useful than a focus on political boundaries. Each of the climatic zones of Central Eurasia induced its inhabitants to follow a closely defined form of life adapted to rigorous conditions. Central Eurasia does not border on any major coastline, and its climate is a continental one, of extremely hot summers and cold winters, with low rainfall and generally low agricultural productivity except in certain special places. The rivers, except for the Volga in Russia and the Liao in Manchuria, do not flow into major ports or navigable seas. These general conditions faced modification by four types of peoples: forest hunters, oasis agriculturalists, pastoral nomads, and caravan traders. None of these people lived in a single contiguous zone, but they all interacted with each other over vast distances in order to support themselves. On the edges of Central Eurasia were the densely populated agricultural regions that supported the major empires. Gradually, from China in the east and Russia in the west, these settlers penetrated the heart of Central Eurasia, dominating the local inhabitants while struggling to adapt their traditional ways of making a living to harsher conditions in the interior.

Timur was the last of the great Central Eurasian conquerors to attempt to dominate the entire region. After invading Persia, the Middle East, and northern India, he planned a major invasion of China. The campaign got under way in December 1404, after six years of preparation, but he died along the route in February 1405. Timur's successors saw greater benefits in trading with China than in military conquest, so Ming China was fortuitously spared the destruction of Timur's armies.

Timur's son and grandson, whose regimes were centered in Herat and Samarkand, sent tribute missions to Ming China, and the Ming dispatched an expedition to collect information about Central Eurasia in 1413. A tribute embassy from Herat was received in Beijing in 1419. The Ming dynasty could not conquer these regions, but it could influence these oases in the heartland of Timur and his successors' empire by offering profitable trade relations. The Ming emperor Yongle even wrote a letter to Shahrukh, Timur's grandson in Samarkand, accepting terms of political equality and free trade relations.[122] After the 1420s, however, Ming influence and interest in Central Eurasia declined. The Central Eurasian merchants sent more missions, carrying more goods at higher prices and demanding valuable products like silver, porcelain, drugs, and coins in exchange for their cattle. Smuggling undermined strict controls on trade and reduced the profit for the Ming and its influence over the trading networks. Official tribute relations with Herat and Samarkand nearly disappeared after the mid-fifteenth century.

The Ming rulers had greater influence over the nearby oases of Hami and Turfan and strong strategic interest in preventing these towns from coming under the control of an aggressive conqueror. They left the local princes alone but stationed small military detachments in Hami. But the rise of the western Mongolian Khan Esen around 1440 threatened these towns, as Esen staged raids and ultimately captured Hami. He even captured the Ming emperor himself in 1449, but the emperor's relatives secured power in Beijing and held off Esen's expansion. Esen's assassination in 1454 ended this brief consolidation of Mongol military power, while Hami and other oases regained their autonomy.

Turfan was close to Hami but in a different geographic and cultural zone, north of the Taklamakan Desert and deeply influenced by Islamic culture. In the mid-fifteenth century, the Moghuls conquered Turfan, building large numbers of mosques, and sought to expand trade with the Ming. Angered by Ming refusals to expand trade, the ruler of Turfan conquered Hami and held it for a decade until the Ming restored its independence. Despite these hostilities, the Ming continued to allow limited tribute missions from Turfan. But Chinese officials constantly complained that the missions were too large, the goods were unprofitable, and the behavior of the envoys failed to follow appropriate rituals.

Ming relations with the Mongols were even more fraught with difficulties than those with the oasis traders.[123] Because the Mongols were pastoralists who subsisted mainly off herds of sheep and goats, they moved constantly from place to place and usually escaped control by a settled administration. As expert horsemen, they could create powerful mobile military forces that raided settlements at will. Traders of Central Eurasia knew that Mongols could be powerful allies, who would protect caravan routes and warehouses of goods in return for access to the products that they wanted. The Mongols did want many Chinese goods, like tea, silk, metals, medicines, and musical instruments, and they were prepared to trade horses, sheep, and pastoral products for them. But the Ming officials, fearing that the militarized tribes would use Chinese goods to build up their wealth, constantly refused demands for trade. Ming refusals stimulated Mongol raids, creating a cycle of instability on the frontier.

Some Mongols did settle in Ming China, enticed by offers to serve in the Ming army and gain grants of land, grain, clothing, and money. Enlightened Ming officials realized that these settled and acculturated Mongols could be valuable border guards, but others objected to creating settlements too close to Beijing as a strategic danger.

Tribute relations with the Mongols in the steppe could provide a useful means of playing one group of Mongols against another, as part of a divide-and-rule policy. The rise of Esen to power threatened to create a united confederation that would seriously endanger Ming power. But Esen's inability to exploit the capture of the Ming emperor, and the fact that he was not descended from Chinggis Khan's lineage, undercut his legitimacy and that of his tribespeople in western Mongolia.

Two other leaders of the eastern Mongols mounted challenges to the Ming in the sixteenth century. Dayan Khan (1464–1532) gained unity by military and administrative consolidation, defeated the western Mongols, and again began raids along the frontier. But the Mongols under his rule once again rejected his legitimacy and sabotaged his dream of a united Mongol threat to the Ming. Dayan's grandson, Altan Khan, revived the Mongols' unity in a more productive and lasting way. He continued the incessant raids while also asking for regular trade relations. He gained a concession from the Ming in 1551, allowing border markets to trade Mongol horses for Chinese silk and, after twenty more years of conflict, achieved the right to send regular tribute missions to Beijing. The Mongols could now build up their economy and living standards with Chinese-manufactured products like porcelain, silk, carpets, as well as tea, silk, and salt, and they established a permanent settlement at Hohhot. The formal embrace of Tibetan Buddhism, marked by the Mongol leader's creation of the title of Dalai Lama for the leader of the Yellow Sect, linked the Mongols to Tibet and encouraged the development of settlements centered on monasteries.

The Chaghatai Khanate and Its Successors

Farther west, beyond the reach of most of the Mongols and the Ming, lay Transoxania, the core of the Chaghatai khanate, ruled by Chinggis Khan's descendants. This region includes the fertile lands north of the Amu Darya River up to the fertile Zarafshan River, and steppes and deserts surrounding them, corresponding to modern Uzbekistan and parts of Kazakhstan, Tajikistan, and Kyrgyzstan. It also includes the major caravan towns of Bukhara, Samarkand, and Tashkent.[124] The rulers here had become predominantly Islamic during the fourteenth century, influenced by the local settled population. The dissolution of the Mongol Empire left many local rulers contending for control of the oases and steppes, but only those who could claim a Chinggisid heritage could legitimately name themselves as khans and gather substantial support. Timur himself could never claim the title of khan but set up puppet Chinggisid khans to support his legitimacy, while calling himself emir, or *gurgan,* meaning son-in-law, because he had married a Mongolian princess.

Timur destroyed Chaghatai control in Transoxania in 1370, and after his death his descendants achieved new heights of political integration and cultural florescence. Herat and Samarkand, as the primary political and cultural centers of the Timurid period, supported substantial numbers of poets, scientists, and traders. Caravan trades along the Silk Road brought new wealth to these cities, linking the oases all the way through Xinjiang as far as Nanjing, the capital of the Ming dynasty. The most famous ruler, Ulugh Beg (1394–1449), built three large madrasas, or Islamic institutes of learning, of which the greatest was in Samarkand. It included a huge astronomical observatory and attracted outstanding mathematicians and astronomers from Iran and Central Asia. The observatory's scientists produced a large work calculating the positions of the stars and planets, the calendar, and theorems of trigonometry. In Herat, poets and artists created a new language, literary Turkic, combining Persian forms with the directness of the vernacular language. Calligraphers and illustrators produced dramatic miniature paintings of battle scenes and romances. The greatest literary work of the period was the autobiography written by the Turkic conqueror Babur (1483–1530).[125] Babur was deeply rooted in the Turkic and Persian culture of Transoxania, although he gained his greatest fame by conquering India near the end of his life.

The Sufi religious order of the Naqshbandi also rose to prominence in Transoxania, receiving patronage from the rulers. These Sufis focused on generating intensive mystical insight by reciting the *zikr,* or invocation of Allah, silently, thus stressing the individual's direct relationship with the unity of God. The founder of the order was a modest man from a small village northeast of Bukhara, but his followers became wealthy landowners and businessmen. Later, the Naqshbandi would extend their networks over a huge expanse of Central Eurasia and the Middle East, from Yemen to Northwest China.

By the mid-fifteenth century, the Timurid rulers faced military threats from nomads to their east, the Kalmyks, or western Mongols, known to the Chinese as Oirats or Zunghars. Other Turkic nomads from north of the Syr Darya River known as Uzbeks moved south and defended the Timurid khan. But when the Timurids lost, many of them abandoned him, moving to the northeast, where they became known as Kazakhs, a Turkish word for freebooters, vagabonds, or adventurers. This collection of tribes consolidated itself into a clearly defined cultural group in the seventeenth century, creating the Kazakh confederation. In 1501, Muhammad, the first Uzbek khan, seized Bukhara and founded a new dynasty, the Shaybanids, which lasted for the entire sixteenth century. Babur, the last Timurid, reluctantly abandoned Transoxania to conquer India. Muhammad Shaybani soon conquered the other major cities of Khiva, Herat, Tashkent, and Ferghana. Although Muhammad had a Chinggisid heritage, claiming direct descent from Chinggis Khan's son Jochi, he was a Sunni Muslim, heavily influenced by the Timurid culture. Under the Shaybanids, economic development occurred based on local agriculture and the caravan trade routes. The tribal Uzbek rulers became partly settled, but they kept themselves separate from the local oasis population. But a critical development in Iran in the same year of 1501, when Shah Ismail established

The Ulugh-Beg madrasa in Samarkand. The Timurid ruler Ulugh Beg built this large Quranic school in his capital of Samarkand in the fifteenth century and over time made it into one of the most significant centers of learning, Islamic religious scholarship, and culture in Central Asia. He taught there in person, while other leading scholars also worked on topics of both religious and secular interest at the institution. Ulugh Beg's observatory, for example, collected data on the position and orbit of planets and stars that was unrivaled at the time in its detail. Under the Timurids, the cities of Samarkand and Herat attracted eminent cultural figures from Persia, Arabia, and Central Asia. (Marc Deville)

the Safavid dynasty, cut off much of Central Asia from the rest of the Middle East. The Shi'ite Safavids and the Sunni Shaybanids fought each other to a standstill, dividing the formerly united Persian and Turkic cultures into rival religious sects and linguistic definitions. The Naqshbandi Sufis became more influential in Transoxania, building up the wealth of their shrines by creating large endowments *(waqf)* whose income they invested profitably, while gaining more gifts from their patrons. Ultimately, repeated attacks from Iran destroyed the Shaybanid Uzbeks, ending their hundred-year consolidation of the Transoxanian core. During the seventeenth century, small states, of which Bukhara and Khiva were the dominant forces, divided up the territory.

East of Transoxania lay Moghulistan, later known as East Turkestan, or Xinjiang.[126] Its geography in general resembled Transoxania, dominated by vast deserts, small rivers, and numerous oasis towns. But these towns lay at the foothills of mountains north and south of the Tarim basin, and they supported their agrarian population by channeling melted snow from the surrounding mountains down to their fields. The silk routes had crossed this region since ancient times, so the oases were always loosely connected, but each town had a strong local identity, and rulers could seldom enforce any stable unity. North of the Tarim basin lay the Tianshan Mountains and the steppes of Zungharia, the source of repeated invasions by Turkic and Mongol pastoralists, and to the east was China, the largest military and economic power. The main economic linkages of the region were centripetal, extending outward away from the blank center of the Taklamakan Desert. The easternmost towns, Turfan and Hami, faced China, the northern Ili valley faced the Russian forest and Kazakh and Zungharian steppes, and the western towns had close connections over the Pamir Mountains with Transoxania and southward to Tibet and even India. The rich fields of the oases were attractive targets for nomadic state builders, but the fragmentation and harsh conditions of transportation made it nearly impossible for one ruler to control the entire region for long.

Under the Mongol Empire, the region belonged to the Chaghatai khanate, but the khanate divided in the mid-fourteenth century along religious lines, when the western khan converted to Islam while groups in the east maintained Buddhist, Christian, and shamanist traditions. But the first Moghul khan converted to Islam in order to centralize his power against the rising influence of Timur.

Timur's repeated invasions failed to consolidate control, as the local families expanded Islamic ties to the east as far as Turfan. Timur's death spared Moghulistan from the immense demands he would have placed on it to finance his war against China but left the region fragmented among rival khans for the next three hundred years, until its final conquest by the Qing in 1760.[127]

By comparison with Transoxania, which lay closer to the sophisticated Persian and Turkic cultures, the eastern khans kept closer ties to their Mongol nomadic heritage and were despised as backward "donkeys." But some, like Khan Yunus (r. 1416–1487), moved back and forth between the Persian and Moghul worlds. He studied for a period in Iran, then took control of Moghulistan and Turfan, but local nobles resisted his efforts to make them settle in towns and take on alien Persian ways. At the end of his life, he moved back to Tashkent to enjoy the elegant culture of an advanced city. His grandson Babur grew up in the Ferghana valley, 350 kilometers to the east, but he still retained Turkic and Persian traditions. When his rivals ejected him from Ferghana, he raised a large army and went on to invade India and found the Mughal Empire. Continual warfare between local khans did not, however, damage the local economy, as numerous caravans still traveled through the region from Samarkand heading for Turfan, Hami, Ming China, and back.

In the seventeenth century, new nomadic confederations arose in northern Xinjiang and Kazakhstan who would eventually destroy the Chaghatai legacy. The Kazakhs, Kyrgyz, and Qalmaqs (Oirats) provided the ground on which the large Zunghar confederation built its powerful state. In the oases, certain Sufi masters of the Naqshbandi order became politically influential. Known as the Makhdumzadas, they took power in the south but soon divided into rival factions known as the White Mountain and Black Mountain sects, fighting each other continuously. In 1678–1680, encouraged by this divisiveness and supported by the Dalai Lama, who had named their leader Galdan the "heavenly khan," the Zunghars seized the Tarim basin and Turfan, installed the White Mountain leaders, and subjected the local rulers to heavy exactions in order to build their large military state. Conquest by the Zunghars ended the independent history of Moghulistan. To this day, Xinjiang has been under the rule of a succession of outsiders: the Mongol khans, followed by Manchu conquest, then Chinese warlords, and then the modern People's Republic of China.

The Zunghar Empire

The Zunghars were the last major nomadic power to emerge from the steppes of Mongolia to challenge the expanding influence of the settled regimes of Qing China and Muscovy. Although they resembled earlier steppe empires in many respects, they went further toward genuine state building than their predecessors. They promoted agriculture by moving farmers from the southern regions to areas north of the Tianshan; they drafted artisans from as far away as Sweden to instruct them in metallurgy and weapons making; they drew maps and built towns for trade as well as fortifications.[128] Their rulers did not come from the Chinggisid line, but they created a new line of legitimation by obtaining designations as khan from the Dalai Lama in Tibet. The Zunghar Empire, from its consolidation under Galdan in the 1670s until its extermination by the Qing in the 1750s, lay at a central crossroads of consolidating states to the east, north, and south. The rulers desperately sought allies and resources from all sides—Mongols to the east, Tibet to the south, and Russian to the north—to secure their position, but they ultimately fell to combined Qing and Russian expansion. The tsarist and Manchu empires discovered that they had common interests in excluding the volatile peoples between them so as to foster profitable trade relations and secure a stable border. Central Asia remained divided between these two empires until they both collapsed in the twentieth century.

The western Mongols, a group of tribes known generally as Oirats to the Chinese, or Kalmyks to the Russians, or Qalmaqs to the Persians, had joined Chinggis Khan's conquering confederation but later rebelled against Kublai Khan. They had never coalesced into a single independent formation. They rose again to dominance under the leadership of Esen Khan (d. 1454).[129] Esen first moved east, taking Turfan, Hami, and Gansu, and even captured the Ming emperor in 1449. But he did not try to conquer China and quickly returned to the steppe. When he defied Mongol custom by proclaiming himself khan, despite his lack of Chinggisid heritage, his followers quickly rebelled. The great leaders of the eastern Mongols, Dayan Khan and Altan Khan, focused their efforts on extracting resources from the Ming garrisons in Northwest China, stimulating the Chinese to build the Great Wall and accept regulated trade relations. In the 1570s, Altan Khan also reintroduced and consolidated the position of Tibetan Buddhism among the Mon-

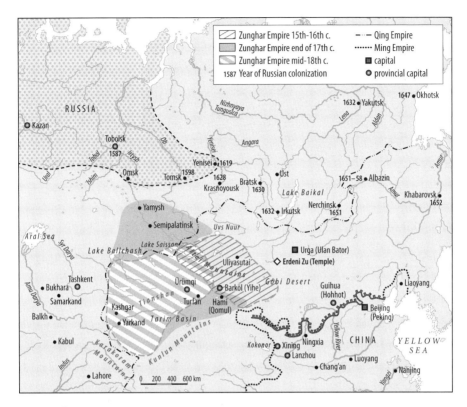

The Zunghar Empire

gols by creating the leader of the Gelugpa Buddhist sect as the Dalai Lama and establishing regular contacts with monks, building monasteries at his new capital of Koke Khota (modern Hohhot).

During most of the sixteenth century, the western Mongols remained divided and isolated from the two empires and the eastern Mongols surrounding them. But when Russian Cossacks began moving into Siberia, they looked for profitable contacts, sending a trade embassy to Moscow in 1607. They brought horses to the Siberian garrisons to exchange for paper, cloth, and cash. The Russians, however, demanded complete submission to the tsar in return for regular diplomatic relations, while the Mongols offered only conditional loyalty, so no permanent alliance could form. But the Russians gained their first solid information about the large Chinese Empire from these Mongol contacts. One group of the western

Mongols, the Torghuts, broke away from the others and migrated thousands of miles westward to the Volga River, where they sought Russian protection. The unification of the Oirats began in the early seventeenth century when they agreed to cease raiding each other and join together for common defense. The Tibetan Buddhist Zaya Pandita (1599–1662), an adopted son of the Oirat leader, contributed to their consolidation by devising an alphabetic script for the Oirat language, translating Tibetan texts into Mongolian, and aiding diplomatic and commercial contacts with Tibet. Zaya Pandita's Tibetan contacts offered the Oirats a powerful alternative legitimating force to the claim of Chinggisid descent and laid the ideological basis for the Zunghar state. Batur Hongtaiji (r. 1635–1653), although he could not call himself a khan, took further steps to constructing the new state by conducting military expeditions against the Kazakhs and into Kokonor, in Qinghai. Like his counterpart in Manchuria, Hung Taiji, Batur Hongtaiji developed the military forces that laid the basis for administrative centralization. He renewed relations and cooperated with the Russians to exact tribute from the Kyrgyz, while encouraging trade conducted by Central Asian merchants, called Bukharans, through the Russian city of Tobolsk. He tried to obtain weapons and farm tools to develop cultivated lands under his control and built a small city on the Irtysh River, where he gathered artisans from China, Transoxania, Mongolia, and Russia.

In 1640 the major khans of eastern and western Mongolia gathered in a large conclave to settle their differences and coordinate legal customs. Seeing rising threats from Russia and the Qing, they tried to create a socially unified formation, based on Tibetan Buddhism as the official religion, but they could not agree to allow individual khans to subordinate themselves to a single ruling authority. This "fatal individualism" of the khans ultimately doomed them to defeat by the coordinated bureaucratic states around them, but they made an effort to respond to the rising pressure. They needed a single dynamic leader to pull them together before they fell separately under Russian or Qing domination. Batur was not that leader: upon his death in 1653, the Zunghar confederation fell apart. But his nephew Galdan returned from a Tibetan seminary in 1670 with the promise of creating a powerful military and state formation.

As described earlier, the Kangxi emperor launched four expeditions against Galdan, and his successors dedicated themselves to exterminating the Zunghars

Dawaci Khan, one of the last rulers of the West Mongolian Zunghar people, initially fought against the troops of the Qing and finally ended up offering to serve them by intervening in a succession dispute on behalf of the khanate, a fateful decision that brought about the destruction of his state. This portrait, which was painted under Qing rule, portrays him as a loyal subject and official in the service of Emperor Qianlong. (Ethnologisches Museum, SMB/Waltraut Schneider-Schütz)

and their state. With the elimination of the Zunghars, all of Mongolia and Xinjiang passed under Qing control.

Economic Changes in Central Eurasia

Many authors have argued that the Central Eurasian trade routes called the Silk Roads declined irrevocably in the early modern period, and they have connected the decline of the continental trade with the rise of European maritime trade.[130] But the silk routes did not decline; they simply shifted direction, as they had many times in the past. Timur's capital of Samarkand lost population, but Bukhara maintained its size, and the new city of Khoqand in the Ferghana valley prospered. The Mughals in India had enormous demands for horses, stimulating large-scale drives of horses southward in exchange for Indian textiles. The Qing also purchased strong horses from the Kazakhs, as did the Russians. Russian penetration eastward to Orenburg opened up new market demands that provided profits for Bukharan merchants.[131] The fur trade on the Chinese border also drew traders through Mongolia, as the new settlements at Urga and Hohhot developed around monasteries. The rise and fall of empires and khans, and their associated wars, certainly disrupted commerce, but the caravans revived during interludes of peace. In some regions, also, agricultural production increased with the aid of stimulus programs from the ruling empires, like the Zunghars, Russians, and the Qing. As far as we can tell, the population increased as well. Although there are few clear quantitative data, it seems implausible to suggest a large-scale decline in the absolute amount of trade, but the relative proportion of Central Asian production in global production did decline.

Of all the regions discussed in this chapter, Central Eurasia experienced the greatest political and cultural disintegration. Once the heartland of the great nomadic conquerors who moved out against the settled societies around them, it became a divided territory dominated by the large empires of Russia, China, and Safavid Iran. The western half turned almost exclusively Islamic, while the eastern section mixed together Islamic settlers, Buddhist Mongols, and Chinese immigrants. The powerful expansion of the settled empires eliminated most opportunities for autonomous rule, but the economic exchanges that had always crossed the region continued in newly regulated forms. Central Eurasia's greatest political contribution to the wider world was its continual influence on settled life, through the conquest of India by Babur and the conquest of China by the Manchus and their Mongolian allies. Pastoralism, oasis agriculture, and local religious sects continued to preserve a distinctive cultural region that spanned borders and disrupted the efforts of the agrarian empires to hold them apart.

4. Japan

THE MONGOLS attempted to invade Japan twice, in 1274 and 1281, but they were defeated by disease, a typhoon, and the fierce resistance of the warriors, or *bushi,* of southern Japan. Although they failed to conquer the islands, they accelerated a process that led to complete political disintegration. The Kamakura shogunate, or warrior government, based on a fragile balance between the court in Kyoto and the military rulers in Kamakura, fell apart in the mid-fourteenth century, plunging the country into decades of civil war. Two rival emperors fought each other with warrior allies, until the Muromachi period (1392–1490), which restored a fragile unity controlled by the military ruler in Kyoto. The disintegration reached its nadir in the Onin War of the mid- to late fifteenth centuries, but in the late sixteenth century, the warriors slowly put back together the elements of a centralized state.

The Tokugawa shogunate (1603–1867) created a new political regime, based on a similar duality of emperor and military ruler but much more deeply rooted in local society and structured so as to guarantee long-term stability. During the first half of the Tokugawa, up to the mid-eighteenth century, the country benefited from peacetime conditions; its population grew, agricultural production expanded, and commercial networks tied together the country domestically, even though it was relatively isolated from the outside world. Although Japan did not expand territorially on such an impressive scale as Ming–Qing China or tsarist Russia, it achieved equal, if not superior, levels of urbanization, agricultural productivity, and cultural and commercial integration. Tensions within the Tokugawa structure, however, became more apparent in the late eighteenth century and ultimately brought down the shogunate in 1868.[132]

Japan's four main islands—Hokkaido, Honshu, Shikoku, and Kyushu, from north to south—lie mainly in a mild temperate zone, with adequate rainfall and plentiful forests.[133] The small plains and rivers supported dense peasant populations. The islands' climate favored productive agriculture and the formation of small domains by rural lords, but their geography did not foster a centralized po-

Kunashir

Hokkaido

Otaru

Hakodate

Matsumae

Minmaya

Hirosaki Hachinohe

Noshiro

SEA OF JAPAN

Akita Miyako

Honjō Morioka

Ichinoseki

Tsuruoka

Sado Yamagata Sendai

Niigata Yonezawa

Ullŭng-do Nagano Aizu

Takeshima Wajima Iwaki

Takada Nikko

Oki Toyama Utsunomiya

Kanazawa Matsumoto

Honshu Fukui Kōfu Edo Chōshi

Matsue Tottori Gifu Sakura

Obama Kyōto *Fuji* Odawara

Tsushima Hamada Okayama Himeji Nagoya Fuchū

Fuchū Hiroshima Kōbe Osaka Tsu Toba

Shimonoseki Takamatsu Sakai Hamamatsu

Fukuoka Kokura Wakayama

Hirado Matsuyama Tokushima *Izu and Osagawara Islands*

Gotō Islands Saga Funai Kōchi

Nagasaki Kumamoto Saganoseki *Shikoku* Oshima

Nobeoka

Yatsushiro Miyazaki

Kagoshima *PACIFIC OCEAN*

Yamagawa

Yakushima *Tanegashima*

0 50 100 150 200 250 km

Japan in the Tokugawa (Edo) period

litical structure. Valleys separated by mountain passes formed worlds of their own. The climate, crops, and commercial connections varied greatly between northern Honshu and Hokkaido, which had deep snows, long winters, and harsh famines, and subtropical Kyushu, connected by maritime links to the Ryukyu Islands, Taiwan, and Southeast Asia. The most densely populated regions, with the best growing conditions, lay in western Honshu along the Inland Sea and the Kanto plain around Edo (modern Tokyo). A form of central authority, tied to the emperor in the Kinai plain (modern Kyoto, Nara, and Osaka), had existed since the seventh century AD, but the emperor's court usually had only limited authority beyond the capital. Weakening of the central government and rising conflict over resources could easily lead to constant destructive warfare between the lords.

The Japanese people also faced many natural disasters. Fires constantly swept through the wooden cities, earthquakes struck repeatedly, and typhoons, famines, and epidemics often hit the islands. Disasters challenged the ability of lords and rulers to relieve the people, and if these became too frequent, rebellions or resistance movements challenged the rulers' authority. In general, when the government was unified, Japanese rulers held such superior military force that few major rebellions broke out. Close communal organization of villages, or city guilds, helped the people work together to address collective crises. Although Japan, unlike China and Russia, was relatively invulnerable to invasion by external powers and seldom challenged by large peasant revolts, it still had more than enough internal rivalries to create its own form of chaos.

The Kamakura period, which lasted from AD 1185 to 1333, is named after the city where the first shogun, Minamoto Yoritomo, located his headquarters, in eastern Japan, a considerable distance from the emperor's palace in Kyoto.[134] The ancient population and cultural center of Japan had been in the Kinai plain, including Kyoto, Nara, and Osaka. Of a total population of about seven million people in 1150, 1.4 million lived in Kinai and 1.6 million in the Kanto plain, whose center is modern Tokyo. Yoritomo was the first ruler to displace the capital from the cultural heartland to Kamakura, located at the southern end of the Kanto region.

Yoritomo, however, did not replace the emperor in Kyoto but styled himself as shogun, the emperor's leading military officer, or "Barbarian Subduing Generalissimo." He called his government the *bakufu,* or "tent government." Although he claimed to be a servant of the emperor, in fact his government dominated over the court. His followers, the bushi, or samurai, vowed unconditional loyalty to their lords, and in return they received grants of land. Economic disintegration supported local military power, as independent manors, collecting their own revenues, broke away from the centralized bureaucratic administration. Military governors appointed by the shogun became more independent from the center. They could pass on their positions to their descendants, control most of their estate revenues, and escape surveillance from Kamakura. In fact, the shoguns themselves were under the control of regents belonging to the Hojo family, who controlled large estates around Kamakura. Hojo Masako, the "Nun Shogun," held the real power in the regime until her death in 1225.

But the court in Kyoto still remained the center of cultural prestige, and it preserved the remnants of an earlier administration of elite nobles and civilian bureaucracy. Court and bakufu each needed the other: the court relied on the warriors to suppress local uprisings, while the warriors invoked the emperor as their symbol of legitimacy. By the thirteenth and fourteenth centuries, however, most political authority had already slipped away from the central government in Kyoto into the hands of local military elites.

In 1274 and 1281, the Mongol armies of Kublai Khan launched invasions with over 140,000 troops. Aided by the "divine wind" *(kamikaze),* a typhoon that destroyed the Mongol fleet, the samurai held them off, but their victory eventually tore Japan apart. Unlike the profitable civil wars of the previous century, driving off foreign invaders gave the warriors no opportunities to gather loot. Samurai fought not only out of loyalty but for personal gain and expected tangible rewards for victory. Veteran soldiers petitioned for relief, complaining that they had waited for months and received nothing in return for service.[135] Buddhist priests also claimed a great deal of credit for the victory, as their intensive recitation of sutras had brought down the divine wind. The shoguns in Kamakura, however, maintained tight control over their capital city, and the divided factions around the emperor in Kyoto were unable to challenge them.

Competition between rival factions at court, at the bakufu, and between the Buddhist sects began to tear the shogunate apart. Emperor Go-Daigo in the 1330s led a revolt against the shogunate in an effort to restore imperial power.[136] From 1331 to 1392, two rival emperors and their followers fought each other all over the

Himeji Castle, which lies over 80 kilometers west of Osaka, is one of the few fortress complexes to have survived from the Warring States (Sengoku) period in Japan. The castle was built in the four-teenth century at a strategically important point controlling access to both the Seto Inland Sea and the overland routes between eastern and western Japan. Up to the beginning of the seventeenth century, this stronghold was repeatedly expanded until it finally comprised no fewer than eighty-three separate buildings. The Tokugawa shogunate had most of the castles of the former warlords *(daimyo)* torn down, but Himeji was spared and handed over to a local prince as a reward for having supported the Tokugawa shoguns in their conquest of Japan. Up to the present day, the castle has withstood bomb blasts and earthquakes and is now one of the most important UNESCO World Heritage Sites in Japan. (© Blaine Harrington III)

country. The civil war brought rising waves of violence around the country, as bandit gangs of fifty to one hundred horsemen committed robberies and assaults everywhere. Some of them were desperately poor people, but others were local land-owners fighting to keep or expand their holdings.[137] Freed from the tight disci-pline of the warrior regime, young men engaged in stone-throwing brawls, or they exhibited nonconformity by wearing masks and strange clothing, causing others to fear them as demons. A local writer described "assaults in the night, armed rob-beries, falsified documents, easy women, galloping through the town, panics for

The samurai were warriors whose sole purpose was to fight for their masters; they dominated the military and political culture of Japan from the twelfth to the seventeenth century. As this colorful picture from the seventeenth century shows, they customarily wore boots, armor, and elaborately decorated helmets, and they rode their horse into battle to engage in hand-to-hand fighting with long swords. (De Agostini Picture Library/A. Dagli Orti)

no reason, chopped-off heads, monks who defrock themselves and laymen who shave their heads . . . parvenus who are turning the world upside down."[138] This process of *gekokujo,* or lower-class people overturning the status of superiors, affected all classes and regions. At the same time, principles of equality challenged the inherited hierarchical structure. Landowners formed leagues, called *ikki,* that united warriors and peasants in federations defined by freely sworn vows, and these ikki challenged the power of the military governors. They also arbitrated disputes among their members and helped landlords to suppress peasant uprisings. Along the seacoast, other uprooted sailors and warriors became pirates, launching attacks on the coasts of Korea and China to gather grain and kidnap local people for ransom.

The peasants, however, organized their own village leagues, called *so,* to resist rent demands from their lords. They also increased their cultivation and yields, preserving the surplus for themselves. They drew up secret documents swearing community solidarity, blessed by local gods, when they "drank the divine waters of unity."[139] Then they addressed petitions to the local tax collectors, claiming harvest losses and asking for tax reductions. Soon these leagues broadened their activities to extend beyond petitions to demonstrations of force and rent strikes.

The shogun restored his power, but he moved to Muromachi, a district of Kyoto, where he and his successors resided from 1392 to 1573. In this period, called the Muromachi, or Ashikaga shogunate, the dual power of shogun and emperor disappeared, because the court in Kyoto was impoverished and powerless. The shogun opened trade relations with Ming China in 1392, declaring himself a tributary of China. Not only did this relationship offer profits from trade, it confirmed the shogun as the supreme sovereign of Japan. But within Japan, even the shogun himself suffered a reduction in authority, because only his deputies, the military governors called *shugo,* had local authority. They began to turn themselves into genuinely autonomous territorially based lords, or daimyo. While the shoguns lived in impotent elegance in Kyoto, heavily influenced by the highly aesthetic fashions of the court, the daimyo gradually divided up the country.[140] Local lords along the coast profited from growing international trade, allying with powerful merchants to export gold, sulfur, and swords to China in exchange for copper coins. As more coins flowed into Japan, the economy became increasingly commercialized. Monasteries and merchants used the market to free themselves from the grip of warriors. Zen priests managed large cargos shipped to the China coast, and merchants formed guild organizations, called *za,* uniting those people in one locality who practiced the same craft or trade. Moneylenders and sake brewers grew rich from financial transactions, lending money and paying taxes to the bakufu and the lords for their luxury expenses.

By the mid-fifteenth century, these contradictory pressures once again tore Japan apart. The population increased to seventeen million despite civil war. The guilds established far-reaching merchant networks like their German contemporaries in the Hanseatic league. Merchant elites controlled new towns, like Sakai on the Inland Sea, the gateway to Kyoto. But peasants rebelled against heavy taxation and the abuses of brewers and millers.[141] The villagers and Buddhist temples hired warriors to protect themselves, and the village leagues expanded over larger territories. Each family fought to protect its relatives, and men established domination over women. In order to preserve family property, law codes gave land to only one son and no longer to women. The remaining sons left to seek their fortunes with roving military bands. The shogun became only one among a group of equally powerful military lords, and he controlled only Kyoto, while bandits roamed the country and pirates attacked the coast. The murder of the shogun by his rivals in 1441 touched off a national crisis that lasted over one hundred years.

Beginning with the Onin War (1467–1477), the country fell into incessant internecine warfare.[142] Military factions, with armies of up to one hundred thousand men on each side, fought in the capital city. The rough foot soldiers in these armies pillaged, burned, and looted houses and temples, destroying nearly all of Kyoto, while poverty-stricken emperors had to peddle their calligraphy to survive. Ancient families and large armies were annihilated. The Japanese call this period the age of "Warring States," but "bastard feudalism," the European term for this period of social upheaval, also fits Japan. In Mary Elizabeth Berry's words, the war created a "culture of lawlessness" that "wrenched apart one political and social universe without quite destroying it or substituting something new."[143]

By the early sixteenth century, the people of Kyoto were sick of war, and new Buddhist sects emphasizing the need for peace and material prosperity gathered support. The followers of the Lotus sect, descended from the thirteenth-century monk Nichiren, rejected the claims of lords and city officials for taxes, stressing the possibility for prosperity in this world rather than praying for reincarnation in the future. They built twenty-one large compounds in the city, with heavy walls topped by watchtowers and surrounded by moats, making small fortresses for the believers. In the 1530s, they expanded control over Kyoto and neighboring villages, but they alienated other Buddhist sects with their intolerance. They particularly attacked the Amida sect, torching its buildings and denouncing its beliefs. For a while, they created peace in the capital by driving out the shogun's administration, repressing other warriors and sects, and taking over the city. But the monasteries on the hills of Mount Hiei overlooking the city mobilized warriors to defeat them in 1536. Once again the victors torched their enemies' temples, slaughtered thousands of people, and banished the Lotus sect. The townspeople of Kyoto had not brought peace any more effectively than the warriors who oppressed them.[144]

Cultural Change during the Ashikaga Period

During the turbulent Ashikaga period, the rough warriors embraced Zen, one of the most austere and mystical sects of Buddhism. While they also enjoyed war stories celebrating disciplined fighters, they supported a highly aesthetic, inwardly focused spiritual practice. Zen's basic principles were "A special transmission outside the scriptures; No dependence on the written word; Direct pointing at the soul of man; Seeing one's nature and attaining Buddhahood." Zen teachers, instead of reading sutras or conducting elaborate ceremonies, focused on their students' individual spiritual development. Students could gain enlightenment only when they meditated on logical paradoxes *(koan)*, or suffered beatings by their teachers. The texts of Zen consist not of scriptures but of cryptic anecdotes about famous masters. Yet unlike monastic Buddhism, the enlightened soul need not leave the world; he can live as he did before, while utterly transformed within. The simplicity and practicality of Zen appealed first of all to the samurai. Supported by the shogun and local lords, Zen Buddhists spread their teachings in local temple schools, which raised literacy in the countryside to a remarkably high level.

Despite its individual focus, Zen developed into a major institution in the fourteenth century, under the leadership of the Five Mountain temples in Kamakura and Kyoto.[145] The monks managed estates for the lords, lent out money, and promoted commercial and cultural relationships with China. The bakufu protected and promoted Zen monasteries, while also collecting taxes from them. Zen masters served as important diplomatic envoys and even as ship captains. They spread Chinese-style poetry, landscape painting, and Buddhist and Neo-Confucian treatises in Japan.

Zen originated in China, where it was called Chan, meaning "concentration," and its popularity in Japan came from newly restored contact with China. The Mongol invasions had stimulated Japanese shipbuilding, and Japan resumed official trade with Ming China in 1401. The shogun celebrated his new prosperity by establishing a great Zen monastery and dressed himself in Ming clothing. In 1394 he built Japan's most beautiful secular structure, the Golden Pavilion in Kyoto.

The famous stone garden of the Zen Temple of Ryōan-ji, in Kyoto, contains no plants, only moss-covered rocks and beds of fine gravel symbolizing the ocean. The Zen Temple, of which this garden forms a part, was constructed in the fifteenth century, though the garden is thought to have been laid out only a century later. Its natural forms symbolize the Zen aesthetic of extreme simplicity, in conjunction with their deeper spiritual implications. (© Michael S. Yamashita/CORBIS)

This small three-story building, with a Zen meditation room and a bronze phoenix at the top, harmonized effortlessly with the landscape garden and pond beneath it. It was burned down in the Onin civil war and later restored. It lasted until 1950, when a crazed monk burned it again, and was restored to its original style. The Silver Pavilion, modeled on the Golden Pavilion, was built in 1482 by a shogun who became a Zen monk. It survived the Onin War, although it was never covered in silver leaf. It is only a plain wooden structure overlooking a meticulously crafted small garden. It now represents the aesthetic style of modesty and austerity known as *wabi,* or *sabi,* where beauty lies beneath the surface. The Japanese also developed their own gardens on the model of the Chinese landscape garden, which was a miniature portrayal of nature. The ultimate refinement is the Ryoanji garden, which has no plants at all, only sand and rocks to depict the endless expanse of sea.

A Buddhist procession; this form of religious procession was just one of many ritual activities that took place regularly in the cities of Japan during the early modern period. Horses and people pulled a large holy shrine pavilion on wheels, followed by flag-bearers, monks, and members of the local populace. These kinds of religious ritual generated a lively atmosphere of collective rejoicing in celebration of the changing seasons. (Art Resource/Scala, Florence. Photo © The Newark Museum 2014)

The Zen aesthetic that permeated Japanese society during these troubled times was responsible for many of the greatest masterpieces of the visual and architectural arts. Black-and-white brush paintings depicted a great landscape in a few well-defined strokes. The Zen painter Sesshu (1420–1506) practiced extreme abstraction, using roughly splashed brush strokes to hint at larger meanings. *No,* a slow ritual dance theater, also suggested spiritual worlds beyond the stage, and it attracted popular audiences by alternating with *kyogen,* the raucous, bawdy comedies. Popular picture scrolls displayed in bright colors the agonies of Buddhist hell. Perhaps the best-known piece of sculpture, the Great Buddha of Kamakura, is impressive only for its size, not its aesthetic quality. Much more striking are the vigorous realistic wooden statues of court nobles, military leaders, and Zen monks.

Other sects besides Zen also spread their influence widely through the countryside, building thousands of temples and nunneries up to the end of the sixteenth century. The Pure Land, or Amida sect, unlike Zen, appealed to a broad range of classes, including outcaste groups, beggars, and women. It used vivid pictures of hell and promises of paradise to encourage its followers to beg for the Buddha's mercy.

Nichiren, however, the founder of the Lotus sect, attacked the teachings of the Amida sect as dangerous and evil. He blamed the Mongol invasion on the heretical doctrines of the popular sects, and he insisted that the bakufu should support only his sect as the true one. His sect also attracted a great deal of support from the lower classes, and as we have seen, they rose up during the civil war period to claim independent authority.

Wandering preachers who also worked as entertainers, healers, and prostitutes transmitted a simple Buddhist message: recite a mantra of a few sacred words with true devotion and you could be saved. These entertainers also distributed booklets of prayers, encouraging the development of literacy and mass publication. Because Japan, unlike China, could use a syllabic alphabet for simple texts, it was much easier to spread information to a mass public through the written word. Even though the country was politically divided, Japanese of many classes could find common connections through these religious practices, songs, festivals, and new customs like ritual bathing.

Even after holding off the Mongol invasion, the Japanese were perfectly capable of committing collective social suicide. Nothing seemed to hold the country together in 1500, and its future looked bleak. The twilight of the true samurai had arrived. Yet the warring lords on their estates were laying the foundation for a new powerful state. Local political and administrative consolidation created the building blocks for much greater centralization in 1600 by the Tokugawa than the Kamakura shogunate had ever achieved.

The Unification of Japan, 1550–1600

In the sixteenth century, known as the "Age of Warring States," regional lords (daimyo) and their military servitors (samurai) fought incessantly, while Westerners brought Christianity and gunpowder weaponry, domestic and foreign trade flourished, and Japanese armies intervened in Korea. By the early seventeenth century, the new Tokugawa shoguns had expelled foreigners, ruthlessly suppressed

Christianity, and nearly shut off foreign trade, inaugurating the so-called Period of Seclusion *(sakoku)*. This phase of Japanese history, called the Tokugawa or Edo period, lasted until 1868. Japan was not, however, entirely cut off from the world. It still had relations with China and Korea, and it kept track of developments in Southeast Asian and maritime regions. Its domestic commercialization and gradual bureaucratization paralleled that of other Eurasian states.[146]

The constant violence of the mid-fifteenth century, in the long run, laid the groundwork for unification. New men rose from obscurity; inferiors overthrew their superiors. Warring lords built thousands of castles across the country. These new lords, known as the Warring States Daimyo, often came from obscure origins, and they did not owe loyalty to the bakufu or the court. They collected vassal warriors around themselves when they gained charisma from success in battle. The daimyo placed their castles in strategic locations favorable for military defense and the accumulation of supplies. They also surveyed the lands they controlled and invested heavily in increasing agricultural and commercial production to support their domains. The castles soon became centers of commerce supplying the new military elites. Nearly everyone, including the peasantry, was armed, but within their domains, the lords forged powerful tools for local administrative control. They bought off the most powerful warriors and by 1591 required them to live in the castle towns. With these armed men under their control, they could suppress the independent village leagues and force the peasantry to register land, pay taxes, and provide corvée labor to build more forts and transport supplies. Legal codes defined each domain as a separate "country" *(kuni)* with independent authority from the shogun.[147]

The scale of military competition expanded dramatically. Masses of peasants using pikes and bows replaced the skilled elite mounted archers of earlier times. These foot soldiers made the samurai swordsmen obsolete. Firearms were brought by the Portuguese in 1543 and first used in 1575. Japanese artisans quickly learned how to meet this new demand. The new weaponry accelerated the trends toward larger investments in offense and defense. The use of cannons required building bigger fortresses, and the effectiveness of muskets in battle drove the warriors to create larger armies. Armies grew in size from 30,000 to 60,000 in the early sixteenth century to 250,000 to 280,000 at the end of the century. Around 250 daimyo rulers contested incessantly for supreme power in an intense elimination tournament.

Yet despite the warfare, foreigners and Japanese prospered in trade. Some merchants joined the pirates and smugglers along the China coast; others ran important cities, like Sakai, through their guilds. After the Jesuit Francis Xavier arrived in 1549, Christianity began to take hold in the west and south, supported by lords looking for foreign aid. The population grew from about ten million in 1450 to nearly seventeen million in 1600, and arable land expanded modestly by about 25 percent.[148] However, this land was cultivated more intensively, as paddy rice became the main crop. The Champa rice that had come to China earlier arrived in Japan around 1400, allowing double cropping in the south; cotton cultivation began on a significant scale in both the Kinai and Kanto plains. Local markets proliferated, and the rate of urbanization rose. Daimyo themselves had to use cash to pay their suppliers and retainers. Osaka became the key commercial center where samurai collected to spend money and merchants gathered to supply their needs.

A powerful warrior, Oda Nobunaga (1534–1582), began to form a winning coalition. He consolidated his position in central Japan, then marched triumphantly into Kyoto in 1568 and seized Sakai in 1569. He crushed the independent village communes and commercial cities, brutally enforcing a military-dominated social order. His principle of rule, "rule by force," demanded complete loyalty from his followers and total submission by his enemies. He burned to the ground three thousand buildings in the huge Mount Hiei monastery and slaughtered the resident men, women, and children. He even built his own navy to subdue a rival coastal lord. But Nobunaga was killed before he could claim to be shogun of unified Japan.

Toyotomi Hideyoshi (1536–1598) completed the unification by extending military control to southern and northeastern Japan. Hideyoshi had no family lineage at all; he lived only by the sword. At first an enemy of Nobunaga, he then allied himself with Nobunaga and expanded his base in central Japan. By 1590, he had subordinated all the major lords in the country. Hideyoshi gathered his followers into large coalitions, concentrating them in large numbers in attempting to induce his enemies to surrender. He fought few major battles, but he won those he did fight decisively. Instead of eliminating those he defeated, he reduced the size of their domains and left them under close supervision, using surplus lands to reward his followers.

Hideyoshi's administrative reforms had more lasting impact than his battles. In 1588, he ordered the Great Sword Hunt, stating that "the farmers of the various provinces are strictly forbidden to possess long swords, short swords, bows, spears, muskets, or any other form of weapon."[149] All metal weapons would be melted down and cast into a Great Buddha. Daimyo and samurai gave up the gun but kept their honorific swords. Thus, Hideyoshi ensured that no mass army could resist him. He stated, "this is a measure specifically adopted to prevent occurrence of peasant uprisings [ikki]."[150] He then froze the social order. He prohibited farmers from going into trade or leaving the villages and samurai from doing hired labor. Samurai were separated from the land, so they could not hold independent fiefdoms, and farmers were bound to the soil like serfs. Unlike Ming China, Japan's military rulers could enforce reliable registration with a comprehensive land survey. Taxes were assessed according to the productive potential of the land, measured in *koku,* a unit roughly equivalent to one year's per capita grain consumption. Of the national total of 18.2 million koku for twelve million people, Hideyoshi controlled approximately two million koku in his own domains, plus gold and silver mines. He stepped up production from mines in order to enlarge the currency supply.

Hideyoshi pressed hard on the peasantry, but he left the lords alone. Daimyo owed soldiers to the shogun in proportion to the size of their domains, but they were otherwise free. Unlike Peter of Russia, Hideyoshi stopped short of nationalizing the army; daimyo maintained their followers, but the shogun could confiscate and rearrange their fiefs. His final campaign destroyed the castles that had sprouted like mushrooms during the century of civil war. By 1615, daimyo had only one castle each. Hideyoshi supported foreign traders, but he feared foreigners and their Christian followers, because they supported the daimyo of western Japan. He banned proselytizing in 1587, when he seized Nagasaki, and crucified many Japanese Christians when he became suspicious of the disorder caused by quarrels between the Franciscans and Jesuits and the foreign influences on them. He began to put controls on foreign and domestic commerce in order to suppress piracy.

Near the end of his life, Hideyoshi announced, "My wish is nothing other than that my name be known throughout the three countries [of Japan, China, and India]."[151] In 1592, he launched an almost inexplicable campaign against Korea. Was he trying to divert the attention of his domestic rivals, or was he driven by a megalomaniacal ambition to conquer East Asia? As in 1895, Japan's intervention on the continent brought disastrous results for everyone. When a Japanese army of over two hundred thousand men took Seoul, Hideyoshi envisaged an easy conquest of Beijing, but the Korean admiral Yi Sunsin, with his famous armada of "turtle-clad boats," the first armored ships in naval warfare, decimated the Japanese navy, while Korean guerrillas harassed the occupying troops. Chinese troops crossed the Yalu River and quickly drove out the Japanese army in 1593, inflicting a humiliating defeat. Hideyoshi attacked again in 1596 but only suffered further losses until his death in 1598. The consequences for Japan were short-lived, but Korea was devastated, and the fiscal strains on the Ming aided the expansion of the Manchu state. For the next three centuries, Koreans, the true Confucians, hated both sets of barbarians: the Japanese and the Manchu conquerors of the Ming.[152]

Tokugawa Ieyasu (1542–1616) put the finishing touches on the structure that Hideyoshi had begun. Unlike his predecessors, Ieyasu came from a prestigious military family. At Hideyoshi's death, he had the largest holdings in the country, 2.5 to 3.0 million koku. Then he carefully maneuvered to make himself the supreme leader, assembling a coalition of eastern daimyo supported by the rich Kanto plain. His opponents, supporting Hideyoshi's heir, collected in western Japan. At the critical Battle of Sekigahara on October 21, 1600, eighty thousand supporters of Hideyoshi's heir faced off against Ieyasu's roughly equivalent forces for the ultimate prize: the title of shogun. Ieyasu's victory, and his claim of descent from Minamoto Yoritomo, the first Kamakura shogun, entitled him to claim the shogunate in 1603. He concluded the civil war in 1615 when he captured Osaka castle from the last holdouts. Ieyasu then moved the capital of the bakufu government from Kyoto to the small fishing village called Edo (now Tokyo) in his domains in the Kanto plain. It grew to become the largest city in the world by 1700, with over one million people, including the shogun's retainers and officials, merchants, daimyo, and their attendants, artisans, and construction workers.

Japan's unification was the work of these three military men, but they were aided by other trends, some of which were shared with the rest of Eurasia. The climate probably became warmer in Japan in the sixteenth century, allowing farmers to increase their yields and extend cultivation northward in Honshu. The warriors had more prosperous sources for their extractions. Even more important, Japan's maritime trade expanded notably, as Ming China developed an "insatiable appetite" for Japanese silver.[153] In exchange Japan imported floss for its silk industry and learned new technologies, including the abacus for calculation, improved shipbuilding, and ceramics. When the Ming lifted its prohibition on overseas trade in 1567, resolving the piracy issue, Japanese and other merchants could travel freely to Chinese and Southeast Asian ports. The Portuguese could also enter this large intra-Asia maritime trade with bases in Macau and Nagasaki. As we have seen, Europeans made the greatest military contribution by introducing matchlock guns in 1543, and the Japanese quickly improved on the Western designs. Oda Nobunaga used alternating lines of musketmen in 1575 to win his battle, and other daimyo soon copied him. Although the early guns still fired slowly and uncertainly, they definitely hastened the unification of Japan.

Tokugawa Institutions

The first shoguns set up an institutional structure, known as the *bakuhan* system, of extraordinary complexity and durability.[154] It lasted for over 250 years, and it balanced the court in Kyoto, the shogun in Edo, and the over two hundred feudal lords against each other in a system of control that combined feudal and bureaucratic elements. The shoguns first seized much of the lands of the daimyo who had opposed them, making their own domain the largest in the country. They controlled over one-quarter of Japan's agricultural production. They also controlled the major cities of Edo, Kyoto, Nagasaki, and Osaka, as well as major mines. The other daimyo had to follow the shogun's restrictions on castle building and relations with foreigners, but they were nearly autonomous within their domains. Ieyasu's victory was based on a coalition of forces, so he could never go so far as to eliminate his daimyo allies.

The *sankin kotai* hostage system required all the daimyo to maintain costly residences in Edo and to spend up to a year there, closely watched by the shogun's inspectors and spies. When they returned to their domains, they had to leave their wives and children behind as hostages to ensure their good behavior. Not only did it keep the daimyo under close watch, but traveling with their retinues to and from Edo used up much of their income. Daimyo had been divided into three classes depending on their loyalty to Ieyasu. The twenty-three *shimpan daimyo,* relatives of the shogun, provided heirs when the Tokugawa line was empty; the 145 *fudai daimyo,* loyal but unrelated, formed the linchpin of regional administration; and the ninety-eight *tozama daimyo,* mostly hostile to Ieyasu, secretly nursed their grudges. After much land confiscation and domain transfer, the shogun himself held 6.8 million koku, the fudai and shimpan 9.3 million koku, and the tozama 9.8 million koku.[155] Two of the most powerful tozama daimyo, Satsuma and Choshu, led the Meiji Restoration movement that overthrew the bakufu two and a half centuries later.

To be a daimyo required a minimum of 10,000 koku, but the wealth of daimyo varied greatly depending on their size and the productivity of their lands. Of the 145 fudai daimyo, fourteen held more than 100,000 koku, while thirty-one had the minimum of 10,000 koku.

The peasantry gave over two-thirds of their agrarian production to their lords, probably the most intensive agrarian extraction rate in the world. The disarmed and immobilized peasantry were nearly helpless in the face of the lords and their arrogant sword-carrying samurai, but thousands of peasant protests did occur. These were petitionary movements, in which village headmen and designated representatives asked the lords to reduce their demands in times of harvest failure. The petitioners often paid for these impertinent requests with their lives, but by invoking ideals of benevolence, they could partially limit the lords' extractions.[156]

The shoguns appointed the daimyo's heirs, but within the domains, the lords had complete power over justice, tax collection, and internal affairs. Shogunal law evolved from vassal oaths into formalized codes, which emphasized strict frugality and a static, agrarian economy, much like the first Ming emperor had. The emperor himself, the source of legitimacy for the shogun as military ruler, received large land grants and a lavish new palace in Kyoto, but he was kept out of any access to power.

Japan's state structure puzzles analysts accustomed to European institutions, inspiring contradictory phrases like "bureaucratic feudalism" or "integral bureaucracy."[157] On the one hand, the vassal oaths, independent lords, service ethic of the samurai, and military ideology evoke the European Middle Ages, but the growing bureaucratization, pervasive control measures, and commercial growth look like phenomena of absolutist regimes. Yet Russia, too, baffled Western visitors with its combination of service nobility and apparent absolute power granted to the tsar. These examples ought to undermine our natural assumptions of sharp oppositions between "feudal" and "modern" (bureaucratic) society and lead us to reconsider the real nature of state development in the West, which also blended medieval and centralizing elements.

The military leaders needed a new ideology to legitimize their rule during peacetime. Chinese Neo-Confucianism offered the most convincing answers.[158] In its Japanese version, it stressed the strict social hierarchy dividing *shi* (scholars in China; samurai in Japan), merchants, artisans, and peasants and the obligations of filial piety, meaning obedience of inferiors to superiors within the family and the polity. Unlike China, however, the shoguns enforced strict barriers of social mobility between the classes. They forbade samurai from engaging in trade or agriculture, and they issued regulations to ensure that each class in all aspects of daily life—food, housing, clothing, and decoration—stayed within its allocated status. Samurai were entitled to the great privileges of carrying swords, serving as administrators, and even bearing a surname. But they were no longer the dynamic warriors of the past. The scholar Hayashi Razan (1583–1657) identified the samurai with the Confucian "gentleman" and stressed the transformation of men of war into literate scholar-officials and loyal bureaucrats. The samurai themselves were divided into a large number of ranks. Depending on their rank, their stipends could make them nearly as wealthy as the shogun's retainers or scarcely different from a poor peasant.

Villagers, the second highest group in the four-class hierarchy, still had rights of self-governance. After paying taxes, they kept up their own shrines and irrigation works, and they enforced discipline on each other in collective responsibility units of five families each.

Artisans and merchants or townspeople *(chonin)* were nominally the least respected people, even though their wealth might exceed that of the lower samurai. Since foreign trade had been nearly shut down, they had little opportunity to move around or accumulate wealth outside their sponsors among the samurai. They, too, were organized in groups that enforced standards of quality and prices and held collective responsibility for their members. Even the outcastes had their own corporate groups to keep discipline, while also exercising some self-governance.

Cultural Transformation and Confucianization

Confucian popularizers, like Kaibara Ekken (1630–1714), explained the classical texts simply for rural people, women, and children and wrote practical works on agronomy and childbearing. Japan's active publishers disseminated these ideas in thousands of copies. Printing and literacy spread widely, and schools proliferated, but not every rough warrior could make the transition.

From 1701 to 1703, the episode of the forty-seven *ronin* (masterless samurai) epitomized the changes of the century, inspiring plays, tales, and, later, films. When Asano, the backwoods daimyo, was insulted by the urbane Kira, protocol officer at the bakufu, Asano drew his sword and slightly wounded Kira. It was a capital offense to draw a sword at the shogun's court, so Asano was sentenced to perform ritual suicide *(seppuku)*. Asano's retainers became ronin, whose primary duty was to avenge their lord's death. They carefully bided their time, feigning dissoluteness to throw their enemies off guard. Twenty-two months later, they stormed Kira's mansion in Edo, cut off his head, and presented it to their lord's tomb. The bakufu was thrown into extensive debate. The ronin had admirably followed the traditional code of loyalty, but they had disrupted law and order. Finally, they were not condemned as criminals but allowed to perform honorable seppuku. The courage of the ronin won them great acclaim from both samurai and commoners, at a time when the growth of commercialized pleasures led many to be concerned about the softening of the nation's moral fiber.

Such a mismatch between China's bureaucratic state and Japan's special hybrid system stimulated vigorous controversy. The controversial Wang Yangming (Yomeigaku) school became especially powerful in Japan. Yomeigaku followers advocated the purity of individual will against restrictions by ceremonial codes or domain laws. The native Japanese religious cults, systematized as Shinto, as well as the Buddhist sects, offered alternatives to Chinese Neo-Confucian orthodoxy and possibilities for syncretism. The Chinese, Koreans, and Dutch who were allowed to send trade and tribute embassies kept open an important window on the outside world. Beneath the surface of the isolationist, repressive shogunal regime in the seventeenth century there bubbled an effervescent intellectual culture. Japan was never truly isolated in the so-called sakoku ("closed country") period.

The Tokugawa period created many of the conditions facilitating Japan's rapid breakthrough into the industrial age. In this way, the historiography of Japan has paralleled that of Russian scholars who find in seventeenth-century Muscovy the germs of Peter's reforms. Even without the stimulus of foreign wars, extensive foreign trade, or religious controversy, Japan still had an active cultural life and growing economy, and it gradually created a literate, mobile, inquisitive population. Rather than stopping halfway on a road leading from feudalism to an autocratic state, it creatively balanced local autonomy and central control.

Japan's "seclusion" from the continent was not so damaging economically: traders still went to China via Kyushu and Okinawa, but most important, internal trade and communication networks developed rapidly. State and commercial communications coexisted and aided each other, as private letter deliveries in Ming China followed the same routes as government couriers. Printing spread more unevenly. Because China had long had printed books, the Ming–Qing period developed regional distribution networks for a broadly based reading public, but Japan also expanded printed materials for both urban and prosperous rural readers.

Printing did have broad cultural effects in China and Japan, but they were less dramatic than Europe's, because East Asia started from a higher level of literacy. Unlike some Europeans, East Asian literate elites did not see printing as a threat because it would spread dangerous knowledge to illiterate masses, and the printed word did not create separate states based on different spoken languages. The wide circulation of maps and guidebooks, and the ability to distribute one's own poetry among circles of friends, created aesthetic networks, travel businesses, and a sense of participating in a common national culture.[159]

The Late Tokugawa Period

In eighteenth-century Japan, as in China, commercial networks spread all over the country, but unlike in China, the population did not grow. Foreign trade was highly restricted, and frontier expansion was slight. By the 1790s, serious tensions surfaced in the form of social unrest, foreign encroachment, crop failure, and intellectual debate, and beginning in the 1850s, disputes over foreign and domestic policy tore apart the shogunate. While Chinese reformers put the empire back together after its midcentury crisis, Japanese reformers overthrew the shogunate in 1868 and launched the Meiji Restoration that set Japan on its astonishing rise to world power.

The seventeenth-century unifiers had imposed a rigid military and bureaucratic structure on the country, repressed Christianity, and severely restricted foreign contact. Despite their reactionary efforts to freeze society, they unintentionally promoted change. The military rulers had removed the armed warriors from the land and concentrated them in castle towns, in order to watch over them. But this concentration of people made the three hundred castle towns into dispersed centers of local commerce. The samurai, as spendthrift consumers, attracted large groups of merchants and craftsmen to serve them. By 1700, Osaka and Kyoto each had a population of four hundred thousand, nearly equal to London and Paris. Because so many lords and samurai spent half their year in Edo, it grew into a huge urban conglomeration of nearly one million people, the largest city in the world. Of the total Japanese population, 5 to 7 percent lived in cities greater than a hundred thousand, compared with 2 percent in Europe. Japan became one of the most urbanized societies in the world.

Because the samurai living in towns had to cash in their rice stipends in order to buy urban products, Osaka became the central grain marketing center of the country, with merchants serving the shogun's agents. Three urban centers dominated the country, each with its own economic niche: Osaka as wholesaler, manufacturer, and financial center; Kyoto outstanding in fine silk and elegant crafts; and Edo as the military–bureaucratic center collecting the shogun's retainers and visiting lords (daimyo), who demanded luxury goods and entertainment.

Because the shoguns forced the lords to leave hostages in the capital, lords and their retinues crowded the main road to Edo on Honshu Island, the *Tokaido,* inspiring innkeepers and peddlers to supply their needs at regular stages. The maritime route across the Inland Sea likewise tied Honshu, Shikoku, and Kyushu. These and other major interregional trade routes bound the country together economically, despite the inspection stations and custom dues collected at the border of each domain. There was no national currency: Edo used gold and Osaka silver, while the countryside used copper coins, so major exchange houses dealt in sophisticated financial instruments to adjust currency rates.

New merchants, like the house of Mitsui, supplied clothing, uniforms, and household goods to the shogun, lords, and retainers. They wrote their own laws, which carefully controlled times of work, dress, food, and relations with customers so as to enforce disciplined service to the firm. In the nineteenth and twentieth centuries, they would clothe and provide ships for the Japanese army. Like Mitsui, the Sumitomo family of Osaka began as copper refiners and later developed into powerful financial cliques, called *zaibatsu*.

Arable land also expanded in the dynamic seventeenth century, as peasants pushed clearance of the lower reaches of rivers and also intensified production on existing lands. Rice cultivation moved farther north, while double cropping of rice extended further south. Cash crops like tea, mulberry, and cotton also expanded, and the total population nearly doubled, to thirty-one million by 1721. Although the shogun's and lords' taxes were quite heavy initially, the ruling elite living in cities knew little about techniques of farming, so peasants were able to keep the surplus they gained from improvements. Over time, taxes as a percentage of output declined from 60 percent in the seventeenth century to 33 percent in the eighteenth.

Even the limited foreign trade still kept a vital lifeline to the Chinese market open. Chinese techniques of silk weaving, mining, and ceramics making always provided new inspiration for Japanese adaptations. The sweet potato, brought to Japan, like China, from the New World, helped to guard against famine in the eighteenth century.

The dynamic growth of the seventeenth century peaked and leveled off during the following century of "social stasis." Shoguns fruitlessly issued streams of sumptuary legislation restricting the clothing, food, and housing of townspeople and ordered merchants not to "exceed their station," but as in Ming China, the nouveau riche, aping the superior culture of the court and lords, could buy themselves the status of connoisseurs. Despite its distinctive history, in many aspects of material life and commercial culture Japan had caught up with Ming and Qing China. Unlike China, with its vastly diversified regional economies, Japan's culture was more tightly focused on the two largest regions of Kinki (Osaka–Kyoto) and Kanto (Edo), but the mass consumer culture spread through regional and village marketing networks around the country. Cultural unification followed economic networks.[160]

The population of Japan, however, followed a strikingly different pattern from most of the rest of the world. From 1600 to 1720, aggregate population had more than doubled, from twelve to over thirty million people. From 1720 to 1860, it hardly changed at all. The production capacities of the archipelago seemed to have run into an ecological barrier. Nearly all easily accessible trees had been cut down, and new cultivable land was scarce. Severe crop failures caused devastating famines. But the key mechanisms holding down population growth were not famines but population control by villagers.

Japanese village communities could enforce population controls, because they were tightly bound networks of prominent families supervising dependent kinsmen, tenants, and landless laborers. The whole village paid taxes, making everyone responsible for everyone else's obligations. The government tried to enforce its ideal of a self-sufficient, harmonious community *(kyodotai)* with controls on migration and trade, as it aimed to restrict each of the four classes—samurai, merchants, artisans, and peasants—to their own profession. Lacking new land, villagers intensified production on their existing fields, but this farming system was highly vulnerable to fluctuations in the weather; households that increasingly specialized in cash cropping were at the mercy of grain markets as well. Landholdings fragmented into diverse sizes, and the uniformity of the agrarian community broke up into landlords, tenants, and landless laborers. All families practiced deliberate restriction of births to adjust their populations to limited resources. Men left home for long periods of time to labor elsewhere; induced abortions and substantial infanticide reduced fertility. In eastern Honshu, one of the poorest regions, many villagers practiced infanticide despite efforts by local scholars to denounce the practice.[161] Chinese practiced similar demographic controls, but the Japanese were driven to greater extremes because they lacked room to expand. The shogun's government, or bakufu, did try to encourage settlement of Japan's northern frontier, on the island of Hokkaido, but ran into conflicts with the native Ainu tribes there, who were offered protection by the Russians. Only fisheries offered some chance to escape land constraints.[162]

Fiscal Crises

The bakufu and daimyo faced severe fiscal crises in the midst of these tensions between burgeoning commerce and limited agricultural production. They were not able to raise effective taxes on the new wealth generated by commercial growth, because they did not live in the countryside with direct supervision over the peasantry. Wealthy farmers could conceal their yields and hide their illicit trading from intrusive inspectors. Most important, Japan, unlike Russia but in some ways like China in the eighteenth century, faced no immediate military threats to drive more intensive extraction. The samurai were not needed as warriors, so they spent their time and money in the cities on aesthetic, sexual, and material consumption, borrowing money from merchants to finance an expensive way of life.

As the samurai fell heavily into debt, merchants extended their grip over the lords' domains. Lords repudiated their obligations and the shoguns issued more coins, bankrupting many merchants and debasing the currency, but they only postponed the crisis. Shogun Yoshimune (r. 1716–1745) launched a reform effort guided by the leading Confucian statecraft scholar of the day, Ogyu Sorai, but it had only modest effects. Tensions grew along with prosperity throughout the rest of the century. Rural people petitioned against heavy taxation, smashed moneylenders' shops, and in 1764 rebelled against corvée levies for postal stations.

The urban merchant class, for its part, prospered and kept much of its income. In the flourishing time of the Genroku period (1680–1720), the special urban culture of the kabuki theater, the courtesan quarters, music, and fine foods drew in not only samurai but commoners as well. The shoguns issued repeated sumptuary regulations to restrain these upstart commoners, to no avail. Commoners in the wealthy cities could eat the same food, wear the same clothes, and even marry into samurai families.

Despite the shogun's conservatism, intellectual life in isolated Japan was vibrant, as scholars tried to place Japan within the East Asian order. On the one hand, shoguns and scholars created an increasingly unified cultural community, centered on particular Japanese features, such as the emperor system, Japan's topography, and religious traditions. On the other hand, Chinese influences became stronger than ever, placing Japan in a larger East Asian order that defined cultural norms in universalist terms.

By sponsoring land surveys of the entire cultivated area of the islands, and by creating the first maps covering all of Japan since the eighth century, the shoguns encouraged the population to think of themselves as a unified whole.[163] The sankin kotai system of traveling lords created a cultural hierarchy centered on Edo and spread Edo speech and culture out to the provinces. Publications in Edo of everything from farming manuals to novels were distributed to people in villages throughout Japan. Mass travel for pilgrimages mixed men and women together and brought together people from diverse provinces. Hundreds of thousands went annually to visit the central Shinto shrine of Ise. The market towns created a special culture of their own, known as the "floating world" *(ukiyo)*. It included the kabuki theater, the Bunraku puppet theater, popular fiction, woodblock prints, and varieties of entertainment dedicated to pleasure, offering a sharp contrast with pedantic Confucian sermons. The popular classes drew in the samurai to their culture, but the samurai also influenced the commoner public, as newly rich merchants tried to copy the refined traditions of the tea ceremony, with its Zen origins, flower arranging, Chinese classical scholarship, and group poetry writing. In aesthetic circles dedicated to these arts, amateurs from all classes mixed together on an equal level, defying the shoguns' efforts to preserve rigid boundaries and hierarchy.[164]

Attitudes toward China demonstrated this enduring ambivalence. Confucianists like Ogyu Sorai saw Japan as a society based on Chinese classical texts; Motoori Norinaga, by contrast, denounced the corrosive influence of Chinese teaching and espoused the unique emotional linkage of the "native Japanese heart" to the Way of the Gods, as expressed in its most ancient poetry and its Shinto cults. Others stressed Japan's political differences from China: it had a single imperial line, it had never been invaded, and it was, in their view, closer to the ancient Confucian ideals than China itself. Later nationalists turned these arguments for Japanese superiority into militarist claims to dominate Asia, but in the Tokugawa these were mainly defensive arguments against the dominance of the Chinese classical tradition. "National studies" scholars defined Japan as a unique polity *(kokutai)* superior to all others and under threat from foreign influence. By contrast, Dutch studies scholars used the slim porthole of Nagasaki to obtain books on Western medicine and science. The awareness of Europe's existence seen on global maps showed that Japan was only a small group of islands, not the center of the cosmos.

As in China, the shoguns saw writing as useful for moral indoctrination, but Japan, unlike China, had a syllabic alphabet, so literacy was easier to promote. Eighteenth-century education was found mainly in private academies for samurai and wealthy townsmen. Later, education began to spread more widely through temple schools. By the mid-nineteenth century, up to 50 percent of the male population and perhaps 10 percent of the female population had become partially literate.[165] A booming and diverse publishing industry supported the demands of these newly educated readers, who sought almanacs, travel guides, manuals on etiquette and medicine, comic books, and romantic stories. Anyone, no matter how lowly, could use this "library of public information" to improve him- or herself.

National Consciousness and Social Tensions

This does not mean that Japan had a fully formed national consciousness by 1750. Most people still identified only with their hometown or domain, and there was wide diversity of tastes in food and local dialects. People were divided from each other both by the enforced status system and the geographical divisions of the domains. Yet there was a growing sense of a common experience among the educated urban and rural public and even a new sense of the importance of public opinion for guiding the government. Confucian philosophy supported the idea that rulers should respond to the needs of their subjects by keeping open public channels of communication. When severe famines or official abuse caused general suffering, critiques appeared, sometimes in satirical form, invoking the welfare of "our Japan" *(waga Nihon)*. In this ideology, "Japan" was a region of uniform cultural values distinct both from mainland East Asia and from the "barbarian" tribespeople of Hokkaido in the north and the Ryukyus in the south.

These tensions would become sharper in the nineteenth century, exacerbated by new foreign contacts, major famines and revolts, and popular movements. Oshio Heihachiro, for example, an Osaka policeman inspired by Wang Yangming's dedication to the people, led an urban uprising in 1837. New religions, enthusiastic pilgrims, ecstatic dancing, and the cult of Maitreya (the same deity inspiring China's White Lotus movement) indicated a search for saviors and outlets for emotion. Ominous signs of the wider world generated more intensive debates over strengthening coastal defenses and keeping the country sealed. Learning of China's loss in the Opium War, the Japanese became even more wary of the West. Outside the central government, the still unsubdued domains of Satsuma and Choshu enacted economic reforms that made them powerful rivals of the weak shogunate. None of these tensions burst into open conflict, however, until 1853, when the American commodore Matthew Perry steamed into Edo Bay to demand the opening of trade.

Tokugawa Japan had developed a surprisingly dense, rich, dynamic social fabric marked by intensive commerce and agriculture and creative artistic and intellectual production within a rigid institutional frame. It was communication intensive, with a well-educated populace, and it had sophisticated financial and commercial institutions that prepared it for a new explosive outburst when the industrialized world cracked its shell.

5. Korea

THE KOREAN peninsula, about 240 kilometers wide, extends southeast from the Manchuria highlands for approximately 1,000 kilometers, from latitudes 42 to 35 degrees north. It covers an area of 218,000 square kilometers, about three-fifths the size of Japan and two-thirds the size of Italy. Mount Paektu, an extinct volcano nearly 3,000 meters high, is the highest peak in Korea and a sacred place for the Korean people. From it flow two streams, which become the Yalu and Tumen Rivers, which empty into the Yellow Sea and the East Sea, respectively. These rivers and the mountain define the northern borders of modern Korea, whose boundaries were established during the fourteenth century.[166]

Four-fifths of the peninsula is mountainous, and ranges divide the peninsula from east to west, limiting travel through high passes and fostering regional divisions and fragmentation. The northern part contains high mountains extending along the eastern coast, while the southern and western sections have lower plains and river valleys, which support rice agriculture. Even though only 15 to 20 percent of the land is arable, the fertile valleys can support a large population. Korea has a coastline over 8,000 kilometers long, but the shallow Yellow Sea, with many tidal flats, does not support deep harbors, while the east coast, bordering the deeper East Sea, has several excellent harbors.

The continental climate shifts sharply between bitterly cold winters, mild springs, and hot and humid summers. The summers bring heavy monsoon rains every year in July, along with typhoons. The mild climate of the south supports paddy rice agriculture, as monsoon rains arrive conveniently during the growing season, and fishing flourishes along the rivers and coasts.

For most of its early history, Korea was not united under a single state, and its boundaries under the Koguryo state (37 BC–AD 668) extended north into Manchuria. After the seventh century, the Silla state (668–918) and the Koryo dynasty (918–1259), from which is derived the Western word for Korea, controlled most of the territories of the modern two Koreas, except for parts of North Korea. Korea

·[178]·

Korea, circa 1750

fell under Mongol domination in the thirteenth century. Only the Choson, or Yi, dynasty (1392–1910) established the borders that the two Koreas maintain today.

Situated between the vast empires of China and the mobile tribes of Manchuria to the east and the Japanese islands, 120 miles across the sea to the west, Korea has always suffered or profited from close contacts with its neighbors. Despite invasions from both Manchuria and Japan and active trade relations with Chinese and Japanese, the Korean peoples have maintained a distinct identity for many centuries, but their evolution has closely followed that of the surrounding regions of East Asia.

The Mongol Period and the New Choson Dynasty

After an extended period of resistance, during which Mongol forces devastated much of the country, the military elites of the Koryo dynasty decided to surrender to the Mongols in 1258. The Mongols forced Koreans to take part in their attempted invasions of Japan in 1274 and 1281 and forced the Koryo king to marry into the Yuan imperial house. Korea's peaceful submission subjected the country to heavy demands for tribute of gold, silver, cloth, grain, ginseng, and falcons, as well as young women and eunuchs. Powerful families profited from the alliance with the Mongols, creating large estates independent of the control of the king. When revolts broke out in China in the mid-fourteenth century, however, the Yuan began to lose power, and Koreans allied with the Mongols came under attack. King Kongmin (1351–1374), even though he himself had nearly entirely Mongol blood, declared independence from the Yuan, ended cooperation with the Mongols, attacked Yuan commanderies, and recognized the Ming dynasty in 1368. He attacked powerful families who dominated the military, and he allied himself with a Buddhist monk, Sin Ton (d. 1371), in order to carry out radical reforms of the government. They taxed concealed lands, returned lands to their rightful owners, and freed many slaves, but their actions enraged the powerful elite families, who forced the execution of Sin Ton in 1371 and the assassination of King Kongmin in 1374.

At the same time, Korea suffered invasions both from Chinese bandits in the north, called Red Turbans, and Japanese pirates, called *waegu (wakō),* along the southern coast. The military commander Yi Songgye controlled the dominant force defending the country. When King U (r. 1374–1388) ordered him against his will

Porcelain vase from the Choson period. The Choson dynasty produced exqui-
sitely crafted, delicately painted white porcelain vases, which are among the
finest achievements of Far Eastern porcelain manufacture. Their simple, elegant
forms, their discreet decoration, and their fine gradations of color represented
the sober Neo-Confucian ideals of the Korean state. (RMN-Grand Palais/
Martine Beck-Coppola)

to carry out a suicidal attack on Ming country, Yi turned his forces on the capital, ousted the king, and soon proclaimed himself the ruler of a new dynasty, only the third in Korea's long history. This dynasty, the Choson, would last for 518 years, until it was conquered by Japan.

Although Yi himself was a military man from obscure origins, his supporters included prestigious Confucian officials, strongly influenced by the Song Chinese philosopher Zhu Xi. They promoted, with his approval, the rebuilding of the National Academy, the creation of a national shrine to Confucius, support for student fellowships, and scholarship on the Confucian classics. They also led an assault on the power of Buddhists, who had strong influence in the Koryo state. Most of the monasteries had their land confiscated, and their slaves were taken over by the state. Neo-Confucian principles, based on the metaphysics of *li,* or "rational principle," and qi *(ki),* or "material force," dominated the Choson period even more than they did in China. Neo-Confucian morality also affected the family structure, by eliminating the rights of women to hold property, subordinating secondary wives and concubines to the primary wife, and putting the primary wife strictly under the control of her husband and mother-in-law. She could almost never obtain a divorce, could almost never leave the inner quarters of the family compound, and had to wear a hood in public.

The examination system, as in China and Vietnam, determined many appointments to official positions, but unlike China, access to the exams was determined largely by heredity. The *yangban* classes, designating those eligible for the two highest types of degrees, in civil and military positions, were the dominant social group, dedicated to ensuring their purity by limiting access to the elite. They were exempt from corvée labor or military service, allowing them to devote themselves full time to studies. They married only among themselves and lived separately from other people. Every three years, fourteen hundred candidates who passed provincial examinations competed for the highest degree, and two hundred of them passed.[167] Sons of concubines fell into an inferior status and were banned from taking the examinations. Civilian yangban ranked higher than military yangban. Outside the yangban rank, there were other degrees, including those for the "middle people" *(chungin)* or skilled workers, and the "miscellaneous exams" *(chapkwa),* including technical specialists such as lawyers, doctors, accountants, and translators. Each of these ranks tended to form exclusively hereditary groups in order to limit access to privileged positions. Genealogies attested to their descent from illustrious ancestors. Regular censuses listed each household and each social status, whether one of the aristocratic classes, commoner, or slave. Although Japan had its outcaste people *(burakumin)* and China had a small population of "mean people" *(jianmin)* and enserfed peasants *(nubei),* slavery *(nobi)* included up to 30 percent of Korean society. In the south, up to 50 percent of the agricultural labor force were slaves. Slaves were personal bond servants of their masters, who mainly belonged to the yangban elite, or government slaves who performed corvée labor and paid taxes. They performed duties ranging from personal attendance to agricultural labor. Their status was hereditary, determined by the mother's status, and they could be bought and sold on markets. As in Japan, there were also outcastes, working in occupations like butchering, tanning, and wickerwork.

The peasantry in Korea also faced restrictions that were rare in China. The majority of peasants were tenant farmers working for the yangban, and they were fixed to their land. The state attached identification tags to each of them, listing their name, date of birth, class status, and residence and required them to carry these tags at all times. The mutual responsibility system, like the Chinese *baojia,* ensured that one household could not leave, because others would have to pay its tax obligations. The land tax, at one-twentieth of the harvest, adjusted for productivity and weather, was fairly low, but tenant farmers shared one-half of their crops with the landlord, and they also owed tribute taxes consisting of special local products, paid to the state, as well as military and corvée labor.

The dominantly agrarian economy had very limited commercial activity. Most handicrafts were produced for government use in special workshops, and all taxes were paid in kind or in labor services. The government artisans produced weapons, court robes, utensils, and paper. A few artisans worked for yangban families, making luxury goods like brass ware, horsehair hats, and leather shoes. Only a small number of licensed shops were permitted in the capital, and the government suppressed private markets. Peddlers carried ordinary goods to the countryside for the use of the common people. Currencies, made from mulberry bark, copper coins, and iron, circulated only for the payment of taxes. The main medium of exchange was cotton cloth.[168]

Rulers and Reforms

Despite the primitive economy, several strong rulers enacted significant changes during the fifteenth century. King Taejong (r. 1400–1418) established a grand new capital at Hanyang, modern Seoul, replacing the Koryo capital of Kaesong, by using the forced labor of over two hundred thousand workers. The new city was dominated by official residences and palaces, with major roads running to symmetrically placed gates. Official markets and inns provided for foreign envoys and the needs of the resident population. The northeast section of the city included the National Academy and the national shrine to Confucius. The mountain ranges surrounding the city provided auspicious geomantic influences and defense citadels. The king confiscated Buddhist property and put in place the fiscal system of the dynasty. He carried out land surveys, promulgated law codes, and established relations with China and Japan. He also initiated the identity tag *(hopae)* system that would classify the entire population into strictly limited status groups and bind the peasantry to the land.

The most glorious reign of the Choson dynasty was that of King Sejong (r. 1418–1450), who expanded the military and cultural power of the state on all fronts. He established the Hall of Assembled Scholars, gathering the most illustrious scholars to advise him on policy and carry out research based on the Chinese classical tradition. They compiled books on agriculture in order to promote new techniques of fertilization, water control, and seed selection, and they prepared detailed maps of each province of the country.

In 1443 Sejong assigned the scholars the task of creating an alphabet for the Korean language, stating, "The sounds of our language differ from those of China and are not easily conveyed in Chinese writing. In consequence, though one among our ignorant subjects may wish to express his mind, in many cases he after all is unable to do so."[169] Promulgated in 1446, this simple alphabet, called *han'gul,* of twenty-eight letters—seventeen consonants and eleven vowels—fit the spoken Korean language very closely and made possible extensive literacy. Koreans had also developed highly the art of movable type, and the king sponsored the printing of large numbers of primers and introductions to the life of the Buddha, the eulogies of his ancestors, and guides to Confucian moral relationships. The established scholars, however, protecting their exalted positions, fiercely opposed the use of the *han'gul* alphabet and tried to restrict its dissemination. As in Japan and Vietnam, alphabetic texts and native character systems reflected popular traditions that escaped supervision by the narrow Chinese-influenced policemen of culture. At the same time, translations of Chinese texts into Korean helped to spread the basic principles of Buddhism and Confucianism. Korea, then, followed other countries of the early modern period by establishing broader cultural integration through popular literacy and the spread of moral traditions in the vernacular language.

Foreign Relations

In its foreign relations, the Choson dynasty continued its founder's policy of pursuing friendly relations with Ming China, despite some Chinese reluctance, while suffering sharp conflicts with Japan. Under the principle of *sadae,* or "serving the great," the Choson elite regarded China as the preeminent political and cultural power and eagerly sought tributary relations with the empire. Ming rulers, at first suspicious of the lowly origins of Yi Songgye, allowed tributary missions at least three times per year to celebrate imperial birthdays and the winter solstice, and these missions conducted extensive commercial and cultural exchanges. Koreans could export local products like horses, ginseng, furs, and straw mats in exchange for silk, medicines, books, and porcelains. Over forty-five thousand horses produced from state-operated ranches moved to Ming China between 1392 and 1422.

Manchuria was an important source of horses for the Choson dynasty, so it established markets to trade with the local Jurchen tribes, and "tame" Jurchens were invited to come to trade in the capital. Under Sejong, the dynasty took control of its northern regions away from "wild" Jurchen tribes by establishing garrisoned forts along the Yalu and Tumen Rivers and clearing new land. Sejong thus secured the boundaries that mark off North Korea from China today.

Sejong also moved to wipe out the pirate marauders centered on the Japanese island of Tsushima, but he offered trading privileges to the Japanese rulers of the island, thus beginning the first official trading relationship with Japan. The Japanese shogun agreed to suppress the pirates in return for a printed copy of the Buddhist Tripitaka, in 6,467 volumes. Japanese established trading settlements in southern Korean ports, and Koreans eagerly imported copper from Japan in exchange for silk. The ports in South Korea were part of an extensive maritime network that reached as far as Siam.

Usurpation and Purges, 1450–1519

During the century and a half after Sejong's reign, however, political stability and economic security declined, culminating in the devastating invasions of the Japanese at the end of the sixteenth century. King Sejo (r. 1455–1468), the son of Sejong, usurped the throne from his twelve-year-old nephew, setting off a cycle of recriminations and purges that lasted for nearly a century. King Sejo executed six officials of Sejong's court who protested the usurpation, making them into martyrs for Confucian propriety. A vigorous military man, he attacked Jurchen tribes in Manchuria, introduced the Chinese ever-normal granaries to stabilize grain prices, and attempted to promote commerce by putting iron cash into the market. He also supported Buddhism and abolished the troublesome Hall of Worthies, the notable scholars who remonstrated against his policies. Although Sejo caused dissent with his usurpation, his policies did strengthen the state and economy.

The same cannot be said of Yongsangun (r. 1494–1506), a capricious, violent man, reminiscent of the later paranoid tsar of Russia, Ivan the Terrible. Sexually abusive and paranoid, Yongsangun killed anyone who disagreed with him, and he began large-scale purges of the bureaucracy. Confucian scholars felt that it was their duty to remonstrate, or constantly remind the ruler of his flaws, in order to make the ruler fulfill his duty of benevolence toward the common people. They also believed in writing honest histories that provided tools for moral reflection. Yonsangun rejected this built-in limitation on his power. When the scholar Kim Chongjik wrote that Sejo had usurped the throne, the enraged Yonsangun in 1498 had Kim executed, sliced his body in eight parts, and distributed one piece to each of Korea's provinces, posted with signs calling him a traitor. In addition, he purged all of Kim's disciples in government offices. Once again in 1504, he purged officials, but this time he had gone too far. The bureaucrats deposed the king and sent him into exile, where he soon died in suspicious circumstances. Korean kings could exact brutal vengeance on their critics, but unlike in China, the elite class had the power to depose them if needed.

Further purges and executions followed in 1519 and 1544, and these left deep divisions among the literati class that would break out in factional struggles later on. But the spirit of Neo-Confucian moral investigation never vanished. The two greatest philosophers of the Choson period, Yi Hwang (Yi Toegye) and Yi I (Yi

Yulgok), conducted vehement and arcane debates with each other over the relative importance of the two fundamental Neo-Confucian principles of li and qi, attracting numerous disciples. Both sides reinforced the dominance of the Zhu Xi Neo-Confucian orthodoxy in Korea. Unlike Japan and China, where the Wang Yangming school rose as a serious rival to the Zhu Xi school in the sixteenth century, and some scholars flirted with Buddhism and Daoist inspirations, Korean scholars remained firmly within the boundaries of Song orthodoxy.

By 1575, different factions among the yangban competed vigorously for appointments in the ministry of personnel. These groups, linked by kinship relations, marriages, master–disciple relations, and friendships, became hereditarily distinct groups, called "easterners" and "westerners," each of which claimed to be morally superior to the other. King Sonjo (r. 1567–1608) exacerbated factional strife by shifting support from one side to the other to assert his own power. He purged over seventy of the eastern officials in 1589 but rejected the warnings of a western faction official about the Japanese invasion. Later, the eastern faction, which came to dominate, split into northern and southern groups, and the northern faction itself split into greater and lesser factional units. Each of the factional groups disputed vociferously about the correct mourning rituals for members of the royal family and appointments to high office, but none of these were really based on moral principle. The victorious faction, in the words of a French missionary, "sits at a sumptuously prepared table, and savors the best morsels at his pleasure," while the defeated faction, "covered in tatters, spitefully grinds his teeth and shows his fist, like a man who is promising himself a spectacular revenge."[170]

The yangban also evaded taxes and military service, as they expanded their estates at the cost of smallholder peasants. Commoners with yangban protection could also bribe their way out of military service, leaving military units hollowed out and underpaid.

Hideyoshi's Invasion

Because of factional infighting, complacency, and inattention to world events, the Choson elite was woefully unprepared for the catastrophic series of invasions that afflicted Korea in the late sixteenth and early seventeenth centuries. When Hideyoshi, the military unifier of Japan, announced his ambition to conquer China, he requested Korean permission to cross the peninsula with his large army. The Korean elite, as loyal vassals of the Ming, angrily refused but failed to make any serious preparations against an attack. The king rejected the warnings of the western faction's ambassador to Japan about Hideyoshi's planned invasion. When Hideyoshi invaded in 1592, he easily overwhelmed the Korean troops. Japanese samurai had been fighting each other for two hundred years, and they had acquired European gunpowder weaponry, including mobile hand-carried firearms, while the Koreans had only obsolete cannon. Within three weeks, Hideyoshi had reached Seoul, causing the king himself and many of the residents to flee. Ming China intervened, driving the Japanese troops back until a truce was negotiated in 1593.

The only Korean military hero in these desperate times was Admiral Yi Sunsin (1545–1598), who built a fleet of "turtle ships," or ironclad armed boats equipped with cannon, with which he destroyed over four hundred Japanese ships in more than ten battles, cutting off the Japanese supply lines to the southeast Korean coast. Korean guerrilla forces, or "righteous armies" *(uibyong),* also harassed Japanese troops behind the lines, causing a stalemate that lasted from 1593 to 1597. Hideyoshi still claimed victory, even though he withdrew his troops, demanding the daughter of the Ming emperor as one of his wives, the restoration of trade between China and Japan, and Japanese occupation of the southern part of Korea. China agreed only to recognize Hideyoshi as "king" of Japan but no more. Negotiations broke off, and Hideyoshi began a second invasion in 1597, just as Yi Sunsin was unfairly dismissed from his command and sent to jail. Meanwhile, grain supplies in Korea ran short, stimulating banditry, peasant uprisings, and the destruction of registers by slaves who took this opportunity for liberation.

In new battles between Chinese and Japanese forces, the Japanese won a great victory, sending back thirty-eight thousand ears of enemy soldiers to be buried in the notorious "Ear Mound" in Kyoto. But once Yi Sunsin returned to his command, he took control of the southern seas, winning seventeen out of his eighteen battles, once again cutting the Japanese supply line. Yi died in battle, but Hideyoshi died in the same year, forcing the Japanese to withdraw once again. The Japanese took back with them captured Korean ceramicists and thousands of volumes of books for the Tokugawa library.

Koreans could celebrate a great victory, claiming that "the dragon banner waves haughtily in the west wind," but the economy had been devastated, nearly two million lives had been lost, and temples and towns had been burned to the ground.[171] Documents as well had suffered so much destruction that accurate measures of the economic loss are impossible, but we know that agriculture did not recover to its sixteenth-century level until the early eighteenth century.

Just as the Koreans and Chinese were fighting off Japan, the tribal leader Nurhaci (1559–1626) had begun to conquer the other Jurchen tribes of Manchuria. Nurhaci offered to help the Korean king recover his territory, but his offer was refused. Koreans loyally supported Ming China as it resisted Nurhaci's rise, but the Korean and Chinese forces lost to Nurhaci in 1619. One faction of the court, however, continued to support the Ming general Mao Wenlong, who continued to raid Nurhaci's territory. At the same time, internal revolt by disaffected military officers in Korea caused upheaval in the capital, and soldiers who lost after the suppression of the revolt fled to Manchuria to join Nurhaci. In 1627, with the aid of these soldiers, Nurhaci crossed the Yalu River in his first invasion of Korea. He captured Pyongyang and Seoul, burned the royal storehouses, and pillaged the countryside, forcing the king to swear allegiance as a younger brother of Nurhaci against the Ming. The Manchus demanded that Koreans pay heavy tribute of gold, silver, cloth, and cavalry to support their campaigns. When the Koreans resisted, a Manchu army of 120,000 men once again invaded in 1637. It was led by Nurhaci's successor Hung Taiji, who had now declared himself emperor of the Qing dynasty. Once again, the court tried to flee to its only refuge on Kanghwa Island, but the roads were blocked, and they suffered a siege in a mountain citadel for forty days. The king had to surrender his investiture from the Ming, send hostages to the Qing court, and swear to adopt the Qing calendar, which counted years according to the reign name of the Manchu emperor. For the next two and a half centuries, Korea was a reluctant tributary of the Qing, whom they regarded as barbarians. They sent tribute missions but delivered scathing reports in private back to Seoul and continued to use the Ming calendar in private documents. Although the Manchus had not devastated the country to the degree that Hideyoshi had, they had inflicted deep humiliation on the officials and military officers, and they had not gone away. As the Manchus went on to take Beijing and establish the expansive and glorious Qing, Koreans nursed their grudges and looked back to the Ming with nostalgia. Forced into the role of "younger brother" to a neighbor whom they did not respect, they reinforced their cultural distinctiveness by embracing Neo-Confucian norms with a vengeance. Choson Korean elites took pride in being the purest practitioners of Zhu Xi's norms and rituals, viewing the Qing as decadent.

The first Westerners arrived in Korea accidentally in the wake of military struggle. One Catholic priest accompanied Hideyoshi during his invasion. Visitors to China brought back information about Christianity, included a précis written by Matteo Ricci. Three Dutch mariners were shipwrecked on the coast in 1627; one survived. Because of his expertise in cannon casting, he obtained a military post and married a Korean woman and took a Korean name. In 1653, a Dutch yacht was shipwrecked on Cheju Island, and the crew lived for thirteen years in the kingdom as lower military officers. Henrik Hamel, the secretary on board the yacht, wrote a detailed journal that is still a valuable source on this period.[172]

Factionalism and Social Change

Factional struggles continued after the recovery from the invasions, as elite families disputed fine points of Confucian rituals and, most important, the control of land. Access to power allowed the winners to accumulate large landholdings, but yangban out of power fell into tenant status. The number of slaves steadily declined in the eighteenth century as the government workshops closed down, and slaves fled from their masters. The number of yangban rose, but many of these new entrants to the elite had purchased their status, and few of them were wealthy. The examination system no longer provided even a limited channel of upward mobility: success in the exams depended on patronage, bribery, and lineage status, not on knowledge of classical texts. Even the successful candidates had no guarantee of getting a job with their degree, and the students staged protest riots.

The tax system also diverged substantially from economic reality, despite efforts at reform. The invasions had created a fiscal crisis, by destroying registers of slaves, commoners, and land. Registered land had dropped to 46 percent of the pre-invasion level by 1646. As the yangban elite evaded even its own limited taxes, many miscellaneous levies fell on the backs of the common people, for activities like producing salt, raising fish, or owning boats. They also owed local tribute taxes and levies to escape military service. In a great reform effort, known as the *tae-dong* system, officials shifted many tax levies to landowners and converted tribute payments into rice, cloth, and cash. In many ways, this reform corresponded to the late Ming and early Qing reforms aiming at simplification and equalization of tax burden, although it was much less monetized. It substantially changed the distribution of burdens on the agricultural population and for a while lightened them. But officials could not resist adding further taxes, just as in Qing China. They made farmers pay a military service tax and they established a "righteous granaries" system similar to the Qing ever-normal granaries. But instead of stocking the granaries with purchases and voluntary contributions, Korean officials forced peasants to contribute, in theory for the sake of disaster relief. In fact, the peasants often never got their grain contributions back. By the late eighteenth century, the state collected ten million Korean bushels per year of grain, nine times the amount of the land tax.

Economic Development

As extreme Confucianists, the Korean elite were much more hostile to the development of commerce than either the Chinese or Japanese. They banned foreign trade outside of tribute missions to China and Japan, imposing genuine isolation on the country. The stereotypical description of Korea as the "hermit kingdom" applies reasonably well to this period. Yet internal developments did promote commerce and a limited amount of agricultural growth, and the state found it necessary to mint cash coins despite its reservations.

The taedong tax system required officials to obtain goods by depending on commercial agents. They set up shops and regulated markets in the capital for exchange of basic products. In the provinces, markets opened only once every five days, but a network of these periodic markets allowed farmers to travel to markets daily. Peddlers could circulate among them while riding packhorses, selling household goods, dried fish, needles, and combs. Guilds of moneylenders, innkeepers, and others supported the peddlers. Buddhist monasteries also produced important crafts for sale. Farmers intensified production of food crops by adding fertilizer, eliminating fallow fields, converting dry rice fields to paddy, and transplanting rice seedlings. They developed commercial agriculture, focusing on tobacco and cotton, and they introduced new crops like the potato and sweet potato. The population grew from about ten million in 1650 to fourteen million in 1810, indicating that new crop production could support more people, but this was a much slower rate of growth than that of China, and living standards may not have changed much.[173] In the nineteenth century, Korean agricultural yields were at least 30 percent or more less than those in China and Japan.

Seoul, the biggest city, grew to a size of two hundred thousand people, much smaller than Edo or Beijing, but the government presence in the city generated commercial demand. Some kings shut down the minting of cash, fearing inflation. The result was to inflict damaging deflation on the markets for over thirty years, but after 1731 King Yongjo agreed to resume minting coins. Yet there was only one denomination of cash coins, no paper or silver currency, no bills of exchange or banks. Private merchants still managed to conduct trade in defiance of official restrictions, which tried to limit privileges of trade to six shops in Seoul.

Although the Choson dynasty is often regarded as stagnant culturally and economically, there were significant changes within the limits of traditional norms. Koreans debated similar issues to those of their colleagues in Japan and China: how to cultivate morality within a bureaucratic system; how to reconcile different religious traditions, including Buddhism, Christianity, and Confucianism; and how to apply Confucian moral principles to practical statecraft. Outside of turbulent court politics, scholars founded *sowon (shuyuan),* or academies, where they could discuss critical issues with like-minded people independent of factional strife.[174] Some proposed to relieve peasant poverty by limiting landownership, without going so far as to confiscate the holdings of the wealthy. Some even proposed that the barbarian rulers of the Qing had useful lessons to teach Korea. Both Jesuit learning, or Western learning, transmitted through Beijing, and the Empirical Studies movement of Qing China *(kaozheng)* had their echoes in Korea. The distinctive Korean school of Sirhak, or pragmatic studies, focused on specific uses of classical learning combined with empirical research to study administrative, economic, and scientific problems. They criticized negative effects of the taedong reform, as it had fostered a wealthy commercial class and led peasants to lose their land. Wang Yangming's ideas attracted followers despite the condemnation of the Zhu Xi school.

Contradictions of the Eighteenth Century

During the reign of King Yongjo (1724–1776), Choson literati demonstrated their peak achievements and limitations. The king tried to settle incessant factional struggle by announcing a doctrine of impartiality, modeled on the Yongzheng emperor's denunciation of personal cliques. Sirhak scholars who gained access to government under his patronage compiled large encyclopedias of knowledge, including agricultural texts, legal codes, and military science. Chong Yagong, the greatest of the Sirhak scholars, promoted Western engineering techniques, explored Catholic doctrines, introduced smallpox vaccination, and promoted egalitarian agricultural communities while resisting commerce. Pak Chega outlined the elements of an economic doctrine approving increased consumption, the circulation of wealth, foreign trade, and greater production. Pak Chiwon, a fascinating writer who satirized the yangban class, also wrote a detailed description of his experiences on a tribute mission to Beijing, which described corrupt officials, haggling at the border, dissident scholars, and intimate friendships.[175]

By contrast, King Yongjo himself is best known for killing his own son. A neglectful father, he could not comprehend the disruptive behavior of his son, who was clearly mentally ill. Lady Hyegyong, Prince Sado's wife, wrote a gripping memoir describing the thoughtlessness of his father and the gruesome acts committed: "In [1757], Prince Sado began to kill. . . . He came in with the severed head [of a eunuch] and displayed it to the ladies-in-waiting. The bloody head, the first I ever saw, was simply a horrifying sight. As if he had to kill to release his rage, the Prince harmed many ladies-in-waiting."[176] The king had to act, but he responded brutally. He confined the prince in a small iron box and starved him to death. Yet despite his incompetence as a father, King Yongjo is regarded as one of the greatest kings of the dynasty.

With this bizarre incident, we conclude our sketch of the Choson dynasty in the mid-eighteenth century. It produced brilliant scholars, vicious courtiers, and both ruthless and benevolent kings, and it supported millions of hardworking peasants and traders. In some ways a pale echo of the more dynamic societies of China and Japan, Korea had still followed parallel processes creating stronger cultural integration, economic growth, and social transformation. In the century to come, Korea, like its neighbors, would face the tremendous challenges of industrialized Western powers and fall into a time of unprecedented dysfunction and ultimate collapse. Yet it still preserved a distinctive version of the East Asian cultural tradition.

6. Vietnam

MODERN Vietnam extends for over 1,500 kilometers along the coast of the Indochinese peninsula, from latitude 23 to 8 degrees north. Its population is heavily concentrated in two large fertile deltas, those of the Red River and Mekong River, which are linked by a mountain chain and a small strip of coast. It has a land area of 330,000 square kilometers, almost as large as Germany and somewhat smaller than France.[177] In the fourteenth century, however, the Mekong delta was very sparsely populated and under the control of the Cambodian empire of Angkor. The Indic Champa polities controlled the coastal strip of central Vietnam and part of the south, with a capital near Qui Nhon. The densest population and strongest state, known as Dai Viet, occupied the Red River delta. Chinese dynasties had occupied this region from the first until the tenth century AD, when Vietnamese kings finally threw off Chinese rule, establishing their own regimes. The Ly and Tran dynasties, lasting from the tenth through fourteenth centuries, created foundations for Vietnamese culture that both borrowed from China and affirmed its distinctiveness. Buddhism of the Mahayana school became the predominant high-culture religion, while local spirits reinforced local power. Chinese political theory was adapted to affirm that the Vietnamese kings were true "emperors" who ruled the south by virtue of receiving a heavenly mandate, while Chinese rulers controlled the north. The Ly and Tran dynasties introduced the Chinese examination system to recruit some of their officials, initiating the creation of a small class of Confucian-educated literati who aided the centralization of the realm. The Tran rulers and princes also excelled in military tactics, as they successfully repelled three invasions by the Mongols from 1258 to the 1290s. General Tran Hung Dao is celebrated in street names and memorials all over Vietnam today.

After the expulsion of the Mongols, the Tran polity disintegrated in a major economic and political crisis during the fourteenth century. Dai Viet suffered invasion by the early Ming ruler Yongle in the early fifteenth century, but the great military leader Le Loi drove out Ming troops, establishing a new dynasty and a

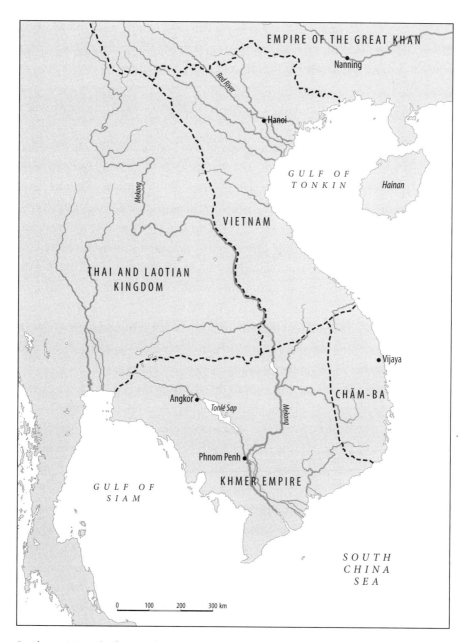

Southeast Asia in the fourteenth century

newly consolidated regime. This polity expanded to the south, nearly eliminating Champa, but fell victim itself to internal fragmentation from the mid-sixteenth century onward. In the late eighteenth century, China again intervened while a large military uprising, the Tayson Rebellion, threw the country into upheaval, until a new leader, Nguyen Anh, once again established central authority and a new dynasty in 1802.

Pierre Gourou, eminent French geographer of Southeast Asia, once dubbed Vietnam "the least coherent territory in the world."[178] A central theme in Vietnamese is the repeated cycling from a centralized polity unified at the elite level to long periods of internecine warfare and local decentralization and back to centralization. A second dominant theme is the growing influence of Chinese cultural and administrative practices, introduced by rulers to foster increased bureaucratic control, at the same time that they fought off invasions from the north. Vietnam never, however, became a miniature model of China, and it retained many practices distinctive to Southeast Asia. A third theme is the interplay between lowland, densely settled agricultural regions, the uplands that surround the river deltas, and the broad trading networks along Vietnam's very long coast.

During its first three centuries as an independent polity, the Dai Viet rulers drew on Chinese Confucian institutions derived from the Tang and Song to reinforce their legitimacy. The Ly imperial clan built its own ancestral temple, wrote its genealogy, and enforced patrilineal succession, while it employed writers of classical Chinese to staff its administrative posts. It held examinations to select those with the best Chinese classical learning. But this Chinese veneer did not extend far beyond the small family elite. All of its taxes and manpower came from the capital region. Beyond this area, personal ties and blood oaths defined loyalties much more than bureaucratic position. Buddhist monks and local notable families had far more influence than Confucian scholars. Even some of the examinations, far from enforcing Zhu Xi's Neo-Confucianism, supported syncretic religions by testing knowledge of Confucianism, Buddhism, Daoism, and shamanism. The Tran dynasty (1225–1400) took a few more steps closer to Chinese customs, giving significant official positions to those who passed examinations, but Buddhism and aristocratic values still predominated. Fourteenth-century rulers asserted: "Our country has its own definite principles. The northern and southern countries [China and Vietnam] are different. If we adopt the plan of the pale-faced students [of China], disorder will immediately follow."[179]

During the fourteenth century, Dai Viet suffered major environmental and political collapse, more extended than that of Yuan and Ming China. Population growth in the preceding centuries, perhaps doubling from 1.2 million in 1200 to 2.4 million in 1340, had put severe strains on the agricultural production and institutions of the Red River valley.[180] Nearly all land had been cleared, agricultural productivity was not rising, and the irrigation structures were fragile. Peasants fled from tax and corvée burdens, while private landowners sheltered villagers from taxes in return for coerced labor. Lawless gangs led by defrocked monks proliferated in the mountains and forests. The state lost income, as starving peasants joined rebellions, which disrupted production and threatened the capital. The population may have dropped to 1.6 million in the delta by 1400.[181] Cham kings in the south took advantage of disorder in the north, killing the Tran king and sacking the capital of Hanoi in 1377.

Rise of the Le Dynasty

An adventurous court official named Ho Quy Ly, who came from a family of Chinese immigrants, took advantage of the crises that shook the Tran state for his own interests.[182] As a royal adviser, he persuaded the reigning emperor to abdicate in favor of his son and then appointed himself as regent for the young heir to the throne. Then he forced the young emperor to abdicate and named himself emperor of a new Ho dynasty in 1400. He ruled for only seven years, but he initiated important reforms in the tax system, limited landholdings by powerful local families, and began to strengthen his military forces. But the Ming dynasty took advantage of Vietnam's weakness and invaded in 1407, claiming to restore the Tran to power. They captured Ho Quy Ly and took him back to China. The Ming invaders did win support from thousands of officials and wealthy landowners who had been attacked by Ho Quy Ly.[183] However, outside the capital, in the southern edge of the Red River delta, a wealthy landowner named Le Loi (1385–1433) named himself the "Pacification King" and organized his villagers and regional supporters to drive out the Chinese. The region from which Le Loi came, Thanh Hoa

Province, was a frontier, primitive compared with the wealthy capital, but it contained skilled military men, regarded by the sophisticated people of the capital as fierce, illiterate believers in exotic rituals like monkey sacrifice to prevent eclipses. Le Loi had close contacts with the rugged hill peoples, called Muong, on the periphery. He may even have had Muong ancestry himself.

Le Loi had no cultural prestige but gained status when Vietnam's most famous scholar patriot, Nguyen Trai (1380–1442), joined him. Trai had obtained a doctoral degree in the examination system and joined the dynasty of Ho Quy Ly. When Chinese troops occupied Hanoi, he was confined to house arrest, but he escaped to join Le Loi in 1418. As the Vietnamese version of the classic scholar–strategist famed in the ancient Chinese novel *Wars of the Three Kingdoms*, he wrote important military texts and poetry to inspire the soldiers to fight for the victory of the nation. His "Proclamation on Defeating the Wu" is the most renowned statement of Vietnamese independence from China. In one poem, "Written after the start of troubles," he wrote, "The realm has borne the clash of spears and shields. The people weep and wail—what can be done?"; in another he celebrated the power of heaven's support for popular resistance to the Ming: "Wood stakes in rows on rows stem not the tide, sunk iron chains yet fail to shackle waves, The people's strength, like water, tips the boat / No rugged terrain frustrates Heaven's will."[184]

Generations of Vietnamese have been taught to revere Nguyen Trai as the emblem of Confucian moral values of righteousness, dedication, and integrity, but his alliance with Le Loi was an awkward marriage of convenience. After Le Loi took power and named himself emperor, Nguyen Trai served him as a high official, but he offended many of his colleagues by denouncing them for compromise and corruption, and the emperor himself grew suspicious of Trai. After the emperor withdrew his support, Trai wrote bitterly, "Ask to be put in charge of streams and hills! For you know naught about the world of men. . . . Hide out like one who fishes or cuts wood. Stop speaking of the country—is it yours?"[185] He was executed after being charged unfairly with killing the son of the Le emperor, but his reputation was later rehabilitated. His poetry, written in the native Vietnamese script, or *nom,* marks a significant contribution to Vietnamese literature.[186]

Le Loi defeated the much larger Ming army through a brilliant strategy of guerrilla warfare, forcing the Ming to withdraw in 1427. Le named himself emperor of the new Le dynasty (1428–1788). Nguyen Trai portrayed him as a man with true kingly virtue backed by a heavenly mandate, in order to win over support from the Confucian scholar elite of the capital. But the literati were divided, as in every dynastic transition in China, between personal connections and cultural respect for the failing Tran, on the one hand, and recognition of the role of crude but effective military force in restoring peace to the country, on the other. Those who did rally to the Le dynasty enjoyed substantial respect and prosperity, and the dynasty did finally bring a lasting period of peace to a country that had suffered nearly a century of upheaval.

The new scholar elite blamed the collapse of the Tran on the decadent influence of Buddhism, and they launched a determined campaign to impose Chinese Neo-Confucian values on the country. Le Loi's tomb followed the model of the Ming emperor Yongle. From the 1440s, as in Korea, the Vietnamese examinations became completely orthodox enforcers of the Zhu Xi school. Le Thanh Tong (1460–1497), regarded as the greatest emperor of Vietnamese history, heavily imposed Ming institutions, including a national census, a survey of the entire country, a new national history, a Confucian law code, and a strong central administration with the same six ministries as China. The Chinese dragon replaced an "eel-like water creature" as the emperor's emblem.[187] He promoted agriculture by encouraging land clearance and dike inspections, while he penalized landlords who tried to concentrate their holdings. He also expanded the territory southward, shattering the Champa state in 1470, razing its capital, and settling it with military colonies. He forced all Cham captives to take Vietnamese names and wives in order to "correct themselves" into proper moral subjects. Tolerance of cultural diversity declined in the face of proselytizing Confucian moralism.

Economic Growth in the Fifteenth Century

Vigorous economic growth took off in the fifteenth century after the restoration of order. Most of this growth was centered on agriculture, as the Le rulers disdained commerce and tried to limit foreign trade. After Ming armies withdrew, farmers moved back into lands they had fled and continued to clear more lands on the edges of the delta. New rice strains from Champa, which ripened more quickly and resisted drought, continued to spread through the delta, raising productivity. The population of the delta rose to around 2.5 million by the end of the fifteenth century, and northern Vietnam's total population reached over four million people.[188] The number of villages and market towns increased, generating demand for a larger volume of currency. Vietnam depended heavily on Chinese copper cash, but it was often in short supply. Ho Quy Ly had tried to coerce merchants to use only paper money, as did the early Ming emperor, but this experiment failed in both places.

The Vietnamese state gained from this expansion in agriculture, as it broadened its tax base and allowed the state to increase the number of officials, schools, and military personnel. The enlarged army, up to over 250,000 men, was the key to the successful invasion of Champa in 1471. The army also used handguns and artillery derived from Chinese models, which the Cham lacked. This conquest marked the decisive beginning of the "advance to the South" *(nam dian),* which lasted for the next three centuries, culminating for Vietnamese national historians in the unification of north and south under the Nguyen dynasty in 1800. Vietnamese settlers from the north followed the troops, bringing more intensive agricultural techniques learned from China, along with uniform and pervasive Chinese administrative techniques: tax registers, law codes, examinations, and woodblock printing.[189]

In the sixteenth century, however, the Le state fell apart. A series of Buddhist rebellions based in the hills surrounding the capital broke out from 1511 to 1521, and one of the rebel leaders killed the emperor and briefly seized the capital, showing that many marginal settlers rejected the expansive Le state.[190] Once again, farmers fled the tax rolls, vagabonds proliferated, and military adventurers took power. Mac Dang Dung (d. 1540), a general from the Le family, founded his own dynasty in the capital, which lasted from 1527 to 1592, and gained recognition from Ming China, but the Le emperor and his followers fled first to Laos, then consolidated their own regime south of the capital in Thanh Hoa Province. They finally recaptured the capital in 1591.

This extensive period of division and warfare inflicted further disasters on the population, reducing agricultural output and causing harvest failures and disease.[191] Even after restoration of the Le dynasty, the country remained divided between two powerful families of military lords, the Trinh in the north and the Nguyen in the south, who continued to battle each other through the eighteenth century. During this time, northern and southern Vietnam, divided at the seventeenth parallel of latitude, slightly north of the twentieth-century border, followed separate paths.

In the north, the Trinh military lords, like the Tokugawa shogun, claimed to rule on behalf of the figurehead Le emperor. Military culture dominated over civil Confucian customs, but the regular examinations continued to recruit literate scholars, and gradually the civil officials gained some authority back from the military officers. But the number of officials was quite small, and the examination system was corrupted as the government sold official positions and access to examination degrees. Villagers still evaded taxes and found state exactions burdensome.

At this point, Catholic missionaries arrived, bringing opportunities offered by a new religious doctrine.[192] The number of believers rose rapidly, up to two hundred thousand or three hundred thousand during the eighteenth century. Christianity appealed most to the poorest, marginal, and mobile elements of Vietnamese society, who could find no respected place in local village cults. The Pure Land sect of Buddhism also revived, and Neo-Confucian scholars attempted to disseminate their learning to the villages with popular printed texts. A new, competitive, uncertain cultural environment replaced the confident Confucian missionary program of the mid-fifteenth century. Northern literati continued to admire Chinese culture as the source of "manifest civility," but they proudly identified themselves as a distinctly civilized culture, the "people of the south." Unlike Koreans, they felt no gratitude toward the Ming or Qing as defenders of their territory, nor did they openly embrace the ethic of serving the greater power. But they recognized the dilemmas of a small state on the border of a massive empire, and they knew how to use this asymmetrical relationship to their advantage.[193]

The New Society of the South

In the south, a very different polity and society developed, a distinctly "new way of being Vietnamese."[194] The Nguyen lords controlled a much smaller population and smaller army, but they successfully held off repeated Trinh invasions by taking advantage of the south's unique location. They had close ties to maritime traders, and they learned from the Portuguese how to use cannon on ships. Originally they were military colonizers from Thanh Hoa in the north who took over former Cham territories, and they aimed to restore themselves to power as the true subjects of the Le emperor. But they developed a strong regional identity over time, as they gathered refugees who increased their population.[195] Chinese emigrants who had fled south at the fall of the Ming dynasty and Buddhist contacts with China reinforced direct contact with the northern empire.[196] The immigrants developed major port cities like Hoi An as key nodes linking the south to maritime trade that extended from Japan to Southeast Asian seas.[197] During the eighteenth century, heavy Chinese settlement along with Vietnamese expansion cleared the vacant Mekong delta, making it into a second highly productive agricultural zone and a vibrant commercial community.[198] Through a series of vigorous military campaigns, the Nguyen destroyed the remnants of the Cham state and seized the lower Mekong delta, the location of modern Saigon or Ho Chi Minh City, from the Khmer Empire in 1674. The Nguyen relentlessly nibbled away at Cambodian control in the south for the next century. Although the Nguyen considered themselves superior to the primitive Khmers and Cham peoples, because of the civilizing processes borrowed from China, they created a new cultural amalgam mingling Southeast Asian and East Asian features. They called their society Dang Trong (the interior) by contrast with Dang Ngoai (the outside), the more established regime of the north. Because Mahayana Buddhism rivaled Confucianism in cultural strength, military domination was greater than in the north, and because trained scholars were scarce, syncretic movements, including both polytheistic cults and Christianity, flourished. Christianity had even greater appeal in the open frontier of the south than in the heavily controlled, if troubled, society of the north. Maritime trade became essential to the state, providing up to a third of its tax revenue, and Chinese and other emigrants were welcomed. The export rice trade, supplying Japan with its greatest foreign trade, made the region prosper first in Hoi An, where there was a substantial resident Japanese community. During the eighteenth century, the rice trade shifted farther south, and the city of Saigon began to boom.

The northern scholar Le Quy Don was shocked by the wealth of the south, calling it "the world's most fertile land."[199] Gradually, as their society and economy diverged from the north, the Nguyen rulers developed a concept of a distinct, independent regime. By the mid-eighteenth century, although they professed loyalty to the Le emperor as the ruler of a united Dai Viet, they used a title indicating claims to a distinct kingship. They requested recognition from the Chinese court as a separate vassal state, but the emperor refused.

Literary Culture of the Eighteenth Century

The eighteenth century was one of great cultural achievements, a high point in classical learning and literature. The encyclopedic scholar Le Quy Don (1726–1784) was one of Vietnam's most important writers, excelling in history, philosophy, and poetry. He traveled on a tribute mission to China, and he wrote classical Chinese poetry in an outstanding style, but he also served in government in the south and wrote a detailed record of the culture of the new frontier occupied by the expanding Nguyen lords.[200]

In this moving poem, he meditated on the limits to imperial ambition as seen in the failure of the Ming emperor's invasion:

> FORT CO-LONG
> Four hundred years—these walls have crumbled since.
> Bean stalks and melon vines now sprout and thrive.
> Limpid blue waves wash off King Trần's fierce wrath.
> Spreading green grass can't hide Mu Sheng's shamed face.
> Gold oxen, after rain, plow up some swords.
> Cold birds, by moonlight, moan amidst the ruins.
> Why must the empire's bounds forever stretch?
> Nine districts formed the realm of Yao and Shun.[201]

Le Quy Don refers to a fort built in northern Vietnam by the Ming general Mu Sheng in the early fifteenth century, when the Yongle emperor invaded the country. General Tran Gian Dinh defeated Mu Sheng, forcing him to retreat to Fort Co-long in 1408. Contemplating the ruined fortress, the poet describes how natural growth buries the weapons of war. In the last line, he invokes the mythical Chinese emperors Yao and Shun as examples of rulers who did not try to expand their domination toward the south.

The poet Ho Xuan Huong (ca. 1775–1820), a concubine with a classical education, became a brilliant open exponent of women's longing and sexuality, using the native Vietnamese nom script with literary flair and nuance.[202] As one of the very few great women poets in the East Asian literary tradition, she knew how to use allusion and double entendre to express both resentment and passion that contradicted rigid patriarchal norms. For example, in the poem "On Sharing a Husband," she writes: "Screw the fate that makes you share a man / One cuddles under cotton blankets; the other's cold / Every now and then, well, maybe or maybe not. / Once or twice a month, oh, it's like nothing."[203]

But the most famous writer of all Vietnamese literature is Nguyen Du (1765–1820), the creator of Vietnam's national epic, the *Tale of Kieu*.[204] He had traveled to China and greatly admired the classical tradition, but during the Tayson Rebellion he retreated from politics. He returned to serve the new Nguyen dynasty, but he despised the crudity of the new military rulers from the south and expressed nostalgia for the lost classical world. *The Tale of Kieu,* one of the only world epics whose protagonist is a woman, tells the story of the beautiful Kieu and her true lover, a young scholar whom she must abandon when she is sold as a prostitute. She rises to great influence as the consort of a bandit king but eventually returns to her lover in calm, chaste resignation to the mysterious forces of heaven and fate. Combining deep classical knowledge with the pungent folk wisdom expressed in nom, *The Tale of Kieu* epitomizes the history of the Vietnamese people, their passion, suffering, and endurance.

Collapse and Reunification under the Nguyen

The collapse of both the Trinh and Nguyen regimes and the recreation of a united Vietnam in the late eighteenth century falls outside the time period of this volume, but it deserves brief treatment. Unlike the other regions discussed here, which consolidated and expanded upon the achievements of the early eighteenth century, the Vietnamese polities experienced dramatic upheaval. A major uprising known as the Tayson Rebellion broke out and eliminated Trinh rule; the Nguyen lords marched north aiming at conquest; Qing China intervened to restore the Le emperor; and the Tayson leaders ambushed and drove out the Qing armies from Hanoi. They proclaimed a new dynasty, but the remaining Nguyen lord of the south overthrew the Tayson and proclaimed his own dynasty, the Nguyen, in 1802.[205]

Modern Vietnamese historians exalt the Tayson as a revolutionary "peasant movement" and trace the origins of the Vietnamese Communist party to its mobilization of the peasant masses against both the "feudal" Le regime and the Chinese invasion. But the Tayson in fact were neither revolutionary nor particularly peasant in orientation. They were political opportunists who took advantage of major tensions in the Nguyen regime and drew on multiple discontented classes for political and military support.

Three brothers from the village of Tay Son, a small town in the highlands near the city of Qui Nhon in southern Vietnam, began the Tayson uprising in 1773. They attracted support from upland peoples who resisted the Nguyen state and from lowland farmers pressed by heavy taxation. The Nguyen had extended their rule very far south from their capital at Hue, but their control over the southern region was fragile. They had spent heavily on military campaigns against the Khmers and Siamese, and they had built elaborate palaces in the capital. But foreign trade had declined rapidly, and copper imports from Japan and China, essential for supporting the currency, had been cut off. The Nguyen tried to force the population to use its own zinc coins, but the population rejected these measures. Qui Nhon in particularly suffered from heavy labor exactions for transporting rice from the rich Mekong delta. Upland peoples likewise faced increased tax burdens in this region.

The Tayson brothers, Nguyen Nhac, Nguyen Hue, and Nguyen Lu, built on this unrest to form large armies. Nguyen Nhac, a tax collector and betel nut trader who knew the local administration well, captured the city of Qui Nhon with a deceptive maneuver, staging a false surrender that allowed him access to the city, then escaping captivity and letting his followers storm the town. The Tayson armies, feared for the loud hissing sounds they made during attacks, quickly overwhelmed the lax local Nguyen forces, but they surrendered to invading Trinh forces to preserve themselves in 1775. For the next ten years they drove south against the remaining Nguyen troops, while Nguyen Nhac occupied Cha Ban, an old Cham capital, and proclaimed himself emperor. They then turned against the Trinh and advanced north, taking Phu Xuan (Hue) and Thang Long (Hanoi) in 1786. Nguyen Hue, the strongest military leader of the three brothers, turned against Nguyen Nhac and proclaimed himself emperor in 1788. But the refugee Le emperor called in Chinese troops. Nearly two hundred thousand Chinese troops crossed the border and occupied Hanoi in 1788, but during Tet, the Vietnamese New Year's, Nguyen Hue ambushed the troops and drove them in a humiliating defeat.[206]

The Hall of the Mandarins in Hue, the imperial capital of the Nguyen dynasty, drew heavily—if also on a smaller scale—on Chinese ritual architecture. Dragons on the roof and shades of yellow symbolized imperial power, while in the halls the foremost scholars prepared ritual garments for taking part in courtly ceremonies. (Photo by Peter C. Perdue)

Nguyen Hue entertained vast ambitions of marrying into the Qing court and even invading the southern provinces of Guangxi and Guangdong, but he died in 1792. After his death, the Tayson movement lost momentum, while the small group of Nguyen lords in the south led by Nguyen Anh gained allies from the French and Siamese to plot their return to power. For the next ten years, Nguyen Anh tenaciously moved northward against weakening Tayson resistance until he captured Thanh Long in 1802 and proclaimed his new dynasty, the Nguyen.

Although the Tayson were not a revolutionary peasant movement, they were part of a series of dramatic changes that linked Vietnam to the eighteenth-century world, shared by many other regions. The Vietnamese move to the south (nam dian) included clearance of land on sparsely populated frontiers stimulating de-

A Tayson soldier. William Alexander, an eighteenth-century English painter, visited Vietnam and made sketches of the typical fighting men of the region. These were peasant boys, often barefoot, without uniforms, who were dressed in turbans and equipped with rudimentary firearms. The troops of the Tayson were probably dressed in very similar fashion to this man. (British Library)

mographic growth, like the Chinese expansion under Qianlong. The growth in the Chinese merchant community of Saigon created a new geographic orientation southward toward the maritime world shared by island Southeast Asia and its many participants, including the Dutch, French, Portuguese, and, later, British. Highland peoples and the Cham peoples conquered by Vietnam who joined the Tayson paralleled the ethnic character of frontier uprisings seen in both eighteenth-century Russia and China. The Tayson also invoked many Confucian ideals, using the slogans of "righteousness" *(nghia;* Chinese, *yi),* "virtue" *(duc;* Chinese, *de),* and the "Mandate of Heaven" *(menh troi;* Chinese, *tianming)* to legitimate their revolt, but they combined these notions with supernatural appeals to local Vietnamese traditions, including magical swords, mysterious lights, and slaying of giant snakes.[207] They drew on support from many marginal elements of a mobile, diverse, unruly society, including pirates, bandits, merchants, religious leaders, and ethnic minorities. The Vietnamese peasantry in general served the Tayson as sources of soldiers and taxes, as they were forced to pay increased burdens during a time of unceasing warfare. Ultimately, the Tayson contributed to the strengthening of state control over rural society. They attempted and failed to impose a universal identity card system on the population, copied from ancient Chinese institutions. But the Nguyen dynasty that succeeded them imported a stronger Chinese model of bureaucracy adapted to Vietnamese conditions that enabled it to survive for the next century.[208] By 1802, Vietnam, like the other East Asian societies, was a unified country with unprecedented levels of commercial prosperity, cultural integration, and bureaucratic centralization, reasserting its traditions just as the challenges from Western powers loomed ominously ahead.

7. Comparisons, Connections, and Convergences

ACROSS this vast region, spanning Russia, Central Eurasia, and East Asia, there were common trends shared by nearly all the societies, others that were distinctive to a single region, and others that were confined to only one national or imperial unit. In addition, interactions between the different parts of the region by military, commercial, and ecological forces caused them to respond to common challenges, even if they did not respond in the same way. Even though this region spans many climatic zones, a huge variety of languages and cultures, and three major religious traditions (Christianity, Islam, and East Asian Buddhism and Confucianism), we can still discover certain broad trends that affected all of it to some degree.

Certain global trends, like climatic change, had a definite impact on the formation of states and societies at several critical periods. The Little Ice Age, beginning around the thirteenth century and lasting in the Northern Hemisphere until the twentieth century, was a period of lower temperatures that affected agricultural productivity and population growth. China's annual temperature was about one degree centigrade lower than average from the fifteenth to nineteenth centuries. The coldest period occurred from 1620 to 1740, accompanied by heavy rainfall and floods in the south, with warming from 1740 to 1830.[209] Just as the Medieval Optimum, a earlier time of warmer temperatures, favored the expansion of population and the consolidation of core cultures in places like Kiev and Song China, the cooler temperatures of the Little Ice Age put extra strains on agrarian populations and on the states that relied on them. Despite efforts to link the outbursts of pastoralist nomads to desiccation, there is little evidence of direct connection between the Mongol and Timurid conquests and climatic change.

The seventeenth century, however, stands out as a time of crisis across the entire region, corresponding to the nadir of the Little Ice Age. Major volcanic eruptions punctuated the seventeenth century, causing exceptionally cool summers. There is no direct connection between cold weather and economic or political distress, but times of high grain prices in Europe, however, do correlate closely with severe weather conditions. In China, cold summers delayed the transplanting of crops, killed fruit trees and fish in ponds, and lowered agricultural yields. The Time of Troubles in Russia, the Ming–Qing transition, the collapse of the bakufu into warring states in Japan, and increased conflict in Korea, Vietnam, and Central Eurasia all occurred around the early seventeenth century. These military upheavals do not have one single cause, but similar patterns do appear. The underlying factors include climatic change, population pressure, fiscal limitations, decline in silver flows, and blocked mobility of aspiring elites.[210] In each region, however, specific military and state formations modified the general upheaval. Climate itself did not absolutely determine political change: it only put strains on ruling structures that forced them to respond. The Manchus, for example, developed more effective famine relief policies in southern Manchuria than the Ming during the early seventeenth century, increasing the strength and attractiveness of their regime. Human societies were becoming more resilient in the face of climatic shocks. Frontier expansion increased the supplies of arable land, and increased intensity of cultivation, including fertilizers and new seeds, could increase productivity on existing lands.

Most of the region followed parallel processes of population growth and decline. The world population rose slowly from around 350 million in 1200 to 421 million in 1500, stagnated in many places in the seventeenth century, then rose more rapidly to 900 million around 1800.[211] China, the largest population unit, followed this trend quite closely, rising significantly in the Ming from over 60 million in 1400 to possibly 150 million in 1600, declining up to 30 percent during the Ming–Qing transition, and growing steadily to reach 300 million in 1800. Japan followed a somewhat special trajectory. It grew despite constant warfare in the sixteenth and seventeenth centuries and experienced slow growth during the eighteenth century.

The trajectory of global trade and its impact on the Eurasian continental trade is a subject that needs further exploration. One conventional assumption—that the rise of maritime trade between the New World and Asia damaged the classic caravan trade of the silk routes—needs reexamination. Caravans continued to carry Chinese goods like silk and tea across Central Eurasia through oasis towns into Russia and the Middle East; political upheavals often disrupted the trade, but it revived periodically. As the Ming negotiated trading licenses with Mongolian pastoralists, and the Russians penetrated Siberia and Central Eurasian territories, the two expanding empires generated further demands for trade under their control. After the treaties of Nerchinsk and Kiakhta, regulated trade at border towns subordinated the independent Mongols, but the volume of trade increased. India under the Mughals and Safavid Iran also participated in these wide-ranging trading networks.[212] Japan, once again, followed a special path, opening itself to commercial links both with China and with maritime Asia in the sixteenth century but closing down much of the free trade in the seventeenth and eighteenth centuries. Still, Japan maintained links to maritime Asia through the southern islands and the Ryukyus and allowed tribute missions from Korea and very limited European contact. Curiosity about foreign peoples persisted, and Japan was never entirely isolated. Korea kept its own trade under tight control, but tribute relations with Japan and China still kept it in touch with East Asian developments. Vietnam fostered greater ties with maritime trading communities, ranging from Japan to Southeast Asia, as the wealth of the southern region grew.

Frontier expansion was a key element in the formation of the major states and societies across the region and, in fact, the globe. Almost everywhere, settlers backed by powerful bureaucratic states moved into sparsely settled borderlands, subduing resistance by native peoples, turning forests into fields, exploiting mountain resources, and creating new dense agrarian settlements. The world had a little over twice the population in 1800 that it had in 1500, but its human footprint was many times larger. Both tighter centralization by expanding empires and greater concentration of capital by commercial organizations, often with state charters, pushed trading networks outward into mountainous, forested, desert, and maritime regions. These pioneering soldiers, settlers, and traders dramatically transformed the ecologies of the frontier region. As John Richards states, "The global scale and impact of human intervention in the natural environment during the early modern period were unprecedented in history."[213] Russia thrust into huge territories to the east, as its fur traders moved rapidly across Siberia, into Alaska and down the coast of North America; China under the Qing conquered and penetrated decisively the Manchurian forests, Mongolian steppe, and Xinjiang's deserts and grasslands, while also controlling trade routes to Tibet; Japanese moved northward into Hokkaido in pursuit of fish and furs and southward to the Ryukyus for tropical products; Vietnam dramatically altered the structure of its polity by incorporating a large, dynamic new trading and agricultural delta in the south. Only Korea failed to take much advantage of this outward push. The Central Asian regimes attempted to control trade routes themselves by grasping for resources wherever they could: the Zunghars looked to exploit pastoral products, minerals, tea, silk, and furs to build their state during their century of flourishing.

State formation, including the construction of new administrative apparatuses, the proliferation of paperwork and officials, and the rationalization of tax collection, was a common goal of all the major actors in a complex game of Eurasian geopolitics. On the positive side, the expanding states needed new methods to gather and concentrate the new resources gained from military expansion. On the defensive side, they needed to protect their gains from rival powers who challenged their control. The fifteenth century was a time of consolidation and expansion of administration, marked by greater paperwork, imposition of bureaucratic codes, and standardization of promotions and salaries in Ming China, Le Vietnam, Choson Korea, and Russia. Often, it was frontier commanders and ethnic groups who succeeded best at amassing military force and creating innovative institutions. In the seventeenth century, the Manchus, located strategically next to the Mongols and the Chinese borderland, combined the elements of all three cultures to create a powerful military and administrative regime designed for warfare, administrative consolidation, and accumulation of wealth. Muscovy, also located in a marginal zone by reference to the richer Kievan state and Byzantium, used its frontier position to dominate its rivals by mixing nomadic pastoral military technologies, personalist Central Eurasian politics, and European administrative structures. In Vietnam, likewise, frontier commanders like Le Loi and the Nguyen lords focused on military goals first, flexibly accommodated minority peoples from the highlands, and adapted Confucian bureaucratic techniques from China to the Buddhist, fluid, and commercialized regions of the south. The military founders of the Tokugawa, emerging from centuries of internecine warfare, maintained the imperial court in Kyoto but built a newly centralized shogunate in Edo to rule the country. Korea and the Central Eurasian regimes had a less continuous type of state formation. The Choson regime restored itself after Hideyoshi's invasion but did not conduct major reforms to resolve endemic problems of factionalism, elite privilege, and economic stagnation. The Zunghars and Shaybanids attempted to consolidate their gains but faced too many rival powers to achieve a stable state.

States expanded and commercial networks grew within limits determined by transportation costs. Rivers, inland seas (for example, the Baltic, the Mediterranean, and the Inland Sea of Japan), land routes, and open sea stand in descending order of convenience, cost, and security. The relative importance of these different forms of transportation determined the nature of each state's linkages to its neighbors. China and Russia, using their enormous rivers for large-scale transportation of basic goods, could dominate large areas, but they also invested heavily in land transportation for military goals. Japan's Inland Sea was the key focus of commercial exchange, but its coastal connections, like those of Korea, were limited to a few southern ports and islands. None of the empires ventured large-scale voyages into the open sea of the Pacific: the Chinese, Russians, Japanese, and Vietnamese hugged the coastlines, following predictable paths of winds and currents.

History is not only a story of winners, even though they dominate the written record. Let us not forget those who suffered most in this period: the independent nomads of Central Eurasia, the hill peoples of China, the enserfed Russian peasantry, the Japanese community-bound villagers and, to some extent, women everywhere. State builders were most afraid of people who were free to move, and they tried with varying degrees of success to register their populations and control migration.

The populations targeted by the state had only limited options of resistance, through protest and flight. The peoples of the hills, the coastal regions, the grasslands, and the internal frontiers of marshes and deserts often did their best to use geography to avoid the intrusive hand of the state. They developed alternative social formations on the edges of the consolidating empires, in order to preserve equality, autonomy, fluidity, and freedom.[214] Russian peasants in general rarely staged open revolts, but the Cossacks of the Ukraine and the settlers of Siberia asserted their independence from serfdom and military service repeatedly. In the core of Russian lands, they found themselves increasingly bound by law and landlord oppression. In Japan, peasants could organize petitionary movements to beg for reductions of taxes in times of famine, but they had been disarmed by the Tokugawa shoguns, so they could never engage in serious armed conflict against their samurai superiors. Tokugawa Japan succeeded even better than Russia in tying down villagers to tightly organized communities collectively liable for taxation. Russian villagers could flee to the sparsely settled frontier, but Japanese peasants, except in Hokkaido, had little freedom to move. The Korean state also instituted widespread controls over its relatively immobile peasant population, including the most extensive identity card system on the continent. Chinese farmers retained their weapons and enrolled in militia units for self-defense, and the great diversity of the Chinese landscape offered them many opportunities for both escape and revolt. China had sophisticated bureaucratic record-keeping methods, but both the Ming and the Qing were unable to prevent substantial mobility, and many millions of villagers escaped registration. Vietnamese villagers likewise experienced very diverse conditions of mobility, from the tightly bound communities of the northern delta to the loose and mixed confederations of the south.

The position of women, by modern standards, changed very little during this period. Nearly everywhere, women suffered under patriarchal domination and had little freedom to choose their marriage partners, their residences, or their means of living. Except for the prominent Russian empresses of the eighteenth century, women never held high political positions. Yet there were large variations geographically and temporally in the degree of their subordination. Women in pastoral societies always had higher status that those in agrarian settled societies, as they played vital economic roles in taking care of animals, and the mobility of pastoralists required them to be active. As mothers and wives of khans, they often had considerable political influence. In Russia, elite women's status changed sharply under Peter's reforms, as he abolished their seclusion in harems and began to provide opportunities for education in Western culture, with tutors from France and Germany. Chinese women benefited from the commercialization and new mobility of the sixteenth to eighteenth centuries, which gave them opportunities to travel on pilgrimages beyond their households and also left them at home when their husbands went on trading voyages. A new cult of sensibility in the eighteenth century recognized the importance of sentiments of love that contested with obligations to family and children. Women in some elite families gained a high level of cultural prestige, with classical learning rivaling that of male scholars, and they could spread their achievements through letters and poetry circles.[215] Foot binding, however, a painful and crippling practice unique to China, which kept women in seclusion, spread downward through lower social classes, severely restricting their freedom. Itinerant Buddhist preachers could find enthusiastic audiences among women confined to the home.

Japanese women faced many of the same patriarchal restraints as their Chinese counterparts, although they did not bind their feet. They, too, were almost always confined to the household, but many peasant families supported the education of their daughters at rural schools and provided them with lavish clothing. Up to 10 percent of women gained some knowledge of the Japanese syllabic script and Chinese characters. In exceptional cases, some women escaped the bonds restraining them. Ema Saiko (1787–1861), one of Japan's finest poets and painters, developed her great talents with her father's support and inspired many women disciples. Some new religious sects supported by the merchant class embraced women preachers. Jion-ni Kenka (1716–1768), a Buddhist nun, gave free lectures to men and women in Edo that attracted up to one thousand people.[216] In Vietnam, women had greater rights to inheritance than their East Asian neighbors to the north, and the astonishing poet Ho Xuan Huong indicates that they had cultural outlets that were much more open than the other East Asian societies. Korea, of all the societies here, seems to have been the most rigid and confining for women both at elite and commoner levels, but Lady Hyegyong's memoirs give us a brief glimpse of the emotional undercurrents of this repressive patriarchal society.

· · ·

Besides these general trends, there were also common trends among culturally defined regions. We may divide them into three parts: the Russian Orthodox and Slavic culture; Central Eurasian pastoralism, caravan, and oasis culture; and the East Asian agrarian, bureaucratic, Buddhist and Confucian culture.

David Christian has argued that northern Eurasia, especially Russia, faced particular problems of agrarian production that affected the ability of states to rule.[217] Because the Russian plains stretched over large flat areas, military conquerors faced few barriers to expansion. Conversely, the cold climate, sporadic rainfall, and low agricultural productivity supported only a sparse settled population, meaning that state builders did not have access to large amounts of resources through coerced labor or taxation. Until the rise of Muscovy, Slavic settlers in these plains and forests generally lived in small communities lacking powerful leaders. The Muscovite state created the first continuous tradition of agrarian autocracy, drawing on both Byzantine and Mongolian precedents. By concentrating the dispersed resources of Eurasian lands in the hands of a few powerful families and, finally, an autocratic tsar, Muscovy could expand over huge areas and support a powerful military apparatus.

Many scholars have debated the causes of the rise and fall of nomadic empires in Central Eurasia, in both ancient and modern times. From Ibn Khaldun's concept of *asabiyya,* or solidarity, to Owen Lattimore's description of the high impact of nomadic culture on Chinese states, historians and theoreticians have recognized special characteristics of nomadic regimes that bordered the major settled societies of Eurasia.[218] The most convincing general explanations, however, avoid simplistic environmental determinism or the ascription of unchanging psychologies of "need" and "greed" to pastoral peoples. Instead, they focus on particular historical sequences that generated progressively larger and more durable states over the last two millennia. Nicola di Cosmo, for example, describes four different means of obtaining resources used in succession by nomadic state builders from the first century BC to the eighteenth century AD: tribute, trade partnership, dual administration, and regular taxation. Kublai's Mongol Empire initiated regular taxation, which spread to Timur, the Ottomans, the Zunghars, and the Manchus. The Zunghar state was the final independent Mongolian regime to challenge control of Central Eurasia, and it combined all four methods of resource extraction in its desperate search for revenue. It exacted tribute from oasis dwellers and Siberian forest peoples; it looked for trading profits from the Qing, the Russians, and Central Asian traders; it enacted different administrative structures for settled and nomadic peoples; and it taxed certain oasis agriculturalists whenever possible.

The Qing, however, perfected these techniques in its own way at a much more effective level. The Qing rulers could exact tribute as gifts from visitors to the court on diplomatic missions, and it promoted trade on a large scale with Central Eurasians, Russians, and Europeans. Dual administration was a key feature of the Qing state in the frontier areas. But in taking over the Ming fiscal system and perfecting it, the Qing drew on the vast resources of agrarian China, far exceeding the capabilities of the rival Zunghar regime. As a Central Eurasian regime with strongly

Chinese characteristics, the Manchus knew how to secure domination of both the steppe and settled regions.

Ming and Qing China, however, were also East Asian regimes. The East Asian mandarin regimes of China, Vietnam, and Korea shared a long tradition of centralized bureaucratic government, based on salaried officials selected through more or less meritocratic examination systems. In each of them, scholars and officials debated recurrent issues of administrative practice that have a very modern ring: how to ensure that state officials are insulated from the pressure of personal ties or special interest groups, how to keep bureaucrats in touch with the needs of the population they served, and how to ensure equitable distribution of the nation's wealth among the poor.[219] The pressure of "feudalization" meant that influential families or factional groups tied to regional and commercial interests could distort policy decisions so as to undermine the public good. Bureaucratic apathy could replace emotional involvement in the welfare of the people with standardized practices, for example, by distributing famine relief according to fixed quotas instead of personal need. Officials and scholars who debated these questions tried to reconcile the increasingly impersonal procedures of large states with the need for personal connections more characteristic of smaller societies and those based on bonds of military and charismatic authority. Some argued for a return to the spirit of the "feudal" period of ancient Chinese history, when warrior kings acted for the welfare of their own populations, guided by sages schooled in texts of the golden age. Others tried to institute "community compacts," where villagers met in banquets with leading notables to reinforce social solidarity. To a lesser extent, the reconciliation of bureaucratic and personal authority was a theme of Russia and Japan, where new administrations had emerged from individual military formations. The Russian tsars who attacked noble families tried to impose more uniform administration, as the shoguns compiled national codes and imported Chinese texts on moral learning and administrative practice.

In summary, centralized bureaucratic government, with all its contradictions and flaws, inexorably progressed across the region, bringing greater standardization of administrative practice as well as elite and popular culture and supporting extensive commercial exchange. The large empires of Russia and China and the smaller states of Japan, Korea, and Vietnam all penetrated their societies more effectively, while expanding their territorial dimensions and generally experiencing population growth and cultural dynamism. None of them were static, many of their institutions were resilient and adaptable, and most of their subjects prospered. But these were contingent outcomes of many diverse factors of military, environmental, and cultural interactions, which were vulnerable to reversal in the subsequent century.

·[two]·

The Ottoman Empire and the Islamic World

Suraiya Faroqhi

Introduction

IN any work on world history dealing with the period from 1350 to 1750, it is inevitable to first address the question of how and why such a time span comes to be a subject of study. In Turkish history, by analogy with French practice, it is customary to have what is generally called the "modern" epoch begin in 1453—the year of the Ottoman conquest of Constantinople. This epoch (also often referred to as the early modern period) lasts until the radical reformation of the Ottoman state and its institutions in the mid-nineteenth century, marked by the proclamation of the much-studied "reorganization order" *(Tanzimat fermanı)* issued in 1839.

As a result, the period presents historians of the Ottoman Empire with several problems. According to the traditional time divisions used in Turkish historical scholarship, this means including part of the medieval early phase of the Ottoman Empire, a polity that first came to prominence as a regional princedom *(beylik)* in Northwest Anatolia around 1300. Yet prior to the mid-fifteenth century, source material is so scarce that many themes can be treated satisfactorily only when dealing with the period after 1453; indeed, Ottoman archives only really begin in this period.[1] Accordingly, the stress must necessarily lie on the later end of the spectrum. But we may console ourselves with the observation that rigidly demarcated eras are, after all, only artificial historical constructs.

As regards the end of the period under consideration here, the Russo-Turkish War, fought from 1768 to 1774, may justifiably be regarded as a historic watershed. Under the terms of the peace treaty of Küçük Kaynarca (1774), foreign ships were granted the right, hitherto denied, to enter the Black Sea.[2] In addition, the so-called independence of the Crimea that was provided for in this same treaty set in train a political process that culminated shortly thereafter (1783) in Russian annexation of the region. Clashes with the tsarist empire from the 1760s onward resulted in many failed harvests and disruption to trade routes both on land

and at sea. This situation led to serious shortages in Istanbul, which, including its suburbs, had a population of some 420,000 in 1829 (older statistics are generally problematic). In a wider context, this war signaled the start of an enduring economic depression, which effectively precluded any possibility of Ottoman military or political victory in the conflicts of the later eighteenth century.

Furthermore, the years after 1770 witnessed the growing integration of business activities in the great Ottoman centers of commerce like Istanbul, Saloniki, Izmir, and Aleppo, into financial networks mostly controlled by the French. Only the revolutionary wars that followed the proclamation of the French Republic in 1792 and continued, with only brief interruptions, until 1815, served to reverse this trend, at least for a spell.[3] It therefore seems appropriate to consider the grave political crisis in the last quarter of the eighteenth century, together with the growing economic integration into the periphery of a European economy around the same time, as a clear borderline between epochs, for which the year 1774, the date of the Peace of Küçük Kaynarca, may stand as a symbol. During the last quarter of the eighteenth century, it is also clear that the Ottoman state began to lose its grip on power both internally and externally. In consequence, in order to explore all the ramifications, I shall in this chapter extend our end date by around a quarter of a century.

Historiography and the Ottoman Empire

Historical research on the Ottoman Empire is currently in a state of flux. Whereas up to about twenty years ago it was customary to contrast a brief period of initial growth (1300–1453) and an even briefer phase of ascendancy (1453 to the end of the sixteenth century) with a centuries-long decline (from the late sixteenth century to the First World War), this way of looking at things has, at least among scholars, lost much of its credibility. As elsewhere, there is a tendency among modern historians of the Ottoman Empire to question the primacy of war and foreign policy. Conversely, the growth of interest in such aspects as art history and cultural history has left its mark. In such areas of study, although the exercise of power still plays an important role, it is no longer the only aspect worthy of consideration. Accordingly, as has also been the case with historians of India, the last few decades have witnessed a positive reevaluation of the eighteenth century. Nowadays, the architecture of this period, along with many of the new departures in poetry, are no longer simply dismissed as "debased classical forms" but instead treated as independent initiatives, the first signs of a momentous change that would ultimately result in the creation of an "Ottoman modernism."

As regards the seventeenth century, and to some extent the eighteenth as well (at least up to the 1760s), historians far prefer to talk in terms of a series of crises, from which the Ottoman state and society nevertheless largely recovered, albeit often only with great difficulty. In other words, the assumption is no longer of some "constant state of crisis." Historians thus have reassessed the supplanting in the provinces of strongly centralized forms of government by more decentralized arrangements from the late eighteenth century onward: commentators are now at pains to stress that the various provincial magnates in the eighteenth century were relatively well integrated into the Ottoman state structure and, if anything, played a major role in the survival of the empire during the crises it faced later in the century.[4] And in no way should the spheres of influence of these dignitaries and magnates be interpreted as prototypes of the corresponding modern nation-states, a view commonly held in the 1950s.

This change of attitude undoubtedly has to do with the fact that not only in American and European historical scholarship but also in many intellectual circles within Turkey, the centralized nation-state is no longer necessarily seen as the *non plus ultra* in political history. There are a number of writers now active in Turkish journalism who question the orthodox view that safeguarding the state is the sole political goal and instead have demanded a greater role for democratic consensus. In this context, one is less tempted to accept territorial expansion or its opposite as the only valid criteria for determining a state's "heyday" or "decline." Admittedly, in literature aimed at a broader readership, there is little sign of this change as yet. When all is said and done, the established pattern of thinking, with its various ramifications, is just too convenient and comfortable a mode of discourse to slip into when discussing Turkey's EU accession and other contemporary problems, for Turks and foreigners alike.

By contrast, historical research is not exclusively determined by political and cultural trends that typify the period when they arose; if these trends were absolutely dominant, history would have to be banished from the circle of strictly scientific disciplines on the grounds that it was a branch of scholarship merely designed to legitimize existing power structures. However, in Ottoman history, the gradual discovery of central and local archives and the discussion of their contents have determined the direction of much research. For the period from around 1450 onward, grand viziers, chief ministers, and above all treasury administrators have left behind considerable volumes of documentation. Yet also the kadi registers (local magistrates' records), which exist in many of the larger cities, mostly from about 1570 onward, have enabled historians to write relatively detailed city histories and also to throw new light on the dispensation of justice—stimulating fresh debate about Max Weber's concept of "Kadi justice."[5] Between 1940 and 1970, most documents that drew the attention of historians related to the period between 1450 and 1600, while it was European archives that they consulted when looking at nineteenth-century history. Yet the ongoing cataloging of the Ottoman state archive, which has placed undreamt-of quantities of material at the disposal of researchers, is primarily concerned with the nineteenth century. As a result, this era now exerts an enormous fascination for historians. But researchers who have devoted themselves to the long-neglected "transitional period" of the seventeenth and eighteenth centuries have also got their money's worth: the correspondence between the central authorities and local functionaries, which increased in leaps and bounds from the mid-eighteenth century onward, and the extensive documentation of the practice of tax farming are now available for study in quantities that simply did not exist before.

For a long time, historians of the Ottoman Empire tended to regard only those colleagues who worked from primary sources in the archives as serious professionals. However, since 1990 there has been a reevaluation of narrative sources, and a number of chronicles plus other works with a historical focus have been published in critical editions. These works have also enabled scholars to engage critically with narrative sources; some colleagues have even discussed pertinent questions in front of a broader public.[6] Historians are thus attempting to process a broad spectrum of sources and cast a critical eye over them. Nowadays, as compared with thirty years ago, researchers are much more attuned to the fact that everything written down in an archival document is not necessarily true. Yet in spite of close collaboration between art history and history, the study of material culture—let alone any integration of the as yet limited results of Ottoman archaeology—remains the Cinderella of our profession.

1. *Geography and Resources*

IN its first phase, the Ottoman Empire occupied both banks of the Sea of Marmara and the Aegean. The oldest provinces were Rumeli and Anadolu: the former occupied roughly the region we now call Thrace, which lies partly within Greece and partly within Turkey, while the latter corresponds to modern western Anatolia. The Aegean region and the southern slopes around the Sea of Marmara have a Mediterranean climate, but in the immediate vicinity of Istanbul the weather is too cold and damp to grow olive trees.

Ottoman expansion in the Balkans and on the Anatolian plateau in the course of the fourteenth century meant that regions with continental climate and cold winters soon formed part of the empire's heartland: in this context, such regions as the recently conquered principalities in the areas now covered by Bulgaria, Serbia, and Bosnia might be cited, plus, from the sixteenth century onward, much of Hungary. In central Anatolia, which prior to the Ottomans had been ruled by the Karaman princedom and even earlier, in the thirteenth century, by the Seljuks of Rum, the Ottomans encountered dry steppeland. In contrast, the mountain ranges that fringed the southern and especially the northern sides of the peninsula were cooler and, particularly in the Black Sea region, extremely rainy. In these colder zones, nomads and merchants who relied on the camel as a means of transport first had the onerous task of breeding hybrids that were more suited to this type of climate—crossing one-humped dromedaries with two-humped Bactrian camels. Meanwhile eastern Anatolia, with its excessively cold winters and brief summers, presented a major challenge to Ottoman armies, which frequently had to cross this region during the many conflicts of the sultans with the Safavid rulers of Persia. In the seventeenth century, it was famously said of winters in Erzurum that a cat attempting to spring from one roof to another would freeze solid in mid-jump, dropping to the ground only when the spring thaw came.[7]

It was only with the conquest of Egypt and Syria (1516–1517), followed by Iraq in the 1530s, that the Ottomans first came across warmer climate zones and above all desert regions. To some extent, these climate zones always remained alien and unfamiliar to them—even the experienced Ottoman traveler Evliya Çelebi (1611–after 1683) described the caravan routes of the Arab and Syrian deserts as a strange and hostile environment.[8]

Even so, in Anatolia and the Balkans alike, adaptation to summer heat was generally more highly developed than protection against the cold: where house design was concerned, for instance, the inclusion of lots of windows ensured a through draft, and in the seventeenth century, wealthy people could have ice-cooled drinks delivered from specially equipped depots. But as for hearths, even when provision was made for them in the construction of the house, they usually heated very poorly, while the use of glowing coals in open basins increased the risk of fire. In these conditions, furs were not necessarily a luxury, particularly in the cold winters of the Little Ice Age.

In the coastal regions of Anatolia and parts of the Balkans, several areas were still comparatively densely wooded; the great fleets of the sixteenth century were possible only because the sultans could call on these huge stocks of timber, especially from the forests of northwestern Anatolia. In addition, the timber could be ferried to Istanbul relatively cheaply by sea; this is the reason why, in that vast city, only the mosques and associated institutions were built of stone, while almost all dwellings (with the notable exception of the sultan's palace) were made of wood. In the long term, this intensive exploitation led to deforestation, such as along the coast of the Gulf of Izmit and in the immediate vicinity of Istanbul. However, large tracts of predominantly virgin forest still remained in the more remote areas of Anatolia, especially because the sultans made efforts to regulate the building of sawmills and felling there.[9] There were also extensive forests along the southern coast of Anatolia; as far back as the late Middle Ages, these had been a source of timber for Cairo, a role they continued to fill in the Ottoman period.

Both freshwater and seawater resources were used for fishing and (in the latter case) for salt extraction: for instance, anchovies was a staple food in Trabzon (Trebizond) during the seventeenth century.[10] Fish traps were widely used on lakes, with those exploiting them paying a levy. But the use of the Mediterranean as a source of salt was even more significant—not only people but livestock depended on it. After the capture of Cyprus in 1570–1573, the Ottoman authorities also controlled the important salt extraction industry on this island.

Only very few rivers were navigable; although troops and military supplies were ferried up the Danube to the frontier province of Hungary, the Iron Gates (the deep gorge between Romania and Serbia) and the constantly shifting course of the middle reaches of the river hampered its use. Dangerous shallows on the Tigris and Euphrates entailed the use of flat-bottomed barges or even rafts made from inflated animal skins. Shipping was very active on the Nile; the port of Bulaq played a vital role in provisioning Cairo. In southern Anatolia, the Seyhan and the Ceyhan were navigable, though the commercial significance of these rivers was negligible as the region was only sparsely populated. Undoubtedly, the relative lack of navigable waterways hampered the development of city life, trade, and industry.

· · ·

Dietary habits, and hence the use of the agricultural potential offered by the various regions of the Ottoman Empire, were often quite different from today's norms. In the sixteenth century, for example, clarified butter was the cooking and eating fat of choice: this was supplied to Istanbul from the regions north of the Black Sea. In contrast, olive oil, now much sought after as a foodstuff, was then mainly used to make soap and as fuel for lamps. As a result, there were far fewer olive groves in, say, western Anatolia than there are now; however, in northern Syria and on Crete (which was brought under Ottoman rule in 1645–1669), olive cultivation continued to play a major role in the local economy.[11] Peasants and tribesmen frequently grew cotton near the Aegean and Mediterranean coasts, as well as in northern Syria, at least partially as a commercial crop. Citrus fruits were being grown in a few places in Anatolia from as early as the sixteenth century, although this area did not develop into a major citrus-growing region until after the Second World War.

Grape cultivation, though, already comprised a significant part of the economy by the sixteenth century; in a civilization where sweets were highly prized but sugar was rare and expensive, raisins and grape syrup were, alongside honey, the principal sweeteners. Even in the late eighteenth century, vineyards were not an uncommon sight in the area immediately outside the capital, though these had all disappeared by the mid-twentieth century. It is therefore untrue to claim that the Islamic proscription against wine put a stop to viticulture. In general, most of the fruit and vegetable cultivation we know about took place in the environs of the major cities, though this may in part simply be down to the sources, because vegetable plots in villages for personal use generally had no taxes levied on them and so do not appear in the relevant records. Yet the staple diet of most Ottoman subjects was wheat and barley, which were both used in bread making. The frequently hilly terrain forced Anatolian farmers to use simple hook plows, though heavier, more sophisticated moldboard plows, which turned the soil, were a familiar sight in certain regions. The shortage of water meant that in many cases, farmers tilled their fields only once every two years. Because of the extensive labor it entailed, plus the large amount of water required, rice remained quite a luxury, at least in the sixteenth and seventeenth centuries: although there were large expanses of paddy fields in the region around Plovdiv (Ottoman: Filibe) and northeast of Ankara, these apparently could never meet the demand for rice.[12] Consequently, even in the kitchens of the better-off subjects of the sultan, rice was used only sparingly, say, in soups or desserts.

Lack of water also accounts for the low yields recorded. As late as the nineteenth century, in the arid regions of Anatolia, it was not uncommon to harvest four grains for every seed sown (ratio of seed corn to harvest was 1:4). In the late sixteenth, and also in the nineteenth century, many regions of the Ottoman Empire suffered from prolonged periods of drought and seriously depleted harvests (the 1590s were also notorious in Italy for their lack of rain and poor harvests).[13]

Large-scale irrigation was often used for horticulture rather than agriculture— excepting, of course, the long-established irrigated farming in Egypt's Nile Valley. According to local conditions, water mills operated either all year round or only during certain months; in Istanbul, where water was notoriously short even in the seventeenth and eighteenth centuries, millstones were driven by horsepower.

In order to ensure ample reserves for the army, the fleet, the royal palace, and the capital, the sultans decreed that all provincial cities should acquire grain only from their own districts; if this ruling had been applied consistently, it would have hindered the growth of towns in the provinces, because the respective administrative districts were very small. However, this regulation appears not to have been enacted consistently; for instance, in the late sixteenth century, Ankara was taking in deliveries of grain for bread from several surrounding administrative districts. Conversely, at least before 1600, the sultan's administration appears to have enforced the ruling far more strictly in the regions along the Aegean coast of Anatolia; this would explain the sparse population of towns in this area at that time. Istanbul got most of its grain from the regions on the west coast of the Black Sea, as well as from Moldavia and Wallachia (that is, modern eastern Bulgaria and Romania). Merchants resident in Istanbul were responsible for trading in grain; they were under such stringent state supervision that they can be regarded as quasi–state functionaries.[14] As the prices paid were generally low, this gave landholders little incentive to invest and expand.

If Ottoman subjects got to eat meat at all, it was mostly in the form of mutton. At least in the larger cities, the less well-off clientele could buy boiled and roasted sheep's heads from shops specially dedicated to the purpose, plus prepared dishes made from the poorer cuts of these animals. Fat from the internal organs was used to make tallow candles. By contrast, in the sultan's palace, the preferred meat was chicken. Meat eating was evidently a kind of status symbol; to meet this demand, an ingenious bureaucratic system ensured a ready supply to the capital and its many important civilian and military officials. Certain members of the wealthier classes *(celeb)* in the Balkans were required to send to Istanbul a certain quota of sheep, which were sold on at prices laid down by the state *(narh)* to butchers there.

Butchers slaughtered the animals and sold them to consumers, again at prices fixed by the sultan's officials. During the sixteenth century, these were often so low as to eventually drive many butchers into bankruptcy. By the late eighteenth century, though, butchers could earn a good living; supplying meat to the military corps of the Janissaries at prices below the market average earned them a special subsidy known colorfully as the "butcher's compensation" *(zarar-ı kasabiye)*.[15]

2. *Administration of the Ottoman Empire*

FROM the point of view of the Ottoman elite of the sixteenth and seventeenth centuries, the western Balkans had far less to offer than the Aegean in terms of provisioning the heart of the Ottoman Empire, if only because of the great difficulties presented by rounding the Peloponnese. The historical sources relating to this region are correspondingly few. Bosnia was the sole exception, because it was seen as a valuable source of troops, which sultans and viziers successfully deployed in their wars against the Habsburgs. Hungary mainly came within the purview of the Ottoman center insofar as frontier forces needed to be stationed there; this situation may explain why the Ottoman authorities put no significant obstacles in the way of exporting oxen to Christian Central Europe, a trade that flourished especially in the sixteenth century.[16]

Farther east lay Wallachia and Moldavia, Christian principalities under Ottoman control, whose rulers paid a handsome tribute for their investiture. These two principalities were the scene of frequent clashes, for the region lay within the sphere of influence of the kings of Poland–Lithuania, the Habsburgs, and later the Russian tsars. These principalities became famous as Istanbul's breadbasket, a role they fulfilled in peacetime, at least during the eighteenth century. The regions north of the Black Sea were sparsely populated and of interest to the central administration and the capital's inhabitants primarily as the source of butter, skins for leather tanning, and above all slaves. Some grain grown in the Crimea also helped to supply the inhabitants of Istanbul.

Crossing the Black Sea, on the borders of Persia lay eastern Anatolia; only the southern half of this area, around Diyarbakir on the Tigris, supported enough agriculture to produce surplus grain. Even today the north, close to the Black Sea shore, is characterized by extensive mountain forests, while there were only limited agriculturally productive areas around Erzurum, Erzincan, and Van. But even the grain grown in the southeast rarely made its way to Istanbul, as the central authorities used this region to supply the Ottoman garrisons in southern Iraq.[17]

Agriculture in Mesopotamia had recovered only to some degree from the crises of the late Middle Ages; yet Baghdad was still an important center, and Ottoman governors of the eighteenth century and their female relatives continued to construct many notable buildings there.

Thanks to its abundant agricultural potential and its geopolitical position, the region between Ayntab (modern Gaziantep) in the north and the Egyptian border, which for simplicity's sake I define here as the northern frontier of (Greater) Syria, was one of the empire's key provinces. Yet the useful strip of land was narrow and soon petered out into the Syrian desert, where the sultan's writ scarcely ran. In consequence, it makes sense to discuss Syria under the rubric of "frontier regions."

Syria's productivity was due to the precipitation that fell on the mountains of Lebanon (Cebel Lübnan) and other high ground, feeding small rivers that made possible the oasis farming around Damascus, famous for its apricots. In the steppeland regions, though, the rainfall was enough only for cereal cultivation. In particular, as a relatively prosperous province, Syria was required to provide extensive resources for the pilgrims' caravans on their way from Damascus to Mecca during the hajj, before they set out to cross a very special kind of border zone, namely, the Syrian and Arabian deserts. Farther south lay Egypt, in the imaginations of Ottoman officials the quintessential symbol of abundance: the constant (if usually vain) hope was that other, more recently conquered territories might turn out to be a new Egypt. Yet outside the Nile delta, the fertile land was confined to a narrow strip.

Border guards were stationed in the far south; between the First and Second Nile Cataracts, written correspondence has come to light from these military units, in both Arabic and Turkish. Aside from the garrisons, a few isolated Coptic villages were dotted along the southern border of the Ottoman Empire. There, African slaves were made into eunuchs; shariʻa law forbade castration and so was banned within the sultan's realm.[18] Along the Red Sea, the Ottomans established the province of Habesh (Ethiopia) in the sixteenth century; this was under the control of the Ottoman official representative in Jeddah, the port of Mecca, while the interior was occupied by an independent kingdom, into which Ottoman governors would occasionally try to extend their rule.

While there were no formal, ruler-straight boundaries in the Sahara and Sahel (such as those that came to be drawn after the "Scramble for Africa" in the late

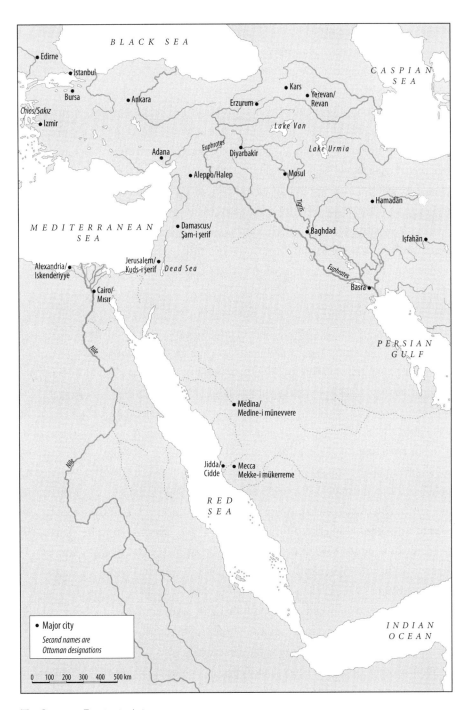

The Ottoman Empire in Asia

Within the map:

BLACK SEA

CASPIAN SEA

● Edirne

● Istanbul

● Bursa

● Ankara

Chios/Sakız

● İzmir

● Kars

● Erzurum

● Yerevan/Revan

Lake Van

Lake Urmia

● Adana

Euphrates

● Diyarbakir

● Mosul

● Aleppo/Halep

Tigris

● Hamadān

MEDITERRANEAN SEA

● Damascus/Şam-i şerif

● Baghdad

● İşfahān

Jerusalem/Kuds-i şerif ●

Dead Sea

Alexandria/Iskenderiyye ●

Euphrates

● Basra

● Cairo/Mısır

Nile

Nile

PERSIAN GULF

● Medina/Medine-i münevvere

Jidda/Cidde ●

● Mecca Mekke-i mükerreme

RED SEA

INDIAN OCEAN

nineteenth century), several central African kingdoms such as Bornu maintained relations in the sixteenth century with the Ottoman sultan.[19] The Mediterranean coast of North Africa (Maghreb) was a completely different world, accessible to Ottoman governors and troops from Istanbul only by ship. These circumstances made it hard for the Ottomans to maintain control there, for while over the course of the sixteenth century merchant vessels gradually began circulating in the winter months as well, the Ottoman navy retained the old custom of laying up in harbor from November to early May. This situation also explains why the Istanbul government was ready, even as far back as the sixteenth century and still more so later on, to accord local military commanders and sea captains a fair degree of autonomy. Unlike in Egypt, these commanders were obliged to pay only a minimal tribute as a form of concessionary tax acknowledging Ottoman authority. Otherwise, all taxes levied within North Africa were paid directly to the local military.

Expansion and Islamization

The different significance that the Ottoman administration accorded to the various frontier regions may be explained largely through the history of the empire's expansion. Early on, the sultans' sphere of influence expanded particularly rapidly in southeastern Europe. As early as the mid-fourteenth century, the Ottomans had established a foothold on the Balkan peninsula; in 1526, when victory at the Battle of Mohács paved the way for the conquest of the kingdom of Hungary, the grand vizier Ibrahim Pasha had just conducted a rather difficult military campaign to put down an uprising by the supporters of a former regional principality in eastern Anatolia.[20] Accordingly, the empire's westward expansion proceeded far quicker than its counterpart in the Anatolian east, not least because scarcely any formally organized or stable long-term polities existed in the late medieval Balkans. Because of its influential nobility, even Hungary, by European standards a medium-size kingdom, displayed strongly centrifugal tendencies that seriously hampered resistance to the Ottoman takeover. In contrast, both the Turkmen princes who ruled Iran in the fifteenth century and the Safavid dynasty that came to power in the region after 1500 prevented the Ottoman sultans from realizing their ambition to achieve lasting gains well beyond the current

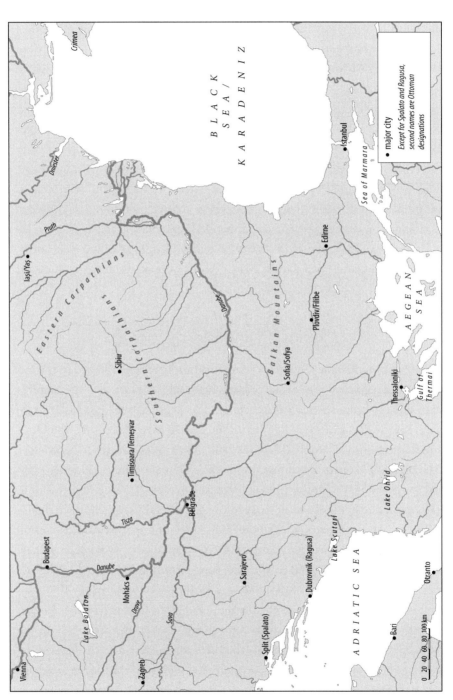

The Ottoman Empire in Europe

● major city
Except for Spalato and Ragusa,
second names are Ottoman
designations

BLACK SEA / KARADENIZ

Crimea

Dniester

Pruth

Eastern Carpathians

Iași/Yaş

Southern Carpathians

Sibiu

Danube

Tisza

Timișoara/Temesvar

Budapest

Vienna

Lake Balaton

Mohács

Drave

Zagreb

Sava

Belgrade

Sarajevo

Split (Spalato)

Dubrovnik (Ragusa)

Lake Scutari

Lake Ohrid

ADRIATIC SEA

Bari

Otranto

Balkan Mountains

Sofia/Sofya

Plovdiv/Filibe

Edirne

Istanbul

Sea of Marmara

Thessaloniki

Gulf of Thermai

AEGEAN SEA

0 20 40 60 80 100 km

Turkish–Iranian border. However, the situation was different in the southeast, where Sultan Süleyman I (r. 1520–1566) succeeded in bringing Iraq under enduring Ottoman rule from the 1530s onward.[21]

Yet for many centuries, the epicenter of the Ottoman Empire was the Aegean, on both its eastern and western shores. The realm of the sultans thus established itself on the farthest frontier of the Islamic world and over the course of the fifteenth century proceeded to expand, principally into the Balkan peninsula. It would therefore be unrealistic to impute modern Turkey's orientation toward Anatolia to earlier eras. This geopolitical constellation also meant that, up to the capture of Syria and Egypt by Sultan Selim I in 1516–1517, the Ottomans ruled largely over Christian subjects. During this period, it was by no means uncommon, especially among irregular forces and fortress garrisons, for Ottoman troops to maintain their adherence to Christianity.

In the late fifteenth century, when the first truly significant Ottoman chronicles were written, the upper echelons of Ottoman society—in much the same way (mutatis mutandis) as their Christian adversaries—saw themselves unequivocally as championing the spread of the one true religion, which in their case, of course, was Islam. Nevertheless, it is highly uncertain when and how the notion of the sultans as steadfast champions of the faith first arose and how quickly and in what particular social circles the idea spread. The debate over whether the early Ottomans should be regarded primarily as opportunistic raiders, long-term conquerors, or warriors for Islam has been going on for a long time; however, in the absence of source material, all conclusions are more or less hypothetical. It is also entirely feasible to imagine that, for many fighters, extending the control of a Muslim sultan or Islam, on the one hand, and personal enrichment, on the other, were by no means mutually exclusive—quite the opposite, in fact. After all, as well as seeking salvation in heaven, many of the Christian knights who took part in the Crusades were also after booty and temporal power.

In line with the new ideology, from the late fifteenth century on, Ottoman chroniclers portrayed their sultans in such a way as to suggest that they had always been in conflict with the infidel. Episodes that did not fit with this image, such as alliances with Byzantine heirs apparent or even the marriage of Sultan Orhan (r. 1326–1362) to Theodora, the daughter of the Byzantine emperor John VI Kantakouzenos, were therefore glossed over.[22] In actual fact, in many cases the sultans of this early period seem to have gone to great lengths to integrate local elites into their system of rule regardless of religion. Thus, aside from the afore-mentioned irregular and garrison forces, in the fifteenth century it was perfectly possible for minor aristocrats in the Balkans to serve in the Ottoman army as cavalrymen *(sipahi)*. The sultans made them so-called *timar* holders by granting them taxation rights, usually over a village, a favor that raised them above the mass of ordinary imperial subjects, in return for performing cavalry duties. Initially at least, the sultans did not require the sipahis to embrace Islam, and in some cases it took several generations for full Islamization to occur.[23]

Even so, by the beginning of the sixteenth century, the granting of special priv-ileges to Muslims was a well-established practice, while the distinction between Muslims and non-Muslims remained a cornerstone of the Ottoman state and so-cial system up to the mid-nineteenth century and in many cases beyond. All major offices of state were occupied by Muslims, although it was still possible for some non-Muslims to wield a fair degree of power in practice. For instance, in the six-teenth century, the highly influential palace physicians were very often Jews, or to cite a later example, in the eighteenth century, a high-ranking Ottoman could secure a lucrative tax-farming concession only by having one of the capital's major moneylender bankers (in this period, generally Armenians) stand surety. As such, it was perfectly possible for non-Muslims to pursue successful careers, as evidenced today by the luxurious homes in Christian Balkan settlements from the late eigh-teenth and early nineteenth centuries.

Nevertheless, Muslim preeminence was striking: they were to be found at the head of all manner of listings, and right up to the early nineteenth century dis-paraging comments about non-Muslims were quite common even in official docu-ments. A non-Muslim was not entitled to testify against a Muslim in front of a *kadi*—a legal shortcoming that may well have fostered the growth of written busi-ness transactions, as these played down the role of oral testimony. In addition, all adult non-Muslim males had to pay a poll tax known as a *ciyze* in Turkish (*jizya* in Arabic), and up to the early nineteenth century, the Ottoman authorities pre-scribed particular colors of clothing or special forms of head covering for Chris-tians and Jews, so that they could easily be identified in public. However, forced conversions were rare, though not entirely unknown; pogroms, in contrast, were extremely uncommon.[24]

In recent research, Islamization in the capital has once more become a hot topic. This phenomenon manifests itself in practical terms in Muslims taking over inner-city districts where Christians or Jews once lived, worked, and prayed. It is particularly associated with the history of the construction of the Yeni Cami (New Mosque) on the southern shore of the Golden Horn. When building work began on the mosque in the late sixteenth century under the regency of the *valide sultan* (mother of the sultan) Safiye, a Jewish quarter was razed and its former occupants resettled on the remote outskirts of the city. But after the building work ground to a halt for decades, the area's Jewish inhabitants returned. They were expelled for a second time following a major fire, and the mosque complex was finally completed in 1660, effectively Islamizing an entire central city district.[25]

Historians of southeastern Europe are especially interested in the processes that led to the conversion of various population groups in the Balkans. One particular measure enacted under the "Islamization campaigns" that occurred during the reign of Sultan Mehmed IV (r. 1648–1687) was the edict that the long-established Jewish palace doctors could continue in office only if they adopted Islam. Also, on the famous hunting parties conducted by this ruler, it became something of an established ritual for non-Muslims to be brought forward for conversion in the presence of the sultan. However, contemporary research has finally managed to consign the supposed forced conversion of the Bulgarian population of the Rhodope Mountains by the seventeenth-century Ottoman authorities to the realm of myth.[26]

Subjects and Officials

As well as discriminating between Muslims and non-Muslims, Ottoman administrations, especially during the sixteenth and seventeenth centuries, drew a clear distinction between taxpaying subjects (*raiyat;* plural: *reaya*) on the one hand and military and civil servants of the sultan, plus their family dependents *(askeri),* on the other. The *askeri* were exempt from most, though not all, taxes. This distinction became a fundamental principle of the Ottoman system of rule from the second half of the fifteenth century at the latest: at that time most officeholders—not, however, shari'a or Quranic scholars *(ulama)*—found themselves in a position of dependence vis-à-vis the sultan that bordered on slavery.

The sultan could have them killed without due judicial process; this prerogative only disappeared almost a century after the end of the period under scrutiny here, in 1839.

Ordinary subjects, in contrast, had to be condemned by a kadi or sometimes a governor in a properly constituted legal process. In addition, the sultan was the legal heir of his servants—against the right enshrined in the Quran, which protected the inheritance of subjects, except in cases where no legal heirs existed or where the deceased had been careless enough to leave behind undischarged debts to the state treasury. Especially in cities that were remote from the sultan's seat of power, like Cairo, for instance, some merchants in the sixteenth and seventeenth century not only amassed significant fortunes but also spent them on magnificent stone houses and left their property to their descendants.[27]

It is therefore untrue to claim that Ottoman subjects generally tried to conceal their wealth for fear that it might be confiscated. After the end of the period under consideration here, during the crises of the late eighteenth and early nineteenth centuries, it certainly was not unheard of for the treasury to summarily seize the estates of wealthy subjects. But the fragility of property was much more a feature of the later period and not typical of the whole of Ottoman history.

Judges and Teachers

How did members of the Ottoman governmental apparatus attain their positions? In the case of judges and the closely associated numerous professors at the colleges where law and theology were taught *(medrese),* it is fair to say that a kind of self-recruitment system operated, as every Muslim had the right to pursue such a course of study. Graduates of these schools were granted an important privilege: only in very exceptional cases was corporal punishment meted out to them. In order to get appointed as a kadi, a young man had to spend many years teaching at these academies, so as to gain a thorough theoretical knowledge of Islamic law before engaging with its practical application.

In addition, there were a number of eminent legal and religious scholars whose legal opinion *(fetva)* was sought by opposing parties in disputes. Although these opinions were not binding on a kadi, the judges responsible generally took them very seriously and the party that presented such a document had a good chance of winning the case. Kadis and tutors alike were locked into a strict hierarchy, in which a person's advancement depended on his having attended the top colleges in Istanbul, Bursa, or Edirne. As a result, the best that scholars from the empire's Arab provinces could hope for was a career in their home region; they were debarred from rising to the uppermost echelons in the empire's heartland.

Aside from the special case of legal and religious scholars, commentators in the sixteenth century were adamant that the strict hereditary separation of office-holders and taxpayers formed one of the pillars of the Ottoman state.[28] While the timars themselves could not be inherited, candidates for these grants often had to prove their descent from timar holders and other officers of the sultan in order to secure such a tax concession. In border regions, timars could also be granted to military men from the subject classes who had distinguished themselves through acts of valor. However, as long as there were people who remembered the lowly origin of someone thus favored, the timar holder had to reckon on being denounced as an "interloper" and being stripped of the honor. As firearms increasingly came to the fore in the seventeenth century, the military significance of timar holders as cavalrymen declined sharply; however, especially in remote regions, they continued to function as local administrators until the early nineteenth century.[29]

Yet between the fifteenth and the early seventeenth century, there was one further—this time undisputed—method of joining the ranks of Ottoman officials. Both members of certain military units and other dignitaries were often recruited through the so-called child tribute *(devşirme)* system, in which Christian peasant families from the Balkans and Anatolia had to hand over a certain number of their young sons to be converted to Islam and to serve initially as laborers for Muslim farmers in Anatolia. Once they had learned Turkish and become fully acculturated in Islamic society, most of these young men were advanced as candidates for the Janissary corps, into which they were inducted as soon as places became free. In the meantime, they were kept busy on other tasks, including civilian duties, such as providing unskilled labor for the construction of the great Süleymaniye mosque complex in Istanbul (1550–1557). Large detachments of Janissaries were stationed in the capital and in Cairo; they wore uniforms long before this became a widespread practice in European armies. When their military service came to an end (it is hard to determine the exact length), many Janissaries were granted a timar—though this was not necessarily viewed as an advancement.

While the official position was that these troops were not allowed to marry during their period of active service, in practice married Janissaries were often tolerated as early as the fifteenth century. From the seventeenth century on, it became increasingly common for sons to follow in their fathers' footsteps. Among garrison troops, marriage and integration into the local community seem to have been the norm right from the outset. Although it was occasionally claimed in early literature that those who entered the sultan's service through the child tribute system lost all contact with their families, we now know that the opposite was frequently the case: a successful former Janissary like the architect Sinan (c. 1490–1588) was allowed to bring his relatives to live with him in the capital or alternatively to secure various advantages for them in their home region.

When the number of Janissaries was significantly increased in the late sixteenth century, while their pay sharply decreased because of the central government's lack of resources, there began a momentous process of teaming with the tradesmen and artisans of the major cities, notably Istanbul, Cairo, Damascus, and Aleppo. Officers of the Janissary corps would sometimes claim to be associated with this or that shop owner—in other words, they began to operate a protection racket. Less powerful members of the corps turned to business and commerce themselves. In Istanbul, transport and trading in wood, fruit, and vegetables were the principal activities; even as businessmen certain Janissaries did not refrain from acts of violence.

Conversely, traders as well as artisans regarded it as an advantage in many respects to belong to one of the military corps stationed in their city: although membership cost a fair amount in fees, the advantage was that one was exempted from various taxes and no doubt found it much easier asserting one's rights in disputes by being able to call on the assistance of the relevant corps. As a result, in late eighteenth-century Cairo, almost all Muslim craftsmen and merchants were nominal members of military corps; this process was also well advanced in Istanbul, Damascus, and Aleppo.[30] In this way, then, the Janissaries became city militias, which, for all the parades they continued to hold in their hometowns, enjoyed little success on the battlefield against European armies in the eighteenth century. Furthermore, the papers that a Janissary needed to show to collect his pay were negotiable and circulated during the eighteenth century as a kind of bond.

In the late sixteenth century, the Ottoman military high command changed its principal force to musket-armed infantry, relegating timar holders to a subordinate position; however, the new soldiers were engaged only for the duration of a campaign and had no claim on the privileges due to regular servants of the sultan. Many of these temporary recruits sought a more permanent integration into the Ottoman military apparatus by staging a rebellion to draw the attention of the empire's leaders to their demands. The rebels were frequently described as *celalis*. In the almost sixty-year period between the death of Sultan Süleyman I (1566) and the reign of Murad IV (1623–1640), such rebellions were particularly frequent and serious, but they were not unheard of even in the late seventeenth century. In this period, the ringleaders sometimes managed to recruit whole armies, which occupied and sacked even such major cities as Bursa or Ankara, in some cases more than once. But for reasons that are still unclear, the Balkans were largely spared these upheavals.

The Ottoman elite attempted to tame the rebel leaders by offering them commands on the empire's frontiers, where they could take the fight to the Habsburgs. In the opinion of some Ottoman historians, this "integration policy" stands in stark contrast to the violent suppression of provincial rebellions in France during the reigns of Louis XIII (1610–1643) and Louis XIV (1643–1715).[31] But it is pertinent to ask whether, say, the brutal crushing of the Anatolian military rebellion by Vizier Kuyucu Murad Pasha at the beginning of the seventeenth century was really so different from its French counterparts.

The Sultan's Court and Top Imperial Bureaucrats

Recruitment for the sultan's court was more stringently regulated than it was for the military. As long as the child tribute system still held sway, young people who appeared to the relevant officials to show particular promise were brought into the palace as pages. Young prisoners of war could also be recruited in this way. Some pages were selected as personal servants to the sultan; they were responsible for maintaining his clothes and personal arms and so came into daily contact with their sovereign. After thorough training, which gave them the polish of an Ottoman gentleman, former pages were then sent to the provinces as high-ranking military officials and civil servants. On leaving the palace, these young men, often without being consulted beforehand, were married off to girls who had also served at court but who had failed to attract the sultan's interest. The most successful graduates of the palace school could rise to become commanders, governors, or even viziers.

Communal education in the palace precincts fostered in many Ottoman officials a highly developed esprit de corps, as well as an extreme sense of loyalty to the sultan (a fact often remarked upon by foreign observers). There are hardly any documented instances of high officials who had undergone a palace education resisting execution by their rulers, though many of them would have had ample opportunity to do so. Unfortunately, no statements by Ottoman officials revealing their thoughts and feelings on this question have yet come to light. But to judge from the behavior of those concerned, they simply accepted the often life-threatening intrigues between officials, which mostly fought for influence on the sultan, as an occupational hazard. In other words, it became an integral part of their worldview that they were helplessly exposed to the whims of their ruler.

From the late sixteenth century on, ever more members of the ruling elite were no longer recruited centrally, but they received official posts after having first served in the households of powerful dignitaries in Istanbul or the provinces. In these households, alongside the children of the head of the household, young slaves and sometimes even the sons of clients were raised, for whom the dignitary in question would, where possible, secure positions in which they could both better themselves and at the same time promote the interests of their patron—for loyalty to patrons and to one's former teachers were among the fundamental values of the Ottoman elite. Among the military serving in Egypt, household education was a central factor in the recruitment of the upper classes.[32] Marriages between the daughters of powerful heads of household and ambitious young men in Mamluk households were not uncommon. In this context, some of these women even managed to amass a fortune and wield political influence.

The Ottoman government apparatus was headed for the most part by the grand vizier, who took the position of the ruler's absolute representative, although he could be (and frequently was, in practice) dismissed at any time by the sultan. The grand vizier and a number of lower-ranking viziers formed the sultan's council (*divan-i-hümayun*); however, the influence of this body was generally much greater in the sixteenth century than in later periods. The *Şeyhülislam* (supreme religious authority) was responsible for matters pertaining to religious law and the appointment of kadis. From the seventeenth century on, there were a few occasions on which this high official declared it lawful for the sultan to be deposed; in these instances, he played a decisive role in the change of ruler. Otherwise, the number of high officeholders who comprised the central administration in Istanbul was extremely limited. In the early days, the head of the chancery *(nişancı)* was an influential figure, but from the seventeenth century onward, functionaries from the circle around the grand vizier increasingly began to fill key bureaucratic roles. In particular, the chief of clerks *(reisülküttab)* became more of a specialist for foreign affairs; for relations with European states, he relied on the support of officially appointed interpreters, who often worked as diplomats as well. Financial administration under the *defterdar* (chief finance director) was also a key state function. The body of civil servants under him, which in earlier times had been inchoate, expanded visibly and became more organized in the mid-sixteenth and again in the eighteenth century.[33]

The Role of the Sultan

Domestic and foreign observers alike consistently viewed the sultan as an indispensable element in the structure of the Ottoman Empire; in practice, the role played by the ruler varied enormously from one period to another. Over the first two and a half centuries (1300–1566), it seems that the sultan was expected to personally head up the administration and expand first the principality and then the empire through his conquests. At least, this is the impression we gain from Ottoman chronicles, though, as already noted, most of these date only to the years immediately before and after 1500. What the expectations were for sultans in earlier periods will probably remain a mystery to us forever.

On the death of his generally not very old father, the eldest son often had the advantage of being the only grown-up among his fellow princes. Yet until the late seventeenth century, succession was in principle open to all sons of the ruling sultan. This situation institutionalized disputes over who should succeed, which princes battled out during an aging father's lifetime. Süleyman (I) the Magnificent intervened personally in the conflict among three of his surviving sons, yet in opting

بروروز پیروز مسرّت اندوز که طایر زرین جناح وقت صباح جمال دل غروزیله

بروزکاه هندی پروزایدوپ جهانی روشن واهل زمانی شادوشن انتشیدی مهرسپی
مجدواقبال سرورپی سعادت وجاه وجاه جلال الدین تجلّی انیکله دیجورعمن نوریسورودن سجود بااولان
نکته دلاوتسلّی وداورمرادآور سلطان مرادداد کنتر شاه خاور کبی مغرب حقافزادک
انیکله مشوتش ومدهوش اولان سیه بوش لان دروزنده خان عدل بی کلوب قضای قلوبدن
خاکاکم مسلوب ومقارنت شکل اول مقدمه لایکّ امرانی بی بو منتج مطلوب اولدی یعنی
خمس وخمسین وثمانیایه محمدنایه اون التبتی کوفی قاصر الاسلام مسدلتین عزواحدتهام

Mehmed II ascended the Ottoman throne in 1444. This miniature from 1616 shows the sultan as a grown man; in truth, when he came to power he was only around twelve years old. His father, Murad II, had abdicated in favor of his son and retired to the West Anatolian city of Manisa. However, when the Ottoman Empire found itself embroiled shortly afterward in a new war with the European powers, at the urgent request of the grand vizier, Murad II returned to the throne and ruled until his death in 1451. (Roland and Sabrina Michaud)

for the future Selim II (r. 1566–1574) he was far from choosing the one who had displayed the most military talent. In contrast, the Ottomans, unlike many princely dynasties in medieval Anatolia, never adopted the practice of dividing up the kingdom as a solution to succession disputes.

Süleyman's great-grandfather, Mehmed (II) the Conqueror (r. 1444–1446; 1451–1481), issued an edict whereby a sultan should kill his brothers as soon as he had ascended the throne in order to avoid any further conflict.[34] Until the mid-seventeenth century, sultans more or less adhered to this decree.[35] Even so, this measure was not uncontroversial, especially when young children were involved who had played no part in the succession dispute. Far from it, in fact: after the death of Murad III (r. 1574–1595), when a succession of children's coffins were carried out of the palace gates, protests broke out among the general population. In all likelihood, the lack of any legitimacy in Islamic law for fratricide was a major reason for the rules of succession being gradually altered in the seventeenth century, for it was during that period that religious law took on a practical significance that it had not necessarily had in former times.[36]

Henceforth, after the death of a ruling sultan, he was succeeded by the eldest member of the dynasty: in practice, this meant that the new sultan was often a brother or nephew of his predecessor. At the same time, the education of Ottoman princes underwent a change: up until the late sixteenth century, it was customary for them to be sent off to Anatolia in the company of their tutors and often their mothers as well, where they were prepared for the struggle to ascend the throne.[37] But sultans in the seventeenth and eighteenth centuries were raised in a remote corner of the royal palace and prior to their succession had no experience whatsoever in the business of government. Their investiture was therefore an occasion to introduce them to Istanbul's people and for them to formally take possession of their capital. To this end, a ritual was established in which a sultan who had just come to power was ceremoniously girded with a sword in a sanctuary outside the city gates of Istanbul. Among these later sultans, only Murad IV turned out to be a successful military commander, retaking the captured city of Baghdad from the Safavid Persian ruler Shah Abbas I.[38] Although other sultans, including Mehmed III (r. 1595–1603), Mehmed IV (r. 1648–1687), and Mustafa II (r. 1695–1703), accompanied Ottoman armies on campaign, they played only a limited role (or none at all) in directing the fighting in the field.

However, in the seventeenth century, this shortcoming was far less important than it would have been, say, prior to 1566. After 1600, the Ottoman government apparatus was organized to cope with a sultan who was mentally unstable, a child, or a thoroughly responsible adult who nevertheless chose to take relatively little interest in the business of government. For one thing, over the course of the sixteenth century, the empire's financial bureaucracy had, at both the central and a provincial level, developed into an important organization with a career structure. Also, functionaries like the grand vizier, various provincial governors, commanders of the Janissary corps, and personages at the palace such as the sultan's mother (the valide sultan) had by then acquired so much power as to obviate the need for sultans to take an active part in government. Indeed, from the point of view of certain high officeholders, such involvement was positively unwelcome.

In earlier scholarship, it was customary to follow some contemporary commentators, who regarded these developments at court, and especially the incipient marginalization of the timar cavalry and the rise of the custom of purchasing offices, as symptoms of decline. In the last two decades, however, a different interpretation has gained widespread acceptance: we now know that various contemporary reports about abuses and reforms were not the work of impartial observers but were written as polemics in conflicts between different coteries of officials.[39] In light of this information, these documents therefore need to be examined critically. Modern historians also now recognize that during their careers, successful palace functionaries like the chief eunuchs or the valide sultan had plenty of opportunity to amass a wealth of political experience. Accordingly, their interventions were by no means as uninformed or disastrous as earlier commentators used to claim.

The most telling difference between the rule of the Ottoman sultans and their counterparts in early modern Europe lay in the absence of any established, constitutionally privileged aristocracy and of an assembly of the different privileged estates. This difference struck the Habsburg envoy Ogier Ghiselin de Busbecq as a positive attribute when he visited the court of Süleyman the Magnificent in the mid-sixteenth century at the behest of his emperor, Ferdinand I (r. 1503–1564).[40] Yet as regards the safety of life and limb of officials and courtiers, this distinction (though extremely important in terms of constitutional law) had only limited practical significance: to be sure, many viziers ended up being executed, but much the same also happened at European courts during the Renaissance. One only has to think of the many victims of England's King Henry VIII (1491–1547).

The readiness to see the Ottoman state system not as a form of "Oriental despotism" without any legislative framework but as a variant of absolutist rule has opened historians' eyes to many interesting aspects whose significance was once lost on them. For instance, Ottoman rulers of the seventeenth and eighteenth centuries were seriously hamstrung in their exercise of power by alliances between military corps stationed in the capital and groups of legal and religious scholars, as well as court officials. Experienced contemporary observers were well placed to analyze exactly when and in what form political problems might arise for a particular sultan or grand vizier from such combinations of interest groups. Alliances of this kind brought about the downfall of several sultans; nevertheless, the state bureaucracy continued to function, albeit sometimes with difficulty. These observations suggest that the events of the seventeenth and eighteenth centuries should be viewed less as decline and more as bureaucratization and the development of political routines.[41]

Tax Farming as a Fiscal Measure

Turning now to the provinces, it was ultimately a vital function of the Ottoman central authorities to ensure the loyalty of dominant elites in what were often far-flung provinces. Up to the seventeenth century, lower-ranking provinces (*sancak, liva*) were placed under the jurisdiction of the so-called *sancakbeyi* (district governors), who in times of war commanded the sipahis of their region. They in turn followed the orders of the *beylerbeyi,* the governor-generals of the major provinces. But from the mid-seventeenth century on, the clear distinctions between these offices were eroded as governors hardly ever resided in their provinces, being replaced largely by local magnates who in most cases were granted the right to raise taxes in lieu of the absent governor. Yet throughout the eighteenth century, a lively official correspondence kept the central administration regularly informed about developments on the periphery of the empire; expansion of this reporting system was especially high on the agenda in the final years of our epoch, around 1750.

In many regions, a decentralized system developed from the late sixteenth century on, as the central authority increasingly went over to contracting its revenue

gathering out to tax farmers. In principle, this form of tax collection, which ensured the exchequer a relatively regular income, had already become widespread
in the fifteenth century, with several prominent aristocratic families from the Byzantine period retaining their positions as tax farmers during the reign of Mehmed
the Conqueror. Yet from the late sixteenth century it appears that a monetized
economy gained a firm foothold in the empire, largely (though by no means exclusively) as a result of the import of Spanish silver from the New World to the
eastern Mediterranean. The sources give no indication of the amount of money
in circulation at this time, but the spread of markets and trading point unequivocally to the advent of a money economy.[42] On the other hand, the central government's need for ready cash became more acute, for wars of the time were increasingly being fought by mercenaries armed with muskets, who required regular
payment. The services of the sipahis, for which no money changed hands, were
now seen by the central authorities as very much second-string, prompting them
to transform many of the former timar lands into tax farms.

In the long term, although the profits made by the tax farmers entailed a loss
to the state coffers, as well as higher taxation for the sultan's subjects, the Ottoman
authorities were still prepared to accept this state of affairs in view of the relatively
secure flow of hard cash it yielded. Even so, the treasury tried all kinds of measures to boost the state's income. For instance, the appropriate officeholders were
prepared at any time to accept higher bids for a tax farm that had already been
allocated—usually for a period of three years—forcing the incumbent leaseholder
either to give up his source of income or to raise the amount he paid. The treasury also used its tax farmers as providers of interest-free credit: when the army
needed, say, tent canvas or sacks, these people were required to put up the money
and simply deduct it from the payments due at the end of the fiscal year. This arrangement must have left many suppliers out of pocket for long periods.

As well as taxes, resources belonging to the sultan were farmed out to leaseholders: this was particularly the case for mining operations, and sea salt extraction on the Mediterranean coast was also leased out. In order to secure a healthy
yield for the state coffers, the tenants were each apportioned clearly defined areas
within which they had a sales monopoly for the salt or alum from their mines. In
the same way, nomad herdsmen were supplied with a quota of salt, which they
were obliged to buy from the salt leaseholder at a price set by the vendor often

with no regard to the current market rate. Sometimes this quota was so large that the buyers could not use all the salt. Similar problems arose when dyers or tanners were compelled to buy quantities of alum (aluminum sulphate, used to clean fleeces and hides) that in no way matched their requirements. Under these conditions, smuggling was rife.[43]

New forms of finance were devised when, during the Ottoman–Habsburg War of 1683–1699, the central authorities in Istanbul found themselves urgently in need of a much larger revenue stream: this was the origin of the lifelong tax-farming system (known as *malikâne*), first introduced in 1695, and which could occasionally, by means of supplementary payments by the original leaseholder, also be passed down to descendants.[44] An "ideological" justification was quickly found for the new practice: it was claimed (at least officially) that because the new proprietors would be concerned to ensure lasting productivity, they would treat those beholden to them well. In contrast, the short-term lessees were never in office long enough to develop any interest in longer-term yields. In addition, the official view now maintained that only members of the political class (askeri) were able, or had any incentive, to protect taxpayers. This effectively excluded prosperous subjects from access to lifetime tax farms.

In actual fact, high-ranking members of the Ottoman state apparatus or even princesses, who all acquired a taste for these malikâne sinecures, hardly ever lived in the regions where their tax-farming operations were located. Accordingly, they delegated the day-to-day management to agents known as *voyvodas,* who enjoyed no security of tenure and who were therefore inclined to follow the old-style tax-farming practice of concentrating on short-term gains. Plus, as already noted, potential leaseholders of large properties required surety from a moneylender or banker; because these latter players were undertaking a substantial risk in standing bail, it is fair to assume that they too shared in the profits. This arrangement therefore enabled those who were not members of the Ottoman political class an informal way of gaining a stake in these lifelong tax farms. Yet the material interests of the voyvodas and the guarantors in all probability meant that such long-term considerations as the protection of taxpayers receded into the background. Thus, for instance, it is recorded that producers of printed cotton cloth in the northern Anatolian city of Tokat in the late eighteenth century frequently found themselves on the run from tax collectors.[45] So, especially where the commercial sector was concerned, the tax farm system, including those farms leased out for life, represented a considerable hindrance.

The Rule of the Magnates

In the provinces, tax farms for life were an important factor in the rise of a class of landed notables *(ayan):* this process led by around 1750 to a situation where, as already noted, Ottoman authority in most parts of the empire was exercised not by centrally appointed governors but rather by intermediary notables and magnates and, in the larger cities, generally by the army garrison stationed there. Many notables also owed their power to the fact that they devolved the tax burden that was demanded from a province to settlements and from there down to individual families, as this type of arrangement gave them numerous opportunities to exercise protection and consolidate their power within a locality. An important factor in this was mediation between the central government and local communities; this intermediary position had the potential to bring influence to bear in favor of provincial inhabitants, though in practice the magnates and notables were always concerned first and foremost with fostering their dynastic interests.

Though rare, attempts by local magnates to found their own principalities did occasionally happen. Most of these attempts failed in the preparatory stages, and it is likely that lifelong tax farms played a key part in keeping provincial magnates loyal to the central authority. Assuming that a local independent power base had been established, all the notables living in the area in question could hardly have retained their tax farms, as the sultan was the sole source of legitimacy where these were concerned. Moreover, the magnate who had appointed himself prince would have constantly tried to seize the resources of any rival families on his territory. As a result, Ottoman rulers usually had no difficulty in mobilizing competitors to any magnate who dared to try and assert his independence to act against them. The sultan only needed to brand the person concerned a rebel, condemn him to death, and then set his enemies on him. Also, any magnate who flirted with the idea of independence could have no way of knowing whether he himself would still have recourse to his original tax farms after he had staged his rebellion. All this meant that the most significant tax farmers were effectively compelled to become stakeholders in the Ottoman project for life.[46]

Nevertheless, very few magnates still attempted to establish independent principalities, for the most part in the Arab provinces. None of them succeeded. Shortly after 1600, for example, Canbuladoğlu Ali Pasha, whose power base was the area around Aleppo, tried to set up a separate state. Some years later, it was the turn of a Druze prince called Fakhr ad-Din II (c. 1572–1635) who beat off all rivals to assert power in his home region around Beirut, which flourished under his rule, albeit briefly. In both cases, the rebels forged an alliance with the grand duchy of Tuscany. Fakhr ad-Din II even fled to Italy for a spell, spending several years in exile there. Following his defeat at the hands of Ottoman forces, the Druze prince and some of his sons were executed. The youngest, however, was brought up at the court in Istanbul and went on to have a successful career in the sultan's service.

Architecture, Festivals, and Ceremonies as Symbols of Power

Ottoman power was intimately bound up with the construction of substantial stone buildings, a tangible reminder of the sultans' claim to legitimacy. Indeed, this association was so strong that the regimes that succeeded Ottoman rule in the nineteenth and twentieth centuries, from Mecca to the Balkans, set great store by tearing these edifices down, or at least letting them fall into ruin. As well as Ottoman rulers, military commanders of the fourteenth and fifteenth centuries, such as Hacı Evrenos, who conducted successful campaigns in the Balkans, had a number of caravansaries, aqueducts, bridges, and of course mosques erected in their name.[47] Not only did such activity gain them religious credit but another motivating factor was undoubtedly its value as a visible demonstration of power—sometimes even in open rivalry to the Ottoman sultan.

The oldest section of the sultan's palace in Istanbul (the Topkapı or the Cannon Gate Palace), which is located on the site of the ancient Greek city's acropolis, dates back to Mehmed the Conqueror: a kiosk decorated with faience tiles harks back to Iranian models, whereas the gate to the second courtyard and a loggia with a view over the sea are clearly inspired by Italian forms. Commentators have concluded that this architectural eclecticism was the sultan's way of immortalizing his victories over Prince Uzun Hasan (of the Aq-Qoyunlu, or White Sheep

General view of the Sultanahmet mosque (completed 1617). Built by the architect Mimar Mehmed Ağa, it was controversial at the time, because the young sultan had no military victories to his name for the building to commemorate. In the eighteenth century, however, many Ottoman rulers preferred this mosque for their public Friday payers, and today it is regarded as Istanbul's principal mosque. It has a total of six minarets (only five are visible in this photo). (Photo by Suraiya Faroqhi)

Turkoman tribes), who ruled over part of Persian territory, and his conquests of former Genoese and Venetian territories.[48] As for victory over the Byzantine Empire, the greatest prize lay there for all to see right outside the gates of the palace—the church of Hagia Sophia, transformed into Istanbul's main mosque as soon as the Ottomans seized control of the city in 1453.

Mehmed the Conqueror built two further palaces, one in Istanbul and another in the old capital of Edirne: neither has survived, though in the case of Edirne, written and pictorial records are extant. It may be that the palace in Edirne was a political concession to those who wanted a capital city close to the border and who spurned the ancient seat of the Byzantine emperors as an "accursed place."

At the same time, wrangling over the future capital of the empire also sparked a debate (albeit a less clearly formulated one) about the role of the sultans. Was it justified to regard Mehmed the Conqueror and the Ottoman rulers who came after him as the new *kaysar-i Rum,* the successors of the Roman and Byzantine emperors, or should they rather take the simple piety and military prowess of the early Ottoman sultans and their companions as their model? The image of the global conqueror with an eclectic taste in art, which Mehmed II cultivated through such acts as inviting Gentile Bellini and other Italian painters to come to Istanbul, was evidently frowned upon in some quarters. Indeed, Bayezid II (r. 1481–1512) pointedly had the paintings commissioned by his father removed and deliberately styled himself as a devout and almost saintly monarch.

A second attempt at presenting the sultan as a ruler of the world, and hence as the successor to the emperor and pope, was made during Süleyman the Magnificent's first years in office. The swift conquest of the Knights Hospitallers' stronghold of Rhodes and shortly thereafter the kingdom of Hungary raised hopes among some commentators who were close to the court that Sultan Süleyman might be the "millennial ruler" who would have dominion over the whole Earth just before the Second Coming of Christ and the Day of Judgment. Incidentally, similar expectations were also raised at the court of the Holy Roman emperor Charles V (1500–1558). The grand vizier Ibrahim Pasha, Süleyman's alter ego and confidant during his early reign, had an ornate and precious gilded helmet adorned with four crowns fashioned for his master in Venice, which bore a striking resemblance to the papal tiara. In the event, Süleyman never wore the helmet, as crowns were not a traditional part of a Ottoman ruler's regalia, but even so the artifact was carried with the Ottoman armies on campaigns in Central Europe as a symbol of the sultan's authority. But then the grand vizier fell into disfavor and was murdered, and when further conquests in Europe failed to materialize, the helmet was eventually melted down. Only a few engravings and a recently discovered fragment of vellum testify to an image of a sultan who was to reign supreme over Christian kings and the pope alike.[49]

The four-crowned helmet was a stage prop for military campaigns, but the real place for regal ceremonial displays was the Topkapı Palace, which was further extended, notably during the reign of Süleyman the Magnificent. This had the effect of cutting the sultan off even more completely, not only from his subjects but also from his own dignitaries. While up to the second half of the fifteenth century it had been common practice for the ruler to give evidence of his continuing good health by dining in front of an assembled troop of Janissaries in the palace courtyard, in the sixteenth century this ceremony was confined to the two main religious feast days of the year *(bayram)*. The sultan's isolation was further exacerbated in the second half of the sixteenth century, when the ruler's quarters were moved from the third courtyard of the palace, where he had resided hitherto in the company of his pages, into the harem. This meant that, even for the viziers, he was accessible only with great difficulty. At audiences with foreign envoys, it became the custom for the sultan not to speak or to say only a few words and for the ambassadors to hold all substantive political negotiations with the viziers or with the chief secretary of the grand vizier. By the mid-seventeenth century, palace ceremonial duties had evidently become an onerous burden for many sultans—hence, possibly, their frequent extended stays in Edirne, ostensibly on hunting parties. However, the Janissaries clearly regarded the sultan's absence as a threat for reasons that had little to do with military affairs. From the seventeenth century on, many Janissaries began supplementing their meager pay by taking up a trade. Many soldiers of this period can best be regarded as armed artisans who were constantly worried about their livelihoods. If the court had moved permanently to Edirne, the Janissaries would no doubt have lost a large portion of their clientele. After Mustafa II was deposed in 1703, his successor Ahmed III had to promise that he and subsequent sultans would henceforth remain in Istanbul.[50]

Court ceremonial also changed after 1703: the sultan spent less time in his palace, preferring instead to stay in villas on the shores of the Bosphorus, which prosperous city dwellers at that time, Ottoman princesses included, had had built as summer residences.[51] It was also around this time that sultans began appearing more frequently in public, along with their sons, at ceremonial occasions, perhaps as a way of demonstrating that the dynasty's continuing survival was assured.

Likewise, public festivals were another method of confirming the legitimacy of the sultan's rule. The occasions for these celebrations were typically princesses' weddings and the circumcisions of princes. Military triumphs were also celebrated, usually by lighting up the major cities, though overall such festivities were far fewer than those relating to the imperial succession. As the princesses and princes in question were all very young, it is fair to claim that these festivals, too, were designed to symbolize the dynasty's continuity. The ruler was the focus of attention on these occasions, with gifts being handed over to him in the main, rather than to the children or young people whose day it was.

The Influence of Persian Tradition on Courtly Culture

In the thirteenth century, Persian was widely used as a written language both at Anatolian princely courts and among educated town dwellers. The first attempts to employ Turkish as an official language came only in the late Middle Ages; the first uses of Turkish in literature also date from the fourteenth century. Over the following hundred years, accounts of the sultans' heroic deeds sometimes were composed in Persian. For the most part, though, the chronicles that were such a rich source for historians to gauge how the Ottoman elite regarded itself were written in Turkish. Even so, among the educated classes, there soon developed a literary form of Turkish that was heavily laced with both Persian and Arab loan words—the latter mostly coming into Turkish via the Persian. Without the appropriate schooling, this register of language was unintelligible, and the chronicler and writer Mustafa Alî (1541–1600) lauded it as a significant cultural achievement. In contrast, there were also authors, such as the travel writer Evliya Çelebi, who despite having been raised and educated at court still continued to write in an elevated form of the vernacular.

The use of Persian by educated Ottomans was relatively unaffected by political factors; as a result, despite the succession of wars against the Safavid rulers of Iran in the sixteenth and early seventeenth centuries, Persian remained the language of choice for the educated elite in Istanbul and was indispensable for anyone involved in the literary world. It was through studying the Persian classics that a knowledge of prosody was acquired, a skill every educated person was expected to have. An Ottoman admiral whose fleet was wrecked during a storm in 1554 and who had to make his way home via Persia recounted how on one occasion his ability to extemporize Persian poetry saved him from execution.[52] And among the dervish order of the *Mevlevi,* to which many of the ruling elite belonged or with which they at least sympathized, the reading and textual exegesis of the works of the mevlana Celaleddin Rumi (1207–1273), which were written in Persian, were required tasks.[53] Consequently, a Persian dictionary became part of the indispensable "standard equipment" for the library of every learned person. Yet in the long term, Ottoman authors increasingly moved over to writing their works in Turkish, even if in many cases this was still a "Persianized" form of the language larded with many foreign terms.

The Central Role of Religious Institutions

Religious foundations financed both Muslim worship and the education system; in any midsize city, there would be around fifty to a hundred of them, while in major cities and especially Istanbul, they numbered in the several thousands.[54] In the culture of the Ottoman ruling elite, it was considered good form to establish such pious foundations. Thus, in these institutions and the often monumental buildings that housed them, their practical use for the Muslim faithful was inextricably bound up with the prestige of those who had endowed them. They not only allowed devout Muslims to conduct their religious observances in imposing surroundings but also provided employment for a multitude of people, from professors down to cleaners. In Istanbul, Edirne, and Bursa, all three capitals or ex-capitals, it was often ruling sultans who financed important mosques and schools, in order to promote the practice of the Islamic faith.

In contrast, it was comparatively rare for rulers to found mosques in the provinces. Yet it was common practice, once the Ottomans had conquered a region, for a variety of dignitaries to erect mosques in the name of the ruling sultan, or at least to convert an existing church into a sultan's mosque, say, by adding a minaret: this was the case on Crete in the mid-seventeenth century, and in Kamenets Podolski/Kamaniçe in the Ukraine in the 1670s. This practice explains the occasional presence of mosques dedicated to Ottoman rulers in small and remote places, especially on the Balkan peninsula. Lavish new buildings, though, were rarely built in the provinces, although Süleyman I did order a magnificent new mosque complex to be constructed from the ground up in Damascus. It also became increasingly common in the fourteenth and fifteenth centuries for the consorts of Ottoman sultans, as well as princesses and their husbands, to found religious institutions in the provinces. For example, the mosques of Princess Selçuk Sultan and her consort Mehmed Bey in the Greek city of Serres, both built in 1492, testify to this.[55] In later periods, such exalted figures preferred to build in Istanbul or its environs. In addition, many mosques were endowed by prosperous inhabitants of provincial cities.

The size and the holdings of the individual foundations were commensurate with the political and social standing of the persons who had established them: a sultan was in a position to erect a vast complex comprising a mosque, colleges, a large refectory, and a Quranic school, together with accommodation for dervishes, while at certain periods sultans' mothers would endow complexes that were every bit as lavish as those built by their sons. Viziers tended to be responsible for more modest buildings, though these could be elaborately decorated. On the other hand, ordinary subjects of the sultans could also get involved in this activity: small institutions were set up, for instance, to supply the oil for use in the lamps in a mosque or to ensure that the founder's former servants had a roof over their heads in their old age. Some people also established institutions to carry out tasks that nowadays fall within the purview of city authorities—thus, a heavily used road might be repaired using a foundation's funds.

Among institutions providing welfare, public kitchens *(imaret)* played a particularly prominent role. In the capital, these were not primarily intended for the poor but rather catered to the students and tutors from the many theological and Islamic law colleges in the city, as well as serving as guesthouses for officials who had come to Istanbul on business. This situation explains why the menus that have survived contain some luxurious dishes; even the kitchens of some lowly Anatolian imarets did not stint on using valuable spices, including saffron and pepper. Often it was members of the sultan's family who would provide the funding for setting up these public kitchens: for example, Hürrem sultan, the wife of Süleyman the Magnificent, better known in European sources as Roxelana, put up the money for an ancient institution of this kind in Jerusalem to be rebuilt. Here, too, theology teachers and students were the principal beneficiaries, while women were let in only after the males had been served. It is reasonable to assume that the poor normally received only leftovers, though they probably had better prospects in smaller foundations that in the grand institutions.

Often, buildings with a commercial purpose were also linked to religious institutions; especial mention should be made in this context of caravansaries and *bedestan*s (covered, domed market halls).[56] Caravansaries on the main arterial routes were the subject of frequent descriptions by foreign travelers, but at least as important were similar buildings in the cities, which served as housing and storerooms for traveling merchants. In other similar structures, craftsmen plied their trade, often taking over an entire building to house members of their guild. While travelers often stayed overnight for nothing in the caravansaries along the main highways, rent was paid in the town guesthouses, generally to a religious institution that maintained the building as a source of income.

Covered market halls had stone walls, while their domes were built of stone, brick, and lead. As such, they offered much better protection than the customary wooden shops; they were designed primarily to store and sell valuable goods. These buildings, too, generally belonged to religious institutions, which demanded rent from merchants using them, though in practice many were not able to do so, or refused payment. Furthermore, covered markets were a symbol of sophisticated urban living: they were built when a town's star began to rise and disappeared again if it fell on hard times.

The water supply was also in the hands of religious foundations, particularly in Istanbul, where there are few natural springs or streams within the city precincts. In the Byzantine era, therefore, a large number of underground cisterns were built; yet because the variety of Islam practiced by the Ottomans requires believers to make their ritual ablutions before prayer in running water, after 1453, the cisterns were abandoned in favor of reservoirs outside the city, from which water was channeled via aqueducts into Istanbul and distributed through faucets and fountains. Because a mosque could not—and cannot—function without water, it was vital to establish which institutions had a legitimate claim to this or that amount of water. To achieve this, maps showing Istanbul's water system were drawn up; these maps, especially from the eighteenth century, have survived in a well-preserved state. Right up to the nineteenth century, running water in private houses was regarded as a great luxury; the famous architect Sinan had to defend himself against charges of siphoning off water that rightfully belonged to a religious institution into his own house.[57]

Institutional funds that were set aside for these religious and welfare purposes were the subject of a series of provisions devised by legal and theological scholars down the ages. On the one hand, such funds had to fully belong to the person making the endowment, and, on the other, these resources had to be as enduring as possible. Because in the Ottoman Empire ultimate ownership of all fields, meadows, and woods *(miri topraklar)* devolved to the sultan, this form of property could be endowed only if the ruler had agreed in advance to assign full legal rights over it to the potential benefactor. Accordingly, only sultans and in exceptional cases some of their closest confidants were able to transform land that had been used as fields or meadows into pious foundations. Conversely, pieces of land with houses on them, plus gardens and vineyards, were considered the private property of subjects, meaning that their owners could sign them over to pious foundations without much ado. As gardens and vineyards were often located in the vicinity of towns, most institutional property was to be found there.

Some forms of movable property (chattel), such as books, were also suitable donations to pious foundations. In the eighteenth century, a library, along with a building specially constructed to house it, was a favorite endowment, especially among Istanbul benefactors. More contentious was the endowment of sums of money, as this entailed lending the amount in question to solvent individuals in return for a modest rate of interest (10–15 percent). This form of endowment became commonplace in Istanbul from the late fifteenth century on and appeared shortly thereafter in the larger cities of Anatolia and the Balkans. The principal objections of theological scholars to this form of endowment concerned the ephemeral nature of money, which could be lost or lose its value.

Furthermore, around the mid-sixteenth century, the inevitable circumvention of the Islamic proscription against usury that this practice entailed became the subject of debate. However, the most eminent legal and theological scholar of the day, Ebusuud Efendi, concluded that a ban on cash foundations would be so devastating for Muslim communities that tolerating this practice was the lesser evil.[58] In the eighteenth century, this form of endowment became popular as a source of relatively cheap credit even among artisans, who frequently established their own guild foundations. Yet cash endowments never gained a foothold in the Arab provinces.

Though non-Muslims could not found religious institutions, they were free to set up charitable foundations; even so, a number of monasteries from the Byzantine period survived with help from a mixture of long-standing endowments and more recently acquired resources. Sometimes, at least in the sixteenth century, priests and monks even managed to persuade sponsors to finance magnificent frescoes: this was the case, for instance, at the Monastery of the Transfiguration of Christ at Meteora in Thessaly. However, Sultan Selim II seized the land belonging to countless monasteries, thereby forcing the monks to buy it back, in part through the sale of other valuables. Although in practice non-Muslim places of worship could be repaired but not enlarged or built from new, pragmatic considerations often determined practice on the ground. Thus, Jews who had settled in Istanbul and above all Saloniki after being expelled from Spain in 1492 were permitted to build new synagogues.[59] Those churches that after the conquest had remained in the hands of the Orthodox Church frequently were converted to mosques more than a century later on the initiative of a sultan, a vizier, or a dervish sheikh. So it was that Orthodox Christians in Istanbul lost the Church of the Monastery of Theotokos Pammakaristos, which had been the seat of the ecumenical patriarchate but in 1591 became the Fethiye mosque on the orders of Murad III.[60]

In order to function, religious institutions required a written culture: a document, often in elegant calligraphy, set forth in black-and-white the intention of the benefactor, which later administrators were obliged to follow, insofar as this was possible. When Ottoman sultans conquered regions that had formerly been under the control of Muslim rulers, it was the custom for those institutions that the new ruler was prepared to recognize to be recorded in special ledgers. In addition, larger institutions kept account books, which now form a key source for studying the history of wages and prices; sometimes the history of a significant building can even be traced from the records of estimates submitted for the cost of carrying out incidental repairs.

Ottoman Legal Culture

Because the Ottoman Empire was an Islamic entity, the sultans and their ministers applied religious law *(sher'i, sheriat)*. In principle, legislation enacted by the sultan in his capacity as supreme ruler *(kanun)* was meant only to plug the gaps that religious law, formulated in the early period of Islam, inevitably left when applied to the world of the sixteenth and seventeenth centuries. What that entailed in individual instances is the subject of just as intense a debate among historians today as it evidently was at the time among the Ottoman elite. A particular problem was posed by the fact that, according to sultanic kanun, supreme ownership of agriculturally usable land lay with the sultan, whereas Islamic law unequivocally favored the private property of individuals. Ebusuud Efendi, the leading legal authority (Şeyhülislam) under Süleyman the Magnificent, succeeded in formulating a ruling that legitimized this de facto situation. Süleyman's rule also saw the creation of a statute book that, on the basis of the authority to punish *(tazir)* that had long been vested in the sultan by scholars of Islamic law, sanctioned the prosecution of offenses for which religious law demanded such stringent proof that in practice any criminal proceedings were impossible.[61] And yet kanun was never a hard-and-fast set of official, semiofficial, or even unofficial statutes. Because of changes in the way the empire was administered, legal ordinances of the early eighteenth century were by no means the same as the kanun from the time of Süleyman the Magnificent.

Over time, however, the influence of kanun law receded and greater emphasis was placed on religious law. At the end of the seventeenth century, Sultan Mustafa II (r. 1695–1703) even went so far as to decree that all reference to kanun should cease forthwith and that religious law should henceforth form the sole basis of all government decisions. However, it is unclear how this worked in practice. For example, it certainly was not the case that agriculturally useful tracts of land that came under the supreme ownership of the ruler were suddenly converted into private property around 1700, while administrations of the eighteenth century clearly continued to appeal to kanun. It is therefore doubtful whether this edict really represented a victory of religion over pragmatic secular rule. It is probable that Mustafa II was merely intending to counter the influence of the powerful viziers' houses during his rule by raising the profile of his former teacher and later Şeyhülislam Feyzullah Efendi and the religious law he represented. The toppling of Mustafa II and Feyzullah Efendi in 1703 effectively annulled the orders of this sultan, for no Ottoman sultan was bound by the edicts of his predecessors. Nor does it appear that his immediate successors, Ahmed III and Mahmud I (r. 1730–1754), revived this ruling.

3. *Ottoman Society*

IN the early modern period, our best date range for studying the demographic history of the Ottoman Empire is between around 1480 and 1600. For it was during this period that extensive records were kept that were designed to provide information on taxpayers and taxes. As we have already seen, it was common practice at that time to grant certain military and administrative officials the right to levy particular taxes in the area under their jurisdiction (these assignments were known as timar or, for larger tenures, *zeamet*). Because the Ottoman treasury expressed the size of the timars it allocated in monetary terms, it first had to prepare data on how much revenue a village or urban tax was likely to yield. Ultimately, timars were less about handing over command of a region than about assigning the control both of goods and services expressed in monetary terms and of cash payments. Because the tax income from a village or a town could change over time, new records were supposed to be drawn up every thirty years, in principle at least—in practice, this time span varied considerably. In these records, specially designated officials wrote down the names and paternal names of the heads of all households liable for taxation, in cities and in the countryside. The records also enumerated a whole series of taxes for which local taxpayers were liable.

These exhaustive Ottoman tax registers (called *tahrir* or *tapu tahrir*) or detailed fiscal surveys *(mufassal)* each covered a single province (sancak, *liva*) and, in addition to taxpayers' names, also listed the names of villages or city districts. This makes them a key resource for studying the history of settlement.[62] And because they also noted the recipients of taxes, such as timar holders, endowment trustees, or administrators of crown land, the registers are an invaluable source of information on how the state structure operated in the provinces. However, because all registers in the period were solely concerned with taxes, those who were tax-exempt were often left out.

Certain problems with the registration system were inevitable because of the difficulty involved, for one thing, in including nomads and semi-nomadic peoples. Also, although it was not uncommon for widows in the Balkans to be the heads of households, they appear in the records only in exceptional cases. Those in the service of the sultan often were not mentioned either, because they were exempt from many taxes; in garrison towns, as much as 20 percent of the population may have fallen into this category. In addition, many registers went missing; none exist for Istanbul, though it is unclear whether this is because the registers have been lost or whether the city enjoyed the privilege of exemption. Finally, it is fair to assume that in some instances, people in the provinces must have made fanciful declarations to officials from outside the area who were charged with gathering information.

A further complication is added by the fact that we have information about family sizes only in a very few instances, making it extremely unreliable to employ the number of known taxpayers as a base for estimating overall population size. All the same, these registers, a number of which have been printed or analyzed in the meantime, do offer some overview of the Ottoman population of the Balkans, Anatolia, and Syria. However, there are so many imponderable factors that there has only ever been one attempt to estimate the total population of the Ottoman Empire, and that was over fifty years ago.[63] This study found that, in around 1520–1535, there were some six million inhabitants of the Ottoman Balkans and Istanbul, while Anatolia and Greater Syria accounted for a further 5.7 million. No figures were available for Egypt and western North Africa. According to this estimate, therefore, the whole population of the Ottoman Empire's central provinces, including the cavalry army that was financed by those who lived in this region, numbered some eleven to twelve million. Istanbul is included within this as a city of around four hundred thousand inhabitants, although there are no official records to corroborate this. All these figures are highly problematic, and the author of this estimate conceded that the actual count might be of the order of 10–15 percent higher; if this is remotely correct, then that would mean a population of some fourteen million. However, the population increased quite dramatically over the sixteenth century.

The registers of Ottoman taxpayers stop shortly before 1600, because around this time the administrative assignment of tax-collecting rights was supplanted by the tax-farming system. As the sums to be collected were no longer determined by the central authority but rather were set by the offers made by prospective tax farmers, from the point of view of the treasury, it was no longer worth investing any time and money in compiling these tomes. For the seventeenth and eighteenth centuries, then, estimations of the Jewish and Christian population of the empire are reliant on the registers that provide information of the special tax (*cizye*) levied on non-Muslims. As a supplement to the general tax register, these documents are even useful for the fifteenth and sixteenth centuries, insofar as they exist for this period and are used circumspectly. Because neither the Orthodox nor the Gregorian Armenian Church nor the various Jewish communities collected demographic statistics, little source material regarding census figures has come to light from these quarters. Thus, all estimates of the non-Muslim population of the empire, too, are to be taken with a pinch of salt.

As regards the Muslim population for the period after 1600, we have only a series of tax registers that list the sums of cash (*avarız*) owed by various groups of taxpayers. Within a single province, all the groups listed as *avarızhane* ("tax-liable households") paid the same sum. But within an impoverished settlement, such a group would consist of far more people than in a prosperous one. Only if a document should happen to note how many taxpayers belonged to an avarızhane in this or that district—and that is indeed often the case—do these data give us a clue as to the size of the overall population. In the Balkans in the late seventeenth century, a marked decline is noticeable in the number of houses registered as liable for paying avarız. Yet it is unclear what conclusions should be drawn from this; in the absence of clear indications of a sharp decrease in population, it is perfectly possible that this restructuring was simply the result of a smaller number of taxpaying units but with more people in each. Perhaps this measure was a response by the treasury to the poverty that the Ottoman–Habsburg War of 1683–1699 and ensuing conflicts in the early eighteenth century (up to 1718) undoubtedly occasioned.[64] But neither can we entirely rule out population declines.

These problems explain why it is so difficult to give an estimate of the entire population of the Ottoman Empire. The situation is somewhat better regarding regions or individual cities, however. For instance, at the start of the sixteenth century, there were a total of 6,531 households in the Anatolian city of Bursa (comprising some 32,000 people, not including those who were tax-exempt, and perhaps just under 40,000 if these were factored in). The Balkan cities of Saloniki and Edirne (Adrianople) had 4,863 households (comprising 24,000 people) and 4,061 households (comprising 20,000 people), respectively, if one likewise disregards the tax-exempt employees of the sultan; yet in Edirne, where the sultans maintained a residence, there must have been a considerable number of these.[65]

The Family in State and Society

For the early period of the Ottoman Empire, the only family about whom we can make any pronouncements, and even then with the requisite caution, is the royal family. Yet sources are even lacking where the sultans, their partners, and their offspring are concerned; just isolated bits of evidence lead us to the conclusion that we cannot indiscriminately apply the better documented circumstances of the seventeenth and eighteenth centuries to earlier periods. Thus, the North African Arab traveler Ibn Battuta (1304–1368/1369, or 1377) recounted that, during his visit to the still small but already truly dynamic Ottoman principality, he was received in the absence of Sultan Orhan (r. 1326–1362) by one of his wives—a gesture that would have been unthinkable in later periods.

Up to the mid-fifteenth century, Ottoman sultans often married princes' daughters from both Anatolia and the Balkans—although the princes that subsequently ascended the throne were, in the main, the sons not of these princesses but typically of slave women.[66] Moreover, foreign princesses who were married to sultans did not in all cases convert to Islam; for example, the Serbian princess Mara, wife of Murad II (reigned, with breaks, 1421–1451), remained an Orthodox Christian. Others, though, did embrace Islam and immortalized their names by endowing religious institutions.

However, from the second half of the fifteenth century to the end of the Ottoman dynasty after the First World War, no more marriage alliances were forged with foreign royal families. The reasons for this can only be guessed at. On the one hand, Sunni dynasties from which suitable brides might have been found lived only in far-off realms. Iranian princesses, to whom there was much easier access, were unacceptable because of their Shi'ite faith. On the other hand, the sultan's harem had become a strictly hierarchical organization dominated by slaves. The sultan's daughters and sisters were usually married off at a young age, perhaps because, as freeborn Muslim women, they did not quite fit in, and this kind of thinking may henceforth have conditioned attitudes toward foreign princesses also. Apparently, the Sunni rulers of Central Asian principalities never seriously considered any dynastic alliances with the Ottomans.

The many Balkan campaigns, plus the brief war against the Black Sea Cossacks in the seventeenth century, saw large numbers of slaves, both men and women, fall into Ottoman hands. The same was true of the Habsburgs. Relationships—or, after release, marriage as well—between Ottoman masters and these captives were by no means rare. The well-known dervish sheikh Şahidi from the small southwestern Anatolian town of Muğla, who lived during the early sixteenth century, recounted that his grandfather, while on campaign (date unspecified) in the Arabian lands, had fallen in love with a young Christian girl and had eloped with and later married her. Whatever the truth of this anecdote—allegedly, the girl in question had long been a secret Muslim—Şahidi's account shows that such relations with Christian or former Christian women were by no means regarded as shameful.[67] This was also true of later periods.

Many ethnicities were represented among leading families of the Ottoman elite, whose members, as we have seen, were married off to former slave women of the sultan after completing their education at the royal palace. One interesting example is the Spanish nobleman Gutierre Pantoja. Taken into Ottoman captivity sometime before 1620, he rose through the ranks as a page at the Topkapı Palace and went on to serve in the Ottoman navy. During the war against Crete (1645–1669), he was taken prisoner once more, this time by the Venetians, and after several adventures was finally able to return to his family in Spain. Pantoja has left us the only account to come to light so far of such a marriage, and in the first person. The bride originally hailed from Ukraine or Russia and, as a newly converted Muslim, had been in the service of a female member of the sultan's court, who arranged the marriage for her in loco parentis. Unfortunately, though, Pantoja's report was given in the context of a trial by the Inquisition, which he had to undergo before he could resume his place in "normal society" back in Spain. Because of the many subterfuges he had to resort to in this situation, there can be little doubt that he suppressed a great deal of information that we would have found fascinating.[68] If the couple had had surviving sons, there would have been no impediment to them in turn pursuing careers in the service of the sultan and, in spite of their mixed Spanish and Russian-Ukrainian background, being looked upon as normal Ottoman officials.

In other cases we find, at least in the seventeenth century and sometimes even earlier, coteries of officials who had been brought to Istanbul through the *devşirme* system and who all came from the same region.[69] Others were imported as slaves, for instance, Abkhazians (Abaza) from the northeastern coast of the Black Sea, who after 1600 began to play a role in the upper echelons of Ottoman society. The households of dignitaries played a decisive role in the organization and internal cohesion of such groups of compatriots. The members of these coteries provided one another with mutual support and together vied with other organized groups for high office. There were so many connections between households that after the death or fall from grace of, say, a vizier, his servants were taken in by other households or even by the sultan's palace. Sometimes even larger factions would coalesce, with officials from the Balkans opposing their rivals from the Caucasus. This furnishes us with yet more proof that the child tribute system and slavery did not in the least produce a society of atomized individuals, in which every official had only himself and the sultan to rely on.

Despite the recruitment of outsiders, these kinship groups retained their importance, even in the highest ranks of the Ottoman elite. When, toward the end of the sixteenth century, the Serbian patriarchate of Pec was restored, the grand vizier Sokullu Mehmed Pasha appointed his brother (or possibly nephew), an Orthodox priest, as the new patriarch. And the court dignitary Gazanfer Ağa, originally a Venetian, who as a eunuch had no possibility of starting his own family, had his sister come to Istanbul, where, having converted to Islam, she made a good match, for there was no shortage of people eager to be related to this influential courtier to both Murad III and Mehmed III (r. 1595–1603).[70]

What information is there concerning marriage and family life among Ottoman subjects? We know very little indeed about the rural population—the overwhelming majority.[71] However, there are several important studies on the female inhabitants of the large and also smaller towns, based on kadi registers. Women could appeal to the kadi, because Islamic law regarded all women, including those who were married, as legal subjects (and continues to do so today). Townswomen would regularly appeal to the local court—and sometimes even to the sultan's council—in cases where their husbands had deprived them of the inheritance due to them. In addition, there were quite a few cases in which women "bought" divorces by renouncing any claim on money owed to them in the event of being repudiated by their spouses, sometimes even paying their husbands an additional sum to have them disappear from their lives. By contrast, repudiation on the part of the man is seldom recorded: it appears rather that the main reason divorced women went to court was to protect themselves against possible stalking by their ex-husbands. For reasons that we can no longer fully comprehend, the kadi registers for Aleppo in the eighteenth century have a particularly large stock of information on women. This, then, has shed some light on their role in the forging of links between various prominent families and on certain "typically female" activities, such as gathering in communal public bathhouses.[72]

Inheritance registers indicate that monogamy was the norm, at least within the urban centers of Anatolia and Istanbul. Women's careers and work are seldom mentioned, though particularly in towns that had a significant textile industry, some information on women earning their living in this field has come to light.[73] In Bursa, for instance, silk spooling was usually women's work, while in Istanbul there were embroiderers who worked not only for their own households but for outside clients as well.

Migrations, Voluntary and Forced

Even in the fifteenth century, it was common practice for sultans to order forced migrations of populations in areas they had just overrun; this practice, along with the people who were affected by it, was known as *sürgün*. In the case of Constantinople/Istanbul, Mehmed II was evidently concerned with making the former capital of the Byzantine emperors, heavily depopulated by the death, flight, and enslavement of its former inhabitants, into a thriving center of commerce and political life once more. As a result, because the economic viability of new settlers was especially important, Christians and Jews were brought to the city, despite the fact that Istanbul was expressly planned as a Muslim metropolis. At this early stage, Istanbul clearly was not a very inviting prospect, and there seems to have been some resistance against this forcible relocation. To remedy this situation, the sultan founded a large pious institution not only to benefit students and teachers but also, as already noted, to give people employment opportunities.[74] Several viziers followed his example, albeit on a more modest scale.

But at least from the early sixteenth century on, Istanbul became a magnet for inhabitants of the empire and foreigners alike. In spite of its frequent plague epidemics, immigration there must have been significant enough to spur city authorities into taking the first measures, in the late 1590s, to limit the number of new arrivals. The restrictions were further tightened in the late eighteenth and early nineteenth centuries, without really having any long-term impact on immigration, both from within the empire and from Venetian colonies like Dalmatia and Crete. In the seventeenth century, employment opportunities in the city's naval shipyards attracted those who had once built ships for the Venetian navy on Crete and who had lost their jobs when the yards at Chania were closed. It appears that Cretan workers were looked on so favorably by the Ottoman arsenal authorities in Istanbul that they actually displaced many Muslims who had formerly worked in this sector.[75] In addition to economic migrants, hard times in particular drew many poor provincial people to Istanbul, where they hoped to find greater security and maybe also alms: the administration, meanwhile, expended a great deal of effort to drive these poor migrants back to their home provinces as quickly as possible.

Forced settlement and relocation of subjects was also not uncommon in the provinces. In the fifteenth century, for example, members of the elite from the newly conquered city of Trabzon (Trebizond) on the Black Sea coast were obliged to restart their lives in the Balkans. The Ottoman authorities also embarked on a similar large-scale resettlement program after taking Cyprus from the Venetians (1570–1573). Prior to this, the island had suffered massive losses when large numbers of inhabitants were sold into slavery following the capitulation of the Venetian fortresses; a register of prisoners of war from this period contains around twelve thousand names. The Ottomans planned to ship in large numbers of new settlers especially from central and southern Anatolia. It was left to the individual villages or city districts to determine which of the sultan's subjects would be relocated: preference was given to families who did not own sufficient farmland. But fractious neighbors or people who had committed minor offenses could also reckon on being deported to Cyprus. Leaving aside the hot climate and particularly recurrent problems with swarms of locusts, the island's reputation as a temporary penal colony must also have played a part in many of the new settlers vanishing after only a brief sojourn there.[76]

The Ottoman authorities clearly preferred relocations ordered by the sultan rather than those undertaken by private initiative, because peasants were, in principle, tied to the land. Without the express permission of the local official, who might be a timar holder or a steward of crown land or of a religious institution, peasants were not allowed to leave their cottages and villages. However, they were not serfs but were, as they always had been, under the authority of the local judge who was appointed by the sultan. The analogy with the late Roman "colonate"—a peasant legally tied to the land but who could not be bought or sold—is not so far-fetched.[77] Furthermore, any official who had tracked down "his" absconded peasant was required to prove his claim on the person in question to the judge, and given the lack of family names, such proof was by no means easy to establish. De facto migrations on the sole initiative of the migrants were therefore not uncommon. Yet when the authorities wished to coerce people to relocate, it was in the logic of the system to rely on a sultan's edict to that effect.

The geographical distribution of subjects was, then, to a large extent the result of migrations. There are, however, scarcely any demographic maps, and the only map based on Ottoman tax registers, which encompasses the entire Balkans in around 1520, is already over fifty years old.[78] This shows that the eastern half of the Balkan peninsula was relatively thinly populated at that time by Muslims, a significant proportion of whom were nomads or semi-nomads *(Yürük)*. In contrast, the Christian population was concentrated in the western mountainous region. It is hard to ascertain what determined this distribution. Because most Balkan principalities of the late Middle Ages have left behind very few records, we do not know to what extent the plague epidemics of the time were responsible for drastic falls in population or how the countless conflicts that took place in the pre-Ottoman period explain the flight of some populations into the mountains. It is equally hard to ascertain to what extent the Ottoman wars of conquest shaped this pattern of settlement.

A long-running and—thanks to the very sketchy sources—similarly inconclusive debate surrounds the ethnic origins of many Muslims in the Balkans. For the modern state of Bosnia-Herzegovina, the facts are relatively straightforward:

the overwhelming majority of the Muslims living there are indigenous people who speak a Slavic language, although there was clearly also a limited amount of immigration from the heartlands of the Ottoman Empire. Yet many educated Bosnian Muslims used Ottoman Turkish as their second language; in fact, the second language was so widely used that a regional dialect developed. Likewise, a significant proportion of Muslims on the island of Crete appear to have been local people; these people continued to speak Greek, and only the educated learned Turkish. In Bulgaria, although there were natives who had converted to Islam, there was also an influx of nomadic and semi-nomadic peoples as far back as the fifteenth and sixteenth centuries. However, the Ottoman authorities had only a very limited interest in the distinction between those who were born as Muslims and those who were converts; there are hardly any other sources on this question. Moreover, during the early modern period, it was customary in many Christian societies both within and outside the Ottoman Empire to use the expressions "Turks" and "Muslims" as synonyms; hence, these terms should in no way be interpreted as denoting ethnicity.

A "retreat to the mountains" was also noticeable in some regions of Anatolia when the military uprisings of the late sixteenth and early seventeenth centuries led to the razing of many villages on the plain; these settlements were too vulnerable to inflated tax levies and attacks alike. Their inhabitants may well have emigrated to less easily accessible areas, where tax collectors would have found it hard to track them down. Others probably moved to the cities, especially Istanbul, while the young men among the refugees would have tried their luck as soldiers.

Over the course of the seventeenth century, in many parts of the empire, notably central Anatolia, the tax revenues from harvests plummeted, which suggests that the settled population there must have slumped. Where Anatolia is concerned, the relation of nomads and semi-nomads to the settled populace has always been problematic, because nomadic groups often eluded inclusion in the tax register. However, unlike their rivals in neighboring Iran, the Ottoman central administration persistently refused to accord tribal groupings any stake in power at the heart of the empire. The leaders of such nomad groups therefore had the opportunity to be active only at a provincial level, and their political aspirations were correspondingly limited. Because farmers were considered the better taxpayers, from the late seventeenth century on the sultan's government tried to promote settlement, sometimes by coercion.[79] However, officially organized settlement programs only truly became effective in the nineteenth century.

As regards the provinces that make up present-day Palestine, as the presence of any central Ottoman authority began to dwindle from the late sixteenth century on, villages on the fringe of the desert became prone to frequent attacks by Bedouin tribesmen. As a consequence, many settlements were abandoned. However, around the same time, new settlers established themselves on the coastal strip, which since the Crusades had been kept deliberately depopulated by the Mamluk sultans for military reasons.[80] We may clearly assume that in western Anatolia and Palestine, the population of regions favorably situated for transport were able to survive, whereas areas of marginal agriculture were abandoned; in central Anatolia, though, there were many lost settlements while only Izmir's growth compensated for this decline.

Toward the end of the era under consideration here, following the loss of the Crimea to Russia (1774–1783), a migration of Muslims began from the regions that the Ottoman Empire had lost to the territory that still remained under the control of the sultan. While most of the populace quit their homelands only in the late nineteenth and early twentieth centuries, the Crimean Tatar aristocracy had already emigrated to Istanbul by the end of the eighteenth century.

Trade in the Sixteenth and Seventeenth Centuries

From the outset, Ottoman government practice was geared toward a monetary economy. As accounts from the sixteenth century prove, there was a whole series of taxes and duties to be paid in cash, not only on paper but also in actuality. This practice undoubtedly promoted the spread of markets and annual fairs. Moreover, even a timar holder who received no money from the central authorities and paid over very little to them was obliged to equip himself and his armed retinue. To do this, he needed a market where he could sell surplus stocks of grain that he had collected as tax in kind, purchasing in exchange clothes, weapons, or horses. This explains why, in registers dating from the early sixteenth century, there was at least one market officially registered for each district. And with the growth of the population and commercial enterprise over the following eighty years, the number of markets multiplied.

Although many taxes were paid to Istanbul in the form of silver, the productivity of the Ottoman silver mines was very limited, and locally extracted precious metals were under strict state control. Only very few people had access to the silver that flowed into the country through foreign trade. Therefore, as in other early modern empires, the subjects were forced to sell their goods at the place where the majority of silver was to be had: in the capital. All the products from the length and breadth of the Ottoman Empire arrived there, as evidenced, for example, by an exhaustive register from 1640 listing the range of goods that were available in Istanbul, together with their prices. A Moroccan ambassador who visited the city in the late sixteenth century remarked how impressed he was by the cornucopia of goods that could be bought there.[81]

In general, the Ottoman elite took a somewhat skeptical attitude toward exports. The top priority was always to supply the extremely large internal market. But first and foremost, it was the demands of the sultan's court, the army, the fleet, and also of the inhabitants of the capital that had to be met; an eminent scholar of this period has characterized this attitude as "provisionism." Only those goods that were left over after local needs had been met were made available for export, and neither native nor foreign merchants were permitted to export goods that were regarded as strategic war materiel.[82] However, the definition of what constituted strategic goods changed over time: thus, in the sixteenth century, the export of cotton was usually proscribed, among other reasons in order to secure the navy's supply of sailcloth. But in around 1600, the authorities first relaxed this prohibition and then dispensed with it altogether, perhaps because there were many fewer naval engagements in this period but possibly also because more cotton was being produced by that time anyway, and conversely the need for extra earnings had become far more acute. Under such circumstances, tax revenue from the export of cotton would have been most welcome.

Fiscal interests were always a prime consideration, even in those areas where taking a longer-term view would have suggested that it were more prudent to forgo some immediate gains in order to hopefully reap more substantial tax income once economic growth had ensued. So, for instance, the western coastal regions of the Black Sea bore the brunt of the burden of supplying Istanbul's needs. But as we have already seen, the grain growers of this area received only very modest payment in return; here, then, immediate fiscal considerations hampered long-term investment in the farming sector. Along with a pronounced tendency to justify such harsh measures by appealing to tradition, "provisionism" and "fiscalism" were the unswerving precepts that Ottoman officials adhered to when it came to intervening in the economic activities of their subjects.

This "provisionism" of the Ottoman elite also explains why set prices dictated by the authorities *(narh)* were an integral part of daily life in the empire: for certain years—not just in Istanbul but also in Edirne and Bursa—there are very detailed registers that stipulate both the prices and the quality of commodities.[83] However, in provincial towns, these prescribed prices mostly affected only a very limited range of goods; in all other cases, the relevant guild masters must have agreed on the prices that could be charged locally. A comparison of prices listed in extant registers and other sources indicates that by present standards, houses were relatively cheap, whereas clothes and riding animals like horses or camels were extremely expensive. By contrast, in Anatolian villages in the sixteenth century, donkeys and two-wheeled carts were comparatively plentiful and so could be had for next to nothing. Nor did implements like looms cost much either. Even so, well into the eighteenth century and in many places later still, even houses belonging to better-off townspeople were quite modestly equipped with consumer goods.

In the Ottoman court and among the upper echelons of officialdom, in contrast, conspicuous consumption of luxury goods was evident. Because, for the most part, such goods, including Iranian silk, Russian furs, English woolen cloth, and Florentine or Venetian brocades and velvets, came from far-off regions, long-distance traders occupied a privileged position in the empire.[84] For instance, they were generally not required to sell their wares at officially set prices but were free to strike private deals with their clients. Yet that was the case only for wholesale commodities; and when Venetian merchants attempted in 1600 to open a shop in the Istanbul bazaar where they could sell their fabrics directly to customers, local competitors quickly spoiled their plans.

It would be unrealistic to assume—as much of the earlier literature did—that the Muslim inhabitants of the Ottoman Empire completely shunned trading with "infidels" or even spurned mercantile activity altogether, preferring to leave this to the Christians and the Jews. Merchants from all three great monotheistic faiths are known to have regularly visited the trading hub of Venice in the sixteenth and seventeenth centuries. Moreover, throughout this period, the Ottoman state apparatus was perfectly willing to lend diplomatic support to demands for compensation lodged by Ottoman subjects who had been robbed of their goods while on the way to Venice. In the peace settlement following the Cyprus war of 1573, the doges and the sultan had agreed that the Venetians should assume responsibility for the safety of merchant ships in the Adriatic. This is the reason why, in 1615–1617, the Venetian government even engaged in a brief conflict (the War of Gradisca) against a Habsburg archduke in order to drive the so-called Uskoks—allegedly Croatian Habsburg frontier guards from the eastern Adriatic but actually well known for engaging in piracy—away from the coast and force them to settle further inland.[85] The alternative would have been an intervention by the sultan's fleet, which the Venice Signoria wished to avoid at all costs.

The administration in Istanbul evidently took the protection of Ottoman merchants beyond the borders of the empire so seriously because it regarded any act of aggression against its subjects as an attack on the sultan himself. Conversely, no attempts were ever made to protect indigenous producers against the competition from imported goods. Because the Ottoman elite regarded low prices on the internal market as a fundamental prerequisite for the sultan's enterprises, no measures that might have led to even a temporary hike in the price of particular commodities were ever enacted.

Religious Life and Culture in the Cities

In the eyes of the Ottoman central authorities, the cities were an indispensable part of the fabric of the empire, as it was here that tax collectors stored the revenues they had gathered in the form of commodities and here that the sultan's subjects held their markets, where grain was traded for cash. But the practice of religion and representation of the sultan's power were also more straightforward in cities than out in the open countryside. Accordingly, mosques with a *minber* (a pulpit) and a minaret *(cami)* were almost exclusively confined to towns; these were the only places where Friday prayers could take place and the name of the sultan could be mentioned by the preacher in a solemn allocution, a significant sign of authority throughout the Islamic world. The inhabitants of villages most likely prayed in a simple prayer room *(mescid)* or in a dervish convent *(tekke, zaviye)*.

Alongside the mosques, in most cities there were also colleges for the training of legal and religious scholars *(medrese)*. However, graduates of these schools in provincial towns had only limited career prospects: they were generally excluded from careers in the central administration, which were reserved for those who had studied in Bursa or Edirne or, best of all, in Istanbul. The best these second-rank graduates could hope for was a job as a prayer leader, administrator, or preacher in a local religious institution.

Dervish convents were more widespread; these not only were the permanent home of devotees of these mystical groups but also threw open their doors to townspeople to take part in prayer sessions after hours. Dervish hermitages were also widespread in the countryside, with the entire populace of certain villages in some regions considering themselves the descendants of a dervish saint. As some of these lodges acquired significant libraries, they also provided people with access to written culture. Especially among the followers of the mevlana Celaleddin Rumi (Mevleviyye), the recitation of religious poetry as well as music making and dancing became regular features of the ritual. The Mevleviyye incurred the wrath, particularly in the seventeenth century, of orthodox legal and religious scholars, who strongly disapproved of these activities, but in the following century they flourished anew under the protection of the music-loving sultan Selim III (r. 1789–1807). For the most part, dervish lodges were founded at the initiative of a single man who had gained the reputation of being a saint in his locality (in very rare cases it might even be a woman). In other instances, after the death of a saint, his disciples and descendants would establish a permanent institution: thus, the order of the Bektaşiyye in the present-day city of Hacibektaş was founded long after the death of the mystic Haci Bektaş Veli. And in the early days of the Mevleviyye order, a female descendant of the mevlana Celaleddin Rumi was active in the northern Anatolian city of Tokat, where she founded a lodge. The position of the principal of the order (*Şeyh,* or sheikh) would usually be passed down from father to son. The treasurer of the attached religious endowment was also a hereditary post and could therefore, if necessary, be vested in female offspring.

Many sheikhs legitimized their position by commissioning extensive family trees, in which they documented their spiritual ancestry as well as their corporeal lineage, ultimately tracing their descent from the Prophet Muhammad or from

The former dervish cult center in Hacıbektaş. This shows a general view of the complex in this central Anatolian town, which once served as a religious center for the Bektaşiyye and (briefly) the Nakşbendiyye dervish orders. The building is now a museum but is still sometimes used for religious purposes. It comprises assembly rooms, the mausoleum of Haci Bektaş Veli—the Sufi mystic who gave the Bektaşiyye order and also the town its name, a mosque endowed by the Nakşbendiyye dervishes in the early nineteenth century, and a graveyard. Inscriptions indicate that the buildings in the complex date from the sixteenth to twentieth centuries. (Photo by Suraiya Faroqhi)

one of his original followers. These texts do not mention women, though: like many Venetian family portraits of the sixteenth century, the family trees of dervish sheikhs reflect a worldview in which males descended solely from other males.

Many dervish lodges in Anatolia, Syria, and Egypt date from before the Ottoman period. When Ottoman sultans assured these institutions of their continued existence, their main impulsion in doing so was doubtless a personal sense of piety. For it can be presumed that holy men were greatly revered at the early Ottoman court; certainly, this is a well-documented phenomenon in the late sixteenth century. Besides, the fundamental principle of religious institutions was that they were founded for all eternity; this ensured them special protection under Islamic law, with local legal and religious scholars undoubtedly weighing in on their behalf.

Furthermore, the early Ottoman sultans had good reason to solicit the good-will of well-established religious personalities; as descendants of a minor Anatolian prince from the fringes of the Islamic world, their legitimacy had no firm religious basis. As a result, the sultans were at pains to forge close contact with one or another dervish lodge. Admittedly, in the last years of his rule, Mehmed the Conqueror took a quite different line, seizing the property of many religious institutions in order to grant their income as timars. However, his successor Bayezid II thought it advisable to quickly rescind this measure.

But the Ottoman government had other pragmatic reasons for wishing to promote long-established dervish lodges. Hospitality was a highly prized virtue in Islam, and many dervish sheikhs clearly practiced it of their own accord, out of a sense of religious duty. But above and beyond this, at some unspecified stage, the sultans began to make those dervishes whose institutions lay close to the main arterial routes responsible for taking in and entertaining travelers. In return, they were exempted from paying certain taxes. In a world where there were no inns, accommodating travelers was an important social function, and even as late as the eighteenth century, the heads of several dervish lodges were still very concerned with pointing out that they had performed this duty or that their rivals had failed to do so. Under Ottoman rule, newly founded dervish communities were also required to fulfill these same obligations.

Orthodox Christian city dwellers in the Balkans and elsewhere formed communities centered on their churches. They also had a central organization in the form of the ecumenical patriarchate of Istanbul and the patriarchates of Antioch (modern Antakya), Alexandria, and Jerusalem. Because the center of their religion lay within Ottoman territory, in disputes with other Christian denominations Orthodox Christians could often count on the support of the sultan's administration, for example, in the extremely frequent conflicts over usage of the Church of the Holy Sepulcher in Jerusalem. For ultimately, the other Christian denominations represented in the Ottoman Empire—the Gregorian Armenians and the Catholics (who formed a tiny minority of Ottoman Christians)—had their religious headquarters in Echmiadzin (on Safavid Persian territory) and Rome, respectively; moreover, Catholics were often regarded as subjects of the pope, the "archenemy" of the Ottoman sultan. In the eighteenth century, the Greek-speaking hierarchy consolidated its control over the Orthodox Church even in the Arab-speaking provinces of the empire. Impelled, among other things, by the wish to maintain some form of independent voice, the Orthodox Christians of Aleppo reacted to this attempt by the church to impose centralization by seceding to the Catholic Church.[86]

Particularly in the eighteenth century, but also in earlier times, Orthodox city dwellers founded schools for their children, often with the cooperation of their local churches. Although the opposite is sometimes claimed, such institutions were by no means proscribed by the Ottoman authorities—quite the opposite, in fact: the import of books from Venice printed in Greek was expressly permitted. However, there was no requirement for Orthodox priests to have been educated in seminars or theological faculties, and the numbers of those who studied at the patriarchate's college in Istanbul were limited. Hence the frequent digs in the accounts of Western travelers at ignorant Orthodox priests.

The Jews of the Ottoman Empire lived almost exclusively in the larger cities, primarily in Saloniki, Istanbul, and (from the seventeenth century on) in Izmir as well. While Mehmed the Conqueror had resettled the long-established, Greek-speaking Jewish community of the region in Istanbul, many of the Jewish inhabitants of the other cities of the Balkans and Anatolia, who were predominantly from Spain, Portugal, and Italy, also moved there. The newcomers came from communities with very different religious and legal traditions. Especially in Istanbul, over the course of the sixteenth century, the ensuing differences of opinion led to bitter clashes between the followers of various rabbis.[87] Much information about the religious life of the Ottoman Jews has come from the many legal pronouncements made by local rabbis, some of which have since become available in modern translations. Besides, book printing was common among the Jews; indeed, prior to the eighteenth century, they were almost the only Ottoman subjects to practice this art. Even so, only works with a religious content were deemed worthy of printing.

Around the mid-seventeenth century, the millenarian tendencies that had been evident for around the hundred years preceding among Muslims and Christians, both within and outside the Ottoman Empire, also gripped the Ottoman Jews. In Izmir, Sabbatai Zevi proclaimed himself the Messiah, and although this claim was fiercely rejected by local rabbis, he still managed to attract a loyal following in several Jewish communities in the Ottoman Empire and abroad. It was not uncommon for these followers to give up their ordinary work in order to do penance and wait for the end of the world. After Sultan Mehmed IV gave Sabbatai

Zevi the choice of execution or conversion to Islam, Zevi opted for the latter.[88] A number of Zevi's acolytes followed his example, forming a unique community that emigrated en masse to Istanbul after the Greek annexation of Saloniki in 1912, and which in some instances still retains its special identity.

Occasionally the legal depositions of the rabbis also contain indications of social conditions and attitudes that in all likelihood also pertained beyond the bounds of the Jewish community. For instance, there is the account of a young man who was able to break off his engagement because it retrospectively came to light that his bride-to-be was one of those who had been forcibly resettled *(sürgün)* by the sultan.[89] We may assume that non-Jews also shied away from forming liaisons that forced the non-sürgün to remain at the place where his or her partner was obliged to remain in perpetuity.

Living and Working Conditions among the Urban Populace

It was a peculiarity of Ottoman city planning that business and residential districts were usually separate from one another; the center of the city, close to the central mosque, was the site of the shop-lined streets and the covered, domed market halls *(bedestan)*.

The shops of craftsmen pursuing the same trade were often, though by no means invariably, to be found in the same street, specially assigned to them. In the residential quarters, the rich and poor frequently lived cheek by jowl, but during the seventeenth century at the latest, some neighborhoods were favored by the prosperous. Members of a particular religious or social group often lived close to one another, but these demarcations were not universally rigid, with Muslims and non-Muslims living in the same area in some towns over the long term. New Muslim quarters tended to spring up around recently founded mosques. Newly built non-Muslim quarters, as already discussed, had somehow to circumvent the fundamental problem that Islamic law allowed the repair of non-Muslim places of worship but expressly forbade any new construction.[90]

Most inhabitants of Ottoman towns practiced a trade or earned their livelihood from their gardens, vineyards, or other farming activities. In the larger towns, the majority of tradesmen were organized into guilds, which, at least from the

Street in Elmalı in southwestern Anatolia. The houses here are thought to date from the late nineteenth or early twentieth century but display many characteristics of West Anatolian urban building styles of previous eras: lower floors made of quarry stone, timbered upper storeys, oriels, and many windows that look out onto the street but are set at such a height that the occupants can look out but passersby cannot see in. (Photo by Suraiya Faroqhi)

seventeenth century on, were typically run by a guild warden and various assistants. There were also merchants' guilds, but they were less prominent. Unfortunately, we do not know how or to what extent the guilds were active in the countless smaller settlements where economic activity also went on but that were basically semirural in character. Local records prior to 1850 mostly relate to the larger, or at least midsize, conurbations.

Nor is much known about how the guilds came into being. From the books that were frequently copied in artisans' circles we may surmise that, at least in "ideological" terms, there was some connection to the fraternities (ahis) that had played an important role in Anatolian towns in the late Middle Ages. Although the objectives of these groups were strongly characterized by Islamic culture and ethics, several guilds (especially in Istanbul) encompassed members of different faith communities. Furthermore, after the mid-fifteenth century, there is scarcely any mention of *ahi* activity, whereas the guilds entered the record only from around 1550 on. This latter situation is no doubt partly explained by the lack of source material, but it is also fair to assume that the guilds developed only gradually from informal gatherings into organized groups. All these observations indicate that the *ahis* certainly did play a role in the creation of guilds, especially where tanners all over the empire are at issue, and the tanners of Sarajevo in particular. But where most Ottoman guilds were concerned, their influence was mainly indirect and should not be overplayed.[91]

After around 1600, guild wardens not only had to pass muster with the master craftsmen under their wing but also, at least in Istanbul, had to be officially appointed by the central authorities.[92] We also know of cases from the eighteenth century where military men waived their army pay in return for being appointed as a guild warden; this is doubtless related to the aforementioned gradual encroachment by the military into trade and commerce. But even in such instances, wardens could hope to remain in office for a protracted period only if they succeeded in gaining at least the passive endorsement of the master craftsmen. Artisans frequently appealed to the kadi to rule on conflicts with rival guilds. In addition, the wardens and "experienced craftsmen" of any artisans' organization (ehl-i hibre) had to be prepared to divulge any information on guild customs and standards to the kadi, in case any customers should complain about the quality of goods supplied by this or that craftsman. This is how scribes attached to the kadi came to write down these guild rules and regulations, which were normally transmitted only by word of mouth.

The guilds in the empire's Arab provinces present historians with particular problems. It is thought that no organizations of this kind existed in Syria and Egypt during the Middle Ages. Yet by the seventeenth century they were widespread, not just in major cities like Cairo or Aleppo but also in relatively small places like Jerusalem. In this center of Muslim, Jewish, and Christian pilgrimage, guilds are so well attested in the kadi registers that they have given rise to short monographs on a whole series of organizations of this kind.[93] There is nothing in the records to indicate that the guilds were formed on the direct orders of the central Ottoman administration. But beyond this, little can be said about their precise genesis, largely as a result of the vague terminology employed in the registers: one and the same expression might refer to a simple craft or to a well-organized guild. This problem must remain unresolved until new sources come to light.

Among the nonguild subjects who practiced a trade, two classes of people should first be mentioned: apprentices and journeymen (*kalfa;* though these do not appear universally, either in space or time). Only master craftsmen had a voice in the guilds. And leaving aside the women who were engaged in various branches of the textile industry, in the fifteenth and sixteenth centuries the silk and cotton center of Bursa employed significant numbers of slaves. Elsewhere, though, the use of slaves in the trades was uncommon.[94] However, in the last quarter of the sixteenth century there arose a "profit squeeze": on the one hand, the increased demand for Persian raw silk in Europe caused the price of this material to skyrocket, but on the other, thanks to the generally poor economic situation and to pressure from the Ottoman elite, the manufacturers of Bursa silk goods were not in a position to compensate for their losses by raising prices. But before long the manufacturers solved the problem by switching over to using a nonslave workforce, a strategy made possible by the growth in population during the sixteenth century. Alongside the cultivation of silk moths that was just beginning in the region around Bursa and the concomitant changeover to less expensive types of raw material, these freeborn workers were largely to thank for the recovery of the Bursa silk industry in the period after 1600.[95]

Wars made heavy demands on both agricultural and craft production; the military revolts of the late sixteenth century had already visited mass poverty on several regions. In addition, with the cost of waging war continuing to increase throughout the sixteenth, seventeenth, and eighteenth centuries, higher taxes and heavily reduced public consumption in the wake of warfare brought an ever more frequent recurrence of serious economic depression. For example, during the Great Turkish War of 1683–1699 and the War of 1714–1718, the infrastructure was so badly neglected that commerce between the regions largely stagnated. So, after the Peace of Passarowitz (1718), Sultan Ahmed III (r. 1703–1730) and his grand vizier Ibrahim Pasha initiated a policy of reconstruction, with the main focus on securing the trade routes. This period also saw the founding of many pious foundations and the reconstruction of dilapidated mosques and schools, measures undoubtedly also designed to create employment. And many branches of trade and commerce did indeed recover, and for two decades after Passarowitz, something of an economic boom is evident in the Ottoman Empire, albeit on a limited scale.

Village Society

In many provincial centers like Ankara and Bursa in Anatolia, Aleppo and Damascus in Syria, and Cairo in Egypt, there was clear evidence of qualitatively and quantitatively significant industrial activity, the fruits of which were traded beyond the respective regions, despite the impediments noted above. Manufacturers and traders in these cities were also adept at making the villages and small towns of the surrounding areas into suppliers. Thus, the craftsmen of Ankara dyed and fulled angora wool that had already been spun, and in some cases even woven, by home workers in the surrounding villages, while, from the seventeenth century on, rural areas around Bursa produced a large proportion of the raw silk that was processed by the city's artisans. The villages and hamlets around Aleppo, meanwhile, were home to soap boilers, whose products were also important to the dyers of the town.[96] In such instances, the market-driven and monetary economy of the cities also embraced certain village inhabitants. By contrast, the rural population in outlying areas was engaged in much more of a subsistence economy, providing only for themselves or at most for the nearest provincial capital. High transport costs made it impossible either to provide relief to areas farther away from the coast in the event of famine or to involve them in supplying Istanbul during the fat years.

The basic unit of production and society in the countryside was the peasant family with their plot of land *(çift)* held in fee. Although the peasants could not sell their land, with the consent of the local government official they were allowed to assign it to a third party. Yet the sum paid for such pieces of land was lower than the price that could be obtained when selling gardens or houses over which one had full ownership. If a peasant left behind several sons when he died, the law required that they took over the enterprise on a communal basis. However, things were often quite different in reality: many families managed farms that formed just a small part of the standard *çift* leased out within a particular area. Although it was officially forbidden to subdivide farms, as leasehold property was not governed by the inheritance provisions of Islamic law, during periods of population growth, such arrangements were by no means unheard of. If a family had no sons, then, at least from the late sixteenth century on in some regions, daughters could also take over the land.[97] Interestingly, the authorities justified these concessions to farming families by claiming that it would be unjust to deprive surviving dependents of the fruits of the labor that the deceased farmer had invested in his land. In the Balkans there were also widows who continued to farm the land of their dead husbands.

Current historical research assumes that the larger estates *(çiftliks)* that developed from the seventeenth century onward in Anatolia and the Balkans were economically less significant than was once thought. In particular, they cannot be universally linked to the export of agricultural goods to Europe. Certainly, the owners did partly cultivate grain for Istanbul, but in many instances they were only power holders who had taken over the landholding rights from local farmers and reemployed them as sharecroppers or day laborers.[98] For a labor force that could be called on year-round, the owners of the çiftliks frequently employed slaves; in the wake of the military campaigns of the sixteenth century, these were occasionally so cheap that they could sometimes even be found working on the estates of prosperous large farmers. But for all this, the family farm remained the predominant unit in Anatolian agriculture, especially since the central government persistently refused to legally recognize the loss of peasants' rights to their land.

Alongside these settled tenant farmers, there were also, particularly in central and eastern Anatolia and in regions bordering the Syrian desert, nomads and seminomads who raised livestock such as sheep, camels, or even horses, depending on climatic conditions. Because nomads were hard to tax, they rarely entered the records, and little is known about their lifestyle. Settled farmers would often barter arable crops with nomads in exchange for animal products. This took place chiefly at markets held by the farmers and herders on summer pastureland. Certainly it is very wide of the mark to postulate any permanent conflict between "the desert and the sown." However, the Ottoman archives are so full of complaints by settled farmers about infringements committed by nomads that it would be naive to paint the relationship as an idyllic one.

The farming community in Egypt presents a special case. Following the Ottoman conquest in 1517, the *iqta'* system of tax farming introduced by the Mamluk sultans was abolished, and at least for some time taxes were collected instead directly by state officials. Later, as in other Ottoman provinces, the authorities resorted to the traditional method of tax farming; the timar system was never introduced here. Other practices were also retained from the Mamluk period: for instance, in some settlements it was customary for artisans, whose services farmers often called upon, to be paid with a share in the harvest, so disengaging them from the open market. On the other hand, during this period, as the population gradually began to recover from the crises of the fifteenth century, there were also merchants who, for instance, invested in sugarcane cultivation, thereby forging new connections to the market in several regions.[99] In economic terms, then, at least the first hundred years of Ottoman rule appear to be characterized not by recession but rather by a modest degree of expansion.

4. *The Ottomans and the World Beyond*

THERE can be no doubt that the expansion into the Balkans, the expulsion of the Venetians from the eastern Mediterranean, and the later long-running conflict with the Habsburgs represented decisive aspects of early Ottoman history. Yet neither should we forget that Iran, North Africa (and to a lesser extent Central Africa, too), and the countries bordering the Indian Ocean, at least during the sixteenth century, played an absolutely key role in Ottoman politics and trade. "East" and "West" are inextricably linked in this regard: for instance, Ottoman expansion into the Red Sea and occasionally the Indian Ocean as well was conditioned, at least in part, by Portuguese attempts to bring trade in this region completely under Lisbon's control and, if possible, to also conquer the holy sites of Mecca and Medina. And the Ottoman advance into North Africa is closely bound up with Spanish expansion (promoted particularly by Charles V) toward Tunis and the attempt by the last representative of the Portuguese House of Aviz, Dom Sebastian (r. 1557–1578), to extend his realm to Morocco. Only with regard to Iran was the "European connection" of little significance, as all attempts to create an economic or political alliance between the shahs of Persia and the European powers to oppose the Ottoman Empire yielded little in the way of concrete results.[100] As for the Far East, the Ottoman elite rarely entertained direct contacts with this region; the Chinese porcelain that was so highly prized at court and among the wealthy came to Istanbul via several middlemen; plus, the Ottomans' sources of information on China were very scant.[101]

Rivalry with the Mamluk Sultans and Reaction to Portuguese in the Indian Ocean

Between 1485 and 1491, Sultan Bayezid II and his Mamluk counterpart, the sultan Al-Ashraf Sayf al-Din Qa'it Bay (r. 1468–1496), were at war with one another.

This was almost certainly related to the fact that, following his defeat in the accession struggle, Bayezid's brother Prince Cem had initially been granted political asylum in Egypt from 1481 on. For the time being, though, this conflict ended in a stalemate.

However, the position of the Mamluk rulers of Egypt and Syria was placed in real jeopardy only when Vasco da Gama, with the aid of an Arab pilot, landed on the west coast of India. From the fifteenth century on, the sultans of Egypt had increasingly come to monopolize the trade in Indian spices, thereby offsetting the sharp decrease in tax revenues brought about by plague epidemics and other setbacks within their own domain. Besides, by the late fifteenth century, many Mamluk subjects had found ways of concealing their wealth from the depredations of official tax inspectors. Venetian traders, who at this period supplied most European markets with spices, found ways and means of manipulating the market to their advantage, despite the Egyptian sultan's monopoly, by buying very little or nothing at all when prices rose too high. Even so, the income from the monopoly on the spice trade accounted for a large part of the sultans' budget. In consequence, even the limited amount of pepper and other spices that the Portuguese began to bring back to Europe via the sea route threatened to undermine the financial foundations of Mamluk rule. In Venice, merchants and the government alike quickly grasped that, in the matter of the spice trade, the Ottomans were the rising power and adapted to this new situation.[102]

Wars against the Ottomans also posed a threat to the rulers of Syria and Egypt because their rule relied heavily on the recruitment of military slaves, who, according to the dictates of Islamic law, had to be non-Muslims at the time of their capture and enslavement. These young men, who were shipped to Egypt mostly from the as yet still non-Muslim regions to the north of the Black Sea, were trained in the arts of war and then freed. Subsequently, their former owners were keen to maneuver their freed protégés into positions where they were responsible for collecting taxes and wielding local political power. Because only freedmen could marry and raise children, the Mamluks had only freeborn offspring. But because freeborn people were debarred from entering the elite, which was entirely and exclusively recruited from among former military slaves, the Mamluk leadership could not perpetuate itself without a constant supply of new blood. An embargo on access to the non-Muslim world, and particularly to the areas north of the Black Sea, therefore had the capacity to plunge this entire system into a deep political crisis. By the late fifteenth century, the coastal regions of the Black Sea had come under complete Ottoman control, after the Genoese had been expelled from their former bases and attempts by the Polish king to gain a foothold in this region had failed. Thus, by around 1500, Istanbul had the ability to directly destabilize the rule of the Mamluk sultans. A further problem for the Mamluks was posed by the fact that their crack military forces were cavalry units, who had very little experience in the use of firearms. By contrast, the Ottomans had created the "gunpowder empire" par excellence, with their fearsome artillery playing a key role even as early as the siege and conquest of Constantinople in 1453. The penultimate Mamluk sultan Qansuh al-Ghawri had created a unit equipped with artillery, but it was crucially not deployed in the decisive battle (1516) against Sultan Selim I.[103] Also, the Mamluk sultans had no battle fleet, which was prohibitively expensive because of the notorious lack of timber in Egypt. As a result, they sought Ottoman help in opposing the Portuguese, who had begun to encroach on the Indian Ocean from the late 1400s on. But the naval commanders who were dispatched from Istanbul to Yemen soon found themselves in open conflict with their colleagues from the Mamluk army. After they had conquered Egypt, the Ottomans immediately annexed Yemen as well.

Another source of tension was the situation in eastern Anatolia. At the beginning of the sixteenth century, the Dulkadir principality, whose main cities were Maraş (modern Kahramanmaraş) and Elbistan, and whose ruling dynasty also had interests in central Anatolia (long since Ottoman territory), was a Mamluk vassal state.[104] The same was true of the small principality of the Ramazanoğulları in and around Adana, which, thanks to its strategic position on the trade and pilgrimage routes to Damascus and Mecca, was of great importance to the Ottoman sultans. Selim I's conquest of the Mamluk kingdom in 1516–1517 also brought these two territories—and with them the whole of Anatolia—under Ottoman control. But before long a revolt broke out in the former possessions of the Dulkadir, which was finally quelled only in 1527; at around the same time, shortly after the death of Selim I in 1520, his governor in Egypt revolted, attempting to establish his own sultanate. This rebellion was also ultimately unsuccessful.

After the Ottoman conquest of Syria, no more Mamluks were recruited for this territory. Alongside dignitaries who were directly appointed by the authorities in Istanbul or who occasionally "bought" a governorship by leasing the appropriate taxes, the central government also frequently turned to the members of locally well-established families who lived in fortified settlements on the fringes of the desert and who periodically conducted bloody feuds against one another. In contrast, in Egypt the Ottoman sultans continued to fall back on the institution of military slavery. Still referred to as Mamluks, these troops organized themselves into "political households," which could be garrisoned in the palace of a dignitary. Occasionally, though, less prominent officers simply set up such "households" in their own barracks. In the mid-eighteenth century, these households managed to largely monopolize the tax resources of Egypt. But because the Mamluks no longer supplied Egyptian sultans after 1517 but operated strictly within an Ottoman context, modern historians tend to focus on the differences from the situation pre-1517, rather than stress the elements of continuity.

The Ottomans were drawn to the Indian Ocean primarily through Portugal's intervention in the area. Around the mid-sixteenth century, Ottoman fleets or flotillas appeared off the west coast of India on several occasions, and some mosques in this region received financial assistance from Istanbul. Nevertheless, there was never any decisive set-piece battle with the Portuguese, nor did the Ottomans seek to conquer any Indian territory. Relations with the Mughal emperors who ruled over northern India during this period were also extremely limited; a report prepared by Admiral Seydi Ali Re'is, who visited the court of Emperor Humayun, excited little interest among the ruling elite back in Istanbul.[105] The sultans sent envoys to the Mughal court only from the mid-seventeenth century on, but even these apparently performed mainly ceremonial tasks. By contrast, a number of rulers from Southeast Asia, notably the sultans of the kingdom of Aceh in northern Sumatra, tried to solicit military support from Sultan Süleyman the Magnificent against the Portuguese; and at least one Ottoman envoy by the name of Lütfi attempted to convince the sultan of the benefits of heeding this call.[106] But after Süleyman's death his successors decided against further intervention in the Indian Ocean, though a number of individual Ottoman soldiers definitely did enter the service of Southeast Asian princes as advisers in the use of firearms.

Control over the Hejaz and the
Protection of Muslim Pilgrims

However, undoubtedly the most significant side benefit that Selim I brought to the Ottoman Empire as a result of his conquest of Egypt in 1517 was control over the Hejaz, with its twin pilgrimage cities of Mecca and Medina. The pilgrimage (hajj) to Mecca was, and is, obligatory for all Muslims who have the wherewithal to undertake it; any ruler who gave the faithful the means to fulfill this religious duty would gain significant prestige from having done so. Because the Ottoman sultans did not descend from the line of the Prophet Muhammad, religious status was something that they first had to earn. Accordingly, protection of pilgrims to Mecca henceforth constituted a mainspring for the legitimacy of Ottoman rule within the Muslim religious community *(ummah);* viewed from a purely secular perspective, this service to religion was at the same time of enormous political benefit.

During this period, provisioning the inhabitants of Mecca and Medina along with the pilgrims was feasible only from Egypt. Accordingly, the Sharif, a prince who was directly descended from the Prophet and who had previously ruled the holy cities under the aegis of the Mamluk sultans, immediately pledged his allegiance to Selim I and so was permitted to stay in office. As the Ottoman sultans did elsewhere when dealing with vassal Muslim rulers, the established dynasty was allowed to retain its exclusive claim to rule over its domain. Even so, from the many claimants to the throne within these dynasties, the sultan in Istanbul had the option of selecting those candidates most congenial to him. This arrangement remained in force right up to the end of the Ottoman sultanate after the First World War.[107]

From a material standpoint, the Hejaz was a "loss-making proposition," as neither agriculture nor trade there generated much income. Instead, every year large quantities of money and grain from Egypt, Syria, and later Anatolia and even the Balkans had to be expended on feeding the inhabitants of the holy cities. For without these subsidies, the general lack of resources would have either left pilgrims unable to buy provisions at the markets of Medina and Mecca or seen local rulers clamoring for compensation to defray the real or alleged expense of catering to the pilgrims, as often happened before 1517. The infrastructure for these supplies was provided by pious foundations in Egypt, which in some cases dated from the period of Mamluk rule but which were greatly bolstered and expanded by Selim I and Süleyman. Even so, there were frequent complaints in Mecca that provisions had been better under the Mamluk sultans.

The Ottoman sultans also followed Mamluk tradition in taking upon themselves the task of protecting pilgrims' caravans: in practice, this not only entailed providing military hardware, including field artillery, but also paying subsidies to Bedouin tribesmen in the vicinity of the pilgrimage routes. Officially, these payments were intended as compensation to the Bedouin for selling food to the pilgrims and sharing their precious water supplies with the newcomers. But in practice, they were also about buying the Bedouins' loyalty to the sultan through gifts and persuading them not to attack and plunder pilgrim caravans. Evidently, the Bedouin regarded these grants as their rightful dues and did not shy away from attacking pilgrims if they were dissatisfied with the sum they received. Conversely, though, Ottoman officials considered such acts of aggression as serious crimes that deprived the perpetrators of their status as Muslims, so allowing the full force of the law to be brought down upon them.

This arrangement worked reasonably well as long as the political situation was relatively stable and the requisite financial resources could be found. But when this was not the case, as, for instance, during the Ottoman–Habsburg War of 1683–1699, when all available funds were diverted to the Balkan front, the safety of the pilgrims could no longer be guaranteed. This situation was exacerbated by the fact that the Mamluks, who controlled Egypt's resources at that time, showed themselves increasingly reluctant to support pilgrims' caravans leaving Cairo.[108] But even caravan commanders who were not Mamluks, attempted to save money by paying only part of the promised subvention to the Bedouin. In addition, during the first half of the eighteenth century, great upheavals took place among the nomadic peoples of the Arabian Peninsula. Small tribal groupings who had lost their grazing grounds to stronger competitors were particularly inclined to try and recoup their losses by attacking pilgrims. Right at the end of our period, in 1757, there was a particularly devastating attack on pilgrims returning from Mecca to Damascus, which claimed the lives of many people, including one of the sultan's sisters.

The Ottoman rulers also demonstrated their control over the Hejaz through grand construction projects. In Mecca and Medina, they had the main mosques rebuilt, adding the domes and slender minarets that had characterized Ottoman sultans' mosques since the fifteenth century. In the late 1500s, all the buildings around the Great Mosque in Mecca were torn down to create the same kind of clear space surrounding the monumental mosques in Istanbul. The sultans also financed the repair of watercourses and in the same vein created stopping places for pilgrims with ample water supplies and simple rooms. Inscriptions immortalized the good intentions of the ruler who had endowed the building. Clearly, Ottoman sultans saw the establishment of ordered civic life in the pilgrim cities as an important touchstone for the legitimacy of their rule.[109]

Conflicts with the Shi'ites of Iran and Anatolia

Ottoman rulers of the fourteenth and fifteenth centuries had sometimes tolerated or even actively supported dervishes, whose practices and beliefs did not necessarily accord with Sunni Islam. It is thought that some dervish orders incorporated into their rituals certain elements of nature cults that still clung on in the religious observance of Anatolian peasants and nomads. But at the beginning of the sixteenth century, Shah Ismail I (r. 1501–1524), who came from a renowned family of dervish sheikhs from the western Iranian city of Ardabil, ascended the Safavid throne of Persia. At the same time, he remained the leader of a dervish order with a widespread following in both Iran and Anatolia. This event, which threatened Ottoman rule in Anatolia, brought about a sea change in the sultans' attitude toward heterodox practices. Henceforth, they styled themselves as staunch defenders of Sunni Islam, both within their own borders and elsewhere in the Islamic world.[110]

The rift between Sunni Muslims and Shi'ites went back to the early history of Islam: it originally turned on the question of whether, as the Shi'ites maintained, the direct descendants of Muhammad were the only legitimate claimants to the leadership of the faith (caliphate) or whether, as the Sunnis maintained, other leaders could also be considered rightful successors. A particular bone of contention was the legitimacy of the Prophet's first three successors. In the sixteenth century, this old antagonism was so strongly politicized by both Ottoman and Safavid rulers that both sides adduced influential legal and religious scholars to condemn their respective opponents as non-Muslims. As a result, throughout the sixteenth century, persecution of real or assumed heterodox dervishes became very much the order of the day. In particular, membership in the Safaviyye order, which had been founded by ancestors of Shah Ismail, was punishable by death or at least enforced exile.[111] Under these circumstances, many heterodox dervishes took refuge in the long-established order of the Bektashis, who were regarded as close to the Janissaries and therefore relatively safe. But admitting these outsiders only led in time to the Bektashis in their turn being suspected of heterodoxy.

The young shah Ismail I, who in 1501 founded the Safavid dynasty that was to rule Iran until 1722, embraced an extreme variant of Shi'a, which revered the fourth caliph Ali, a son-in-law of the Prophet Muhammad, as an almost godlike figure. This belief found widespread resonance among the nomadic and semi-nomadic population of Anatolia.[112] The Şahkulu Rebellion of 1511–1512 in south-western Anatolia, which the Ottomans had great trouble in suppressing, clearly took its inspiration from Ismail I; the leader of the uprising was in his turn revered as a prophet. As well as being motivated by religious concerns, the followers of the shah were driven by political convictions—the central Ottoman administration, located in far-off Istanbul, granted nomadic tribes only minimal involvement in the political process.

During this period, several Anatolian tribes emigrated to Iran, and the administration in Istanbul undoubtedly saw this migration as a threat, quite apart from encroachments by Shah Ismail's forces into Anatolia at this time. Yet Selim I's victory at the Battle of Çaldiran in 1514 put an end to any further Safavid advances. Selim swiftly followed this up by occupying Azerbaijan and eastern Anatolia, and while the conquest of Tabriz proved a temporary victory, Erzurum and Diyarbakir were incorporated into the Ottoman Empire in perpetuity.

The religious conflict between the Safavids and the Ottomans lost some of its edge after 1600, when Shah Abbas I (r. 1587–1629) repudiated the extreme views of his predecessors and adopted the more widespread tenets of the Shi'a faith. But his contemporary Ottoman counterpart, Sultan Ahmed I (r. 1603–1617), followed Sultan Süleyman in favoring a narrative that presented the Ottoman ruler as the victor over the heretical Persians. As a result, the strident religious and political rhetoric continued unabated throughout the seventeenth and eighteenth centuries, and the attempt by Nadir Shah in 1736–1744 to establish the hybrid form of Shi'a and Sunni he called Jaf'ari as the fifth orthodox school *(mahzab)* of Sunni Islam ultimately foundered on Ottoman opposition.[113]

Countering the migration of heterodox nomads to Iran, Sunnis from both Iran and the Caucasus decamped to Ottoman territory. Legal and religious scholars sought a sphere of influence in which they did not have to compromise their convictions. Moreover, in both the early sixteenth and the late seventeenth century, the Safavid rulers tried to bring political pressure on their Sunni subjects to convert, a move that prompted further waves of migration to the Ottoman Empire. The role played by the Persian language as a cultural medium in enormous territories between Istanbul and Delhi enabled some immigrants with a literary education to be easily absorbed into the Ottoman civil service.

The often inhospitable terrain of eastern Anatolia may be one reason why the territories that Selim I conquered in this area were, in the main, administered indirectly with the help of local, often Kurdish, chiefs. The Ottoman authorities required of these local rulers that they profess loyalty to both Sunni Islam and the sultan: in the event of war they would provide both military and logistical support. Larger cities in the region and fortresses—notably, Erzurum, Diyarbakir, and Van—were controlled by governors appointed directly by the central administration. But elsewhere the sultans were content to install well-known and respected tribal personalities as governors; this practice gave rise to certain families who established a tradition of occupying particular posts. However, as with the Tatar khans and the sharifs of Mecca, the sultan's approval was always needed for such appointments. A memorandum by one of these candidates has survived from the sixteenth century, in which the author seeks to demonstrate that he possesses all the necessary qualities to take on the governor's position formerly occupied by his father.

Around 1600, Aziz Efendi, who in his post in the central Ottoman administration was well versed in corresponding with Kurdish princes, compiled a collection of advice for his successors; this work succinctly but comprehensively encapsulates the reflections of an experienced Ottoman bureaucrat of the period.[114] Aziz Efendi emphasized the Sunni orthodoxy of the frontier princes and stressed their key role in the event of conflict breaking out against the Safavids and so underlined the importance of making concessions to them in small day-to-day matters. In general, Ottoman politics of the early modern period seems to have proceeded quite cautiously: thus, in many cases the great tax registers—a vital source of information for Ottoman bureaucrats and modern researchers alike— were introduced into eastern Anatolia only toward the end of the sixteenth century, while some regions such as Cizre east of Mardin were never actually audited for taxation purposes.

North Africa and the Ottomans

The process by which the regions west of Egypt came under Ottoman control is inseparable from Spanish and Portuguese expansion in the area. Hayreddin Hızır (more commonly known in European sources as Barbarossa and in Turkish as Barbaros Hayreddin Pasha; c. 1466–1546) and his brothers had originally been fighting independently against Spanish military commanders in what is now Algeria; having concluded the Reconquista on home soil, the Spanish were now attempting to take the fight to the Muslims of North Africa. The fortress of Algiers was Hayreddin's most important base, but in 1519 he voluntarily placed himself and his forces under the command of the Ottoman sultan Selim I and subsequently Süleyman, thus effectively making Algiers an Ottoman province. In 1533, Sultan Süleyman appointed this experienced seafarer, renowned for his many victories in the Mediterranean, as grand admiral of the Ottoman fleet; from then on, he operated out of Istanbul. The situation in Tunis was more complicated; in the sixteenth century, the Hafsid dynasty there had been able to assert its rule only through outside help. This enabled the Holy Roman emperor Charles V to besiege and take the city, which the Spanish held until its capture by the Ottoman commander Sinan Pasha in 1574. Tripoli had already become an Ottoman province in 1551.

Even so, the Ottoman central administration experienced great difficulty in trying to rule the newly conquered territories through its usual method of appointing governors. North Africa could be reached only by sea, and the western Mediterranean was not under the sultan's control. After some initial successes, the Ottoman attempt to capture the key fortress of Malta failed in 1565. As a result, in these three far-flung provinces, a system of government by the military and naval commanders quickly became the norm; they in turn soon began to appoint the local governors, who were known as *dey* (or *bey* in Tunis from the mid-seventeenth century onward). This process began in Tunis, where the Ottoman *deys* were replaced by a commander named Murad Bey, whose descendants subsequently occupied the position. This dynasty was toppled by Husayn ibn Ali in 1705, who established his own line of succession. In Tripoli, the militia of the *kuloğlu,* comprising sons of immigrant soldiers and indigenous women, was a potent political force. Although all these regimes (Turkish: *garb ocakları,* meaning "western military units"; French: *régences*) acknowledged the supreme authority of the sultan, in matters of day-to-day politics they were autonomous; even wars between Tunis and Algiers were not uncommon.

Even so, the administration in Istanbul managed to exert some (albeit loose) control over Algiers in particular, as the troops stationed there were recruited from Anatolia. Unlike in Tripoli, kuloğlu here were not permitted to join the army, meaning that in the event of trouble, the sultan had the ability to cut off the supply of fresh troops.[115] Clashes between the rulers of the North African provinces and the central authority were often sparked by political problems. For instance, in the seventeenth and eighteenth centuries, the *garb ocakları* refused to recognize the treaties that the sultan signed with European powers unless they too had ratified them. Barring ratification, they believed themselves perfectly justified in attacking the ships of the country in question or raiding its coast in search of slaves. If diplomatic complaints were then lodged in Istanbul, the Ottoman central government would try, with more or less success, to assert its authority. But from the point of view of non-Ottoman shipowners, it was often more practical to get their own governments to reach accord with the garb ocakları: this certainly happened in the case of the Netherlands. Occasionally, Dutch governments, along with French and English kings, would deploy naval units to bring pressure to bear on this score. The people in the most perilous position were the inhabitants of southern Italy: until the late eighteenth century, their masters, the Spanish crown, concluded no treaties either with the Ottoman central government or with the garb ocakları.

Alongside agriculture and trade, the plunder seized by the corsairs constituted a major source of income in the three Ottoman North African provinces. The captains of the corsair ships formed a kind of Muslim counterpart to the Knights of St. John on Malta. People were an especially prized booty, as they could be released on payment of ransom, exchanged for prisoners, or—particularly if the captives were youths or craftsmen—put to work in North Africa. Occasionally, particularly promising young slaves were given as gifts to dignitaries in Istanbul, who in turn sent them to the palace as pages, where they were brought up in the sultan's service. Some slaves were eventually freed by their masters and made a name for themselves serving on corsair vessels; this was precisely the background of a number of influential people in Algiers. In addition, there were volunteers who had joined up with the corsairs as a way of escaping the domination of European aristocracies and the extremely limited chances of advancement these societies offered. In all these cases, adopting Islam was the key to successful assimilation. Yet prisoners-of-war who continued to anticipate returning home mostly refused to convert, and for this group there were priests and monks to look after their pastoral care.[116] Religious orders such as the Trinitarians made a specialty of ransoming prisoners, advancing the money to buy their release and then subsequently being paid back by the families.

This society of military men and seafarers was chiefly composed of immigrants, but in parallel with it there existed an indigenous society of artisans, merchants, farmers, and nomads. The manufacture of headgear—the well-known fez—flourished in Tunis, with the products also becoming popular in Istanbul from the eighteenth century on.[117] South of Tunis, olive oil was grown for export to Marseilles; in the eighteenth century, most of the olive oil cultivation was in the hands of the governing bey, who collected the relevant taxes in kind. During the seventeenth and eighteenth centuries, it was quite common for the bey to organize large armed processions at more or less regular intervals around his domain, a custom also observed, mutatis mutandis, in other Ottoman provinces, especially those with a large tribal population. On such occasions, the bey's authority was confirmed by the fact that the nomads who had acknowledged his rule had a chance to demonstrate their loyalty anew by paying their tributes.[118]

The Crimean Tatars

Among the Muslim princes who paid homage to the Ottoman sultans, the khans of the Crimea occupied a special position, thanks to their military strength and their relative proximity to the Ottoman heartlands. By the end of the sixteenth century, this khanate represented the last relic of the Tatar Empire, which had been founded in the thirteenth century by Chinggis Khan's successors on the territory of present-day Russia and Ukraine, with all the other khanates already having been overrun by the tsars. Even so, the Crimea was no longer an independent principality, following Mehmed the Conqueror's seizure of the region in 1478. The former Genoese region of Kaffa/Feodosia became the directly ruled Ottoman province of Kefe, which gave the sultan a relatively tight control over the Crimean Tatar princes.

These princes always came from the ruling family of the Geray; yet the sultan could still choose from among the many members of this clan, as indeed was the case with other dependent principalities. Several of the Tatar princes had spent part of their youth in Istanbul and were therefore able to secure themselves the necessary patronage; in addition, these sojourns in the capital effectively turned them culturally into Ottoman gentlemen.[119] In the eighteenth century the Gerays were regarded as the noblest family in the Ottoman Empire after the royal family, and some contemporaries even took the view that if the ruling dynasty should die out, then the Gerays would have to take over the succession. From the perspective of Istanbul, the Tatar khans—not least because of their Sunni faith—were important allies, albeit ones whom it was vital not to let become too powerful. Thus, for example, although Gazi Geray (1554–1608) took part in many of the sultan's campaigns, his request to be named prince of Moldavia was consistently refused by Istanbul. Dignitaries under the khans were known as *kalga* and *nureddin,* some of whom were well placed to inherit the throne.

In the sultan's armies, Tatar troops were invaluable as a vanguard whose sacking and pillaging activities were designed to spread terror throughout the enemy's territory; the destruction wrought by these forces around Vienna in 1683 are a prime example of this tactic. Only very occasionally, though, did Ottoman viziers assign a significant role to these troops in set-piece battles or even sieges. For some inhabitants of the Ottoman central provinces, the wide-ranging campaigns of the Tatars took on an almost mythical status; thus, in the late seventeenth century the travel writer Evliya Çelebi seriously claimed to have advanced with a Tatar horde to the gates of Amsterdam.[120]

Ottoman sultans were only marginally involved in many of the conflicts between the Tatar khans and the Russian tsars; it was not uncommon for the khans to wage war entirely at their own initiative. Several attacks on Moscow by the Tatars, during which they burned down large parts of the city, took place entirely without the participation of Istanbul. Accordingly, the sultan's direct intervention to oppose the seizure of the khanate of Astrakhan by Tsar Ivan IV (r. 1533–1584) was something of an exception. For this campaign, there were even plans afoot to create a Don–Volga canal to ferry Ottoman troops directly to relieve Astrakhan.[121] Yet the project never came to fruition, and the sultan's forces soon withdrew without having seen any significant action.

In the border region between the Kingdom of Poland–Lithuania and the khanate, conflicts between the Tatars and the Cossacks who served the Polish king were a frequent occurrence throughout the sixteenth and seventeenth centuries.[122] On both sides, cattle rustling was a prime objective, because the forces involved lived entirely from their livestock; prisoners were also taken to be sold as slaves. Registers have survived from the northern Anatolian ports of Sinop and Samsun, listing the taxes *(pencik)* levied from slave traders based there; many of these slaves ultimately ended up being sold in the region around Istanbul. For instance, Hürrem Sultan (better known in European sources as Roxelana or *la rossa;* d. 1558), who rose to become the wife and key adviser to Sultan Süleyman the Magnificent, first arrived at the Topkapı harem as a slave from Russia or the Ukraine.[123] The central region of the Crimea, with its more favorable climate, was characterized by a thoroughly urban civilization, as evidenced by the imposing eighteenth-century palace of the Tatar khans at Bahçesaray, which is still standing today. Within the towns, Islamic law was administered by judges (kadis), some of whose registers for the eighteenth century have been preserved.

The Ottomans and Latin Christendom

There is an immense body of secondary literature on the relations between the Ottomans and Latin Christendom. It is impossible to do justice to this material in just a few pages, even if one were to restrict oneself to treating the problems only from the Ottoman perspective.

By way of introduction, however, a few words should be said about the Ottoman attitude toward the border, especially as it impinged on the Christian world. As we have seen, the late Middle Ages saw the Ottoman Empire expand rapidly into southeastern Europe, and this was in part attributable to the actions undertaken by a series of "marcher lords" *(uç beyleri),* such as the Evrenos, Köse Mihal, and Malkoç dynasties, under the aegis of the early sultans. As far back as the fourteenth century, these marcher lords had aligned themselves with the Ottoman rulers and embarked on conquests throughout the Balkans. Certainly, though, the extent to which any one of them was beholden to the sultan of the day depended on individual circumstances. The connection might be extremely loose, especially after Timur the Lame (Tamerlane) took Sultan Bayezid I Yıldırım (r. 1389–1402) prisoner during the Battle of Ankara in 1402, sparking a struggle for the succession among his sons that lasted for more than ten years. From the fourteenth century on, these marcher lords were established on estates throughout southeastern Europe; for the most part, they transformed these holdings into pious foundations, which played a major part in spreading Ottoman culture and Islamizing the surrounding conquered regions.[124] During this period, therefore, it would be misleading to talk in terms of a fixed, linear border; indeed, it was often the case that the Ottomans established a presence in a territory that belonged to this or that principality long before the territory as a whole had been captured.

Nor did the areas bordering the Ottoman Empire in Central Europe during this period have stable frontiers: for instance, for a spell in the fifteenth century the Hungarian king Matthias Corvinus had his residence in the city of Vienna, which he had just conquered but which his successors then promptly lost to the Habsburgs once more. And at the beginning of the sixteenth century, although the borders of Bohemia and Hungary were by no means annulled by a personal union that existed from time to time between the two crowns, their significance did nevertheless decline. In addition, sovereign power over people continued to be as important as territorial borders "on the map" for long after the period under consideration here. This power could sometimes lead to a condominium of two rulers over one and the same territory. In some regions of Ottoman-controlled Hungary, such an arrangement was struck with the Habsburgs: Hungarian noblemen who had fled to imperial territory continued to collect taxes from "their" tenant farmers, regardless of the fact that the latter were also having to pay money to Ottoman administrators. This double taxation system may well explain why certain areas of Hungary in the seventeenth century were very thinly populated.[125]

As already noted, the victorious struggle against the "infidels" and the resulting expansion of the Islamic world was a prime mover for the sultans, at least from the mid-fifteenth century on. Conversely, unfavorable peace settlements represented a distinct threat to a sultan's authority: the loss of Hungary in the Peace of Karlowitz in 1699 is, then, thought to have been a key factor in the deposing of Sultan Mustafa II (r. 1695–1703) four years later.

The wars of the period were presented in fifteenth-century Ottoman chronicles as glorious episodes legitimizing the rule of a particular sultan; the authors of such accounts were not concerned with an exact chronology or precise details about the respective opponents. Documentation in the various Balkan territories was similarly sketchy, especially since Byzantine writers paid little heed to events in the provinces. Byzantine chronicles also offer little in the way of chronological information or insight into the transition from Byzantine to Ottoman rule.[126] Relevant sources can be found in the archives of various monasteries throughout southeastern Europe, on Mount Athos and also the island of Patmos. Because these religious orders recognized the authority of the Ottoman sultan relatively early on, they were in a position to request privileges and even occasionally to offer asylum to aristocratic refugees from the Balkans. Yet such arrangements also indicate that, during the last days of the Byzantine Empire, many monasteries and priests chose not to accept the Byzantine emperor's assurances of protection and instead to reach their own accommodation with the Ottomans.

Conquests in Southeastern and Central Europe to 1526

Around 1350 there were a large number of principalities in the eastern Mediterranean region, which in part were the result of conquests by the Venetians and the allies of the latter after 1204 (the Fourth Crusade). The territory of present-day Bulgaria also played host to a series of petty principalities about which very little is known: even the reconstruction of Ottoman conquests here presents serious difficulties.[127] Mehmed the Conqueror overran the Kingdom of Bosnia and incorporated its lands into the Ottoman sphere of power. The Serbian principality of Tsar Stephan Dushan (r. 1331–1355) disintegrated shortly after his death, whereupon Belgrade became a frontier fortress of the Kingdom of Hungary.

János Hunyadi successfully defended it against Mehmed the Conqueror in 1456, but by 1522 it was in Ottoman hands, taken by the new sultan Süleyman the Magnificent.

By 1261, the Byzantine emperor Michael VIII Palaeologos had regained control over Constantinople from the Latin Empire (1204–1261). Yet Byzantium was scarcely able to defend its Anatolian possessions from this point on, and in due course these were all taken by the Ottomans; Nicaea/Iznik, which during the Latin Empire had served as the Byzantine capital in exile, fell into Ottoman hands in 1329. Sometime after 1360, the sultans gained control of Gelibolu/Gallipoli, after an earthquake had destroyed the city walls. Up to the sixteenth century, this port was the most important base for the slowly growing Ottoman navy. In the Peloponnese, the small Byzantine principality of Mistra, which remained allied to Constantinople, vied with other local rulers for supremacy, while the Acciaiuoli family, which originally hailed from Florence, exerted a more or less firm control over Athens from 1388 on. Saloniki was the second most important city of the Byzantine Empire, although the Commune of the Zealots that developed there (1341–1350) brought it a brief period of autonomy. After first being overrun by the Ottomans, Saloniki was recaptured by the Byzantines, but because the emperor realized that he would be incapable of defending his prize against the Ottomans, he transferred the city to Venetian control in 1423. But by 1430, the Ottomans overran the city for the second and final time.[128]

There was a long preamble to the capture of Constantinople by Mehmed II in 1453. Leaving aside some attempts to besiege the city during the early days of Islamic expansion, the first significant blockade was carried out by Bayezid I in the late fourteenth century. Construction of the fortress of Anadoluhisarı, close to Istanbul but on the Anatolian (Asian) side of the Bosphorus, also dates from this period. In addition, all attempts by the penultimate Byzantine emperor, John VII Palaeologus, to mobilize large-scale military assistance from Latin Europe for the defense of the city failed, despite the fact that he had recognized the authority of the pope as the head of the Christian communion at the Councils of Ferrara and Florence in 1444, and hence the de facto unification of the Roman and Orthodox churches. On the one hand, it soon proved impossible to accomplish the reunification of the churches on the ground in Constantinople; opposition to his move was led by Gennadios Scholarios, whom Mehmed the Conqueror later appointed as the ecumenical patriarch. On the other hand, attempts to launch joint Western and Central European crusades against the Ottomans (for example, in 1396 at Nicopolis and in 1444 at Varna) had ended on both occasions in a humiliating defeat for the Catholic princes leading the expeditions. In consequence, preoccupied with their own problems, most were now disinclined to get involved in far-off Constantinople. The death of Enea Silvio Piccolomini, Pope Pius II, shortly before a crusade he had organized to reconquer Constantinople was due to set sail (1464) finally put paid to all attempts to wrest the city from Ottoman control.

Accordingly, during the siege of 1453, there was only a small contingent of Genoese and Venetian soldiers among the defending force. The city was taken by storm and subsequently plundered, with only the northern suburb of Galata spared, because the mainly Genoese leaders of this settlement had remained neutral during the siege and promptly recognized Ottoman authority following the fall of the main city.[129] Thus, it is wrong to assume any unified approach on the part of the Genoese to Mehmed II; this discrepancy arose from the very loose structure of the Commonwealth of Genoa, which was dominated by various powerful clans. The leading men of Galata would therefore have been able to plausibly claim that they had nothing to do with the Genoese who were fighting on the Byzantine side. The deployment of large-caliber cannon enabled the sultan to destroy the walls on the land side of the city, a feat that no attacker had ever achieved before. The discovery of the grave of Eyüb Ansari, a follower of the Prophet Muhammad, soon after the fall of the city gave the sultan the occasion to build a shrine on the Golden Horn, which soon became a center of settlement. The principal town of a separate district in Ottoman times, Eyüp now forms part of Greater Istanbul.

In their conquests in the Balkans, the sultans sometimes engaged the services of members of the local nobility, who had been brought as young prisoners to the Ottoman court and who, after conversion to Islam, forged careers for themselves in the service of the sultan. Mahmud Pasha, the long-serving yet ultimately executed grand vizier under Mehmed II, was originally a member of a branch of the aristocratic Angelos family, which had settled in Serbia and which in the past had provided a number of Byzantine emperors. This dignitary's aristocratic background doubtless played no small part in the many military and diplomatic successes he achieved in the Balkans.[130] Such cases demonstrate that sultans often considered

Mehmed II's siege of Belgrade in 1456. This siege of what was then the southernmost fortress of the kingdom of Hungary ultimately failed after the Hungarian commander János Hunyadi reached the city with a relief army and took over its defense. The Ottomans finally took the city in 1521, under the command of Sultan Süleyman the Magnificent (r. 1520–1566). Following his conquest of Rhodes in 1520, this was the second major military campaign led by the sultan. (Topkapı Palace Museum, Istanbul)

the family connections of high officeholders to be extremely important, notwithstanding the fact, as already mentioned, that these dignitaries were in a relationship of dependency not far removed from slavery vis-à-vis their masters. Or to put it another way: it would be wrong to assume that viziers and other high officials had simply forgotten their origins in the Balkans.

The Conflict with the Habsburgs
and the French Alliance

Shortly after ascending the throne, the young Hungarian king Lajos II (r. 1506–1526) entered into an alliance with the Habsburgs, which was sealed with a double marriage: while (after some false starts) Anna of Hungary married the future emperor Ferdinand I, Lajos himself wed Maria (1505–1558), the sister of Charles I and Ferdinand I. In the event of either of these two dynasties dying out, the other would gain the right of succession. However, by this stage, Hungary was an elective monarchy, and a strong faction among the magnates lobbied for an indigenous ruler. So, when the childless Lajos lost both his crown and his life in the Battle of Mohács against the Ottomans in 1526, these magnates chose Janos Zapolya as their king, whom Sultan Süleyman was prepared to recognize. But Zapolya did not live long either, and Ferdinand I mobilized his own, not inconsiderable, support among the Hungarian aristocracy. The resulting armed conflict led to the partition of the former Kingdom of Hungary into three parts: Transylvania (in Magyar and Turkish: Erdel) became an autonomous principality, which was mostly under Ottoman suzerainty until it was ceded to the Habsburgs under the terms of the Peace of Karlowitz in 1699; Central Hungary was administered as a province of the Ottoman Empire by governors directly appointed by the sultan; and Ferdinand gained a narrow but relatively densely populated strip of land in the north, the so-called Royal Hungary for which, however, he had to pay a tribute to the sultan. In the Peace of Zsitva Torok (1606), the Habsburgs believed that they had been relieved of this obligation, though the Ottomans took a different view, and the matter was finally resolved to the satisfaction of both parties only in 1612 (or, according to other sources, in 1616).[131]

The confrontation with the Habsburgs presented the Ottomans with a new set of challenges, as for the first time on the European continent, their armies were faced with those of a rival global empire, even though Charles V's voluntary abdication in 1555 had split the Habsburgs into two separate dynasties. Even so, the Spanish and Austrian branches of the family were not only related by blood but were also pledged to offer one another total support. Moreover, as an early modern, absolutist state, the Habsburg domain in Austria and elsewhere could deploy far greater resources against the Ottomans than had ever been available to the small Balkan principalities in the fourteenth and fifteenth centuries.

The rivalry between Charles V and Francis I of France (r. 1515–1546) involved a whole series of contentious issues, such as the control of Italy. To create a counterbalance to the Habsburg forces ranged against him on France's borders—in Spain, in the Franche Comté region, and in the Netherlands—Francis I sought an ally in the third major power on the European continent, namely, the Ottoman sultan.

After an exhaustive debate, the last contribution to which appeared in 2008, historians have been able to ascertain that the accords negotiated between the French ambassador and the grand vizier Ibrahim Pasha in 1535–1536 were never ratified in law. On the French side, it is clear that these earlier draft agreements were invoked during the discussions in the second half of the sixteenth century that led to the first legally valid accords being signed in 1569. On the Ottoman side, the chancellery of that time evidently did not have sufficient documentation at hand to say with certainty that no such earlier accords had ever existed.[132] Nevertheless, what is beyond dispute is that joint Franco-Ottoman operations did take place from the 1530s on, particularly against the Duke of Savoy, who at that period was a Habsburg ally. In 1543, French and Ottoman units teamed up to besiege the city of Nice, while the Ottoman fleet overwintered at the French naval base at Toulon. However, Francis I came under intense diplomatic pressure for having concluded a pact with the "archenemy of Christendom," and no further joint military operations were staged thereafter.[133]

Even so, diplomatic relations between France and the Ottoman Empire remained generally very cordial until the mid-seventeenth century. But when, during the long struggle between Venice and the Ottomans over control of Crete (1645–1669), Louis XIV sanctioned his noblemen to fight on the Venetian side and also allowed a number of French aristocrats to campaign alongside Holy Roman Emperor Leopold I in the Ottoman–Habsburg War (1664), this was regarded as a hostile act at the sultan's court. Relations sank to an all-time low, exacerbated by the less than diplomatic behavior of some envoys. Yet until Napoleon I's occupation of Egypt in 1798, there was no direct war between France and the Ottoman Empire: Istanbul continued to regard the French king as a potential adversary of the Habsburgs and hence as a diplomatic asset. Even the *renversement des alliances* in 1756—that is, the pact that was concluded between the Habsburgs and France's Bourbon rulers—had no dramatic consequences for Ottoman diplomacy in the period under consideration here.[134]

The Encounter with Genoa

In the fourteenth and fifteenth centuries, Genoa had established a significant presence in the eastern Mediterranean, founding Kaffa/Feodosia and Tana as important trading bases on the northern coast of the Black Sea. Ships that had called at these two ports were responsible for bringing the bubonic plague epidemic known as the Black Death to Europe, via Italy, in 1348. On the southern Black Sea coast, Amasra was also a Genoese possession; and in the years following the restoration of the Byzantine Empire in 1261, Genoese traders seized the opportunity to secure a dominant role for themselves in the mercantile enclave of Galata north of the Golden Horn, where all foreign merchants were now obliged to settle. After all, because of their active participation in the Latin Empire (1204–1261), the Venetians were for the time being persona non grata at the Byzantine court. The Genoese were also active in the principality of the Komnenos dynasty in Trebizond; for a long while, there was a commonly held view in Anatolia that any unidentified but definitely non-Muslim ruins were *ceneviz* (Genoese). In the Middle Ages, the slave trade in the Black Sea region was a lucrative source of income for Genoese merchants; despite papal bans, they also supplied slaves to Mamluk-ruled Egypt.

Yet the most important Genoese possession in a region where the Ottomans gradually asserted their control was the island of Chios, just off the Anatolian mainland. Close to the modern coastal towns of Eski Foça and Yeni Foça (Phokaea), there were major alum deposits, which the Genoese began to exploit from as early as the thirteenth century. Alum was widely used in dyeing and tanning, and because the technology of the period required that only the highest-quality alum be used, the extremely pure deposits found in this region were of crucial importance to the Italian textile industry. In the fifteenth century, Genoese merchants also used Chios as a base for their long-distance trade throughout the eastern Mediterranean.

Nevertheless, because of the conquests of Mehmed II, the Genoese lost their decisive influence in both Galata and Trebizond, along with all their bases on the Black Sea. Mehmed the Conqueror also tried to choke off the alum trade; the precise political aims of this action remain unclear. But because extensive alum deposits were found shortly afterward at Tolfa near Rome, exports of this mineral from the Ottoman Empire to areas under the rule of Latin Christendom declined sharply anyway. Only the Venetians continued to occasionally buy shipments of alum from the Ottomans, as they did not want the pope to have a monopoly on a mineral that the burgeoning dyeing industry in Venice in the sixteenth century urgently required. The Genoese, meanwhile, adjusted to the new political landscape first by participating to a limited degree in Ottoman tax-farming arrangements but then by largely withdrawing from the eastern Mediterranean. In spite of this, though, a handful of merchants from the city were still resident in Anatolia in the seventeenth century. The Genoese withdrawal also caused Chios to lose most of its commercial importance.

This island, which from the mid-fifteenth century on had been a small enclave in an otherwise Ottoman-controlled Aegean, was not directly administered by the Genoese state but rather was governed by a consortium of merchants known as the Maona. The members of this group, who all belonged to the Giustianini clan, were responsible for paying tributes to the Ottoman sultan, a duty that they continued to observe, albeit with increasing difficulty, right up to the Ottoman occupation of Chios in 1566. Unlike Venice in a comparable situation, the Genoese state had largely relinquished any role of protecting its subjects in the eastern Mediterranean.[135]

Venice, Dubrovnik/Ragusa, the Spanish Habsburgs, and the Mediterranean

When the Ottomans established their control over the eastern Mediterranean in the late fourteenth and especially the fifteenth century, the colonial system of the

Venetian Republic was the only significant power in the region. Despite repeated Ottoman attempts to take them, a number of key bases remained firmly in Venetian hands for the entire duration of the Republic, such as the island of Corfu (Kerkyra) and a narrow strip of the Dalmatian coast. In general, though, the political history of the eastern Mediterranean was characterized by a progressive displacement of Venetian power by the Ottomans; in other words, the decline of Venice was not solely the result of the rise of "new" powers such as England, France, and the Netherlands.

In addition to the smaller towns and fortresses along the Adriatic coast that the Ottomans soon ran across during their campaigns in Albania and for the most part promptly captured, the Venetians had also managed to assert their control over the major port of Dubrovnik. But from the fourteenth century onward—it is impossible to determine the exact date—this site was under Ottoman suzerainty, albeit with certain special privileges, according to which officials of the sultan were not permitted entry to the heavily fortified town.[136] Instead, they collected the taxes owed to them at the city gates. In its many clashes with Venice, the city council of Dubrovnik could often count on the sultan's support.

Merchants from this city also maintained an extensive trade network right across the Balkans; until the Ottoman conquest, this had mainly revolved around the export of metals from the peninsula's many mining operations. However, the sultans banned this trade, as copper, lead, and silver were military-related commodities. Undaunted, Dubrovnik's merchants managed to come to terms with these changed circumstances, switching by the sixteenth century to trading in wax, wool, animal hides, and leather as their leading export goods.[137] One major import that came to the Balkans through Dubrovnik was finished woolen cloth from Italy. Dubrovnik traders were active throughout the length and breadth of the peninsula; their ships frequently called at Rodosçuk/Rodosto in Thrace (present-day Tekirdag), the last major port before Istanbul. But from the late sixteenth century on, they came under growing pressure from English and Dutch competitors, while their occasional provision of ships for Spanish naval actions brought heavy losses. By the seventeenth century, trade was profitable only during times of war, when Venetian and Ottoman ships could not venture out. A major earthquake in 1667, whose traces can still be seen in the city, only deepened the crisis. Nonetheless, right up to the Napoleonic period, the city administration still managed to raise tributes to pay to the sultan and so retain its autonomy.

For the central administration in Istanbul, Dubrovnik's special status had the advantage that, because of its international trade, the city brought in far more in tribute payments than might have been expected from the duties levied in any other Ottoman port on the Adriatic. Finally, the merchants of this city—who were Catholics but by definition neutral—were free to visit Italy during wartime and supply goods from there to Istanbul. Furthermore, the city was a hotbed of the latest news, where Ottoman viziers could gather information about political developments in Europe, and European courts, including Spain, tried to sound out Ottoman intentions.

There were also some Venetian possessions that dated from the division of the Byzantine Empire after 1204. The largest of these was Crete, where the Venetians clung on until the middle of the seventeenth century; Candia (modern Iraklion) was turned into a formidable fortress, and the reports kept in the Venice state archive from the Venetian governors of the city, who gloried in the title of Duca di Candia, are a principal source for the late medieval history of this region. The Ottoman invasion and conquest of Crete in the mid-1600s was generally a very swift affair.[138] But the siege of Candia lasted for a full twenty-five years, and a sizable Ottoman settlement of troops and their families grew up outside its walls, which finally moved into the citadel after it fell.

On the Peloponnese, the Venetians controlled Koron and Modon and also, on occasion, the city of Monemvasia, which the Ottomans named Menekşe ("violet"); these bases were all lost to the Ottomans in the wars of the late fifteenth and early sixteenth centuries. In addition, for around a century, Venice ruled Cyprus: in 1468, the Signoria had arranged a marriage between a Venetian nobleman's daughter, Caterina Cornaro, and the king of Cyprus. But when he died, followed shortly after by his son, the Venetian government prompted the widowed queen, as an "adoptive daughter of the republic," to transfer sovereignty of the island to Venice, although Caterina employed delaying tactics for some time. Cyprus remained in Venetian hands until it was overrun by the Ottomans in the war of 1570–1573. In the Aegean, the island of Tinos was a Venetian possession right up to the eighteenth century; however, in 1715 the peace settlement at the

Ottoman mosque in Rethymnon (Crete). The minaret of this mosque is one of the few that can still be seen in Greece today, but at the time of writing, this particularly tall example is undergoing restoration in the old town of Rethymnon, a historical conservation area. After the conquest, many churches were converted into mosques, but this is a new building. (Photo by Suraiya Faroqhi)

end of the Great Turkish War forced the Venetians to hand back the Peloponnese, which they had seized during this conflict.[139] Tinos also fell to the Ottoman Empire at this time, ending once and for all Venice's role in the eastern Mediterranean.

The Venetian presence in this region was based on trade: as far back as the Mamluk period, it was primarily Venetians who imported pepper and other spices to Europe; they also brought back with them a taste for decorative motifs and concepts of town planning that still today give Venice its special character. Moreover, the great importance of this trade prompted Venice to effect a quick volte-face when it became clear that the Ottomans were about to supplant the Mamluks as the major power in the region. While Vasco da Gama's voyage to India and the attempts of the Portuguese king to monopolize the import of spices to Europe made inroads into Venice's trade at the start of the sixteenth century, from around 1530 it was evident that Portugal's efforts to establish a monopoly in the Indian Ocean had basically come to nothing. This helped revive the import of spices through the Red Sea to Egypt and on from there to Venice; this trade flourished up to around 1600, when the Dutch established a far more effective monopoly.[140] As for merchants in Cairo (already under Ottoman control), they were well placed to weather this crisis, as it was in around 1600 that coffee consumption in the Ottoman Empire grew to the extent that trading the commodity became a viable commercial proposition. In Europe, however, this was not yet the case, with the result that the Venetians fared far worse from the Dutch intervention. Even so, the Venetians continued to play a key role in the trade in angora wool and finished goods made from it in the decades around 1600.

Besides, up to the seventeenth century, Venetian merchants exported woolen cloth to the Ottoman Empire; this was a new industry for Venice, which had begun to develop only after 1550. Yet production costs were relatively high in Venice, not least because of the high level of taxation, and the collapse of the Ottoman market sparked by the financial crisis of the late sixteenth and early seventeenth centuries, plus competition from English textiles, brought about the decline of this manufacturing sector, which by 1650 was no longer a significant contributor to the Venetian economy. As often happened in early modern history, the Venetian woolen industry was a flash in the pan that appeared from nothing and then disappeared without a trace within a century.[141]

A stone pinnacle of a minaret surmounted by a crescent moon in Rethymnon (Crete); the minaret is set into a wall, and is no longer part of a mosque. (Photo by Suraiya Faroqhi)

All things considered, then, it is reasonable to talk in terms of an interdependence of the Ottoman and Venetian markets that lasted until the middle of the seventeenth century. The Ottoman–Venetian connection thus endured longer than one might have anticipated looking at the trade crisis Venice faced around 1600; at the start of the seventeenth century, the number of merchants from the Ottoman Empire in the city was still so significant that the Signoria was prepared to spend large sums on converting an old palazzo into a "Turkish" accommodation *(Fondaco dei Turchi).*[142] Around the midcentury mark, though, a definite slump was noticeable, which may also explain why Venice was prepared to engage in such a protracted struggle to hold Candia: with fewer commercial positions to defend, political and military considerations came to the fore.

Over the course of the sixteenth century, the duel between the Ottoman and Spanish Empires was fought out in the waters of the Mediterranean: in 1538, the Ottoman fleet won a dramatic victory off Preveze in the Adriatic. By contrast, the siege of Malta in 1565 was a signal failure, in which Spanish support for the island was decisive. The next great naval engagement also played out in the Adriatic, at Lepanto (Turkish: Inebahtı) in 1571—or, more precisely, off the Curzolari Islands.[143] Although this victory by Philip II's half brother Don John of Austria could not save Venice from losing its sovereignty over Cyprus, and a new Ottoman fleet was built and launched in no time, the heavy loss of experienced seamen was in all likelihood a much more serious blow. Henceforth the Ottoman fleet relinquished its offensive capability and began to play a more defensive role, as well as being used in support of ground operations. Also, the psychological effect of Lepanto, carefully nurtured by a skillful propaganda offensive, was enormous throughout the whole of Catholic Europe, and especially in Venice. Yet after 1580, a disengagement of the warring empires became evident, with the result that the historical sources, at least on the Ottoman side, are less extensive for this period. In general, historical research has to date conducted a very one-sided analysis of the Spanish–Ottoman conflict, by largely ignoring Ottoman perspectives on the war.[144]

The protracted Spanish–Ottoman conflict brought constant danger to the inhabitants of Italy's coastal regions. However, at least in one case, Ottoman rule seems to have provided a tempting alternative to the life of oppression suffered by the "have-nots" in Spanish-controlled southern Italy: in 1599, the Dominican theologian Tommaso Campanella—later famous for his utopian (or, from a modern viewpoint, nightmarishly dystopian) treatise *The City of the Sun* (*Civitas Solis*)—attempted to foment an uprising in Calabria, which with Ottoman help was intended to expel the Spanish from the region. Curiously, though, no Ottoman sources on this episode have ever come to light.[145]

Relations with England and France

From an Ottoman standpoint, relations with England and France were inextricably bound up with their rivalry with the Habsburgs. In the case of France, it was the personal clash between ruling dynasties that made Francis I appear an attractive ally. As for England, trade considerations first and foremost prompted London to dispatch envoys and merchants to Istanbul. According to its royal charter, members of the Levant Company, founded in 1581, were granted a monopoly on English trade in the eastern Mediterranean; this institution also paid the salary of English ambassadors to the Sublime Porte. However, their actual appointment was in the gift of the monarch, beginning with Elizabeth I (r. 1558–1603) and subsequently passing to her successors. Toward the end of the sixteenth century, though, the queen's ministers also attempted to instigate direct contact with the Ottomans with an eye to being better prepared to face the Spanish threat. In this context, Elizabeth and female members of the Ottoman royal household exchanged letters and gifts. In their correspondence, the English sometimes claimed that Protestants and Muslims should make common cause in opposing the "idolatrous" Spanish. It is not recorded whether this charm offensive had any effect in Istanbul. Whatever the case may be, after considerable resistance by the French, the first accords were signed in 1581, regulating the rights and responsibilities of English subjects residing on Ottoman soil. Henceforth, English traders had no need to sail to Istanbul under the French flag or to pay consular fees to French envoys. Over the following years, the crushing victory over the Spanish armada in 1588 would doubtless have kept alive Ottoman interest in Elizabeth I's realm: after all, Istanbul was very interested at this time in supporting any initiatives that might hinder a buildup of Spanish naval forces in the Mediterranean.[146] Conversely, during the English Civil War in the mid-seventeenth century, it was the supporters of King Charles I who went cap in hand to Istanbul to try to secure funds from the sultan for the royalist cause—albeit in vain.

This encounter also had repercussions on the cultural front, at least on the English side. Over the course of the seventeenth and eighteenth centuries, a large number of English travelers of diverse outlooks and interests made their way to the Ottoman Empire. While some commentators attempted to collect and disseminate relatively well-documented information on the country, others produced more or less entertaining pieces of pure fiction, and there is some evidence to suggest that these latter works helped establish a stylized self-image for elite members of the early British Empire, which began to develop after 1700. The term *imperial envy* has been suggested to describe the ambivalent attitude in evidence in these works.[147]

However, the main reason for the English presence in the eastern Mediterranean was to purchase Iranian raw silk in Aleppo or Izmir: weavers at Spitalfields in London wove this into fine fabrics, but even more important was the selling-on of raw silk to continental Europe, which yielded large profits. By contrast, the aforementioned export of English woolen cloth was, despite its damaging effect on rival products from Saloniki and Venice, only of secondary importance for the English merchants. Nevertheless, this trade meant that ships on the outward journey did not have to take on ballast, plus it furnished the Levant Company with a useful defensive argument. For, despite the large amounts of ready cash that the resale of raw silk earned for the country, die-hard mercantilists still repeatedly accused the company of weakening Britain by taking gold and silver out of the country to pay for this commodity. Because the silk trade was of such paramount importance to the English, the trading houses concerned withdrew from the Mediterranean at the beginning of the eighteenth century when wars in Iran brought an interruption in silk exports. Instead, they turned to the competitively priced silk that was now becoming available from Bengal and China.

In doing so, the English merchants left the field open to their rivals the French, who bought a wide range of goods from the Ottoman Empire and likewise could offer woolen cloth in return. The French had taken longer to establish regular commerce with Ottoman ports (in French: *échelles du Levant*); only under Louis XIV and his finance minister Jean-Baptiste Colbert did this finally occur. There was no French counterpart enterprise to rival the English Levant Company. However, members of the Marseilles chamber of commerce did have a de facto monopoly, as all goods from the eastern Mediterranean that were not imported through Marseilles attracted a surcharge duty of 20 percent. This regulation was lifted only temporarily during the wars of the eighteenth century, when Louis XV's navy was unable to protect French merchant vessels from privateers in the service of the English.

Accredited merchants who visited the ports of the eastern Mediterranean at the behest of their principals in Marseilles were counted as members of the local French *nation* and hence came under the strict supervision of the resident French consul in each port.[148] It was expected that these mainly young men would emigrate without their families and would not marry native Christian women during their stay, for Ottoman regulations required that the husband of any Ottoman subject became one of the sultan's subjects. These young traders were also meant to return home again after a relatively short time.

In practice, however, the consuls found it impossible to enforce the official directives. Often the merchants were in conflict with the consuls and so disinclined to obey their strictures; a frequent bone of contention was the fees that were supposed to be paid to the consuls by the traders. Also, many of the *nations* of Marseilles merchants settled in the Ottoman provinces had very tense, uneasy relations with the envoys of the French king. In actual fact, then, there was often greater room for maneuver for French subjects than the regulations anticipated. Several Frenchmen, especially in Izmir, married local Catholic women whose families had the requisite wealth; meanwhile, the Ottoman authorities were generally prepared to treat these people and their offspring as French subjects. As a result, some long-running French dynasties grew up in the Levant, whose members either were actively involved in commerce or took on the role of French consuls.[149] In the latter case, the candidates would first undergo a period of training in France before returning with their newly acquired office to the Levant.

Like their English counterparts, French merchants in the Ottoman Empire also sold woolen cloth, most of which was produced in Carcassonne and other areas of the Languedoc. Official agencies monitored quality and price; for example, a French ambassador in the eighteenth century even forced the traders to agree prices among themselves so as to forestall a slump in the market.[150] It is doubtful whether such official dirigisme was beneficial to the Carcassonne weaving industry in the long run, though: when the Ottoman market was hit by a serious crisis in the late eighteenth century, the mills in this city were so dependent on sales through the Marseilles merchants that they were unable to find alternative markets, and textile manufacturing disappeared without a trace.

The Greek and Armenian Trading Diasporas

The early seventeenth century saw merchants from the Netherlands arrive in Istanbul for the first time. Up to the Peace of Westphalia in 1648, the Netherlands was, apart from an armistice from 1609 to 1621, at war with the Spanish Habsburgs. The Ottomans saw this conflict as a good reason to establish relations with the Dutch. It is even conceivable that the sultans had scheduled their actions in the Mediterranean over the preceding century so as to prevent the Spanish army from ever being able to bring operations against their kings' rebellious Dutch provinces to an end—a classic example, first, of the fact that global politics were already being conducted in the early modern period and, second, of an army winning all its battles and yet still losing the war.[151]

The tendency toward mercantilism in official economic policy that was evident in many European countries during the seventeenth century usually prevented Ottoman merchants from operating within the realm of Latin Christendom, notwithstanding the fact that the principle of reciprocity was enshrined in many of the accords reached with Western nations. Venice was one of the few exceptions that proved the general rule. As well as any official decrees that were enacted to this effect, there was also an undercurrent of local xenophobia and envy: thus, despite having the support of the French king, an attempt by Ottoman Armenians to establish a trading colony in Marseilles in the early seventeenth century came to nothing.

In contrast, Amsterdam embraced the principle of free trade much more wholeheartedly, with few restrictions, and in the eighteenth century the city played host first to Armenian and later to Greek merchants, who settled in the Netherlands for the long term. For the Armenians, the most important commodity was mohair from the region around Ankara, already well known from trade with the Venetians. The textile industry in the Dutch town of Leiden, which flourished until the early eighteenth century, used mohair to weave the worsted cloth known as *greinen*. For their part, the Greek Orthodox merchants focused more on cotton.[152] Even after 1730, when the cloth mills of Leiden went into rapid decline, mohair imports were still of interest to the Armenians of Amsterdam, for during the many wars in which the French crown was involved at that time, they could resell mohair to the mills of Amiens and other northern French towns without having to pay the usual 20 percent supplementary duty. Moreover, these latter enterprises preferred to source their mohair from Holland because of the better cost–performance ratio, while their owners railed bitterly against the monopoly of Marseilles.

Over the course of the eighteenth century, it became clear that in the trade with Amsterdam, the Armenians were increasingly beating their Dutch competitors hands down; their better business contacts in Ankara and Izmir enabled them to offer higher-quality goods at more competitive prices. The Dutch authorities responded to complaints from Amsterdam by putting in place some (admittedly limited) protectionist measures for local traders; it went against the grain for contemporaries of Adam Smith to do away with free trade altogether. Two very important conclusions may be drawn from this development: first, a trading company in the European mode was not necessarily superior to an "old-style" mercantile diaspora; furthermore, it is wholly incorrect to portray the Armenians as isolated *pedlars* operating with no strategic market information and with no access to credit and warehousing facilities. Second, this development indicates that it is wrong to regard all non-Muslim merchants of the Ottoman Empire across the board as "compradors," that is, as agents and brokers for European principals, who were obliged to defend Western interests against those of the Ottomans.[153] Quite the contrary: as soon as the institutional framework permitted, the non-Muslim Ottoman subjects of the period discussed here were more than willing to compete against Western European merchants.

Alongside the merchants who traded with the Netherlands, historians have identified two further distinct types of Greek Orthodox diaspora. On the one hand, there were the traders who sold goods produced in the Ottoman Empire on Habsburg territory, and on the other, there were those who concentrated on the internal market within the Holy Roman Empire. Members of the latter group often settled permanently in Vienna or Budapest, especially given that, toward the end of the period treated here, Empress Maria Theresa and Emperor Joseph II demanded that all merchants resident long term on Habsburg soil should swear an oath of allegiance to them. Moreover, the term "Greek Orthodox" is used here because their shared faith represents the only common denominator for this otherwise truly disparate group of traders; also, many of their number with some degree of formal education tended to use Greek as their everyday language. However, as far as ethnicity is concerned, this mercantile diaspora was far from homogeneous.

The development of both these diasporas should be seen within a wider context: during the eighteenth century, Orthodox traders had established a thriving market across many parts of the Balkans. Among other things, this was stimulated by the transition in this same period to large-scale manufacturing in certain regions of the Habsburg Empire, especially Bohemia and the environs of Vienna. As a result, the demand for semimanufactured goods like leather and red-dyed cotton yarn increased enormously. Tanned hides for export came particularly from the territory of modern Bulgaria, while much of the thread for weaving was produced in the small town of Ambelakia in Thessaly in present-day northern Greece. Yet the traders who controlled the distribution and sale of these goods often lived on Habsburg territory, where they also concluded the agreements that founded their companies.[154] Alongside the land route through the Balkans, they also often had goods transported by sea; Trieste, which the Habsburgs developed into their principal Mediterranean port at this time, played a key role in competing with nearby Venice. A colony of Greek Orthodox merchants settled here, too.

In the same way, there were also entrepreneurs, of both Orthodox and non-Orthodox origin, who undertook to set up dyeing operations "in the Turkish manner" on Habsburg territory. While most factories of this kind operated only for a short period, the dyeing of red yarn became a well-established industry in Habsburg lands, as well as in southern France. This development increasingly squeezed the market for the Ambelakia product around 1800; no alternative market for this manufacture ever appeared, and the story of red yarn can be taken as just one more example of the many proto-industries that never developed into full-blown industries.

In Poland–Lithuania, the dominant mercantile diaspora that imported Ottoman goods was that of the Armenians: in the eighteenth century, they maintained regular connections with Lvov (Lviv). Yet there were also Polish traders who came to buy goods directly from the Ottoman Empire. In the seventeenth century, it became the vogue among Polish noblemen to dress in the so-called Sarmatic style, which incorporated many Ottoman elements; this generated a demand in the Polish market for textiles and also ceremonial weapons.[155] Fabrics made from angora wool were also greatly sought after; consequently, in this period, the central Anatolian town of Ankara had connections, albeit often only indirectly, with Venice, the Netherlands, and Poland.

The Conflict with the Austrian Habsburgs and the Role of Poland to 1683

Although it is unconventional to introduce a discussion of Ottoman–Habsburg and Ottoman–Polish relations in the early modern period with an account of trade, the wars that will serve as the subject of this section formed only part of a much broader picture. Following the three-way partition of Hungary in around the mid-1500s, the next great war between the Habsburgs and the Ottomans broke out in 1593. The only major set-piece battle of this long confrontation took place at Mezökeresztes/Haçova in 1596, where the Ottomans were the victors.[156] Sultan Mehmed III was present on the battlefield, though he did not command the army. For the most part, this conflict was fought by besieging fortresses, so that artillerymen and sappers became the most important components of the opposing forces. At the Peace of Zsitva Torok in 1606, the Ottomans gained a number of fortresses; overall, however, their principal gain from this war was a consolidation of the empire's borders.

The Ottomans did not intervene over the entire course of the Thirty Years' War (1618–1648), although the Bohemian nobility urged them to help right at the outset. Evidently, the decisive victory of Habsburg troops under the command of Ferdinand II at the Battle of White Mountain in 1620 persuaded the Ottomans that intervention on their part would not have been a productive move. In the years that followed, Sultan Murad IV was clearly preoccupied with regaining Baghdad from the Safavids, while the reign of his successor Ibrahim (r. 1640–1648) was dominated by the war with Venice over control of Crete.

Thus, for over half a century, both major powers had other priorities. Accordingly, the next clash occurred only in 1664. In spite of a Habsburg victory at St. Gotthard an der Raab, the peace treaty signed at Vasvar panned out favorably for the Ottomans, because foreign policy in the Holy Roman Empire at that point was focused on the struggle against Louis XIV. The interests of the French crown and the Ottoman sultan converged once more, though diplomatic relations between the two states were anything but good. For the first time, this conflict afforded an Ottoman commentator the opportunity to write an extensive description of Vienna, when the travel writer Evliya Çelebi accompanied the ambassador Mehmed Pasha to the Habsburg court, where the latter man was due to conclude a peace between the two empires. Evliya Çelebi combined his own observations with Ottoman and even some Habsburg folklore to produce an instructive and sometimes amusing text.[157]

We know very little about the motives that impelled the Ottoman grand vizier Kara Mustafa Pasha to stage a second siege of Vienna in 1683, over 150 years after Süleyman the Magnificent's first failed attempt in 1529. The successes of Imre Thököly, whom the Ottomans had installed as the "king of Middle Hungary," and of the Hungarian "malcontents" doubtless played a role here. It is also fair to assume that the Ottomans learned only too late that King John Sobieski of Poland, who was originally an ally of Louis XIV, had changed sides at the beginning of 1683 and was now lending Leopold I military support.[158] This situation may explain why the Ottomans, when they were on the point of launching an all-out assault against Vienna, made no preparations to intercept the relief army that was bearing down on them.

The ensuing defeat at Kahlenberg and the lifting of the siege in the fall of 1683 were far more perilous for the Ottomans than the retreat in 1529 had been. This time, the Habsburg side had the opportunity of carrying the fight to Ottoman Hungary. In 1686, Allied troops captured the city of Buda, the principal Ottoman fortress in Hungary, and all attempts to redress this loss foundered on the powerful Habsburg armies, soon under the command of Prince Eugene of Savoy. In the 1690s, the Ottoman war effort was further compromised by a leadership struggle, when the Şeyhülislam Feyzullah Efendi tried to directly interfere with the running of the state and the conduct of the war. This exceeding of his authority was heavily criticized by Ottoman legal and religious scholars and by the military. After the Ottoman defeat at the Battle of Senta/Zenta in 1697, peace negotiations began that were to culminate in the Treaty of Karlowitz (1699), which deprived the Ottomans of all their Hungarian territory save the Banat of Temesvar.[159]

Without the Polish alliance, Leopold I would have been unable to stop the Ottomans from taking his capital. Yet the Poles and Ottomans had come into contact with one another long before these events. Conflicts were frequent: as early as the fifteenth century, the sultans had prevented the Polish kings from extending their influence to the Black Sea. In the seventeenth century, Polish monarchs continued to try to establish a presence in Moldavia (Turkish: Bogdan), while many noblemen from this region maintained close relations with the Polish court.

In the later sixteenth century, when Poland became an elective monarchy, the sultans often exerted a powerful influence on the elections: for instance, Prince Alexandre Édouard from the House of Valois—the later King Henry III of France—won election to the throne of Poland in 1573 primarily as a result of the Ottomans declaring that they would not accept as king any candidate from the House of Habsburg or anyone closely associated with that dynasty. In the seventeenth century, the Ottomans led several campaigns against the fortress of Hotin on the territory of Poland–Lithuania, finally conquering it. Also, Kamenet Podolski/ Kamaniçe and the surrounding region became one of the last territories to be overrun by the Ottomans (1672); as usual, the cathedral there was transformed into a mosque.[160] However, Podolia was one of the shortest-lived Ottoman provinces, as the Peace of Karlowitz in 1699 obliged Sultan Mustafa II to give up this territory once more. Right at the end of our period, in 1768, Sultan Mustafa III (r. 1757– 1774) declared war on Tsarina Catherine II of Russia, because the First Partition of Poland was seen in Istanbul as a serious violation of Ottoman interests. What role French foreign policy may have had in this move is still the subject of debate.

Between the Habsburgs and the Romanovs' Rise to Power

It is still unclear whether the growth that many Ottoman industries and trading enterprises experienced in the mid-eighteenth century may have lulled the empire's government into a false sense of security, leading it to overestimate its own potential and to underestimate that of Russia under Catherine the Great. After all, as recently as the early eighteenth century, attempts by Tsar Peter I to extend the Russian Empire's rule to the shores of the Black Sea had ended in abject failure; furthermore, we still do not know what prompted the Ottoman commander Baltacı Mehmed Pasha to spare Peter's army after he had encircled it and had it at his mercy in 1711.

An Ottoman ambassador around the mid-eighteenth century who had viewed the Russian armory at Kula—driven almost entirely by water power—gave a vivid account of the growing mobilization of resources that the tsar and tsarinas of this period were able to set in train, even in the face of considerable internal opposition. Yet it seems that his report went largely unheeded.[161] Consequently, the entry of a Russian fleet into the Mediterranean through the Bosphorus in 1770—British naval commanders assisted in this action—came as a complete surprise; while the destruction of the Ottoman fleet at Çesme near Izmir unleashed panic in this city and sparked a pogrom against Christians in the region. The appearance of the Russian fleet also triggered an uprising in the Peloponnese, which the sultan was able to suppress only with the help of Albanian mercenaries. Yet when payment for these troops was not forthcoming, they seized the local sources of tax revenue and harassed the civilian population of the region; the situation became so anarchic that the Ottoman central authorities had to organize a military campaign to expel the mercenaries from the peninsula.[162] So it was that the ongoing conflict with Russia transformed structurally weak points of the Ottoman Empire into full-blown trouble spots: in 1821, the Peloponnese was one of the flashpoints of the rebellion that ultimately led to Greece achieving statehood in 1830.

However, most confrontations between Ottoman forces and those of Catherine II were played out in the principalities of Wallachia and Moldavia; these traditional breadbaskets of Istanbul were devastated on several occasions by the armies of both sides. Up to the mid-eighteenth century, the provisioning of Ottoman troops with food and equipment had often been somewhat better than that of their opponents. However, during the Ottoman–Russian War, this advantage was lost in an all-pervading sense of misery, with even the Russian troops lacking the most basic provisions. Furthermore, the sultan's army was largely composed of militia-like units. For, as we have already noted, over the course of the seventeenth century, many members of the Janissary corps became artisans and merchants, for whom military service was just a sideline. Accordingly, the Ottoman troops could do little to resist the disciplined tsarist forces, making the Ottoman Empire's defeat a foregone conclusion. Finally, the experienced diplomat and major political writer Ahmed Resmi was given the unenviable task of negotiating and signing the unfavorable Treaty of Küçük Kaynarca (1774). His record of this event furnishes us with an impressive picture of his frustration, not least with his superiors in Istanbul.

"A Tenacious Defense"

It has often been claimed that in the eighteenth century the Ottoman Empire was one of those states whose power, in contrast to such "coming" states as Great Britain, France, and Russia, suffered a rapid decline.[163] Indeed, Russia's increasing mobilization of its huge resources—in manpower, timber, metals, and, above all, water power—must have presented the Ottoman Empire, whose resource base was far more limited, with an almost insuperable challenge.

There is no question that the sultans' empire in 1730—let alone in the annus horribilis of 1774—was far less powerful and prestigious than it had been toward the end of the sixteenth century. Conversely, new research has shown that the Ottomans were well placed to put up a "tenacious defense" to the mounting problems they faced (as we have seen, much like the situation outlined in a classic study of the decline of the Venetian republic). Overall, then, it makes little sense to sweepingly dismiss the years between the death of Süleyman the Magnificent (1566) and the final demise of the empire after the First World War as an undifferentiated period of decline.

In the late sixteenth and early seventeenth centuries, the Ottoman regime underwent a fundamental change: while in former times, the activities of the sultan played a central role in the state, during this later period a system of government evolved in which bureaucrats, pashas, the valide sultan, and the Janissaries manipulated the levers of power. For a long time, it was usual for historical commentators to ascribe all the empire's problems to the political inexperience of the sultans of the seventeenth and eighteenth centuries. Yet in the "new-style" regime, the active participation of the sultan was by no means essential—in fact, those who genuinely wielded power did their best to discourage it. The only reason viziers and tax farmers still needed their ruler was as a figurehead to legitimize the whole system.

On the other hand, during the reconstruction of the Ottoman regime from the mid-sixteenth century onward, and again after 1718, the country's civil service was vigorously expanded, and even a patrimonial system such as this functioned according to a set of well-established rules. Thus, although contemporary European sources frequently give this impression, it makes no sense to construe the Ottoman system of rule as a chaotic mess, in which "despotic caprice" and "machinations" were the sole driving forces. No doubt, the practice of buying office was widespread, although it is fair to say that even contemporaries had no clear idea of where the legitimate use of patronage ended and corruption began.

It would be equally wrong to impute political naïveté indiscriminately to all members of the court and to simply condemn them all as corrupt schemers. Anyone who had attained high office in the palace had learned to judge his or her moves shrewdly within a strictly hierarchical system. Of course, there were some instances where the internal politics of the palace saw people appointed to offices to which they were unsuited, but such unfortunate cases were hardly confined to the Ottoman elite.

Similarly, it has been claimed that the viziers of the Ottoman Empire made a crucial error in not taking on board the major changes in strategy and tactics that occurred on the battlefields of the Seven Years' War (1756–1763). From a purely military standpoint, this criticism is justified, but there were some important political and economic reasons behind this decision. Therefore, it would be wise to recall the judgment of the Marquis de Bonnac, who as a long-serving French ambassador to the Sublime Porte from 1700 on was a painstaking observer of how the Ottoman Empire functioned. Bonnac famously described the Peace of Passarowitz of 1718 as "une paix honteuse mais qui étoit devenue absolument nécessaire" ("a shameful but absolutely necessary peace settlement") and hence agreed with the grand vizier Ibrahim Pasha, who also believed that the Ottoman Empire urgently needed a "pause for recuperation."[164] Even so, the Ottoman administration did not use the ensuing period of peace to build up a modern army but rather concentrated its energies on a diplomatic offensive and above all on improving the country's infrastructure. The prosperity (albeit moderate) that the country enjoyed between 1720 and 1760 may well have established a template for the Ottoman system's ability to weather all the various crises in the years that followed.

The Ottoman system of rule also displayed a high degree of legitimacy when faced with momentous political challenges. The participation of provincial elites in the exercise of power, the allegiance of the Muslim urban population to the sultan through their incorporation into the new militia-style Janissary corps, and the role of the ruler as the guardian of the Islamic faith all doubtless played a central role in this context. Because the only way for legal and religious scholars to make a real name for themselves was in the service of the sultan, this meant that at least the most influential families were closely bound up with the sultan's court and its potential for patronage. In addition, some dervish sheikhs, especially from the Mevleviyye, Bektaşiyye, and Nakşbendiyye orders, made key contributions to stabilizing the power of the sultan. Even non-Muslim elites were prepared to mostly live with the system. For in spite of occasional Islamization campaigns, they were generally free to practice their religion in daily life, nor were they prevented from earning a living or, in some cases, from amassing some considerable wealth. These various factors explain why the Ottoman system of rule survived major crises, such as the military revolts around 1600 and the war of 1768–1774, which otherwise might have spelled the end of the empire. Undeniably, the army, and later the militias, also represented a central support for Ottoman power, yet it would be wrong to assume that the sultan's power resided in military might alone.

5. Safavid Iran

IN recent years, the relationships between the Safavids and their neighbors have become a popular subject for research.[165] In this context, India has attracted a great deal of attention, no doubt in part because of the many Persian artists and writers who visited not only the Mughal Empire but also the south of the country between the sixteenth and eighteenth centuries.[166] By contrast, the relationship between the Safavids and the Ottomans has been relatively neglected, and the few monographs on this subject that do exist concentrate mainly on political and religious conflicts. Certainly, these clashes helped both sides define their own identity more clearly: since the founding of their empire in 1501, the dynasty of Shah Ismail I (r. 1501–1524) declared itself a Shi'ite state, thereby drawing a sharp distinction with the Sunni Ottomans.

Nevertheless, the cultural connections with the Ottoman Empire—in other words, the westward expansion of Persian culture—are at least as significant as the military entanglements. In the Islamic world, Iranian poetry and book illumination constituted closely connected forms of expression of central importance to the self-awareness of an educated elite both within and outside the Safavid Empire. Cultural links were forged even when political conditions were unfavorable. As regards the literary connections between Persia and Central Asia, it has already been noted that in the seventeenth century, the Sunni–Shi'a division did not cause any form of "iron curtain" to descend between the literati of the two societies.[167] However, this division did play a major part in Persian–Uzbek politics, because the Uzbek khans strongly identified themselves as Sunni. As for the Safavid–Ottoman wars, while their long duration and the bitterness with which they were contested undoubtedly made cultural contacts more difficult, these contacts endured and were carefully nurtured all the same, as can still be seen from surviving texts and works of art.

Linguistic barriers were of little significance. When Shah Ismail I established his rule over Iran, he had to create a balance between, on the one hand, the

Turkic-speaking clans and their princes, who at that time constituted the entire army (the qizilbash, Turkish for "red head," after the color of their headgear), and, on the other, the long-established population from whom the majority of civil administrators were recruited. This also entailed a skillful multilingual aptitude: Shah Ismail I wrote poetry in a Turkic language, which he and his military commanders doubtless also used in everyday parlance. But the administrative language, in which most literary works were also written, was Persian (Farsi), which was also the language of refined education at the courts of both the Mughal emperors of India and the Ottoman sultans. For instance, Sultan Selim I (r. 1512–1520), who was an implacable political and military adversary of Shah Ismail I, wrote poetry in Persian. It would therefore be wrong to claim that the Safavids distinguished themselves as Persian speakers from the Turkish-speaking Ottomans.

In political history, the peace accord that was signed with the Ottomans at Qasr-i-Shirin (Zohab) in 1639 marked a division between two historical periods. In this treaty, Shah Safi (r. 1629–1642) renounced claims to the area now covered by Iraq; the Ottoman–Iranian border that was set at that time, despite a further series of wars in the early eighteenth century, is largely identical to the present-day frontier between Turkey and Iran. The late seventeenth century therefore witnessed a protracted period of peace and a corresponding economic upturn; the traditional claim that the death of Shah Abbas I (r. 1587–1629) ushered in a long period of political and economic decline is disputed by a number of modern historians.[168]

Our discussion here embraces the era up to the collapse of Safavid rule in the wake of the Afghan conquest of Isfahan in 1722. This was followed by the rule of Nadir Shah (1688 [or 1698]–1747), who in the mid-eighteenth century regained and unified all the former territory of the Safavids and even extended Persian rule to northern India; this chapter of Iranian history came to an end with the assassination of Nadir Shah in 1747.

Important Sources

Among our primary sources, the Persian chronicles play a central role: these were created at the courts of the various dynasties that ruled Iran from 1350 to 1750. For the Mongol period, we have the *Jami al-Tawarikh,* compiled at the behest of the grand vizier Rashid al-Din Fadl-Allah (murdered in 1318). Among the texts from the era of Timur is the *Zubdatu't Tawarikh* by the Persian historian Hafiz-i Abru. But the template that many later authors strove to emulate was the work known as the *Rawzat al-Safa* by Mir Khwand (1433–1498), who was active at the court of the Timurid emir Husayn Bayqara (r. 1469–1506). Mir Khwand's grandson Ghiyas ad-Din Muhammad Khwandamir (1475–1534) reported from his own first-hand experience of the founding of the Safavid Empire; Mir Ahmad Munshi al-Qummi (chronicle of 1591), Mahmud Natanzi (1598), and Mirza Beg Junabadi (1629) all wrote histories of the rule of Shah Abbas I and also treated his predecessors.

A key source for the early seventeenth century is the work of Iskandar Beg Munshi (d. 1633/4), who compiled a world history that, although unfinished, does contain a completed chapter on the history of the Safavids (who by then had already been in power for over a century).[169] From the later years of the Safavid dynasty and the years immediately after their fall, a number of manuals of administrative practice are of especial interest, notably the work of Mirza Rafi'a. This work was dedicated to Soltan Husayn (r. 1694–1722), the last Safavid shah to rule from Isfahan; however, it may have been written only when he had already lost his throne. The author of the work known as the *Tadhkirat al-Muluk,* who was active around 1725, almost certainly wrote this work for the Afghan conquerors who had just deposed the Safavids from the throne. In all probability, this treatise, which presents the administration of the preceding centuries as more systematic than it actually was, was designed to suggest continuity between the old and the new dynasties and hence to legitimize for Iranian readers the regime that had just taken over.

Because of the destruction resulting from foreign incursions, particularly the disruption that ensued after the end of Safavid rule in the mid-eighteenth century, the central archives of the various dynasties that ruled Iran between 1350 and 1750 have not survived. Moreover, because of the decentralization of the legal system, the relevant documents in this realm were not stored in public archives but remained within the families of the kadis that had once been in charge; these circumstances were often detrimental to their preservation. However, the archives from the shrine of Sheikh Safi al-Din (1252–1334) in Ardabil have been preserved and even stretch back as far as the Mongol period.[170] In addition, because of the frequent occupation of northwestern Iran by Ottoman troops, a great deal of information is also to be found in the Ottoman archives. In particular, the Ottoman administration of Tabriz, which lasted for around five years (1725–1730), generated a large amount of documentary material.

For the sixteenth century, the accounts of several European travelers are a supplementary source of some significance. The Venetian envoy Michele Membré takes pride of place among these as a result of his excellent knowledge of Turkish.[171] For the seventeenth and eighteenth centuries, the various Catholic missionaries who were active in Isfahan, attempting to convert the resident Armenians there, produced a wealth of source material. Of especial note among these are Raphael du Mans and the Polish Jesuit Judah Krusinski, who wrote eyewitness accounts of the end of the Safavid Empire. But the most famous foreigner to write about Iran in the seventeenth century was undoubtedly the French Huguenot Jean Chardin, who because of the revocation of the Edict of Nantes ultimately emigrated to England and became Sir John Chardin. Between 1667 and 1677, he traveled to Iran on a number of occasions, mostly staying in Isfahan.[172]

Ottoman spies, envoys, and travelers have also left behind reports offering a different, and extremely interesting, kind of outsiders' perspective.[173] The archives of Topkapı Palace contain many reports by spies from the second half of the fifteenth century; these provide information on the affairs of the White Sheep (Aq-Qoyunlu) Empire, which for a brief period (1468–1490) ruled over most of Iran.[174] Of especial importance are the descriptions of Tabriz, Qazvin, Urmiya, and Hamadan in the travel journal of Evliya Çelebi (1611—after 1683), who was a relative and friend of high Ottoman dignitaries and who visited western Iran in the company of an Ottoman ambassador in the 1650s, shortly after the Peace of Qasr-i Shirin in 1639. As a member of the Ottoman elite brought up in the palace, this author had learned Persian; in addition, he was fluent in Azeri Turkish, as his many quotations in this language indicate. Although he was a devout Sunni Muslim, Evliya was quite willing to engage in discussions with Shi'ites. For example, he gives an account of a debate with unnamed Iranian acquaintances that focused on the question of why it was not possible in Iran for a female descendant of the Prophet to marry a first-generation Muslim, whereas the Ottomans permitted such relationships, at least in principle. This dialogue gives us an insight into the problems that educated subjects of the shah and the sultan deemed worthy of discussion. Also of interest is a passage in which the author recounts a discussion about forms of torture allegedly practiced in Iran; he himself took the view that the lesser punishments allowed under shari'a law should suffice, while his opponents argued that human wickedness made a more severe form of deterrent necessary. The Ottoman chroniclers who reported on the many campaigns conducted by pashas and viziers on Safavid soil also provide us with valuable information; a prime example is Matrakçı Nasuh's richly illustrated account of Sultan Süleyman's conquests in Iraq.[175]

Iran under Timur, the Timurids, and the Aq-Qoyunlu

The successors to Chingghis Khan in Iran, the so-called Ilkhans, also adopted Islam after a few generations. Ghazan Khan (r. 1295–1304; converted to Islam in 1295) was the first ruler of Iran from the Mongol dynasty to do so, and he set about reorganizing his empire according to Islamic precepts. At this time, the region under the control of the Ilkhans also encompassed almost all of Anatolia: tradition maintains that even the early Ottoman sultans were initially vassals of the Mongol rulers of Persia. However, after 1335 this empire suffered a swift decline under Ghazan Khan's successors. Around the mid-fourteenth century, the originally Mongol but at that stage already Turkish-speaking Jalayir asserted their control over Baghdad and briefly also in western Iran. Their rule collapsed again shortly afterward but is known above all for its patronage of the poet Salman Sivaji and for the richly illustrated manuscripts commissioned by some of these princes. These upheavals also ended the suzerainty of rulers based in Iran over the petty principalities of Anatolia. In the late fourteenth century, however, this connection to a major realm that included Iran was restored, when Timur the Lame founded a new Mongol empire, which he ruled from Samarkand.

Timur was originally a leader of the Mongol Barlas clan; in 1370, he was proclaimed ruler of the Ulus Chaghatai, a Central Asian nomadic principality that had come into being from the fragmentation of the Mongol Empire.[176] In a series of campaigns, he first overran Khwarazm, the region to the south of the Aral Sea, and the Iranian province of Khorasan, where he installed his son Miran Shah as governor in 1380–1381. Soon after, Timur conquered Herat in present-day

Afghanistan; after a brief interlude, this region was brought under the jurisdiction of the central administration of the newly formed empire. In 1383–1384, he also tore down the fortifications of Kandahar and incorporated this city into his realm.

In western Iran, however, the all-conquering Timur installed vassal rulers. Tabriz was the scene of a bitter struggle for supremacy, as the Jalayir dynasty, with their seat in Mesopotamia, also laid claim to this important city; it was also sacked in 1385–1386 by Timur's rival Tokhtamysh, khan of the White and Blue subdivisions of the Golden Horde. Timur responded to a rebellion in the newly conquered city of Isfahan by massacring its populace in 1387, while the central Iranian province of Fars was also placed under the control of a son of Timur after the local ruling dynasty had been eradicated. In the same year, 1393, he deposed the Jalayir in Baghdad for the first time. Timur also led a pillaging raid into northern India in 1398, which culminated in the massacre of the inhabitants of Delhi, whereupon the princes of this region acknowledged him as their sovereign. In 1401, Timur's second conquest of Baghdad, which the Jalayir had recaptured in the meantime, also ended in the wholesale slaughter of its people.

In the west, Timur launched an assault against the Syrian possessions of the Mamluk sultans in 1400–1401: Aleppo surrendered, while Damascus was overrun and sacked. After putting the inhabitants of the Ottoman city of Sivas in northern Anatolia to the sword, Timur triumphed over the Ottoman sultan Bayezid I Yıldırım (r. 1389–1402) at the Battle of Ankara in 1402 and established his sovereignty over the petty princes of the region. These rulers now returned to their localities, from which Bayezid I had evicted them a few years earlier. Despite the heavy casualties they incurred, these two campaigns were not aimed at establishing permanent control over Anatolia and Syria. Rather, they were designed to punish the Ottoman sultan and the Mamluk rulers for failing to acknowledge Timur's supremacy and for refusing to extradite those of his opponents who had taken refuge in the territories of the two monarchs concerned. Timur also planned a campaign against China but died in Otrar in 1405 before he could set this in motion.

One important prerequisite for Timur's conquests was the mutual assimilation of the conquering Mongol descendants of Chingghis Khan and the various Muslim peoples that they came to rule over from the thirteenth century on. Nor did this process end after the rule of the Mongol khans had largely collapsed in the mid-fourteenth century. On the one hand, the Mongols who had settled in the Near East and western Central Asia had all adopted Islam; Timur did not hesitate in justifying his campaigns by claiming that they were in defense of the Islamic faith or its Sunni branch.[177] On the other hand, the Mongols had abandoned their original language; as reports by envoys and other visitors to the court of Timur indicate, those around him all spoke a variety of Turkic.

Likewise, the political and social objectives of Timur's reign differed fundamentally from those of Chingghis Khan and his immediate successors. At least in the early phases of their campaigns of conquest, one of the principal aims of the latter had been to secure new pasturage at the expense of the settled population, whereas Timur's income relied on tax contributions from local peasants and city dwellers. Even so, many cities in Iran and elsewhere were still razed to the ground, despite the damage this caused to trade and manufacturing.

Therefore, there were clear limits to the degree of assimilation between rulers from a nomadic background and urban elites; for example, hardly ever did a member of the Persian-speaking ruling class make it into the military aristocracy; nor are there any recorded instances of, say, the son of a military commander studying Islamic law and theology in order to pursue a career as a kadi. Yet in the legitimization discourse conducted by Timur and particularly his successors, there are several allusions to Mongol and Islamic laws, whose contradictory aspects clearly were of no concern to the speakers.

Timur founded a dynasty: his youngest son, Shahrukh (1377–1447), succeeded in asserting sovereignty over the provinces that had once been directly controlled by Timur, but only after a series of wars lasting over fifteen years. The change of leadership was problematic as neither the Mongol nor the Iranian–Islamic tradition had any hard and fast rules about succession: all princes were free to stake a claim, which inevitably led to conflict over who should take the helm. Only two of Timur's sons outlived their father, and one of these, Miran Shah, was dead by 1408, but because Timur's grandsons were also entitled to make a claim on the throne, the accession of Shahrukh was by no means a foregone conclusion. Matters were complicated still further by the fact that, shortly before his death, Timur named one of his grandsons as his heir. Although this prince was in no position to assert his rights, as long as he was alive Shahrukh was able to gain legitimacy for his rule by claiming that he was representing the young man's interests and so carrying out the wishes of his deceased father.

Timur, and later his successor, drew support for his power primarily from the emirs, high-ranking military commanders who invariably came from the Turkish-speaking community. Their vernacular was Chaghatai, which later evolved into the Uzbek language; in any event, the majority of these commanders knew Persian as a second language. In a practice that was already widespread during Timur's reign, under Shahrukh the sons of emirs generally inherited these positions from their fathers, and they would often transfer from serving in the retinue of one prince from Timur's family to that of another. Timur's sons and grandsons were dispatched to the provinces at an early age, where, depending on individual circumstances, they attempted to establish what was frequently not a very sound power base for the coming accession struggle.

In the main, Timur's high-ranking commanders had already been part of his retinue when, in the years before 1370, he was still engaged in establishing his rule over Ulus Chaghatai. This personal allegiance to Timur was more important than membership of the ruler's own Barlas clan. Nevertheless, Timur was still prepared to grant certain moderate privileges to the Barlas. The emirs commanded armies whose soldiers were drawn from the regions that they were governing at the time. As required, nomads and peasants were obliged to provide support; in some provinces, there may also have been a provision, dating from the time of the Ilkhans, to recruit from among these groups when the army needed more manpower. It may be that the numerous allusions to regional army divisions in the chronicles of the period refer to military units that were assembled in this way.[178]

This kinsmanlike closeness to the ruler proved especially advantageous when high-placed officials were suspected of planning a revolt or actually took part in one. While princes and other relatives of Timur could usually count on clemency even after attempted rebellions, gruesome punishments were visited upon those who were not part of the inner circle. Iranian officials were in a particularly dangerous position, as Timur and his emirs from Ulus Chaghatai already regarded them with some disdain.

Although Timur and his emirs lived as nomads, taking their families and livestock with them in the baggage train of their armies, the ruler's power rested largely on the fact that he actually excluded the nomadic clans from any positions of high political office for the duration of his reign. In his immediate domain, namely, Ulus Chaghatai, this meant that he withdrew so many resources from the clan leaders, including tax-raising powers, livestock, and potential fighters, that they were no longer in any position to rebel against him. Conversely, his constant campaigns of conquest, which were aimed not necessarily at extending his sphere of influence but simply at consolidating his power, were often a lucrative source of revenue for less prominent clan members. Outside Ulus Chaghatai, nomadic clans were often pillaged every bit as brutally as the settled populace, with Timur using their livestock to provide fresh supplies for his armies. As a result, only relatively few of the clans from this "outer region" joined Timur's retinue for any length of time; in eastern Anatolia, western Iran, and Mesopotamia, the dominant Karaquyunlu, Aq-Qoyunlu, and Jalayir retreated before the advance of Timur's armies, only to reappear as prominent players on the political stage after his death.[179]

Shahrukh was regarded as a ruler who, unlike his father, made no attempt to micromanage the administration of his realm right down to the smallest detail. Instead, he relied on a few trusted confederates among his emirs and on the advice of his wife Gawharshad—at least until she fell from favor for one-sidedly promoting the interests of one of her grandsons. This system functioned satisfactorily, so long as the ruler was surrounded by a large number of emirs who had formerly served his father. But over time they died, and in most cases their sons could take over only part of their power base. The surviving older emirs arrogated many of the remaining resources to themselves, and this concentration of power in a few hands became the source of much discontent. The frustration felt by young princes and emirs in a society where the central authorities had no monopoly over arms erupted time and again in revolts. In 1447, Shahrukh died while trying to crush one of these insurrections.

Administrative duties and the raising of taxes were the domain of officials who worked in governmental bodies known as divans *(diwan);* under both Timur and his successors, the title of vizier denoted (in contrast to its meaning in later periods) an official in a divan, often only middle ranking. There were two such divans at the ruler's court, one of which dealt with military affairs, while the other was concerned with correspondence and tax matters. In the first of these, the personnel spoke Turkic, whereas Persian was the official language in the latter. A divan also operated in each of the main provincial centers. We know quite a lot about the functioning of these bodies, as the authors of chronicles and other documents often came from this milieu.

In the reign of both Timur and Shahrukh there were frequent investigations into the embezzlement of funds by emirs and financial experts. It appears that Shahrukh intervened only after repeated complaints began to point to a major scandal; investigations would often entail financial bureaucrats making life difficult over a long period for subjects and members of the administration alike. Minor cases of fraud were evidently tolerated but could still be used against the person responsible at a later date. Occasionally difficulties with the bookkeeping system could lead to accusations that subsequently turned out to be unfounded. So, during the reign of Shahrukh, the son of an emir who had been dismissed due to an alleged misappropriation of funds is said to have taught himself proper accounting methods and proved that the missing sum, for which his father had been deemed responsible, was in fact only a minor discrepancy.[180]

Shahrukh preferred Herat as the seat of government; Shiraz and Timur's former capital of Samarkand functioned as important regional centers. As a way of legitimizing their rule, the Timurids placed special emphasis on Sultaniyeh, the ancient royal residential city on the road from Qazvin to Tabriz, where many Mongolian rulers of the fourteenth century were buried. The most important places were home to garrisons, under the command of the respective city governor. In theory, these dignitaries, who were called *darugha,* were subservient to the higher-ranking provincial governors, who were often Timurid princes or prominent emirs. Yet the darughas could ensure the security of the towns they had been charged with protecting only if Timur did not order them to leave on campaign. Another way in which Timur consolidated his own power was by ensuring that his officials never had too clearly defined or secure areas of responsibility. Usually city militias received enough training in military techniques, especially archery and the use of a slingshot, to hold any besieging force at bay for a while. For constant preparedness in defensive warfare was vital. During the accession struggle in which Shahrukh eventually prevailed but also in the endless border skirmishes and rebellions that occurred during this period, the ruling elites of cities in the Timurid Empire had to try to predict who would come out on top and to take the eventual victor's side. Such a decision meant sealing the city off from the enemies of the prince or emir they had elected to support.[181] Wrong decisions could result in heavy losses. The wars, burnings, and pillagings that Isfahan had to endure during the fifteenth century at the hands of Timur, the Timurids, and the Aq-Qoyunlu are vivid examples of this.[182] The situation was made even worse by the fact that not all the wars that an emir chose to fight at the frontier had the support of Shahrukh. It was therefore all too easy for a city to find itself caught between two fronts.

In spite of this unstable internal situation and the problems that the increasingly independent Karaquyunlu in Azerbaijan under their leader Prince Kara Yusuf were making for the Timurids, the princes of this dynasty still managed to provide the wherewithal for diplomatic and cultural activities. In consequence, missions from various Timurid princes paid regular visits to the Ming court of China, which had succeeded the previous, originally Mongolian, Yuan dynasty in 1368. At the Chinese court, these tribute missions—for this was how the role of ambassadors was construed by the emperor and his officials—had always been regarded, no doubt with good reason, as attempts to secure Persian merchants' permission to trade directly with China, from which they were otherwise debarred.[183] In particular, the horses that these missions brought with them were so highly prized by the Chinese court that the envoys from Iran were always granted an audience, despite misgivings in some official quarters.

Ulugh Beg (r. 1448–1449), the eldest son of Shahrukh, was renowned for his patronage of art and culture. His base was in Samarkand, which he had ruled as an autonomous prince even before the death of his father in 1447 and where he employed a number of astronomers and mathematicians. Ulugh Beg built an observatory at his palace and had astronomical tables drawn up that became well known throughout the Islamic world; he may even have been personally involved in their preparation. However, his defeat in the accession struggle and his death shortly thereafter brought this brief cultural flowering to an end. One of Ulugh Beg's scholars, the astronomer Ali al-Din Muhammad Qushji (known in Turkish as Ali Kuşçu), was appointed by Mehmed the Conqueror as a professor at the newly founded university of Aya Sofya in the recently conquered Ottoman capital of Constantinople/Istanbul. The Timurid emir Husayn Bayqara, a son of Timur's great-grandson, who ruled in Herat after the death of Shahrukh, was also a keen patron of the arts and sciences. Writers and miniaturists at his court created important works, while the poetry of Husayn Bayqara's vizier Mir Ali Shir Nava'i established Chaghatai as a literary language. The poet Jami, who wrote in Persian, was active in Herat around this time, too, and was also persistently urged to come to Istanbul but never made the move.[184]

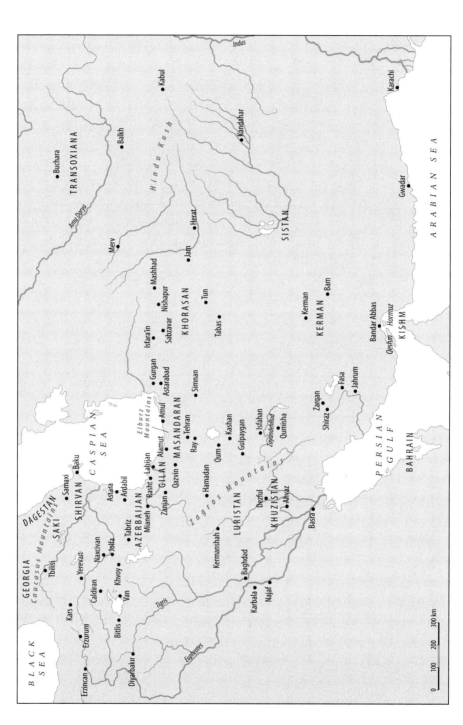

Iran in the Safavid period

In the late fifteenth century, the Turkoman princes who became known as the White Sheep dynasty (Aq-Qoyunlu) ruled over the whole of Iran (with the exception of Khorasan) and eastern Anatolia. Under the leadership of Kara Othman, this dynasty had gained territory from their Turkoman rivals the Karaquyunlu (Black Sheep), as they had consistently supported Timur in his Anatolian campaigns and remained loyal to Shahrukh when he secured the succession. In 1467–1468, Kara Othman's grandson Uzun Hasan (also called Hasan Padishah; 1425–1478), who ruled first from Diyarbakir and later from Tabriz, conquered a large part of Iran from the Karaquyunlu and the Timurids; the latter were left only with Transoxania and Khorasan.

This expansion made Hasan Padishah—who styled himself as a renewer of the Islamic faith and even attempted to wrest control of the Hejaz and the Muslim holy sites from the Mamluk sultans—into the archrival of the Ottoman sultan Mehmed the Conqueror. The ensuing war between Mehmed and the Aq-Qoyunlu ended with the defeat of Uzun Hasan at the Battle of Otluk-Beli (also known as Bashkent, in eastern Anatolia) in 1473; the tribal structure of Uzun Hasan's army and his lack of firearms made his army vulnerable. However, it was only much later, after Shah Ismail I had brought the rule of the Aq-Qoyunlu in Iran to a definitive end, that the Ottomans were able to incorporate the Anatolian provinces of the defunct empire into their own territory. In the early phases of Safavid rule, though, the western borders of the new realm largely corresponded to those of the preceding Aq-Qoyunlu Empire; only Selim I's victory over Shah Ismail I in 1514 established the Ottoman–Safavid frontier further east.

The succession to Uzun Hasan was ultimately settled after a five-year struggle between his sons; this conflict decisively weakened the Aq-Qoyunlu empire: with the death in 1490 of the successor Yaqub Bay, whose wealth largely depended on the silk trade to Aleppo and Bursa and who furnished Tabriz with some imposing public buildings, the decline of an empire that had, albeit briefly, been so powerful began in earnest. However, the tax regime imposed by Hasan Padishah—who on his mother's side was related to the Comnenus dynasty of Trebizond/Trabzon and whose daughter became the mother of the future first Safavid shah—remained in force in this region long after the overthrow of his rule by the shah and the sultan.[185]

The Safavids and Their System of Rule

The Safavids have been called the "Dervishes in the Anteroom of Power."[186] In the fifteenth century, in both Iran and eastern Anatolia, where nomadic groups wielded considerable power and princely control was only very limited, there was room for political activity by dervishes and their leaders. Among these, the descendants of Sheikh Safi al-Din (d. 1334) were particularly prominent, in both western Iran and Anatolia. While Sheikh Safi had been Sunni, his successors assimilated themselves with the nomads, who had incorporated elements of a number of Near Eastern religions into a belief system that they themselves regarded as Shi'ite, although this view was not necessarily shared by legal and religious scholars (ulama) from that faith. Sheikh Junayd (d. 1460) attracted a large following among the nomads in Anatolia and also established family connections to Uzun Hasan. These ties stood his grandson Sheikh—and, from 1501, Shah—Ismail I in good stead, when he proclaimed himself ruler of Iran, although he also had a significant following in the far western corner of Anatolia.

A series of documents give a reasonably good account of the history of the much-venerated shrine at Ardabil, the burial site of Sheikh Safi al-Din. The story begins in the fourteenth century, in other words long before Shah Ismail I founded the Safavid Empire; the surviving texts and records note various gifts, endowments, and sales of property to benefit this institution. Members of the Mongol aristocracy (who meanwhile had converted to Islam), among them a daughter of Ghazan Khan and also the renowned vizier and generous patron Rashid al-Din Fadl-Allah, also contributed to the construction and fitting out of the grave complex. Information for the fifteenth century is scant, but we do know that one of the wives of Sheikh Haydar (d. 1488), a stepmother of the founder of the Safavid dynasty, endowed a number of villages for the benefit of the shrine.

After Shah Ismail I had established his rule over Iran, Ardabil became a family shrine for the Safavids, with prominent members of the dynasty being buried there and many shahs visiting it to pay their respects. Accordingly, donations were forthcoming not just from members of the ruling family but also from men and women from the political elite, who alongside their charitable intent were doubtless also keen to proclaim their closeness to the ruling dynasty. In around 1600, the Ardabil complex became a major property owner, especially after Shah Abbas I had assigned all his urban and rural landholdings to this institution, as well as to the Mausoleum of Imam Ali Ridha in Mashhad; a specially appointed bureaucratic organization was responsible for administering this endowment. Because this income far exceeded the institution's charitable and administrative expenditure, during the seventeenth century the shrine was in a position to purchase new real estate. It survived the Ottoman occupation of 1725–1730, though not without incurring some damage.[187] However, under Nadir Shah it declined in importance, due to this ruler's interference in pious foundations in general but also because a specifically Safavid shrine no longer possessed any particular significance for rulers from other dynasties.

The Borders of the Safavid Empire

While the heartland of the Safavid Empire is roughly coextensive with the modern state of Iran, the territory ruled by this dynasty extended considerably farther east. Kandahar, situated in present-day Afghanistan, was one of the most important frontier fortresses, which the Safavids had on several occasions to defend against attacks by the Mughal emperors of northern India. Herat, likewise now in Afghanistan, was an important center, namely, of the Safavid province of Khorasan.

Another frequently disputed border separated the Safavid realm from the area ruled over by the Sunni Uzbek khans, with its centers at Bukhara and Samarkand. In 1587, the city of Mashhad was captured by the Uzbeks and reconquered by Shah Abbas I only in 1598. On the western frontier also, at least at certain periods, the Safavid Empire similarly extended farther than present-day Iran. Until the defeat of Shah Ismail I by Sultan Selim I at Çaldiran in 1514, the Safavid–Ottoman border was situated, as we have already seen, deep within the territory of modern Turkey, near Erzincan. Thus, the current Turkish border city of Van belonged to the Safavid Empire until Sultan Süleyman I took in it 1548; in the Peace of Amasya (1555) it formally became part of the Ottoman Empire and shortly thereafter was developed into a formidable border fortification.[188] In addition, at least for several decades the Safavids were in control of Iraq until it was overrun by Sultan Süleyman I. In the early seventeenth century, Shah Abbas I did succeed in wresting this province back from the Ottomans, only to lose it again soon after to Murad IV.

The arrival of Süleyman I (the Magnificent) in Qasr-i Shirin, Iraq. This miniature, which was painted during Süleyman's lifetime but some twenty-five years after the events depicted, forms part of a world chronicle, of which only fragments now survive. For educated Ottomans, the entry of the sultan into Qasr-i Shirin, famous for its palace ruins dating from the Sassanid period (224–651), must have signified a connection to the literary renown of this dynasty. As a result of their conquest of Iraq in 1533–1534, the Ottomans not only took control of Baghdad, the old capital of the caliphate, but also gained access to the Persian Gulf. (Roland and Sabrina Michaud)

Henceforth, Iraq remained under the rule of the Ottoman sultans right up to the collapse of the empire in 1919–1922.

By contrast, most of the principalities of the Caucasus were vassal states of the Safavids. For the ruler of Iran, Georgia was a valuable source of military slaves *(ghulam),* who since the second half of the sixteenth century had also come to play a significant role in the upper echelons of provincial administration; career opportunities such as this persuaded many Georgian noblemen to voluntarily relocate to the heartland of the Safavid Empire. The religious center of the Armenians was also sited within Safavid territory, namely, in Echmiadzin. But because this site lay close to the Ottoman–Iranian border, it appears that the priests who resided there in the seventeenth century were obliged to play host to any number of high-ranking travelers passing between the shah's and the sultan's territories.[189] In eastern Anatolia and modern northern Iraq, there were also autonomous dominions, whose mainly Kurdish rulers largely supported the Ottomans but who in some cases also acknowledged the authority of the Safavids.

Territorial Conflicts with the Ottomans

Throughout the whole of the sixteenth century, there existed between the Ottomans and the Safavids an almost permanent state of war, punctuated by a few brief interludes of peace. Several different factors played a part in this. One major bone of contention was sovereignty over the numerous Muslim and Christian rulers of the Caucasus. When Ottoman armies appeared in the region, the sultans were able to lay claim to the leadership role; but as soon as these forces withdrew, the resulting power vacuum, as we have seen, was filled by the Safavids. Furthermore, the Ottoman rulers attempted to annex Tabriz and the province of Azerbaijan into their empire: this city was occupied several times but on each occasion recaptured by the Safavids.

Farther south, the dispute centered around control of Iraq and Baghdad, formerly the capital of the caliphs: this region had originally been in the hands of the Jalayir dynasty before being conquered by Shah Ismail I in 1508. From the Safavids' perspective, as well as from a religious viewpoint, the loss of this territory shortly afterward to Sultan Süleyman I was a serious blow. For Iraq was the last resting place of Imam Ali (c. 598–660), the son-in-law of the Prophet Muhammad, and Ali's son, Imam Husayn (626–680), whose mausoleums (in Najaf and Karbala, respectively) were, and continue to be, visited by hundreds of thousands of Shiʿite pilgrims every year. Nevertheless, the Safavids were prepared to renounce all claims to this region if this concession would ensure them a lasting peace with the Ottomans. Given the military superiority of the sultans' armies and the difficulty in keeping control over Iraq, religious considerations appear to have taken a backseat to realpolitik.[190]

An eighty-year period of peace set in after the Peace of Qasr-i Shirin in 1639. But in the early eighteenth century, after the Safavid dynasty had been severely weakened by a number of revolts, both Tsar Peter the Great of Russia (r. 1682–1725) and the Ottoman sultan Ahmed III seized this opportunity to invade northern Iran, with both claiming that their intervention had been in response to an "invitation" by Shah Tahmasp II (r. 1722–1732). The shah, whose military strength was very depleted, ended up ceding control of Jalin and Mazandaran to the tsar; these two provinces just south of the Caspian Sea had already been occupied by Peter's forces anyway. In 1723, Ottoman armies from Baghdad and Erzurum invaded Persia, quickly gaining control over Tabriz, the main city of northern Iran, which over a period of five years they built up into a regional center of power for the sultan (1725–1730). This occupation was carried out in agreement with Tsar Peter, but after his death in 1725 the Russian forces initially withdrew from the region, with all their conquered territory being restored to the shah. In 1730, the military commander Nadir—who came from the Turkic-speaking clan of the Afshars and who at that time, at least formally, was in the service of the shah—forced the Ottoman armies into a retreat. This episode undoubtedly played a part in the toppling of Sultan Ahmed III and his vizier Damad Ibrahim Pasha shortly thereafter.

In waging war, the Safavids used different tactics than their Ottoman adversaries. Their army consisted chiefly of cavalry, and though familiar with firearms, they rarely used them. Constructing fortresses or besieging those of their enemies was also of secondary importance. Rather, mobility was the key quality of the Safavid army, which was well versed in the tactic of luring its opponents into terrain where there were few resources and then attacking them once they were exhausted and desperate. This strategy was effective against the nomad armies put in the field by internal rebels against their rule and by the Uzbeks. It also proved its worth in Azerbaijan, as evidenced by the protracted resistance of the city of Tabriz to Ottoman onslaughts. In this situation, the Safavids required large numbers of horses; as a result, the shah's stables and the stud farms scattered right across the empire were always a key concern of the Safavid central administration.[191]

The Safavid Claim on Power

As this brief discussion has already demonstrated, the clash between the Safavids and the Ottomans was partly a product of territorial rivalries; yet it also involved a whole constellation of customs and attitudes that we might characterize—using a somewhat anachronistic expression—as political and religious ideology. Sunni and Shi'a Islam had existed from the earliest times in the history of the faith; the origin of their divergence was the question of whether the caliphate should be restricted to the direct descendants of the Prophet Muhammad through his daughter Fatima and her husband, Imam Ali—or possibly also the offspring of Imam Ali with another of his wives—or whether influential men from the Prophet's retinue had had the right, after Muhammad's death, to appoint one of their own number as caliph at their discretion. The Shi'ites took the former view, the Sunni the latter.

Long before the Safavids came to power, Shi'ite religious and legal scholars had repeatedly declared that the descendants of Muhammad had been deprived of their rightful inheritance, and frequently even murdered, by a succession of usurpers like the Umayyads and the Abbasids. Foremost among these martyrs from the Prophet's family was Fatima's and Imam Ali's son Imam Husayn, who was killed doing battle against the Umayyad caliph Yazid at Karbala in Iraq in 680. Commemoration of his martyrdom continues to play an important role in the religious calendar of the Shi'ites, and also in a more diluted form for some strains of the Sunni faith, to the present day. In Safavid Persia, elaborate memorial processions with graphic tableaus of the death of Imam Husayn and recitations of elegiac verse were essential elements of the ceremonies staged by the shahs to demonstrate their devotion to the family of the Prophet. Most of the descriptions of these rituals were written by European observers, that is, outsiders; however, there are two accounts by the Ottoman traveler Evliya Çelebi, who basically describes the same scenes. Evidently, as a Sunni Ottoman, he was also conscious of reporting something "alien and exotic," which he viewed with disapproval yet also a certain degree of fascination.[192]

The first four caliphs after the death of the Prophet Muhammad—Abu Bakr (r. 632–634), Umar I (r. 634–644), Uthman (r. 644–656), and Ali (r. 656–660)—are regarded, without exception, as exemplars by the Sunni. However, where the Shi'ites are concerned, the first two caliphs in particular are pure usurpers, while Aisha, one of the wives of the Prophet, is also included on this blacklist because of her opposition to Ali. The Safavids included a ritual cursing of the "usurpers" in their ceremonies, which was also extended to the caliph Uthman. Occasionally, the Safavid rulers also demanded such observances from their supporters. For the Ottoman sultans, however, it was precisely this denigration of the first three "righteous caliphs" and Aisha that was totally unacceptable; the Peace of Amasya (1555) and the treaty in 1590 that the Ottomans concluded with the young shah Abbas I each contain a passage forbidding this cursing. Yet it is difficult to determine how effective these regulations were in practice. In the mid-seventeenth century, this contentious issue was still the cause of diplomatic incidents: for instance, when Evliya Çelebi visited Urmiya in an official capacity in 1655, he had to restrain his entourage from responding with violence to the cursing of the first caliphs. He also admits to having himself once had a muezzin beaten up after the man had, in standard Shi'ite fashion, included a curse on all the enemies of Ali in his call to prayer.[193]

One widespread branch of Shi'a Islam, the so-called Twelvers, who had formed the majority in Iran since the sixteenth century, believed that the twelfth imam disappeared into occultation; his followers commonly described themselves as Imamis. Since his disappearance, the Imamis—or at least many of their legal and religious scholars (ulama)—took the view that the Islamic community had been ruled not by legitimate religious leaders but by rulers whose power was strictly limited to the "wordly" realm. As a result, it was a point of deep controversy among the ulama of Iran in the sixteenth century whether it was even permissible under these circumstances to observe Friday prayers, as these included a sermon by the preacher in which it was customary to invoke the name of the "rightful" ruler. Accordingly, in the first century of Safavid rule, relatively few Friday mosques were built. However, as the supposed descendants of the Prophet, the Safavids claimed the position of legitimate rulers, and so over time it became a proof of loyalty to the dynasty if a scholar ruled that holding Friday prayers was admissible. As an outward sign of his right to rule, Shah Abbas I had both a court mosque and a Friday mosque built in a new quarter of Isfahan that he had recently founded.[194]

Yet pronouncements by legal and religious scholars were just one aspect of Shi'ite religiosity. A form of devotion had developed among the often nomadic or semi-nomadic clans that placed the son-in-law of the Prophet, Imam Ali, so strongly in the foreground that the significance of the Prophet Muhammad even began to pale in comparison with this "Lion of God." Such sects had already existed in the Middle Ages, and orthodox theology had coined a term, *ghulat* ("extremists"), for people espousing this view. The Sunni, meanwhile, liked to peddle the apocryphal tale that the supporters of the Safavids and/or Anatolian heterodox Shi'ites held ceremonies at which women were present and where, at a given moment, the "lights were extinguished." Evliya Çelebi also mentioned this alleged ceremony but honestly admitted that, despite having traveled to Iran several times, he himself had never personally witnessed it.

Accordingly Shi'ite religious and legal scholars living in Lebanon—Ottoman territory—in the sixteenth century often took a very guarded attitude to the new regime in Iran. Yet a prominent member of this community, Sheikh Ali al-Karaki (d. 1534), emigrated to the Safavid Empire, perhaps in the hope of converting the shah and his court to views that would be more acceptable to mainstream Shi'ite theologians. However, it was only during the reign of Shah Abbas I and especially his successor Shah Safi that the Safavid rulers came to fully espouse the teachings of the orthodox Shi'ite ulama. Although the differences between Sunni and Shi'a continued to be played up in both Ottoman and Safavid propaganda, the tension abated noticeably after this religious and political turnabout.

Besides, instances of Shi'ites who suffered persecution on Ottoman soil and so migrated to the Safavids are more extensively documented than there are recorded cases of "everyday tolerance." Thus, Baha al-Din al-Amili (1547–1621), an eminent religious dignitary from Isfahan, once journeyed incognito to his homeland of Syria; while presenting himself to strangers as a Sunni, many religious scholars in Damascus knew perfectly well who he really was, yet no one ever betrayed him.[195]

Safavid legitimacy rested to a large extent on the shahs' claim to be representatives of the Mahdi—that is, the Islamic leader whom it was prophesied would appear at the Day of Judgment. Safavid rulers also occupied the role of the principal sheikh of the dervish order, a tradition that was traced back to Sheikh Safi al-Din. In this context, from the early sixteenth century on, the Safavids maintained that they were descended from Musa al-Kazim, a descendant of the Prophet and the seventh imam of the Twelvers; in particular, Shah Abbas I made great play of this connection. In the shah's realm, all those attempting to distance themselves from the Safavids by disseminating potential alternative symbols of veneration could reckon on a heavy punishment. For instance, one popular form of religious and political opposition was the recounting and spreading of myths and stories concerning Abu Muslim (d. 755). His revolutionary activities in Khorasan had paved the way for the expulsion of the Umayyads by the Abbasids, yet he was murdered shortly after the establishment of the new dynasty. Discussions about the relationship of the Safavids to the religious and legal scholars of the established Twelver Shi'a (Imamis) frequently lighted on the question of whether Abu Muslim should be regarded as a friend or foe of the descendants of the Prophet Muhammad. This discussion hinted at the politically hot topic of whether the Safavids should remain true to their early religious-revolutionary image or instead adopt the less "activist" views of the Imamis. Shah Abbas I, who, as already noted, wanted to follow the latter approach, construed the mention of Abu Muslim as a direct attack on his policies.

Adherents of Islamic mysticism (Sufis) were tolerated so long as the palace was certain of their loyalty. But among the ulama, the question of whether the Sufis' ceremonies, including the practice of music and dance, were acceptable remained a topic of fierce debate right up to the end of the Safavid dynasty; the parallels with the debates in Istanbul during the seventeenth century over the legitimacy of religious dance and spiritual music are striking. The rulers of Iran tended to switch their support from one side to another, thereby assuring themselves of the continuing loyalty of each.[196] This also enabled the shah to claim that he was acting impartially.

In common with many dervish sheikhs of this period, the Safavids also appointed deputies, the so-called *khalifa*s. Their task consisted of spreading the order to places that were often far removed from the established regional dervish centers or to strengthen the loyalty of supporters in existing "cells." Khalifas were frequently dispatched to Anatolia in the sixteenth century, where they would present secret adherents of the Safavid order with a characteristic piece of headgear known as the *taj*. Whenever the Ottoman–Safavid conflict spilled over into the open or threatened to do so, these meetings could become extremely dangerous both for the envoys from Iran and for their Anatolian hosts. Anyone who was caught could expect to be summarily executed.[197]

The reaction of the sultan's government to the khalifas was colored by a fear of espionage that was every bit as acute as latter-day manifestations of similar anxieties. In the often strained atmosphere between the two empires, the Ottoman sultans regarded the shah's subjects, who wanted to visit the tombs of Imam Ali and Imam Husayn in Iraq, with deep suspicion. Yet little could be done to prevent them from entering Iraq in peacetime, while it was the sultans' bounden duty to allow safe onward passage to pilgrims to Mecca. After all, the hajj is one of the fundamental duties of all Muslims who have the wherewithal to make the journey, and the sultans' legitimacy was largely contingent on their much-trumpeted protection of pilgrims. However, the Ottoman administration ordered that Iranian pilgrims should, wherever possible, be conducted to their destination through sparsely populated regions; there were also some instances of "suspicious" Iranians being lured into ambushes and killed. If the Ottoman side was concerned to maintain good relations with the shah's regime, the authorities could always blame such incidents on brigands. The account of an Iranian woman pilgrim who traveled to Mecca in the early seventeenth century testifies to the fears of the author and her companions when they had to stop over in Erzurum and Erzincan—it is noteworthy that their sojourn in Aleppo, though, also under Ottoman control, was far less worrisome.

In his own verse, Shah Ismail I presents himself as a reincarnation of earlier prophets and as a kind of demigod—a concept that the ulama in both the Shi'a and the Sunni tradition make no allowance for. Yet the veneration of the shah as a mythical or divine being was widespread in Anatolia and continued to be so long after the death of Shah Ismail I in 1524. For example, the poet known as Pir Sultan Abdal, who is thought to have lived in the region of Sivas in the seventeenth century, wrote a series of ecstatic poems in which he predicted his execution (which indeed seems to have followed shortly afterward) and expressed his desire to ascend to heaven to join his shah. It remains unclear whether he was referring to the then ruler of Iran or to some demigod figure in the afterlife.

In contrast, since the reign of Sultan Bayezid II, Ottoman rulers had unequivocally defined themselves as the guardians of Sunni Islam against "Shi'a heresy." There were even some legal and religious scholars in positions of great influence who maintained that the Shi'ites might not even be Muslims.[198] Likewise, a politicization of the Shi'a–Sunni split in the service of dynastic politics is also evident on the Iranian side. Thus, Ismail I promoted Shi'a as a kind of established state religion, although it is thought that the majority of the populace of the Safavid Empire during his reign were Sunni. Anyone wanting to climb the career ladder in government had first, at least for form's sake, to proclaim himself an Imami, in other words to embrace so-called Twelver Shi'ism. Yet in the early sixteenth century a purely pro forma conversion seems to have sufficed in many cases. In other instances, though, far more intense pressure was exerted.

In consequence, during this period, quite a large number of people were prompted by their Sunni convictions to emigrate to the Ottoman Empire. These emigrants included not just scholars but also military commanders, say, from the Caucasus region, who took up arms on behalf of the sultan when the Ottoman army appeared in their homeland. When these forces withdrew once more, those concerned had no option but to decamp across the border. Thanks to their extensive linguistic and geographical knowledge, many individuals from this background found ready employment in the Ottoman bureaucracy, not always to the delight of their homegrown competitors.[199]

Qizilbash and Ghulam

The early expansion of the Safavids' religious–political project to Anatolia, which we have already touched upon several times, was driven by some very practical considerations. For although it is assumed that the Ottomans, just like the Safavids, initially rose to power from a tribal background, even by the mid-fifteenth century the sultans ruled over an empire in which nomadic and semi-nomadic peoples were able to exercise power only at local level at best and—particularly important—play only a very minor role in the Ottoman armed forces, compared with the holders of military prebends (timar) and the Janissaries. As regards the successive capitals Edirne and Istanbul, power there lay in the hands of a decidedly sedentary bureaucracy, which included a significant number of religious and legal scholars.

By contrast, in the sixteenth century, the core of the army in Iran was made up of tribal groupings known as the qizilbash. During the reign of Shah Ismail I, some of these fighters believed so fanatically in their ruler's supernatural powers that they were prepared if need be to go into battle unarmed. However, his defeat at Çaldiran may well have weakened the charisma of the young ruler; indeed in the ten years after this setback, up to 1524, he shied away from any further conflict. Some of the names of qizilbash clans, such as the Shamlu, the Takkalu, and the Dhu'l-qadr, hint at connections with Anatolia and Syria. Over the following decades the qizilbash continued to form the principal support for the Safavid dynasty; up to the time of Shah Abbas I, important governorships were almost always filled by members of this group, and even after his reign they were still well represented among top administrative officials.

During the sixteenth century, the shahs' wives also included some members of qizilbash families; likewise, in this same period, many daughters and sisters of current rulers were also married to prominent members of the qizilbash. The women of the Safavid dynasty founded kinship groups that were admittedly less close-knit than those on the male side, but no less significant for that. Thus, the sons from such unions were entitled to call themselves "royal prince" *(mirza);* in this regard, Safavid practice in the sixteenth century differed markedly from that of the Ottomans, who made every effort to prevent the development of multiple branches of the ruling family descended from a nonruling prince.[200] Even so, a member of the qizilbash aristocracy, who was also a royal prince, could easily get caught up in a conflict of loyalties if (as not infrequently happened) his clan rebelled against the shah. Presumably, the same dilemma also faced any high-ranking representative of the qizilbash who had been appointed as a prince's tutor (as also often happened in the sixteenth century) if his fellow clan members chose to stage a revolt.

Shah Tahmasp I (r. 1524–1576) and especially Shah Abbas I attempted to establish royal households that were independent of qizilbash influence by raising an elite of military slaves, whose recruitment had some similarities with the Ottoman practice. In the latter domain, from the fifteenth century onward, the great majority of state servants who were not legal or religious scholars were regarded almost as slaves of the sultan. In Iran, though, these ghulam were drawn not from the populace of the central provinces, as was usually the case in the Ottoman Empire, but from the non-Muslim principalities of the Caucasus—especially Georgia—which lay within the Safavids' sphere of influence. This practice satisfied Islamic law, which forbade the enslavement of even the non-Muslim subjects of a Muslim ruler, so long as they did not rebel against their master.

Here as well, Islamization was the prerequisite for a successful career. Nevertheless, the shah was occasionally prepared to tolerate practices that harked back to the Christian past of his ghulam. Successful ghulam vied with prominent qizilbash for high office, including governors' posts, but could never entirely overcome their rivals; modern historians are divided over the extent of their influence. What is beyond dispute is that, together with the Shi'ite religious scholars, the ghulam formed the principal support for Shah Abbas I in his efforts to consolidate central power.

The Safavids also employed servant women from Georgia, sometimes in important positions. For instance, Eskandar Monshi recounts the tale of a woman called Gulcahra who was in service in Iran with a family with close links to the Safavids but who after the death of Shah Tahmasp I (1576) returned to Georgia in the retinue of a high-ranking official named Sama'an. When her new master had to travel to Istanbul, the women of the Georgian court also sent Gulcahra to the city, where she quickly came to prominence in the service of Safiye, the mother of Sultan Mehmed III. When war threatened to break out once more between the Ottomans and the Safavids, the Ottoman grand vizier Dervish Pasha dispatched her as an envoy to Shah Abbas I, where she tried (and failed) to broker a peace settlement at the last minute.[201]

Right up to the late sixteenth century, in terms of domestic policy, the primary aim of every shah was to secure the allegiance of both the qizilbash and the settled populace of Iran, together with its legal and religious scholars. Such integration could be sustained only by the personal efforts of individual shahs, and the deaths of Shah Ismail I (1524) and Shah Tahmasp I each sparked years of civil war; the rise to power of the very young Shah Abbas I (1587) also took place under somewhat irregular circumstances.[202] For Abbas's father and predecessor, Muhammad Khodabanda, was still alive; however, his near blindness meant that he could perform only limited regnal duties and could not effect the integration of important political groupings. From the reign of Shah Abbas I on, three rather than two groups had to be incorporated within the Safavid elite, as by this stage the ghulam had also risen to prominence alongside the qizilbash and dignitaries from the settled Persian population. Remarkably, although ostensibly a more complicated undertaking, this actually worked far better than in earlier times. In the seventeenth century, the succession was no longer accompanied by outbreaks of civil unrest and instead became a matter of routine.

Rulers, Dynasties, Princesses, and Palace Life

As we have seen, the political system of Safavid Persia was strongly geared toward the personality of the shah. Of course, any shah's first task was to operate successfully within the many-branched dynasty into which he had been born. In this respect, Shah Ismail I was a special case, inasmuch as he was descended from a line of dervishes, who had certainly had political ambitions and contacts to ruling dynasties but who had never formally ruled a polity in their own right. Sheikh Junayd, the grandfather of the first Safavid shah, had already moved to Anatolia in order to win supporters from among the nomadic clans there and had been killed in 1460 in a skirmish near the Samur River against the Shirwanshah dynasty. Ismail's father, Haydar, also fell in battle, while another branch of the family performed their traditional role as sheikhs of the Safaviyye dervish order at the shrine in Ardabil. Evidently, it was only after the death of his elder brothers that the shah Ismail (at that stage still very young) got the chance to even contest the accession. Any connections to palace culture that the future shah had are most likely to have come through his mother, Aliyya Begum, who was one of Uzun Hasan's daughters.[203]

Unlike the Ottomans, whose successors were born to slave women and whose wives, if they came from foreign dynasties, hardly ever bore future sultans, the family connections of many of the mothers and sisters of Safavid shahs are extremely well known. During the sixteenth century, the women of the dynasty played an especially active role: in this period they were not so closely confined to the harem as became the norm in the seventeenth century.[204] Some of these women had had a good education, notably Mahin Banu Khanum, who mastered the highly prized art of calligraphy. As a daughter of Shah Ismail and Tajlu Khanum, this princess was a full sister to the second shah Tahmasp I; she remained unmarried. In the second half of the sixteenth century, it was by no means uncommon for women members of the dynasty to accompany the ruler on horseback on hunting expeditions and sometimes even on military campaigns, too.

Yet male and female members of the ruling family alike operated mainly in dynastic politics. In the sixteenth century, princesses received a thorough grounding in such a role, being placed in their childhood under the protection of a guardian from the ranks of the qizilbash. In this context, Mongolian tradition may well have played a role, in which the aura of the ruling family also surrounded its female members. A few examples will suffice to illustrate this point: the chronicles, which otherwise are extremely unforthcoming about women, mention Tajlu Khanum, because this spouse of the empire's founder occasionally attempted to insert another of her sons on the throne in place of the heir apparent Tahmasp. In contrast, Mahin Banu (also known as Shahzada Sultanom) became an adviser to her brother Tahmasp after he ascended the throne. During the reign of Shah Ismail II (r. 1576–1578), his sister Pari Khan Khanum tried to fulfill the same role; there are even suggestions that she planned to usurp the throne herself.[205] She was also active in diplomacy, sending an envoy to Istanbul to try to obtain permission for her to donate Persian carpets to the mausoleums of Imam Ali and Imam Husayn in Ottoman-occupied Iraq (which in the event she was not granted). Under Shah Muhammad Khodabanda, who as already noted was hampered in his duties as a ruler because of his eye condition, his wife Khayr al-Nisa sometimes acted as de facto head of state.

It also seems to have been common practice for Muslim rulers in the second half of the sixteenth century not to personally go on the hajj to Mecca but instead to send female family members to show the flag for the dynasty at this holiest of sites. For instance, the shah sent his mother, the Mughal emperor Akbar one of his wives, and the Ottoman sultan Murad III at least one princess and maybe even more.[206]

Because the wives of the Safavid dynasty were also touched by the aura of royalty, they found themselves in extreme danger during conflicts over accession—although they were not murdered or rendered unfit for political life by being blinded nearly as frequently as royal princes were. For instance, Shah Abbas I had all his sons killed during his lifetime and ordered their sons—his own grandsons and sole successors on the male side and hence likely heirs apparent—imprisoned in the palace. After the shah's death, however, during the reign of his grandson and successor Shah Safi, many women from the palace harem were also killed in 1632; the sources give a figure of forty. Likewise, following the death of Shah Abbas I, the grandsons of the deceased ruler by his daughters, that is, his potential successors on the female side, were also either assassinated or blinded. Under Shah Safi, a purely patrilineal system of succession was brought in: henceforth, only the offspring of Shah Ismail I from the male line could ascend the throne, and the Shi'ite clergy, who stressed the legitimizing role of descent from an Imam, confirmed this privilege.

Hence, the political role of Safavid princesses was largely finished after 1632; in this later period, any women close to the ruler who managed to secure influential positions did so in their capacity as former slaves and concubines, who in time became the mothers of reigning monarchs. So, around 1629–1632, the role of women in the Safavid palace began to take on a remarkable resemblance to the system that had long since been established in the Ottoman Empire: an avoidance of multiple family branches but also the rise of the mothers of rulers to become the most important women at court.

In this context, the palace eunuchs also gained considerable political influence as the go-betweens for the queen mother resident in the harem. These individuals found themselves in the paradoxical position of being reviled at the Safavid court as "nonmen" and yet at the same time having access to high positions of power. Thus, in the seventeenth century, princes were typically raised by the palace eunuchs, while the other key roles of the latter also included administration of the royal treasury and the arsenal. In some cases, they even rose to become grand vizier. So Saru Taqi (d. 1645), who in this capacity served both Shah Safi and his successor Abbas II (r. 1642–1666) for many years, was a eunuch who exploited his access to the royal harem, then a center of political power struggles, as a way to carve himself out a political career.[207]

Forming part of the palace in the wider sense were a series of key institutions, such as the treasury and the royal stables and stud farm, already mentioned in the context of the Safavid army. The workshops attached to the court *(buyutat)* were also of enormous importance. These included, most significantly, the royal library, which was not only a repository of priceless books but also a center of book production. As was also the case in the *nakkaşhane* of the Ottoman court in the sixteenth century, the artists employed in the library of the Safavid palace were often responsible for creating templates that were later transposed by porcelain and textile specialists into their own respective media.[208]

Safavid palaces were geared toward ceremony that continued to make the monarch a very visible presence and was not, as happened in Istanbul from the mid-sixteenth century, designed to conceal him from profane public gaze. Therefore, a central role was accorded to banquets, which the ruler himself attended. The actual meal was preceded by a solemn procession of guests, sometimes including foreign ambassadors, bearing extravagant gifts. These occasions were often held on open terraces *(talar)* supported by a series of slender columns, a characteristic motif of Safavid palace architecture. These ceremonial banquets took place in full view of many people, especially because the palace of Shah Abbas I in Isfahan was situated right next to a large public square, which in turn opened onto an extensive bazaar.

Some commentators have seen this relatively easy access to the shah as a remnant of the egalitarian tradition prevalent among nomad groups, which saw the ruler as primus inter pares. However, a new study has shown that the accessibility of, say, Shah Abbas I—strictly graded according to the guest's rank—far from mitigating his tendency toward centralization and urge for absolute power, actually played into these, as the ruler could be seen standing in the midst of the cream of society and in the lavish banquets gave clear evidence of his generosity, in Iranian eyes a principal virtue for a ruler.[209]

The Power and Spreading Influence of Religious Scholars

Alongside the kadis and the preachers in the Friday mosques, the ulama also included a numbers of successors to the Prophet Muhammad as well as a group of specially qualified legal and religious scholars known as the *mujtahid;* these belonged almost exclusively to the sector of the population known as Iranians (Tajik) and not to the qizilbash.

At the beginning of his reign, Shah Ismail I regarded the establishment of the Twelver Shi'ite (Imami) faith as a key political objective. To this end he created a completely new office, known as the *sadr;* holders of this position were charged with spreading the new leader's faith throughout the country and combating tendencies that he deemed potentially heretical. Gradually, though, as this objective was achieved through the widespread adoption of the Imami religion, the political importance of this dignitary waned. Henceforth, his role was confined to overseeing pious foundations, whose incomes largely funded religious and legal scholars.[210]

The kadi court was responsible for administering justice for "common" subjects and sometimes also for emirs. Even so, in the seventeenth century the shahs sought to create a counterbalance to this system by establishing the appeal court of the so-called *diwanbegi*. Because this dignitary was an emir, it can be assumed that his views did not always accord with those of the legal and religious scholars (ulama). In the earlier years, appointments to the kadi court were one of the sadr's responsibilities, although other officials may also have been involved. It seems that, at least in the case of Isfahan, appointments to this post could be assumed either by a high religious officeholder or even by the ruler himself. It was not uncommon for sons to follow their fathers into this position. However, in the case of the Isfahan official known as the shaykh al-Islam, who in the early Safavid period was responsible for formulating case law in accordance with the beliefs of the Imamis, as well as performing similar tasks to those of the sadr, the Safavid shahs preferred to install people of their own choosing, in some instances Shi'ite immigrants from the Ottoman realm.[211]

Yet the role of the kadis clearly differed considerably from one age to the next and between towns. Thus, it has been observed of Tabriz in the late eighteenth century that the city's most powerful individuals did not occupy any official positions; the post of kadi there had become merely an honorary title. This situation explains why, as already noted, no kadi archives have survived from the Safavid Empire or the reign of Nadir Shah.[212] In the late seventeenth and early eighteenth centuries, many mujtahids appear to have cast doubt on the claim of the Safavids to be the hidden twelfth Imam's representatives on earth; in the view of these opponents, this role should properly have been filled by clerics. Such a marked self-confidence probably has to do with the fact that, in enacting his centralization policy, Shah Abbas I was heavily reliant on the support of the ulama, a trend continued by his successors. Accordingly, a mujtahid played a key role at the ceremonies that marked the accession of Shah Safi, while several years later a respected descendant of the Prophet was even appointed as grand vizier.

In the seventeenth century, the Safavids frequently married off princesses from their family to descendants of the Prophet and members of the religious hierarchy; for instance, even as late as 1712, ten years before the demise of the dynasty, a marriage was concluded between the director of the great pious foundations of Imam Reza in Mashhad and a daughter of Shah Sulayman (r. 1666–1694).[213] Given the persistent, if diluted, aura of power that surrounded even the female members of the Safavid dynasty, one consequence, almost certainly not foreseen at the outset, was that the male offspring of these unions, who in truth should have enjoyed special protection as descendants of the Prophet, often had their eyes put out to render them unsuitable as heirs apparent. But at the time when these marriage alliances were made, the main concern of the Safavid rulers was to forge closer ties between the ruling dynasty and the ulama.

Important developments also took place within the religious domain after 1600.[214] A series of scholars who were responsible for laying the foundation of Shi'ite theology were active during this period: for example, Muhammad Baqir Majlisi (1627–1698 or 1699) compiled and provided commentary to a major anthology of pronouncements of the Prophet Muhammad and his successors, as seen from the perspective of the Imamis. After the fall of the Safavids, many Shi'ite scholars emigrated to the Iraqi pilgrimage cities under Ottoman control, where, in spite of the ongoing tensions between the Ottoman sultan and Nadir Shah, life seemed less precarious. There, the theologian Aqa Muhammad Baqir Bihbihan (1705–1803; or in other sources c. 1705–c. 1793) formulated the intellectual framework for the remit of the mujtahids, to whom, thanks to their understanding and insight, he accorded the right and duty to assume leadership of the Muslim community.

Following the demise of the Safavids, the close ties between the ruler and the ulama were interrupted. Even under Nadir Shah but also in the period thereafter, secular rulers and the religious hierarchy often found themselves at variance with one another. But Bihbihan's definition of the role of the mujtahid enabled the Shi'ite ulama to keep functioning effectively in these changed circumstances.

Power, Money, and Bureaucracy in the
Center and the Provinces

It had been common practice in the Timurid and Aq-Qoyunlu Empires to dispatch young princes as titular governors to the provinces, where, equipped with their own court, they were meant to learn the art of kingship. In the sixteenth century, the same kind of princely education was also commonplace among both the Safavids and, until the 1570s, their Ottoman rivals. During this period, young princes from the dynasty of Shah Ismail I were given a guardian from one of the qizilbash clans; the bond of loyalty that customarily existed between a student and his tutor meant that the princes were linked to a particular clan. Conversely, a prince who became shah could, as head of the Safaviyye Sufi order, lay claim to the special devotion of the qizilbash.

As potential rivals, the princes in the provinces presented a problem to the ruling monarch; one well-known example of this is Alqas Mirza, who was driven by a clash over the succession with his brother Shah Tahmasp I to take refuge with the Ottoman Sultan Süleyman I. Süleyman attempted, albeit unsuccessfully, to use Alqas to make territorial gains from the Safavids and promptly dropped him when these efforts came to nothing.[215] Cases like this prompted Shah Abbas I to henceforth have princes educated in the royal palace. This enabled succession disputes to be kept to a minimum, but with the drawback that all new shahs thereafter had only minimal experience in the business of ruling and so had to rely on their courtiers. Conversely, this practice did mean that Safavid rule became more institutionalized; thus, until the crisis of the Afghan invasion in 1722, Shah Soltan Husayn managed to hold on to power for decades, despite the fact (to go by the accounts of many contemporary observers) that he showed little interest in the business of government.

Under the Timurids, the titular governor of a province (often called in the sources a *hakim;* pl. *hukkam*) was usually a high-placed emir; he was typically supported in this role by a "city captain" known as a darugha. The Safavids continued this practice; under their rule it was customary, especially in important centers like Isfahan, to directly appoint governors and their darugha. In this later period, a greater tendency to specialization is evident, meaning that the city captain no longer had access to the finances of the city that he controlled. Also, the shah could at any time take control over a particular area of responsibility; when Shah Abbas I, for instance, made Isfahan into his seat of government in the late sixteenth century and set about expanding the city, he assumed personal responsibility for various administrative tasks, even some relatively routine ones.[216]

Under both the Timurids and Safavids, special departments (diwan) were responsible for raising taxes; yet collection of these revenues was farmed out, a practice that also spread quickly in the Ottoman Empire of the sixteenth century. In fiscal terms, some provinces counted as the personal possession of the Safavid ruler (*khassa*, sometimes also *khalsa*). In the course of the seventeenth century, this practice was extended to cover more and more of the empire. Under the rule of the Timurids and also the Aq-Qoyunlu and the Karaquyunlu, the taxes from a larger region were generally allocated to a prince or a Turcoman emir, who would use it to pay his bureaucrats or armed forces. Beneficiaries of this kind of hereditary tax allocation enjoyed immunity: other tax collectors were not allowed to enter the area assigned to him.[217]

This arrangement, which was also practiced on a more limited scale by the Safavids—especially when religious and legal scholars were concerned—was known as *suyurghal*. In the Safavid period, this form of allocation seems to have been regarded as the preserve of the ulama; occasionally, even religious foundations are described as the suyurghal of their directors. Whereas a suyurghal was hereditary, the tax allocations called *tuyul* were granted in recompense for particular services rendered and were strictly linked to fulfillment of the task in question; these were therefore not intended to be hereditary. Nevertheless, in practice these conditions were not always observed. At the local level, tax collection lay in the hands of official called *kalantar;* in exceptional cases, such as the Armenian quarter of New Julfa in Isfahan, this task could also be assigned to a non-Muslim.

Alongside these officials who worked closely with the central government, there were also individuals who came from the urban elite and who fulfilled a number of different functions, which in other states were performed by a centrally directed agency. One of these influential people was the *naqib,* who might best be described as the legal representative of the descendants of the Prophet Muhammad. It was his task to ensure that the numerous descendants of the Prophet really did receive income from the many institutions that had been established over the centuries to benefit them. Conversely, he was also called upon to pass sentence on these people if they were accused of some transgression. In addition, the naqib also seems to have had a say in the raising of taxes owing from city guilds.

Cities as Political and Religious Centers

Before Shah Ismail I founded his dynasty, Tabriz and Herat were the main regional centers. Tabriz had an illustrious past, as the seat of the Il-Khanate and the Aq-Qoyunlu. Yet even by the mid-seventeenth century, when the Ottoman traveler Evliya Çelebi was resident in this city for some months, the formerly towering mausoleum of Ghazan Khan had been damaged by an earthquake and was falling down. Even so, Evliya enthusiastically admired the city's beautiful sights, especially the mosque founded by and bearing by the name of Aq-Qoyunlu ruler Sultan Hasan.[218] Tabriz was also favored as a residence by the early Safavids. After Shah Ismail I captured Herat, he put artists from the former Timurid palace of Husayn Buyqara to work on the Safavid residence in Tabriz. However, it soon became apparent that the region was too exposed to Ottoman attack. For when Sultan Selim I entered the former capital of the Ilkhans in 1514, his booty included the artists from the Safavid palace in Tabriz: those who survived the long march were taken back to Istanbul, where they arrived in around 1516.[219] However, those artists who wanted to return to Iran were able to do so once Sultan Süleyman had succeeded to the throne in 1520.

Under Ismail I's successor Shah Tahmasp I, the Safavids made Qazvin, south of the Elburz Mountains to the northwest of Tehran, their capital. There they built not only a large palace with gardens but also mosques and a centrally situated square, characteristic of major Iranian cities. Evliya Çelebi reports that by the mid-seventeenth century a mosque there, named for its founder Sheikh Dühük, was held sacred by Sunni Muslims as well as by Shi'ites. But what most impressed the traveler was the so-called Müşebbek mosque, both in terms of its size and the excellence of its design; he particularly drew attention to the inlay work on the dome and the private box where the ruler of the day attended prayers.[220] However, the Ottoman traveler avoided even mentioning most of the buildings from the Safavid period.

Shah Abbas I preferred the city of Isfahan, further to the south, which he graced with the addition of a whole new district, including a principal mosque, a new

palace, and the famous park known as the Chahar Bagh. These new city quarters
became the seat of the government, while the old city center was turned over to
craftsmen and merchants. Official population figures do not exist for this period;
however, European visitors estimated that in the seventeenth century, the capital
popularly called a name meaning "half of the world" was home to around half a
million people, at least when the court was in residence there. This made Isfahan
larger than any European city of the same period, probably even including Istanbul.
Yet some extrapolations put the figure at a maximum of just 100,000, even in the
late sixteenth century.[221]

Furthermore, many cities in the Safavid Empire were renowned as religious
centers. Both Sheikh Safi, for whom the Safaviyye order is named, and the founder
of the dynasty, Shah Ismail I, were buried in Ardabil; because many people wanted
to have their own final resting place near to these two greatly revered figures, an
extensive cemetery formed part of the complex. But an even more exalted status
was accorded to Mashhad, site of the mausoleum of Imam Reza. Mahin Banu
Khanum, whom we have already encountered as a calligrapher and adviser to her
brother Shah Tahmasp, donated jewelry, weapons, and Chinese porcelain to this
shrine. Shah Abbas I even undertook a pilgrimage on foot from Isfahan to
Mashhad, a distance of over 1,000 kilometers. It seems that the shah was concerned
with promoting this pilgrimage site at a time when the Ottomans had reconquered
Iraq, making visits to the shrines of Imam Ali and his son Imam Husayn a much
more difficult proposition. Conversely, as we have already briefly touched upon,
the Iranian ruler had just managed to win back Mashhad from the neighboring
Uzbeks. They had sacked the shrine several times, as they regarded the complex
as a specifically Shi'ite devotional site that could have no claim to protection by
a Sunni ruler.

By contrast, in the sixteenth century, the Fatima Masumeh shrine in Qom—a
city better protected from foreign incursions—was the object of devotion for the
princesses of the Safavid dynasty, who withdrew there to pray from time to time;
both Tajlu Khanum and Mahin Banu Khanum helped furnish the shrine. Later
members of the Safavid dynasty preferred to be interred at this pilgrimage site.

Most Safavid shahs displayed a high degree of mobility, even if not all of them
traveled around quite as frequently as Shah Abbas I. Perhaps this fact—together
with need to promote trade, of course—explains the high priority that Iran's rulers

gave to the expansion of caravansaries along the main arterial routes through the region. In addition, along the road that ran from Isfahan to the monarchs' summer palaces on the Caspian Sea, a number of small pavilions were constructed for occasional use by the shah as hunting lodges.[222] The inhospitable natural conditions in the Great Salt Desert (Dasht-e Kavir) of central Iran only increased the need for public investment: cases are recorded where a recently built caravansary had to be abandoned and replaced by a new one in a different location because the water supply was insufficient.

The End of the Safavids

The last Safavid ruler to govern Iran in its entirety was Shah Soltan Husayn (1694–1722). He continued the policies of his predecessors, which aimed at supporting the established clerical hierarchy of the Imamis through pious foundations and the implementation of shari'a law but also through opposition to forms of Islamic philosophy and mysticism deemed dangerous by religious scholars. While this policy did not prevent the shah from maintaining friendly relations with those scholars who called for philosophical ideas to become an integral part of the public discourse of the age, antiphilosophical tendencies, especially directed against the Sufis, still predominated. Members of the dynasty spent large amounts setting up schools in which the orthodox position of the religious hierarchy was passed on to future generations.

It is also fair to assume that the intermittent attempts undertaken in the late seventeenth and early eighteenth centuries by Iran's rulers to put administrative pressure on non-Shi'ites to convert must have had the support of the majority of the established Shi'ite hierarchy. In any event, this policy was actively promoted by the influential head of the legal and religious scholars, Muhammad Baqir Majlisi. However, if we are to believe the Ottoman envoy Dürri Ahmed Efendi, who visited the shah's court in 1720 and 1721, many Persian Sunni subjects were alienated from their Safavid rulers, a situation no doubt exacerbated by this policy, and so gave the representative of the Ottoman sultan a hero's welcome in many of the places he visited.[223] The Sunni Lesgians, who lived in the northwest of the country, even staged a revolt, which among other things was provoked by the heavy-handed rule of the local Safavid governor, and sought Ottoman support. This insurrection was probably one of the reasons behind the decision to dispatch Dürri Ahmed Efendi, whose linguistic skills and knowledge of the country made him a tailor-made candidate to lead a "fact-finding mission" and possibly also to win over future recruits to the sultan's cause.

Under such circumstances, the support of the religious hierarchy could not really hope to compensate for the fundamental weak points in Safavid rule, notably current economic problems: especially serious was the steady draining away of the country's precious metal resources to India, a phenomenon that had been around for centuries but that was exacerbated around 1700 by the involvement of English and Dutch trading companies (the East India Company and the VOC, respectively). By now, these enterprises were no longer particularly interested in exporting Iranian silk, and they transferred their capital to India instead. The lack of demand for raw silk also had a negative impact on the finances of the shah and on the country's entire economy.[224] Natural disasters and failed harvests caused a sharp reduction in revenue, which the shah's treasury tried to make up for by raising tax rates. Food riots in Isfahan even had to be put down using military force.

As the situation deteriorated, the ruler Soltan Husayn found it impossible to quell an insurrection that broke out on the borders of the Safavid Empire, at Kandahar in present-day Afghanistan.[225] Mir Ways Ghilzay had established independent rule there in 1709; subsequently, in 1721 his son Mahmud, who was a Sunni rather than a Shi'ite, launched attacks against the empire's central provinces, and as the Safavid forces failed to drive him back, he penetrated even deeper into the Iranian interior, laying siege to Isfahan in 1722. After several months, the city was forced to surrender. Mahmud Ghilzay proceeded to proclaim himself the new ruler of Iran, as Mahmud Shah, and took his predecessor Soltan Husayn captive. In 1729, the former shah was put to death by Mahmud's successor Ashraf. However, one of Soltan Husayn's sons, Tahmasp Mirza, had managed to escape and likewise had himself proclaimed shah in the former capital of Qazvin. Yet Tahmasp II was quickly expelled by forces loyal to the new ruler.[226] The following years saw the appearance of several pretenders with more or less fictitious connections to the outgoing dynasty.

This period witnessed the rise of the later ruler Nadir Shah, who came from a humble background but who by 1727 had risen to become the *Itimad al-dawla* of Tahmasp II—the Persian grand vizier. Nadir Shah succeeded in bringing the

Pashtun Ghilzays' rule over Iran to an end. In 1732, this by now powerful military commander deposed his sovereign, replacing him with a prince who was still a baby. Evidently, even at this late stage, Nadir Shah believed that, as a man with no connections to the preceding dynasty who had come to power only "at the point of a sword," he would not be acknowledged as shah without acquiring further legitimacy.

The new ruler attempted to gain this legitimacy through various means: primarily by marrying off one of his sons to a Safavid princess but also by soliciting support in 1736 among respected figures from both the settled and nomadic communities, in accordance with the ancient Mongol tradition. Subsequently, after embarking on a major pillaging raid into northern India and defeating the Mughal emperor Mohammad Shah, he proclaimed himself as the "Great King" to whom both the Indian ruler and the khan of Uzbekistan should be subservient. In this context, Nadir Shah was fond of citing both the Timurid tradition—after all, Timur had also pillaged far and wide in India in his time—and his own Afshar heritage, namely, a tribe that spoke a Turkic language. His propagandists sometimes even spoke in terms of a "clan" of great rulers, which was thought to include the Ottoman sultans in the west, Nadir Shah, and, as the successors to Timur, also the Mughal dynasty of India.[227]

However, the most ambitious of all Nadir Shah's undertakings was surely the attempt to reconcile Sh'ia Islam to the Sunni tradition. This project may even have been intended—although this is hotly disputed—to bring Iran fully back into the Sunni fold. In political terms, Nadir Shah clearly hoped that this move would divest the clash with the Ottoman sultans of the religious dimension that it had always had, to a greater or lesser extent, under the Safavids. Instead, within the framework of Sunni Islam, a fifth school of religious jurisprudence (madhhab or mahzab) was to be established that would be named for the imam Jafar and would be recognized as just as orthodox as the four existing schools—the Hanafi, the Hanbali, the Maliki, and the Shafi'i. In line with this, it was hoped that the Ottoman sultans would establish a special prayer space for the new school at the Great Mosque in Mecca, like those that had long existed there for the other four schools.

The differences between the traditional Sunni law schools did not, and do not, prevent their followers from recognizing one another as devout orthodox Muslims, and Nadir Shah hoped that this would henceforth also be the case with the fifth school. Yet the project foundered on the opposition of the Ottoman sultan Mahmud I (r. 1730–1754) and that of the ulama of Istanbul, who rejected the project not least because of its inherent violation of tradition. Even so, the shah and the sultan concluded a peace treaty in 1746, thereby ending almost two and a half centuries of mutual vilification as apostates and heretics that sometimes flared up into open conflict.

Similarly, the Shi'ite hierarchy also dismissed out of hand any absorption into the Sunni community. At two meetings convened by Nadir Shah in 1736 and 1743, several legal and religious scholars from the two traditions had initially reached a provisional agreement, but this gesture was most likely conditioned by fear of the dreadful punishments that might otherwise be meted out to them—the shah became notorious for this in the final years of his reign. In theological terms, the founding of a new school of jurisprudence would mean recanting everything that constituted the core faith of a devout Twelver Shi'ite.[228]

The Economy

The possibilities and limitations of agriculture in Iran are strictly determined by its topography: a broad range of mountains, where most population centers are located, runs from the northwest to the southeast. Immediately south of the Caspian Sea is a narrow strip of land with a subtropical climate, which is separated from the rest of the country by a steep mountain range; even in the Safavid period, this region was relatively densely populated. In contrast, because of the extremely hot climate, the coastal strip beside the Gulf of Basra has comparatively few inhabitants. Beyond the main mountain range lies an arid region comprising deserts and salt lakes, which has to be crossed to reach the far east of the country, where there are also some scattered upland regions. This area contains some extremely favorable terrain for farming, especially around Mashhad, the most important city in the northeast of the Safavid Empire. There, such as around Sistan in the far southeast, independent farmers had established themselves, far from major arterial roads used by Ottoman, Uzbek, and other forces in their invasions.[229]

In other regions, though, both under the Aq-Qoyunlu and the Safavids, the land was controlled by magnates, who often also played a role in the government of the empire as a whole. Frequently, these powerful figures had assumed tax-farming responsibilities over the farmers of the region, while channeling only a relatively small proportion of the funds to the central administration. In addition, the shah would occasionally divert these tax payments to his military commanders, who in return were obliged to supply troops for any campaigns the ruler saw fit to undertake. It is debatable whether the Safavid shahs were regarded as the overlords of all the country's agriculturally productive land. Private individuals endowed religious foundations, which in accordance with Islamic law they could furnish only with goods that were their full property, meaning that the shah must at least have granted such potential founders the land on which the future institution would be built. Moreover, Shah Abbas I appears to have drawn a distinction between the holdings that he considered his private property and those that belonged to the dynasty. In 1606–1608, he signed over his entire personal stock of real estate to a religious foundation without touching the land that belonged to the crown.

In many regions, as in the vicinity of the long-standing capital of Isfahan, land was made suitable for farming only by ingenious irrigation systems. To minimize the water loss through evaporation, the culverts for these systems were often dug underground, requiring an experienced and trained personnel to maintain them. In wartime, these channels often became unusable, forcing farmers to suspend operations for long periods. The cultivation of silkworms, another important source of income for the Safavids, was very conflict sensitive: both Ottoman pillaging raids and the scorched-earth policy that some Safavid rulers employed in times of invasion must have put silkworm farmers in a desperate position.

As in the Ottoman Empire, the plot of land held in fee (virgate) was the basic unit both in terms of cultivation and for taxation purposes. Even the terminology shows resemblances: the commonest word in Iran for such units (*juft*) corresponded to the usual Turkish term *çift;* in both instances, these designated a plot of land that could be plowed by a team of oxen and that was large enough to ensure a livelihood for a single family. In fertile areas, therefore, the *juft/çift* was often smaller than in mountainous regions or on arid steppeland.[230] In addition, in both the Safavid and Ottoman Empires, the practice was widespread of having revenue sources that were, strictly speaking, payable to the central financial administration allocated directly to particular designated groups or individuals; while this avoided the transport of large sums of cash, it also made accounting much less transparent and increased the likelihood of disputes.

As we have already seen, nomadic tribes played a far more significant political role in the Safavid Empire than they did in the sultan's realm: ultimately, they were far more numerous in Persia, because the country's topography made it far more difficult to turn them into settled communities than in Anatolia. For the years around 1900—figures do not exist for the period under consideration here—it has been estimated that city dwellers made up less than 10 percent of the total population of Iran, while farmers accounted for around 60 percent. In these circumstances, tribal groupings must have comprised more than 30 percent of the population. According to geographical conditions, these groups specialized in raising either horses, camels, or sheep. Sheep provided the wool that nomads and settled communities alike used to weave the famous Persian carpets.

Trade

Alongside legal and religious scholars, merchants were some of the most prosperous and respected of Iran's city dwellers. However, in many areas of trade, officials who were responsible for the shah's coffers and who operated in the ruler's name and on his account competed against nonprivileged traders from the subject classes. Even so, the merchants' profit margins must have been extremely healthy, for a stall in the covered marketplace that Shah Ismail I created in his first capital of Tabriz attracted a daily rental charge of thirty local dinar. Nor, evidently, was the bazaar laid out in Isfahan by Shah Abbas I ever empty. Especially after the monarch made this city into his capital, many foreign traders began to beat a path to it: beside merchants from the various Christian communities, these also included Indians, Tatars, and Arabs, who clearly saw it as advantageous to offer their wares outside the royal palace.[231] However, for the period in question here, not much is known about the Muslim traders of the Safavid Empire, in contrast to the Armenians. This is because neither the chroniclers nor the compilers of biographical encyclopedias treating the lives of the ulama paid the mercantile class much heed.

Evliya Çelebi has provided some useful insights into the commercial life of Tabriz in the mid-seventeenth century. Although the town, as the author himself concedes, had suffered great damage during the preceding Ottoman occupation, by the time Evliya visited Tabriz, the reconstruction program ordered by Shah Abbas I was largely complete. The traveler mentions two hundred caravansaries, many of them probably in the immediate vicinity of Tabriz, and seventy other mercantile buildings within the city precincts. He also marveled at the great domed bazaar where wealthy merchants conducted their business, which he compared with the widely renowned business center of Aleppo. Evliya recounts of Hamadan that the city was home to three caravansaries made of brick or stone, and he singles out for particular praise the complex built by an Ottoman pasha. He also talks about eleven mercantile buildings in the same city and a bazaar that supposedly contained two thousand shops; this was frequented by traders from both India in the east and the Ottoman Empire in the west. Meanwhile, Urmiya, which the author calls Rûmiyye, was only a midsize town in the eyes of Iranians who knew the empire well, but even so, Evliya was entranced by the many shops that the proprietors often decked out with flowers, as well as with the rich merchants and the large bazaar that boasted several domes. His account indicates that the latter specialized in silk fabrics.[232]

Evliya's descriptions are fundamentally optimistic, but especially in the second half of the seventeenth century, internal trade in Iran began to suffer as a result of a shortage of metal for coinage—a situation that, as already noted, was made worse at this time by the activities of European trading companies. The Dutch, in particular, rather than buying Iranian silk, now went for silk from China or Bengal. And to ensure that they had the necessary ready cash to hand, they exported the money that they had made by selling woolen fabrics and other merchandise in Iran. But because the Safavid Empire was reliant on foreign trade for gold and silver, and cashless transactions were very rare, these changes in the world market also became a source of problems for internal trade.

In connection with his account of the country's trading centers, Evliya also describes the system of market inspection, which both in Tabriz and Urmiya was carried out very strictly: all foodstuffs were sold by weight, and the stalls were fitted out with scales with standard weights, which the merchants could not tamper with. People who used false weights ran the risk of brutal corporal punishment, including blinding.[233] Counterfeiters and coin clippers could reckon on a death sentence.

The Export of Silk

A considerable proportion of the raw silk produced in Iran was destined for export. Since the fifteenth century, traders from Europe and the Ottoman Empire eagerly sourced silk from northern Iran, which the weavers of Spitalfields in London and their counterparts in Istanbul turned into fabric of both high and middling quality. The foreign earnings that Shah Ismail I amassed from this export trade prompted his rival Sultan Selim I to ban the import of Iranian silk into his territories and imprison traders who were subjects of the shah and happened to be on Ottoman soil at that time. He also impounded their stocks of raw silk. For a brief spell, the merchants and silk weavers of Bursa still managed to get hold of supplies through Aleppo. But when Selim I conquered the city in 1516, this last marketing opportunity for Iranian raw silk in the Ottoman Empire was also closed off.[234]

However, Sultan Süleyman the Magnificent soon revoked this ban. Aside from the consideration that this compromising of the livelihoods of subjects who had no direct involvement in the conflict violated Islamic law, the plight of the unemployed silk weavers of Istanbul and Bursa may well have had a bearing on this decision. Yet when the ban was lifted and the silk trade revived, it appears that most of the Iranian merchants who came to sell raw silk in Bursa, Tokat, or Aleppo were no longer Muslims but Armenians.[235] It may well be that these traders were better placed to sell their wares on Ottoman territory, because as Christians they were not tainted by the suspicion of playing a dual role as agents of the Sufi Safaviyye order. In any event, the so-called Persian merchants (*acem tüccarları*) who were extremely active on Ottoman soil in the seventeenth and particularly the eighteenth century and who were represented by their own consuls (*şehbender*) were mostly Armenians.

During the frequent Ottoman–Safavid wars, raw silk was always a favorite booty item for Ottoman forces; in the long term, these disruptions may well have contributed to driving up the cost. But the price rises on the Ottoman market in the late sixteenth century, insofar as they were not caused by currency devaluation, were primarily the result of increased demand for this commodity on the European market. English merchants were at the forefront of this clamor for raw silk, first via Aleppo and, from the seventeenth century on, via Izmir, too.[236]

In 1619 Abbas I seized the entire silk production of his empire to swell his own coffers, a situation that lasted until the shah's death in 1629. Armenian traders were expected to take over the marketing of the commodity; they had already gained experience in this area and continued to play an important role after the monopoly on this trade was lifted. At the height of his conflict with the Ottomans, the shah planned to have the whole raw silk production of Iran exported by the sea route by European traders, a move intended to seriously compromise the sultan's economy.

However, this project came to nothing: for a start, the English and Dutch merchants could not raise the necessary capital to fund such a large-scale venture. Armenian middlemen preferred to sell a portion of the raw silk in Aleppo and other markets on Ottoman territory. Although homegrown silk production in the Ottoman Empire had begun in the early seventeenth century around Bursa and on the Peloponnese, there was still a large demand for the Iranian product. Plus the Armenian traders could get a better price when the European companies competed with one another to buy the goods either at Aleppo or within Iran itself. Ultimately, Shah Abbas I lost interest in the enterprise when he was no longer at war with the Ottoman sultan.

Most modern historians concur in identifying a decline in the importance of Iranian silk on the world market in the second half of the seventeenth century. In this situation, Dutch traders operating in Iran tried reducing the amount of silk that they had contracted with the Safavid treasury to purchase. Conversely, in Isfahan the Iranian authorities often had problems supplying the quantities of silk stipulated in their contracts with Europeans. Conflict seemed preprogrammed into the system.[237]

In contrast, Armenian traders attempted to open up new markets by initiating contacts with the court of the Russian tsar and by trying to establish an alternative route for silk exports through Russia: Tsar Peter I took a personal interest in this undertaking, as he planned to establish a homegrown textile industry. But as the customs registers for the border town of Erzurum show, the long-established trade route through northern Anatolia also continued to be important in the seventeenth century. However, after 1722, the conflicts arising from the collapse of the Safavid dynasty hit northern Iran particularly hard, and Iranian raw silk promptly disappeared from the Erzurum customs records. The English merchants who throughout the seventeenth century had exchanged Iranian silk for woolen goods in Aleppo now sought alternative sources of income.

The Role of the Armenians in Foreign Trade

The Armenian traders who played a central role in exporting Iranian silk originally hailed from the city of Julfa in northern Iran. Shah Abbas I forced them to move and had Julfa razed to the ground, perhaps to prevent the émigrés from returning to their homeland or simply within the context of the scorched-earth policy, which formed part of the Safavid military strategy against Ottoman incursions. Following their arrival in Isfahan, the Armenians were resettled in their own newly established part of the city, which they named New Julfa after their former home and which lay across the river directly opposite the new quarter founded by Shah Abbas I. Here they were allowed to erect a series of richly decorated churches, which in a special act of conciliation were occasionally visited by seventeenth-century Iranian rulers. New Julfa was controlled by the most prosperous of the Armenian merchants, whose main role was to pay tax levies to the shah's treasury but who also occasionally were called upon to represent the interests of their community. It may have been the intention of the Safavid rulers to integrate these wealthy merchants into their governmental apparatus, to form a fourth center of power alongside the ulama, the qizilbash, and the ghulam. As a result, the rich Armenian merchants were made beholden to the shah's household, while, correspondingly, the community enjoyed the ruler's protection.

According to a manual of administration compiled in the mid-eighteenth century, in the century before, the Armenians had become an important source of finance for the royal household through the gold and silver that they earned from their export of raw silk.[238] However, some historians play down the significance of this text, because its author was merely reporting supposed facts in hindsight; he was writing at a time when the Safavids had already fallen from power and hence was already relatively remote from the events of the seventeenth century. But in this particular case, his account is borne out by an edict issued by Shah Safi in 1629, which also emphasizes the major contribution made by the Armenians to the empire's economy.

Over the course of the seventeenth century, though, life became more and more difficult for these traders in Isfahan. The treasury's problems mounted to the point where it increased the tax burden. In addition, the rulers and their advisers often attempted to deflect the people's discontent over economic misery onto convenient scapegoats. Rich non-Shiʻites, in particular the Armenian community, often bore the brunt of these repressive measures. Leading figures from this community often came under official or semiofficial pressure to convert to Shiʻa Islam, and many fell in line with this. With the siege of Isfahan in 1722, the situation became truly untenable for many Armenian traders, not least because the endless conflicts of this period caused the Iranian raw silk market to collapse. Many of those who could still salvage some possessions emigrated; Armenian émigrés from Isfahan appeared at this time both in India and in Venice.

Textile Manufacture

Despite the importance of raw silk as an export commodity, weaving was nevertheless a thriving industry within Iran. Mainly local manufactures were available in the countryside: wool, goat's hair, and cotton provided the raw materials for simple fabrics. Travelers frequently remarked that both men and women were engaged in spinning and weaving; however, virtually nothing is known about the mechanisms by which the producers distributed their textiles to local inhabitants, neighbors, or family members. In particular, foreign observers often noted the huge extent of Iranian textile production.[239] Midsize towns produced cloth for their immediate environs, whereas Tabriz, Mashhad, Yazd, Kashan, Kerman, and above all the capital Isfahan supplied the supraregional market as well as the Safavid ruler's court; in addition, a numbers of weavers worked exclusively for the export market. In the Ottoman Empire, the terminology of silk cloth weaving, such as the word *zerbaft* for gold brocade, is largely of Iranian origin. It is reasonable to surmise that silk cloth from the empires of the Ilkhans, the Aq-Qoyunlu, and the Timurids also stimulated homegrown Ottoman production. Tabriz was a center of the cotton- and silk-processing industry: in the seventeenth and early eighteenth centuries, velvets and the silk fabric called *deriya,* which looked similar to modern taffeta, were widely in demand.[240] Mashhad was also a center of silk manufacture, while the weavers of Yazd specialized in mixed weaves of silk and cotton. In addition, this city also produced brocade made from brass thread "for the more modest budget," which for the first few months of wear was indistinguishable from gold brocade.

Kashan produced silk fabrics, mixed weaves, and also carpets of high quality; velvet from Kashan often appeared in diplomatic gifts from Iranian dignitaries. This city became especially renowned for its silk fabrics decorated with images of animals and also people, for in the Iran of the sixteenth to eighteenth centuries, the Islamic ban on representing living beings was valid only in a religious context.[241] Kerman was particularly famous in the seventeenth century for its painted cotton textiles; and since Shah Abbas I had moved his capital to Isfahan, the textile manufacturers of this city had a large and deep-pocketed circle of customers in the Safavid court, for the court needed large quantities of expensive fabrics especially for the many honorary garments that the rulers distributed at state occasions and other special events. However, in this respect, the shah himself and his innermost circle at least in part were "self-caterers," for as we have seen, the palace had its own workshops. Brocade weaving also flourished in Isfahan, with producers making it from both silver and gold thread. Likewise, elaborately dyed and painted cotton fabrics from the city were also much sought after by foreign visitors.

Traditional Persian clothing also included fabric belts with intricately embroidered ends; during the seventeenth century, these were also greatly in demand in Poland, as they formed part of the so-called Sarmatic costume then popular among the country's noblemen. Meanwhile, prosperous qizilbash put on their own ostentatious show with the taj, a red turban surmounted by a tall conelike structure, which symbolized their membership of the Sufi Safaviyye order. This headdress could sometimes be decorated with precious stones; this was certainly the case whenever the shah attempted to persuade a foreign potentate such as the exiled Mughal emperor Humayun, who was resident at the Safavid court from 1543 to 1545, to wear the taj. For all its symbolic value, this style of headgear was still subject to the vagaries of fashion. But because it had become a distinctive symbol of the Safavids, it was viewed with great suspicion on Ottoman soil and could bring its wearer some unpleasant encounters. Thus, during the Ottoman occupation of Tabriz around 1600, its inhabitants thought it wise to hide their taj, but as soon as the city was retaken by Shah Abbas I in 1603, the contentious headgear reappeared. However, when the Safavid dynasty came to an end, the headdress so strongly associated with the defeated regime disappeared once and for all.

Other pieces of prestigious clothing were the twill fabrics known as *shal,* which were produced from the wool of a particular type of goat or from the finest lambswool and which had intricate decorative patterns woven into them. They were used as belts or for turbans. From the seventeenth century on, these fabrics are clearly identified in the sources; coarser, cheaper versions were made for the local market. Before the advent of the jacquard loom, though, shal cloth was renowned as a luxury item that was extremely difficult to manufacture. Nevertheless, the producers faced stiff competition from similar fabrics imported from Kashmir; evidently, this form of weaving only really got going in Iran once it was already firmly established in India.[242]

The Widespread Impact of the Arts

A particularly noteworthy form of textile production was the manufacture of both woven and knotted carpets. Sadly, no unequivocally Iranian-produced carpets have been preserved from medieval times; thus, although this art form undoubtedly goes back much further in time, we know about it at firsthand only from the late fifteenth century, with examples becoming more numerous after 1500. At least a few miniature paintings give us some clue about the carpets made in the Timurid period: at that time, it seems the vogue was for small patterns of the kind familiar to us from surviving contemporary silk fabrics.

The large and elaborate carpets from the early Safavid period, of which a few original examples have survived, present quite a different picture. Some of these not only have inscriptions giving their exact date but there are also a few cases where the producers are mentioned by name. Magnificent pieces such as these were clearly destined for shrines or palaces; yet there survive hardly any of the smaller carpets of this early era produced, say, for the houses of the more prosperous inhabitants of Isfahan or Tabriz or for nomads' tents.[243]

From the sixteenth century on, Persian carpets were characterized by patterns in which elaborately curved scroll decoration predominated, contained within a basic grid framework. In some cases, two or even three of these grids were superimposed on one another. Figures of animals or people could be incorporated in this basic pattern so long as the carpet was being made for a nonreligious setting. For instance, there are examples of wild animals attacking their prey, a familiar

Medallion carpet with lions, tigers, gazelles, and (possibly) billy goats depicted on the inner panel; the imagery probably represents a hunting scene. In the corners, birds are seen cavorting, while the borders consist of peacock-like birds and fishes or reptiles, which are evidently in the process of seizing prey. Iran, late sixteenth century. (Museum für Islamische Kunst, SMB/Gerhard Murza)

Garden carpet. While this genre was already known of in the Safavid period, only very few examples have survived, with most extant carpets of this type coming from the late eighteenth or early nineteenth century. Stylized flowers depict planted borders, while bands represent waterways in which fish are seen jumping. Northwestern Iran, circa 1800. (Museum für Islamische Kunst, SMB/Reinhard Friedrich)

motif from the Sassanid period. But mythical beasts also make an appearance: these include winged fairylike figures (Persian: *pari*) as well as dragons, derived from Chinese ornamentation. In addition, there are several depictions of everyday people, such as figures hunting on horseback. Occasionally, carpets would be produced illustrating episodes from a literary work. Another design, of which surviving examples date mostly from the eighteenth century, was inspired by the traditional layout of Iranian gardens, with watercourses, flower beds, and straight paths. By examining the way the decoration is arranged and the knotting techniques, experts have attempted to ascribe the surviving carpets to particular places of manufacture. However, there is still a great deal of uncertainty in this regard.

Carpets were among the diplomatic gifts that Iranian envoys brought with them to Istanbul and elsewhere. Some Persian prayer rugs, which were carefully stored at the sultan's palace, have been preserved in excellent condition.[244] These Iranian carpets had an important influence in the development of Ottoman carpet manufacture: for while the Anatolian tradition favored geometrical patterns and mostly continued to produce such carpets, in the second half of the sixteenth century, the sultan's court began to demand carpets in the Persian mode, decorated with sinuous scrollwork but without any depictions of people or animals. Around 1600, the meeting of these two traditions gave rise to the type of Turkish carpet known as Ushak (from its place of manufacture, in western Anatolia), which is characterized by a basically abstract pattern but replete with elaborate arabesques.

In the period under discussion here, Persian carpets were not yet being exported to Europe on a large scale; among the goods dispatched by English and Dutch merchants in the seventeenth century, these textiles, which became very highly prized after 1800, are scarcely mentioned. However, one exception are the so-called Polonaise carpets, which were occasionally commissioned by wealthy Polish buyers in the early modern period; some of these incorporated the coat of arms of the purchaser as part of the design. Polonaise carpets were usually enhanced with gold and silver thread; the original impression must have been one of great opulence, but unfortunately their effect has been dulled over time by the oxidation of the metallic thread. Likewise, the silk carpets produced at many points during the Safavid period must have made a totally different impression when first created than the one they convey nowadays, as textile colors on silk fade much more rapidly than on wool.

Book Illustration

In contrast to their Ottoman counterparts, Iranian palaces were richly decorated with figurative frescoes and pieces of porcelain. Yet only very few examples dating from before the seventeenth century have survived. By contrast, there is a relative abundance of illuminated manuscripts from the fourteenth century on; it is unclear whether the lack of any older examples is down to the Mongol invasions that took place after 1200 or whether this art form became established in Iranian culture only under the Ilkhans and successive dynasties.[245]

Our conception of Iranian painting is therefore heavily based on book illustration. While some experts surmise that the stylistic characteristics of book illuminations and fresco paintings that originated from the same school of painting were broadly similar, it would be unwise to draw any sweeping conclusions from this observation. In any event, because book illustration, unlike frescoes, was a portable art form, the global spread of Persian culture may be attributed largely to dissemination of illuminated manuscripts.

Alongside the works of poets and occasionally also chroniclers, stories from the epic poem known as the *Shahnameh* by Firdawsi were favorite themes of illustrated manuscripts commissioned by Persian rulers. Firdawsi was a tenth-century

"Polonaise carpet." This style of carpet, which was decorated with interlaced foliage and which often incorporated an abundance of gold and silver threads, acquired its name because a number of them were woven to order for wealthy Polish clients. Isfahan, mid-seventeenth century. (From *Die Orientteppiche im Museum für Islamische Kunst Berlin* by Friedrich Spuhler, Berlin: Staatliche Museen Preußischer Kulturbesitz, 1987.)

poet who enjoyed the patronage of Mahmud of Ghazni (971–1030).[246] The *Shahn-ameh* recounted the legendary adventures and heroic exploits of the pre-Islamic rulers of Iran. This subject matter provided a rich source of illustration; Safavid rulers were especially fond of commissioning extensive cycles of illustrations from the work. The prince and later shah Tahmasp I, for instance, had some particularly magnificent examples produced at his behest; in his youth, Tahmasp took a great interest in painting, although religious convictions later caused him to turn his back entirely on this art form.

Shah Tahmasp's disdain for painting in the latter years of his reign may be one reason why one *Shahnameh* originally produced for him found its way to Istanbul, as a present for Sultan Selim II on his accession to the Ottoman throne. Unfortunately, it went missing from the palace library sometime after 1800 and reappeared in the 1960s, when its then owner dismembered it to maximize his profit from the sale of the individual sheets. In scholarly literature, it carries the name of the man who was responsible for its mutilation: the Houghton *Shahn-ameh*. During the second half of the sixteenth century, Persian works often served as models for imitation; this accounts for the occasional appearance of so-called *shehnamecis*, whose job it was to immortalize the deeds of the Ottoman sultans in Persian verse forms in the style of Firdawsi; some of these versifiers were more accomplished than others.[247]

While the major *Shahnameh*s were so extravagant that usually only rulers and princes commissioned them—moreover, some of these were never completed—there were also less opulent manuscripts that were likely produced not to order but rather with an eye to a more or less unknown market. Especially in Shiraz, where the production of illustrated manuscripts went back to the fifteenth century, this industry continued for more than a century. Many illustrations were lavishly executed using expensive colors, especially blues derived from lapis lazuli, while their design was often of the highest quality; these exist alongside much less exalted "cheap versions." A large number of manuscripts from Shiraz were acquired by Ottoman buyers, and a significant proportion of all the surviving books produced in Shiraz can now be found in Istanbul.[248]

Aficionados with less money to spend could also purchase individual album pages, which especially after 1600 were produced by master illustrators, who often signed their works and sometimes even left marginal notes on the scenes that they had drawn or painted. For example, Shah Abbas I's court painter Riza-yi Abbasi was painted by his younger colleague and follower Mu'in. But many of these works were concerned not with portraying a specific person but rather with capturing typical aspects of the human condition, such as youth and old age. This style of album sheet also spread from Iran to Istanbul, where the poet and miniature painter Levni (d. 1732) produced portraits of young Persian men in elegant poses for his patrons at court and in the city.[249]

Collectors would often assemble their sheets into albums, which sometimes were masterpieces of the book illustrator's art in their own right. There are instances of Persian miniatures finding their way to India, Central Asia, or Istanbul and being presented in a lavish setting by their new owners. The bindings of the albums, in leather or papier-mâché, afforded them ample opportunity to do so and also to add more decoration to the individual pages. Multicolored paper could be embellished with stencils, but the most elaborate settings were illustrated freehand with drawings or miniature paintings; the colors of these were generally muted, so as not to distract the viewer from the central illustration. Sometimes, verses that had a more or less obvious connection to the subject of the miniature were also incorporated into the framing. In this form, some album pages migrated from one collector to another and ultimately found their way into public libraries.[250]

Faience

Iran had a long tradition in the manufacture of fine faience, and the masters of this craft had extensive experience in producing work inspired by Chinese models. For a while, the master potters of the sixteenth century continued the tradition established under the Timurids; the inspiration for this clearly came from Chinese export wares from the first half of the fifteenth century. In the following period, patterns that were derived from Persian manuscript illustration became popular; while in other areas, designs tended to spread from Iran to the Ottoman domain, in the sixteenth and the seventeenth centuries, we find pieces that were produced in Iran but that were clearly inspired by contemporary manufactures from Iznik in northwestern Anatolia.

However, over the course of the seventeenth century, the style of Persian faience changed fundamentally, and it is this more recent phase, involving the production of blue-and-white-patterned tableware, that will concern us here. In this instance, too, Chinese models were the source of new inspiration. When Shah Abbas I and his prominent ghulam Qaracaqay donated their collections of valuable pottery to the shrine at Ardabil, where these treasures went on public display, this was probably the first occasion on which a significant number of the Safavid shah's subjects would have seen certain designs devised by Chinese master potters.[251] The centers of Iranian faience manufacture were situated not only in the west of the country but also in the northeast, namely, in Mashhad, where Qaracaqay and his successors ruled as governors for a long time.

Some Chinese porcelain patterns were brought to Iran through trade. For instance, a standing male figure on a blue-and-white plate from the Safavid period was found to be closely related to designs that are typical of so-called Kraak porcelain, a type of Chinese porcelain produced specially for export to Europe. This porcelain first arrived in Iran in the first half of the seventeenth century aboard ships of the Dutch East India Company. Patterns that sold well were quickly copied by the shah's subjects. We may assume, therefore, that a Chinese dish inscribed with the motto "Sapienti nihil novum," which given its Latin text was obviously made to order for a European client, was the model for various Safavid pieces, on which illegible lines of script had been transformed into purely decorative elements.[252] Chinese influence is particularly evident in depictions of birds and landscapes.

Poetry

The poet Hafiz (c. 1320–1389), whose work is still widely read both within Iran and abroad, was active in Shiraz at the beginning of the period under discussion here.[253] Although his father died when he was still a boy, the young poet managed to complete his schooling at a college for Islamic law and theology (madrasa). Subsequently, he worked from time to time as a copyist and became renowned for his excellent knowledge of Arabic; he also occasionally taught at a madrasa himself. Otherwise, little is known about his life; he may have had close connections with dervish orders. We do have evidence, though, that several princes invited him to attend their courts—for instance, Ahmad Jalayir summoned Hafiz to his palace. Yet Hafiz turned down all these invitations, possibly because he was already under the patronage of a prince of the Muzaffarid dynasty in his hometown of Shiraz. Timur brought this principality to a swift end two years before the poet's death.

Hafiz's poems were collected into a single volume *(diwan)* only posthumously; many later manuscripts contain texts that Hafiz's copyists and publishers added in at their own initiative long after his death. Philological attempts to uncover and restore his original text are therefore evident from an early stage: a century after the poet's death, for example, one of Husayn Bayqara's sons personally worked on an edition that was intended to correct the numerous copyists' errors that had accrued to Hafiz's work. Many calligraphers and miniature painters were also inspired by the poet's works. People's fascination for his poems is based at least in part on the fact that readers can, on one level, take them as a celebration of the joys of earthly existence, but they can also be read as an allegory of humanity's mystical connection with divinity. Particularly in the Ottoman Empire, from the sixteenth century on, commentators delved deeply into the meaning of Hafiz's poetry; mystical interpretations were favored not least because they got round the problem of how a devout Muslim could have sung the praises of wine.

The outstanding literary figure of the fifteenth century was Nur al-Din Abd al-Rahman Jami (1414–1492).[254] Similarly, only the sketchiest details of the author's life are available; however, we do at least know that Jami was a leading member of the Naqshbandi dervish order and that he completed the hajj to Mecca from his home in Herat. Greatly esteemed as a writer of prose, he published a biographical anthology of the great figures of Islamic mysticism and became known for his good knowledge of the Arabic language. As a poet, he was regarded as a worthy successor to Hafiz and as the last exponent of "classical" Iranian verse.

Poets appear to have had a hard time under the Safavids. At least during the later years of his reign, when he espoused orthodox Shi'ite theology, Shah Tahmasp I was clearly no longer had any interest in "worldly" poetry. This lack of patronage forced many authors to emigrate to India or the Ottoman Empire. Nor was it uncommon for a poet who had originally been a loyal follower of the Safavids to suddenly find himself as an Ottoman subject thanks to the vagaries of war. This happened, for instance, to the poet Fuzuli (d. 1561), who is now especially revered for his poems in Turkish but who also wrote a *diwan* in Persian.[255] At a time when Iraq was still part of the Safavid Empire, Fuzuli had repeatedly condemned the Ottomans as "unbelievers." But when Sultan Süleyman conquered this region in 1534, for reasons unknown the author did not leave for Safavid territory. Although he remained a devout Twelver Shi'ite throughout his life, he chose to stay in his home province and sought, with moderate success, patrons among the Ottoman elite, beginning with Sultan Süleyman and his son Prince Bayezid. Fuzuli received a small stipend from the religious foundations that funded the mausoleums of the Prophet Muhammad's descendants in Iraq. Even in the seventeenth century, during his trip to the Safavid Empire, Evliya Çelebi reported hearing Fuzuli's poetry being recited at a memorial service in Karbala for the Prophet's murdered grandson Husayn—prompting him to make a tart remark about Fuzuli's "disagreeable" text.[256]

The Safavids and the Ottomans

The history of Iran can be considered from several different aspects. However, the interconnections between the inhabitants of the principalities and monarchies that ruled successively over this region and their Anatolian neighbors are worthy of closer scrutiny than has hitherto been accorded them. Twice, first under the Ilkhans and then under Timur, Anatolia was ruled at least for a short time from Iran; conversely, the many Ottoman attempts to control northwestern Iran and the Caucasus from Istanbul all came to nothing.

In the early phase of their history, Jalayir, Karaquyunlu, Aq-Qoyunlu, the Safavids, and the Ottomans—at least as far as the Ottomans' Anatolian provinces were concerned—all belong to the "successor states" that were established in this region after the collapse of Timurid rule, often by princes from a tribal background. This common origin manifests itself in often very telling details, such as the names of particular forms of taxation. Yet among the many successors of Timur, the Safavid and the Ottoman dynasties emerge as the most significant by virtue of having both developed mechanisms through which the rulers could contain succession disputes and thereby ensure the continuation of their respective dynasties. Such forms of organization were absent from the other principalities and realms. On the Safavid side, until the late sixteenth century, reverence for the ruler as the head of a dervish order and representative of the hidden twelfth imam constituted an important factor in legitimizing the dynasty's rule, although this did not prevent the outbreak of long-running wars after the death of Shah Ismail I in 1524 and

Shah Tahmasp I in 1576. By contrast, apart from a brief spell in the sixteenth century, the eschatological element is missing in the legitimacy discourse of the Ottoman sultans, who mostly confined themselves to emphasizing their role as guardians of Sunni Islam and especially of the holiest sites of Islam and the hajjs.[257]

The introduction of a "counterbalance" to the qizilbash emirs in the form of slaves (ghulam) of the shah from the Caucasus, especially under Shah Abbas I, was undoubtedly one important reason why the succession became a far less traumatic affair in the seventeenth century, thereby consolidating the rule of the Safavids. For the Ottomans, "preventative" fratricides by newly ascended sultans from the mid-fifteenth to mid-seventeenth centuries may well have helped limit wars of succession; while from the late fifteenth century onward, the class of "quasi-slaves" from which viziers and governors were frequently recruited represented a stabilizing factor, somewhat like the ghulam in Iran. Moreover, in the seventeenth century, the rulers of both realms insured themselves against rebellions by their respective sons by having them brought up within the confines of the palace, cut off from the outside world.

In both cases, this measure meant that rulers came to the throne who were completely inexperienced in the business of government; but in both countries, this discrepancy was compensated for by the growth of a much more thoroughly organized bureaucracy. Even so, one could argue that Safavid officials struggled more with this arrangement, because they were less institutionalized and less of a presence in the provinces than their Ottoman opposite numbers.

In the circumstances under which both the shahs and the sultans ruled, the institutionalization of the civil service was intimately bound up with control over the country's legal and religious scholars (ulama). Despite all their efforts, the Safavid rulers appear to have been less successful in their attempts to integrate the Shi'ite religious hierarchy into the state apparatus than the Ottomans were in co-opting the Sunni scholars. Perhaps Shah Abbas I and his successors simply did not have enough time: for while the Ottomans were pushing through this program in the eighteenth century, the Safavids were on the brink of collapse. In any event, in eighteenth-century Istanbul, it was only very small factions of the ulama who were ever prepared to make common cause with any rebels. Likewise, in provincial Iran, the kadis do not appear to have played the same stabilizing role as their counterparts in the Ottoman Empire of the seventeenth and eighteenth centuries. At least hypothetically, this difference might explain why the two dynasties, after such similar beginnings, went their separate ways.

Yet political events played only a peripheral part in the spread of Iranian culture from east to west—especially, though by no means exclusively, in its Timurid form, as exemplified at the court of Husayn Bayqara. In Ottoman *diwan* literature and in miniature painting, Iranian influences set the predominant tone for a long period. In this context, we have enumerated various cultural border crossers. But this is merely a sample, and countless other artists, poets, and scholars could also be cited, not to mention "ordinary people" who have left no record behind.

Translated from the German by Peter Lewis

·[THREE]·

South Asia and the Indian Ocean

Stephan Conermann

Introduction

THE TREATY of Tordesillas, which was concluded in 1494 between the rival maritime powers of Portugal and Spain, effectively divided the world into a Portuguese and a Spanish half. While Portugal was primarily interested in controlling the sea route along the African coast to India, for Spain securing the territories in the west that had only recently been discovered by Christopher Columbus was paramount. After difficult negotiations, the dividing line between the spheres of influence was set at 370 Spanish miles (approximately 1,770 kilometers) west of the Cape Verde Islands. That corresponded to a longitudinal measurement of 46° 37′W.[1] Generally speaking, the history of South Asia and the Indian Ocean has hitherto been presented in the light of this European meta-history, namely, the successful exploration, conquest, and annexation of the world from the end of the fifteenth and beginning of the sixteenth centuries. The Treaty of Tordesillas can therefore in this context act as a symbol for the hubris and the fantasies of omnipotence, which characterized Europe from this period onward, alongside thoroughly palpable economic successes.

However, it is also possible to read the period from 1350 to 1750 quite differently. In his book *After Tamerlane: The Global History of Empire since 1405,* the Oxford historian John Darwin put forward an interesting interpretation. Darwin's intention was to clarify exactly how it came about that European states, which over the course of history were to come to be defined as the "West," managed to dissociate themselves from the international system of the early modern period and begin to dominate Islamic and Asian empires, and in some cases even partially seize control of them. What, he asks, were the reasons for this special European role, and how are we to evaluate the consequences for the world as a whole of European imperialism and colonialism? If, Darwin maintains, we take an overview of Eurasia at the end of the fourteenth century, we see that European states scarcely play any role in the intertwined economic, cultural, and political networks that existed there. It would therefore be wrong to look at this point for the systemic origins of a special line of development for Eurasia in the Middle Ages. Rather, considered from a global perspective, Europe's position in around 1400 looked decidedly bleak. It was Muslims who controlled world trade, while the most significant polity of this era was China, which exhibited a political and cultural unity that was not even evident in embryonic form in Europe at this time. Even so, it cannot be denied that, from a European perspective, a noticeable trend toward expansion took place in the period from 1480 to 1620. Yet this must be viewed in the context of global history. As a consequence of this enlarged perspective, which of course is very often directly related to the dates 1492 and 1498, European successes are relativized, as it becomes clear that the Europeans did not enjoy a monopoly of expansion in the early modern period. The European irruption into the wider world thus brought little that was new to the world, except perhaps for a form of organized violence that was unknown before this era.[2] After they were unable to secure a monopoly over the black pepper trade, for a long while Europeans played the role of an alien presence in the Indian Ocean, which basically centered around the granting of the right to unmolested passage in return for payment. Therefore, if the element of coercion is discounted from this perspective, the difference between Europe and Asia diminishes. Some commentators even assign the Mughal Empire a central—though not a leading—role within the global network of economic relations that existed in premodern times. Ultimately, it was the Mughal Empire that developed into the greatest imperial power of the early modern period and that above all succeeded in establishing a global network that spread beyond the Indian Ocean to create a global network of economic contacts.[3]

Even though the Indian Ocean as a cultural and above all an economic sphere has been the subject of intensive academic interest for some decades, its history has still been far less thoroughly researched than that of the Atlantic or the Pacific.[4] In the process, the period between 1500 and 1800 has sometimes been regarded as an early phase of modern globalization.[5] For example, in his two seminal works on the world of the Indian Ocean, K. N. Chaudhuri advances the thesis that the "capitalistic" long-distance trade in both luxury and basic goods formed the basis for an economic unification of the region, which transcended geographical and cultural borders.[6] In Chaudhuri's view, urban centers and ports were the prerequisite for a supraregional division of labor. Chaudhuri, who expressly took the work of Fernand Braudel as his template when structuring his studies,[7] while

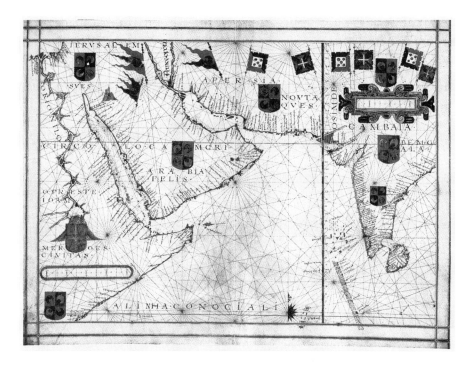

Northwestern section of the Indian Ocean, from the atlas by Fernão Vaz Dourado, circa 1576. Fernão Vaz Dourado (1520–c. 1580), the son of a high-ranking Portuguese official and an Indian woman, was a Portuguese cartographer whose extremely accurate maps were prized by seafarers and used by diplomats to determine frontiers and spheres of influence. (From *Novos Mundos—Neue Welten: Portugal und das Zeitalter der Entdeckungen: Eine Ausstellung des Deutschen Historischen Museums Berlin in Zusammenarbeit mit dem Instituto Camoes, Lisbon, und der Botschaft von Portugal in Berlin,* edited by Michael Kraus and Hans Ottomeyer, Dresden: Sandstein Verlag, 2007.)

also following to some extent the ideas of Immanuel Wallerstein, differentiated four enduring driving forces that operated in the period extending from the rise of Islam in the seventh century through to the establishment of European hegemony over the region in the late eighteenth: first, the spread of Islam and the associated establishment of a unified symbolic and semiotic cosmos; second, the strong political and cultural presence of Chinese civilization; third, the periodic migration of nomadic groups from Central Asia; and fourth, European maritime expansion after 1500. The potential for travel, people's mobility, economic exchange, climatic conditions, and historical developments all combined to create a network of extensive interdependencies and connections. Conversely, we also find local religious, social, and cultural networks.

In a similar vein Michael Pearson—likewise following Braudel's example—has examined the "deep structure" that created long-term continuity, primarily among coastal communities around the Indian Ocean.[8] Although on the one hand, we can identify very different neighboring societies—the list ranges from East African farming communities and traders with connections that transcended regions to members of courtly societies—Pearson maintains that there are a series of other factors that argue in favor of the unified nature of the Indian Ocean as a realm of interaction. These include topographical similarities; wind flow; the incessant circulation of people, ideas, and goods; structural similarities between harbors, modes of seafaring, and navigation; common religious patterns; and the organization of overseas maritime trade.

Kenneth McPherson places the idea of overlapping cultural areas in the foreground.[9] In doing so, his intention is to counteract any conception of a common cultural realm. Alongside the Mediterranean, he sees first and foremost the Arabian Sea, the Gulf of Bengal, the South China Sea, and the island world of Southeast Asia as separate unified entities. This concept has been challenged by Pierre Chaunu in particular, who sees in it the danger of an unreliable essentialization of realms that are intrinsically heterogeneous.[10] Research in this field conducted by Niels Steensgaard also leads him to the conclusion that the Indian Ocean as a whole, both at a middling level but above all on a micro level, displays far less coherence than, say, the Baltic or even the Mediterranean.[11] When all is said and done, he claims, long-distance trade in mass-market goods remained only marginal in relation to total trade within the region.

The American social historian Immanuel Wallerstein, however, takes quite a different line of argumentation. For him, from a European perspective and with regard to the global economy of the early modern period, the Indian Ocean represents an "external area." Such external areas form, in his view, a constituent part of other global systems that are not geared toward Europe. As such, their connections to the supraregional European economic system can be disregarded, particularly because these systems that existed outside Europe may be categorized as relatively simple and as being restricted to trade conducted by a few rich merchants. Andre Gunder Frank, Bary Gills, Samuel Adshead, and Janet Abu-Lughod subsequently put forward several good arguments against Wallerstein's position.[12] These scholars take the view that even prior to European expansion in the sixteenth century, the Afro-Eurasiatic realm had developed into a close-meshed network of economic and cultural interactions.

Finally, there are a series of commentators who follow the later Fernand Braudel in postulating three mega-economic regions east of Europe in the period 1500–1800: the Islamic World, South Asia, and China. All three, it is claimed, allied with the European economic system to form an impressive superworld economy; however, far from being self-contained, this entity was, rather, fragile and unstable. Another, likewise extremely interesting, viewpoint comes from India.[13] The premise here is that the Indian Ocean formed an autonomous global system in its own right, with the Indian subcontinent at its center. According to this interpretation, although Europeans certainly gained access to this network from 1500 onward, right up to the eighteenth century they never managed to take over this system or even to achieve dominance within it. India's central role was based on its strategically favorable medial position between West Asia on the one hand and Southeast Asia and the Far East on the other. In addition, India had the potential to offer a wide spectrum of trade goods at very reasonable prices, while also itself having a very large demand for consumer goods, minerals, and metals. Ultimately, it was also Indian merchants who, thanks to the segmentation of Asian trade, dominated the trading networks and their nodes. According to Paul Bairoch, as a result of its highly differentiated mercantile and banking system, India was responsible for producing no less than 25 percent of global trade goods in 1750.[14]

For their part, C. A. Bayly, David Ludden, P. J. Marshall, and David Washbrook have all emphasized that analyses of the modern global system fail to take account of the uniqueness of the mercantile world of the Indian Ocean before 1770 and that these analyses marginalize the internal dynamism of non-European societies—including the capitalistic developments that are in evidence there.[15] There is clearly a need for studies with a polycentric approach, which take into consideration the multilateral character of the many-layered connections that existed in the Indian Ocean in the premodern period. The key concepts of a history of the worlds within this region should be openness, interdependence, and adaptation, as well as the porousness of spatial and political borders. A "mental remapping" of regions thus requires that we diverge from a relatively immobile and essentializing form of geography, which focuses on characteristic traits such as values, languages, material practicalities, or forms of marriage ("trait geography") toward a way of seeing that places at the forefront the analysis of processes such as mobility, migration, development, conflict, colonialization, and hybridization. In this way, regions can be conceptualized both as dynamic and as open-edged entities connected to one another, in which integration and fragmentation coexist alongside one another. Maritime regions in particular possess extremely blurred and mutable borders. Another research imperative is to discover answers to such questions as the following: How far did the maritime world of the Indian Ocean extend? How far did it stretch into the interior? What regions were included or excluded, and with what degree of intensity? In what direction did the currents of circulation flow? And how did these currents bind the world of the Indian Ocean together, or divide it, or help open it up? Above all, the aim must be to work out what the basic features of this circulation were.

Epochs

The spread of Islam and the establishing of Muslim political, economic, and religious networks from the seventh century on virtually transformed the Indian Ocean into an Islamic inland sea.[16] In the eleventh century, three major, intersecting regions began to crystallize: the Arabian Sea and the Gulf of Bengal, which are sometimes bound together under the umbrella term "Indian Ocean," and the South China Sea. Hand in hand with this came the development of global ports and the creation of a north–south gradient: on the one side stood China and India, where high-value goods were manufactured; on the other were tropical regions that had only cheap unprocessed raw materials and goods to offer. The shift from the thirteenth to the fourteenth century may be seen as a high point of this development, a stage when Muslim networks, which extended across the Indian Ocean far into the hinterland of the respective coastal regions surrounding it, formed the most important dynamic factor of the Eurasiatic trading system. The documents found at the Cairo Genizah tell us a great deal about the Muslim and Jewish mercantile networks of the twelfth century, which spanned the Indian Ocean.[17] Yet the heterogeneity of Islam must always be borne in mind. Furthermore, it was not just religion that offered ready-made templates of identification.

An intensification in maritime trade becomes evident from the fifteenth century on at the very latest. It is linked to the growth of a monetary economy and a growing market orientation on the part of agrarian and industrial production in various regions. In addition, this period witnessed a reorganization of the principal trade routes. New nodal points and networks were established, while the rhythm of circulation began to change. This manifested itself not in any increase in direct transportation of goods from one end of the region to the other but rather in an intensification of the circulation of consumption within individual regions. In Europe, maritime trading companies dealing in short- and middle-distance trade came into being, which had the distinct advantage of reducing the duration and the capital outlay required for individual ventures. Moreover, the north–south trade in goods between India and East Africa also grew stronger at this time. An impetus toward urbanization becomes apparent even on the East African coast.

Prior to the beginning of the sixteenth century, Europeans played only a subordinate role, with the only connections to Eurasian trade arising through the Mediterranean. Yet even after 1500, there is no question of any European dominance. Over the succeeding 250 years, the European presence varied from place to place and from age to age, but overall European influence over the Indian Ocean remained strictly limited. Generally speaking, Europeans found themselves obliged to fall in line with existing trading structures. Later, in the phase of early modern globalization, the Indian Ocean found itself incorporated, via the Atlantic, into a more comprehensive system of barter, though these connections were primarily of an indirect kind. Even so, this phase brought with it a series of seminal changes. These included the spread of Christianity and of Portuguese as a trade lingua franca, as well as the creation of Indo-Portuguese communities and the rise of new ports under European control (for example, Goa, Manila, Batavia, or Pondicherry), plus the growing volume of European trade around the Cape of Good Hope. A decisive factor in this change was, of course, the inclusion of the American realm through the import of precious metals, especially silver. With this, the Europeans finally had at their disposal a commodity that was greatly sought after in the Indian Ocean.

Among the factors that must be taken into account when making any attempt at periodization are indigenous political processes of transformation, such as the demise of the Vijayanagara Empire, the rise of the sultanate of Golkonda, or the

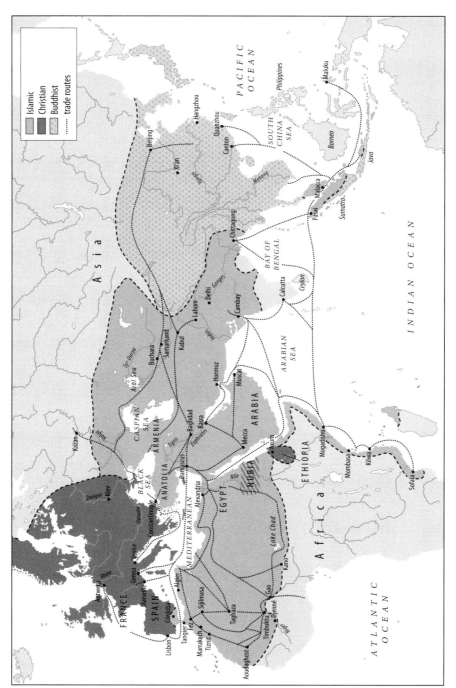

Trade routes and religions in Eurasia and Africa in the fifteenth century

Islamic
Christian
Buddhist
trade routes

PACIFIC OCEAN

Asia

Beijing
Xi'an
Hangzhou
Quanzhou
Canton

SOUTH CHINA SEA

Philippines

Maluku

Borneo

Java

Sumatra

Malacca

Pasai

Chittagong

BAY OF BENGAL

Mekong

Delhi

Lahore

Cambay

Calcutta

Ceylon

INDIAN OCEAN

Samarkand

Sry Darye

Buchara

Aral Sea

Kabul

Indus

Ganges

CASPIAN SEA

ARMENIA

Hormuz

Muscat

ARABIAN SEA

ANATOLIA

Baghdad

Basra

Tigris

Euphrates

Mecca

ARABIA

Damascus

Black Sea

Kiev

Dnieper

Constantinople

Alexandria

Nile

Axum

ETHIOPIA

Mogadishu

Mombasa

Kilwa

Sofala

Africa

NUBIA

EGYPT

Lake Chad

Kano

Gao

Djenné

Timbuktu

Taghaza

Sijilmasa

Audaghost

Tiznit

Marrakech

Tangier

Fez

Lisbon

Cordoba

SPAIN

FRANCE

Antwerp

Ghent

Genoa

Venice

Marseille

Algier

MEDITERRANEAN

Kazan

Volga

Danube

ATLANTIC OCEAN

transformation of the Mughal Empire after 1707. In addition, Portuguese attempts in the sixteenth century to control the trade in Asiatic spices to Europe should be seen only in conjunction with the opposing measures taken by local protagonists like the sultanates of Aceh or Oman. The internal interrelations and interactions within the European East Indian companies should also be studied in greater depth than hitherto. Although in the "Age of Commerce" (fifteenth to eighteenth centuries)[18] agencies originating in Europe certainly played their part in the expansion in the manufacture of goods, in the monetary economy, and in long-distance trade, they were neither responsible for instigating these developments nor were they able to gain a stranglehold over them.

The rhythm of the monsoon season conditioned complementary ecosystems. Subtropical rainforest regions on the coasts of India and the Indonesian archipelago supplied pepper, cloves, and other spices. Teak came from the west coast of India, while hardwoods came from East Africa. Arabia was the source of breeding horses, dates, and dried fish. In the main, revenue was collected in the form of taxes and not as maritime excise duty. The capitals of the regional empires were situated inland, with the result that it was not uncommon for ruling elites to be prejudiced against trade and seafaring. Nevertheless, wealthy landowners had a strong interest in maritime trade. It would take until the nineteenth century before a fundamental change brought about an end to this global trade within the Indian Ocean and establish in its place a new system, this time controlled by Europeans. Expressed in terms of the Christian calendar, the "European" century occurred between 1770 and 1914–1918 because, as Jürgen Osterhammel observes, "Never before had the western peninsula of Eurasia ruled and exploited larger areas of the globe. Never had changes originating in Europe achieved such impact on the rest of the world. And never had European culture been so eagerly soaked up by others, far beyond the sphere of colonial rule."[19] Thus, it was only in a long eighteenth century, which following Osterhammel we can determine as having begun in the 1680s, that European influence began to make itself felt worldwide— and not merely in the Atlantic region.[20]

1. South Asia

IN 1350, Muhammad ibn Tughluq (r. 1325–1351) established a patrimonial empire in South Asia, which at least nominally extended from the northern frontiers of India to the Deccan Plateau.[21] As sultan, he exercised power through the belief of his followers in his authority. This came about by means of an official recognition of his power by the caliphate, which by this stage was based in Cairo. Furthermore, shari'a law was basically regarded as the highest form of authority, yet in the consciousness of contemporaries, it exerted more moral authority than legally binding power. It was the supreme duty of a sultan to ensure the spread of a Muslim value system but above all to care for the material well-being of his subjects. Muhammad ibn Tughluq had a standing army at his disposal, with whose aid he could rapidly quell insurrections and rebellions and conquer new territories. There existed in the capital Delhi a ministry of war, whose head was responsible for maintaining the armed forces in state of constant readiness and for ongoing recruitment. He determined rates of pay and soldiers' ranks and during campaigns was required to look after accommodating and supplying the troops. Both in Delhi and in the provinces, he could call on a supporting cast of helpers. Every individual soldier was placed on a list of salaried retainers and at regular intervals was paid a fixed sum in cash from the state budget. To this end, a number of central regions of the empire were placed under the direct rule of the sultan; the revenue generated by these regions flowed straight into the state's coffers. The higher echelons of the civil service were granted a fixed income from certain landholdings. As well as the main army in the capital, the governors of the provinces also maintained contingents of troops. If unrest arose, it fell initially to local forces on the ground to quell it. If that proved impossible, troops from the neighboring province or the main standing army was called in to help. The army, which was theoretically split into ten divisions, was composed of soldiers from the most diverse ethnic groups. Alongside "Hindus," Turks, Iranians, and Afghans also served in Muhammad's forces.[22]

The principal factor in maintaining the army was an efficient financial bureaucracy. The vizier, as the right hand of the sultan, had supreme command over all internal affairs of the empire, and three state officials answerable to him were entrusted with administering all financial matters. We know from a contemporary manual on administration that the revenues of the sultanate were made up primarily of eleven different forms of tax, provided for by Islamic law. They included, for example, the poll tax *(jizyah)* imposed on Christians and Jews, "followers of the book"; a compulsory tax paid by every Muslim; excises on landownership; and above all a toll on any booty seized during military campaigns or raids. These were supplemented over time by numerous additional taxes that had no foundation in shari'a law. All state income and expenditure were the subject of punctilious bookkeeping. Daily and annual accounts were kept, along with a register for each province and every tract of land held in fee from the sultan. Unfortunately, none of these documents have been preserved.

Muhammad ibn Tughluq had his own administrative staff, but despite the central control over finances and troop contingents, provincial governors were given a free hand to act more or less autonomously. They were basically charged with performing the following functions: to act as the supreme executive power; to protect the populace from external threat; to support scholars and Sufi mystics; to provide food and accommodation for local troops; to facilitate the work of financial officials; and to protect the peasantry from exploitation. The numerous rebellions staged by governors in the fourteenth century suggest that only a very limited personal relationship of dependency existed between the ruler and his governors. Because, as a rule, Muslims initially represented a small minority in the regions they controlled, the business of local administration was left to the indigenous population, who only had to pay the levies imposed on them on a regular basis. It is difficult to ascertain what the general position of the "Hindus" was under Muhammad ibn Tughluq, but we can fairly assume that they were in large measure permitted to lead their lives, govern themselves, and practice their religion without hindrance. In the main, it was even possible for them to occupy positions within the central bureaucracy and make a career for themselves. At first, the administrative staff comprised long-serving individuals, who retained their positions through changes of ruler. In addition, Muslim migrants with a degree of bureaucratic experience—such as those who had fled in the face of Mongol invasions—were always welcome, because they were personally beholden to the sultan, given that they owed their positions to his protection alone. Finally, among the administrative staff, the number of Afghans, who had been resident in northern India for a long time by this stage, increased steadily.

The most common and widespread form of practical power in Muslim-controlled India during the reign of Muhammad ibn Tughluq was the so-called rule by consent. In practice this means that those who wield power of any kind in turn show themselves willing to submit to a supraregional ruler and to align themselves with the framework of the patrimonial state through the payment of tributes. Because the ruling echelon of Muslims comprised only a vanishingly small proportion of the total populace, complete destruction of the indigenous ruling and social structures was neither possible nor even planned by the Muslim authorities. In the central areas of northern India around Delhi, the direct influence of this ruling elite was naturally far stronger than in the more outlying regions. Although these peripheral areas had been conquered, in practice all this meant was that a governor with a unit of troops was stationed there and that the administrative-military cadre, controlled centrally from Delhi, had a foothold there. As a rule, local lords continued to exercise power in their regions, just as long as they paid the levies imposed on them. Basically, this amounted to a voluntary subjugation, without any direct threat on the part of the Muslim authorities. This mostly came about through tactical considerations, as local rulers calculated that they would receive tangible political advantages from cooperating with the Muslims, while at the same time not having to sacrifice too much of their own autonomy.

During the reign of Muhammad ibn Tughluq, there was a network of different control mechanisms that the sultan used to supervise his administrative staff. Alongside the attempt to monitor the holders of sinecures and governors through independent officials who were mandated solely to the relevant administrative department in Delhi, it was always open to the ruler to dismiss even the most respected dignitaries of the empire. However, the most important instrument for overseeing both the ruler's subjects and affairs of state was the espionage department *(diwan-i barid)* especially established for this purpose. A contemporary manual lists the duties of the leader of this department:

He must strive to settle any grievances. If a judge or a governor should, either through carelessness or partiality, issue an edict against a person that runs counter to Shar'ia law or offends the sense of natural justice, he should make every effort to pursue this matter there and then, so it can be properly investigated and put right again. He should always endeavour to check the state of state or religious affairs. Whenever he receives a report about something that contravenes the wishes of the ruler, he should inform the ruler without delay and await his orders, so that the seed of rebellion might not even get the chance to germinate in the heads of insurrectionists.[23]

The official who headed this department had at his disposal a network of informers and spies who provided him with relevant information about the aims, undertakings, and personal affairs of all the leading figures of the empire.

Despite all these stabilizing factors, though, the patrimonial empire still disintegrated. The early years of Muhammad ibn Tughluq's reign witnessed ambitious, large-scale projects such as the creation of a second administrative center at Daulatabad in the south of the empire or the attempt to introduce a new currency. But contemporaneous with this, a period of great drought led to a devastating famine in the northern provinces of the realm. A campaign against the rebellious governor of Mabar in 1335 ended in a catastrophe, as the emperor's army was almost entirely wiped out by an outbreak of cholera. Over the years that followed, too, epidemics and famine raged across large tracts of the country. Even in Delhi, the economic situation was so disastrous that in 1337 Muhammad ibn Tughluq relocated his royal residence to the region around Jaunpur and Awadh, which had been spared the ravages of the famine. The sultan now sought to restore the former position of the sultanate of Delhi though economic reforms. However, the lack of trust was simply too great. In 1344, Afghan emirs, in alliance with a group of the region's administrative officials, rose up in rebellion in Gujarat. The empire threatened to disintegrate once more. The ruler himself duly set off on campaign to the region with an army to quell the uprising. But this enterprise proved difficult, as the rebellion spread from Gujarat to Daulatabad. In the event, Muhammad ibn Tughluq managed to restore order only superficially. When an emir staged a new rebellion in Gujarat and the sultan mobilized again to crush it, the provinces around Daulatabad seceded once and for all, to form the Bahmani sultanate (1347), a state entirely independent of Delhi.

As various pretenders to the throne became engaged in a power struggle in Delhi that lasted for many years, many emirs in the provinces took the opportunity to secede. This, then, was the prevailing state of affairs when Tamerlane (or Timur the Lame, d. 1404) crossed the Indus with a large army in the summer of 1398. He easily defeated the forces of Sultan Mahmud Shah (r. 1399–1414/1415), occupying and sacking Delhi. The invasion was a short-lived affair, however; as early as New Year's Day on 1399, Tamerlane's troops withdrew. Even so, they left the Delhi sultanate in a state of anarchy, with the ruler of Delhi now just one among a whole host of feuding petty princes.

Following Tamerlane's invasion, a number of other Muslim successor states came into being on the territory of the Delhi sultanate:[24] Malwa (1401–1531), Gujarat (1396–1572), Jaunpur (1394–1476), Khandesh (1399–1599), and Multan (1444–1524). In most cases, these regional empires took over the bureaucratic system of the former central power, while each evolved their own social and artistic characteristics. Delhi itself fell in 1444 to the former governor of Multan, Sayyid Khizr Khan (the dynasty he founded, the Sayyid, was named for him).[25] Mahmud, the last of the Tughluq dynasty, had died the year before. Yet Khizr Khan and his successors continued to enjoy the status only of provincial princes. Control of Delhi and the territorial claims associated with it were by now worth so little that the last of the Sayyids, Ala ad-Din Alam Shah (r. 1445–1451), ceded the city without a fight to Bahlul, an Afghan from the clan of the Lodi, and confined himself to reigning over Badaun alone until his death in 1478. Bahlul (r. 1451–1489), during whose reign many Afghans came to settle in northern India, was able to extend Delhi's sphere of influence again to some extent, above all through his conquest of Jaunpur. The reign of his successor Sikander Lodi represented a high point; in 1504 he ordered the new capital of Agra to be built. Under Ibrahim Lodi (r. 1517–1526), however, a new round of revolts and insurrections erupted.

Non-Muslim India

Even during the reigns of the sultans Muhammad ibn Tughluq and Firuz Shah, Muslim rulers only ever controlled parts of South Asia. Although they succeeded, at least temporarily, in conquering the smaller "Hindu" principalities on the Deccan, the Yadava Empire of Devagiri, the Kakatiya dynasty in Warangal, and the Pandyan kingdom of Madurai, the whole of the south of India remained beyond their control. Here, in the fourteenth century, an independent "Hindu" empire came into being, namely, Vijayanagara.[26] Its capital was the city of Hampi (also known as Vijayanagara) on the southern bank of the Tungabhadra River.[27] The early Vijayanagara ruler Harihara II (r. 1377–1404) already held sway over most of the area south of the Krishna. Despite several crises and setbacks, the rulers of Vijayanagara managed to consolidate their power and were able successfully to repel attempted invasions by the Muslim sultanates of the Deccan Plateau. In particular, the reign of Krishna Deva Raya (r. 1509–1529) is widely regarded as a political, economic, and cultural high point. He was succeeded by his half brother Achyuta Deva Raya. When he in turn died in 1542, Sadashiva Raya came to the throne as a boy; true power, however, lay with the regent Rama Raya, Krishna Deva Raya's son-in-law. As soon as Sadashiva was old enough to lay claim to power in his own right, Rama Raya had him summarily incarcerated.

Rama Raya attempted to continue the expansionist policies of his father-in-law, especially against the Muslim empires in the north, yet his endeavors ended in a catastrophic defeat. At Talikota in January 1565, he lost a decisive battle against the combined forces of the Deccan sultanates. The Vijayanagara ruler was taken prisoner and immediately beheaded. The Muslim troops sacked and destroyed Vijayanagara and expelled its populace. The royal family fled, and the next regent, Tirumala Deva, subsequently tried to repopulate and revive the capital but met with no success and was forced to move the court to Penukoda. The Vijayanagara Empire survived until around 1650 but had long since lost its position of hegemony in the south of India.

Vijayanagara's rulers maintained an extremely efficient administration, which they had inherited from their predecessors. The king wielded supreme authority. He was supported by a chancellery and a series of ministers, with all the more senior courtiers being required to undergo military training. As a rule, all senior advisers and officers received their salary in the form of cash payments. Tax revenues came through the medium of major landowners, who collected them within their own domains. Overall, the empire was subdivided into five main provinces, each usually headed by a governor from the ruling family. At a local level, as with the Delhi sultanate, the state bureaucracy operated on a consensual basis, with communities being largely autonomous where internal affairs were concerned. Only strategically important regions were placed under the control of a governor appointed directly from Hampi.

The capital was wholly dependent on its water supply system. This precious resource was channeled through numerous canals into huge reservoirs, which were then drawn on to irrigate the surrounding fields and supply the population. Sugarcane, rice, wheat, coconuts, pepper, ginger, and cardamom were all grown locally. In addition, a thriving textile industry developed. Spices, cotton, jewels, ivory, coral, and incense were all exported to China. In return, ships from the Far East brought a wide range of cargoes to the many ports of Vijayanagara, including Mangalore, Honavar, Bhatkal, Barkur, Cochin, Cannanore, Machilipatnam, and Darmadam. Other ships sailed from these ports to the entrepôts of the Red Sea, with the result that goods from Vijayanagara reached even Venice. Cotton thread was sold to Burma and indigo to Persia.

The reports given by one particular traveler from the mid-fifteenth century tell us a great deal about society in Vijayanagara at the time.[28] In 1442, the Timurid ruler Shahrukh (d. 1447) dispatched the scholar Abd ar-Razzaq as-Samarqandi (d. 1482) of Herat to southern India, to take gifts to the governor of the Muslim community in Calicut to reward him for his earlier voluntary submission to his rule. As-Samarqandi complied with his ruler's request, but his journey took him not only to Calicut but also to the capital of Vijayanagara. This emissary returned to Herat only in December 1444.

Significantly, the Timurid ruler's envoy gives no evidence of having harbored any pronounced feelings of superiority toward his hosts. Of course, many of the practices and customs of the "Hindus" seemed remarkable to him, but he never takes a supercilious attitude toward the "infidels" or makes disparaging remarks about them. One reason for this uncommon tolerance may have been the fact that, as a result of the intellectual and administrative convergence with Muslim concepts of organization that Vijayanagara experienced up to the late fifteenth century, many phenomena and institutions would have seemed familiar to the envoy. In the mid-1980s, Burton Stein was one of the first historians to advance the thesis that Deva Raya II's (r. 1424–1446) impressive victory over the Gajapatis was primarily due to his deliberate policy of incorporating Muslim mercenaries

Woodcut (1527) showing a view of the harbor at Calicut. This map comes from a companion volume to a maritime chart *(Carta Marina)* produced by Lorenz Fries (1491–1550). Alongside an introduction to various aspects of nautical life, Fries also provided the reader with an index and an alphabetically arranged chapter containing shorter or longer descriptions of 120 listed ports. The illustrations were the work of Albrecht Dürer's pupil Hans Baldung Grien. (Sign. Mapp. I, 9 m-2)

within his army and equipping them with Arab horses.[29] Furthermore, Deva Raya placed these non-Hindus in positions of high authority and allowed them to build mosques and cemeteries and to practice their faith openly. In so doing, he departed radically from the practice of his fellow "Hindu" rulers and established a flourishing major empire that was fundamentally geared toward expansion and one that, in its structure and pretensions, did not differ greatly from the Islamic sultanates of the period.

Philip B. Wagoner expanded on Stein's interpretation,[30] arguing that the founding myth of Vijayanagara, which is repeated in various sixteenth-century sources, represented an attempt to directly proclaim its legitimacy through the Delhi sultanate. For this myth no longer paints a picture of a hostile Muslim ruler to the north of Vijayanagara. Rather, the authors present Vijayanagara as a successor state to the Delhi sultanate and the "Hindu" rulers as the legitimate and hence equal heirs to the Islamic sultans. Wagoner also demonstrates that this same notion occurs in various Telugu-language sources from the sixteenth century. Ultimately, according to his thesis, as a result of more than two centuries of close contact with their Muslim neighbors, the courtly elite that set the tone in Vijayanagara seems to have assimilated many Islamic elements into their own culture, transforming them in the process. This fruitful adoption of aspects of foreign culture is evident in such diverse realms as architectural forms, dressing habits, and the titles that rulers adopted, as well as more generally in military and administrative matters. Particularly noteworthy is the adoption of the traditional Muslim royal title: from the mid-fourteenth century on, the rulers of Vijayanagara officially styled themselves "the sultan among Hindu kings" or sometimes even simply "sultan."

The Rise of Babur

Babur's father, Umar Sheikh Mirza (d. 1494), had managed to establish a small principality in the Ferghana Valley.[31] He legitimized his rule primarily through the fact that he was directly related to Tamerlane, the figurehead of all Muslim rulers in Central Asia. During the period when Babur was alive, no hard-and-fast rules existed for royal succession, with the result that there was a constant state of feuding among the pretenders to the throne. Even so, in this case, they all had a common enemy, in the shape of the Uzbek ruler Muhammad Shaybani Khan (d. 1510). Following the death of his father in 1494, Babur, who was still only a boy at that stage, became embroiled in the confused power struggles that took place among the most diverse parties in Central Asia, ending up spending the next ten years living the nomadic life of a warlord. After two attempts to establish control over Samarkand had failed, he decided to gather his strength and marshal his forces by withdrawing over the Hindu Kush mountain range to Afghanistan. He eventually succeeded in taking Kabul, which he developed into the seat of his power. At the beginning of the sixteenth century, the Uzbek Confederation, under the leadership of Muhammad Shaybani Khan, threatened to overrun this region. However, before this conquest was completed, Shaybani Khan was defeated and killed in 1510 by Shah Ismail Safavi (d. 1524). Babur exploited the ensuing power vacuum in Central Asia, finally managing at the third attempt to take Samarkand, though he was forced to relinquish it again just six months later.

Over the course of the following years, Babur undertook several campaigns against India. Because the situation seemed favorable to him, he embarked on his first such campaign in the winter of 1525–1526, at the head of an army of twelve thousand men. In no time, he had defeated every army that opposed him. Finally, on April 21, 1526, he lured Ibrahim Lodi into launching an attack against his army, which occupied a well-prepared defensive position in the vicinity of Panipat. This engagement, which ended in victory for Babur and the death of his adversary, represented a turning point in the history of South Asia. It may be seen as the beginning of the period—lasting until British rule in 1858—when the successors of Tamerlane held sway over large parts of the subcontinent, though initially, this did not involve any real control over the region as a whole.

One major problem was a group of Rajputs, that is, "Hindu" local rulers who had formed an alliance, under the leadership of Maharana Sanga, to oppose the invading forces. At the Battle of Khanwa on March 17, 1527, Babur definitively crushed the Rajputs. Despite his continuing precarious political situation, Babur now set about consolidating and extending his reign from Agra. At first, this entailed pacifying the region through a series of military campaigns and engagements and compelling the local potentates to recognize his authority and pay taxes. Vaguely defined tracts of land were assigned at the ruler's discretion to be held in fee by his officers, who were responsible for establishing and maintaining order there. In the regions under his direct control, Babur introduced a new system of taxation, based on estimates of the former income generated by clearly delimited territorial units. At the same time he made considerable efforts to improve the transport network in his new realm.

On December 19, 1528, in the presence of Iranian, Uzbek, Rajput, and Afghan emissaries, many Timurid and Chaghatai–Mongol dignitaries, various sheikhs of the Naqshbandi Order, and scholars from Samarkand, along with many of his own family members from Central Asia, Babur held court, accepting his subjects' homage and in return distributing honorary vestments of office, gifts, and sinecures. Basically, this ceremonial occasion may be regarded as the true beginning of the Timurid–Mongol claim to hegemony over northern India. After two more turbulent years in power, Babur, the "founder" of the Mughal Empire, died on

December 21, 1530.[32] His first resting place was a garden near the site of where the Taj Mahal was subsequently built. However, sometime between 1539 and 1544, his body was removed to Kabul, where Babur was buried in a simple tomb on a hillside.

His son and successor, Humayun (d. 1556),[33] found it impossible at first to consolidate the ruling alliance that his father had fashioned and failed to defend the structurally unsecured empire against its internal and external enemies. In 1540, a major defeat at the Battle of Kannauj against the forces of Sher Shah Suri (d. 1545), who had established a form of principality from his power base at Bihar, forced Humayun to flee the subcontinent. The rulers of the Sur dynasty, who now assumed power in Delhi, holding it until 1555, laid the foundations of enduring administrative structures. However, their internal feuding enabled Humayun, who after an epic journey had finally taken refuge at the Safavid court in Persia, to return to India and regain power. Although he reigned for only one more year thereafter, the effective and successful bureaucratic policies of the Suris saw him rule over what was now a very well-organized and territorially greatly expanded region.

Difficulties of Consolidating Power under the Sur Dynasty

But to what extent did the power base of the Pashtun Sher Shah, who ruled over Delhi from 1540 to 1545, differ in institutional terms from that of the Lodi dynasty?[34] The decisive structural change that Sher Shah was able to bring about within the aristocratic Afghan military society in Hindustan must be seen as a wholly new departure in the history of northern India. Admittedly, this reading of events is based almost exclusively on the report by the scholar Abbas Khan Sarwani (d. sometime after 1586), who in around 1580 wrote a history of Sher Shah's rule. By the fifteenth century, the society of the Afghans who had emigrated to Hindustan was so deeply segmented that even during its period of rule (1451–1526), the Afghan Lodi dynasty found it hard to legitimize its realm to other Afghan tribes. The power of the Lodis was far from absolute; in view of the strong position of other families, they should rather be regarded as "first among equals."

Clan affiliations and family groupings largely determined the picture of society at that time. The aforementioned historian Abbas also gives an account of the powerful rivalries between the Afghan tribes in Hindustan. Sher Shah was the first ruler who managed to suppress this destructive tendency. Abbas identifies in the relationship between Sher Shah as the patron and his men the basis for his military success. He successfully separated out tribal structures and questions pertaining to the exercise of power. Under Sher Shah, clan loyalties no longer influenced the practical business of ruling; instead, the sultan's rights eclipsed any tribal rules. This break with existing traditions of rule and with the Lodi dynasty proved a key factor in the rise of Sher Shah. The fact that he did not join Sultan Muhammad, the last son of a Lodi ruler, in his failed uprising prevented Sher Shah from ultimately being consigned to social oblivion. Because Sher Shah was a member of the small and insignificant Sur clan, his chances for advancement within the traditional and long-established clan system of the Afghan nobility would have been extremely limited, in any event.

Sher Shah therefore needed to put in place a new system of tribute and loyalty for his political career. Before he could gain the respect of the aristocracy, he first had to establish his own power base. In doing so, he did not rely on tribal loyalties but instead, even from an early stage, presumably around 1520, set about laying the foundations for an independent power base in the region around Sasaram, when he took over the jurisdiction of two of his father's districts. There, he sidelined the major landowners *(zamindaran),* ended the system of forced labor, and appointed paid employees from outside. He hired Pashtun tribesmen, whom he promised a fixed wage to supplement the booty they seized by their own efforts in conflict. He subjected his soldiers to harsh discipline in camps and in a constant regime of drill.

It was not just the organization of his army but also the success deriving from this that made Sher Shah attractive as a patron. In order to ensure the correct distribution of salaries to his troops, he devised an ingenious system of monitoring, which was subsequently also adopted by the Mughals. It is thought that some soldiers received their pay directly from the state's coffers, whereas the majority were paid by army officers from the profits of their landholdings in fee *(iqta'at).* To make sure that these soldiers received the money due to them on a regular basis, the practice of branding horses was introduced and made compulsory. In this way, it became possible to precisely determine which officers were responsible for paying which soldiers under their command. Sher Shah thus ensured that much easier instances far easier for him to control gained precedence over unjust treatment and the threat of unrest among the soldiery that resulted from it. The vertical hierarchical structures that Sher Shah made the basis of his authority are markedly different from the horizontal system employed by the Lodi rulers, who always found themselves in direct competition with their own allies, the nobility and the warlords. By contrast, Sher Shah did not rely on clan structures but instead—with the aid of military units, which initially relied on farming, plus a new upper echelon of bureaucracy—created a new centralized power structure. But to keep his troops loyal and biddable, Sher Shah had to make sure that he had independent finances at his disposal.

The question of the origin of these finances is therefore key. In his early years, Sher Shah undoubtedly owed the considerable income he acquired to his abilities as a military commander. He was able to claim his share of the booty from his service under a variety of leaders, while in addition governing the districts belonging to his father. In assessing his financial resources, the years between 1529 and 1539 are crucial. Because, as a result of his membership in the Sur clan, he had no chance of preferment under either the Lodi or the Mughals, in 1529 Sher Shah entered the service of a more modest empire, namely, the Nuhani (Lohani) sultanate in southern Bihar. There, precisely thanks to his distance from the complex structures of the Afghan aristocracy, he was entrusted with a position of responsibility, in being appointed legal guardian of the young prince Jalal Khan, who had not yet come of age. After the death of the sultan and his wife, Sher Shah duly became provisional regent of the sultanate. But although this brought him independence, he was unable, at least at first, to acquire the resources of the Nuhani clan. According to Abbas's reports, the main portion of Sher Shah's wealth derived from the property he seized from emirs and sultans. A good example of this is the battle in which he prevailed over the king of Bengal, in which he acquired not only treasure but also large numbers of horses and elephants. Thereafter, Sher Shah found himself in a far more secure position than before to deploy the resources of the Nuhanis for his own diplomatic purposes. In doing so, his independent power increased to such a degree that the Nuhanis and their successors ended up fleeing to Bengal. They found allies there, but in another battle Sher Shah was to emerge even stronger as the victor once more.

Alongside war booty, marriages and alliances with rich widows also contributed greatly to Sher Shah's prosperity and his rise to prominence. He gained control over such resources when he married Lad Malika, the widow of a military commander to whom the Lodis had entrusted care of the provincial treasury in the fortress at Chunar. Sher Shah appropriated not only this horde but also all the surrounding districts *(parganas)* and in this way was able to secure and extend his nearby home and power base. Shortly afterward, under similar circumstances he married Guhar Gosain, the widow of Nasir Khan from the Nuhani clan. He also formed a union with a woman who hailed from the highest aristocratic circles of Hindustan, Bibi Fateh Malika. Her decision to defend herself and her wealth from the Mughals with Sher Shah's assistance signaled a key political breakthrough moment for him. Her wealth allowed him to launch an attack on Bengal, during which he overran and captured the city of Gaur in 1538, thereby securing massive riches for himself.

Sher Shah was now in a position to purchase people's loyalties, something he needed if he was to achieve his final ascent to the peak of power. Sher Shah's military success was closely bound up with his style of military leadership. One of the key innovations that he had introduced to the prevailing military landscape was the distribution system that he used among his forces. By the end of the 1530s, his name was synonymous with victory, wealth, and good pay, as well as with well-disciplined and therefore reliable soldiers. Not only did Sher Shah have a powerful army, but its reputation had also grown to such an extent that it acquired its own momentum, attracting warriors who were only too keen to be recruited to its ranks. Furthermore, the personal control over his power base that Sher Shah cultivated was another of the main preconditions for his rise. In contrast to the Lodi dynasty's system of governance, Sher Shah successfully contained the latitude previously enjoyed by the elites and hence curtailed their power.

In the phase of consolidation after 1539, Sher Shah's principal task consisted of securing his system of army pay even when less war booty was flowing into his coffers. By making it more heavily dependent on agricultural resources and introducing a new system of remuneration for soldiers, he still managed to maintain his most important instrument of power even in the absence of war booty. One essential element of this system was the branding of horses mentioned previously. Following the victory at Kannauj in 1540, where Sher Shah brought Hindustan and all its land resources under his control, circumspect management of the finances of the empire in conjunction with the systematic exploitation of its

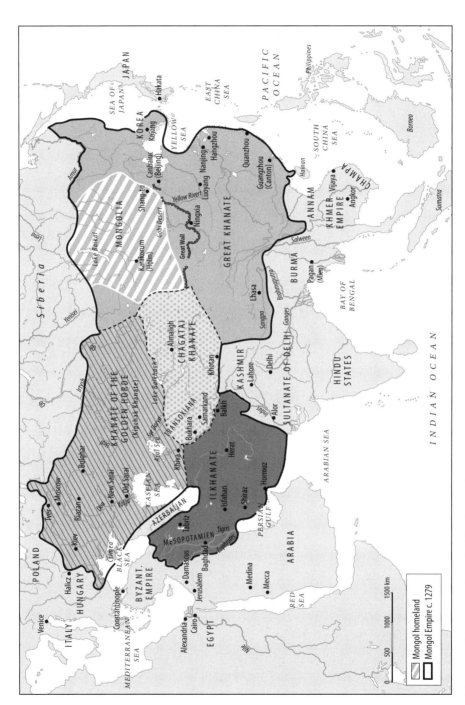

The Mongol Empire at the end of the thirteenth century

POLAND
HUNGARY
ITALY
Venice
Haliez
Kiev
BYZANT.
EMPIRE
Constantinople
MEDITERRANEAN
SEA
Tver
Moscow
Riazan
Bulghar
Don
New Sarai
Old Sarai
Volga
Crimea
BLACK
SEA
Jerusalem
Damascus
Alexandria
Cairo
EGYPT
Nile
RED
SEA
Medina
Mecca
ARABIA

KHANATE OF THE
GOLDEN HORDE
(Kipchak Khanate)
CASPIAN
SEA
Volga
Irtysh
Ob
Ob
Yenisei
Lena

SIBERIA

CHAGATAI
KHANATE
Almaligh
Syr Darya
Lake Balkhash
Amu Darya
Aral Sea
Khiva
Bukhara
Samarkand
TRANSOXIANA
Balkh
AZERBAIJAN
Tabriz
MESOPOTAMIEN
Baghdad
Tigris
Euphrates
ILKHANATE
Isfahan
Shiraz
Herat
Hormuz
PERSIAN
GULF
ARABIAN
SEA

Khotan
Kashmir
Lahore
Delhi
SULTANATE OF DELHI
Indus
HINDU
STATES
INDIAN OCEAN

MONGOLIA
Lake Baikal
Karakorum (Holin)
Gobi Desert
Great Wall
Ningxia
Yellow River
Shang-tu
Canbaluc (Beijing)
Korea
Kojong
YELLOW
SEA
Luoyang
Nanjing
Hangzhou
GREAT KHANATE
Lhasa
Songpo
Brahmaputra
Ganges
BURMA
Pagan (Mien)
Salween
BAY OF
BENGAL
Quanzhou
Guangzhou (Canton)
Hainan
SOUTH
CHINA
SEA
ANNAM
KHMER
EMPIRE
Vijaya
Angkor
CHAMPA
Borneo
Sumatra

EAST
CHINA
SEA
PACIFIC
OCEAN
Philippines
SEA OF
JAPAN
JAPAN
Hakata

Amur

0   500   1000   1500 km

Mongol homeland
Mongol Empire c. 1279

agricultural resources were enough to ensure regular payments to the military and the stabilization of power. Sher Shah introduced administrative innovation to the management of estates, which later were to inspire the Mughal emperor Akbar's agrarian policies.

Likewise, the composition of Sher Shah's army warrants closer attention. In his report, Abbas hints that Sher Shah's troops were exclusively Afghans, thus allowing him by the 1530s to become the sole Afghan warlord in northern India. Yet even Sher Shah's own family history indicates that the assumption of a purely Afghan army is highly improbable, despite the fact that a strikingly large number of Afghans—albeit from insignificant clans—were appointed as commanders. Except for a brief period, the Sur clan had served never under Afghans but under the Turkbachchas—descendants of Turkmen or Mamluk slaves. It was while in the service of this clan that Sher Shah's father had come into possession of the two parganas, one of which, Sasaram, was to form the power base of his son. Sher Shah's alliances with non-Afghans are reflected both in the tactical unions with rich widows and in the makeup of his army.

However, Sher Shah's connections with the Rajputs are particularly significant. There are even some indications that his mother came from a Rajput family. Reputedly, friendly relations to one or more of the local Rajput families around Sasaram are believed to have made a significant contribution to Sher Shah's early successes. The personal access he enjoyed to individual members of this family enabled him indirectly to recruit fresh troops. In this regard, his Rajput friends acted as middlemen, securing Sher Shah access to the human resources of diverse ethnic groups, not just the Rajputs. It may even be the case that in the pre-Mughal period, concepts like "Afghan" or "Rajput" signified not so much ethnic as military identities and were not used to denote clearly delineated population groups. Here we may point to the fact that the name "Pashtun" (Afghan) was adopted by all "Hindus" of the military caste when they converted to Islam. They were then adopted into Afghan clans and gained acceptance there. Contemporary sources also bear witness to this form of conversion, which is not like a religious conversion in the modern sense but was conducted on practical grounds of employment and military efficiency.

For what at first sight might appear to be a switch of religious faith was in most case merely a means of notifying others of military recruitment or career success. Socioreligious identities were created on the military employment market. One exception in this regard is the Rajputs. Thanks to the high esteem in which they were already held, as a group with a long-standing military tradition, they had no need of an identity change. Status, ethnicity, and social background were scarcely of any significance in Sher Shah's army. The caste system, which plays a key role in the social history of India, had lost its significance within the army, with many of Sher Shah's commanders being slaves in the process of emancipating themselves. Through the creation of a unit, a disciplined group that was not just some loose agglomeration, ethnic and social conflicts ceased to play a major role anymore. The most important institution of authority under Sher Shah was not the clan, a particular tribe, or the royal court but the army encampment.

There remains the question of how stable such authority was. Older Indian political science regarded the treasure horde as an essential element of royal rule. A hidden treasure trove was seen as the center of a future kingdom, nor did the riches even need to be distributed to engender genuine political solidarity. Yet Sher Shah, who after his victory over the king of Bengal had a large quantity of treasure at his disposal, also legitimized his authority by dividing up his riches. In this way he made them appear inexhaustible, thereby securing himself widespread prestige and recognition. Yet we might still ask how in practical terms a union of the most diverse religious and ethnic groups could possibly be effected. There were in fact profound differences of opinion in matters of lifestyle between Islamic scholars on the one hand and especially the Rajputs of Central India on the other. It remains an open question for historical research to determine how a social balance could have been achieved in these circumstances.

The Mughal Dynasty's Legitimation of Power

The concept of rule that both the founder of the Mughal Empire, Babur, and his son Humayun represented brought together influences from the Mongolian, Turkish, and Islamic traditions.[35] Babur legitimized his authority by establishing a personal link back to the Mongol ruler Chinggis Khan (d. 1227) and the founder of the Timurid dynasty Tamerlane. For the position of those leaders had gone far beyond merely that of a successful military or political leader. The reverence felt for the house of Chinggis Khan ensured its members a widely recognized birthright to power. Thus, even the mighty Tamerlane did not assume the title "khan" but exercised his power in the capacity of emir. The most obvious difference between the Mongolian and the Islamic tradition was the fact that the khan was a military and political leader who wielded absolute power, while the decisions of an Islamic leader were circumscribed by the requirements of shari'a law.

Tamerlane's conception of power was conditioned by religious concerns. A central element was the idea that the offices within an earthly realm symbolized those in the kingdom of God. Just as God was the sole ruler of heaven, so only one person could rule over God's realm on Earth. Even though his authority was not unlimited and consultation of capable advisers was usually required, the ultimate power to command and to make decisions still rested with the ruler alone. Tamerlane himself adopted the title of "the Proclaimer and Renewer of the Faith of Muhammad," thereby not only linking his personage with the two immediately preceding holders of the title, the Mongol rulers Mahmud Ghazan Khan (d. 1304) and Öljeitü (d. 1316), but also creating a connection to the Umayyad and Abbasid caliphs. Following the death of a Timurid ruler, the country was customarily divided up not among tribes, as was true among the Mongols, but instead, according to territorial considerations, among his successors. Although women could not become rulers themselves, they could from time to time wield considerable power, acting, for instance, as regent in the absence of the ruler. As we have already seen from the example of Babur, among the Timurids it was also perfectly possible for a minor to accede to the throne.

Although Babur, like Tamerlane, believed implicitly in the will of God, he also governed with practical and political rather than religious considerations uppermost in his mind. The Timurids had never recognized the caliphs' suzerainty in religious and hence legal affairs, but at the same time as Babur conquered the subcontinent, the last caliph, Al-Mutawakkil III, was deposed by Ottomans in Egypt. Recognition of the supremacy of the Ottoman sultan was out of the question. As a ruler from the house of Tamerlane, Babur believed in the inherited right of the Timurids to power. After he had consolidated his rule in Kabul, in 1507 Babur took on the title *padshah* and in so doing threw down the gauntlet to the other regional powers. Babur regarded the suzerainty that he claimed for himself as indivisible. Even so, he continued to observe the principle of dividing up territorial power among his sons. Such a combination—ruling authority invested in a single person on the one hand and divided territorial power on the other—presents a

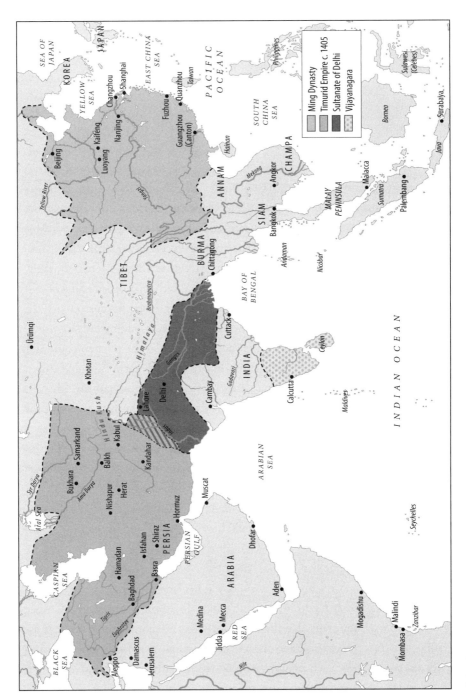

Asia, circa 1400

permanent risk for continuing hegemony. So it was that the Mughal Empire was faced with a severe test straight after the death of its founder.

Theoretically, Babur's son Humayun was swiftly proclaimed ruler. The practical division of the country with his three brothers turned out to be more problematic, however, and was the first and last experiment of this kind by the Mughals. The attempt was made all the more difficult by the precarious position the empire found itself in, still in the process of consolidating and surrounded by external enemies who remained very strong. An initial agreement was made but soon dissolved, especially because Humayun's brother Kamran turned against the new padshah. The development of the state under Humayun was strongly colored by his mystical mind-set. The ruler arrogated to himself a position that corresponded to the sun as the center of the cosmos. Courtiers were organized into twelve departments surrounding the ruler, which were supposed to correspond to the signs of the zodiac. Humayun set especially great store by the notion that the temporal ruler was God's shadow on Earth. Humayun even evolved a new court etiquette, in which the symbolism of light and the sun played a central role, leading some people to think that Humayun was attempting to claim divinity for himself. For example, the ruler took to concealing his crown beneath a cloth. Whenever he revealed it, his courtiers were expected to react by exclaiming, "The light has shone!" The fact that Humayun saw his authority as a personal possession is also made clear through an anecdote that told of how the ruler once rewarded a water carrier who had saved his life by endowing him with royal authority for a few hours. And yet in practice Humayun was unable to impose his principle of total sovereignty even within his own court. At times, the position of the aristocracy was so strong that it could exact a high price for lending Humayun its support—for instance, in his struggle against his brother Kamran—and effectively blackmail him.

The Orchestration and Development of Power under Akbar

The huge changes that the imperial system of the Mughals made to the social fabric of the subcontinent continued to influence the reign of succeeding rulers even after the collapse of the Mughal Empire.[36] At the start of the nineteenth century, particularly in matters of agricultural organization and taxation, rulers harked back to concepts first devised by the Mughals. Their systems of currency and coinage, as well as weights and measures, were revived both by the British and by the independent principalities. Forms of social interaction and legal traditions were retained, while the aesthetic of the Mughal period became an important point of reference in art and architecture. In the military sphere, too, Mughal methods of recruitment, administration, and discipline of soldiers had considerable influence. Their system of numerical ranks and of distributing parcels of land as remuneration was likewise adopted later by the Rajput rulers and the French.

Yet more than any individual measures, what endured most tenaciously was the myth of the imperial authority of the Mughal rulers, which lived on well into the eighteenth century in India. Even the British East India Company (EIC) perpetuated the fiction of Mughal suzerainty right up to the Indian Mutiny of 1857. One result of this was that, even a century after the demise of the Mughal Empire, moves to attain independence were hardly in evidence at all. One might well ask how and why the Mughal rulers were in a position to fabricate symbols and rituals that facilitated the creation of an all-embracing network of authoritarian and hierarchical relationships or how they could win over powerful social groupings to their cause, subordinate them hierarchically, and still forge a sense of social cohesion.

At the beginning of his reign, Akbar (r. 1556–1605), Humayun's son and successor, had to contend with opposition, but he ultimately managed to consolidate his power by restructuring the relationship between himself and the country's elite.[37] He not only to a large extent created an equilibrium between the various different ethnic groups within the ranks of his army but above all generated a sense of common identity. By introducing the positions of military commander (*mansabdar*) and imperial administrator (*amir*), he created offices of great prestige, which acted as powerful magnets for ambitious men from all backgrounds. Akbar himself cultivated an approachable charismatic style of leadership that was unique among Indo-Muslim rulers. With the help of symbols and rituals, he established an image that presented the ruler as the incarnation of the empire. Yet he began to formulate this ideology in words only after appointing the scholar Abul Fazl Allami (1551–1602) as his adviser. By associating himself this closely with the destiny of the state, Akbar made his position unassailable. Any criticism of the ruler was tantamount to calling the whole system into question.[38] Through explicit reference back to Tamerlane as his ancestor, Akbar justified his power, first and foremost in the eyes of his Muslim subjects, who accepted his appeal to the memory of Tamerlane as vindication of a legitimate monarchy. A complex courtly ritual served to exalt the ruler, a personage to whom the nobility felt not only beholden on a personal level but also intimately connected. By the end of the reign of his son and heir Jahangir, in 1627, this system of regulative symbols and rituals was well established.[39]

Although particularly the highly specialized and systematic bureaucratic apparatus of the Mughal Empire may appear impressive, the real heart of the system was the firm bonds of loyalties and interests that linked the ruler and his servants. Central to this was a certain shift in values among the military nobility, who came from a variety of different backgrounds, whereby the conventions of individual, tribal-, or status-based honor had to be reinterpreted as a more impersonal sense of being beholden to the empire. Being in the service of the Mughal ruler, and hence the empire, and potentially even promotion and personal advancement within the hierarchical system soon became the external manifestations of a new code of honor that was evolving.

The way Akbar was perceived publicly was initially characterized primarily by the symbolism of rulership. An early and unequivocal expression of Akbar's political autonomy was his decision to make not Delhi but the village of Fatehpur Sikri the site of the new capital of his empire. Akbar fostered a close relationship with Salim Chishti (d. 1571), a respected Sufi sheikh, who lived in Fatehpur Sikri and who played a key role in the development of Akbar's ideology.[40] After Salim's death, at the ruler's behest the village was developed into the capital, following well-thought-out plans. Alongside the palace, central features of the new city were a grand mosque and the tomb of Salim Chishti, which became a site of pilgrimage. With this project, Akbar on the one hand emphasized the role of Indian Islam as a combination of legalistic religion and mysticism, while on the other managing to make a connection between the sanctity of the tomb of the Sufi sheikh and his own personage and royal authority. After Chishti's death, his sons were also strongly urged to enter into Akbar's service so that Akbar might become party to the "mystical qualities" surrounding these family members and benefit by association with their renown. Akbar extended this connection to the Chishti Order (Chishtiyya) by making a pilgrimage to the grave of the founder of the order in

Sketch of the Mughal ruler Akbar (r. 1556–1605). Akbar is widely regarded as one of the most important rulers of the Mughal period. He consolidated the empire through a series of wide-ranging administrative reforms. In addition, he attempted to create a new syncretistic form of religion that was more fitting for the Indian subcontinent than Islam. To this end, he established a kind of monastic order with himself as its spiritual leader. (Roland and Sabrina Michaud)

India, Moinnuddin Chishti (1141–1236), at Ajmer. When a dispute broke out there over a donation made by Akbar, the ruler assumed personal control over the shrine.

Furthermore, by making Fatehpur Sikri into a new capital free from all existing political connections, Akbar undermined any influence that particular social groups might have exerted on the old structures of authority in Delhi. Yet the Mughal ruler also expended a good deal of his resources on extending and strengthening three strategically important fortresses in Agra, Allahabad, and Lahore. This was intended to enable him and his royal retinue to travel throughout his empire and to oversee military operations personally. But in 1585, the new capital at Fatehpur Sikri was abruptly abandoned, as Akbar moved his residence to Lahore for military reasons. Soon after, he revived the lifestyle of his forbears, coming up with the idea of a court camp of tented accommodation, from which he would conduct his affairs of state. He effectively created a truly mobile capital involving all the essential elements of administration and courtly life. There is a suspicion, though, that security concerns were not the only reason for Fatehpur Sikri being abandoned. The decision may also have helped the Mughal ruler to break free of court ceremony and protocol—which in the meantime had grown extremely well rehearsed and rigid and which, while designed to under-line the stature and power of the ruler, in truth succeeded only in making him seem passive—and to give fresh impetus to the image of an active and aggressive ruler. Akbar's court camp contained all the elements of regal authority and re-sembled Fatehpur Sikri even in the external design of the tents. The camp was gigantic and meticulously organized, with the structures of the ruler's camp being mirrored on a smaller scale by those of the dignitaries who traveled with him. The fact that the ruler's court camp was a genuine capital of the empire is indicated by coins minted at this time, which have not the name of a city on them but instead descriptions such as "camp of good fortune" *(zorb muʿaskari-i iqbal)*. Whereas Akbar's predecessors set great store by their sovereignty over Delhi—just as control of Samarkand and the political support of the populace there played an especially key role for the Timurids—the Mughal ruler invested all his authority in his person and dynasty exclusively.

This fact is reflected in the ideology of the dynasty, which, as we have seen, the aforementioned scholar Abul Fazl Allami was largely responsible for formu-lating and disseminating. Gifted with a rich imagination and a wide-ranging intellect, he was an outstanding ideologue and propagandist. Abul Fazl constructed an intellectual framework that was intended to legitimize the rule of Akbar and dispel the claims of rival parties right from the outset. He claimed that the ruler and his family had a divinely inspired right to rule over mere mortals, who were endowed only with lesser qualities. This dynastic formula, which represented Abul Fazl's conceptual reworking of Akbar's political and personal ambitions, was spread by the scholar at court, in his personal correspondence, and above all in his work *Akbar-Nama*. At the heart of this treatise, published in 1595, stands an ideology that places Akbar in particularly close proximity to God. To corroborate this assertion, Abul Fazl cited the appearance—attested over subsequent generations—of a hidden light that shone from within Akbar's brow (or forehead) but that could be perceived only by especially spiritual people. This mythologizing played its part in ensuring that, in his lifetime, Akbar possessed greater esoteric authority than the *muqtahidun,* the most holy Sufi masters of this era, or even the Mahdi.

In a fabulous myth contained within the *Akbar-Namai,* Abul Fazl told of Akbar's forefathers. These are said to have included not only the first man, Adam, and fifty-one generations of Christian and Muslim prophets but also the first known Turkish–Mongol personalities. To try and make this ideology more intelligible and more accessible to humans, Abul Fazl brought together two widespread and familiar doctrines: the ancient origin myth of the Mongols (as elsewhere in his work, Abul Fazl tells the story of a pure woman, who gives birth to the founding fathers of a ruling dynasty; in Akbar's case, a divine light causes her to conceive) and the illumination philosophy of the Persian mystic Shihab ad-Din Suhrawardi (d. 1193), which Abul Fazl openly acknowledges as a source for his *Akbar-Nama*. In his complex theory, this latter scholar outlines the idea subsequently taken up by Abul Fazl of a heavenly light passed down to man by the angels by means of a hierarchical system. Akbar, Abul Fazl maintained, was imbued with an especially large quantity of this light, which due to its power had to be kept hidden, and this was proof of his proximity to God.

Such details help pave the way for an ideology that could embrace "Hindus" and other non-Muslims and that counteracted the religious and ethnic tensions that had characterized previous Indo–Muslim realms. Abul Fazl succeeded in couching Akbar's publicly enacted religious practices and a dynastic claim to power that went back to the time of Tamerlane in a single ideological framework, which found widespread acceptance among the elite of the Mughal Empire. If we view Akbar's "Divine Faith" in this context, all theories about its derivation from diverse religions and ideologies are rendered redundant. After 1583, Akbar did not conduct any more orthodox Muslim rituals and instead began to worship the sun. To this end, he invented many new rites and conducted discussions with acknowledged holy men of various sects. He practiced sexual abstinence, which for a ruler was extremely uncommon, and even had his hair tonsured, so that his soul might float free up to heaven when he died. Akbar was soon able to enthuse a number of his closest officials for the new religion. This form of bond is referred to as "imperial discipleship" and is commonly thought to have considerable political efficacy. From a certain point in time on, every week a group of twelve men would be inducted into Akbar's circle of followers. This was deemed an especial honor and represented both a closer connection to the ruler and an extraordinarily reliable and loyal form of affiliation. The initiation rite included a declaration whereby every Muslim was required to renounce orthodox Islam and henceforth to agree to venerate Akbar directly. In addition, the new initiate had to swear a personal oath of loyalty to his ruler. This rite became a way of binding the elite directly to the throne as well as having the advantage of taking the most diverse subjects together through the process of common acceptance of a new ideology, an act that eclipsed old ties. The idea of the ruler as an enlightened being also spread beyond the court and was even absorbed into the folk traditions of the rural populace. This principle was upheld under Jahangir (r. 1605–1627); the new ruler demanded from his subjects the same degree of reverence that his father had been accorded.[41] In this respect, though, his claims went beyond those of Akbar, insofar as Jahangir considered himself a greater prophet than Muhammad and saw the holy men of his age not as spiritual teachers but as competition.

So, with the help of Abul Fazl and his ideology, Akbar managed to create a new imperial identity. In the early seventeenth century, most of the elite of the Mughal Empire were almost entirely dependent on pursuing careers in the service of the empire, while only a minority—for example, the Rajputs, plus a few Afghans and Indian Muslims—still owned their own landed estates, to which they could have returned in times of crisis. A military–administrative elite had grown up, constructed on the model of Islamic military slavery. This approach allowed different ethnic groups to be incorporated into the army and to be brought up as reliable warriors serving dynasties of sultans. Some noblemen and high officials of the Mughals, despite being freemen from a legal point of view, elected to have themselves classified in a manner akin to military slaves. Even the term "slave" *(bandah)* was employed. This use of terminology denoting a social relationship between a slave and his master suggests that normative connotations influencing this development had arisen over centuries of military slavery in the Muslim world. A social hierarchy was also evident in the question of inheritance law—both Akbar and Jahangir claimed any property belonging to their deceased "slaves" for themselves, a practice definitely not in accordance with the Islamic inheritance law.

Two further, more profound connections evolved from this relationship between the ruler and his elite: first, the spiritual discipleship already mentioned; and second, service as a family tradition, which was almost more important than the former in the early sixteenth century. The expression *khanazad* ("son of the household"), which originally denoted an actual direct connection with the court, became a term that people applied with pride for service lasting several generations but in which no direct connection to the ruler ever necessarily came about. This concept filtered down to influence even the lowest ranks of any particular group of servants and could on occasion be a powerful complement to Abu Fazl's dynastic ideology. As long as the ruler was resident at court, this kind of relationship could be sustained relatively easily, for which reason Jahangir mostly resided at court instead of personally embarking on military campaigns. In order to give commanders stationed in far-flung outposts of the empire a sense of close contact and maintain their pride in their service as khanazad, a powerful symbolism developed. Thus, the ruler's seal was treated with just as much reverence as the ruler himself.

The network of social relations that the Mughals fashioned between master and slave, lords and their retinues, or the ruler and family traditions proved to be an extraordinarily sustainable way of controlling the empire. People's capacity to identify the person of the ruler behind mere symbols was invoked through an imperial ritual. Yet the basis for the Mughals' power lay in a more deep-seated quality—namely, the impulsion to attain greater honor through subjugating oneself to the personage of the ruler and his dynastic authority. This desire transcended social barriers and ensured that the elite of the Mughal Empire could never countenance any shortcomings, either in the system of norms surrounding their personal code of honor or in the matter of their service to the ruler.

The Relationship to Native Elites

The relations between the Mughals and the Rajputs formed one of the cornerstones of Mughal rule.[42] These connections served to integrate an independent cultural group, which actively promoted the aims of the empire, into the political system. The region inhabited by the Rajputs was a strategic transition zone between the larger cultural centers in Gujarat and those on the northern Indian plain, through which many trade routes led. The key factor here was the loyalty that underpinned the relationship between the Mughals and the Rajputs. To illustrate this phenomenon, we may cite three separate instances mentioned in an essay by Norman P. Ziegler, taken respectively from the genealogies, the clan histories, and the administrative chronicles of the Rathor Rajputs of West Rajasthan in the mid-seventeenth century.

In his work, Ziegler gives a general definition of loyalty as a sense of connection and willingness over a protracted period to act in the interests of the object of loyalty and in doing so to willingly make moral, emotional, and material sacrifices. Similar to the forging of one's own identity, loyal relationships are, he maintains, founded in the social matrix. An important reference point was the local political culture, through which political situations were defined and which offered a subjective orientation. In making his assertion, Ziegler made the following assumptions: first, loyalty has to do not only with questions of identity, that is, of the self in connection with others, but also with the perception of right and wrong, as defined in cultural terms. It is therefore about integration as well as concepts of locality and membership but also about common values and social institutions. Second, loyalty is based on common interests shared between an individual's personal goals and the objects of his or her loyalty. It is the product of individual identification and pacification. Third, loyalty in a wider sense is dependent on conceptualizations of systems of order and of myths and symbols through which this order is defined and that address larger goals. Fourth and finally, loyalties in premodern societies are governed by a multitude of primary and secondary groups and are subject to competing norms and standards, from which they derive both their plurality and their potential for conflict.

During the Mughal period, the Rajputs defined their identity with the aid of two primary entities: brotherhood and alliances formed through marriage. In this, the concept of brotherhood corresponds in the widest sense to a patrilinear unit of ancestry represented by the clan and to a connection via the bloodline of a male ancestor with a forefather. But in reality, this kind of clan was usually not an integrated group; the real functional units were therefore smaller brotherhoods spanning three or five generations. These had a very close, unbreakable bond to their country, which they described as their home and their origin and construed as the basis for their livelihood and strength. Both brotherhoods and ties through marriage persisted under the Mughals—they were highly significant for the Rajputs' own conception of themselves. Yet these connections did not account for all alliances. As a result of the structural characteristics of these groups, the loyalties within a region could be very complex and embrace the most diverse institutions or organizational principles. Even so, the dominant institution was blood relationship. This can be demonstrated particularly well through the example of the partially independent brotherhoods of the Rathor Rajputs, which to a large extent were able to elude the control of more powerful groups and which had only limited contact with the Mughals. The predominant criteria within this group were unilineal descent and the principle of equality among brothers, and there were only minimal differences in rank, with even the leader of such a brotherhood being only a "first among equals" and dependent on the will and the assent of his brothers.

Other communities display a stronger differentiation; here, wealth and power were also key determining factors. Moreover, they were influenced by two further institutions: lordship and clientship, defined by hierarchical relationships and by a general feeling of loyalty between groups or individuals and a higher instance. Kinship by blood and ancestry played a role here only within the ruling families, while for the rest of society their relationship of patronage represented the means by which they accessed land and positions of authority. Those in this kind of clientship situation were generally designated in contemporary texts by the term *cakar* ("servant"). Yet this conveys more the sense of a military subordinate who was granted rights over a particular tract of land. This type of relationship between a local ruler and his cakar was based on an arrangement of mutual obligation: the client pledged his loyalty and promised to fulfill particular duties, while the patron offered him in return protection and recompense.

Under the strategy of indirect rule, in which the Mughals claimed the right to name successors for regions under their control and supported these successors with weapons and resources by allocating to them a sinecure *(jagir)*, clientship developed into a significant institution, which supplanted affinity as an organizational principle. Local rulers were able to centralize their administrations to such a degree that in the early seventeenth century the first Rajput states came into being, in which there was a clearly defined and institutionalized locus of power, which could apply rules and sanctions and enforce them. Over the course of the sixteenth and seventeenth centuries, the Mughals granted local rulers more wide-ranging power over their regions and hence over access to land, the most important source of privilege and remuneration. As local rulers now grew more powerful, they attempted to switch social bonds and to base these on patronage relationships rather than on blood relationships. These endeavors met with fierce resistance, in which the very basis of the ruler's claim to authority was called into question. These kinds of undercurrents, which even in the Mughal period kept erupting to the surface, did not just play a local role but also had an influence on the supporters of the Mughal throne. The sea change in these social relationships gave rise to more bureaucracy in local principalities. Even back in the early Mughal period, authority over a village was secured not by a spoken guarantee but through written title deeds. In order to break down the traditional ties and structures, in later years local rulers would displace their various clients within their catchment area and no longer entrust them with administration of their home villages.

Alliances through marriage provided another institutionalized form of access to land, status, and prestige. In addition, these were more stable than the relationship between patron and client, as a marriage not only was regarded as a pact between two families and their associated brotherhoods but also signified a spatial and territorial alliance through the custom of the *sala katari,* in which the bridegroom gave the brothers of his bride particular items of clothing or pieces of land as gifts. The system of loyalty and identity formation that was widespread among the Rajputs was a network formed of common ancestry (within the brotherhoods) and hierarchical, binary relationships (within a kingdom). These bonds were complemented on every level by alliances through marriage.

The Rajputs were able to transfer many of these local patterns directly over to their contacts with the Mughals, with whom they not only entertained patron–client relations but to whom they were also linked by marital alliances. This explains the loyalty the Rajputs showed toward these foreign rulers. Nevertheless, the various systems could sometimes come into conflict with one another. This became clear above all in the differences between an equal social ranking and a hierarchy, as well as in land matters. Likewise, conflicts could arise between the demands of the brotherhood and those imposed by service or the desire for personal achievement. The disunity among the Rajputs over principles of social organization was reflected in a corresponding conflict about norms of behavior and values. Yet the reason for the very stable relationships of loyalty that the Rajputs nevertheless maintained with the Mughals may well be found in their culturally conditioned belief in rank, order, and authority.

In the traditional literature of the seventeenth century, the code of behavior of the Rajputs was laid down in principles that represented the dharma, a canon of social graces that were seen as innate. A Rajput could maintain or enhance his position in the caste system only if he acted in accordance with these principles. General rules stipulated that a father's death should be avenged, that a Rajput should be prepared to fight and die in his master's service, and that it was forbidden to kill members of one's own clan. The third and first rules of this code of conduct relate to the brotherhood, and for individuals who defined themselves through this group, they contained the promise of mutual support above all against external forces. Control over a country was made possible through the preservation of a sense of community. The cultural understanding of the brotherhood as a unified, communal entity also gains in significance with regard to the system of revenge, which ensured that the balance of power was maintained. Such a balance could also be achieved through marriage alliances, which established new social connections.

The second rule of dharma (that is, the obligation of service to a master) is closely bound up with the perception of the kingdom in the Rajput tradition. This was transformed in myth into a wedding between the king—who himself was at one and the same time the earthly representative of God, master, and husband—and the country as his bride. The king was assigned the role of great benefactor, who was expected to protect the country and provide like a father for all his subjects. This honor was due to him in return for services that he had rendered to a deity. Likewise, to serve the ruler was regarded as a mark of respect, as an act of subjugation and self-sacrifice. By these means, a Rajput could fulfill the moral task with which he was entrusted, namely, to protect and preserve his country and its people. The relationship between patron and client was thus incorporated into a myth of salvation, which among the Rajputs even generated an internal categorization: anyone who was less devoted to his master was seen as a lesser Rajput.

One further important factor conditioning the growth of strong and enduring loyalty between Rajputs and Mughals is the fact that even a Muslim could be perceived as a Rajput. The Rajputs regarded themselves as a divided caste, embracing both "Hindu" and Muslim Rajputs. The latter had to wield at least as much power and authority as his "Hindu" counterpart. Because Muslims could thereby gain entry into the social system of the Rajputs, it was possible for a "Hindu" Rajput to serve a Muslim master. And yet within the ideological system, contradictions arose, which became evident in the relationship between service for a patron and the brotherhood's system of norms. Especially as local rulers began to gain increasing control over status and land during the Mughal period, the patron–client relationship was often given precedence over the laws of the brotherhood.

During the Mughal period, the Rajputs formed part of a complex process of change and transition, as the region became ever more closely integrated into the affairs of northern India. Not only were local social and political structures affected, but so were the values and ideals against which the Rajputs measured themselves and their deeds. So it was that they found themselves confronted with decisions about the nature of their formation of identity, their obligations, and the focus of their loyalty, all of which gave rise to conflicts. Loyal relationships with the Mughals were based primarily on the fact that the latter's ideals and aspirations resembled those of the Rajputs and that the Mughals did not seek to alter the cornerstones of the traditional social order of the Rajputs. The policies that the Mughals practiced, of supporting local leaders, entering into marriage alliances, and granting land as reward for service and loyalty, enjoyed considerable support in the local ideology. In this sense, through their submission to Mughal rule, the Rajputs were able to realize their own ideals. The alliance between the

Rajputs and the Mughals may therefore be described as a product of identification and obligation, which were generated through personal contacts and associations, and in harmony with the local customs and ideals that were set forth in local myths and symbols.

Tribal Communities

The interaction between tribal communities and agrarian society in medieval India was a great deal more important than both contemporary reports and modern research might lead us to believe.[43] The structure of the Mughal state was based on the fact that the elites had farming surpluses at their disposal, which they systematically collected and distributed. The structures of village communities played a decisive role in the growth and survival of this system. These structures were characterized by two central features: on the one hand their extreme social stratification and on the other the key position occupied by the small peasant farmer in agricultural production. However, these basic parameters, which modern research has set to try to understand Indian agrarian society in the Middle Ages, fail to take into account certain essential elements. One such factor is the role of tribal communities, whose participation in this socioeconomic process was vitally important for the stability of society. Although vast tracts of the empire remained unexploited by the farming system, they were almost certainly inhabited nevertheless. In all probability, these areas were used by people for whom cultivation of the land did not yet constitute a livelihood. And even in regions where the state agricultural system was well established, other ways of life and other socioeconomic systems must have existed. Examples of this are Fhakkar and Janjuha tribes who lived around Lahore. The central state's control of their region was only nominal. The fact that such regions and their statistics are given both in the official chronicles of the government and in the biographies of rulers (for instance, Abul Fazl Allami's second work, the *Ain-i-Akbari*) was intended to suggest a unified structure for the whole empire, and this assumption has influenced modern scholarship, too.

The definition of a tribe and its outstanding characteristics is difficult and contentious. But even in the absence of a precise definition, we can still identify the existence of certain groups who, although they were forced to become settled farmers in some cases, made their living through herding livestock. In addition, these social groupings were characterized by a particular sense of community that was quite distinct from the social hierarchy of the rest of the populace. It is also extremely hard to say what the relationship was between the various social categories of the time (tribe and caste or peasantry and landowners). Accordingly, modern researchers have largely ignored the category of "tribe" and simply assigned the people in question to categories that fit the image of the classic agrarian system of the Mughal period better. Thus, the terms "landowner" *(zamindar)*, "indigenous leader," "peasant," or "caste member" have often been applied to describe tribal people, thereby unwarrantably simplifying a complex situation. The existence of tribal cultures within the Mughal Empire would signify a social distribution of power that would also have influenced the nature of the central state. As a result, in both medieval and modern sources, tribal societies are described only in a very simplistic way, while their existence and contribution to society and the economy are ignored.

Even so, despite this paucity of source material, an attempt has been made to investigate the structural dynamics behind the transformation of tribal societies in medieval India, particularly in the Punjab region. While the description of livestock herding generally hints at the existence of tribal societies, there were also some regions where certain tribes pursued other forms of economic activity. This development can be traced in a longer-term study of the history of these tribes. In this, processes of becoming sedentary and of forming social strata become evident. One example is the tribe of the Jats, who evolved quite distinctly in different regions of the Punjab and who can therefore hardly be studied as a homogenous grouping. In areas with favorable agricultural conditions, some Jats abandoned their herding lifestyle and turned to settled farming. This process was protracted and characterized by several interim stages, where livestock herding and crop growing were carried out in tandem. We may surmise on the evidence of contemporary sources that the Jats had their own very particular form of social organization and that under the name "Jat" in the Punjab many different social units existed, which had retained a strong tribal identity and whose livelihood was not solely focused on farming. Conversely, it can be demonstrated that at least from the seventeenth century on, the Jats were designated as farmers. This was above all the case in the regions of the Punjab, where the climate and the kind of soil promoted the process of sedentism. The natural environments in which the various groups of the Jat lived had an effect on the changes that their society underwent, giving rise to fundamental differences and specializations.

Over time, the other tribes living in the Punjab also experienced a similar kind of assimilation process. We may cite here the example of the Ghakkar, whose leaders ended up serving in the central administration of the Mughal Empire as mansabdaran. The city of Gujarat was built by Akbar precisely in order that the Ghakkar should give up their previous way of life. Similar structures are also evident among the Khokhar tribe. Parts of the Bhatti tribe even remained nomadic right up to recent times, while other Bhatti families are cited in the *Ain-i-Akbari* as being *zamindaran*. However, this alone does not constitute sufficient proof that they participated in the structure of the differentiated village communities, as time and again the designation *zamindaran* was simply applied to powerful tribal leaders. Conversely, the fact that many of the regions controlled by the Bhatti lay in areas that were renowned for intensive and commercially viable agriculture may well indicate that they did integrate into agrarian society.

At any one time, different groups from a single tribe might find themselves at different stages of integration into the agrarian society of the Mughal Empire. Those who were already fully integrated presumably exchanged their tribal identity for a form of caste status in a hierarchical society. There were also some groups who even at the height of the Mughal Empire's power retained their tribal identity, yet who were so affected by the political changes taking place in their surroundings that changes to their social structure became inevitable. However, this kind of social transformation could happen in a number of different ways. Nomadism and livestock herding usually occur in combination with one another and up until now have been studied as such, with researchers keen to stress the instability of such a way of earning a living, as well as the inability to produce a surplus on a regular basis. The need for agricultural products and manufactured goods fueled a constant process of sale and purchase; for this reason, the contacts between the tribal groupings with sedentary society were of great importance, because they could to a large extent influence the tribes' ideals and their economic considerations.

Between nomads and village communities, there grew up relationships of mutual dependence that overlay social and economic differences. In this regard, tribal

societies emerged as mercantile middlemen between various rural or urban settled societies. The most famous of these tribal traders were the Lohanis, who even
prior to the reign of Babur were transporting goods between India and Kabul.
They journeyed across India in regular cycles, coordinating their routes with the
trading patterns of the various settled communities through which they passed.
Other likewise mostly Afghan tribes also traveled around more restricted areas
in the same way. For the tribes of the Punjab, direct trading and bartering relations were easier to maintain with the local village inhabitants. In some areas, a
surplus of products from pastoral herding was generated, thus enhancing the significance of the tribes for the economy of the empire, as well as the importance
of local trade connections. The exchange of goods could also sometimes have a
power-politics background, with the livestock herders either placing themselves
under the jurisdiction of the local authorities or conquering and subjugating them.
Similarly, regular raids were carried out by the tribes in some regions. Instances
of tribal societies dominating village communities are the Ghakkars, the Juds, and
the Janjuhas.

By the end of the seventeenth century at the latest, thanks to the expansion
and the powerful position of the Mughal Empire, such a model of rule was scarcely
imaginable any longer. The central state attempted to protect the sedentary population, because the empire was dependent on the revenue generated by agricultural surpluses. Even though the historical sources provide scant evidence, it is
probable that the shepherd tribes subordinated themselves to the local settled
farming community, being employed by the latter as seasonal agricultural labor
or as armed forces for the state. The commercialization of agriculture and the
cultivation of extensive areas of farmland greatly increased the demand for
manpower. Regular raids were, according to the sources, carried out primarily
by the Bhatti tribe, who were notorious for their attacks even in the time before
the Mughal Empire. They had at their disposal six thousand mounted warriors,
plus a large number of foot soldiers. The Jats also used this method to supplement their livelihood, which could not be met simply through a life of pastoral
herding.

Other tribes also conducted regular raids on villages and highways. Yet in the
prevailing circumstances, the development of sedentism was a natural progression,
because it presented the most opportunities in the long term. The growth of

commercialized agriculture under the Mughals facilitated the transformation of formerly nomadic tribal societies that lived through herding livestock and their integration into the agrarian system. The monetarization of the economy and the growth of trade also ensured that a greater number of people were able to earn a living from the same area of land. The agrarian society must have been in a position to assimilate the former tribal societies or alternatively may have had urgent need of them as a labor force. Such a situation commonly arises, particularly at times of economic upturn. The tensions that erupted in the Punjab in the eighteenth century can at least in part be traced back to this process of assimilation. As a consequence of the close economic ties that existed by then, structural changes in the tribal societies also affected the settled and commercialized farming community of the Punjab. Although in the long run they were unable to withstand the structures and the dominance of the Mughal Empire, the tribal societies of the Punjab were still an economically significant and militarily influential power.

Bureaucracy

Another important theme is the connection between the nominal rank of the military officials of the Mughal Empire, their wages, and the actual strength of their troops.[44] Under Akbar, officers or their rank was designated by a numeral and the suffix -i (for example, *hazari,* meaning "of one thousand"). This form may be called the "single service rank." During the reign of Jahangir and Shah Jahan (r. 1627–1658),[45] the word *zat* ("person") was added to the single service rank, supplemented by another numeral and the word *suvar* ("horseman," "ordinary soldier")—this usage may be termed the "double service rank." At the same time, the third service rank also evolved, characterized by an indication of how many of the horsemen had two or three horses at their disposal *(suvar sih aspa du-aspa).* Ordinary officers had the possibility of being promoted to the rank of 5000/5000 (that is, a service rank of five thousand, with five thousand horsemen under one's command). Apart from a very few exceptions, only princes of the ruling family could climb any higher in the ranks. There is much disagreement on the question of whether the personal salary of an officer and the associated earnings were linked to a troop contingent. The classic view taken by scholars, which has its origins in a work of 1903 by William Irvine *(Army of the Indian Moghuls)*, works from the assumption that an officer with a double rank had to manage two contingents: on the one hand horsemen, who were linked to his personal income, and on the other additional cavalrymen, who were connected with the suvar rank and who had to be paid from the funds allocated to that. But if we are to believe another account, from India itself, an officer's personal rank was an entirely private matter. According to this interpretation, an officer with a double rank had to employ only a single contingent.

Information from newly discovered documents on the promotion of a Mughal officer would appear to lead us to the conclusion that state service and the titles linked to it changed over the course of successive generations of rulers. Four distinct phases can be identified in the history of the service rank: in the first phase, under Chinggis Khan and Tamerlane, the numerical rank of an officer could be taken as a military fact; in other words, an officer "of a thousand" really did command a thousand men. From the final years of Tamerlane's reign to the early part of Akbar's, the effective strength declined below the nominal. Thus, officers at this time commanded far fewer men than their title might lead one to believe. This discrepancy was acknowledged in the third phase. Accordingly, it was at this time that the single rank was changed to a double one. This meant that while an officer designated as commanding one thousand troops was not downgraded in name, the new designation, which gave the number of warriors who were actually under his command, allowed his military significance to be portrayed accurately. The term *Akbar-Nama* for this innovation reveals that it was introduced during Akbar's reign, in its eleventh year in fact, while the *Ain-i Akbari* indicates that this new regulation was put into effect only gradually. Once it became compulsory for horses to be branded, it became far easier to enact such provisions. In the last phase, under Shah Jahan, a reorganization of the empire and state finances took place—a change that must have affected the sector accounting for the largest proportion of state expenditure, namely, the civil service. On paper, Shah Jahan had an army that he could not afford in reality and whose effective military clout was far less than its nominal strength. The ruler solved the problem through a compromise: the size of the contingents corresponding to any particular rank was decreased, but along with it so was the remuneration due to the officers. Henceforth, state servants were required to assemble only a third or sometimes even a quarter of the troops indicated by their rank, while their personal salaries were cut by an average of one-third. Meanwhile the funds that were paid in addition for the contingents were reduced by up to one-sixth, with the provision for being cut still further if they fell short of the mobility, for example, if there were too few horses and too many men for a protracted expedition. In addition, note that position of various service ranks of cavalrymen within the contingents had changed over the course of the successive Mughal administrations. While, under Akbar, the *bar-awardi*, a man who was poor but nonetheless deemed suitable for military service, was the most widespread military group supported by the state, the designation *sih-aspa do-aspa*—that is, a trooper of triple rank with two or three horses—still did not exist during Akbar's reign. Yet it was precisely those horsemen who were of prime importance during the reign of Shah Jahan.

Against this background, some clarification of the posts of *faujdar* or *faujdari* during the Mughal period is called for.[46] The term *faujdar* itself was used as far back as the Sur dynasty and denoted a military commander. The Mughals then incorporated the title of faujdar into their administrative system and used it as the basis on which to crate, in the form of the so-called *faujdari,* an organ for stabilizing the local bureaucracy. Central authority was thereby strengthened and the installation of mansabdaran (military commanders) facilitated. The arrangement of the granting of earnings from landholdings was not compromised by the creation of the office of faujdar. After a province had been captured by the Mughals, a high-ranking nobleman *(subah-dar)* would take over its administration. He was supported in his duties by other aristocrats of lesser stature *(amir* or *hakim),* who functioned as hands-on leaders of the administrative units into which the province had been divided. A number of these districts *(pargana)* were, according to the *Ain-i Akbari,* run by particularly bold, respected, and upstanding noblemen, who were designated as faujdar. Their office combined the duties of a bureaucratic official with that of a military commander. In bureaucratic jargon, a hakim was called a faujdar from the fortieth year of Akbar's reign on. By that time, the administrative unit of the faujdari was fully established, as Akbar created a network of military bases, some of which were combined as faujdari. These military posts made the work of the local administration more efficient and direct, because the troops stationed there by the faujdar would, in an emergency, allow a direct intervention to take place.

There is much debate among scholars as to how large a faujdar's area of responsibility was. Chronicles and administrative documents demonstrate, however, that the faujdari represented an independent administrative unit and that the specific territorial extent could vary. Under Akbar, each administrative unit was relatively large and normally encompassed a province, though it could sometimes cover a larger and very occasionally even smaller area. In the fortieth year of Akbar's reign, the administration of the empire was unified and structured more clearly. The functions and duties of a faujdar were now fixed, as was the area under his control. According to the *Ain-i Akbari,* a faujdar could govern several parganas, though these could not all lie within the same province. Also, a *sarkar* could be governed by several faujdar. It was under Jahangir that the administrative unit of a faujdar came to be called a faujdari. However, references in the memoirs of the ruler (the *Tuzuk-i-Jahangiri*) allow us to draw only some very imprecise conclusions about the size of the administrative unit that was apportioned to a faujdar—the examples cited there relate exclusively to particularly high-ranking noblemen, who later became known as *faujdari-i-umdah* and who in some cases governed more than one province. Likewise, under Aurangzeb (r. 1658–1707), the size of the areas placed under the control of a faujdar was no longer as uniform as it had been under Akbar. Sources attest to instances in Gujarat in which a faujdar had responsibility for a single pargana. From this, we may conclude that the faujdari constituted a distinct administrative unit, existing independently of the financial division into sarkar and parganas. Whereas under Akbar and Jahangir, a faujdar normally governed a province, the units became smaller under later rulers.

This development might indicate that the faujdar functioned more in the sense of a civil servant than a military commanded and that the state was therefore beginning to show an increasing interest in the maintenance of law and order. Yet there is also a connection here with the problem of the growing number of mansabdaran who had to be provided with official posts. The responsibilities of a faujdar were manifold, and he received his order direct from the Mughal court. Within his domain, he exerted an influence over the military, the police, the dispensation of justice, and financial matters. His principal task, however, was to uphold law and order; in emergencies, he could even enforce the laws of the empire with the help of troops that he stationed at the military bases. According to reports in the *Ain-i Akbari,* the role of the faujdar was to support the civil authorities, for instance, controlling the illegal manufacture of weapons at blacksmiths' forges, suppressing revolts, ensuring the streets were safe, and investigating thefts. In this last matter, the faujdar was personally liable for locating the stolen goods. A faujdar was also an integral part of the justice system, leading the trial proceedings at court. Judgments were delivered by a judge and the relevant ministry in agreement with the faujdar. The legislative bases for judgment were shari'a law and the opinion of the legal officers. In cases where shari'a law was not involved and only the finances or the general regulations of the empire were concerned, the faujdar alone was empowered to pass judgment himself. A faujdar was also responsible for levying taxes on the zamindaran. The faujdar thus played a key role in local administration, combining the role of military commander with that of the senior civil servant of a faujdari administrative unit.

Social Structures in Agriculture

Historians have attempted to reconstruct the patterns of distribution of the income earned by the various social strata of mansabdaran in the Mughal Empire. The statistical analysis that A. Jan Qaisar offers in a seminal article is based on two premises concerning the administrative apparatus of the empire:[47] whenever an official was granted a salary and given a sinecure *(jagir),* then his claim was exactly commensurate with the amount that was entered as a *jama* or *jamadami*— that is, the expected yield of a particular region—in the imperial ledger relating to his *jagir.* However, the actual income *(hasil)* was generally quite different; this discrepancy between *jama* and *hasil* eventually led to the introduction of a so-called monthly scale. For the twentieth year of Shah Jahan's reign, figures for the total amount of income demanded from the various ranks of the mansabdaran as well as for the expected earnings from the whole empire have been preserved, allowing us to work out the percentile share of these officials and hence a pattern of distribution. The sources in this instance are official tables of salaries and a list of the mansabdaran from the rank of 500 zat upward, as well as figures for the empire's jamadami in the *Padshah-Nama,* the official history of Shah Jahan's reign. The income of a mansabdaran comprised the following elements: the zat and suvar ranks were calculated separately. Zat ranks were divided into four categories, according to whether the suvar rank of the mansabdar was the same size, half as large, or larger than his zat rank or whether it even amounted to less than half of the latter. As far as the suvar rank was concerned, this was multiplied by 8,000 dams, or in the case of the *do-aspa-sih-aspa* mansabdaran by 16,000 dams.[48] The result of these statistical investigations is that 5.6 percent of all mansabdaran (that is, 445 of 8,000) in the year in question laid claim to 61 percent of the total estimated earnings of the empire. At the head of the hierarchical bureaucracy of the Mughal Empire, just seventy-three princes and noblemen (0.9 percent of all mansabdaran) controlled 37.6 percent of the estimated income of the empire as a whole. On the other side of the equation, 7,555 mansabdaran (94.4 percent) were entitled to receive just 25 to 30 percent of the expected yield, with the result that a large proportion was left over for the state coffers.

Studies in the last few decades have shown not only that the hitherto widespread, generalizing model of Oriental despotism must now be regarded as outmoded but also that the socioeconomic structures of Asia were extremely diverse, even within an individual country.[49] Up till now, scholars researching the history of India mostly employed an abstract standard model relating to farming practices across the whole of Asia. Indian agrarian society in the precolonial era was seen as an undifferentiated mass of peasant farmers who lived in family-based village structures, tilled farmland according to long-established custom and practice, and in the process were solely subject to the political–military authorities and their taxation demands. The concept of private landownership was seen as irrelevant and underdeveloped, with the cultivation of the land being regarded not as a right but rather as a coercive duty imposed on the peasantry. The village communities could subsist for themselves and so stave off their own decline, but they were a hindrance to any further development. As a result, only superficial changes occurred in the composition of the exploitative class and in the way in which the produce that the farmers had to hand over was determined and collected. The general organization or the context in which the goods were produced remained unaffected. Only the changes in the amount of the yield and the way in which it was produced influenced how it was distributed and what proportion the producer ultimately received.

In his work *The Agrarian System of Mughal India* (1963), Irfan Habib produced the definitive study on the theme of land rights during this period. One key factor that emerges from this study is the clear delimitation, taken from the contemporary sources, between the right to own agricultural land *(milkiyat)* and the right of use pure and simple. The first category encompasses in practice the right to make hereditary claims on ownership and lease of land and was in most cases granted to peasant title bearers *(raiyati)* or major landowners (zamindaran). Milkiyat under the Mughals did not, however, correspond to our modern conception of ownership of land. The *raiyat* could not simply dispose of his land, because cultivation of the land was also a duty, while the right to hereditary usage was not always observed in practice. Yet studies by Nurul Hasan and B. R. Grover have shown that land sales by raiyati definitely did occur.[50] As long as peasants paid taxes, these authors demonstrate, they were never driven off their land and were certainly in a position to sell it. Whereas Habib discusses differences only in income between the various social classes, Grover reveals that there was a clear hierarchy in the distribution of land rights: peasants who cultivated or leased their land were pitted, on the one hand, against tenants (so-called *pahikashtkari*) who owned land in regions distant from where they lived and, on the other, against people who tilled part of their land and leased out the remainder. In his study, Habib distinguishes between various strata of the rural population—zamindaran, rich farmers, and poor farmers—but does not further investigate these different classes. Extrapolating from the situation in Maharashtra in the nineteenth century, one might ask whether a certain social asymmetry also existed in the late seventeenth century, in which leaseholders or pahikashtkari could in practice be richer than the local zamindar.

To date, little has been written in the scholarly literature about the lowest echelon of agrarian society (that is, people without any ownership or property rights). Habib's work does contain some details about peasant laborers and village serfs in India. Peasant laborers were engaged tilling the fields of farmers and zamindaran, *dhanuks* husked rice, while other groups worked as guides and porters. Because the untouchables, a significant sector of "Hindu" society under the caste system, were excluded from usage rights, many people must have had no land of their own. Although there were large unexploited tracts of territory, there was a lack of capital. The problems of the landless were also exacerbated by socio-anthropological factors.

The kind of village community that owned land communally and shared out the fields in rotation—hitherto largely the model for research into Indian society under the Mughals—is now, according to Habib, no longer to be found. The *Smriti* literature contains clear indications of privately owned land and inheritance provisions, whereas by contrast, officials of the British Raj in the nineteenth century spoke of communal ownership and periodic distribution. For the British, property meant more than just the right to take possession of land or sell it; it also entailed the right to administer and lease property. In the northwestern provinces of India in the nineteenth century, tenant farmers were required to pay their rent not to an individual owner but into a communal fund, which was used to cover the costs incurred by the village and to meet the tax demands of the state. This situation also pertained to the raiyati villages. Habib's view is that the rise of manufactured goods was a major contributory factor in the decline of the kind of classic village community described here. Some villages had no established council as such but were represented instead by elected inhabitants. In cases where an established council did exist, though, this position was often handed down across generations or—where it attracted a salary—sold on.

In studying the organization and the economic basis of Indian agrarian society, it is important not to concentrate exclusively on the rural population but rather to include precisely those groups that operate between the state and the broad mass of the populace and who in so doing exerted a significant influence on the distribution of goods. Researchers have treated this aspect to the extent that certain inferences may be drawn concerning the conditions of agricultural production and the social and economic status of the producers. Yet more recent studies have called details previously known about the mansabdaran and the *jagirdaran* into question. These administrators could lay claim to the yield of a particular area but not to the land itself. On the one hand, it is now argued that reimbursement in the form of agricultural yields was highly practical for the Mughal bureaucracy. On the other, some claim that the jagirdaran, who, after all, did not need to have any long-term interest in the region assigned to them, contributed to the impoverishment of the peasants, a phenomenon that became especially apparent during the financial crisis that occurred during Aurangzeb's reign. The crown lands of the Mughals *(khalisa)* never amounted to more than one-fifth of the entire territory under cultivation, meaning that the large majority of the empire's territory was open to virtually uncontrolled exploitation. Mass migrations and the abandonment of farmland were the results of such a policy, which bestowed large profits on the jagirdar, who was appointed for only a brief period, while doing great harm to the state, which relied heavily on the farming economy. Later, when many jagirdaran sold their rights to agricultural yields, and these then became hereditary over time, an economic upturn and peace duly ensued in the provinces.

The most significant findings of the latest research have to do with the rights of the zamindaran.[51] Contrary to earlier assumptions, these officials were found to have been present throughout the territory of the empire, in both the *jagir* and the khalisa regions. The zamindaran were not a homogeneous class, but they did all share particular special rights and privileges that affected agrarian society. Any structural change among the zamindaran class thus had a direct influence on the whole of society. While tribal leaders and mid-ranking zamindaran were entitled to collect agricultural yields and to govern smaller regions, the direct zamindaran, who were virtually identical to the raiyati, were the true settlers of virgin territory. A certain degree of political authority flowed from this right. Yet we cannot make the assumption that these were static groups. Above all, the erstwhile potentates made tribute payments, were appointed as mansabdaran, and were awarded their own lands as leaseholds. A mid-ranking zamindar could be promoted to *sadr zamindar,* in which role he became responsible for dispensing justice within several parganas. And if he advanced to the rank of *ta'aluqdar,* he found himself in a superior position to the other zamindaran, who had to pay their contributions to the state through him. Sooner or later, such a ta'aluqdar would usually claim the regions that lay within areas under his control. Yet it was also possible for a zamindar to lose his status; repeated sales and partitioning of a zamindar's landholdings could see his personal share of territory grow so small that he was reduced to the status of a common landowner. Land law under the Mughals was complex. It is a commonly held view, for instance, that the rural populace fared better under local tribal leaders than under the mid-ranking zamindaran, because the former supposedly had a longer-term interest in the land and its inhabitants. The mid-ranking zamindaran, in contrast, often sold their proportionate rights to yields. Different regulations governed zamindaran in Bengal, where they paid the state a fixed sum, which apparently was not linked to the expected yields from their lands. In this way, the zamindaran there could increase their share by simply upping the rate of production. Although, over time, the sale and transfer of rights saw the zamindaran become a more heterogeneous class, the foundations of their authority, namely, the caste system, remained as firm as ever.

Alongside the zamindaran, religious dignitaries also formed part of the medial group between the state and the general populace. These included both Muslim religious scholars and "Hindu" Brahmins. They could also lay claim to income payments but had no claim on ownership of the land apportioned to them (though this is verifiable only for the Muslim dignitaries). Despite the fact that they are accorded great significance in contemporary sources, religious dignitaries had very little land and as a consequence had only very limited political influence.

Where the composition of the rural population is concerned, one should consider categories such as the degree of independence or dependence of ownership rights as inappropriate, because one sees the relative proportions of the various categories as unresolved and therefore liable to produce an unreliably generalizing result. Even so, some provisional assumptions can still be formulated. The Mughal Empire had a class-based society, characterized by the existence of different, clearly structured ownership rights and a complex form of stratification. Cultivation of the land was not just a right; it was also a duty. Conflicts could arise if too much of the agricultural yield was collected. In such instances, the theoretical subjugation of the peasantry also became evident in practice—many simply abandoned their farms. The obligation to cultivate crops was imposed particularly during the period of mass migrations under Aurangzeb. Generally speaking, with regard to their socioeconomic organization, peasants in the Mughal Empire were freer than serfs in Europe or other regions, such as Assam. New historical data support the assumption that the rural populace split into two categories. On the khalisa estates, the personal freedom and property rights of the peasantry were usually respected, while on the jagir estates, which were bound up with special claims on revenue, the jagirdar had no interest in the land itself and in many cases acted to all intents and purposes like a despot. Correspondingly, there were two categories of raiyati, with those in the crown lands being relatively independent, whereas those in the jagir estates would have to be considered more as semi-slaves. Therefore, the question of how political and administrative power over the peasantry was exercised is key.

Zamindaran and raiyati villages must also be differentiated from one another. It needs to be investigated whether zamindaran, driven by enlightened self-interest, played a protective role, shielding the peasants from excessive taxation demands by the state. We can, however, state with certainty that different social strata formed there than in raiyati villages, where other forms of property rights were in force: the rights of the zamindaran were alienable, for instance, while a different structure operated in the raiyati villages. Changes in the structure of occurred on two levels. At the local level, it was mainly about controlling the means of production and about authority. Vertical changes occurred either through economic pressure or other stimuli—mostly, though, they were driven by the sheer will to survive in hard times. According to Habib, such a situation also led to an increase in productivity—the populace had not grown significantly, he claims, while the area of land under cultivation had been greatly expanded. Although massive burdens were the predominant feature of rural peoples' lives, there were still a (very) few incentives to keep farming. Noteworthy in this regard were the tax concessions given by the state to anyone who recultivated fallow farmland. And for many peasants, the sheer status enjoyed by a regional ruler or zamindar may well have been sufficient incentive for them to occupy and till unclaimed land. The state supported "settlers" such as these with loans, while wealthy local people also extended credit. In this way, capital gained great influence over the production of primary goods, and there developed far earlier than was once assumed a dependency on credit lines and market forces. In the case of a price increase, though, not only the middlemen profited; the example of tobacco growing demonstrates that farmers adapted quickly to changing demands. The cultivation of new cash crops must have ensured them profit, too.

In the Mughal Empire, although villages sold the produce that they grew, they rarely brought in any goods. As a result, in contrast to Europe, the same intensity and nature of mutual exchange between the countryside and the city did not materialize, nor did the resulting specializations and divisions of labor. Yet a large financial sector arose as a distribution apparatus, which spread the income from farming in such a way that everyone received their share. Middlemen and merchants, for example, met their own needs not through being producers themselves but through providing services. However, the influence of money stopped short of the villages—only when taxes were demanded in hard cash and the farmer sold his products to raise it did rural people participate in this form of economic activity.

In general, recent studies point to an inherent dynamism within the agrarian society of the Mughal Empire. Before the Mughal era, the difference between the city and the country appears to have been less pronounced. Revenues then were normally collected in the form of produce and used directly, meaning that there was no need for any special structure to distribute goods in this way. If these suppositions are true, then under the Mughals, Indian commerce developed from the level of loosely connected subsistence units into an economy with internal trade and a large financial sector. Yet all the evidence suggests that taxation demands were so heavy that they prevented the agricultural producers from participating in the growth of the economy.

As we have already seen, the zamindaran occupied an important position in the political and cultural life of India;[52] their social significance increased still further under Mughal rule. They also had an enormous influence on the rural economy—in view of its expansion, the state's bureaucracy had to rely heavily on the work of the zamindaran. The cooperation with the zamindaran helped secure Mughal authority, though conflicts of interest were not uncommon. On the one hand, the connections of the zamindaran to the court contributed to the cultural synthesis between the diverse traditions present in the empire, while on the other, the zamindaran also supported separatist and local currents. Yet in the final analysis, the contradictions between a centralized empire and the claims of the zamindaran were too profound and so contributed to the rise of structural problems within the Mughal Empire even before the incursion of the Western powers into the subcontinent.

As mentioned earlier, the Mughals applied the term "zamindar" to people of very diverse ranks, including certain powerful and independent tribal leaders as well as somewhat insignificant middlemen at the village level. This conceptual leveling and simplification can be interpreted as a deliberate wish of the Mughals, at least officially, to reduce influential local leaders to the status of simple intermediaries. Even during the era of the Delhi sultanate (1206–1526), the legal structure of agriculture and the associated balance of power changed fundamentally, and this process only accelerated during the Mughal period. In the empire, three nonexclusive categories of zamindaran existed: the independent tribal princes, the intermediate, mid-ranking zamindaran, and the direct zamindaran. At least one zamindar could be found in almost every pargana in the Mughal Empire. Tribal princes were the autochthonous and autonomous leaders of their regions and exercised almost sovereign power. The sultans had tried constantly to divest these princes of their power and forced them to make tribute payments. This sparked numerous uprisings, and it was found necessary to exert military force to subjugate the independent tribal leaders. By the time of Akbar's reign, the majority of the empire was the sphere of influence of such princes, who had become independent after the end of the sultanate.

To consolidate his power, Akbar likewise demanded tribute and military support. Yet he and his successors added various points to the procedure, so creating a different relationship between the zamindaran and the central government: For one, Akbar was the first ruler to involve the powerful tribal princes in the structure of government and administration. Thus, when a local prince was granted an important *mansab* (rank), he also acquired the rights over a jagir. The revenues from this land far outstripped his original sources of income, while the influence of a tribal leader was strengthened by his potential to raise a large body of troops. Men in the service of tribal princes as well as clan members profited similarly from lucrative state positions.

Second, in return, the Mughals gained influence over the tribal princes, whose status and titles were now dependent on the ruler's goodwill. In individual cases, the ruler even claimed the right to a say in questions of succession. This not only helped strengthen the control of central government over the local princes but also imbued them with a sense of personal obligation to the ruler. Furthermore, the Mughals insisted that either the local prince in person or a close relative should be permanently in attendance at the Mughal court.

Third, although the sultans had also demanded military support from the local princes, the Mughals were the first to develop a system whereby even local potentates without a mansab were prepared to perform military service. This system was very important for maintaining the Mughals' hold on power; in all important campaigns, the forces of their vassal lords played a key role.

Fourth, the Mughals appear to have weakened the power base of the tribal princes from the inside. In forging close ties to their vassals, they created a new class of partners and in some cases were even offered direct imperial mansabs.

Fifth, one especially important element in the new development of the agricultural system was the fact that the home provinces of the tribal leaders were treated like a personal sinecure. Theoretically, then, local princes had thereby to bear the title of a jagirdar and were subordinated to the imperial income regulations. However, they could still bequeath their rights. Although this ruling was mainly enforced in the case of princes who were mansabdaran, the Mughals also tried to transform the tribute due from the other local leaders in such a way that it would come into line with the corresponding shares of actual revenues from the jagir. But many princes continued to make irregular tribute payments *(pesh-kash)*. In attempting to also align the peshkash with the jagir-specific payments, the Mughals gathered information on particular tribal leaders' spheres of influence and in so doing strengthened their theoretical and actual control.

Finally, unlike their predecessors, the Mughals managed to persuade local potentates to obey imperial laws. And just as important as their observance and implementation was the freedom of trade and transit. Tribal princes could be forced to take action against rebels on their territory, while the Mughal ruler also asserted the rights of those who complained at court about infringements by local rulers.

Because positive economic and military developments prevented a social fragmentation of the Mughal Empire into individual, small domains ruled by local princes, the central state was in a position to ensure a large measure of peace and security. This in turn fostered trade and commerce, at the same time that increasing purchasing power stimulated the growth of economic infrastructures and large tracts of fallow land were put under cultivation. It is true that the Mughals owed the firm control that they had gained over the local princes to several military campaigns, but even so they had also managed to build up over time a relationship of loyalty with these rulers and so could often count on voluntary cooperation. The contradiction between imperial and local claims on authority, however, could never be fully resolved. Not every tribal leader could be granted a high mansab or a lucrative jagir. When the Mughal ruler could no longer satisfy the wishes of the local princes, they in their turn sought to transform the jagirs that they had already controlled outside their original home provinces into regions with hereditary rights. The fact that pressure had constantly to be exerted on the zamindaran considerably weakened the military might of the Mughals. Over time, an increasing number of insurrections broke out, so that by the end of the seventeenth century the advantages of a centralized system were no longer clearly apparent.

The category of the mid-ranking zamindaran was broadly defined, encompassing all those who collected tribute payments from the direct zamindaran and paid them to the imperial treasurer, the jagirdaran, or the tribal princes. The tasks of this group included preparing data for the estimation of the payment level, gathering in the anticipated sum, and expediting the cultivation of unused land. Mid-ranking zamindaran provided key support for the Mughal administration in collecting rural taxes and enforcing imperial law. In return, they were granted freedom from certain obligations, tax-free estates, and other concessions. Even so, in many cases they were concerned only with expanding and securing their own power, with some handing over the taxes they had collected to the central authority only after force had been used against them by the Mughals. The exploitation of the rural populace increased, with many mid-ranking zamindaran using every opportunity to try to ascend to the position of local prince. On average, mid-ranking zamindaran received a sum in the range of 2.5 to 10 percent of the taxes they collected. In most cases, they were entitled to pass down their rights to their heirs, though the state could always intervene in or otherwise influence matters of inheritance. Normally, mid-ranking zamindaran wielded power over smaller areas, for example, a village. In order to meet the wishes of the high mansabdaran and noblemen, who did not belong to the zamindaran class and who hence had no heritable territorial rights, the Mughals introduced the system of sinecures attached to particular people, thus enabling permanent rights to be attached to the office of the jagirdaran. Yet the state system of the Mughals was dependent on the zamindaran to such a great extent that the Mughals could never completely suppress this latter grouping, not even when they rebelled against the ailing central state.

The direct zamindaran were the proprietors of property rights over farmland and domestic land. Their number included not only peasant landowners but also owners of property within villages. As a result, every part of the empire belonged in the final instance to a direct zamindar. The rights of this class were hereditary and sellable, and the Mughals saw it as their duty to protect this stratum of society. For example, they promoted the registration of deeds surrendering property, so that in cases of dispute, unambiguous claims could be asserted. The rights of the direct zamindaran were granted to a large number of people, among other reasons in order to expand the proportion of land under cultivation. Sometimes, land (usually uncultivated) was granted free of any taxation *(madad ma'ash)* for charitable purposes; after some time had elapsed, this could become zamindaran land. Unlike the peasant landowners, the zamindaran leased out their land. Generally speaking the tenant, so long as he paid his rent regularly, enjoyed a really secure status, as well as a measure of hereditary title to the land. Yet the zamindaran had the right to prohibit their tenants from abandoning their estates and instead to compel them to cultivate all the land in their possession. In places where the direct zamindaran did not collect the yield from the land, this was levied directly by the farmers themselves, and 10 percent was deducted as the landowner's share to be paid to the direct zamindaran. Direct zamindaran were charged with supporting the central bureaucracy in enforcing the law and to summon up troops. Thus, in their social position, direct zamindaran found themselves squeezed between their superior zamidaran and the state on the one hand and on the other the peasantry, with the result that they often came into conflict with both sides when trying to assert and secure their own position. It could sometimes happen that the direct zamindaran passed the pressure exerted on them from above down to the peasantry below them, but in most cases they were to be found leading the peasants' revolts in protests against constant increases in taxation from the higher echelons of society. In some cases, the position of the direct zamindaran was undermined by their mid-ranking counterparts, when, for instance, the latter introduced a new class of landowner in order to strengthen their own position in the provinces.

As a result of the various classes of zamindaran, a hierarchical structure developed in the agrarian economy, in which various rights were in force and pressure was transferred down the pecking order. Time and again, these conditions hampered greater progress. Although the central government tried to ensure that a peasant never had to pay more than 50 percent of his total crop yield, when the influence of the central government waned and the pressure on the jagir increased, a farming crisis ensued, which was only to grow worse over the course of the eighteenth century. Despite the general loyalty that the zamindaran showed toward the Mughals, numerous conflicts of interest existed between both the zamindaran and the state and among the various zamindaran themselves. In the long term, these contributed to the weakening of the administrative and military authority of the state. Attempts by the Mughals to solve these problems had only a short-term effect. With the death of Aurangzeb in 1707, the central government became too weak to maintain the fragile balance of power. The government by then was simply too dependent on the zamindaran to be able to change the structure of the agrarian economy.

The Reign of Aurangzeb

Opinions are divided in assessing the reign of Aurangzeb. This is first and fore-most due to the fact that the Indian historian Jadunath Sarkar (1870–1958) has, right up to the present day, by virtue of his monumental study *A History of Au-rangzeb* (five volumes, 1912–1924), enjoyed a kind of monopoly of interpretation on the second half of the seventeenth century. Sarkar saw in this potentate a reli-gious fanatic who wanted to reverse the development toward tolerance and mul-ticulturalism instigated by his predecessor. This fundamentalism, in conjunction with a pointless and economically disastrous policy of conquest in the Deccan, led to the collapse of the empire, according to the eminent historian. Several convincing arguments have been advanced in recent years against this interpretation. In par-ticular, critics have accused Sarkar of having relied too heavily on the witness of contemporary historians, who as a rule embarked on an interpretation of their age with a clear parti pris agenda in mind.[53]

The first twenty years of Aurangzeb's reign were very unsettled.[54] From his residence in Shajahanabad, the ruler tried to drive forward the expansion of the empire through costly military campaigns. In Bengal, for example, where the au-thority of the central government was never fully recognized, Aurangzeb's army commander Mir Jumla did manage, albeit with heavy losses, to conquer Koch Bihar and Assam at the beginning of the 1660s, but these areas were lost again within four years. In addition to such futile military adventures, many local uprisings also broke out. In the northeast, Afghan tribes rose up against the Mughal troops stationed there. Although Aurangzeb personally marched there at the head of an army and occupied the region for a spell, peace was restored here only in around 1685. At the same time, the death of the maharaja Jaswant Singh in Merwar in 1678 unleashed a full-blown Rajput war. In this instance, too, the ruler intervened in person, advancing to Ajmer. Aurangzeb's son Akbar exploited the difficult po-litical situation to break away from his father, declare his independence, and ally himself to the rebellious Marathas on the Deccan. Thereafter, Aurangzeb made peace with Rana Raj Singh, one of the key protagonists in Merwar. Indigenous groups continued the struggle, and in 1707 Ajit, the son of Maharaja Jaswant, en-tered Jodhpur in triumph.

Aurangzeb (r. 1658–1707) in old age, reading the Quran. In 1681, Aurangzeb led a campaign to the Deccan to restore peace and order there. Unfavorable circumstances and likely also personal reasons prevented him from ever returning north during the remainder of his lifetime. British historiography is fond of portraying Aurangzeb as a sanctimonious ruler whose fundamentalist religious policies played a key role in the decline of the Mughal Empire. Researchers have since revised this negative image. (Roland and Sabrina Michaud)

By 1680, it appeared advisable for Aurangzeb to change the theater of war and move against the two remaining independent sultanates on the Deccan, Ahmadnagar and Bijapur. In addition, he found himself opposed by the Marathas, under whose protection his son had placed himself. The "Hindu" Marathas originally came from the northwest region of the Deccan Plateau.[55] Many Maratha troops and tax collectors were in the service of the sultans of Ahmadnagar and Bijapur. Maratha society, which was predominantly rural, was ruled over by local dignitaries, who controlled their own forces, had the right to raise their own taxes, and had at their disposal extensive family networks. In the struggles against the forces of the Mughal Empire from the 1620s on, they performed the role of commanders in the military units of the sultanates. Between 1646 and 1656, one of these dignitaries, a man by the name of Shivaji, succeeded in establishing an independent principality within the sultanate of Bijapur. Shivaji's murder of the Bijapuri commander Afdal Khan won Shivaji great renown. Khan was universally hated among the Maratha groups, after he had dared to desecrate the holy shrines at Tuljapur and Pandharpur. This coup attracted many other Marathas to Shivaji's ranks. By the time he had notched up notable successes against the forces of the Mughals at Surat (1664) and Poona (1663), if not before, Shivaji had become a serious anti-Muslim leader on the Deccan.

Aurangzeb's first move was to dispatch an army with his uncle Shayista Khan at its head against Shivaji. This campaign ended in catastrophe for the Muslim forces. Jay Singh, the next commander, was more successful. In 1666, he managed to compel Shivaji to sue for peace. Under this agreement, the Marathas had to relinquish twenty-three of their thirty-seven forts to the Mughals. Nevertheless, they were still permitted to regularly collect a quarter of all the tax revenues of Bijapur. The Marathas used this privilege to exact as much tax income as possible from the regions that they overran. The result of this was that these regions were completely bled dry by the time the Mughals annexed them once more. Shivaji went in person to the court of Aurangzeb. There, he was endowed with a high rank, with the intention of absorbing him into the mansabdar system as a zamindar. However, when Shivaji refused to acquiesce in this plan, Aurangzeb had him incarcerated. He was able to escape, though, and make his way back to the Deccan. From 1669 onward, the Marathas launched a new series of attacks on the Mughals. Among other campaigns, they sacked the port of Surat in 1670. In 1674, Shivaji adopted the formal title of "king" *(chatrapati)*. Six years later he died, the first supraregional Maratha ruler. His son and heir, Shambaji (d. 1689), was able to rule unchallenged over the Deccan for a short while, as Aurangzeb's forces were tied up fighting the Afghan tribes in the north of the empire.

At the beginning of the 1680s, in light of the continuing lack of success of the forces dispatched from Delhi and Agra against Bijapur and the Marathas, the Mughal administration on the Deccan began to show clear signs of dissolving. Accordingly, in 1681, Aurangzeb decided to relocate his court to Burhanpur. This was duly accomplished the following year. The Mughal ruler was to spend the remaining twenty-five years of his life there, primarily fighting against insurrectionists and other rebels on the Deccan. At first, this campaign of his was very successful. Despite the inefficiency of the Mughal bureaucracy in the south of the subcontinent, which contemporaries often mocked, Aurangzeb was able to take Bijapur and eight months later Golkonda as well. The whole Deccan was transformed into a single province, with its capital at Aurangabad. Subsequently, Aurangzeb succeeded in capturing Shivaji's son Shambaji, whom he executed.

In the wake of these initial successes, Aurangzeb decided to remain in the Deccan and combat the growing destabilization of the region by waging a series of small wars of attrition against the rebels. His principal opponent remained the Marathas, whose resistance did not diminish even after the death of their leader. The Mughal leader staked everything on defeating this enemy. For this reason, for a long time henceforth the ruler's encampment became the actual administrative center of the empire. Only in 1696 did Aurangzeb finally choose Brahmanpuri (now renamed Islampuri) as his new capital. Even then, however, the ruler continued to live exclusively in his tent. In 1699, defensive walls were built around the city. Shortly thereafter, Aurangzeb left his most important minister, Asad Khan, in Islampuri as acting head of government and went off to fight a six-year-long war of attrition against the mountain strongholds of Maharashtra. He returned only in 1707, sick, exhausted, and ultimately unsuccessful, and died on May 3 of that year from an illness he had contracted.

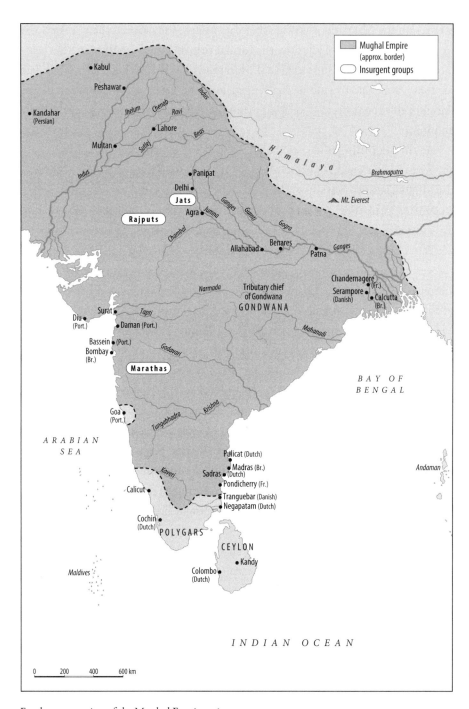

Furthest expansion of the Mughal Empire, 1690

Political, Social, and Economic Disintegration

In seeking to identify reasons for the breakup of the Mughal Empire after the death of Aurangzeb, it becomes clear that there are no individual, monocausal grounds but rather that many different causes were responsible, some of them inherent within the system and some external. Moreover, they tended to exacerbate one another. The stability of this complex empire with its subtle administration was of necessity guaranteed only if certain conditions pertained. I shall outline below, on the basis of findings from the latest research, various structural weak points of the Mughal system of rule.

The demise of the jagirdar system, which was closely bound up with the structure of medieval village communities in India and with both the local and the central administration of the Mughal Empire, may be pinpointed as one important weak point.[56] Although Mughal bureaucracy had at its disposal a comprehensive and multilayered system of checks and balances, a systemic crisis still arose, signs of which became apparent even in the first half of the seventeenth century, a period generally characterized by stability. One feature that became especially obvious was the beginning of the major problem concerning the discrepancy between the availability of jagir estates and the rapidly increasing number of officials who were due recompense. In the short term, some technical administrative solutions were found to alleviate this problem, but these only served to worsen the situation in the long run. The objective of amassing a greater body of revenue for the upper class and the state to draw on was, at different times, pursued more or less intensively through various strategies, but neither the expansion of the empire's territory (in conjunction with extending the proportion of land under cultivation or ensuring that it became more productive) nor trading in nonagricultural produce and demands for higher yields at the expense of the lower classes succeeded in improving the situation in the long term. The reason for this may be sought in the Mughal Empire's social system, which remained static and ossified despite the continuous growth of the privileged upper class.

The fundamental problem, namely, the imbalance between the revenue that was needed to maintain the state and actual income, could not be solved in this way. The internal structures of the agricultural system prevented any real change from taking place. Although land was still available within the territory of the

Mughal Empire, the use of undeveloped areas by landless peasants—who often came from the lowest rungs of the caste system—was blocked by the privileged rural population. The central government did not manage to break the predominance of the mid-ranking castes. Certainly, several initiatives were undertaken to improve farming, but these were not aimed at the lowest echelons of society. The Mughals' system of production only functioned so long as the local representative of central authority could control the zamindaran. Yet because government officials were increasingly poorly paid, the number of troops declined along with the quality of military equipment. This made it more difficult for the jagirdaran to collect taxes, and the ensuing loss of income was reflected in lower earnings for the officials charged with collecting them. This downward spiral was only hastened by revolts on the part of the provincial population. Alongside a social system that hampered the growth of farming and the problems of the local administrative apparatus, various other aspects also contributed to the crisis of the jagirdar system. The growth of the ruling class was huge, with countless claims to official state positions being lodged, and when these were dispensed, several factors had to be taken into account, including questions of who was related to whom and the traditional authority wielded by local rulers, whose support for the Mughal Empire needed to be solicited. At first, Shah Jahan and Aurangzeb were able to withstand the intense lobbying on the part of various special-interest groups regarding the dispensing of public offices, but discontent soon spread, particularly among the nobility, who suffered from shorter-term appointments and delays in the provision of jagiri, and accordingly their loyalty to the empire started to wane.

In order to raise the amount of disbursement available to the military, both Shah Jahan and Aurangzeb extended the crown lands in the subcontinent. The state laid claim to those estates that were especially productive and straightforward to govern, while the mansabdaran had to make do with the more difficult regions. Given that there was no actual shortage of farmland in the Mughal Empire, some scholars take issue with the thesis that there was any crisis at all in the jagirdar system. As a rule, rural administration functioned well more often than badly. Nevertheless, law and justice could no longer be enforced and taxes on farm yields no longer reliably collected. The assertion that increases in taxation and the unscrupulous and unsustainable behavior resulting from ever more frequent changes of jagiri were largely responsible for the crisis of the Mughal Empire is countered by the thesis that a normally functioning administrative apparatus would have quickly uncovered and prevented such an abuse through its multilayered levels of monitoring. The assumption that a hereditary rural aristocracy like the zamindaran would have protected the peasantry from being oppressed by the state or its officials may also be refuted. The ever more frequent change of jagiri by the jagirdaran should not be underestimated: the result of this was that 80 percent of the country was held in perpetuity by a handful of powerful mansabdaran, while in the course of the eighteenth century, jagiri even became heritable. A growing attitude of despotism toward the lower classes was a direct result of declining control by the administrative authorities. The gradual but fully consistent growth in power of the zamindaran could have profound consequences at a local level. Yet little research has so far been done on how this process contributed to the strengthening of the zamindaran. A direct causal link exists between the strength of the zamindaran and the weakness of the jagirdaran. As a result of their inability to protect the landowners from exploitation, the reputation of the Mughals suffered considerably. A fragile social balance, which had been created by the acknowledgment of the Mughals as a central authority guaranteeing safety and stability, was now upset, making way for local authorities to come to the fore.

The next problem area concerned the frequent revolts staged by the peasantry and various tribes within the Mughal Empire. In his brief study, Gautam Bhadra cites two representative examples from the Kamrup-Goalpara region in the northwest of India.[57] In this work, he also discusses the *paik* system, which played a significant role in the agriculture of Assam and Koch Bihar but which was severely disrupted by the bureaucratic reforms of the Mughals. The *paikay* were peasants who also did service as soldiers of the nobility or armed servants. In payment, they received farmland that was not liable to any taxes. People in other occupations paid their dues in the form of services for which they received a small parcel of land. In this arrangement, four peasants were usually grouped together in a collective. While one of them was doing his or her service, the others would till their land. There were different social ranks among the paikay; archers, for example, generally came from the lower castes and were treated accordingly, being granted fewer privileges than, say, trained artists. A disruption of such a system, which was firmly embedded within the community, had the capacity to adversely affect both the nobility and the peasantry and provoked a swift and violent reaction.

The Mughals had no interest in preserving the paik system. Conflicts therefore arose between the Mughal system of a centralized military and the associated payments policy, in which salaries were paid either in cash or in the form of harvest yields, and a local system based on service, which had at its core a decentralization of (military) power. Over the course of this conflict, three strands of general dissatisfaction can be identified: emanating first from the normal raiyati (peasants); then from the paiks, namely, a particular group of raiyati and soldiers; and last from the local nobility. Thanks to the broad distribution of armed and well-trained paikay throughout the affected areas, these local revolts had the capacity to develop into a very effective resistance against the central power.

The Mughals' humiliation of the local aristocracy appears to have been a key factor in sparking rebellions. The hierarchical structure of society had a special significance for the historical development of this border region. Immediately before being overrun by the Mughals, the principality of the Koch, who at this time had only just evolved into a ruling caste, had recently come into being as a polity. The nobility and populace of the region were very attached to their princely house, which over time had become a symbol for their social mobility and authority. The feeling that these local authorities had effectively been dishonored by the Mughals provided a powerful catalyst to revolt. In addition, the structure of this society, in which both the peasantry and the leadership belonged to one and the same caste, contributed to widespread mobilization and a swift formation of a sense of common cause against the Mughals.

As regards the causes of the rebellions, two tendencies can be identified. On the one hand, there was a tradition of regular revolts by the rural populace and their leaders against the central power. On the other hand, it appears that it was primarily people who pursued a specialized trade who became the prime movers of the insurrections. The regional peculiarities of the revolts should also be noted. Revolts in border regions only recently conquered by the Mughals, such as Assam and Bengal, were by no means uncommon. The social and taxation systems were quite different there than in other parts of India. The wide distribution of tribes ran counter to the political order of the region, so that revolts could easily be sparked there. A cycle of violence and reprisal and the fact that punishment as a symbol of authority were enacted both by the representatives of Mughal power and by the rebels make it clear quite how perilous and prone to periodic collapse the writ of the Mughals in this region was. Despite the fact that such rebellions were regularly put down, they still kept occurring so frequently that they became a touchstone for the failure of the Mughals to properly integrate the border regions into the central structure of the state.

The revolts staged by the rural population in the Mughal Empire during the eighteenth century have hitherto been studied largely for their significance to the collapse of the empire as a whole.[58] Important aspects, such as the specific history of the region in question and the social strata that got involved in these uprisings, have largely been neglected, as have the reactions of the urban population. Muzaffar Alam has analyzed the events surrounding the rebellions of zamindaran in three northern Indian regions (Moradabad-Bareilly, Awadh, and Banaras). Of central importance in his analysis are questions concerning the nature and the context of the confrontation between the zamindaran and the central government, concerning the participation of other social groups, and concerning the conditions that made these uprisings against the Mughals possible in the first place. He also investigates whether the initiative came from the ranks of the zamindaran or from the rural populace themselves. This study is based on Persian sources. The zamindaran of the regions being studied came from various castes and communities, although Rajputs always formed a majority. In addition, though, the position of zamindar was also held by Jats, Brahmins, Muslim sheikhs and *sadat* (that is, descendants of the Prophet Muhammad), as well as (later) Afghans and, especially in the province of Banaras, Bumihars, Kayasthas, and Kurmis. Not all of these groups took part in the uprising against the central power; the local faujdari were usually assigned to suppress these revolts, though less frequently the provincial governors also became involved. Alongside military means, the Mughals also made use of their strong administrative structure, co-opting local leaders directly into the service of the state by creating new official positions. In many cases, though, there was no question of adopting this kind of solution, and the armed forces of the central government experienced great difficulty in suppressing the rebels. The successes of the central government against the rebels were only temporary and showed at best only a marginal military and strategic superiority on the part of the Mughals. The threat posed to the Mughals by the uprisings of the zamindaran may be gauged by the size of the armed bands commanded by the zamindaran and by the number of fortresses that were under their control.

At certain times, as many as twenty-five strongholds could be under their control, and in one case a report mentions a rebel unit of up to eleven thousand men. It is impossible to estimate how many local peasants followed the zamindaran, because most of these leaders initially commanded their own armed contingents.

The strength that the zamindaran gained through their alliance with the rural population was often compromised by internal social conditions. The zamindaran distinguished themselves from one another according to caste, clan, and provenance and fought not only against the central government but also, first and foremost, against one another to assert their own interests. In the process, the rural populace suffered any number of raids, sackings, and depredations. The victims of these power struggles between local potentates would often call on the Mughal rulers for help. In some cases, zamindaran who found themselves threatened by the revolts of other zamindaran would even align themselves with the central authority. The same factors that could lie at the root of internal conflicts between the zamindaran could, however, also generate sympathies and an esprit de corps. To try and combat this cohesion between zamindaran from a particular caste or clan, the Mughals attempted to dissipate such powerful connections at a local level or to disrupt them by appointing new zamindaran from different castes or clans. Conflicts could also break out within a caste or clan. The Mughals were also quick to exploit such rifts by favoring one family over another.

The revolts of the zamindaran were a manifestation of the rage felt by local members of the ruling class, who had many resources and armed means at their disposal. In this regard, it is enlightening to take an overview of the funds that were available in the rebellious regions. We may gauge the prosperity of a region from thriving trade, as evidenced by, among other indicators, the founding of several new towns within an area. Particularly in Banaras, at least three major cities came into being in the late seventeenth century, with significant markets for local produce. An expansion of economic structures of this kind must have been based on a significant growth in commercial agriculture and with it a rise in the prosperity of local zamindaran. In part, the opening up of new trading possibilities went hand in hand with an expanded cultivation of the land, which in turn generated increased revenues. At the same time, violent rebellions erupted in this region, seriously threatening Mughal sovereignty there. Further examples from other regions also demonstrate that greater wealth and the attendant increase in the power of the local zamindaran provide an explanation for the rebellions that they led. Not least, the revenues generated by agriculture helped the zamindaran grow prosperous. In many cases, they passed on far less of this wealth to the state than they were actually liable for, given the level of income raised within their region. Often, this illegally retained money ensured the zamindar concerned a rapid rise to power and wealth. Although the unreliable data on tax revenues do not necessarily reveal anything about the level of production of goods within a region, because they might just as easily simply attest to the relative strength or weakness of the zamindar who collected the respective taxes, by comparing overall revenues from the seventeenth and eighteenth centuries, we can nonetheless identify a clear boom in agricultural activity in the regions studied.

The impetus for the unrest was thus provided by the zamindaran within the regions in question. They were rich and powerful and were seeking autonomy or at least a greater share of tax revenues. Yet most of them were not in a position to bring together diverse local groupings under their leadership. This meant that a communal revolt of zamindaran from different clans and castes was only a very rare possibility. In those instances where they managed to prevail over the Mughals, they laid waste to the region and terrorized merchants, village dwellers, and other zamindaran. In consequence, at least part of the rural population turned to the Mughals and fought on the side of the central government. Unfortunately, the reaction of the urban population in these regions is not documented, but in other regions we know that they also aligned themselves with the Mughals. In particular, the merchants had profited from the security of the empire and the farming system. The social structure in the countryside was severely disrupted by the rebellions. The zamindaran not only were the leaders of the uprisings staged by impoverished village dwellers but also used the impoverished to further their own interests.

Karen Leonard has put forward a theory to explain the familiar narrative of the collapse of the Mughal Empire from an economic perspective.[59] Though a connection is often made between the economic factors and the tensions within the Mughal bureaucratic system, these other theories do not take sufficient account of a circle of people who in this context appear to be of the utmost importance: the bankers of the leading financial and commercial institutions (the so-called Great Firms). Leonard defines these as financial enterprises that often had a head office and several branches, enabling them to provide their services across a wide area. They were engaged in various branches of commerce and industry and also had some influence of the practical politics of the empire but were also ultimately reliant on the state: in order to maintain the progressive monetary and credit system throughout the huge expanse of the Mughal Empire, these financial services had to function in a very flexible way and relied on political stability. The period of creeping decline that affected the Mughal Empire was at the same time a phase of growing involvement on the part of the financial institutions in the realm of direct tax levies on a regional and local level. In this way, especially between 1650 and 1750, they were able to occupy positions of political power throughout the empire. In this process, Indian bankers found themselves cooperating closely with regional powers, including the East India Company. However, when the EIC duly assumed political control over the whole of India, from 1750 onward, the indigenous financiers were systematically replaced. They lost their significance in the political system, which in turn meant that their role was subsequently almost entirely forgotten by historians. Yet at the same time, there is the general assumption that financial institutions must have been of enormous significance particularly for bureaucratic empires. Precisely with regard to the multiethnic and multifaith Mughal Empire, we may therefore surmise that financial and political connections were crucial for the cohesion of the state. In this, the Mughals were certainly especially dependent on the officials of the central administration, though merchants or bankers who operated in the cities also played a decisive role by supplying goods and providing means of payment. In sum, the Mughal Empire was based on a finely balanced network of alliances and structures. When external powers such as the EIC began to compete with the Mughal Empire for credit and other financial services provided by Indian bankers, this equilibrium was disturbed and the banks became ever more powerful.

According to Leonard's thesis, the later Mughal rulers paid too little attention to this important development, however. While bankers rarely belonged to the ruling class of aristocrats and high officials, their influence means that they must be counted as part of the country's strategic and political elite. Their role as state treasurers was especially important. A small number of Great Firms supplied the financial wherewithal to meet immediate state expenses, such as official salaries, allowing these to be paid regularly and so freeing them from any direct dependence on the rises in taxation. Close connections between the Great Firms and the state also came about through the personal loans taken out by certain officials or noblemen. The Mughal rulers never managed to eradicate this practice, in which the jagirs were put up as security. Another aspect of banking activity, indeed one that made up the lion's share of the business, was the transfer of money on behalf of the state. Three further branches of business linked the leading bank enterprises with the Mughal Empire: they were involved in the *Karkhanas* (that is, the royal manufactories); they were contractors in the construction of official buildings; and, finally, they traded in jewelry, precious metals, and gemstones. Of especial importance was the role played by the Great Firms in collecting revenues—by 1750, this activity was under their control to all practical intents and purposes. In this role, they extended credit to the state, which in return granted them full control over the income they collected. The rates that the bankers set were soon more important economic criteria than the taxation demands of the Mughal ruler. It is irrelevant whether this development is now regarded as a symptom or a cause of the progressive weakening of central Mughal government: whatever the case, the Great Firms grew ever more powerful in the realm of tax raising, while at the same time they began to invest more heavily in local businesses.

This shift in interest was conditioned by the lack of protection that the Mughals were able to offer providers of financial services in the second half of the seventeenth century, a period when serious disruption to commercial enterprise was caused by a series of major rebel raids. In particular, attacks on Surat, the richest harbor of the Mughal Empire, inflicted considerable damage on the Great Firms. Their connections to the ruler, which were actually very good and direct by then, were severed, and several merchants and bankers simply quit the region. Between 1650 and 1750, the major Indian banks regrouped and reorganized, relocating from the urban centers of the Mughal Empire to the regional independent kingdoms and to the trading centers of other powers, while at the same time expanding their trade and credit transactions with the Dutch and the English. A brief digression here might serve to make clear why the role of the great Indian banks prior to 1750 has often been overlooked by historians up till now: the relations between the Great Firms and the East India Company changed decisively after 1750, when the EIC not only began to employ its own bankers to transact its business but also took over financial services for Indian rulers and hence started to play a role in the collection of taxes. In their privileges and assignments, the indigenous banks were almost entirely supplanted by the EIC, which thereby gained great influence over the state system.

According to this Great Firm theory, then, the changed loyalties and interests of the great Indian banking houses, which disengaged from the central government and began to move increasingly toward smaller kingdoms or to foreign powers, notably the EIC, proved to be the decisive factor in the downfall of the Mughal Empire. Granted, these financial enterprises were not directly incorporated into the administrative structure of the state, but even so, not just the Mughal treasury but also individual officials at all levels were dependent on them. A comparison with the role played by bankers in imperial China reveals a clear contrast. Merchants and bankers in China were strictly controlled, and new systems of money transfer were monopolized. Certainly, attempts at control were undertaken from time to time in the Mughal Empire, but these regularly foundered on the power and autonomy of the financial institutions and the tension between the short- and long-term aims of the Mughals and the bankers. Leonard identifies the distinct advantage of the Great Firm theory as residing in the fact that it relates both the demise of the Mughal Empire and the rise of the EIC to economic factors and so emphasizes their inextricable linkage. In addition, by virtue of the good state of source material here, the theory can potentially be easily put to the test. It should be the goal of scholarship in this field, she claims, to examine the heterogeneous category of the great Indian financial institutions and to analyze them and their activities in light of this theory.

External trade, too, underwent a fundamental change over the course of the eighteenth century.[60] New, powerful mercantile cities like Bombay, Madras, and Calcutta came into being, and the export of goods geared itself increasingly to China, whereas before the countries bordering the Persian Gulf or the Red Sea had been the principal importers of Indian goods. This development hit merchants in the traditional trading centers hard; some moved to other towns, where new structures developed as a result of the cooperation between the English and Indians. This trade was dominated by the employees of the East India Company, who engaged in business as private traders. Developments such as these can be seen as a direct consequence of the extensive political collapse of the Mughal Empire.

Research in the field of Indian export activity in the eighteenth century is hampered by the absence of the primary source, namely, the customs records produced by the Indian administration at this period. Moreover, the papers of individual Indian merchants have been only sporadically preserved. Most information in this area therefore derives from the reports written by European trading concerns, and in particular two newsletters from Gujarat, which also furnish us with information on the daily life of the region. In some instances, the account books, manifests, or family histories of Indian merchants have been preserved in the legal documents of the European settlements. However, these documents are only of limited use in this case, because they never go into great detail about Indian society.

The concept of "Indian trade" must first be defined anew for the eighteenth century, because "India" did not exist at that time as a political or territorial entity and because, even by the early decades of the eighteenth century, Mughal administrative control over their empire had largely dissolved. The situation was even more complicated when viewed from an economic and social perspective. Large parts of rural India were not connected to the highly developed trade network, which primarily covered the coastal regions and the major cities such as Delhi and Agra. A mutual relationship of dependence must have grown up between the various centers of trade, with agricultural and artisanal products from the heart of the empire being sold in the ports and shipped abroad. Monetary and financial credit structures also tied the towns into sophisticated networks of interrelatedness. Within individual regions, the economic connections were closer still, even between cities whose administrations were hostile to one another. Frequently, a sense of social interconnection also linked the individual coastal cities, though trading between them was often far from simple, due to the existence of different local customs. For example, by the mid-eighteenth century, trade between the two largest provinces, Gujarat and Bengal, had become so difficult that conditions similar to those governing foreign trade were imposed on financial transactions.

The most important trading region of the Mughal Empire was the province of Gujarat, with its principal port at Surat.[61] The goods that were exported from here, primarily textiles and indigo, were produced in the villages surrounding the Gujarati capital of Ahmadabad and three other large cities. Rich merchants mainly from northern, central, and northwestern India had settled in Surat. At the beginning of the eighteenth century, the port was in a very favorable position, and Indian maritime trade was recording healthy profits. Immediately after the death of Aurangzeb in 1707, however, the political situation in the empire became so uncertain that trade suffered serious disruption. Although the businesses in Surat, Ahmadabad, and other large cities had normalized once more by around 1710, in the first two decades of the eighteenth century the formerly highly secure main trade routes, especially in the areas around Delhi and Agra, had fallen into disarray. Armed peasants, often led by their zamindaran, made the roads a dangerous place; according to the account given by a Dutch traveler at the time, such marauding bands could comprise as many as five thousand men. This had two consequences for trade: on the one hand, no goods from the heartland could be transported to Surat and sold; while on the other, the flow of products from Surat above all to the north of the country also dried up. As a result, their production was also shut down. Furthermore, the market for Indonesian spices disappeared, driving specialized merchants to ruin.

As a direct result of this political decline, the province of Gujarat also collapsed. It was cut off from the centers of production and had lost most of its consumer markets. Farther damage was caused by the attacks carried out by the Maratha army on its major cities, including Surat. Mughal forces succeeded in holding on to the most important urban centers of the province, but presently the officers of the Mughal army and the governors of the various regions—driven to penury by their dwindling income from the surrounding land—began plundering the merchants' coffers. Public order was maintained longer in Surat; it was only after 1720 that the leading officials of the Mughal administration there also lost their integrity after having been deprived of most of their livelihood by the Maratha attacks. Even more serious problems were caused by disputes among the leading officials of the city administration, which saw the steward of the port, the bailiff of the citadel, and the admiral of the Mughal fleet at loggerheads with one another. In the thirty years after 1720, the merchants in Surat came under increasing pressure from all sides, with the various stewards who governed the port during that period posing a particularly grave threat. In 1732, the city's traders staged a successful uprising against this official, but this failed to improve the situation for their successors.

Moreover, for two years, the port of Surat was blockaded by warships of the EIC. The motives of its representatives in taking this action were complex. They

wanted to protect their private trade networks and to stop the Mughals from imposing taxes on every private British mercantile transaction, but they were also
concerned to put on a show of strength in times of political crisis and—to para-
phrase the words of the official justification of the blockade—to protect the privileges originally bestowed on them by the Mughals. In order to bring the damaging siege to an end, the merchants of Surat managed to win the port steward
over to agreeing that English trade, whether official or private, should no longer
be subject to any official control.

By the end of the first half of the eighteenth century, the economic landscape
of Gujarat had changed radically, then. Trade in Delhi and Agra had ground to
a complete standstill, while in Ahmadabad three-quarters of the city lay in ruins.
Only Surat had managed to maintain a little of its former prosperity. The great
merchant fleet had almost disappeared, the strong connections to West Asia were
now considerably weakened, and the formerly wealthy merchants had lost most
of their influence. According to some estimates, Indian trading activity in Surat
had shrunk to one-third of its original volume, though this was also a natural consequence of the expansion of English trade.

A quite different development that affected other regions can be observed from
the example of the Malabar Coast, which had never been part of the Mughal Empire. The principal harbor of this narrow strip of territory was Calicut, though
Cochin, which lay farther south, was the preferred port of call above all for ships
of the Dutch Vereenigde Oostindische Compagnie (VOC), which was headquar-
tered there. The main trade good was pepper, most of which was sold by a heterogeneous group of Indian, Arabian, and private European merchants. In the late
1720s, for a variety of reasons, the price of pepper in Cochin suddenly soared. The
collapse of Surat and the closure of trade routes to the north, together with the
fall of the Safavids in Persia, meant that more and more traders now found themselves obliged to buy their goods in Cochin. The rise of a new, powerful kingdom
in the south of Cochin brought an end to the heterogeneous and fragmentary state
of the Malabar Coast and the power of the merchant class that lived there. The
new regional rulers monopolized the pepper trade and closely controlled its production and distribution, with the result that the merchants practically became
state employees. This development on the Malabar Coast differed in many respects
from that which occurred in Gujarat. In Cochin, it had to do not with a struggle

against a crumbling administration but with establishing a new centralized structure. Accordingly, the demise of the mercantile classes there did not signify a retrograde step but simply the advent of a new kind of trade, in which profits devolved to the state.

In the north of the Malabar Coast, which was dominated by the port of Calicut, things developed quite differently. The armies of Mysore, one of the successor states of the Mughal Empire, conquered the region and over the following years destroyed trade there, first by extorting money from the merchants, then by attempting to impose monopolies, and finally by plundering the city's wealth. As the great trading and port cities declined, so Alleppey was able to establish itself as a new harbor in the south. Toward the end of the eighteenth century, the principal trade routes for pepper ran not to the north of India but to Muscat or China. It even appeared that India's pepper trade with West Asia had been weakened.

In eastern India, meanwhile, trading centers had become established on the western arm of the River Ganges. The most important harbor there was Hooghly, the main port of Bengal. There, Shi'ite merchants with connections to Persia formed the most influential group among the trading community. The political collapse of the Mughal Empire, which set in motion significant changes in Gujarat and other provinces, began to compromise Bengal only in the 1740s. There is evidence to show that an economic downturn was affecting Bengal even prior to the Battle of Plassey. While Hooghly lost its foremost position as a trading city over time as a result of the oppression of government officials stationed there and their attempts at extortion, Calcutta grew in popularity as a port thanks to the freedom it offered and the protection provided by the British there. In addition, Hooghly was captured by the Marathas in 1740 and remained under their control for a long time. The collapse of other regions must also have had an influence on Bengal. In particular, Bengal had enjoyed a thriving trade relationship with Gujarat. Hooghly was an important trade port on the route from Surat to western India, but particular goods destined for the Chinese market were, at least in part, shipped via Hooghly. The demise of the Indian fleet had a strong influence on developments in the city. The remarkable rise in the private transport of goods by the English that accompanied Hooghly's decline resulted in Calcutta outstripping it as a trade hub. However, toward the end of the eighteenth century,

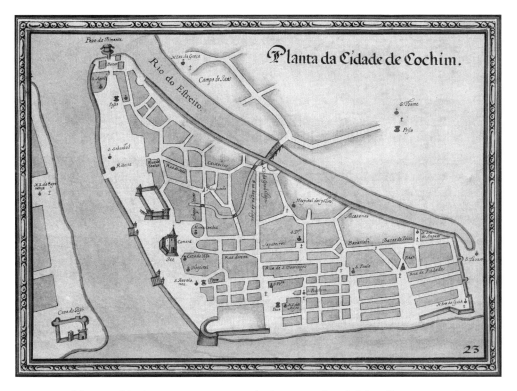

Map of the city of Cochin, circa 1648. In 1502, the Portuguese founded their first commercial settlement here, in a town sited on a natural harbor on the Malabar Coast. The following year, they constructed a stronghold containing a small wooden church. In the second half of the seventeenth century, the Dutch took over control of the region; they seized the town of Cochin in 1663 and successfully incorporated it into the profitable trading network of the Vereenigde Oostindische Compagnie. (Bayerische Staatsbibliothek, Munich, Cod. icon. 162)

English shipping concerns turned their attention increasingly to Eastern markets, foremost among them China.

Three quite distinct phases of development may be identified for Bengal in the eighteenth century. The first was the decline of the dominant port of Hooghly, which was supplanted by a newly evolving English trade hub. We may assume that the various forms of political pressure that operated in other areas of India also played a role in Bengal, albeit a less decisive one. Second, in the second half of the century, the trade structure was dominated by English traders, and only those Indian merchants who acquiesced in this foreign dominance were able to do business there. During this phase of development, trade began to turn increasingly to the East rather than the West. Finally, in a third phase from 1780 onward, the influence of the Industrial Revolution resulted in a slump in the region's remaining trade with Europe. Furthermore, these new developments also came to have a decisive influence on the internal market in India.

Because of a paucity of source material, this kind of pattern of development cannot be identified for the Coromandel Coast region. Political weakness and the great political and economic pressure that resulted—which arose in the country's other great trading centers over the course of the eighteenth century—had been a fact of life on the Coromandel Coast for around a hundred years by this stage. It may well be for this reason that English settlements such as Madras, which was already a flourishing port by the end of the century, came to prominence more rapidly. Originally, the Coromandel Coast was ruled by two powers. The north was governed by a Muslim dynasty and manufactured simple fabrics, which were much in demand across large parts of Asia. The only port of any significance in this region, at Masulipatnam, was home to Mughal and Komati merchants.[62] The south was divided politically into a number of smaller areas, which were under the control of the "Hindu" kingdom of Vellore. Patterned textiles were the main trade goods here and were sold primarily to Southeast Asia. Yet no important trade center existed in the south. With the arrival of the English and the Dutch in the seventeenth century, therefore, trade positively flourished here and was even extended to the Philippines. Masulipatnam continued to thrive as well, leading to the conclusion that political structures that were not geared toward sustainability did not fundamentally harm the region's trade. However, over the course of the eighteenth century, even trade on the Coromandel Coast declined. One possible cause for this could be that the well-organized and wealthy EIC ultimately proved too powerful competition for the Indian merchants. In other regions, this factor did not play a role, with the only danger to the merchants there being the private traders operating under the banner of the EIC and their own government. Conversely, we might conjecture that after the final collapse of the weak Indian political structures in the eighteenth century, the survival of certain trading structures on the Coromandel Coast was the real peculiarity.

This region was ravaged by three conflicts: the Muslim powers in the north fought against the "Hindu" areas to the south; the conflict between the Mughals and the Marathas was also played out along the coast; and finally the interventions by French and English forces and the clashes between them further added to these confusing conflicts. Masulipatnam was occupied by the English from 1759 on, although the poor and shortsighted administration of the region endured, forcing Indian merchants and producers to flee inland. The branches of trade that were established in Madras, the regional capital of the victorious English, continued to flourish even after the great upheavals of the eighteenth century, while Bombay also experienced a boom, which had its origins in the emigration there of many merchants from Surat. Whether in Madras, Bombay, or Calcutta, prosperity for Indian traders was ensured only through cooperation with the English. In actuality, then, prosperity was subject to complete control by an external power; nevertheless, it was more secure and palpable than trade under the crisis-hit Mughal administration. Indian merchants were happy to put up with this restricted freedom. Only the Muslim shipowners from the former great centers of trade did not survive the momentous changes. The close trade contacts with West Asia dissolved in the course of these developments, with the new end points of the trade routes now lying in the Far East.

2. The Indian Ocean from the Fourteenth to the Sixteenth Century

IN 1989, Janet Abu-Lughod's book *Before European Hegemony: The World System, AD 1250–1350* appeared, in which the author argued convincingly that an early Eurasian "world system" (a deliberate linguistic allusion to Immanuel Wallerstein's work) had already developed in the thirteenth century in the form of the "Pax mongolica."[63] A closely woven network of supraregional trade relations was able to form both along the Silk Route as well as across the Indian Ocean, facilitating manifold cultural interactions. This network was controlled by Muslim merchants, although the leading political power in the region at this time was China. Yet after the reign of the Xuande emperor (r. 1425–1435), this major power renounced any engagement in central and southern Asia and henceforth pursued an isolationist policy.[64] In view of the costs and the unsatisfactory results of endeavors that had been undertaken up to that date, all forms of expansionist ambition were rejected and all contact with non-Chinese restricted to trade and vassalage. Yet even in this realm there were some qualifications. In 1440, it was decided to limit the missions from Hami in Xinjiang Province to Beijing, which hitherto had taken place almost every month, to just one per year. The Eurasian trade network came under threat not only from the deposing of the Yuan dynasty by the Ming in 1368 and the ensuing loss of control over the Far Eastern regions and access to the East China Sea but most seriously from the devastating plague pandemic in the mid-fourteenth century.[65] Nevertheless, by 1300 three fundamental historical processes had taken place, which were to shape the history of the Indian Ocean as a supraregional trade zone over the next two centuries.[66]

The first of these concerned East Africa. The Islamization of the East African coast saw a completely new economic area, which was rich in raw materials, suddenly incorporated into the overseas trade network.[67] The east coast of Africa, whose northern part was known as the "Land of the Blacks," while farther south it was referred to as the "Land of Sofala," was thereafter regarded by the Arabs as an integral part of the Indian Ocean. Whereas, before the twelfth century, the "Land of the Blacks" had only had a very marginal connection to supraregional trade, in the period that followed, Muslim merchants began to settle along the coast, particularly in the towns of Zayla, Mogadishu, Mombasa, and Kilwa—all places that the famous Islamic traveler Ibn Battuta visited in the mid-fourteenth century and described in his account of his journey. These Arab traders duly married into the indigenous population and founded offices of their trading concerns in these towns. We also know, from semilegendary reports, that Muslim merchants from other regions also gravitated to the east of the African continent, because life there appeared to be more lucrative and secure. From the thirteenth century on, the newly settled Muslims established a large, coherent area of control around the town of Kilwa, whose influence extended at times even as far as Sofala. In the fourteenth century, this generated a clear increase in trading activity right along the East African coast.

The second process saw the same development occur in the Southeast Asian region.[68] As a result of the consolidation of Muslim control over the Indonesian island realm and especially the Straits of Malacca, this area, which was rich in lucrative trade goods, became firmly tied into the intercultural trading network of the Indian Ocean, which was dominated by Muslim merchants. Islam reached Southeast Asia by the same route by which it arrived on the coast of East Africa. We know that Muslim merchants and sailors were present along the whole west coast of the Malay Archipelago and on Sumatra from the seventh century onward. Here, too, the founding of local Muslim sultanates from the thirteenth century on, the most powerful of which clustered around the Straits of Malacca, sparked an upturn in trade. In the ensuing period, the influence of Islam was so strong that by the sixteenth century, most of the inhabitants of Indonesia and the Malay Archipelago had adopted this faith. From Southeast Asia, Muslims maintained a thriving trading relationship with China via Canton.

Third, from the late thirteenth century, the Mamluks of Egypt controlled the Red Sea, which now, in place of the Persian Gulf, assumed the role of a trading hub between the Indian Ocean, North Africa, the Muslim heartlands, and Europe.

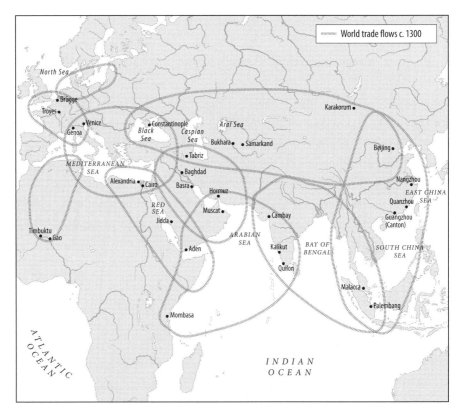

Trading regions in Asia and Africa, circa 1300

By 1350, then, as a zone of trade and commerce the whole Indian Ocean, including East Africa and Southeast Asia, had become a single entity whose trade routes were more than ever being determined by Muslim merchants and seafarers transporting trade goods on their vessels. Quite how "normal" maritime traffic across the Indian Ocean became may be gauged from the fluency with which the Russian merchant Afanasy Nikitin (writing in 1472) could reel off data for passages from the Persian port of Hormuz to India.[69]

In the period that followed, namely, from the middle of the fourteenth to the beginning of the sixteenth century, commercial traffic across the Indian Ocean ran relatively regularly and unimpeded. Sea routes that used the monsoon season to their advantage had been devised and were soon being plied by traders every bit as naturally as the sometimes difficult coastal routes to and from the countless ports on the Indian coast. During this period, neither the range of products being transported nor the nautical knowledge of the Arab sailors changed at all. In those days, the vast economic zone that we now call the "Indian Ocean" was divided up into three smaller overlapping regions of maritime trade.[70] The first of these stretched from the Red Sea, the Persian Gulf, and the East African coast to the west coast of India. The most important trade centers within this first economic zone were the aforementioned towns of Sofala, Kilwa, Mogadishu, and Mombasa, together with Aden, Muscat, al-Karazi, Diu, Surat, Cambay, Daybul, and above all Calicut—all forming knots in the net of navigable seaways. Within the second "circle," which encompassed the whole Indian subcontinent, the Gulf of Bengal, and the west coast of the Malay Archipelago, the trade routes ran via Rajamundri, Satgaon, Shatijam, Mataban, Tahawi, and Tanasari. Finally, the third great trading zone comprised the Indonesian island realm and the east coast of China up to Canton, with the Straits of Malacca forming the key entrepôt for goods of all kinds.

The continuity of trade on the Indian Ocean even remained guaranteed when, over the course of the fifteenth century, the great realms around the Indian Ocean steadily fragmented into much smaller spheres of influence controlled by local potentates. While Muslim sultanates had come into being, as we have seen, along the East African coast and the Straits of Malacca, the northern part of the Red Sea was still controlled by the Mamluks, who at the same time by dint of their hegemony over the sharifs of the Hijaz also held sway over large parts of the west coast of Arabia. The south coast and the southern tip of the Arabian Peninsula, with the key ports of Aden, ash-Shihr, and Zafar, were initially in the hands of Yemenite Rasulids (until 1454) but later came into the possession of the Tahirids from Khorasan (in the case of Aden) and the Cathirids (in Zafar and ash-Shihr), whereas on the west coast the sultanate of the Hadariba had consolidated its control. Sovereignty over the Persian Gulf was largely divided between three loosely connected groupings. Mesopotamia was ruled by members of the Shi'ite Musha'sha'iya. The hinterland and parts of the northern coast of the gulf were the domain of first the Timurids and later the Turkmen

Confederation of the Aq-Qoyunlu ("White Sheep"). Meanwhile, the important trading port of Muscat and the Strait of Hormuz were under the control of the rulers of the "sultanate of Hormuz" or its vassals in al-Qaf and al-Bahrayn.

On the Indian subcontinent, too, following the demise of the Delhi sultanate, a number of regional politically connected polities had grown up around their respective local rulers. Thus, after the breakup of the Bahmani sultanate, in 1490 Muslim rulers could be found in Gujarat, Golkonda, Ahmadnagar, Bengal, Bidar, Berar, Bijapur, Malwa, and Multan, in addition to "Hindu" realms in Vijayanagar and Orissa, plus—outside the subcontinent—the Buddhist Sri Lanka. Yet this picture of political disruption is deceptive. Throughout this period, the Indian Ocean continued to constitute a coherent geopolitical macrocosm. The coastal regions were largely under the control of Muslim regents, who all had a vested interest in ensuring that the well-established and flourishing maritime trade continued to run smoothly. The Indian Ocean remained the connecting link between the abutting Islamic, Indian, Southeast Asian, African, and Chinese cultures.

What kinds of goods were being transported across the Indian Ocean in this period? First and foremost, it continued to be a case of an exchange of finished products for raw materials. Everyone had certain goods to offer that were rare elsewhere and therefore much in demand. The Muslims of North Africa, Asia Minor, and Persia primarily sold, alongside grain and horses, manufactured goods like metalware, textiles, carpets, and weapons, some of which had been made in Europe. The East African coast was the source of amber, gold, precious stones, ivory, valuable hardwoods, and of course also slaves. India and Sri Lanka supplied pearls, bamboo, betel nuts, pepper, cinnamon, and gemstones, while the Southeast Asian island world was the principal supplier of much sought-after spices and perfumes. From China came tea, silk, porcelain, ginger, sugar, and drugs. Ibn Battuta reported seeing Chinese hens that looked like ostriches and, like the much-admired porcelain, were destined for the Indian market. Carpets were carried from Aksaray to Syria, Egypt, Anatolia, and India. Silks were imported from Nishapur, while melons came from the region around Bukhara. Rice, grain, and cotton were shipped from India to Zafara and Oman, while honey and betel nuts were transported in the opposite direction. One of the most important trade goods was horses, which were dispatched in their thousands to the subcontinent from Persia, Yemen, and Oman.

Islamic Worlds?

For the entire period under consideration here, the question arises to what extent the "Islamic world" formed an entity. Here, it is not so much a matter of formal adherence to a religion but rather a question of a common identity, of a transregional, semiotically coded nexus of commonalities of meaning and lifestyle. For example, where the Muslims in India were concerned, was this a case of an Islamic diaspora or even of Muslims in exile? If we take the common definition of exile as the enforced banishment, expulsion, or resettlement of people on religious or political grounds or emigration chosen voluntarily but under the threat of religious or political coercion, we quickly ascertain that such a phenomenon evidently did not exist in the premodern Islamic world or at least that the issue was never broached openly.[71] Of course, people knew the feeling of being far from home, and in such contexts the Arabic term *watan* was widely used—a word that closely equates to the Latin term *patria,* conveying the sense of a place on Earth where one is at home and the full force of which only a person who has become alienated from that place can fully appreciate.[72] Other expression found in the sources, such as *jins* and *asl,* are not differentiated from *watan* and likewise denote an individual's or group's "origin," in particular their "place of birth or residence." All three terms are, according to normative lexicographical findings and to the consistent linguistic usage in literary and historical sources—in other words, extremely diverse kinds of text—at this stage still completely unpolitical concepts. Spatial separation from home territory could occasionally evoke yearnings that subsequently recur in the familiar topos of a "longing for home" in the Arabic-language body of literature. The learned Baghdad writer, poet, and historian Abu I-Faraj al-Isfahani (d. 967) gathered together sixty-seven anecdotes relating more or less centrally to this theme and published them in his *Book on the Behavior of People Who Have Been Separated from Their Homes and Their Families.*[73] The basic tenor of all these stories is set by various kinds of homesickness, which was a familiar feeling among Muslims in the premodern period, even though we possess very few narrative accounts of this phenomenon. By contrast, a concrete feeling of exile in the contemporary sense is scarcely present in the texts that have come down to us. This may for one thing have to do with the fact that banishment as a punishment—in contrast to both the ancient world and the modern period—was

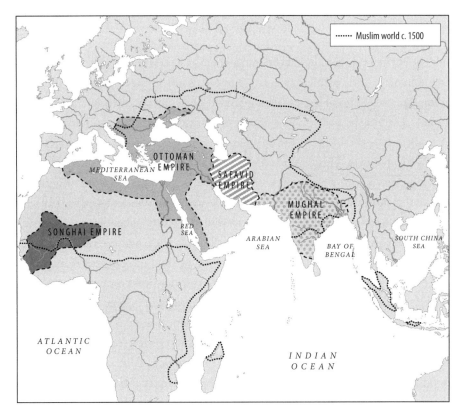

The Islamic world, circa 1500

unknown. Second—and this would appear to be a far more important factor—
Muslims who remained within the Muslim sphere of power during the Middle
Ages evidently never felt truly alien, exiled, or ostracized, even when fate conspired
to keep them moving from place to place, never to return to their homeland. Two
biographies serve to illustrate this point.

The first is of Ibn Battuta (1304–1368/1369), one of the most famous world
travelers in history, who was born into a Berber family resident in Tangiers and
embarked on a pilgrimage to Mecca in June 1324, after having apparently undergone a solid basic education in his hometown in the Maliki madhhab (school)
of Islamic law.[74] He would finally return to his homeland twenty-five years later.

His extensive journey took him through a large part of the Islamic world. For example, he stayed for no less than twelve years in southern Asia. After returning to Fez in 1349, however, he found his urge to travel was still not sated, and so he set off on two further expeditions, one to Muslim Spain (al-Andalus) and the other to Sudan. Around this time, the Marinid ruler of the Maghreb, Abu-Inan Faris (r. 1349–1358), got to hear of Ibn Battuta's accounts of the remarkable things he encountered on his travels. Accordingly, he ordered him to dictate his adventures to the court secretary Ibn Juzayy (d. around 1356). Even so, Ibn Battuta's writings contain a number of contradictions, while many claims are clearly dubious. For instance, it seems highly unlikely that Ibn Battuta actually undertook the journeys he describes himself as having made to the Bulgars, to Oman and Yemen, or to eastern Anatolia. We also learn very little about the traveler's personality from his reports. He seems to have had a deep-seated aversion toward the Shi'ites, he was extremely ambitious, and he had a string of wives. Upon arriving at a royal court, he expected to be granted the patronage of the ruler and complained if he was not accorded the attention he considered was due to him. Although Ibn Battuta journeyed throughout the Islamic world, he never appears to have encountered any difficulties in communication or in fitting in. Everywhere he went, he seemed to integrate himself effortlessly into the new environment. Throughout his writings, no experiences of alienation or exile are reported; even in India, he felt at home in the Mughal ruler's entourage and remained there for almost a decade.

The second biography concerns the renowned universal scholar Ibn Sina (c. 980–1037). Under his more familiar name of Avicenna, Ibn Sina had an equally remarkable life and career.[75] He was born near Bukhara, where his parents had settled some years before. His father had been the Samanid governor of Kharmatyan. Once the whole family had moved to Bukhara, Ibn Sina received an outstanding education, which included above all the Greek sciences, in particular medicine. Accordingly, as a young man, he was appointed to be a physician at the Samanid court of Nuh ibn Mansur (r. 976–997). In addition, he obtained a position in the imperial bureaucracy. When the Qarakhanids marched into Bukhara in 999, Ibn Sina moved to Gurganj in Khwarazm to work as a doctor and governor for the Ma'munid ruler there, Abu I-Hasan Ali ibn Ma'mun (r. 997–1009).

Sometime later, for reasons we do not know, he moved to Gurjan, to work at the court of the Ziyarid emir Qaboos ibn Vusmgir. But because this ruler died shortly before his arrival, Ibn Sina spent several months in the retinue of the emir's son Manuchihr ibn Qaboos before moving on to Rayy, where he offered his services to the Buyid ruler Majd ad-Daula Rustam and his mother Sayyida. However, in 1015, the ruler's brother Sams ad-Daula attacked and captured the city. At the behest of the new ruler, who was suffering from a serious disease, Ibn Sina set off via Qazvin to Hamadan, where the seat of Sams ad-Daula's government was located. He cured the ruler, who named him his vizier in gratitude. Ibn Sina remained in this post right up to Sams ad-Daula's death in 1021. The new emir, Sama ad-Daula, wanted to retain this experienced man and so after his enthronement asked Ibn Sina to stay on in his role. However, Ibn Sina had already initiated contact with his Buyid counterpart Ala' ad-Daula in Isfahan. Once his connections to this enemy court became known, Ibn Sina spent four months in prison, and only Ala ad-Daula's victorious entry into Hamadan prevented worse from happening. Ibn Sina was saved and worked until his death in 1037 for the new ruler in Isfahan.

From their accounts, neither Ibn Battuta nor Ibn Sina appear to have experienced any fundamental problems in integrating whenever either man moved or was forced to move from one Sunni Muslim society to another. How are we to explain this genuinely surprising fact? The following thoughts are nothing more than a provisional attempt to find some starting points for interpretation, which might then be verified, modified, or disproved in detailed studies. The field of cultural semiotics provides a helpful approach to interpreting this phenomenon.[76] Following the work *Philosophie der symbolischen Formen* ("Philosophy of Symbolic Forms," 1923–1929) by Ernst Cassirer (1874–1945), the proponents of cultural semiotics proceed from the following premises: "Using the procedures of text production, ritualization, genre formation, grammaticalization, and monumentalization, every culture stores certain patterns of action which have proven themselves important over the course of the culture's evolution. It is these patterns which maintain the identity of a culture and retain the structural information which determines the culture's further development." A culture interpreted as a system of symbols thus consists of "individual and objective users of symbols, which produce and receive texts and through which, with the aid of conventional codes, messages may be conveyed that enable users of symbols to overcome their problems." Therefore, it is a fundamental task of cultural semiotics to decipher the coded text of a culture.

We may work from the assumption that Ibn Battuta and Ibn Sina, as representatives of premodern Muslim modes of perception and behavior, experienced no great difficulties in integrating during their numerous changes of location, because they operated within the cultural-semiotically unified Muslim global community *(ummah)* and within the bounds of the Muslim sphere of power. What does ummah signify in this context? Normally, ummah designates the supraethnic faith community of Islam. Yet, although the religious, ethical, and ethnic connotations of the term are already defined in the Quran, it remains multilayered and multifaceted. Ultimately, ummah has three levels of meaning. First, ummah denotes the global community of all Muslims. This meaning predates all other connotations and forms the basis of the Muslim conception of the world. In premodern times, it was perfectly natural for people quite unreflectingly to regard themselves primarily as a member of a faith community instituted by God, the *Jamaʿat al-muʿminin*. Second, almost antithetically to the preceding, ummah, in its plural form *umam,* can also be used to describe other groups of people not characterized by their adherence to the true faith but rather defined by their heathen nature and barbarity and shunned as a result. Finally, ummah in a nonreligious sense can signify an ethnicity or a people. Throughout the Middle Ages, many authors use ummah in this latter sense, with pre-Islamic, Islamic, and non-Islamic peoples alike being described as ummah. There is much evidence to suggest that this third level of meaning can be traced to the influence of Greek works. In particular, it was Muslim geographers who, when compiling their own works, drew heavily on Arabic translations, say, of the "Guide to Geography" by Ptolemy (c. 100–170) or the *Geography* by Marinos of Tyre (c. 70–130).

In this case, I am using ummah as a functional term, which stands for a culturally closed mental Muslim realm, whose members communicate with one another by reference to a common system of symbols. Our task is to determine the codes from which the culture of the premodern ummah was assembled, in order to thus gain a better insight into how individual Muslims effortlessly got their bearings within the Islamic world. A multitude of coded entities might be taken as the basis of an investigation: cities, Sufi centers, rulership, bureaucracy, social life, or infrastructures. These are all well worth an intensive cultural–semiotic analysis, because as signifiers they were responsible for conveying meanings that were instantly and often quite unconsciously understood by all those in the know. One of the most important codes in all Muslim societies was the attempt to put the divine law (shari'a) that had been developed by legal scholars into practice. Admittedly, this process met with complete success only in a very few instances, particularly because secular law played a much greater role than religious proscriptions in many areas of life. Nevertheless, within Islamic law, it was the realm of practical theology *(fiqh)* as opposed to speculative theology *(kalam)* that gave the artifacts and mind-set of Muslim communities their distinctive flavor.

Of course, even in the premodern period, it would be incorrect to talk in terms of *the* Islamic law as a monolithic entity, either in theory or in practice; even so, we are justified in talking about a system of symbols that was recognizable to, and could be deciphered by, all Muslims wherever they lived and at whatever period and which was valid throughout the entire ummah.[77] The elements that were important for everyday life were not so much the highly complex principles of legal interpretation, which it took a lengthy process of training to master, but instead the various branches of the law. It is under this rubric that we discover in the statute books of all the Islamic schools of law the most significant decrees, which derive from records of the dicta or actions of the Prophet Muhammad (and the Prophet's comrades) and thereafter are hallowed as divine law either by virtue of being acknowledged as such by scholars, by their appearance in the Quran, or through independent reasoning or conclusion by analogy. Differing opinions among the scholars of any particular school of law on how to categorize principles of legal interpretation and the precepts that developed from them are just as frequently encountered as divergent views between different schools of law.

Nevertheless, the core for all Muslims is universally the same and authoritative. This concerns, first and foremost, their religious duties. The attainment of ritual purity, the giving of alms, fasting during the month of Ramadan, praying five times a day, and the pilgrimage to Mecca—the Five Pillars of Islam—are hard-and-fast spiritual obligations that help to forge a sense of togetherness and from which a whole host of artifacts derive that convey signs interpretable by all Muslims: mosques, madrasas, Quran schools, clothing, script forms, and so on. Equally socially characteristic and immediately identifiable as Muslim from al-Andalus

(Spain) to India are the obligations owing from one person to another, as proscribed by God and enforceable by the kadis (Islamic judges). These matters involve quite everyday forms of communication, constantly and universally present, and concern questions of marriage and inheritance, provisions for which went hand in hand with rules for how a man and his wife should conduct themselves. Furthermore, alongside passages on the lawful treatment of slaves, Islamic handbooks on law also contain instructions on the proper conduct of trials. To how great an extent the principles of divine law that are expressed in these works actually affected social intercourse between people may be gauged from the sections on the law of property and the code of obligations, which are always treated exhaustively. These have to do with elementary things such as buying and selling, deposits, cession of goods, surety, leasing, endowments, or gifts. And finally, a chapter of these books was devoted to the punishments that were imposed by God on specific crimes (adultery, calumny in cases of adultery, theft, and so on). It is of no interest to us here whether these injunctions deriving directly from God were actually enacted and observed in the individual Muslim societies of the premodern period. Rather, what I would wish to emphasize is simply the fact that Islamic law created a universally binding system of symbols for all Muslims, which instantly placed coreligionists from very different backgrounds on common ground and forged a link between them. Everywhere they went, Ibn Battuta and Ibn Sina encountered Islamic legal codes that were familiar to them and provided them with a sense of security and self-confidence, dispelling right from the outset any potential for feelings of alienation.

To sum up, I might raise the following point for discussion: within the Islamic sphere of influence, people hardly ever experienced feelings of alienation despite quite differently structured societies. This has to do, on the one hand, with the fact that the modern concept of alienation does not commute easily to the Muslim premodern period. There was no imperial capital, for instance, from which a person could be ostracized to the periphery, but instead there were countless centers, all competing with one another, within an overarching religious community (ummah). Although thoroughly dissimilar secular ruling legal practices held sway within the individual local polities, the cohesion of the ummah relied on legal principles that were fundamentally accepted as universally normative by the individual. These codes, which of course in real life went unobserved by many, functioned as a system of symbols that created a supraregional, semiotically unified space, within which a Muslim, who was indeed in a position to decipher the codes at any time, might feel at home.

The World of Seafaring and Navigation

In 1343, Ibn Battuta planned to embark from the port of Calicut, on the Malabar Coast, for China.[78] Unfortunately, he never set sail, as a storm arose that smashed the boats in the harbor to pieces. Ibn Battuta had no other choice but to continue his journey to China as an Islamic envoy by other means. Whether he ever reached there or not need not concern us at this juncture. Rather, the questions that concern us here are as follows: what sea route Muhammad ibn Tughluq's emissary might have used to travel from Delhi to Calicut and thence to China; what life on board ship was like; what cargo was being carried on his passage; what nautical knowledge was widespread at this time; and, finally, what trade routes Muslim sea captains used when navigating their vessels in these waters. From the various sources that have come down to us, it is difficult for historians to form a coherent picture of maritime (predominantly mercantile) activity in the area of the Indian Ocean in the period from 1350 to 1520. Alongside finds of coins and other archeological artifacts, we also have at our disposal a considerable number of travelers' reports and chronicles. For example, the renowned Marco Polo (d. 1324), the Russian Afanasy Nikitin—who was active in the Indian Ocean between 1469 and 1472—the Venetians Josaphat Barbaro (d. 1494) and Nicolo di Conti (d. 1496), the Genoese Girolamo da Santo Stefano (d. sometime after 1510), and Ludovico di Varthema from Bologna (d. 1517) have all left colorful accounts of their voyages, supplemented by the reports of the Portuguese seafarers Duarte Barbosa and Tomé Pires (d. around 1540) on their voyages to Burma, Hormuz, and India.[79] Furthermore, we are also able to draw on Chinese source material, together with numerous Persian, Ottoman, and Arabic chronicles and memoirs. Yet the most valuable sources are the detailed "sea mirrors" written by three Muslim captains from the end of the fifteenth and the beginning of the sixteenth century, as well as a Malayan "Sea Codex," commissioned by Mahmud Shah (r. 1488–1530), one of the rulers of the sultanate of Malacca.

Goods and passengers were transported on ships, of which two basic types plied the waters of the Indian Ocean at this time: first, the traditional Arab *dhow* and, second and predominantly, Chinese seagoing junks.[80] When Ibn Battuta was making preparations for his voyage in Calicut, he had the opportunity to view the Chinese ships lying at anchor in the harbor there at close quarters:

> The Chinese vessels are of three kinds; large ships called *junks,* middle sized ones called *zaws,* and small ones called *kakams*. The large ships have anything from twelve down to three sails, which are made of bamboo rods plaited like mats. They are never lowered, but they turn them according to the direction of the wind; at anchor they are left floating in the wind. A ship carries a complement of a thousand men, six hundred of whom are sailors and four hundred men-at-arms, including archers, men with shields and arbalests, that is men who throw naphtha. Each large vessel is accompanied by three smaller ones. . . . These vessels are built only in the town of Zaitūn in China [Quanzhou], or in Ṣīn-Kalān, which is Ṣīn al-Ṣīn [Canton]. This is the manner after which they are made; two parallel walls of very thick wooden planking are raised and across the space between them are placed very thick planks secured longitudinally and transversely by means of large nails, each three ells in length. When these walls have thus been built the lower deck is fitted in and the ship is launched before the upper works are finished. The fitting-out of the ship is then completed. . . . On the side of the planks are the oars, which are as long as ships' masts. Ten to fifteen men operate each of these oars, and one remarkable feature is that they stand up to row. In the vessel they build four decks, and it has cabins, suites and salons for merchants; a set of rooms has several rooms and a latrine; it can be locked by its occupant, and he can take along with him slave-girls and wives. Often a man will live in his suite unknown to any of the others on board until they meet on reaching some town. The sailors have their children living on board ship, and they cultivate green stuffs, vegetables and ginger in wooden tanks. The owner's factor on board ship is like a great Emir.[81]

Mahmud Shah's "Sea Codex" furnishes us with interesting details about the complement of these vessels; they were mostly crewed by Muslim sailors, and the Malaccan ruler's main impulsion in having this work compiled was to ensure the safety of these Muslim seafarers:

The application of laws of the sea is intended to prevent arguments and disputes, to dissuade seafarers from simply following their own whims and personal desires, and to avoid any difficulties or misfortunes that may arise on junks or other ships.[82]

Aside from the ship's owner, who usually remained back in the home port, the highest authority on board was the captain, whose orders had to be followed unquestioningly even if he was only a young man. Alongside and below the caption, the coxswain was required to rule on matters of custom and practice on board ship. The helmsman had charge of the anchor and also gave the signals. He and the coxswain between them had executive authority over the ship's crew. The crewman who was responsible for setting the sails was also responsible for all affairs on deck and for matters concerning the crew. A watchman, who took full personal responsibility for everything that occurred during his period on watch, also appointed other crew members to watch over the cargo and any slaves who were being carried on the voyage. On land, he accompanied the captain and ensured his safety. Finally, ordinary sailors performed all the necessary tasks on board, aided by passengers who had paid nothing for their voyage but were working their passage instead. Four areas on board were subject to special rules: only officers had access to the ship's operations room, and it was also forbidden for people to enter without permission the room where those on watch rested. Likewise, no one was allowed to loiter in the region of the anchor capstan or to set foot in the cabins opposite the captain's cabin, which were reserved exclusively for his servants.

Arab dhows, too, were constructed from wooden planks, though in their case, these were held together by fibers from the date palm. Seagoing vessels of this kind had an average length of around 30 meters and could carry a cargo of up to 150 tons. Their main mast—most dhows had two masts—could sometimes reach a height of 25 meters and their yardarm a breadth of 30 meters. The mainsail seems to have mostly been rectangular and therefore did not have the triangular lateen-sail form that it usually takes today. Depending on the strength of the wind, the yardarm was raised or lowered instead of reefing the sail, a practice that was not yet known at that time. At the stern was the main rudder, as well as the high bridge of the vessel, while the bow had room for the sea anchor and a small stone anchor for securing the ship while in port. The cargo was generally covered with a tarpaulin or bamboo mats. For going onshore, every dhow also had a ship's boat, and on board the main vessel, there was always a barrel of freshwater.

During the voyage, vessels frequently put into harbors in order to repair damage they had sustained on the open seas. At the end of a long voyage, the dhow was pulled up onto dry land to prepare it at leisure for the next season's sailing. At sea, of course, much depended on the training and the routine of the crew. So, for instance, manipulating the mainsail was anything but straightforward, especially as the yardarm had to be lowered and turned around the main mast when jibbing. Adverse winds were countered by using varying sizes of sail, plus the aforementioned raising or dropping of the yardarm, though when the wind was gusting in different directions, this necessitated pushing the yardarm forward or backward as well. The crew of an average oceangoing dhow comprised experienced sailors, with many of them skilled in particular duties on board. Abul Fazl Allami gives an account of a ship's crew in his *Ain-i-Akbari:*

> The number of sailors on a ship varies according to its size. On large ships, there are twelve different types of sailor: 1. The captain (or shipowner), who determines the routes. 2. The pilot (or captain). He must be familiar with the deeps and shallows of the ocean and have a good knowledge of astronomy. He is the person who pilots the ship to its port of destination and protects it from danger. 3. The head of the common sailors. In nautical language, sailors are called *khallasi* or *kharva*. 4. the *nakhuda-khashab*. He supplies the passengers with firewood and straw and helps guard the cargo during the voyage and later when the ship is unloading. 5. The petty officer. He oversees the docking and disembarking of the ship, and often works for the pilot. 6. The quartermaster, who is in charge of the ship's provisions. 7. The *karrani*—man who can write, and who keeps the ship's logs, as well as distributing water to the passengers. 8. The helmsman. He steers the ship in accordance with the captain's orders. Some ships have more than one helmsman, but never more than twenty. 9. The *pangari,* who keeps watch from the crow's nest and calls out when he sights land, or another ship, or a storm approaching, etc. 10. The *gunmati,* who is one of the sailors and is responsible for baling out water that has seeped into the ship. 11. The on-board marksman, who is deployed during sea battles. The number of sharpshooters depends on the size of the ship. 12. The sailors. They set the sails and haul them

in. Some of them also serve as divers, who repair leaks underwater or release the anchor if it has stuck fast somewhere.[83]

Often, the merchants traveling on a ship would pose a particular problem. As a matter of principle, the captain did not have the authority to give them orders, but usually his commands as sea were followed without question. One of the "sea mirrors" contains the advice that the captain should listen to any complaints that might arise and according to the individual case come to a reasoned decision, though the safety of the ship and its crew would always be paramount. The sea mirror advises that his best course of action would be to take a long look at the merchants before the ship set sail so as to save himself from any unpleasant surprises on the high seas.[84]

So that life could take a regular course on the oceans, a whole series of special regulations were put in place, the flavor of which we can judge from Mahmud Shah's "Sea Codex": small transgressions on board were punished with seven blows with a stick. But if, for instance, any intimate relations should develop between a married woman and a single man (sailors frequently took their wives on board), the captain would sentence both of them to death. If both were unmarried, each would be beaten one hundred times, before being forced to marry. But if they refused to marry, they could be absolved from doing so by handing over a large sum of money. If a single man committed adultery with the wife of a crew member, and if the crew member killed the adulterer in anger, this crime was forgiven and no legal consequences ensued. Furthermore, the crew member had the right to demand that his wife be put to death for her infidelity. If he chose to spare her life, though, she became the property of the captain. In cases where a male and female slave had intimate relations and were caught in the act, both were subjected to the punishment of bastinado (foot whipping), which took place at the capstan under the supervision of the captain. As well as for the crimes outlined above, the death penalty was commonly imposed for involvement in any conspiracy to murder the captain, the officers, or pilots. Wearing a dagger with the intent of carrying out a mutiny was also punishable by death.

If a ship took people who had been shipwrecked or stranded on board, a particular sum was demanded from them in return. Passengers were carried by contract. If they wanted to disembark at any port other than the one specified in the contract, then the captain had the right to demand monetary compensation from them. Generally speaking, no one was allowed to come on board until he had paid the requisite fees and taxes to the harbor police; these customs duties commonly entailed handing over a tenth of commodities such as betel nuts, coconuts, and salt. Merchants carrying goods with them to sell were obliged to first present them to the responsible customs officers for inspection.

If a captain wished to make an unplanned landing, he was required to hold a general council and get the assent of his entire crew. However, once a ship made port, the first thing a captain did was to find the chief of the harbor police there to settle customs formalities with him. Thereafter, he had the sole right to conduct business in the port for the first four days. Subsequently, the merchants on board were allowed to disembark for two days and, after them, the rest of the crew. If goods were offered to the crew, no one was allowed to outbid the captain. In any event, slaves could not be bought without the prior agreement of the captain.

After the captain, the most important man on board was undoubtedly the pilot, for he alone had the necessary nautical knowledge to guide the ship safely into its port of destination. On smaller ships, it was not uncommon for the captain to also be the pilot. Mahmud Shah's "Sea Codex" recounts that the large seagoing junks even boasted a "grand navigator," an "assistant navigator," and a "sail navigator," with the last having full responsibility for rigging the ship when the vessel weighed anchor.

Normally, before the start of a voyage, the captain would conclude a contract with the shipowner, in which his salary, the itinerary, and the precise amount of cargo were all specified. Once the ship had left its home port, the *mu'allim* had full responsibility for the voyage going smoothly. The "maritime law" as documented by Mahmud Shah stipulates the following:

> The pilot has command of the ship. . . . If the pilot should neglect his supervision of the ship with the result that he and the rest of the crew are endangered or even suffer shipwreck, then he should reckon with the death penalty unless God should see fit to show mercy to His servant. In order that the ship might complete its voyage as planned, the highest duty of the pilot is to diligently observe and take account of the winds, storms, tides, the motions of the moon and stars, the seasons, the position of bights and shallows close to the shore, coral reefs, sandbanks, or stretches of coastline without any freshwater. He must have

a profound knowledge of all these matters, so that the crew might confidently place their safety and security in his hands, both on land and at sea. Every mistake on his part should be avoided whenever possible. At the same time, he should not neglect to pray to God and the Prophet to keep him free of all dangers. The pilot occupies a similar position to that of the imam, and the same authority should be accorded to him. If he should want to leave his ship—wherever that might be—he should not be granted permission to do so. The law and seafaring custom requires that this should be so.[85]

Of course, as stated in one of the sea mirrors, the most important thing for a pilot was to possess sound nautical knowledge, both in theory and in practice:

Be aware that the basic qualifications required of a captain are rationality and a great deal of experience. . . . Knowledge of the sea lanes and sailing with the monsoon are matters of experience, whereas knowledge of the celestial constellations, the bases for reckoning by them, and calculating latitude by studying the stars and other such things belong to the realm of reason. Measuring longitude and distances, though, call for both experience and reason.[86]

It is a fortunate circumstance that some of these captains were sufficiently ambitious as to write down their seafaring knowledge and leave them for posterity in the form of maritime handbooks or sea mirrors. Accordingly, we have the works of three pilots written between 1400 and 1550, which furnish us with detailed information about Arab seafaring and the customary sea routes across the Indian Ocean.[87] Broadly speaking, this maritime knowledge can be divided into six separate areas: the study of landscape features, the management of the ship and its crew, precise observation of the monsoon season, the art of taking compass bearings, estimation of the elevation of stars, and calculation of the distance traveled. As regards sea routes, the pilot Ibn Majid identified three categories, according to degree of difficulty: (1) coastal sailing; (2) the direct sea route between two ports, not involving any change of course; and (3) the route from port A to port B involving a change of course on the high seas.

Journeys along the coast, which undoubtedly must have been the first form of navigation in the Indian Ocean—though it is impossible to say precisely when people began sailing from place to place—demanded good eyesight on the captain's part, a good deal of experience, and a thorough knowledge of the coasts, especially the various physical features that acted as landmarks. Such features could include coastal formations, the color of the water at different points, reefs, sand-banks, currents, tides, winds, or topographical characteristics—in other words, phenomena that were useful both for recognizing a stretch of coast again and for avoiding typical danger spots. The exhaustive sea mirrors conscientiously list all the details of particular coasts that are worthy of attention, even including certain kinds of birds, fish, and types of plants to be found there. If a ship ventured into shallower waters, the sea depth was always sounded out with the aid of a plumb line. A little container was fastened to the end of this line so that the nature of the seafloor might be determined.

Although, in principle, these sailors needed relatively few technical skills, the potential for danger was, as can readily be imagined, considerable, not least because people began—primarily in order to save time—to leave the coast and find a more direct route to a distant overseas port. However, this required an ability on the captain's part to hold a steady course over a long period. At first, this seems to have been achieved through knowledge of navigation through star sightings, though this technique was supplemented from the thirteenth century on and ultimately largely supplanted by use of the compass. The compass rose, though known about in this period, entered widespread use in the Indian Ocean only somewhat later.

The Arab compass consisted of a magnetic needle, a magnetic stone, and a compass dial marked with thirty-two directional bearings. All three elements were located in a housing fixed on the afterdeck, which must have been clearly visible to the helmsman. In contrast to European compasses, the thirty-two characters on the compass dial, which corresponded to thirty-two separate points on the ship, were star signs—they roughly accorded with the points at which certain stars rose or fell. With the aid of such compasses, Arab seafarers could, by holding their course and skillfully using various trade winds, steer a safe passage to ever-farther-flung coastal ports. Yet no one dared rely on this technique alone; the compass was a very delicate instrument. It could become demagnetized as a result of a faulty magnet or be rendered useless by strong magnetic fields or even excessive cold. It was also perfectly possible that small errors might have been made when installing the needle, dial, or magnet in the housing on the rear deck, which over time must inevitably have led to navigational deviations. Likewise, instances also occurred of the compass dial shifting during the voyage, unnoticed by the captain or the helmsman. In order to gain some control over the compass readings and, in cases of doubt, put himself in a position to correct any irregularities that might arise, the pilot would execute a series of star sightings to help him determine the ship's position. In the fifteenth and sixteenth centuries, this meant first and foremost the vessel's precise latitude, because Arab sailors at this time, just like their European counterparts, faced insurmountable difficulties in determining longitudinal position.

Generally speaking, sailors naturally looked for the most direct sea route between harbors, though this was not always available. Sometimes, taking a zigzag course to get to one's destination was unavoidable; in these instances, the interplay of compass readings, plotting one's own position by the stars, and estimating the distance already traveled worked best when sailing in a southerly or northerly direction. The latter had to do with the calculation of position. Unlike the Europeans in the Mediterranean, who navigated according to the position of the sun at its zenith, Arab sailors in the Indian Ocean oriented themselves by the altitude of fixed stars, that is, according to the varying distances of these stars from the horizon, which were different from one latitude to the next. Their elevation was not, however, expressed in degrees, as was otherwise customary in Arab astronomical texts of the period, but in *isba'* (an isba' corresponded to one finger's width). This peculiarity was due to the fact that Arab captains formerly used to reckon the elevation of stars by holding their hand out outstretched toward the horizon. Of course, this finger's breadth was later standardized, with 224 fingers making up a complete circle of 360° (and one isba' therefore corresponding to roughly 1°36'). Likewise, the outstretched hand was also supplanted by a standardized instrument with the passage of time. The use of this instrument required a calm sea and as clear a sky as possible. The person who did the measuring need be, according to Sulaiman al-Mahri, wide-awake, sober, and in good physical shape. Furthermore, pilots were advised to compare their results with earlier measurements. To this end, the captain carried tables with him showing the altitudes of the polestar at significant points.

One major problem for Arab seafarers of the fifteenth and sixteenth centuries was the calculation of distances traveled.[88] Time intervals were usually given in *zam,* a unit that originally corresponded to the length of a watch, namely, three hours. It a peculiar feature of Arab maritime navigation that distances at sea were also measured in this unit. Several different calculations were advanced to ascertain the distance that a ship steering a constant course would have to travel in order to move the measured altitude of the polestar on by one isba'. This was found to correspond to eight zam or, to express it conversely, a distance of one zam was, given a steady course, equivalent to raising the measured polestar by 118 isba'. On a strictly northward or southward course, this was of course no problem, whereas in other directions the calculations remained very imprecise. At this stage, there was a lack of trigonometric knowledge and of possible ways of working out the speed of a ship. In addition, the characters on the compass dial, which served to determine a ship's heading, accorded only very approximately with the actual risings and settings of the stars.

By contrast, the calculations of favorable times to sail in accordance with the regular monsoon periods were far more precise. In all the sea mirrors we find copious amounts of information on this subject, whose principal difficulty resided in fixing exact dates. The lunar year that the Arabs used otherwise proved unsuitable for determining voyage time, because of the annual adjustments that were necessary. Accordingly, for this purpose, Arab scholars fell back on New Year's Day in the Persian 365-day calendar, using this as the starting point from which to calculate the days, ignoring any divisions into months. Thus, for example, Sidi ali Re'is worked out that the most favorable embarkation date for a voyage from Gujarat to Malacca was Day 300.[89]

To summarize: in the period from the fourteenth to the sixteenth century, despite all political fragmentation of the various (predominantly Muslim) countries bordering on it, the Indian Ocean continued to act as a mercantile entity. Transregional trade was conducted overwhelmingly by Muslim merchants, who over the course of the centuries developed a sophisticated maritime culture that allowed them to sail their vessels safely on long ocean voyages. Thanks to the three extant sea mirrors and the Malay "Sea Codex" of Mahmud Shah, but also through a careful reading, say, of the reports of Abd-ar-Razzaq as-Samarqandi, Ibn Battuta, Sidi ali Re'is, and Afanasy Nikitin, we cannot only build up an accurate picture of the possibilities and the limitations of Arab seafaring and the navigable

routes across the Indian Ocean but also amass a great deal of detailed information about what cargoes were carried where on what ships and, above all, what
life on board these vessels was like.

The Perspective of the Mamluk Empire

Clearly, as we have already noted, the Mongol period was a time of accelerated
consolidation. In the thirteenth and fourteenth centuries, a global realm of transport and communication developed, setting in motion momentous processes that
covered the whole spectrum from political and military reaction via commercial
changes to transfers of culture and technology. Even Europe eventually managed
to hook up with this transregional network. In the period between 1250 and 1517,
the interface between the Mediterranean and Europe, the Silk Route and the
Indian Ocean, was formed by the so-called Mamluk Empire in Egypt and Syria.

Without a doubt, this polity represented a unique social model with an extraordinary degree of polarization.[90] A predominantly Arab populace was ruled
by an elite of freed military slaves who were of exclusively Turkic origin. This elite
attempted constantly to regenerate itself through a self-imposed set of rules. For
instance, the only people who could become Mamluks were those non-Muslim
Turks who had been born outside the Islamic sphere of power as freemen but then
enslaved and brought to Egypt, where they were forcibly converted to Islam, ultimately given their freedom, and finally educated in the knightly tradition. Only
people who fulfilled these criteria could be a member of the ruling elite with all
its attendant political, military, and economic privileges. Within the Mamluk
ruling caste, the smallest social unit was formed by the substitute family that gathered around any particular lord and liberator. This family carried the name of its
master and went extinct only upon the death of the last of its members. According
to the Mamluk ideal, loyalty to one's lord and solidarity with one's comrades who
had assembled around the same patron (in practice, this devotion had its limits
when it came to power struggles) were unbreakable bonds that lasted a lifetime.
They gave deracinated individual Mamluks a sense of homeland and social stability. The flip side of this esprit de corps, however, was the intense rivalry that
existed between Mamluk families, the ensuing internal conflict among the Mamluk
ruling caste, and especially the inevitable fall from power upon the death or vio-

A Mamluk ship with archers; galanty show figure, Egypt, fifteenth century. In this leather artifact, a merchant ship with a large rudder and four sails can be seen sailing from right to left. As well as the captain, the other figures that are depicted are three archers and a skipper holding a quadrant. Several ancient manuscripts mention Egyptian shadow-play theater, but very few such figures have survived to the present day. (Museum für Islamische Kunst, SMB/Georg Biedermeiser)

lent overthrow of any of the family heads. Yet despite the tensions that were pre-programmed into this system, the model of the Mamluk "one generation mili-tary aristocracy" seems to have acted as a major force in promoting stability in Egypt at this time, not least because of its simplicity. At least, it is fair to assume that the longevity of Mamluk suzerainty over the indigenous populace of Egypt and Syria was partially or even primarily attributable to the Mamluk principle of constant renewal. And the subject here is a historically unique model of a society: Once a person starts to study the 250-some years of the Mamluk Era in Egypt and Syria (1250–1517), one characteristic of that period stands out immediately—the very unusual polarization of its society. A predominantly Arabic population was dominated by a purely Turkish-born elite of manumitted military slaves who sought to regenerate themselves continuously through a self-imposed fiat.

As an economic power, together with Genoa and Venice (and, to a lesser extent, also Barcelona), the Mamluks controlled the regions surrounding the Mediterranean and the Black Sea. Yet Egypt and Syria also acted as a transhipment center for many products that were transported across the Indian Ocean to the ports on the Persian Gulf and the Red Sea and thence on the land routes farther into the interior of the Middle East. In addition, goods came overland via the Silk Route to the Levant, from where they were shipped across the Mediterranean to Europe. The Mamluk Empire thus functioned through the entire era under consideration here as a kind of pivotal point between Europe, North Africa, Central Asia, sub-Saharan Africa, and South Asia.[91]

The so-called Karimi merchants played a key role in this process.[92] The social makeup of this group of powerful and influential traders, who had already built up an extensive network during the twelfth century and who controlled long-distance trade with India and Southeast Asia via the Red Sea, is very difficult to comprehend.[93] In the thirteenth and fourteenth centuries, the wealth of the Karimi merchants was proverbial, and even the legendary figure Sinbad the Sailor may have had his origins in this grouping. Their trading houses were located in Alexandria, Cairo, Aden, Qus, and Mecca, as well as along the most important trade routes in the Hejaz and Yemen. Political influence went hand in hand with their economic success. Thus, for example, they acted as mediators between the Yemenite Rasulids and the Mamluks. However, for a number of reasons, particularly the nationalization of the spice trade, the trading network of the Karimi merchants finally collapsed in the mid-fifteenth century.

From around 1350 onward, it became increasingly difficult to transport goods from east to west and elsewhere along the overland routes. Voyages across the Indian Ocean were, by contrast, remarkably trouble-free. Egypt's importance as a transit country remained undimmed, with the Red Sea now developing into a busy entrepôt for mercantile activities. Even Mecca and the sharifs of the Hejaz took part in this Red Sea trade. The great majority of the goods that were brought across the Indian Ocean were unloaded and valued in the port of Jeddah. From there, valuable commodities were transported to Alexandria, from where they found their way across the Mediterranean into Europe.[94] The Portuguese official Duarte Barbosa (1480–1521) gave the following account:

> If you leave the land of Prester John [that is, Christian Abyssinia] and the coast of *"Arabia felix"* and cross to the other side of the Red Sea, which they also call "Arabia," you will come across a harbor known as Suez, to which the Moors bring all the spices from India, along with herbs and other goods from Jeddah, the port city of Mecca. They put these goods in small boxes, load them onto camels, and transport them overland to Cairo. From there, other merchants take them to Alexandria, where they are in turn bought by the Venetians.[95]

From Jeddah, ships would sail back to Calicut, laden with large quantities of copper, mercury, copper acetate, saffron, rosewater, scarlet cloth, silk, and taffeta, not to mention huge amounts of gold and silver. Of necessity, the extended and intensive maritime traffic in the Mediterranean and the Red Sea went via the ports of Aden, Alexandria, and Damietts. However, both these seas were not the only trade routes open to Egypt. The overland route from Egypt to Syria and the Near East as well as those to North Africa and Biladut-Takrur played an important part in the blossoming of Egyptian trade. Finally, Mecca, with its annual pilgrimage, was a key center of transregional trade.

Although the Mamluk period has been thoroughly researched, hardly any studies have looked at Mecca, the central Muslim place of pilgrimage, during this era. Latterly, however, John L. Meloy has published a monograph on this subject.[96] Meloy's concern is not to locate Mecca as a central nodal point in the network of transregional pilgrimage activities but rather to make the basic political and economic environment of the sharifs the centerpiece of his treatise. This family, which traced their ancestors back to the Prophet Muhammad, had controlled the Hejaz since the late twelfth century. Their power derived from control over the pilgrimage sites of Mecca and Medina but also from the strategically favorable position of the Hejaz, as it was particularly in their port of Jeddah, accessed via the Red Sea, that the mercantile worlds of the Indian Ocean and the Mediterranean met. From the late fourteenth to the sixteenth century, when the Portuguese began to encroach on the trade with Asia, trade in the Red Sea continued to expand and laid the foundations of Mecca's prosperity. Yet the sharifs' exercise of power in the Hejaz had always been premised on achieving a modus vivendi with the Mamluk sultans in Cairo. In response to the massive upheavals of the fifteenth century, the Mamluk rulers resident in Cairo exploited their favorable geopolitical position and seized control over the import and export of certain lucrative goods carried by overseas trade. The rulers of Mecca could not avoid being affected by these attempts at monopolization.

John L. Meloy relates the story of the city within this area of conflict: on the one hand, the prosperity that is bound up with the steady stream of trade flowing into Mecca and, on the other, the Mamluk sultans' claims to hegemony, whose constant urge was to acquire a share of the profits of long-distance trade. The city's socioeconomic conditions were based primarily on a combination of pilgrimage, cattle husbandry, patronage, and protection. For the sharifs, politics represented a tightrope walk, because they needed to both satisfy Mamluk ambitions and respond to the many claims asserted by the tribal alliances and local dignitaries. Paraphrasing a quotation by C. Snouk Hurgronje, Meloy encapsulates the history of the city in the fifteenth century as "the loss of Mecca's isolation within the context of Mediterranean–Indian Ocean trade."[97]

Shortly after the death of Sharif Muhammad ibn Barakat in 1497, a combination of internal tensions and external events brought about the collapse of the power structure within Mecca. Another factor in its demise was the series of attacks undertaken by the Portuguese in the Indian Ocean and the Red Sea, which in the long term led to the commercial decline of the region. Even the military campaigns undertaken by the penultimate Mamluk sultan of Egypt, al-Ashraf Qansuh al-Ghuri (d. 922 AH/1516), could do little to reverse this decline. Sharif Barakat ibn Muhammad (d. 931 AH/1525) did manage to consolidate his control over the Hejaz for a while, but even he had ultimately to fall in line with the new great-power constellation occasioned by the rise of the Ottomans.

Aden and Indian Muslims

One group of important protagonists in the economic network that extended from the Indian Ocean into the Red Sea were the Rasulid rulers of Yemen, who were of Turkmen origin.[98] The last Ayubbid regent of Yemen had abandoned the region in 1229 and gone to Egypt and Syria, leaving power there to devolve to one Umar ibn Ali b. Rasul. After he was formally recognized by the Abbasid caliph of Cairo in Baghdad in 1235, he assumed the title of "al-Malik al Mansur" ("victorious ruler") and in so doing founded an economically and politically very successful ruling dynasty, which lasted until 1454. The authority of the Rasulids, who had their main urban centers at Zabid and Ta'izz, rested principally on legitimate military control and to a lesser extent on the support of local groups, families, and tribes. Over the course of time, the Rasulid rulers, who after the fall of Baghdad to Mongol forces in 1258, even arrogated a caliph title to themselves, extended their direct sphere of influence eastward as far as Zafar. In contrast, the north of the region remained largely in the hands of the sharifs of Mecca or the Mamluk sultans.[99] Over the entire period, the port of Aden formed the heart of the suprare-gional trade network controlled by the Yemenite rulers. As a central transhipment center for the spices that were transported across the Indian Ocean and up the Red Sea to the Near East and thence to Europe, Aden played a vital role in creating the economic stability that ensured that social order was maintained.[100] Yemen's key exports included horses and agricultural produce. In the medium term, though, the Rasulids were unable to sustain the position of political and economic independence that they had attained in the thirteenth century. A series of Zayditi imams succeeded in establishing power bases in the highlands in the fourteenth century, because the authority of the Mamluk sultans did not extend to these remote regions. In 1324, the Zayditi were even able to occupy San'a for a spell, and three years later, the Rasulid ruler was seized by the Mamluks while on the pilgrimage to Mecca. Although his successor an-Nasir Ahmad (r. 1401–1424) once more managed to bring stability to his country, the realm dissolved again after his death. On major cause was an outbreak of bubonic plague. For a whole generation, merchants gave Aden a wide berth and headed straight for Jeddah.[101]

Thanks to new documents on the administration of the port of Aden discovered by Éric Vallet, historians have been able to reconstruct the Rasulids' connections to India and their involvement in the Islamization of the coastal regions there.[102] The sources reveal that the harbor administration appears not only to have taken over the collection of excise duty on import and export goods but also assumed responsibility for officially receiving merchants and accommodating them in a manner appropriate to their status. Maritime and commercial connections existed between Yemen and the Indian coasts that can be traced back as far as the first century AD. At the start of spring, ships would set out from southern India,

Malabar, and Coromandel and make for the ports of the southern Arabian Peninsula, particularly Aden, al-Shihr, and Zafar. In the months of July and August,
they would then return to India. This traffic was used among other things for the
shipping of commodities for the slave trade; merchants, pilgrims, and scholars also
favored these routes. From it, there developed a regular annual trade route, with
the arrival of the ships in the Yemenite harbors being designated as the "Indian
season." Under the Rasulids, the harbor administration at Aden would distribute
diverse gifts to the most important merchants in the name of the sultan, including
valuable textiles and horses. In addition, the port authority used the merchant
ships to send donations to Muslim dignitaries in India.

A list of these donations has been preserved; it is believed to date from the
early 1290s and was in all likelihood drawn up by the governor of Aden, who headed
the city administration.[103] It is organized according to six Indian coastal regions
and gives for each a detailed account of the number of donations and their intended recipients, together with their places of residence. The extremely systematic character of the list is striking. In general, no one person is singled out for
special favors and privileges in the regional donations. Each preacher and kadi receives the same number and size of gifts, with the sole exception of the kadi and
the preacher of Tana, who are each given a valuable robe in addition to their other
presents. This may be a hint at their special status. Textiles from Sousse and turbans are sent to every region except Malabar. It is also noteworthy that the religious dignitaries from the northern regions (Gujarat) each receive 2 *bahar*s (240 g)
of madder. This doubtless has to do with the textile industry there, which had a
particular requirement for this commodity. By contrast, gold is sent to the four
central and southern regions of India. There is no doubt that both gold and madder
were lucrative goods in the internal market in India, so their sale every year would
have represented an important source of revenue for the religious dignitaries.
The giving of these donations appears to have been extremely strictly regulated
by the harbor authorities in Aden. The fact that the list is no isolated one-off
but instead represented common practice may be gauged from its frequent use by
Rasulid secretaries; the documents have quite demonstrably been edited and
brought up-to-date several times. A century later, nothing had changed with
regard to this practice, and donations were still being administered by the Aden
port authorities.

As for the Indian communities, it would seem that adherents or congregations following a particular Islamic school of jurisprudence were the beneficiaries of the Rasulid donations, especially the Shafiʻites, a school to which most of the Sunnis in southern Yemen and the Tihama region had allegiance. This might suggest a preference for southern Indian communities who were predominantly Shafiʻite. However, conflicting with this assumption is the knowledge that the Sunnis in Gujarat, as a result of influences from Iran and Central Asia in the twelfth and thirteenth centuries, were overwhelmingly adherents of the Hanafi school of Islamic law. Conversely, then, this would seem to indicate that membership of a particular school of jurisprudence was not after all the determining factor in patronage by the Rasulid sultans.[104] Another possible basis might be material support for a large number of Yemenite scholars in Indian exile, as well as the further development of such existing groups. The Yemenite biographer al-Janadi (d. 1331) mentions in this context several legal scholars who emigrated to India to earn a living and to expand their knowledge. India must have been a land full of promising potential for these Muslim scholars, because certain locations there were already renowned as part of the Muslim system of knowledge transference. Not least, they had the opportunity to become followers of Ibn Battuta, who was active at the Delhi court. However, al-Janadi's descriptions neither give any differentiated geographical information about where the Muslim legal scholars from Yemen settled (he confines himself to talking about "India" [*bilād al-Hind*]), nor does he call their emigration "pleasing to God," as he regarded India as the "Land of the Unbelievers."[105] According to Zayn ad-Din, the Muslim historiographer of Kerala, the Yemenites played a decisive role in the growth of Muslim communities in the south of India. On the one hand, conversion to Islam took place independently on the part of the indigenous community, promoted by their most respected leaders adopting the faith, while on the other, the religion was transmitted by these religious dignitaries from Yemen. Yet the familiar sources on the Rasulid era cannot confirm that the Yemenite scholars actually made a major contribution to the Islamization of India as a whole. Moreover, their emigration during this period was still only on an individual basis and could not be described as collective mass migration.

Therefore, there is no evidence to suggest that any politically motivated exodus took place or that particular social groups were attracted to India. The only verifiable act (according to al-Janadi) was a direct intervention by the Rasulid sultan al-Muzaffar Yusuf (1295) in appointing a Muslim judge after being asked in a letter from a community in Tana to do so. It is likely that other Muslim communities on the west coast of India behaved in a similar way, as is demonstrable also in the case of Calcutta (Kolkata). The requests for annual donations by the Rasulids were also issued in the name of preachers or judges from the community, who were already well established and respected in the region. This procedure also held good for the Indian communities mentioned in the *Nūr al-maʾārif*. According to this, the contributions by the Rasulid court occurred only at the request of the local Indian communities and represented a substantial material foundation for them. In return for the patronage, the sultan's name was invoked alongside those of the caliphs and the great imams of the past as a benefactor and great lord in the local Friday sermon. This can be seen as the first symbolic proof of sovereignty in India. In this light, the patronage would then have been primarily politically motivated.[106]

According to the current state of source material, nothing points to a close connection between the Yemenite sultans and Indian Muslims prior to the reign of al-Muzaffar Yusuf. For this period, there are only isolated indications and incomplete descriptions. We know that at this time, the northern regions of India had, since the reign of the Ghaznavids, offered up prayers in the name of the sultans of Delhi. For the rest of India, under the sway of diverse "Hindu" kingdoms, there is evidence that, at the beginning of the thirteenth century in the major settlement of the al-Qass (that is, Gujarat/Cambay/Somnath/Bhadresvar), the name of the Abbasid caliph was invoked instead. We know from Ibn Battuta that a small community in the southern port of Kulam was likewise still paying homage to the Abbasid caliph in the fourteenth century. This was probably also the case for other southern Indian communities, as it was in the cities of Gujarat and in far-flung China, too. This connection was maintained by the successors to the Rasulids and served as a conclusive argument for legitimation against the Mamluks and for asserting the independence of their sultanate. Furthermore, the continuing veneration of the dead caliph Mustaʿsim Biʾllah in Friday sermons in Calcutta is well documented. We can therefore reasonably assume that the Rasulid court exploited this direct connection to the Abbasid caliphate for its own legitimation.[107]

The conditions for the development of patronage in India remain unclear. It seems probable that, from the 1260s on, the Muslim communities began to coalesce in order to profit from the Rasulid donations. This process seems to have become well established by the end of the thirteenth century. And yet, with the exception of a letter written by the merchants of Calcutta,[108] the aforementioned practice is not touched upon in the primary sources. Neither the donations by the harbor administration of Aden nor the exact role of Sultan al-Muzaffar Yusuf are mentioned. A century later, though, during a difficult period for the Rasulids, the successor on the Rasulid throne, al-Afdal al'Abbas (r. 1363–1377), wrote a eulogy to his forebears in which he confirmed that al-Muzzafar Yusuf commissioned the building of the Friday mosques in China and at Hormuz and that homage continued to be paid to him in those places—a dynastic legend that is confirmed in no other source. Similarly, contemporary witnesses from the time of al-Muzzafar Yusuf do not corroborate these statements either. However, in al-Janadi's work, we do find a report of the sultan intervening with the Chinese emperor—most likely the Mongol Great Kublai Khan (r. 1260–1294). This concerned the matter of the emperor's proscription against Muslims being circumcised, a practice that, following a letter from al-Muzzafar Yusuf and the dispatch of a precious gift to Kublai, was finally permitted.

Accordingly, the Rasulids' presentation of themselves might well have had less to do with simply appearing as defenders of the faith and more to do with laying claim to political sovereignty. This strategy by the Rasulids of using religion to legitimize their claims during the second half of the thirteenth century must be seen in conjunction with the rival pretenders to their own throne, namely, the Mamluks in Egypt and Syria. This rivalry is evident in a letter written by the Mamluk sultan Baybars I to al-Muzzafar Yusuf while on the hajj of 1269. This contains an appeal by Baybars to the effect that a ruler is duty-bound to undertake jihad and that therefore a precondition to Muzzafar's claim on power would be an attack on the Tatars. Without question, especially after losing control over Mecca in the 1240s, Sultan Baybars felt it incumbent on himself to lay claim to and ultimately to achieve sovereignty over Yemen. It seems likely that the constant reference to the Abbasids by the Rasulids, along with their fostering of patronage in India, was a direct response to the Mamluk challenge to their legitimacy.[109]

So, did the Muslim communities in India venerate the Rasulids and the deceased Abbasid caliph voluntarily? The geographical listing of the Rasulid donations noted above exactly reflected the borders of the great "Hindu" kingdoms, before the entire west coast of the *Bilād al-Hind* fell into the hands of the sultanate of Delhi. During the second half of the thirteenth century, these "Hindu" dynasties were in conflict with one another. This was particularly true of the great realms in the center and the south (Pandya/Hoysala and Yadava). Each of these empires therefore had a pressing need for large quantities of horses for the cavalry, and Muslim merchants played a key role in the import of these animals. The "Hindu" princes also vied with one another in their commercial interests to forge a link with the Yemenite administration. The Rasulid donations to Muslim dignitaries of the region also created good contacts with the most important members of the Muslim communities, who in many cases were traders or shipowners. The result was that Yemen secured for itself a privileged position in trade matters.[110]

By the end of the fourteenth century, the number of communities left that paid homage to the Rasulid ruler al-Malik al-Ashraf had dwindled by three-quarters of its peak figure to just eleven. The explanation for this lies in the growing competition from the sultans of Delhi over the course of the fourteenth century, as well as from the rulers of Hormuz. Gujarat, which was attacked by Ala' ad-Din Khalji in 1300, gradually came under the control of the Turkic-origin elite. The regency of Muhammad ibn Tughluq represented a historical turning point in this regard. The sultans of Delhi now became the subject of veneration, beginning with the construction of the main mosques in the large cities of Gujarat. Their military campaigns took them ever farther south, to the kingdom of Pandya. The Yemenite chronicler Ibn 'Abd al-Majid cites the 1313 expedition of Malik Kafur as a key date, after which the subcontinent came under the control of Turkic-origin rulers. It was also around this same time that the Rasulid patronage in Gujarat and Konkan came to an end.

Very few traces of this rupture can be identified, except for an account written by the Catalan Dominican friar Guillelmus Adae (William Adam), who in 1316 sailed from India to the coast of Abyssinia. Adam reports that the most important ports of northern India (Cambay and Tana) saw the Yemenite sultanate as their enemy. He also mentions the city-states of the Gulf region—Qays and

Hormuz—as rivals to the Rasulids. Since the 1330s and the victory of the princes of Hormuz over Qays, these rulers' ambitions had been growing. However, little is known about this period, especially how the Gulf princes managed to bring these ambitions to fruition on a commercial level on the Indian coast. In the ports of Gujarat and Konkan, they would have had to deal with the new rulers of India. Competition between the Rasulids and the lords of Hormuz appears to have been at its strongest in the Malabar region, which was in the hands of various minor Tamil dynasties.

For most of the fourteenth century, the rulers of Hormuz were named in the Friday sermon in Calcutta. Calcutta was first mentioned as an important port by Ibn Battuta in 1340. Close connections developed between this city and the major cities of the Gulf. This was underlined among other things by the financial support that the princes of Hormuz, in their struggle against Qays, received from the Sufi community (more of a network, in truth) of the Kazaruni, who subsequently settled in Calcutta and cultivated a decisive influence over the rulers of Hormuz. This grew ever stronger until the late fourteenth century, when the merchants of Calcutta and the kadi switched their allegiance to the Rasulid sultan.[111]

The political context of this period (1393–1398) is significant. In the face of attacks by Tamerlane, the rulers of Hormuz faded into the background while the power of the sultans of Delhi waned dramatically. In this highly unstable political situation, the Rasulid sultanate, which had been spared any assault by Tamerlane, came to represent a secure partnership for the Muslim merchants of India. Even so, we should not be misled by the letter that has come down to us from the traders of Calcutta: the Rasulid sultanate possessed the aura it did at this period only thanks to a fortunate boom period. By the beginning of the fifteenth century, the Yemenite rulers were in dire straits. Growing tribal uprisings in many parts of their empire severely weakened its power. In particular, the Rasulid secretaries angered and alienated the merchants and shipowners of India through their interference in the trading affairs of Aden in 1420. In 1422, the provost of Calcutta responded by taking direct responsibility for all trading affairs between southern Indian ports and those on the Red Sea. The upshot was that the port of Aden was now circumvented and the Rasulid rulers lost control. This trend continued, and by around the end of the 1420s, the Rasulid ruler seems to have been noticeably weakened, with no connections any more to Calcutta or other Indian ports.

Even in the absence of any precise information on the end of the Rasulid patronage in the chronicles, it is clear that this was at an end by the first decades of the fifteenth century. To be sure, it had survived the fall of the Abbasid caliphate in 1258 and made a concerted attempt to adapt to the changing geopolitical landscape. But despite the enormous territorial gains by the sultans of Delhi, the Rasulid presence in southern India did not vanish entirely. This was doubtless due to the decisive factor of commercial links, not least on the import of horses. In general, we may conclude that Rasulid influence endured as long as the port of Aden remained important as a stopover and as a point of contact for intermediary trade. Over the course of the fifteenth century, it lost this character. Insofar as the Rasulids continued to appeal to the old caliphate of Baghdad, they also aligned themselves with the old political conception that drew a distinction between the "domain of Islam" *(dar al-Islam)* and the "domain of the unbelievers" *(dar al-kufr)*. On the basis of this distinction, the elites of the Muslim communities of India had continued to cleave to that seat of power, which in their eyes offered them a clear possibility of identification. Veneration of this or that ruler at Friday sermons did not have to do with acknowledgment of sovereignty but rather represented above all a structural element for orientation of the Indian Muslim religious and political sense of identity. The recourse to Rasulid patronage, and also the demise of this phenomenon, should be understood in this context.[112]

From the thirteenth to the fourteenth centuries, the Yemenite sultanate was responsible for bringing about profound changes in the models the Muslim communities of the Indian coastal regions turned to when forming their sense of identity. This century-long period, which witnessed the collapse of the Abbasid caliphate, was also characterized by the self-assertion of the Sunnis, especially those who inhabited lands bordering the Indian Ocean. Neither the Ismailis nor the Ibadi, marginalized in the mountain regions of Yemen and Oman, respectively, were able to exert any significant influence on northern India or East Africa during the thirteenth century. A century later, Ibn Battuta portrayed the region of the Indian Ocean as a uniformly Sunni world. In the long term, the profound political transformations that occurred on the Indian subcontinent in the fourteenth century did not favor the Rasulids. The regional and independent sultanates that gradually came into being sought legitimacy by styling themselves as staunch defenders of Islam. This process began in the principality of Madurai in the ancient kingdom of Pandaya in 1334, followed by Bengal in 1336. In the aforementioned letter from Calcutta, its authors explicitly mention existing groups in the region—in Bengal, Hormuz, and al-Samutra—where the name of the regional sultan was the one invoked in the Friday sermon. The competition between all these new states that arose during this second great phase in the rise of Islam was immense. In the transition between the thirteenth and fourteenth centuries, this manifested itself not only in India but also in the heartland of Islam, at the holy sites of Mecca and Medina. Bengal was at the forefront of this development, when its sovereign commissioned the building of a magnificent, and up to that date the largest, madrasa in Mecca in 1410. In the ensuing years, other Muslim rulers from India followed suit by erecting their own monuments in the holy city. It is certain that by this stage the Rasulid sultanate no longer represented the indispensable link for Indian Muslims that it once had, as a kind of compensatory presence for the lost caliphate of Baghdad. Its historical role as the connection between the "old world" of Islam and the "new world" of India was now at an end.[113]

3. The Indian Ocean from the Sixteenth to the Eighteenth Century

BY the end of the fifteenth century, a network of several dozen generally Muslim trading bases had grown up between the East African coast, the Indian Ocean, and the Near East, facilitating not only regular trade contacts but also an intensive transfer of new technologies, of a welter of new ideas, and of many different groups. Europe participated in and profited from these interactions from the periphery, through the Mediterranean and the trade routes that ran through Eastern and Southern Europe. The beginning of the sixteenth century saw the simultaneous occurrence of various important developments and events: the discovery of America, the rounding of the Cape of Good Hope, the growth of the three great Muslim empires of the Safavids, Ottomans, and Mughals, and finally the rise of new trading enterprises and such commercial practices as monetization and the commercialization of farming. Of course, all this does not represent some abrupt break with the past, but even so there is clear evidence of a process of ongoing acceleration and consolidation. The world was changing, though there were as yet no signs, such as those that appeared in the nineteenth century, say, of European predominance. The following overview will sketch the most important political players in and around the Indian Ocean region in this period: the Mughal Empire, the non-Muslim ruling confederations of India, the Ottoman Empire, the Safavids, and the European powers.

The Perspective of the Mughal Empire

In presenting the economic history of South Asia in the Middle Ages, the lack of statistical sources means that the focus must fall on the commercial structure and the role played by Indian merchants in the maritime trade of the sixteenth and seventeenth centuries.[114] In the eighteenth century, though, the South Asian economy underwent a significant change, as trade in the Indian Ocean came increasingly to be dominated by European trading companies and by the exchange of goods with Europe. One important constant is the centuries-old distinction between, on the one hand, commercial activities oriented toward the coast and, on the other, onshore trading, with the former mostly being conducted by Muslims, while the latter was controlled by "Hindus."[115] Generally speaking, European trade in the Indian Ocean integrated itself into these traditional structures, which were thereby strengthened and enriched. Major upheavals came only with the encroachment of the British Empire into the region.

At the end of the fifteenth century, India's merchant navy was largely in the hands of Muslim traders from Gujarat. They were active principally in the Indian Ocean and dominated the sea routes between Cambay and Malacca. Indian merchants also sailed regularly to the Red Sea and the Persian Gulf, while the Arabian Sea was under the control of Arab traders. The east, between China and the Malay Archipelago, was dominated by the Chinese, while Indonesia was primarily visited by Malay and Japanese vessels. The rise of Malacca as an entrepôt for Indian, Chinese, and Javanese traders represents one of the most significant developments in the history of the Indian Ocean in the fifteenth century. Indian and Chinese merchants were mainly interested in acquiring Indonesian spices there but also traded with one another, with the Indians importing silk and porcelain. Chinese merchants bought huge quantities of pepper, some of which undoubtedly came from Malabar, plus in all likelihood they also had an interest in Indian opium, sandalwood, and incense. However, the trade between the Indians and the Chinese in Malacca was only of minor importance, because the rulers of the Ming dynasty in China were concerned with imposing strict limits on foreign trade and were intent on sealing their country (the "Middle Kingdom") off from the sea. Indian merchants did not venture into the China Sea; their ships were not sufficiently stable, nor were they equipped to fight off attacks by the many pirates who plied those waters. Moreover, the demand for Indian goods in China was simply too small to warrant such voyages. By contrast, Indian textiles of various different qualities were highly sought after in Southeast Asia, and there were direct trade connections with Sumatra. By the late fifteenth century, the inhabitants of the Moluccas had begun to specialize in the production of spices and had become dependent on Indian textiles and Javanese grain. This trade was conducted almost exclusively by Javanese merchants, who also shipped spices to Malacca.

Painting of a Portuguese boy, Mughal school, northern India, seventeenth century. While this portrait is ostensibly a thoroughly naturalistic portrayal of a youth dressed in European clothes, certain details point to a stylized depiction of this handsome young man. In any event, one remarkable feature is the completely nonideological and unprejudiced representation of this "alien" person. (Museum für Islamische Kunst, SMB/Ingrid Geske)

Toward the end of the fifteenth century, Indian traders were well represented in the Indian Ocean, with a strong presence in Malacca and with firm trade links to Java and Sumatra.[116]

In a westward direction, two main trade routes were used by Indian merchants, one running via the Red Sea to Cairo and Alexandria and the other through the Persian Gulf to Basra and Baghdad. Although the freight traffic between the Red Sea and India's west coast was dominated by the Karimi merchants, Indian ships also regularly sailed to the ports of southern Arabia. In the Persian Gulf, Hormuz and Muscat were the principal destinations of Indian vessels, while merchants from Gujarat settled in Persian cities and in Arabian ports along the Red Sea. Even so, internal trade within Persia remained closed to Indian traders because of the country's unstable political situation. Historical sources indicate that the position of Hormuz as a transhipment port was comparable to that of Malacca in the Indian Ocean, though Indian ships played only a minimal part in the trading activities there.[117] The east coast of Africa was also regularly visited by Gujarati merchants in the fifteenth century, who while en route to the Red Sea may well have traded Indian textiles for gold and ivory.[118]

In the period before the arrival of the Portuguese, Arab and South Asian traders generally worked hand in hand. Indian merchants were more or less free to settle in the Arab lands, while Arab traders were welcome visitors to the west coast of India. The most important Indian port at the time, Cambay, was notable for its large settlements of Arab and Persian merchants, which went back as far as the tenth century. Toward the end of the fifteenth century, as Cambay's harbor slowly silted up, a great rivalry developed between the ports of Surat and Diu to capture its trade; both were already important centers for trade with the Red Sea.[119]

The principal export commodity of the South Asian merchants consisted of coarse fabrics, which found a ready market in Indonesia and the Red Sea region, selling mainly to poorer people. Finer textiles had no viable market in these locations; it was for this reason that the Dutch East India Company (VOC), with its textiles purchased from the Coromandel Coast, never really posed competitive threat to the Gujarati weavers and traders of coarser materials. Even in the seventeenth and eighteenth centuries, the trade in luxury goods represented only a very small fraction of total trade in the region. India exported rice, pulses, wheat, and oil, all of which were sought after in Malacca, Hormuz, and Aden. Coconut palm products, turmeric, and ginger were also traded, although where such commodities were concerned, being commonplace around the Indian Ocean region, only small profits could be expected. Conversely, India also exported large quantities of relatively low-priced goods that were urgently in demand in the consumer markets where they were sold. For instance, Bengali merchants traded in sugar and raw silk and Gujaratis in raw cotton, while Malabar exported pepper. Indigo, meanwhile, was exported from ports in both Bengal and Gujarat but also from the Coromandel Coast. These stable economic structures all changed dramatically when India lost its role as the primary shipper for the spice trade, a development that saw the textile trade grow enormously in importance over the course of the seventeenth century.[120]

Indian merchant shipping was able to hold its own against the growing influence of European trading companies in the sixteenth and seventeenth centuries, not least because the cargo rates charged by Europeans were in some cases twice as high as those of Indian concerns. In addition, Indian trade relied on a traditional system of social connections. In most cases, in order to avoid any complications, merchants used the ships that were available within their own community. Dividing cargoes up across several vessels minimized the risks that traders incurred. The Indian system operated far more smoothly than that of the Europeans. Investment in transport was extremely uncommon in India at this time, though, as ships were privately owned, expensive, and a risky venture.

Indian shipping at this stage was largely Muslim in character; "Hindu" merchants rarely arranged for the transhipment of goods on their own ships. Prosperous Indian merchants tended to travel with their cargoes, while others preferred to send agents. The captains of the ships, often of Persian origin, were independent traders in their own right, yet often also acted as agents for other merchants or on behalf of the shipowner. However, most Indian merchants were small businessmen who mostly only had one or two bales of cloth to trade and who conducted their trade in various ports. The fact that they were so numerous prevented the wealthy merchants from gaining a monopoly. For a long time, contracts were not regarded as binding. So long as a weaver returned in full the money that a merchant had paid in advance for his wares, the weaver was free to then sell his textiles to the highest bidder. Contractual law and custom was developed further only under the influence of the British East India Company in the 1730s.

India's overseas trade was based on a system of cooperation and trade-offs between merchants. The shipowners and other traders had to rely on middlemen, who were responsible for supplying a harbor with particular commodities. These individuals then undertook to sell the goods on or supply them and were indispensable to both Indian and European businessmen. Money changers also formed part of these networks, which were powerful entities. Middlemen at a local level were an unavoidable fact of life, and even toward the end of the period under discussion here, such structures still remained intact. The Indian mercantile world was governed by an unwritten social code, which enabled everyone to work in the profession allotted to him and to earn a living. Innovations such as centralized production were not catered for.

As long as peace reigned in the ports and duties were regularly paid, administrations seldom interfered in trading activities. South Asian rulers, including the Mughals, were never particularly interested in maritime trade and mostly left regulation of this business to local administrators. There was no naval force to protect the Indian mercantile fleet. Local bureaucrats would sometimes attempt to exploit this unregulated situated for their own ends. Yet this happened only infrequently, because the ethos of an emir precluded him from involving himself too much in mercantile affairs. High-ranking dignitaries participated "at a distance" through investments. Unlike the other South Asian traders, Muslim merchants made full use of their wealth and became local worthies on the political stage.

The availability of money, which the merchants needed in order to conduct business in the coastal towns, was a constant problem; for this reason, interest rates fluctuated with the season according to the arrival and departure of the merchant ships. Prices were set somewhat arbitrarily, which made it extremely difficult to calculate the costs of transactions. Both the merchants and the manufacturers of trade goods, however, learned to live with such uncertainties. The markets in the Indian Ocean region were unpredictable; the expectation of a good hajj pilgrimage year could lead to a boost in production, whereas news of political unrest in the Ottoman Empire or the Persian Gulf could have a negative influence on manufacture and trade.[121] The purchase of goods for overseas trade occurred in various different ways. The prosperous merchants, who undertook annual voyages, normally worked on the basis of cash before delivery, while other traders simply spontaneously bought what was available. However, even when faced with stiff

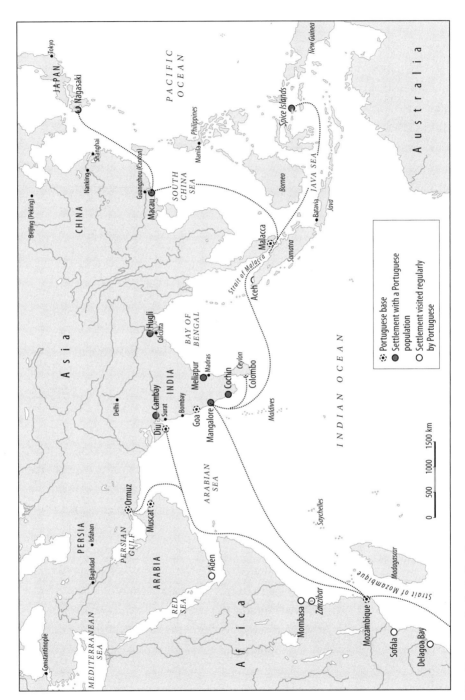

The Portuguese in the Indian Ocean

competition, Indian merchants would observe strict social bounds. Business was always organized within the framework of the family, with trading partners from outside this domain (who even so had at least to come from the same social group) only ever being accepted as a short-term stopgap measure. Cooperation, including that between Hindus and Muslims, was generally very unpopular.

Above all, it was the almost simultaneous rise of the great empires of the Ottomans, Safavids, and Mughals that influenced India's seaborne trade in the sixteenth century. However, it is not easy to determine what precise changes took place at this time. The connections in overland trade that the great empires created and secured were certainly of the utmost significance. By the late sixteenth century, the Red Sea had become India's principal consumer market, especially for textiles. This situation changed only marginally when maritime trade with China resumed in the mid-eighteenth century. Muslim shipowners from Gujarat, meanwhile, were at the forefront of opposition to Portuguese attempts to wrest control of Indian Ocean trade, while other traders were not so dependent on the free traffic of cargo. Over time, though, the Portuguese reopened up the harbors they had seized to ships from Gujarat, which accounted for the greater part of customs revenues. Furthermore, the private trade conducted by Portuguese officials also made them reliant on cooperation with the Indians. This unofficial trade was overwhelmingly financed by Indian merchants, who in return were granted excise-free carriage of their cargoes by ships flying the Portuguese flag. Until the eighteenth century, the market in India was not dominated by European trade. At most, the European trading companies would attain a temporary predominance in the trading of certain commodities.

Initially, maritime trade in South Asia simply continued earlier trends—though the rise of the Yarubis in Oman saw the appearance of pirates in the Arabian Sea, who mainly attacked vessels from Gujarat.[122] The rise of the British EIC and the Dutch VOC likewise influence Indian seaborne trade. At first, however, the collapse of Portuguese restrictions led to freer trade, though this was curtailed once more by the VOC, which proved far more thorough in enforcement than the Portuguese had ever been. By the mid-seventeenth century, the VOC had succeeded in imposing a very effective monopoly over the spice trade, and after 1618, almost no ships from Gujarat sailed to Sumatra again. The only markets left open to them now were the Red Sea and the Persian Gulf, where they traded in textiles.

The decline of southern Asian seaborne trade began long before the collapse of the Mughal Empire. Shipping in Bengal, for instance, reached its zenith in the 1670s, before suffering a noticeable setback. A similar thing happened in Gujarat in the early eighteenth century. Indian traders had flooded the markets in the Indian Ocean with goods; between 1698 and 1710 merchants from Gujarat undertook a series of wholly unprofitable voyages. The demise of the port of Surat in the Mughal Empire and the gradual disappearance of the fleet that used to tie up there were the most significant commercial developments in the Indian Ocean. Soon afterward, the trade being conducted from Bombay (Mumbai) by the British, which was primarily directed at China, brought about further momentous changes in the structure of business in the Indian Ocean.[123]

The economy of South Asia during the Mughal period and up to the eighteenth century was characterized by the coexistence and partial commingling of a subsistence economy with the commercialized sector.[124] Large sections of the populace lived in villages and supported themselves with their own produce and through traditional mutual obligations. This system was specifically Indian; in other parts of Asia, say in China, the commercialization of life had already become a reality over the course of the tenth, eleventh, and twelfth centuries through the existence of informal markets. Nevertheless, trade in goods in India was a complex and multifaceted business. Shortfalls or overproduction in subsistence farming were compensated for by commercial activities. A leading characteristic of this kind of trade was its relative one-sidedness. Goods flowed from the villages to the cities, supplying them with ample foodstuffs, raw materials for manufacture, and finished products. Although local markets were held regularly, regional trade was far more complex. Most official buildings in India were surrounded by a marketplace, with the result that larger cities had several small markets and a central market. These not only supplied local inhabitants with their immediate needs but also served as hubs for traders from other regions who purchased their goods here. Villages in the environs of towns were often, for technical administrative reasons, reliant on these markets, while conversely the cities were dependent on the land. The fact that taxes were collected in hard cash increased the pressure on people to amass corresponding amounts of cash through trading activity.

Some cities developed specialized markets for dealing in goods acquired from supraregional trade or even from overseas commerce. In part, officialdom even promoted such markets by means of offering tax concessions on goods purchased there. In cases where cities were themselves manufacturing centers, they regularly exported their goods to other regions and at the same time became favorite commercial centers. Examples of such major trade hubs were Hooghly, Masulipatnam, and Surat, in which, above all, goods for resale were purchased. Supraregional trade did not just deal in luxury goods, even though transport costs made goods more expensive anyhow. Foodstuffs and plain textiles accounted for the majority of mercantile activities, which could span huge distances and which for cost reasons were mainly transacted by the sea routes. Trade was dominated by certain regions. Bengal, for example, exported far more than it imported. Particularly the west coast and Gujarat were supplied from ports on the Coromandel Coast with both imported luxury items and locally manufactured goods.[125] Luxury textiles, imported goods, and cotton were the main branches of trade in Gujarat, while in exchange foodstuffs and raw materials were imported to the region. By contrast, the North Indian heartland was primarily an import region, with only salt, indigo, and grain being exported, along with luxury products from Kashmir.

The example of the grain trade demonstrates clearly how some regions, such as Bengal, had production surpluses, while others ran deficits. In built-up areas, the population was reliant on imported foodstuffs. Grain, most likely comprising various different kinds of cereals, was also traded between regions with surpluses. Gujarat was the main importer of grain; here, in contrast to the highly developed production and commercial sector, the land not very productive. The textile trade was only very peripherally characterized by the purchases made by Europeans, with most fabrics being sold by Indian or other Asian merchants within India itself or in western and Central Asia. Goods were made not exclusively for home consumption or for overseas trade but rather in different grades of quality for different groups of consumers. Bengal was also of enormous importance in the trade in textiles, primarily silk and cotton. Fundamental relationships of dependence existed in the supraregional trade in intermediate products or raw materials. The silk industry in Gujarat was dependent on the import of raw silk from Bengal, but large quantities of Bengali silk were also exported annually via Agra to Persia and Turkey. Bengal, in turn, imported cotton from the region between Surat and Burhanpur. Dyestuffs for textile manufacture, which were grown only in certain regions, were also popular trade goods. Some cotton fabrics were dispatched to villages in the regions of Agra, Ahmedabad, and Masulipatnam that specialized in dyeing, as well as to some places in Bengal itself. Relatively little is recorded about the trade in minerals, but we do know that South Asia had mined sufficient iron, saltpeter, and diamonds to supply its needs. Malabar's supraregional trade in pepper and spice was of great importance. The slave trade should also be mentioned: Bengal was the site of regular slave markets supplying the whole of India.[126]

Scant information is available about the sheer volume of overseas trade. Statistics showing an increase in population may reasonably allow us to conclude that this was occasioned by economic growth. Though European exports to the region rose steadily, they always remained only a small proportion of the total trade conducted in any individual production center. We might therefore expect that, proportional to growing investment by Europeans, the total volume of goods traded might also have expanded. Hitherto, it has been assumed that the prices of consumer goods remained stable in India until the 1660s and that only the relative cost of gold and silver changed. It was further surmised that copper grew ever more expensive and that with the import of silver to Bengal, the price of silver fell, thus raising the general price level of the currency, which was based on silver reserves. However, more recent studies have shown that grain prices also rose, particularly in Hindustan, in the Punjab, and in Gujarat. Moreover, the changes supposedly brought about by the import of silver are no longer taken as documentary fact—certainly, the export of grain from Bengal seems to have been unaffected by the ensuing price adjustment that allegedly took place. We must therefore conclude that Bengal at this time, in comparison with other regions, was still able to produce and sell goods at a competitive price. The integration of markets was still not very advanced at this stage, and supraregional trade was based above all on the basic differences between the buying and selling price in the different regions. The difference in the wheat prices between Agra and Gujarat was commensurate, say, with the high transport costs. In all probability, the European trading companies were unaffected by rising prices on local markets, because they were in a position to sharply lower their transport costs. Yet price rises in the Mughal Empire were almost certainly not so much the result of changes in the money supply but rather were triggered by real economic factors. The taxation system and the state bureaucracy must also have exerted a strong influence on the economy. The rate of urbanization rose over the course of time, as did population figures, so that even leaving trade with Europe aside, a steady price increase could have been foreseen. Internal trade was hampered by various factors, including the lack of a uniform system of weights and measures, currency, and taxation.

The Infrastructure of Trade

In premodern South Asia, different forms of markets existed, from the small village *hât* markets to the international trade hubs of Surat or Agra. The markets can be divided into four categories:

- Centers for overseas or inland trade via land or sea routes. The differences here were primarily ones of scale. Ports focused on international trade.
- Smaller bazaars, *manîs,* or large markets, where locally produced goods were sold mainly for local consumption.
- Seasonal special markets, where merchants sold goods to one another but where consumers were also allowed to buy.
- Isolated village markets, where the surpluses of local production were exchanged between producers or consumers.

There were many cross-linkages between the first three categories, while the fourth type was probably hard to distinguish from the seasonal hât. As a result of their favorable geographical and political position, the great commercial nodal points developed rapidly. They were often centers of administration as well and so had countless markets of diverse categories to call on to attract merchants from many surrounding regions.

The merchants themselves were distinguished by their function and their prosperity and even prior to the advent of Europeans were for the most part specialists. Ports in particular were home to a class of extremely wealthy and powerful merchants, some of whom owned large mercantile fleets and who operated across many branches of trade and commerce. Riches could be amassed only with the help of good connections to politics and bureaucracy, and accordingly political errors rather than commercial misjudgments were more often the cause of a person's fall from prosperity. Some of the small traders were traveling salesmen whose limited sales just earned enough to make a living. Although in particular the middlemen of the European trading companies often pursued their own business

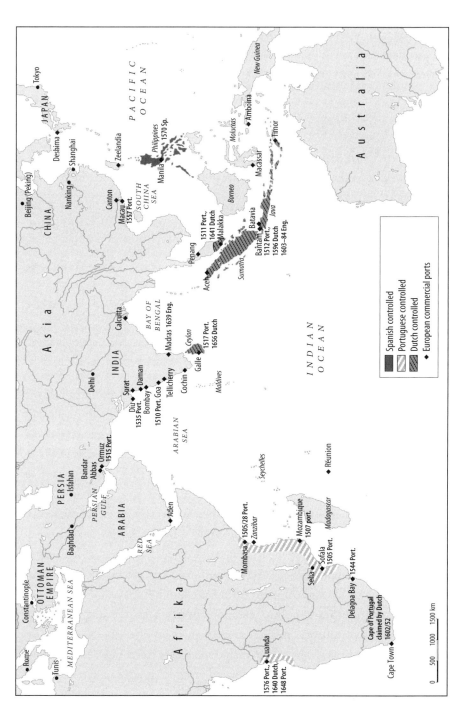

European expansion before the eighteenth century

interests, intermediaries *(dalal)* were highly specialized. Every group of goods had its own middlemen, and some dalals were even appointed by the government, as in Bengal, to work in a particular area of expertise. Hindu traders came from a very few castes, while Muslim traders were especially active in Gujarat, in the Deccan, and in Bengal, and Armenians operated throughout the empire. Business was usually confined to members of a person's own caste or social group. However, Hindus often handled financial dealings for Muslim traders, whose ships were also used by Hindus for overseas trade.

Goods were either sold directly at the great trade hubs and city markets or were supplied on the basis of a contract. In the second half of the seventeenth century, most goods in long-distance trade were acquired in this way. Prepayment was required from the merchants on conclusion of a contract, because the resources of the producers would not otherwise have stretched to meet increasing demand. Moreover, this form of forward contract also served to counteract the inherent instability of the market and price fluctuations. The contractual system operated on a hierarchical basis and was used by the government, the European trading companies, and rich merchants alike, who mostly engaged the services of various middlemen.

One key aspect of this expanding world of commerce was the development of an extensive banking system, which grew in significance from the eighteenth century on as certain mercantile dynasties began to specialize in the financial sector. One typical instrument was the system of *hundi* or notes of exchange, which guaranteed the repayment of a specified sum at a specified location after a specified period. These notes of exchange became the standard means of payment in major transactions, especially in long-distance trade. Professional money changers developed over time into credit grantors, though their most important source of income was the deposit business. This entailed them accepting bank deposits, which had to be paid out again when required but which in the meantime were invested by the creditors. A ruse much favored by bureaucrats was the illegal investment of state funds, for which they pocketed the interest that accrued. One highly speculative financial instrument was the ship mortgage bond, which was used to invest at high rates of interest in a ship's cargo. Important creditors for major transactions were the state and the aristocracy, but money lending took place on a smaller scale on the lower strata of the economy as well. Here, a clear relationship of subservience and dependence existed between small traders and local money-lenders. Interest rates could vary considerably from region to region, with the result that finance remained very inconsistent in the Mughal Empire. Similarly, there was no unified postal system, and official documents were regularly carried by private couriers.

Transport opportunities were efficient and diverse in the Mughal Empire, with even sudden spikes in demand being catered for. The main modes of transport were pack oxen and camels; two-wheeled oxcarts were the fastest, safest, and cheapest conveyances for both goods and people. A very few merchants traveled on horseback. Waterborne transport on rivers and canals was the most important and cost-effective means of transport for inland trade. Goods that were handled in large quantities could be transported in this way. In northern India, the major route was the River Ganges with its tributaries, while in the northwest of the country, the Indus formed the main transport artery. Relative security and a generally well-maintained infrastructure, especially along the central axes from Surat to Agra, Gwalior, or Masulipatnam, expedited people's journeys. Even so, the journey from Surat to Agra on a lightly laden oxcart could still take from thirty-five to forty days. The waterways were usually slower, and travel times depended on how high the water levels were in the rivers, which were crossed by stone bridges. Larger bodies of water were crossed with the aid of ferries or pontoon bridges. The frequency of places for travelers to stay varied enormously from region to region; hostels and boardinghouses were sometimes erected by the government and sometimes financed by the villages that lay along the main routes. Larger hostels consisted of several rooms, halls, and terraces, as well as small shops and service providers, while smaller accommodation facilities were just a simple collection of huts.

The organization of land transport, which was controlled mostly by the nomadic Banjaras, did not always run smoothly. Above all, the heterogeneity of this group, who had no single leader, could become the basis for violent clashes. There were even some circumstances in which caravans came into conflict when they encountered one another. Traveling merchants and their goods were relatively well protected in large groups, so for this reason caravans were often extremely large, while ships also sailed in convoys. But in general, traveling in a small group was not unsafe either. Even bands of highwaymen appear to have operated within the parameters of social sanctions and codes and often contented themselves with token payments from travelers. In some parts of the country, travelers received a stamp from the governor, which entitled them to compensation in the event of losing their valuables. The only real threats to trade were pirates off the west coast and attacks by the Marathas, a problem rife in Gujarat in particular following the death of Aurangzeb. There is nothing to indicate that the incipient demise of the Mughal Empire restricted inland trade.

While the majority of the populace in the Mughal Empire either consumed their own produce or were engaged in local barter arrangements, there was nevertheless a large and growing commercial sector within this subsistence economy. Almost half of all yields had to be paid out in the form of tax revenue to the state. The producer of goods had only limited capacity to purchase goods himself but those who profited from taxes—ruler, officials, merchants, and so forth—were responsible for most domestic demand. The basic conditions for successful commerce were peace in the empire and a good infrastructure. Although the economy grew, and prices and the volume of trade also increased, the underlying structures always remained the same. The growing demand could always be met, with the result that innovations were never necessary and so never happened.

The Perspective of the Ottoman Empire

The various protagonists in the Indian Ocean also included the Ottomans.[127] Before the sixteenth century, the Ottoman Empire had shown no interest in the Indian Ocean. The attention of the rapidly expanding empire had up until then been firmly fixed on the Mediterranean as a key sphere of communication. That all changed with the general mood of dynamic optimism that took hold of Europe following the discovery of the New World. After the Turks had conquered the Mamluk Empire in 1517, thereby bringing the pilgrimage sites of Mecca and Medina under their control, they began to extend their feelers farther eastward. If they were to secure a share of the lucrative trade across the Indian Ocean, it was vital above all for them to confront the Portuguese.[128] In this, they had one major advantage: Europeans were obliged to take the longer route when transporting goods, around the Cape of Good Hope, whereas the Ottomans could use the old trade routes via the Red Sea and the transhipment hubs in the Levant and Egypt. New types of ships were tried and the necessary nautical skills acquired. In addition, numerous maps, travelers' reports, and geographical treatises of the age testify to a general sense of intellectual curiosity, of a desire to learn more about the regions around the Indian Ocean. Within just a short space of time, ships were sailing regularly to Hormuz, Calicut, and Aceh, where Ottoman traders had established settlements. In the sixteenth century, the Ottomans quite clearly belonged to the winners in the international struggle for control of commercial traffic between South and Southeast Asia on the one hand and the Near East and Europe on the other.

Key figures in this regard, under the reign of Sultans Selim I (r. 1512–1520) and Süleyman I (r. 1520–1566), were people such as Piri Reis (1470–1554/1555) and Selman Reis (d. sometime after 1538). When he was still in his youth, Muhiddin Piri bin Hacý Mehmed, who later attained the rank and title of admiral *(reis)*, accompanied his uncle Kemal Reis, a renowned Ottoman corsair, on a voyage into the Mediterranean and took part in the ensuing war against the Venetian Republic.[129] In 1495 his uncle joined forces with the regular Ottoman fleet. On Kemal's death in a shipwreck near the island of Naxos in 1511, the multilingual Piri moved to Gelibolu and began writing a nautical treatise *(Kitab-ý Bahriye),* which he completed in 1521. Already, in 1513, he had drawn a world map, which he officially presented to Sultan Selim four years later. From 1516 on, he was active as a captain in the Ottoman navy in the Mediterranean and in the water around the Arabian Peninsula and also took part in the victorious campaign against the Mamluks. In his later years, he was a Turkish governor in Egypt, wrote poems, and compiled instructions on how to sail in verse form. In 1547, Piri Reis was named supreme commander of the Ottoman fleet in the Indian Ocean *(Hind Kapudan-i Derya)* and admiral of the fleet in Egypt *(Misir Kapudan-i Derya),* with his headquarters at Suez.

On February 26, 1548, he managed to recapture the port of Aden, which had been occupied by the Portuguese. In 1552, he seized Muscat, which had been established as a base by the Portuguese in 1507. Shortly thereafter, he took the island of Kish. In 1552–1553, he proceeded to besiege the island of Hormuz with a force of thirty-one ships and over eight hundred men. The population of the island offered him a large hoard of treasure, which he accepted in return for lifting the siege. On his return to Suez, the news reached him that a powerful Portuguese fleet was blocking the entrance to the Persian Gulf. On learning this, Piri Reis transferred the captured treasure onto three ships and sent most of his fleet (twenty-eight ships) back to the safe haven of al-Basra. With the remaining three ships, he attempted to break through the Portuguese blockade, which he managed with the loss of one of his vessels. However, following his arrival in Egypt, his political rival for the post of governor there reported to the sultan simply that Piri had returned with only two ships out of his original fleet of thirty-one. He saw fit to mention neither the preservation of the vast majority of the fleet in Basra nor the treasure on the two ships that made it to Cairo. Sultan Süleyman reacted by ordering the death penalty for Piri Reis, who was publicly executed in 1554 at the age of eighty-four.

Selman Reis, who was born on the Greek island of Lesbos, entered the service of the Mamluk Empire at an early age.[130] His excellent nautical knowledge earned him a rapid rise through the ranks of the newly formed Mamluk fleet. By 1515, he had command of a squadron of fifteen ships, which he was ordered to take to Yemen to attack the positions held by the Portuguese there. This venture was a failure, but just before the Ottoman victory over the Mamluks, he did successfully defend Jeddah against European attack. When the Turks assumed power, he was taken as a captive to Istanbul but was subsequently released and taken to Cairo in 1524 by the new Ottoman governor of Egypt, Ibrahim Pasha (d. 1536).[131] Selman Reis then devised a comprehensive plan of action for Ottoman operations in the Indian Ocean, in which he proposed establishing bases in Yemen and down the East African coast and expelling the Portuguese from both Hormuz and Goa.[132]

As the Europeans continued to launch attacks on ships and harbors in the Red Sea, Selman Reis was named as supreme commander of an Ottoman fleet of eighteen ships. An expedition to Yemen was very successful, allowing Selman to establish a base for his fleet at Kamaran. In the years that followed, the Ottomans came to play such an important role in the Indian Ocean that a series of local rulers on the South Indian coast and along the Persian Gulf sought their help. The first phase of Ottoman dominance lasted until a defeat against Portuguese units off Diu in 1535. In the second half of the 1540s, after a decade of violent clashes throughout the Indian Ocean region, Portuguese–Ottoman relations finally reached some measure of stability. In contrast to the Ottomans, the prime concern of the Portuguese was always to ensure that merchants could go about their business without any hindrance.

Despite a serious defeat, again off Diu in 1546, and the fact that after his glorious conquest of Aden in 1548 and Muscat in 1552 Piri Reis had to give up the latter again in 1554 and had also failed in his siege of Hormuz,[133] the Ottomans still succeeded in building up an extensive trade network in the Indian Ocean during this period. Commercial links extended at this time from the east coast of Africa and the west coast of India via Ceylon to Siam and Malacca. In particular, the grand vizier Sokullu Mehmed Pasha (d. 1579) devised truly global plans for the Ottoman Empire. His best-known project was his intention, through the digging of a Suez canal and one between the rivers Volga and Don in Russia, to create a direct sea route between Central Asia, the Red Sea, and the Indian Ocean.[134] Yet a fatal setback for these plans occurred in the west, at Lepanto at the mouth of the Gulf of Patras. On October 7, 1571, quite against expectations, the Ottoman fleet suffered a devastating defeat there against an alliance of Christian Mediterranean powers, assembled by Pope Pius V (d. 1572) and led by Spain.[135] Although the victory was never properly exploited and the league disintegrated, the aura of the invincible Ottoman fleet was destroyed by the engagement at Lepanto. The Ottomans went on to conquer Tunis in 1574, but their dream of being the predominant naval power was at an end. Furthermore, the loss of so many experienced commanders, captains, and ordinary seamen on the Turkish side at Lepanto could not be recouped for many years.

In 1580, Philip II of Spain (r. 1556–1598) gained control of Portugal and with it the Portuguese holdings in India *(Estado da India)*.[136] Henceforth, the Portuguese influence in the Indian Ocean declined steadily. Yet at the outset of the seventeenth century, the Ottomans changed their priorities, especially because protracted infighting between different factions at the court in Istanbul had hampered the evolution of a long-term foreign policy in the Indian Ocean region. Gradually, the view began to prevail that in view of the state's tax revenues, the Ottomans' precarious participation in the spice trade should be abandoned,[137] especially after the defeat at Lepanto had spelled the demise of an active policy to expand the fleet.

The Perspective of the Safavid Empire

Even before the establishment of the Silk Route, long-distance trade had played a significant role on the Iranian plateau for many centuries, given the region's pivotal location between the Indian subcontinent, Central Asia, Russia, and the Mediterranean. Although silk is most commonly associated with China, for a long time

Iran was also an important producer of raw silk and silk fabrics. The most lucrative market for Persian silk was in the Afro-Eurasian world, in a region that, according to Marshall Hodgson, obtained its cohesion from common cultural forms and a closely knit trade network.[138]

A study by Rudi Matthee has as its subject the dynamic crosscurrents between political authority and mercantile activities in the Safavid period, when the ruling elite—in a complex interplay between the royal court, indigenous and foreign merchants, and trading companies—began to engage in transregional and intercontinental commerce. In his study, Matthee focuses on the production, distribution, and export of silk from the regency of Shah Abbas (r. 1587–1629) to the 1720s.[139]

Iran not only traded in silk but also produced it itself. From the Mongol period, there is evidence of thriving silk production in Khorasan, which then from the thirteenth century on also spread to Mazandaran and Gilan. Tabriz, the capital of the Il-Khanate, increasingly became the nodal point of different trade routes, which were also used by Europeans. For a period in the fourteenth century, the flourishing exchange of goods between Iran, the Mediterranean, and the Indian Ocean was severely disrupted by political upheaval and the ravages of the Black Death. After the death of the ruler of the Il-Khanate, Abu Saʿid, in 1336, the empire fragmented, while trade dwindled to a minimum as a result of a European boycott of the market at Tabriz. Political uncertainty in the Black Sea region and the rise of the Mamluks, meanwhile, saw the center of commercial activity shift to the Mediterranean. The conquest of Lesser Armenia (on the southern coast of Asia Minor) by the Mamluks, the destruction of the port of Aya, and the rise of the Ottomans all resulted, up to the beginning of the sixteenth century, in Iran becoming somewhat isolated.

In 1500, then, there were four Muslim powers between the eastern Mediterranean, the Red Sea, and Persian Gulf: the Ottomans, the Safavids, the Mamluks, and the Mughals.[140] The main adversaries of the Safavids were the Ottomans, who by 1480 had overrun all the former territory of the Byzantine Empire. The Persians failed to halt their advance toward the Black Sea in the war of 1514, and in the years that followed, the Ottomans also conquered the Levant, Egypt, and the Arabian Peninsula. Mesopotamia, too, came under the control of the Turks, who even advanced as far as Tabriz on two occasions. Questions of territorial sovereignty were finally settled by the Treaty of Amasya in 1555, which apportioned Iraq and Eastern Anatolia to the Ottomans and Azerbaijan and the southeastern Caucasus to Iran.

The Iranian silk trade continued in the face of these political upheavals, though the main centers for dealing in this commodity shifted after Tamerlane's death in 1405 from Sultaniya to Tabriz, Ardabil, and Kashan. Caspian silk continued to be shipped to Italian weaving mills but also increasingly to the first Ottoman capital of Bursa (especially in the second half of the sixteenth century).[141] Yet during the first two decades of Safavid rule in Persia (that is, up to the 1520s), war, epidemics, and marauding bands of brigands made the caravan trade extremely difficult. Relations between the Ottoman Empire and the Safavids reached a low point after the Battle of Çaldiran in 1514, as Istanbul sought to deprive the Safavids of their state income and so sparked an economic war (for instance, by denying entry to any Muslim–Safavid merchants). Henceforth, Iranian traders tried diverting their trade routes through Mamluk territory, though this move was generally also blocked by the Ottomans. The route through Russia was problematic as well, and the situation began to improve only following the death of the Ottoman sultan Selim in 1520. Later, between 1538 and 1555 and on several other occasions up to 1590, ongoing tense relations and occasional military clashes between the two states, as well as internal problems, the Ottoman–Venetian conflict of 1570–1573, and various local rebellions in Anatolia, continued to make the overland silk trade route to the west very difficult. Yet at the same time, the demand in Europe for Persian silk continued to grow. Although the caravan trade functioned only to a limited degree, it never stopped entirely, largely thanks to the role of Armenian merchants operating between Iran and the Mediterranean, especially from the mid-sixteenth century on.

The Armenians operated as family concerns, and their networks stretched as far as the ports of the Mediterranean.[142] By the end of the sixteenth century, they had secured a monopoly over the supply of Persian silk and worked as brokers for both the local markets and the European trading companies. At the same time, the ports of the Levant, such as Aleppo, grew in size and gained in importance, especially in response to European economic expansion.[143] The European demand for silk continued to increase over time, a situation that led in the midterm to it being processed in Italy as well. Silk became a luxury good of the urban elite in the West, and merchants used every conceivable means of acquiring this valuable commodity. In the sixteenth century, the European trade in Iranian silk was conducted via the route that ran through Anatolia and Mesopotamia.

A northern trade route also ran past the Caspian Sea to the Volga basin. This stable political center, which was established with the rise of Moscow in the fifteenth century, enabled trading to continue uninterrupted.[144] The boycott by the Ottomans caused Shah Ismail to instigate contact not only with the Portuguese but also with Russia. Many different protagonists were interested in this route, including Iranian Armenians, Russians, Indians, and also the English, who formed the Muscovy Company to exploit this route. Another reason for its popularity was the fact that the old trade routes through the Levant were already dominated by other merchants, notably the Venetians. However, efforts by the English to become involved were not very successful, because Russia was increasingly afflicted by political unrest in the final third of the sixteenth century, because poor infrastructure hampered both transport and trade, and because Russia placed restrictions on foreigners' freedom of movement.

Because silk and silk products were increasingly in demand in India, too, merchants began using the sea route across the Indian Ocean. Caravans journeyed from the Caspian provinces to the Persian Gulf. In the fifteenth century, the growing importance of sea transport saw Hormuz become an entrepôt for South Asian and Southeast Asian trade.[145] Hormuz also excited interest by the Portuguese, who in the long term entered into an alliance with the Safavids.[146] Initially, though, they took over the customs station on Hormuz and made it difficult for the Safavids to gain direct access to the open sea.

Silk was transported from the production sites in Persia to the trading centers, where it was loaded onto mule or camel caravans.[147] Engaging the services of a particular caravan had a great deal to do with its leader's reputation and trustworthiness. The caravans were led by so-called *qafilah bashi*, who expected not only a fee but also gifts. Often the racial background of the preponderance of merchants who comprised a caravan would determine its leader (a Turk, an Armenian, and so on). The journey time, conditions, and goods carried were all stipulated in advance in the contracts drawn up between the merchants and the caravan organizers. From Isfahan, the goods were carried to the Persian Gulf. When cargoes were shipped and what times vessels arrived were dependent on the Indian monsoon season.

The decision by the English and Dutch to become involved in the Persian Gulf had to do with competition in the spice trade, to which end they had created their respective great overseas trading companies, the English EIC and the Dutch VOC.[148] Unlike the VOC, with its tightly organized network in Asia, the EIC had no unified chain of command. Yet the English company was more closely regulated by its government than the Dutch, although their inferior arrangements for accessing credit hampered competition with the VOC. In the course of exploring the western Indian Ocean, the Dutch came across the Persian Gulf before the English, in 1607. Silk was not their main motivation in doing so, as they preferred the Chinese commodity. Ultimately, however, the Dutch market was also supplied with Iranian silk. The Dutch decided officially to become involved in the silk trade in 1622. As the EIC had done six years previously, the VOC obtained permission to conduct business throughout Persia.[149]

Shah Abbas, meanwhile, had made an attempt to control the trade in silk.[150] In the event, though, the monopoly that the Safavid ruler hoped to achieve proved scarcely any impediment to market forces. It was clear that Iranian merchants did not have to necessarily purchase their silk from the court but could simply source it directly from the places of manufacture. In 1622, a joint Safavid–English force conquered Hormuz from the Portuguese. The port was officially moved from the island of Hormuz to the neighboring mainland. Thereafter, the Persian Gulf was also open to British trade. No sooner had Safi I (r. 1629–1642) come to the throne than the export monopoly was abandoned and the merchants could once more take delivery of the silk directly at the Caspian Sea. The driving force behind this decentralization was the Armenian merchants with their excellent connections to the Iranian court. This loosening of control, however, did not mean a completely hands-off attitude toward the silk trade by the state. Naturally, it maintained overall control over the cultivation and distribution of this valuable commodity. For the Europeans as well, this more relaxed trading did not mean that they did not have to pay any duties, especially when they found that their concept of bartering found no widespread acceptance.

The 1640s saw a number of changes in the way Iranian silk exports were organized. The Levant became a more attractive proposition and as the only profitable destination began to attract the interest of the Safavids. Foreign companies gradually quit Iran, as they became disaffected by the country's poor infrastructure and trading conditions. Henceforth, they preferred to concentrate their efforts on other regions of Asia, for instance, the Indian subcontinent. Even so, political relations with Isfahan were not broken off entirely, for there was still advantage to be gained from securing trading rights and privileges. The English withdrew in the midterm from the Iranian silk trade, whereas the VOC still remained tied to a contract. This presented some problems, because the Iranians wanted to restrict the agreed exemption from tariffs just to silk purchased from the court, a clause that the Dutch did not accept. But little ultimately was done to prevent them from trading anyway. For all the weaknesses of the Safavid state, it is astonishing that it did not insist, by pointing to its contractual obligations, on the VOC buying a fixed amount of silk from it. The best explanation is that the Persians were hamstrung by a combination of fiscal necessity and their limited economic and political options. The Safavid government was sorely in need of hard cash but was incapable of coordinating the lucrative Levant route with the maritime route.

Under Shah Suleyman I of Persia (r. 1666–1694), the Safavid state found its coffers empty.[151] This circumstance can be attributed both to the long years of conflict with the Ottomans and to the habit of transforming entire regions into crown lands. Besides, the influx of silver from abroad began to dwindle, so that the state had urgent need of new sources of revenue. In 1669, Shaykh Ali Khan Zanganah, who had a special interest in the silk trade, was appointed grand vizier to try to remedy this situation.[152] The most important development at this time was the growing significance of the connection with Russia. Treaties marked the beginning of a regular trade in silk between the countries. This exchange of goods was, however, more of a private venture than a measure imposed by the government. The Armenian traders in particular pursued their own interests in this enterprise. Yet for all the privileges they were granted, they did not focus their activities completely on the northern route, because they were accorded far more freedoms when trading with the Levant. The early eighteenth century was marked by economic downturn and political impotence. Internal unrest and external threats even began to jeopardize the silk trade at this time.

In conclusion, we may record that although Hormuz developed into an important port on the Persian Gulf, the European trading companies never succeeded in securing for themselves a greater share of the Iranian silk trade. Matthee cites three reasons for this:[153] (1) political factors, as the state did not allow foreigners any greater shares; (2) environmental and logistical hurdles, as the production sites were located in the remotest northern provinces, to which Europeans as a rule had no direct access; and (3) poorly equipped European enterprises, which found it hard competing with local traders. Their aim was to do business with private silk growers, which was impossible in Iran with its state monopoly. Limited price flexibility and lack of control over production ultimately forced Europeans to look elsewhere for silk. Iranian silk was an attractive proposition to them only so long as it was cheap and easy to get hold of.

European Perspectives

When the Portuguese landed on the coast of Malabar in the late fifteenth century, their clear objective, aside from Christian missionary activity, was to control European trade in spices, especially pepper, from the Indian Ocean region.[154] As an experienced maritime power, the Portuguese first and foremost needed bases on the coast to pursue their activities. Their cause was helped by the fact that they were well organized, that they did not shirk from using force as a way of attaining their goals, and that, in their three-masted carracks and galleons, they had ocean-going ships that were ideally suited to the new waters they had discovered.[155] Their fleet was clearly superior to that of any Asian power, while their fortified land bases enabled them to build up a serviceable strategic infrastructure. They made Goa the seat of their administration.[156] They asserted their interests against opposition from local rulers and in 1509, off Diu, were able to defeat an armada dispatched by the Mamluk ruler of Egypt. He feared the profits that would accrue from a spice trade under Portuguese control, a trade that would circumvent the existing Arab-controlled trade route to Europe.[157]

With the arrival of the Portuguese, the structures of Indian foreign trade changed. Monopolies in trading in a particular commodity had not existed hitherto. Now, even within Asia, the Portuguese defended their monopoly of the spice trade with undisguised aggression. From the outset, they made it clear that they had little interest in a peaceful exchange. Indian rulers had always been primarily interested in long-distance trade because of the fees that they could levy on merchants in return for their protection. The Portuguese concentrated on controlling the sea routes and hence also seaborne trade within Asia, the misleadingly named "country trade." The superiority of their fleet put them in a position to demand protection payments. However, their presence did nothing to compromise overland trade, a factor that would later, in the sixteenth century, force them into the embarrassing position of having to lower their pepper prices and level of imports into Europe in face of the competition posed by caravan traders. In line with the so-called *cartaz* system, Indian merchants were obliged to obtain a trade license from the viceroy of Goa whenever they wanted to leave port.[158] The sultans of Bijapur, too, and even the Mughal rulers had to acquire Portuguese licenses for the passage of their merchant ships from Surat to Mocca. Although corruption and poor administration made the cartaz inefficient, it remained one of the main sources of income for the Portuguese in the Indian Ocean.

By 1520, the Portuguese had succeeded in establishing an official shipping route known as the *Carreira da India*.[159] This term was applied to the regular voyages from Lisbon to Goa and back, which were dependent on prevailing trade and monsoon winds. Portuguese trade in Asia was booming at the start of the sixteenth century, although it was subject to regional variation. This initial success of the *Estado da India* was due to the fact that here the Portuguese crown was able, to a far greater extent than anywhere in Europe, to participate directly and intensively in economic life and to fund and maintain a network of royal manufactories throughout Asia.[160] The organization in Lisbon that ordered all overseas trade was the Casa da India. The liabilities arising from the Indian trade that had to be covered by an outflow of money from Portugal remained negligible in the first half of the sixteenth century. This situation changed radically and enduringly in the second half of the century. Henceforth, until well into the eighteenth century, the Portuguese, Dutch, English, and French paid their dues with silver coins of Spanish origin. From this point on, the world economy was permeated by a stream of silver flowing from the mines of Spanish America.[161]

The Portuguese trading system functioned very well, but from 1530 onward the ships of the crown were increasingly replaced by privately owned vessels. This also signified a decline in royal capital being invested in cargo. Two decades of crisis ensued, which led to a further shrinkage in the level of royal involvement. Yet this does not imply that the period from 1550 on was a phase of general decline in commercial activity. Beginning in the middle of the sixteenth century, private trade conducted by Portuguese officials, soldiers, and priests began to gain a firm foothold; this was often carried out in collaboration with Indian and African partners. In many places, in fact, local practices were even adopted. After the sixteenth century, the risks increased for the Portuguese in the Indian Ocean because of the threat posed by the Dutch and English, with the result that trade in this region became a crown monopoly once more. This points to a fundamental problem facing all trading empires: the profits frequently did not flow into the same coffers that had to bear the infrastructure costs of the colonial system. Because the volume of private business far outstripped crown and monopoly trade, reference is often made to a "shadow empire" or "informal empire."[162] As Wolfgang Reinhard has written, "Over the course of the seventeenth century, the importance of Portuguese India for the motherland was eclipsed by Brazil. The first Europeans to take over their role in world trade were the Dutch."[163]

The large trade zone around the Indian Ocean was fed with goods from all the abutting regions: from East Africa and the coasts of Arabia and Persia and Mozambique came slaves, ivory, amber, gold, and ebony, while southern Arabia provided horses, sugar, pearls, camelhair fabrics, and fruits the grew in arid zones.[164] Dyes, carpets, and silk were imported from Persia, silverware and other manufactured goods from Europe. The main trade hubs were Hormuz, Aden, and the ports along the coasts of Malabar and Gujarat as far as Goa, while Diu and Cochin can be seen as the nodal points of Portuguese West Asia.[165] Yet Akbar's conquest of Gujarat posed a constant threat. In southern India, in the wake of the sultanates' victory on the Deccan, Vijayanagara ceased to be a trading partner.[166] Sri Lanka represents an exception within the Estado da India, because here the Portuguese—especially because of the lucrative trade in cinnamon—enacted a systematic policy of conquest.[167]

Only some twelve to fourteen thousand Portuguese lived in the Estado da India.[168] This population deficit was overcome through marriage to baptized native women from the upper castes. Proper Portuguese communities had the right to self-determination, based on the model of towns in the mother country. Between 1497 and 1700, a total of 1,149 ships, carrying 721,705 tons of cargo and 300,354 people, left Lisbon, of which 960 ships with 598,390 tons of freight (83 percent) and 292,227 people (97 percent) arrived in Asia. In the opposite direction, 781 ships set sail with 537,215 tons of cargo and 193,937 people on board,

Sword hand guard *(tsuba)* engraved with the image of a Portuguese merchant ship, sixteenth century. This hand guard was clearly manufactured in Japan and is designed to stop the user's hand from slipping forward onto the sharp blade when thrusting. The Portuguese motif is remarkable, showing a *nau* (carrack) in full sail and with a small female figurehead. The indirect influence of Portugal's Estado da India extended to the Far East. (From *Novos Mundos—Neue Welten: Portugal und das Zeitalter der Entdeckungen: Eine Ausstellung des Deutschen Historischen Museums Berlin, in Zusammenarbeit mit dem Instituto Camoes, Lisbon, und der Botschaft von Portugal in Berlin,* edited by Michael Kraus and Hans Ottomeyer, Dresden: Sandstein Verlag, 2007.)

of which 666 ships, with 441,695 tons (82 percent) and 164,012 people (84.6 percent), docked in Lisbon.[169]

The Dutch VOC, founded in 1602, began to appear in the Indian Ocean in the seventeenth century, followed shortly afterward by the British EIC, both of which wanted to secure a share of the spice trade for themselves.[170] To begin with, both companies dispatched their ships to the Spice Islands and Indonesia, where they reckoned on only a weak Portuguese presence. However, they quickly discovered that trade in the Indian Ocean region functioned only in the context of local conditions. On many Southeast Asian islands, spices could profitably be exchanged only with textiles woven in India, particularly from the Coromandel Coast and Gujarat, because the people there were not yet experienced in handling money.[171] Over time, the Dutch took over the trade within Asia from the Portuguese, but the principal long-term goal of both Northwest European trading companies was to control direct trade with Europe. The Dutch proved extremely successful in developing a stable trade in textiles—even as early as 1606, the king of Golkonda granted them a *farman* allowing them to build a "factory" in Masulipatnam, in return for small payments to the king.[172] In the north of the subcontinent, though, the VOC found it harder making headway, because the Portuguese continued to have influence at the Mughal court. Accordingly, it was 1617 before a permanent Dutch trading post was opened in Gujarat. The federally structured VOC—to which the Dutch legislature the States General had granted a monopoly of Dutch trade between the Cape of Good Hope and the Straits of Magellan, together with the right to wage war, conclude treaties, take possession of land, and build forts—eventually, in the wake of several European conflicts, began to openly oppose the Portuguese and made plans to seize all their major strongholds along the trade routes.[173] Within a short time, they did indeed manage to do so, thanks to their superior fleet. Between 1636 and 1646, Goa was blockaded every trading season by the Dutch, who also wanted to take over the cinnamon trade from Ceylon and the export of pepper from Malabar. With the conquest of Columbo (1655–1656) and Cochin (1659–1663),[174] the VOC finally achieved its goal. Ultimately, the Dutch victory over the Portuguese was no great surprise, as it was only natural that Europe's most advanced economy should also gain hegemony over the Indian Ocean in the seventeenth century.

The English East India Company followed a quite different strategy in the first half of the seventeenth century but was just as successful.[175] There was only a very limited market for pepper in England—trade in pepper was not an especially lucrative business. And so the EIC began to expand its trade links to Indian ports, in order on the one hand to ship other commodities back to England but on the other to realize a profit by selling Indian goods on the islands farther east. Trading posts were set up in Gujarat, on the Coromandel Coast, and finally in Bengal.

As early as 1607, plans had been drawn up to sail to the port of Surat and investigate trading opportunities there. William Hawkins, one of the EIC's captains, duly reached Surat in 1609 and spent several years at the Mughal court of Jahangir. Yet trading privileges were granted to the EIC only in 1612 through an imperial edict, which was designed to protect the company's interests from Mughal officials. The main concern of the English while developing their trade network was the danger posed by the Portuguese through their political presence at the Mughal court. The EIC therefore strengthened its fleet and tried to dispatch permanent envoys of its own, such as Sir Thomas Roe (1581–1644),[176] to the Mughal court.[177] In 1613, a permanent settlement was finally established in Surat, from which several products were to be shipped directly to England. However, the majority of the freight was intended for the east of the country and for internal Asian trade. Prior to this, other important English settlements had already been set up at Masulpatnam on the Coromandel Coast and on Java. When the Mughals expelled the Portuguese from Hooghly in Bengal, the trading capital of the eastern provinces, in 1633, both the English and the Dutch were able to form trading networks in a region that was renowned as the breadbasket of the empire and was later to become the center of Mughal textile production.[178]

The structure of the trade organized in India by the commercial companies from northwestern Europe did not fundamentally change in the sixteenth and seventeenth centuries. The pattern was always for a main settlement to be established in an Indian port or in the vicinity of one, connected with other trading stations inland, at locations where sought-after goods were produced. The main trading stations were partially independent of one another but always cooperated. The VOC had set up posts above all in Surat, Cochin, Pulicut, Negapatam, Masulipatnam, and Hooghly, until the EIC gained the upper hand there in the second half of the eighteenth century. But because the headquarters of the VOC was already located on Java, it did not have to search for a site for one on the Indian subcontinent.[179] In this regard, the EIC was of necessity the more dynamic enterprise of the two, as it did not have such a base at its disposal and therefore focused all its efforts on gaining a firm foothold on the Indian mainland. Besides, it wanted to avoid making payments to local middlemen by controlling local trade itself. In 1639, the British captured Madras; in 1665, Bombay was transferred from the English Crown to the EIC; and in 1696–1699, a fortress was erected in Calcutta.

So firm was this principle that trade should be conducted independently of local rulers that the EIC even found itself waging war against the Mughal Empire in 1687–1688, a conflict the company lost. Yet even this did not compromise its urge to participate in local commerce.[180]

In the eighteenth century, India's foreign trade expanded noticeably, particularly through the involvement of the Dutch, the English, and also the French. France had developed into a remarkably successful trading power in the Indian Ocean in the 1730s.[181] Its first attempts to gain a foothold, in 1684, were hampered by the fact that other powers were already well established there. In 1671, a heavily armed French fleet sailed into the port of Surat, but stiff competition from other nations meant that the French were initially unable to fortify their position. In 1673, though, the port of Pondicherry in Bijapur fell into their hands and would later become the center of French commercial activities in the region. From a long-term perspective, however, the French could not assert their presence on the subcontinent because their trading company was heavily dependent on the crown and had been created first and foremost not to turn a profit but rather out of geopolitical considerations.

As well as building up trading settlements, the European commercial companies used strategies such as the naval blockade. In those places where Europeans were obliged to conduct business under Mughal rule, the blockade of native ships was their answer to their inferior military position on land. In the frequent conflicts between the companies and the representatives of the Mughals, which mostly erupted over the payment of tolls, the first move by Mughal forces was to try to disrupt the flow of vital supplies for the European settlements, whereupon the European ships would barricade the ports. However, both sides normally were intent on reaching quick solutions that did not involve bloodshed.

When such differences of opinion arose, Indian trade that passed through the English settlements also played a significant role. In 1717, the English had received a farman from the court in Delhi, empowering them among other things to carry their goods toll-free throughout the empire in exchange for an annual payment of 3,000 rupees. The indigenous merchants simply bought themselves licenses from the East India Company and so circumvented the Mughal taxation system. The period between 1710 and 1760 may be regarded as a phase of undisturbed growth and continual prosperity for the EIC.

European trade with Asia would not have been possible without the discovery of South American silver mines. There is a close connection between monetary liquidity in Europe and the growth of intercontinental trade.[182] All the same, trade between Europe and Asia was very unbalanced, with the result that fears arose in England that the import of goods and the outflow of large quantities of silver abroad to pay for them might become a source of economic instability. No comprehensive study has yet been made of the influence that the massive import of precious metals had on the Indian market. According to some commentators, the expected economic effect of the steadily increasing influx of precious metals was neutralized by the demand of people in the East for luxury items made from gold and silver. To date, no evidence has shown either major movements in Indian prices or precise import figures for precious metals or the requirements of the Indian currency. All we know for sure is that silver from India was often exported to China.

Alongside the profits from sales to Europe, the VOC above all was able to record handsome additional income from the import of spices to India. By contrast, the only extra source of income for the EIC was the sale of crude metals such as iron, zinc, and lead, along with a few European luxury goods. The main problem facing European trade with India was always the financing of the return cargo on ships. After all, most profits were made from the import of Indian goods to Britain. In the sixteenth century, Portuguese trade had been based primarily on the export of black pepper to Portugal, which represented an extremely lucrative business. Getting hold of pepper in Asia required no complex structures or particular experience, while in Europe the markets were already established and the groups interested in trading the commodity many and varied. Pepper also served as ballast, stabilizing the ships on their return voyage to Europe. Indian textile later supplanted pepper as the most commonly imported good. The English sold fine cotton fabrics and printed textiles in particular, both at home and in North African markets. By the end of the seventeenth century, the market for textiles was so well established that even luxury products of this kind could be sold and soon came to determine demand. Other important Indian export products were indigo, saltpeter, and Bengali raw silk. In particular, the saltpeter trade was closely associated with the military strategy of Holland and England, because it was a key component in the manufacture of gunpowder, a rapidly growing sector.

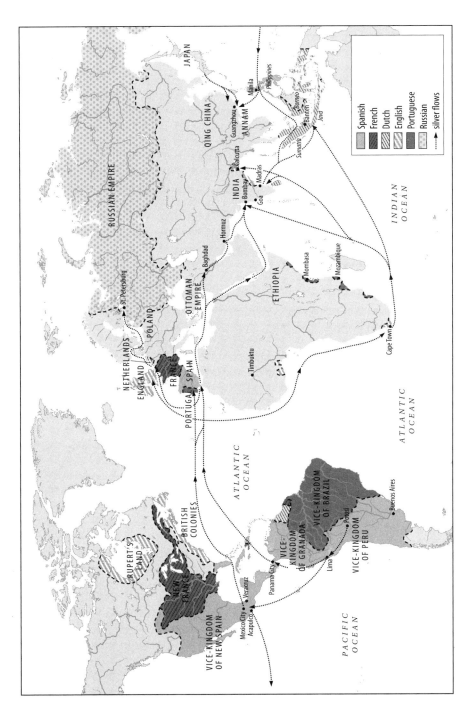

Silver routes in the early modern world

The first great boost to European trade with India came with the formal arrival of the VOC and the EIC on the scene. Private trade by European individuals also helped generate economic competition. Many branches of commerce, which had previously been served by Indian traders, were now taken over by Europeans. One revolutionary development was to organize trade within an impersonal firm, an innovation that departed in equal measure from traditional patterns of business in both Europe and Asia. Both trading companies had always set great store by building a system that was independent of the randomness of time and personnel. Imported goods therefore had to be standardized, quality controls were introduced, and regular deadlines for delivery were agreed. All this was completely unknown in the Indian market, especially matters concerning quantities of goods and contractual commitments. These were normally based on the principle of prepayment, which gave both weavers and traders a measure of security. However, merchants seldom worked directly with weavers, operating instead through middlemen.

It was only in the mid-eighteenth century that trade with Europeans took on significant proportions for Indian rulers, with a majority of their income now derived from taxes levied on the trading companies and private European merchants. This trade was particularly extensive in Bengal, one of the wealthiest provinces of the Mughal Empire, where the textile industry in particular profited from the purchases made by Europeans.[183]

4. South Asia and the Indian Ocean in the First Half of the Eighteenth Century

IN the period between 1707, the year when the Mughal ruler Aurangzeb died, and 1757, when the British took control of Bengal, Southeast Asia underwent a gradual process of transformation. The Mughal Empire found it impossible to administer large parts of regions that had formerly been more or less under its central control. Yet by no means did this signify that the empire was breaking up and dissolving into independent areas. Rather, it was the case that Mughals found themselves having to relinquish a whole series of right while still nominally retaining suzerainty—with one exception. In other words, all henceforth independently operating principalities continued to officially recognize the suzerainty of the Mughal ruler. There is no question of any "collapse" at this stage, especially given that the Europeans who arrived in Southeast Asia, according to Reinhard Schulze, "encountered economic prosperity, a clear growth in population, embryonic political institutions, societies in which commercialization, agricultural activity, and urbanization were woven into a complex network, patterns of cultural reinterpretation that were based on a separation of worldly and religious fields of knowledge, and very specific processes of social change, which for instance in the context of a renomadization led to new forms of social integration."[184] Where the Mughal Empire was concerned, then, it was not a case of "degenerative decline" but rather one of "renovating" change, according to Michael Mann. This development amounted to the transformation of a central imperial federation into a loose alliance of states without this change in any way being associated with an economic or bureaucratic decline. Says Mann: "Quite the contrary, for reterritorialization basically also meant the continuation and reorganization of the structures of the Mughal Empire, which revealed their strength in the emerging territorial states and made a major contribution to consolidating the newly established dynasties."[185] In neither the late seventeenth century nor the mid-eighteenth century was it foreseeable, despite the British successes in Bengal, that the East

India Company, and with it Britain, would rise to become the dominant power in South Asia at the beginning of the nineteenth century.

Ultimately, the Mughal Empire was also a patrimonial state with the classic fault lines that are typical of such a ruling confederation.[186] Some of these problem areas have already been highlighted: (1) the collapse of the jagirdar system, which was closely bound up with the structure of medieval village communities in India as well as with the local and central bureaucracy of the Mughal Empire; (2) the frequent peasant and tribal uprisings; (3) the new kind of revolts that occurred among the rural populace in the eighteenth century; (4) the growing involvement of financial institutions in the realm of direct tax collection on both a regional and local level; and (5) the fundamental transformation of foreign trade that took place with the rise of new trading centers, such as Bombay, Madras, Pondicherry, Chandernagore, and Calcutta. Other factors include the concentration of economic activities on a local level, which went hand in hand with an intensification of the relations between city and countryside in the form of exchanges of people and goods; a commercialization and monetization of farming on the southern Deccan, in Bihar and Bengal, and in parts of Gujarat and Maharashtra; and the centralization of tax collection through administrative and fiscal reforms, together with a simultaneous renunciation of rights, a transformation of large areas into a tax-free zone, and the emergence of hereditary ownership of large estates.[187]

From a political point of view, the period from 1716 to the end of the century was characterized by numerous successful attempts initially to form new ruling confederations and then by individual potentates to expand their own control. The fact that twice within a space of only twenty years, troops from Iran captured the Indian capital is symptomatic of the military and structural weakness of the Mughal Empire. On the first occasion, in the late 1730s, the founder of the Persian Afsharid dynasty, Nadir Shah (r. 1736–1747) led a campaign against the Mughals, passing through Ghazna, Kabul, Peshawar, Sind, and Lahore on his way into India.[188] At the Battle of Karnal on February 13, 1739, he defeated the Mughal emperor's army. Thereafter, he marched at the head of his troops into Delhi and put the city to the torch. Muhammad Shah (r. 1720–1748) begged for mercy, and so the Persian ruler finally contented himself with plundering a hoard of treasure (including the "Peacock Throne" and the Koh-i-Noor diamonds) and withdrew back to his homeland.

After the death of Nadir Shah, Ahmad Shah Durrani (1722–1772) succeeded in establishing an empire in Afghanistan that extended far into the northeast of modern-day Iran, eastern Turkmenistan, the whole of Pakistan, and the northwest of India.[189] From the 1750s on, the Afghans made repeated incursions into northern India. In 1757, they overran and sacked Delhi, while in 1761 they scored a major victory over the Marathas at the Battle of Panipat. Although they nominally accepted the sovereignty of the Mughal emperor, this was only on condition that they were henceforth given control of Punjab, Sind, and Kashmir. After Ahmad Shah's death in 1772, the Durranis moved their capital from Kandahar to Kabul and used Peshawar as their winter headquarters.

Meanwhile, during the reign of Baji Rao I (r. 1720–1740), the Marathas had managed to extend their sphere of power decisively.[190] Malwa, Gujarat, Rajasthan, Bengal, and Orissa were annexed. With the Marathas, it was less a question of well-organized leadership and administration and more one of a loose confederacy of diverse groups with compatible aims. Their defeat by the Afghans was more significant in that it helped the British gain a foothold in the region rather than fatally weakening the Marathas. Their expansion continued under Balaji Baji Rao (r. 1740–1761) and Madhav Rao (r. 1761–1772).

The power vacuum that arose in Punjab as a result of the invasions was filled in the first half of the eighteenth century by, among others, the Sikhs, who were able to assert their authority over the Durranis and local Muslim groups in a series of skirmishes.[191] In order to defend themselves against persecution by Aurangzeb and his successors, the Sikhs had formed their own troop contingents, which over time evolved into twelve warlord principalities, all very different as regards their size, organization, and power. Ultimately, these were to conduct a kind of guerrilla war against the Mughals, with varying degrees of success. It would be 1801 before a proper Sikh Empire was established.

In the north of the subcontinent, from the 1720s the Shi'ite governors of Awadh (the *nawwab*), who were of Persian origin, exploited the structural weakness of the center in order to agitate for independence.[192] Under Sa'adat Khan Burhan al-Mulk (r. 1722–1739) and his successor Safdar Jang (r. 1739–1754), Shi'a Islam was made the official religion and the administration and taxation systems centralized. Faizabad acted as the capital and developed into a lively intellectual and economic center. Around the turn of the century, British influence increased, and after the Battle of Buxar in 1764, Shuja ad-Daula (r. 1754–1775) was forced to broadly accept British dominance.

The East India Company had by this time already gained a firm foothold in Bengal. Ever since 1704, the Mughal governor there, Murshid Quil Khan (d. 1725), a Brahmin who had openly converted to Shi'a Islam, had wielded actual power from Mushidabad.[193] He dissolved large numbers of Mughal benefices and converted the payment of taxes and donations to hard cash. Especially under Alivardi Khan (r. 1740–1756), the authority of the Mughal governors was consolidated in Bengal. He scored a victory against the Marathas, but his successor Siraj ad-Daula was then destined to suffer defeat by the British and their commander, Sir Robert Clive (1725–1774) at the Battle of Plassey on June 23, 1757,[194] despite the fact that Siraj's forces were bolstered by the presence of French troops. In British historiography, this engagement was and still is regarded as the beginning of the East India Company's rule over Bengal.

As in the other cases, the existing ties between the center of the Mughal Empire in Delhi and the governor based at Hyderabad on the Deccan, Mir Qamar ad-Din Khan Siddiqi (1671–1748), began gradually to loosen at the beginning of the eighteenth century.[195] The provinces, which Qamar ad-Din Khan had ruled since 1724 in the name of his own dynasty, encompassed the whole Deccan Plateau and bordered on the East India Company's spheres of influence, as well as those of the French on the Coromandel Coast. The new ruler reformed the administration and within a short time consolidated his control, with the result that for a while the course was set for both internal and external stability.

In South India, around the time of the predominance of the empire of Vijayanagara and Mysore, a ruling confederation coalesced around the Wodeyars.[196] In the course of the seventeenth century, they managed to annex large parts of what are now Karnataka and Tamil Nadu and become the leading power in this region. After Kanthirava Narasaraja (d. 1714) ascended the throne in 1704, he was able to secure and expand his own power under the nominal sovereignty of the Mughal ruler. Despite some internal and external problems, his successors Krishnaraja Wodeyar I (r. 1714–1732), Chamaraja Wodeyar VI (r. 1732–1734), and Krishnaraja II (r. 1734–1766) were largely able to sustain this momentum. In the 1750s, Haider Ali (d. 1782), a successful and charismatic commander who had scored victories against the Marathas, assumed practical power in Mysore. Unlike the previous rulers in this region, he was a Muslim.

. . .

Long before the fourteenth century, seafarers, merchants, holy men, and migrants had crossed the Indian Ocean in search of goods and commodities, new regions to explore, or possible places to settle. Over the centuries, these permanent movements transformed the Indian Ocean into a zone of interaction crisscrossed by a whole series of different trade networks. Mercantile activities were at the forefront of these developments, especially the transporting, purchase, and sale of products over long distances. In the process, commercial activities also involved the exchange of knowledge, different forms of faith, and ideals. In this way, the Indian Ocean evolved into a highly complex realm of economic, social, and political activity, which was linked directly or indirectly to all areas of Europe, Africa, and Asia.

The history of South Asia and the Indian Ocean as a single unit is still best treated as an economic history. Of course, it is possible to think of other analytical approaches as well, for example, considering it as an environmental history,[197] in the context of "traveling concepts,"[198] or against, say, the background of migration, mobility, or conflicts. But to date, no substantial studies have really pursued these avenues of inquiry for the region being examined here. Accordingly, we will stay with the economic angle. If we look at the period under consideration here, we can basically distinguish three levels of trade, with each defined by the length of the route by which goods were transported.[199]

First, in all parts of South Asia and around the Indian Ocean, apart from the most thinly populated, there was a very active commerce between the villages and the district capitals or alternatively between one group of villages and another. The connecting link in this form of exchange of goods was the weekly markets or traveling salesmen. Agricultural products, industrial raw materials, textiles, and pottery formed the main part of this local barter economy. A day's journey on foot or other slow methods of transport determined the range of this type of trade—20 to 30 kilometers at most.

Above this level and quite considerably removed from it was regional trade, which was conducted chiefly by major traders and large-scale markets. Goods that came into circulation here met the demands of regions in which particular foodstuffs, industrial goods, and products were in short supply thanks to the local climate or the peculiarities of the regional geography. The distance between regional markets varied enormously, and trade was usually conducted overland, on rivers, or across the sea. For instance, the camel caravans that set out from the northern cities of China and crossed the Gobi Desert unloaded their wares in Turfan, Urumchi, or Kulja. These urban bazaars in turn supplied other northern or western regions in Central Asia. The merchants would cover several thousand kilometers on their annual journeys, but even so they were still part of only a regional network. The same category included merchants who transported their goods by sea from Muscat to the ports of Gujarat—a distance of 1,800 kilometers, which was nevertheless incomparably safer and faster than overland routes.

The third level was what is commonly designated as the true premodern form of interregional trade. This commerce in goods had a transcontinental dimension and was very strongly characterized by the nature of the particular goods being traded. The articles that were carried on this trade route were important commodities greatly in demand around the world: silk, brocades, fine cotton, porcelain, jewels, spices, and thoroughbred horses. In addition, transcontinental trade had two distinguishing characteristics: on the one hand, when shipping luxury goods, one always needed a balance of mass-market goods to offset the risks of making a loss. On the other hand, because the purchase and consumer markets were so distant from one another, the transport of these goods, which were exported from China, Southeast Asia, and India to the eastern or western Mediterranean, was handled by local trade emporiums. At each of these entrepôts, commodities could be split up into smaller portions or handed over from one intermediary to another.

It is virtually impossible to gauge the extent and the quantitative dimension of trade in South Asia and across the Indian Ocean up to the fifteenth century. Unfortunately, the trading organizations have preserved very few of their books and documents; the same is true of private merchants. Before the era of double-entry bookkeeping, estimates of profits could have been made only by contemporaries who were completely familiar with the business books in circulation. This material is sadly no longer at our disposal. Europe became acquainted with a form of double-entry bookkeeping from 1494 on, when a treatise on the subject was written by the Italian Franciscan friar Luca Pacioli. "Double-entry" bookkeeping denotes that every transaction is recorded twice. Thus it was that a single accounting record came to contain a note of the basic credit and debit involved, so preserving every single transaction twice over, albeit in different accounts. In each case, the precise value is recorded in both the credit and the debit columns. We also have evidence that, from 1426 on, inventories, stocktaking, and sales records were also kept. Until the emergence of the great European bureaucratic trading companies in the sixteenth century, it is impossible for historians to estimate even approximately what quantities of goods were exchanged within the Eurasian region. However, we may work from the premise that from the tenth century on, the great majority of goods that were exchanged at a transcontinental level represented only a negligible amount of the total volume of goods bought and sold. Very few ports on the Indian Ocean produced export goods on a truly grand scale. Most articles had to be carried overland from far away to the trade hubs on the coast. The transport of goods, no matter whether by beast of burden such as donkeys, camels, horses, or oxen or on wheeled vehicles, was a complex affair. There were too many variables governing the success or failure of any enterprise, and by no means were all of them under the control of the traders or carriers. Before they could derive any profit from trading, shipowners in the Indian Ocean had to overcome a whole series of adversities either born of chance or inherent within the system. Storms, reefs, shallows, and piracy were the seafarer's worst enemies, not to mention situations in which a ship's master docked in a foreign harbor only to find that there was not enough cargo available to transport home.

As before, in spite of numerous instances of political instability, devastating waves of epidemic, and the encroachment of European trading companies, in the final analysis developments in commerce in South Asia and the Indian Ocean from the mid-fourteenth to mid-eighteenth centuries were characterized more by continuity than by ruptures. In a comprehensive and very detailed article, the Dutch historian Rene J. Barendse has convincingly summarized the interaction between South Asia and Europe in and around the Indian Ocean from the fifteenth to eighteenth centuries, in which he accords the traditional emphasis on the significance of Europe only secondary significance.[200]

As a result of the complex relations between Asia and Europe, the focus must lie on the connections and not the dichotomies. It is sensible to talk in terms of a constantly changing and adaptable social and economic network. The basic structure of commercial exchange consists of South Asia sending goods (textiles, pepper, sugar, and so on) to the Levant and North Africa. The point of connection between Africa and the Near East was the Swahili Coast, where gold, ivory, and slaves were exchanged for textiles, weapons, and porcelain. Egypt and Syria functioned in many regards as the heart of the supraregional interconnections. Long-distance trade in the Indian Ocean was based on interlinked trade routes within smaller maritime regions. The network was tantamount to an interlacing of maritime connections between interlinked ports. The essential difference between the premodern global system and the modern one is the absence of any hegemonial core. In addition, there were many sites of production on an equal footing and several major entrepôts. Finally, no firm core or system of hierarchically structured manufacturing processes existed. In general, no interventions from a political sphere stood in the way of trade. It was self-reliant and operated according to its own set of rules.

Taking our cue from Barendse, eleven theses may be formulated in conclusion:

1. The history of premodern great empires cannot be viewed in isolation, but rather parallels and connections must be highlighted—not only as regards Indo-Persian culture but also in connection with trade and other links across both land and the Indian Ocean.
2. Economic developments took place within the framework of global trade. In this, both the Indian Ocean and South Asia, as well as Europe, were important players, intimately connected with one another. The Mediterranean and the Indian Ocean cannot be considered as separate realms.
3. In the sixteenth century, a continuity rather than a rupture can be identified in the matter of the range of products, commercial traditions, and trade routes.
4. The Pacific twenty-first century cannot be read back onto the sixteenth century. The European hegemony that crystallized over the course of the "long" nineteenth century should likewise not be understood as a teleological process that had its starting point in the discovery of America and the first rounding of the Cape of Good Hope.
5. The massive transformation of the pattern of consumption is less to be ascribed to the East India trading companies and more to the behavior of consumers in Europe.
6. South Asian ruling confederations and their trade should not be seen as static entities over time. Rather, cyclical patterns and underlying dynamism can be discerned in many cases.

7. State and trade in the Indian Ocean and South Asia are closely bound up with the agricultural systems of cultivation and tribute, maritime history, and the claims and requirements of port cities. Every trade center had a major influence on patterns of trade.

8. The Indian Ocean did not constitute a unified commercial realm but instead reveals a complex structure. There were different markets for different goods with different routes. Various networks existed in parallel and also overlapped.

9. The economic behavior of the various players who were engaged in trade around the Indian Ocean and South Asia were guided in their actions by thoroughly rational motives.

10. The Mamluk Empire, the Ottoman Empire, the Safavids, and the Rasulids were important protagonists whose role has hitherto not been sufficiently well appreciated by historians.

11. Islam provided Muslim merchants with a system of symbols that enabled them to move effortlessly between North Africa and the island world of Southeast Asia.

Translated from the German by Peter Lewis

·[FOUR]·

Southeast Asia and Oceania

Reinhard Wendt and Jürgen G. Nagel

Introduction

AS REGARDS their natural environment, as well as their historical and sociocultural background, the defining characteristics of Southeast Asia and Oceania would at first sight appear to be diversity and heterogeneity. This chapter, however, will endeavor to present this region in a way that does not simply catalog the histories of the individual constituent areas but instead highlights the elements that these areas have in common. Without ignoring the manifold differences that exist, the emphasis will be on coherence. Overall, the intention is to reveal that this is a region containing a whole series of shared elements that not only lend it an internal coherence but also clearly distinguish it from the wider world beyond.

Chronologically, this chapter falls within the period from the mid-fourteenth to the mid-eighteenth century. Several significant dates around the mid- to late fourteenth century, such as the founding of Ayutthaya in 1350 or of Malacca in 1377, or the accession of the Ming dynasty in China in 1368 (whose repercussions were felt as far away as Southeast Asia), or the settling of New Zealand by Polynesian peoples, could have been taken as meaningful points from which to start our investigation. However, particularly where Oceania is concerned, beginning our review in the mid-fourteenth century is problematic. For although it would be entirely wrong to talk of static cultures in that region, it is nevertheless true to say that the pace of change there was slower than in other areas. It is therefore essential to look back to the period before 1350. It is also necessary to begin our review somewhat earlier in the case of maritime Southeast Asia, given that Majapahit was founded there in the 1290s, the last of the Indian-influenced empires to emerge in the region. And at the other end of the timescale, because some consideration of the Second Age of Discovery and in particular the voyages of Captain James Cook are a turning point vital for an understanding of the history of Oceania, we also propose to briefly treat periods that extend beyond 1750.

1. Space and Culture

TOGETHER, Southeast Asia and Oceania form an extremely heterogeneous region.[1] Its landscapes range from towering mountains to extensive atolls in the vast expanses of the Pacific; it contains rainforests, in Southeast Asia, but also wide tracts of desert, such as in the heart of Australia. The mainland and the islands, the plains and mountains, and the coasts and interiors form often stark contrasts.

Both Southeast Asia and Oceania are embraced by what is now referred to as the Pacific Rim. This geographical designation encompasses a region that, as even just a cursory glance at a map will show, mainly comprises water. This expanse of water separates islands and landmasses but also connects them and represents the living environment for seafaring peoples. The oceans form transportation routes, which both lend the region cohesion internally and give it access to the world outside. Not for nothing have Denys Lombard and Anthony Reid, say, attempted to follow in the footsteps of Fernand Braudel in portraying either the South China Sea at the very least or, more widely, all the seas of maritime Southeast Asia as a kind of Mediterranean. The overriding importance and ever-present nature of the sea is reflected in the very name "Oceania."

To the north, Southeast Asia is separated from the Indian subcontinent and China by a chain of mountain ranges that form an extension of the Himalayas. Nevertheless, it is connected to these regions by various major rivers: the Irrawaddy, the Chao Phraya, the Mekong, and the Red River. These all rise in the Himalayas, giving Southeast Asia its characteristic topography of river valleys and mountain chains running on a north–south axis. These waterways also give rise to the extensive low-lying swampland and deltas that are among the most fertile agricultural areas in the whole of continental Southeast Asia.

The Kra Isthmus, the narrow land bridge that connects the Malay Peninsula with the Asian mainland and separates the Indian Ocean from the South China Sea, is the place where continental Southeast Asia changes to maritime Southeast Asia; highly different climatic and sociocultural conditions are also in evi-

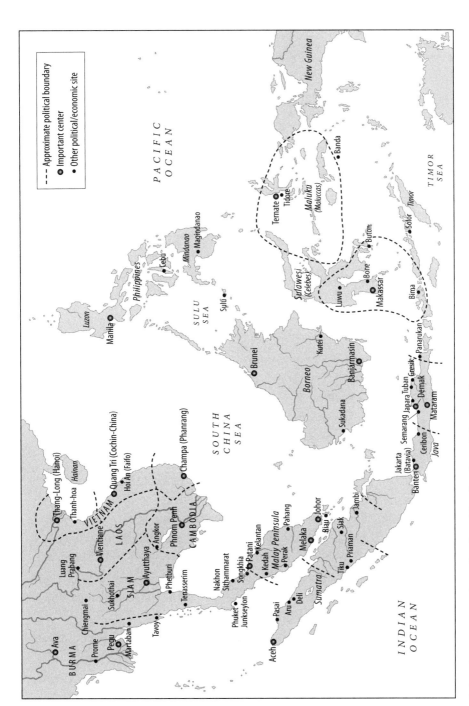

Political centers in continental and maritime Southeast Asia, circa 1600

dence south of this transition point. Maritime Southeast Asia is characterized by a vast mass of islands numbering in the tens of thousands. They range from the tiniest islets to landmasses that are virtually continents in their own right—Borneo, for instance, is the world's third largest island. The southern coastlines of Sumatra, Java, and the Sunda Islands have high cliffs dropping sheer into the Indian Ocean, as does the eastern seaboard of the Philippines into the Pacific. To the north and west, however, the chains of mountains gradually give way to coastal plains. Mountains often tower over the lowland regions. At 4,101 meters, Kinabalu on Borneo is the highest mountain in Southeast Asia. This peak rises more or less sheer from the shoreline of Sabah. Biogeographically, the Malay Peninsula, Sumatra, Java, Bali, Borneo, and the Philippines—in other words, the western parts of maritime Southeast Asia—belong to the mainland, to which they were joined by land bridges during the last Ice Age, when sea levels were much lower than now. This was not the case, however, with the eastern islands, which have many features in common with Oceania and Australia. The original vegetation of Southeast Asia was the locally varied tropical rainforest, whose diversity of species declines the farther away one travels from the equator. Mangroves, which can withstand great variations in tide level and salt water, thrive along the coast, and extensive swamps have developed in the river deltas.[2]

The Pacific Ocean extends from west to east across a distance of 12,000 kilometers. It covers a total area of 180 million square kilometers, occupying a third of the Earth's surface. Across its huge expanse can be found both landmasses of almost continental dimensions as well as countless other islands—large, small, and minuscule. New Guinea, New Zealand, and New Caledonia all have high mountain ranges, deep valleys, broad plains, and wide rivers. The Sepik River winds for 1,126 kilometers through New Guinea. Glaciers and a permanent covering of ice characterize particularly the far south of New Zealand's South Island (Fjordland), where the mountains reach heights of 4,000 meters and more, but snow also falls on the mountainous regions of New Guinea, which in some places soar high above the rainforest—at Gunung Jaya to a height of 5,033 meters.[3]

Australia truly does constitute a continent in its own right, from a European perspective the fifth. With the exception of the Great Dividing Range, which marks the point where the continent runs down to the eastern seaboard of the Pacific, and some other mountain ranges in the northwest, Australia is characterized chiefly by vast plains with little variation in altitude. The interior of the continent has no rivers emptying to the sea. The lowest point of the entire region under consideration in this chapter can be found there, at Lake Eyre, a salt pan 12 meters below sea level. In addition to the deserts of the interior, Australia also has extensive areas of scrubland, bush, and hard grass, as well as fertile coastal plains and tropical rainforests.[4]

The islands of the Pacific Ocean are all of volcanic origin. On the so-called high islands like Fiji, Tahiti, or Hawaii, this provenance can be clearly seen. Some peaks on these islands reach considerable altitudes, for instance, 1,844 meters on Samoa and 2,400 meters on Tahiti. And Mauna Kea on Hawaii ascends to 4,205 meters above sea level. Erosion has carved out deep valleys, and the sediments washed downstream have formed a series of plains of varying breadth. The soils are fertile and mineral rich, with precipitation, streams, and rivers providing a steady supply of water. Most islands are surrounded by reefs, with only occasional channels for ships to pass through. The constant prevailing winds mean that the high islands all have a well-watered side with correspondingly lush vegetation and a drier side with poorer plant life. In cases where volcanoes disappeared entirely over time, either through erosion or rising sea level, only the reef remained. Accretion of corals saw these reefs grow ever wider. Flat atolls arose, which have hardly any elevation above the sea and which frequently form a chain surrounding a lagoon. Some of these reefs were lifted up by seismic activity and came to form a third type of flat island. Atolls and other low-lying islands are prone to water shortages, especially the farther away they are from the equator. Streams and other watercourses are very rare, while sources of freshwater are generally found only below normal sea level and can be accessed only when the tide is on the ebb. Such islands are not particularly fertile and are comparatively poor in plant and animal species.

Southeast Asia and Oceania belong almost entirely to the tropical climatic zone, between the Tropic of Cancer in the north and the Tropic of Capricorn in the south. A warm, humid climate with high temperatures and plentiful rainfall prevails above all near the equator. However, altitude and topography can give rise to marked local differences. As a rule, the farther one moves away from the equator, the cooler and drier it becomes and the more pronounced the contrast between the rainy or monsoon season and the dry season. These extremes are the

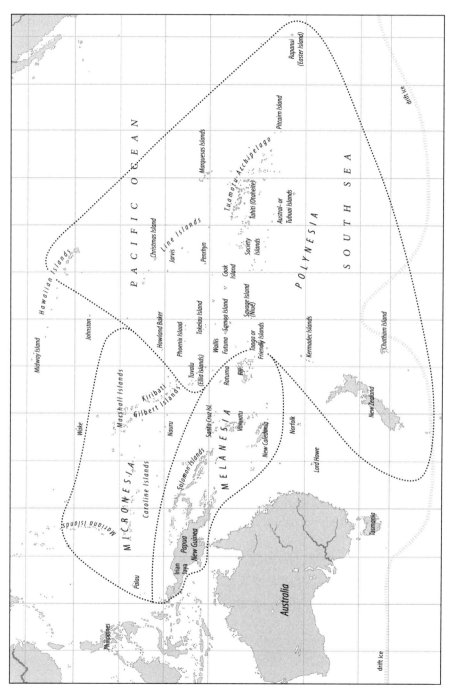

The major regions of the Pacific Rim: Polynesia, Micronesia, and Melanesia

result of the system of winds, which according to the time of year blow from different directions. North of the equator, the months between October and April are characterized by northeasterly winds, and by northwesterlies south of the equator. From May to September, the prevailing winds south of the equator are southeasterlies, while to the north southwesterlies are in the ascendant. These winds pick up moisture as they blow over the warm waters of the ocean and release it when they pass over land. Precipitation is especially high in those areas where rain clouds encounter mountains, while drier regions are found on the leeward side of these ranges. The great landmass of Australia has a continental climate with vast temperature differences between day and night, especially in the interior.[5]

Both Southeast Asia and Oceania are characterized by volcanic and seismic activity. These events have caused terrible destruction but have also given rise to fertile soils and created the characteristic landscapes of the region. The Pacific islands exist only as a result of volcanic activity; notable volcanic peaks include Mayon on the Philippines, Merapi on Java, and Taranaki on the North Island of New Zealand. Hot springs and geysers, which the Maoris learned how to exploit as heat and cooking sources, are found particularly on New Zealand.

Climate, Catastrophes, and Ecology

Daily life and land usage in Southeast Asia and Oceania were determined first and foremost by the constantly recurring periodic succession of rainy and dry seasons. The cycle of trade winds lent shipping and long-distance foreign trade a seasonal rhythm. Profound climate changes had the effect of impairing agricultural production, seriously affecting the food supply and sparking political upheaval. The marked cooling of temperatures that set in worldwide from the fourteenth century on (the "Little Ice Age") had the capacity to produce such effects, as did the so-called El Niño event, in which high pressure in Southeast Asia combines with areas of low pressure over the eastern Pacific to create a sudden warming of the seas off the Peruvian coast in December, as well as extreme drought conditions on the western side of the ocean. If this phenomenon reoccurred frequently, the ecological consequences could be devastating. For example, major unrest in Vietnam during the period under consideration here has been traced to causes such

as this, which may also have been a further contributory factor to the destabilization of the kingdom of Angkor. Furthermore, Anthony Reid and Victor Lieberman
identified similar climatically determined crises in Southeast Asia in the second
half of the seventeenth century as well.[6]

The Black Death began to ravage Eurasia in the fourteenth century. Yet Southeast Asia was only indirectly affected by the epidemic; it suffered no population
losses and, on the contrary, experienced it as an impulse toward development. As
communications along the so-called Silk Road were severely compromised by the
death and illness brought by the bubonic plague, the sea route became the only
viable alternative communication channel between China, Southeast Asia, the
Near East, and the Mediterranean, and thanks to its geographical position Southeast Asia profited hugely from this enforced change.

Both Southeast Asia and Oceania were afflicted on a regular basis by natural
disasters such as periods of drought, floods, volcanic eruptions, tropical cyclones,
and tidal waves (tsunamis). In particular, the coastal plains and the low-lying islands of the Pacific were—and still are—largely defenseless in the face of the destructive power of tsunamis. With typhoons, it is not only the hugely increased
wind speeds but also the heavy rainfall that accompany them that bring widespread destruction. However, flooding and volcanic eruptions can, in the middle
and long term, also have some positive consequences. On Sumatra, Java, Bali, Sulawesi, and the Philippines, lava and other volcanic rock have, over time, become
transformed into mineral-rich soils. Likewise, floods, while threatening settlements
and farms, also brought downstream soil and mud that settled into layers of sed-
iment, forming fertile floodplains.[7]

The most significant factor in changing ecological conditions, though, was
human intervention. Originally, dense forest covered the whole of Southeast Asia.
People exploited this resource, felling trees on a large scale and bringing about a
profound change in the natural environment. Slash-and-burn farming techniques,
for instance, were continuously employed, at ever-increasing distances from villages, to turn virgin forest into arable land. When fields could be reached only
after a long trek on foot, people simply moved on and established a new village at
another location, leaving behind them secondary forest or grassy steppeland covered in scrub. Population growth and trade in natural resources accelerated this
trend, as cultivated land came to occupy ever-larger tracts of land. Demand for

forest products, especially particular woods, also radically altered the natural vegetation over time. In places where forest had been clear-felled, all the nutrients soon leached out of the soils, and damage caused by erosion increased. New species were brought to the region as a result of regional and international exchange of plants, a development that also left its mark on the ecosystems and landscapes of Southeast Asia.[8]

Hunter-Gatherer Societies

Southeast Asia and Oceania are no less diverse in sociocultural terms than they are in their geography.[9] New Guinea provides an instance of particular heterogeneity; there developed on this island countless village communities isolated from one another, along with a great diversity of religious beliefs and a multiplicity of forms of artistic expression. The region being examined in this chapter embraced a wide spectrum of social structures, from the egalitarian to the aristocratic and the centralized. Repeatedly, internal dynamics as well as external influences engendered social and economic changes and gave rise to complex and highly fluid conditions.

The region's many varied ecological systems provided a living space for a variety of nomadic hunter-gatherer societies. People from these cultures lived by using bows and arrows, spears, or blowpipes to hunt down wild animals. Traps consisting of pits or snares were also widely used by hunters. Fish were caught either by hand (with spears) or with nets. The hunter-gatherer diet was supplemented with insects or mussels, together with berries and fruit gathered from the forests. In addition, roots and tubers were dug up with digging sticks. Honey was obtained by smoking bees out of their hives. Hunting and gathering societies existed in the tropical rainforests of New Guinea, the highland regions on the Philippine islands of Mindanao and Luzon, and the arid and semiarid zones of Australia. Even so, both the Australian Aborigines and the later white settlers generally tended to prefer the climatically more favorable zones on the coast, along rivers, or in the more rainy areas of the continent. In the dry areas of Australia, the aboriginal groups occupied strictly delimited domains, in which they knew all the streams and rivers and either permanent or seasonal watering places. The men hunted for game, but in the main Aborigines of these regions lived on plants, which the women

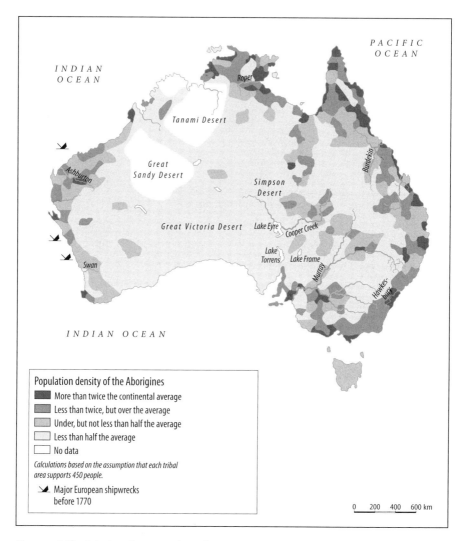

Centers of Aboriginal settlement in Australia

and older children gathered or excavated. Tools were made from wood, stone, bones, and other materials available from the bush. Nets and fish traps were woven from grass or plant fibers. Pelts and skins were the only materials from which clothes could be made.[10] The so-called sea nomads, the "foragers of the oceans,"[11] did live as well as hunters and gatherers. From their houseboats, they originally fished with spears and harpoons, later supplanting these with nets and rods. Onshore, they collected mussels and other seafood.

These peoples did not live in some hermetically sealed microcosm but rather were involved in regional or supraregional bartering relationships. Many gathered natural products such as rattan, copal, or swallows' nests in the forests or harvested sea cucumbers from the ocean and exchanged these goods for food, metal goods, or jewelry. Even the Aborigines were reliant on bartering to some extent. In Southeast Asia, these races often lived in uplands regions, for which reason they are sometimes referred to as "montagnards." Yet such peoples were by no means exclusively hunter-gatherers; they also included settled farmers.

Agrarian Societies

Most of the inhabitants of Southeast Asia and Oceania were closely connected with the farming economy. In Southeast Asia, rice, as the staple foodstuff, determined the fundamental structure of all agricultural activity. Wherever it grew successfully, rice had become established as the preferred staple diet by the fifteenth century. However, a few other crops also became widespread. As a consequence of the different natural conditions that pertain in each area, a clear distinction should be drawn between the two principal regions of Southeast Asia and Oceania, despite the fact that some prehistoric and early historical migrations had already linked them in certain regards. The fragmented island world of the Pacific had its own group of plants that was useful to humans, while both the quantitative and qualitative limitations on agricultural land precluded the use of large-scale cultivation and, furthermore, put a natural ceiling on population growth. In Southeast Asia, on the contrary—on both the mainland and the numerous large islands—ample amounts of high-quality farmland were at peoples' disposal, thus enabling intensive, large-scale agriculture to be practiced, which in turn was able to supply a steadily increasing population. In addition, the climate also favored the introduction of irrigation-intensive cultivation methods. The only places where there was some correlation between the two areas were on the smaller islands of the Philippines and the Malay Archipelago, which geologically were closer to the volcanic and coral islands of the Pacific and which permitted no extensive mass cultivation of irrigation-intensive crops.

In terms of culture, the two major regions were most closely related in the transitional realm between the nomadic or semi-nomadic hunter-gatherer societies and settled farming cultures. In extensive, thinly settled mountain and forest zones, slash-and-burn agriculture dominated in various forms. The most radical variant was found among the Hmong of Siam, which entailed cutting down the primary vegetation in order to achieve the maximum short-term yield. This method required that each group practicing it moved en masse to a new location every fifteen years, because the land they tilled in this way fell victim to desertification. A more ecologically sustainable approach involved leaving behind selected trees from the primary vegetation to act as protection against soil erosion and drying out; this form of cultivation allowed a periodic regeneration in a rotation cycle of around ten years. Using this method, groups such as the Karen of Burma and Siam were able to become more settled. Often, slash-and-burn was combined with mixed sowing, in which different grains like dry rice or millet were combined with squash or legumes plus, depending on the particular region in question, batatas, melons, or edible grasses and later even with maize or chili peppers. In addition, on fire-cleared fields, various vegetables were sown among legumes.

These kinds of cultivation methods were suited to groups of only a limited size, however. Most of the populace of Southeast Asia was organized into sizable social units pursuing a rural-agrarian mode of existence, which demanded more complex cultivation methods. The staple foodstuff rice was probably the strongest unifying element in farming throughout Southeast Asia, especially because it also spread to South Asia and the Far East. Two distinct cultivation methods characterized rice-growing areas. Dry rice cultivation is based either on the less labor-intensive mode of sowing—to which category, in principle, the use of rice in mixed-sowing techniques in slash-and-burn tillage also belongs—or on the more productive method, which involved planting out seedlings on plowed fields and was widespread on several Philippine islands and in northwestern Sumatra. Wet rice cultivation *(sawah)* is thought to have been practiced in Southeast Asia from the eighth century on and in all likelihood began concurrently in Vietnam and Burma, as well as on Java. Subsequently, it spread to all areas where there was enough water. This technique is based on planting out seedlings in flooded fields (paddy fields) and requires complex irrigation systems. In mountainous regions like the north of mainland Southeast Asia, central Java, or the highlands of Luzon, arti-

Rice-growing terraces of the Ifugao people, northern Luzon. Hemmed in between the Cordillera Central and the Sierra Madre, the rice terraces of the Ifugao agricultural-ists are located in the north of the Philippine island of Luzon. The onerous work of hewing these terraces out of the mountainsides began as far back as two thousand years ago. Throughout their history, they have constantly had to be repaired and improved, and this remains an ongoing task. (Photo by Reinhard Wendt)

ficial terraces were constructed on a grand scale to facilitate wet rice cultivation, because this was the most efficient way of all of growing this crop. Given sufficient irrigation, it yields two crops every year.[12] Using drystone walls totaling several hundred kilometers in length, the Ifugao people of Luzon transformed steep slopes up to an altitude of 1,700 meters into a huge rice-terrace landscape. A system of canals channeled water to the paddy fields here, which were cultivated using simple digging sticks.

Moreover, a rice culture based on irrigation also entailed a more complex form of society than gathering wild plants or slash-and-burn agriculture. An irrigation system had first to be constructed and then constantly supervised, and instruments of power were needed to properly administer it. In addition, this cultivation method helped foster economic relations within a society. Because construction, maintenance, and supervision involved some expenditure, this meant either that barter relationships were intensified or that an exchange on a monetary basis was organized. Aside from Indian and Chinese cultural influences, one of the essential bases for the formation of states in Southeast Asia was the need to put in place an effective apparatus, in the form of wet rice cultivation, for feeding a growing populace.

Alongside rice, other cultivated crops played a regional role as staple foods. In arid zones, primarily in the highlands, millet was grown in parallel with dry rice and in many locations probably preceded the cultivation of rice. On the less fertile islands of the eastern Malay Archipelago and the Philippines, sago filled the role of rice, supplemented by taro and yams. As well as growing agricultural crops, people also kept livestock such as water buffaloes, chickens, or pigs. These were a good source of protein but did not form part of people's everyday diets, being reserved for slaughter only on feast days or in the context of certain ritual observances.

As well as fulfilling a basic domestic subsistence function, in many cases, the more complex forms of agriculture were geared to export. Staple foods, primarily rice, were the subject of intensive trade even at this early stage, with Java and Siam as the chief exporting countries. By no means were all Southeast Asian societies at this time self-sufficient. In addition, the wealth of the region was based in large part on luxury agricultural commodities. From an early stage, spices like pepper from Sumatra and Borneo, cloves and nutmeg from the Moluccas, and sugarcane from Java, Siam, and Cambodia were harvested for the Asiatic and the global market alike. Farming in this region also supplied raw materials for industry such as plants used as dyes or cotton, which was widely cultivated.

Thus, from the earliest times, the cultivation of cash crops formed an integral part of Southeast Asian agriculture. Although this form of farming here was not solely prompted by the appearance of Europeans, it was fundamentally influenced by European intervention, in two phases. First, a clear intensification of demand became noticeable, which stimulated the expansion of farmland without, however, fundamentally altering farming structures in the region. Subsequently, the Southeast Asian farming economy experienced increasing interference by Europeans in production, which manifested itself in the introduction of new cash crops for the global market and in changes in working practices, especially the development of a plantation system employing indentured agricultural laborers or slaves.

The precise timetable of this development varied according to specific location and commodity. Both nutmeg production on Banda and, in part, clove production on Ambon were brought under the control of the Dutch as early as the beginning of the seventeenth century.[13] Generally speaking, modern plantation commodities such as sugar, tobacco, rubber, or indigo—including the attendant mass import of a labor force to produce them—did not exist in this region in the early modern period. The trailblazer for this development was sugar production on Java, which was run by Chinese entrepreneurs and funded by the Dutch East India Company (VOC); even by the late seventeenth century, this enterprise was experiencing a massive boom. Under the influence of European demand, dependence on cash crops increased both among farmers and among secondary groups such as merchants and dockworkers. Furthermore, this arrangement in the agricultural economy also favored the introduction of a monetary economy in societies that had hitherto encountered this phenomenon only peripherally.

In Oceania, the transitions from hunter-gatherer societies to a farming economy were much more fluid, which is not to say, however, that in comparison to the "highly developed" rice-producing Southeast Asia, this region had only thoroughly "primitive" forms of farming. This view gained currency solely from the erroneous first impressions of the first European travelers to the region. The natural configuration of the land in Oceania necessarily meant that farming activities there were primarily focused on tree fruits, including palm products, and roots and forced farmers to fall in line with the rhythm of dry and rainy seasons. Among indigenous agricultural crops, taro was the most significant, but this encountered a highly successful rival when the potato was introduced from South America. Yams and sago were also grown here, while the breadfruit tree provided a staple food.

The development of a farming economy here began in prehistoric times with rudimentary attempts to regulate existing sources of freshwater; following the creation of artificial irrigation systems, there gradually arose an intensive form of agriculture, whose surpluses ensured the survival and expansion of a growing populace. Fields were created by means of slash-and-burn clearance and, in more upland terrain, by terracing. The domestication of a species of pig indigenous to Oceania provided not only a further source of food but also an important means of barter, which enabled agriculture here to expand beyond a narrowly circumscribed subsistence farming. Agricultural activity intensified and expanded in many locations throughout Oceania from the end of the first millennium on. In Polynesia, the boom in population numbers that took place between AD 1000 and 1500 led to an exponential increase in the area of land under cultivation. In many places, woodland gave way to a three-field system involving the rotational planting of sweet potatoes, breadfruit, and taro. Likewise, on New Guinea, from around AD 800, the widespread system of swamp irrigation was steadily supplanted by a rotational fallowing system that exploited the nitrogen-fixing properties of ironwood plants (Casuarinaceae). In some regions, and for certain crops, there developed a highly sophisticated form of garden or terrace agriculture with artificially controlled irrigation, especially on New Guinea but also on various islands in the Fiji Archipelago and in the New Hebrides (Vanuatu).

Although animal husbandry did not play nearly so prominent a role in Southeast Asian and Oceanian farming as it did in parts of Europe, Asia, and Africa, where indoor breeding of livestock and herding set the tone, it was still significant. In most cases, livestock husbandry was a small-scale undertaking, concentrated on individual households and involving only smaller animals. Indeed, in Oceania, only three animal species were ever domesticated: pigs, dogs, and hens. In Southeast Asia, too, it was not common practice to raise large domestic animals such as buffaloes or cattle; these were mostly used as draft animals in tilling fields. Occasionally, though, cattle would be traded or sent in tribute payment. It was much more usual to encounter poultry of all kinds in villages. The consumption of meat, a comparatively rare occurrence in everyday rural life, often took on a ritual character, because slaughtering was generally construed in spiritual terms as the sacrifice of the life of an animal. The distribution of meat as a precious foodstuff around an entire village community is also to be understood as a ritual act, expressing the symbolic redistribution of wealth. Pigs, which were domesticated at a very early date throughout the region, played a special role; in many places, they had a prestige and cult function, as, for example, among the Batak of Sumatra, the Papua of New Guinea, and various Oceanic civilizations. Keeping pigs was largely proscribed in Islamized areas, where they were often supplanted by goats. In contrast to Islamic expansion, Hindu dietary proscriptions on the consumption of meat could scarcely assert themselves.

As a rule, cultivable land was available in abundance, for a long time even on the densely populated island of Java. Agricultural land was administered by the village community; land that was currently in use was in the individual possession of the person farming it, but if it fell fallow, it could be taken back into communal ownership at any time. Also, anyone was free to annex land that had not yet been reclaimed for farming. Even the power of the aristocracy held little sway over this informal arrangement. The nobility continued to "grant" land to new settlers or in some centrally organized states was given direct access to farmland as a way of actively managing the state's economic activity. But at root, because of the mismatch between available land and the limited labor force, the competitive struggle for available manpower was more urgent than it was for land. Herein lies one of the bases for the many different systems of personal bondage that existed in early Southeast Asia, ranging from voluntary debt bondage to the sale of slaves captured on raids specifically undertaken for this purpose.

In the Pacific, too, the organization of landownership relied on the same foundations of communalism and reciprocity. The one fundamental difference between here and Southeast Asia lay in the fact that available space in Oceania was strictly limited and that these comparatively small areas displayed extremely varied natural conditions (for example, shoreline, swamp, woodland, and arid fallow land). Individual villages mostly possessed social clusters reflecting this structure. Within village communities, land use was organized according to need in such a way that all households or families had a share in all forms of land. Here also, the person using or cultivating the land was regarded as the owner, with the result that concrete landownership tended to be extremely short-term and flexible. Even so, in most cultures there was still an elite in whom formal landownership was vested and who basically fulfilled the role of a distributive and administrative instance. Yet this elite was, as a rule, characterized by the pragmatic and flexible way in which it handled questions of landownership.

Rural life was organized in village communities, which, against this background, displayed a basically egalitarian structure, as well as a patriarchal orientation as regarded the division of labor in farming. Households comprising a family or at least a part of a clan formed the smallest social units and at the same time constituted the individual "enterprises" cultivating the land. Although there were usually village chiefs, most decisions, especially those relating to farming, were taken collectively. There was no contradiction between this and the fact that the village community was ultimately dependent on a ruler or an aristocrat. This connection, though, was based on the principle of personal fealty and not on the matter of landownership. It was not invariably the case that inherited status guaranteed a person the right to occupy a position of leadership. Age also played a role, as did personal competence, charisma, or military success. References to an original homeland, a migration movement, or particular epochal events often played a key role in asserting identity.

More complex social hierarchies arose in cultures in the lowland regions than in the highlands. These initially developed at a local level and were dominated by the heads of clans. These chiefs endeavored to maintain their own authority and that of their kinship group and to expand the region they controlled. Armed clashes were commonplace. As a result of endemic diseases fostered by the humid, tropical climate, population density in Southeast Asia throughout the entire period under consideration here was low. According to Reid's estimates, some twenty-three million people were living in the region in 1600.[14] The principal aim of wars, therefore, was to acquire people and their manpower by means of deportation and forced resettlement. For example, no substantial political entities existed on the islands that later came to be known as the Philippines in the precolonial period. People there lived in small, scattered village or clan-based communities led by a *datu,* a chief or tribal leader. Beneath him were arranged aristocrats, freemen, and bondsmen. Some of those in the lower echelons of the hierarchy were required to pay tribute in the form of a portion of their harvests, while others had to do military service or be designated as serfs. The Spanish chronicler and lawyer Antonio de Morga went so far as to call them slaves. However, it is more accurate to characterize them as partial leaseholders or villeins.[15] Their manpower was the most significant capital held by the elite within a village community, but in many cases there were blood ties that transcended the boundaries between different echelons and social groups. Social gaps do not appear to have been unbridgeable, and strict class divisions were unknown. Each village was inhabited by a group bound together by familial affinities, whose members stood in a relationship of mutual dependence on one another. Yet the scattered nature of these communities hampered communication between them, and when contacts were made, they were often hostile.

In the center of these village communities were patrimonial palaces, such as the *kraton* on Java or the *kadatuan* on Sumatra, presided over by a *ratu* or *datu,* as their titles were known in Malay. As a result of wet rice cultivation and the ensuing supraregional trading connections it fostered, a number of these petty principalities saw their power increase and their influence expand. They were able to bring neighboring communities to heel by force of arms and loosely annex them. However, they rarely succeeded in forming firm power structures that went beyond simple payment of tributes or in establishing lasting dependencies. In this context, the organization of Buddhist or Hindu kingdoms appears to have become an exemplar, setting a model for the establishment of other forms of supraregional authority. Later, Confucian and Islamic organizational principles also helped foster the rise of powerful empires with expansionist tendencies.

Urban Societies

Unlike Oceania, Southeast Asia was, in many places, a highly urbanized region. The coastal zones in particular were dominated by countless ports, but significant urban centers were to be found in the interior as well. The development of cities occurred at a far later date here than in the surrounding major regions of China and India; archeological evidence points to the first urban settlement on the Malay Archipelago appearing only in around 1200 at Kota Sina on Java.[16] Yet during the period that is the subject of this study, Southeast Asia experienced a rapid urbanization that was every bit as impressive as contemporary developments of the same kind in both Europe and China in the early modern period.

However, the phenomenon of the city in Southeast Asia is far removed from the customary European parameters. Any definition that relied on particular architectural features or institutional structures as key characteristics would be too skewed toward old European concepts, especially because no uniformity is evident across the entire Southeast Asian region. The only features that lend themselves to a homogeneous definition are local agglomerations in settlement on the one hand and centralized functions on the other.[17] Estimates of the populations of Southeast Asian cities are, at least for the precolonial era, extremely difficult and can convey only a general impression of the order of magnitude rather than hard-and-fast figures. They generally rely on inconclusive European observations, which in retrospect turn out to be open to interpretation. Because Southeast Asian societies have left behind no written records relating to many different areas of their social and cultural life, historical scholarship is forced to turn to European sources for this information, even though these contain a plethora of misunderstandings and distortions deriving from their authors' cultural dissonance. A variety of accounts, comprising both firsthand reports by the internal bureaucracy of the European East India companies and retrospective publications by travelers, form an important basis of research into the history of Southeast Asia. According to the estimates that Anthony Reid has compiled on the basis of such material, there were several large cities in the region during this period, numbering between 50,000 and 100,000 inhabitants.[18] For Java alone, he identifies six cities in this category—Batavia, Semarang, Demak, Japara, Tuban, and Surabaya. On the Malay Archipelago there were another five that can be assumed to have exceeded the 100,000 mark, at least on occasion: Banten, Melaka, Aceh, Macassar, and Brunei. On the mainland, alongside Ayutthaya, Reid's estimates cite Pegu and Phnom Penh, as well as the Vietnamese royal cities of Thang Long and Ki Long, as being of this size. In the period preceding the one under review in this study, Angkor in its heyday is even thought to have boasted a population of half a million.

One of the principal factors bedeviling the observations of European travelers, and hence any estimates based on their reports, was the great degree of flexibility evident in Southeast Asian cities. Within these metropolises, buildings could be rapidly displaced from one location to another, plots reassigned to a new owner, while in major trading centers controlled by a politically strong central power, whole population groups could suddenly be shifted at will like figures on a chessboard. Thus, when the British East India Company established its factory at Macassar on Sulawesi, the sultan granted it an inner-city plot where the palm trees were felled in return for a compensation payment and whose inhabitants were resettled in another sector *(kampung)* of the city.[19] Viewed from the outside, cities in this region were founded quickly but by the same virtue could also suddenly decline in importance or be ceded to other rulers. In extreme cases, they could even be displaced to another site at relatively short notice, for instance, when they were threatened by attack, as reported by English travelers to Sumatra in 1634.[20]

The familiar cityscape of the region scarcely bore any comparison with European conceptions of the city. Built from light materials such as bamboo and palm leaves, a feature dictated both by the prevailing tropical climate and the ready availability of these building resources, cities in Southeast Asia presented a seemingly insubstantial and sprawling aspect, with no clear demarcation from the surrounding countryside. The internal layout was rambling, giving many European visitors the impression of an "inhabited forest." City walls, such as those erected by the sultan of Banten, were rare; instead, the characteristic skyline was formed by imposing rulers' prestige buildings and religious edifices, often the only stone structures within a city. Despite this lack of clear demarcation, the combination of centralized authority and a greater than average density of settlement still warranted the designation of "city" regardless of any Eurocentric perspective.

The centralizing function of such settlements allows us to create a typology of Southeast Asian cities. In this region, two principal types of city can be identified: centers of power on the one hand and centers of economic activity on the other. The textbook distribution was that the former occurred in the interior, whereas the latter were to be found principally on the coast. Thanks to the vital maritime trade routes that passed through the region, many major trading ports ("emporia") sprang up, whose marketplaces guaranteed a free exchange of goods between independently operating traders, as laid down by the local rulers.[21] The participation of rulers in this thriving trade, be it through the collection of excise duty or through mercantile activity of their own, helped lay another foundation stone for the growth of these cities, alongside their favorable geographical position. Particularly on the Malay Archipelago, these cities became the nucleus of city-states commanding extensive spheres of influence.²² In this way, economic and political centralization could be concentrated within a single city. Conversely, some centers of power located in the interior, whose appeal was based primarily on being the seat of the aristocracy and on the usually attendant concentration of important religious cult sites, were by no means devoid of economic activities. These centered mainly on their control of, or at least influence over, farming in the surrounding region and to a lesser extent on playing a facilitating role in trading ventures.

The openness of Southeast Asian cities, which was a key feature of their topographical position, was also reflected in their populace. A typical urban settlement exhibited what was in every regard a profoundly mixed, diffuse metropolitan society. Segregation within cities along linguistic, ethnic, or religious lines was not an invention of colonialism but an integral part of regional city tradition. Considering the negative connotation of the term, perhaps it is more appropriate to talk in terms of people "belonging" to certain quarters of the city. The concentration of particular groups in certain city quarters (kampung) was not only the norm in Southeast Asia but also voluntarily entered into by all parties concerned. From the point of view of rulers, the possibilities of control made this arrangement highly desirable, whereas from the perspective of the "aliens"—in many cities, the total number of incomers from abroad far outnumbered the indigenous population—this practice afforded them a clear measure of protection. Familial and ethnic relations and the sense of solidarity deriving from such connections formed a central security system. Ethnicity in this sense was clearly an assigned attribute but one that was effected mutually by involving the parties concerned and that was based on an interplay between political decisions taken by those in power and the desire for cultural solidarity by a community that considered itself an ethnic group. Accordingly, we cannot discount the possibility that the formation of ethnic groups manifested itself differently from city to city.

This phenomenon was commonly observed in emporia and in cases where diaspora groups settled in a particular location. In such cases, these were exiled, dispersed social groups, who integrated themselves to some degree as a minority into a foreign culture without sacrificing their cultural self-awareness. They were characterized by wide-ranging networks of connections and an enduring relationship to their country of origin but also in the long term by the development of a hybrid culture of their own, such as that of the *peranakan* Chinese in Southeast Asia. Their dispersal may have been caused by persecutions, but sometimes they were purely economic migrants.[23] In particular, diasporas of merchants—in both the pre- and postcolonial period—were directed to occupy specific settlement sites and in return were granted extensive autonomy in administrative and legal terms. Examples of the sheer variety and imprecision of ethnic categorization are provided by the many Chinese diasporas, which often demarcated themselves further within their own community according to place of origin and religious orientation, as did the "Malays" found in most port cities, a group that, the farther away it settled from its true place of origin, the Malay Peninsula, the more it embraced all manner of Indonesian ethnicities. This also held true for the "Buginese-Macassar" diaspora in the east of the Malay Archipelago, which was regarded by Europeans as a homogeneous unit but in fact was made up of two distinct cultures of southern Sulawesi, who in their homeland had traditionally been enemies of each other.

The most important port cities also had their own hinterlands. Alliances between their rulers and elite groups in the surrounding region gave them access to political networks, while immigration widened their social contacts, and their supplying of export goods as well as of provisions for urban society broadened their range of economic relations. These multifarious connections are especially clear in the case of Malacca, which both during its own independent period of florescence in the fifteenth century and under Portuguese rule in the sixteenth century entertained close relations of all the kinds outlined earlier to its own hinterland, which fell into abeyance only following the Dutch conquest in 1641, when the city itself went into decline.[24] In cases where such city–hinterland relations continued, city-states arose, which typified the Malay Archipelago during this period. These city-states only rarely ruled over a clearly delineated territory but rather were characterized by their *focal urbanism,* which held sway over the metropolis itself as well as large tracts of the agricultural hinterland and all international trade that passed through the region. In this way, the city-state was able to realize a profit from both these forms of economic activity, which in turn was invested in the welfare and continuing growth of the urban population.[25] The city itself formed the focus of such an entity, which from the perspective of European newcomers was defined as a kind of territorial state, whereas from a Southeast Asian perspective represented a power structure composed of alliances and flexible hierarchies.

Furthermore, the importance of religion for urbanization in Southeast Asia should not be overlooked. A close relationship existed between the traditional centers of power, which developed as either Hindu or Buddhist polities. The rulers, who were responsible for instigating the growth of cities, derived their legitimacy from religion and assumed all central religious functions. Through this connection, such cities acquired, alongside their formal religious centrality—for instance, as places of pilgrimage or as the sites of major temples—a spiritual significance in their own right. This form of gain in significance was alien to Islam, but even so the Islamization of maritime Southeast Asia also played a significant role for urbanization there. The expansion of economic centrality, the increase in the power of local sultans, and the establishment of Islam first as the religion of the ruling elite and shortly thereafter as a popular faith were all so closely interlinked that they lent one another impetus, thus making it almost impossible to identify the original cause.

In some regions, the ecological and cultural conditions did not favor urbanization. The peoples of the rainforests and highlands—both on the mainland and in island Indonesia, Oceania, and the Philippines—lived in settlements that did not have enough population density and were too remote from centers of state power and supraregional economic networks to stimulate urbanization. In regions such as this, the growth of cities, if it happened at all, was sparked only by colonialism.

Much earlier, indeed immediately after they first appeared in the early sixteenth century, Europeans acted as a catalyst to city development in urban Southeast Asia. However, it was uncommon for this to be a form of simple transplantation of European models to Asia. Rather, in this precolonial period, European models assimilated themselves into existing city models and brought about a gradual change from the inside. When the Portuguese seized Malacca, they did so primarily with the aim of continuing to run a typically Southeast Asian emporium under their own auspices, in order to skim off any surpluses for their own benefit.[26] In 1571, the Spanish chose a place that lay in a well-protected location, where the Pasig River flowed into a large tidal bay, as the site of the capital of the Philippines.

Some two thousand people lived in precolonial Maynila, yet within half a century the populace of Manila, as the city was now known, had increased to almost fifty thousand. The VOC conquered many ports in order to curtail their activities as free-trading entrepôts for goods on which the Dutch claimed a monopoly, while continuing to allow them to perform all their other functions unimpeded. New settlements founded by Europeans, such as Batavia, were the exception rather than the rule, as were the mixed-race Eurasian elites that inhabited them.[27] Even then, such cities, as can be clearly seen in the case of Batavia, ultimately took on unmistakably Southeast Asian characteristics.

Maritime Living Environments

Southeast Asia and Oceania are characterized by heavily indented coastlines and a fragmented patchwork of islands, combined, in many places, with a very inaccessible interior. The upshot of this was not only that the main settlements developed primarily on the coast and along rivers but also that the principal trade and communication routes were by water. Living with and on the water therefore left far more of a mark on both economic and cultural activities than in other parts of the world. From the Korea Strait to the Cook Strait, the key role of water is the most striking common denominator in a major region that is otherwise hallmarked by its extreme heterogeneity. In this respect, it is no coincidence that precisely here there developed living environments in which the term "maritime" denotes far more than merely living at the waterside.

Societies in which a maritime orientation characterized many different aspects of daily life existed at various different levels of intensity but may still be divided into two basic types: first, those that practice a sedentary mode of existence on land but that derive their livelihood primarily from the sea, such as the fishing societies that existed throughout Southeast Asia and to an even greater extent in Oceania; second, those in which social life in its entirety had been transferred to the sea.[28] These could have a nomadic character, as with the Bajau people, who lived between Sulawesi, Borneo, and the Philippines; the Orang Laut in the Strait of Malacca and the Riau-Lingga Archipelago; or the Moken people, who lived off Siam and Burma but are particularly associated with the Mergui Archipelago and the Andaman Sea. Alternatively, this second group could have a sedentary aspect, like the so-called floating villages in Halong Bay off North Vietnam. In addition, such features also apply to various pirate groups and approximate to the way of life of many merchants who habitually accompanied their cargoes to their destinations.

These communities plied their trade mostly beyond the range of written documentation and even aside from the major trade and traffic routes. Even so, their significance beyond their own living sphere should not be underestimated. They worked as fisherman and foragers of maritime produce such as trepang, agar-agar, or tortoiseshell. As such, they were repeatedly to be found in the most important ports of the region, where they also performed the role of middlemen, trading such commodities as birds' nests, wax, and other forest products from Borneo, which they brought to Macassar. As a result of increasing demand from China, the Bajau from Sulawesi became the acknowledged experts in trepang (sea cucumber). They also traded in some processed goods. In this way, these boat people exploited certain market niches, displaying the rudiments of commercial enterprise and fostering trade contacts right down to the end user; as such, then, they led a far more complex economic life than mere subsistence based on fishing.

Because of their mobile lifestyle, it is difficult to assign the sea nomads to particular polities. The Bajau from the southern coast of Sulawesi aligned themselves variously with the rival states of Boné and Macassar. Their northern cousins off the Sulu Archipelago were regarded by the dominant Tasong ethnic group there as the property of the sultan, which probably had more to do with the slaving expeditions organized by the sultanate than a general classification. Internally, the sea nomads were acephalous societies, organized by family group forming ships' or house communities. Some sea nomads had stilt houses in the shallow waters of coral reefs or off volcanic islands, though in the precolonial period these were never their primary place of domicile; until at least the nineteenth century and in many places up to the early years of the twentieth century, they lived mainly on their boats. These were highly specialized forms of craft, which had just enough room for the core family and were oceangoing as well as being suitable for navigating shallower inland waters. It is fair to assume that these societies usually built their own vessels, although there is some evidence to suggest that they also had boats constructed in the main shipbuilding centers of the region.[29]

The types of vessel used in the region were suited to all manner of different functions and equipped to handle a range of natural conditions.[30] Over time, a huge diversity of different craft were developed, too many and varied to describe in detail here. As the very simplest form, dugout canoes were the most practical of craft and were found throughout the region; they were widely used for day-to-day transport of goods and people on rivers and near coastal waters. The lack of natural resources in certain regions dictated that boats could not be made by hollowing out entire trees, but comparably simple craft were still used there, such as tree-bark canoes in Australia. Greater stability was required for sailing the high seas. Outrigger canoes, which had a float offset to one side of the main hull where the occupants sat, minimized the danger of capsizing. Twin-hulled or multihulled craft offered even greater security. Basic forms of both of these were used throughout the Pacific but also in the eastern Malay Archipelago region, for example, the kora-kora of the Moluccas. In both locations, the first Europeans to document their travels encountered whole fleets of such vessels, sometimes numbering hundreds of boats, with some of these evidently so substantial, even from a European perspective, that they warranted the designation "ship."

Rowing boats and sailing ships alike were found in the region's waters. In Oceania, these were mostly single-masted craft, usually equipped with a lateen sail. In addition, especially in Melanesia, trapezoid sails were also used, not to mention certain elaborate local variants. The plethora of islands here was reflected not only in the great diversity of boat types but also in the variety of sails. In Polynesia, tacking into the wind was a completely normal navigational technique, while in Micronesia, the whole mast was usually switched about when necessary. Rowing vessels, which were commonly associated with Polynesia, could also reach a considerable size. Oared ceremonial boats were also found in Southeast Asia; notable among these is the Siamese royal bark.

While the dugout canoe represented the basic form of ship construction in the Pacific, in Southeast Asia ships were more commonly built with keels and planking. Initially, shipbuilding was carried out by each individual seafaring people. There was a great variety of local boat- and shipbuilding traditions throughout the region, and practitioners were highly regarded, not just as specialists at their own trade. Particularly in Pacific societies, master boatwrights belonged to the elite. However, regional centers presently arose where particular expertise evolved

Model of a Prahu Paduwakang, a traditional merchant vessel used by the Bugis. The Bugis, a people native to the southwest of the island of Sulawesi, were renowned for their nautical skills and their trading activities. This was evidenced in a dense trading network, which covered the entire Malay Archipelago. From the seventeenth century on, these routes were plied predominantly by sailing ships of the Prahu Paduwakang type. These multimasted vessels were the largest ships ever built at the wharves on Sulawesi. In the twentieth century, this ship type was developed into motorized vessels ("Pinisi") that are still widely used around Indonesia. (Tropenmuseum, Amsterdam, coll. no. 668–123)

in shipbuilding techniques. In the Malay Archipelago, for instance, shipbuilding centers came into being at Madura in eastern Java and in southern Sulawesi, where the products were of such high quality and gained such a reputation for excellence that they were bought beyond the immediate region. Manufacture was based on generations of accumulated expertise within shipbuilding families; ships were generally constructed as one-offs, without any set plans being laid down beforehand. Genuine family traditions developed from this practice, which, however, did not come to form a hermetically sealed system. Time and again, outside influences were adopted, as among the Bugis of Sulawesi, for example. Among the many different successful types of freight-carrying sailing boats in Indonesia—generically known as *prahus*—the *prinisi* of Sulawesi were the most widespread. It was this type of sailing vessel that was also used by the first Europeans to settle in the region, thus introducing external influence into its further development. Thus, from what had originally been a purely Sulawesian type of ship, there developed the so-called Macassar schooner, a European–Indonesian hybrid, which Buginese workshops turned out in increasing numbers to supply the market the length and breadth of the Malay Archipelago.[31] Another external influence that came to bear on ship design in this region was widespread copying of features from Chinese junks. Thus, a hybrid shipbuilding culture can be said to have developed from an early date on the Malay Archipelago.

Fishing formed the initial basis for all modes of existence in maritime areas, including those that were not completely reliant on the sea. Even cultures that were oriented toward farming used fish to supplement their supply of basic foodstuffs, provided they were in the vicinity of a seacoast, a lake, or a river. Above all, however, many coastal dwellers specialized in catching fish. In doing so, they deployed a wide range of fishing techniques, depending on particular environmental circumstances and social organization. Implements of all kinds were used, from simple hooks and harpoons, through nets of various sizes and shapes, right up to complex weir systems. Likewise, fishing could be undertaken on an individual basis but was commonly organized by the family or village group. Its position vis-à-vis hunting and gathering was fluid. On the one hand, extensive gathering of marine produce took place, as practiced by the sea nomads, as well as simple fishing in the shallow waters around countless estuaries or off gently sloping beaches. On the other hand, fishing was also undertaken far out on the ocean in large groups. A specialized form was the whaling that took place on Lamalera in the Solor Archipelago, which involved the entire village; although it resulted in only very few kills per year, these still ensured the survival of the community for months on end.[32]

A characteristic feature of the region was the transport of goods by water. This was conducted both across the sea routes linking islands and mainland coastlines and on rivers in the interior. In many regions, rivers were either the only or at least the most effective means of transport. On the mainland, major waterways like the Mekong represented the vital communications artery for entire civilizations.

Local vendors used them to carry their goods from place to place, while specialized traders relied on them to forge links between centers of production in the interior and export hubs on the coast, as, for example, the vital link that saw pottery exported from the Siamese city of Sukhotai throughout the whole of Asia. On some tropical islands, the rainforest was so dense that transportation of any large goods was impossible overland and so shifted to available waterways. This enabled trade emporia such as Banjarmasin on Borneo, which was a major pepper exporter, to come into being even though it was some distance from the coast. On the high seas, there was a system of supraregional trade links, which taken as a whole formed a kind of maritime Silk Road, enabling goods to be carried by sea between the Far East and Europe.[33] The people who were engaged on all these various routes represented not just a mode of conducting trade but in many cases a genuinely maritime mode of existence.

A broad spectrum of different organizational forms developed in seaborne trading, ranging from joint ventures controlled by influential investors to comparatively minor peddlers. Merchants of this latter type tended to accompany their shipments, sometimes on very long voyages, from their point of departure to their destination port. Voyage times were dependent on monsoons, and often ships were forced to wait for long periods for favorable winds. At particular transport nodes, such as on the Malay Peninsula (Malacca), large numbers of merchants would wait on the right trade winds to continue their journey and so contributed to the prosperity of their host port. Quite coincidentally, this modus operandi made long stretches of living on board cargo ships inevitable. Despite the fact that research has long since shown that by no means was all trade throughout Asia conducted in this way, it was still widespread and represented a key factor of maritime life. On such a voyage, it was not uncommon for one and the same person to assume the role of both the skipper (*nachoda*) and the merchant. In Indonesia in particular, a group of maritime experts arose combining the roles of shipowner, merchant, and navigator.

For longer voyages, and on the larger cargo ships, large and complex crews were indispensable. To regulate their activities and organization, a body of maritime law came into being, which on the Malay Archipelago formed part of the oral tradition of *adat* law; in consequence, it was only rarely committed to paper. The sole written documents to come down to us are the *udang udang laut* of 1656–

1672 from Malacca and the regulations codified in 1676 by Amanna Gappa, head of the Wajorese merchant community in the port of Macassar.[34] These legal documents, which may be regarded as typical of the mainly orally transmitted rules of maritime transport in Southeast Asia, regulated such matters as the position of the nachoda (literally "king on board" in the language of Malacca); the composition and responsibilities of ships' complements; the incorporation of merchants, cargo rates, and routes; the principles of potential forms of business and organization; the distribution of capital, turnover, profit, and loss; and how to handle debt. Because both of these documents were drafted at the instigation of merchants, we may assume that the mercantile affairs were uppermost in their minds when codifying legislation and that the maritime adat statutes as a whole would have contained further provisions governing life on board ship. In view of the long voyages, crossing many frontiers, and the complex crewing arrangements, long-distance cargo ships constituted a maritime world in their own right.

Against this background, people in the region acquired a high degree of competence in navigational matters. Undoubtedly, this occurred initially on merely an individual basis and over time gradually gave rise to a specialist cadre in the form of the nachodas as well as to navigators offering local piloting services. Repeatedly, European captains newly arrived in the region and equipped with only the most rudimentary local knowledge came to rely on these skilled pilots. At the same time, it is clear that certain ethnic groups known collectively as "seafaring peoples"—and not just among Europeans—displayed especial expertise in this realm. The most well-known example of this in the Malay Archipelago is the Bugis of Sulawesi, who were disproportionally well represented among the local nachodas and ships' crews and who attained a dominant role in shipbuilding. Because Southeast Asia represented an interface with other seafaring cultures, expertise also came from outside into the region, in the shape of Arab and Chinese navigators who plied these waters.[35] While most Southeast Asian sailors relied first and foremost on their own experience, additional technical aids were introduced by the Arabs and the Chinese, who around 1500 were at the cutting edge of nautical development.

The significance of knowledge gained through experience was especially apparent in Oceania. Vast distances between often tiny islands did not deter the peoples of the region from venturing out onto the high seas and sailing successfully

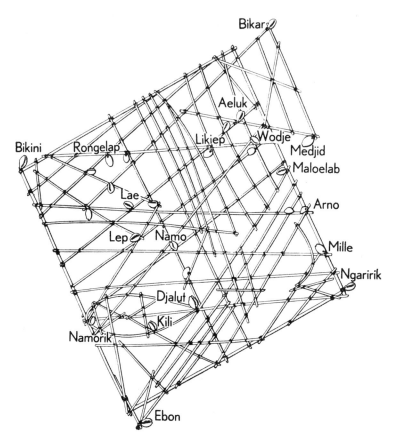

A stick chart made by Marshall Islanders. It was not only the observation of water, waves, and winds that helped the Polynesian peoples navigate the Pacific. These stick charts represented an important navigational aid; on these, the ribs of coconut leaves and cowrie shells symbolized different currents and islands. (From *Südsee: Inseln, Völker und Kulturen* by Clara B. Wilpert, Hamburg: Christians, 1987.)

around the Pacific, for the most part entirely without relying on any navigational aids. The sole exceptions in this regard were the stick charts used by inhabitants of the Marshall Islands.[36] These were lattices made from the midribs of coconut fronds and cowrie shells, which provided a schematic representation of fixed locations in the oceans, mostly islands, and showed the ocean swell patterns around them. It is likely that stick charts were not used directly for navigation while at sea but were intended either for training navigators on land or, in their larger forms, as general directional aids. Above all, though, they performed a mnemotechnical role, helping to preserve experientially gained knowledge and hand it down from one generation to the next.

Finally, a maritime mode of existence that operated in something of a twilight zone was that of piracy. However, a basic problem of definition precludes a clear view of the history of this group, because people were quick to impugn their rivals or enemies as pirates. In particular, Europeans slandered any native seafarers whom they clashed with as "pirates" or "smugglers," and so their accounts of such matters should be treated with the utmost caution. Undoubtedly, groups did exist that specialized in piracy, making the South China Sea, the Sulu Archipelago between Indonesia and the Philippines, and the Strait of Malacca in particular extremely dangerous places to sail through. Of necessity, little is known about them and their way of life, because they either inhabited the coastlines of little-visited islands or, like the sea nomads, lived on board their ships. But tales of the permanent struggle waged against piracy by states, colonial authorities, and trading companies and the role that pirates played in the regional slave trade seeped into the collective consciousness, as represented by official histories.

Forms of Political Organization

The Ming dynasty's accession to power in China entailed a significant break in the political evolution of large swathes of Asia. This event also influenced Southeast Asia in many ways, not least through the spread in the use of gunpowder, which had been used in China since the Song dynasty. From the mid-fourteenth century on, these developments heralded the demise of classical empires, the growth of new cities, and a new political beginning in the region. This upheaval was reinforced by the momentous demographic changes that were brought about by the appearance of major epidemics and a noticeable worsening of the world's climate.

However, it was not just in this situation of political change that the enduring influence of neighboring empires made itself felt. Southeast Asia was a region surrounded by the most significant major empires of Asia: the "Middle Kingdom" of imperial China, the empire of Japan, and the leading powers of the Indian subcontinent, first and foremost the Hindu realm of Vijayanagar and the Muslim Mughal Empire. Among these, China was the undisputed neighboring superpower.

From his capital in Beijing, the Chinese emperor regarded the states of Southeast Asia as a constituent part of his sphere of influence, while in their own interest these states often willingly subjected themselves to the Chinese system of tribute payment. Nevertheless, China's system of rule in the region remained unchanging and inflexible. Only Vietnam represented something of a special case, for although its ruling elite were schooled in the traditional Confucian manner, Vietnam did not simply adopt China's political system.[37] States in the region had a somewhat different relationship with India, which assumed the role of a big brother where culture was concerned. In terms of power politics, the various Indian empires did not expand their influence into Southeast Asia but instead confined themselves to exporting models of rule and systems of religious belief as the basis of empires that were to develop independently in the region.

The Indian legacy in the formation of empires in Southeast Asia manifested itself in the inseparable symbiosis of Hinduism and Buddhism with the political growth of kingdoms. In concert with the "great kings," religious institutions exercised a decisive influence on the structure and development of states. Hindu temples and the Brahmin priestly caste that administered them, as well as Buddhist monasteries and their monks, were at the very heart of political life, alongside the increasingly complex bureaucratic state apparatus. Conversely, secular rulers found themselves exalted to an almost divine status. In Champa and among the Khmer, the ruler was treated as the "reflection of the divine founder of the dynasty," while in Siam he was regarded as a bodhisattva. Contact with the king was possible only through indirect means, mediated by officials or priests. Following rulers' deaths, their sepulchres took on the role of temples. The ruling class provided the clergy with estates and other material wealth and facilitated major religious building projects; in return, the clergy gave spiritual legitimacy to rulers. Unrestricted absolutist rule was based on this foundation. This was true of the kingdoms of Siam, Cambodia, and Burma, as well as the Indianized states among the islands off the Malay Peninsula—notably, the state of Majapahit on Java, where a Hindu–Buddhist empire assumed political dominance from the similarly Indianized but solely Buddhist kingdom of Srivijaya from the fourteenth century on.

At the other end of the state-typological spectrum, too, religious developments and state building were inextricably bound up with one another. Especially in maritime Southeast Asia, city-states arose that had at their core an urban center with autonomous rulers but that also commanded a sphere of influence in surrounding areas. After Aceh had converted to Islam at the end of the thirteenth century, one after the other of the fledgling states of the Malay Archipelago also adopted this new religion: Malacca (1410), Banten and Cirebon (1525; thereby becoming the first cities on the coast of Java to do so), and Macassar (between 1603 and 1607). By 1460, two Muslim island sultanates, Ternate and Tidore, whose political structure was very akin to that of the city-states, had joined the growing phalanx of Islamic states in the region. By the mid-sixteenth century, Islam had gained a foothold on Sulu, parts of Mindanao, and in isolated pockets on Luzon, all in the Philippines. The people who first brought Islam to Southeast Asia were merchants, most of whom came from India initially but also from Persia and the Arabic world; these were later joined by converts from the respective regional large cities on each of the islands concerned. These merchants and others undertook missionary work in support of itinerant Sufi preachers and "holy men."

Despite the supposed independence of the Islamization process from any state influence, it was primarily the new rising political centers that provided a perfect fit with the structure of Islam, which had as its prerequisite strong rule that nevertheless at the same time displayed cultural tolerance and openness to free trade. In addition, the potential for a new constituency of allies among the faith community must have seemed a very tempting prospect to many a ruler in the region, especially given the uncertain times that then prevailed, characterized by constant regional struggles for supremacy and the appearance of new European military powers. Evidently, the figure of the Ottoman sultan, as at least a putative ally beyond the horizon, helped introduce a measure of calm into interstate relations in Southeast Asia. Although an actual alliance with the foremost Islamic powers in the west never became a reality, military know-how certainly filtered through the Islamic networks—which were based on trade and the hajj pilgrimage—to the east of the Malay Archipelago. Islamization of subjects lagged clearly behind rulers' conversion. Though extensive regions of maritime Southeast Asia came to be thoroughly Islamized, this came about only gradually. The official dates of conversion relate only to the ruling elites and tell us nothing about how firmly the new religion was anchored among the ordinary populace.

The period of upheaval in which the region found itself is particularly apparent in the rise of the small sultanates. Traditionally, a tense relationship existed between the coast and the interior, between statehood based on control of farming surpluses and statehood based on control of trading rights. The former primacy of the first definition of nationhood within the political structure now changed radically. The integration of centers on the coast into territorial states, hitherto only minimal, now grew much stronger in the wake of a number of movements, all of which influenced one another. The dwindling power of centralized polities in the interior went hand in hand with religious expansionism and the spread of trade on many levels. This led to a new political landscape, far more geared to small entities, in which alliances and power hierarchies played a decisive role to an even greater extent than before.

This change was also evident on the mainland. The trading boom of the fifteenth and sixteenth centuries blurred the strict dichotomy between agrarian–inland and mercantile–coastal oriented states. Now, realms arose that, on the one hand, continued to be based on a farming economy by means of control of the interior but that, on the other, had a stake in the expansion of seaborne trade though their involvement in centers of power or commerce on the coast. Thus, new political centers arose—notably, Ayutthaya in Siam, Phnom Penh in Cambodia, Pegu in Burma, or Mrauk-U in Arakan—as the germ cells of new state formation. Public income was distributed on a wider basis. The new states behaved very differently, though, vis-à-vis contact with the outside world. Burma was more inclined to adopt an isolationist stance, while Siam and its new metropolis of Ayutthaya presented a much more cosmopolitan face, actively seeking contact with foreign powers, entertaining diplomatic relations, and even engaging the service of Portuguese mercenaries. These two extremes represented different strategies of self-assertion in an era when growing European dominance became ever more apparent, although continental Southeast Asia remained largely unaffected by it.

In the process, the traditional significance of religion, far from being obscured, was actually revitalized by political developments, particularly within Buddhism's sphere of influence. In the mid-fifteenth century, Buddhist rulers made a concerted effort to search out the roots of their faith, to reform monastic orders, to have copies of the written canon made, and to intensify contacts with India and Sri Lanka. Therefore, priests and teachers were invited from there to Southeast Asia, and sacred artifacts and texts were acquired. As a result, in the second half of the fifteenth century, the region witnessed a Buddhist renaissance; a network of contacts arose that has prompted some commentators to talk of a new Buddhist "ecumenical movement."[38]

Alliances and loyalty hierarchies were at least as essential for the configuration of the political map of this area as the internal power structure and the typology of state forms. State power in the literal sense was not clearly circumscribed. Hard-and-fast political boundaries were to be found only in a few of the larger kingdoms; in smaller states or island realms, it is more meaningful to talk in terms of zones of influence. Srivijaya, which was for a long time thought of as a major power, now tends instead to be regarded as a kind of "Hanseatic League of the East."[39] In the sixteenth century, hegemony over the eastern Malay Archipelago was divided between the city-state of Macassar and the island sultanate of Ternate, despite the fact that each of these states had very little formal territorial control. Malacca found itself in a similar situation at the same time regarding the western side of the archipelago.

Thanks to environmental conditions, formation of any major empire in Oceania was even more restricted, with the result that here, too, the hierarchical organization of spheres of influence came to play an important role. By contrast, at the regional level of the islands and archipelagos, central dynasties developed that sometimes, as on Pohnpei (Ponape) and Lelu in Micronesia, even produced "urban" centers: walled settlements at the seat of the dynasty, with 1,000–1,500 inhabitants. At Pohnpei, this central dynasty was fragmented by a series of revolts that broke out around 1350 and was supplanted by five smaller ruling houses.[40] On Hawaii, a political system evolved that researchers refer to as *stratified chiefdom*. This system derived its dynamics from the competition between individual chiefs and was further aided by the isolated location of Hawaii. At best, these conditions could give rise to a polity that in its complexity was comparable with conditions in parts of Southeast Asia. As such, this afforded both the possibility of diversified power structures, favored by the fragmented structure of the terrain, and a complex conception of statehood, which embraced aristocracy, ruling dynasties, and the ritual aspects of rule. In addition, there were countless acephalous societies such as the Aborigines in Australia or the Papuas on New Guinea who had absolutely no formal power structures.

European colonialism as a special form of state formation appeared in Oceania only toward the end of the nineteenth century, while this same process began on the Southeast Asian mainland a few decades previously. The earliest colony in the region was the Philippines, where the Spanish were present from 1565 on, establishing themselves as the colonial power there right up to the Spanish–American War of 1896–1898. Alongside the capital of Manila, which was developed into a central colonial metropolis, Spain's power base derived from, on the one hand, cooperation by converted regional potentates and, on the other, the ongoing expansion of the Catholic mission. The influence exerted by other European expansionist powers during this era remained confined primarily to the economic realm. Their contribution to the formation of colonial empires only really began toward the end of this period. Even the core areas of British India (Bengal) and the Dutch Indies (Java) were brought firmly under the control of the countries' respective East India companies only in the second half of the eighteenth century. The first outposts of European colonialism in this period in maritime Southeast Asia were the area around Batavia, various islands of the Moluccas, and a growing number of individual ports, which began to display many features of colonial cities even before the onset of territorial colonialism. Moreover, Java also experienced an initial expansion of indirect rule, especially in the aftermath of the "Chinese rebellion" of 1740, when a revolt by Chinese farm laborers sparked a pogrom that cost the lives of two-thirds of all the Chinese living in Batavia at the time.[41]

Not every form of political organization manifested itself in the shape of rigid, enduring forms of states. At a level below that of stable systems of rule, there also existed flexible or independent forms of organization. Egalitarian societies settled principally in inaccessible regions like rainforests, upland zones, or on the sea and organized themselves into family and clan units. Small-scale ethnicities, although loosely attached to the great centers, could display great changeableness in their political organization. There might occur a change between two different forms, however short-lived, as among the Kachin in the highlands of Burma, who were acquainted with both egalitarian and aristocratic structures. Alternatively, a whole spectrum of forms could arise within one and the same ethnic group, such as the Karen in Siam, who lived in loosely connected village communities, including principalities with a Burman–Buddhist character.[42] Far more remote from state control, in contrast, were diaspora groups, who developed their own local administration within an overarching state structure.

Gender Relations

Uniform gender relations did not operate either within Southeast Asia or Oceania. As a general rule, it is fair to say that a specific division of labor was commonplace between men and women. Hunting, fishing, house building, and war waging were some of the activities reserved for men. In the main, men also tilled the land, preparing it for cultivation and bringing in the harvest. Women planted rice or edible tubers and tended gardens and fields but also looked after small children, cooked, weaved, and fed the hogs. In both parts of the overall area being discussed here, however, kinship groups and lineage relationships played a central role, with descent being either patrilinear or matrilinear. That said, in Southeast Asia, the handing down of rights and responsibilities occurred predominantly through the father's line. Yet there were some exceptions. The Minangkabau people on Sumatra, for instance, were organized along matrilinear lines, although the mother's brother frequently occupied an important position. Under Chinese, Indian, and European influence, matrilinearity was steadily suppressed. It was not uncommon for hybrid forms to develop. For example, the Javanese were familiar with bilateral lines of descent.

Matriarchy held sway across large areas of Oceania. There too, though, the maternal uncle was endowed with a series of responsibilities, which would have devolved to a father under a patrilinear system. Although the father's line of descent was key on Tonga, even there female descendants were accorded a higher social status than male ones. But in marrying off the highest-ranking women to Fiji, the men found a solution ensuring that they could retain top positions. A different situation pertained on Samoa, where similar rules of descent were observed. There, the most important noble titles were acquired by women. And because any even remotely coequal men were generally too closely related, the women tended to marry high-placed Tongans.[43]

Matrilinear rules of descent, however, did not necessarily mean that women also exercised greater social or political power. Their actual status was extremely varied throughout the region. While a higher degree of female autonomy was characteristic of certain parts of mainland Southeast Asia,[44] in Melanesia, for example, women were considered unclean. There, men lived communally in the men's house, determining political questions among themselves, carrying out central ritual activities, and bringing up boys to be warriors. Women, by contrast, lived with their daughters in individual family houses scattered around the settlement. They were not initiated into many aspects of religious life, nor were they permitted to take part in important ceremonies. In Australia, too, women were excluded from obtaining spiritual knowledge, to which only initiated men were party. Yet in Polynesia women were allowed to possess spiritual powers; in line with this, they also occupied a social and political position that was equal with that of men.

Marriages were sealed according to specific rules that determined conduct within kinship groups. As well as stating explicit preferences, these rules specified criteria that ruled out certain candidates. Marriage in Oceania was mostly exogamous, that is, the bride had to come from another clan. In the matriarchal conditions prevailing among the Minangkabau, the same applied to the bridegroom. In other areas—for example, among the Lahu of Burma and Siam—the bridegroom moved into the house of his parents-in-law, where he worked off the bride-price. In the Philippines, Christian missionaries fought long and hard against this practice. The Shan in Burma practiced polygyny, while polyandry was widespread among the Batak on Palawan.

Forms of Artistic Expression

The natural and sociocultural diversity of the region, along with both external impulses and internal developments, are mirrored in the broad spectrum of forms of artistic expression.[45] One feature that unites Southeast Asia and Oceania is that most of these had a sacred or ceremonial purpose, putting people in touch with their ancestors or with spirits and deities. It was a religious undertaking to create a work of art, and as such artistic expression followed a set pattern. Although the names of individual artists remain unknown, their work was highly prized, and in Oceania artists even comprised a special social echelon, as the mediators between the here and now and the beyond.

Sculptures and carvings in and from wood often had a zoomorphic or anthropomorphic form and were, as a rule, steeped in religious-spiritual significance, though they could also sometimes be an expression of status and power. Often they embodied the community's ancestors, putting humans and their souls in contact with their forebears and the spirit world. Snakes, dragons, and buffaloes were common motifs. The snake derived from the realm of Indian culture, while the dragon was of Chinese origin, frequently functioning as a symbol of a ruler's power. According to a widespread Southeast Asian conception, the buffalo was a creature that straddled the underworld and this world. The horns that adorned many houses in the region were an allusion to this spiritual role of the buffalo.

Yet the ancestors also inhabited the here and now in human form. They were depicted in this guise on domestic shrines and were given a human face on masks, sacred ceremonial staffs, as well as everyday secular items such as taro-crushing sticks, weapons, shields, or spear-throwers. Both the anthropomorphized figures produced by wood-carvers from the Gulf of Huon in New Guinea, which are reminiscent of cubist sculptures, and other so-called primitive objets d'art from Oceania were later to influence the expressionist and surrealist art movements in Europe.[46]

The key role played by the ancestors as the founders and enduring supporters of a civilization was clearly evident in their carved depiction on the door lintels and load-bearing house posts. The roof of a house literally rested on them, and they formed the pillars and supporting beams of the community. For example, among the Maori the ancestors were (and still are) symbolically present in both the structural fabric and the decorative carvings of the communal "big house" (wharenui). An image of the head or full body of an ancestor (iwi) was set at the apex of the roof joists of the porch at the front gable end of the big house. The joists themselves represented the ancestor's arms, while the interior space of the gable was his chest. The beam forming the roof ridge was conceived as his backbone, while the joists of the rear gable were the ancestor's legs.[47] By contrast, the ceremonial men's house, such as that built on the middle reaches of the Sepik River in New Guinea, depicted the Earth Mother. These structures, which could measure up to 25 meters in length and 18 meters in height, were supported on massive stilts. The central roof post did not simply mark that part of the house that was reserved for the male elders of the tribe but also represented the ancestors and indicated the place where they were thought to be present.[48]

Weaving was often a sacred activity and was reserved for women.[49] Yet the textiles that they produced had not merely a ceremonial but also a social function. For instance, if an endless spiral chain was used on the loom, this symbolized the

Maori gathering house in Rotorua, North Island, New Zealand. The gathering houses of the Maori symbolize the presence of the ancestors in their intricate interior carvings and in their whole method of construction. The large central column is the seat of the ancestor's head and torso, while the weatherboards on the front gable end of the building represent his arms and the interior of the meeting house his rib cage. (Photo by Reinhard Wendt)

continuation of life. Among the Batak, pregnant women wrapped themselves in certain cloths that were supposed to protect them from harm. Almost universally in Southeast Asia, the dead were covered in protective shrouds to prepare them for their journey into the afterlife. In a social context, textiles were designed to display group cohesion or status.

The main fibers used in weaving were silk and cotton, while a particularly fine cloth known as *piña* was manufactured on the Philippines from the fibers of the pineapple. Reserve-dyeing techniques were widespread and have continued to the present day. These include batik cloth, in which wax is applied to those parts of the fabric that are meant to remain color-free. This procedure is repeated for each individual color. If dye-resistant bindings are applied to the warp or weft threads prior to dyeing, the results are so-called ikat fabrics. Many of the external influences that came to bear on Southeast Asia are reflected in the patterns applied to textiles. For example, Javanese batiks include Indian floral motifs, Chinese-inspired portrayals of birds, and geometric patterns from the Islamic tradition.

Basketwork from plant fibers or fabrics made from tree bast *(tapa)* is characteristic of Oceania, symbolizing femininity and fertility. Some of these textiles had an exclusively ritual function, while others were worn as matlike skirts or loincloths. Fine mats woven, say, from pandanus leaves were treasured family possessions. They contained genealogical information and recounted the origins of the family. Tapa was manufactured above all from the inner bark of the paper maple and breadfruit trees. Once all vestiges of the external bark had been stripped off, the inner bark was cut into strips, softened or moistened, and hammered with a wooden mallet until smooth and pliable. This process also widened the strips considerably, producing whole lengths of fabric that, when stuck together, could result in fabrics measuring several meters in both length and width. The beaten bast fibers were dyed, painted, or printed with designs.[50]

Gold jewelry was widespread in Southeast Asia. The Balinese considered it a mark of beauty to file their teeth, while a popular custom in Burma, Siam, and Vietnam was to blacken them. Dayak women also indulged in this practice, in addition to gilding their teeth. In Oceania, colorful feathers from tropical birds were prized as fine ornamentation and valuable possessions. They were often used to make masks and headdresses. Particularly impressive were the feather top pieces from the highlands of New Guinea, whose raw materials derived from several species of parrot and, first and foremost, the bird of paradise. Captain James Cook found that red feathers from the Tonga islands were valuable as goods for barter in other parts of the Pacific. On Hawaii, they were incorporated into magnificent feather capes and helmets worn by high-ranking personages on ritual occasions or during conflict.[51]

As far as architecture was concerned, stone was generally not used as a building material in either Oceania or Southeast Asia. This was not just the case for simple windbreaks woven by Australian Aborigines or the Aetas on the Philippines to act as a shelter from sun, rain, and storms. Right across the region, wood was the construction material of choice for building dwellings, while even rulers often had no choice but to use it for their palaces. The humid climate and attacks from insects soon destroyed such edifices.

The only cases where this general rule did not apply were the residences of powerful rulers or sacred buildings, such as temples, pagodas,[52] mosques, and churches. The stone-built temple complexes at Pagan and Angkor testify to the extent of these respective empires and to the influence they exerted. They also, while emphasizing the contacts that Southeast Asia had with India, clearly bear witness to the creativity and potential of the local rulers and the artists and craftsmen they employed. This was also the case at the temples in Prambanan and Borobudur in central Java, which were built as early as the ninth century. The three great temple towers at Prambanan are dedicated to the Hindu "trinity" of principal deities: Brahma, Vishnu, and Shiva. Not far from this site lies the Buddhist temple at Borobudur, built just a few decades earlier and designed in the form of the quintessential Buddhist motif of the mandala. Four almost square plinths with double-walled galleries running round their perimeter are surmounted by three further plinths, this time circular and studded with small stupas. The whole edifice is surmounted by a single, large stupa at the center. Pilgrims walking through the galleries are confronted by friezes with scenes showing the life and path to enlightenment of the Buddha. As they progress up the building, they steadily detach themselves from the earthly realm and enter into the higher spheres.

Indian influences are reflected in the principal religious buildings of both the Hindu and Buddhist empires of this region. At first, it was a simple matter of imitation, but later the Indian models were adapted to local tastes, developed further, and assimilated into the traditions of a particular area. It was a similar story where the influence of Western architecture was concerned, as can be seen above all on the Philippines but also in Batavia. On the Philippines, the Spanish are initially thought to have erected buildings in the local way. Then, subsequently, they took to following familiar European–Spanish traditions, introducing stone building methods, tiled roofs, and other innovations. However, the moist, humid climate and frequent earthquakes demanded that they adapt buildings to suit local conditions. In consequence, a hybrid Spanish–Philippine style of architecture developed. The load-bearing timber frame was adopted from the traditional native style of house but with stone or brick walls (which had only a decorative, nonstructural function) cladding the ground floor. There could sometimes be a gap of up to 30 centimeters between the masonry and the wooden frame. This guaranteed the building enough flexibility to withstand earthquakes. The upper story

General view of the temple at Borobudur in central Java, with its nine terraces surmounted by the main stupa. The Borobudur temple can be seen as the Buddhist cosmos manifested in stone. The four square and three round platforms, crowned by a great stupa, grow progressively narrower as they proceed upward. Pilgrims, who ascend the platforms in a clockwise direction and walk through their galleries of images, gradually leave the world of passions and desires behind them as they climb and ultimately enter Nirvana. (Photo by Reinhard Wendt)

was given a wooden surround, into which were set large sliding windows, which could be opened almost to their full extent to let a cooling draft blow through the house. Further openings were made below the windows, which replaced the traditional "window to the ground" and were designed to promote the circulation of air. Official secular buildings in Manila such as the city hall tended to follow European models more closely. The same was true of the capital's magnificent stone-built churches. Yet in the provinces, the appearance of churches departed from this pattern: indigenous construction materials like coral were used, and builders were frequently obliged to resort to bamboo or wood. Where Chinese master builders were involved, Far Eastern decorative elements were often added.[53]

In Oceania, there is also evidence of stone architecture serving a religious or military purpose. For example, in the case of the *marae* on Tahiti, these were large stone temple complexes that included living quarters for the priests and buildings housing religious statues. Likewise, stone temples were also found on Hawaii. The early thirteenth century saw the construction of the royal city of Nan Mandol in Micronesia. This city is sometimes called the "Venice of the South Seas" because it is built on almost a hundred artificial islands created in a lagoon on the east coast of Pohnpei. These islands provided space for the houses of the political elite, as well as the workshops of leading artists and burial plots.[54]

With the aid of textual and picture sources, as well as archeological finds, we can gain an impression of what everyday architecture of the region, now long disappeared, must have looked like.[55] This broad category includes both the great longhouses and the simple wind shelters erected by the Aborigines. Stilt houses on seacoasts or on the banks of rivers or lakes are one cultural element that is common to both Southeast Asia and Oceania. Sentani Lake in New Guinea was the site of some particularly fine examples of the Oceanic variant of this type of building. There, ceremonial or chiefs' houses were erected on stout pillars made of ironwood, carved into the shape of spirits, ancestors, or cultural heroes.[56]

Spaniards like Antonio de Morga reported that in the Philippines the houses stood high above the ground on stilts,[57] were built of bamboo or wood, and were roofed with palm fronds. This method of construction not only saved them from being flooded or infested with rats but also ensured good circulation of cool air and created space beneath the buildings where small livestock could be kept or domestic tasks carried out (out of the heat of the sun), such as husking or grinding rice. Most houses had two or three small rooms, comprising a kitchen and combined dining, living, and sleeping quarters, and sometimes in addition another room that was used as either a bedroom or storeroom. The floor in the living room was made of polished hardwood boards, while the bedroom was floored with strips of split bamboo, set at a distance of 1–2 centimeters apart. This created a "window to the ground," which acted like a natural air-conditioning unit. The walls were made of a latticework of bamboo filled in with nipa palm fronds. No nails were used in the construction of these houses. Lianas and cords made from natural fibers were used to lash together posts and beams.[58]

Literature and Music

Whereas literature in Oceania was universally in the oral tradition, in Southeast Asia external influences had stimulated the development of written forms of transmission either just before or around the start of the period under discussion here. Genres firmly in the oral tradition included epic poems, anthems, songs, stories, and sagas but also folk theater, shadow plays, and puppetry. This last form of dramatic performance, whose roots lay in the great Hindu epics of the Ramayana and the Mahabharata, became highly significant, especially on Bali and Java, but was also widespread in mainland Southeast Asia. The marionettes for the shadow plays were made from buffalo or cattle hide and manipulated by sticks attached to the limbs. These *wayangs* survived on Java as legacies of the Hindu period even during the time of the Islamic sultanates and became an integral part of their identity.

Written literature in Southeast Asia came into being as a result of stimuli from India, China, the Islamic world, and Europe. Yet throughout the region these external influences were adapted to local conditions and given an indigenous flavor. In addition, homegrown vernacular forms of literature evolved. The texts in question were of both a religious and a secular nature and written in either prose or verse form. They included, for example, inscriptions commemorating the dedication of a temple or praising the exploits of rulers.[59] It is thought that Javanese literature has the longest tradition of all in the region, stretching as far back as the ninth century. Its golden age came in the thirteenth and fourteenth centuries, when its influence also spread to neighboring regions. Echoes of Javanese literature can be found as far afield as Siam and Cambodia. Only slightly more recent than old Javanese literature are the translations of or commentaries on Buddhist writings that were produced in the Burmese kingdom of Pagan. These were written in either Pali or Sanskrit. Other texts with a religious flavor were the poetic works composed in Burma from the fifteenth century on, which took their inspiration from earlier Pali literature. These stories and verse epics had as their subject episodes from the life of Buddha. Siamese literature, which developed from the fourteenth century on, was also inspired by religion but was used for ulterior purposes—for courtly uses, for political means of legitimizing rule, or for entertainment.

The earliest traces of a Malaysian literature appear in the tenth century and display clear signs of Islamic influence. However, the classical period for works from this literary canon began only in the seventeenth century. Because the Malay language was spread far and wide in Southeast Asia by merchants and Muslim scholars, these texts had a resonance far beyond the region where they originated.

A written literature began to appear in Vietnam around the turn of the tenth century. The texts in question were scholarly tracts, written in Chinese or at least using Chinese characters. Alongside these were tomb inscriptions, religious texts, and official proclamations. In the late thirteenth and early fourteenth centuries, there were devised here not only a book-printing technique, using wooden tablets, but also a Vietnamese written language in which verse epics and prose texts were composed. Particularly characteristic of Vietnam are works of a nationalistic character documenting historical developments and political events.

On the Philippines, although written material existed, composed in a writing system borrowed from Sanskrit over a number of stages as well as in Arabic script, an indigenous form of literature arose only under colonial rule and Christian–Spanish influence. Thus, missionaries used religious dramas—mostly called *comedias* regardless of their content—to disseminate Christian doctrine in an entertaining way. While these plays followed Spanish models, they were written and performed in Philippine languages. In an attempt to attract a bigger audience and hold their attention for longer, tales of adventure and love were incorporated into the *comedias*. These performances were met with great enthusiasm by Filipinos. Over time, they themselves began to write them, giving free rein to their imaginations, building in elements from European chivalric tales as well as native war dances or acrobatic stage-fight sequences culled from Chinese operas. A similar development took place in the singing of the story of Christ's Passion. Introduced by Spanish missionaries, the practice of portraying Christ's crucifixion and resurrection through a kind of recitative, with the various roles taken by different singers, spread out throughout the Philippines. At the start of the eighteenth century, handwritten and printed text books began to appear in Philippine languages, initially translated from Spanish originals but later written by native authors. One such tale of the Passion was Gaspar Antonio Belen's *Mahal na Passion ni Jesu Christong P. Natin na Tola*. This work is regarded as the first truly significant work of Philippine narrative poetry. This particular tale also had its Spanish antecedents, but Belen did not simply translate these sources. While remaining faithful to the basic tenor of the story, he gave the biblical characters Filipino traits. Indigenous epic traditions were combined with new forms of capturing, conveying, and preserving stories adopted from Europe. So, where their content was concerned, the Philippine *pasyon* were Christian, but in their epic structure they were decidedly Southeast Asian.[60]

In Southeast Asia and Oceania alike, song and dance as well as the performance of epics or shadow plays were accompanied by music. Gongs were characteristic of both maritime and mainland Southeast Asia. Expanded into entire ensembles, in which gongs of different sizes were mounted horizontally on wooden sound boxes and were supplemented by vibraphones and xylophones plus wind and string instruments, they formed gamelan orchestras, which became typical of Java and Bali. The songs that Australian Aborigines intoned during ritual activities and to mark births or deaths in the community were accompanied by the deep-sounding didgeridoo, a wind instrument in the shape of a large hollow tube.

The Historical Tradition and Historiography

The historical tradition always formed a core element of the literary canon in the written cultures of Southeast Asia. Whether they were embedded in different religious–cultural contexts or independent of the various written traditions, a great diversity of forms emerged that nevertheless exhibited certain fundamental similarities. The key forms of written transmission of history consisted of chronicles, annals, and dynastic journals, as well as mythical tales. Accordingly, the narrative accounts show evidence of a marked blurring of the boundaries between history, legend, and fairy tale, while diary entries kept at the courts of ruling dynasties tended to stick closely to facts.

On the Southeast Asian mainland, Buddhist and Hindu traditions left their mark on historiography, which was influenced both by Indian mythology and by conceptions of the written word that had become established through the major texts that formed the literary canon of the great Indian religions. Texts with historical resonance were just one of many forms within a great stream of text production that had a long tradition clearly dominated by religious writings. This dominance had a demonstrable impact on the business of writing history. Yet it was also the case that regional forms of historiography were strongly colored by events on the ground, notably the kind of rule that pertained there. The outcome of all of these influences was a pronouncedly independent Southeast Asian historiography.

Against this background, two forms of classical literature with historical resonance arose in Burma. Historical events lay at the root of a special variant of poetry known as *mawgun*, while alongside this there also existed a historical ballad form called *egyin*. Furthermore, from the early sixteenth century, a partially compilatory form of chronicle literature had also evolved, which reached its peak in the comprehensive chronicle of the *U Kala* at the beginning of the eighteenth century.[61] Contemporaneous with these developments, various chronicles also began to appear among the Mon. In Laos, historical portrayals were considered the foremost literary productions of their age. Meanwhile, over the course of the Ayutthaya period (1351–1767) in Siam, the courtly annals *(phongsawadan)* began to detach themselves both linguistically and in terms of their content from the older religious traditions, which had placed the history of Buddhism *(tamnan)* at their center, ultimately dispensing entirely with such accounts.[62] The growing importance of the Siamese court was also exemplified by the fact that an increasing number of historical events from recent times began to be portrayed in the form of eulogistic verses.

In Vietnam, literary historical writing constituted an important part of scholarly literature. Under Confucian influence and imitating Chinese models, chronicles became the central category of national historiography. The extensive compendia of historical scholarship that were produced were another form of Vietnamese history writing that owed much to Chinese tradition. Toward the end of the fifteenth century, Vu Quynh (1455–1497) compiled an anthology of fairy tales, legends, sagas, and chronicles. This tradition was continued during the civil wars that raged in Vietnam in the sixteenth and seventeenth centuries, in the writing of sweeping descriptions of the country, with extensive sections devoted to its history. The precarious circumstances of the period meant that these accounts were written anonymously, particularly because a close connection was usually drawn between contemporary political demands and historical references. In the eighteenth century, Le Quy Don (1726–1784) dedicated a thirty-volume history of Vietnam to the Le dynasty, which by then had consolidated its power. This work had a clear political motivation, for while ostensibly being about historical event, it was actually designed first and foremost to lend legitimacy to the current regime.

In maritime Southeast Asia, the writing of history was not solely determined by the imported Islamic tradition. Rather, this reshaped older native modes of expression. The particular form of the region was Malay historical writing, which was practiced throughout the whole archipelago.[63] This situation was further stimulated by the fact that the Malays did not represent a clearly circumscribed cultural group but were a hybrid ethnicity encompassing all those who used the Malay language, the lingua franca of maritime Southeast Asia, and who—at the latest from the fifteenth century—followed Islam. The only exception was the Philippines, as a result of Spanish colonial policy. Therefore, Malay historiography not only differed from chronicling on Java, in Macassar, or among the Bugis but also, unlike the countless oral traditions of the region, was not associated with a concrete ethnicity, having instead a universal character. Its geographical focal point was the Malay Peninsula and on Sumatra. In addition, Borneo played an important role. Beyond this core area, chronicles in the Malay language began to appear as far east as Sumbawa and the Moluccas and as far west as southern Siam.

Malay chronicles exhibit a particularly close link to the relevant ruler. Like many other pieces of historiography, they performed the role of conferring legitimacy—they were written at the direct behest of the sultan and passed down as the property of the ruling house. As a rule, they embraced the history of a whole dynasty. As such, they comprised two essential components: the genealogy of the royal family and its founding legends were indispensable elements of all such texts. Later accretions to this core template were myths concerning the realm's Islamization. Indian and Islamic elements would occasionally combine to form new founding legends. More recent developments in Malay historiography focused on events that lay less far back in time and generally occupied shorter time spans. Many colonial conflicts were chronicled here, meaning that modern historians are not compelled to write the history of European–Asian interactions on the Malay Archipelago solely by relying on European sources. Accounts might be couched in verse form *(syair),* in which case the report essentially concentrated on a single, seminal event, or alternatively were presented within the framework of a chronicle in prose *(hikayat),* which encapsulated a longer period of history.

From the outset, oral traditions were a key component of Southeast Asian and Oceanic historiography. In the preliterate cultures of the Pacific as well as in the hinterland of Southeast Asia, they remained right up to the colonial period the basis of a collective consciousness of history. But in literate cultures, too, oral transmission was not to be underestimated. First, courtly chronicles accounted for only part of the entire historical record of a society, and second, historical accounts were frequently supplemented by nonwritten elements. We need only point here to the significant role played by mnemonic techniques and improvisation among the educated elites in both Buddhism and Hinduism. In their cultural environment, written testimony was free to be accompanied by performative accounts. Thus, on Bali, for instance, historical narratives migrated from being written texts to pieces of performance art, and back again.[64]

Contemporary European authors likewise contributed to the historical tradition of any given period.[65] In most cases, this occurred within the context of the myriad of travel reports and descriptions of the activities of the Estado da India, the Dutch and British East India companies, or missionary orders. Frequently, the authors would include cultural and historical information together with regional reports and legends that they gleaned in situ in their own accounts. Although their writings served the purpose primarily of recounting the European presence in this region, as part and parcel of this process they also assumed something of the character of an applied geography treatise and hence themselves became a constituent part of Southeast Asian historiography. Shortly after the Portuguese conquest of Malacca, Tomé Pires (1465–1524/1540), who visited the region from 1512 to 1515, compiled his *Suma Oriental,* the first overview of European knowledge about Asia. Over two hundred years later, the Calvinist curate François Valentijn (1666–1727) trod in Pires's footsteps when he wrote the monumental work *Oud en Nieuw Oost-Indiën* (1724–1726), the fruit of the seventeen years he spent in Asia. As in Pires's book, each sphere of influence that was treated in Valentijn's tome was seen very much from the perspective of European history, but Valentijn did recount the history of numerous Southeast Asian regions with an attention for detail that has seldom been matched.

Other authors, in particular missionaries, published works devoted entirely to the history of particular regions of Southeast Asia. For example, in Rome in 1650, the Jesuit Alexandre de Rhodes published a history of Tonkin *(Relazione de*

Tunchino), while in 1688 two historiographical books by the same author, the young priest Nicolas Gervaise (1662–1729), who had worked as a missionary in Siam from 1681 to 1685, appeared in Paris: *Histoire naturelle et politique du royaume de Siam* and *Description historique du royaume de Macaçar*. Like most of his contemporaries, Gervaise turned his attention to the culture and the history of the country, which he knew from firsthand experience. But above and beyond this, his example also showed that European authors, relying on reports and other source materials, were perfectly prepared to write historical accounts of places unknown to them—in Gervaise's case Macassar, which he had never personally visited. A plethora of printed and unprinted sources of European provenance came from the Spanish Philippines. They were compiled mostly by monks, who recounted the missionary work of their fellow brothers but at the same time managed to convey valuable ethnographic information from different regions of the archipelago.[66] Yet one of the earliest and most absorbing descriptions of the Philippines came from the pen of a government official: Antonio de Morga described the first phase of colonial rule on the islands in the late sixteenth century. Morga was at pains both to do justice to the traditional way of life on the Philippines and to praise the achievements of the Spanish colonists.[67]

The frequent confusion of local history with the history of the colonial presence in a region was maintained in the professional writing of colonial history that took place in the nineteenth century and after. Even following decolonization, the history of Southeast Asia largely remained the history of Portuguese, Spanish, Dutch, and British involvement in the region. And even when scholarly treatment of the topic of Southeast Asia—above all in philological subjects—did not concentrate on colonialism, external influences were the first aspects that were emphasized, as is abundantly clear in the designation "Indochina." For a long time, the Indianization of Southeast Asia was a favorite topic of European scholars.[68] However, toward the end of the colonial period, the first backlash against this tendency was spearheaded by authors like Job van Leur and Bernhard Shrieke. Precolonial societies not only started to become a fundamental subject of interest for historical research but were also increasingly recognized as autonomous cultures worthy of study on their own terms. More recent studies, albeit from different perspectives, see Southeast Asia as a significant independent region within a developing global system. Anthony Reid adopted an integrated approach that took account of social, economic, and cultural history when he revealed the dynamic contribution made by Southeast Asia, aside from all European influence, to the "age of commerce" (1450–1680).[69] Likewise, with his concept of *ReOrient,* André Gunder Frank sought to reintegrate Southeast Asia into the dynamics of the ongoing globalization process.[70] In a similar vein, attempts to interpret the Indian Ocean as a single, coherent maritime realm in the spirit of Fernand Braudel's treatment of the Mediterranean also invested the region with a new sense of autonomy.[71]

By contrast, the discovery of the historicity of Oceania came somewhat later. This had in large measure to do with the exclusively oral tradition that governed the region. First, it prompted scholars working from a European perspective to adopt an ideological approach, which took as its premise the idea of "peoples without a history," while, second, right up to the twentieth century it hampered the development of specialized areas of study, as cultural studies were for a long time consigned merely to the realm of philology. Even so, as early as the nineteenth century, the first piecemeal efforts were made to collect and record elements of the oral tradition, as exemplified in the work of Charles Hardie, who was active on behalf of the London Mission Society on Samoa.[72] Nevertheless, even here, colonial history, with its restricting perspective, set the tone for a long time. A real change was heralded only from the mid-twentieth century onward, largely thanks to the efforts of Australian and New Zealand historians, aided by the rise of the new discipline of ethnohistory in the United States.

2. Contacts and Interactions

THE CLASSIFICATIONS of Southeast Asia, Oceania, and the Pacific Ocean are concepts that were coined outside of the region, names that reflect exclusively European viewpoints. "Southeast Asia" denotes a culturally multilayered and geographically diverse area between India and China, realms that, when viewed from the outside, appeared historically and politically more compact and unified. The concept appears to have first been used by German ethnologists and geographers in the early twentieth century. In 1923, Robert Heine-Geldern pointed out the ethnic, linguistic, and cultural commonalities of the region.[73]

In the early modern period, European perceptions and terminology conceived of the region as the "East Indies," while later the term "Hinterindien" ("Far India") became current in German scholarship. In the nineteenth century, the French christened their possessions in Vietnam, Laos, and Cambodia "Indochina" *(Indochine)*. Magellan and his crew almost perished after becoming becalmed as they tried crossing the sea that lay between the New World and Asia. The term "Pacific Ocean" derives from these experiences, while the designation "Oceania" likewise alludes to the vast expanse of water here. In this study, "Oceania" and the "Pacific" are used interchangeably. However, that is by no means common practice. Sometimes Australia is not counted as being within the region, while other studies exclude Hawaii.[74]

The French explorer Jules-Sébastien-César Dumont d'Urville divided the Pacific conceptually into three regions: Micronesia (literally: "little islands"), which lies to the north of New Guinea and east of the Philippines; Melanesia (literally "black islands," after the dark color of their inhabitants' skin), comprising New Guinea and the archipelagos adjoining it and running in the direction of Fiji; and Polynesia (literally "many islands"), which is located within the triangle bounded by Hawaii, Easter Island, and New Zealand. Later, with Indonesia the "Indian islands" were added.

Thus, European conceptions live on in the names of the regions of Oceania as well as Easter Island, New Zealand, and the Philippines. A host of similar examples could also be cited. Such a strong terminological legacy from the Age of Exploration is uncommon elsewhere and can be regarded as a kind of cohesive element unifying Southeast Asia and Oceania. Conversely, these appellations serve only to fragment a region that has a whole series of tangible things in common, both within Southeast Asia and Oceania, respectively, and across both regions as a whole.[75]

Time and again, then, there have been people, goods, and ideas that have crossed boundaries within the region. Austronesian peoples opened up and populated the entire region. Their languages are spoken in an area extending between Taiwan, Easter Island, and Sumatra. This factor alone links Southeast Asia and Oceania. Moreover, eastern and southern Southeast Asia exhibit many connections to the neighboring Pacific islands. Melanesian peoples not only inhabit the west of Oceania but also live on New Guinea, the Moluccas, and some of the Lesser Sunda Islands. Even though they were of a very loose nature, therefore, there were definite contacts between the Lesser Sundas and the northern coast of Australia.

Certain cultural forms of expression, which admittedly are also widespread in other regions of the world and may indeed have their origins there, can be seen as a touchstone for this kind of supraregional connection. The so-called X-ray style of art, which depicts invisible organs within the bodies of animals, along with the spiral shape as an ornamental feature, and above all sculptures of human forms in a crouching position, are found not only throughout Southeast Asia and Oceania but also in the Far East and the West Coast of North America. They may be ascribed to particular forms of society and presumably did not develop in isolation from one another but in concert.

The X-ray style appears in hunter-gatherer societies as a form of hunting charm. Examples of this occur in the far north of Australia and the west of New Guinea. The widespread use of the spiral pattern from Borneo to Australia and from New Guinea to the Marquesas and, even farther afield, to America, can be traced back to Chinese influences. Squatting human forms are, as a rule, an artistic expression of settled farming societies. These can be traced back to the position adopted by embryos in the womb and are associated with fertility, survival, and rebirth, as well as with warding off evil and affirming life. Countless variations and abstractions in the portrayal of such forms may be observed, while the motif also appears in drawings and engravings. Some figures are clearly shown squatting, while others are standing with bent knees. Among the Batak on Sumatra, but also on the Cook and Marquesas Islands, representatives of different generations are depicted, one above the other, on "ancestor poles." In graphic depictions, such as Aboriginal rock art or on shields in New Guinea, the squatting figure or so-called hocker was increasingly stylized and ultimately evolved into a pure ornamental pattern composed of hooks, spirals, and curved lines.[76]

Alongside these factual connections, there are also attributions of a conceptual nature that highlight commonalities across the region as a whole or at least in part. Modern concepts such as the "Pacific Century" or the "Pacific Rim" and institutions such as Asia-Pacific Economic Cooperation, in which the states bordering on the Pacific exchange information on economic, environmental, or cultural questions, start from the premise that there is a degree of coherence across the region. Southeast Asia shares many common features of flora and fauna; moreover, the similarities that characterize the region in this regard are also what distinguish it from neighboring regions.[77] Victor Lieberman's comparative study of political and institutional developments in Burma, Siam, and Vietnam in the period under discussion here also reveals many parallels in the history of mainland Southeast Asia that set it apart from the surrounding areas.[78] Anthony Reid reaches similar conclusions with regard to maritime Southeast Asia: communications between the islands linked their inhabitants. By contrast, external contacts with China or India played a comparatively minor role. If one delves beneath the surface of Buddhist, Hindu, Chinese, and, later, European characteristics, one quickly discovers cultural similarities of a purely Southeast Asian nature.[79] The German historian Bernhard Dahm identifies in this capacity for cultural syncretism, selective adaptation, and creative integration of external influences a trait that links all the peoples of Southeast Asia.[80] Behind the Christian *pasyon* of the Philippines, the Hindu plays of Bali, or dramas in the Muslim tradition, the Filipino musicoethnologist Ricardo Trimillos has identified a wealth of structural affinities that point to common epic traditions.[81]

A Common Sense of Dynamism: Internal Expansion and the Input of External Agencies

Southeast Asia and Oceania were shaped as a region, in whole or in part, by the dynamism of internal agencies. Yet external influences also had a shaping and cohesive function. Among the earliest expansionist tendencies to arise independently within the region, and that served to extend it, were the Austronesian and especially the Polynesian settlement of the Pacific. Their objectives were the islands in the vast expanse of ocean between Hawaii, Easter Island, and New Zealand. Over the course of the period under scrutiny here, Burma, Siam, and Vietnam rose to become major empires that bound mainland Southeast Asia into a single cohesive unit. In island Southeast Asia, a similar role was performed by Majapahit.

Southeast Asia and to a lesser extent Oceania did not constitute hermetically sealed regions. Rather, they represented points of departure, transit zones, and objectives for supraregional and even intercontinental contacts. Merchants from Southeast Asia established far-reaching trade networks and forged commercial contacts that helped lend the region internal cohesion. At the same time, they turned their gaze beyond the region, crossing its borders by venturing into the Indian Ocean and even as far as the east coast of Africa. They also sailed to China, Korea, and Japan.

Furthermore, Southeast Asia assumed a mediating role between the east and west of Eurasia. Both the South China Sea and the Indian Ocean were the sites of heavily used trade routes, and these all converged at the Strait of Malacca. Southeast Asia thus constituted an integral part of the "Maritime Silk Road,"[82] on which merchants from a wide variety of nations plied their trade along a chain of commercial ports, forging links between them. Janet Abu-Lughod considers this phenomenon as a late medieval world system, in which Chinese, Indian, and Muslim mercantile circles effectively fashioned a transcontinental exchange network, with Southeast Asia to a large extent playing the role of middleman.[83] For all its size, the Pacific may be regarded here as a kind of frontier region as well, which not only isolated people but also brought them in contact with one another. The Polynesians explored the Pacific almost in its entirety, and the Melanesians and the Micronesians opened up certain parts of it, while the Chinese, the Malays, the Indians, and the Arabs also ventured around its periphery at least.

Last, one factor of enormous importance was the allure of spices in particular but also of other natural products from Southeast Asia, for example, sandalwood and other tropical woods, plus resins, trepang (sea cucumber), mother-of-pearl, and tortoiseshell. The Chinese and the Japanese were drawn to the region by these goods and their economic potential, as were the Indians, Arabs, and Europeans from many different countries. European encroachment on the region embraced the whole globe, coming not just from the west—that is, from their staging posts in Africa—but also from the east, across the Pacific from America.[84]

Chinese traders had been coming to the region, and setting up bases there, from long before the beginning of the period under discussion here. These formed the nuclei of the diaspora communities that developed in Southeast Asia, with Chinese merchants acclimatizing to native practices and customs and, in turn, having a lasting effect on the local economy and culture. They imported porcelain, silk, tea, and lacquered goods and exported back to China not only spices and other natural products but also silver. After the Mongols superseded the Song dynasty, in the second half of the thirteenth century they launched attacks against the land borders across the north of continental Southeast Asia as well as its coastal frontiers to the south. Although they were unable to gain any lasting foothold, they still managed to destabilize existing empires to such an extent that deep-seated political change set in throughout the region.

In the early fifteenth century, the Chinese state once again attempted to bring stronger pressure to bear on Southeast Asia. The Ming dynasty sought to develop a naval force that would not only dominate the South China Sea but also project China's influence as far as the Indian Ocean. This policy found expression in the total of seven voyages undertaken by the fleets of Admiral Zheng He (1371–1433/1435) between 1405 and 1433. Zheng He's naval units each comprised up to a hundred vessels and crews numbering some thirty thousand men, including not just sailors and soldiers but technicians and experts in administration as well. The junks were armed with cannons and small firearms and equipped with magnetic compasses; these fleets were impressive for their sheer size but also for the huge distances they covered. Although Zheng He's expeditions remained a one-off in the annals of Chinese seafaring, they were every bit as remarkable as the achievements of the European Age of Discovery that ensued over the following centuries. In addition to exploring the Malay Archipelago, the coasts of Siam, India, and Sri Lanka, Zheng He also ventured as far as the Persian Gulf and sailed down the eastern seaboard of Africa as far as Mozambique. For the most part, he established friendly contact with local rulers, but whenever he encountered stubborn resistance to Chinese suzerainty, he was not averse to using armed force, as, for example, on Sri Lanka in 1411. However, there is no evidence to corroborate Gavin Menzies's thesis that Zheng He's fleets might even have reached America at this time.[85]

As a result of these endeavors, some regions became dependent, albeit in a very loose way, on China. The Middle Kingdom regarded Southeast Asia as an integral part of its tribute system. Visits by delegations from the region to the Chinese imperial court were seen as gestures of submission; at the same time, though, they also helped establish beneficial commercial links. Accordingly, the "gifts" that China bestowed in recognition of its homage were often far more valuable that the "tribute" brought to Beijing by the envoys. As such, the whole system may be regarded as a very special form of foreign trade. In political terms, what China was laying claim to amounted to nothing more than a kind of informal sovereignty; even so, this did not preclude the occasional direct intervention. In the first half of the fifteenth century, for instance, Vietnam was occupied for a while, while at the end of the period being examined here, Burma was also the subject of Chinese intervention, from 1765 to 1769.

From the west, meanwhile, merchants from India had been coming to Southeast Asia from as far back as the last few centuries BC in search of gold and spices and offering textiles in exchange. At first, these traders were Tamils, but they were later joined by merchants from Gujarat, Bengal, and other parts of the subcontinent. The intensification of these contacts in the Christian era both strengthened economic exchange between the regions and saw the transfer of certain elements of culture and religion. Buddhism and Hinduism played a decisive role in the establishment and stabilization of extensive empires in both mainland and island Southeast Asia. Sanskrit became the language of official inscriptions, Indian calendrical systems became widespread, and Brahmin rituals became an established feature at royal courts. Indian influences were also felt in local justice systems, as well as in architecture and crafts. Siam and Burma maintained contacts with Sri Lanka over many centuries. Monks from the island traveled to the region and helped stabilize Buddhism and the empires based on this religion. As with Chinese influences, Indian influences were also metamorphosed and adapted to local conditions by the Southeast Asian capacity for cultural syncretism. However, unlike the case with China, no political influence was exerted on the region by India. Only the extreme northwest of mainland Southeast Asia—namely, those areas of Burma that faced the Bay of Bengal—were to come under the sway of the Mughal emperor of India in the seventeenth century.[86]

Even in the pre-Islamic period, Arab traders were already a familiar sight in the ports of Southeast Asia. As Muslims, they maintained these contacts, and once Islam had also taken root in India, Arab merchants were joined by their coreligionists from the subcontinent both in conducting commercial activities in the region and in spreading the Islamic faith there. The first indications of the presence of Islam in the region are found at Aceh in northern Sumatra in the late thirteenth century. Chinese sources hint at even earlier influences. Muslim communities quickly gained a foothold on the coasts of Sumatra, the Malay Peninsula, and Java and thereafter on mainland Southeast Asia as well. Once Islam became established as the predominant religion in Aceh around 1300 and in Malacca at the start of the fifteenth century, its influence began to grow steadily, and Islamic sultanates came into being.[87]

Europeans were present in the region from the early sixteenth century on. In 1511, the Portuguese admiral Afonso de Albuquerque conquered Malacca, the hub of all long-distance trade between South Asia and the Far East. A year later, the first Portuguese fleet set sail for the Moluccas, the famed "Spice Islands" where cloves and nutmeg came from. Portuguese explorers first set foot on Chinese soil in 1514, while in 1543, Portuguese sailors were shipwrecked on the coast of southern Japan. Portugal thus set up a series of bases stretching from the Moluccas to Nagasaki—all part of the Estado da India, which had its nerve center at Goa.[88]

In 1522, the first Spanish vessels reached the Moluccas from the east, across the Pacific. There, they took on board spices, which they sold at a considerable profit back in Europe. However, across the vast combined region of Southeast Asia and Oceania, the Spanish lacked the necessary financial and human resources to compete seriously with rival European powers for control of the Moluccas. Accordingly, they settled for establishing hegemony over the country and peoples of the Philippines—an act tantamount to empire building—and sold their "claims" on the Spice Islands to Portugal.[89]

Following the model of the Portuguese, the Dutch, too, with their monopolistic East Indies Company erected a system of bases in the region, which was centered on Batavia and spanned a huge distance from India via the Moluccas to Japan. Initially on Ambon but later on Java as well, they took the first steps from a purely trading interest to exercising dominion. This same approach was subsequently adopted by the English and the French. However, prior to 1750, although these instances bear all the hallmarks of a global, transnationally structured trading empire, we can identify only the embryonic beginnings of colonial empire building.

European merchants did not just realize a profit from exporting spices or valuable textiles back to their native lands. At least as significant and lucrative (though not more so) was trade within Asia itself, the so-called country trade, in which they also had a hand. Southeast Asian spices were used as a commodity in India for the purchase of fine textiles, while in China they were exchanged for porcelain or tea. Such "intermediary trade goods" helped curtail the outflow of precious metals, which remained the most important form of currency used by Europeans on the Asiatic markets. In particular, China's "silver hunger" gave rise to a constant drain on this commodity, which ultimately let flow American silver not just via the Atlantic and Europe but directly across the Pacific to Asia. Procedures such as this integrated Southeast Asia for the first time into a realm of economic interaction of truly global dimensions.[90]

Furthermore, the Spanish and Portuguese in particular were not just interested in improving their balances of trade through acquiring lucrative trade goods. They were also concerned to win souls for the Catholic faith and so actively promoted missionary work. The private mercantile companies of the Dutch and the British stayed aloof from such activities, fearful that these might have an adverse effect on their core economic business. The French, in their turn, opted for promoting religious missions as a way of pursuing their secular ambitions. But just as Buddhism, Hinduism, and Confucianism were all integrated into local lifestyles, so Christianity found itself assimilated into Southeast Asian culture, and in time it took on its own unique character there.

This capacity for cultural syncretism, which manifests itself here once more, also became apparent in other "innovations" that the European presence brought with it. Foodstuffs from America, which the Spanish and Portuguese just happened to have on board their ships, spread rapidly throughout the region in Southeast Asia, without European involvement. Characteristic local foods were developed from them. For example, on Java and elsewhere, people smoked tobacco blended with cloves; likewise, spicy chili pepper varieties from the Americas entered local kitchens in Southeast Asia in the form of hot sauces like *Sambal Oelek:* the generic terms *ke-tsiap* and *kecap* are the roots of the word "ketchup," a foodstuff that became popular only much later among Europeans and Americans.[91]

The dynamic processes of an economic and political nature that arose within the region and came to bear on it from outside had some far-reaching ramifications. An increased demand for local goods, an expansion of production, and an intensification of trading activity all gave rise to new branches of industry and new transport infrastructure. The coastal cities in particular experienced a boom. The demand for food grew, a development that promoted the cultivation of rice and the trade in this vital commodity.

Market Economies and Trade

At first sight, the entire region was characterized by an agrarian economy. The most striking common factor in this enterprise was the cultivation of rice, the use of which determined the material and cultural living conditions in many places even though, according to varying environmental factors, different methods of cultivation prevailed. On closer inspection, then, surplus production in both the agrarian and industrial sectors came to form the basis for a remarkable level of trading activity, which was as typical of the region as the rice-growing cultures. Trade routes created a multifarious interconnectedness within the region. Often, these networks were strengthened and in part completely restructured by external influences from India, China, and ultimately Europe. Farm produce formed the backbone of regional trade links. At least in years with good harvests, it was rice that became a key trade commodity, transported over long distances. At a very early stage, some sectors of the agrarian economy developed a market orientation. In this process, special importance was accorded to cash crops, even before the arrival of Europeans (though their appearance undoubtedly provided lasting stimulus to this sector). From early on, pepper, cloves, and nutmeg, as well as dyestuff and aromatic plants, were grown to meet supraregional demand. With the advent of the Europeans, these were further supplemented by plantation crops like sugar, tobacco, coffee, and tea. Yet the systematic collecting and marketing of marine and forest products like trepang, rattan, and birds' nests also occurred in response to a market demand.

Trade was able to build on a dense network of transport routes, which in accordance with the physical topography of the region were predominantly seaborne. Even in the interior, rivers and canals were used out of preference. Boats and ships of every conceivable type were indispensable forms of transport. Their use characterized the lifestyles of entire peoples who largely specialized in the art of seafaring, for example, the Bugis of Sulawesi. Only in Japan and on Taiwan (Formosa) were there road networks, maintained at least in part by the state.

The so-called Maritime Silk Road formed the real trading axis of the region. Despite the fact that it has generally been ignored by historians down the ages, this represented a vital alternative to the actual Silk Road, which ran across country from China through Central Asia and on to the Near East but which was largely inaccessible for Southeast Asia. The route of the main seaborne trade axis, by contrast, began in the ports on the South China Sea, ran along the Chinese, Vietnamese, and Malay coasts to the Strait of Malacca, from whence it continued on to Bengal and the shore of the Indian subcontinent to the delta of the Indus River. There, it divided into two principal routes, running respectively to the Persian Gulf and the Red Sea. Unlike the later routes followed by the European East India companies, this sea route always hugged the shoreline and, in common with the overland Silk Road, could be interrupted at any time to allow local markets abutting on it to take advantage of the exchange of goods.

Two sets of straits along this route acted as decisive hinges between the maritime worlds of the South China Sea and the Indian Ocean: the Strait of Malacca, with the port of the same name, and the Sunda Strait between Java and Sumatra, controlled by Banten (Bantam). Ports such as these used the advantage of their location to become entrepôts, thus enabling their rulers to skim off a share from the profits generated by long-distance trade. Later the Dutch, with Batavia, and the British, with Singapore and Penang (Georgetown), also got in on the same act.

This system maintained only loose ties at best to Oceania. While they are barely identifiable in the early modern period, the highly fluid conditions pertaining on the eastern flank of the Malay Archipelago means that their existence was by no means improbable. For later periods, enterprises such as the trepang fisheries on the northern Australian coast run by seafarers from Macassar are well attested.[92] In the open Pacific, the massive distances involved hampered the growth of any intensive trade contacts between the scattered archipelagos. Within these limited regions, however, there was a lively exchange between peoples all intimately acquainted with the sea, which often centered on ritual encounters. The most well-known example of this is undoubtedly the traditional "Kula trade" conducted by the Trobriand Islanders, in which an exchange of goods took place within a geographical ring a few hundred kilometers in circumference; though the goods had ritual significance, the exchange was also of economic importance. This phenomenon was described only at the beginning of the twentieth century by the Polish-British anthropologist Bronislaw Malinowski.[93]

As regards the actual goods traded, a European perspective tends to overstress the importance of luxury items. In actual fact, the day-to-day business of trade was characterized by mass-market goods, foremost among them foodstuffs, with rice at the head of the list. The three thousand different varieties of this commodity that were reputedly traded could be transported over long distances with no deterioration in quality. Export-oriented cultivation put not only instantly utilizable food onto the market but also a whole range of lucrative cash crops, quite apart from any spices: oilseed rape, cane sugar, raw silk, indigo, and hemp. Most textiles in the region were imported goods. Fine woolen and cotton cloth came from regions of India close to the sea, while prestigious silk products hailed from China. Ceramics were also imported from the Middle Kingdom, both in the form of luxury items (porcelain) and as mass-market goods (Zhangzhou or Swatow ware). Additionally, in some areas of Southeast Asia, slaves were a lucrative trade commodity, even though slaving expeditions and the level of commercialization of the trade never reached the proportions of the transatlantic slave trade.

Spices traded on the world market came mostly from this region. However, some of the larger emporia also offered imports from other Asiatic markets, for instance, cinnamon from Sri Lanka (only inferior related substitutes were available from within the region). Likewise, there was no truly equivalent alternative to Cassia cinnamon, highly prized in China. Other lucrative goods in maritime long-distance trade included various dyestuffs from forest zones, precious and aromatic woods from the Malay Archipelago, and rubber, which even at this early stage was being tapped in limited quantities on the Malay Peninsula.

For a long time, scholars of Southeast Asian history made the basic assumption that trade within the region was organized exclusively through the so-called peddlers. According to this interpretation, all merchants accompanied their cargoes personally to their destinations and sold them on markets whose conditions—for example, level of supply and demand and price trends—they had no advance knowledge of and no effective way of anticipating. Accordingly, such traders were incapable of developing any specialism but rather were obliged to continue accompanying their goods overseas in order to respond appropriately to developments on the ground. Thus, they were in no position to withstand European competition when it arrived. This viewpoint may be traced back to the work of Job C. van Leur; subsequently perpetuated by Niels Steensgaard, it became something of a research paradigm.[94]

Several case studies in more recent research, though, have collated plenty of evidence to corroborate the widespread existence of this "peddling trade" but have also found clear signs of more complex commercial links, typified by credit systems, overseas trading posts, and extensive fleets of cargo vessels. Yet while the crude characterization of the whole of Asian trade in this period as peddling trade has largely been refuted by these findings, the idea of peddlers as such is by no means absurd. The trading system of Southeast Asia that European expansionist powers encountered in the sixteenth and seventeenth centuries was, rather, a juxtaposition or, more precisely, a blend of "traditional" and "modern" elements—a kaleidoscopic reality every bit as complex as the corresponding situation in Europe at this time. Asian merchants operated within networks; in other words, they were generally enmeshed in a complex series of commercial relationships comprising business partners and their own families. Links of this kind gave rise to highly complex organizational forms like merchants' associations, which were very close in spirit to the principles of the European East India companies. Thus, Turks, Armenians, Arabs, Persians, and Abyssinians were regularly engaged in the merchant fleets fitted out by Gujarati traders for voyages to Malacca, the epicenter of the Malaysian spice trade.[95] Even voyages undertaken by individual ships might be the result of investment by a whole host of individual interests. Some merchants focused exclusively on their role as investors. Indeed, it was precisely during this period from the fifteenth to the seventeenth centuries that comprehensively structured financial systems developed, facilitating the provision of credit throughout the entire region. Various groups among the mercantile diaspora played a key role in this process. The Armenians and, to an even greater extent, the Chettiar community of southern India became renowned for their acumen in providing merchant banking facilities.

While it always remained somewhat in the shadow of trade and farming, a not insignificant industrial sector also existed in the region in this period. Mostly, farming and industry went hand in hand; in addition, a number of export-oriented specialisms also developed. Textiles and ceramic products played a key role, as did precious metals—both in the form of raw materials and as finished goods. Nor should simpler goods be omitted from this list, goods that enabled peoples living far from the commercial centers to nevertheless participate in far-reaching exchange processes, as was the case with the rattan products made in the rainforests of Borneo. Another important sector of industry was shipbuilding, which spawned an innovative branch of specialization particularly on the Malay Archipelago but which was also present at least as a subsidiary industry or conducted to meet a community's own needs on all coasts throughout Southeast Asia and Oceania. Industrial activity did not invariably, however, give rise to specialization and hence to an internal differentiation within societies; although, as in Japan, there arose within many of the city-states within Southeast Asia a caste of artisans, such a development did not occur in the upland regions or the rainforest. Meanwhile, on the Pacific islands, at least the beginnings of a social structure based on the division of labor were in evidence. Even so, it is indisputably the case that even outside the main commercial centers of the region, goods were being produced for more than just a local market.

Textiles from China and India were imported into Southeast Asia predominantly as luxury items. Although these were significant as a trade commodity, they were beyond the reach of many inhabitants of the region. Generally, garments for everyday use were woven in the home. However, there was also a form of individual manufacture that was not geared solely to everyday usage.[96] Eastern Java, Bali, and Sumatra were significant exporters of textiles in the sixteenth century. From the early fifteenth century on, Javanese fabrics had been popular in northern Sumatra, while striped cloth from the Javanese region around Panarukan and Pasuruan was much in demand in Malacca at the end of the sixteenth century. Bali and Sumbawa manufactured brightly colored fabrics, which were sold by

Javanese merchants as far afield as the Moluccas. In addition, traditional batik textiles formed the premier export product of Java; nevertheless, these proved unable to compete in the supraregional market, due to the fact that the very specific dyeing method used to make them was too labor intensive and costly. The Philippines, Luzon, Cebu, and Panay—which, as comparatively dry regions, were ideally suited to cotton growing—supplied the tropical islands of the archipelago with cloth and finished items.

The production of ceramics was also market oriented. China was both the pioneer and the foremost model in this field. Under Chinese influence, Vietnam began to turn out black-and-white and blue-and-white glazed pottery. And in the Siamese kingdom of Sukhotai, two independent styles of ceramics developed, both of which became popular throughout Southeast Asia. Archeological finds indicate that goods such as these were exported throughout the region; domestic ware from Chinese production centers, which was loaded on board seagoing junks from southern ports in bulk orders of ten thousand or sometimes even a hundred thousand pieces, dominated imports to the region.[97]

Yet the most important export goods in maritime Southeast Asia were agricultural. For a long time already, pepper came not solely from India but also from Southeast Asia. From the beginning of the sixteenth century, pepper cultivation spread from a few centers on the coast of Sumatra, Java, and the Malay Archipelago to encompass large tracts of Sumatra, Malaysia, Borneo, and Vietnam. Around 1670, Southeast Asia reached the zenith of its pepper production, with an output estimated at some 8,000 tons. Until the end of the eighteenth century, the cultivation of cloves and nutmeg was largely confined to the Moluccas. The necessary hike in output here to meet global demand was met by making cultivation of the crop steadily more intensive. Whereas up to the fourteenth century, in all likelihood the collection method was to forage peppercorns from wild-growing plants, the following centuries witnessed an increasingly systematic monoculture on plantations; thanks to Dutch monopolistic policies, this system managed to preserve the Moluccas as the sole site of cultivation right up to the late eighteenth century.

European demand for goods like these was not, however, the factor that determined their export-oriented cultivation. Despite the fact that Portuguese sources claim that the cultivation of formerly wild-growing cloves in the Moluccas began only with the arrival of Europeans on the Malay Archipelago,[98] Indian and Chinese manuscripts from the first century AD already hint at the use of Moluccan cloves in their cultures. Many sources indicate that imports to both countries continued during the European Middle Ages; this import trade has been shown to be a major contributory factor in the rise of maritime Southeast Asian states like Srivijaya in western Indonesia. Over and above this, there was the famous transport of spices across the land route to the Levant and Egypt. Given this long-standing demand in both Asia and Europe, plus the limited cultivation potential on the small Moluccan islands, it seems highly probable that cloves were being grown as a cash crop from as early as the fourteenth or fifteenth century, notwithstanding the fact that, in the absence of any European chronicler at this stage, there are no written records to corroborate this assumption. So, it seems that the Europeans did not stimulate any new market in this regard in Southeast Asia but rather tapped into an already existing one to a greater or lesser degree. In the sixteenth century, only around one-quarter to one-third of the cloves exported from Southeast Asia were shipped to Europe. The vast majority of buyers were Asian, including the Arabs, who also supplied spices to East Africa. The European share in the estimated total production was extremely small. Even though, in many instances, the paucity of hard-and-fast source material means that only conjecture is possible, we may still confidently speculate that there was always an extensive demand within Asia for these commodities and that the Europeans only gradually encroached on this market.[99]

However, the massive intervention of Western European trading companies into this market finally changed the whole structure of the business and stimulated a clear rise in the quantities of spices being exported. The Europeans latched on to existing conditions in two key regards. First, as players in the market, they participated in particular sectors, thereby lending them an additional Europe-oriented dimension. Beginning with the aforementioned spices, they prompted a drastic increase in production of commodities that were greatly sought after in Europe as luxury items. In the course of this development, a change in the structure of demand in Europe caused growers in general to switch over to plantation farming, a move that saw, for instance, coffee and tea cultivation begin on Java and that introduced new growing methods throughout Southeast Asia. Second, products were now geared toward European taste, as can be clearly seen from

Chinese porcelain of this period. In these ways, then, Europeans may unequivocally be said to have brought about a lasting transformation of the regional economic system, albeit indirectly.

Conversely, the new European players assimilated themselves into other sectors of the intra-Asian market. This was particularly true of the trade in textiles, where, in addition to exporting Indian and Chinese fabrics for home consumption, they took a hand in the internal markets within Asia. Their participation in local exchange of goods, the so-called country trade, proved to be essential in injecting new capital into the European companies' trading activities.

Because European goods were only salable in very small quantities in Asia, it was essential—especially in view of the prevailing ideas of mercantilism—that the steadily increasing drain on precious metals in payment for Asian commodities be kept to a minimum. Before precious metals could successfully be supplanted by opium in China, the only method of achieving this reduction was to take part in the lively commerce between the great trading centers of Asia. The transport of Indian textiles to the Malay Archipelago, for example, became the most significant trade route of the European country trade.

Even the first Europeans in Asia, the Portuguese, who were unrivaled in the trade with Asia during the sixteenth century, became involved in part in a form of country trade. Yet this never formed an official part of the Estado da India. The Portuguese state presence had, in the cartaz system, created another opportunity for generating additional income, as the trade in spices and other luxury goods remained stubbornly in the red. This entailed selling passes *(cartazes)* within their trading bases that entitled the bearer to enter and pass safely through Portuguese-controlled ports. Yet it was precisely in Southeast Asia that the trading base system of the Estado da India was much too sparse—with a formal presence only in Malacca, the Moluccas, and Timor and at Macau on the Far Eastern mainland—to alone ensure firm control over all the trade routes in the region. Armed Portuguese enforcement patrols were justifiably seen by those who fell foul of them as a kind of highway robbery. Even so, many indigenous nachodas fell in line with the cartaz system so as not to jeopardize their own trading interests or run any unnecessary risks. Private Portuguese merchant associations were far more heavily involved in the Asian country trade than the royal trading company, and as such they were often under the protection of Asian sultans. Outside

India, large associations of this type existed in Macassar and on some of the Lesser Sunda Islands, especially Flores and Timor.

Likewise, the Dutch VOC, which from a European standpoint superseded the Portuguese as the principal player in Asia, relied on a system of bases. At the outset, it confined itself to establishing commercial "factories" at key trading entrepôts under the control of local rulers. But in 1619, when the VOC governor Jan Pieterszoon Coen seized the settlement of Jayakatra on the Sunda Strait and founded the new city of Batavia on its ruins, he established his own headquarters there, with all the character of a major "emporium." Further Dutch conquests ensued at Malacca (1641), Macassar (1667), and Banten (1684). Nonetheless, both the textile and the pepper trade remained largely free markets, within which the VOC established itself as one of the most powerful buyers. However, by means of treaties with regional rulers and further military conquests, the Dutch managed to secure a purchase monopoly by the 1680s. Alongside its purely mercantile activities, the VOC now emerged as a promoter of new branches of commerce. Some ventures, such as gold mining on Sumatra or various attempts at indigo planting, never got beyond the start-up phase. By contrast, the sugar industry on Java, where the company backed Chinese investors by way of guaranteed orders and fixed prices, thrived under the control of the VOC, enjoying its first heyday as early as the end of the seventeenth century.

Not only taking into account European expansion in the region but also expressly highlighting independent Southeast Asian developments, Anthony Reid calls the period between the fifteenth and seventeenth centuries the "age of commerce."[100] This age was characterized by a hitherto unknown upsurge in commercial activity. Southeast Asian trade experienced the beginning of its own boom in around 1400, stimulated by Chinese and Indian demand. China, by far the biggest market for Southeast Asia, was able to inject more precious metals into the market through its conquests in Vietnam and the Shan States. In addition, the first lasting trade contacts began to evolve with Japan at this time, via the Ryukyu Islands. Europe, too, saw an increase in demand for Southeast Asian spices in the fifteenth century; although, at this early stage, this demand did not in all likelihood stimulate a boom in the region, it did help support developments that were already afoot within Asia. But from the mid-sixteenth century, Japan and Europe entered the Asian market on an equal footing with China and India.

Under these auspices, the Southeast Asian economy experienced a period of major upswing between 1570 and 1630. A decisive factor was an enormous influx of silver, both from China and Japan as well as from the Europeans, who gleaned their supplies of the metal primarily from Spanish America. The discovery of new silver deposits in Mexico, Peru, and Japan around this time brought a significant stimulus to the entire region. American silver increased European buying power in every respect. The Spanish in Manila imported it directly and used it to purchase Chinese goods. However, the bulk of the silver from the Americas was shipped across the Atlantic and used to fuel the economy of Europe, which in turn fueled the Portuguese (and later Western European) trade with the "Far East," by a variety of different means. Most silver eventually ended up in China. At the end of the "age of commerce," Anthony Reid thus identifies a "crisis of the seventeenth century."[101] Manifesting itself in the region in the form of sinking prices, population decline, failed harvests, and political crises, this general crisis continued to cast its long shadow beyond the end of the seventeenth century over the remaining decades up to the end of the period we are discussing here and promoted the ultimate economic triumph of the European powers. For maritime Southeast Asia at least, this crisis is customarily seen as manifested in the military and economic successes of the Dutch. However, this interpretation is not without its critics, given that mention of this crisis is largely confined to European sources, which form the bedrock of Anthony Reid's argument.[102] Reid's interpretation is also very narrowly focused on the spice and luxury goods sector; on the contrary, no serious signs of crisis were evident in many areas of the Southeast Asian economy in the seventeenth century. Nevertheless, there is no disputing either the intensification of trade during the "age of commerce" or the increasing dominance of European trade over the course of the eighteenth century in many sectors. European trade was able to establish a general hegemony by the nineteenth century at the latest, by which time it had also come to assert a far-reaching influence on the conditions of production.

Religion

To an even greater extent than in economic matters, in the realm of religion, Southeast Asia proved to be a crucible of external impulses, which were free to interact there, creating distinct communities. The successive waves of Indianization, Sini-cization, and Islamization and ultimately also the Europeanization or Western-ization of Southeast Asia ensured that all the great religions of Eurasia were im-ported here: Hinduism, Buddhism, Islam, and Christianity. India was both the point of origin of Hindu and Buddhist religiosity and the joint instigator of a progressive wave of Islamization. Likewise, China not only acted as the agent of Buddhism, and partly also of Islam, but also transmitted Confucianism as a state and social philosophy to Japan and to mainland Southeast Asia. Alongside these developments, we may also observe certain common cultural–religious features that derived from states' internal dynamism. The imported faiths, Islam and Christianity included, were capable of being assimilated into existing belief systems, incorporating as they did certain inherited elements themselves. Sub-sequently, through close connections with local traditions and circumstances, they took on their own unique character. This naturally entailed, at the same time, the long-term survival of traditional religious conceptions that had their roots in animism and nature-based religions. Unequivocally, fundamentalist manifestations of Islam or Christianity were not evident at all in Southeast Asia in this period.

The imported faiths encountered a broad spectrum of animistic nature reli-gions. There was no question of any standard form of religiosity in the region; nei-ther the long tradition of these belief systems nor their sheer variety can be sum-marized succinctly. Because there are hardly any written records describing the forms of religion that existed prior to external missionary activity, historical re-search is forced to rely on inferences drawn from isolated relics and on conclu-sions reached by analogy with surviving nature religions. Yet these in turn have not remained uninfluenced by the centuries-old dominance of imported "formal religions." Even so, a whole series of common elements may still be addressed, which are in evidence even beyond the borders of Southeast Asia in Oceania.

The designation "animism"—which is by no means as uncontentious as it once was—derives from the observation that, for all their manifest differences, the forms of religion in question all shared the notion of a "spirit" immanent in humans, animals, and inanimate nature alike. A more apposite summary might be that everything inhabiting the natural environment was ascribed its own autochthonic life principle, which should not be confused with a "soul" in the Judeo-Christian sense.[103] Closer to European conceptions was the presence of the dead, who were generally deemed to live on in the form of spirit beings in the immediate environs of the human world. In order to ensure a propitious communication with them, there arose among the nonmissionized cultures a plethora of ancestor cults and death rituals, which were so deeply embedded in these civilizations that they frequently survived conversion to Christianity or Islam. Alongside the ancestors, in the animistic or nature-religion imagination, a whole range of divinities and spirits, which were organized into various categories, exerted their influence over people's everyday lives. Unavoidable contact with them gave rise to a variety of ritual observances but by no means universally to the growth of religious elite groups such as shamans. Accordingly, while "priest-magicians" (datu) played a central role in the social life of the Batak on Sumatra, the Papua on New Guinea managed without a priestly caste. With or without spiritual specialists, though, magic performed a vital function in social organization throughout the region. Equally significant for the structure of society were the secret societies that were found in many places, which as religion-based entities existed alongside the political structure and exerted a huge influence on it. These secret societies, which were mostly exclusively male associations, had their own symbolism and rituals and generally their own cult sites of assembly as well, such as the "dance houses" on New Guinea.

After the traditional belief systems had been suppressed in Southeast Asia by the various enculturation movements, on the one hand they survived in very few remote locations such as on New Guinea or in the highland regions on the mainland, but on the other hand, some of their central elements proved extremely tenacious. Not just veneration of the ancestors and the concept of spirit beings but also fertility and harvest cults were successfully integrated into all the imported religions. In addition, in most Islamized or Christianized societies, small groups continued to exist that clung primarily to the traditional belief systems of their civilizations.

As regards the missionary movement, which was extensively bound up with economic and political expansion, the original religions that lived on in such areas—far removed from the well-charted trade routes and the power axes associated with them—manifested particular longevity. In maritime Southeast Asia, in spite of the early cross-linking of the island world, many peoples of the interior such as the Batak (Sumatra), the Toraja (Sulawesi), and the Dayak (Borneo) were largely spared exposure to missionary activity right up to the late nineteenth century. Others, like the Orang Asli (Malay Peninsula) or the Papua (New Guinea), were never seriously Christianized or Islamized. This was especially true of the island world of Oceania, where Christian missionary societies were able only to reshape the religious landscape of the region once a strong European presence had been established there. Against this background, it is significant that particularly in Oceania traditional faith models proved especially durable despite all attempts at "modernization." This was also the case with the Australian Aborigines' belief in the idea of the Dreamtime.

The first major wave of enculturation to impress itself on Southeast Asia is customarily referred to as "Indianization," though this is a somewhat diffuse concept that is virtually impossible to pin down in temporal terms. Throughout the whole of the first millennium AD, migration, trade, and the activities of itinerant preachers repeatedly carried Indian cultural currency to the region, which manifested itself in the most diverse of forms.[104] Indianized states may well have been in existence as early as the third century, but they became tangible in historical terms only with the rise of Srivijaya in the seventh century. Where religion was concerned, the term "Indianization," equally vague in this realm, too, can refer to both Hinduism and Buddhism. Religious influences from India spread across the whole of mainland Southeast Asia, extending as far as the Strait of Macassar between Borneo and Sulawesi, thereby dividing maritime Southeast Asia in two in cultural terms until the advent of Islamization. Hinduism, however, which had initially been highly influential, was once more displaced in the fifteenth century. By then, Theravada Buddhism had asserted itself on the mainland, while maritime Southeast Asia witnessed the triumphal onward march of Islam in this century.

The only things that remained of Hinduism were architectural monuments, such as the many lingam pillars, together with linguistic reminders of Hindu origins like the name of the (Buddhist) Ayutthaya dynasty in Siam. Certain rituals also lived on. As had already happened with the traditional nature religions, these Hindu liturgical elements were also incorporated into new religious contexts. This process was aided by a similarity between certain elements of Hinduism and those of animistic religions, some of which have been traced by researchers to a common prehistoric origin ("ancient Indonesian peoples"). This similarity is openly acknowledged in modern times by adherents of animistic religions, notably in debates in independent Indonesia over whether such beliefs should be recognized as legitimate religious communities.

Hinduism on Bali, however, is an exceptional case. It is thought to have arrived there in the eighth or ninth centuries and was hallmarked by East Javanese influences, which grew even stronger from the eleventh century onward, largely through the presence of the dominant neighboring power of Majapahit. After the collapse of this empire, the Hindu elites that fled from Java settled on Bali. In this way, official Balinese Hinduism became closely associated with the ruling elite, whereas popular religion maintained a strong animistic flavor. Ancestor cults, nature spirits, and magical rites continued to play a major role; by contrast, the caste system was not at all prominent. It is therefore more appropriate to talk in terms of a typical Balinese religion rather than an Indian one. The agrarian nature of the island, which was dominated by imposing rice-growing terraces, helped ensure a syncretic blend of animism and Hinduism. The Hindu fertility goddess Devi Sri, for example, was reinterpreted on Bali as the goddess of rice. The Islamization of the region in the fifteenth and sixteenth centuries also helped usher in a further step toward the "Balinization" of Hinduism, because it cut the island off from any potential Indian points of reference. The result was a culture with a rich diversity in its forms of expression across a wide range of genres: festivals, dances, masks, wood and stone sculpture, and painting all began to display typical Balinese stylistic elements. Village life became entirely geared toward religious rites and the temple. Each settlement had three temples with distinct functions; in addition, there were also a large number of small family and domestic shrines. Local rulers gained their legitimacy in the classic Hindu manner, by becoming the focal point of religious life.[105]

The spread of the second religion of Indian origin in Southeast Asia, Buddhism, is shrouded in mysticism. According to legend, the northern Indian Mauryan ruler Ashoka (304–232 BC) was responsible for sending the first Buddhist missionaries. Yet archeological evidence is available only from the fourth century AD. In this instance, too, we may reasonably assume that the faith was spread via the sea routes and was closely associated with trade. Sri Lanka played a decisive role in this, as an important center of Buddhist scholarship; most of the later Buddhist networks that developed in Southeast Asia had some connection with the island. Sri Lanka was the home and epicenter of Theravada Buddhism, which as one of the early schools of the "original" form of the religion (later designated by the term "Hinayana," or "lesser vehicle") promoted an orthodox interpretation of the canonical texts (the Pali Canon). In deliberate contrast to the popular form of Mahayana Buddhism ("greater vehicle"), it adhered to the idea of individual salvation and rejected the veneration of gods and bodhisattvas. Yet even the Theravada doctrine was unable to sustain its orthodox purity over the course of history—either in the form of state Buddhism, which adopted the interpretation of rulers as bodhisattvas and forms of veneration reminiscent of Hinduism, or in the form of a popular Buddhism, which in common with all other religions showed itself ready and willing to incorporate animistic elements.

Nevertheless, Theravada Buddhism came to characterize the life cycle of people throughout the Southeast Asian mainland. As a rule, children became novices in a monastery at the age of seven, and although the majority of them did not remain there throughout their lives, they did complete all their education in such institutions. They learned reading, writing, and the fundamental tenets of Buddhist teaching. The monastery system with its many different branches not only formed the education system of the Buddhist kingdoms of the region but also influenced the political sphere. When novices reached the age of majority, they were required to decide whether to take up the monastic life in perpetuity. Many opted for life within the monastery, and in consequence monks—both in terms of their sheer numbers and through the influence they exerted on society—remained one of the most significant population groups. The borders between monasticism and a secular existence continued to be fluid, however; adults were free to leave or rejoin the monastery at any time.

To an even greater extent than Buddhism, the spread of Islam was intrinsically bound up with long-distance trade in Southeast Asia. Muslim merchants were the prime movers in laying the groundwork for Islamization of the region. Although these traders came from a wide variety of different regions, at the outset it is fair to say that India was the most significant point of origin (though Java was chiefly Islamized by Muslims from Champa and China). Persian Muslims were also involved, resulting in a brief dissemination of Shi'ism. Shi'a Islam was pushed back in the fourteenth century but did nonetheless have a more enduring influence on Islamic mysticism (Sufism), especially in northern Sumatra. Islamic mysticism was widespread, because many of the agents of Islamization were closely associated with Sufi communities. The first Islamic scholars were members of Sufi orders, and it was they who for the most part became the teachers of Islam convert rulers. These scholars were soon joined by others, who set about providing the general populace with religious instruction. These teachers were a mixture of noblemen, merchants, and landowners, and many of them were *hajis* who had undertaken the pilgrimage to Mecca, but only very few were actual Islamic scholars. At their instigation, many schools were founded, which contributed greatly to Islam becoming firmly established among the common people. In turn, the close teacher–pupil bond that was fostered in their schools enabled them to forge a close connection to the major religious orders and promoted the veneration of "holy men." On these foundations, there arose an independent regional form of popular Islam.

In addition, like Hinduism and Buddhism before it, Islam served to legitimize the ruling elite, who defined their role as successors of the Prophet Muhammad, in both a doctrinal and genealogical sense, and as champions of divine law. In doing so, they were able to draw heavily on older ideas. For instance, the orally transmitted adat law, which had conditioned all social life in the Malay world for centuries, was not supplanted by the imposition of shari'a law by the authorities. Rather, the two legal systems, which in all likelihood did have several points of common ground (though the exact nature of the noncodified law that existed prior to the advent of Islam can be the subject of only educated guesswork at best), entered into a symbiotic relationship, leading some scholars to apply the term "Adat-Islam" to the religion as a whole in this region. This designation does not really refer to any direct article of faith or form of Islamic mysticism but first and foremost denotes a religion-based understanding of the law that derived from two equipollent sources.

When Islam encountered the Indian religions of maritime Southeast Asia, they were long-established belief systems and as such were susceptible to a comparatively easy process of reshaping. Concurrently, however, Christianity and Islam met and clashed as expansionist rivals. European expansion and Christian missionary activity went hand in hand. This was particularly clear in Southeast Asia during the Portuguese era. Although the Estado da India had been established primarily on economic grounds, it consistently claimed, as a representative of the Portuguese state, to also be responsible for the promulgation and upholding of the Catholic faith. It was no coincidence that the Asiatic centers of the Estado were also bishoprics. The foot soldiers of this first wave of missionary work were members of religious orders, principally the Jesuits but also the Dominicans, Franciscans, and Augustinians. As the papal nuncio for Asia, the Spanish Jesuit Francis Xavier (1506–1552), an early disciple of the order's founder St. Ignatius Loyola, was active in Southeast Asia in the 1540s and became known as the "apostle of the Moluccas" before turning his energies to the Japan mission. A succession of his Jesuit brothers was active not just in the immediate environs of Portuguese colonial cities but especially at the courts of local rulers. Although they often managed to persuade individual rulers to be baptized, these conversions had no wider ramifications. Only in Vietnam did the French Jesuit Alexandre de Rhodes succeed in laying the foundations for a long-lasting Christian community, despite the fact that he was personally expelled after just a few years in the country.

The Catholic mission on the Philippines met with far greater success. Unlike in the other regions, the missionaries here enjoyed the protection of a colonial power. The symbiosis of colonial and missionary interests here was so fruitful that it became known as the "Philippine model." Success was based on a combination of coercive methods, which in a colonial context could be far more effective, and strategies of enticement, such as offers to provide education and health care and the staging of ostentatious religious festivities, all of which were readily accepted.

Competition for the souls of Southeast Asia between a mystically oriented Islam and Catholic Christianity resulted in a clear winner. From the outset, it was apparent that Islam ultimately had a far greater ability to assert itself. Once particular regions had been Islamized, Christianity found it impossible to gain a foothold, and when the two religions competed directly to convert "heathen" courts, Christianity invariably drew the short straw, at least in the long run. Quite apart from Islam's attraction to ambitious rulers of Indonesian city-states and island sultanates, Catholicism had the distinct disadvantage of being incapable of effecting continuity with the means at its disposal. Its spiritual representatives ultimately remained isolated, being unable to marry into the local population or elites, and for a long time shunned indigenous helpers. Its missionary purpose was focused on conversion, combined with a radical break with all tradition, especially that of the adat, while the prerogative for interpretation remained deliberately rooted in the Spanish motherland. The promoters of Islam behaved quite differently. Certainly they, too, demanded clear indications that a person had renounced

Mosque in the style of a Javanese temple in Bandung, circa 1860–1872. The Islamization of Java from the fifteenth century encountered a civilization largely shaped by Hinduism. While Islam largely displaced this religion, many other cultural elements still survived. Many Javanese mosques, like this example from Bandung, testify to a blending of cultures. The Muslims began by adapting local buildings to their purposes but gradually evolved a typical regional style of architecture, which gave mosques the appearance of traditional Javanese temples. (Tropenmuseum, Amsterdam, coll. no. 60022051)

his or her "paganism," including practices such as the mass slaughter of all pigs kept by a community during group conversions or circumcision for individual converts. But conversely they refrained from all form of iconoclasm, and because the majority of them were simply laypeople eager to promote the cause, they were free to integrate in every respect into the community that was to be converted, including by starting families.[106]

The trading companies of the Dutch and English were the only vectors of Protestantism into Southeast Asia. Thanks to their mercantile character, though, Christianization did not form an integral part of their expansionist aims, unlike the Estado da India. Indeed, so as to avoid conflicts that might have compromised its freedom to trade, the British East India Company expressly forbade all missionary activities within its sphere of influence. The Dutch VOC was somewhat less dogmatic in this regard, for although it appointed pastors *(predikanten)* and religious aides *(ziekentrooster)* only for the pastoral care of its own employees, it did leave the pastors a free hand to engage in missionary activities if they felt a calling to do so and so long as these activities did not disrupt the core business of the company. In the final analysis, the VOC regarded itself as the protector of Protestantism within Asia, a role that it consistently adapted to particular local conditions. For example, it imposed a strict ban on all missionary work in Japan, as this would have placed the already marginal and highly precarious position of the VOC settlement in Nagasaki in immediate and mortal danger. By contrast, on Sri Lanka, it felt free to pursue an official policy of missionary work, which met with some success. In Southeast Asia itself, the conditions and strategies for missionary activity were far less clear-cut, so any efforts at Christian conversion seldom had any lasting effect.[107]

Protestant Christian missionary work in Oceania was far more successful. Based on the activities of missionary societies from England, Scotland, Germany, Australia, and the United States, it appeared only in the nineteenth century. The same is true of Christianized people in Southeast Asia, especially in the Malay Archipelago, who remained largely untouched by Islamization but converted to Protestantism only during the colonial period. These groups included the Batak in central Sumatra and the Toraja of southern Sulawesi.

Everyday Culture

Various aspects of everyday culture within the region under discussion here (or at least across large parts of it) had the effect of forming bonds between communities. Indigenous plants, cultivation techniques, and domestic animals spread throughout the region, creating a common cultural currency. Bananas, for example, are typical food crops both for Southeast Asia and for the Pacific islands. The Polynesians had them on their boats during long-distance voyages and took them to the far eastern extremities of the region. Rice was and remains the most important food crop in both continental and maritime Southeast Asia. Wet-rice cultivation began in what is now Vietnam and spread from there not only to China but to the whole of Southeast Asia. The fast ripening variety called Champa rice, combined with new irrigation techniques, made it possible to harvest two crops in a year. Rice developed from being not merely the most important staple foodstuff of the region into a commodity; in addition, in many places it assumed a central cultic and cultural role. In many countries of Southeast Asia, "eating" is synonymous with "eating rice." If you inquire about a person's well-being in Thailand, for instance, you ask whether he has had some rice. "Bon appétit" in Vietnamese can be translated as "Enjoy the rice." However, as one travels from west to east, from Southeast Asia to Oceania, the consumption of rice decreases, with roots and tubers forming the key constituent of people's daily nutrition.[108]

In contrast, the black domestic pig is just as prevalent in the villages of Southeast Asia as it is in New Guinea or on Tahiti. Until the arrival of Europeans, this animal supplied the bulk of people's intake of meat and protein. At the same time, it also functioned as an indicator of wealth. Consequently, it did not form part of everyday cooking but was reserved for special occasions. Pigs were slaughtered as part of particular rites or when a house was to be dedicated or, alternatively, to give thanks for a good harvest or celebrate the birth of a child or a wedding.[109]

As regards stimulants, Southeast Asia and Oceania can be subdivided into two main areas—one in which chewing betel nuts is widespread and another characterized by the drinking of kava. Both customs have not only a general everyday cultural significance but also a ritual one. The consumption of betel nuts has a stimulating and mildly hallucinogenic or intoxicating effect. The so-called betel morsel has three constituent elements: the nut of the Areca palm, wrapped in a betel palm and dusted with ground limestone chalk. Betel chewing is widespread in the area between Indonesia and western Melanesia. Kava, which has a relaxing effect, is obtained from the root of the plant of the same name, a member of the pepper family, and plays a key cultural role in many significant occasions in the area east of the betel zone, particularly in Fiji, Samoa, or Tonga. The root is either chewed or pounded, mixed with water in a wooden dish, and filtered through a bast-fiber sieve. The resulting drink is served in coconut shells. The kava ceremony connects the participants with their ancestors or in some cases even makes them into ancestors themselves.[110]

Given the enormous significance of water and waterways, both Southeast Asia and Oceania are steeped in legends, metaphors, and symbolism relating to boats and their part in history and the present. For Polynesians, memories remained very much alive of the intrepid early seafarers and the mythical "great boat" in which their ancestors once set off on their epic voyage. In many Austronesian languages, the words for boat, house, and group are semantically related. For instance, in the Tagalog-speaking areas of the Philippines, *barangay* means both "boat" and "village community." Likewise, in some linguistic idioms, *kabang, bangka,* or *banwa* signifies "boat," whereas in others it denotes a social group, and in still others a house. Houses were frequently constructed as boats and had a keel, a mast, or a rudder. The kinds of houses customary among the Toba-Batak, with their curved gable ends, were designed to be reminiscent of the boats in which this people, according to tradition, came to Sumatra from the north of Siam. Boat symbolism accompanied initiation rites or the transition from life to death. Similarly, some decorative elements can be traced back to the basic form of boats. This was true of the widespread half-moon-like motif, whose ends either curve up or are bent downward. In the same way, the elongated triangle shape that forms a key element of whole-body tattoos on Samoa is intended to depict a boat. Political control was often encapsulated in the analogy of a flotilla and its crew. For example, on the South Moluccas, the wider society and the village community alike were construed as a boat's crew.[111] And to this day, the Maori of New Zealand are organized into groupings that reflect their descent from particular boats' crews, while the captains who once navigated across the Pacific from Tahiti to the North and South Islands are regarded as their ancestor chiefs.[112]

Education and Scholarship

The development of education and scholarship arose from the tension between the conflicting poles of religion and politics. As a rule, religious elites were the agencies of the various educational systems that were closely associated with spiritually oriented centers of academic learning. Patrons encountered these institutions first and foremost at rulers' courts, so that the influence of power politics and subsequent manipulation always remained a possibility. The relationship of education and scholarship to the realm of commerce focused above all on the paths by which knowledge was disseminated, which drew on existing trade networks.

In all religious contexts, with the exception of Christianity, transferences of learning from India played a decisive role. Hindu Brahmins and Buddhist monks alike brought not only ideas to Southeast Asia but, most important, texts as the basis of educational systems. These included canonical religious writings as well as reference books and compendia of knowledge. Buddhist countries in particular adopted numerous texts from India such as the Pali Canon and the Sanskrit epics (the Ramayana and the Mahabharata) and integrated them into their own system of learning. The vectors of this sort of transference exerted great influence on the rulers who had summoned them and their elites. In this way, courts themselves became seats of scholarship. In countries like Siam, for example, courtly poets were responsible for creating the entire literary canon. This kind of Buddhist center also existed in maritime Southeast Asia before the advent of Islam. The most important center, which was able to generate some measure of legacy after its demise, was located in the capital of the kingdom of Srivijaya on Sumatra. Accordingly, it is no accident that the development and spread of knowledge did not remain confined to palaces and monasteries but that popularization and dissemination by traveling merchants is also in evidence.

Transfer of knowledge in this way also placed a premium on translation. The strongholds of this activity were also the intellectual centers of the Buddhist kingdoms. In the main, they were monasteries, which were both centers of scholarship and religious training institutions. All of the greatest poets in Burma were educated in monasteries, while in Siam monasteries formed the basis of school education.

Islamic scholarship developed in close concert with Mecca, once more transmitted in large part via Muslim India. Many European commentators refer to travelers coming to Southeast Asia from Islam's holiest city in the Hejaz. This was especially the case in the newly Islamized Aceh, which earned the reputation of being the "verandah of Mecca." In the Malay Archipelago, Quranic schools (madrasas) became the institutional core of an educational system that otherwise was mainly geared to teaching by parents. These schools were heavily skewed along gender lines, with far more boys than girls receiving a school education. The religious education of adults also played an important role, especially during the phase of direct Islamization. As a result of this process, the main ports, which were the bridgeheads of Islamization, also became religious centers.

Fledgling Islamic scholarship in Southeast Asia was dominated by the mystical allure of Sufism. Scholars arriving there imported these ideas and concepts from Arabia and Persia but also from India. In the process, medieval doctrines from the West also gained a new lease of life. These were brought to Southeast Asia by the countless teachers who had studied in Mecca. In the eighteenth century, thanks to ever more intensive transport connections to the Arabian Peninsula, the orientation toward Mecca increased still further, and with it the influence of the changing concept of religious education from the heartlands of Islam. New translations and editions of classic texts were disseminated, prompting a reappraisal of religious texts and something of a renunciation of mysticism, the central role of teachers, and the veneration of holy men.

The renaissance of Confucianism during the seventeenth and eighteenth centuries in Vietnam can be attributed to state influence. There, it was primarily the courts and their bureaucratic elites, who had been schooled following the Chinese model, who were responsible for importing this learning and placing the rigid Confucian written canon once more in the center of scholarship.

To the extent that a colonial education system existed during the period under discussion, it too had a predominantly religious flavor, being organized through mission schools. The Spanish missionaries on the Philippines created a network of schools whose curricula were designed primarily to convert the indigenous population to Catholicism. In organizational terms, the missionaries modeled their schools on the Spanish education system. Above and beyond the school system, though, the Catholic Church was also able to assert its long-lasting intellectual hegemony over the Philippines, not least thanks to its monopoly on the printed word. The University of Santo Tomás, which was founded in Manila in 1619 with three faculties, was the first European-style institution of higher learning in Asia, and when Filipinos came under American colonial rule (from 1898 on), they were keen to emphasize their long tradition of academic education.

By contrast, the educational ventures of the trading companies were strictly in-house enterprises. The children of British East India Company and VOC employees received an elementary education; any civilizing mission aimed at educating the wider community was alien to these purely mercantile institutions.

One exception to this general rule was Sri Lanka, where the missionary efforts of the VOC also involved establishing a number of schools, including a pastors' seminary.

Language and Writing

Language and writing constituted another unifying cultural feature of the region, for a large proportion of the languages spoken in Southeast Asia and the Pacific island world belong to the Austronesian linguistic family. This covers a region extending from Madagascar in the west to Easter Island in the east and makes for many linguistic similarities. At present, it embraces more than a thousand individual languages and two hundred million speakers. The individual tongues are in many cases extremely different but nevertheless so broadly related that several recognizably similar words can be found in widely separated parts of the Austronesian world. Austronesian languages are spoken throughout the whole of Oceania, with the exception of Australia and large parts of New Guinea.[113] However, Austronesian tongues do occur on the north and east coast of New Guinea. The remainder of the island is dominated by Papuan languages, which are also spoken in the east of Indonesia, for example, on Timor and Halmahera. New Guinea is one of the most language-rich areas of the world, with over 700 different linguistic idioms.[114] A third language group in the region is Australian. In the early eighteenth century, before the arrival of Europeans, the "fifth continent" was home to over 250 different languages and 700 different dialects.[115]

Apart from the Papuan languages, then, the whole of maritime Southeast Asia falls within the realm of Austronesian languages. Even so, linguistic landscapes can be extremely varied. For instance, the Philippines are home to more than a hundred separate languages.[116] Conversely, the mainland part of Southeast Asia is far more linguistically heterogeneous. This region is home to Austronesian languages such as Cham, which is widely spoken in Vietnam and Cambodia. However, the predominant language families there are the Sino-Tibetan, Tai-Kadai, Austro-Asiatic, and Miao-Yao languages. Sino-Tibetan languages include Burmese and Karen (and also Mandarin Chinese); they are also spoken in the north of Siam, Laos, and Vietnam. Thai and Laotian are the leading examples of the Tai-Kadai family, which also has some speakers in Burma and Vietnam. The Miao-Yao family basically comprises these two languages. Austro-Asiatic languages occur primarily in Cambodia, Laos, and Vietnam but are also found in Burma and mainland Malaysia. Vietnamese and Khmer are the most significant members of this group.[117]

In situations of linguistic heterogeneity, lingua francas tend to evolve. In mainland Southeast Asia, these tended to be the languages of the politically dominant powers, namely, Burmese, Thai, Khmer, and Vietnamese. In maritime Southeast Asia, Malay achieved supraregional status. It was originally spoken by people living in the south of Siam, along the Strait of Malacca, and on the coast of Borneo. The significance of the Strait of Malacca, as an economic artery not just of the region but also as the vital link between South Asia and the Far East meant that merchants spread Malay far beyond its original home. The modern national languages of Indonesia and Malaysia have their roots in old Malay, though they derive not from the colloquial language used by traders but rather from the elevated-register Malay that was the norm at the court of the sultan of Johore-Riau.

The intensive external contacts of the region led to the import of other languages. Contacts to the Indian subcontinent not only resulted in the adoption of Buddhism and Hinduism but also brought Sanskrit. Likewise, the Chinese language played a key role in Confucian-oriented Vietnam. Muslim traders and preachers brought Arabic to Southeast Asia, where it began to be employed both in commercial life and in religious affairs.

Until the arrival of Europeans, only orally transmitted forms of language were known in the Pacific region, except for Easter Island.[118] Nevertheless, there were sign-based mnemonic systems. For example, Polynesian tattoos were far more than mere bodily decoration. Their patterns signified the origin and social status of the people sporting them. Lines, circles, or dots had a precise meaning. Maoris signed the treaties that they concluded with the British in the nineteenth century with a portrayal of their facial tattoos. Tattoos were also once widespread in Southeast Asia. However, Confucianism, Islam, and Christianity all frowned upon and discouraged this practice.

Rock paintings or petroglyphs by Australian Aboriginal peoples can also be understood as a succession of signs preserving information in graphic form. Rooted in ritual and ceremonial activities, they could be interpreted only by initiates. They gave an insight into mythical stories and the connections of the individual Aboriginal ethnicities to the land and landscape and were also memory aids recalling the migrations of ancestors and cult heroes. Spirals and lines on *tjurunga* stones perform a similar function.[119] While the initiated were able to divine the order of the world from these signs, the symbolism remained unintelligible to outsiders.

In contrast to Oceania, the transference of other cultures to Southeast Asia also brought the spread of writing. Indian influences were especially productive in this regard. Phonographic writing systems were developed for Burmese, Khmer, Mon, Thai, Lao, Cham, Javanese, Balinese, and Sundanese, and these can ultimately be traced back to writing systems from the subcontinent, particularly the *Brahmi* script. Malay could formerly be written with this type of letters, too. The easternmost point reached by Indian-inspired scripts was the Philippines.[120] The most widespread form there was the *Baybayin* writing system, which was used primarily for Tagalog but also for other languages. Writing systems such as this were not directly imported from India, however, but were passed down within the region. Thus, the Thai script derived from a model from Angkor, while Baybayin reached the Philippines via Borneo or Sulawesi. The use of Chinese characters brought about a cultural Sinicization of parts of continental Southeast Asia. Particularly in Vietnam, Chinese script was the most widespread form until far beyond the period under discussion here.

Muslim traders brought Arabic script to Southeast Asia. After the arrival of Islam there, this script was used to spread the tenets of this new religion. From the sixteenth century on, textbooks were written in the Malay language. Although scripts of Indian origin already existed, the Arabian script seemed more suited to conveying Islamic concepts and ideas. Arabic was adapted to accommodate the phonetic peculiarities of the Malay language. The result was a unique script known as *jawi*. The countries inhabited by Malays are called *Bilad al-jawa* in Arabic, while the people living there are referred to as *Jawa* or *Jawi*. *Jawi* script was not just used for writing religious texts, though; official chronicles and popular literature were also written in it. Acehnese, Javanese, Sundanese, and Buginese were also committed to paper in the *jawi* script.[121] It spread east to the Philippines, where it was used in the Muslim south primarily in religious or legal documents.[122]

In the maritime areas of Southeast Asia, Portuguese developed alongside Malay as a lingua franca of economic life following the arrival of Europeans in the region. Subsequently, it spread far beyond the isolated bases of the Estado da India. In common with other languages of European colonialism—Spanish, Dutch,

French, and English—Portuguese was responsible for introducing many loan words into local languages. The increasing use of European languages also served to spread the Latin alphabet, which over time became the most important writing system between Sumatra and Easter Island.

Spanish missionaries on the Philippines initially experimented with the Baybayin script but soon came to rely entirely on Latin script.[123] From the seventeenth century on, within the VOC's sphere of influence, Protestant pastors began writing down religious texts such as sermons, catechisms, or Bible translations in the Malay language, using the Latin alphabet.[124] There were also some attempts by Dutch pastors to write down Malay in Arabic script, but these did not catch on in the long term.

In Oceania, New Zealand, and Australia, on the Philippines, and in Indonesia and Malaysia, the spread of the Latin alphabet was the result of the cultural hegemony that existed during the colonial period. By contrast, Vietnam undertook a largely voluntary change to its writing system. Until the thirteenth century, the only widespread form within the country was Chinese, a logographic writing system. An independent script known as *Chu Nom* was developed, and Catholic missionaries finally worked out, on the basis of the Latin alphabet, a phonographic system of writing involving many diacritical marks. This became the official Vietnamese script known as *Quoc Ngu* in 1945.

3. *Mainland and Maritime Southeast Asia*

THE HISTORY of the creation of empires in mainland Southeast Asia was conditioned by a series of different factors. Not least of these was the cultural and political dynamism within the region itself, which eagerly took up external influences, especially of Indian and Chinese provenance, adapted them, and "indigenized" them.[125] In the west and center of mainland Southeast Asia, it was initially Hindu and then above all Buddhist stimuli that helped lend these empires a religious–cultural foundation and establish stable bureaucratic structures. Over time, Buddhism gained supremacy over Hinduism, which nevertheless still left behind certain traces. For instance, the name of the Indian city of Ayodhya—the domain of King Rama, an incarnation of the god Vishnu—is echoed in the Siamese Ayutthaya. Siamese monarchs were also given the soubriquet "Rama," placing them firmly within this Hindu tradition of the legitimizing of power.

One key factor in the rise of empires in mainland Southeast Asia was wet-rice growing, with its attendant irrigation techniques and cultivation methods, as well as the supraregional trade it generated. This formed the economic basis of state building in the region. Cultural transfers became possible, a growing population could be fed, and the blossoming of agriculture in general and of commerce made it easier for taxes to be levied.[126]

Buddhist Kingdoms

In the early years AD, the sole forms of political organization existing in Southeast Asia were small village communities. Some of these developed an expansive dynamism, however. Rising native clans and princes regarded external stimuli, especially from the Indian subcontinent, as offering an opportunity to extend their realm of influence, consolidate it, and give it some measure of intellectual underpinning. Merchants had been responsible for disseminating corresponding information, and Brahmins and Buddhist monks, who came in response to invitations

The kingdoms of mainland Southeast Asia in the middle of the sixteenth century

from ambitious rulers, not only passed on their belief systems but also conveyed political power techniques and modes of political organization from India. They were appointed as kings' advisers and as tutors to princes. In addition, they instigated a series of cultural transfers such as the introduction of writing systems.

Thus, in the second half of the first millennium AD, a series of large polities following this basic pattern arose in the fertile valleys and plains of Southeast Asia. Their chiefs adopted titles from the Sanskrit, styling themselves now as raja. The initial points of orientation derived from Hinduism before Buddhism in its various guises gained a foothold, ultimately establishing itself throughout the region in the form of the Theravada school. Because different nature religions were absorbed into the new faith according to the region, the precise complexion of Theravada Buddhism varied from kingdom to kingdom throughout Southeast Asia. Yet one feature common to all the various forms was their loose structure. The raja exercised direct control only over a core heartland. The fealty of vassal rulers was ensured through a system of tribute payments; these rulers were required to offer military support when necessary. Even so, these subordinate rulers remained rivals with the potential to challenge the raja's supreme authority. O. W. Wolters dubbed this arrangement "Mandala empires"; as in the Buddhist symbol of the mandala, a leading figure in the center was surrounded by concentric circles of lesser princes who were more or less dependent on the main ruler. To work, this system relied heavily on the personalities involved but overall was extremely unstable.[127]

In order to create lasting, resilient, and spatially more extended structures, it was therefore necessary to establish three key elements: a centralized bureaucracy, more efficient access to income from agriculture and trade, and a religion focused on the head of state. Moves in this direction first became evident in the Cambodian kingdom of Angkor in the ninth century and then a century later in the Burmese kingdom of Pagan. Their rulers claimed to be gods and pointed up their divine status with the aid of monumental sacred architecture. Buddhist monasteries and temples, which formerly had been located principally at sacred sites such as mountain slopes or peaks, were now erected in or very near the centers of political power. A network of religious institutions was thus superimposed on the kingdoms, with the capital and hence the king as its epicenter. Even though the populace suffered from the burdens imposed on it by the construction of these massive temple complexes, in overall terms of political control, a centripetal force had effectively supplanted the centrifugal mechanisms of earlier, inherently more unstable petty principalities.

Nevertheless, rulers only partially succeeded in giving the large empires that they acquired and expanded through conquest a stable internal structure. The control exercised by the central bureaucracy over the peripheries was only superficial. Subjugated rulers remained potential rivals. Time and again, even members of the ruling dynasty, who were entrusted with the control of far-flung provinces, made bids to gain power in their own right.

In clear contrast to this highly unstable actuality is the image of these kingdoms that various ancient sources sought to convey, a view that was for a long time taken at face value by historians. Potentates styled themselves in inscriptions as supreme kings, as maharajas, even as world rulers presiding over well-ordered empires. China regarded Southeast Asia as part of its sphere of influence and so in its annals depicted delegations from the Buddhist kingdoms of the region as tribute-bearing missions from large, powerful countries. Likewise, past research has frequently been guilty of turning simple raiding expeditions into full-blown annexations and transforming loosely independent entities into hierarchically structured systems of provinces and districts.[128]

These internal weaknesses were compounded by external challenges, which plunged both Angkor and Pagan into existential crisis at the end of the thirteenth century. The Mongols (Yuan) established themselves as the new ruling dynasty in China and sought to transform ritual tribute arrangements into direct control. Shan, Thai, and Lao peoples emigrated into Southeast Asia from the neighboring Chinese provinces of Yunnan and Guangxi. The result was fundamental political change and an ending of the old systems.

Yet the new rulers did maintain the existing Indian-influenced culture that they encountered in their new domains. They made strenuous efforts to continue with the centralization of power structures, to organize the military into more effective fighting units, to collect taxes more efficiently, and to improve the main communication routes. However, they did not succeed in settling the matter of their own succession and ensuring a conflict-free transition of power. Repeatedly, the internecine rivalry of pretenders to the throne seriously weakened these kingdoms. Another constant factor in the history of mainland Southeast Asia was the ongoing feuding with neighboring kingdoms. In the period being examined here, Lieberman distinguishes several booms and declines that occurred more or less in parallel across the various regions of mainland Southeast Asia. In the fourteenth century, a general crisis was followed by a phase of expansion by the leading mainland kingdoms, which ended only in the second half of the sixteenth century. Reforms in the seventeenth century led to an overarching consolidation throughout the region, until destabilizing developments once more appeared on the horizon around 1750.[129]

Pagan in present-day Burma fell in 1287 to an attack by the Mongols. At that time, the city covered some 25 square kilometers and contained more than 2,500 Buddhist monasteries, stupas, temples, and other religious edifices.[130] While it continued to exist as a political center, the surrounding country now split into a northern and southern part. In Upper Burma in the mid-fourteenth century, a new empire established itself, with its capital first at Toungoo and later at Ava. This new state immediately had to deal with local potentates bent on achieving autonomy, armed border clashes with Lower Burma, and attacks by Shan peoples from the frontier regions with Yunnan, Siam, and Laos. In 1527, Ava was captured by an alliance of Shan forces. The Burmese elite fled the city and once again made Toungoo the center of the northern territory.

Lower Burma was ruled by the Mon, from their capital at Pegu. The Mon had to fight Siam and to withstand long-running conflicts with the north. In 1539, troops from Toungoo overran Pegu. King Tabinshweti and his son Bayinnaung not only unified the country but also expanded it significantly. At the end of the sixteenth century, Burmese troops invaded Yunnan and conquered the Laotian city of Vientiane as well as Ayutthaya, so extending the borders of the kingdom as far as central Siam. The kings of Lower Burma resided partly in Pegu and partly in Ava.

After a brief phase of weakness, Kings Anaukpetlun and Thalun introduced far-reaching reforms, which over the course of the seventeenth century brought internal consolidation and renewed external expansion. Ava became the sole capital. These kings also fundamentally reorganized the justice system by codifying legal norms in written form and assembling a corpus of case law. A form of land register summarized real estate ownership in the kingdom, while a census made it simpler to organize labor and to collect taxes. A program of building religious monuments and importing relics of Buddha from Sri Lanka was designed to provide religious and intellectual corroboration of central state power. From the second half of the seventeenth century, however, Burma suffered a series of invasions from China. The conquest of Ava by rebels from Lower Burma in 1752 spelled the end of the Toungoo dynasty. Yet a new ruling house was quickly able to establish itself and founded Rangoon as its capital in 1755. The reinvigorated Burmese state began to pursue an expansionist policy once more. In 1767, Burma attacked Ayutthaya and destroyed the city. However, it never succeeded in occupying Siam long term.

The great empire of Angkor in Cambodia, which had existed from the ninth century, was at the height of its power in the twelfth and thirteenth centuries.[131] It dominated large parts of continental Southeast Asia and maintained cultural contacts with the Javanese Sailendra dynasty, which was responsible for the building of the temple at Borobudur. Excavations and the sheer size of the remaining structures at Angkor have led archaeologists to estimate that the capital once had over half a million inhabitants. Sufficient rice to feed a population of this size was produced with the aid of an extensive and technically advanced irrigation system.[132]

The country was spanned by a hierarchically structured network of temples. At their head stood the imperial temples in the capital, which were led by members of the royal family. All temples in the provinces were subordinate to these. A well-organized road system allowed good communication, with frequent hostels to accommodate both officials and pilgrims. This centralized religious and administrative structure made it easier for the country's rulers to control their realm and to gather tributes and other payments. The kings of Angkor were deified. For example, Jayavarman VII immortalized his own features by having them carved into a massive statue of the Buddha Avalokiteshvara on one of the towers at the temple at Angkor around 1200, so that they looked down on observers from all four sides. This temple also contained symbols of the deities of the country's various provinces, as a sign of their integration and subjugation to the central authority. In return, Jayavarman VII dispatched to all parts of the country statues depicting himself in the guise of a Buddha. For a long time the kings of the Khmer adhered to the Brahmin rites, even though Theravada Buddhism had by this stage gained a firm foothold among the general populace. Yet even before the end of the period that is being treated here, the royal household had switched its allegiance to this school of Buddhism.[133]

In the late thirteenth century, Mongol attacks on Angkor fatally weakened the state. Neighboring kingdoms quickly exploited the situation. Mainly as a result of Siamese raids and conquests, Cambodia also lost large parts of its sovereign territory and shrank to around its present size. By 1432, Siamese troops had occupied Angkor. The king and the ruling elite fled. Phnom Penh became the new capital. Khmer power was further eroded by the southern expansion of Vietnam between the fifteenth and eighteenth centuries.

In 1283, ethnic Thai people,[134] who had been emigrating from the eighth century from Yunnan into mainland Southeast Asia, founded the kingdoms of Lan Na and Sukhotai in the north of Siam.[135] Sukhotai had originally been a provincial city in the kingdom of Angkor, but it subsequently asserted its independence and profited from the techniques of governance developed by the Khmer. Sukhotai exploited not only the waning influence of Angkor but also the decline in importance of Pagan to build up its own position. Nevertheless, it was rivaled by other Thai kingdoms. The pressure exerted by the Mongols had temporarily brought about a measure of unity among these polities, but any rapprochement was at an end by the beginning of the fourteenth century.

The more southerly kingdom of Ayutthaya evolved into the new principal power in Siam. It not only consolidated its position on agricultural resources but was also able, thanks to its proximity to the sea, to tap into long-distance trade.[136] In 1438, Ayutthaya successfully conquered Sukhotai and became the political and cultural center of the country. Its army and navy helped it extend its sphere of influence, as it besieged Lan Na, overran Angkor, and established itself on the western side of the Kra Isthmus. This conquest enabled it to conduct trade more easily in the Bay of Bengal and maintain contacts with Sri Lanka, as well as giving it ready access to the tin mined there, an important raw material for weaponry.

Culturally, Ayutthaya took its cue from the Khmer Empire. Its courtly rituals and architecture and especially the concept of a divine monarch were all inherited from the Khmer. As in the other kingdoms of mainland Southeast Asia, the kings of Siam founded their power on personal bonds of tribute payment and loyalty. Although at first, the governance of provinces was entrusted only to relatives, later rulers centralized the country's administration and created a bureaucracy that was divided into a military and a civil domain. Both administrative sectors were headed by a minister and were organized internally into different areas of responsibility both subject related and regional. The kings often appointed to ministerial posts foreigners—Chinese, Persians, and even Europeans—who had no power base within the country. The king was at the head of a hierarchically structured society; not only did he fulfill the role of the highest judge in the land, nominally the entire country was his personal possession, but he also controlled all foreign

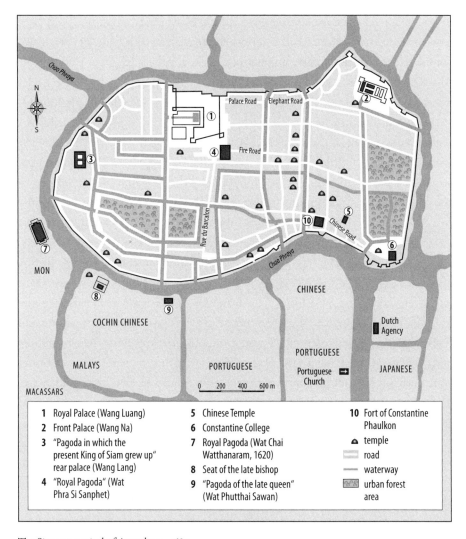

The Siamese capital of Ayutthaya, 1687

trade. In order to ensure that the population was supplied with food and water, the authorities controlled a network of grain stores and took responsibility for maintaining irrigation systems. To do this, it regularly drafted able-bodied men; this workforce was under the control of a specially appointed authority.

Repeated outbreaks of conflict with Burma run like a red thread through the political history of Siam. In 1567, the country suffered a sound defeat by its neighbor, although it quickly recovered from this setback. However, two hundred years later, in 1767, Ayutthaya succumbed to another Burmese assault. The city itself was completely razed, and a new capital arose in the nearby settlement of Bangkok. The country rapidly regained its former prowess. At the end of the period under discussion here, in 1781, Siam grew to its greatest extent yet under King Rama I.

From the fourteenth century on, the most important kingdom to occupy the region now covered by the state of Laos was Lan Xang, the so-called Land of the Million Elephants. Prince Fa Ngum, who had grown up in Angkor and in consequence was a highly cultured person, founded the kingdom in 1353. As part of the Angkor, Therevada Buddhism also spread throughout Lan Xang. In the early fifteenth century, the kingdom gave its support to Vietnam in its struggle against the Chinese. But after changing sides, Lan Xang became the target of attacks by the Vietnamese, and the capital Luang Prabang came under foreign rule. Burma also invaded Lan Xang and in 1574 overran the country's second most important city, Vientiane.[137] Around 1600, Laos managed to free itself from this stranglehold. Its kings during the seventeenth century—Voravongsa, Suriyavamsa, and Soulingavonga—fostered political and economic relations with their neighbors and cemented these ties with marriages. In this way, they created their own buffer zone between Vietnam, Siam, and Burma. The result was a cultural golden age. The country's economic wealth was founded on gold and ivory, shellac (obtained from the lac beetle), and musk. But after the death of Soulingavonga, Laos fragmented into three smaller rival kingdoms: Luang Prabang in the north, Vientiane in the center, and Champassak in the south. These three states were able to maintain their independence as a buffer between the major kingdoms in mainland Southeast Asia.[138]

Vietnam

Vietnam fulfilled the same role for the east of continental Southeast Asia as the Buddhist kingdoms of Pagan, Angkor, and Ayutthaya did for the center, south, and west of the region, respectively. At the start of the period being treated here, the country occupied only the far north of the area covered by the modern Vietnamese state. Factors that played a decisive role in shaping the history of Vietnam include strong cultural influence from China, frequent attempts by this powerful northern neighbor to dominate the country politically as well, counterreactions continually aiming at independence and reaching that goal, and finally a southern expansion that came to a halt really only in the seventeenth century, when it reached the Mekong Delta.[139]

From around 100 BC, Vietnam was under Chinese rule for more than a thousand years, before finally gaining its independence in the tenth century AD. Three hundred years later, the Mongols also advanced as far as the eastern borders of Vietnam, but the country was able to beat off their attacks. During the Ming dynasty, China made one last attempt to conquer Vietnam but failed once again. In spite of these repeated bouts of conflict, though, Chinese influences continued to set the tone in the cultural life of Vietnam. The political leadership followed Chinese models, with Confucian ideas acting as paradigms, while civil servants were recruited on the model of the examination system that the powerful neighbor to the north had developed in accordance with this philosophy. Chinese script also entered Vietnamese life, along with Buddhism, which unlike in the rest of Southeast Asia was not of the Theravada school but which rather took on a highly Sinicized form as a result of Confucian and Taoist elements. Yet in terms of social life, Chinese influences manifested themselves more or less strongly. Above all, it was the upper echelons of society that adhered to Confucian teachings and practices. Moreover, although Chinese culture was adopted on a wide scale, it was adapted to fit local conditions and indigenized. Thus, veneration of local deities continued to be a feature of Chinese-influenced Buddhism in the country, while some Indian influences can also be identified within the religion. As the Vietnamese spread south from their heartland in the north, they took their modified form of Chinese culture with them.

One sign of the urge for cultural autonomy and for distancing Vietnam from China are the various writing systems that were adopted and developed within the country. Homegrown script was introduced alongside Chinese characters, and Christian missionaries instigated a switch to the Latin alphabet, a change that nationalistically minded Vietnamese eventually ensured became the predominant form.

In 1427, Le Loi defeated an invading Ming force and founded the Le dynasty, which at least nominally held sway over Vietnam until the final years of the eighteenth century. Victories in the clashes with China strengthened the country politically. Vietnam also enjoyed economic success at this time, and a new sense of dynamism prompted the country to expand southward. The first enemy encountered during this phase of southward expansion was the Champa kingdom, which had been in existence since the third century. Its populace were distinct from the Vietnamese not only in their culture and religion but also in terms of their ethnicity and language. For one thing, the Champa kingdom had a pronounced Indian character, and for another Islam had taken root there early on. The Vietnamese overran Champa in 1471, despite the fact that Champa had tried to persuade China to join it as an ally, even going so far as to send tribute delegations to the Ming court. Mongol attacks in the late thirteenth century probably weakened Champa to such an extent that the kingdom was unable to withstand pressure from the Vietnamese. The Cham were assimilated and incorporated into the Vietnamese Empire.

Yet this by no means spelled the end of the Vietnamese push toward the south. In 1479 both Laos and northern Siam were attacked. Thereafter, though, internal conflicts put a stop to any further campaigns of conquest, for politically Vietnam was an extremely heterogeneous entity. Its different regions and local rulers found themselves in a state of almost constant conflict. While the House of Le continued, officially, to exercise supreme authority, actual control over the country became the subject of intense rivalry between two powerful family clans: the Trinh, whose power base lay in the north, and the Nguyen, who were preeminent farther south. The Nguyen turned the port city of Hoi An into an important nodal point in international trade, thereby continuing a development that had begun in Champa some time before. The proximity of the north to China led to an even stronger Sinicization of that region. Hanoi became its capital in 1593. By contrast, in the south, Chinese influences were far more subject to indigenization, plus traditions from Champa tended to live on here. In 1659, the Nguyen invaded the Cambodian heartland and annexed parts of the Khmer Empire. They also extended their influence farther south, to the eastern Mekong Delta. After 1630, when contacts with Japan were broken off, which were of huge significance to the port of Hoi An, and when in addition its harbor began to silt up, the Nguyen moved their capital to Hue in 1687 and established Danang as the new entrepôt for long-distance trade. During this same period, the Nguyen also formally disengaged themselves from the sovereignty of the Le dynasty. The Le managed to prevail in the north against internal revolts and also withstood assaults by China in the eighteenth century but was ultimately incapable of challenging an attack launched from the south by the Nguyen, supported by the French. In 1802, a unified Vietnam was proclaimed as an empire with its seat at Hue.[140]

Peoples of Limited "Statehood" in Mainland Southeast Asia

On the periphery of the Buddhist kingdoms and Vietnam were peoples who either led a semi-nomadic existence as hunter-gatherers in the rainforest zones or engaged in sedentary subsistence farming in the form of slash-and-burn agriculture but who in each case lived far beyond the control of the nearest metropolis and its ruling elite. Their world was the remote mountainous region of the deep interior. Geographical conditions made theirs an extremely isolated existence and gave rise to significant linguistic and cultural differences. Even so, it is possible to identify certain common features—a fact that has led Willem van Schendel to coin an umbrella term for the region they inhabited: *Zomia,* a term that denotes "highland" in several Tibeto-Burmese languages.[141] In the south, Zomia begins in the mountains separating Siam and Burma; covers the north of Cambodia, the east of Vietnam, and large tracts of Burma and Laos; and extends farther in the direction of India and China. Many of these people of limited "statehood" therefore were, and in some cases still are, at home on either side of formal state borders and even straddle the frontiers that delimit continental Southeast Asia. Accordingly, right up to the present day, the Karen, Akha, Hmong, and the Yao live not just in Burma, Siam, Laos, and Vietnam but also in the adjacent parts of China from which they once emigrated. Likewise, the Naga and the Chan live on either side of the Burmese–Indian border.

The cultural, economic, and political developments that took pace along the coasts, as well as on the plains and along the major river valleys, never affected Zomia. The people living there adapted themselves to the natural environment. This did not mean that they were unresponsive to innovations, as New World crops such as maize were readily adopted and grown in their fields. Yet wet-rice cultivation remained confined to the valleys. Similarly, Buddhism and Sanskrit, Confucianism and Chinese characters also never reached Zomia. Social hierarchies were scarcely in evidence, and people largely cleaved to animistic belief systems, venerating a multiplicity of nature deities in the form of animals and plants.

The remoteness of Zomia also made it a place of refuge for those wishing to escape taxes, labor duties, or the other constraints, commitments, and norms that were a common feature of life in the lowland kingdoms.[142] The ethnicities of people inhabiting the upland regions can only partially be traced back to the remains of earlier civilizations that were driven into far-flung and inaccessible regions by the advance of expanding empires. The large measure of freedom and self-determination that characterized these cultures was thoroughly attractive, and it is no coincidence that the mountain regions of Southeast Asia became the seat of resistance movements and remain so to this day. It is a lowland metropolitan viewpoint to regard Zomia as some sort of peripheral zone of barbarianism. Even so, the contrast between the valleys and the mountains, between the upland and lowland cultures, played a key role in the economic, cultural, and political development of Siam, Burma, Cambodia, Laos, and Vietnam. Rigidly structured, centrally administered kingdoms came into being on the plains, while the uplands were the home of migrant montagnards with flat social hierarchies. Between these two distinct natural and cultural realms, there always existed an antagonistic relationship of interdependency, which represented a defining and binding element in the historical development of mainland Southeast Asia.

Diaspora Groups in Mainland Southeast Asia

Another set of people with limited statehood but who, unlike the "primitive peoples" of the highlands, were well established in the political and economic centers of the region were the many diaspora groups, which in the period under consideration here could be traced back mainly to communities of traders. Retaining both their cultural autonomy and their contacts to their homeland, while at the same time being highly adaptable in many regards, members of these communities attained high office in the administration of port cities and royal capitals. In mainland Southeast Asia, these communities comprised mainly Chinese. However, at a certain stage, the Japanese also played a prominent role.

The Chinese did not form a unified group, however. In the overwhelming majority of cases, they came from the provinces of Fujian and Guangdong in southern

China. They did not speak the elevated Mandarin form of Chinese but instead used a variety of local dialects. Moreover, these groups comprised not just Han Chinese but also members of the mountain people known as the Hakka. The heterogeneity of the diaspora communities increased as a result of the respective conditions of the localities in which they settled and varied greatly from region to region. Because, over the course of several centuries, the motivation, composition, and number of immigrants changed, the multiplicity of characteristics defining a diaspora community only continued to grow.

It is not known when Chinese peoples first settled in mainland Southeast Asia. In any event, Buddhist pilgrims were among the first people to arrive in the region. They were followed by merchants selling Chinese products at markets and buying in goods from Southeast Asia and India for export. The natural rhythm of the trade winds but also the fostering of political and commercial contacts meant that many of these merchants regularly lived for extended spells in the largest ports in Southeast Asia. In common with other foreigners, they tended to settle in their own separate quarters in these cities and govern their own affairs.

Merchants did not confine themselves to pursuing their own economic interest but also provided an impetus for local developments in a variety of different ways. For instance, they contributed to the expansion of a whole series of port regions, while their purchases stimulated the local economy. In addition, they brought with them cultural and technical expertise and innovation. The diaspora was in no way affected by the Ming dynasty's embargo on foreign trade activity. Because trade with Southeast Asia was vital for the survival of many individual towns and regions along the southern coast of China, this now illegal activity was simply carried on clandestinely. This operation could work only because many Chinese traders remained in Southeast Asia and maintained their contacts to their former homeland. When the trade embargo was lifted again in 1567, it provided the diaspora community with a new impetus, and the numbers of Chinese going to Southeast Asia and trying their luck there increased. Many indigenous rulers welcomed the Chinese presence not just because of the economic benefits that their mercantile activities brought but also because of their political agenda to prevent the rise of a native merchant class. Because the Chinese had no vested interest within their host society, it could also be advantageous for local rulers to entrust members of this diaspora community with the organization of important economic tasks.

Accordingly, many Chinese became harbormasters, tax farmers, or credit grantors. Often they married native women, and they and their children advanced within local elites. This was equally the case in both Siam and Vietnam.[143]

Over time in many places, Chinese merchants themselves began to produce either the goods that they required for export back to China or those that they could readily sell at markets in local towns and cities. In addition, they planted pepper and sugarcane, obtained precious woods from the rainforests, and opened tin mines. In effect, traders became entrepreneurs. For their plantations and mines, they needed large labor forces, which they recruited in China. Not unlike the system of indentured labor that the British ran in the nineteenth century, this workforce was not required to pay for its crossing but instead entered the service of those who had paid for their journey and defrayed the cost through the unpaid work that they undertook.

When Europeans began settling in the region from the sixteenth century on, this opened up new service opportunities for ethnicities such as the Chinese who were prepared to migrate. In this way, the interests of the colonial powers and Chinese entrepreneurs converged. Production on plantations and in mines intensified, as ever-larger numbers of Chinese flooded into Southeast Asia. These emigrants were no longer enticed to Southeast Asia by the opportunities offered by trade. Particularly from the nineteenth century on, the main drivers of migration out of China became poverty and the ravages of war and revolution. As before, even under Western colonial rule, the Chinese in the cities of Southeast Asian kingdoms lived in their own quarters, the precursors of modern Chinatowns. By and large, the Chinese were left to regulate their own internal affairs. They appointed leading members of their own community to act as their representatives dealing with the local authorities, thereby increasing these individuals' prestige and influence. These individuals undertook important tasks for indigenous rulers and colonial authorities alike, for example, in the realm of fiscal administration.

The cultural differences between the various Chinese groups abroad led to the formation of communities that set themselves apart from one another. They each sought a symbolic connection with the ancestors of their homeland, maintaining the traditions that had once been common there and preserving their local dialect. The same family name also signaled a continuing connection to their region of origin. Yet while, on the one hand, the Chinese abroad distinguished themselves from one another according to the region they came from, on the other they maintained complex networks that extended to even the remotest provinces of their host country and beyond.

Throughout mainland Southeast Asia, irrespective of whether it was Vietnam, Laos, Cambodia, Siam, or Burma, a cultural adaptation to the respective local conditions may be observed among the Chinese diaspora. For a long time, it was exclusively men who came to Southeast Asia. They entered into relationships with local women and, if they stayed for longer periods, accommodated themselves to the prevailing lifestyles and circumstances in their host region. This was true to an even greater extent of the children born of these unions. In Siam, for example, these offspring were known as *lukjin,* or "children born in the country." They were required to pay special taxes and wore distinctive clothes, yet they were also exempt from certain duties such as corvée labor. Over time, they gradually became indigenized, taking Siamese names, speaking the language, confessing Theravada Buddhism, and conforming to the social norms of the land of their mothers.

Japanese merchant diasporas grew up in Hoi An in Vietnam and in the Siamese capital of Ayutthaya. The economic basis of these communities was the trade in woods and resins, silk, and spices in the local markets. Like Europeans, the Japanese paid primarily in silver, which in Southeast Asia commanded far higher prices than at home. As Japan became increasingly centralized in the early seventeenth century, the shogunate sought to bring foreign trade under its control. In 1621, all overseas contacts with Southeast Asia were banned. Any Japanese living there were forbidden to return to Japan. Many of them were Christians and lived in exile communities, which over time were assimilated into the culture of their host societies. In Hoi An, this fundamental change in the nature of the Japanese diaspora was one of the reasons behind the city's decline in importance.

Diaspora communities developed first and foremost in the main cities. This fact gave them a multicultural flavor, as it was often the case that such groups lived cheek by jowl with one another. A classic example of a multicultural society of this kind was the Siamese metropolis of Ayutthaya. In its heyday, it was the political and economic center of the kingdom and played host to a great number of foreign merchant communities. By the mid-seventeenth century, the city had around one hundred thousand inhabitants. Alongside the majority of the Siamese population residing there, there were also people from maritime Southeast Asia, like Macassars, Bugis, and Malays; Europeans from various countries; Armenians; Persians; Indians; and, above all, Japanese and Chinese. In the first half of the seventeenth century, there were around a thousand Japanese and several thousand Chinese living in Ayutthaya. Some kings employed samurai bodyguards, not all of whom proved loyal, however. The Chinese were active in commerce and made Ayutthaya the headquarters from which they created a network of business contacts throughout the Malay Peninsula, Kalimantan, and Java. In addition, they acted as moneylenders to local rulers. The influence they thus acquired smoothed their path into important official posts at court and central administrative roles. One person who pursued an extraordinary career was Taksin or Phraya Tak, who had a Chinese father and a Siamese mother and who was adopted by a local aristocratic family. Embarking on a military career, he successfully expelled the Burmese who had conquered and destroyed Ayutthaya and in 1767 ascended the throne as the king of Siam.

European Influence and the Beginning of Colonialism in Mainland Southeast Asia

Unlike in maritime Southeast Asia, scarcely any lasting European presence established itself on the mainland. The Portuguese and the Spanish and the trading companies of the Dutch,[144] English, and French perceived mainland Southeast Asia primarily as a kind of gap between India and the Malay Archipelago, where their main interests lay. The region was only peripherally bound up with their economic activities, with only isolated factories and settlements being founded, among which Ayutthaya was the most significant. Nevertheless, Europeans were responsible for introducing new weapons technology into the region, and their number included several adventurers who entered service with native rulers as soldiers, artillerymen, cannon foundrymen, or military instructors. This development had major implications for internal rivalries within the region. Some of these enigmatic figures even rose to high positions, such as Constantine Phaulkon, a high counselor to the king of Siam in the late seventeenth century,[145] or, a few centuries previously, the Portuguese Felipe de Brito, who founded a small empire of his own in southern Burma. Yet both these men's careers ended tragically. In addition, the missionaries from various different Catholic orders who gradually started to appear in the main cities of mainland Southeast Asia were important vectors of European influence.

In Burma, the Estado da India set up factories to pursue its commercial ends. And a series of local kingdoms employed Portuguese advisers and mercenaries in order to give themselves an edge in warfare. The VOC was also concerned with establishing a mercantile presence in the region.

Ayutthaya also sought to benefit from European military technology and expertise. By the mid-sixteenth century, over a hundred Portuguese artillerymen were engaged in the defense of the city. Siam also maintained economic contacts with Portugal. Because its relations with the Muslim sultanates were strained, the two nations may well have made common cause to give themselves a strategic advantage. Later the VOC showed an interest in installing its representatives in the Siamese-controlled ports along the Kra Isthmus. However, since 1613, their most important trade settlement had been at Ayutthaya.[146] The British East India Company followed the Dutch example and also set up an agency there. The French followed suit in 1656. While also pursuing economic interests, in 1664 the French made Ayutthaya into the center of their missionary work in Southeast Asia, as well as becoming involved and gaining considerable influence in the political life of the region. The French were used by the Siamese as a counterbalance to the Chinese, who had risen to positions of great influence within the court. Constantine Phaulkon, who originally came from Greece, attained an especially exalted post at the Siamese court: as the *phraklang* (minister of the treasury and finance), he was responsible for maintaining contact with foreign emissaries. Phaulkon used this position to forge a close relationship between Siam and France. A formal treaty was drafted to give the agreement a formal legal basis. But after it emerged that this agreement granted France a whole raft of special privileges, a revolt broke out and Phaulkon was executed.

Yet Siam was far from merely being the object of European power politics. For its part, it derived great capital from the presence of Europeans. We have already mentioned the adoption of European military technology, but the interest in Europe and Europeans went beyond just this aspect. Siamese envoys traveled not only to Japan, China, India, and Persia but also to France and the Netherlands. But as in Japan, the conviction steadily grew among Siam's rulers that too close a contact with Europeans brought more risks than opportunities.[147]

European missionaries were active in Siam, Burma, and especially Vietnam. Portuguese merchants or mercenaries in the service of local rulers were the first people to open the way for evangelization. However, their efforts met with little success. Because these missionaries did not have the kind of backup that would have been available from a secular Western presence, they largely confined themselves to strategies of accommodation, by attempting to carve themselves out an accepted role within native societies, steeping themselves in indigenous culture, and trying to search out points of contact for their work in local traditions—all to the end of anchoring the Christian faith in the native way of life. The most striking example of this modus operandi in mainland Southeast Asia is Vietnam.

The first missionaries arrived in Vietnam from Malacca and the Philippines as early as the sixteenth century. In the early 1600s, Jesuits—some of whom had been expelled from Japan along with people from Christian congregations—made a more concerted effort to evangelize the country. In this, the French Jesuit Alexandre de Rhodes (1591/1593–1660) played a leading role. Rhodes paid heed to local circumstances and made strenuous efforts to spread Catholicism in close liaison with native Christians; he also set about wooing the ruling elites with his mathematical and astronomical knowledge. He tolerated private ancestor altars in Christian houses. Despite all this, though, the Chinese Confucian–oriented ruling echelons of Vietnamese society remained aloof. The Jesuit missionaries enjoyed greater success with the simple peasant population. Political repression, social crises, and a clear sense that the classic religio-philosophical systems of Buddhism, Confucianism, and Daoism were on the wane made these social classes receptive to Christianity's message. The Christian faith seemed not just to hold out to them the promise of spiritual regeneration but also to offer distinct socioeconomic advantages.

In order to operate more independently, Rhodes attempted to disengage Vietnam and the rest of Asia except for the Philippines from the sphere of influence of the existing missionary programs that were under royal patronage. Accordingly, he managed to persuade Pope Innocent X to place the mission in Vietnam under the aegis of the Sacra Congregatio de Propaganda Fide. Apostolic vicars— titular bishops without existing dioceses, who reported directly to Rome—were entrusted with the task of evangelizing on the ground. By and by, these vicariates were set up not just within Vietnam but across large parts of mainland Southeast Asia. These positions were mainly occupied by secular priests who were members of the Société des Missions Étrangères de Paris (MEP), who undertook most of the missionary work.

Unlike the Jesuits, the MEP forbade Vietnamese Christians from erecting ancestor shrines—a decision rescinded only by Pope John XXIII in 1964—but did set up a seminary for the training of native priests from Vietnam and other areas of mainland Southeast Asia. This was founded in 1664 in Ayutthaya but as a result of the unstable political situation there in the late eighteenth century was shifted to several locations before finally ending up in the British territory of Penang in 1807. Native Christians, who translated the Gospel into languages that their compatriots could understand, made Catholicism in Vietnam truly viable, even though Rome prohibited the appointment of Vietnamese bishops. By 1640, it is estimated that there were some 120,000 Christians living in Vietnam. By the end of the century, figures of 200,000 to 300,000 have even been cited.

Right from the outset, Rhodes tried to persuade France to become politically and economically involved in the region. His successors also took the view that their position would be greatly strengthened with French state support behind them and so continued to lobby for colonial intervention. These urgings effectively opened the way for French encroachment on Vietnam, at first informal but later formal. Through intense propagandistic lobbying at home in the form of petitions and memoranda to politicians, missionaries prepared the ideological ground for colonialism, and when France finally engaged in Vietnam, they played an active part as intelligencers, interpreters, and middlemen who could liaise with indigenous groups. Because they could offer lucrative trade contracts as well as access to Western military technology, they encountered few problems in finding native groups who were prepared to cooperate with France and make religious and political concessions. From a French viewpoint, indigenous Christians were its natural allies. As a result, the rest of the populace often regarded them as collaborators who had cut themselves adrift from the traditional political and social order and who were undermining the whole Confucian system of values. The period after 1698 therefore witnessed repeated proscriptions of missionary activity and persecutions of Christians. Of course, such hostility provided only a welcome pretext for further intervention.

This overview of European involvement in mainland Southeast Asia would be incomplete without some mention of indirect influences, too. Though foodstuffs and narcotics from the New World were imported by the Portuguese and Spanish, it was native agents who spread them and integrated them into their way of life. Chili peppers, for example, lent Southeast Asian cuisines the spiciness for which they are now renowned. Tobacco became a popular form of narcotic, while potatoes and maize helped feed a rapidly growing populace. It was also primarily via mainland Southeast Asia that New World plants found their way to China; there, over time, they became important staple crops and also played a fundamental role in opening up the mountainous regions of the country to internal colonization.[148]

Hindu Empires

By the fifteenth century, the Indian legacy on the political map of maritime Southeast Asia was only represented in the form of the Hindu empire of Majapahit. Originally, Indian culture influenced the whole of the Malay Archipelago. From the first centuries AD onward, a number of states with a marked Buddhist or Hindu flavor had arisen up to a line running north–south through the Strait of Macassar. These were not the product of Indian power politics but rather of a maritime transfer of culture, which at root was driven by trading connections. Ultimately, as current research is in the process of revealing, the political initiative for the formation of these polities derived primarily from the regional elites.

The last Buddhist major power in maritime Southeast Asia was Srivijaya, with its center at Sumatra. Though the decline of this state entity began in the thirteenth century, its federal structure formed the premise for future developments. On Sumatra itself, the legacy of Srivijaya manifested itself in the formation of a number of small states—a development that continued until colonialism. Meanwhile, Majapahit on Java inherited the mantle of the foremost regional power; accordingly, Buddhist influences were largely suppressed. In a cultural context, only isolated architectural monuments remained, such as Borobudur on Java and a few integrated ruins on the Hindu island of Bali.

The Hindu kingdom of Majapahit was founded in the late thirteenth century with the expulsion of Srivijaya from Java. Its center lay in the east of Java, in the environs of the later metropolis of Surabaya.[149] The state reached the height of its power as early as the mid-fourteenth century. The reign of King Hayam Wuruk (Rajasanagara, r. 1350–1389) saw an expansion that culminated in Majapahit gaining maritime control over the whole of the Malay Archipelago. The *Nagara-kertagama* of 1365, which celebrates this epoch in the form of a heroic epic poem, includes a list of states that paid tribute to Majapahit, which span the Malay Peninsula, Sumatra, Borneo, Sulawesi, Timor, and the southern Philippines. Majapahit adapted a tribute system based on the Chinese model, with the result that its significance resided not in an extensive territorial rule but rather in a sphere of influence with Majapahit at the pinnacle.

Although the Minangkabau were also regarded by the Javanese rulers as vassals, they were actually the most significant rivals to Majapahit on Sumatra. Their home was in the west of the island, in the most important gold-producing region, but following the demise of Srivijaya, their influence extended to Jambi and to other key ports on the east coast. Despite repeated military interventions, Majapahit was unable to drive the Minangkabau back for any extended period. The rise of the Islamic sultanate of Malacca, which brought the east of Sumatra under its control in the fifteenth century, entailed a loss of political influence for the Minangkabau. Chinese and European sources refer to their polity as a kingdom, but it is more likely that they did not constitute a unified political entity of this kind. The Minangkabau coastal state of Indrapura first appeared in the mid-sixteenth century as a pepper exporter.

The start of the decline of Majapahit set in with the death of Hayam Wuruk, as the state never again attained the internal stability it had enjoyed during his reign. Even so, the decisive factor in its demise was its clash with Islam. The ascent of this religion in the region gave rise to a series of kingdoms to rival Majapahit's dominance. In particular, the founding of the sultanate of Malacca at the beginning of the fifteenth century seriously challenged Majapahit's preeminence at sea. In 1447, King Kertawijaya himself converted to Islam, though this remained an isolated, transient episode. Following his murder in 1452, his successors attempted to push back Islam, a task in which they ultimately failed. Further coups d'état ensued. This internal division undoubtedly hastened the demise of Majapahit, all the more so as the kingdom was rocked by succession disputes in the early years of the fifteenth century. As a rule, 1478 is usually cited as the final year in the history of Majapahit; however, there are indications to suggest that the state continued to exist well into the 1530s, albeit in a partial form only.

After the decline of Majapahit, Bali remained the final bastion of Hindu state-hood and religious observance in maritime Southeast Asia. Even before the de-mise of the Javanese supremacy, however, smaller Hindu kingdoms existed on this island. When members of the ruling Javanese royal house fled here in 1478 and founded the Gelgel dynasty, they were able to rely on a Hindu elite that had al-ready been established by the Majapahit conquest of Bali in 1334. Before long, the new dynasty, which was based in the Klungkung region, was ruling the entire is-land and even for a time developed the potential to become a leading regional power, with hegemony over parts of Lombok, Sumbawa, and eastern Java. In the course of its eastward expansion, the dynasty came into armed conflict with the rising sultanate of Goa-Tallo (Macassar). Yet the dynasty's preeminent position came to an end only really in the mid-seventeenth century as a result of internal disintegration, with Bali splitting into several small kingdoms. Although Klung-kung under the Gelgel dynasty continued to claim suzerainty, by this stage this was at best a notional claim.[150] Together with Klungkung in the east, Mengwi in the south and Buleleng in the north were the most significant petty states. They were involved in numerous armed clashes within their own territory but after aban-doning any expansionist claims scarcely came into conflict with Islam again. The Hindu rajas are known to have had Muslim subjects,[151] while many Balinese, pri-marily immigrants, converted to Islam. The fundamental power structure of the island remained intact even during the early colonial period. However, the ten-dency of the Hindu kingdoms to look inward, as well as the marginal role that Bali had come to play by this stage in regional trade relations, resulted in their general isolation from the dynamic developments that were taking place in the Malay Archipelago. It was only in the early years of the twentieth century that Bali was forcibly integrated into the Dutch colonial empire.

The rise of Islam spelled the end of the predominance of the Hindu kingdoms, which fell into decline despite not being conquered by force of arms. Their internal weakness prevented them from engaging in any sustained rivalry with the new power factor of Islam, especially because this relied not on the traditional struc-tures of dynastic empires but rather on trading connections and city-states. Apart from the special case of Bali, the only aspects of Indian influence that ostensibly remained in the Malay Archipelago were tiny Hindu communities and isolated architectural relics. However, bearing in mind the propensity of Southeast Asian societies to integrate, we should not disregard the continued survival of Hindu elements in a cultural context.

Islamic Sultanates

The period between the fourteenth and eighteenth centuries was an era of major upheaval in maritime Southeast Asia. The epoch was bounded by two fundamental shifts in power structures, namely, Islamization in the first half of the period and the increasing European presence in the second. The spread of Islam, which made its influence felt in all realms, began as early as the end of the thirteenth century. The new religion reached the East primarily along the established trade routes and set in train, by the fourteenth century at the latest, a wave of Islamic empire building.

The comparatively small sultanate of Demak on Java was the first historically attested starting point for the formation of an Islamic polity in the Malay Archipelago. This state originated in an early attempt to assimilate Islam during the Majapahit period. In the power vacuum that ensued after the demise of the last Hindu empire, Demak briefly rose to become the strongest military power on Java. The campaigns that it waged in the west of the island brought about the destruction of the last Indian-influenced regimes. Yet the expansion of Demak was soon checked by the rise of Surabaya and the new leading power on Java, Mataram.

But prior to Javanese Islam establishing a political role for itself, the first significant site in this regard in maritime Southeast Asia was Sumatra. This, the largest island of the archipelago after Borneo, was the true cradle of Islamization in the region. The sultanate of Aceh on the northwestern tip of the island experienced one of the earliest conversions to Islam. A paucity of historical evidence makes it impossible to place a specific date on this event, but we may state with certainty that the region around Aceh, Perlak, and Pasai was Islamized by the 1290s. The region formed the first bridgehead for a gradual process of Islamization that eventually spread as far as the Moluccan Islands. The sultanate of Aceh was an expansionist entity from the outset.[152] Mainly through the use of seaborne operations, it asserted its control over the whole of the northeast coast of Sumatra. The sultanate's development was fostered by its favorable position for trade with India.

However, Aceh's attempts to project its power could not be sustained in the long term without coming into conflict with rival sultanates on the Malay Peninsula. Clashes with Johor on the southern tip of the peninsula lasted until the seventeenth century. Even more intense was the rivalry with Malacca, at least until the beginning of the sixteenth century.

Malacca was founded by Hindu Malays from Jambi and Palembang who had retreated in the face of the victorious armies of Majapahit after the ports in the southeast of Sumatra had unsuccessfully attempted to assert greater independence. Prince Paramesvara (1344–1414), who hailed from Palembang and fled via Temasek (the settlement that later became Singapore), is regarded as Malacca's principal founder. Initially under the protection of the Chinese, Paramesvara built up the fledgling state and in the early years of the fifteenth century converted to Islam, as Iskandar Muda.[153] The city and the surrounding region were also Islamized over the course of the next three decades. Malacca's favorable position in the center of the straits that lie between the Malay Peninsula and Sumatra, the principal route from the South China Sea to the Indian Ocean, along with its excellent harbor and plentiful supply of freshwater enabled it to become even more prosperous than Aceh, a situation reflected not only in its economic development but also in the political and religious sphere.

Economically, Malacca quickly became the hub of pre-European overseas trade. Streams of goods from China, the Moluccas, and India all converged here. Both for practical trade reasons, given the long routes, and from political considerations, following China's isolationist stance from the 1430s onward, merchants' societies of all countries involved in the region established branches in the city. The sultan granted them freedom of trade along with extensive powers of self-governance and profited from the excise duties they paid.[154]

Politically, the immediate territory of the sultanate encompassed the south of the Malay Peninsula as well as the eastern part of central Sumatra, including the regions of Rokan, Siak, Indragiri, and Jambi. Yet as a result of Malacca's economic control over important trade routes, its political influence extended far into the east of the Malay Archipelago. Against this backdrop, many commentators regard the sultanate as a successor of Srivijaya.

Even in religious terms, Malacca was able to outstrip its rival Aceh. In this, too, the influence of the trade routes in disseminating Islam throughout maritime Southeast Asia was decisive. Malacca became a center of Islamic spirituality and scholarship and hence also the point of origin of new missionary movements, which were in turn supported by Malacca's maritime contacts both with Muslim-ruled India under the Mughals and the Islamic heartland.

However, the supraregional significance of Malacca was ultimately to prove the sultanate's undoing, primarily as a result of how it was perceived by the outside world. Malacca was seen by the Portuguese as the sole central node of the spice trade and as the principal power in Southeast Asia. Accordingly, from the very outset, it became the target for expansion by Portugal, which was interested less in integrating itself into the Asiatic system of trade and more in controlling it. In 1511, Afonso de Albuquerque (1453–1515), commanding a fleet of seventeen or eighteen ships and a complement of 1,200 men, overran the city of Malacca after a siege lasting several weeks. This spelled the end of the majority of the merchants' societies within the trading emporium of Malacca. The Portuguese wanted to maintain its position as an emporium (trading center), albeit under their control and with exclusive access to the spice trade. Yet owing to the many alternatives open to seaborne traders in the region, this objective of forming a monopoly could not be realized. In consequence, Malacca never again attained the importance it had enjoyed during the fifteenth century.[155]

Alongside Macassar on Sulawesi, Aceh was the main beneficiary of the Portuguese conquest of Malacca. Independent trade with India was, in the main, diverted to its ports, as the Indian-Muslim body of merchants, who up until then had operated from Malacca, relocated to Aceh. The state even experienced a new political revival under Iskandar Muda (1583–1636).[156] Clashes with the Portuguese followed military conquests on Sumatra, especially in the Deli region, on the Aru Islands, and in Johor. However, an attack by Aceh on Malacca failed, as did a lasting occupation of Johor. Even so, initially the state was highly attractive to the West Europeans who began to appear on the scene at this time, as an alternative to Portuguese-controlled Malacca. But because Iskandar Muda refused to relinquish his monopoly on trade, neither the Dutch VOC nor the British East India Company established any enduring presence in Aceh. Despite this, the sultanate was able to preserve its independence until the late nineteenth century. The increasing dominance of the Dutch prevented Aceh from developing a prominent economic position, though it retained its central religious significance—the port was always an important stopping-off point for Muslims taking part in the hajj to Mecca.

The second beneficiary of the decline of Malacca, then, was the mercantile hub of Macassar on the southwestern peninsula of Sulawesi, the urban center of the dual sultanate of Goa-Tallo. Many Asian merchants who wanted to circumvent Portuguese control diverted to Macassar. As a result, it developed into an entrepôt for the Moluccan spice trade. Its sultans derived a considerable degree of power from political control over this trade; their grip on the region was further tightened by a "top-down" Islamization in the early seventeenth century. Macassar's maritime influence extended as far as Lombok in the southwest and the Moluccas in the northeast. After vying with Bali and Ternate to establish political spheres of influence, Goa-Tallo in southern Sulawesi assumed the leading role in the region, a position that even the larger of the Bugis states, such as Boné, Luwu, and Wajo, could do little to challenge. Nevertheless, this hegemony generated considerable potential for political unrest. At first, though, Macassar profited a second time from the conquest of Malacca in 1641, when the VOC wrested control of the colonial city from the Portuguese. The upshot was that a Portuguese diaspora community now settled in Macassar, further strengthening its position as a trade hub for the next two decades and more.[157] However, this role was at variance with the key interests of the Dutch, whom the sultans were not prepared to yield to. Accordingly, the VOC exploited the potential for internal conflict within Sulawesi, allying with the exiled Bugis prince Arung Palacca from Boné. Between 1666 and 1669, the company and its allies embarked on one of its most concerted campaigns of conquest, which culminated in Macassar becoming a Dutch colonial city, while its immediate hinterland became a Dutch colonial possession.[158] The city remained Muslim and continued to be an important entrepôt for trade—albeit no longer in spices—but under Dutch governance did not have the influence it had wielded when it was an independent state.

Banten (Bantam) on the Sunda Strait Java assumed a very similar role. This Muslim sultanate, which was based on a city-state, exhibited much the same power structures as Macassar.[159] After gaining its independence from Demak under the leadership of Hasanuddin (r. 1552–1570), Banten controlled one of the most important harbors of the region but pursued policies that were favorable to trade. This made Bantam an attractive location for many merchants' societies, including the Chinese and not least the Dutch and the English, who at the beginning of their involvement in Southeast Asian trade called primarily at the ports of Aceh and Bantam and founded their first major trading posts on the archipelago there. Banten controlled the western end of Java and even ventured to launch military attacks against Sumatra on the far side of the strait. By the early seventeenth century, the sultan was able to establish a political zone of influence there. Yet the sultanate of Banten was one of the first to come into conflict with the VOC and one of the first to fall victim to it. With the founding of Batavia by the Dutch, Banten lost its sphere of influence. Nevertheless, after the fall of Macassar, its fortunes revived as it played host to many refugees from that city. It was finally overrun, though, in 1682 and incorporated into the VOC's immediate domain.

Thereafter, the principal Islamic state on Java was Mataram. Its rise had begun at the end of the sixteenth century under the first sultan, Sanapati, who reigned from 1584 to 1601. However, Mataram's most significant ruler, not least because of his expansionist ambitions, was Sultan Agung (r. 1613–1646). During his reign, he brought a large portion of Java under his control, with only the far west—with the sultanate of Banten and the VOC's sphere of influence—remaining independent. Mataram had a federal structure; only the heartland around the capital Karta was ruled directly by the sultan's court. There the sultan held complete sway over the territory, which he assigned to members of his retinue to govern. Farther away from the political center, local princes ruled as vassals of the court. The more distant they were, the more they took on the aspect of allies rather than subjects. Under Agung's successors, resistance grew to centralized control. The princes' desire for greater independence might have threatened the continued existence of Mataram as a unified empire were it not for the intervention of the VOC on the side of the court, a move designed to forestall the rise of new, potentially uncontrollable centers of power. In return, the company was granted new trading rights and an expansion of its immediate sphere of influence to Cirebon. From the other side, the rise of Madura weakened the peripheral possessions of Mataram. Furthermore, internal turmoil was now rife within the state. Two wars of succession, in 1706 and 1719–1723, respectively, as well as violent upheavals in the wake of the "massacres of the Chinese" in 1740 rocked the kingdom and paved the way for further intervention by the Dutch.[160] The Treaty of Giyanti (1755) finally divided the state into two spheres of interest, ruled respectively from Jogjakarta and

Surakarta. The VOC retained control of the northeastern coastal strip with such key ports as Semarang, Japara, Gresik, and Rembang. The weakened and fragmented Mataram itself was now finally under the company's indirect control. Over the following century, the region along with the conquered ports of the Malay Archipelago came to form the nucleus of all subsequent Dutch colonialism.

These ports included the smaller emporia that lay on the northeastern coast of Java. The Islamization of eastern Java, including the cities located there, is partly shrouded in mystery and myth. According to some commentators, "holy men" *(wali songo)* were responsible for spreading the faith,[161] and Islamization to some extent went hand in hand with the expansionist policies of Demak between 1527 and 1546. As sultanates, these city-states were rather weak, with the result that they were absorbed into Mataram's sphere of influence in the seventeenth century and in the eighteenth ultimately fell into Dutch hands. However, they were able to retain at least a regional significance as trade ports.

A more significant political role within their region was played by the Moluccan sultanates of Ternate and Tidore, which had been Islamized as early as the 1460s from Malacca.[162] Prior to the rise of Macassar, it is likely that Ternate was able to extend its influence as far as Sulawesi; subsequently, the rivalry with Macassar for preeminence on the eastern Malay Archipelago shaped the political map of the region. Closer to home, there was a constant rivalry between Ternate and Tidore, with Ternate being focused more on the West, while Tidore looked predominantly to the East. The significance of these tiny states on their small volcanic islands resided in their position as the exclusive area for cultivation of cloves. The sultans controlled the market in this spice as a royal monopoly, which they were ultimately forced to loosen their grip on in the face of the overwhelming military threat posed by the VOC.[163]

In the political fabric of the Malay Archipelago, the Islamized states of Borneo played a somewhat peripheral role. The most significant of them—namely, Brunei in the northwest, Sukadana in the southwest, Banjarmasin in the south, and Berau in the east—all converted to Islam in the course of the sixteenth century. In the main, they were ports offering facilities for the export of products from the Borneo hinterland that could be traded overseas lucratively. Thus, Sukadana exported forest goods and diamonds, while Banjarmasin developed into a regionally important entrepôt for the trade in pepper. In theory, they were all tribute states of Javanese powers, but in practice the real power of Banten and Mataram on Borneo was only marginal. After the demise of Malacca, the sultanate of Brunei expanded and rose to become a regional power on the west coast of the island. During the following century, the Sulu sultanate became another small regional power, evidently with the acquiescence of Brunei. Founded by Muslims as early as the fifteenth century and situated in the inaccessible island world between Borneo and the Philippines, the Sulu sultanate was for a long time ignored by the outside world. Because this maritime region had little to offer in the way of export goods, the dynasty that was based on the island of Jolo played a major role primarily in the Southeast Asian slave trade during the eighteenth century.[164] While Europeans regarded Sulu first and foremost as a haven for piracy, its political influence made itself felt as far afield as Sulawesi, Borneo, and the southern Philippines.

The existence of Islamic states in the southern Philippines can be traced to the activities of Muslim missionaries from Ternate. Especially in the sixteenth century, Islam spread across the island of Mindanao. Maguindanao, as the largest Muslim state on the island, proved sufficiently strong to prevent the Spanish from completely overrunning Mindanao. It achieved this both by means of a jihad, proclaimed in the 1650s, and through diplomatic skill and the surrender of peripheral islands to the colonial power at the start of the eighteenth century. Moreover, before the arrival of the Spanish, a Muslim family related to the sultans of Brunei also briefly ruled over the Manila region.

The predominant Muslim sultanates that held sway over much of the region when Europeans first arrived there represented a completely new form of state, which was at root little more than a city-state—albeit a highly prosperous one—but which also established a system of alliances and spheres of influence. A whole series of such polities, such as Malacca, Aceh, and (after 1511) Johor in the west, Demak, Banten, and increasingly Mataram on Java in the east, or Maguindanao and the Sulu sultanate in the north jostled for power, though it proved impossible for any central power structure to assert itself in maritime Southeast Asia after the decline of Majapahit. All these successor states held sway over very small territories; indeed, in the case of many of the city-states, there was scarcely any territory at all to speak of. In addition, the power of these states resided only in extensive systems of alliances and vassalage arrangements. A decisive factor in each new "empire" projecting its own power was the extent to which it developed economic networks. Most sultanates were important hubs for supraregional trade. While Malacca, Macassar, and Banten fell into European hands by very dint of this position, Aceh, Brunei, and Sulu were able to continue to perform this role for a long time as independent powers.

Western Bases and Colonies in Maritime Southeast Asia

The second phase in the shift in power structures was ushered in by the new presence of Europeans in the region. This development began very early in a low-key way and became increasingly dynamic over the course of the seventeenth and eighteenth centuries. Island Southeast Asia was the main focus of European activities in the early modern period, conditioned above all by the demand for spices. The Portuguese were the first Europeans to reach Southeast Asia, in the early sixteenth century. They were looking for cash crops but also brought a new religion with them—Christianity, the last major religion to gain a foothold in the region. In 1511, the Portuguese seized Malacca and shortly thereafter reached the Moluccas. Six years later, they dispatched the first trade mission to China. In 1521, Ferdinand Magellan's voyage across the Pacific (in the service of the Spanish crown) heralded Spain's attempt to gain access to the Spice Islands through the "back door" and open trade with China. Once a return route had been plotted across the Pacific to Acapulco, in 1565 the Spanish began to organize a long-term occupation of the islands they called the "Philippines." The presence of Europeans had a formative influence on the development of the region in two key aspects. On the one hand, the network of Portuguese bases and subsequently the far more effective trade system put in place by the Dutch East India Company, like the diaspora structures, had the effect of binding the region together. On the other hand, the Philippines, which as the sole long-term Spanish possession in the region represented a special case of European dominance, became the scene of progressive colonial penetration and territorial rule. In this regard, it fitted into the development of regional imperial structures. The same is true of the gradual spread of colonial nuclei of the British and Dutch East India companies (Java, the Moluccas, and the Malay Peninsula), though this became truly significant only in the nineteenth century, when it ushered in a completely new epoch of empire building in maritime Southeast Asia.

On the Moluccas, the Spanish met the Portuguese as the only competing power during the initial phase of European expansion. A series of armed clashes did not result in either side gaining clear dominance over the northern Moluccas. Rather, the position of both the Spanish, who retained a settlement on Tidore until 1664, and the Portuguese, who in 1575 were forced by fierce resistance from local elites to abandon the fort they had founded on Ternate in 1522, was extremely precarious. Somewhat more stable was the Portuguese foothold on Ambon, where they were granted permission to establish a factory on the coast of Hittu in 1525. In 1545, they also founded the first Jesuit mission there. By contrast, on Banda the Portuguese were unable to establish any lasting presence. Even so, they did manage to negotiate favorable trading terms with the local sultans, which palpably helped stimulate local nutmeg cultivation to meet the increased export demand. Yet the Estado da India was far from reaching its objective of achieving a monopoly over the trade in cloves and nutmeg.

The trading hub of Malacca remained the center of the Portuguese commerce in spices. After the arrival of Vasco da Gama in India in 1498, the Portuguese were able in short order to secure a number of bridgeheads on the subcontinent through force of arms, which gave them access to Indian textile and spice markets. However, access to the spices of the Moluccas via Malacca was neither cost-effective nor exclusive. The only way to make it pay was to gain control of the city, whose port conducted almost the entire trade in Moluccan spices. Soon after their seizure of Malacca in 1511, the Portuguese constructed a large fortress complex to consolidate their control of the city, port, and the sea-lanes, in addition to building a new city center for Portuguese settlers. Muslim merchants were forced to leave the city; Hindu traders filled their places and developed into the most important local mercantile diaspora. In an attempt to revive and expand trade, large sections of the precolonial administration were absorbed into the Portuguese bureaucracy, and all private traders were brought under its jurisdiction.[165]

As a result of its sparse presence, however—in maritime Southeast Asia only in Malacca and on Timor, Ternate, Tidore, and Ambon—the Estado da India was in no position to control the seaborne trade in spices, despite its ambition to do so. In order to at least secure control of those sea-lanes that in the very broadest sense passed by or near to its possessions in Asia, the Portuguese established the cartaz system of naval trade licenses, a formal method of granting merchant ships protection in return for payment. All independent traders were required to obtain a pass issued by the Estado da India, granting them the right to sail the route in question. Under threat of armed assault, ships were obliged to call at Portuguese-controlled ports and submit to having their passes and cargoes checked. The cartazes represented a totally new phenomenon in Asia, both as a system of comprehensive supervision by a single state and as a system of protection.[166] The takings from excise duties and the issuing of cartazes became an important source of revenue for the Estado da India, soon outstripping all the income generated by actual trade. Meanwhile, trade had begun to focus in the export of pepper, with the result that the Moluccan spice trade was increasingly marginalized within the total trade portfolio of the Estado da India.

The economic and political demise of the Estado da India was no sudden collapse but rather proceeded, despite the continuing existence of the core entity, as a creeping transition to a loose confederacy of Portuguese expatriates, who increasingly pursued their own commercial interests.[167] In addition, the reduced means of the mercantile elites, who from 1570 onward increasingly wrested control of the Estado from the Portuguese nobility, together with their lack of political interest, further impaired its market dominance. Yet a decisive factor in the terminal decline of the Portuguese era in Southeast Asia was the appearance of a new competitor, the Dutch East India Company (VOC), founded in 1602. As a joint-stock company, the VOC was able to bring considerable financial resources and a measure of flexibility to bear on the competitive struggle for control of the spice markets, which the structurally weakened Estado da India could do little to counter. No sooner had the first Dutch ships of the so-called predecessor companies appeared in 1595 than the Portuguese were obliged to abandon their hold on the Moluccas. In 1605, their most important base of Ambon fell into the hands of VOC troops. The culmination of this development came with the conquest of Malacca by the VOC and its allies from Johor in 1641. This overwhelming European competition, which also included the British East India Company (EIC), based on the Indian subcontinent, ultimately forced the Portuguese to retreat to their last bastions of Goa, Macau, and East Timor, which they retained into the age of colonialism.

A pepper and spice market on the island of Banda, mid-seventeenth century. Pepper and other spices had been important commercial commodities in Southeast Asia long before the arrival of Europeans in the region and had been traded at independent markets in their regions of origin. It was at such places that European merchants made their first trading contacts. At the same time, in their reports they provided a picture of Asian commercial activity, such as in this illustration from 1646, which shows a market on Banda, where various produce from the surrounding Moluccas is on offer alongside the indigenous nutmeg. (From *Gewürze: Acht kulturhistorische Porträts,* by Elisabeth Vaupel, Deutsches Museum, Munich, 2002.)

As well as driving the Portuguese from the Malay Archipelago, the VOC also managed at an early stage to prevail against its British rivals. For one thing, in the first decades of the British–Dutch struggle for supremacy, the VOC proved to be far better equipped both financially and in terms of its ships. Moreover, the Dutch were not afraid to take drastic measures to seize control of places that were crucial to their overall strategy. In their conflict with the EIC, the so-called Amboina Massacre was the decisive turning point; in this incident, in 1623, a Dutch military contingent murdered all the occupants of a small British trading post on Ambon Island. Exaggeration of this incident for propaganda purposes in Great Britain could not prevent the EIC from subsequently being driven out of the Malaysian island region and forced to make do with a few small peripheral bases with no real political or economic significance, the largest of which was Bengkulu on Sumatra. Only with the decline of the VOC in the late eighteenth century was Britain able to return temporarily to the archipelago and even establish lasting colonial rule on the Malay Peninsula.

View of Fort Rembang, circa 1770. From 1762 until his death, the Danish artist Johannes Rach (1720–1783) lived in Batavia, where he was employed by the Dutch. He created numerous topographical drawings during his time on Java. This ink drawing, which dates from around 1770, shows the Dutch fort at the eastern Javanese port of Rembang. Native ships lie at anchor off the fortress, alongside two vessels flying the Dutch flag. The presence of a "Pencalang," a boat of Malaysian origin, at the bottom right of the picture indicates that even the VOC resorted to using Asian ship types for regional sea transport. (From *Johannes Rach, 1720–1783: Artist in Indonesia and Asia,* by Johannes Rach, Perpustaken Nasional [Indonesia], and Rijksmuseum [Netherlands], Jakarta: National Library of Indonesia, 2001.)

Nor did the VOC take any less strict an approach to its Asian rivals. Trade treaties that secured the VOC a buyer's monopoly were wrested from the sultans of Ternate and Tidore under threat of military intervention. In order to gain exclusive access to the rare commodity of nutmeg, Governor-General Jan Pieterszoon Coen seized the Banda Islands in 1621 with a band of mercenaries, had the indigenous elites executed, and sold a sizable part of the population into slavery. Henceforth, nutmeg production was conducted by Dutch settlers and their slaves. In addition, the VOC managed to market nutmeg products from the Banda Islands in Europe as the only genuine ones.[168] The company also conquered all major ports whose activities in the spice trade they deemed as threatening their own position: Malacca in 1641, Macassar in 1667, and Banten in 1682. Out of the major trading centers, only Aceh was able to retain its independence, though it did sacrifice some of its economic centrality.

Overall, however, the Dutch success in maritime Southeast Asia did not rest solely on the use of military force. The conquests of the seventeenth century were costly campaigns, which moreover could be won only with the aid of regional allies. As such, for a commercially based organization, these were practicable only in exceptional circumstances. The secret of the VOC's success lay, rather, in a considered and flexible strategy that weighed all options and costs in the balance and chimed in remarkably well with the complex web of existing political and economic structures in Southeast Asia.[169] Employing this approach, the VOC developed a system of trading posts, trade and protection treaties, and military and political alliances (which, if the need arose, could be backed up with military action, such as the destruction of "illegal" plantations or the pursuit of alleged "smugglers"). Over time, all these various strategies enabled the VOC to become the most significant economic power in maritime Southeast Asia, yet with none of the huge outlay and investment of a territorial colonial power.

Dutch colonial cities arose on the site of the cities that were conquered. Though these cities had lost their role in the free spice trade, they still remained thriving harbors and retained all the characteristics of Southeast Asian urban life in their internal configuration. The most important of these VOC cities—also, in marked contrast to the rest, the most visually striking—was Batavia on Java. Newly founded by Coen in 1619 on the ruins of the conquered city of Jayakatra, Batavia was expanded by the company into the center of its Asiatic trading empire. This empire stretched from Batavia not only to Japan but also westward to the Indian subcontinent and the Arabian Peninsula. Batavia, too, was home to a variety of ethnic groups and diaspora communities. Yet in contrast to elsewhere, the most remarkable features of Batavia were the leading economic position of the Chinese, a situation consciously encouraged by the Dutch, and the mixed-race culture that developed from relations between Dutch men and Asian women. Over time, the descendants of such unions developed into the most important stratum of colonial society.[170]

Dutch power in Southeast Asia was initially concentrated on cities such as this, together with a few islands in the Moluccas. Over the course of the eighteenth century, the VOC realigned its sphere of influence on Java by bringing most of the principalities that existed in the northeast of the island under its indirect jurisdiction. The company's efforts to achieve this were greatly aided by the internal weakness of the main indigenous power on Java, Mataram, and the conflicts that erupted after the revolt of the Chinese in 1740, when native rulers attempted to expand their own domain. Through a clever combination of alliances with the most dynamic of the warring factions and targeted military campaigns of its own, the VOC was able to bring Java, as far as possible, under Dutch control by the mid-eighteenth century. In general, it was the case that European influence in maritime Southeast Asia, whose significance cannot be overstated, consisted first and foremost of a European agency arriving in the region and starting to dominate certain very specific but important aspects of its economic life from within.

The aims of the Spanish on the Philippines were to engage in the lucrative spice trade, exploit sources of precious metals, and create for themselves a springboard to the Far East and Southeast Asia, where they identified huge untapped potential for trade and missionary activity. In 1521, while searching for a western passage to the Spice Islands, Ferdinand Magellan had also set foot on one of the islands that was later to form part of the Philippines and claimed it for Spain. However, he was killed when, in an attempt to win allies, he tried in vain to demonstrate the superiority of European weaponry in a local dispute. In the wake of Magellan's voyage, Spanish seafarers explored large tracts of the Pacific during the later sixteenth and seventeenth centuries. Their hopes of finding gold, spices, territory, or religious fulfillment in an earthly paradise did not come to fruition, partly as a result of not immediately finding a return route across the Pacific to the Americas. Only after the Augustine monk Andrés de Urdaneta succeeded, in 1565, in charting an eastward course that ran far to the north across the Pacific to Mexico could the Philippines be developed into the western outpost of Spain's Latin American empire. By 1543, the archipelago was named for the Spanish crown prince, who was later to become King Philip II.

The isolated and scattered villages on the Philippines could offer little resistance to Spain's far superior military forces. Thus, unlike in the Americas, the Spanish largely refrained from using military force in their conquest of the islands. The most important pillar of their power soon became the missionary activity undertaken by religious orders, who in many parts of the country remained the sole representatives of the colonial administration, which made Manila the country's capital in 1571. For the first time in its history, the archipelago was forged, albeit still in a very rudimentary fashion, into a single political unit.[171] Following the model of *Las Indias,* the Spanish Americas, a governor-general headed the administration. The country was divided into provinces.

After an initial orientation phase, in which dreams of spice trading and precious metal deposit evaporated and farming proved distinctly unappealing, the economic interests of the few secular Spaniards who came to the Philippines came to focus on the lucrative transpacific trade. This consisted primarily of exchanging American silver for luxury goods from the East—especially silk—which was brought from the Far Eastern mainland by Chinese merchants.[172] For 250 years, galleons regularly plied the route between Acapulco and Manila, linking Asia with the Americas. In administrative terms, the Philippines were part of the viceroyalty of New Spain (Mexico). Together with their colonial empire in Las Indias and isolated bases on the Carolinas and Marianas, the Spanish embraced the Pacific region so comprehensively that they felt justified in regarding it as their exclusive sphere of interest, which they were entitled to defend against other powers. In effect, the Pacific became a "Spanish lake."

The Chinese soon became indispensable not only in foreign trade but in internal commerce also. Although the indigenous peoples, or "Indios" as the Spanish called them, by analogy with Spanish colonies in the Americas, supported Spanish power with tribute payments, forced labor, and the supply of raw materials and food, their living conditions did not, at least at first, change in any structurally fundamental way as compared with the precolonial period. The traditional social hierarchy also remained substantially intact, as datus and the nobility were subsumed into the lowest echelons of the colonial administration. The farther away from the capital and the few other centers of Spanish activity one got, the weaker the political and cultural influence of the colonial power became, with some parts of the country remaining beyond the control of the central authority in Manila until well into the twentieth century.

Prior to the arrival of the Spanish, the capital was a small homogeneous settlement of no more than two thousand inhabitants. By 1620, however, there were already more than 40,000 people living in Manila. They came from the most diverse ethnic backgrounds. Alongside 2,400 Spanish, there were 3,000 Japanese,

16,000 Chinese, and 20,000 Filipinos. Whenever galleons were being loaded or unloaded, the population of the city increased further, with an influx of hundreds of traders from dozens of countries.[173]

It was only from the mid-eighteenth century on that the Philippines tapped into the global market in an intensive way,[174] as the worldwide demand grew for agricultural raw materials such as sugar, tobacco, Manila hemp, and coconut oil. The galleon trade declined in significance. Over time, the islands were opened to free trade. Land increased in value and more and more new, hitherto unexplored areas were reclaimed for farming, while the internal transport network was expanded and regional commercial centers were created. Yet the Spanish derived minimum benefit from this economic upturn. The international marketing of products from the Philippines was controlled by foreign—especially British—trading concerns. The Chinese acted as middlemen, while mixed-race Chinese-Filipinos, known within the Philippines as "mestizos," developed into the most important landowning class.[175]

As the internal frontier was pushed back, so the culture of the Christian lowland Filipinos spread to more and more areas of the archipelago. As a consequence, the ethnic groups of the mountain regions, where Spanish culture had barely penetrated, and the Muslim population of the south found themselves increasingly forced on the defensive. In order to convert Filipinos to Christianity and at the same time bring them under the umbrella of the colonial state, missionaries were charged with the task of persuading a scattered indigenous population to uproot themselves and move to closed settlement, the so-called *reducciones*. Even while this process was going on, the missionaries began to evangelize among native peoples and redoubled their efforts once the new settlements were in place. From the late sixteenth to the late nineteenth century, the process of founding "reductions" continued unabated, at ever-greater distances from the Christianized centers on Luzon and the Visayas. A half century after colonization of the Philippines had begun, the majority of the population was already Catholic, while missionary activity was effectively complete in the Spanish-controlled areas by 1700.

Members of religious orders deployed a wide gamut of different strategies and techniques in their evangelizing.[176] These ranged from leading exemplary frugal lives through enticement and gentle pressure to blackmail, intimidation, and physical violence—for example, in the desecration and burning of precolonial idols.

If indigenous priests and priestesses refused to submit voluntarily to the new religion, they were forcibly converted and reeducated. However, the power of new religious concepts to win over new converts—coming in the wake of a change in political power—should not be overlooked. Partly by chance and partly planned, Spanish traditions of missionary activity and the experiences gained in converting indigenous peoples in South America fell on extremely fertile ground in the Philippines, with the native peoples more receptive to the lavish, colorful ceremonial and the emotive impact of the Catholic faith. Indeed, a special form of Catholicism developed as a result. The characteristic capacity of Southeast Asian peoples to absorb elements of alien cultures into the framework of their own traditions was also applied to Christianity, giving it over time a distinctly indigenous flavor on the Philippines. Established traditions of faith were endowed with new Christian content, and long-hallowed forms of religious observance were maintained in a new guise.

Diaspora Groups and Maritime Networks

Significant areas of society in maritime Southeast Asia operated outside the higher power structures and state-building processes. In particular, the diaspora communities, as alternative societies, played a major role in shaping the image of the entire region. The sort of mass migration, primarily of manpower, that would have formed the basis of a sizable diaspora, did not exist before the nineteenth century. Even so, the commercial world of maritime Southeast Asia was—to an even greater extent than the mainland—characterized by a diaspora of different groups of merchants, whose influence was felt even in the processes of empire building, because they settled precisely in the new centers of power, where they played a key role as middlemen for European traders.

The largest diaspora group in maritime Southeast Asia was the Chinese. Its members came from the south of the country, mainly from the provinces of Fujian and Guangdong, and included some Hakka people. Commercial links from these provinces to the whole of maritime Southeast Asia had existed since the earliest times. On the main westward route, Malacca was the most important port of call for trade with India, through Indian diaspora merchants who lived and worked there. On the principal eastward route, from early on the Chinese were

A Chinese merchant on Java. The German artist Caspar Schmalkalden (1616–1673) from Thuringia traveled to Asia as a soldier of the VOC between 1646 and 1652. The handwritten report he produced of his journey, which contains historical, geographical, and natural historical descriptions of the countries he visited, also includes several illustrations, such as portraits of the various different ethnicities he encountered. In Batavia, these were largely Chinese, who as traders and artisans dominated the economic life of the VOC's metropolis on Java. Schmalkalden's sketch shows a prosperous merchant, who traded in silks and porcelain. (From *Die wundersamen Reisen des Caspar Schmalkalden nach West- und Ostindien 1642–1652*, edited by Wolfgang Joost, Weinheim: Acta Humaniora des Verlags Chemie, 1983.)

present on the Moluccas, where they were by far the largest buyers of cloves and nutmeg prior to the arrival of Europeans.[177] However, their trading activities were always contingent on the foreign affairs policy of the Chinese central government at any particular period. When, after a brief phase of state-sponsored expansion in seaborne trade in the early fifteenth century, the Ming dynasty retrenched and banned foreign commerce once more, settling in key ports across Southeast Asia became for Chinese merchants no longer simply a matter of fostering business relationships. Many of them decided to settle abroad permanently, simply in order to stay in business. They proved adept at assimilating themselves into local communities. They often adopted the Islamic religion of their host country, married into local elites, and attained important positions in the state apparatus. However, they did manage to retain their autonomy—usually with the support of those in power—and so developed a totally independent culture (peranakan).

In Banten, for example, the Chinese created their own quarter, which was clearly separated from the political–religious center of the city with its Friday mosque and sultan's palace and which effectively acted as a central regional market. The fact that this quarter was developed on a site chosen by the Chinese themselves emphasizes the privileged status that they enjoyed in Banten. Members of the Chinese community also acted as political advisers. They shared the influential post of harbormaster *(syahbandar)* in regular rotation with Indian merchants from the Coromandel Coast.[178] The situation of the Chinese was much the same in independent Malacca, where one of the four harbormaster positions was permanently occupied by a member of the Chinese diaspora community. In Malacca, too, a Chinese quarter was in existence long before the arrival of Europeans.

Chinese merchants or dignitaries who had long gained influence and pursued careers in the local bureaucracy were generally the first people with whom the European East India companies came into contact when they sailed into a foreign port completely unknown to them. In the longer term, too, the European companies often remained dependent on their services as middlemen. This could happen in one of two ways. First, Chinese merchants could offer their services as intermediaries in acquiring goods for EIC or VOC traders that were hard to come by. Second, they frequently performed the role of liaising with indigenous rulers who had monopolized lucrative export markets. Even though the Chinese were initially regarded as unwelcome competition, over time European and Chinese merchants found that their interests often complemented one another or even that there was mutual benefit in cooperating. This was the case not just in ports that were under the absolute control of a local ruler. Cooperation also continued when the Dutch had taken charge of such trading centers and even after they had founded the most important commercial hub in the region, Batavia.

It was not without reason that Sir Stamford Raffles, the later British governor of Batavia, described the headquarters of the VOC as "basically a Chinese colonial town under Dutch protection."[179] Even before the city was founded by Jan Pieterszoon Coen, Chinese traders had settled there; they may even have influenced Coen's decision to change the location of the city, because trade within Asia with groups such as the Chinese merchants' diaspora was an important part of the Dutch strategy to counter the drain on silver resources. The Chinese were present both in the city of Batavia, where they worked in all conceivable trades and services, and in the surrounding region, both as managers and as manpower in the booming sugar plantations. Several of their junks ensured a steady trade between southern China and Batavia.

The active encouragement of the Chinese diaspora by the VOC is clearly evident from the case of Batavia. Within this Dutch mercantile center, the trade with China, which steadily increased in importance thanks to the growing European demand for tea, was conducted primarily through the traders' diaspora community. This community was granted political and legal autonomy in return for a simple poll tax, which was set very high and soon came to account for half of all VOC income in Batavia. In addition, the Chinese were exempted from military service. Beyond the city walls, the VOC licensed Chinese sugar production and guaranteed it a fixed price and volume of sales.

Such policies were not without problems, though. Interculturally, the privileged position of the Chinese met with some reservations from Europeans, while among the Chinese populace itself, the potential for conflict was increased by the uncontrollable influx of new arrivals, especially destitute economic migrants. In addition, when sugar prices collapsed in 1740, the VOC responded by dropping the price paid and the guaranteed sales volume. The ensuing descent of the Chinese rural populace into poverty led to tensions, to which the VOC reacted with deportation plans. The result was a poverty-driven revolt by Chinese peasants, with several thousand coolies marching on Batavia. However, their badly organized and executed attack was successfully repelled on October 8, 1740. Yet this victory did not lift the general cloud of suspicion of collaboration from the Chinese living within the city's walls, despite the fact that most of them had absolutely no contact with their compatriots on the countryside. Europeans carried out spontaneous acts of violence against the Chinese inhabitants. At first, the VOC did nothing to prevent these outrages. Around two-thirds of the Chinese living in the city and its environs were killed during this unrest, which has gone down in history as the "Massacre of the Chinese."

But for all its bloody and sensational nature, the massacre did not bring an end to Chinese involvement in Batavia. The Chinese population was restricted henceforth to a particular quarter and their political influence on the VOC administration noticeably reduced, but even so Chinese economic activity gradually returned to the city. Investment opportunities and the labor market in Batavia still remained highly attractive. In the nineteenth century, the sugar industry experienced a new boom period, far exceeding anything during the VOC era. New branches of industry also came into being, such as textile manufacture, which produced Javanese fabrics using traditional techniques on an industrial scale for the first time, with the result that they came to the attention of a market beyond the immediate region.[180] And because of the absence of any alternative, it was once more Chinese laborers who did all the unskilled work in the docks or on plantations.

Certainly, because of the exceptional position of the Chinese there, Batavia was a special case. But in other regards, it is highly representative: during the period of the VOC, the Chinese diaspora performed similar roles and was accorded similar privileges in many other cities across the Malay Archipelago. In Macassar, for instance, it was primarily rich Chinese who lived in the Dutch-controlled city center.[181] Chinese merchant communities who were intensively engaged in import and export also existed in all the ports of Northeast Java.[182]

Furthermore, the Chinese were not only indispensable partners for the Dutch on the Malay Archipelago; they also performed this function for the Spanish on the Philippines.[183] Chinese–Filipino commercial and cultural contacts stretched back as far as the tenth century. Yet by the time the Spanish settled in Manila, the Chinese colony there was still only small, with just 150 members. The mercantile interests and the daily needs of the Spanish generated a clearly increasing demand for Chinese goods and manpower, however. Even by 1603, there were already twenty thousand Chinese in Manila, as compared with just a thousand Spanish. Despite the central importance of trade, as in Batavia, many of the Chinese immigrants worked in various trades and service industries, while some were engaged in farming. Because the Spanish felt threatened by the economic strength of the Chinese diaspora, though, their rights and freedom of movement were curtailed, and their community was banished to a site outside the city gates. However, those Chinese who had converted to Christianity were permitted to leave this ghetto and work in other parts of the Philippines.

Even so, mistrust and hatred of the Chinese remained rife among the Spanish. They fomented public opinion against the Chinese by casting them as the scapegoats for the Philippines' economic woes. And because the Chinese regarded the Filipinos as culturally inferior barbarians and also frequently exploited them in economic terms, this propaganda fell on fertile ground. The Spanish, in constant fear for their security, monitored and systematically discriminated against the Chinese in commercial life and in general. On several occasions, they refused new immigrants entry and countered rumors of plots and attempts at revolt with bloody pogroms, notably, in 1593, 1603, 1639, 1662, and 1762–1764. For their part, the Chinese tried to hold their ground, hatching conspiracies and staging uprisings, which in turn provoked further Spanish reprisals.

Alongside the Chinese and sundry others who settled in the region before the nineteenth century—Arabs from the Hadramaut, Persians, and Armenians—the most prominent foreign presence in maritime Southeast Asia comprised various groups of Indian merchants. The economically strongest of these were Muslims from Gujarat. Others included the Chulias (another Muslim group) from the Tamil-speaking south of India and Hindu groups referred to variously by Malays and Indonesians as Kelings and Chettiars, depending on their caste. Indian merchants focused primarily on trading in cotton and other textiles. Goods they imported from the subcontinent included tropical hardwoods, tin, rubber, medicinal plants, pepper, and spices. Because onward transport of these commodities was organized mainly by local seafarers and merchants on the Malay Archipelago, the Indian traders all tended to settle around Malacca as the key entrepôt for the east–west sea route. In the city itself, the Gujarati had long constituted the largest merchant diaspora group. After the Portuguese seized control of Malacca, most of the Indians went to Aceh, though some relocated to Johor or Kedah. Because they traded more widely in a diversity of goods—unlike the Europeans, who largely concentrated on the spice trade alone—they rarely came into conflict with this latter group; this enabled them not only to survive alongside Europeans but also to become key partners in the role of intermediaries for the British East India Company in particular.

The seafaring peoples of the Malay Archipelago played an important role in this context. The conditions of long sea voyages and the advantages of networks also saw the growth of communities of such peoples in key trade hubs, although they were not so widely dispersed as the Chinese, Indians, or Armenians. Yet despite the fact that their diaspora experience was less pronounced and the range of their networks narrower, it was precisely they who had an integrative function in the region, even acting as a counterbalance to the processes of empire building. Prior to the arrival of the Portuguese, Malays were prominent in this role, constituting the most important foreign trading power in the region between the Malay Peninsula and the Moluccas. And even during the period of European intervention, they continued to ply their trade in many regional ports, not unlike the Minangkabau on Sumatra.

The Bugis of Sulawesi were probably the most important group of this kind in the whole of the Malay Archipelago. They were experienced sailors and successful maritime traders, who served all the ports in the region. Yet their presence as a diaspora group relied not solely on trading but also on the particular situation in their homeland. The Bugis' conflict with Macassar and their ambivalent attitude to the VOC led to a pronounced split of the region into different factions and repeatedly forced members of the Sulawesi elite into exile. Not all of them were as fortunate to carve out a career from this situation as Arung Singkang (1700–1765) from Wajo, who through marriage and conquest created a new power base on the east coast of Borneo, which he used as a launching pad for several attempts to overthrow the regime in his homeland. In the 1730s, he gained a fearsome reputation as the commander of a pirate fleet.[184] Far more typical was the economic dominance of the Bugis on the Riau Islands, where as well as trading they increasingly came to control mining activities. On this basis, the Bugis diaspora developed into the most powerful indigenous economic force on the western Malay Archipelago. From the 1720s on, they exerted great political influence in the sultanate of Johore-Riau, where a Bugis occupied the second-most important office of state *(Yamtuan Muda)*. Exclusively Bugis settlements arose around Selangor and Kelang on the Malay Peninsula from the late seventeenth century on. At the same time, many settlements founded by the Bugis flourished on the east coast of Borneo, a fact exploited by Arung Singkang. The Macassar people found themselves in a similar situation. Because the conflict lines in Sulawesi cut right across ethnic groups, they found themselves in the same initial predicament as the Bugis, but being less numerous, they were not in a position to bring the same economic power to bear. In the long term, therefore, a common Buginese–Macassarese diaspora arose,[185] perhaps also conditioned by their close similarity between the two groups from a European perspective.

Changes in the Economic Structure

As a result of these political, social, and ethnic developments, the economic structure of the Malay Archipelago was also fundamentally altered. The boom of the "age of commerce" was first and foremost connected with the growing demand for cash crops and the increasing orientation of their production to the world market. The cultivation of such crops was intensified—be it pepper on Sumatra and Borneo, cloves on the Moluccas, or nutmegs on the Banda Islands. The gathering of wild forest crops and produce from the sea—which in contrast to spices were almost entirely destined for the Chinese market—also became more intensive. This increased demand also partly dictated a change in cultivation priorities. For instance, higher prices on the Chinese market ensured that pepper cultivation on Java was scaled down in favor of sugarcane plantations. Likewise, the trees from which gum benzoin aromatic resin was gathered were now no longer confined to the mainland but were increasingly planted in northern Sumatra, too, specifically for export. Finally, there were constant efforts—though vigorously opposed by the VOC—to extend the area where cloves were cultivated.

The growing significance of cash crops led to a hitherto unknown accumulation of capital and concentration of wealth in a few hands, with certain individuals or families amassing a considerable fortune. As regards economic–geographical considerations, the power of the export centers and trading posts increased markedly. Likewise, their growing importing power, noticeable especially in the textile market, formed the basis of their huge significance in maritime Southeast Asia. These commercial centers became prosperous and spread the wealth of the boom phase. From such places, imported Indian textiles reached the farthest corners of the spice-growing islands. At the same time, the trading centers contributed to a further restructuring of the agricultural sector. Being in a position to import all the food they required, their demand stimulated the orientation of agricultural production toward export, particularly in the rice-surplus regions such as Java. Indirectly, this development also prompted farming regions such as the Moluccas to specialize still further in cash crops and hence to become ever more dependent on their trading networks. Entire village communities shifted from subsistence farming to an export economy and from a system of barter to a monetized economy.

Insofar as trading centers did not come under the control of the European expansionist powers, control over these processes of accumulation remained to a large extent in the hands of local rulers. One clear manifestation of this can be seen in the fact that most of the sultans in maritime Southeast Asia minted their own coinage and injected mainly gold coins, sometimes with a wide circulation, into the economic process. The golden *mas,* for instance, was widespread throughout the Malay Archipelago; in many places, its value was initially set at the same level as the Spanish peso *(Real de a ocho),* though as trade contacts with Europeans grew, its value generally collapsed, sinking to a half or in extreme cases even a quarter of its former purchasing power.[186] The reasons for this included a decline in the proportion of precious metal in the mas, failed monetary policies, and increasing European pressure on indigenous markets. Alongside the mas, the only other coin with supraregional currency was the peso. Even in the absence of a central governing authority, the ever-closer interconnectedness of the region helped create what was in effect a rudimentary monetary union. The Dutch were not in a position to impose their own currency on the region and so, despite their monopolistic ambitions, fell in line with this existing situation.

There is no question that the Europeans played a key role in the economic upheavals that affected maritime Southeast Asia. This was even true of the Portuguese, despite the fact that they never managed to gain a dominant position in Asian commerce. Nevertheless, in certain sectors, they still managed to deploy sufficient additional purchasing power to stimulate the dynamic processes of intensification and concentration already noted. Spanish importing of silver and gold on the route from the Americas to Manila further hastened these processes. Above all, however, it was the Dutch who succeeded in diverting certain commodity flows to meet the particular needs of European markets. Yet in all such cases, the sectors in question, the spice trade first and foremost, were of a very manageable scope. But in larger sectors, notably the textile market, attempts to impose controls came to nothing. The indirect influence of Dutch trade policy should not be underestimated in this matter. Thus, their attempt to gain complete control over the trade links to the Moluccas partially undermined the position of the ports in Northeast Java, which were forced to export the rice surpluses generated by their surrounding regions to the Far East.

Yet the greatest and most lasting influence exerted by the East India companies was in the restructuring of the market-oriented agricultural economy. While sugar production on Java, say, still remained mainly in thrall to Chinese demand, increases in rubber production on Sumatra and the Malay Peninsula are primarily attributable to European requirements. This was true to an even greater extent of tobacco, coffee, and (at a later stage) tea; indeed, tea was introduced in the first place into maritime Southeast Asian agriculture only by Europeans.[187] These commodities represented the first decisive steps toward a plantation economy. The true breakthrough in this area came in the nineteenth century, when the Dutch colonial administration instigated a state-organized plantation system.

In organizational terms, the Europeans borrowed from the Southeast Asian model, by placing ports at the center of their own commercial systems in the region. This trend began with Portuguese Malacca and was continued in Dutch Batavia and Spanish Manila, all of which became centers of extensive trade networks embracing other ports. Here, too, the prime mover was the desire of the controlling authorities to acquire a monopoly. Yet this access was exploited not solely in order to create profitable basic conditions but also to divert commodity streams entirely to Europe. In this regard, the emporia (trading ports) can primarily be seen as "closed" entities. But in many other aspects, the ports under European control did continue to be devoted to the free movement of goods. The fundamental model of regulation, protection, and fostering of certain groups remained intact—and with it the basic role of a port under European administration to act as an emporium.

One of the indirect influences of Europeans on regional trade structures was the displacement of Asian trade routes by excessive attempts on the part of European powers to assert their dominance. While the Dutch in particular were indeed able to dominate certain regions, they were hardly ever in a position to impose a complete monopoly. Even in the Moluccan spice trade, new areas of cultivation, new routes, and new entrepôts kept on springing up.[188] The great significance of these "illegal cultivation" and "smuggling" activities for internal trade within Asia may be gauged from the frequency and intensity of the VOC's efforts to combat such activity. Nor did the potential for evasion necessarily focus only on ports and cities. For example, the small rocky island of Bonerate between Sulawesi and Sumbawa became a base frequently used by "smugglers," especially in the trade network of the Bugis.[189] Also, small settlements sprang up to act as new emporia, such as the Buginese-dominated ports on the east coast of Borneo.

Just as the internal structural developments in maritime Southeast Asia were not solely the work of Europeans, neither was the region's integration into the global market. Rather, their particular contribution lay in lending impetus to processes that were already in train before their arrival. The European centers in the region served as hinges joining maritime Southeast Asia to other major economic regions of Asia. Trade connections to China were facilitated by the Chinese diaspora in Java and other Indonesian ports and via the Manila–Macau connection. The Dutch "country trade" was one of the links to the West, the Indian subcontinent, and the Persian–Arabian region that never fell into disuse but that was constantly revitalized by the advent of new products. Via Asia the connections to an increasingly European-dominated global market were faster and more direct, thus meeting an ever-growing demand. Indeed, the real significance of the European influence on maritime Southeast Asia between the sixteenth and eighteenth centuries can be said to reside in this acceleration of globalization.

Peoples of Limited "Statehood" in Maritime Southeast Asia

As on the mainland, there were countless peoples in maritime Southeast Asia who were characterized by the total lack (or relative absence) of state structures, a socioeconomic and political existence on the periphery of the main centers of power, and an adherence to animistic forms of religion. Various gradations of the "peripheral" must, however, be distinguished here. Thus, the Batak on Sumatra or the Toraja on Sulawesi manifest more complex societal structures than, say, the "headhunters" of Borneo, but even so, until their ultimate colonial penetration in the nineteenth century, they continued to operate on the margins of the dynamic new world while not remaining completely untouched by it.

For instance, the sultans and chieftains of the most remote islands in the far northwest or southeast of the Malay Archipelago existed on the border between statehood and "tribal society." However, regions such as the Aru Archipelago, the Kai Islands, and Tanimbar were fully integrated into both the empire-building processes we have touched upon and the networks of seaborne trade. In most cases, they were vassals of larger sultanates, to which they paid tribute. Although the written sources are unclear on this point, there is some evidence to suggest that they also developed into places of origin of regional cash crops, whenever increasing European attempts to impose monopolies caused indigenous farming and trade to take evasive measures and relocate. In this sense, the integration of peripheral locations may in all probability even have increased as the European presence grew.

Even with those ethnicities living in forested or mountainous areas or on highland plateaus in the hinterland of dynamic coastal regions, and who were ostensibly seen as inaccessible and remote from any state structure, their marginal location did not necessarily equate to total isolation. The Orang Asli, for example—a modern umbrella term for various peoples in the interior of the Malay Archipelago—had retreated to the highlands during the Indian waves of settlement in the first millennium AD. Yet they continued to maintain constant contact with the coastal region, exchanging forest products such as hardwoods or resins for Southeast Asian trade goods like textiles and metalwares. The rise of the Muslim sultanates signified not just a growth in the demand for Orang Asli products but also an increased risk of enslavement. For this reason, they withdrew even farther into the interior, to areas largely untouched by the various campaigns of conquest.

The Batak were reputed to live a particularly isolated existence in the interior of Sumatra—a perception that rests largely on the reported experience of Europeans, who first set foot in the land of the "Batta" in 1824. Yet before the age of colonialism, none of the expansionist powers ever succeeded in absorbing the Batak heartland around Lake Toba into their realms. Islam reached most Batak only in the nineteenth century, when it was in direct competition with Protestant missionary efforts. Nevertheless, the Batak forged long-standing trade links with the commercially powerful kingdoms on the coast.[190] This may be a principal reason why some Chinese and European accounts suggest that the Batak were vassals or tribute-paying peoples to a state entity.

The inhabitants of the rainforests of Borneo, who are usually referred to by the Malay umbrella term of "Dayak," were largely inaccessible to most foreign visitors to the island, thanks to the poor transport conditions within the primeval forest. But the forest products and pepper that were exported from Borneo and that, via the major emporia of the region, eventually found their way to China or into the communities of the Chinese diaspora, indicate that even the Dayak were clearly also involved in the trade networks of Southeast Asia. During the eighteenth century, the areas settled by the Dayak were considered tribute-paying regions of Banjarmasin, whose primary source of wealth was the export of the pepper harvested there. The Dayak also came into contact with the "outside world" through their role as pirates.

The Toraja, who lived in the central highlands of southern Sulawesi, had retreated to this more remote area following repeated attempts by Macassar and the Bugis sultanates to conquer them and convert them to Islam. The Toraja regarded Islam as the faith of their traditional enemies, despite the fact that the Bugis considered them to be subjects of the state of Luwu.[191] The political status of the Bajau was also unclear, though highly relevant to regional development; this nomadic people plied the sea routes between Borneo, Sulawesi, and the Philippines. As subjects and warriors of either Macassar or Sulu, they were also involved in the power politics of the region. In addition, as suppliers of marine products, they formed an important part of trade networks, particularly those catering to the Chinese market. This situation did not substantially change under Dutch control, except for the ports in which they sold their wares. Like most peoples of this kind, they were largely invisible to the representatives of the European commercial powers and so do not appear in most of the written records of the period. However, they played a significant part in the processes that lent maritime Southeast Asia its unique aspect—a combination of empire building and seaborne commercial links.

4. Connections to Japan and China

IN the history of the world, interactions between regions play an important role. Because the Far East was of overriding importance to the region under discussion here, this part will treat Southeast Asia's contacts and connections to Japan and China in greater detail. This will include an overview of Japan's maritime trade network in general, because its special relationship to the Southeast Asian region can be explained only through reference to such structures.

Japan's Maritime Contacts with the Outside World

In both cultural and economic terms, Japan was in constant contact with China in the age under discussion here, as well as in the preceding period. China was the origin of the kanji—the characters that the Japanese used to give their language written form. Likewise, the art of calligraphy and drawing with ink were also adopted from China, together with stylistic elements of architecture and garden design. In addition, China was the source of Confucianism, which helped shape Japan's social system and its system of values, and of Buddhism, which was to become the country's most important religion, alongside the native Japanese religion of Shintoism. Zen Buddhism became particularly significant; although this, too, was a Chinese import, in Japan it took on a unique and distinctly Japanese character and played a decisive role in shaping the country's spiritual and cultural life.

Commercial links with China existed at both a central and a regional level. However, because China regulated and restricted trade, merchants often sought illegal ways of doing business, with their activities—at least from an official Chinese perspective—taking on the form of smuggling and piracy.

In the thirteenth century, after the Mongols had not only overrun the Chinese Empire but also occupied the Korean Peninsula, Japan also found itself facing an invasion. From 1268 on, the new "Chinese" (Yuan) ruling dynasty commanded

Japan to submit to its sovereignty. When this submission was not forthcoming, Mongol invasion fleets were sent against Japan in 1274 and 1281. On both occasions, a combination of Japanese defensive action and storms—the famous "divine winds" *(kamikaze)*—drove back the invaders. Even so, these conflicts compromised Japan's cultural and economic links to China only for a limited period. During the reign of the Ming dynasty, who succeeded the Yuan, the Ashikaga shōguns agreed to be subsumed under Chinese dominion within the framework of the tribute system. The recompense that Japanese delegations received when they traveled, laden with gifts, to the Chinese imperial court to pay homage was sufficiently lucrative to justify acceptance of this subservient role. In exchange for raw materials such as gold, copper, and sulfur, plus manufactured goods like swords, fans, sunshades, and lacquer goods, the Japanese returned home with copper coins, raw silk and manufactured silk goods, cotton thread, and porcelain.

This official trade was organized by the shogunate and the main Zen temples. In addition, several individual principalities, notably Daimyate in western Japan, conducted trade with Chinese partners on their own initiative. Piracy also continued during this period, with large flotillas of ships raiding ports on the Chinese coast. These corsairs were by no means only Japanese but comprised a wide mix of nationalities, including Koreans, Chinese, Southeast Asians, and later even Portuguese. China took this as an excuse to ban the Japanese in general from their territorial waters. This was one of the reasons why Japanese–Chinese contacts dwindled in the fifteenth and sixteenth centuries and finally died out altogether. Furthermore, the power of the Ashikaga shogunate also declined in this period, ushering in a phase of constant military clashes between various warlords (daimyo), all vying for supremacy in the country. Fewer and fewer official delegations traveled to the Chinese court. Attempts by the daimyo to establish commercial contacts were shunned by the Chinese as they lacked the sovereign authority the shōgun had and so could play no part in the tribute system.

Korea frequently functioned as a kind of bridge for cultural and economic contacts to Japan. But there were also plenty of commercial links with the Korean Peninsula itself, though many of them took the form of smuggling or piracy. Official communication with Korea was via the island of Tsushima, which on the one hand formed part of Japan but on the other was bound by a kind of tribute system to Korea. Toyotomi Hideyoshi, who in the late sixteenth century managed to almost completely unify Japan once more after the "warring states" period, launched attacks against Korea in 1592 and 1597. Both invasions were thwarted by Korean resistance and Chinese intervention. The Tokugawa shōguns, who finally succeeded in bringing the civil wars in Japan to an end and in imposing central control over the country from Edo (Tokyo), resumed commercial contacts with Korea.

A new group of players appeared off the coast of Japan in the sixteenth century, in the shape of Portuguese navigators. They found themselves welcomed for a number of reasons. For one thing, acting as intermediaries, they were able to conduct the commercial exchanges with China that were so important to Japan. In the fragmented political landscape of Japan, which was characterized by intense rivalry between competing warlords, profits gleaned from trade could immeasurably strengthen an individual's standing. Consequently, Japanese daimyōs were keen to attract Portuguese sailors to their ports. The warlords in the south had a clear geographic advantage in this regard, given that their lands bordered on the South China Sea. In addition, some of them—for example, Omura Sumitada in Nagasaki—also gained strategic benefits from this relationship, not merely by allowing Christian missionary activity but by converting to Christianity themselves (and thereby obliging all their subjects to convert also). One useful side effect of conversion for Christian daimyōs was a growth in trade through their friendly contacts with the Jesuits. The new faith was also welcome in terms of internal Japanese politics, as a counterweight to various Buddhist sects that had gained positions of considerable political and military power in certain parts of the country. Finally, many daimyōs were also interested in fostering contacts with the Portuguese because Portuguese familiarity with firearms gave them access to a military technology whose benefits were obvious in times of almost permanent conflict.

Japan in this period did not simply permit foreign trade but was itself also actively engaged in it. The period between 1543 and 1639 was therefore characterized not only by the presence of Europeans but also by a greater openness in general on the part of Japan, with a corresponding network of contacts beyond its borders. True, China regarded actual Japanese pirates and those it perceived as such as a threat and closed its ports to merchants from the east. Nevertheless, long-distance trade with Southeast Asia and even further beyond was still possible, and so Japanese merchants established their own trade communities there in a series of port cities. Some daimyōs made handsome profits from foreign trade; the Christian missionary work of the Jesuits thrived particularly in the south on the island of Kyushu, while the advent of firearms contributed to the emergence of a few very powerful daimyōs. Ultimately, by 1600, one of these warlords, Tokugawa Ieyasu, was able to assert dominance over his rivals and found a new shogunate.

Now the contacts with the West were seen in a different light. What had once been perceived as useful was now regarded as a threat, because it appeared to pose a danger for the newly won unity of the country and Ieyasu's own hold on power. In order to cut the other daimyōs off from a significant source of income, the shōgun Ieyasu monopolized overseas trade and introduced strict regulations for it. Catholic Christianity, with its competing loyalties to priests and the pope, jeopardized the authority of the central power and through its intolerance to other religions threatened to foment dangerous civil unrest. Accordingly, persecutions of Japanese Christians and foreign missionaries, isolated incidents of which had already occurred in the late sixteenth century, now increased. When Spanish Franciscans, who advocated different forms of evangelizing than the Jesuits, came to the Japanese islands from the Philippines, the Japanese view of Europeans became more complex. Yet a more negative attitude began to creep in after Dutch and English seafarers appeared and gave their assessment of the practices and intentions of the Spanish and Portuguese. The information that the shogunate received about European colonial rule in the Americas and also in Asia led it to the conclusion that missionary activity was simply preparatory work for a military invasion. Finally, a socially motivated rebellion, which was instigated mainly by Japanese Christians, led to the expulsion of the Portuguese and all missionaries and sparked a bloody suppression of Christianity.

Japan thus voluntarily severed all the contacts it had once sought. Even so, trade was too important to ban entirely. The shogunate therefore ensured that it kept open a small window to Europe; a phase of controlled isolation ensued. With the aim of reducing the daimyōs' income, the shōgun also controlled the relations with the Chinese and Koreans; like links with Portuguese before them, these contacts could now take place only under strict supervision and monitoring at designated sites. The Dutch, for their part, were confined to the artificial island of Deshima in Nagasaki Harbor; trade with China was also restricted to this port, while commerce with Korea continued under the Tokugawa shogunate to be conducted via the island of Tsushima.

The Ryukyu Islands

The Ryukyu Islands—nowadays the Japanese prefecture of Okinawa—lie between Japan to the north and Taiwan to the south.[192] For centuries, they formed an important supraregional trade hub, which not only forged contacts between China and Japan but also allowed both countries to foster indirect links with Southeast Asia and beyond, as far afield as the Americas and Europe. For the Ryukyu Islands themselves, this brought a considerable economic boom. Merchants from there set up trading posts at various places in continental and maritime Southeast Asia. They profited from the restrictions that both China and Japan had imposed on their foreign trade. The first unified empire to come into being on the Ryukyus arose in the twelfth century. Although it collapsed several times over the following centuries, it was repeatedly reconstituted.[193] As early as the fourteenth century, the Ming rulers of China began to entertain relations with one of the subkingdoms of the islands within the framework of the tribute system. This arrangement proved so lucrative that the Sho dynasty was able to reunite the islands as a single monarchy in 1429. Shuri Castle just outside the trading port of Naha became the center of the kingdom. Its foreign contacts extended as far as Siam, Melaka, and Java. Moreover, it was not just goods that flowed along these lines of communication; knowledge and ideas were transmitted through these channels, and there was also a degree of human interchange.

The trade with China that the tribute legations made possible was restricted to certain occasions and times. Delegations traveled to China not just whenever a Chinese emperor died and a new one ascended the throne but also when a new king was about to be installed on the Ryukyus and new rights to trade were being sought. But because merchants were also keen to trade outside these periods, illegal activities ensued, including smuggling and piracy, which were indistinguishable from one another in the Chinese view of things anyway. The Ryukyu Islands had profited from the fact that the Ming dynasty had, at least officially, largely repudiated foreign contact and turned its gaze inward after the great expeditions of Admiral Zheng He in the mid-fifteenth century. When these restrictions were finally loosened in 1597, it hit the islands hard, and their significance as a hub in communications between the Far East and Southeast Asia declined.[194]

Hideyoshi's attempts at the end of the sixteenth century to invade the Korean Peninsula also had far-reaching consequences for the islands. He expected the island kingdom to furnish him with logistical assistance for the operation, but this help was not forthcoming. In response to this snub, the Tokugawa shogunate, which was established shortly thereafter, pressed the daimyo of Satsuma on Kyushu to launch a military campaign against the Ryukyus. Satsuma's troops suppressed the Shuri kingdom in 1609 and obliged it to pay tribute. Formally, though, Satsuma allowed it to retain its autonomy so that trade could continue to operate through the usual channels. The possibility thereby opened up for Satsuma to conduct its own foreign trade through the Ryukyus independently of Edo.[195]

The Chinese emperors, meanwhile, continued to regard the Ryukyus as a tribute-paying vassal kingdom, while at the same time it was formally subservient to the Tokugawa rulers in Edo. It was required to give evidence of both loyalties by sending regular delegations to the respective courts. Every two years, a tribute ship had to be dispatched from the Ryukyus to Fujian on the Chinese mainland, the site of one of the island kingdom's trading bases. In the Japanese context, the Ryukyus were obliged—just like the Chinese and the Dutch—to dispatch envoys to the court at Edo. This was invariably the case whenever a new shōgun came to power in Edo or there was a new king in Shuri. The shogunate also required the representatives from the Ryukyus to dress in the Chinese manner. This made clear that they were not regarded as Japanese but as Japanese vassals.[196]

China's Southern Coast and the China Sea

The mid-fourteenth century was also an important period of change in the maritime history of China. Especially in this context, the ascent of the Ming dynasty to power in 1368 constituted the decisive break that shaped the history of both China and Southeast Asia. Fundamentally, China had always had an ambivalent relationship to the South China Sea, to seafaring, and to foreign maritime contacts. While the populace of the southern coast was completely at home with the sea and seafaring, the central administration, irrespective of which dynasty it belonged to, generally followed an entirely different direction, which was geared toward the country's interior. This led to repeated, sometimes long-lasting, periods in which the Chinese Empire cut itself off from the sea. Shortly before the ascent of the Ming, however, southern China experienced a period of relative tolerance of foreign trade on the part of the Yuan dynasty. Economic expansion and the absorption of new nautical knowledge saw the province of Fujian (Fukien) and its major metropolises of Guangzhou (Canton) and Xiamen (Amoy) become the maritime center of gravity for the whole of the South China Sea. The province formed the key interface between the East China Sea and the South China Sea, and it was here that the network of sea routes known as the Maritime Silk Road— which became an important alternative to the famous Central Asian land route to Europe—had its origin. And it was from here that numerous Chinese navigators and traders took the opportunity of profiting from a supranational maritime trading system, which has been described by many commentators (Fernand Braudel, André Gunder Franck, Janet Abu-Lughod) as an early global system of commerce.

The Ming dynasty's seizure of power represented a fundamental change in China's maritime contacts to Southeast Asia,[197] notwithstanding the fact that this did not occur suddenly but rather was a protracted process lasting several decades. Private seaborne trade was tolerated for several years more before finally being outlawed in the fourteenth century. The lack of interest by a dynasty that was solely oriented toward land-based power politics was not the principal decisive factor in this move, though; rather, first and foremost, it was the mistrust of the Confucian bureaucratic elite toward anything mercantile and any contact whatever with outside "barbarians." Such profit-oriented trade contacts seemed impossible to reconcile with the moral ideals and the supposed cultural superiority of China.[198]

Where the state itself was concerned, China still remained active in seaborne trade for a while, as the first Ming emperor revived the old tradition of tribute relations and his successor extended these to the maritime sector. High-ranking court officials were dispatched at the head of great fleets to overseas rulers to demand their subjugation, along with extensive tribute donations, to the "son of heaven." The extent of these donations reached such proportions that it is legitimate to designate this realm, too—in contrast to the far more intensive and fragmented tribute contacts to land-based neighbors in Asia—as a form of trade. The most obvious manifestations of this short-lived phase of Chinese seaborne expansion were the voyages of exploration undertaken by Zheng He. Yet even during his lifetime—in 1433 to be precise—this form of maritime foreign contact was curtailed, in all probability both for financial reasons and because of the growing landward orientation of the second Ming emperor, who died in 1424.[199]

With this speedily executed withdrawal from policies premised on sea power, the Ming dynasty definitively ushered in an age of maritime isolation. The state-owned fleets of junks were scrapped, private sea trade was banned long term, and tribute missions from major and minor rulers overseas were noticeably reduced. For the people of southern China, inasmuch as they were involved in maritime trade and maintaining overseas contacts, this development forced them into illegal activity and helped strengthen Chinese settlements abroad. The new restrictions imposed by the Ming had the effect of making the overseas bases of Chinese mercantile dynasties, which had been in existence for a long time, into true diaspora communities. These formed the nuclei of a Chinese diaspora in Southeast Asia that had its roots in southern China and that continued to grow in extent and economic significance. In economic terms, a shift became apparent, from bilateral trade that concentrated on luxury items toward a more complex set of trade networks involving a broad palette of goods, including everyday items of mass consumption. However, on a level branded as "smuggling" in official parlance, there were still plenty of opportunities to circumvent China's self-imposed isolation, thus guaranteeing the continued existence of foreign trade outlets for South China as well as a permanent connection between the diaspora communities abroad and their mother country. In view of this, the strict trade embargo could not be maintained in the long term, even under the Ming. Over the course of the sixteenth and seventeenth centuries, the strictures were therefore cautiously though systematically relaxed, and the most important ports opened once more to Asian merchants. From 1567 on, certain licensed Chinese vessels were also able to ply their trade perfectly legally.[200]

Thus, a Chinese source of 1618 describes two routes to Southeast Asia regularly used by Chinese merchant ships. The more westerly of these ran along the coast of southern China to Indochina and the Malay Archipelago and from there to Siam or Sumatra, Java, Bali, Timor, and finally southwestern Kalimantan. The easterly route ran from Southeast China to Taiwan and Luzon (Philippines) and from there down into the Sulu Sea, to Sulawesi and the Moluccas. In each case, the length of the route and the monsoon conditions seldom allowed more than one port to be called at on any single voyage. Manila, which offered access to the transpacific trade, and Batavia, which was opened to Chinese junks by the VOC, followed in the 1730s by Macassar and at the beginning of the nineteenth century by the Dutch ports on the north coast of Java, were all particularly lucrative ports of call on these routes.

Against this background, the Chinese historian Ng Chin Keong draws a direct connection between the development of Chinese seaborne trade with Southeast Asia from the late sixteenth century onward and the expansion by European trading powers in the region.[201] Chinese products like silk, porcelain, and tea were much sought after in Europe, and the demand only increased. Chinese junks, which unloaded goods of this kind in great quantities, as well as supplying all manner of everyday consumer goods, were most welcome at the European trading posts. Europeans also obtained large quantities of utilitarian pottery, precious gold thread, or paper directly from the Chinese Empire via this route.

On their return journey, the same junks took back local Southeast Asian products with them, which in turn were eagerly snapped up by consumers back home for use in Chinese cookery or medicine. These included, first and foremost, trepang and agar-agar, birds' nests, and various products from sharks. Other goods regularly in demand by the Chinese from Southeast Asia included turtles, wax, and rattan. In order to free themselves from dependence on European contractors, Chinese traders swiftly developed their own networks for purchasing such commodities, buying them directly from the people who gathered them.

The cargo of a Chinese ship generally comprised goods belonging to several merchants or trading houses. The owner or captain of a junk would offer any spare capacity on board to prospective shippers before he set sail, and would also accept commissions to purchase particular goods at the port of destination and bring them back with him. Junk captains could also act as agents for several investors. Alongside the merchants and their servants, the ships frequently transported another kind of passenger: workers trying their luck on the Malay Archipelago or those who had already been recruited as contract laborers back in their home region. During the seventeenth and eighteenth centuries, though, such emigration from China came to concentrate entirely on Java, in particular on the sugarcane production that had been set up there by Chinese investors.

Ever since seaborne trade began to be conducted from the port of Fujian, this commerce was in the hands of noble families, who invested their money in shipping enterprises and dispatched the younger or lowlier members of their clans, or even their servants, overseas. In the transitional phase between the Ming and the Qing dynasties, the Cheng family assumed the leading role among the trading houses of southern China. Their dominance came to an end when the Manchu introduced the system of the Hong merchants in the early eighteenth century. Within this centrally regulated, but in practice locally operating, system, overseas trade in Xiamen was restricted to a very limited number of merchants approved by the emperor—the so-called ocean firms *(yang-hang)*. These specialized in overseas trade and belonged without exception to traditionally wealthy and influential merchant families.[202]

Officially, only very few ports remained open to foreign trade during the Ming and Qing dynasties. For a long time, the role of the central trade hub was filled by Xiamen, which as the place of origin of most of the Hong merchants had by this stage eclipsed Guangzhou on the Pearl River. That city managed to regain its former status only in the eighteenth century when, as the sole port open to Europeans before the First Opium War (1839–1842), it became the main conduit for the tea trade with Europe—and hence also the point of entry for the influx of Indian opium into China. From 1698 on, the British East India Company had maintained a factory in Guangzhou (Canton) under the control of special Chinese authorities and strict regulation of its trading activities. Though trade with China was also open to other European powers under similarly restrictive conditions, none of them was as significant as the British presence in Canton.

Ultimately, in 1760, a whole series of existing regulations were grouped together to form the so-called Canton system, which in essence was based on a dual monopoly. On the Chinese side, a small group of well-established and capital-rich mercantile dynasties—the Hong merchants—were granted privileged access to European traders, much like the older trade model operating in Xiamen. On the European side, the East India companies were given exclusive rights to transcultural trade by the Chinese state. However, they were confined to the "Thirteen Factories" enclave—a tightly restricted and guarded compound outside the city walls, in which the Hong enterprises had their offices and warehouses. Despite these restrictions, trade in Guangzhou was lucrative enough for all European companies to acquiesce in the trading regime imposed by the Chinese. This even remained the case when the relevant authorities became increasingly autonomous and corruption became part of everyday dealings with the Canton system. Only when, in the early nineteenth century, the opium trade—which was, strictly speaking, illegal but which was conducted openly and intensively all the same—began to spread like wildfire did tensions between the Qing rulers and the Europeans escalate. The overwhelming military superiority of the British in the ensuing Opium War finally put an end to all of Beijing's attempts to subjugate the maritime-oriented provinces of southern China to centralized state control.

Taiwan

The island of Taiwan (Formosa) off the coast of southern China came to the attention of the neighboring and the long-distance seafaring powers alike only at a relatively late stage. Taiwan was already occupied in the pre-Christian era by Malay–Polynesian groups, who lived by fishing, hunting, and slash-and-burn farming. Later periods saw migration from the Chinese mainland, especially during the Han dynasty. Nevertheless, the numbers remained inconsequential, and no lasting contacts resulted. Even after the imperial authorities had embraced the entire region, at least theoretically, as part of its system of tribute payments, no practical interest was taken in the island, and so it remained outside the Chinese heartland. Indeed, there are only isolated, vague references to Taiwan in the official sources. For private maritime trade, too, the island was of little interest, though there may well have been intermittent trading posts on Taiwan from the twelfth century on. However, its unfavorable position with regard to monsoons and the leading role played by the Ryukyu Islands as a mercantile relay station had a negative impact on its development. Taiwan remained a "geographical barrier" (Roderich Ptak), which had more of a dividing than a linking function.[203]

Yet the island came more into China's purview as a result of the economic rise of Fujian. Merchants from that city circumvented the Ryukyu network and increasingly came to regard Taiwan as part of their own sphere of influence. Even so, during the Ming period, Taiwan was still in no position to form a bridge between diverse cultures. Only toward the end of that dynasty did general interest in Taiwan grow as it slowly started to develop into a commercial link and a focus of interest on the part of supraregional and global players.²⁰⁴ This development really came to the fore in the late sixteenth century, when Taiwan began, in however low-key a way, to enter into the geopolitical field of conflict between different rival global powers. The Portuguese Estado da India undertook only a few exploratory voyages to the island, concentrating its efforts otherwise on Macau. And though China as a state continued to show no interest in Taiwan, the liberalization of overseas trade that had been going on since the 1560s made it easier for Fujian merchants to settle on the far side of the much-used Taiwan Strait. Following the political unification of Japan, merchant shipping from Kyushu, and most particularly from Nagasaki, increased markedly, and took in Taiwan as a way station. In 1626, on the north of the island, the Spanish founded an outpost of their Philippines colony; however, although missionaries were occasionally dispatched there, it remained largely insignificant. It may be that Spain's interest in Taiwan had something to do with an envisaged conquest of China—a plan that was certainly discussed in Spain in the late sixteenth century but was shelved at the very latest after the loss of the armada off England in 1588. It is more probable that commercial considerations were uppermost in the founding of the base on Taiwan, but for all that it still proved a dead end.

Finally, the Dutch VOC embarked on the first comprehensive program to colonize Taiwan when, after two earlier failed attempts, it founded the fortified colony of Zeelandia in the southwest of the island in 1624. In 1642, the VOC also absorbed the Spanish outpost. The aim was to establish a key base for the trade with Japan, and the Dutch succeeded in this, at least for a short while. Not least, the export of local Taiwanese goods like wild animal skins, which were much in demand in Japan and saw Zeelandia develop into a hunting settlement, underpinned this enterprise. The reckless attitude displayed by the Dutch soon wrought ecological and social damage, but even so, the way in which this venture tied the island into supraregional trade links was a new departure in the economy of the island. Thereafter, the island can be seen as an exponent of an early phase of globalization, playing as it did the role of an interface between different maritime areas.

Yet the influence of the Dutch, which was geographically limited in any event and hardly warrants the oft-used label of "the Dutch era in the history of Taiwan," did not last long. The end of the Ming dynasty on the mainland in the mid-seventeenth century also heralded the demise of the colony of Zeelandia, as these larger political developments saw the island come under the rule of the Zheng clan. This clan comprised supporters of the Ming dynasty in the south of the empire. Following the expulsion of the Ming from Beijing by the Manchu Qing dynasty in 1644, southern China became the last redoubt of the old dynasty, which after long years of fighting was also finally lost, forcing the Zheng to withdraw to Taiwan. Under the leadership of Coxinga (Zheng Chenggong; 1624–1662), the Dutch were finally driven from the island in 1662. The Zheng clan proceeded to gain territorial control over other areas of the island and established its first complex polity, along Chinese lines. Hand in hand with this came a palpable Sinicization of Taiwan's political and cultural life. In addition, the island was opened up for agricultural development, a process that the Dutch had instituted only in the immediate environs of Zeelandia. But even more important than farming for the continuing survival of the Zheng state were its external economic contacts to the southern Chinese mainland, Japan, and Southeast Asia. The intermediary role of Taiwan, which is completely comparable with that of Fujian one to two centuries before, was thus institutionalized to some extent.

Even the rule of the Zheng was a relatively brief interlude for Taiwan, despite the profound rupture it represented. In their self-image as heirs to the Ming and representatives of the true Chinese Empire, the Zheng then embarked on a military campaign on the mainland under the leadership of Coxinga's son, Zheng Jing (d. 1682). However, they were no match for the army of the Qing, and their inevitable defeat on the mainland heralded the end of their reign on the island, too. In 1683, the Qing dispatched an expeditionary invasion fleet to Taiwan, whose troops overran the Zheng state within the space of just a few weeks. In the same year, an official act of state incorporated Taiwan into the Chinese Empire, and a year later, it was made into a prefecture of the province of Fujian. Culturally, these events strengthened the process of Sinicization in the coastal and lowland regions. The influence of the expanded Chinese bureaucracy also made itself felt, as did immigration from the mainland, which increased in the eighteenth century, bringing not only Han Chinese but also Hakka people to Taiwan. One result of this influx was that Buddhism and Confucianism gained ground on the island.

The culture of the indigenous people, who were referred to as "mountain tribes" or even just "barbarians," remained largely undisturbed under the rule of both the Dutch and the Zheng. Both employed indirect methods of rule over these Austronesian native groups. Although this situation did not change fundamentally under the Qing administrators, the aboriginal population found itself steadily reduced to the position of a minority by the ongoing Sinicization. In many parts of the island, especially near the coast, processes of acculturation could be observed, whereas in remote mountainous regions in the interior, traditional languages and forms persisted. A form of political organization also existed in those areas, but it was based on the extensive autonomy of village communities. According to later testimonies, these communities, which are described in early Chinese sources as partly acephalous and partly segmentary, had leaders (variously called "chiefs" or "captains") and council assemblies but boasted egalitarian decision-making processes in both the political and the judicial spheres.[205]

Politically and economically, Taiwan was increasingly marginalized under the Qing. The court in Beijing regarded the island as just another outlying region, comparable with Mongolia or Tibet, and so invested little in its administration, economy, and infrastructure. Furthermore, as a result of the more trade-friendly policies of the Qing on the southern Chinese mainland, the role of a hinge between the China Sea and the Pacific and between the Far East and Southeast Asia shifted back to Fujian once more, with its trading center at Xiamen, and subsequently in the late eighteenth century to Guangzhou.

European Influences

Although the maritime Far East did not play a central role as a transitional area between Southeast Asia and the Eurasian mainland for those who took part on the European expansion during the early modern period—this role remained the preserve of maritime Southeast Asia and the Indian subcontinent—many of the developments we have discussed are still closely related to the appearance of Europeans in Asia. European involvement in the maritime Far East began in 1543, with a shipwreck of Portuguese sailors on the southern Japanese island of Tanega. Six years later, the Jesuit Francis Xavier (1506–1522) arrived in Japan, to preach Christianity in Kagoshima. His arrival signaled the start of an epoch of Japanese history that is customarily referred to as the "Christian century," thanks to the intensive absorption of religion, science, and technology that took place then. Japanese delegations were sent to seek an audience with the pope in Rome, as well as with the Spanish kings Philip II and Philip III. Merchant ships sailed as far as India. The only people the Japanese kept at arm's length during this period, as suspected pirates, were the Chinese. This enabled the Portuguese to play an indispensable role as middlemen in the exchange of goods between the two countries.

Christian missionary successes began in earnest after Alessandro Valignano (1539–1606), who supervised the Far Eastern Jesuit mission from Macau, devised his strategies of enculturation for Catholicism. By means of a deliberate assimilation of the lifestyle of the host country, the missionaries managed to gain access to influential circles in Japanese society. The Jesuits' close relationship with the mercantile community as well as the aforementioned different interest groups in the internal political sphere in Japan combined to make the Christian mission to the country highly successful during the sixteenth and seventeenth centuries. Yet this came about only because Christianity was able to find fertile ground in these specific historical circumstances—which possibly also explains why it lost ground again so rapidly once these circumstances changed.

While the competing efforts of the Spanish and English to forge trading links with Japan amounted only to flashes in the pan, thanks to their close connection with the Jesuit mission, the Portuguese were present in Japan for around a century. Ultimately, however, this link was to seal their fate. With the unification of the realm under Toyotomi Hideyoshi and the founding of the Tokugawa shogunate in 1602, Christianity as a political factor became a potentially disruptive threat to the bloodily won unity of the country. In a series of decrees (1587, 1612, 1615), Christianity was banned. Immediately after the first proscription in 1587, nine missionaries (the "martyrs of Nagasaki") were executed, followed in 1634 by the killing of nine more who had been sent from Manila. Japan experienced a wave of persecution of Christians, which culminated in the failed Shimabara uprising, brutally suppressed by troops of the shogunate, with Dutch help, in 1638. In 1639, the Portuguese were expelled once and for all from Japan.

Only the Dutch East India Company had managed to successfully present itself as a non-Christian organization and enemy of the Portuguese. From 1639 on, the VOC was Japan's sole European trading partner. Its employees were obliged to live and work in almost total isolation and were watched over at every step on the small artificial island of Deshima in Nagasaki Harbor. In the port, an arm of the Japanese bureaucracy was set up specifically to administer this relationship. It monitored the activities of the Dutch and took on specially trained interpreters in order to smooth official contacts and facilitate trade agreements. Around two hundred Japanese women and men were dedicated to the task of looking after the small group of Dutch, who never numbered more than fifteen to twenty. They were spied on and their communications deliberately hampered. The Europeans were prohibited from learning Japanese; they were expected to rely constantly on the interpreters. Trade was allowed to be conducted only through a specialized guild of merchants in Nagasaki, and only one Dutch ship was permitted to enter the base in any single year. The only direct contact that the VOC employees had with Japanese culture took place on the annual journey north to Edo to pay formal homage to the shōgun.

Nevertheless, scholars such as Engelbert Kaempfer (1651–1706), Carl Peter Thunberg (1743–1828), and Philipp Franz von Siebold (1796–1866) were still able to use their stay on Deshima to fundamentally broaden Europe's knowledge of this mysterious country. A large number of interpreters and pupils, to whom they were able to impart Western knowledge, for example, on medical and pharmaceutical matters, instructed them in return on traditional Japanese subjects. The physician Engelbert Kaempfer in particular made Sino-Japanese medicine and pharmacology the focus of his work. The strictly controlled court visit to Edo not only was used for observation and the secret gathering of information or materials but also provided an opportunity to meet with Japanese experts and exchange opinions with them.

Unlike in China, where there was little interest in the Europeans who had settled to trade in Macau or Guangzhou, for the Japanese Deshima also represented a fascinating window on Europe. In order to ward off destabilizing influences from abroad, this window was admittedly opened only a crack, but what came into the country through this gap Japan was able to regulate to its specifications. The gap proved large enough to at least convey basic information on the world outside Japan. In this way, the shogunate gained insight into the main developments taking place in international politics, into the rise of the European powers,

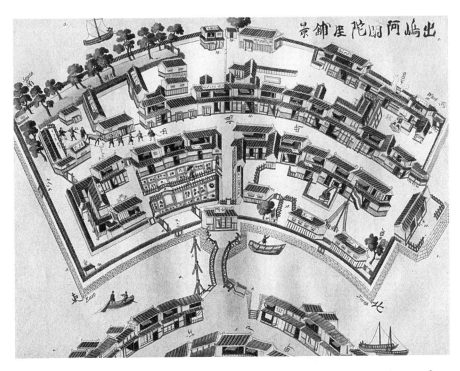

出嶋阿関陀庄舗景

Japanese adaptation of a map by Isaac Titsingh. The artificial island of Deshima in the Bay of Nagasaki spreads out like a small fan in this ground plan. The island's only link to the mainland city was via a bridge, where traffic could be easily monitored. A handful of Dutch traders lived in barracks on the island, watched over by a large Japanese population. Even so, a degree of cultural exchange was still possible. Japan was interested in acquiring knowledge from the West and was also eager to gain some impression of conditions beyond its borders, but not at any price. Consequently, all contacts were strictly regulated so as to serve Japanese interests. This map was originally produced by the great scholar Isaac Titsingh (1745–1812), who between 1779 and 1784 was the head of the Dutch delegation on Deshima, and it was later copied by Japanese cartographers.

and into Western achievements and the shogunate's own shortcomings. There came into being a circle of specialists, with relative close contacts to the Dutch, who developed an awareness of where Japan lacked knowledge in comparison to the West. One of the things to emerge from this constellation of specialists was a body of scholarship called "Dutch learning" *(rangaku)*. This was not simply concerned with absorbing European expertise but was also interested in the methods and perspectives of Western research. Over time, this approach began to rival the traditional, Chinese-influenced attitude to learning. By 1720 at the latest, when the ban on importing European books was lifted, the loosening of Japan's cultural ties to China became increasingly apparent. Despite its official policy of isolation, therefore, the country maintained a limited exchange of information with the Dutch—a factor that may well have contributed to the rapid rise of Japan after 1868. Japan's controlled insulation protected it from European influences while still allowing it to perceive the wider world and, despite a series of internal crises, to undergo a remarkable process of development in terms of its infrastructure, its economy (now based on the division of labor principle), its trade, and its banking and educational systems. The Dutch presence in Nagasaki Harbor survived the bankruptcy of the VOC in 1799, continuing under direct Dutch government control until 1860.

Zeelandia on Taiwan was actually intended to perform the role of a permanent port of call and supply station. Following its founding in 1624, the settlement at first developed entirely along these lines but finally foundered on the political developments already described, which the company did not have the power resources to withstand. Even so, the Dutch did leave their mark on Taiwan in some measure. Alongside its function within the trade connection between Batavia and Nagasaki, Dutch commerce in the new colony rested on two main pillars. On the one hand, products from Taiwanese flora and fauna, such as the pelts and horns of the indigenous red deer, rattan, or medicinal plants, proved to be highly lucrative export goods, while on the other the company also promoted large-scale rice and sugarcane cultivation both for the colony's own use and as a source of additional revenue. The VOC's colonial project—which thoroughly warrants this name, at least in the regions surrounding its two fortresses on the coast—was not without its ecological consequences and also caused social displacement. Despite the relative brevity of the Dutch presence on the island, the stocks of wild game were dramatically depleted, the woods close to the coast extensively felled, and not least a process instigated whereby all indigenous forms of life were increasingly driven inland.[206]

Like the Dutch in Japan, the Europeans in China were perfectly prepared to submit to a restrictive regime in order to secure access to lucrative markets. A lack of power and the prospects of the profits to be made in particular product sectors justified this approach. State-regulated trade between the Europeans and the Chinese began with the admission of Europeans into at least one port and the founding of the British factory in Guangzhou (Canton) in 1698; this interaction culminated in the firm framework of the Canton system. Trade centered mainly on tea, which experienced a rapid increase in demand in Europe in the eighteenth century; at this stage, before the first attempts by the British to establish tea plantations in northern India, China was the only place where tea could be obtained. In addition, silk goods, porcelain, and other Chinese luxury goods were highly sought-after export commodities. Within the parameters of the Canton system, the Europeans could export only a limited amount of goods, and in order to develop their business they were obliged to use state-licensed Chinese monopolists (the Hong merchants) as trading partners and remained subject to constant monitoring by Chinese officials.

Thus, during the eighteenth century, in the realm of commerce at least, it is more appropriate to talk in terms of a long-lasting and mutually beneficial business relationship than it is to speak of European influence on China. Yet the central authorities in Beijing increasingly took no part in this. This all changed with the import of opium from the second half of the eighteenth century on; opium was produced primarily in India, where it was sold by the East India Company and imported to southern China—strictly speaking illegally but within the framework of the Canton system—by private British trading houses. The Chinese authorities tried to counter the devastating consequences of opium consumption with ever more drastic measures, which ultimately led to the First Opium War, at the beginning of the colonial phase in Asia. This coercive form of influence, however, lay beyond the era of the East India companies.

Portugal played the role of trailblazer for the trading companies where forging relations with imperial China was concerned. At the start of the sixteenth century, the Estado da India made several attempts, including the use of force, to gain access to the Chinese mainland but likewise did not have enough military power to force the issue. Instead, an agreement was reached through negotiation. In 1557, the Chinese government allowed the Portuguese to found a trading post on the Pearl River delta at Macau, which up until then had been a small fishing village; the first Portuguese ships visited there in 1516. Although China retained ultimate sovereignty over Macau, the agreement provided for sufficient local autonomy that the base soon developed into a proper colonial town, which functioned alongside Goa and Malacca as one of the key political, religious, and economic centers of the

Estado da India. Macau became the hub for Portuguese trade with Japan, the center for purchase of Chinese goods, and the base for Catholic institutions coordinating missionary work in China and Japan. In the long term, Macau remained the only Portuguese base in the Far East, though it declined in the face of competition with Guangzhou and the redrawing of the major trade routes by the West European companies and the trading houses of Fujian. Its decline was also hastened by the failure of the missionary efforts, especially in Japan.

However, the Jesuits were able to gain some degree of influence in China. While their initial missionary successes in Japan fell victim to the centralization and homogenization policies of the Tokugawa shogunate, they managed to establish a lasting presence in China, an achievement that was ultimately attributable to the same methods of acculturation that they had employed in Japan. The difference was that these methods were applied more consistently in China. The missionaries not only assimilated themselves superficially into the customs and mores of the country but also deliberately sought access to the Confucian class of officialdom. Their conspicuous erudition and their readiness to engage with the Confucian canon of learning led to a situation where at least their most significant representatives were regarded no longer as missionaries but as scholars of equal stature. Some Jesuits managed to rise officially to high-ranking positions in the ranks of the mandarins and to influential posts at the court in Beijing, particularly in the scientific realm. In this way, the German missionary Johann Adam Schall von Bell (1592–1666) became director of the imperial office for astronomy and devised a calendar reform for the Chinese administration.

Alongside their strategy of assimilation, the Jesuits also profited from the fact that China did not instrumentalize their religion and that the missionaries disseminated their faith somewhat diffidently. Although Christian communities arose that were not inconsiderable in either size or duration, the role their founders played in Chinese–European relations in the realms of science and literature was generally much more highly regarded. Ultimately, it was an internal church dispute—the so-called Chinese rites controversy—that put an end to this development. At the beginning of the eighteenth century in the Vatican, after decades of conflict, the critics of the policy of accommodation finally gained the upper hand, with the result that two papal bulls were issued, the first in 1707 and the second in 1742 (entitled *Ex quo singulari*), in which all participation by Jesuits in the

"Chinese rites" of ancestor worship and the official veneration of Confucius was banned. In retaliation, the court in Beijing refused to sanction any Christian mission that did not accept the primacy of the Chinese rites. Yet the Christian communities in the country were allowed to remain and continued to be under the pastoral care of European Catholic priests.[207]

Meanwhile, largely unnoticed by the other European powers, to the north the Russians had reached the shores of the Pacific by the seventeenth century and gradually set about exploring the waters, both close to home and farther afield, off the east coast of Siberia. As an immediate neighbor of China, they thus laid the foundations for an enduring, albeit far from unproblematic, cultural exchange with the Far East. This relationship was given its first tangible expression in international law in the Treaty of Nerchinsk, concluded in 1689.

5. Oceania

OCEANIA was settled in several phases.[208] Some 35,000 years ago, people who spoke Papuan languages reached the area that we now know as Melanesia. Around 4000 BC, the migrations of Austronesian-speaking peoples began. These people embarked on the longest-known sea voyages undertaken by any Stone Age cultures, not only embracing as they did the Pacific but also venturing as far to the west as Madagascar.[209] The Polynesian Triangle alone—with its points at Hawaii, Easter Island, and New Zealand—would, if stood on its end and transposed to Eurasia, stretch from France in the west almost to the Kamchatka Peninsula off Siberia in the east and down to the farthest tip of the Indian subcontinent in the south.

Melanesia, Micronesia, and Polynesia

The Austronesian opening up of the Pacific can be traced through the excavation at different sites of earthenware decorated in a particular, distinctive way; this is known as "Lapita pottery" from the site on New Caledonia where it was first found.[210] People from this culture used stone axes but had no tools made of metal, and they kept domestic animals and farmed. They embarked on their voyages across the oceans in groups of probably less than a hundred. On New Guinea and on other islands of the western Pacific, they encountered people who spoke no Austronesian languages and partially assimilated them, though farther east they ventured into hitherto unpopulated regions. They took animals and plants with them on their voyages, which gave them the wherewithal to survive in their new homelands. On the larger islands that they settled, they cultivated taro on irrigated fields, while on atolls they dug trenches down to the level of the groundwater in order to grow crops.[211]

In all probability, the islands that they came across in the wide expanses of the Pacific were deliberately navigated to and were not simply chance finds by crews

A Lapita potsherd decorated with a human face. The archaeological site known as Lapita, on the peninsula of Foué on New Caledonian, has yielded a distinct kind of pottery that scholars have used to demonstrate the Austronesian discovery and colonization of the Pacific. The distinctive way in which these potsherds are decorated have enabled archaeologists to easily determine what era different pieces of Lapita ware come from. (From *Südsee: Inseln, Völker und Kulturen,* by Clara B. Wilpert, Hamburg: Christians, 1987.)

of boats that had strayed off course. Long before Europeans plucked up the courage to venture beyond the sight of coastlines, the Austronesians set off across the largest of the worlds' oceans in their small craft. On their voyages, they covered hundreds of kilometers without making land. They had no compasses or sextants but instead know how to navigate by star sighting or charting the position of the sun and watching the skies and the ocean currents. For example, the air tended to shimmer above lagoons, or their greenish waters could be reflected in the clouds above. By contrast, cloud banks tended to mass above mountainous islands, announcing their presence long before they came into view. Coral reefs, meanwhile, affected the ocean swell, while water ebbing out of lagoons when the tide went out could change the pattern of currents.

The Austronesian peoples made shorter voyages in outrigger canoes. For longer voyages across the open sea, they used catamaran canoes, with the two hulls joined together by a platform of planks and lashed with ropes made from coconut fibers. These craft were exceptionally seaworthy and yet at the same time spacious enough to carry food crops and domestic animals on board as well as people. Oceangoing canoes could vary in length between 10 and 40 meters and have a complement of up to fifty to sixty people and all their provisions. Shelters on deck offered protection from the waves, wind, and sun. The stepped masts of these craft were fitted with a triangular lateen sail woven from rush matting.

The Austronesians originally came from southern China and first arrived in the Philippines, via Taiwan, before going on to settle Indonesia, the Malay Peninsula, and the east coast of Vietnam. Between 2000 and 1500 BC, some of these peoples then set off eastward across the Pacific in the direction of Micronesia, while others landed on the coasts of the Melanesian islands, which they used as a springboard to reach Fiji, Tonga, and Samoa between 1550 and 1200 BC. Then, around 500 BC, eastern Polynesia was the objective of a further wave of expansion. In this part of the Pacific, Tahiti in particular developed into a dynamic center of culture. From there, the Polynesians settled Hawaii, Easter Island, and finally—at the beginning of the period under discussion here—New Zealand.[212]

There is strong evidence to suggest that Austronesian peoples also reached the mainland of South America from the easternmost Polynesian islands. It was there, scholars now presume, that they encountered sweet potatoes, which came to play a key role in their diet. According to other commentators, though, this crop reached Oceania only after Columbus, via Europe and Asia.[213]

The different environmental conditions encountered, along with the isolation that set in after the first phase of exploration, saw the development of a wide variety of cultures, despite certain general similarities. In Melanesia, the different societies coalesced around concepts of kinship and the clan. Individual family groups traced their descent from a mythical ancestor. They felt themselves bound to a totem that generally took the form of an animal and to which specific taboos adhered. There were no larger political entities than these village communities organized along the lines of kinship. Men, who lived communally in a men's house or who came together to form secret societies, set the tone in the social and political life of the village.

New Guinea, the second largest island in the world, was characterized by an Austronesian-speaking population on the coast and by Papuan-speaking groups in the interior. Reciprocal influences and at the same time the remote circumstances in which the small communities frequently lived, combined to produce a cultural and linguistic variety that is unique in the world. The island world of wider Melanesia beyond New Guinea was also hallmarked by this combination of Austronesian and Papuan language and culture. Yet many contacts existed both within New Guinea and with other Melanesian islands, as well as between those islands. Trade networks and systems of exchange along coasts and rivers and overseas carried goods as well as people and ideas.[214]

In contrast, the traditional societies of Micronesia were hierarchically organized. A considerable social gulf existed between the high-ranking elite groups and the remainder of the populace. Rivalries within the elite were a cause of armed conflict. Aside from a few precipitous volcanic islands, the habitats of most Micronesians were low-lying coral islands. Freshwater and fertile soils were scarce, making fishing the most important source of food and creating a close relationship with the sea.

In contrast to idyllic Western conceptions of them, Polynesian societies were also characterized by more or less acute social divisions. A ruling class, at whose head stood chiefs or kings, dominated political life. The next echelons of society were occupied respectively by the nobility—priests and warriors—and craftsmen and artists. Below these came the mass of common people, and on the lowest level of all were bondsmen. Unified political assemblies or polities developed only on very few islands. The overwhelming picture of Polynesia as a whole was one of fragmented societies, and relationships were characterized by rivalry and warfare. The most important social positions were passed down from father to son, and as a rule kinship, age, and sex had a decisive influence on a person's social status. Marriage and war were the most important methods by which a ruler could improve his own position and that of his kingdom. If he attained an exalted position, he was endowed with mana on a grand scale—a sense of gravitas and power that could be used, even inadvertently, to weaken or otherwise harm others less gifted with this quality. To avoid doing a person harm unintentionally, certain forms of contact with and meeting influential people were taboo.[215]

On Fiji, all social life was regulated by the chiefdoms. Larger assemblages were divided into subgroups, with large families forming the smallest social unit. War was a commonplace occurrence. On Tonga, there arose centralized political structures with a pronounced aristocratic character and a predisposition for expansionism. At the apex of the social pyramid stood the Tu'i Tonga, the ruler, who traced his ancestry to a creator god and who was regarded as sacrosanct. He was aided by a council of high-ranking officials. Beneath them were ranked the strata of priests, artists, warriors, and the common people. For centuries, Tonga waged war against Fiji, Samoa, and Niue, at various times controlling these other islands.

On Tahiti, society was stratified in a similarly strongly hierarchical fashion. In this case, the leadership role was assumed by the nobility. They saw themselves as the descendants of gods, whose cult they were responsible for maintaining. Alongside this role, they also directed the island's social and political life. Princes were supported by a court comprising officials, priests, and warriors. The aristocracy did not need to have any concerns over how to make their living, being entirely provided for by the other social classes. The second echelon of Tahitian society were the so-called landowners, whose ranks also supplied all the craftsmen, priests, and scholars. The ordinary people tilled the fields, fished, and raised animals, thus maintaining the lifestyle of the higher classes. But even beneath them was the servant class, sometimes referred to as slaves, who belonged to the aristocratic families and who were employed in their houses. People on Tahiti lived in scattered individual settlements, each of which was home to large families with up to sixty members. They came under the jurisdiction of different districts, of which there were several on Tahiti, each controlled by a ruling family. Armed conflict was an integral part of everyday life. Many families fought bitter and bloody wars to gain supremacy over Tahiti and the neighboring islands.[216]

James Cook witnessed the preparations being made by the Tahitian king Tu to launch an attack on Moorea. In a bay, he had assembled over three hundred war catamarans, which Cook estimated could carry a total of almost eight thousand men. William Hodges, who accompanied Cook as an artist on this, his second, voyage of discovery, portrayed two of these boats in an oil painting, which he completed on his return from the Pacific. Alongside the craft can be seen a chief in

William Hodges (1744–1797): *War Boats of Otaheite* [Tahiti] *and the Society Islands (with a View of Part of the Harbour of Ohaneneno [Haamanino] in Ulietea [Ra'iatea], One of the Society Islands.* London, 1777, oil on canvas. Captain James Cook set great store in having the knowledge that he gleaned during his voyages around the Pacific captured visually as well as in words. Nor did he stop at simply mapping difficult routes or favorable anchorages; rather, he insisted on keeping an objective and scientific record of various coastlines, along with all manner of flora and fauna, and even portraits of people. Trained artists like William Hodges, who later also worked in India, devoted themselves to the task of painting landscapes, cloud formations, and the skies and light effects of the Southern Seas. They also documented spectacular events such as this scene, in which Tahitian war canoes are being prepared for an attack on the neighboring island of Moorea. (National Maritime Museum, Greenwich/Ministry of Defence Art Collection, BHC 2374)

his ceremonial war garb with a tall headdress. The German naturalist Georg Forster brought a similar headdress with him back to Europe from his travels. It consisted of a woven top hat with a flat disk attached to the front side and was decorated with rare feathers and sharks' teeth.[217]

The situation was much the same on Hawaii. There, too, an aristocratic class had grown up, in which chiefs and high priests enjoyed the highest status. They inherited their positions. Over the course of time, the chiefs attained godlike status. Beneath them were ranged warriors, artists, noblemen, and commoners. The social structures were more open on the Marquesas Islands, however. There, chieftains' positions were not passed down from father to son, and even women could perform this role. In addition, it was quite normal for people to marry outside the bounds of their social class.

Within Polynesia, Rapa Nui, known to Westerners as Easter Island, followed a particularly independent line of development, which may be partially explained by the island's extreme isolation. The closest neighbors are people living on the Gambier Archipelago, 2,600 kilometers away, or in South America, some 3,600 kilometers distant from Easter Island. The erection of the huge stone statues for which the island is renowned is still shrouded in mystery. Some of these figures weigh more than 80 tons, and they stand at between 4 and 20 meters tall. They had to be transported several kilometers from the quarry where they were made to the sites where they were installed. They have generally been interpreted as ancestor figures raised to the status of gods. They were set up on platforms that also served as the burial sites for chiefs. Altogether, there are 250 such platforms on this small island and around a thousand statues. None were put up later than the seventeenth century. The reason for this break in tradition is reckoned to have been a conflict between two ethnic groups who originated from immigrants who arrived on the island at different times. As wood and food became scarce, war broke out. The more recent immigrant group eventually prevailed and ended the production of the famous figures.[218]

New Zealand

New Zealand was the last region of the Pacific to be colonized by the Polynesians.[219] They called it Aotearoa, the "land of the long white cloud," and referred to themselves as Maoris. The name "New Zealand" derived from the Dutch navigator Abel Janszoon Tasman, the first European to explore the region. New Zealand is the largest and most temperate landmass in Polynesia, ecologically far more diverse than the tropical islands of the region and with large climatic variations between the North and South Islands, as well as between low-lying plains and highland areas.

The Maori most likely settled the islands in several waves of migration, the first of which is now dated to no earlier than the thirteenth century AD. The newcomers found New Zealand to be extensively forested. The animals and plants that they brought with them on their voyages evidently did not survive, and so they had to make do with what they found on the islands. They pursued a hunter-gatherer lifestyle, catching fish, gathering mussels, and snaring animals and birds. Some of the later migrants had viable crops with them when they landed, some of which were wholly unsuited to the new environment, while others thrived only in certain parts of the islands with a mild climate. Even so, farming gradually spread, and within a few centuries, the newcomers had fundamentally changed the ecology of New Zealand. The first change was that the indigenous megafauna was wiped out; hunting was largely responsible for this, but so were depredations by the dogs and rats that the Maori brought with them. Another, later cause was the slash-and-burn method of agriculture, which further reduced the remaining habitats of the large animals. Extensive areas of grassland developed on the South Island, while on the North Island, ferns and scrub vegetation replaced the woodland. Sweet potatoes became the staple diet; these thrived especially well throughout North Island but could also be grown in the northern half of South Island.[220]

The centuries between 1500 and 1800 in the European calendar are considered the classical period in the history of Maori civilization. Their political structure was akin to that of the Polynesian islands. Family groups combined to form larger tribal units led by a chieftain. Around fifty different such groupings can be identified. They each trace their ancestry back to one of the boats that their ancestors once navigated across the ocean from Tahiti to New Zealand. The chief also occupied the most exalted position in the group's genealogy. His rank was therefore hereditary in principle, though in practice he could be usurped by those who had distinguished themselves in political life or in war.

The meeting houses were the focus of community life; at the same time, though, these were symbolic places, which recalled the groups' origins across the ocean and the social structure. Men met there to discuss matters of political and military importance. The meeting houses symbolized the totality of the community's ancestors and were usually decorated with elaborate carvings, which are now recognized as one of the most significant works of art in Oceania. The ancestors were present whenever the fate of the living was discussed and decisions reached. Ramparts of stone or earth protected the settlements during the many violent conflicts that broke out, as different ancestral groups vied for land or control of fishing grounds.

The first British settlers landed at the Bay of Islands in 1792, spearheading the development of New Zealand into a colony of the British Empire and another "New Europe" in the Southern Hemisphere. Whalers established bases, and missionaries also gained a foothold. The Maori sought contact with the newcomers of their own volition, obtaining from them practical knowledge and weapons to help them gain an advantage in the internecine power struggles.

Australia

The first people to arrive on the "fifth continent" came from Southeast Asia some 50,000 years ago. Adapting to the environmental conditions they encountered, the people who later became known to white settlers as Aborigines developed modes of existence characterized by extreme hardiness and tenacity. Yet their society was by no means static. In a process that may have taken anything up to 10,000 years, the Aboriginal peoples took possession of the entire continent. Favored living environments included the banks of lakes or rivers or seacoasts. The first signs of human life in the Australian interior can be traced to around 26,000 years ago. Although the first tribes had common roots, they began to diverge over time. The hundreds of different forms and dialects of the Aboriginal language bear clear witness to this development. The various climatic and environmental conditions that existed in, say, the cool, damp region of Tasmania in the south, in the tropical north, in the arid interior, on the coast, or farther inland presented all kinds of challenges to the Aborigines. The survival strategies that they devised in these different regions were correspondingly diverse. In small groups never numbering more than a few families, they led a nomadic existence, ranging far and wide across the continent in search of hunted or foraged food. Different groups would occasionally meet to exchange gifts or resolve conflicts either peacefully or violently. Yet more settled communities developed in the more fertile regions.

Tools and weapons were developed, such as the boomerang, whose history goes back some 20,000 years. Sporadic contacts with the outside world in the north are thought to have brought not only the semidomesticated dog known as the dingo to Australia but also more advanced tools and innovations in boat-building techniques. Trace of cultural exchange can also be identified in the visual arts and music, as well as in the form of foreign loan words in Aboriginal languages.[221]

Aboriginal culture was firmly rooted in and with the natural environment. The people lived in their environment in the sense that it supplied everything they needed for their survival. And they lived with it, inasmuch as they found the spiritual world that characterized and guided their whole existence reflected in nature. For those who knew how to interpret the signs of the landscape, it was a storybook containing not only the history of how natural phenomena, animals, and people came into being but also maxims for social order and appropriate behavior. This storybook was the creation of mythical beings with human or animal form, whose activities had helped fashion the landscape or who themselves had been petrified into notable landmarks. The memory of such events lived on at sacred sites, which were linked by paths. The elders of a group were the keepers of this communal memory, making it visible through dances, petroglyphs, or sand paintings and preserving its content in stories or songs, which were passed down from one generation to the next. This not only helped to perpetually reinforce the identity of the group, it also facilitated communication with the spirit beings, who inhabited nature and upon whose goodwill humans relied. The elders were not just the ones who led the ritual observances; they were also the repositories of authority within any given group, dispensing justice and ensuring order was maintained. Noninitiates and women were excluded from this knowledge and from the authority it endowed.[222]

The fact that the Aborigines lived with nature and saw it as spiritually charged did not mean that they did not alter it. Over the space of several millennia following the arrival of the first humans, more than 85 percent of large mammals disappeared from the fifth continent. The most likely cause of this was the deliberate fires started by the Aborigines to make the gathering of roots, larvae, or insects and the hunting of animals easier. Besides, useful food plants sprang up reinvigorated after being subjected to fire. The downside of this was that it decimated trees and scrub vegetation and deprived the megafauna of its habitat and food sources. What resulted was a savanna and scrubland terrain, interspersed with eucalyptus trees, an environment that characterizes large tracts of Australia today.

Eucalyptus is indigenous to Australia and withstands attacks from worms and termites, as well as droughts and even fires.[223]

Up to the end of the period under discussion here, namely, the late eighteenth century, Europeans were only occasional visitors to isolated points on the coast of Australia. This all changed in 1770, when James Cook explored and charted the east coast of Australia. He made land at a spot just south of the modern city of Sydney, which he named "Botany Bay," before setting sail north once more, passing the Great Barrier Reef, and navigating through the Torres Straits. Cook brought back reports of a fertile land and painted a friendly picture of its native inhabitants, which was clearly influenced by contemporary notions of the "noble savage." On the strength of these favorable reports, Botany Bay (in 1788) and shortly afterward Sydney were chosen as convenient "disposal sites" for convicts deported from Britain, who could no longer be packed off to the newly independent American colonies. These consignments of convicts laid the foundation for the British colony of New South Wales.

Yet the British expected more from their new possession than simply a solution to their convict problem. They also had an eye to raw materials such as timber for shipbuilding. Moreover, strategic considerations also played a role in the occupation, as Britain was keen to deter the French, who had already sent several voyages of exploration into Australian waters, from gaining any foothold there. Matthew Flinders's circumnavigation of the continent in 1801 not only provided an accurate picture of its coastline but also underpinned British claims to this part of the globe. At Flinders's suggestion, the continent was now named "Australia."

Over the coming decades, the fifth continent played host not just to convicts but increasingly to voluntary settlers. As a result, European interest in Australia grew. White immigrants took the view that the indigenous Aboriginal people had failed to exploit their land, and as a consequence these immigrants came to look upon it as virgin territory, *terra nullius,* which they were entitled to dispose of as they saw fit. This conception was formally overturned only in 1992 by a ruling of the Australian High Court. White encroachment destroyed the Aborigines' physical and psychic relationship with the natural world. Many of them died because their immune systems—like those of Native Americans—were unused to European diseases, because European colonists and livestock herders robbed them of their land, and because in many cases they were systematically persecuted by the incomers. In the final years of the eighteenth century, there were estimated to be around 300,000 Aborigines living in Australia. By the early twentieth century, their number had shrunk to around 60,000.[224]

The Second Age of Discovery and the Role of Europeans

The first time Europeans became aware of the Pacific Ocean was in 1513, when the Spanish explorer Vasco Núñez de Balboa crossed the Panama Isthmus and stood on the eastern fringes of this ocean. At around the same time, in their exploratory voyages to the Moluccas, the Portuguese had also reached the far western edge of the Pacific, though because they arrived there from island Southeast Asia, it is likely that they were not immediately aware that they had ventured into a hitherto unknown vast ocean.[225] Like America before it, the Pacific was something of an unpleasant surprise for Europeans sailing across the Atlantic Ocean in the hope of reaching Asia, as it represented yet another hindrance on the westward passage to the riches of the Orient. Because the Panama Isthmus lies on an east–west axis and the new ocean appeared to open out beyond it toward the south, Balboa christened it the *Mar del Sur,* or "Southern Ocean," and claimed it for Spain.

Accordingly, the first people to venture forth to explore the uncharted expanses of this ocean and its island chains in the early sixteenth century—effectively treating it as a "Spanish lake"[226]—were Spaniards or Portuguese navigators in the service of Spain. But the first Europeans to discover quite how vast an expanse the Pacific covered were Ferdinand Magellan and his crew. They took three months to voyage from the southern tip of South America, where they finally found a passage around the American continent, to the Marianas. During that time, they were often becalmed, and their provisions and freshwater were almost at an end when they finally made land. As a result, Magellan named the ocean *Mar Pacifico* (literally, "the still ocean"), which presumably was intended to convey a sense of threat rather than sound inviting. After the Augustinian monk Andrés de Urdaneta discovered an east–west passage across the northern Pacific in 1565, the Spanish had a return route to their American possessions—a factor that made exploration of the Pacific far more straightforward and allowed them to establish territorial control over the Philippines along the same lines as their colonial rule in South America.

In undertaking their voyages of exploration, the Spanish and Portuguese were driven not just by the search for precious spices but also by the dream of discovering the legendary realm of Ophir, King Solomon's fabled land of gold. Names that are still in common use today testify to this desire: for example, New Guinea, named for the area of Africa from which gold was exported to Europe, or the island group of the Solomons, in the western Pacific. Another constant key factor in exploration was the ambition of individual navigators to chart new sea passages, discover unknown lands and islands, and find sources of lucrative trade goods. Later, such motivations were supplemented by chiliastic visions—the utopian or millenarian urge to find lost paradises. For instance, many people speculated that the place where, according to ancient European notions, a *Terra Australis* was located was the site of an unspoiled land, where they might convert the inhabitants to the true faith and establish God's kingdom on Earth. In 1606, Pedro Fernández de Quirós called the main island of the New Hebrides Espíritu Santo: this name recalled the *Austrialia del Espíritu Santo,* the southern land, which Quirós wished to discover and name in honor both of his patrons, the Austrias (the Spanish Habsburgs), and of his religious convictions. One of Quirós's captains, Luis Váez de Torres, detached himself from the expedition and sailed farther westward; in 1606, he discovered the strait running between Australia and New Guinea, which was full of dangerous reefs and shallow and which today still bears his name.

The Spanish found neither gold nor a new continent, however, while the dreams of an earthly paradise also came to nothing. Yet they did manage to incorporate the Pacific into a global network of trade contacts. The silver that their galleons took from Acapulco to Manila, and that then made its way from there into the Chinese market, not only caused that country's economy to boom but also linked the Pacific via America and via Asia with Europe.[227] The Iberians regarded the Pacific as a mare clausum, in which they had the sole claim to all navigational and commercial rights. The English and the Dutch, however, refused to accept this edict, attacking Spanish ships and laying waste to cities both on the Pacific coast of South America and on the Philippines.

In 1688, following a voyage diagonally across the Pacific in search of booty, the pirate, adventurer, and explorer William Dampier landed on the northwest coast of Australia. He encountered Aborigines there and left behind one of the earliest descriptions of these indigenous peoples. Dampier saw them as the most wretched people on Earth; according to him, apart from their human form, the Aborigines were more like animals than human beings. To his great surprise, they showed no interest whatsoever in the goods and gifts offered by the Europeans.

The Dutch not only settled parts of island Southeast Asia but also in the seventeenth century "discovered" for Europe parts of Australia and the southeast Pacific. Though their activities were commercially motivated, military and strategic considerations, which had to do with the country's secession from Spain and its global struggle for independence, also played a decisive role. For example, Oliver Noort circumnavigated the globe between 1588 and 1601 but in the course of this voyage also attacked the Spanish port of Valparaiso in Chile, waited in vain in Philippines waters to ambush Manila-bound silver galleons, and then proceeded to sack local settlements, raid Chinese junks, and launch an assault on Manila itself, which was beaten back by determined Spanish resistance. Over the following decades, the Dutch regularly blockaded Malacca, Macau, and Manila; attacked Portuguese, Spanish, Chinese, and Japanese ships; established themselves as the leading European power in Southeast Asian and Far Eastern waters; sent out their feelers from there toward the Pacific and Oceania; and sounded out both the eastern and western passages across the Pacific toward the Spice Islands, China, and Japan.[228]

Jacob le Maire and the brothers Jan and Willem Corneliszoon Schouten rounded Cape Horn and made the voyage across the southern Pacific to Southeast Asia. In 1642, Abel Tasman set sail from the Dutch base on Mauritius in the Indian Ocean and headed east. He did not sight the Australian mainland, because it lay to the north of his chosen route, but he did come across the island that bears his name today. He, however, named it Van Diemen's Land to honor his employer, the governor of the Dutch East India Company (VOC). Tasman ultimately ended up at the Dutch port of Batavia, but before this, his voyage had taken him in a wide arc across the western Pacific, where he came across Aotearoa and called it New Zealand as well as the islands of Tonga and Fiji. On a subsequent voyage, he sailed along the northern coast of Australia, an area he called New Holland.

Occasionally, Dutch ships would also reach Australia by chance, for instance, when conducting voyages of exploration in island Southeast Asia. Thus, without realizing it, the Dutchman Willem Janszoon was probably the first European to set foot on Australian soil, when he landed on the northwest of the Cape York peninsula in 1606. Moreover, it was a reasonably common occurrence for ships on the long voyage from the Cape of Good Hope to Batavia to be shipwrecked by storms on the inhospitable west coast of Australia. The first of these mishaps took place in 1616, when Dirk Hartog landed on the island that was subsequently named for him. Two mutineers from the vessel *Batavia,* which ran aground on a coral reef in 1629 in dramatic circumstances, were put ashore close to the modern settlement of Kalbarri. They were the first Europeans to remain permanently in Australia.[229]

None of these chance or deliberate discoveries led Europeans to anticipate a flow of attractive economic trade goods from Australia. Accordingly, further voyages of discovery were abandoned. Even so, the vision of a *terra australis incognita* continued to cast its spell. Quirós was inspired by this notion, as were Le Maire and the Schouten brothers. Likewise, Jacob Roggeveen set off on a voyage in search of this fabled land in 1721–1723, at the behest of the Dutch West Indies Company, a sister organization of the VOC. After rounding Cape Horn, he came across an island on Easter Monday, 1722—a date that inspired him to call his discovery "Easter Island." Roggeveen and his crew were astonished to see the monumental sculptures made of tufa, which were worshipped by the native people.

Ultimately, the vision of a southern continent was the key inspiration behind the European penetration of the Pacific region in the eighteenth century, in which England and France played the leading role. The rivalry between these two major powers, which was played out not just in terms of strategic power but also economically, formed a constant backcloth to these endeavors. Defeat by Britain in North America and India in the mid-eighteenth century served to stimulate French interest in the Pacific region, which was still free of colonial possessions, and the mysterious fifth continent. Both French and English armchair theoreticians had put forward a welter of ideas about the appearance and character of Oceania and Australia. For example, the Scottish hydrographer Alexander Dalrymple wrote in 1770 that the landmass north of the equator must of necessity be balanced by one in the south in order to maintain the equilibrium of the Earth and facilitate its steady rotation. In addition, pieces of evidence adduced by those who had traveled in the Pacific pointed to the existence of a large landmass: these included sightings of large groups of offshore islands, which from previous explorers' experience usually indicated the presence of a big landmass behind, as did frequently changing winds, flotsam in the water, the lack of a swell, flocks of birds, and cloud formations. These theories prompted an urgent demand for explorers to locate the fifth continent and take possession of it.

There ensued an intensive exploration fever known as the Second Age of Discovery, an era characterized by the scientific research undertaken during the voyages. In 1764 and 1766, respectively, the French mathematician and naval officer Louis-Antoine de Bougainville set off on his two renowned voyages to the South Seas. The English, keen to assert their role as the world's foremost sea power, followed suit; Samuel Wallis undertook an exploration of the southeastern Pacific that was more meticulous than that of any navigator before him, during which he discovered Tahiti in 1767. Bougainville arrived there shortly afterward. Henceforth, the island became the principal base for a series of Pacific voyages; it also became the epitome of an idealized Western view of the "South Seas paradise." James Cook, too, landed on Tahiti several times on his three voyages of discovery across the Pacific between 1768 and 1779.

Cook is seen as the prototype of the kind of scientifically minded explorer who characterized the second half of the eighteenth century. The region that he explored was immense, covering the entire expanse of sea from Antarctica in the south to the Bering Straits in the north and from the Magellan Straits in the east to Australia in the west. In practical terms, Cook demonstrated that the long sought-after Northwest Passage around northern Canada—which would have represented the shortest route from England to China—was constantly icebound and impassable. In addition, he conducted such a systematic exploration of the South Pacific that he could not possibly have missed finding a large landmass. Consequently, his voyages demonstrated empirically beyond all doubt that the fabled *terra australis incognita* did not, in fact, exist or at least was confined to the landmasses of Australia and New Zealand.

The voyages of Bougainville and especially Cook marked a turning point in the history of European expansion, as these were the first scientifically driven voyages of discovery. Not only were the expeditions the subject of meticulous preparations, but a large complement of scholars also came along on the voyage. On Cook's voyages, these scholars' tasks included taking hydrographic and topographic measurements, such as taking depth soundings in bays to ascertain their suitability as anchorages or ports or in passages that were difficult to navigate. Coastlines were fixed on nautical charts and a whole range of astronomical, anthropological, botanical, and zoological studies undertaken. All those involved scrupulously documented their findings in detailed written accounts and drawings. This was far from being science freely conducted for its own sake, however: the data that were collected were used by the British Empire to help it corroborate its dominant role in world affairs.

The cargoes that were brought to Mexico by the Manila galleon and then transported further on to Europe—namely, spices from the Moluccas, silver and silk from Japan, tobacco from the Philippines, and Chinese luxury goods—had a major impact on the European balance of trade and mode of living. World-weary social critics in Paris, London, and elsewhere found their imagination suddenly piqued by the promise of the Pacific. Commentators believed that the "noble savage" of legend, living in a paradisiac natural state, had finally been located in the island world of Oceania. This myth was just one in a long history of European imagined ideals. Ever since Columbus's discovery of America, non-European societies had been treated as templates onto which potential alternatives to the European social order could be projected. Tahiti and its people now seemed to be a perfect example of just such an alternative form of existence. There, it seemed, society still existed in its unspoiled natural state, much as Jean-Jacques Rousseau had described it. The people were welcoming and friendly, there appeared to be no class differences, and everyone took a share in the natural riches that the tropical environment offered in abundance. Furthermore, Europeans were enthralled by the physical beauty of the people there, which put them in mind of the ideal human forms of classical antiquity. Easy sexuality and free love held out the promise of a world untrammeled by stifling constraints and conventions.[230]

Entranced by such delights, Bougainville christened Tahiti "New Kythera," after the Greek island that was dedicated to the cult of Aphrodite, the goddess of love. The botanist and Rousseau acolyte Philibert Commerson eulogized the island, writing that it was free of all vices, prejudices, want, or disputes. He went on to claim that the native people there were the most fortunate on Earth and could feed themselves from the fruits that Nature brought forth without any effort on their part. They were not ruled by kings, Commerson maintained, but by caring family heads, and the only God they worshiped was Love.

In actual fact, the society of Tahiti and other Pacific islands was by no means free of constraints, violence, or social hierarchies. For example, the women with whom European sailors came into contact generally did not belong to the local elite. Sexual favors were a ruse employed to get hold of rare trade goods, and the women might have offered their services under pressure from their fathers, brothers, or even husbands.

The "noble savages" of Polynesia were described, drawn, and painted, and some ultimately even traveled, at their own behest, to Europe. Omai was the most famous, though not the first, of these. Thought to have been born in around 1753 and a member of the Tahitian middle class, Omai was tall and slim, though was not particularly handsome and above all did not have the light skin color of the Polynesian nobility. In 1774, he came to England somewhat by chance, finding himself on board a ship that was part of Cook's second voyage but had been forced to return home. In England, the wealthy private scholar and botanist Joseph Banks, who had been with Cook on his first voyage, took Omai under his wing. He introduced the Tahitian to the king and his consort. There followed a string of invitations to visit the houses of aristocrats and scholars; Omai learned to dance, ride a horse, ice-skate, and fire a gun, and he was taken to several theater performances, concerts, and horse races. He particularly enjoyed polite conversation and seemed to confirm the popular image of a natural man and "noble savage," displaying friendliness, intelligence, natural grace, and effortless gallantry toward women (he was even involved in a few dalliances during his stay). In short, he presented a highly favorable contrast to the stiff English gentleman. Omai traveled back to the South Seas in 1776. In the interim, he had identified so strongly with his English hosts that he passed himself off as a European in his old homeland and attained a high status with his newly acquired skills and manners. He is thought to have died in around 1780. He lived on for a while in Europe as a literary device, used by writers to criticize or castigate Western society.

Far more ambivalent, right from the outset, was the image of the Australian Aborigine.[231] Dampier, as we have seen, considered Aborigines the most miserable people in the world and noted their lack of interest in European goods. Cook was also struck by their lack of acquisitiveness, but more in keeping with modern attitudes he interpreted this in a positive light. In his view, the Aborigines needed nothing because Nature either furnished them with all they required or rendered superfluous many of the things that Europeans considered indispensable. He regarded them as happier than Europeans. In contrast, from the late eighteenth century on, colonialism saw them first as foremost as "troublemakers" who stood in the way of white land acquisition and exploitation.

For a long time, the contacts between Europeans and the people of Oceania were only sporadic and brief. This situation changed only with the voyages of James Cook. Thereafter, visitors from the West arrived more frequently, and the exploitation of the natural resources of the Pacific gathered pace. Whales and seals were hunted and sandalwood trees felled. Captain William Bligh was given the task of taking breadfruit tree saplings from Tahiti to the Caribbean; the plan was to cultivate the fruit, which required very little care, as food for the slave workers on the sugarcane plantations. This first attempt to transfer breadfruit failed in 1792, when the famous mutiny broke out on board Bligh's ship HMS *Bounty,* but the following year trees were successfully transported to Jamaica. In doing so, the Europeans managed to incorporate the Pacific, too, into the system of global plant transfer, which had gone hand in hand with expansion from the very beginning.

From a European perspective, James Cook is the epitome of the enlightened, rationally minded, and humane explorer. But the Maori and Aborigines see him in a very different light. From their standpoint, he brought violence, displacement, and death.[232] Europeans imported diseases that the immune system of Oceanian people could not cope with. On some islands, up to 90 percent of the populace succumbed to such illnesses. Moreover, the natural and cultural landscapes of the region were fundamentally changed, reformed, and not infrequently destroyed forever. Missionaries landed on a succession of islands and preached a new religion. Carpetbaggers and adventurers set themselves up as advisers to indigenous rulers. Little by little, Oceania ultimately found itself parceled out into colonies.

Yet where these contacts were concerned, it was not just the Europeans who determined the course of events. Particularly in Polynesia, certain rulers were keen to exploit the opportunities that these new contacts provided. European firearms helped intensify the wars between rival Maori groups on New Zealand. In Fiji, meanwhile, newly acquired military technology enabled a chieftain by the name of Seru Cakobau to assert control over the whole archipelago. Chief Pomare did the same on Tahiti, while on Hawaii King Kamehameha I relied on the support of European advisers to unify the whole island group under his rule at the turn of the eighteenth century.

Translated from the German by Peter Lewis

·[FIVE]·

Europe and the Atlantic World

Wolfgang Reinhard

Introduction

UNTIL the fifteenth century neither the inhabitants of the Atlantic side of Africa nor the people living in the lands not yet called America nor the inhabitants of "Latin" Europe west of a line running from St. Petersburg to Trieste knew anything of one another. Furthermore, even those inhabiting particular areas of these three continents knew little or nothing about those in other regions. Admittedly, thanks to its consciously cultivated cultural unity, the comparatively small continent of Europe represented something of an exception in this respect. Yet Europeans had little inkling that within a few hundred years they would impose a common economic and cultural system on the peoples of these other two continents.

However, this dominance of Europe in the Atlantic realm, which was firmly established by 1750, is still reflected today in the imbalanced state of historical research, with inescapable consequences for the basis of the present study. While there is a wealth of documentary source material in the case of Europe, for the precolonial era in both the "New World" and in those parts of Africa beyond the influence of Islam, a written culture was wholly absent. Certainly, alongside the physical evidence—comprising archeological and linguistic discoveries from both continents—there is also a rich oral tradition recounting the history of African peoples, which in recent years has been systematically gathered and collated into oral histories. Yet it has since become clear that, while these texts undoubtedly do recount historical events, these were often altered to meet the requirements of the particular community at the time when they were first recorded. Of course, written accounts are also colored by the historical awareness of their originators, but once written they remain for all time as testaments to an age and are not, like oral history, subject to constant revision. To be sure, there exists an extensive colonial history of Latin America from the premodern era, in which the colonized people also have a voice, along with all manner of travel reports and other sources of European origin on Africa from

Europe supported by Africa & America.

In 1792, the painter and poet William Blake used the ancient motif of the Three Graces to symbolize Africa and America's amicable support of Europe. That such a situation might prevail and endure was the fervent wish of Johan Gabriel Stedman in the afterword to his book, for which Blake provided the illustrations. However, in voicing this naive aspiration, Stedman was knowingly contradicting his experience of brutal violence and slavery in Suriname in 1772–1777, the actual subject of his text. (IAM/World History Archive)

the sixteenth to nineteenth centuries. But because the precolonial peoples of Africa and the Americas did not themselves possess a written language, European historians effectively regarded them as having no history. Research into these peoples was left to the anthropologists, who from time to time provided thoroughly historical, informative insights into these cultures.

Grossly oversimplified, since the premodern historiography of the Middle Ages and the early modern period, historical research within Europe has passed through three phases, which overlap in terms of time: a form of nationalistic history that held sway from the early nineteenth century on and focused primarily on political events and elites was followed, initially from the late nineteenth century but especially after the Second World War, by a growing acceptance of a structural form of history that took account of social and economic factors. This, in turn, was superseded, from the 1980s on, by the so-called cultural turn: grounded as it is in linguistic and semiotic theory, this approach has made it its primary objective to investigate the actual historical significance of academic history's findings. As the "new European" scholarship in North America rapidly caught up and ultimately assumed the leading role, after the Second World War modern academic history began to take an interest in Africa, Central America, and South America, doubtless influenced by contemporary geopolitical considerations. Research institutes specifically focused on these regions were established, professorships endowed, and scholarly journals founded in England and the United States, followed by France, Spain, and Germany. In addition, African history was introduced as a subject of study at newly founded universities in colonial Africa. Shortly thereafter, as African countries gained their independence, history began to be employed in a way that had long since been evident in Latin America: historians were called on to produce national histories of the various countries for the purposes of political pedagogy. In Africa, this sometimes entailed romanticizing precolonial conditions. Indeed, such nationalistic forms of history are still in demand there, despite the fact that the 1970s, both in Africa and in the West, saw a fundamental shift in structural history toward grand hypotheses critical of colonialism such as dependence theory. In spite of further innovative initiatives, including attempts to disengage African history entirely from the paradigm of European academic history, indigenous historical research was unable to match the lead taken by Europe and the United States. For even the founding fathers of African historical research, at least, were mainly Europeans, alongside a few Africans who had been educated in Europe. And even today, it is still the case that the leading research centers and places of publication of the most influential journals on Latin America are all to be found in England and the United States; in the case of Africa, it is England and France. Even the concept of an "Atlantic history" developed as the result of an exchange of ideas between the United States and Europe.[1] In contrast, the study of history in many Latin American and especially African countries is hampered by an absence of institutional continuity and a lack of resources. As one commentator has written: "Many of our colleagues in Africa . . . are struggling even to survive from one day to the next."[2]

I. *Atlantic Africa*

ACCORDING to our current knowledge,[3] Africa was the cradle not only of hominids in general but also of the species *Homo sapiens;*[4] the sub-Saharan region, apart from its highland areas, and especially on the side of the continent facing the Atlantic, offered somewhat inhospitable environments for human habitation. The deserts in both the north and the southwest are followed, from north to south and from west to east, by areas of thornbush savanna, known in the north as the Sahel, with just 100–400 millimeters of rainfall annually, and then by moist savanna, with 400–1,500 millimeters of rain. However, the rainy periods are concentrated in just a few months, with the amount falling varying greatly from year to year, making sufficient rainfall a fundamental requirement of existence in Africa. And even in the areas of tropical rainforest, which cover the Congo basin and a strip along the Guinea coast, the lush vegetation conveys a misleading impression, as the layer of humus in the soil that can support cultivation is extremely thin. If it is cleared for cultivation, the high rate of chemical exchange within the soil, conditioned by the humid heat in this region, causes all the nutrients to quickly leach out and leave it barren.

This state of affairs meant that farming in sub-Saharan Africa was only rarely carried out with the aid of a plow; rather, it was almost exclusively done by human labor, through the use of digging sticks and hoes; deep plows would have made the soil quality only degrade even faster. Despite highly developed techniques of hand cultivation, then, yields remained correspondingly low. The most important food crops were various strains of millet, plus (in the area between Niger and Senegal) rice,[5] yams, and plantains, the last supposedly an early introduction from Asia. Animal husbandry, especially of large livestock, was also very limited; accordingly, no close functional connection was created between arable and livestock farming through the use of animal motive power, especially draft animals, or by using their manure for soil improvement. At most, animal husbandry was carried out in order to supplement diet with dairy products and meat. In the Sahel and the northern savanna region, there existed a cultural division of labor between arable farmers, who lived predominantly along watercourses, and livestock herders, who pursued a more or less nomadic existence on the tracts of land in between. Farther south, roughly between the latitudes of 10° north and 10° south, while livestock farming was not entirely precluded by the presence of trypanosomiasis spread by the tsetse fly, it was severely hampered by this disease.[6]

This illness manifested itself as sleeping sickness among humans and among livestock (especially horses and cattle) as the disease nagana pest, which was generally fatal. Africans were also prey to several other more or less deadly diseases—above all, malaria and yellow fever. Epidemics and famines occurred on a regular basis, claiming countless lives. John Iliffe is quite correct in his assertion that Africans' great contribution to world history was to have succeeded in cultivating a part of the world that was in many regards a particularly hostile environment. The fact that the end result sometimes struck visitors from other continents as meager and that cultural and political development suffered several setbacks should in no way compromise history's acknowledgment of African achievements.[7]

African societies produced a broad spectrum of ornate textiles in great quantity, ranging from woolen and cotton fabrics in the north to textiles woven from plant bark and, above all, from the fibers of the raffia palm in the south. Basket weaving and pottery were highly developed, and alongside elaborate wood carvings, works were also produced in copper, bronze, and brass in the lower Niger region, using sophisticated casting techniques such as the lost-wax process. First and foremost, though, the Africans were past masters at extracting iron from ore and processing it in bellows-powered blast furnaces. Trades were usually the preserve of specialists, who among the societies of the northern savanna organized themselves into guilds. This was sometimes a sign of a group's privileged status but could also result in collective discrimination. Thus, in some places, blacksmiths were close to the kings, by dint of their reputation for possessing magical powers, while in Islamic-influenced societies, they were stigmatized and ostracized.[8]

Food and manufactured goods were bartered. However, where transport relied on human porters, as in the central tsetse-fly belt, for a long time trade seems to have remained predominantly a local affair. By contrast, there existed since ancient times a thriving trade exchanging rock salt from the Sahara with millet and gold from the Sudan, as well as a trade in cola nuts from the southern rain forest, highly prized as a stimulant. The trans-Saharan trade route used caravans of camels or donkeys; reports tell of trains of up to 20,000–30,000 camels carrying salt. Communities specializing in mercantile activity played a key role in this enterprise: the Dyula in the west and the Hausa in the east. Over and above the basic business of barter, textiles, copper artifacts, or particular species of shells could take on the role of proper currencies. Despite a paucity of resources, Africa's production of manufactured goods was richer and more varied than once thought. Trade with Europeans was not a necessity but rather a luxury for African societies.[9]

This framework of ecological and economic conditions was paralleled by cultural and mental configurations, beginning with the contrast between, on the one hand, the forest and scrubland as threatening wilderness, the haunts of wild beasts, evil spirits, and hostile magicians, and, on the other, the settled lands that were carved out of this wilderness as the epitome of civilization and culture. These settlements were inhabited by exogamous ancestral clans governed by systems of either matrilineal, patrilineal, or bilineal descent. Matrilineal ancestral clans predominated in the tsetse belt with its basic systems of herding, whereas patrilineality seemed to go hand in hand with more developed forms of animal husbandry.

Throughout, the family or household constituted the basic social unit. Individuals in the modern sense counted for nothing; without families they were barely capable of surviving. It was essential to have many children—hence, the African obsession with male virility and female fertility. Women married and gave birth apparently as soon as possible but with gaps of several years between the births; these gaps were occasioned by the practice of prolonged breast-feeding, which in turn was driven by the lack of alternative sustenance for young children. Besides, this feeding method was a way of combating the extremely high incidence of child mortality, a statistic that reduced average life expectancy to just twenty-five years or less. But it also precluded the possibility of any rapid population increase.

In contrast, most men married late, because to do so they needed to be able to pay the bride's father a bride-price for the work potential and fertility that the family was losing in relinquishing their daughter. In this way, the practice of polygyny asserted itself as ideal and became widespread: it gave rise to the household of the so-called big man, surrounded by his wives and their children, grown-up married and unmarried sons, younger brothers, poor relations, clients, and slaves.

In many places, households of this kind, comprising anything between ten and fifty members, became the fundamental building blocks of society.

However, even under pain of punishment for adultery, this habit of men marrying late gave rise to the kind of broad-minded sexual mores that even the earliest Arab travelers to the region commented on. But above all, competition to secure brides made generational conflict between men a permanent feature of African societies. It was institutionally controlled by the system of age sets in conjunction with the practice of circumcision and initiation rites involving torture by the established men of the clan. Time and again, the propensity for this system to spawn notorious violence among sexually frustrated young men was exploited in the formation of special warrior societies characterized by their bloodthirsty brutality, such as the *imbangala* in sixteenth-century Angola. Conversely, there was little respect shown to elderly men and their life experience. Whenever a person began to show signs of incipient weakness, he rapidly became a figure of fun.

Africa was and remained politically decentralized. Even its foremost ancient empires were not rigidly organized. Most Africans lived in local communities that never exceeded 1,500 square kilometers in area and a population of between three thousand and thirty thousand. These settlements were based on ancestral clans or groupings of these, legitimized in myth by overwhelmingly specious genealogical connections. Yet population growth and increasing prosperity through trade could (as could the control over important cults and cult sites) lead to a situation where the chiefs of such local communities developed into rulers of extensive empires. In the Sudan, such rulers achieved military superiority by fielding a mounted army, especially after the Muslims had introduced saddles, stirrups, and snaffle bits to the region. Farther south, warfare seems to have been conducted less efficiently, at least until the establishment of standing armies that owed sole allegiance to individual kings.[10] However, it was perfectly possible for empires to come into being not just through conflict but also through peaceful confederation.

Empires could grow up around urban centers or conversely give rise to the formation of towns. Such towns are not always easy to distinguish from large villages; perhaps the main distinguishing features were that their inhabitants no longer lived exclusively off the land, they were home to specialized artisans, they became centers of commerce, and "public buildings" were erected there, first and foremost (naturally enough) royal residences. But in any event, the prerequisite for the formation both of cities and of empires was the production of sufficient agricultural surpluses to feed town dwellers and the political and religious elites. Because Africa had trouble in achieving such surpluses, cities and empires arose here later than elsewhere. However, it is incorrect to claim that Islam was responsible for introducing city culture to Africa, though it undoubtedly contributed to its rise. Ancient urban settlements have been uncovered in the northern savanna region, along with cities both on the fringes of and deep within the west African forest belt, such as Ife, Oyo, and Benin (which are thought to have flourished from the twelfth century onward). In the southern savanna, cities developed within the Kingdom of Kongo from the fifteenth century on.[11]

While some African empires developed complex institutions, these were far removed from the impersonal stability that characterizes modern states—in consequence, the misleading term "state" should be avoided when referring both to premodern Africa and for Europe at the same period. As family enterprises, these empires were largely dependent on the personal competence of each individual ruler. Their weakest point was the matter of succession, which was extremely difficult to administer and regulate under the prevailing conditions of polygyny and matrilineality. Certainly, the many wives of the ruler could serve to strengthen ties of loyalty with vassals. But the problem remained of which son of which wife should accede to the throne. And under matrilineality, it was the nephews rather than the sons in direct line of inheritance anyway. In short, this system gave ample opportunity for serious conflict within the ruling elite; there could be no question of dynastic unity. Accordingly, the borders of these empires were not fixed but fluctuated according to how strong the center of power was at any one time. In Benin, the king's sole authority to impose the death penalty delineated a core zone of unequivocal, direct rule. Outside this zone were regions that were controlled by deputies of the central power who operated under its supervision. Further beyond these, in turn, were other areas whose ancestral rulers were left in place and simply required to pay a tribute and finally those from which tribute could be exacted only by launching military campaigns, such as in the period when Dahomey was still somehow dependent of Oyo.

Yet the stability of African empires rested not solely on military force and political institutions but just as much on the specific religious properties of royalty, as manifested in traditional myths and ritual practices. The legendary founder of the Lunda Empire, for instance, was believed to derive his charisma from the magical aura that surrounded him of being a particularly effective hunter. More often, though, this charisma rested on the ruler's ability to bring about regular rainfall and fertility.[12] Even the historical founder of the Songhay Empire, Sonni Ali (1464–1492), was descended from a family of magi kings and was regarded as a powerful magician, despite being a Muslim, at least in name. His successes would only have enhanced this reputation.

Certain aspects of the royal ritual pertained throughout Africa. At the start of a king's reign, a fire would be lit and carried by means of torches to areas under royal control; these flames would be allowed to go out only on the ruler's death. Likewise, as a superhuman figure, the king was required to conceal his natural bodily functions. Thus, whenever he ate or drank, all those present had to throw themselves to the ground and look down, for it was thought that anyone who saw the king eating would be able to kill him thereafter. In some places, the king would remain constantly behind a screen and communicate with his subjects only through a particular dignitary. The king also led the rainmaking ceremony; among the Vili, this ritual would conclude with the monarch shooting an arrow into the sky. The common good depended on the king's good health and bodily perfection. If he showed any weakness, or if natural catastrophes ensued that he had clearly been unable to avert, he could be killed or forced to commit suicide. The sole purpose of the kingdom was to ensure its inhabitants' well-being.

African kings did not exercise unlimited power but were dependent in a number of different ways on dignitaries and aristocrats. Some monarchs attempted to free themselves from such ties by appointing their bodyguard and servants exclusively from among clients and slaves who had no roots within the realm and who were therefore solely answerable to the king. However, to do this required amassing the necessary wherewithal. In many African monarchies, such as Dahomey and Asante, and among the Bakongo and the Lunda, we also encounter the extraordinary institution of a kind of female co-regency. The "king's mother"—not his mother in any biological sense but rather the holder of an office that in the case of the dynastic mythology of Dahomey descended from the mother of the country's first king—ran her own independent court with her own instruments of power and played a role in political decision making, especially the question of the succession. In Dahomey, she was appointed for life by the king from among the wives of his predecessor.[13] African women sometimes enjoyed considerable independence and played a significant role in commerce, society, and political life, particularly when such roles were validated by religion and myth.

Africans, both male and female, saw themselves as inhabiting a world that was permeated by mysterious powers, a kind of magical universe. As we have already seen, no area of life could be disengaged from this realm and be seen as entirely secular. In common with most premodern religions, African religions were also closely bound to particular peoples, clans, or groups. As a result, there may have been as many as three thousand separate African religions, many of which, however, shared certain characteristics. Each religion only accepted members of the group from within which it arose. Even so, it was not uncommon for the creator of the world or the earth goddess to be co-opted as ancestors of the particular people. Under these circumstances, it was almost impossible to switch religion; rather, elements of other religions were adopted and adapted. This was to become a problem for both Islam and Christianity. However, "conversion" was also pointless in such circumstances, because Africans viewed religion not as a set of doctrines but as a way of life. This is why there is not a single word in African languages for "religion." Nor should the esoteric knowledge amassed by shamans and priests be equated with religious dogma in the sense of the Christian tradition.

Religion was a community affair, not a matter of individual faith. Not only were the elite within a community, with the king at their head, intimately bound up with it, but so were the dead. Worshipping the ancestors and treating them as an integral part of the community were essential elements of African religions. The ancestors existed as the "living dead" in a kind of afterlife but were thought to be constantly present, because there was no barrier between the spirit world and the life of the community. In consequence, they were included within ceremonial rites, as they were thought to look after their descendants, exerting good or malign influence over them and interceding on their behalf with the gods. Their souls could also be reborn within their successors—this was thought, for instance, to explain the resemblance between grandfathers and their grandchildren. The ancestors also represented an important way of legitimizing power; in some places, they were regarded as the true owners of the land. Kings were able to communicate with them through mediums; the graves of kings, and their upkeep, were of great significance to the community.

Even so, the apparent affinity of Africans to the Christian notion of the afterlife was extremely limited. Heaven and hell were alien concepts to them, because they were unable to reconcile themselves either to some insuperable "spatial" barrier between the here and now and the afterlife or to the linear concept of time implicit in the idea of the finality of the individual human life ending in death. There did seem to be some notion of repayment for good or evil deeds in the beyond, but this was eclipsed by concern for the well-being of the community in the here and now and the relationship between the good conduct of its members and the influence of omnipresent mysterious powers on their existence, in practical terms on rainfall and fertility, drought and disease. Natural disasters were therefore seen as originating not just from evil supernatural forces but also from individual transgressions and social disorder. In this respect, African religiosity was explicitly focused on this life and overcoming practical difficulties; as such, then, it was an important—perhaps the most important—instrument for dealing with an inhospitable and often downright hostile environment. Kings who failed in their role as guarantors of communal well-being could be killed, while witch doctors who failed to conjure up rain were also summarily executed.

For this reason, veneration of the creator of the world and supreme deity stayed within strictly defined bounds. The concept appears to have existed in all African religions, sometimes taking a female form but overwhelmingly (even in matrilineal societies) a male one. But more important in dealing with the problems of everyday life were the other deities, a whole pantheon of gods and goddesses, who in Yoruba theology were known as *orishas* and among the Fon as *Vodun*. In common with other polytheistic systems, these gods were responsible for various aspects of life, including agriculture, blacksmithing, war, and love. The system was not dualistic, as there was no devil, and the powers of evil were not clearly personified. Rather, good and evil, salvation and disaster were integral features of the gods and the ancestors themselves. There were even ancestors who had been wicked people during their lifetime. Above all, the "trickster" deity evident in most cultures not only loved playing practical jokes but was also capable, for no apparent reason, of visiting great harm on people. It was thus especially important to appease such deities with ritual observances.

Alongside the actual gods and ancestors, the world was also peopled with a whole range of spirits. In addition, objects of the most diverse kind could become repositories of the mysterious powers of the magical universe. In former times, such objects were called "fetishes," whereas nowadays (by analogy with the belief systems of North American Indians), the term "medicine" is preferred. The fact that the old Kingdom of Kongo became liberally sprinkled with crosses as a sign of the country's Christianization was in large part driven by this association with the salutary power of certain objects.[14]

The principal way of gaining the favor of all these powers was to offer sacrifices. Almost everything could be sacrificed: various objects, fruits, animals, and even in extreme cases people or at least human blood. Occasionally these sacrifices would be accompanied by a short prayer, in which the persons offering the sacrifice presented their request. Though this ritual could be conducted in temples or other cultic sites, it was not obligatory, and similarly priests, elders, and rainmakers could be involved but not by necessity. The most important communal ritual was a dance to the rhythmic beat of drums and bells, accompanied by singing. This rhythmic stimulation was designed to enable a particular god or spirit to take possession of the dancer. The "possessed" dancer, equipped with the appropriate clothing and other attributes, thus became a living god, displayed gestures and behaviors that were typical of the god in question, and could even sometimes convey important messages from the deity.

The protection of the gods and ancestors and of the spirits and "medicine" was urgently required to counter the ubiquitous forces of evil, in particular the black magic practiced by both male and female witches. A person could become a witch by birth; after all, we have already noted the existence of evil ancestors. But witches could also be people possessed by evil spirits or those who had invoked neutral magical powers for evil purposes. Personal or collective misfortune helped fuel suspicion of witchcraft, especially against neighbors who might stand to profit from it or to whom one at least could impute the motive of envy. Suspected witches were subjected to trials by poison and other "ordeals." Some peoples had secret societies whose members donned masks and engaged in witch hunts, cruelly torturing their victims to death.[15]

Through comparing the detailed reports of Capuchin missionaries in the seventeenth century with modern ethnological findings, it has been possible to reconstruct more accurately the complex religious system of the ancient Kingdom of Kongo. From this, the personified or impersonal powers of the magic universe emerge as having three distinct dimensions:

1. The *mbumba* dimension of the earth and water spirits, which were key in determining people's relations to nature, life, and fertility. Their mediums could be either men or women. There appears to be some connection to matrilineal ascription of inheritance and rank in this bilinear or dual-monolinear society.
2. The *nkadimpemba* dimension of the sky spirits, whose mediums were exclusively male. This dimension was connected to social and political relations within the community and to the patrilinear ascription of dietary taboos, freedom, or bondage. Witch finders came from this realm.
3. The dimension of the ancestral sprits, which could be oriented toward both matrilineal and patrilineal systems.

All three dimensions exhibit separate functional hierarchies, with women able to become chiefs in the *mbumba* dimension. The king's authority was dependent on him legitimizing himself within all three dimensions, especially because he did not exert exclusive control over any one of them. Significantly, the Portuguese were successively integrated into all three dimensions: as ancestral spirits because they were white skinned, as the ancestors, who dwelt underground, were also reputed to be; as water spirits, because they had arrived from overseas; and as representatives of the supreme sky spirit.[16] While these details cannot be universally applied, they do make plain the complex mental structure of the African religious and political world.

Peoples and Empires

The kind of generalizations that have been made thus far are only possible because Atlantic Africa displays a considerable degree of cultural and doubtless also genetic similarity. If we follow Christopher Ehret's language-based approach,[17] we discover that almost all the peoples of this region speak languages belonging to the Niger–Congo family, or—insofar as they live south of the Sudan savanna region—variants of its most important subgroup, namely, the Bantu languages. While Afro-Asiatic languages were spoken in the Sahara by Arabs, Berbers, and the Tuareg, the only group in the savanna speaking these was the Hausa, with Nilo-Saharan languages evident only in the heartland of the Songhay on the Niger and in the empire of Kanem-Bornu around Lake Chad. Only in the far south do we encounter the Khoisan languages of the San (formerly pejoratively called the Bushmen) and the Khoikhoi (equally pejoratively once known as Hottentots). The San were hunter-gatherers like the pygmies of the Congo basin rainforest, though the latter lived in a symbiotic relationship with settled Bantu farmers and adopted their language. The Khoikhoi were cattle herders, who were organized into patrilineal clans.[18] Indicators such as the relatively minor differences between Bantu languages and the predominantly sparse settlement of the savanna region south of the Congo basin may point to the comparatively late spread of Bantu-speaking groups, to the detriment of the Khoikhoi.

It may conceivably be for this reason that the history of the similarly thinly, albeit somewhat more heavily, settled area between the Sahara and the rainforest, with its confusing mass of peoples and languages, presents us with a far more dynamic picture. Or is this, rather, attributable to its early contact with the Islamic world? Alternatively, our knowledge may simply be skewed by greater availability of source material in this case. For, while the rest of Atlantic Africa presents no writing systems or written transmission of history prior to the arrival of the Portuguese, for this region there is no shortage of eyewitness accounts or proper historical documentation in the Arabic language, or at least in Arabic script.[19] The zeal with which scholars in the post–Second World War period sought to fill the gaps in the written record with the African oral tradition (oral history) has since been supplanted by a more cautious approach. For as a rule, unlike in many written sources, oral history has no fixed original text but instead only several versions subject to constant alteration. Besides, fixed points in time in the past have little significance for Africans, and so the oral tradition frequently aims not to recount historical actuality but rather to attempt to establish norms. Stories of African founder kings probably have very little to do with demonstrable historical events but are key documents in corroborating the idea of African kingship.

Of course, written sources not only have to be checked (as always) for their bias but in addition in the case of Africa must be examined closely to determine how far the foreign author has understood the alien culture or perhaps misunderstood it from the perspective of his own. Thus, for example, the common moral

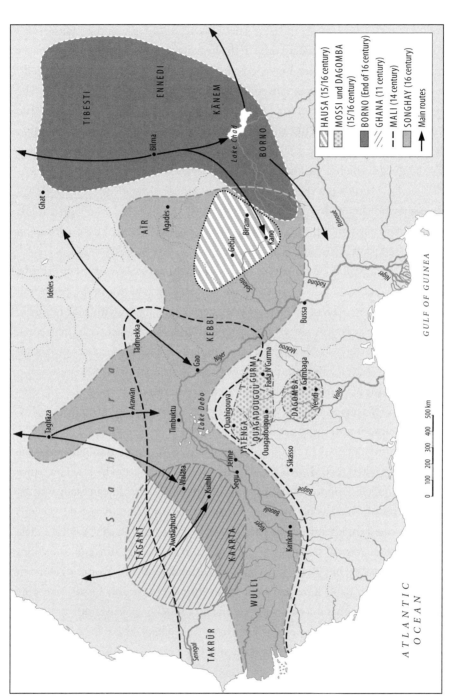

Kingdoms of the Sahel from the eleventh to the sixteenth century

outrage shown by Muslims and Europeans alike at African "promiscuity" in most instances really only indicates that they have failed to grasp the problems of African family and sexual relationships. However, such texts may sometimes come from informed observers and conscientiously include statements from Africans themselves. Greater certainty can only be obtained not from comparing various sources of the same kind with one another but above all through a comparison of the oral tradition, written sources, and both ethnographic and archeological finds. Thanks to such opportunities, we know more about West Africa and the Kingdom of Kongo than we do about the Congo basin rainforest area or the Lunda Empire.[20]

Since ancient times, economic, political, and cultural communication in the region between the desert and the Guinea coast had been oriented toward the north, across the Sahara. As a result, its focal point was the ecologically favored savanna. This northward orientation began to change to a southward one only during the course of the seventeenth century, as the forest region gained in importance by dint of the arrival of Europeans on its coast.

The Kingdoms of Mali and Songhay

By the mid-fourteenth century, in the Western Sudan and Upper Guinea, Mali, the empire of the southern Mandé people, the Mandinka, had already reached and passed its zenith. Arab travelers gave accounts of its power and prosperity, costly pilgrimages to Mecca organized by its rulers caused a stir, and it was preserved for posterity on a map included in the Catalan Atlas of 1375. With its heartland on the upper Niger, it stretched eastward for 2,000 kilometers from the Atlantic coast to the borders of modern Nigeria, and for almost 1,000 kilometers from the southern Sahara to the northern fringes of the rainforest. Local rulers who were not members of the ruling family recognized the king's suzerainty and paid tributes; vassal princes were required to send their sons to court as hostages. The ruler's power rested on the one hand on his formidable army of archers and cavalrymen and on the other on his control over the goldfields of Bambuk and the fertile inland delta of the Niger, where royal slaves were settled as farmers, creating surpluses of cereals. Other captives from the regular campaigns to the south were sold on the far side of the Sahara, in exchange for suitable warhorses for the king's army. The trade in horse and metal was a royal monopoly. The king and the ruling elite were all Muslims, although this did not prevent them from retaining "objectionable" traditional customs, such as the religious role of the king as the source of his legitimacy.

The Mandé merchants of the empire, the Dyula, were more deeply Islamized, because as city dwellers and traveling adventurers they had disengaged themselves from the settled agrarian lifestyle and its cultural horizons. The Dyula not only played an important role in mercantile centers like Djenné, Timbuktu, and Gao but also ventured beyond the borders of the empire, principally to the south, in order to trade in the gold and cola nuts from the forest region. From the north, alongside grain from Niger and salt from the Sahara, they also imported metalwares, textiles, spices, and horses from the far side of the Sahara, while the goods they brought from the south included (alongside the gold and nuts) slaves and ivory, plus cattle, hides, and finished leather items from the savanna. They generally traveled in armed groups and set themselves up in business in suitable towns along the route or alternatively founded their own settlements, such as Kankan (in Guinea), Bobo Dioulasso (in Côte d'Ivoire), and Begho (Ghana). Although their own Arabaic education may have remained limited, within their retinues were ulama, who were revered by them and non-Muslim Africans alike as bearers of the written culture and not least as producers of heavy amulets comprising written verses from the Quran. In this way, for centuries after the demise of the Mali Empire, a Muslim network continued to spread across large tracts of West Africa, which proved to be of decisive importance in the quiet spread of the Islamic faith.

From around 1360 on, the Mali Empire disintegrated as a result of the customary conflicts over succession. Former vassal states became independent, principal among them the Wolof Empire in Lower Senegal. In the north, the cyclical shift of power between the Sahel and the desert entered a new phase. Whenever powerful empires encroached on the desert, the nomadic tribes living there kept their peace, but when these empires crumbled, the pressure from the north began to increase once more. In 1433, the Tuareg captured Timbuktu (a town they had originally founded), which then proceeded to take on an ever increasing role as the intellectual hub of West African Islam, especially after the black ulama were replaced by Sanhaja Berbers from the Almoravid tradition. By 1550, the city boasted more than a hundred Quranic schools, and as late as 1600 Sudanese Islamic

Djenné (Mali), which is situated in the fertile inland delta of the River Niger not far from Timbuktu, was an economic and cultural metropolis of the Mali Empire and later the Songhay Empire. Its Great Mosque, which dates from the thirteenth century, was rebuilt at the beginning of the twentieth century. It is the largest building in the world constructed in the Sudanese mud-brick architectural style and has space for thousands of worshipers. It has to be restored after every rainy season. (Photo by Merrick Posnansky)

scholarship came to be regarded as superior to that of the Maghreb. But the demise of Mali also left the "heathen" Mossi from the upper reaches of the Black Volta River free to launch raids from the south on Niger with complete impunity. A small rump of the former Mali Empire, on an arm of the Niger south of Djenné, did manage to assert its independence but vanished from history around 1600.

Just as Mali had once taken over the mantel of the Soninke Empire in Ghana, so it in turn was now supplanted by Songhay, a former vassal state around Gao downriver of the bend in the Niger, which also achieved independence in the fourteenth century. Its power resided on its control over the best region for horse rearing east of the Niger and its army of mounted lancers but also on its deployment of a "battle fleet" on the Niger, comprising the boats of fishermen who worked the river. Sonni Ali used these forces to overthrow Timbuktu and its Tuareg rulers, along with

Djenné and the Fulani of Massina. The Mali and Mossi Empires also came under severe pressure but were never overrun by Songhay. Sonni Ali was nominally a Muslim, occasionally observing his prayer and almsgiving duties, but at the same time was regarded as a powerful magician who consulted soothsayers, worshiped "idols," and offered sacrifices to trees and rocks.

In the conflicts over the succession that followed his reign, the throne was usurped by one of Ali's commanders—the Soninke Askia Muhammad Touré (1493–1528), who gave his rule the stamp of legitimacy by opting for the purer Timbuktu form of Islam and undertaking the hajj to Mecca; Askia Muhammad was responsible for Islamizing the Songhay court and ruling elite. Even so, his successors still retained elements of traditional kinship at their capital Gao. The historian J. D. Fage even surmises that there was a long-running conflict between traditionalist and Islamic factions at the Songhay court.[21] Askia Muhammad extended the empire into the Sahara as far as the Aïr Mountains and the salt mines of Taghaza, as well as eastward, where he controlled a tract of Hausa territory that included Kano and Katsina up to 1515. At that time, Songhay, though situated somewhat farther east, was at least as large as the Mali Empire. Taking its cue from Mali, it increased the number of slaves engaged in the royal agricultural and manufacturing enterprises but also supplied the slave markets of North Africa. Political power lay in the hands of the many princes (thanks to the practice of polygyny) and the Songhay nobility who thronged the capital Gao. Anyone who managed to assert authority there in the frequent succession struggles gained a distinct advantage through the support of Songhay's elite troops. However, the most important claimant was the *Kurminafari,* a prince who, as vice-regent and supreme commander of a slave army raised by Askia Muhammad, had control over the governors and vassals of the western provinces, as well as over the empire's breadbasket.

In spite of the recurrent conflicts over who should ascend to power, the Songhay Empire remained basically stable; its demise was caused by an external influence. The sultan of a reunified Morocco, Mulay Ahmed al-Mansur (1578–1603), was keen to gain control over the trans-Saharan trade in gold, salt, and slaves. By 1582, in return for help in the war against his "heathen" neighbors, the king of Bornu to the southwest of Lake Chad had already become a vassal of the sultan. On several occasions, Mulay Ahmed demanded that Askia relinquish his hold on the salt mines at Taghaza, which in any event were already worked out and had been abandoned and replaced by others. When Askia Muhammad refused, the sultan dispatched southeast across the Sahara a force of several thousand musketeers, half of whom perished en route. Even so, this depleted army still managed to rout a numerically far superior Songhay force at the Battle of Tondibi on the Niger north of Gao in 1591. Apparently the Songhay cavalry—in common with other West African warriors—had unwisely forsworn the use of firearms as "unchivalrous." A *pashalik* was established in Timbuktu and the garrison greatly bolstered by the arrival of elite troops from Morocco. Askia suffered a further defeat, and Gao fell to the sultan. The Songhay Empire duly collapsed; all that remained was a puppet king in the north and an independent rump state down the Niger in Dendi, which fostered stronger ties to African traditions once more.

Yet Mulay Ahmed's prestige as a trans-Saharan caliph of the west immediately dissolved amid further wars of succession. There arose in Timbuktu, under nominal Moroccan sovereignty, an autonomous military republic under the control of a hereditary fellowship called the *Arma,* which elected its own pasha. Together with the trade center of Djenné, Timbuktu and the surrounding region were plundered and terrorized. Yet this period also witnessed a new, unstoppable advance by the Tuareg, who by the eighteenth century controlled all the territory around the bend in the Niger and brought the independent reign of the Arma to an end. The Bambara established the empires of Segu and Karta on the upper Niger, while in the upper Volta region, clashes with the Mandé warrior state of Gonja saw the Mossi empires of Yatenga, Ougadougu, and Dagomba expand their territory—despite the almost constant state of conflict that existed between the kings and their chieftain nobility, which was finally decided in favor of the monarchy only in the eighteenth century by a slave army equipped with muskets. All of these empires were originally "heathen" but over time and under the influence of the Dyula took on the standard half-Muslim character—so long as the matrilineal system did not stand in the way.

The Empires of the Guinea Region and Kanem-Bornu

The northern hinterland of the upper Guinea coast in the region of present-day Senegal and Gambia was covered by a patchwork of empires of the Wolof,

Tukolor, and above all the Malinke peoples, which were characterized by their pronounced social stratification. Where families of the former Malian aristocracy remained in charge, only sons of the wives of the dynasty could become king. Below them were the regular aristocracy, marked out by special apparel and a highly developed warrior ethic, who did not engage in any commercial activity, followed by the castes of various artisans, then free and indentured peasants, and finally slaves. The area farther to the south was dominated by rebellious, acephalous groups of autonomous communities; however, since the sixteenth century these had been partly integrated into new empires founded by a new wave of Mandé conquerors, the Mane.

Beginning in the late seventeenth century, the area north of Senegal and Futa Jalon on the upper Gambia River saw the emergence of the first instances of jihad movements instigated by hard-line Muslims, of the kind that would reshape Sudan in the nineteenth century. Elements of the Sanhaja Berbers of the southwestern Sahara were resident there as peaceful and devout "Marabout clans" under the protection of Arab nomads who had migrated to the region in the fifteenth century but who were regarded as bad Muslims. In 1673, the ascetic Awbek ben Ashfaga began preaching jihad, attacked the "heathen" Wolof and Tukolor, and attempted to establish an Islamic state with a statutory system of *zakat* donations. However, following military defeats, the movement quickly disintegrated. It was a different situation in Futa Jalon, which since the fifteenth century had been infiltrated by Fulani herders, who initially lived in peaceful cooperation with the settled farmers of the region, albeit as pariahs at the bottom of the social hierarchy. However, their growing prosperity, primarily through the expansion of their herds (possibly the result of European demand for hides), led to conflicts, in which an alliance of nine ulama elected a leader and embarked on a jihad against their neighbors, which lasted from 1725 to 1776 and culminated in the formation of a closed Muslim community. Captives were sold as slaves to the Europeans, a trade that may well have caused the conflict to go on for as long as it did.

In central Sudan and lower Guinea between the Volta region and Lake Chad, the coast and its hinterland played a greater role, for even then this was the most densely populated area of Africa, which also had the highest degree of "urbanization." Yet even here, the savanna zone had an advantage in terms of development. Like Ghana and Mali, the empire of Kanem north of Lake Chad owed its early Islamization to trans-Saharan trade, which here turned primarily on slavery. In the fourteenth and fifteenth centuries, internal conflicts led to the center of the empire shifting to Bornu southwest of the lake. From there, an aristocracy of mounted lancers, who unlike the Mali and Songhay also had access to armor, ventured south on slaving raids. However, despite embracing the same "knightly ethos" as these states, the leaders of Bornu did not always share their contempt for firearms. Quite the opposite: Mai Idris Aloma (1569–1600) got hold of muskets from the Ottomans, along with instructors, and used them to arm his bodyguard of slaves. The heartland of the empire was, once again, administered by royal slaves, while its farther reaches were controlled by military vassals, who were kept in check by the royal guard. In this way, Bornu rose to become black Africa's strongest military power, which notwithstanding all the customary dynastic disputes lasted for almost a thousand years.

Admittedly, no merchant class comparable to the Dyula arose in Kanem-Bornu, perhaps because attractive goods like gold were not available. This role was filled in Bornu by its immediate neighbors to the southwest, the Hausa, whose ironworking centers developed in the course of the fifteenth and sixteenth centuries into walled cities, which swore their allegiance to Islam. Like their neighbors, their rulers and nobility rode out on slave-hunting expeditions and vied for supremacy. Yet alongside this, the Hausa states developed a textile and leather industry supplying the whole of North Africa via the central Saharan trade routes, while slaves who settled around the cities cultivated food crops, cotton, and indigo and prepared leather for working by liming and tanning it. Traders from Ragusa (Dubrovnik) living in the Hausa city of Kano in the late sixteenth century regarded it, alongside Cairo and Fez, as one the three great metropolises of Africa.

A succession of important groups occupied the lower Guinea coast or its hinterland. Running from west to east, these were the Akan west of the lower Volta and the Ewe to its east, who were succeeded by the Aja in the region east of the Volta where a gap appears in the rainforest and the savanna runs right to the sea, and adjoining this territory were the Yoruba, followed by the Edo west of the Niger, the Nupe to the east, while farther to the south were the Ibo (or Igbo) and the Ibibio and finally the Efik. Although these people created the most diverse communities, some nevertheless exhibit significant cultural similarities, principally in the notion of the family and in religion. Islamic influence reached these regions only toward the end of the period under consideration here, with the result that there were no taboos impeding these cultures' magnificent depiction of the human form. The first small empires here grew up in the less densely wooded zones bordering the savanna, which were easier to clear-fell and yet which also still had plentiful supplies of timber and places of refuge in the nearby forest.

The oldest of these empires was the Yoruba city-state of Ife, which was located on a small goldfield and could trace its origins back to the ninth and tenth centuries. From the twelfth to the fifteenth centuries, Ife was an important kingdom, boasting an ironworking industry, and was renowned for its production of highly sought-after blue glass beads and impressive terra-cotta sculptures. From the thirteenth century on, these were joined by the famous bronze sculptures. In contrast to Nupe, where in the fifteenth century a warlike empire arose that temporarily overran parts of Yoruba territory in the following century, Ife seems to have been peaceful and only culturally dominant throughout its existence. Not least, it was also a religious center, from which the kings of other realms claimed to trace their descent and who sought ritual legitimization from the *Oni* (rulers) of Ife through symbolic artifacts, such as the royal swords of Benin and Oyo.

Benin itself is thought to have originated at around the same time as Ife. Extensive systems of earth ramparts testify to the early settlement of its heartland. In the fifteenth to sixteenth centuries, the empire expanded and remained a major power up to the eighteenth century. The Portuguese recounted tales of its impressive capital, where court artists (a hereditary role) continued the great sculptural tradition of Ife. The king, who in Benin had the title of *oba,* was interested in firearms but tried to avoid being converted to Christianity, which the Portuguese demanded in return. Accordingly, trade with Portugal came to nothing. Benin engaged in the slave trade with Europeans but was careful to keep it under strict control, because it needed slaves of its own to develop its manufacturing. This was, broadly speaking, also the case in all the larger West African communities, who were far from being mere henchmen in the European slave trade, as has sometimes been claimed. The oba even employed freedmen as administrative chiefs, in instances where he had been unable to secure the fealty of vassals through marriage ties. Around 1600, however, the *uzama,* the aristocracy comprising Edo chiefs from the capital and the provinces, assumed effective control by taking command of the army; henceforth, the oba was confined to ceremonial duties.

The savanna kingdom of Oyo, farther to the north, in the heartland of the Yoruba, was overthrown by Nupe in the sixteenth century. Its ruling dynasty fled south to Borgu. After several decades, they in turn had assembled a heavily armed cavalry force, which they used to strike back against Nupe. Over the course of the seventeenth century, Oyo expanded to become the foremost Yoruba power, which with the exception of Benin subjugated almost all neighboring kingdoms and ultimately the Aja kingdoms in the west as well, including Dahomey. In this way, Oyo reached its greatest extent in 1730. Not untypically, the empire was organized into four concentric zones: in the center the capital of the *alafin* (ruler), and beyond this the confederate Yoruba cities, whose rulers (likewise originally installed by the Ife) remained in office and were tied to the alafin through blood ties or marriage. Other peoples who lived in more far-flung parts of the empire were governed, alongside indigenous chiefs, by tribute commissars *(ajele),* who were themselves supervised by royal envoys *(ilari).* Finally, tribute was exacted from the Aja through military expeditions. Oyo, too, was characterized by the customary tension between the ruler and the nobility, especially the seven *oyo mesi,* who were both army commanders and royal electors and who enjoyed the support of the *ogboni* secret society. In the eighteenth century, this group managed to depose an alafin and force him to commit suicide; however, they had a vested interest in preserving central power and not arrogating it to themselves.

While the smaller Aja kingdoms closer to the coast, such as Allada and Wydah, together with the Akan realms of Denkyira, Akyem, and Akwamu, fell strongly under the influence of the slave trade, and in part owed their rise to this activity, the interior witnessed the growth of larger communities with a tough warrior ethos, which were able to keep dependency of this kind within bounds.[22] In the seventeenth century, Dahomey arose as an offshoot of Allada and in turn was able, dependence on Oyo notwithstanding, to subjugate the coastal lands and replace their kings with "officials," while in other conquests, existing chiefs were left in place. Yet the limited extent of the empire, along with the forces of the founder clan, which could be rapidly mobilized, plus the regular army of the court, equipped with firearms and the renowned yet infamous bodyguard of fearsome female warriors, enabled Dahomey to control its territory with an almost "modern" intensity and efficiency. The fertile clearing in the rainforest was used for the systematic expansion of agriculture and textile manufacture, while foreign trade (which was not exclusively in slaves) was a crown monopoly. Likewise, the circulation of cowrie shells as currency was strictly controlled by the royal court. By all accounts, there was even a road-building program. Religion was also centered on the king, who in large measure was free to name his own successor. In practice, a kind of primogeniture operated in Dahomey—something of a unique achievement in polygynous Africa and one that helped foster political stability.

Much the same can be said of the principal Akan kingdom of Asante, a federation of six dominions created around 1680. In 1701, it freed itself from Denkyira's suzerainty and proceeded to conquer territory in all directions. By the mid-eighteenth century, its musketeers had even defeated the cavalry forces of the savanna kingdoms of Gonja and Dagomba, which were likewise annexed. In 1820, the kingdom covered more than 250,000 square kilometers, which were divided into zones in the usual fashion: (1) the center, comprising the six original dominions, where in the interim the king of Kumasi had risen from the status of first among equals to become overall monarch, or *asantehene;* (2) the subjugated Akan peoples, who paid taxes; and (3) the vassal states of the north, under the control of Asante envoys, which were obliged to pay an annual tribute in the form of slaves. Slaves and free settlers alike were drafted to systematically develop farming and commerce in the center of the empire. When European powers refused to provide the "development aid" the Asante requested, they simply took it upon themselves to purchase silk cloth from the Hausa, which they then unpicked and combined with homegrown cotton to create new fabrics. Asante was also a thriving trading state with a well-developed road network; it exerted some influence over the cola nut trade to the north, but its main concern was to gain control of the trade to the south, with the Europeans, in gold, slaves, and ivory. And it was primarily gold that made Asante rich. A gilded stool became the quintessential symbol of Asante kingship. Over time, free "officials" from the principal families, appointed by the king, gradually supplanted the original chiefs, who were also neutralized by a calculated "divide and rule" policy. These officials were of a "patrimonial" nature—in other words, as members of the royal household, they received no actual salary and remained dependent on the grace and favor of the ruler, before whom they were required to regularly appear. Under some circumstances, though, they could hand their positions on to their sons. There already existed a clear career path in the Asante bureaucracy or military. With the help of literate Muslims, who were otherwise kept at arm's length, a chancellery and a treasury were created. A system of runners ensured good communications, while security was in the hands of royal courts and a kind of secret police *(ankobea)*. Ideological conformity, meanwhile, was fostered by a ruler cult. Asante foreign expansion was effected through a combination of skilful diplomacy and a much-feared army conscripted from among its subject peoples.

It was a completely different picture, however, in the area of half-land, half-water, around the Niger delta and the rivers to the east. In particular, the Ibo/Igbo retained the village as the largest political unit, despite their great population density, their remarkable creative skills in the production of wood carvings and ironwork, and their extensive trading networks using huge canoes. Their villages were divided into hereditary family units and their dependents—so-called houses. The only supravillage institutions were religious centers like the famous Ibo oracles and the highly developed secret societies, particularly prevalent among the Efik. Decentralized systems of this kind, however, proved extremely susceptible to exploitation by the slave trade and consequently suffered great upheaval. Villages became towns, the "houses" businesses, and the chiefs kings.

Along the coast beyond the Niger delta, right down to the mouth of the Congo, similar kinds of small trading kingdoms sprang up. Yet of all these, only Loango is thought to date from before the European encroachment, as the Vili who inhabited that region traded their sea salt for copper and iron from Bungu in the interior. However, they forged contacts with the Teke kingdom farther up the Congo only as a result of the slave trade. Otherwise, northern Central Africa seems to have been made up of only small communities of subsistence farmers, though this is no reflection on their quality of life.

Kingdoms in South Central Africa

It is only on the southern fringes of the rainforest that we encounter larger kingdoms once more. In the sixteenth to seventeenth centuries, on the middle reaches of the Kasai River, eighteen clans of the Mongo and Kete peoples combined to form the kingdom of Kuba, which boasted considerable wealth and highly developed institutions and became widely renowned for its wood carvings and raffia basketwork. Up to the colonial period, it seems to have enjoyed a relatively undisturbed and peaceful existence. By contrast, for the Kingdom of Kongo in the north and the Kingdom of Ndongo (between Kuba and Kongo) and their successor states, the opposite seems to have been true. The Portuguese presence brought the first momentous change to Kongo and Ndongo and ultimately caused their decline, while successor communities arose precisely as a result of this process, in which the slave trade was not the sole factor but undoubtedly played the most significant part.

In the fourteenth century, the Bakongo from Bungu migrated across the Congo and conquered the Kimbundu, who lived on the opposite bank. They brought with them their sophisticated metalworking skills and founded the central settlement of Mbanza Kongo as the residence of their ruler, the *manikongo*. Further expansion in the fifteenth century saw the rise of the Kingdom of Kongo, founded on perhaps just a dozen exogamous matrilineal lineages of the Bakongo, known as *kanda*. Yet the foremost lineage was that of the Mwissikongo, from whose leading figures endorsement for all important decisions was required. They chose the strongest candidate from the royal family as ruler and appointed the twelve members of his council, among whom the most significant roles in the seventeenth century were the judge (as chairman), the chamberlain, and the secretary. Four of the twelve were women, either former kings' widows or aunts or sisters of the reigning king, including the *nzimbupungu,* the co-regent (the only one whose identity we know was an aunt of the king). The court comprised relatives of the king and of the provincial governors; the loyalty of important chiefs who did not belong to the ruling clan was secured by allowing them each to provide one of the king's wives. The council appointed important Mwissikongo as governors of the eight main provinces, and they in turn appointed the chiefs of the subprovinces, the districts, and the subdistricts. The governors potentially represented the most dangerous rivals of the king. As a result, these posts were filled ideally by relatives of the monarch. In addition, the restriction to just a three-year term of office for governors was strictly observed and lines of communication assiduously fostered by permanent representatives of both sides. Even so, the governors had an interest not in seceding but at most in a steady turnover of rulers, just as long as the system of royal distribution kept operating; a significant proportion both of the tributes collected by the gover-

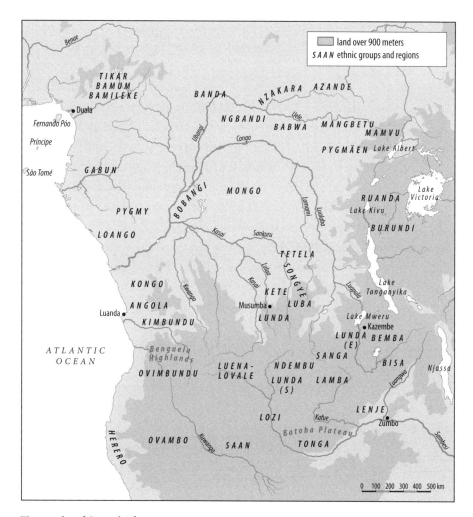

The peoples of Central Africa

nors and of the luxury goods acquired by the court through trade was demonstratively redistributed by the king among the members of the ruling elite.

The Portuguese reached the Congo in 1483 and began intensive contacts with the manikongo in 1485–1486. Soon after, in 1491, three ships arrived carrying priests, artisans, and soldiers as "development aid workers." The manikongo and the ruling elite had themselves baptized, and the victor in the succession struggle,

·[767]·

Afonso (1506–1543)—who as the son of a queen who was not a member of the Mwissikongo clan was eligible to succeed according to only European but not African law—engaged enthusiastically with Christianity and Portuguese culture. The intention was to subject the kingdom to a thoroughgoing cultural change. However, when the lure of Africa for the Portuguese was eclipsed by the "discovery" of India, and once the sugar plantations of São Tomé, and soon after Brazil, began to signal their inexhaustible demand for slaves, and the Portuguese had founded a town in Luanda in 1575, Portuguese interest in Africa dwindled to being solely about the slave trade. Yet the Kongo monarchy had become so heavily involved with the Portuguese by this stage that it found it impossible to keep slavery in check. Armed conflict broke out against Luanda, which ended in 1655 with crushing defeat for the Kingdom of Kongo at the Battle of Mbwila, at which most of the Mwissikongo elite were killed. The kingdom dissolved into its separate parts, though right up to the late eighteenth century, a succession of pretenders to the Kongo throne set themselves up as king in the run-down capital of São Salvador, as it is now called.

It appears that the aforementioned cultural influence of the blacksmiths caused the fixed wooden cult objects *(lunga)* of the lineages to be replaced by movable iron ones *(ngola),* a practice that engendered mobility in the region. In any event, the Kimbundu king of Ndongo, which lay some 160 kilometers inland from Luanda, as guardian of the *ngola a kiluanje* shrine, was able to establish his own realm and initially refused to be baptized, asserting his independence, despite his participation in the slave trade. Ultimately, though, this was all in vain. In 1618, the residence of the Ngola (from which the name "Angola" derives) was destroyed by the Portuguese, and the Ndongo kingdom, which was already heavily depopulated, also collapsed.

Yet although the effects of the Atlantic trade were becoming evident ever-deeper inland, African empires, scarcely influenced by slavery, were still able to form in the heart of southern Central Africa, particularly around modern Shaba and Katanga. The beginnings of these realms have, admittedly, come down to us only through oral sources, which are difficult to interpret, with the result that even the dating presents problems. On the Lualaba River in the east, the chiefdoms of the Luba, who were renowned for their naturalistic wood carvings, coalesced in a predominantly peaceful process into kingdoms that entertained hardly any outside contacts.

Things were different with the politically more creative Lunda on the Kasai River to the west. Here, with help from the Luba territories, one of three lineages vying for leadership was able to assert itself and displace its two rivals. By the seventeenth century, the fifteen central village communities had become a centralized monarchy that harbored ambitions to expand. With a complex apparatus of dignitaries, this kingdom was able to control the expanding Atlantic slave trade. The Lunda kingdom conducted manhunts, not solely for the purpose of supplying the slave trade, but also to augment its own population. Far-reaching expeditions in all directions involving only a few hundred warriors succeeded either in establishing Lunda colonies or in integrating local chiefs into the Lunda hierarchy through the tribute system. In the eighteenth century, one of these *kazembes* founded a kingdom in the Luapula Valley south of Lake Mweru that was larger than that of his overlord, to whom he continued, however, to pay homage as before. In this way, the loose Lunda system of rule stretched from the lower Kwango to Lake Tanganyika. The capital in the open woodland some 100 kilometers east of the Kasai River was protected by a ring of ditches and ramparts 30 kilometers in circumference. Within this, successive kings erected their own fortified palaces; next to these lay the kings' tombs. Western visitors were deeply impressed by this complex, not least by its cleanliness in comparison with Luanda.

One of the two displaced Lunda lineages moved west, its numbers swelled by rootless people from other tribes, and over time their leaders relinquished the original Lunda title *kinguri* in favor of that of *kasanje*. Ultimately, bands of nomads known as imbangala emerged from this migration, who "cultivated the land with the spear"—in other words, lived by plundering other peoples. The children of the imbangala were not killed, as was widely rumored, but instead given up to be raised communally, because family and ancestral community had been completely supplanted by a magical and heavily armed society of warriors, into which people were inducted by initiation. This society was characterized by both its military efficiency and its extreme brutality. Although the imbangala came from pure African roots, on their migration west they encountered the Portuguese slave trade and found that they were ideally suited to becoming its main supplier.

Aside from anomalies of this kind, however, the history of Atlantic Africa in the period 1350–1750 may be broadly summarized by the common denominator of "empire building," in which both increasing population density and trade played a part. Long before the advent of Europeans, Africa had established a far-reaching network for the exchange of goods, with offshoots that extended as far as the Mediterranean; on their arrival, all Europeans needed to do was to tap into this existing network. Yet they were to change this system and with it large parts of Africa beyond all recognition.

2. *Latin Europe*

EUROPE likewise presents a varied picture but in contrast to the other two continents can nevertheless be defined as unity in diversity.[23] It is true that European history since the Middle Ages is hallmarked by a peculiar sense of restlessness—rocked by crises, yet highly productive at the same time—and a process of increasing differentiation, which toward the end of our period gave rise to a world of sovereign states with considerable confessional and national contrasts. Even so, this world still calls itself the "European state system" and combines constant political conflicts with continuing fundamental similarities. In both political and economic terms, Europe still continues to present common structures. But above all, Europeans share a common culture, both apropos the real and mental basic parameters of their existence and with regard to the practical manifestations of their religious, intellectual, and cultural life.

Yet up to around 1750, strictly speaking this was true only of that part of Europe west of a line running from St. Petersburg to Trieste, which circumscribed the sphere of influence of the Latin culture conveyed through the Catholic Church. At that stage, Russia had only just begun to integrate its Eurasian empire into this Europe, while southeastern Europe likewise was, as part of the Ottoman Empire, still more of a contact zone to a different world. For this reason, we will confine ourselves here to considering "Latinate Europe," as it was only this entity that was involved in the formation of a shared Atlantic world—first and foremost its western colonial powers of Portugal, Castile, the Netherlands, France, and England and more indirectly the other countries of southern, central, and northern Europe. It is no coincidence that the easternmost outposts of the European world trade network in the seventeenth and eighteenth centuries were located on the one hand in Courland and on the other in Trieste.[24]

Life Chances and the Meaning of Life

Over these five hundred years, Europeans were under constant threat and acutely aware of being so. Because the here and now had little protection to offer them, they hoped for help from the hereafter.[25] For them, shortages of goods were not some abstract economic concept but a bitter daily reality. Over and above this, the apocalyptic horsemen of hunger, plague, and violence could strike at any time and did so frequently.

Although, in general, the climate of Europe in the Middle Ages was warm and dry, beginning in the fourteenth century, there were a number of dramatic spells of intense cold and rainfall, leading to ruined harvests and famine. Then, from the sixteenth century on, a general cooling occurred, which has somewhat exaggeratedly been described as the "Little Ice Age" and was to last until the nineteenth century. Alpine glaciers advanced, pushing back the boundaries of where settlement and agriculture could take place. This was the context in which repeated bouts of cold and rainfall occurred, with catastrophic consequences.[26] Because food production was based primarily on individual subsistence farming or beyond this at most on regional markets—transport by land of basic foodstuffs over greater distances foundered on the prohibitive cost—the inevitable upshots were famine and widespread economic crises. When the cost of cereals, a staple food, skyrocketed, the demand for other goods plummeted, thereby also causing unemployment. In many instances, a direct connection can be shown empirically between inflated corn prices and extremely high rates of mortality.

No less frequent was another kind of recurrent catastrophe, namely, the various different plagues that hit the continent, primarily the "Black Death" bubonic plague that swept over Europe from 1347 to 1351 and is thought to have claimed the lives of between one-third and one-half of all Europeans.[27] Until the eighteenth century, when the plague made its last appearance (in 1720–1721)—albeit confined on this occasion to southern France—any modest growth in Europe's population was repeatedly annulled by famines and epidemics. According to more recent estimates,[28] the continent's population developed roughly as follows:

- 1350: 75 million
- 1450: 55 million

- 1500: 80 million
- 1600: 100 million
- 1700: 120 million
- 1800: 190 million

It took until the sixteenth century for population figures to climb from the low point they reached after the fourteenth century. The seventeenth century again suffered a stagnation born of crisis, before a definite upturn in the eighteenth, which was to culminate in a continent-wide population explosion, despite the fact that new crises hit once more in the mid-nineteenth century. This is explained both by a decrease in mortality and by a concurrent increase in the birthrate, caused (among other things) by a change in marriage patterns.

The area west of the St. Petersburg–Trieste line was characterized, in the main, by a particular pattern of marriage behavior, with a uniquely high marriage age across different cultures—around twenty-six years old for men and twenty-four for women—and a correspondingly uniquely high quota of single people. This resulted in fewer children, as this pattern meant that women utilized only some 40 percent of their childbearing potential.[29] Basically, people got married only when the man was able to secure a position as an independent farmer or as a master craftsman. Gradually, though, the spread of home working in the countryside for the textile industry and the growth of opportunities in paid employment saw people begin to marry younger, without any of the former preconditions. As a result, numbers of children also began to climb.

This was accompanied by a drop in infant mortality. Prior to this, the average European had a statistical life expectancy of just twenty-five to thirty years, a remarkably low figure explained by the fact that many children died while still babies and by the fact that barely half of them lived until the age of fifteen. Admittedly, anyone who did make it to this age could generally reckon on a further forty years of life—a life-expectancy figure of fifty-five comparable to that of modern India. In these circumstances, then, death was a constant feature of daily life and was personified in the form of the grim reaper; meanwhile, through their depictions of dances of death and textbooks on the art of dying (artes moriendi), art and literature of this period give ample evidence of religious attempts to come to terms with the experience of death.[30]

In these conditions, the "normal" European family consisted of the parents and just two or three children.[31] The number of children living in a household was kept down not just by mortality but also by the fact that the late marrying age saw the emergence of youth as a separate stage of life in bachelorhood: young people were often sent away from home to take up temporal positions in service ("life cycle servants"). Consequently, domestic servants, maids, apprentices, and journeymen became attached to families elsewhere, away from their birth families. The European family unit therefore was formed not, as in other parts of the world, through ancestry and lineage but primarily through marriage and the establishment of a household. This fulfilled not only the needs of a rural society, long since epitomized by the tenant farm tied to a manorial domain, as well as those of urban industry with its family-run firms of artisans, but also the precepts of the Latin church. For according to its teachings, the sacrament of marriage was originally based on the consensus and sexual union of two partners, free of the obligation to involve the wider family, as happened in other societies. Even if de facto the parents and later the authorities also had to give their approval in this matter, the late marrying age also favored a free choice of partner, because the likelihood was that the parents would already be dead or at least absent.

Significantly, European family names are more often derived from places and occupations rather than from ancestral lineage. Christian disregard for blood ties necessarily also led to a relative devaluation of the wider ancestral entity, the kinship group, a feature that once again is reflected in European languages in the interculturally striking harmonization of terms for paternal and maternal relatives, between blood relatives and relatives by marriage, and between "real" and ritual relatives, especially godfathers and godmothers. As a religion with the salvation of the individual at its heart, Christianity does not acknowledge any religious credit accrued by ancestors; as a community religion, it accords the family no cultic status; as a missionary religion, it apportions no significance to ancestry; as a monotheistic religion, it has no ancestor cult; as a religion with ordained offices, it recognizes no hereditary charisma; and finally as an ascetic religion, it accords no religious significance to fertility. Yet east of the St. Petersburg–Trieste line, different kinds of socioeconomic conditions counteracted these principles, whereas the Christian principles mentioned before largely chimed in with those of the west. Over the long term, then, this situation promoted the growth of individuality and mobility and that openness to family planning and the forging of new social ties that were to become characteristic traits of Western culture.

The Role of Women

Yet these developments still lay far in the future. Premodern Europe was much more a closed than an open society, with a tendency for a somewhat rigid assigning of status, especially where the role of women was concerned.[32] Only men could become priests, but otherwise Christianity recognized no theologically based qualitative distinction between the sexes. Yet precisely because Christianity was not a family religion, it left cultural scope for rules deriving from other sources, which just as they did in the rest of the world, prescribed that in Europe there should also be a strict division of labor between the sexes, organized within a patriarchal system where the paterfamilias held sway. These rules also included the right to corporal punishment of a wife by her husband. Law, politics, and war were all male affairs, from which the "weaker sex" was permanently excluded, or just passively involved in, as a dependent legal subject under the guardianship of the husband, or as a prince's daughter married off against her will in order to help seal an alliance or peace treaty, or as a victim of rape by foreign or even friendly forces.

Alongside the "biological slavery" of having to give birth to many children, there was also the high likelihood that in doing so, the woman would succumb to medical complications, such as puerperal fever. For sure, there were several examples of important female rulers and independent women making a living for themselves through business (and the latter by no means confined to the widows of master craftsmen). But they remained just as much an exception as the girl who, having been sent to a nunnery against her will in order to reduce dowry claims on the family's wealth, then rose to become a powerful abbess or a revered scholar. The Reformation introduced the possibility of divorce but in practice was reluctant to implement it. Nor did the new role of pastor's wife bring any significant change. Women in this role did not really do anything different than what most women had been doing for centuries, namely, running the household not under but alongside their husbands. Women's labor and organizational skills were indispensable to the running of farms and craftsmen's workshops; widowers were far less able to fend for themselves than widows. In this subordinate

role—which, because of women's indispensability, was still a powerful and sometimes even dominant one—women enjoyed the universal protection of the law,
also with regard to her own property, but to varying degrees according to the
particular jurisdiction.

Bonds of affection certainly played some part in marriage, but men married
first and foremost in order to establish a household; in certain cases, it was only
retrospectively that husbands would come to love their wives in their role as dili-
gent housewives and mothers. But there was no question of love as passion in such
arrangements; this was regarded as prostitution.[33] The growing separation between
peoples' working lives and family lives among the rising bourgeoisie in the eighteenth century relieved women of this class from the need to earn and thereby
created the conditions for a stronger emotionalizing of the relationship between
man and wife. It was only at this stage that the natural differentness of the female sex was "discovered." On the one hand, this development did have the capacity to allow the woman to degenerate from a partner of her husband to his play-
thing, but on the other, it allowed women to confirm their advantages, which had
been praised since the Renaissance, through intellectual and practical emancipation. A watchword of the Enlightenment was that "reason should not be the preserve of one sex or the other."[34]

Society of Estates

Yet inequality was by no means confined to the relationship between men and
women. Rather, in both a vertical and horizontal sense, it was enshrined as a self-
evident principle in the laws and customs of premodern Europe. Man's equality
in the eyes of the God of Christendom—who was often depicted as disregarding
rank and personage to condemn even popes and emperors to perdition in scenes
of the Last Judgment—only rarely took any concrete political or ideological form.
Instead, it was thought that this God had ordained each and every person's position and role in the world and given all their appointed "status" or "estate." Even
the angels and the saints in heaven and the devils in hell were categorized into
different ranks. And each rank had its own specific "honor"[35] graded according
to a person's estate. This honor was upheld by a person fulfilling the duties that
attached to his or her rank and was compromised by any infringement against

Jesus Christ as Pantokrator (ruler of the world), seated on two rainbows and surrounded by two representatives each of the three estates, into which ancient learning traditionally grouped the human race: first, the pope with a priest; second, a king with a prince; and finally, two peasants. In each case, Latin inscriptions set forth the common task that underpins their respective estates: humble intercession for the men of God; protection by the nobility as the duty of the ruling class; and tilling the land with the hoe (middle high German: *Karst*) as the lot of the peasantry. At this stage, town dwellers (burghers) were not yet in evidence. (bpk—Bildagentur für Kunst, Kultur und Geschichte, Berlin)

these obligations. Thus, a lord was obliged to protect his subjects, and they in turn had to extend "advice and help" to him in this task.

Likewise, a paterfamilias was duty bound to ensure the sexual propriety of the women in his household, while bakers were obliged to bake bread of prescribed sizes and weights, and so on. The whole fabric and security of society rested on this practice of people observing their rank. As a result, vertical and horizontal mobility were originally regarded as illegitimate in the Middle Ages and even later were still viewed with suspicion. Accordingly, while endogamy was not enshrined in law, it certainly was the norm. But what did develop within this society of orders, alongside the growing social differentiation that accompanied the division of labor and the potential for wealth creation set in train by the burgeoning monetary economy, was the alternative of stratification according to property, income, and profession. These were the beginnings of the modern class-based society, although it only really gained a firm foothold through the industrial economy of the nineteenth and twentieth centuries. In such a society, mobility reigned supreme.

The social world of premodern Europe was organized vertically into three estates: the priesthood, the warriors, and the peasantry.[36] This arrangement supposedly derived from an ancient pattern of formal social order common to all Indo-European-speaking cultures. The First Estate was originally the Catholic clergy, whose members had a monopoly on conducting ritual religious observance and on drawing a living from this activity. They also enjoyed precedence of rank over the laity and three legal privileges: the *privilegium canonis,* a higher degree of protection within the criminal law; the *privilegium fori,* a special legal status to appear exclusively before ecclesiastical courts; and the *privilegium immunitatis,* exemption from the worldly duties of the laity, such as compulsory military service, the obligation to fill certain positions, and the liability to pay taxes. Small wonder, then, that strong anticlerical resentment began to build up among the laity, which finally erupted during the Reformation. Conversely, many people sought the lesser ordinations, in order to enjoy these privileges. The ordination and the celibate lifestyle, together with highly distinctive vestments, created a clear demarcation.[37]

Being a priest was not a hereditary office but rather, thanks to the commitment to celibacy, was obliged to recruit via mobility from other estates. Even so, this mobility was channeled through family connections and class distinctions.

Certain livings, for example, German bishoprics, were reserved for the aristocracy.[38] These could remain in the hands of a particular family and be passed on, say, from an uncle to his nephew. In eighteenth-century France, there seems to have existed among the clergy a kind of class distinction between well-remunerated aristocratic bishops and highly educated but poorly paid pastors from a bourgeois background; it is no coincidence that some of the leaders of the French Revolution came from this latter group. Because the clergy also embraced members of religious orders, women could also attain membership by becoming nuns.

In places where the Reformation took hold in the sixteenth century, the clergy as an estate founded on religion was abolished. Henceforth, its priests had to become married functionaries appointed only according to need within a community. Thanks to their steadily increasing level of academic qualification, they also became prominent members of the up-and-coming academic professions—a new upper echelon of the middle class with which they became inextricably linked and from which they swelled their ranks, at least in places where internal recruitment via the appointment of pastors' sons was not the norm. As a result of the abolishment of religious orders and other institutions of the old church, this new professional clergy was far less numerous than the Catholic priesthood.[39]

Technically speaking, the nobility formed the Second Estate,[40] although in social and political terms it was universally dominant, even within the priesthood. In most countries, the aristocracy comprised just 1 percent of the population; only in Hungary, Poland, and Castile did they make up a higher proportion. Throughout Europe there was an exclusive higher nobility comprising just a few dozen or at most a hundred families, who were for the most part fabulously wealthy and endowed with titles such as count, prince, and duke and who were not infrequently invested with special powers of dominion. The great majority of the aristocracy was made up of the minor nobility, which had developed in the Middle Ages, in part from lords' bond servants. Its precise organization varied from country to country; likewise, its economic power varied considerably.[41]

Nobility was an ascribed quality, which in contrast to membership of the clergy was acquired through birth and which in some cases goes hand in hand with a proto-racist consciousness of having inherited outstanding attributes. Anyone who had had nobility conferred on them only recently by a monarch or who had simply acquired noble status through prolonged pursuit of an aristocratic lifestyle on the basis of a large fortune was keen to retrospectively fabricate a spurious family tree. In such families, questions of descent continued to play a major role. Mobility across class was hushed up. Aristocrats could be recognized by their bearing and by the lifestyle of a major property owner; engagement in certain activities, notably artisanal or mercantile, could lead to the loss of one's noble status (derogation). In the Middle Ages, the aristocracy became a warrior caste characterized by its embodiment of certain legitimizing ethical and religious ideals—in other words, knights. The knightly code of chivalry was based on certain, particularly warlike, virtues: bravery, loyalty, magnanimity, and so on. The most important symbol of knighthood was the right to carry a sword. This caste once held a monopoly on military service, but in the age of mercenary soldiering that followed, what remained was a natural claim to officers' posts in various armies. In several countries, aristocratic privileges consisted of a special legal status, tax exemption, and a claim on particular estates reserved for the nobility. However, since the late Middle Ages, middle-class arrivistes had challenged the nobility's sole claim to positions of great authority in the service of princes. Even so, the aristocracy remained the ruling class, because the immediate concern of these bourgeois social climbers was to crown their achievement by being raised to the aristocracy.

The remainder of the population made up the Third Estate, tellingly referred to in Castilian Spanish as *estado llano,* or "the plain estate." In practice, this class was divided into the bourgeoisie and peasants, with the peasant being completely devoid of privileges (and often more or less in a condition of serfdom), whereas "bourgeois" was not (in contrast to its modern usage) intrinsically a general class designation like aristocrat or peasant but rather was applied to signify a citizen of a particular town. Hence, one could only be a citizen *of* Augsburg or Zaragoza, in other words, someone who shared in the privileges of this or that town, but not a "bourgeois" per se. In addition, the Third Estate was the real place where the class society as we know it began slowly to develop, through stratification according to income and property, as well as classification into different professions. In the countryside, alongside peasants with varying degrees of ownership rights and wealth there was a sharp increase in the number of those who belonged to "subpeasant classes," without any possessions to their name. This was not unconnected to the growth of rural home working (for example, for the textile industry). In the towns, meanwhile, in addition to the existing stratification into patricians, merchants, artisans, domestic servants, and the poor, people began to be differentiated according to hundreds of different activities.

As in other caste- and order-based societies, in Europe too there existed below the three estates and their subdivisions something approximating to a Fourth Estate, composed of marginal groups, which were on the one hand a tolerated or even necessary constituent element of the social fabric but on the other were consistently excluded from the normal structure of the estates. These included the Jews, who lacked the most essential and basic quality of Europeans at that period, namely, membership of the Christian church. Ever since the high Middle Ages, their communities in towns and villages had been subjected to bouts of violent persecution on the basis of groundless claims that they had desecrated the host, committed ritual murder of Christian children, and poisoned wells. During the years of the Black Death, these attacks escalated into mass pogroms, often fomented by the authorities in response to peoples' fears.[42] Central European Jews *(Ashkenazim)* fled to Bohemia and Poland, especially with the onset of mass expulsions from German towns and territories. The Jews were expelled from England at the end of the thirteenth century and from France in the fourteenth. The countries of the Iberian Peninsula followed suit in 1492 (Spain) and 1496 (Portugal); the Jews there *(Sephardim)* emigrated to the Ottoman Empire and to the northern (non-Spanish-administered) Netherlands. The states that made up Italy tolerated the presence of Jews expelled from the Spanish possessions of the duchy of Milan and the kingdom of Naples, but even so Jews were confined to ghettos in Venice in 1516 and thereafter in Rome, too. Following the pogroms in Poland in the seventeenth century, large numbers of Jews flooded back into Central Europe once more. A few of their number were destined to gain social and economic advancement as financiers at princely courts *(Hoffaktoren),* but most eked out a miserable existence as "rural Jews." They were allowed to settle in England again in 1657. In 1700, there were estimated to be around 750,000 Jews in Europe, of whom 300,000 were still resident in Poland. The overwhelming majority lived in a state of being merely tolerated and with limited rights.

Other marginal groups were itinerants, including Roma who had emigrated to Europe in the fifteenth century, and the so-called outcasts, such as hangmen, knackers, and prostitutes, who despite their indispensability were socially ostracized, especially in the German-speaking lands. In addition, a growing number of the poor became vagrants—among this group, it was often hard to distinguish between unemployed people seeking work, beggars, and criminals.[43] The emergence of this group was accompanied by an increasing popular fear of such people and brutal methods enacted by the authorities to control the problem from the seventeenth century on, by attempting to lock them all up indiscriminately in penitentiaries and workhouses. Most authorities had more than enough problems dealing with poverty within their own area.[44] For most premodern Europeans were poor, not just in the sense of the modern definition of relative poverty, which falls short of the average standard of living in failing to satisfy certain basic needs that society regards as normal. Rather, people then lived on the edge of absolute poverty. If this boundary is crossed, it means that even the necessary minimum of goods and services to ensure a person's physical survival is lacking. Above all, cereals, which were eaten in the form of porridge or bread, or in the case of Italy as pasta—the staple European diet—were no longer readily available. Moreover, the second staple element of the European food culture, meat, was completely out of the question in these circumstances. Insofar as they were not the victims of individual cruel twists of fate, such as being ill, or crippled, or old, or orphaned, in the normal run of events, these poor people may well have pursued a perfectly happy existence, both subjectively and objectively. But every personal crisis or collective catastrophe saw them plummet into grinding poverty, in extreme cases even into death by starvation, because they had no resources to fall back on. Up to the nineteenth century, it is thought that, with regional variations, some 50–80 percent of the population found themselves in such a position.

For Christians, sinful earthly existence was fundamentally imperfect. Real life would begin only after death in the bliss of heavenly existence. Faith of this kind not only made poverty and misfortune bearable but could even lend them meaning as a perceived punishment for sins committed or as a divine trial. Furthermore, Christ himself had identified with the poor (Matthew 5:31–46), so that a certain idealization of individual poor people went hand in hand with the voluntary poverty of whole religious communities, the so-called mendicant orders. But at the same time, the growing number of itinerant poor were regarded as a problem and threat. Certainly, living standards rose for a spell in Europe after the Black Death, owing to a rise in the cost of labor and a drop in the price of food. Yet from the fifteenth century on, the population began increasing once more, with a concomitant rise in the number of poor, food prices soared, and actual earnings fell (in the sixteenth century even below the cost of basic provisions). In normal times, private acts of charity plus countermeasures on the part of the authorities may well have helped at least keep on top of the situation, but this was not the case in periods of crisis.

The first line of welfare defense that people could call on was the social network of relations within small groups in which each and every European was integrated. Family and relations, friends and neighbors, employers and colleagues all fell into this category and were, with decreasing intensity, even obliged to help. Relatives and acquaintances could be relied on to advance small loans. A dense network of credit relations played its part in lending coherence to society. However, to aid the poor, there were only limited resources to hand for this kind of collective self-help in times of crisis.

Integration within manageably small groups and networks in which people all knew one another ("face-to-face society") formed the basis of Europeans' existence at this time. Although under these circumstances the significance of agnate ancestral kinship (lineage) was reduced to being just one important possibility among several, kinship as such still continued to form the social husk of the nuclear family. Attached to this were networks of brothers-in-law and godfathers, neighbors and compatriots. Social transactions could be balanced and based on reciprocity. This was tantamount to dealing with "friends." But often these transactions boiled down to a person's dependence on someone more powerful, the relation of a "client" to his "patron," who could grant him "protection and help." This was also the kind of assistance that was expected of saints, say, the one after whom one was named or the patron saint of a region. This was why people often chose particularly powerful saints like the Virgin Mary or John the Baptist as their patron saints. Integration into a family, a small group, and networks served to provide a communal security against fear. Insurance existed on only a very limited scale at this time; only in the eighteenth century did it develop into a broad-based attempt to use mathematical rationality to counteract the vicissitudes of fate.

It has recently been suggested that the term "society of orders" should be replaced by "group society."[45] We have already seen that only in the case of the clergy membership of one of the three estates could be said to denote the same thing throughout Europe, whereas in all other instances national, regional, and local patterns played a key role. For the horizontal inequality of Europe was even more pronounced than its vertical inequality. No regime, community, or city was quite like any other. Each had a legal status that was valid for it and it alone. This is what is meant by the terms "privilege" and "privilege society," for a privilege is—in contrast to the modern concept of the law, with its claim to universal applicability—nothing but a law in favor of singularity, a law that grants this group or person rights that others do not have. Even individuals, or rather individual families, could be privileged in this sense, that is, endowed with a specific personal legal status. This has already been mentioned with regard to the clergy and the aristocracy.

Settlements

On average, 90 percent of Europeans lived on the land in this period, overwhelmingly under the sway of a local lord since time immemorial and, from the high Middle Ages on, predominantly in a village,[46] whose buildings were by now as stable and fixed as the settlement as a whole. Clustering together in this way meant living communally not just under the informal control of one's neighbors but also within the structured order of an organized community, which everywhere enjoyed a greater or lesser degree of autonomy and had its own officials. In southern Germany, the village fence performed the same function as a wall in a town—namely, the demarcation of a legal precinct.[47] The open-field system, in which every farmer cultivated a strip in commonly held fields and which entailed crossing other people's plots in order to farm it, necessarily required communal arrangements.

Yet only a very small number of farmers had unrestricted ownership in the modern sense of the land they worked; rather, they were subject to the system of dual ownership, to the feudal system in its widest sense (as opposed to the narrower meaning of the term, denoting a system of lords holding lands in fee). An actual lord, generally a nobleman or alternatively an institution, held ultimate ownership over a tract of land, while a farmer had the use of it—a right that could in practice be legally framed in vastly different ways.[48] Throughout most of Europe, the farmer, who originally was just as much the "property" of the landowner as was the piece of land, was by now beholden only to the so-called freehold manorial system—that is, he was obliged to pay specified fees to the landowner, either

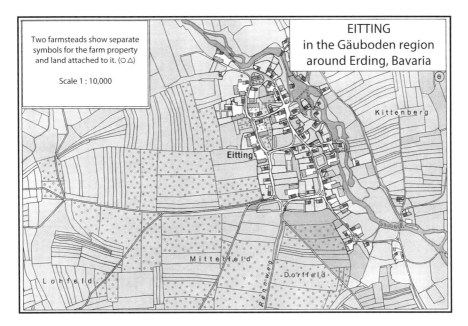

Typical European agricultural field system, in Eitting, Bavaria. (From *Bayerischer Geschichtsatlas*, edited by Max Spindler, Munich: Bayerischer Schulbuchverlag, 1969.)

in the form of money or in kind (that is, produce). In most cases, he had long-term tenure of the land, nor was it uncommon for farmers to bequeath it or even sell it—naturally after some payment to the landowner. This system also had the capacity to develop into a modern tenant-farming arrangement; this was overwhelmingly the case in England, for example. By contrast, east of the River Elbe, from the fifteenth century on, there was an increasing tendency for lords to tend their own land, employing tied farmers as the vast majority of their workforce; in this way, the manorial system became a squirearchy, with its practice of so-called secondary serfdom.[49]

Correspondingly, the extent of communal autonomy also varied considerably. Where farmers were free, or where control over land, the courts, the tithe system, and the country lay in several hands, the potential arose for the development of widespread self-determination through elected officials, albeit with large farmers wielding most authority. In contrast, under a squirearchy, the lord appointed the officials and left the community little freedom to maneuver. In countries where central authority was quick to develop, such as England and France, at least the judicial system resided more or less in the hands of royal officials. Across large parts of Europe, most people's daily lives were played out against the backcloth of the rural community.

In the main, these rural communities also constituted parishes. The church was not just the topographical center of the village but also its cultural and social focal point. People's lives were regulated by the rhythm of the ecclesiastical year, with its festivals and services marking significant rites of passage. Originally, the pastor would, through his background and his limited range of knowledge, have had much in common with the farmers in his parish; before the Reformation, educated theologians were seldom found in the countryside. Yet even after priests, primarily Protestant pastors, became social outposts of the bourgeoisie in the country, thanks to their academic learning, they did not become merely instruments of higher church authority but also continued to act as helpers and arbitrators. The church cared for the poor and later often also provided a school for the children of the village. The laity were also involved in church affairs, taking over responsibility for the church building and frequently forming fraternities serving not just spiritual purposes but also social and sociable ones.

Most people never ventured beyond this stable environment, with which they could identify emotionally. Certainly, there were already some long-distance travelers during this period;[50] in addition to those people whom we have already mentioned who had been unwillingly uprooted, merchants and pilgrims should also be cited—the latter almost being the tourists of the Middle Ages and the early modern period. Later, these groups were also joined by itinerant craftsmen (journeymen) and students making their way to famous universities and still later by young aristocrats taking the "Grand Tour" through Europe.[51] Admittedly, the roads in this period left a lot to be desired; the most comfortable option was therefore often to travel by water, which was also a means of transporting goods cost-effectively. Only in the eighteenth century did the systematic construction of metaled country roads begin to augment the age-old civil engineering skill of bridge building. This was the result of private initiatives in England, whereas in France it was at the king's instigation. Now the postal service, which had been growing from the sixteenth century on, could carry people as well as letters in its coaches; the journey time from Paris to Lyon shrank from ten days to just five. Yet most common people remained rooted to their localities; the scope of their wanderings, including their potential choice of marriage partner, was overwhelmingly confined to the villages in their immediate vicinity.

Moreover, this period also witnessed the beginnings of the "flight from the country" toward towns. Rural people were already being enticed away from land to the cities in the Middle Ages, drawn not only by the sheer appeal of city life but also by the prospect of higher wages, better food, greater security, and improved welfare in times of crisis. Over the course of the fourteenth and fifteenth centuries, around one-quarter of all villages were abandoned; this statistic is attributable not only to the population losses that occurred as a result of the Black Death but also to migration to towns.[52] Although the boom in the founding of European cities was over by this stage, the network of towns was still being extended through the building of so-called lesser towns and markets, with the result that most villages had such a market within reachable distance. This was followed in the sixteenth century by major infrastructure projects initiated by burgeoning modern states, such as mining towns, fortresses, refugee settlements, and royal residences. It is significant that capital cities like Vienna, Berlin, Turin, and Copenhagen experienced their largest population increases in the eighteenth century. But most towns were, and remained, small; many scarcely differed from villages in their pronounced agricultural orientation. Even as late as 1700, there were still no more than 130 towns and cities with between 20,000 and 100,000 inhabitants. Very few were larger than this; Paris, London, and Naples were the three largest conurbations at this time. Yet despite the overwhelmingly rural character of Europe, some heavily urbanized zones had developed since the Middle Ages—notably, the trading and textile towns of the Netherlands and northern Italy. In the fourteenth century, Ghent, with sixty thousand inhabitants, was the second largest continental city north of the Alps (after Paris). By 1650, 55 percent of Holland's population were city dwellers; in the Veneto region of northeast Italy in the eighteenth century, this figure was as high as 86 percent.

Generally, European cities were walled settlements with their own jurisdictions and a degree of communal autonomy,[53] which, however, amounted to complete independence only in the case of Italian city-states such as Florence, Milan, and Venice. Elsewhere, their autonomy differed only by degrees from that of villages. In addition, towns formed the focal point of their surrounding regions, not

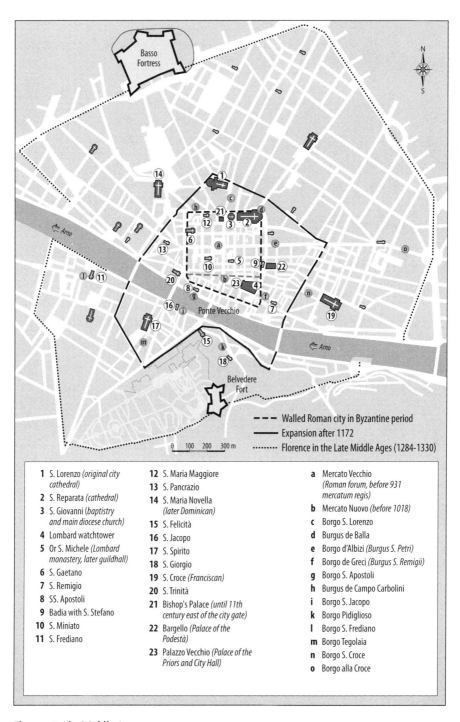

Florence in the Middle Ages

Basso Fortress

N

Arno

Ponte Vecchio

Belvedere Fort

– – – Walled Roman city in Byzantine period
—— Expansion after 1172
········· Florence in the Late Middle Ages (1284-1330)

0   100   200   300 m

1 S. Lorenzo *(original city cathedral)*
2 S. Reparata *(cathedral)*
3 S. Giovanni *(baptistry and main diocese church)*
4 Lombard watchtower
5 Or S. Michele *(Lombard monastery, later guildhall)*
6 S. Gaetano
7 S. Remigio
8 SS. Apostoli
9 Badia with S. Stefano
10 S. Miniato
11 S. Frediano

12 S. Maria Maggiore
13 S. Pancrazio
14 S. Maria Novella *(later Dominican)*
15 S. Felicità
16 S. Jacopo
17 S. Spirito
18 S. Giorgio
19 S. Croce *(Franciscan)*
20 S. Trinità
21 Bishop's Palace *(until 11th century east of the city gate)*
22 Bargello *(Palace of the Podestà)*
23 Palazzo Vecchio *(Palace of the Priors and City Hall)*

a Mercato Vecchio *(Roman forum, before 931 mercatum regis)*
b Mercato Nuovo *(before 1018)*
c Borgo S. Lorenzo
d Burgus de Balla
e Borgo d'Albizi *(Burgus S. Petri)*
f Borgo de Greci *(Burgus S. Remigii)*
g Borgo S. Apostoli
h Burgus de Campo Carbolini
i Borgo S. Jacopo
k Borgo Pidiglioso
l Borgo S. Frediano
m Borgo Tegolaia
n Borgo S. Croce
o Borgo alla Croce

Florence in the Middle Ages

just in their capacity as trading centers and markets but also in a cultural sense, as spiritual centers richly appointed with churches and monasteries. For example, no fewer than 264 Italian cities in the fourteenth century were also bishop's sees. Religion also meant education, bringing schools and sometimes even universities to towns. Finally, as states began to develop, towns became the site of law courts and later of bureaucracies. Towns were not like islands of alien culture in a rural setting but were intrinsically bound up with the surrounding countryside. To be sure, as members of city confederations, urban dwellers were personally free and privileged, unlike the majority of peasants. But even so, in most towns, only a minority enjoyed full citizens' rights; the majority were disenfranchised citizens, sometimes comprising transient groups from rural backgrounds, such as female domestic servants. Conversely, wealthy burghers and urban institutions began to acquire land in the country and assume the role of lords of the manor, while also running the rural economy through their control of the food market. Powerful cities dominated their environs; this was the case for the major towns of Flanders, while imperial cities such as Berne, Lucerne, and Ulm gained control over large territories. In addition, Italian metropolises like Florence, Milan, and Venice subjugated rival cities within their purview and in doing so created real city-states (albeit, as always, without granting these new subjects any political say).

Nature and Religion

While Europe remained relatively thinly populated, environmental problems still reared their head in this period. In the towns, it was a question not merely of often woefully inadequate hygiene and waste disposal, as well as the ever-present danger of fire, but also of water pollution from tanning and dyeing or, in London, of air pollution from countless coal-burning fireplaces. Coal was now increasingly being used as a fuel, after deforestation saw stocks of the universal fuel and raw material wood dwindle.[54] In northern Germany, the Lüneburg Heath came into being after the saltworks in the town of Lüneburg had used up all the trees in the surrounding forest. Ultimately, these works had to import the firewood they needed from far-off Mecklenburg. The same thing happened at saltworks in Bavaria and France. Glassworks required even more wood for their operations. In addition, there were also the demands of the building trade and of shipbuilding. To erect the Frauenkirche

(Church of Our Lady) in Munich, twenty thousand tree trunks were felled, while the construction of a midsized ship used up to four thousand. As early as the thirteenth century, total deforestation of the Po Basin was causing the regular flooding that still occurs there today, as the ground became saturated with rainwater. Around this same time, the first corrective measures were attempted, with bans imposed on tree felling, followed by reforestation projects in the fourteenth century.

However, the forests yielded not only timber but berries and mushrooms, too, as well as serving as a foraging site for fattening up pigs and as a hunting ground, often hotly disputed between peasants and their lords. But the woods were also looked upon as wilderness, as a formless chaos in contrast to cultivated territory, and as the haunt of all forces that were inimical to man: the forest was home to robbers and giants, witches and evil spirits. The poet Dante Alighieri even placed the gates of hell in a wild woodland setting.[55]

This juxtaposition of the exploitable natural world and the feared supernatural world is typical of the religion of premodern European man, which was characterized by an irresolvable tension between immanence and transcendence. As long as 90 percent of people remained attached to an agrarian culture, they struggled to comprehend the fundamental achievement of prophetic Judaism and the Christianity that devolved from that faith, namely, the invention of transcendence. Whereas the pre-Judeo-Christian world was inhabited by gods or was itself deified, it was now regarded as the creation of a God who existed in a realm beyond this world and independent of it. Having left the world both to be governed by its own laws and to be formed by humans, God continued to exercise his control over the world indirectly, through human beings devoted to him. In this way, the world had been made fundamentally worldly.

But for premodern Europeans, it also remained the playground of magical forces, filled with many evil and only a very few benign spirits. Inasmuch as people did not simply live out their lives in an apathetic state, they cultivated a devout piety in order to gain protection from God and his saints in this perilous situation. They implored the divine powers to intervene directly to influence the forces to which they were exposed in their daily lives: weather and storms, fruitfulness and harvests, illness and plagues, life and death. People expected immediate practical effects to flow from the Holy Mass and the other sacraments of the church and from the blessings they received and the prayers they addressed to God, the

Virgin Mary, and the saints. As such, although their conception of religious deeds diverged from magic in theological theory, in practice it was very similar indeed. Their piety was reified, masses were counted, and indulgences quantified. Devotion was "haptic"—in other words, fixated on bodily contact with the saints, as evidenced by the countless relics of saints. It was not enough that the Eucharist was already theologically subjected to a degree of objectification through the doctrine of the real presence of Christ in the bread and wine (transubstantiation). Through the introduction of the Feast of Corpus Christi and the adoration of the living Christ in the Host, God himself was reified into a kind of superrelic and a visual contact with him, which would at least bring salvation, assured.[56]

For good reasons, premodern Christianity was therefore for most people a religion of fear or at least of the overcoming of fear.[57] God was primarily perceived as a judge weighing up the transgressions of sinners, while his son, Jesus Christ, who had come down to Earth to save sinners, was also often likewise tellingly depicted in his role of judge on Judgment Day. Objectified in the premodern sense, this signified that people could count on an immediate material reward or punishment in the here and now for committing good or evil deeds. Thus, if a town was hit by a storm, then the cause was deemed to lie in the immoral or spiritually outrageous conduct of a section of its population, for instance, in homosexuality or in the practice of "papist worship" in the Holy Mass. This mind-set provided ample excuse for the authorities to castigate debauchery or to enact the "Reformation," which would doubtlessly meet with God's favor.

To be sure, natural disasters could just as easily be ascribed to the work of the devil, especially to the black magic practiced by his male and female servants, wizards and witches. The fear of witchcraft lurked beneath the surface of many premodern cultures, including that of Europe, and in times of crisis could lead to panic reactions, particularly once a whole demonology of witches was available from the fifteenth century on. During the heyday of the European mania for witch hunting, from the late fifteenth to the late seventeenth century, it is estimated that some 50,000–100,000 "witches" and "wizards" lost their lives (millions are still sometimes falsely claimed to have perished, based on a false extrapolation dating from the eighteenth century).[58] Yet there were some theologians who maintained that this fear was founded on a fundamental overestimation of the power of Satan, which flew in the face of the Christian doctrine of the ultimate authority of God.

But most premodern Europeans (including Martin Luther), beset by fear, preferred to believe de facto in a dualistic universe and in a religion based on the existential struggle between God and the devil, in which humans were required to take sides.

In any event, it is true to say that Europeans in 1750 were, almost without exception, adherents of some form of Christianity. Only a minority of the elites were at that time beginning to disengage from traditional religious belief under the influence of the Enlightenment, a process that would soon take on far more significant proportions. Yet widespread de-Christianization arose only during the twentieth and twenty-first centuries.

From Cultural Transfer to Cultural Autonomy

Defining Europe as "Latinized" is the shortest possible expression of the basic fact that down to the seventeenth century, European elite culture relied exclusively on continuous transfer from the sources of classical antiquity and Judeo-Christianity.[59] Therefore, for any problem arising, Europeans tended to search for a solution either in the Bible or in the collected works of Aristotle. This only slightly simplified state of things constitutes the unity of European culture. However, inside this essential unity there was still room enough for varieties and development. Because of some of these developments, Europe became slowly emancipated first from the authority of antiquity and finally also from the authority of Christianity. Therefore, beginning in the seventeenth century, enlightened Europeans started to found their from now on autonomous culture on the capacities of autonomous human reason as its new unifying principle.

European culture had neither a homogenous origin nor a stable, unified character but nevertheless still exhibited certain basic common features. It is hard to determine what elements of Celtic and Iberian cultures or those of the Germanic and Slavic tribes it may have absorbed in the period prior to the influence of the Roman Empire, not least because, up to the eighteenth century, it was steeped throughout not just in Christianity but also in the legacy of classical antiquity. More precisely, it was characterized by the cultural heritage of ancient Israel, Greece, and Rome as transmitted by the Catholic Church, which was preserved in the

Jewish Bible, the so-called Old Testament of the Christian Bible, as well as in Greek and Roman literature. The Roman components predominated, with the legacy of ancient Greece initially being conveyed mostly in the form of its reception in ancient Rome, while the Jewish elements were those that had been adopted by the Roman church.

For a long time, the Roman church was the sole transmitter of culture; its priests were the only ones who could read and write and, more important, the only ones who could read or write Latin.[60] The Latin language predominated, whereas the knowledge of Greek and ancient Hebrew was limited, expanding only from the fifteenth century on, under the influence of the Renaissance and humanism. At this time, the number of ancient texts that were known about in all three languages increased considerably, and the ancient tradition began, at least partially, to free itself from church paternalism. For the rise of the Renaissance and humanism was intrinsically bound up with the development of an urban secular culture as an alternative to an ecclesiastical culture. While this development also saw vernacular languages begin to play a greater role and to generate their own literatures, its main effect was to strengthen the connection to classical antiquity. The classical tradition was to continue to dominate education right up to the twentieth century. Accordingly, until the eighteenth century, whenever new problems appeared, educated Europeans would usually ask themselves what ancient writers and the Bible had to say on the matter—some appropriate dictum could almost invariably be found in this vast body of work.

In both its content and its language, therefore, European culture lived through constant transference. Its lingua franca, Latin, was a foreign language, as were the three "sacred languages" of Hebrew, Greek, and (again) Latin. For over a millennium, Europe's culture was based on translation, a process that made Europeans into first-rate philologists and interpreters of texts; first and foremost, scientific acuity at this time was deployed in textual exegesis. It was only from the seventeenth century on that Europeans started to rely on their own powers of reasoning and empirically verifiable experience began to supplant ancient and Christian authorities. It was only then that Europe severed the umbilical cord from its mother cultures and began to give precedence to its own languages—in short, to gain its cultural autonomy.

Up to that point, this common grounding in antiquity had engendered and kept alive a certain sense of unity in European culture. In addition, the Catholic Church acted both as an intermediary of this culture and more generally as a common vector of communication. Beyond primary groups, communication creates more far-reaching networks of similarities in consciousness, attitudes, moods, and values. Modern mass communication is European in origin, where it goes back to the church, whose example later organizations followed. A uniformly educated clergy taught a uniform faith, with the Bible and its associated ecclesiastical literature as a uniform textual foundation. The Bible formed the basis of this European cultural uniformity and not just in a religious context. It exerted a huge influence on art and literature and was adduced to underpin arguments or legitimize positions. Yet Christianity was not just a book-based religion; it was also steeped in ritual. In other words, the Europe-wide imposition of largely uniform religious rites only served to strengthen still further the sense of mental commonality. At the very latest, the rise of the mendicant orders in the thirteenth century enabled centrally directed mass sermons to be held, which were designed to promulgate not just certain forms of devotion but also particular political attitudes. Growing literacy and later the media revolution of the printed book lent massive new scope to the potential for communication. Their initial effect was to ensure the success of the Reformation and of subsequent confessionalization, while later they underpinned that of other mass movements, be they revolutionary or nationalistic.

When it was still a sect of Judaism, Christianity had no fully worked-out theological framework. But as it spread throughout the Roman Empire, it was transformed and systematized by Greek and Roman thought. Thus, from the simple, unexplained juxtaposition in the New Testament of God the Father, God the Son, and God the Holy Ghost, Greek ingenuity developed the authoritative doctrine of God as three-in-one, the dogma of the Trinity. Furthermore, the biblical opposites of transcendence and immanence, of God and the world, and of good and evil were identified with the Greek dualism of spirit and flesh and of soul and body, which already played a major role in the works of Plato. Subsequently, Roman legal thinking created from this a systematic theory of the relationship between the church and the secular world. It also, far beyond the bounds of Christendom, established an ontological bipolarity within European thought that has still scarcely been resolved to this day.

Knowledge and Humanism

Another factor that continues to resonate down to the present day was the reception and transmission by Muslim scholars from the thirteenth century on of the universal works of the Greek thinker Aristotle, who became the key philosopher of the Western world. His reception within Europe then took place largely according to a new method of academic enquiry, scholasticism, and within a new milieu, namely, universities. The first universities of Bologna and Paris, founded respectively in the late eleventh and early twelfth centuries, were followed by numerous other new such institutions in the thirteenth and fourteenth centuries and also spread to Central and Eastern Europe with the founding of Prague University in 1347. Further universities were founded, predominantly in the German-speaking lands, by ambitious princes in the fifteenth century, such as Freiburg im Breisgau in Habsburg-controlled territory in 1455, or in cities such as Basel (1459). In 1378, there were at least twenty-eight universities in Europe, while by 1500 this figure had grown to at least sixty-three. Alongside traditional colleges, by the late Middle Ages, the division (introduced in Paris) into four faculties was also widespread: arts (comprising the basic quadrivium of four philosophical foundation subjects), theology, law, and medicine (the last faculty was by no means universally adopted). The teaching staff now comprised a cadre of increasingly professional university lecturers, replacing the old system of a smooth transition from advanced student with a remit to teach to tutor. However, the growing number of institutions of higher learning brought with it a decline in quality and above all among the students a trend away from a universal outlook toward nationalism or even regionalism. This was in line with the interests of the cities and princes who in the main were responsible for endowing these new universities. From as early as the thirteenth century, from time to time study abroad was forbidden.[61]

Europe's universities were long to remain the principal conveyors of knowledge. They form an intrinsic part of the urban milieu, where a substructure of church, community, and private schools had also developed. On the one hand, there were Latin schools, which originally primarily trained future priests, while on the other, there were the forerunners of the later junior high schools, in which teaching focused on reading, writing, and above all arithmetic in preparation for a mercantile career. Yet it was by no means a given for people to go on from these to university, nor was it the norm to complete a course of study through graduation. The university had opened up new opportunities for social advancement alongside a career in the church; nevertheless, it seems that the vertical and horizontal mobility this new institution set in train was initially held in check. Only in the fifteenth century did bourgeois lawyers begin to compete with the old aristocratic classes, and only then did the phenomenon of the European "peripatetic academic" become commonplace, as, for instance, German students traveled south to study in Italy.

There they not only became acquainted with the ever more important academic discipline of Roman law but also coincidentally got to know of a new school of thought that had arisen in Italy during the fourteenth century—Renaissance humanism.[62] Given that there have been many "humanist" movements throughout history, this particular designation indicates that we are dealing here with a particular form of the tendency, which is temporally, and not infrequently also objectively and personally, bound up with the art of the Renaissance and which spread throughout the whole of Europe in the course of the fifteenth and sixteenth centuries. While it cannot be denied that the urge to present an entirely fresh image and to compete with established scholars led to a great deal of vain, self-conscious posturing and misleading polemicism on the part of the adherents of this new movement,[63] it is still accurate to claim that Renaissance humanism began with the poet and writer Petrarch (1304–1374). Among other Italian cities, Florence came to play an especially important role, primarily because of the close connection to the Renaissance art that had also experienced such a brilliant efflorescence there, but also thanks to its ancient tradition of humanist republicanism,[64] which still continues to make its effects felt through thinkers like Niccolò Macchiavelli (1469–1527).[65] Florence's prominent role is also owing to the particularly pronounced adherence of Florentine humanists to Platonic philosophy and Neoplatonic esotericism, as represented first and foremost by the philosopher Marsilio Ficino (1433–1499), who was active at this time in an academy established under the patronage of the Medicis.[66] In conjunction with the humanism of the cities, both in Italy and particularly north of the Alps, courtly humanism also played a crucial role.[67] However, like Petrarch before him, probably the most significant and undoubtedly the most influential humanist of northern Europe, Desiderius Erasmus of Rotterdam (1469–1536),[68] set great store by retaining personal independence from such patrons.

The figure of the free intellectual and artist surviving solely on the fruits of his labor represented an entirely new role on Europe's cultural stage. The novelty of this role also resided in the fact that it could be filled only by someone exercising individual skill. Of course, individual talents had also existed in the Middle Ages, but it was only now that important personages were celebrated, say, by means of an equestrian statue, or that they vaunted their own achievements, as the proud creator of an artwork, for example. Only now do the names of most artists and writers become known as a matter of course. The edifying and instructive lives of the saints of medieval times were now superseded by the biographies of great men (less so women), as well as by those of artists and writers.[69]

The "humanists" of the Renaissance were first and foremost literati, in other words, experts in and teachers of the *Studia Humanitatis,* the curriculum comprising grammar, rhetoric, history, poetry, and moral philosophy. Seen in the context of the seven "liberal arts" of the Middle Ages, this represented a shift of emphasis toward literary and rhetorical subjects. The ability to produce perfect Latin texts and poems and to deliver perfect orations in Latin played a central role. There was a concerted effort to replace the crude Latin of medieval times, now decried as "barbaric," with a more refined form based on classical models such as Cicero. Hand in hand with this came a purer form of Latin script, so-called *Antiqua,* which had its origins not in antiquity but in the court of Charlemagne. All modern European written and printed scripts come from this. In terms of content as well, Latin authors of the classical period, joined by an increasing number of Greeks, were now seen as the authoritative models, as masters not just of the art of writing but also of the art of life. It was widely held that people became fully rounded human beings only through the *Studia Humanitatis*—a conviction that has persisted in the humanistic grammar schools of Europe right up to the present day. For from the fifteenth century on, humanism asserted its preeminence throughout the entire higher educational system.

Revival of Antiquity or the Renaissance

This reverence for antiquity on the one hand and upward revaluation of the present on the other automatically led to the intervening "Middle Ages" (the very concept was invented at this time) being downgraded to a period of "darkness." But this new consciousness of historical distance also engendered a new attitude to history. For the first time, the past was seen as fundamentally different. However, this did not entail a downgrading of Christianity, as previously thought. The new literary–artistic enthusiasm for ancient mythology and its pantheon of gods only occasionally resulted in a full-blown new heathenism, while the craze for esoteric things of all kinds, including the Jewish Kabbala, often only amounted to a search for an ultimate revelation that would complement Christianity and make it acceptable to all people. Most humanists regarded themselves, like Erasmus, not only as Christians but even as better Christians, because they were also determined to purge Christendom of all its medieval malpractices. In this respect, they were close to the evangelical Reformation; indeed, humanism was its necessary prerequisite. However, in contrast to both the Reformation and the traditional medieval Christianity, the humanists were also imbued with a deep sense of anthropological optimism. Whereas, once, even a prominent pope such as Innocent III (r. 1198–1216) had issued one of the customary tractates on spurning worldly things and on the misery of human existence, in contrast the young philosopher Giovanni Pico de Mirandola (1463–1494) published a life-affirming speech about the dignity of man, in which he assigned humanity the role of continuing the creator's work through its own creativity.[70]

Antiquity therefore was considered beautiful and ideal and was later designated "classical," as it reflected nature most consummately. A new sense of communion with nature, then, supported by an appeal to classical models, sparked a rebirth of the visual arts, known in Italian as the *rinascità* and later in French as the Renaissance. The Gothic style of architecture that was then blossoming was rejected; instead, examples of late medieval realism in sculpture, such as the work of Claus Sluter (c.1355–1406) and Tilman Riemenschneider (c. 1460–1531) and Northern painting especially after Hubert and Jan van Eyck (c. 1370–1426 and c. 1390–1441, respectively), were deemed to be closer to Italian Renaissance ideals. There was much reciprocal influence between Flemish and Italian artists at this time.

The focal point of the Renaissance was in Florence, where Filippo Brunelleschi (1377–1446) developed the architecture of pure geometrical forms and Leon Battista Alberti (1404–1472) laid its theoretical groundwork. The new realism in painting had begun there already, with Giotto (c. 1266–1337), and reached its ze-

In Florence, the center of the early and high Renaissance, a palace (known today, after its subsequent owner, as the Palazzo Medici-Riccardi) was built for the ruling Medici family in the mid-fifteenth century. Thanks to its harmonious aspect—columns in the ancient tradition combine with Romanesque arches in the medieval idiom to create a balanced whole—the palace's square inner courtyard is widely regarded as one of the most beautiful of the Renaissance period. (Alinari/ Bridgeman Images)

nith in the introduction of single-point linear perspective. In sculpture, it was the Florentine artist Donatello (c. 1386–1466) who first achieved perfect classical form in his works. The high-water mark in the Florentine Renaissance was represented by Leonardo da Vinci (1452–1519), Michelangelo Buonarotti (1475–1564), and Raphael (Raffaelo Santi; c. 1483–1520).[71] Of the many Northern artists who were influenced by Italian Renaissance art, the most significant was the Nuremberg painter Albrecht Dürer (1471–1528).

Many of the leading Italian artists of this period were distinguished by their remarkable versatility, as sculptors, painters, and architects; the talents of some even extended far beyond the realms of art. In particular, Alberti[72] and Leonardo[73] embodied this *uomo universale*. Leonardo not only was an acute observer of nature but also used his observations to draft blueprints for complex machines and plans for ideal cities. In this, he was following a tradition of mostly anonymous "amateur constructors" who in medieval times had made certain extraordinary technological breakthroughs.[74] While the discovery of certain ancient texts had helped the natural sciences and medicine broaden their knowledge base, for the same reason these disciplines remained in some cases wedded to mistaken ideas for a long time. In addition, these realms were also strongly influenced by Neoplatonist and esoteric modes of thought; in some instances, this was perfectly capable of resulting in valuable new insights. For instance, it is possible that even the purely speculative heliocentric model of the universe devised by Nikolaus Copernicus may go back to the Neoplatonic cult of the sun.[75] But at this stage, the empiricism of the modern scientific method was still a long way off.

Nineteenth-century historians like Jules Michelet (1855) and Jacob Burckhardt (1860) attributed the "discovery of the world and of humanity" to the Renaissance. Such an interpretation effectively made the Renaissance the first epoch of a secular modernity that was sharply distinct from the medieval period—quite falsely, as we now know. It transpires that the Middle Ages were more "modern" than we once gave them credit for and that the Renaissance was actually more "medieval," in particular more Christian. Furthermore, aside from innovations in art and humanism, it turns out to be well-nigh impossible to determine any common characteristics of the period.[76]

The Reformation and Confessionalization

Likewise, from the eighteenth century on, the ecclesiastical Reformations instigated by the German monk Martin Luther (1483–1546)[77] and his many successors—of whom the Geneva reformer, the Frenchman Jean Calvin (1509–1564),[78] was the most successful—were wrongly claimed by their heirs to mark the beginning of the modern world. Certainly, there is no denying that the Reformation unleashed major conflicts and changed the face of Europe forever.[79] New Lutheran churches sprang up in Central and Northern Europe, while the more strictly reformed Christianity of Calvin radiated out from Geneva to embrace France and Southern Europe but above all left an indelible stamp on the Anglo-

Saxon world through its adoption by Scottish and English believers.[80] Yet if the Reformation can be thereby said to have had modernizing effects, these were actually at complete variance with the will of the reformers themselves, who intended to bring about the exact opposite, namely, to return the church to its original purity. In this respect, therefore, the Reformation may be said, rather, to represent the ultimate conclusion of centuries of opposition to the Catholic Church and of efforts to reform it. It was the intention of the Reformation not to found new churches but to win over the existing one to the reformists' way of thinking. Its central tenet, that no deeds on the part of humans could ensure their eternal salvation, which could be effected only through God's grace *(sola gratia),* was not new. It only became a radical and explosive new idea through the conclusions that were drawn from it, namely, that salvation should be based on faith alone *(sola fide)* and that everything that was needed to attain it could be taken directly from the Bible *(sola scriptura).* This effectively made the entire existing church apparatus superfluous. It also, in theoretical terms, should have spelled a definitive end to the traditional objectification of religion; in practical terms, though, this was still out of the question. Consistent spiritualization of religion remained the preserve of only tiny minorities of believers. Luther himself, for instance, was absolutely convinced of the omnipresence of the devil.

The reaction of the Catholic Church at the Council of Trent (1545–1563)[81] was appropriate as it was effective, not just by clearly differentiating itself in theological terms from the Reformation but also by instituting reforms of its own aimed at creating a purified version of its previous religious practice. The systematic construction of magnificent church buildings and lavish ritual observance formed an integral part of the Catholic Church's offensive to assert its identity and regain lost territory. The new Lutheran and Reformed (that is, Calvinist) churches would find themselves in conflict with the Catholic Church for centuries thereafter. In these circumstances, the key objective for all the competing churches was to secure their own membership and keep members in line through strict controls. To this end (often in collaboration with the secular authorities), they employed more or less the same social techniques as one another, beginning with a newly formulated credo as a yardstick of orthodoxy, which could even be used to swear in pastors, teachers, and other functionaries. Thanks to the key role played by such *confessiones,* such efforts, which continued on in some places right up to the eighteenth

century, are now known as "confessionalization,"[82] and the period that is characterized by them is known as "the confessional age."

Although Reformation and confessionalization built on humanism and the
Renaissance and to a large extent took over their achievements, in contrast to those
movements they were initially, and equally across all confessions, characterized
by a profound anthropological pessimism. This was not confined by any means
to the ecclesiastical realm but also, for example, characterized political thought
too, even in the case of an utterly nonecclesiastical philosopher such as Thomas
Hobbes (1588–1679). In this regard, we are more justified in speaking of a return
to the Middle Ages than of a common dawn of a new age on the basis of the Renaissance and Reformation.

An invention of the fifteenth century represented—both for the Reformation
and for confessionalization—one of the most important guarantors of their success: printing with movable type, the second media revolution in history after the
invention of writing. The spread of cheaper paper in the Middle Ages enabled mass
communication to be based on an entirely new foundation. Key texts could now
be cheaply reproduced and disseminated in identical form and in large numbers.
This standardization of language played a major role in the formation of unified
national languages, in Eastern Europe even initially creating a common national
language. The printing of a new Bible translation during the Reformation or confessionalization period could often act as a catalyst in this respect. Massive propaganda to promote the cause, sometimes via the foundation of publishing houses
for this express purpose, was as much a hallmark of confessionalization as was
massive censorship, both before and after publication, to try and suppress the appearance of rival tracts.[83]

A confessionalized education system was designed, in the eyes of the particular church and secular authority in question, to produce orthodox subjects, or
at very least orthodox elites. Dissenters were frequently expelled; even as late as
the eighteenth century, this was the fate of Protestants in Salzburg. There were
also attempts to suppress contact with dissenters beyond national borders; studying
abroad, for instance, was extensively banned for this reason. Careful records were
kept on participation in church rites, such as receiving the sacraments and attending
services, and absentees were punished. Particular emphasis was placed on "distinctive rituals" such as the cult of the sacraments and veneration of saints among

Catholics, the Eucharist with bread and wine among all Protestants, and the rejection of all religious imagery among Calvinists. Old and new institutions alike were all deployed to control a church's flock: among Catholics, Lutherans, and some Reformed churches, this took the form of visitations to the congregations by ecclesiastical and secular heads, while among some autonomous Calvinist congregations, it took the form of a strict control of matters of faith and moral conduct by a group of church elders (a consistory or presbytery).

Naturally, these measures did not always meet with success, but nevertheless the aim of spreading modes of orthodox thought and behavior commensurate with the denomination in question had been largely achieved by the eighteenth to nineteenth centuries. The upshot of this was that there were now different confessional cultures in Europe. The Catholic joy in sensuality not only gave rise to countless lavishly decorated churches and monasteries that were artistic masterpieces but also produced entire landscapes shot through with religiosity, by virtue of the many chapels and wayside shrines that were erected. Lutherans and above all Calvinists had no truck with such things: their world was a far more austere place. Yet German Lutheranism at least compensated for this by indulging in the production of some world-class church music, by no means confined solely to the works of Johann Sebastian Bach (1685–1750). Catholicism retained Latin as the language of liturgy, while Protestants, as we have seen, used the vernacular. Even so, the Lutherans, who retained parts of the Mass, mixed this with some elements of Latin.

Above and beyond this, the confessions also differed where other details of daily life were concerned. Because the "Gregorian" calendar reform of 1582 announced by the pope was unacceptable to many Protestants (the course of the year was still universally determined by the ecclesiastical calendar), German Protestants accepted it only in 1700, while England and Sweden finally fell into line in the mid-eighteenth century. This meant that for a long time, the different confessions calculated time differently. Baptismal names also diverged, because Catholics were obliged to take the names of saints, whereas these were strictly forbidden for Calvinists. The universally standardized system of Jesuit schools and colleges can be said to have hallmarked the behavior of Catholic elites, as did the religious observances practiced by the "Marian congregations," which this same order established all over Europe. Corresponding phenomena on the Protestant side characterizing the whole culture of worship were the religious awakening movements that began with German Pietism in the seventeenth century,[84] which in one variant or another also expanded worldwide over time. The Anglo-Saxon Methodist movement in the eighteenth century was particularly significant in this regard.[85] This no longer placed Protestant orthodoxy at the center of worship but emphasized instead the personal devotion of the individual and its ramifications in a person's life as a whole. Even today, Catholics and Protestants differ in certain aspects of their attitude and even in their mode of speaking.

These confessional cultures overlapped or even converged with national and regional cultures, frequently emphasizing their differences. The cultures concerned here could sometimes be variations in artistic styles or ways of life but more often took the form of distinct national literary and bureaucratic languages, which had been growing since the fourteenth century. Beginning with Petrarch, it was not uncommon for leading humanists to also be successful authors in their native tongue, as well as nationalistically minded champions of its use.

Nevertheless, for all these confessional, national, and regional differences, there remained certain fundamental cultural similarities. This was particularly the case in music, where the compositions of a J. S. Bach, and of his Protestant predecessors and contemporaries, would have been unthinkable without the prior achievements of Italian composers such as Claudio Monteverdi (1567–1643), Alessandro Scarlatti (1660–1725), and Antonio Vivaldi (1678–1741). In Italy, the polyphony of the Renaissance was superseded by sophisticated new modes of instrumental and choral music, which placed a premium on impact and emotion. Here, then, was the birthplace of the concerto, the cantata, and not least a completely new form of music—opera.[86]

Philosophy and the Sciences

Indeed, there can be said to have existed a residual Latin–Christian common currency comprising both ways of living and the legacy of antiquity, which in its improved humanist form was more than ever setting the tone in European culture. Modes of thought remained essentially the same the length and breadth of the continent, because they all derived from a common tradition of form and content. In addition, educated elites continued to operate, as they always had done, in one common lingua franca or even two: initially, of course, this was Latin, but from the seventeenth century on this was supplemented or in some cases even supplanted by French. For the political hegemony of France at that time was reinforced (and vice versa) by a cultural dominance whose intensity can only be compared with the Italian Renaissance, and it was never matched by other countries that took the leading role in Europe at various periods: Spain in the second half of the sixteenth century, the Netherlands in the mid-seventeenth century, and England in the eighteenth.

Communication between the elites, in particular among scholars, therefore continued to be as strong and vibrant as ever. Nothing stood in the way of a Europe-wide dissemination of intellectual achievements in the seventeenth century, even if—or precisely due to the fact that—these did not emanate from universities. Since the foundation of the Royal Society of London for the Promotion of Natural Knowledge in 1652 and the Académie Royale des Sciences in Paris in 1666, academies, as federations of independent or tenured researchers, began to play an increasingly important role, especially in the sciences. The eighteenth century saw a proliferation of new establishments: in 1700, and again in 1744, in Berlin; in 1724 in St. Petersburg; in 1728 in Uppsala; in 1739 in Stockholm; in 1742 in Copenhagen; in 1747 in Olomouc (Olmütz); and in 1752 in both Göttingen and Haarlem.[87]

One of the cofounders of the first Berlin Academy was Gottfried Wilhelm Leibniz (1646–1716), who had immersed himself in the new natural sciences in Paris and London and become a member of the Royal Society. As a lawyer and politician, a historian and theologian, a philosopher and mathematician, and even a sometime inventor, Leibniz played a leading role in many different fields of knowledge and epitomized like no other the universal polymath scholar of this age. He was universal not just by dint of his worldwide correspondence but first and foremost because the notion of a philosophical world system stood at the very heart of his thinking, a system that could square the new mechanistic interpretation of the world with the existence of spirituality and a transcendent God. His mathematical achievements, such as infinitesimal calculus, mathematical logic, and the binary system, can be explained, at least in part, by this worldview.[88]

The new mechanistic view of the world emerged from the natural sciences of the late sixteenth and early seventeenth century, which shunned all esoteric or speculative dimensions in favor of mathematical clarity and empirical verifiability.[89]

In contrast to Johannes Kepler (1571–1630), whose astronomical observations were still accompanied by speculation about the nature of the universe, the physicist and astronomer Galileo Galilei (1564–1642) gave credence only to results that could be proven mathematically or empirically. Admittedly, this approach sometimes led him to miscalculate, and he became embroiled in a momentous conflict, less with Roman astronomers than with the theologians of the Inquisition.[90] After Francis Bacon (1561–1626) had established the theoretical foundations of the inductive–empirical scientific method, René Descartes (1596–1650) attempted, in his 1637 work *Discours de la Méthode,* a complete philosophical and mathematical refoundation of science on the basis of systematic doubt. Descartes's system heightened traditional Western dualism into a strict division of mind and matter. The universe appeared as a machine made up of tiny parts, which obeyed hard-and-fast laws. According to this mechanistic worldview, both human and animal bodies—and even the state, in the philosophy of Thomas Hobbes, say—were conceived of as machines. This mode of thought still resonates down to the present day, at least in popular conceptions of science in Europe.

Leibniz's countervailing view was not the only one put forward in this period. The worldview of his equally famous contemporary and rival Isaac Newton (1643–1727), as expressed in his 1686 treatise *Philosophiae naturalis principia mathematica,* at least still entertained the possibility of a transcendent God. In just a few, relatively simple, mathematically formulated laws, Newton had managed to explain the mechanical workings of the universe in all its great diversity, from the motions of the planets down to the fall of a stone under the effects of gravity, and to thereby render them predictable. A series of new observations and experiments corroborated the findings of his *Principia,* which remained unchallenged as a valid scientific model until Einstein. True, Newton's system also functioned perfectly well without the presumption of a God, but the force of gravity that underpinned it all remained unexplained, leaving open the possibility of interpretation of a divine hand in the matter. In any event, Newton retained a continuing interest not just in theology but also in esoteric ways of perceiving nature (for example, alchemy).

Inspired by Descartes and the Danish astronomer Ole Romer (1644–1710), the Dutch scientist Christiaan Huygens (1629–1695) developed a forward-looking wave theory of light (*Traité de la Lumière,* 1690). It evolved from his practical work as a constructor of telescopes and as an astronomer, along the same lines as Galileo but largely independent of him. Huygens was also responsible for inventing the first pendulum clock (patented 1657), whose spread allowed ordinary Europeans to measure time exactly for the first time—a fundamental prerequisite of the modern world.

Hardly any of these pioneers were university professors, while those few that were occupied their posts only temporarily and not in the subjects where their major achievements lay. They were mavericks who enjoyed royal patronage and belonged to academies: Newton, for instance, was president of the Royal Society. The universities at this time had faded into the background and were to experience a resurgence as research institutions only in the nineteenth century. Even so, there were some notable exceptions in Italy and the Holy Roman Empire, where the new universities founded at Halle in 1694 and at Göttingen in 1737 served as innovative models. In these institutions, some subjects were radically overhauled. For example, in jurisprudence, Roman law took a backseat to the study of current legal practice, while history, political science, and finance were all established as independent disciplines. Use of German became far more prevalent in teaching. The most influential philosopher and jurist of the German Enlightenment,[91] Christian Wolff (1679–1754), taught at Halle, although he was banished from the realm between 1723 and 1740 by the Prussian king Friedrich Wilhelm I by instigation of the local Pietists who accused him of determinism. The reforming universities had, by and large, lost their autonomous status and become state institutions geared in their constitution and range of courses toward the needs of the expanding modern state. Besides, German law and the German language tended to deter foreigners from coming to study there.

The Enlightenment

In Germany and Italy, Russia and Spain, monarchies in the guise of "enlightened absolutism"[92] had gained effective control over the new cultural movement of the "Enlightenment," which had arisen in the late seventeenth century and which reached its zenith in the second half of the eighteenth.[93] Accordingly, it was in its original birthplace of England and France where its emancipatory power was most keenly felt. The Enlightenment there was associated with a new trend toward anthropological optimism. In his 1652 treatise *Leviathan,* Thomas Hobbes was still maintaining that the natural state of mankind before the formation of states was a "war of all against all." Yet by 1689, in the *Second Essay on Government* by John Locke (1632–1704), this primordial state had changed into one of general mutual beneficence. At the same time, through his theory of cognition, which combined physical sensory perception with syllogisms based on learning and experience, and his advocacy of tolerance, Locke articulated some of the key agendas of the Enlightenment. True, he continued to believe in the essentially rational basis of Christianity, but the key difference now was that faith had to justify itself to reason and not vice versa.[94]

The classical definition of the Enlightenment, though, was formulated only by Immanuel Kant toward the end of its golden age, in 1784: "Enlightenment is humanity's departure from its self-imposed immaturity. Immaturity is the inability to use one's own intellect without the guidance of others. This immaturity is self-imposed when its cause is not lack of intelligence but failure of courage to think without someone else's guidance. *Sapere audere!:* Dare to know! That is the slogan of the Enlightenment."[95] In other words, human reason was making a clean break with the authority of the church and antiquity, and European culture was freeing itself from more than a thousand years of constant dependence to assert its autonomous creativity. The linear thought pattern, which held that direct divine guidance would ensure the world's salvation, was secularized into a belief in perpetual progress and trust in the power of human reason, science, and technology to guarantee boundless improvements in people's quality of life.

However, the "trial of Christendom" was instigated and prosecuted not by the English but the French, specifically against the Catholic Church. Pierre Bayle (1647–1706) inaugurated this process with his *Historical and Critical Dictionary* of 1696–1697,[96] while the hugely gifted polemicist Voltaire (François-Marie Arouet; 1694–1778) took it to its apogee.[97] This quintessentially French anticlerical assault should not, however, obscure the fact that it was not only Protestant churches that managed to come to terms with the Enlightenment: the Holy Roman Empire, Spain and Italy, and even in rudimentary fashion the Vatican, played host to a Catholic Enlightenment, which could point to its own respectable achievements.

However, the ongoing "Querelle des anciens et des modernes" in France from 1687 on turned on the question of whether the authors of modern literature were in fact superior to the ancients. Antiquity continued to be regarded as "classical" but lost its exclusive claim on being some universal intellectual yardstick.[98]

The English discourse on the Enlightenment was picked up and disseminated both by Voltaire and by other representatives of the French High Enlightenment, notably Charles-Louis de Secondat de Montesquieu (1689–1755)[99] and Denis Diderot (1713–1784).[100] The latter was the driving force behind the monumental compendium of Enlightenment knowledge and thought, namely, the *Encyclopédie, ou dictionnaire raisonné des sciences, des arts, et des metiers,* which was published over a twenty-year period from 1751 to 1772.[101] In common with this, the influence of the French High Enlightenment was principally felt in the period after 1750, notably in the works of Gotthold Ephraim Lessing (1729–1781)[102] and Jean-Jacques Rousseau (1712–1778),[103] who embodied the nature-loving and emotional strain of Enlightenment thought. For the Enlightenment was by no means just about cold rationality but had just as much to do with a very conscious—sometimes downright contrived—form of naturalness. Even the esoteric tradition of European thought lived on in an enlightened guise, primarily in the phenomenon of freemasonry—which originated in England in around 1720 and presently became enormously popular throughout the continent—and other secret societies.[104]

Giovanni Battista Vico (1668–1744)[105] expressly opposed the linear causality and progressive thought that played a central role in enlightened rationality. With his understanding of the dialectical course of history, he helped the merely probable assert its right once more against the hegemony of the inevitable. His model of developmental cycles *(corsi e ricorsi)* made him a pioneer of comparative social psychology and history.

The liberation of humanity from the yoke of authority was meant to set in train a progression to a greater "humanity," toward a greater sense of empathy and sympathy with one's fellow man. Indeed, the humanizing of the justice system and improvements to welfare and education,[106] with both private and state initiatives encouraging the latter to adopt a much more practical character, were signal achievements of the Enlightenment, even though this also frequently entailed, as in the case of the universities, greater state control. New forms of communication developed and spread, largely tailored to the needs of the up-and-coming bourgeoisie but no less attractive to the clergy and the aristocracy and also ultimately extended, in the spirit of popular education, to peasants and the lower echelons of society.[107]

Fundamental to this program was elementary schooling for all, with the aim of introducing general literacy. In any event, literacy increased to such an extent that a range of periodicals sprang up—these included "moral weeklies," which aimed at disseminating Enlightenment ideas in easily digestible form; "intellectual journals," which combined this same agenda with news and advertisements, the first newspapers; and finally high-flown (scientific) periodicals. The fight against censorship in England had already been largely won by 1694, though elsewhere it took another hundred years and more to resolve. Unlike previously, there was now a new tendency toward individual and silent reading, with books and periodicals often being supplied by "reading clubs." French salons, English gentlemen's clubs, and other "societies" not only fostered a sense of conviviality but were also the setting for the serious debate of topical issues of the day. Many of these societies came to be very efficiently organized and assumed a campaigning role, styling themselves as "political," "mutual," or "economic" clubs and working systematically toward all manner of practical improvements, ranging from agricultural reform to intensive efforts to spread the Gospel in order to raise public morality: these were all manifestation of the Enlightenment. The first such developments took place, once more, in England. In France, meanwhile, some of these societies developed into full-blown provincial academies.[108]

Subsequently, these institutions gave rise to modern clubs and societies on the one hand and to political parties on the other. The Enlightenment, which reached its high point only after 1750, represented a cultural revolution, which, in spite of all the peaks and troughs of history, thereafter laid down an enduring basis for the scientific–technological culture that Europe was to spread throughout the world, including people's awareness of being masters of their own destiny, whether that was in fact true or not.

From Aristocratic Rule and Community Autonomy to the Early Modern State

Around 1350, the concrete political order of Europe was characterized not by state control,[109] and only to a limited extent by the rule of kings, but rather, initially at least, by thousands of aristocratic dominions on the one hand and by urban and rural corporations on the other. Some municipalities, primarily certain Italian and

Swiss cities, were subject to no superior authority, or at most only a nominal one, but instead themselves exercised authority over others, but in most municipalities, political life was played out between the differently weighted poles of dominion and cooperative. Either as a result of manorial privilege, or through their own articles of incorporation, or through an interplay of the two, these communities acquired their own authority, which held sway only over those belonging to the community in question and only within its own domain. For this authority consisted first and foremost in dispensing justice; political and administrative acts were also generally couched in these terms. However, at first, justice was likewise a matter for the municipality or its overlord. Below municipality level, the basic building block of this political world was not the legally responsible individual, as in modern times, but the household, more specifically the male head of the household (or in exceptional cases even the lady of the house). Frequently, though, the clergy and the nobility were not subject to the law of the municipality. This whole edifice was nothing other than the political face of Europe's decentralized social and economic structure.[110]

Of course, almost everywhere in Europe, there were superior political entities with a far wider scope of competence, both factually and in geographical terms—right up to kings, the Holy Roman emperor, and the pope. But in practice this responsibility was exercised only in exceptional cases and moreover was very patchily distributed. Just as, in one and the same village, different powers were vested in different authorities, or different households were answerable to different masters, so did there also exist various higher governing instances whose realms of competence were not coextensive but rather overlapped. Judicial, administrative, military, financial, and ecclesiastical authority all lay in different hands and were correspondingly unevenly distributed in geographical terms. Thus, for example, even in as allegedly centralized a country as France under the ancien régime, the various authorities responsible for administering a village could be located in several different towns.

The result of this was first that the internal borders of the countries and empires of Europe were as important, or even more important, than the external frontiers, indeed, that there was absolutely no qualitative difference between the two. In many countries, tolls were levied at both internal and external borders. Accordingly, most maps up to the seventeenth century showed no "national" external borders. Second, contrary to earlier ideas, even in the Middle Ages, there were clearly defined linear borders, sometimes marked with boundary stones and the like. Yet talk of premodern border zones rather than modern border lines is still justified because, as mentioned, the borders of various authorities were not coextensive. A locality could, for example, belong to one domain ecclesiastically but to entirely another politically.[111]

Political discourse of this period was similarly ambiguous. The concept of "patria" could, for example, denote one's own village or town, a small tract of land, or a larger region like the territory of a particular clan or a kingdom—and sometimes even the realm of heaven. People were also conscious of belonging to the single great domain of Christianity.[112]

Over the course of the development of the modern state, which represents the main political content of the four centuries under consideration here and which was already well advanced by 1750, the concept of "patria" came to be monopolized by the modern notion of "fatherland," which in most cases derived from medieval kingly rule and was ultimately embodied in the modern nation-state. In the process, the internal borders had to disappear or be stripped of their former significance, while at the external frontiers that were established, either all the various different borders that once existed were now subsumed, or at least the preeminence of the political border was now asserted. Internally, centralized government and its imposition on the countryside were institutionalized, in other words changed from personal rule to a system comprising initially courts and later other authorities. Even so, at first these authorities could not manage to consistently centralize the traditional decentralized regime. Rather, it was much more the case that they themselves came under its sway and were absorbed into the local regime and its special interests, whenever representatives of central government assumed regional authority on the ground and found themselves allied with local oligarchies by dint of marriage.

The Church and Law

The first centralizing political body in European history was the Catholic Church. Indeed, it is reasonable to see it as the first European state, given that it offered a template in many respects to all those that came after it. The decisive factor was that, as the vector of Latinate culture in the tradition of the Roman Empire and its legal system, it developed into a hierarchically organized ruling polity that was, first and foremost, a church wielding legal authority rather than one promulgating the virtues of spirituality and Christian love. As a result, ecclesiastical posts that were originally conceived as purely functional were transformed into a legalistic, regimented career structure. For instance, a deacon was downgraded from a person independently responsible for church welfare activities to a preparatory stage for a person aspiring to become a priest. For sure, Judaism and Islam are also legalistic religions, but the Catholic Church surpassed both of these to become organized and centralized to a degree that has no parallel in world history. The politicization and even militarization of the papacy in the Italian wars and the Crusades are part and parcel of this development.

Both in their theoretical pretensions and in their institutional practice, the church and the papacy had a distinct advantage over the up-and-coming secular states of Europe. The papal claim to absolute authority within the church *(Plenitudo Potestatis),*[113] along with its centralism, its bureaucratic apparatus, and its tax-raising powers, enabled the church to become, in the Middle Ages, a model for the modern state. Even secular powers found themselves obliged at first to recruit their leading personnel from the church. Hand in hand with this development came the widespread inculcation of the concept of the ecclesiastical office, which effectively made priests the first appointed officials to inhabit objective roles that transcended their position as individuals. Innovations in the secular domain were usually devised and tried out first in this legal institution of the church. At a time when most monarchies except England were still states based on personal alliances, the church, with its ecclesiastical provinces, bishoprics, archdeaconates, and parishes, was already well on the way to becoming a "territorial state." In this, the monastic "Disciplina" of well-organized monastery communities was able to serve as a model for all manner of political systems, from straightforward control over subjects to utopian blueprints for completely regulated commonwealths. Representative bodies for the secular "estates" took their cue both from the synods and councils convened by the church and from the practices of canon law.

Roman law, which was first codified in the sixth century, was rediscovered in its entirety in the eleventh century. Yet it had been preserved throughout in the uninterrupted tradition of the Catholic Church as a legalistic entity, whose "church fathers" were often lawyers as well, such as St. Ambrose or Pope Gregory I. As a result, the church also played a decisive role in the judicial revolution of the eleventh and twelfth centuries, in which archaic law and justice were supplanted by modern, scientifically founded regulations and procedures.[114] Up until then, secular law had been local and group based, a practice rooted in faith and custom. Verdicts were given by laymen on the basis of previous legal experience and were final, generally with no possibility of appeal to higher courts. Nothing was codified; all law and justice were dispensed orally.[115]

Now, however, the law was disengaged from religion and moral concerns; henceforth, justice was required to stand the test of rational scrutiny. Consequently, some theologians even took the view that secular legal directives were not binding on a person's conscience.[116] Ecclesiastical courts developed a civil process procedure that was taken over by secular courts. And in criminal law, the archaic accusation process ("Where there is no plaintiff, there can be no judge") was replaced by the inquisition process, a carefully regulated system of investigation and questioning on the part of the official authorities, leading to prosecution and the hearing of evidence. It was not uncommon for torture to be used to extract confessions. Church proceedings against heretics were merely a special instance of this investigation procedure. Using the church as a model, the law that was in force in many countries now began to be codified. Civil and criminal proceedings alike were mostly written down and conducted in a highly professional way, with the law and judicial system becoming the monopoly of academically trained jurists. Dispensing justice became the domain of full-time professionals. Under these circumstances, an appeal system became possible and relevant.

Both the fully professional dispensation of justice subject to the appeal procedure and, ultimately, the codification of the law were possible only on the part of the authorities. As such, the "judicial revolution" entailed a major boost to the growing power of the state. The systematic and nationwide expansion of royal justice enhanced the authority of the crown in England, France, and Castile, just as the expansion of papal justice throughout the Catholic Church put the pope's theoretical claim of absolute authority into practice.

Academically trained lawyers represented a new, up-and-coming group who, acting in the service of popes and kings, had a vested interest in increasing their power.[117] For unlike many of their aristocratic and ecclesiastical predecessors in the service of princes, they did not lead an independent existence; rather, they were completely reliant on their paymasters for their position and advancement. While on the one hand this does represent the beginnings of the modern monopoly of lawyers as the state class, on the other the continuing decentralized structure of the political world also facilitated the growth of bodies of royal lawyers with a strong claim on autonomous status in England, France, and Spain. Sometimes, these groups even dared gainsay the monarch on the question of what benefited the common good, and—in England and France, at any rate—even espoused the cause of revolutionary resistance to the crown in the seventeenth and eighteenth centuries, respectively.

Above all, though, a state of rivalry now existed between spiritual and secular authority. As early as AD 494, Pope Gelasius had countered the ecclesiastical authority of the emperors of the Eastern Roman Empire, which was consonant with the Christological Monophysitism of many of the Eastern Orthodox churches assuming a single divine nature of Christ, by promulgating the Roman doctrine of the "Two Powers," which was analogous to the theological tenet of the dual nature of Christ as both divine and human. In other words, it was by God's will that bishops and emperors ruled over the world each in their separate domains.[118] Certainly, Western emperors and kings had also, up to the eleventh century, wielded unchallenged ecclesiastical authority, but thereafter the church had largely successfully pressed its claim for freedom from secular power and had even begun to campaign in favor of a quasi-theocratic supremacy.

The dual nature of Christ, the divine and the human, was meant to correspond to the two sides of humanity, the spiritual and the worldly. In typical Roman fashion, a dual distinction was derived from this, of "Spiritualia" and "Temporalia" (spiritual and temporal matters) in property law, and of clergy and laymen in legal affairs relating to the person. Each fell, quite separately, under ecclesiastical or secular jurisdiction, respectively, albeit with overlaps that were predisposed to cause conflict. These areas of contention concerned not just the clergy's privileged status, which was established hereby and which has already been touched upon, but also the question of marriage law, which the church gained jurisdiction over due to the fact that the institution of marriage was one of the sacraments. Besides, the church laid claim not only to preeminence by virtue of having jurisdiction over more important matters, but also—by pointing to Christ's kingly status—to a kind of suzerainty of the pope (as Christ's vicar here on Earth) over the world as well. Extreme proponents of this position taught that all power emanated from the papacy. According to this doctrine, it was in the pope's gift to install or depose princes and also to exercise sovereignty over heathens who had still not even heard of Christianity. These ideas reached their high-water mark in the thirteenth and fourteenth centuries but in the long run prevailed only really within the church, primarily in the form of an expansion of papal justice as well as massive intervention on the part of the pope in the distribution of livings and the all-embracing imposition of taxes.

In other words, despite everything, Latin Christendom retained its fundamentally dualistic structure, fraught as it was with tension, and by dint of which it differed from all political systems in the world. Even though neither the church nor the state were natural champions of human freedom—indeed, the very concept of "freedom" originally had the negative connotation of "dissoluteness"—nevertheless the simple fact that every European was required in one way or another to serve two masters left potential scope for freedom both in theory and in practice, because these masters were seldom in accord with one another. Conversely, the church and papacy were also institutional guarantors of the overarching cultural cohesion of Europe, because papal ecclesiastical authority was just as much a pan-European phenomenon as papal politics; the papal *Concilia* of the high Middle Ages were impressive forums of European commonality.

Political Theory and State Formation

By contrast, while the Holy Roman emperor was intermittently able to lay claim to hegemony over Europe—the final instance being the reign of Charles V (1519–1556)—in reality the office was nothing more than an honorific title of the German king. The decision to pursue individual variants of state formation throughout Europe rather than to try to impose a unified system was taken in the high Middle Ages at the latest. By that stage, leadership had long since passed to Western European kings on the one hand and to Italian city-state tyrants and the rulers of the larger German principalities on the other. Admittedly, what retrospectively, when viewed in the round, nevertheless still turned out to be a purposeful overall development was neither in fact planned as such nor, when viewed in terms of the individual events that resulted, even had the appearance of a process with any consistent direction. To the contrary, there was no end of ups and downs or even of developments totally at variance with the main thrust, as obviously no one set out with the stated aim of creating the modern state. Equally obviously, any number of kings and princes bent all their efforts toward trying to maximize their own power both within their own realms and abroad. When favorable conditions prevailed and suitable contingent historical events transpired, such polities were able to develop into successful state models, either leaving their many rivals behind or subjugating them.

Once the medieval reading and interpretation of Aristotle had demonstrated that community could be founded on a secular basis, the formation of states from the fifteenth century on became a subject of more intensive reflection and theoretical legitimization.[119] Niccolò Macchiavelli laid bare the ground rules of such political machinations. Jean Bodin (1530–1596) provided a theoretical justification for monarchy through his new concept of sovereignty as unlimited absolute power, which stood above the law and which thus manifests itself primarily through legislation. Thomas Hobbes, meanwhile, saw the state as emerging from a compact designed to end the "war of all against all" and accordingly granted its sovereign almost unlimited powers; in doing so, he was already implicitly moving away from the idea of a ruler in the flesh toward an abstract concept of the state. In contrast, John Locke saw law and property safeguarded primarily through the separation of powers according to the English model, an idea that Montesquieu adapted and popularized on the Continent. In this model, princes moved away from being the master and the embodiment of a concrete community, increasingly becoming instead the holder of the highest office within an abstract institution, namely, the state, as epitomized in the "enlightened absolutism" of the eighteenth century.

Favorable conditions for such a development were a monarchy that was already hallowed or outstanding in some other regard and the recognized role of the monarch as the guarantor of the law—a role that could be exploited to gain power through the expansion of justice. But undoubtedly the most important advantage resulting from this development was the dynastic continuity of highly able rulers, as, for instance, in Brandenburg–Prussia in the period 1640–1786. This is shown by considering the opposite situation: fundamental weakness in the ruling

Non Est potestas Super Terram quae Comparetur ei ("There is no power on Earth to be compared to him")—this description in the Book of Job of the sea monster Leviathan was used by the English philosopher Thomas Hobbes as the motto of his eponymous 1651 treatise on government. Hobbes applied the term to the state, which was created by its citizens through a social compact. Accordingly, the book's frontispiece depicts the crowned figure of the state as being composed of over three hundred individual people. As the sovereign bearer of both temporal and spiritual power, Leviathan carries both a sword and a bishop's crozier, while in both the landscape below and the vignettes left and right, symbols and activities of the two forms of authority are portrayed. His innermost secrets still remain hidden behind the curtain in the center but, it is implied, will be revealed in the book itself. (IAM/World History Archive)

dynasty, as in France after 1559, or a dynastic crisis like that in Austria in 1740 unfailingly entailed an internal or external threat to state building. For the main driving force behind this was an ambitious ruling dynasty working in conjunction with ruling elites such as lawyers.

In the long term, a decisive factor was armed conflict with foreign rivals, as this could be successfully endured only through mobilizing one's own country. Yet the "military" revolution of the early modern period was less innovative than has often been claimed,[120] rather merely representing a developmental stimulus in the history of the traditional Western culture of violence. What was genuinely new were the changes that took place in infantry tactics and fortress construction, both prompted by the swift advances in firearms technology. However, such advances, together with the mercenaries increasingly employed to fight wars, cost far more in royal revenues than a ruler had at his disposal and could live on in normal times. And because this shortfall could be made up only by exacting extra funds from subjects—in some instances even in the form of subsidies from the taxation of subjects of an allied nation—this had the effect of boosting the role of politics in state affairs, either by requiring consensus via the participation of subjects' representatives in councils of all the estates or through coercion on the part of a so-called absolutist monarch, who could push through the necessary granting of funds without any agreement by an estates' convention (either sidelining these bodies or countermanding their decisions) merely by citing his responsibility for acting as he saw fit for the common good. In the latter case, this coercion procedure involved extra costs, but in either case the new tax-raising and tax-collecting apparatus saw costs rise inexorably. What was in operation here was a regenerative, self-perpetuating process, the "coercion–extraction cycle,"[121] which was by no means confined to Brandenburg–Prussia but also, for instance, played a decisive role in the formation of states in the so-called Hundred Years' War between England and France; in the case of England, this took the form of an expansion in the representation of the estates through Parliament, while in France it manifested itself in the crown assuming direct tax-raising powers that bypassed the estates but in which they willingly acquiesced.

Targeted structural changes within states began to take place only under the aegis of the Enlightenment in the eighteenth century. Up until then, monarchs had simply been happy for subjects to show obedience, in other words to remain

calm, and pay their taxes. That was already asking a great deal, as Europeans had
shown a tendency toward rebelliousness, particularly when they were required to
do things that they regarded as illegitimate. Granted, medieval rulers had been
subject to no checks and balances in fulfilling their duties. But for one thing, these
duties—maintaining peace and justice—were not very extensive. Second, there
were no instruments at first to administer such duties intensively in the sense of
modern statehood. Third, the medieval ruler was constantly subject to the strictures of both divine and natural law, as well as to the basic laws of the land, even
in cases such as France, where the monarch stood above the law in all other respects. But even when, in marked contrast to this, he was subject to the positive
law of the land, as in England, this did not make a great deal of difference. For
such a body of law was not very extensive, and who was prepared to compel the
monarch to observe it? This was also true of laws of a higher order, but there it
was a question of fundamental principles of justice and equity, whose violation
would constitute grounds for violent resistance. Fourth, in European eyes, authority
was always a reciprocal relationship, in which the ruler and the subject alike had
rights and responsibilities. Any prince who neglected his legal obligations and duties stood to lose the loyalty of his subjects. Fifth, the most important right of the
subject was the inviolability of his property. Such a right to unrestricted ownership
of private property is a peculiarity of the European legal culture. In consequence,
intrusion into the property of subjects, particularly through taxation, was possible only with their agreement, an arrangement that has theoretically endured
to the present day, even if silent acceptance on the individual's part is taken to be
implicit agreement. The numerous uprisings by both the aristocracy and the
common people against expanding state intervention, especially with regard to
the burden of taxation, that characterize European history from the fourteenth
to the eighteenth century, readily found a cause in this grievance.[122]

To shield himself against the accusation of unlawful exercise of power, the medieval prince ruled with the aid of a council comprising the good and the great of
the land, together with legal experts, whose participation was designed to lend
his actions the imprimatur of consensus. To this end, when important matters
were under discussion, the council was expanded to include representatives of other
bodies throughout the country. Another reason why consensus was vital was because, until relatively late in the modern period, there was no real apparatus of

coercion, meaning that decisions by the ruler relied on the willing acquiescence of subjects to implement them. Alongside the privy council, the royal court (curia) embraced certain household offices such as treasurer, chancellor, and lord stewart. A steady process of institutional growth and differentiation, "a going out of court," made the court dissolve into autonomous bodies and saw the rise of the familiar central state authorities; thus, the chancellory was in charge of the old system of rule by charter, while subsequently secretariats ran the more recent system of rule through official correspondence. This same process saw the growth of the treasury as the central authority responsible for economic and financial affairs, the highest military offices, the supreme courts—constituted along collegiate lines—and the occasional conventions of the estates. Meanwhile, the rump of the royal councils became supreme governmental caucuses ruling alongside the monarch; it became commonplace in many places during the seventeenth and eighteenth centuries for these to be divided into departments with different areas of jurisdiction. However, the predecessors of modern cabinet ministers generally had only a few assistants at their disposal and no extensive bureaucratic apparatus.

Estates' conventions represented the country but not in the sense of a modern parliament. They consisted of those subjects, or representatives of those corporations—primarily cities and church institutions—that were endowed with the right in common law to at least be granted an audience by the ruler in certain affairs pertaining to the country's governance. In some instances, though, they even had the right to codetermination. They differed from modern democratic representatives in representing their own individual interests, or at most their interests as a group, unlike modern parliamentarians, who (in theory at least) represent the common interest of the people. Insofar as they were representatives of corporations, they were empowered only to follow instructions and were obliged, should unforeseen developments occur, to seek guidance from their clients. Nevertheless, either on a common-law basis, as in England, or in revolutionary ferment, as in France, modern parliaments were able to develop from these institutions. Within their legislative period, parliaments are convened for a set length of time, determined in advance. By contrast, for a long time estates' conventions were one-off events, which had no independent right to assemble but rather had to be convened by the monarch.[123]

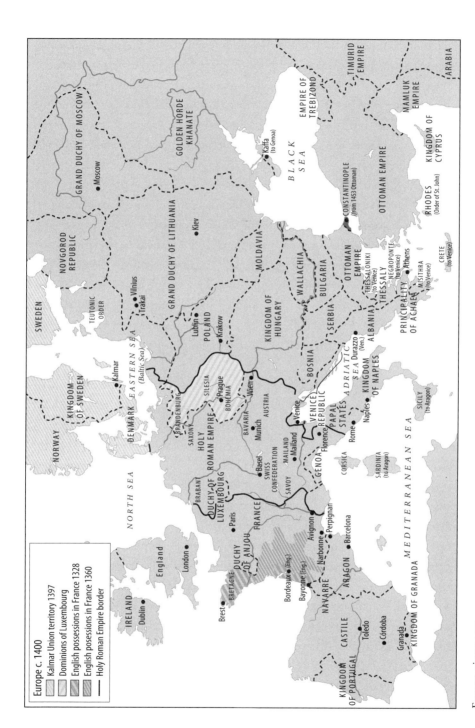

Europe c. 1400

- Kalmar Union territory 1397
- Dominions of Luxembourg
- English possessions in France 1328
- English possessions in France 1360
- Holy Roman Empire border

NORWAY

SWEDEN

NOVGOROD
REPUBLIC

GRAND DUCHY OF MOSCOW

Moscow

GOLDEN HORDE
KHANATE

TEUTONIC
ORDER

Kalmar

KINGDOM
OF SWEDEN

DENMARK

EASTERN SEA
(Baltic Sea)

GRAND DUCHY OF LITHUANIA

Vilnius
Trakai

Kiev

Kaffa
(to Genoa)

B L A C K
S E A

EMPIRE OF
TREBIZOND

TIMURID
EMPIRE

ARABIA

NORTH SEA

IRELAND

Dublin

England

London

BRANDENBURG

SAXONY

SILESIA

Lublin

Krakow

POLAND

BOHEMIA
Prague

Wien

AUSTRIA

MOLDAVIA

KINGDOM OF HUNGARY

WALLACHIA

BULGARIA

SERBIA

BOSNIA

CONSTANTINOPLE
(from 1453 Ottoman)

OTTOMAN EMPIRE

MAMLUK
EMPIRE

KINGDOM OF
CYPRUS

RHODES
(Order of St. John)

OTTOMAN
EMPIRE

THESSALONIKI
(to Venice)

THESSALY

NEGROPONTE
(to Venice)

PRINCIPALITY
OF ACHAEA

Athens
(to Venice)

MISTHRA

CRETE
(to Venice)

ALBANIA

Durazzo
(Ven.)

ADRIATIC
S E A

KINGDOM
OF NAPLES

Naples

SICILY
(to Aragon)

SARDINIA
(to Aragon)

CORSICA

PAPAL
STATES

Rome

Florence

Venice

VENICE
REPUBLIC

Mailand

GENOA

SWISS
CONFEDERATION

SAVOY

Basel

Munich

BAVARIA

HOLY
ROMAN EMPIRE

DUCHY OF
LUXEMBOURG

BRABANT

FRANCE

DUCHY OF ANJOU

Paris

BRETAGNE

Brest

Bordeaux (Eng.)

Bayonne (Eng.)

Avignon

Perpignan

Narbonne

Barcelona

NAVARRE

ARAGON

CASTILE

Toledo

Córdoba

Granada

KINGDOM OF GRANADA

KINGDOM
OF PORTUGAL

MEDITERRANEAN SEA

Europe, circa 1400

Estates' conventions, including English parliaments, were often seen as irksome bodies, not least because, while their remit also included the creation of political consensus and the formulation of legislation, their most frequent concern was to approve the imposition of taxes. For the growing authority of the state could not, as we have already seen, finance its further expansion through its own means but required the consensus of its subjects to draw on their funds. As a result, a clear connection arose between the estates' conventions and wars. The heyday of the estates was between the fourteenth and sixteenth centuries. From the seventeenth century on, though, many monarchs were sufficiently powerful to raise taxes without the estates' involvement and to largely dispense with their services—albeit never entirely, not even in France or Prussia. Only Denmark witnessed the long-term introduction through legal statute of an estateless "absolute monarchy" in 1660–1665,[124] while conversely, in England, corporate joint rule by Parliament was formally instituted in 1689.[125]

England, France, Burgundy, and the Holy Roman Empire

In the relatively small country of England, the Norman Conquest and the introduction of a single royal administration of justice (the "common law") had helped further strengthen the monarchy, relatively centralized since Anglo-Saxon times. However, the financing of the long-running conflict (Hundred Years' War) with France had also seen Parliament endowed with increasing responsibilities, which only expanded further as a result of the crises that ensued in the late fourteenth century. In 1381, the pressure of the taxation burden sparked a major peasants' revolt, while in 1399 conflict with the crown led to King Richard II being deposed. The fifteenth century saw bloody wars of succession (the Wars of the Roses) between the Houses of Lancaster and York (both branches of the ruling dynasty), as well as internecine feuding within the latter. These were brought to an end only by the victory of the Tudor ruler Henry VII (1485–1509), as champion of the Lancastrian cause, over the last representative of the House of York and marriage to his niece. Because the high aristocracy mainly comprised members of the ruling dynasty, large sections of it were caught up in this conflict and destroyed by it. This brought such an increase in the holdings of the crown that the energetic Henry VII scarcely had need of Parliament any longer, especially after the end of the war with France in 1453.[126]

In France, despite modest beginnings, thanks to the consistently shrewd policies of the ruling dynasty a strong monarchy had also developed, which even managed to make the papacy dependent on it in the fourteenth century. From 1309 to 1378, the popes chose to reside in Avignon. They were all of southern French origin and had an entirely French court and college of cardinals.[127] Yet for a long time, the English king had held parts of southwestern France as a fiefdom. When the French king Louis X died without an heir in 1316, the throne was occupied by his two uncles, until the royal line of Capet finally died out in 1328 and was succeeded by the House of Valois; both of these developments were sanctioned by the legalistic construct of Salic law, a form of agnatic succession that excluded not only women but also male offspring of the female line from ascending the throne. A primary aim of this was to debar Edward III of England, a grandson of King Philip IV of France, from any claim on the French throne; his ensuing attack on France in 1337 sparked the Hundred Years' War (1337–1453), which was accompanied by a succession of regional popular uprisings. From 1340 to 1802, English monarchs also retained the title of "king of France." After initial English successes, the French gradually rallied, and an interim lull ensued in 1377, prompted among other things by the internal difficulties of both ruling dynasties. In France, the dukes of Orléans and Burgundy vied for controlling influence over the mentally ill king. England exploited this dynastic struggle by invading again in 1415 and overrunning large parts of France. A turnaround in fortunes came with the intervention of the visionary Joan of Arc, who in 1429 led an army that relieved the siege of Orléans and took the dauphin to be crowned at Reims. However, she was captured by the English in 1431 and burned at the stake as a witch. As in the question of the "Salic Succession," these dramatic events signaled a growing sense of French national consciousness. By 1453, the only remaining English possession on French soil was the port of Calais (until 1559).[128]

In 1363, the French king (John II) granted his youngest son Philip the Bold the duchy of Burgundy in appanage. Through a mixture of marriage, inheritance, and other means, Philip and his three successors in this post wrested complete control over not only the duchy and its "upper territories" but also of the "Low Countries"—in other words, most of the modern Benelux states. Because these regions, especially Flanders and Brabant, were, alongside northern Italy, the most highly developed and richest part of Europe at the time, Burgundy became a powerful political entity, which played a decisive role in the conflict between England and France, as well as setting the tone in matters of courtly culture and administration. Even so, the rulers of Burgundy failed in their attempt to gain a royal crown or to establish a land bridge through Lorraine to their northern holdings. When the last duke of Burgundy was killed in battle against the Swiss Confederacy in 1477, their duchy reverted to French ownership.[129] The French king Louis XI (r. 1461–1483) was also able to secure Provence and further stabilize his monarchy. With the accession of Louis XII (r. 1498–1515), the House of Orléans, former rival to the Burgundians, became France's ruling dynasty.

The German king Maximilian, as the husband of the heir Maria of Burgundy, was able to secure the remainder of the Burgundian lands for their son Philip. Unlike many other countries, the "Holy Roman Empire," which since 1515 had the words "of the German Nation" added to its official title, had remained an elective monarchy, even though in general members of a particular dynasty tended to be elected, as was customary then. The princes who were enfeoffed to the crown, among them many bishops and abbots, enjoyed a considerable degree of political independence. Between 1338 and 1358, seven of these principalities—Mainz, Trier, Cologne, the Rhineland Palatinate, Saxony, Brandenburg, and Bohemia—had secured for themselves a monopoly as electors of the king and future emperor. Royal exercise of power was henceforth possible only as a hegemony arising from a personal power base—that is, the king's own authority as a princely ruler. Emperor Charles IV (r. 1346–1378) from the House of Luxembourg, for example, was very successful in wielding power from his base in Bohemia. At first, even the final regaining of the emperorship by the Habsburgs in 1438 did little to overcome the periods of weak rule that had set in after Charles IV's death. The tenacious reign of Frederick III (1440–1493) laid the groundwork for the acquisition of the Burgundian legacy by Maximilian I (r. 1493–1519). But the Italian policy of the latter was as unsuccessful as his stewardship of the empire. In the meantime, the Imperial Diet had evolved out of periodic meetings of the estates of the empire; during the sixteenth and seventeenth centuries, the quasi-institutional structures of this body were to take definite shape. However, the Imperial Reform of 1495, which theoretically could have ushered in a complete restructuring of the moribund empire and formed a modern state from it, failed because neither the emperor nor the larger estates had any interest in creating such a uniform entity. On the contrary, the dual marriages concluded in 1496 between the heirs to the Spanish and the Burgundian thrones and their respective sisters, as well as those prepared from 1491 on by Maximilian between the Habsburg and the Bohemian–Hungarian heirs and their respective sisters, which finally took place in 1521–1522, were to result in the world empire of Charles V and the Austro-Hungarian Habsburg monarchy.[130]

The Swiss Confederacy, formed in 1291 as a counter to Habsburg power, refused to be bound by the Imperial Reform of 1495. Up to the nineteenth century, the Swiss Confederacy embodied a premodern state of decentralized autonomy of small rural republics and city-states. Following a final round of military conflict in 1499, it gradually grew apart and developed separately from the Holy Roman Empire up to 1648. The military successes of the Swiss assured them a high reputation on the market for mercenary soldiers and, until the defeat at Marignano against the French in 1515, also a brief role as a major power in northern Italy.[131]

Italy, Iberia, Scandinavia, and East Central Europe

In Italy, the authority of the Holy Roman Empire covered only the area north of the Papal States, and even there it was little more than nominal. The most prominent of the many polities within this region were the Ghibelline signorias of the Visconti of Milan, which around 1400 almost constituted a northern Italian kingdom, and the Kingdom of Naples under the House of Anjou. Sicily had fallen to the House of Aragon in 1282. The republics of Florence and Venice, ruled by oligarchs, opposed the dominance of Milan. Florence, which ruled over most of Tuscany, acquiring Siena too in 1555, had been under the informal control of the Medici family since 1434. After two brief interludes of republican rule, the Medici formally gained power over the territory as a duchy in 1531 (and a grand duchy from 1569), a position it maintained until the dynasty finally died out in 1737. Venice remained a republic, even after it acquired extensive territories on the mainland in the first half of the fifteenth century, and set itself up in opposition chiefly to Milan, which the Sforza family inherited from the Visconti in 1450.[132] Meanwhile, the power of the Papal States had been bolstered by the decision of the Avignon popes to return to Rome in 1377, but the lasting effects of the schism meant that it was the mid-fifteenth century before the pope, as sovereign prince of the territory, could begin to energetically assert his authority against the Signorias and communes. Naples was weakened by conflicts within the House of Anjou, until it came under the control of the king of Aragon and Sicily in 1443. The Peace of Lodi in 1454 created a system of relative stability between the five principal powers on the Italian peninsula—Milan, Florence, Venice, the Papal States, and Naples—with other polities such as the republic of Genoa and the duchies of Savoy and Ferrara-Modena playing a subsidiary role.[133]

This equilibrium was disturbed by French attacks on the region from 1494 onward; France's kings laid claim to inheritance rights over both Milan and Naples. This instigated a series of wars that also involved the Holy Roman emperor, Spain, and the Swiss Confederacy, which came to only a provisional end in 1516, with Naples and Sicily still in Spanish hands but with Milan now under French rule. This was the first occasion on which these local clashes turned into Europe-wide conflicts. This period also witnessed the beginnings of a European power structure; in retrospect, then, the five leading Italian players at this time could be regarded as prefiguring the pentarchy of powers that dominated Europe in the eighteenth to nineteenth centuries.

On the Iberian Peninsula, the *Reconquista* was by now largely concluded. Only Muslim-controlled Granada remained as a fiefdom of Castile until it was also captured, in the course of the campaign to unify Spain, in 1492. Aragon, Castile, and Portugal had been vying for supremacy in the peninsula since the eleventh century. Aragon consisted of four largely autonomous regions: Aragon itself, Catalonia, Valencia, and the Balearic Islands, together with the Italian possessions of Sicily, Sardinia, and (from 1443) Naples. Aragon exercised an economic and political hegemony over the whole of the western Mediterranean. Its ambitious monarchy, however, was straitjacketed by the extensive rights enjoyed by the kingdom's estates. In Castile, the former partial kingdoms that made up the territory were more fully integrated, and the power of the crown was expanded with the support, in turn, of the high aristocracy and the cities, though it found itself repeatedly weakened by recurrent disputes over the succession. The situation was similar in Portugal, where a new dynasty ascended the throne in 1385. The alternative was a Castilian succession, so that even at that early stage, it was uncertain whether a union between Castile and Portugal or one between Castile and Aragon would take place. Renewed feuding over the Castilian throne ended with the defeat of Portugal and the joint reign of Isabella of Castile (1474–1504) and Ferdinand of Aragon (1479–1516), who had married secretly in 1469. However, this personal union was finally transformed into a truly nationwide union dominated by Castile by the Bourbon monarchy only in the eighteenth century.[134]

Questions of dynastic unions also dominated the agendas of late medieval Scandinavia and eastern Central Europe. A personal union of the three northern kingdoms of Denmark (which also at that time ruled over southern Sweden), Norway, and Sweden came about toward the end of the fourteenth century; this process, set in train by the energetic Norwegian–Danish female regent Margaret I in 1389, was confirmed by the nobility of the three realms at Kalmar in 1397. The territory of the Kalmar Union stretched from Swedish Finland in the east to the Norwegian territories of Iceland and Greenland in the west. The first split in this union came in 1448, and it was shattered finally by the accession of the Swedish king Gustav I Vasa in 1523. Even so, Denmark and Norway remained linked until 1814, as did Sweden and Finland until 1809.[135]

In Poland, the independence of the partial principalities was annulled by the kings of the fourteenth century. Following the death of the last member of the Piast dynasty and a brief interlude when Poland was ruled by the king of Hungary, the heathen grand duke Jagiello of neighboring Lithuania had himself baptized and in 1386 married the youngest daughter of the Hungarian monarch, Hedwig, who was the heiress to the Polish throne. This personal union was transformed into a unified kingdom only in 1569. Although in principle an elective kingdom, Poland–Lithuania was under the sole rule, right up to its demise in 1572, of the Jagiellon dynasty.[136] When Lithuania converted to Christianity, this divested the Teutonic Order, which had been at the height of its power in the fourteenth century, of the whole basis for its existence and confronted it with an adversary that it was unable to match. After losing large tracts of territory up to 1466, it was obliged to recognize Polish suzerainty and, after the transformation of East Prussia into a secular duchy by the Protestant convert and grand master of the order, Albrecht von Hohenzollern, became a Polish fiefdom in 1525.[137]

After the demise of the Hungarian Arpad dynasty, a branch of the House of Anjou ascended the throne of Hungary in 1308 and consolidated the crown's power. Sigmund of Luxemburg, crowned king of Germany in 1411 (and Holy Roman emperor in 1433), had married the eldest daughter of the last of the Anjou line and so occupied the Hungarian throne from 1387 to 1437. The same branch of the Habsburgs who succeeded in the Holy Roman Empire inherited his title, but after they died out, Matthias Corvinus (r. 1458–1490), the son of the indigenous regent of Hungary, was elected king. Corvinus's rule was so overbearing that, after he died without leaving an heir, the country's elite was only too glad to elect a weak Bohemian king from the House of Jagiello, who was the brother of three kings of Poland, to the Hungarian throne. Prior to this, from 1440 to 1444, their uncle Ladislaus III had ruled simultaneously as king of Poland and Hungary. Following the defeat of his son by the Ottomans in 1526, as a result of the marriages concluded in 1521–1522, the Habsburgs acceded to power in part of Hungary and in Bohemia, while the Turkish sultan restricted the legacy of the indigenous rival candidate to Transylvania and occupied central Hungary himself.[138]

The Papacy and National Churches

The action of frustrated cardinals in shunning the pope who had just been crowned in 1378 and electing their own candidate, who took up residence in Avignon, had far-reaching ramifications for ecclesiastical politics.[139] Because the Great Schism could not be resolved in any other way, a desperate measure was attempted by deposing both popes and having the Council of Pisa choose a new one. This new pope (Alexander V) was recognized in most countries, but his successor (the antipope John XXIII), allegedly a notorious corsair, met with resistance, and two rival "popes" from Rome and Avignon, respectively, each with a limited following, continued to lay claim to the papacy. Accordingly, the Council of Constance was convened at the initiative of the German king Sigmund from 1414 to 1418; this synod deposed two popes, persuaded another claimant to stand down, and chose another who gained universal recognition and was able to take his rightful place in Rome. The Great Schism provided an ideal new impetus to the criticism that had long been leveled at papal authority, particularly at its financial aspects. If the papacy refused to carry out the necessary reforms, then the council would be obliged to take on this task. In this regard, then, it declared its supremacy over the pope and passed a resolution to hold regular future meetings of general synods with the long-term aim of instituting church reform.[140]

Unsurprisingly, the papacy rejected these moves out of hand, and in 1431 the pope attempted to dismiss the Council of Basel as soon as it met. But in doing so, he succeeded only in increasing general support for the council and found himself forced to compete with the kudos that it gained by approving comprehensive reform measures by himself conducting successful negotiations with the Orthodox Church over reunification in 1439. But in the long run, the pope gained the upper hand; the council gradually dissolved up to 1449, with the attempt to create a generally binding church constitution having failed. Even so, popes continued to fear the power of the church councils.[141]

The real beneficiaries of this situation were Europe's secular princes, who were able to play the council and the pope against each other. In 1438 the king of France adopted the council's resolutions against papal sinecures and tax payments to Rome, while at the same time recognizing the authority of the pope. The German princes then took up the resolutions but tried to remain neutral, until the Holy Roman emperor finally imposed a Rome-friendly compromise on them in 1448. Both the organization of reforming councils by individual nation and the agreements on church ordinances reached with particular nations—often referred to as "concordats"—indicate that the universal sovereignty of the papacy was being supplanted by the age of national and territorial churches. The newly strengthened secular rulers also attempted to gain control of the churches within their domains and to prevent "foreign" authorities from "interfering," even if these simply took the form of the neighboring prince-bishop whose see encompassed the territory in question. The same stricture applied to the pope himself. These developments were not necessarily to the detriment of religious life within any particular territory, as many princes began to tackle the reforms that the pope and his bishops had failed to implement. Thus, it was the "Catholic kings" Ferdinand and Isabella who, together with various bishops, set in train a successful revitalization of the Spanish church at the end of the fifteenth century.[142]

The Protestant "Reformation" was nothing more than a continuation of these church reform policies but was made immeasurably more intense by the radical theological agenda underpinning it. Because Luther's theology, as we have seen, rendered the whole ecclesiastical apparatus of salvation redundant and declared the pope to be the Antichrist, this instantly divested the whole clergy and the established church authorities, not least the religious orders and the wealthy landholdings of the church, of their entire raison d'être. Now secular rulers found themselves even more justified than before in taking control of the churches within their territory and appropriating church property—in some cases to finance their new Protestant churches and the welfare and education systems that had formerly been the responsibility of the church, but in many others with no other motive than to swell the state's coffers. The Reformation gained a foothold in Sweden because the crown wanted to boost its finances through seizure of land and other property held by the bishops; in England, meanwhile, Protestant theology really did not come into it at first, with the main concern being to effect a split from Rome and to dispossess the church. Only those Protestant churches that arose in defiance of the ruling prince, as happened in many of the areas of continental Western Europe touched by the Reformation, developed autonomous structures. Wherever rulers were won round to the Protestant cause, however, they assumed the mantle of the supreme religious authority in the land.

Catholic princes likewise continued to wield the religious authority they had exercised before the Reformation, a process that was now made even easier for them by the fact that the old established church was dependent on their support in its struggle against its new rivals. Thus it was that confessionalization was carried out in all three Christian denominations by church and secular authorities working in conjunction with one another but mainly with the latter predominating—with the sole exception, as already noted, of Western European Calvinists. Although Catholic princes did not, unlike their Protestant counterparts, generally dictate which faith their subjects were to follow, they otherwise controlled the church within their territories through exactly the same means and institutions as the Protestants. This arrangement meant continuing security for the churches, but for the princes it represented a threefold political advantage: first, a strengthening of the national or territorial identity of, say, a Catholic Spain or Bavaria or of a Protestant England or Saxony; second, disposition of church resources—in spite of their claim for immunity, the Catholic clergy were taxed and sometimes even dispossessed with the agreement of the pope, as, for example, when funds were required to fund the Huguenot Wars; and third, a new sense of unity and social discipline inculcated in the minds of their subjects.

·[831]·

The process of confessionalization, which began in 1530 and was conducted by churches and many developing states right up to the eighteenth and nineteenth centuries in some cases, albeit with varying degrees of intensity, could be viewed as a constituent part or the first wave of a Europe-wide tendency toward social disciplining. This phenomenon was originally ascribed to the influence of "absolute monarchy,"[143] whereas nowadays we consider schools, the army, and factories in the nineteenth and twentieth centuries as the key institutions that educated the citizens of Europe in disciplined behavior. Yet even the ancien régime, like cities in the Middle Ages, attempted to regulate daily life not solely by means of church discipline but also through a whole range of so-called police ordinances.[144]

Wars and Crises

Whereas the monasteries had once been the epitome of discipline, now it was the standing armies that the monarchs of Europe steadily equipped themselves with, as their finances grew, from the mid-seventeenth century on. There, a hodgepodge of unruly mercenaries was transformed into a body of uniformed soldiers, perfectly drilled through parade-ground exercises; it was deemed as vital that they should have more to fear from their own officers than from the enemy. The growing state monopoly on power weaned people away from their former tendency, born of a decentralized political order, toward self-help and occasional use of force, for while "private" violence declined in this period, "state" violence increased correspondingly: the number of wars reached a peak in the seventeenth century. At this stage, these were not the out-and-out "clashes between nations" that were to characterize the eighteenth and nineteenth centuries but to a large extent were still "nation-building wars,"[145] fought to determine the political organization of European countries.

The most significant long-running conflict in Western Europe took place from 1521 to 1755, between the German and Spanish Habsburgs on the one side and the French House of Valois on the others; from 1589 the Valois were supplanted by the Bourbons. Unexpected royal deaths in Spain and Portugal meant that Charles, the Duke of Burgundy and grandson of the emperor Maximilian, acceded to the Spanish throne in 1516. In 1519, he was chosen by the imperial electors as Emperor Charles V of the Holy Roman Empire, whereupon he invested his brother Ferdinand with control over the German lands belonging to the Habsburgs. As early as 1521, a series of wars broke out with France over the French share in the Burgundian inheritance on the one hand and over French claims on Milan on the other. While the French kings were in no way conscious champions of a modern nation-state, they nevertheless were still waging a "nation-building war" inasmuch as they had thwarted Charles V's realization of a Europe-wide empire. This peripatetic ruler of several countries was the last monarch to try to bring about a universal empire in the sense of complete hegemony over the European continent.[146]

However, by gaining control over Milan and Naples, Charles did at least manage to secure Spanish rule in Italy right up to the eighteenth century. At that stage, Naples and Sicily fell to a subsidiary branch of the Bourbon dynasty, Lombardy became an Austrian possession, and Savoy, with the acquisition of Sardinia, rose to become a kingdom in its own right. The popes attempted to assert their independence between France and Spain, until the powerful state churches of these two countries appropriated their income and consigned them to insignificance.[147]

Yet within the empire, Charles failed in his attempts to suppress the Reformation, which, to the contrary, ensured the imperial estates a greater degree of independence. In 1556, he abdicated as emperor in favor of his brother Ferdinand, who the previous year had negotiated the Peace of Augsburg with the princes of the empire, which brought about a lull, albeit only temporary, in the clash between the confessions.[148] In 1618, the attempt to replace the Catholic monarchical system of Bohemia with a Protestant one based on government by the estates sparked a war that spread ever wider and that finally, as a result of the intervention of the Swedish king Gustavus Adolphus II in 1630 and of France in 1635, ended in the defeat of imperial forces. The Peace of Westphalia in 1648 stabilized relations between the confessions and transferred all important decisions to the Imperial Diet, which since 1663 had become a standing congress of deputies. The independence of the estates was strengthened, which in the case of the more powerful amounted to a state of quasi-sovereignty, while the weaker elements and the princes of the church, as the clientele of the emperor, along with his residual powers as the supreme legal authority and as liege lord, formed the rump of the remaining imperial power base within the empire. Because the Peace of Westphalia was under-written by the former combatant nations France and Sweden, commentators have been keen to see in it the beginnings of a balanced international system of power predisposed toward peaceful coexistence—the so-called Westphalian system. But in the light of ensuing European conflicts over the following centuries, this view is as untenable as that of the Holy Roman Empire as a federal state. When com-pared with the constituent elements of a modern federal state, those of the em-pire did not have remotely the same stature or legal status.[149]

For the emperor, his authority over the Habsburg monarchy of Austria was more important than that over the empire. The former comprised the Austrian ancestral lands on imperial soil as well as the kingdoms of Bohemia and Hun-gary together with their external possessions. The greater part of Hungary, along with Transylvania, was recaptured from the Ottomans between 1699 and 1718. The three constituent parts of Austria–Hungary and the union as a whole was gradually provided with a standardized bureaucracy; however, this process was driven forward with real urgency only in the eighteenth century under the pres-sure of the challenge from Prussia, for despite the competence shown by the em-press Maria Theresa during her reign (1740–1780), the succession of a woman had sparked a monarchical crisis.[150]

In 1740, the Prussian king Frederick II (r. 1740–1786) annexed Silesia, which belonged to the Bohemian crown, and asserted his control over the territory in three wars (1740–1742, 1744–1745, and 1756–1763), which ultimately drew in all the major powers of Europe and their overseas possessions. Brandenburg had aug-mented its heartland in the east of Germany through the acquisition of the duchy of Kleve-Mark (Cleves) on the lower Rhine in 1614 and the duchy of (East) Prussia in 1618. In 1660, the elector of Brandenburg secured Prussia's release from its Polish fiefdom to become a sovereign territory, and in 1701, its first king ascended the throne. Prussia's energetic fiscal and administrative policies were primarily geared toward the development of a powerful army.[151]

In the context of the Austrian–Prussian wars, the "diplomatic revolution" of the Austrian–French alliance of 1755 represented the final cessation of the long-running conflict between the Houses of Habsburg and Bourbon.[152] Charles V had assigned control of Spain and the Italian and Burgundian lands, while at the same time loosening their ties to the empire, to his son Philip II (r. 1556–1598), who in addition gained Portugal through inheritance in 1580. With its highly modern centralized administration and unbeatable army, Spain was the foremost Catholic power in Europe but in the long term found itself overstretched—and not just financially—by its wars with France, the Ottomans in the Mediterranean, the rebellious Low Countries, and England. Exacerbated by plagues and rebellions, Spain's decline set in in earnest in the seventeenth century. Portugal seceded from Spain in 1640, while the northern Netherlands finally gained their independence in 1648, and Italy was lost after the abject end of the Spanish branch of the Habsburg dynasty in 1701 had put a branch of the Bourbons on the throne; the Austrian succession in Spain could not be pushed through internationally. Spain had declined from the leading power of Europe to its pawn, though in the late eighteenth century it was to take major steps toward modernization.[153]

In France, the power of the crown had reached its zenith during the first half of the sixteenth century,[154] but a series of underage and insignificant rulers from 1559 on and a dozen civil wars (the Wars of Religion) against the powerful Calvinist minority of the Huguenots from 1562 proved a serious setback to the nation-building process and saw France eclipsed on the international stage by Spain.[155] The accession to the French throne of the Catholic convert and former Huguenot leader Henry IV (r. 1589/1593–1610) ushered in an internal consolidation and a new robust foreign policy. The country was unified, because all the major fiefdoms had by now reverted to the crown, and the Huguenots had been guaranteed religious tolerance in the Edict of Nantes of 1598. However, this was revoked in 1685. Above all, the prime minister Cardinal Richelieu (in office 1624–1642) and thereafter the long-lived, ambitious, and energetic ruler Louis XIV (r. 1643/1651–1715) succeeded in making France into Europe's politically and culturally dominant power in place of Spain.[156] A series of wars brought eastward expansion at the cost of the Holy Roman Empire. Alsace became French in 1635–1684, while Lorraine was finally incorporated only in 1766. Nevertheless, a succession of international alliances were formed against Louis XIV. The War of the Spanish Succession (1701–1714), which was contested mainly between Louis on one side and the Holy Roman emperor together with the naval powers of England and Holland on the other, ended in an ostensible victory for France but left its monarchy exhausted and able to engage in successful power politics on the international stage again only in the mid-eighteenth century.

England as the Dominant Power

This left the way free for England (and, from 1707 and the Act of Union with Scotland, Great Britain[157]) to become the dominant force in Europe. Yet Britain fulfilled this role primarily with an eye to its growing overseas empire and without any great European ambition as the guarantor of a balance of power within continental Europe. Even so, it in turn (after France) became the dominant cultural model. Under the Tudors, the British monarchy grew in strength but lacked the means to pursue an expansionist policy. The politically and financially motivated split with Rome ultimately also developed into a Protestant Reformation, which was rolled back briefly under Mary Tudor but finally stabilized under Elizabeth I (r. 1558–1603) as the established Anglican Church, with a reformed theology but retaining the traditional doctrine of the apostolic succession. England became the foremost Protestant power in Europe and the most significant adversary of Spain, which sent a great armada against it, to no avail, in 1588.[158]

Ireland, which since the Middle Ages had been a subsidiary territory of the English Crown, was colonized in the sixteenth and seventeenth centuries by Protestant English and Scots. In terms of culture, the Catholic Irish were regarded as barbarians who were to be civilized and converted to Protestantism. In the northeast and the southeast (Ulster and Leinster), they were largely displaced by Protestant settlers from England and above all Scotland, with repercussions that are still felt today. Resistance was answered with brutal violence and banishment to the far west of the island. By the eighteenth century, the British territory of Ireland, then, had also become a Protestant nation, though in actuality only where its ruling political elite was concerned.[159]

England's Parliament was co-opted by the Tudors to help safeguard the Reformation and as a result had gained in significance. When the Scottish Stuart dynasty acceded to the throne in 1603 after Elizabeth died with no offspring to inherit the crown,[160] parliamentary opposition mounted, which demanded legal checks on royal power in matters of finances and the dispensing of justice, as well as calling for a "purification" of the established church by ridding it of all remaining vestiges of Roman influence (hence the term "Puritans" for the advocates of this policy). In response, the Stuart monarch Charles I (r. 1625–1649) dissolved Parliament in 1629 and proceeded to secure additional funds for the crown without any parliamentary approval. At this stage, an "absolute monarchy" seemed an imminent prospect in England, too.[161] Yet when Charles attempted to introduce Anglican confessionalization on Calvinist Scotland, using church homogenization as a way of imposing political conformity, he became embroiled in an armed conflict with the Scots, which he did not have the wherewithal to suppress. In 1640, he therefore had to recall the Parliament that he had suspended since 1629 in order to approve new taxes. But when, in turn, Parliament revived its calls for reform, conflict was inevitable, escalating into a civil war between Parliamentarians and Royalists,[162] which ended in 1649 with the execution of the king, on the charge of having subjected his own people to tyranny by waging war on them, and with the establishment of a parliamentary republic (the Commonwealth).

However, from at least 1647 on, there was no unanimity of purpose in the parliamentary ranks. The first split came with a conflict between moderate Presbyterians in Parliament, whose aim was a synodal church constitution and who were not averse to a compromise with the crown, and the radical Independents, who had as little time for Presbyterian synods as they did for Anglican bishops. The Independents had their power base in the Parliamentarian army, which under the influence of the mass movement known as the Levelers[163] had already begun to discuss the idea of an egalitarian and democratic constitution with universal suffrage—albeit only for men. Although the English Revolution cannot in general be interpreted as some form of socioeconomic class war, it is nevertheless true that the clash between different social and economic interests did play a major role in it. But first and foremost, the conflict was to do with political and religious differences, with a considerable degree of fortuitousness also playing its part.

Thus, a purging of Presbyterians from Parliament by the army could not prevent further conflicts. For the republican government, promoting the interests of the city of London, sought to disband the army and thereby avoid paying the soldiery what it owed. The result was a coup and the imposition of a military dictatorship by the New Model Army's supreme commander Oliver Cromwell (r. 1653–1658), whose rule witnessed the first political union of the British Isles (between England, Scotland, and Ireland). His Protestant expansionist policy laid the foundations of a new rise to predominance by England. However, the Lord Protector ran into both the old problems English kings had experienced with Parliament and new problems with the republican constitution in the form of unrest within the army. Only Cromwell in person had the stature to deal with such difficulties.[164] Also, because for the majority of the political class in England, only a monarch had the authority to unify the nation, they offered Cromwell the crown accordingly in 1657, which he declined. As a result, after his death in the following year, the restoration of the Stuart monarchy proved inevitable, a step that was duly enacted in 1660.

Despite new restrictions placed on the power of the crown, the old conflicts soon arose once more, only this time exacerbated by the Catholic faith of King James II. As a result, in the "Glorious Revolution" of 1688–1689, James's daughter Mary and her husband, William of Orange, who as stadholder of the Netherlands already occupied a quasi-monarchical position, were invited to come and establish a Protestant monarchy under conditions set by Parliament. The English crown thus became a constitutional office, bound by law and the constraints of parliamentary consensus, most effectively in questions of how to finance foreign policy and wars. Even so, in this executive role, William III (r. 1689–1702) still proved a strong ruler. The "cabinet" of ministers occupying the most important offices of state, which developed in the eighteenth century, remained dependent on the crown and became an executive arm of Parliament only in the nineteenth century.[165]

The Netherlands and Poland

In his role as stadholder of the Netherlands, William III had already come to embody the spirit of European resistance against Louis XIV, who had invaded Holland in 1672. Precisely a century before, in 1572, his ancestor and namesake, William of Orange (or William the Silent; 1533–1584), had assumed the leadership of the Dutch rebellion that broke out in 1566 against Spain. The immediate catalyst for this revolt was the persecution of Calvinists, but it was directed against the entire foreign policy of the Spanish king Philip II, who wanted to turn the Netherlands into a strictly controlled and heavily taxed overseas colony. While the southern provinces of the Spanish Netherlands remained Catholic and returned to Spanish sovereignty, the northern territories banded together in 1579 to form a Calvinist alliance (the United Provinces), which deposed the king in 1581 and then sought in vain for a new ruler. Thus, the alliance of the seven northern provinces reluctantly became a corporative republic, which continued to elect its stadholders from the House of Orange-Nassau in lieu of monarchs, though at times it was quite content to do without any head of state at all. After an armistice in 1609, the war against Spain erupted once more in 1621 and finally ended with the independence of this newly "invented" nation in 1648.

In the interim, the former leading economic role of the southern Netherlands had shifted north, from Antwerp to Amsterdam, which became the most important port for foreign trade and also the center of European world commerce. For a brief while, the Netherlands even took on the mantle of the foremost cultural model in Europe, between the dominance of Spain and France. The Netherlands of this "golden age" was based on an urban culture that stressed the importance of orderliness and cleanliness and praised civic and domestic virtues, giving women an unheard-of freedom of movement and setting great store by caring for children. Its comparatively high standard of living led, among other things, to a unique blossoming of painting, with ownership of paintings becoming widespread among the prosperous middle classes. This cultural boom produced a master of world stature in the form of Rembrandt van Rijn (1606–1699).[166] Although the Netherlands was at root a community founded on a strict Reformed Church faith, in practice Jews and Catholics, nonconformists, and free thinkers all enjoyed a measure of tolerance unmatched elsewhere in Europe.[167]

The Dutch were heavily involved in maritime trade with the Baltic, which became a theater where northern and eastern European nations fought out their rivalries. These clashes arose not least over the tariffs imposed on exports from ports on the southern coast. The Jagiellon dynasty in Poland–Lithuania died out in 1572 and was followed by a succession of elected kings until, with the crowning of Sigismund III (r. 1597–1632), a grandson of Sigismund I, the Swedish House of Vasa acceded to the throne. Although, on the occasion of a royal election in 1505, control over the legislative process had devolved to the Imperial Diet, despite religious divisions and occasional rebellions by the politically dominant nobility, the country expanded to its greatest extent, and was at the height of its powers, around 1600. However, Sigismund's claims to the Swedish throne sparked wars with Sweden, while Russia's attack on Livonia saw Poland go to war with the tsarist empire also. Finally, a series of major uprisings and attacks by both Russia and Sweden in the mid-seventeenth century ushered in the demise of Poland–Lithuania and the advent of the chaotic "aristocratic republic" of Poland, whose

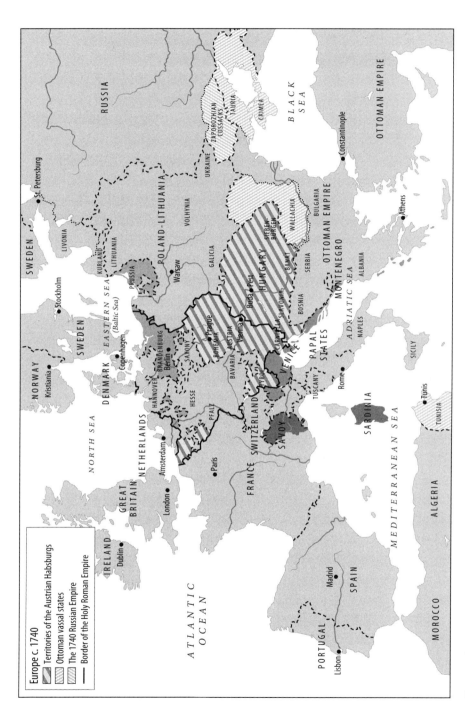

Europe, circa 1740

Europe c. 1740

- Territories of the Austrian Habsburgs
- Ottoman vassal states
- The 1740 Russian Empire
- Border of the Holy Roman Empire

RUSSIA

ZAPOROZHIAN COSSACKS

TAURIA

CRIMEA

BLACK SEA

OTTOMAN EMPIRE

Constantinople

UKRAINE

VOLHYNIA

WALLACHIA

BULGARIA

SEVEN-BÜRGEN

BANAT

SERBIA

OTTOMAN EMPIRE

MONTENEGRO

ALBANIA

Athens

SWEDEN

St. Petersburg

LIVONIA

KURLAND

LITHUANIA

POLAND-LITHUANIA

Warsaw

GALICIA

HUNGARY

Buda • Pest

SLAVONIA

BOSNIA

Stockholm

SWEDEN

PRUSSIA

EASTERN SEA
(Baltic Sea)

ADRIATIC SEA

NAPLES

NORWAY

Kristiania

DENMARK

Copenhagen

BRANDENBURG

Berlin

SAXONY

BOHEMIA

Prague

AUSTRIA

Vienna

CARINTHIA

TYROL

VENICE

PAPAL STATES

Rome •

SICILY

NORTH SEA

HANNOVER

HESSE

PFALZ

BAVARIA

SWITZERLAND

TUSCANY

SAVOY

SARDINIA

Tunis

TUNISIA

MEDITERRANEAN SEA

GREAT BRITAIN

NETHERLANDS

Amsterdam •

London •

FRANCE

Paris •

ATLANTIC OCEAN

IRELAND

Dublin •

ALGERIA

MOROCCO

PORTUGAL

Lisbon •

SPAIN

Madrid •

ultimate fate toward the end of the seventeenth century was to be partitioned entirely among the neighboring powers.[168]

After Sweden had rejected the succession claim of the Catholic Polish king, using this as a pretext to make Lutheranism the established state faith, it was finally able, thanks to extensive political and military reorganization in the seventeenth century, to expel Denmark, weakened through a series of defeats, from the southern Swedish mainland and to itself take on the role of a major power, in successful wars against Poland, within Germany, and against Russia. However, both of the "Northern Wars" (1655–1661 and 1700–1721) ended with a crushing defeat to a grand coalition of adversaries. Thereafter, the exhausted country changed from being a strong, occasionally absolute, monarchy and adopted a parliamentary system in the so-called Age of Liberty (1720–1772).[169]

The Early Modern State

Prior to 1750, in most European countries, a strengthened monarchy had managed to assert its monopoly on power by means of both a greatly expanded central administration and regional bureaucracies that often relied on local cooperation. In line with this, they also progressively widened their jurisdiction, disciplined their subjects, and brought the churches within their domain under state control. Certainly, there were some exceptions to this general trend. The Swiss Confederacy and the Netherlands retained the premodern condition of local autonomy as the principle informing the systems that formed them into confederations and shunned in the process the customary pattern of nation building of other polities in the early modern period; when one considers the relative tolerance that characterized the Netherlands, this was a thoroughly positive alternative. In England, Poland, and Sweden, the corporative monarchy remained the dominant force—the *dominium politicum et regale,* as the lawyer John Fortescue termed it in the fifteenth century. Wherever the estates' assemblies developed an interest in power politics, as in England, there arose a highly promising variant of the early modern state, but where this was not the case, as in Poland, the path led inevitably to political oblivion.

England and France, Austria, and, as newcomers to the international stage in the eighteenth century, Russia and Prussia dominated the interstate sphere as the principal powers, whether in wars that ranged across any and every theater or in diplomatic activities, especially at peace congresses—a form of political interaction between states that had occurred occasionally from the fifteenth century on but that became an increasingly regular phenomenon after 1648. In their military and political machinations, the great powers frequently used weaker third-party states, or parts of them, as pawns, with no consideration for the interests or wishes of those concerned. The main players in this were diplomats, a species of princely state official that rose to prominence in this period, after other powers began in the sixteenth century to follow the age-old example of Venice and the papacy and keep permanent representatives at foreign courts. As yet, no formal training existed for this role, and diplomats relied on their reading of history and their experience to get by. The essential qualifications were an aristocratic title and an independent source of income, as the remuneration left much to be desired.[170]

Diplomatic immunity and extraterritoriality formed the recognized bases of this realm of *Ius Publicum Europaeum* that developed within the system of European power brokerage; this is sometimes misleadingly referred to as "international law." Following studies by Spanish theologians in the sixteenth century, the key contributions in this area were made by the Dutch scholar Hugo Grotius (1583–1645). The freedom of the seas outside limited territorial waters formed a key element, alongside rules governing conduct in war and peace, which were regarded as a kind of legal transaction. Ultimately, on the principle that treaties were made to be observed, both interstate transactions and internal settlements recognized between nations, such as decrees on succession, also became a constituent part of international law—admittedly, never irrevocably, as to this day it remains an inherent problem of international law that it lacks universal jurisdiction with sufficient enforcement powers. Its implementation is possible only insofar as states agree with one another to do so.

By and large, the development of the modern state was far advanced by 1750. Even so, we should continue to qualify polities at this period as "early modern states," given that they were lacking one fundamental constituent of modernity—namely, the political equality among all citizens of a state. Certainly, vertical and horizontal inequality had been eroded somewhat but still remained the norm. The traditional society of orders still reigned supreme, and the individual continued to form part of the polity not directly, as nowadays, but as a member of his or her family or of various corporations, above all their municipality. Only with the French Revolution did a decisive change come about in this state of affairs.

From Subsistence Economy to a Manufacturing Economy

By 1350, Europe had largely progressed beyond the stage of a subsistence economy in the sense of a closed system of production and consumption within the same household or on the same estate.[171] Yet the existing system of payment in cash or in kind, of markets, and of trade and commerce was still geared, not only ideologically but also overwhelmingly in practice as well, to supplying individuals. In the main, this meant providing for the basic needs of a modest standard of living, which all too often was not far removed from the bare minimum needed to survive. The concept of economic growth through industrial and commercial productivity was unknown. Instead, there was assumed to be a pool of goods that remained constantly the same and could be distributed in such a way that everyone had enough to live on, as was only right and proper.

Nevertheless, the agrarian economy of Latin Europe,[172] which had developed during the early Middle Ages, displayed many promising features. The northern Alpine open-field system of cultivation was somewhat unusual in the history of civilization in combining arable farming and animal husbandry. It was based on the cultivation of rye and oats alongside the pasturage and housing of cattle and horses; hay was cut for fodder, and the animal's manure fertilized the fields. In turn, livestock husbandry brought with it utilization of the motive power of draft animals (often horses), enhanced by the advent of the horseshoe and collar, to pull heavy new moldboard plows and harrows. This both facilitated the successful cultivation of cereals and enabled goods to be transported by cart. Added to this was the simple but extremely versatile technology of watermills and windmills, whose spread was promoted largely by the vested interests of landowners as the holders of milling rights; indeed, this was a major factor behind the growth of the entire system. For banal lordship formed a key element of the manorial arrangement, which, through its control over peasants' holdings, comprised the social aspect of the system. In the Mediterranean region, it was impossible to cultivate spring grain, while deep plowing eroded the soil; so, instead of rye, farmers there stuck with wheat. Arable farming and animal husbandry, then, may have been more firmly separated here, but even so the Europe-wide connection between a cereal-growing and breadmaking culture on the one hand and a meat culture on the other was maintained. This found its symbolic expression in the Christian ritual of the Eucharist.

In spite of only a modest yield—the ratio of seeds sown to crops grown and harvested in the fourteenth century oscillated between one in three and one in seven—the system still generated enough surpluses to feed the populations of the cities as well as the clergy and the feudal landowners—at least partially, as many town dwellers were engaged in farming themselves, even if this involved only growing produce in their gardens or keeping chickens and pigs. Conversely, the cities attempted not just to control the surrounding countryside politically but also to spread their economic influence there as well. In some cases, and not just in Tuscany, this meant that the great majority of cultivated land was in the hands of urban dwellers.[173]

Above all, the demand generated by the cities was responsible for introducing considerable changes in farming practices. Its initial impact was seen in the growth of islands of intensely high productivity, first in viticulture, which was widespread thanks to demand from religious institutions and the largely favorable climate that still existed;[174] second in the open-field system through the practice of growing crops that reinvigorated the soil on fallow land during the summer months, notably on the lower Rhine and in northern Italy; third in the market gardening of vegetables and fruit in the environs of major cities; and fourth in the cultivation of "industrial plants" for urban textile manufacture—for example, woad for blue dyeing in Thuringia, the Netherlands, northern and southern France, Piedmont, and Tuscany and madder for red dyeing in the Palatinate, Silesia, the Netherlands, and northern France.

Furthermore, in the medium- to high-altitude ranges of hills, poor arable farming was soon abandoned in favor of dairy farming on upland pasturage, which produced cheese, butter, and meat for the consumer market. In addition, cattle from rich grassland areas on the North Sea coast and from Hungary were herded into more heavily urbanized areas and fattened up as required for slaughter. This "ox trade" was a well-organized Europe-wide business. The pig may have been the meat animal of choice of the smallholder, but in woodland within the catchment area of large cities, pigs were likewise fattened up in large herds with beechnuts and acorns. Moreover, as a result of the church's edict that people should forgo the consumption of meat on Fridays, there was also a lively trade in fish, with salted cod from Norway and pickled herrings from the North Sea and the Baltic, as well as inland with freshwater fish from the belt of intensive stew-pond fish farming in Central Europe, which extended from Bohemia to the environs of Lyon. Finally, there was large-scale farming of sheep for wool for use in cloth manufacture in England and the Mediterranean; in Spain and Apulia (southern Italy) this trade was sponsored and organized by the ruling classes as a lucrative source of taxation.[175]

Because of the population losses that occurred in the fourteenth century, urban demand declined in terms of sheer volume of goods, but as a result of higher wages the demand for quality increased correspondingly. Above all, people were now able to afford more meat. In consequence, farming was abandoned in unproductive areas, prompting a new rise in the number of deserted settlements.[176] This was offset by an intensification in market gardening, with whole regions of fruit and vegetable growing springing up; even onions and garlic were exported in this period. But first and foremost, there was an expansion in pasture farming, with the "cerealization" of late medieval agriculture now being supplanted by a new "grazing economy" that lasted into the modern era. In England, meanwhile, it was not just unproductive farmland that was released from its ties to the open-field system and turned into grazing land for cattle and sheep, surrounded by hedges and fences, in a judicially sanctioned process of dispossession known as the "enclosures." When farmsteads were uprooted and moved into enclosed land, traditional villages disintegrated in a new round of rural desolation.

Yet following a long period when the prices of manufactured goods and wages increased while the cost of basic foodstuffs had fallen, they began to converge once more toward the end of the fifteenth century, crossed over in the first half of the sixteenth century, and then proceeded to diverge in the opposite direction. The cause was the renewed increase in the population, which also ensured that, while grain cultivation became more worthwhile once more, the well-rehearsed demand structure was not allowed to regress.

Trade and Mining

The urban economy was based on trade and manufacturing, comprising a mix of retail commerce, overseas trade, small-scale craftsmanship, and large concerns, with the last giving rise to banking and the provision of credit facilities. Even so, right up to the nineteenth century, this domain was hedged around, at least in part, by ecclesiastical and state restrictions, such as the Catholic Church's injunction against earning interest on loans (usury) or the English Crown's proscription of joint-stock companies. Manufacturing, meanwhile, took the form of small workshops with just a handful of craftsmen (or even just the single artisan).[177] The sector was, on the one hand, differentiated and specialized in terms of both horizontal and vertical division of labor (for example, spinners, weavers, and dyers in the cloth trade, or goldsmiths, silversmiths, blacksmiths, and armorers in metalworking) but, on the other hand, punctiliously regimented by the corporate nature of the virtually ubiquitous guilds. The basic impulsion was to create an order that guaranteed everyone a livelihood.

As a result, there arose not only a system of quality control and a hierarchy of master craftsmen, journeymen, and apprentices but also a deliberate restriction on the number of master craftsmen and their coworkers and on production methods, such as the number of looms a master weaver could have. Other practices included a widespread tendency to buy raw materials and sell finished goods communally, plus a ban on speculating with raw material stocks or semifinished goods and regulations governing salaries and working time. There were recurrent instances of resistance to technological innovations that threatened people's jobs. The craft guilds took a social, political, and religious role to be an integral part of their duties. They fostered a strong feeling of conviviality and provided welfare in cases of emergency; being a member of a guild was sometimes a prerequisite for being granted citizenship and could also entail sharing responsibility for the defense of the town. Guilds all had their patron saint, along with specially dedicated chapels, masses, and feast days.[178]

The most important trades were building[179] and food production, which were universally based on the principle of self-sufficiency. The textile[180] and metalworking trades, in contrast, often concentrated in clusters of workshops supplying a large market, which created marketing problems for individual artisans. This gave rise not only to the communal approach taken by the guilds but also to the new organizational form of "outworking." In this system, a well-funded large-scale manufacturer—the so-called putter-outer—would assume overall organization of production, buying raw materials and distributing them in turn to the individual craftsmen involved in various stages of the finishing process. In some instances, he would also provide the craftsmen with their tools and plant. Ultimately, the putter-outer bought the finished product from the artisans and marketed it. While, at first, the cities tried to suppress the activities of rural craftsmen as un-welcome competition, it now often proved advantageous, especially in the tech-nically not very demanding cloth-making industry, to outsource production to the countryside, either so as to get around restrictive practices imposed by the guilds or sometimes in collaboration with them, whereby the spinning was done in the countryside, while the dyeing and weaving were done in the town.

Home working in the country created new life chances for the rural lower class, and work was often divided up among family members, with women spinning, men weaving, and the children doing ancillary tasks. Whenever this generated a greater population density than local farming could reasonably feed, we use the term "protoindustrialization." However, this term is misleading insofar as many protoindustrial regions precisely did not, as was once claimed, immediately go over to an industrial mode of production in factories but on the contrary suffered dein-dustrialization.[181] In the long-prominent sector of woolen cloth manufacture, for instance, out of the principal areas specializing in this textile branch, only En-gland, not Flanders, Brabant, Tuscany, or northern Italy, experienced a smooth transition to industrialization. Likewise, the linen weavers of northern Germany, Westphalia, the Netherlands, and Silesia and the Swabian and northern Italian manufacturers of fustian—a popular blend of linen and cotton—had no direct industrial successors.

Textile manufacture may well, in many cases, have developed close to where its raw materials were produced, but an industry that was far more firmly rooted to a particular location was mineral extraction, such as the refined salt mined from deposits at Lüneburg, Salzungen, Reichenhall, and Hallein, and similarly the sea salt refined from the Mediterranean at Chioggia.[182] One decisive factor could be whether a particular site still had enough fuel in the vicinity to drive the salt-refining process. If the woods in an area had been clear-felled, it sometimes happened that salt water was channeled to a new site in a heavily forested region, as occurred even as late as the eighteenth century in the eastern French region of Franche Comté, when salt mining was transferred from Salins to Chaux.[183] The first large-scale plants developed in the ore-mining sector. Not only manufacturing trades but also European agriculture were heavily dependent on iron tools, while princes' armies required steel armor and later bronze cannons, with the church needing bronze bells, and commerce gold, silver, and copper as coinage—quite apart from the luxury items made from precious metals that were much in demand by the church and wealthy individuals alike. Consequently, mining expanded rapidly. Among other places, iron was especially plentiful in the Forest of Dean in Gloucestershire, England, in the Siegerland and Upper Palatinate in Germany, in the Austrian region of Styria, and on the island of Elba. Copper was found in Upper Hungary and in Sweden, tin was found in Cornwall, and silver was found predominantly in the Erzgebirge (Ore Mountains) of eastern Germany and the Austrian Tyrol. The only way in which small mining enterprises could compete was in opencast pits. Sinking deep shafts, the technically complex facilities required to drain mines of groundwater and to wash and grade the extracted ore, required much more capital, organization, and technical know-how than small operations could afford. As a result, the mining sector saw the development of large concerns, financed by capital from city institutions and employing hundreds of wageworkers with no affiliations to guilds, who even at this early stage begin to manifest some of the problems and modes of behavior associated with the modern proletariat.[184] By contrast, the metalworking industries, including armaments production, found themselves decentralized in the outworking system; leading centers of this industry included Milan, Liège, Nuremberg, and Cologne.

Trade and Credit

The capital that was invested in mining was generated by the outworking system and by long-distance trade. Only the long-distance traders, not the guild-based traders in local and regional markets, were generally regarded as merchants; the former often possessed a socially far more exalted guild or corporation of their own, with a clear affinity to the urban nobility. Not infrequently, these merchants were elevated into this class or at least vied with it for political and social supremacy.

The activities of the foremost merchants could embrace the whole of Europe and even stretch beyond this sphere to take in Russia or the Near East and were soon to expand overseas.[185] At this stage, many of them visited in person the trade fairs,[186] of which no fewer than 171 in the year 1585 alone, from Spain to the Baltic, may well have had a supraregional flavor; the thousands of other fairs that were held were local annual fairs. Large family concerns like the Medici of Florence or the Fuggers of Augsburg maintained extensive networks of branches staffed by agents.[187] They were organized as temporally limited companies (with the designation *societas* or *compania*), with active partners and pure investors both from within the family and outside taking a share of the risks and the profits. Some of them were already incorporated as companies with limited liability.

In the north of the Holy Roman Empire, a network of merchants' leagues had developed, which had their origins in collectives formed by long-distance travelers, above all sailors, and their collective settlements abroad. Ultimately, the councils of the cities in question became identified with this network, the German Hanseatic League, whose trading activities took in Bruges, London, Bergen, Stockholm, and Novgorod. Lübeck, the town to profit most from this system, became the head of the league. From 1356 on, irregular meetings of the Hansa were held to review common interests; to serve these, political and military means were often deployed. The Hansa's victory over the Danish king in 1370 represented the high-water mark of its power, but by the fifteenth century its demise had begun. This was brought about less by any significant decline in the cities' commercial activity and more by the fact that others began to outstrip them, including the Italians and southern Germans but particularly the Dutch, who began to intervene ever more successfully in Baltic trade. In addition, this period saw nascent nation-states becoming much stronger; over time these polities had outgrown the collegiate structure of a decentralized world, which in some respects was reminiscent of the Swiss Confederacy. This all created sharper conflicts of interest between the cities of the Hanseatic League, with Hamburg usurping Lübeck's preeminent position. By the seventeenth century, the League was at an end.[188]

Alongside the North Sea–Baltic trade system, and in existence well before it, the north–south axis of European trade routes was of key importance. This ran from London via Bruges (later Antwerp and Cologne) to Frankfurt and from there to Nuremberg or via Augsburg to Venice, which was the source of goods from the

East, not least spices. Insofar as it was possible, the preferred mode of transportation was by the more cost-effective sea and river routes. But land transportation, especially across the Alpine passes,[189] was also highly professional and well organized. Parallel with this, there was also a trade axis that ran from the Mediterranean via Lyon to Flanders; by the seventeenth century, no fewer than seventy-two German trading firms had offices in Lyon. Frankfurt, with its fairs, was a hub for European trade, thanks to its location on the axis to Nuremberg, from which important trade routes ran overland to the east. With the onset of European overseas expansion, Lisbon and Seville both gained in significance, though they did not put the Mediterranean ports and their connection to the Middle East out of business immediately. However, "colonial goods" found their way into the European market not so much directly via Portugal and Spain than through Antwerp,[190] which was supplanted as the hub of European world trade by Amsterdam in the seventeenth century, and Amsterdam in turn by London in the eighteenth.

Partnerships were designed not just to generate capital but also to share the often quite substantial risks involved. In addition, ever since the thirteenth to fourteenth centuries, merchants had the option of taking out insurance. Indemnity of this kind began as shipping insurance in northern Italy[191] and in the towns of the Hanseatic League. However, one major problem was the multiplicity and the variable quality of European coinage at the time. From early on, professional exchange brokers appeared on the scene to overcome this difficulty, while the fourteenth century saw the development of public city exchanges, which soon began to offer facilities for clients to make deposits in precious metals and currency, thus becoming the world's first deposit banks. Around the same time, the introduction of letters of exchange and the potential to deposit or withdraw in different currencies at different locations and times witnessed the advent of cashless transactions and the creation of bank money. Regular exchange fairs enabled people to settle debts. The exchange system also began to be used to conceal loans, a facility that had long been indispensable for commerce. Because of the ban on usury, interest-bearing loans were permissible only by hypothecating property as security or as annuity from real estate. Yet the exchange mechanism, with its variations in time and currency, suddenly opened up new possibilities.[192]

In the fourteenth century, the traditional providers of credit, the Lombards, the southern French, and the Jews, were displaced in many places by indigenous operators. In Nuremberg, for instance, the city's leading families conspired to conduct a pogrom against the Jews and expel them.[193] Given this prevailing anti-Jewish trend, in the second half of the sixteenth century, church-run pawnshops *(monti di pietà)*[194] were established to extend small loans to poorer people, which were vital to their survival. However, the most lucrative business where lending was concerned was with the papacy, the princes, and the municipalities. Up to the Reformation, huge sums levied in the form of church taxes, plus income from the sale of indulgences, were transferred to Rome. Thereafter, in the sixteenth century, the popes devised a modern system of credit, which was reasonably solid in comparison to other princes.[195] In Spain and France, meanwhile, royal bankruptcies increased due to the escalating costs of waging wars. Even so, there was no shortage of willing lenders, albeit offering high interest rates. Plus, as the holders of prospecting rights, princes were constantly engaged in mining activities. In this way, the Fuggers were able to acquire many silver and copper mines in the Tyrol as well as Spanish mercury deposits as securities, having first acquired the capital they needed to extend loans from their involvement in the textile industry. Pure trading concerns like the Hanseatic League or the Great Ravensburg Trading Society declined in importance, because they did not get involved in this combined trade in metals and credit. The so-called early capitalists were thus wholesale merchants, entrepreneurs, and bankers all rolled into one.[196]

However, this early capitalism of the sixteenth century was something of a dead end and not only because (as in the case of the Fuggers) credit extended to princes often culminated in serious losses. More important, progress was hampered by the fact that profits were not invested into developing the business but were sunk in acquiring property, aristocratic titles, and social advancement. Yet it is only possible to speak in the loosest metaphorical terms in this context of a "betrayal by the bourgeoisie" *(trahison de la bourgeoisie)* of its supposed historical duty, namely, to further capitalism, because their behavior was completely in accord with the cultural dictates of the period. Although at first sight, profit might appear as an end in itself, on closer inspection it turned out to be subservient to other aims, primarily the social advancement of the family.

In his capacity as a merchant, mining entrepreneur, and banker, Jacob Fugger of Augsburg (1459–1525) was the foremost representative of early capitalism in southern Germany. He was notorious for the role he played in the sale of indulgences, a practice condemned by Martin Luther, and renowned for his financing of the election of Charles V as Holy Roman emperor. We owe the existence of this double portrait of Fugger working with his accountant Matthäus Schwarz to the fact that the latter was something of a fop and was fond of having himself portrayed in different clothes. The archive drawers in the background are labeled with the names of important branches of the Fugger banking firm, including Ofen (Budapest), Cracau (Krakow), and Antorff (Antwerp). (bpk—Bildagentur für Kunst, Kultur und Geschichte, Berlin)

Yet the increasing need for credit by developing nation-states spawned a new generation of financiers. In the eighteenth century, international networks of Jewish and Protestant banking firms played a key role in this business. The foundation of public or "state banks," such as in Genoa in 1586, Venice in 1587, Amsterdam in 1609, Hamburg in 1619, and the Bank of England in 1694, did little to alter this system.[197] Only the corporative parliamentary guarantee to fund public debt on allotted tax revenue, an arrangement that England adopted from the Netherlands in the late seventeenth century, paved the way for the modern system of stable state credit. To their detriment, the French and Spanish crowns could not go down this route.

The Coming Industrial Revolution

In the seventeenth century, and continuing to a large extent also in the eighteenth, economic development went down these preordained paths. This had to do with a general trend that can also be charted from looking at the way populations and prices developed. Disregarding short- and midterm economic cycles, the depression of the fourteenth and fifteenth centuries was followed by a dynamic period of growth over the "long" sixteenth century, although the so-called prices revolution associated with this age was very modest compared with later inflationary periods. By contrast, across most of Europe, the seventeenth century was a period of stagnation, and if one also takes into consideration the wars and demographic catastrophes that occurred, some countries can even be said to have been in deep crisis. Yet there seems to be little evidence of any general "crisis of the seventeenth century."[198] The late seventeenth and early eighteenth centuries, then, show signs of a new upturn, which was ultimately to culminate in the self-perpetuating boom of the Industrial Revolution of the late eighteenth and early nineteenth centuries.

The sense that this represented a revolutionary step toward the modern age is less evident in the still-gradual and at most cumulative revolutionary development of production and technology than in the radical change toward reflection on economic matters in the context of the Enlightenment. For a mode of thinking oriented purely toward subsistence, not only the charging of interest but also any profit over and above one's own modest means of subsistence were reprehensible and rendered a person liable to eternal perdition. Up to the sixteenth century, successful merchants would therefore try to mitigate their "sins" by making religious and social endowments, despite the fact that in the interim, at least, the accumulation of capital in the service of social advancement had been theologically legitimized. Concern with making a profit, though, was greed, the cardinal sin of avarice *(avaritia)*. Just as reprehensible was luxury of any kind, which was tolerated in only modest measure in the very highest echelons of society, as a status symbol.

However, in 1428, in Florence, the center of Italy early capitalism, the humanist Poggio Bracciolini pointed out (for now, only in a very coded way) that it was only the surplus gained through avarice that made cultural activities and good works, not to mention the livelihood of the entire community, possible in the first place. Then, in 1530, the German humanist Konrad Peutinger, who had close links with the leading merchants and financiers of Augsburg, quite openly defended these firms against attacks by the Imperial Diet. Peutinger argued that their risk taking and their heavy investment of capital made a major contribution to general prosperity and to tax revenues, in other words to the public good, and that therefore they should remain unregulated, because the sole motivating factor inducing a person to take risks was the high level of potential profit. In 1564, the military author Leonhard Fronsperger went so far as to claim that self-interest was the prime mover behind all human undertakings.

Even so, in the seventeenth century, the up-and-coming study of "political economy" began questioning more insistently than ever how the general prosperity of the community might be increased. As long as the concept of economic growth was absent, this could be achieved only through the redistribution of wealth, in other words through reallocation to some at the expense of others. Strictly speaking, then, "mercantilism" was both theoretically and in practice an ideology of economic war, given that its key tenets were to buy raw materials cheaply and sell finished goods dearly, with an eye to building up precious metal reserves in one's native country. This aim was to be promoted through the imposition of tariffs, legislation, and, if necessary, even the use of force. The three Anglo-Dutch Wars (1652–1654, 1665–1667, and 1672–1674) were the first purely trade wars in history.

Mercantilism rehabilitated the demand for luxury and made its pursuit a legitimate economic aim.[199] Now, Bernard Mandeville (in his polemic *The Fable of the Bees, or Private Vices, Public Benefits;* 1714) was able to turn existing economic morality on its head and claim that vices, and not virtues, were the prerequisite for economic success. In contrast, in 1758, François Quesnay *(Tableau économique)* and the physiocrats broke with the traditional fixation on the distribution of goods and became the first to maintain that production, specifically agricultural production, was the source of all prosperity. Finally, Adam Smith *(An Enquiry into the Nature and Causes of the Wealth of Nations;* 1776) expanded this viewpoint to embrace all production and in doing so refuted Mandeville's cynicism—for while Smith also identified human self-interest and acquisitiveness as the root of general prosperity, he mitigated it by advocating moral sensibilities and state regulation.

Indeed, the growth in population gave rise to some very promising agricultural innovations, for as the price of food increased, so did the value of farmland and its yield. Land was reclaimed once more and settled, while in many places the open-field system was replaced by variations of an ingenious system of crop rotation. Because this effectively made the open-field system dispensable, enclosures increased, above all in England. Hand in hand with this came technological advances, just as had happened in manufacturing. In the Middle Ages and the early modern period, practically minded technological "amateurs" had invented or improved a whole series of devices, including spectacles, watches, and book printing, along with numerous machines. These included devices that adapted mills to all kinds of new tasks: sawmills, fulling mills, forges, and so on. In the meantime, it became extremely worthwhile to continue this process of technical innovation in a more systematic way, especially because the new realm of empirical natural sciences, which had made great strides since the seventeenth century, could now supply a firm scientific footing to new inventions. Diderot and Jean Le Rond d'Alembert's *Encyclopédie* was therefore much more than a compendium of Enlightenment philosophy; it was also a richly illustrated practical handbook of technology.

The epicenter of economic innovation was England, where agriculture had left the old feudal system far behind, commercialized it to a great extent, and was therefore open to any innovations that promised to increase profit margins. Distribution and communication were systematically improved through road and canal construction. Urbanization was already far advanced; by 1750, 11 percent of the country's population was living in London. The level of wages was relatively high, and in contrast to other countries, a modest degree of prosperity was evident across broad sections of the population, producing a regular demand for a wider range of goods to satisfy both basic and more refined needs.[200] Yet whether this phenomenon was the result of an "Industrious Revolution" in households, with the combined industry of men, women, and children contributing to a steady increase in supply and demand, remains a moot point.[201]

Whatever the case, the upshot was groundbreaking improvements in the textile and metalworking industries. A shortage of wood hastened its replacement by coal; in 1709, the technique of smelting iron ore using coke was invented. One result of this was that an increasing number of iron tools, machine parts, and items for everyday use of a superior quality were turned out. Another was that coal mining increased hugely, prompting James Watt's innovative improvements to Thomas Newcomen's original steam engine in 1769; henceforth, steam engines were not just used for pumping groundwater from mines but were installed to provide the motive power in textile mills.

The eighteenth century saw the creation of so-called manufactories in the textile industry, especially in the production of luxury fabrics such as Gobelin tapestries, as well as in the production of porcelain, a technique copied from the Chinese and perfected in Europe in 1708. Here, unlike the previous practice of guild-based artisans and home working, workers were brought together under a single roof, in order to ensure better quality control; however, the actual working methods in manufactories were thoroughly traditional. Manufactories often came about as the result of princes' initiatives. In France, for example, the production and sale of luxury textiles and mirrors were designed to improve the balance of trade, while Prussia provided its army with uniforms and armament. Lesser German princes followed suit in establishing their own porcelain manufactories. Overall, however, the profitability of these "factories without machines" was low, as, unlike in outworking, they were unable to respond sufficiently flexibly to the market.

By contrast, the factories that began to appear in England were based on the optimal deployment of newly devised textile-making machines. In 1733, weaving speeds were greatly increased by the introduction of the "flying shuttle," while the invention of the "spinning jenny" in 1764 responded to the growing demand for thread. Conversely, the resulting glut of thread was cleared by the advent of the automatic loom in 1787. Obviously, a steady demand for the finished product by consumers was guaranteed. At first, the motive power for these machines, transmitted via shafts and belts, was supplied by waterwheels, an age-old technology in Europe, meaning that the first factories were sited on inland waterways with millraces. But with water power increasingly supplanted by steam power from Watt's engines, industry became independent of waterways and was free to establish itself in towns with good transport connections.

Even though textile and iron production still accounted for only 3 percent of Britain's gross domestic product in 1780, it transpired that this decisive development had set the country irrevocably on the path toward the modern world. In the same way that the Enlightenment had helped people make themselves the masters of their own fate in theory, so the up-and-coming scientific–technological industrial culture enabled them to do so in practice. Although both these aspirations were to prove questionable in the long term, the Enlightenment and the Industrial Revolution did for the first time offer people the chance to build a better life for themselves here on Earth and escape the state of fear and misery in which the great majority of them had languished in the period 1350–1750.

3. The New Atlantic Worlds

THE ANCESTORS of the first inhabitants of the "New World"[202] migrated from Asia via the area around the modern Bering Straits only during and after the last Ice Age, most probably in several waves separated by long intervals. Accordingly, the first Europeans to land there encountered a genetically, linguistically, and culturally diverse picture, with people displaying both Mongoloid and Caucasian features, and hundreds of language families and cultures encompassing all forms of social organization from hunter-gatherer societies to highly organized communities with impressive scientific, artistic, and political achievements—all, that is, except nomadic herdsmen. Animal husbandry did not extend beyond turkeys, mastiffs, and bees in Middle America and llamas, guinea pigs, and ducks in South America. Conversely, the breeding and cultivation of agricultural crops had reached a high level of sophistication. Maize, beans, and squashes formed the staple diet of people in North America, while these and potatoes were the main foods of people in South America.

The far north and south of the twin continent, together with the mountainous areas of western North America, California, and parts of eastern South America were all home to hunter-gatherer societies. Across the vast majority of the rest of the Americas, variations of a mixed economy and lifestyle were practiced, combining cultivation of crops with hunting and gathering. In tropical South America, manioc was the most important cultivated crop. Embedded within the Americas were zones of more complex cultural development: the Mississippian culture in the east of North America, the Pueblo culture in the southwest of North America, and the Chibcha culture in the highlands of Colombia. But the main peoples who should be mentioned in this context were those living in the area occupied by present-day Mexico, who from the fifteenth century on were largely under the control of the Aztecs, along with the Maya in Guatemala and the Yucatán, and finally the Inca and their predecessors, principally the Chimù, who inhabited the west coast of South America and the high Andes in the area between modern Ecuador and northern Chile.

These last areas were most probably home to most of the inhabitants of the double continent, despite the fact that the areas in question are far from being the most hospitable or cultivable. Especially the highlands of Mexico were prone to repeated catastrophic shortfalls in supply, which some historians have not implausibly linked to a strain of heroic pessimism evident in the Aztec religion. The Inca Empire, whose extraordinary level of organization meant that no one was ever in danger of starvation, was characterized by an optimistic worldview. This empire, which covered some 2 million square kilometers, was the only one in the ancient Americas that warrants this designation in terms of its political organization. The so-called Aztec Empire confined itself to simple hegemony over a number of city-states; its rule may be defined as nothing more than a system of plunder for the benefit of the central power.

The hydraulic engineering projects undertaken in Mexico and by the Chimù, the imperial roads built by the Inca, and the numerous temples and secular buildings erected by various cultures testify to a highly developed technical knowledge, which ranks alongside such remarkable intellectual achievements as the Mayan calendar. Yet it was only Mesoamerican cultures, and not those in the south, that had writing systems, while the American cultures' technological expertise extended as far as the working of precious metals but remained predominantly in the Stone Age. The wheel was known about but not used—after all, there was little use for it in the absence of draft animals.[203]

Although some formal affinities have been identified between these cultures and those of East and Southeast Asia, there is still no proof of any cultural influences crossing the Pacific.[204] Perhaps it is just a question of fundamental elements of ancient Asiatic culture deeply embedded in people's psyches and manifesting themselves in parallel on both sides of the Pacific, as though preprogrammed. Likewise, from the Atlantic Seaboard, the only evidence of foreign incursion are the Viking settlements on Greenland and their expeditions to Newfoundland and Labrador after AD 1000. Yet despite all speculation and fraudulent claims to the contrary, these settlements never developed any further.[205]

The Atlantic Ocean and European Expansion

Transatlantic contacts, which for a long period of history were not even possible, have since their inception made the Atlantic Ocean into one of the world's most important transport routes. Today, some 70 percent of all maritime transport is conducted across the North Atlantic, with much the same applying to air transport and financial transactions.[206] The economic, cultural, and political ties between the countries on both sides of the Atlantic are extremely close, especially between the United States and Western Europe. Yet the appearance of Europeans in Asia was prompted by Atlantic trade, namely, by the precious metals transported from the Spanish Americas, the driving force that enabled Europeans to expand their economic activities worldwide in the first place.

Conversely, five hundred years of transatlantic commerce also serves to show how diffuse and fraught with tension this process was and how inconsistent and contradictory its results were and still are. Atlantic trade certainly involved a growing intensification of contacts over long distances but precisely for that reason by no means entailed a general homogenization and alignment between the parties concerned; to the contrary, the exact opposite was, and is, often the case. No one today would dispute the existence of the phenomenon of Atlantic history, but anyone engaging in this field of study finds him- or herself compelled to fall back on diverse categorical constructs.

Running from north to south, we could, for instance, differentiate between a British, Spanish, and Portuguese Atlantic, but in doing so we would immediately be forced to concede that the British Atlantic was, at least up until 1763, a French Atlantic as well, and that in the seventeenth century the Caribbean, which fell within the Spanish Atlantic area, became the stamping ground for all the European seaborne powers, and finally that both this "internationalized" Caribbean and the Portuguese Atlantic to the south also became an African Atlantic from the seventeenth century on.

Under these circumstances, it may be more profitable to follow David Armitage's cue by distinguishing between different concepts of Atlantic history according to their degree of generality.[207] According to this theory, *circumatlantic history* describes the transnational history of Atlantic trade activities, such as the forced migration of African slaves in connection with the plantation economy. *Transat-*

lantic history, meanwhile, is based on a broad comparison between different countries and empires, such as the Spanish and the British. Finally, *cisatlantic history* consists of applying "Atlantic" historical insights to national or even regional individual cases, in determining the specifically Atlantic character of, say, West African or Irish history or in exploring the Atlantic basis for the rise of the cities of Salvador and Seville or Nantes and Liverpool.

In this regard, then, the discussion of the Atlantic and its history takes on a predominantly metaphorical character, merely becoming a shorthand way of referring to the relations between the countries bordering it. For sure, its maritime traffic and the conditions behind it are important themes in their own right,[208] but these cannot, and could never have been, considered in isolation. Europe as a whole can, thanks to the favorable climatic effect of the Gulf Stream, be regarded as a gift of the Atlantic. And yet the ocean is anything but "the big pond" in the center of some "global village," as it has sometimes, somewhat trivially, been portrayed. Rather, the Atlantic continues to be a formidably hostile environment, to humans and shipping alike. Anyone encountering the ocean for the first time on the far western fringes of Europe experiences a perfectly justifiable sense of terror when confronted with the raw power of the elements. Even nowadays, the most modern, well-equipped vessels can vanish without trace in North Atlantic storms.

Thus, in the light of this originally separating role played by the ocean, we might open the discussion of Atlantic history with something of a rousing fanfare: "in the beginning was Columbus!" Only after Columbus's expeditions did authors such as Gonzalo Fernández de Oviedo, Antonio de Herrera y Tordesillas, Richard Hakluyt, or Samuel Purchas begin to regard the ocean as being no longer a frontier marking the end of the known world but rather a route that would ultimately connect the peoples of the Earth. For America could not be discovered by sailing ships battling full into the teeth of the fierce westerlies that blow across the North Atlantic. This was possible only either in the high latitudes, with a following wind provided by the easterlies that blow from the North Pole—this, indeed, was precisely how the Vikings reached Newfoundland in the year 1000—or in the trade wind zone farther south; this latter region was reached for the first time by the Portuguese and the Castilian Spanish only in the fifteenth century. Christopher Columbus merely completed what was historically and geographically inevitable. Despite marrying into the Portuguese aristocracy, Columbus switched over to enter

Spanish service; after thoroughly exploring the African coast and its offshore Atlantic islands, which had only just been opened up, he embarked on his expedition to find the Indies. As a Genoese, he was tailor-made for discovering the Americas, combining as he did Italian know-how with Iberian commercial interest and backing. This combination played a decisive role in setting in train the era of European expansion.[209]

But the first place to be affected by European expansion was, as we have seen, the West African coast.[210] The initial driving force was Iberian expansion, as the powers on the Iberian Peninsula sought to continue the Reconquista against the Muslims on the African coast facing them. As early as 1291, the rulers of Aragon and Castile had demarcated their North African spheres of influence. The Portuguese arrived on the scene in 1415 with their conquest of Ceuta. Alongside the struggle against the old adversary of Christianity and the renown and material spoils that would flow from this, economic interests also played a significant role, above all access to gold from Guinea—important as a metal for coinage—that was brought to the North African coast across the Sahara. To effectively outflank the Muslims of North Africa by landing on the West African coast was therefore a strategically very promising move, in both economic and political terms. The first attested mention of the distant goal of "India"—which initially in all likelihood denoted Christian Ethiopia—appears only toward the end of the fifteenth century.

Between 1415 and 1433, the Portuguese dispatched at least fifteen expeditions southward before they finally managed to overcome the nautical and psychological barrier of Cape Bojador. It turned out that the territory beyond this point was by no means uninhabitable, as had been feared. After the first black African slaves fell into Portuguese hands in the 1440s in the region around Senegal, this new "commodity" alone made the West Africa voyage worth the effort and attractive to investors. Consequently, travels to West Africa were continued, with occasional interruptions occasioned by political considerations. The construction of the fortress of El Mina on the "Gold Coast" in 1481 represented the attainment of an economic goal, as the two speaking names attest. Now the aim was to press on to India. In 1482, first contact was made with the Kingdom of Kongo, an encounter that would have momentous consequences, though corresponding efforts to establish relations with the Kingdom of Benin were unsuccessful. Finally, in

1487–1488, Portuguese navigators rounded the Cape of Good Hope. After a decade's pause, which is shrouded in mystery, in 1498 Vasco da Gama landed on the coast of western India, which was to form the focal point of little Portugal's trading interests for the next century—much to the advantage of its Castilian rivals.

By 1312, Genoese sailors had rediscovered the Canary Islands, which had been known about since antiquity. Situated north of Cape Bojador, the islands soon became a bone of contention between various powers, first and foremost Castile and Portugal. Time and again, however, foreign powers tried and failed to overrun them; their aboriginal inhabitants, the Stone Age civilization of the Guanches, were adept at defending their territory. In the first half of the fifteenth century, Madeira and the Azores were discovered by chance by Portuguese expeditions that it is thought had been blown off course and were subsequently settled by Portugal. The Cape Verde Islands were likewise discovered during Portuguese voyages to West Africa in 1456.

Yet not only in the Canaries but on the West African mainland as well, the Portuguese had to contend with rivals from various countries, primarily Castile, which also had easy access to the Atlantic. Because the Portuguese were alone in responding to the pope's call for a crusade after the Ottoman conquest of Constantinople in 1453, in 1455–1456, under the program of spreading the Catholic faith, they were able to secure from the pope a monopoly on expeditions to Africa and on the subjugation and enslavement of Muslims and heathens, which effectively legitimized the country's claims on Africa. Even so, Portugal still had to assert this claim against its rival Castile, which it largely succeeded in doing in the Treaty of Alcáçovas in 1479, following a brief conflict over who should succeed Henry IV on the throne of Castile. In return for recognition of her accession to the throne, Isabella of Castile agreed to Portugal's monopoly on African and Atlantic exploration south of Cape Bojador, at a latitude of 26° north. Accordingly, the Canary Islands, which lay to the north of this latitude, became Spanish and by the turn of the century had been conquered by Castile, with far-reaching consequences.

The Atlantic islands of Madeira and the Azores, the Canaries and the Cape Verde Islands, along with São Tomé and Principe in the Gulf of Guinea proved to be—just as Iceland had for the Vikings—important jumping-off points between the worlds on the two sides of the ocean. The production of cane sugar on plantations was transferred from Palestine via Cyprus, Sicily, and southern Spain to these islands and eventually from there to Brazil, giving rise "along the way" to the trade in African slaves. Also, it was on the Canaries that the Spanish "reconquest" from the Muslims was transformed for the first time into the conquest of heathens—that is, this territory became the proving ground for the process by which the Spanish would soon conquer the Americas.[211] Moreover, the Canaries were situated in the zone of the transatlantic trade winds, meaning that Columbus was able to embark from here and sail effortlessly westward with a steady following wind.

The first Portuguese voyages to Africa were undertaken in vessels that were more like boats than oceangoing ships, which hugged the shoreline in shallow coastal waters. However, by the mid-fifteenth century, a new type of ship, the caravel, had become well established. These were small vessels with a straight keel and a sternpost rudder, and their combination of square sails on the foremast and mainmast and lateen sails on the mizzenmast made them more maneuverable than any ships hitherto. Up to the eighteenth century, all European sailing ships were simply enlarged and improved variants of this basic type, including the Portuguese *nau* and carrack, the Spanish galleons, the Dutch *fluyt,* and the British frigate and East Indiaman. The most radical improvement was the introduction of the practical lug sail in place of the lateen sail on the mizzenmast in the mid-eighteenth century. Such vessels enabled seafarers to break free from the coastal navigation that up till then had been the norm and to venture onto the high seas—all the more so now that they were also equipped with new navigational aids, such as the magnetic compass, instruments for determining their latitude, and mathematical tables. Even so, determining a ship's longitude accurately became possible only in the eighteenth century with the invention of the marine chronometer; by this time, voyages out into the Atlantic, especially into uncharted waters, had rendered obsolete the so-called *portolan* charts that had been useful for navigation in the Mediterranean.[212]

Certainly, the Portuguese and the Castilians benefited greatly from the advances made in shipbuilding and navigation by the Catalans and above all the Italians, even though the precise contribution made by each is impossible to evaluate. But commencing with the loss of the crusader states in the thirteenth century, and resuming after the establishment of Ottoman hegemony over the eastern

Mediterranean in the fifteenth, merchants from the leading Italian cities, in particular Genoa, turned toward the Atlantic, clearly in an attempt to discover a sea route to the Indies. Not that the European trade with the Indies would have been curtailed by the new Islamic powers, but even so it became a riskier enterprise, with costs increasing thanks to the levying of concession taxes, and Venice exercising even greater control than before. Furthermore, Genoa lost its slave market on the Black Sea and its colonies in the Aegean. This explains the presence of Italian merchants and seafarers, especially the Genoese, on the Iberian Peninsula at this time and the prominent role they played in the voyages of discovery. Alongside seafaring skills and capital, they also were well versed in the application of basic colonization techniques, from their experience in the Mediterranean—not just plantation management and the slave trade but also the financing of discoveries and conquests through limited liability companies, plus the funding of colonial administration by means of open-ended joint-stock companies. These basic models still remained in force during the Age of Imperialism. It is no coincidence, for instance, that America was discovered by a Genoese adventurer (Columbus) and bears the name of a Florentine seafarer (Amerigo Vespucci).

However, Columbus's idea of circumventing the Portuguese monopoly on Africa by looking for a sea route to the west was not a new one—in fact, it was just as familiar as the navigational error that lay at the heart of his venture. For, just like the Florentine scholar Paolo dal Pozzo Toscanelli, Columbus had underestimated the circumference of the Earth and so expected to encounter China at the point where he actually—to his great fortune—ran across the New World. Nevertheless, Columbus still succeeded in getting his plan approved in Spain, having presented it in vain in Portugal, England, and France, and then executing it thanks to his remarkable seafaring abilities. Although the Castilian experts had the same well-founded misgivings as the Portuguese, the rulers of Spain, Ferdinand and Isabella, now unburdened of the responsibility for the Reconquista following their capture of Granada in 1492, decided to seize the opportunity of preempting their Portuguese rivals' attempts to discover the passage to the Indies, and at relatively little cost. On October 12, 1492, Columbus landed on a small offshore island of the New World and proceeded to found a colony on the island of Hispaniola (present-day Haiti). Yet in doing so, he had ventured south of the line established by the 1479 Treaty of Alcáçovas, which threatened to stir up conflict with Portugal.

Accordingly, taking their cue from the Portuguese, the Spanish kings simply prevailed upon Pope Alexander VI, who was well disposed toward them, to transfer the newly discovered lands, together with the duty to establish missions there, to Spanish control and to set a line of longitude 100 nautical miles west of the Azores as the western limit of Portugal's monopoly. Taking this de facto demarcation as the basis for negotiation, the Treaty of Tordesillas of 1494 between Spain and Portugal established a new line farther west,[213] at a longitude of 46° 37' west. This meridian ran right through the middle of Brazil, which was discovered in 1500, after the Portuguese Indies fleet had sailed far to the west in order to exploit favorable westerly winds and currents (the so-called *volta do mar*). Thereafter, the whole country was ceded to Portugal.

In three further voyages of discovery up to 1504, Columbus explored the Caribbean, the coast of Central America, and the mouth of the Orinoco. To the last, he remained convinced that he was exploring the East Indies. Only the publication in this same period of the Florentine seafarer Amerigo Vespucci's hugely successful account of his voyage along the coast of Brazil in Portuguese service led to the association of this territory with a completely new world (in the term *Mundus novus*). Subsequently, maps and globes produced by the German cosmographers Matthias Ringmann and Martin Waldseemüller gave these lands the newly coined designation "America."

Columbus and the Spanish crown may originally have had a system of trading bases in mind, like those that the Portuguese established in Africa and around the Indian Ocean. But because the adventurer failed as an administrator and the first settlements proved unviable, the crown renounced his monopoly and opened up further expansion to private initiatives, albeit under the sovereignty of the crown. Each contract *(capitulación)* with a "contractor" stipulated the contractor's rights and responsibilities. He was responsible for raising the capital and the workforce. Because the latter received no salary but were recruited on a commission basis, the pressure to succeed was intense, especially in the matter of plundering, with corresponding consequences for the opposing side. As such, alongside providers of trading capital and seafarers, the venture attracted an increasing number of people who saw it as a way of improving their social status, not least the minor Spanish aristocracy *(hidalgos),* who were steeped in the tradition of the Reconquista and who had also served the crown during the Italian wars.[214] And since the Amerindian labor force had, meanwhile, become a major economic factor, discovery swiftly morphed into conquest.[215]

Following exploration of the northern and eastern coasts of South America in 1499–1506, the period from 1509 on saw the occupation of the Greater Antilles, the northern coast of Colombia, and Panama. In 1519–1522, Hernán Cortés, operating out of Cuba, overran the Aztec Empire,[216] which was followed by Francisco Pizarro's conquest, embarking from Panama, of the Inca Empire in 1532–1534.[217] From these two new centers, the Spanish proceeded to overrun the whole of the Cordillera by the mid-sixteenth century. However, in the south, the Spanish conquest foundered on the opposition of the Araucanian Indians, while expeditions to the south of North America and to the South American lowlands (including a voyage down the Amazon) indicated that these regions were not worth conquering. The southwest of North America was occupied only in the seventeenth and eighteenth centuries, when English and Russian competitors began to appear there. Yet it was not only people beyond the borders of Spanish America, whose conquest would have proved too onerous when weighed against the expected benefit, who remained independent for a long time. At first, "islands" of independence also existed within the Spanish-controlled areas, such as the Inca empire of Vilcabamba, finally destroyed in 1572, and the sovereign territory of the Itzá of Petén, with its capital on an island in Lake Petén, which was finally overrun only in 1697.[218] The Spanish were concerned to suppress these territories because of the influence that these "islands" exerted on discontented subjects within their realm.

In the first half of the sixteenth century, the Spanish and the Portuguese but also the English and above all the French, whose king Francis I, as a sworn enemy of the Holy Roman emperor Charles V, expressly set out to challenge the Iberian monopoly, explored the Eastern Seaboard of North America. However, they soon lost interest when these voyages yielded neither much in the way of booty nor a passage through to the Indies. Yet the presence of French settlements in Brazil prompted Portugal to assert its formal control over the region by 1551.[219] However, the first French and English settlements in North America were founded only in the early seventeenth century.

Just as the Reconquista served as a model for the Spanish conquest of the Americas, so the British colonization of Ireland laid down a template for their colonists in North America. It is no coincidence that the foremost European colonial powers of the early modern period were those that had already had some experience of conquest and colonization in the Middle Ages. However greatly their colonial empires on the far side of the Atlantic may have differed from one another, they were all underpinned by the self-evident intention of transplanting the world that they had already imposed on various territories on European soil to the New World and founding a series of new Europes on the far side of the ocean. This urge still shines through unmistakeably in the many place and country names in the New World that were taken over from the Old or at least allude to such places: Guadeloupe and Santiago, Athens and Rome, Nieuw Amsterdam and New York, New Extremadura (Chile) and New Hampshire.

The Biological Exchange and Its Consequences

No sooner had Columbus set foot in the New World than a momentous process of biological exchange was set in motion, which Alfred W. Crosby has justly dubbed the "Columbian exchange,"[220] even though this process was only in part intentionally initiated by the Genoese explorer and his successors. In any event, there is no evidence to suggest that an exchange of either plants and animals or of people took place at any earlier period in recorded history. Now, though, Europeans brought with them across the Atlantic from their homelands all the familiar cultivated plants and domestic animals they considered essential for living. These included not only wheat and other kinds of cereal, vegetables and fruit trees, flowers and other ornamental plants, but also, coincidentally, all manner of weeds. While it is true that northeastern North America, an area of particularly intensive exchange, still retained its famous richness of species of native American flora—even here, imported Old World species still accounted for only some 18 percent of the total—nevertheless these later species tended to predominate in terms of the sheer biomass of plant material grown.

Although European agriculture found itself in competition with the no less highly developed cultivation techniques of the indigenous peoples of the Americas, it still managed to gain the upper hand. The result was the spread of farming landscapes on the European pattern, with farmsteads and major landowners, and the growth of villages and towns of a Mediterranean or Western European type. In North America, the fence became a central symbol of a newly introduced economic system, which was based on private property, an anomaly in cultural–historical terms. Ultimately, in the nineteenth and twentieth centuries, the savanna (prairie) lands of both North and South America were transformed into the breadbaskets of the global economy.

The domestic animals that were likewise imported from Europe had virtually no competition in the Americas. As early as 1493, horses, cattle, pigs, sheep, goats, and chickens were taken to Hispaniola, with European dogs and cats, and rats and mice following on shortly afterward. Though the importance of horses and bloodhounds for the Spanish conquest of the Americas is well known, less familiar is the role played by the black pigs the Spanish brought with them, which the conquistadors drove along in herds, as a constant source of food during their campaigns. Many of these pigs escaped into the wild and rapidly spread. Similarly, herds of wild cattle and horses also found it easy to forage off the land. Up until then, the Amerindians had scarcely known domestic animals and consumed animal protein only in very limited quantities. However, they soon learned to exploit this new source of food. The early Spanish commentator Juan Ginés de Sepúlveda was already claiming that the introduction of iron, domestic animals, and cultivated crops was worth more than everything that the Spanish had plundered from the indigenous population.[221] Horse trading with the Spanish in North and South America saw the rise of totally new forms of Indian culture, namely, as mounted big-game hunters or livestock herders, who thrived independently until the campaigns of conquest conducted by white settlers in the United States, Argentina, and Chile in the late nineteenth century. The North American Plains Indians, among whom the horse became widespread in the seventeenth and eighteenth centuries, from the southern prairies right up to Saskatchewan, often abandoned a sedentary mode of existence in favor of a life as mounted nomadic hunters. The Indian mounted warriors so familiar from adventure stories and movies were therefore already a product of creative transatlantic exchange.

The adoption of new crops and animals, and especially the imposition of a new economic and cultural mode of existence, is a question of the cultural power differential between the groups involved, except in cases where the advantages of an innovation are self-evident and meet an equally obvious need. Crops that resemble already existing ones but have certain clear advantages over them—such as the new cereal maize or, in Africa, the manioc root as compared with the yam root—are more readily adopted than completely new and unfamiliar plants, such as the potato when it was first introduced to Europe. To be sure, the sedentary farming cultures of the Americas had a wide range of new crops to offer—for example, corn (maize), potatoes, sweet potatoes, manioc, American bean varieties, peanuts, tomatoes, American squashes, peppers, cocoa, tobacco, and many others—without which Europe and the rest of the world would now be unable to feed themselves.[222] Yet their adoption was extremely patchy, depending on the individual plant and the host community.

Today, corn is grown in warmer regions throughout the world. It fills the ecological niche between wheat and rice—that is, it thrives in places that are too damp for wheat yet too dry for rice. Its yield per hectare is double or triple that of any other type of cereal and, in terms of calorific value, 50 to 100 percent greater than that of African millet varieties. Moreover, it grows quickly and needs far less cultivation than rice. Yet it still offers a broad spectrum of carbohydrates and fats, with 75 percent more calories than the same weight of wheat. However, if it is the only staple food in a diet, it does give rise to the vitamin deficiency disease pellagra. As early as 1493, Columbus brought maize back to Europe. In the marginal regions of the Mediterranean, where the summers are wet, it found ideal growing conditions and so was quickly adopted in the northern areas of Portugal, Spain, and Italy. Subsequently, it was also grown in the Balkans, which became something of a promised land for all kinds of American food crops, including peppers. The Ottoman Empire played a role in their spread (though this is still only poorly understood), as witness the fact that in many European languages, maize is known as "Turkish corn." Maize porridge became popular as a peasant staple in Italy (as polenta) in the seventeenth century and in Romania (as *mamaliga*) in the eighteenth. Nowadays, maize is widespread throughout Europe but, in contrast to other parts of the world, contributes to human nutrition only in an indirect way, namely, as animal (poultry, cattle, and pig) feed.

In the sixteenth century, the Portuguese took maize, peanuts, sweet potatoes, manioc, chilis, and several other American crops with them to China and Southeast Asia. Since then, chilis have given many Asiatic cuisines their "typical" spiciness. Maize and sweet potatoes became an important staple for peasants in China in the seventeenth and eighteenth centuries. Today, some 37 percent of China's total foodstuffs derive from crops of American origin, and 80 percent of all the world's sweet potatoes are grown there. The sweet potato grows well on terrain that has too steep a gradient, is too dry, or lacks the nutrients necessary for rice cultivation and yet with the minimum of tending still produces three to four times the yield of rice per hectare. It is also easy to clean and to prepare and is rich in both carbohydrates and vitamins. It is probable that China's population explosion only became possible through this improved nutrition situation.[223] At the beginning of the seventeenth century, potatoes and sweet potatoes reached Japan, apparently from Indonesia. In 1772, the sweet potato saved the population of the Japanese island of Honshu from starvation, after locusts had devastated the rice harvest.[224]

Alongside China, Southeast African countries are now the world's largest producers of maize. As a vital food crop and provider of calorific value, maize plays an even more key role in these countries than it does in Mexico and Guatemala. However, it seems only to have arrived in southern and eastern Africa at a relatively late date, in all likelihood not before the nineteenth century. By contrast, the Portuguese introduced it to the Atlantic regions of Africa as early as the sixteenth century. By 1550, it was already the staple crop on the Cape Verde Islands and São Tomé. In the seventeenth century, the cultivation of millet and rice declined in West Africa in favor of maize. Whereas millet ripens slowly, in freshly cleared forest regions it is often possible to grow two crops of maize annually. The "white man's corn," as maize is known by both the Mandé and the Bakongo, has long been integrated into West African culture and ritual: for example, as the totem of an Akan group, as an impressed pattern on Yoruba earthenware, and as the epitome of Ashanti power in the eighteenth century.[225]

Manioc or cassava was just as important a Portuguese import to Africa, where it has likewise become one of the key sources of nutrition. It in turn yields 150 percent more calories than maize and has several advantages over the indigenous African staple yam root, which was taken to America by slaves: it thrives on poor, arid soils whatever the elevation above sea level; it is resistant to pests and flooding; and despite all this it still produces greater yields than any other tropical plant. In addition, mature roots can be left in the ground for up to four years. Manioc, like maize, was quick to make an appearance in Atlantic Africa, being cultivated in the south of the Congo basin even before the first Europeans were seen there. According to African tradition, the founding of the Kingdom of Kuba in the sixteenth and seventeenth centuries was closely bound up with the introduction of maize, manioc, beans, and tobacco to the region.[226] It may be that in certain parts of Africa, population growth and the establishment of empires—and hence, indirectly, also the expansion of the slave trade—became possible only through the improved nutrition that came from the imported American crops.

American crops that produced vegetable fats also played a vital role in this biological exchange, such as the peanut in Africa, India, and China or the hardy sunflower, which was extensively grown from the nineteenth century on in Russia not as an ornamental but for its oil and which is now taking on a more significant role once more in other parts of the world, not least in Africa.[227] The most important American food crop in northern Europe, the potato, experienced a similarly gradual adoption, being regarded with suspicion thanks to its unfamiliarity and for a long time grown only as a garden ornamental.[228] And yet the potato was capable of producing up to four times the yield per hectare of the principal European cereal variety, rye, and in contrast to maize contained almost all the nutrients that the human body needs. To be sure, cultivating potatoes was a labor-intensive business and presumed the existence of a plentiful and poor population, but it was also ideally suited to feeding such a population. As a new plant, it was not subject to any traditional taxes, such as the tithe given to the church. Furthermore, the regular hoeing of the soil to get rid of weeds supplanted the old practice of plowing fallow land, so contributing to the dissolution of the traditional open-field system. In sum, potatoes were the ideal staple crop for a growing population in the European Age of Industrialization. The first record of potatoes being eaten comes from Seville in 1573. From the seventeenth century on, it became the staple foodstuff of Ireland and the western Alpine region. In other parts of Europe, it became popular only in the late eighteenth century, in part at the instigation of the state authorities or as a result of the crisis brought about by failure of the cereal harvest in the years 1771–1774.

Admittedly, America was also responsible for introducing new weeds. For example, over time the South American water hyacinth *(Eichhornia crassipes)* has choked up lakes and marshes across large parts of Africa with dense mats of vegetation that deprive the indigenous fauna there of oxygen.[229] Plants that have become the source of new drugs also hailed from the New World. A modern commercial pick-me-up drink claims to combine the stimulating effects of the Bolivian coca leaf with that of the African kola nut but in truth contains neither. Yet the very first success for an American plant of this type was the narcotic tobacco, which Europeans came to enjoy in the form of cigars in South and Central America and in pipes in North America. Its botanical designation *Nicotiana* comes from the French diplomat Jean Nicot, who was responsible for popularizing tobacco in the mid-sixteenth century. By 1600, tobacco was well known throughout Europe and Asia. Africa quickly caught up, too, with tobacco becoming one of the most sought-after import goods traded by European merchants from the seventeenth century on. As a recreational drug, it became widespread in Europe around the same time: annual per capita consumption in England increased from 0.02 pounds in 1630 to 2.3 pounds in 1700, while in the Netherlands, where an industry employing fifteen thousand people manufactured clay pipes in Gouda, similar statistics were recorded. Beneficial properties were ascribed to tobacco but so, from early on, were harmful effects. King James I of England personally panned a pamphlet *(A Counterblaste to Tobacco)* against "this precious stinke," and the list of smoking bans imposed in all major countries of the world and many smaller ones as well from 1604 on is impressively long. However, these were all in vain, not least due to the double standards displayed by states (still in evidence today), which at the same time as enacting bans also set up tobacco monopolies or at least were content (as indeed they still are) to profit from taxation levied on the commodity. By 1988, it was estimated that some 5,270 billion cigarettes, first introduced in 1845, had been smoked.

As a whole, though, the exchange of plants and animals may be said to have benefited both the parties concerned and humanity as a whole. On the level of microorganisms, admittedly, the introduction of bacteria and viruses into the New World had catastrophic effects on the indigenous population. As a result of their isolation hitherto, Native Americans had no immunity against the vectors of diseases of Eurasian and later African origin. Consequently, they perished en masse not only from epidemics such as smallpox but also of relatively harmless infection like the flu. Archaeological finds have demonstrated that North American Indians suffered from many illnesses even prior to contact with Europeans; these included arthritis and tuberculosis, as well as nutritional deficiency diseases brought on by an unvaried diet, especially of maize, plus tooth abrasion caused by sand from the stones they used to mill grain and other sundry ailments. Even so, North America was generally a much healthier place than the Old World, not least because it was free from pandemics. Nevertheless, the life expectancy of twenty-five to thirty was no higher than in Europe, with the population being decimated by infant mortality, women's deaths during pregnancy and childbirth, and war. Estimates of the total population of North America prior to 1492 vary between one and eighteen million, though the general consensus is that there were around two million. Taking both parts of the continent together, figures of between eight and a hundred million have been cited, though an estimate of between forty and fifty million seems plausible.[230]

Europeans and Africans introduced smallpox, measles, influenza, bubonic plague, diphtheria, typhoid, scarlet fever, trachoma, whooping cough, chicken pox, malaria, and yellow fever to the New World. From 1520 to 1600, there is evidence of at least seventeen major epidemics sweeping the Americas. In 1518, the first smallpox epidemic killed a third to a half of the inhabitants of Hispaniola or, in any event, those who had not succumbed to the flu contagion that Columbus brought with him in 1493. This same smallpox outbreak went on to decimate the Aztec defenders of Tenochtitlán and also affected South America and the south of North America, before any Europeans had even visited that region. And the Inca ruler Huayna Capac is believed to have died of smallpox in 1525. In 1530, a reliable eyewitness reckoned that the population of Hispaniola had shrunk from 500,000 to just 20,000. Amerindians disappeared altogether from some islands of the West Indies, while in central Mexico and Peru, their numbers are thought to have declined by up to 95 percent. At the low-water mark of 1650, only around four million indigenous people were living in Spanish America, as compared with thirty to forty million in 1492.[231]

The population losses in the region occupied by the Pueblo culture of the North American Southwest and the Mississippi civilization of the Southeast are believed to have been so great that the whole societal structure of the latter collapsed and was replaced by new groupings of survivors. In 1540, the conquistador Hernando de Soto came across abandoned and overgrown cities in the area now covered by the state of South Carolina. However, the first epidemic hit the northern Atlantic coast of America only in 1616–1618, wiping out in short order around 90 percent of the Massachusett and Wampanoag peoples. The area around the Great Lakes was affected in 1633; in 1639–1640 a smallpox epidemic there reduced the twenty-one thousand population of Huron Indians by about half.

The only "return gift" of this kind from the New World to the Old was a new, aggressive form of syphilis,[232] which was first taken back to Europe by Columbus's crews and spread further by Europeans to Africa. The resistance of Africans to certain infections from Europe appears likewise to have been only limited, despite the fact that it never suffered the same kind of catastrophic outbreak as the Americas. Tuberculosis and bacterial pleurisy, possibly along with the plague as well, were completely unknown to Africans. In addition, they were afflicted by new, aggressive forms of various diseases, such as smallpox and syphilis. Amerindians and Africans alike were fully aware that some epidemics were the result of white men's "magic." Yet deliberate biological warfare seems to have been practiced only rarely; one exception was the decision by the British general Jeffery Amherst and Colonel Henry Bouquet to give smallpox-infected blankets to the native population in 1763, during the French and Indian War.[233]

The Spanish Atlantic

Theoretically speaking, the Spanish Atlantic was not a colonial empire but rather an arrangement of subsidiary territories of the Castilian monarchy, all endowed with equal rights, just like Aragon or Naples.[234] In Spain's American possessions, the Indian inhabitants and the Spanish *peninsulares* alike were treated as free subjects of the crown—hence the plans for a cisatlantic federation of kingdoms under the umbrella of Spanish imperial sovereignty; these were drawn up in the eighteenth century but were already being hinted at by the sixteenth-century bishop Bartolomé de las Casas. However, the harsh reality of colonialism looked somewhat different. The linchpin of Spain's American empire was the flota, which once a year brought over a consignment of Spanish manufactures for Mexico and Peru and collected the most valuable of all the colonial raw materials: silver from northern Mexico and Bolivia.[235] Not least, Spain's foreign policy, which projected the country as a major power in Europe, made this type of exploitative relationship toward its colonies a necessity. Spain's overseas possessions were required to turn a profit for the mother country and otherwise support themselves. Yet in practice this meant that not just the needs of the Spanish crown but also those of the Spanish inhabitants of the New World could be met only at the cost of the indigenous peoples. For the crown required money, and the conquistadors and settlers aspired to become rich and live as colonial masters; at best, some of them were urban artisans, but there was no white peasant class in Spanish America.

The Spanish monarch was represented by viceroys in Mexico and Lima (and also in Bogotá from 1739 and in Buenos Aires from 1776). At the same time, these viceroys were de facto governors of the two largest and most important provinces of Mexico and Peru. The thirty to forty *gobernadores* were directly answerable to the Supreme Royal Council of the Indies in Spain, in the same way as the nominal governor of Milan was subject to the Italian council. Even so, several of the governors were ranked higher than others, because like the viceroys they also presided over one of the ten collegial supreme courts *(audiencias)* and/or were captains-general of a military district. The financial authorities *(cajas reales)* in the most important towns remained largely outside of this agglomeration of administrative, judicial, and military responsibilities, as did the church with its five archbishoprics and its thirty to forty bishoprics.

Nevertheless, the governors were conduits of the royal patronage that made the church into another pillar of the Spanish system of rule. The crown received the tithe paid to the church and appointed incumbents to ecclesiastical livings, which it had established and endowed. In addition, it financed and controlled the Indian missions—run by monastic orders, primarily the Franciscans and the Dominicans but later the Jesuits, too—which existed as independent entities alongside the normal church hierarchy. Up to the end of the colonial period there was fierce debate over whether well-established Indian parishes *(doctrinas)* should be transferred from the control of monastic orders to that of ordinary parish priests. But whatever the outcome, the leadership was always Spanish, as right up to the end mestizos and *indios* were ordained as priests only in exceptional circumstances.

Mexico's early Franciscan missionaries had come to the New World imbued with the utopian notion of living alongside the indigenous people in their natural simplicity and innocence and thereby realizing the millennial advent of the kingdom of God on Earth, the apotheosis of the Christian life.[236] Priests from the native elite were also seen as an integral part of this plan. But when it transpired that the indigenous people were by no means putty in the hands of the missionaries but rather continued to practice their old religion under the veneer of Christianity and skilfully learned to incorporate Christian elements into this observance, a severe backlash ensued. From the *junta magna* of 1568 on, the church in the Americas was required to be solely Spanish-led. Linguistic concessions were ascribed to the intellectual incapacity of the natives to learn Spanish and not intended as concessions to their culture. In the theoretical groundwork of the *missiones,* laid down in 1588 by the Jesuit José de Acosta, the inferiority of the indigenous peoples was taken as obvious. Even their participation in the Eucharist was contested. The high-minded ideals of the early days were discarded.

Tellingly, utopian ideals endured and took root only when they were designed to be enacted without the involvement of the natives, namely, in Puritan New England. Today, the Puritans' originally religious concept of a better world on the far side of the ocean is returning across the Atlantic to the Old World in secular guise, that is, in the form of economic and political evangelizing for the American model.

In contrast to the Franciscans, the Dominicans, particularly Bartolomé de las Casas (1474–1566), took issue with Spain's policy toward the native peoples,[237] which was to carry out campaigns of conquest legitimized by the pope's sanction to establish missions and which subjected those whom it conquered to a brutal regime of exploitation, even after the abolition of Indian slavery (1530–1542). The distribution of Native American labor *(repartimiento)* to Spanish settlers, which came into force in 1503, was transformed, along the lines of the Reconquista, into the *encomienda,* namely, the forcible assignment of native workers, who had to provide hard labor and other services to their Spanish lords *(encomenderos)* in return for food and subsistence pay, accommodation, and instruction in the Christian faith.[238] Until the catastrophic results of the population decline became apparent, this labor force did not have to be regarded as an investment that needed some looking after, like regular slaves, because they were wholly expendable and replaceable. This attitude brought horrific consequences.

Nevertheless, attempts by the Dominicans to set up more peaceful missions and alternative methods of settlement were not particularly successful either. Yet their doctrine of the legal–political independence of Indian communities, formulated by Francisco de Vitoria (c. 1492–1546) in Salamanca and energetically promulgated by Bartolomé de las Casas, became the basis of modern European international law. In addition, this order did succeed first in securing a papal bull in 1537, which had as its subject the vital recognition that Indians were rational beings capable of being converted to Christianity, and second in persuading the Spanish crown to modify the encomienda in 1542–1549. Henceforth, this would contain no provision for Spanish settlers to have direct tenure of Indian labor but instead simply required that Indians become tribute-paying vassals of the king through the encomendero—or at least insofar as this was possible in practice.

The important encomienda of the Maya community of Huehuetenango contained more than three thousand inhabitants in 1530, but by 1549 this number had fallen to just five hundred. The goods they produced in 1530 amounted to a total of 800 pieces of woven cotton cloth, 2,000 different items of clothing, and 400 mats, plus unspecified amounts of maize, beans, and other crops and 2,268 turkeys. In addition, it supplied a constant labor force of forty men to work twenty-day shifts in the fields, along with 120 to 200 for the gold mines and thirty women as cooks; this workforce contributed between 44,000 and 82,800 working days per year, even without taking into account the eighty male and forty female slaves. The mines produced an annual yield of 9,000 pesos, while agriculture generated 3,000. Following the crown reforms, the output of this community in 1549 was just 300 pieces of cloth and—now documented precisely—22.5 bushels of maize, 7.5 bushels of beans, a hundred loads each of salt and chilis, twelve dozen chickens, and finally six natives as servants.[239]

The crown also had a vested political interest in letting the encomienda wither on the vine, because the last thing it wanted was for a new class of feudal lords to develop in the Americas. As a result, the encomienda was never associated with the granting of land rights and was endowed for more than a generation only in exceptional circumstances. This factor really did, then, give it a built-in obsolescence, and over time it disappeared. The conquistadors were never allowed to establish themselves as the lords of a region but were promptly replaced by royal officials. The political order of Spanish America was, like many colonial systems of rule in the New World, intended to achieve certain political objectives that could not be realized in the motherland. There thus developed a kind of bureaucratic absolutism, which was based on cooperation with local oligarchies, while the development of a feudal structure or a system of estates in the old European tradition was just as vigorously suppressed as the autonomy of the church.[240] Tellingly, the states that inherited the legacy of this system after independence were characterized by central governments that tried to keep a firm grip on power but

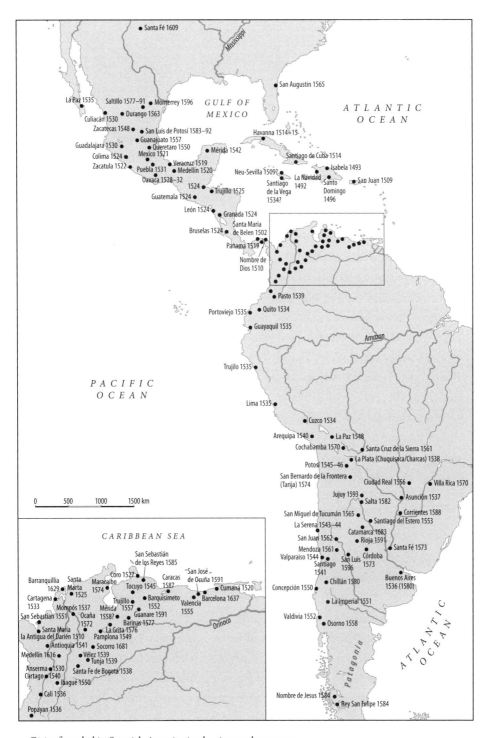

Cities founded in Spanish America in the sixteenth century

with only weak instruments at their disposal and with little ability to assert themselves against local leaders.

At the level below the *gobiernos,* the Spanish crown made the urban-centered administrative division of the country—the royal system known as the *villa y tierra,* which they had better experiences with in Spain than with any system based on aristocratic or ecclesiastical ownership of land—the exclusive organizational principle of the New World. The few hundred thousand Spanish men and women, who by the seventeenth century had emigrated from the not exactly overpopulated motherland to the Americas and remained there,[241] inhabited the two hundred to three hundred towns that the Spanish had founded by that stage.

Even before a statute of 1573 laid down the basic ground plan of Spanish New World cities as a chessboard pattern, many had already adopted this arrangement.[242] While emigration in the eighteenth century remained negligible, the natural growth in population in the same period was considerable. Another factor that came into play was the necessity of securing the empire against competitors; thus, after a further wave of city foundations, their total number increased to over a thousand. As in the motherland, they were governed by a town council *(cabildo)* under the supervision of a royal *corregidor.* The council comprised *alcaldes* (municipal magistrates), *regidores* (councillors), and *alguaciles* (sheriffs), and all of these offices became hereditary over time. Likewise, the encomenderos and later the major landowners too were, in common with all New World Spaniards, citizens *(vecinos)* of some urban settlement.

Policy toward the Indians

This organizational principle was also meant to apply to the indigenous people; the idea was that this would make it easier to Christianize and control them. However, in central Mexico, this arrangement was at variance with the traditional division of the country into city-states *(altepetl)* controlled by the monarchy and/or the aristocracy. The center of each of these regions now became a Spanish *cabecera* (head municipality), while the outlying settlements became *sujetos* of this central authority. Alongside a *gobernador,* who could be appointed or deposed at will, these towns also had a Spanish-style cabildo. In practice, though, the rules of the game tacitly remained those that had held sway before, with members of

Lima—the Quechua name for the Spanish settlement of Ciudad de los Reyes—was founded by the conquistador Francisco Pizarro in 1535 as the capital of the newly conquered territory of Peru, with its location deliberately chosen to give easy access to the sea. The center of the city still displays the classic checkerboard ground plan common to all Spanish colonial towns. Lots owned by individual citizens could comprise parts of a city block or even the entire block. The cathedral and the governor's palace were situated on the central plaza. The fact that even the small section of the city shown here contains four further churches indicates the omnipresence of the church in such settlements. (Archivo General de Indias, Seville)

the ancestral ruling dynasties often being appointed as governors, at least at the beginning of Spanish rule. All in all, what emerged was a clever system of indirect rule by the Spanish minority over the Amerindian majority. Not infrequently, indigenous communities had successfully resisted exploitation by their encomenderos. But the royal *corregidores de Indios* that were universally put in place as supervisors instead of the encomenderos were often no better, as their income was small and their period in office only limited.

The Spanish also imposed this system on the Maya, albeit with the difference that, due to the more decentralized form of settlement there and the continuing existence of independent regions, the population fluctuated constantly and uncontrollably; this also proved to be another way of resisting the colonial power. The Spanish attempted to counter this with the help of the missionaries by setting up the so-called *congregación* system, which consisted of subsuming dispersed settlements under central communities. In Peru, where dispersed settlements were widespread, this policy was instituted on a grand scale in the 1570s and 1580s by the viceroy Francisco de Toledo. Some 1.5 million indigenous people were forcibly resettled into around six hundred *reducciones*—cities and parishes under Spanish jurisdiction. In the process, traditional ethnic groupings were often destroyed, with new ones taking their place in the settlements. The satellite towns around Spanish urban centers, such as El Cercado outside Lima, where Indian manual workers and servants lived, were organized as separate parishes, not unlike the "townships" in twentieth-century South Africa; they were regarded as places where Hispanicization of the Indians had been particularly successful.

The designations "Indios" or "Indians," which were coined when the Spanish first began exploring the region, derived from Columbus's error in believing that he had landed in the East Indies. Despite this, they quickly became convenient catch-all terms used by the new rulers for the aboriginal inhabitants of the region and proved useful for leveling them all into one amorphous mass. Although the previous ethnic, linguistic, and cultural differences between the various indigenous peoples did not disappear, their importance declined. Conversely, colonial rule led not only to far-reaching upheavals of the population but even in some cases to the rise of new "tribes," a process that is also familiar from the history of Africa under colonialism in the nineteenth and twentieth centuries.

Certainly, according to the ideas of the time, a fully Christianized and Hispanicized "Indio" could have become a member of the Spanish ruling society, enjoying all its privileges. This may have happened to members of the native aristocracy who kept their status under the Spanish and half-caste offspring of Spaniards and the indigenous nobility. Some of them moved effortlessly between both cultures. But in general a fundamental cultural divide still remained: the ability of indigenous people to acculturate was questioned, and so their willingness to do so was never encouraged. The result was a culturally stratified society, which in the main amounted to a racial segregation according to skin color, with the Spaniards of European origin at the top, followed by Spaniards born in the Americas, the Creoles (including the whole Amerindian ruling class), then the broad mass of natives, and right at the bottom the black slaves. These categories, then, were the so-called *castas,* despite the fact (or perhaps precisely because) *castizo* originally meant "pure-blood" in contrast to *mestizo* (half-blood). A person's social status was determined by a combination of "order," "blood," and "milk": the milk of indigenous or African wet nurses symbolized enculturation that was not pure European and distinguished Creoles negatively from Spaniards, for example. Indeed, gradually the racial aspect began to come increasingly to the fore.[243]

The crown and the church favored a model of separate development, which, in contrast to the later apartheid system in South Africa, was intended, at least to some extent, to protect the Amerindians. Where it was put into practice, for example, in the so-called Jesuit state of Paraguay, it produced some impressive results. The fringes of the empire were occupied by a chain of regions controlled by different religious orders, which also had the political duty, in part, of securing the borders. Thus, the Jesuit reducciones in Paraguay were charged with helping guard the eastern lands that bordered the high Andes of Peru, where silver was produced—a key heartland of the empire—especially against the expansionist slave hunters from the southern Brazilian São Paulo *(Paulistas).*

In Paraguay, too, the organizational basis of society was formed by the corralling of semi-nomadic natives into reducciones that had a Spanish city constitution but in practice were under the almost unlimited control of the missionaries. By 1732, a total of 141,182 people were living in the reducciones. Entry to Spaniards and other foreigners was forbidden, which was theoretically the case for Amerindian cities also. But overall supervision was in the hands of the royal governor, who was also responsible for appointing priests and corregidores on the advice of the order and was empowered to requisition Indian labor for public works and military service. The economic system directed by the order was neither exploitative nor idealistically communist but rather designed to secure food supplies through arable farming and huge livestock herds and above all by means of the yerba maté tea plantations to generate the necessary surpluses to meet the native tribute payments and settle the bills for the goods that had to be imported. In 1754, the Guarani from seven of the thirty missions rebelled against a Portuguese–Spanish treaty of 1750, which granted their land to their deadly enemies, the Paulista slave hunters. Equipped with firearms by the Jesuit missionaries, the Guarani had successfully defended themselves against the Paulistas in the seventeenth century. This time, the Jesuits refrained from supporting the Indians, a concession that was expressly acknowledged by the crown. The leaders of the revolt were native "officials" like Nicolás Ñeengirú, whom anti-Jesuit propaganda claimed had been installed as "King Nicholas I" of Paraguay. When the Jesuits were expelled from South America in 1768, the reducciones fell into disuse.[244]

Far from imposing forced Hispanicization, the policies of the missionaries centered on the scientific and practical nurturing of Indian languages and the transmission of the Christian Gospel in these tongues. It was this language policy of the church, as opposed to the short-sighted Hispanicization plans of the crown, that enabled Quechua, the ancient language of the Inca Empire, to gain preeminence throughout the high Andes. In Brazil, the Tupi language Nhengatu assumed a similar role. Likewise, Guarani remained as the second official language of Paraguay and in the mid-twentieth century was spoken by 92 percent of the population, as against 52 percent Spanish speakers. However, so long as the ultimate dominance of the *Hispanidad* remained, the utopia of separate development was destined in the long term to strengthen the division of society into racial hierarchies, rather than to alleviate it.

Economy of Spain's Colonial Empire

It was no coincidence that economic policy was fully commensurate with this situation: the economic system was officially tailored to the needs of Spain and saw its principal purpose as channeling money into the coffers of the crown (fiscalism).

The crown retained the mining concession, which it licensed to private enterprises for profit; as well as the quicksilver concession, vitally important for silver mining operations; the salt concession; and the tobacco monopoly. But the entire America trade was monopolized in a broader sense, insofar as it was solely licensed by the crown and from 1503 to 1778 could be conducted only via the royal Casa de la Contratación in conjunction with the guild of principal traders to the Americas (Cargadores de Indias) in Seville (from 1717 on in Cádiz).[245]

In addition, there was supposed to be a ban on all colonial manufactured goods, in favor of Spanish exports of textiles and metalwares, wine, spirits, and other products. However, in the event, this was found to be impractical, given that the imports from Spain could not even remotely meet the demand for basic textiles. As a result, hundreds of workers were employed in textile mills *(obrajes)* from Mexico to Cuzco producing woolen fabrics; sometimes their numbers were swelled by labor forcibly recruited by the authorities and compelled to work in poor conditions.

From the mid-sixteenth century until the gradual dissolution of the monopoly system in the mid-eighteenth, for reasons of both control and security, goods were transported in convoys guarded by warships. Once a year, the Peru Fleet would set sail from Spain, with a stopover in Cartagena, bound for the port of Nombre de Dios (or, from 1593 on, Portobelo), from which their cargoes were transported to the coast of the Pacific, whereas the Mexico Fleet took its cargo via the Antilles to Veracruz. This journey took a total of 70–80 days, with 120–130 needed for the return route via Havana. The cargoes consisted of foodstuffs and manufactured goods, primarily luxury items. But the overwhelming majority of the cargo on the return leg comprised precious metals, principally silver: this accounted for 90–99 percent of goods brought from the Americas from 1531 to 1700 and 77.6 percent in the period 1747–1778. The remainder consisted largely of the dyestuffs cochineal and indigo in the early period, though in the eighteenth century these were supplanted by sugar, cocoa, and tobacco.

From 1545 on, the silver came from the mines at Potosí in the high Andes of the viceroyalty of Peru, as well as from Zacatecas (from 1546) and San Luis Potosí (1592) in Mexico. Before long, the silver ore was being extracted on site by means of the amalgamation process, which consisted of briefly combining the unprocessed ore with quicksilver (mercury), some of which came from Huancavelica in Peru, while the rest had to be imported from Almaden in Spain. Up to the eighteenth century, ore extraction and preparation were undertaken by small contractors, who were required to pay the *quinto* ("royal fifth") levy of 20 percent (later 10 percent) to the crown. Located at an altitude of 4,000 meters, Potosí grew into a city of 160,000 inhabitants, making it one of the largest conurbations in the world at the time. Both there and in Huancavelica, miners were conscripted against their will through the *mita* system of the Incas; these *mitayos* were meant to work for a year in shifts, going down the mine every three weeks, but the pressure put on them by the contractors and the appalling conditions down the mine saw many of them perish, especially in the mining of quicksilver. Over time, though, potential mitayos learned how to evade the draft, with the result that volunteer miners made up the majority even as early as 1603. In Mexico, a conscription system was never in force.[246]

In the period up to 1700, production is thought to have increased by a total of 300 percent; thereafter, it decreased by a third for a spell, but by 1810 it had grown threefold once more. Overall, Spain's American mines are estimated to have produced some 70,000–100,000 metric tons of silver. Factoring in the gold that was extracted, including from Brazil sources in the eighteenth century, the total yield, converted to tons of silver, was between 130,000 and 150,000 tons. Between 1493 and 1800, America was therefore responsible for mining 71 percent of the world's gold and 85 percent of its silver, figures that increased toward the end of this period to 85 and 90 percent, respectively. The silver ingots were registered and stamped or alternatively were minted into *reales de a ocho*. These silver coins of 25.56 grams weight were the key currency of the European world economy; even the US silver dollar derives from them.

Although some of the hoard of silver remained in the Americas,[247] the colonies still suffered from a shortage of revenue, as it seems that on occasion the amount of silver exported exceeded the total weight mined. The quinto, the proceeds from the exported quicksilver, and the surpluses generated by the American monopolies and taxes all flowed back to Spain as crown silver (allegedly some 37 percent of the total, on average), while most of the rest was private silver, that is, payment for deliveries and the transfer of profits. Granted, all the figures pertaining to Spanish America are unreliable thanks to the widespread practice of smuggling, which existed alongside (and within) the flota system. Because the crown was in the habit of requisitioning private silver and compensating the owners with state bonds, a lot of silver came to Spain undeclared. Michel Morineau has found that the supposed dip in silver imports in the mid-seventeenth century never in fact occurred as such but rather that clandestine imports meant that the actual amount remained constant or even increased.[248]

Even so, in the seventeenth century the crown had to switch over to minting copper coinage, as American silver proved to be more harmful than beneficial to Spain. Not only the country's pursuit of great-power status saw this newfound wealth immediately begin to ebb away. The Europe-wide inflation that was triggered, or at least exacerbated, by the sudden influx of Spanish silver created a price differential between Spain and the rest of the continent. This meant that third parties could sell their goods at a large profit in Spain but that the goods that Spaniards bought from them were cheap to them, a situation that in the long term led to the deindustrialization of the Iberian Peninsula. Even by 1600, it is estimated that around half of the private silver had already flowed out of Spain in this way. By 1686, Spain accounted for only 5.6 percent of the American cargoes, behind France, Italy, England, Holland, and Belgium. Instead, silver began to stockpile in the Netherlands, which used it to partially finance its trade with the Baltic, the eastern Mediterranean and the Far East, not to mention its credit business. When Brazil became a major exporter of gold and diamonds in the eighteenth century, the colonial power of Portugal had the same experience, except for the fact that in the interim Great Britain had supplanted the Netherlands as the center of world trade.

From the mid-eighteenth century on, the Spanish colonial empire underwent a profound change. Market-oriented grand estates controlled by Spaniards had, by both legal and illegal means, acquired large tracts of territory, depriving the Amerindian communities, which were growing once more, of land. Despite several famines and epidemics, the Indian population was experiencing a significant upswing again, especially in the north. While the Indian communities, insofar as they were not entrapped by the intermediate trading monopoly of their corregidores, had their own market system, it appears that their output was not significant enough to supply the Spanish cities. In contrast, Spanish haciendas produced wheat, maize, beans, and other foodstuffs and occasionally even meat for the growing cities. They often relied on the labor of indigenous farmworkers who were technically free but in debt bondage to the estate owner *(peones)*. Meanwhile, extensive *estancias* devoted themselves to livestock farming on a grand scale, often on poorer soils. In addition, plantations in the lowlands, generally worked by black African slaves, grew cane sugar, tobacco, cocoa, cotton, and other tropical products.

Around this time, the power of the state also increased under the new Spanish Bourbon dynasty. Bureaucracy became more efficient—that is, both taxes and the Indian tribute payments were collected more consistently. The authorities also expanded their areas of responsibility, curtailing the rights enjoyed by the clergy—whom many Indians, despite abuses, still regarded as their protectors—and attempted to do away with, or at least restrict the influence of, the brotherhoods *(cofradías),* the traditional focus of the social and cultural autonomy of the Indian communities. Little wonder, then, that insurrections grew in frequency and scope during this period.[249]

After independence, the plight of the Amerindians only continued to worsen. The institutions of authoritarian Spanish paternalism, which had at least afforded them some protection, were swept aside along with the brotherhoods. The new liberal regimes wanted to replace the corporative society of the ancien régime with a new individualistic one. While the indigenous peoples may have continued to assert their identity, right up to the present day, this has overwhelmingly been only in a marginalized and defensive mode. For instance, though they have been successful in syncretizing Christianity with their traditional religion, the resulting practice has failed to attract any outsiders—in marked contrast to the Afro-American Candomblé cults of Brazil.

The Portuguese Atlantic

In the beginning, Brazil eked out a marginal existence in the shadow of the Portuguese seaborne Asiatic trading empire.[250] Aside from the redwood and resulting dye for which the country was named, the land seemed to have little to offer by way of trade commodities. Only the presence of international rivals persuaded the crown, in the 1530s, to allocate sections of the coast and its hinterland as *capitanias* (captaincies) to hereditary *donatarios* and finally, in 1548–1551, to found the city of São Salvador de Todos os Santos as the seat of a governor and a bishop. Henceforth, the financial administration of the country was headed by a *provedor mor* and the judicial system by an *ouvidor geral;* between 1587 and 1609, the latter was integrated into the new collegial supreme court of the Relação de Bahia (presumably created on the model of the Spanish Audiencias). Presiding over this court was the newly appointed governor-general, who from 1640 on also sometimes concurrently occupied the post of viceroy, a dual position that was made permanent in 1720. In the meantime, new provinces, organized along the same lines, had come into being, into which, about 1700, a total of four hereditary capitanias and seven regained from the crown were incorporated. However, the northeastern coastal state of Estado do Maranhão (founded 1621) was only in 1774 merged into the Estado do Brasil; prior to this, trade winds and favorable currents had made it very straightforward for this state to keep in direct contact with the Portuguese motherland. Even the two bishops who had sees in this region were under the archbishopric of Lisbon, while the other four bishops in Portuguese America were under the control of the archbishop of Bahia, as were the bishoprics of São Tomé and Angola in Africa—a more than simply symbolic manifestation of the unity of the Portuguese Atlantic.

Portugal's colonial cities were broadly similar to those of the Spanish, with their councils *(câmara)* corresponding to the cabildo. However, in the Portuguese case, its members, at least formally, were elected by and from the ruling elite. In addition, guilds played a significant role, and above all the *misericórdia,* the local charitable brotherhood, which was also an elite organization. Although, as in Spanish America, there were close ties here between the city and the landed gentry, Brazil was never characterized to the same extent by its cities. The rural way of life, especially on a variety of different large estates, always played its own particular role here. Up to the end of the seventeenth century, all the cities, with one exception, lay on the coast.

This one remarkable exception was São Paulo, in the upland region of the south. The Portuguese inhabitants of this settlement had entered into a lasting alliance with an Indian tribe against their enemies. The result was the growth of a mixed-race population of so-called *Mamelucos.* These Paulistas were acquainted with the Indian skills of living in the wild. As a result, they were in the habit of making regular forays into the jungle in bands *(bandeiras)* ranging in size from a dozen to several hundred, and in the company of Indian auxiliaries, in search of slaves and gold. The Amerindian slaves they seized were sold to estates farther to the north but, in contrast to what was previously thought, were also put to work on their own enterprises. São Paulo was quick to respond to the increased demand from the more northerly provinces from the seventeenth century on by producing wheat and meat from livestock, and it even appears that it ultimately began to supply metal manufactures. The most highly prized targets of slave hunting were less the "wild" Amerindian tribes and more the Indians who lived in the Jesuit reducciones in Paraguay, who could be captured together in greater numbers and who in addition were already used to farming. Only after the Paulistas were defeated by the mission Indians in 1641 did this activity abate. It was replaced by a more intensive search for gold, which had, quite literally, far-reaching consequences.

In Brazil, it proved impossible to entirely halt the enslavement of Indians captured in war or sold on by their enemies. A law to this effect of 1609 had to be repealed by 1611 due to resistance by settlers. The Jesuits, who played a decisive role in the Indian missions elsewhere, also managed to gather together Indian groups into mission settlements in Brazil as well *(aldeias)*. But their exclusive control over these settlements was successfully challenged time and again, meaning that it was still possible for settlers to recruit cheap labor from them. This situation proved extremely difficult to regulate. In 1702, twenty-five such villages existed in the state of Brazil, with 14,450 inhabitants, while in Maranhão in 1696 11,000 Indians were living in mission settlements. By 1730, 21,000 were housed in aldeias. By 1700, though, they were outnumbered by around 100,000 white settlers, as well as about the same number of African slaves (by 1670).

By the late sixteenth century, the Brazilian economy was experiencing an upswing, after it transpired that the country offered extremely favorable conditions for the cultivation of sugarcane, which up till then had been grown on islands in the Atlantic. Because sugarcane plantations quickly exhaust the soil, extensive tracts of land must be available to make production viable. In contrast to the cramped Atlantic islands, this was particularly the case in the areas around Pernambuco and Bahia; in Bahia alone, some 11,000 square kilometers of prime sugarcane plantation were ready to be used. The freshly cut cane had to be delivered without delay from the plantations or the fields of smaller-scale growers *(lavradores de cana)* to a sugarcane mill and crushed twice between vertical rollers to extract the juice. The juice was then thickened by cooking, and the crystalline raw

Sugarcane being pressed by means of a vertically mounted roller turned by four horses driven in a circle (elsewhere, this task was performed by oxen, mules, or sometimes water power). The resulting juice was concentrated by boiling it. African slaves are shown operating this sugar press; one even appears to be resting, as no overseer is in sight. (Universiteitsbibliotheek Leiden, 359 G 17)

cane sugar that resulted finally had to be refined. Rum was distilled from the liquid that remained (*melasse;* molasses). Not only the equipment but also the large amount of labor the work required made sugar production a capital-intensive business. The number of sugar mills (*engenhos*) increased from 60 to 350 between 1570 and 1629, while production over the same period grew from around 1,700 to some 13,500 metric tons.[251]

Yet, at least initially, Brazil lacked the necessary manpower for such operations. The sparse Amerindian population was simply unable to supply a large enough workforce. But as the sugar industry boomed, it made sense to switch to using African slaves, as had already been the practice on São Tomé for some while. For right from the outset, Portugal's monopoly on African trade had also given it a monopoly on the supply of black slaves both to Europe and to Spanish America. This trade had been strictly limited up until now but mushroomed rapidly thanks to the demand from Brazil. Up to 1700, the Portuguese are thought to have imported 610,000 slaves from Africa. In 1574, the workforce of the Engenho do Sergipe near Bahia comprised just 7 percent African slaves, but by 1591, this figure had risen to 37 percent, while by 1638, the entire workforce was African. It was claimed that a slave would earn his master his purchase price back in just sixteen months at most in the quantity of sugar he produced; at first, then, there was no incentive to treat the slave workforce at all humanely. As a Jesuit missionary observed in 1627, "A sugar mill is Hell on Earth. Their owners are all damned."[252]

The Dutch Atlantic

As the center of world trade at that time, the Netherlands was also engaged in trading Brazilian sugar. Portuguese merchants were not in a position to enforce their claim to a monopoly on trade with Brazil. It seemed that they did not even have sufficient shipping tonnage, so that during the cease-fire in the war between the Netherlands and Spain in 1609–1621 (Portugal was allied to Spain through a personal union of the two crowns from 1580 to 1640), half to two-thirds of the vessels engaged in trading with Brazil—either licensed or unlicensed—were from Holland. However, according to other historians, the Dutch picked up the sugar only after it had been transhipped in Lisbon or Porto. But even just a third of the Brazilian trade would have constituted around half to two-thirds of all transatlantic Dutch trade, which except for the period around 1700 was reputed to have been even more important than their commerce with the East Indies.[253] Because the crown wanted to reserve the right to refining the sugar for Brazil, there were no sugar refineries in Portugal, while by contrast there were twenty-nine in the Netherlands by 1622, twenty-five of them in Amsterdam. During their conflict with Spain in 1566–1609, the Dutch had managed to transfer the distribution center for Portuguese colonial goods from war-ravaged Antwerp to Amsterdam.

The resumption of the war against Spain in 1621, which coincided with the European economic crisis of 1619–1622, had a damaging impact on Dutch business. The Spanish embargo was more effective than many past historians have given it credit for. Overseas expansion at Spain's expense seemed the best way out—though in practice the Dutch set their sights on the Portuguese seaborne empire, whose constituent elements were more vulnerable than the heartlands of the Spanish Empire to attack by the Dutch fleets and were more attractive to the Netherlands economy as a trading- and plantation-based empire. In the decades after 1621, the Dutch East India Company (VOC) seized almost all of Portugal's Far Eastern trading empire.

At this time, the Dutch founded the long-envisaged West India Company (WIC) to handle trade in the Western Hemisphere. Like the VOC, it was a joint-stock company that had a monopoly over Dutch transatlantic trade and was empowered to wage war and to acquire overseas territories.[254] And in common with its predecessor, its shareholders were organized into economically independent regional chambers, whose directors were appointed by the political powers that be from the ranks of the leading shareholders. The chambers in Amsterdam and Middelburg (Zeeland) had ultimate authority, both regarding the shares in the company's 7 million guilders plus of capital and on the board of directors, who were known as the Lords Nineteen *(Heren XIX),* of whom one member was delegated by the States-General, which had underwritten and partially funded the company. But because the WIC was conceived with a much more overt political purpose than the VOC, traders were more hesitant about getting involved. The company's capital came predominantly from the Dutch interior and from strict Calvinist circles, which in 1619 had gained the political whip hand in the Netherlands, not least from Protestant refugees from the Spanish Netherlands to the south.

However, the WIC was a financial failure; the privateering war it waged brought few dividends, with only Piet Heyn's famous seizure of the Spanish silver bullion fleet in 1628 causing the share price to shoot up momentarily. One apparent way out of the impasse was the decision, alongside the sale and distribution of sugar, to also take over production by seizing most of the Brazilian sugar plantations as well as the transhipment bases on the Guinea Coast and in Angola (the sources of the slaves needed to work the plantations). The period 1630–1654 therefore saw a New Holland established in the sugar-growing region of Pernambuco,[255] which under the governorship of Count Johann Moritz van Nassau-Siegen experienced a golden age, not only economically but also culturally. The count encouraged artists and scientists to settle there, with the latter subjecting the flora and fauna of

Brazil to a thorough investigation never before experienced. In 1637, the Portuguese fort and slave post of Elmina on the Guinea Coast was captured and was to remain in Dutch hands until 1871. Angola and São Tomé fell in 1642. In the period 1636–1645, the WIC, rather than the Portuguese, was responsible for selling 23,163 African slaves to buyers in the Americas.

From 1644, the Brazilians were able to shake off the yoke of Dutch rule,[256] while an expedition from Portuguese Brazil also regained control of Angola in 1648. However, the Dutch remained on the Guinea Coast, and presently, the weakening of the Portuguese hold on that area attracted slave traders from other European countries to settle there, notably the English, French, Danish, and even Germans from Brandenburg. Yet the WIC's decline continued apace, especially after a peace accord was signed with Portugal (by this time, independent from Spain once more) in 1654. In 1664, during the Second Anglo-Dutch War, the WIC lost its fur-trading and settlement colony of the New Netherlands.[257] It had taken over this colony from a predecessor trading company in 1621, but the territory had been greatly increased in 1655, when the governor Peter Stuyvesant annexed the adjoining Swedish colony of Nya Sverige (founded in 1638 by a private Dutch initiative).[258] In 1674, the WIC, which had posted significant losses, was restructured and refloated as a purely (slave-) trading concern with bases in Africa and the Caribbean.

The expansion and internationalization of the slave trade instigated by the Dutch was intimately bound up with the transfer of sugar production to the West Indies. As a result of several conflicts with the Spanish, its enemies had established permanent settlements on the islands of this soft underbelly of the Spanish American empire.[259] The English occupied Barbados in 1627 and Jamaica in 1655,[260] the French took Guadeloupe and Martinique in 1635 and Saint Domingue (modern Haiti) in 1697,[261] and the Dutch landed on Curaçao in 1634 and Suriname in 1667.[262] Because it was perfectly possible to wage war against Spain in this theater while maintaining peace with it in Europe (according to the motto "No peace beyond the line," in reference to the meridian of the Azores and the Tropic of Cancer), an international pirate's paradise developed in the Caribbean in the seventeenth century, in conjunction with French and above all British privateering actions. This anarchy was eradicated only toward the end of the century, when the major maritime powers realized that their interests were best served by restoring order to the region. Prior to this, corsairs had launched a series of large-scale attacks on Spanish ports in the Caribbean, with appalling atrocities.[263]

The few settlers who made their home on these islands initially pinned their hopes on cultivating tobacco. On the one hand, European demand for this commodity was on the increase, while on the other, this crop could be grown on labor-intensive smallholdings with minimal capital outlay. Yet overproduction and competition from a superior product being farmed in Virginia soon brought about a crisis. In this situation, Dutch settlers who had been expelled from Brazil and who had a practical knowledge of farming, plenty of capital, plus ample slaves and shipping tonnage at their disposal succeeded in establishing sugar production employing African slave labor in the Caribbean.[264] In 1645, Barbados had 40,000 hectares of cultivated farmland, in the hands of 11,200 landowners and worked by 5,680 slaves. By 1667, following the "sugar revolution," there were just 745 landowners and 82,023 slaves. In the years 1740–1744, when the zenith of sugar growing on the island had already passed, Barbados was producing 6,891 tons of sugar. At the same time the Lesser Antilles yielded 15,874 tons, Jamaica 16,333 tons, Martinique 15,988 tons, Saint Domingue 42,200 tons, and Cuba 2,000 tons—all of which amounted to an average annual total of around 20,000 tons of sugar produced throughout the Caribbean. Between 1665 and 1833, it is estimated that the juice from some 10 million tons of sugarcane was processed in the West Indies. Even so, the Brazilians still continued to grow this commodity, as did the Dutch, whose plantation colony of Suriname was devoted entirely to sugar.

The Jewish Atlantic

In a symbiotic relationship with the Portuguese and the Dutch Atlantic, a Jewish Atlantic also developed, comprising a global network of Sephardic Jews of predominantly Portuguese origin. Up to the sixteenth century, Portugal and Spain had either expelled their Jewish populations or subjected them to forcible conversion. Moreover, their national inquisitions were set up precisely in order to persecute Jews among the "New Christians" who continued to secretly observe their faith (Marranos). However, unlike the Spanish Inquisition, the Portuguese

Inquisition in the Americas confined itself to conducting just two visitations, in 1591 and 1618, with the result that a comparatively large number of "crypto-Jews" were able to live unmolested in Brazil. The findings of the visitation show that at that time one-third of the owners of engenhos and over 40 percent of the merchants of Bahia and Pernambuco were "New Christians." Under the aegis of the personal union between Spain and Portugal from 1580 to 1640, they could pass themselves off as "Portuguese" even in Spanish America. The Atlantic trading empire of these "Portuguese" merchants and slave traders in Cartagena de Indias, which played a key role in supplying slaves to Peru, has been the subject of an in-depth study.[265]

Because the Dutch practiced a high degree of religious tolerance—for which reason economically important Sephardic communities arose in particular in Amsterdam—the Dutch Atlantic can also be said to be a Sephardic Jewish Atlantic. Living alongside the employees of the Dutch East India Company in Brazil in 1644 were around three thousand private Dutch citizens and some six hundred Jews, partly Portuguese New Christians, who had reverted to observing the religion of their forefathers, and partly emigrants from the Netherlands itself.[266] Following the Portuguese reconquest, because Jews were no longer officially tolerated, the Sephardim were forced to carve out a new role for themselves in the transfer of the sugar plantations to the Caribbean. On Curaçao, where they ultimately came to form a third of the population, the first Jewish community in the Americas, north or south, was founded in 1659 and still exists today. In 1654, the first Jews arrived in New Amsterdam, which later became New York. New studies have shown how the circumatlantic networks of the Sephardim were largely responsible for ensuring that Atlantic global trade surreptitiously remained in Dutch hands for a considerable time, despite the restrictive navigation laws imposed by the British.[267]

Even so, the Jewish diaspora across the Atlantic always remained quite limited in terms of sheer numbers. At the time of American Independence, it is thought that there were only about 2,500 Jews resident in North America. The first synagogue there was built only in 1763 in Newport (Rhode Island). Yet between 1825 and 1925, around four million Jews emigrated to the United States, this time overwhelmingly Ashkenazim from the Russian Empire. In the interim, 40 percent of all Jews have made their home in the United States,[268] with the result that the modern Jewish Atlantic has become part of the Anglo-American Atlantic.

The African Atlantic

The still-extensive production of sugar in Brazil was badly hit by falling prices on the world market and West Indian competition in the final third of the seventeenth century. However, at about the same time, the forays of the *bandeirantes* had not only extended the western border of the country to its present position 3,000 kilometers west of the Tordesillas Line but also discovered the first gold deposits in the region that would soon become known as Minas Gerais; many other such finds were to follow.[269] This discovery sparked the first gold rush in history.[270] In 1711, the principal gold-mining site became Brazil's "Gold Potosí" and was named Vila Rica de Ouro Preto ("rich city of black gold"). The crown divided the plots between itself and the prospectors but passed over its claims and confined itself to taking the quinto levy of 20 percent, which from 1730 on was reduced to 12 percent. The total amount of gold mined between 1700 and 1799, which reached its zenith shortly before the middle of the century, is thought to have been around 172 tons;[271] Michel Morineau, however, has calculated a yield of 852 tons and puts the high point of extraction somewhat earlier.[272]

The mine workers were African slaves,[273] who numbered almost 100,000 in Minas Gerais in 1738. Between 1701 and 1750, 790,200 Africans were brought to Brazil, from 1731 on mainly from Angola. The price of slaves skyrocketed, thereby exacerbating the problems of the sugar industry. Other branches of business thrived, though, particularly the food industry and the manufacture of finished goods to meet the demands of the rapidly expanding population. Tobacco growing also experienced a boom, as Brazilian tobacco found increasing favor among Africans. In 1729, a diamond mine was discovered at Jequitinhonha in the north of the Minas Gerais region. The crown established a monopoly over this enterprise, among other considerations in order to control the amount mined and so prevent the price of diamonds from collapsing. It is believed that a total of 615 kilograms of diamonds were found here in the eighteenth century. In 1763, Rio de Janeiro, the principal port serving the mining region, replaced Bahia as the capital of Brazil.

In the nineteenth century, Brazil diversified into coffee growing. By this time, the focus of sugar production had moved to Spanish Cuba, while plantation farming had spread to the south of British-controlled North America, where it concentrated on the production of cotton to meet the huge demand of the British textile industry. Throughout the course of this century, Brazil imported a further 1.9 million African slaves, while Cuba took in around 780,000.[274] Significantly, slavery was abolished in these two countries only in the first half of the nineteenth century. In the United States, it took a civil war to finally bring the practice to an end. This "plantation America" between the southern states of the United States and Brazil, which arose from the Portuguese and Dutch Atlantic, as well as from parts of the Spanish and British, did not result in a modified transference of European forms of living of the kind encountered in Hispano-American cities or New England villages. Rather, something new emerged—an artificial world, created by the first capital-intensive instance of "agribusiness" in history, and artificial first and foremost in relation to its population of African slaves.

According to the reasonably reliable estimates at our disposal nowadays, 12,521,000 slaves were carried off from Africa by Europeans between 1450 and 1867, 10,160,000 of whom are documented. Probably 10,705,000 arrived on the opposite shore of the ocean, of whom 8,763,000 are documented.[275] Even before the nineteenth century, the number of African forced migrants amounted to more than three times the total number of Europeans who emigrated to America. Accordingly, at least where plantation America is concerned, we must, strictly speaking, talk in terms of an African Atlantic. Today, some islands of the Caribbean are purely African, while on others there is an African majority or at least a significant proportion of the population who are of African origin. Furthermore, out of the 3.5 million inhabitants of Brazil in 1818, one million were counted as whites, 0.5 million as mulattoes, and two million as blacks—Amerindians no longer appeared in this census.

Slavery is a quite generally widespread phenomenon. Many Africans were slave owners, too. In addition, from ancient times they had sold slaves to the Islamic world and to the Mediterranean region, partly via the caravan routes across the Sahara. Therefore, as the first European slave traders to set foot in Africa, the Portuguese were able to tap into an already existing network. As slave trading became the continent's most important export activity, either directly or indirectly, it led to profound changes in African societies. Moreover, plantation slavery in America was vastly different from the traditional slavery practiced by the Africans, the Muslims, or even in Europe.

With the exception of royal estates in West African kingdoms, slaves did not play a key role in the production process but rather were kept as domestic servants who, integrated into family groups, performed a great diversity of roles within the household. To varying degrees, they enjoyed certain rights and were able to engage in independent activities, including social advancement, say, within the military. They were also permitted to marry and, especially in the second generation, could win their freedom and become full members of the family group they had served in. In any event, they were regarded as human beings who, in the terminology of Christian theology, possessed just as immortal a soul as their masters. And at first, this is exactly how they were perceived by Europeans; at this stage, a racist viewpoint seems to have been largely absent. In the early sixteenth century, the pope even consecrated an African by the name of Henrique, the son of a Kongo king, as a bishop. It was the twentieth century before another African became a bishop.

Theoretically, this Christian perspective also applied to African plantation slaves. In practice, even they were accorded a certain degree of self-determination. There were occasional instances of a plantation slave making the transition to a domestic slave attached to a family. But over time, a different attitude increasingly came to the fore, which was more akin to the view of slaves in antiquity, when slave labor had also been a decisive economic factor—namely, regarding the slave as a two-legged chattel, a beast of burden devoid of any individual rights ("chattel slavery").[276] This was despite the fact that Roman law since the age of Justinian had at least defined the slave as a person and imposed sanctions against their willful killing by their masters. Rather, people took their cue from Aristotle's teachings, which held that some people were destined by virtue of their natural inferiority to become the slaves of more superior humans. Alternatively, reference was made to the Bible, specifically the curse that Noah placed on Ham's son Canaan, from whom Africans were believed to have descended. In this way, the entire black race was collectively stigmatized, with the color of their skin being the decisive criterion. Thus, slavery is not a consequence of racism, but rather racism is an ideology that legitimizes the institution of slavery.[277]

System and Extent of Slave Labor

The only truly decisive factor was the slaves' capacity for work. Consequently, two-thirds of the slaves acquired by Europeans were healthy men in the prime of their life, so-called pieces of the Indies *(peças de Indias)*. Women and children were less sought after and were sold at just a fraction of the unit cost of a male slave. By contrast, women and children were highly regarded as slaves by Africans and Muslims, not only because of the great range of services women could perform (including sexual) but also with regard to increasing the available slave population through their fertility. No dowry needed to be paid on slave women, and they came with no ties to their own lineage. As a result, African and European American demands on the African slave market complemented one another.

A volunteer European labor force to work in the Americas could not be raised in Spain or Portugal. Convicts were generally deemed undesirable; only England, in its holdings in the West Indies and North America, made widespread use of this resource. Another category of worker in both the English and French possessions were the "indentured servants" or *engagés*. These workers had paid for their passage to the Americas by signing a contract to work for an employer for several years; in time, they could be sold on to other masters as a kind of slave. Yet with the upturn in the European economy came increased demand for manpower there, making indentured servants too expensive.[278]

Amerindian laborers were exclusively at the disposal of the Spanish, as the conquerors of the areas where the major indigenous cultures had once thrived. Even so, they too still imported black slaves right from the very beginning, primarily to Peru, where they were employed on plantations and in lowland mines, but above all to work as servants and artisans. In contrast to Mexico and the high Andean regions of Peru, around 1600, the population of Lima and other cities of northern Peru was composed of 50 percent Africans. Moreover, the generous emancipation and freedom-buying policies of the Spanish meant that some 10–15 percent of them were already freemen; by 1700, the proportion had risen to 50 percent. By this stage, Spanish America had brought in around 350,000 to 400,000 Africans. The importers were the respective holders of the *asientos,* monopolistic contracts concluded for this very purpose: up to 1640 these were Portuguese traders, up to 1695 Dutch, and up to 1713 a mixture of Portuguese and French. Yet far greater demand was generated by sugar-producing plantation America; due to a dearth of viable alternatives, this sector was firmly wedded to the use of African slave labor. Up to 1700, for instance, Brazil imported 811,000 African slaves, while the West Indies had already brought over 490,000 by that stage. However, British and French North America was still lagging behind, with fewer than 15,000.

The high point of the slave trade in the eighteenth century also marked the high point of slave imports to the Caribbean. While 1.9 million slaves were transported to the thriving territory of Brazil, at the same time no fewer than 3.3 million were shipped to the British, French, Dutch, and Danish islands of the Caribbean, principally by British and French merchants, who had begun to replace the Dutch as the main suppliers around 1700. Between 1700 and 1808, the British carried 2.8 million slaves and the French 1.3 million to America. Slave imports into the whole of the Americas reached a peak in the 1790s, with 75,000 arriving annually. The large islands were at the forefront of this trade, with Jamaica taking the lead: in 1760, its population consisted of 173,000 slaves and just 10,000 whites. By 1770, the size of the average plantation there was 40 hectares, employing 204 slaves. Presently, Jamaica was supplanted as the leading slave importer by Saint Domingue (Haiti); the value of its exports—which by this time, alongside sugar, also included coffee, cotton, indigo, and cocoa—equaled that of all the British and Spanish islands put together. Its slave population totaled 460,000, or almost half of all the one million or so slaves living in the West Indies at that time; the plantations in all the countries of the Americas were employing more than 1.4 million slaves all told. By contrast, the number of free Africans in British and French colonies had remained negligible; in 1780, this group accounted for one-quarter of the number of slaves in Brazil, while in Spanish America there were two and half times as many freedmen as slaves.

Under the British asiento (1713–1739) and above all once the Spanish colonies were opened up to free trade in 1789, the economic upturn this sparked also saw slave imports to these colonies increase once more, reaching a peak in the nineteenth century. In addition to the plantations of Venezuela and the mines of Colombia, the islands of Cuba and Puerto Rico were now the major slave importers. Cuba, which profited from the collapse of the Haitian economy following the successful slave rebellion there led by Toussaint l'Ouverture in 1791, grew to become the region's leading sugar producer, with a slave population of 370,000 by 1860.

From the late seventeenth century on, the rising cost of keeping indentured servants and the rapid growth of the British slave trade led to increasing numbers of slaves being imported to British North America. There, not only did tobacco growing in the Chesapeake Bay area rely on slave labor (in contrast to its cultivation in other regions of the world), but slaves were also put to work on the rice and indigo plantations of the American Southeast. With westward expansion from the 1790s on came a shift to cotton farming. At that point, there were some 700,000 slaves living in the United States; by 1810, there were 1.2 million, and by 1860 almost four million, notwithstanding the fact that, until a ban was imposed on the import of slaves into the United States in 1808, only 389,000 Africans had been transported there.

Consequences in Africa

The opening up of Africa to seaborne trading by the Portuguese and other Europeans had only immediate and far-reaching consequences south of the Congo River, as it radically altered the economic structure there. In West Africa, at least initially, this structure was absorbed into the existing economic system. The gold exports of the Portuguese and the Dutch comprised only a small proportion of the total trade in this metal. Likewise, up to 1600, it is thought that the Atlantic slave trade accounted for only around a quarter of all the slaves exported from Africa. Besides, prior to 1700, slaves were neither the sole export commodity from Africa nor the most valuable. Gold was far more significant, while ivory, skins, and other goods also played a major role. Up to then, the demand from America remained pretty constant. This not only kept prices relatively stable but also enabled Europeans to meet their need for slaves from the normal African trade in this commodity. This traditional slave trade was supplied with people who had already been slaves, plus prisoners of war captured in conflicts between African empires, though these wars were not yet being fought with the specific intention of capturing slaves. Thus, the expansion of Asante (Ashanti) from the late seventeenth century on and the jihad in Senegambia in the eighteenth produced a surge in the sales of slaves. In decentralized societies, kidnapping played an important role, often from neighboring villages.[279] In addition, both types of society also engaged in the deliberate sentencing of actual or alleged criminals to be sold; some people even regarded this as a humanizing of the justice system, as it obviated the death penalty. The sale of debtors also occurred, while starvation even forced some people to offer themselves for sale. The demand and hence the price rose in the eighteenth century. Between 1680 and 1780, Africa's trade across the Atlantic increased sixfold, principally as a result of the export of slaves. This inevitably brought about changes in African societies. A limited conflict or a dynastic war of succession, which did not compromise trade at all, or at most only temporarily, suddenly became a lucrative enterprise by dint of the sale of prisoners of war. Consequently, wars were now even fought for control of the regional trade in slaves. This period saw an expansion of specialized slave-trading networks.

The transatlantic slave trade began with the Portuguese in the Senegal region. Subsequently, the Dutch also set up permanent bases in this area, but the leading players there were the French in Senegal and the British in the Gambia. African merchants were the suppliers of slaves, who in the main had been taken in the course of wars in the African interior, while the intermediaries (some of whom were women) were usually half-castes.[280] In the eighteenth century, the region around the Senegal and Gambia Rivers alone yielded 337,000 slaves, while the total number supplied from here between 1662 and 1865 was 756,000. In the same period, European merchants exported 736,000 slaves from the adjoining region of Sierra Leone to the south, all but 30,000 of whom were also victims of the jihad. However, the areas even farther south, along the Pepper Coast (Liberia) and the Ivory Coast, were almost devoid of slave trade, given their lack of harbors. The Gold Coast (Ghana), where the rainforest gives out for a stretch, was heavily populated with European bases, thanks to the trade in gold that prevailed there up to 1680. The principal trading nations, the Dutch and the British, had their headquarters at Elmina and Cape Coast Castle, respectively. In the eighteenth century, at least 645,000 slaves came from here, out of a total of 1,209,000 from this region. To the east, up to the mouth of the Niger, stretched the "Slave Coast" itself, with the kingdoms of Dahomey, Oyo, and Benin in the hinterland. Whereas Benin banned slave trading until the eighteenth century, a thriving official trade in slaves was conducted here in Dahomey, from the port of Wydah, and then in Oyo, from Porto Novo. In the eighteenth century, 1.2 million slaves came from the Slave Coast, with a total of 1.99 million being transported between 1662 and 1865.

Likewise, another 1.2 million slaves were exported in the eighteenth century from the "houses" of the partially waterborne settlements like Old Calabar, Bonny, and New Calabar that lay on the Bight of Biafra east of the mouth of the Niger; 1.595 million came from this region in all. In the process, the "houses" metamorphosed from family groupings into hierarchically organized slave-trading firms equipped with their own militias, war canoes, and plantations. Their settlements effectively became mini-kingdoms, run by a titular ruler and the heads of the individual houses. Their suppliers were the decentrally organized Igbo (Ibo) people of the hinterland, who used a variety of methods, including kidnapping, their legal system, oracle pronouncements, and secret society collusion, to deliver untold numbers of their kin to the slave market. For example, the cave oracle at Aro "swallowed" those who had been found guilty, only for them to reappear on the slave market. In the eighteenth century, the Igbo are believed to have sold as many as one million of their own people into slavery.[281]

The partially Christianized and partially Europeanized Kingdom of Kongo rapidly became one of the main providers of slaves to Portugal. After initial resistance, the king brought the slave trade under his personal control, supplying slaves from his own household, from raids against neighboring tribes, and increasingly also from the victims of internal conflicts. The taxes he levied on this trade and his hoarding of goods received in exchange for slaves at court helped him consolidate his power. The new Portuguese colony of Luanda lay outside this system and was in competition with it. The disintegration of the Kingdom of Kongo during its conflicts with Luanda went hand in hand with the transfer of the slave trade to newly independent former vassals of the king or to neighboring states on the coast or in the interior, such as Mpinda and Loango.[282] Farther south, within a century, the Portuguese settlers at Luanda had turned the Ndongo kingdom of the Ngola, a thriving and densely populated state in the sixteenth century, into a depopulated wasteland through wars and slave exports. After the initial destruction of this kingdom in 1618, Princess Nzinga founded her independent realm of Matamba on the Kwango River far inland out of the range of the Portuguese; following the example of the Imbangala of Angola, her rule was supported by specially organized bands of warriors. Farther south on the Kwango, the Imbangala themselves had their home in the Kingdom of Kasanje. Matamba and Kasanje soon developed into important intermediaries for the slave trade, as well as dis-

Participants in shipping African slaves to America (in percent)

	15th–19th century	18th century
Portugal	45.9	29.3
Britain	28.1	41.3
France	13.2	19.2
Spain	4.7	—
Netherlands	4.6	5.6
North America	2.5	3.2
Denmark	1.0	1.2
Other	1.0	0.2

patching their troops on slave raids and supplying the Portuguese traders *(pombeiros),* who, unlike in West Africa, had to venture into the interior here. The settlement of Benguela, which was established even farther to the south in 1617, soon evolved a similar system of trade with the Portuguese.

Logistics of the Slave Trade

A succession of other nations—first the Dutch, then overwhelmingly the British and the French—were also active in this part of Africa. By the end of the eighteenth century, the Portuguese, included the Brazilians, were transporting 16,000 slaves from here every year, with the French dispatching 12,800 and the British 11,600. Over the course of that century, Kongo and Angola sent 2.5 million slaves to America, of whom 1.3 million were allotted to the Portuguese. After 1810, in marked contrast to other parts of Africa, a further 1.3 million slaves were still transported from this region. The 5,695,000 Africans who were shipped from Kongo and Angola between 1662 and 1867 (reaching its peak of 340,000 in the decade 1790–1799) accounted for 45 percent of all the slaves exported by Europeans from Africa: 22.5 percent of all African slaves were embarked at Luanda, plus 6.1 percent at Benguela and 6 percent at Cabinda. No other part of the continent is thought to have suffered such a depletion of its population thanks to the slave trade nor to have gone through such momentous changes as a result.[283]

The Europeans attempted to organize the trade through national monopoly companies. However, their costs were too high, and all such companies failed. In the eighteenth century, free trade came to predominate; the Royal African Company now levied a charge for commercial traders to use its bases. Slave ships were by no means simply "loaded" all at once; rather, slaves were normally acquired piecemeal in small groups through various African hunters. It was therefore common practice for ships to lie offshore or cruise up and down the coast for months, further adding to both the cost and the risk factor.

To help spread the risk, anyone who equipped a slave ship usually shared the investment and profits with other slave traders, merchants, and others; even the ships' captains had a stake in the enterprise. In general, slave ships were smaller than normal merchant vessels but had twice the number of crew, in the proportion of one sailor to every seven to ten slaves. The cargo shipped on the first leg to Africa accounted for 55–65 percent of the total costs. In the eighteenth century, the most important goods carried were textiles (making up 56 percent of all cargoes), 63 percent of which (or 36 percent of the total cargo) came from the East Indies; these were especially prized for their quality and their colorfastness. Next, accounting for some 10–12 percent apiece, came liquor and various metalwares, along with other manufactured goods, then firearms and gunpowder (7–9 percent), tobacco (2–8 percent), and iron bars (2–5 percent). European iron was of a better quality and so was preferred as a raw material by African blacksmiths. In addition, the Dutch and English imported cowrie shells from the Indian Ocean to Africa and to Europe, where they were acquired by slave traders from other countries. However, the sudden influx of these shells into Africa, where they had long been widely used as currency, created inflation there. The price of slaves had been rising steadily in any event, but inflation saw a hike from a cost of 10,000–30,000 cowries per slave in 1680 to 160,000 cowries in 1770.

After a voyage of three to four months to Africa and three to six months spent buying in slaves, the slave traders would supplement the provisions of flour and meat that they had brought with them from Europe with yams, rice, beans, and other African foodstuffs, as well as drinking water. Around 200 kilos of food and 65 liters of water were needed per slave on the transatlantic voyage, the so-called Middle Passage, which lasted for several months. On British ships, meals were taken twice a day, one of rice and yams and one a soup made from barley,

During the period in which they controlled the plantation regions of Pernambuco on the Brazilian coast, the Dutch massively increased the import of African slaves to work in the booming sugar industry. At first sight, the slave market in the center of the regional capital Fort Maurits might appear to convey an almost idyllic impression, were it not for the penned-in "merchandise" shown at the edge of the picture and an inspection by a prospective purchaser in the center. This painting from the 1630s is one of a number of realistic works produced by the circle of artists and scientists around the Dutch governor *(stadhouder)* Johann Moritz von Nassau-Siegen. (akg-images, Berlin)

maize, and rusks, sometimes with a bit of meat or fish in it—all of which totaled around two thousand calories. There was also a ration of lemon or lime juice or vinegar against scurvy. Men, boys, and women with children were kept separate from one another and chained up at night for security. During the day, though, they were brought up on deck and washed with salt water, while the crew cleaned out their sleeping quarters. People transported on slave ships had on average just 0.6 square meters of room each.

Because the death of one slave in three hundred meant a decrease in profits of 0.67 percent, the slave "cargoes" were, in the main, treated with care. Even so, the mortality rate was high, though it fell from 20–30 percent in the sixteenth century to 6–10 percent in the nineteenth. The slave traders developed purpose-built ships and worked to ensure a quicker passage and to provide healthier food on board. Insofar as differences between the slaving nations can be discerned, the Portuguese seem to have been better than the Spanish, English, and French, probably because of the much shorter voyage to Brazil. Mortality could occur as a result of a breakdown in provisioning the slaves, when a crossing took longer than expected. Predominantly, though, it was caused by infectious diseases, which the slaves carried with them from Africa and which spread on board ship. The most common were those affecting the digestive tract or unspecified fevers, but occasionally slaves succumbed to outbreaks of measles or smallpox, until the smallpox vaccine came into widespread use here. Given these circumstances, the death rate among crews was higher than on other ships, too.

Within a few days or weeks of their arrival in the West Indies, the slaves were sold individually or at most in small groups, often with a down payment of 25 percent, with the balance of the payment deferred. Now, a large proportion of the crew was superfluous and was paid off. After some fifteen to eighteen months, the ship would arrive in Europe once more, mostly under ballast or at least only partially laden. A simplified formula for this Atlantic system was the "Triangular Trade," first with goods from Europe being shipped to Africa, then with slaves being shipped from Africa to America, and finally with sugar and other plantation goods being carried from the Americas back to Europe. Though this neat designation holds good for the trade as a whole, it was rare for individual ships to be involved in all three transactions. Moreover, direct trade routes back and forth were also common between Europe and the other continents, as well as between Brazil and Africa, though it is true that prevailing winds and currents excluded the West Indies from such direct connections.

The profits of the slave traders fluctuated considerably from voyage to voyage. In the eighteenth century, a third of them even made losses, though others could sometimes make profits of more than 50 percent, while an average profit margin of 10 percent continued to make the business an attractive prospect. While 10 percent margins were not unheard of in other forms of business, this was higher than the average profit. However, Eric Williams's assertion that Great Britain's Industrial Revolution was funded mainly from the profits of the trade in slaves and sugar cannot be corroborated.[284] The slave trade contributed between 0.12 percent (in 1730) and 0.54 percent (in 1770) to Britain's gross domestic product, while if the West Indian plantation economy made any net contribution at all, given the high start-up costs of such enterprises, then it was at most 4 percent. These profits were certainly not enough to stimulate industrialization and probably had little bearing at all on the process.[285] Nevertheless, this trade did have an important influence on the development of shipping, banking, and several branches of manufacturing. Above all, certain ports benefited enormously from the slave trade—foremost among them the French city of Nantes, from which half of all slaving voyages undertaken by the French set sail. Bordeaux, France's second slave-trading port, also made healthy profits from this business, as well as from a whole range of other shipping activities. Much the same was also true of Bristol and later Liverpool, which between 1795 and 1804 is thought to have handled 85 percent of the British and three-sevenths of the entire European slave trade.

Europeans objected to the excesses of slavery, without condemning the trade outright—not even committed Christians and Enlightenment figures spoke out against it. Anglicans, Jesuits, and other Christians successfully exploited the system, as did respected figures like the philosopher John Locke and the statesman Thomas Jefferson. Only in the mid-eighteenth century did concerted and vehement criticism begin to be voiced, by Quakers and Evangelical Christians on the one hand and by Enlightenment freethinkers like Montesquieu on the other.

Plantation Life, Identity, and Spirituality

Life on American plantations was not the kind of patriarchal idyll depicted by Gilberto Freyre.[286] That said, despite excessive exploitation of slaves, neither was it invariably a living hell. The infamous rule that a slave needed to be kept alive only for seven years, the time it took to recoup the outlay on him, is a myth. Rather, a slave who had survived the ubiquitous infant mortality and the Middle Passage and had successfully acclimatized to his new home could look forward to several decades' life expectancy. The fact that the slave population did not reproduce at first must be put down to its demographic composition, especially the reliance on a constant influx of newly imported slaves. The birthrate could hardly grow exponentially when the slave population comprised barely one-third women, many of whom were past their childbearing prime and who in addition were used to long gaps between births and were initially devoid of any family ties. Once a more normal balance in the numbers between the sexes had been restored after imports were stopped, the result was a normal age pyramid and a stability, or even an increase, in the African slave population, which first became evident in the United

States. The reason for this is not that slaves received better treatment there but that there was a general rise in living standards there that affected whites and blacks alike.[287]

On Barbados, both whites and blacks suffered from lead poisoning through their habit of drinking rum that had been distilled using utensils containing this harmful metal.[288] Yet it is doubtful whether the whites were as inadequately nourished as the Africans. Even while they were still in Africa, blacks had lacked vitamins and minerals in their diet (often through having no salt to cook with), which had far-reaching consequences for their health. Studies of the diets of slaves in the Caribbean, Brazil, and North America have revealed similar deficiencies. Conversely, variations in height point to the fact that some slaves at least were quantitatively better fed than they had been in Africa. This may have had to do with how much food they were allowed to grow themselves. It may be that in emergencies, the plantation owner supplemented their food supplies with provisions or possibly supplied a proportion of their daily rations on a regular basis, but in general, slaves were expected, at least in part, to provide for themselves—though they were accorded little free time for this task.[289] Domestic slaves and artisan slaves may have enjoyed a greater degree of latitude and had a better chance of winning their freedom, yet for the overwhelming majority of plantation slaves, their owners were concerned only with extracting the maximum amount of work. For their part, slaves had a latent resistance geared toward keeping their effort to a minimum; sometimes, this resistance manifested itself in acts of sabotage, truculent defiance, assassinations, and insurrections. To teach them a lesson, the white minority punished the black majority for these actions with barbarous cruelty. From the very beginnings of Spain's American empire, slaves who had escaped from their bondage (cimarrones) established and ran independent communities in the jungle.

Despite the fact that a degree of enmity existed between black Africans and Amerindians (sometimes deliberately fomented by the Europeans), this did not prevent runaway slaves and native peoples from cooperating in several cases—a nightmare scenario for the whites. Thus, in the hinterland of the Pacific coast of Ecuador, there arose a mixed African-Amerindian community known as the *Mulatos de Esmeraldas,* with a population of around five thousand. The governor of Quito was forced to sign a treaty with their "kings" to ensure their cooperation. Although the Portuguese, like the Spanish, employed Indian trackers to hunt down the communities of runaway slaves in the rainforest *(quilombos)* and destroy them, there is much evidence to suggest that the famous African slave kingdom of Palmares, which existed in the northeast of Brazil until 1694, included many Amerindian inhabitants. Furthermore, a group of several thousand "Black Caribs," or *Garifuna,* developed from a core of fugitive slaves on the island of St. Vincent in the Caribbean; this group spoke Arawak and had a mixed Amerindian and African culture. The Black Caribs were eventually deported to Honduras by the British in 1797.[290]

In most cases, either by chance or design, slaves found themselves in a mixed community of Africans of different origin and speaking different languages. As a consequence, a more or less universal adoption of the slave owners' language and religion was unavoidable. Yet no slave apostles like the Spanish Jesuit Pedro Claver came to the fore in British colonies, probably because, in contrast to Catholics, British slave owners feared that they would be obliged to free baptized slaves. Besides, Catholicism was better suited than the colder, more distant Protestantism to being combined with latent African religiosity. Here, slaves enjoyed the Old Testament story of a people enslaved in a foreign land and led to salvation by Moses, until the Anglo-American revivalist movement evolved new, more ecstatic forms of Protestantism that were more attractive to Africans.[291] In the matter of religion, as in so many other aspects, the enormous creativity of the African diaspora in the Americas shone through, and the cultural dynamism of the African Atlantic is still a force to be reckoned with today. A prime example of this—though by no means the only one—is jazz music, which has long become accepted as a global cultural legacy. The reconstituting of African religions under the cloak of Catholicism belongs in the same category.

Groups with strong local representation were then free to assume the leadership, especially if they had already been culturally dominant in Africa. For example, the West African slaves who were taken to Bahia in Brazil originally defined themselves, as they had done at home, by region and tribal group of origin—for example, as Oyo, Egba, or Ijesha. From this, there developed the collective term *Nagô,* and finally in the nineteenth century, through cultural exchange with West Africa brought about by many African former slaves returning there, the overarching identity of the Yoruba—a term that had apparently only ever been used in West Africa by outsiders (for example, the Hausa and others) to describe peoples of the western Niger area. Parallel with this, African brotherhoods of the eighteenth century developed in the early nineteenth into cult sites *(terreiros)* that were first given the designation *Candomblé* in 1826. Various groups began to venerate these sites as places of worship of their deities, or orishas; thus, the Oyo worshiped Xangô; the Egba, Iemanjá; the Ijesha, Oxum; the Ife, Oxalá; and so forth. These orishas of Yoruba theology were also joined by the *vodun* of the Ewe and Fon peoples and the *nkisis* of the Angola nation (Bantu), which performed the same roles within their societies. Thus, leaving aside the peculiarities of voodoo and *Santería* in the West Indies, there arose a kind of common denominator of Afro-American religions between Brazil and the United States. Between them, Candomblé and above all Umbanda, further enriched by French spiritism, number millions of devotees in Latin America, with Umbanda gaining an increasing following among whites, too.[292]

Religious creativity on the other side of the Atlantic is attested by the manner in which Christianity was assimilated into the existing mental schema in the Kingdom of Kongo. According to this, then, Christ became the great chief, while the Virgin Mary, like an African queen mother, became his co-regent. However, although the Africans found it difficult to grasp the concepts of resurrection, heaven, and hell, they were fully attuned to the cult of dead ancestors, especially that of former kings. Accordingly, the sacraments and religious observances, even wayside shrines, were revered as especially potent nkisis, while baptism was seen as a protection against witchcraft. In this way, Christianity served as an additional legitimation of royal sovereignty.[293]

One curious consequence of the Capuchin mission occurred in 1704, when the spirit of St. Anthony of Padua took possession of the medium Beatriz Kimpa Vita, who came from Kongo's nobility—an almost commonplace event in Congolese terms. The resulting Antonine movement set about destroying all "fetishes," including crucifixes, and opposed all "sorcerers," including the Capuchins. For they maintained that religious power derived not from prayer and the sacraments but from good intentions *(kindoki)* alone. Beatriz experienced weekly "ascensions," as well as preaching and conducting a form of mass. Her group occupied the capital São Salvador, but after undergoing two abortions and finally becoming pregnant a third time by her "guardian angel," as she claimed, skeptical voices began to be raised, and she herself became beset by self-doubt. At the urging of a Capuchin friar, she was arrested in 1706 by the royal pretender Pedro IV and, after being forced to recant her beliefs, was burned at the stake with her lover. Yet her movement outlasted her and may well have had some influence on American slave revolts.[294]

The economic and political importance of the slave trade for Africa is the subject of much debate. Scholars argue whether it was responsible for a widespread depopulation of large areas of the hinterland of the Guinea Coast or whether these massive losses were confined to the region around the Bight of Benin. There is also doubt as to whether Angola suffered a lasting population catastrophe or whether it recovered quickly and effectively from the depredations of slavery. And, if it is correct that mass transportations and reduced population growth rates caused the population of West Africa to shrink from 25 million to 23 million in the period 1700–1850, instead of increasing to a projected 39.3 million, and that by 1850 the population of sub-Saharan Africa stood at just 50 million rather than 100 million,[295] then does that automatically imply that economic growth was hampered? Indeed, might not this release from the pressure of a growing population under the straitened preindustrial circumstances the continent was then facing, combined with absorption into the European global economic system, even be said to have promoted development? In any event, it is surely no coincidence that certain key locations of the slave trade, such as Ghana and Nigeria, subsequently became the economically and politically most highly developed nations on the continent, as well as pioneers of decolonization. For right from the outset, in their commercial dealings with Europeans, Africans were by no means passive and subservient; they engaged voluntarily in this new trading opportunity, skillfully adopting innovations and assimilating them into their culture.[296]

Admittedly, it is perfectly possible for economic growth to go hand in hand with dehumanization. There is much evidence to suggest that, despite increasing prices, the growing demand for slaves served only to disvalue people's human worth by turning them into mere commodities. Wherever hunting down people and kidnapping them became a daily part of the life of a community, traditional human sacrifice rites tended to degenerate into wholesale slaughter, as in Dahomey. Moreover, Africans simply expanded their traditional slave economy and adapted it to the Atlantic slave trade. In the eighteenth century, there were as many slaves in Africa as there were in America, but in 1850 there were far more in Africa, perhaps almost ten million—another form of Atlantic commonality.

The French and British Atlantic

There were many types of early contact between Europeans and the native inhabitants of North America, and the boundaries between them are not at all distinct. These types of contact occurred in the context of (1) voyages of discovery and trade, occasionally involving shipwreck; (2) the often underestimated temporary presence of tens of thousands of fishermen off the Northeast coast; (3) expeditions that penetrated into the interior and sometimes overwintered with the Indians; (4) missionaries, who formed an integral part of Spanish voyages to the Americas from the very beginning; (5) the trade in furs and skins, which began as early as the sixteenth century; and (6) the founding of settlements.[297]

Although the Iberian powers upheld their claim to a monopoly on exploration of the Americas—even North America—while at the same time failing to enforce it, the English and French were adamant that only actual occupation and settlement of the New World constituted a legitimate claim to ownership.[298] And when both of these nations then proceeded to found settlements, their concern, unlike that of all other processes of Atlantic exchange, was to consciously construct a New Europe overseas. Indeed, the colony of New France in Canada to some extent and quite expressly the Puritan colony of New England were designed to be a better Europe. This Puritan self-image would later come to characterize, in a definitive and enduring way, the mentality of the ruling elite of the principal Atlantic power, the United States.

Yet in the immediate aftermath of their first voyages to reconnoiter the region around 1500, the English confined themselves to fishing off the Grand Banks of Newfoundland. Their predominantly good relations with Spain at the time and England's internal problems led them to desist from any more extensive activities until the late sixteenth century. Francis I of France, on the contrary, spread his long-running conflict with the Holy Roman emperor Charles V overseas. It was in his service that Jacques Cartier ventured as far as present-day Montreal in 1535, in search of the Northwest Passage and deposits of precious metals. However, an attempt to found a settlement on the site of modern Quebec in 1541–1543 failed, like many other early such ventures, not only because of disease and hostile natives but above all because of shortage of provisions in the particularly harsh winters there. Instead of this kind of unattractive undertaking, in the following decades the French preferred to embark on plundering expeditions to the West Indies and to establish bases on Spanish and Portuguese soil (namely, Florida and Brazil); Huguenots played a leading role in both these enterprises, but they were to no avail.

In the meantime, Canada had become an attractive destination for fur traders; in particular, the demand for beaver pelts for new gentlemen's hats that had come into fashion expanded hugely. Tadoussac on the lower reaches of the St. Lawrence River became a major meeting point for French and Indian traders. A trading base founded there in 1600 had to be relocated to Fundy Bay on the Acadian Peninsula (modern Nova Scotia) in 1605. This settlement developed into the town of Port Royal (present-day Annapolis), the oldest French settlement, which nevertheless, due to its exposed position, was temporarily lost to the English in 1613–1632 and 1654–1667. By now the French crown was no longer interested solely in economic gain but was also simultaneously pursuing the political aim of finally establishing a settlement colony of New France in America in defiance of Spanish claims. Even so, for decades the undertaking suffered from basic conflicts of interest. The crown wanted colonization but at no cost to itself. It therefore availed itself of the newly devised financial instruments of regulated- or joint-stock companies with royal assent (charter) and forced noble courtiers and fur traders alike to join together to form holding companies to raise the necessary capital. But because the aristocracy showed little enthusiasm for this venture and the merchants were interested only in the fur trade, the obligation of the *compagnies* that resulted from this process to settle colonists in the New World was largely ignored.[299]

Thus, while Samuel de Champlain (1567–1635) was able to found a fur-trading station and a settlement at Quebec in 1608, by the following year twenty of its twenty-eight inhabitants had died. By 1620, there were around sixty people living there, but hardly any of them were farmers, whose skills were urgently needed. In 1629, New France as a whole numbered 107 inhabitants, of whom seventy-two were living in Quebec and twenty in Acadia; in Quebec at this time, only 8 hectares of land were being farmed. In the meantime, to the south Champlain had explored the land lying between Quebec and the lake that now bears his name and Lake Ontario, as well as all the territory up to Lake Huron to the west, and had also sponsored other expeditions. As early as 1609, on the shores of Lake Champlain, he and his Indian allies had clashed with the Iroquois tribe of the Mohawk; this skirmish, from which he emerged victorious thanks to the fact he was equipped with firearms (then still a rarity in the area), was militarily insignificant but politically of enormous importance. The backdrop to this animosity was the fur trade.

Canada as Contact Zone

Unlike in Cartier's time, the Iroquois were no longer living on the shores of the St. Lawrence; there, Algonquin-speaking groups were the trading partners of the French. Yet of greater importance to the French were the Iroquois-speaking Huron people, who lived between Lake Simcoe and the Georgian Bay inlet of Lake Huron and who exercised a form of middleman monopoly in fur trading over an area extending to Hudson Bay in the north, Quebec in the east, and Lake Winnebago in the west.[300] As a result, Champlain was at pains to win their support and so dispatched the first Franciscan missionaries to arrive in Canada, in 1615, to minister to them. Other tribes, primarily the Mohawk, were excluded from this system. The Iroquois proper, whose homeland lay between Lake Ontario and the Hudson River, found themselves increasingly surrounded by enemies. The confederacy of the Iroquois "Five Nations"—the Seneca, Cayuga, Onondaga, Oneida, and Mohawk (expanded to the "Six Nations" in 1722 by the arrival of the displaced Tuscarora from the south)—is thought to have been formed in the late sixteenth century as a defensive alliance.[301] But now the tables were about to be turned. After beating off a joint Huron and French attack in 1615, the Iroquois Confederacy steadily went on the offensive, for from 1613 onward the Dutch had also established their own fur-trading station of Fort Oranje on the Hudson River (discovered by Henry Hudson in 1609) not far from the present-day city of Albany. The New Netherlands Company that they founded in 1614 was taken over in 1621 by the West Indies Company. In order to do business with the Dutch, who were replaced by the English in 1664, the Iroquois set about annihilating all other tribes who stood in the way between their homeland and Fort Oranje.

Even so, they still had trouble satisfying the growing demand for furs, because their own region had been largely hunted out.

As a consequence, they now began to launch attacks on the fur-trading system of the Huron, the French, and the Algonquin. These assaults were extremely successful, thanks to the firearms they had been able to acquire from the Dutch, while the French and English, just like the Spanish and Portuguese in their American possessions, preferred to withhold such weapons from their native allies. In 1634, the Jesuits had embarked on a major missionary campaign to convert the Huron, which the latter accepted for the sake of the fur trade, although they were perfectly well aware who had brought epidemic diseases into the country, which in 1634–1639 had reduced their people's numbers from 18,000 to just 9,000. From 1641 onward, Iroquois attacks grew more intense. The French colony was also hit, but it was too weak as yet to counterattack. Finally, in 1648 and 1649, the Iroquois carried out two devastating attacks against the Huron with a force of 1,200 men, killing and taking captive their adversaries by the thousands; Jesuit missionaries were also martyred in these assaults. The surviving Huron fled to join their French allies or to the west. Their territory was now empty, leaving the Iroquois free access to the furs.

In 1629, Quebec was besieged into starvation by an English fleet and occupied. Yet when it was returned to France in 1632, Cardinal Richelieu, with his personally controlled Compagnie de la Nouvelle France or Compagnie des Cent-Associés, was able to start afresh. In return for being granted a fur-trading monopoly and other privileges—only fishing remained accessible to all—the company was obliged to settle four thousand colonists there within fifteen years and to support them for the first three years in their new home. As also happened at the start in the English colonies of Maryland and Carolina, a manorial system *(seigneuries)* was set up, which was intended to attract villeins *(censitaires)*. However, initially the official rights of the squires and the duties of the villeins had little significance, because the latter had too many options. They came because this was the only way to acquire the economically most valuable and secure land along the St. Lawrence. The director of the company and the future governor of the region, the royal counselor Jean de Lauson, secured for himself 70 percent of the first 2.7 million hectares. By the mid-seventeenth century, there were sixty-two seigneuries, of which the fifty-two aristocratic squires owned 84 percent. By 1760, the number had risen to 250 seigneuries covering almost 3.2 million hectares. Only in the eighteenth century did the manorial system in Canada appear to take on the same kind of rigid form as in the mother country.[302]

In 1634 a second settlement was founded at Trois-Rivières, followed in 1642 by Montréal, established by a group of idealists, who intended to lead an exemplary Christian existence there in the company of converted Indians. Montréal was granted its own governor and special privileges; by 1663, it numbered 596 inhabitants,[303] out of a total of 3,035 in the whole of Canada, despite the fact that in 1645, instead of the projected four thousand, it had only three hundred citizens. While Montréal fits into the planned pattern, established since the days of Richelieu, of a strictly Catholic New France, it can at the same time be seen as an exception to this template, because the Catholicizing project was largely conducted elsewhere under the leadership of the Jesuits, who first arrived in the country in 1625. Not only did the Society of Jesus run the Indian missions;[304] the Jesuits also opened a school in 1635 and thereafter a seminary in Quebec, the first institution of higher learning to be established north of Mexico. The Jesuits also brought Ursuline nuns and a nursing order to Canada, who set up a girls' school and a hospital, respectively. In 1645, the Jesuit influence was responsible for ensuring that the debt-burdened holding company handed over all the colony's commercial and administrative affairs to a *compagnie des habitants,* run by the principal figures of the settlement, first and foremost the *seigneurs.* Alongside the governors of the three separate settlements, the superior of the Jesuits had a large hand in the day-to-day workings of this company.

Likewise, the Jesuits worked diligently to ensure that the choice for the appointment of an apostolic vicar for the region by the pope in 1657, who was to be promoted first bishop of Quebec in 1674, fell on their confederate François de Laval. Yet the archbishop of Rouen claimed Canada for his diocese, as did the Anglican bishop of London with regard to British America, and tried to make trouble for Laval in Montréal through his own appointee there. Laval's own doctrinal rigor got him involved in a number of conflicts anyway, even ultimately with the governor. The catalyst was his implacable opposition to the sale of hard liquor to the Indians, including excommunicating those who transgressed, plus his demand to have them shot.

A significant proportion of the male populace of French Canada, for instance, in 1666 around five hundred out of a total population recorded by census as 4,219,[305] lived among the Indians as forest rangers or fur and liquor traders and produced a large number of mixed-race children.[306] In doing so, they contributed to the generally extraordinarily good relations between the French and the indigenous population (with the exception of the Iroquois). But the church, which saw this activity as undermining the missionary work, took exception not just to the general looseness of morality but above all to the spread of alcoholism among the Indians. Prior to the arrival of the French, they had had no experience of alcoholic drink, nor did they have the enzymes that help break down alcohol quickly in the body. Yet they took to this new stimulant and indulged in it freely, often to excess. Even the most stringent countermeasures on the part of the French were fated to remain ineffective so long as the fur trade was thriving, for their Dutch and English rivals had no qualms about supplying the Indians in their territories.[307] Plus there were scarcely any influential missionaries in those areas.

Settlements in Virginia and New England

During the Elizabethan Age, England had once more become active on the world stage, setting privateers like John Hawkins and Francis Drake on the Spanish, partly with the financial support of the crown, and embarking on new projects in North America under the leadership of cutthroats who had already earned their spurs with acts of brutality in Ireland, such as Humphrey Gilbert and Walter Raleigh.[308] Gilbert took possession of Newfoundland in 1583, with no immediate consequences. For his part, Raleigh sponsored the founding, in 1585 and 1587, of a base on Roanoke Island (modern North Carolina) on that part of the Eastern Seaboard of North America that the English had named "Virginia," in honor of the "Virgin Queen" Elizabeth I. It was intended as a base for launching privateering raids against Spanish territories but on both occasions had to be quickly abandoned due to the usual problems with provisioning remote colonies. In 1584, Raleigh's close associate Richard Hakluyt had presented a treatise to the queen entitled *A Discourse Concerning Western Planting,* which extolled the advantages of founding colonies in the Americas. According to Hakluyt, they would serve as consumer markets for English woolen goods and as cheap suppliers of exotic commodities and shipbuilding materials, so contributing to a boom in English maritime trade and hence to an undermining of the Spanish enemy. In addition, they could become a dumping ground for England's undesirable and superfluous population and also act as a beacon for the true Anglican faith—with only slight modifications, here was an accurate blueprint for the future British Empire.[309]

However, the British Empire proper was a long time in the gestation. Its beginnings under James I were based on new socioeconomic and ideological developments. On the one hand, under the auspices of economic recovery, commercial stock had in the meantime attracted so much interest that the new colonial–political instrument of the Chartered Company was able to come into its own here as well. On the other, in contrast to the other colonial powers of northwestern Europe, English theologians and jurists began to entertain ideas of universal hegemony of the kind promulgated by Spain—ideas that had been frowned upon a short time ago. Claims to global domination by the "new Solomon" James I and his new chosen people began to be aired, while the heathens, who in their laziness had neglected to follow the biblical injunction to work the land, were divested of all their rights, especially the right to property, by the renowned jurist Edward Coke.

Thus, James I granted the "Virginia Company" (newly constituted on three occasions: 1606, 1609, and 1612) not only the American coast from the Thirty-Fourth to the Forty-Fifth Parallel—thereby legitimizing British claims to the French territory of Acadia—but also (as early as 1609) the whole of the hinterland stretching to the Pacific, a territorial claim that, post-Independence, was readopted by the state of Virginia. The members of the company were courtiers, London merchants, and country squires from Southwest England, who had some personal connection to the colonizing ventures of the sixteenth century.[310] In 1607, the settlement of Jamestown was founded on Chesapeake Bay; however, a similar settlement in Maine at the same time failed. Yet the threat of failure even loomed over Jamestown for many years, thanks to bouts of disease and the usual supply problems. The gentlemen and artisans who for a long time made up the majority of its citizens were neither able nor willing to get involved in the business of agricultural production. The large Indian population around the settlement provided them with food. This may or may not have had to do with the famous romances of "Princess" Pocahontas with John Smith and John Rolfe, but whatever the case, the Indians had a poor opinion of the newcomers.

Primarily through his introduction of tobacco cultivation and processing in 1612–1614, Rolfe became the savior of the Jamestown colony, which consequently became attractive to both new settlers and investors thanks to the high price of tobacco. By 1619, it had around 700 inhabitants and by 1624 no fewer than 1,253 (though only 18 percent of them were women). In 1622, the Indians, oppressed by losing land to various settlements, launched an attack on Jamestown, killing 347 settlers. Their resistance was all in vain; following another war in 1644, which claimed 500 white lives, the tribe was exterminated. As early as 1618, the colony was reorganized. Alongside a governor, a council and an elected general assembly were now established. The assembly, which first sat in 1619, was the first house of elected representatives in American history. However, it appears, at least initially, to have modeled itself less on the British Houses of Parliament than on the shareholders' meetings of the Virginia Company. After the Indian attack on Jamestown, the company was actually dissolved due to financial difficulties, and in 1624 Virginia became a crown colony. From 1634 to 1643, it was divided, once and for all, into counties and parishes on the English pattern. The population increased rapidly: by 1640, more than 8,000 people were living there, by 1653 14,300, and by 1660 27,000, 950 of whom were African slaves. Year on year, around 500–1,000 people emigrated there, with this figure growing to around 2,000 after 1649. About half of this new influx are thought to have been indentured servants, who were treated like slaves and who by the mid-seventeenth century made up more than half of the entire population. In all likelihood, the notorious decline in the status of the African slaves, who had been imported to Virginia since 1619, is attributable not simply to what was happening in the West Indies but also to the arrival of the indentured laborers. Given this kind of composition of the labor force, there must have been a heavy preponderance of men. The economic structure created a decentralized settlement. Ships could land directly at the flourishing plantations, unloading manufactured goods from England and taking on board balls of tobacco.

The northern colonies, which came into existence from 1620 on, presented a different picture. For here the ideological motivation of the strict Calvinists—the so-called Puritans, who found themselves at odds with the established Anglican

Church—played an important role. For the Calvinists wished, as Providence's chosen people, to found a "city upon the hill" in the New World, in other words a Holy Commonwealth that would become a shining beacon of hope for the whole world.

At first, a small group of Nonconformist dissenters, who had emigrated to Leiden in the Netherlands but who found themselves in an economically and politically precarious position there, threatened with assimilation, resolved to decamp to Virginia. After having secured capital and a patent from the Virginia Company, forty-one of these so-called saints, along with sixty-three "strangers," set sail in 1620 on a two-month voyage to America on board the *Mayflower*. However, they made land at Cape Cod, outside the territory of the Virginia Company, and decided to stay there. In order to give their enterprise some form of legitimacy, they drew up the "Mayflower Compact," for which some overinflated and unjustified claims have subsequently been made, either as a prototype contract of dominion or as a key founding document of American democracy. Under the shrewd merchant William Bradford (1589–1657), the colony, which despite agricultural activity had been threatened by starvation, experienced a steady revival and by 1660 numbered three thousand inhabitants. While this extreme Congregationalist group insisted on absolute autonomy for their church congregation, they were generous in the matter of who could become a member.[311]

Yet the most significant settlements in "New England," as this region was dubbed by the Virginia pioneer John Smith in 1616, were the colonies around Massachusetts Bay, which adhered to a form of mainstream Puritanism.[312] Various interests and patents, in which merchants from Dorchester and London played a leading role besides "Puritans" from eastern England, came together in 1629 as a joint-stock company endowed with a royal charter, by the name of the Governor and Company of Massachusetts Bay in New England. The board of the company comprised a governor with a deputy and eighteen assistants, all elected from the General Court of the shareholders ("freemen"), which met every quarter-year. Because, when the company's charter was issued, its place of business was not specified, the influential members, under the leadership of the country squire and lawyer John Winthrop (1588–1649), who became governor in 1629, resolved in 1630 to follow the first four hundred emigrants and move the headquarters of the company to New England. Their decision was prompted by the increasing pressure being exerted on Puritans in England. Thus, the company's constitution also became that of the colony.

Massachusetts also faced a harsh first winter of starvation, but after 1633 the stream of new arrivals increased. By 1634, 4,000 people were already living in the colony. In the third and fourth decades of the seventeenth century, some 70,000 English people emigrated to the Americas, with many going to the West Indies, while others opted for Virginia and around a third for New England, which by 1641 is thought to have had around 12,000 inhabitants. By then, twenty-two new, loosely organized settlements had come into being, including Salem, Boston, Cambridge, and others with names taken from the mother country. An estimate for 1660 yielded a count of 18,000–20,000. The proportion of entire families emigrating was probably greater here than in Virginia. But family-run farms and other rural businesses here did not just generate produce for the colony's own needs. Cereal export from this region began as early as 1634, followed by fish, skins, and wooden manufactures. The consumers of these exports were southern colonies, above all the West Indies, and the Mediterranean region, whose goods began increasingly to be carried in home-produced ships to both England and the Americas from 1641 onward. As early as 1650, Boston merchants were playing a leading role in transatlantic trade.[313]

From 1630, independent settlers who were not members of the company were permitted to become freemen. Even so, from 1631, it was stipulated that they had to be members of their respective church congregations and were required to show documentary evidence that they had undergone conversion to Puritanism. Yet this proved impossible to enforce strictly in practice, meaning that by 1647 non–church members also had obtained the right to vote, at least at a local level. By 1631, this right to vote was the only privilege left to the freemen, who had lost their right to legislate to the oligarchy of the governor and his assistants. Three years later, in the face of Winthrop's opposition, the freemen won back this right. Accordingly, until 1644, the General Court was turned into a bicameral assembly, comprising the House of Deputies and the Upper House of the assistants, both of which were required to approve laws and other resolutions. Local affairs were decided on by township assemblies; elected committees deriving from these bodies also ruled on certain local issues in the meantime. In 1643, four counties were set up as intermediate bodies for the dispensation of justice. From 1641, the colony had been in a position to issue its own statute book; a revised edition came into force in 1648.[314]

Some settlements founded grammar schools. In 1636, a college was established in Cambridge, which in 1639, in recognition of an endowment of £800, adopted the name of its benefactor, John Harvard. This institution offered a broad-based curriculum, though initially this was designed solely for educating future preachers. In 1642, parents in New England were obliged to teach their children reading and writing. Five years later, compulsory school attendance was introduced, funded by the individual communities.

The church in New England was moderately Congregationalist, which meant that its basically autonomous congregations took communal decisions at general synods. But in actual fact, it was an "established church" insofar as its members were originally supposed to be identical with the citizens, and authorities were duty bound to persecute dissenters and people of different faiths. In Boston, for instance, dyed-in-the-wool Quakers were even executed at first. Out of the Covenant of Grace, God's pact with the newly chosen people, there arose the Church Covenant on the one hand and the Civil Covenant on the other. These formed the foundations of the Holy Commonwealth, a common cause espoused by church and state leaders.[315]

Of course, there were many vehement opponents of this regime in Anglican and Royalist England. In 1637, the end of colonial independence seemed imminent, at least for a spell. But the Puritans in New England were also in conflict with the new Puritan regime in the mother country, not due to Massachusetts's claim to be a model for a complete reformation of English society, nor because the stream of emigrants had dried up, but primarily because the colony continued to insist upon its total independence in its internal affairs. Virginia, in contrast, despite its strongly Puritan flavor, remained on the Royalist side in the English Civil War right up to 1652.[316] Ultimately, it was also ruled by Puritan governors, but ones who were just as reluctant as Oliver Cromwell himself to push through the Puritanization of Virginia and the suppression of the governing Anglican Church there. A new wave of immigrants in the 1650s came mainly from Royalist circles.

Alongside the dominant colonies of Virginia and Massachusetts, a whole series of other settlements also came into being up to 1660, in part as a result of schismatic movements in opposition to the Puritan theocracy. The preacher Roger Williams questioned not only the right of civil authorities to exercise coercion in spiritual matters but also the legality of royal land grants; in his view, only purchases from Indians were legitimate. Banished in 1635, the following year he established the settlement of Providence, Rhode Island, on land he had purchased.[317] Three further settlements grew up in the vicinity in 1638–1639, including Newport, founded by followers of Anne Hutchinson, who had been exiled in 1638 for going back to the fundamental beliefs of Calvinism and criticizing the implicit reliance of the Covenant of Grace on righteousness through good works, rather than through faith alone. The settlements that came together to form the colony of Rhode Island were granted a patent by the English Parliament in 1644.[318] By 1674, it had five thousand inhabitants. Connecticut came into being after 1635 through collaboration between Puritan land speculators and migrants from Massachusetts. Its Fundamental Orders of 1639 derived from the statutes of Massachusetts but contained a provision for an annual election of the governor and made no connection between citizens' rights and church membership. By 1663, the colony had more than eleven thousand inhabitants. From Connecticut and various Indian peoples, a group of London Puritans who had failed to find a home in Massachusetts then acquired a tract of land in 1638, on which they founded the settlement of New Haven in 1640. There, an even more rigorous Puritan oligarchy than in Massachusetts was put in place, but the colony remained small and in 1663 was summarily merged with neighboring Connecticut.[319] Finally, from 1623 on, more colonies developed further to the north, on the basis of older legal titles; some of these joined together in 1679 to form the crown colony of New Hampshire,[320] while Massachusetts was able to assert its sovereignty over Maine, which it first proclaimed in 1641, until 1819. In 1660, these territories had around 1,600 inhabitants apiece.

In the south, in 1632, King Charles I had granted land north of Virginia to Lord Baltimore, who in 1634 founded the main settlement of the colony of Maryland, named for the queen. This principal town would presently become known as St. Mary's City, after the Blessed Virgin Mary, as Lord Baltimore was a Catholic and wanted to create a refuge for his coreligionists, albeit only on the basis of religious equality. In addition, it was envisaged that the colony, under the overall sovereignty of its owner (proprietor), would, like Canada, be divided up into manors. In the event, though, a system of major landownership arose, because the many indentured servants had to be given small parcels of land outside the manors at the termination of their allotted period of servitude. Also, the colony's charter foresaw a representative assembly, which by 1650 had developed into a bicameral system like that of Virginia. The religious toleration that was cultivated in Maryland came under threat from radical Catholics but primarily from the inevitable influx of Protestant immigrants, who in time became the dominant majority. Despite conflicts during the English Civil War, Maryland's principle of toleration and the regime of the proprietor were restored by 1657.[321]

Nor did the Dutch colony of Nieuw Nederland on the River Hudson remain simply a fur-trading settlement. Originally, the Dutch West India Company had attempted to promote its settlement through a kind of manor system, but all that now remained of this abortive scheme was an especially pronounced oligarchical political structure. As soon as settlement there was thrown open to everyone, the number of inhabitants increased by 1664 to nine thousand Europeans from various countries, including many Germans and French, together with four hundred slaves. The colony annexed the settlement of Nya Sverige (New Sweden; founded 1638) farther south on the Delaware River, with its four hundred inhabitants, in 1655 and in 1664 was ceded to England, becoming New York.[322]

The Expansion of New France

The reign of Louis XIV in France and the restoration of the monarchy in England gave a further boost to colonization efforts in the 1660s.[323] As states' central power increased, so they sought to exercise greater control over the colonies and to shape them in the image of the mother country. The *Roi Soleil*'s influential minister Jean-Baptiste Colbert was concerned to finally make French Canada a viable, and if possible profitable, proposition. The holding companies were therefore supplanted by a consolidated Compagnie des Indes occidentales, which however was less geared to realizing a profit than acting as an economic and political instrument of control; moreover, it was expressly excluded from getting involved in political or administrative affairs. In French Canada, the representatives of the crown ruled with even fewer restrictions than at home, and attempts to introduce representation for the colonists were instantly stifled. Although, as the king's representative, the governor-general was empowered to intervene in administrative matters, he had to justify his actions in France. His main function was in a military capacity, though, with wars looming against the Iroquois and the British also. Alongside him, the king's intendant was responsible for the functioning of the bureaucracy, the legal system, the economy, and the country's finances. In spite of his brief terms in office, from 1665 to 1668 and from 1670 to 1672, Intendant Jean Talon can be regarded as the founder of the new French Canada. The governor and intendant, along with the Bishop of Quebec, the attorney-general and five (later, twelve) specially appointed councillors, made up the Conseil Souverain, which acted as both the colony's supreme court and its legislature. Remarkably, though, few demands were made on the legal system.

In 1665, a regiment of regular French troops were dispatched to Canada to deal once and for all with the Iroquois problem. The destruction of their villages and stores forced the Five Nations to sue for peace in 1667, a truce that held until a renewed outbreak of hostilities in the 1680s, enabling Canada to move forward in its development. Between 1664 and 1680, almost 10,000 immigrants arrived on the St. Lawrence River—of whom 2,000 were engagés, 1,000 were former soldiers (including Swiss and Germans), and 1,000 were women for the marriage market, recruited with financial inducements to emigrate to Canada in order to compensate for the notorious surplus of single males. Indeed, the French did manage to achieve a more balanced numerical ratio between the sexes and bring about many fruitful marriages. There were bonuses for marrying early and producing lots of children, whereas bachelors were disadvantaged. In the decade 1660–1670, the birthrate is thought to have stood at 6.3 percent. Women gave birth to an average of eight children, and two-thirds of the population were under the age of fifteen. In theory, only healthy French Catholics were accepted as immigrants, while Huguenots were excluded. Most immigrants came from ports on the west coast of France and their environs (up to a radius of around 200 kilometers), with over half of them from the urban lower classes and the women drawn from orphanages. Up to the middle of the eighteenth century, it is estimated that several thousand immigrants arrived, yet even so New France's population count of fifty-five thousand at that time was largely down to the high internal birthrate.[324] The Seigneurie, where minor court cases were heard, the parish community, and the militia organization formed the pillars of rural law and order. During the wars in the late seventeenth and early eighteenth centuries, French Canadian society became more militarized, making the local militia captains the most important arm of the executive.

Arable and livestock farming were promoted and increased in scale. There were also plans to develop woodworking, including shipbuilding and other applications, together with commercial fishing, though these never really came to fruition. Compared with the home country, and with the more favorably placed British colonies, production and transport costs were always prohibitively high in French Canada. Even in the officially sponsored supply of goods to the French West Indies, where plantations urgently needed imported foodstuffs as well as such items as wooden barrels for transporting the sugar they produced, Canada was unable to compete with the British colonies. Accordingly, the main activity in French Canada remained fur trapping and trading, which in 1739 still accounted for 70 percent of Canadian exports.[325]

The further expansion of French North America was also bound up with this question. Although Colbert had forbidden it, he had also allowed for exceptions if another power should threaten to preempt France. Upholding France's claims against England and Spain also meant securing control of new fur-trading regions. In 1671, France had failed to dislodge the English "Hudson's Bay Company," founded the year before, from its fur-trading realm in the north of the country, while in the war of 1686 its seizure of the company's territory had lasted for only a brief spell. Yet it was perfectly free to officially take possession of the area around the Great Lakes. In 1673, the explorer Louis Jolliet and the Jesuit Jacques Marquette—a typical combination among French Canada's frontier pioneers—embarked from the Great Lakes on a journey down the Mississippi as far as the mouth of the Arkansas River, where they retreated for fear of encountering the Spanish. However, in 1682 Robert Cavelier de la Salle ventured right down to the Mississippi delta, claiming the entire region as the French possession of "Louisiana," named in honor of his sovereign. Biloxi was established as the first settlement there in 1699, while Mobile (in the modern state of Alabama) became the territory's capital in 1711. Between 1717 and 1731, the newly created Compagnie d'occident controlled this colony; New Orleans was founded in 1717 and promoted to the capital of Louisiana in 1722. Settlement at this stage was still negligible, but a chain of forts was built in order to secure the Mississippi and

Ohio valleys, with their trade, for France; at this time, the British had barely even reached the Appalachian Mountains.[326]

Meanwhile, Canada was enjoying a fair degree of prosperity, but although the colony was now standing on its own feet financially, French North America still scarcely generated any surpluses. The contrast to the booming French West Indies was so glaring that the mother country could barely summon up any interest in Canada, especially after the imperialist designs of the French crown began to shift to the European theater. In the ensuing wars, the French in America acquitted themselves extraordinarily well, given the numerical superiority of the British, thanks to the earlier militarization of the Canadian population. However, like the Indians before them, they were able to win only individual battles but not wars.

English Proprietor Colonies

With an eye to increasing royal tax revenues, the restored English monarchy made its first task the pursuit of more aggressive trade policies with regard to its colonies; this process had already been initiated by the Commonwealth's Navigation Act of 1651 and was now enhanced by new laws passed in 1660, 1663, and 1673. Non-English ships—which in practice mainly meant Dutch vessels—were prohibited from plying their trade between England and its colonies. Furthermore, so-called enumerated goods—that is, sugar, tobacco, cotton, and indigo—could be exported only directly to England, while all imports to the colonies had to be carried via England. At the same time, levies were imposed on trade between the colonies in order to force them to comply with these directives. While it is true that the colonies profited from this protectionist system, they occasionally also found themselves saddled with additional costs. As a result, the crown and the committees of the Privy Council that were responsible for colonial affairs were, at least initially, amenable to making concessions. In 1662 and 1663, respectively, Connecticut and Rhode Island were granted new charters, with provisions for yearly elections of both chambers and of the governor, by all free men in the territories.

Conversely, Charles II gave away land in North America to meet obligations to various noblemen or to discharge some of his many debts. After the king had granted the area between New England and Maryland, with virtually unrestricted authority (with no question of any assembly being created there), to his brother James, the Duke of York and the future King James II, James proceeded to pass the land between the Hudson and the Delaware on to two old servants of the crown. After several changes of ownership, this became the crown colony of New Jersey in 1702.

First and foremost, though, between 1663 and 1665, Charles II granted to a consortium of eight supporters of his from his early years, including the influential minister Edward Hyde, Earl of Clarendon, and his "kingmaker," George Monck, Duke of Albemarle, the territory of Carolina south of Virginia, named in his honor. He attached the proviso, on the one hand, that the new owners should create a manorial aristocracy there and, on the other, that the settlers should be involved in the legislature. The proprietors duly drafted a constitution in 1665, involving extensive participation by both representatives of the settlers and of the governor and the council that they had appointed. This was followed in 1669 by the Fundamental Constitutions devised by Antony Ashley Cooper (taking his inspiration from James Harrington's tract on political philosophy, *The Commonwealth of Oceana* of 1656), which envisioned a complex social and political hierarchy of property owners. The wholly impractical and unworldly nature of this constitution argues against the alleged coauthorship of Cooper's onetime secretary John Locke (as was once maintained). The settlers, who were disenfranchised by Cooper's constitution, duly rebelled and demanded an order of the kind that had been enacted in other colonies. Land-hungry migrants from Virginia settled in the north of Carolina, where they engaged in mixed arable and livestock farming, while the south was occupied by refuges from Barbados, driven out by the Sugar Revolution; even so, from 1690 on, the growing cultivation of rice in this region meant only that they were caught up in yet another plantation system. In 1701, the proprietors repealed the Fundamental Constitutions and were forced to recognize the existence of two separate colonies, North and South Carolina. As their interest in this region waned, the crown took it over in 1729.

The last of the new proprietory colonies came into being when, with the assistance of the Duke of York, the Quaker William Penn, the son of an admiral and a crown creditor, was granted a charter to settle the southern portion of the duke's American holdings in 1681. There, in the region known as Pennsylvania, his plan was to employ peaceful means to create a safe haven for his persecuted coreligionists.[327] Thus, a carefully constructed, exemplary constitution (which also owed much to James Harrington's influence) was drafted for the colony. Yet Pennsylvania was also meant to be a moneymaking enterprise; over four years, well-planned advertising attracted eight thousand emigrants. The capital of Philadelphia soon overtook New York as the most important city in North America. Yet the pacifism espoused by the Quakers almost led to the loss of the colony. A constitutional compromise, reached in 1701 in the teeth of Penn's opposition, saved the day but also prompted his resignation from politics, though he remained the proprietor of the colony. Ultimately Delaware, which Penn had also acquired in 1682, got its own constitution in 1704, while still remaining under the jurisdiction of the governor of Pennsylvania.

From 1681 on, the Duke of York had called the tune in colonial politics, and in 1685 he ascended the throne as James II. His accession enabled a plan that had been drafted in 1683 during disagreements with the rebellious colony of Massachusetts to be put into action. Ultimately, its claims on Maine and New Hampshire, its shunning of people of other faiths, and its opposition to the Navigation Laws were all manifestations of its desire to assert in practice the de facto independence it had proclaimed in 1629, but this could no longer be tolerated by the crown. Accordingly, in 1684, the charter of the Massachusetts colony was legally revoked and replaced by the Dominion of New England, which, under the leadership of the authoritarian former governor of New York, Edmund Andros, was designed to bring Massachusetts, New Hampshire, Maine, Connecticut, Rhode Island, New York, and New Jersey into one large confederation by 1688. A council was appointed to assist the governor, and representative assemblies were suppressed, or at the very least their powers restricted at a local level. All Christian confessions except Catholicism were officially tolerated, while the Anglican Church was expressly encouraged. New taxes were imposed and the first steps taken toward a formal reassignment of land.

News of the Glorious Revolution of 1688 led to Andros's arrest and the opening of negotiations with the new king, William III. Connecticut and Rhode Island had their old charters reconfirmed, while Massachusetts was forced to accept a new one in 1691. While it now encompassed Plymouth Rock, where the Pilgrim fathers had landed, future voting rights in the colony were now tied to property rather than to membership of a church congregation, freedom of conscience within the framework of English law was introduced, English legislation and its legal system were made binding, and the governor was appointed directly by the crown. Only the council could now be elected, on an annual basis, by the House of Representatives.[328]

The Glorious Revolution sparked anti-Catholic uprisings in Maryland and New York in 1689. Admittedly, the New York insurrection, led by a merchant of German extraction named Jacob Leisler, seems to have been primarily a reaction of the Dutch population against the English oligarchy that had established itself under the colony's authoritarian regime from 1664 on. After Leisler's execution, New York was also granted its own House of Representatives. In 1715, the proprietor of Maryland was restored to full competence.

The formation of the Board of Trade ("The Lord Commissioners of Trade and Plantations") in 1696 created a central authority for the colonies, which was composed of two ex officio ministers and a series of experts. The granting of the charter to found the final and most southerly colony of Georgia (named for the king at the time, George II) in 1732 demonstrated just how centralized conceptions of colonial politics had become in the meantime. A group of prominent trustees wanted to make Georgia into an imperial defensive rampart against incursion by Indians and Spaniards alike, cultivate tropical crops there—above all, cotton—and settle ex-convicts there in the hope of giving them a new start. But only their Common Council, situated in London, would be empowered to pass laws for Georgia, and even then only with the assent of the crown. All administrative powers were vested in this council, and appointment of the colony's governor would have to be confirmed by the king. In addition, an annual report and accounts were to be presented—after all, the venture received financial support from the House of Commons. Moreover, against the wishes of the settlers, the trustees wanted to proscribe major landownership, slavery, and liquor. But as the economy grew stronger, they were forced to allow plantation slavery and the formation of an assembly in 1750. Two years later, Georgia became a crown colony.[329]

Mass Migration and Increased Conflict

Between 1600 and 1775, it is estimated that a total of 552,200 Europeans emigrated to British North America; at the same time 263,200 slaves were also imported.[330]

The immigrants were overwhelmingly English, German, and Swiss, as well as Ulster Scots. Transatlantic networks based on common nationality or a shared religion paved the way for many migrants. German-speaking immigrants lived in Pennsylvania in a cultural bubble. By 1800, some 75,000–100,000 people from Switzerland and the Rhineland had also emigrated there, in part attracted by stories of the soil there producing three times the yield of the poor farmland at home. The great majority of the British immigrants between 1700 and 1775 came from Ireland, with the second-largest group hailing from Scotland, which in the seventeenth and eighteenth centuries was responsible for producing hundreds of thousands of emigrants to the farthest-flung corners of the world. In the same period, just 50,000 people emigrated from England and Wales.[331] At the height of immigration in 1760–1775, some 15,000 people were arriving every year, making a quarter of a million in all, or 10 percent of the total population in 1775. Of these, there were 55,000 Ulster Scots, 40,000 Scots, 30,000 English, and 12,000 German or Swiss. Some 65,000 came as indentured servants; indeed around a half to two-thirds of all immigrants to North America were either designated as this or as engagés.[332] After they arrived, the so-called Redemptioners were later released from their servitude by relatives or friends repaying the shipping company the cost of their passage. This group was supplemented, especially in Virginia and Maryland, by regular shipments of convicts.[333] In addition, British North America imported no fewer than 85,000 slaves between 1760 and 1775.[334] Three-quarters of the British immigrants were men, one half of them below twenty-five years, und most of urban origin. But with the population in 1770 already standing at 1,664,279 whites and 457,097 black slaves, the growth is less attributable to immigration than to a huge increase in the birthrate. As in Canada, living conditions, at least in the northern colonies, were more favorable than in Europe, and it was possible to marry young and start a family. As early as the seventeenth century in Connecticut, life expectancy was already as high as at the start of the twentieth.

This explosive increase in both the white and black population rapidly put the indigenous population in a hopeless position. Unlike for the Spanish, the Indians were regarded not a priori as inferior by the British but rather as independent nations, so in theory at least they enjoyed a higher status than the natives of Spanish America. Yet there, their manpower was needed, whereas in North America they were just considered a hindrance, as the owners of land that the settlers wanted

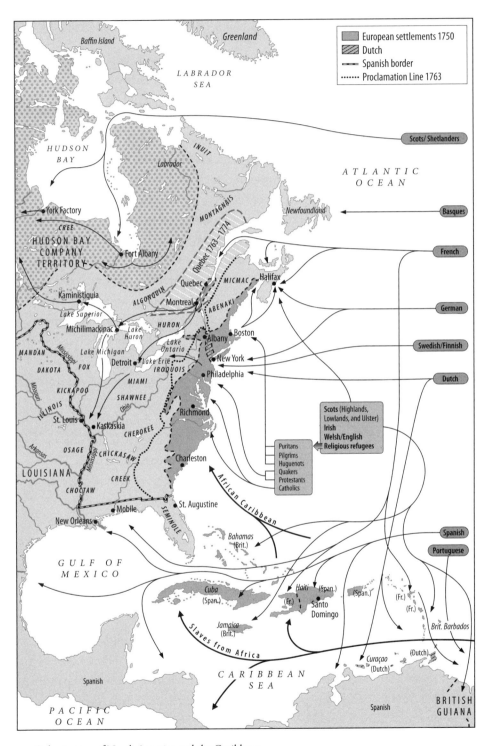

	European settlements 1750
	Dutch
	Spanish border
	Proclamation Line 1763

Greenland

Baffin Island

LABRADOR SEA

Scots/ Shetlanders

HUDSON BAY

INUIT

Labrador

ATLANTIC OCEAN

Newfoundland

Basques

•York Factory

CREE

MONTAGNAIS

HUDSON BAY COMPANY TERRITORY

•Fort Albany

Quebec 1763-1774

French

Kaministiquia•

•Quebec

MICMAC

Halifax

German

ALGONQUIN

Montreal•

ABENAKI

Lake Superior

•Michilimackinac

HURON

Lake Michigan

Lake Huron

Albany•

•Boston

Swedish/Finnish

MANDAN

Detroit•

Lake Ontario

Lake Erie

•New York

Dutch

DAKOTA

FOX

IROQUOIS

•Philadelphia

KICKAPOO

MIAMI

SHAWNEE

ILLINOIS

Ohio

•Richmond

Scots (Highlands, Lowlands, and Ulster)
Irish
Welsh/English
Religious refugees

St. Louis•

•Kaskaskia

CHEROKEE

OSAGE

CHICKASAW

Puritans
Pilgrims
Huguenots
Quakers
Protestants
Catholics

•Charleston

LOUISIANA

CREEK

CHOCTAW

•Mobile

•St. Augustine

New Orleans•

SEMINOLE

African Caribbean

Bahamas (Brit.)

Spanish

GULF OF MEXICO

Portuguese

Cuba (Span.)

Haiti (Fr.)

(Span.)

(Span.)

(Fr.)

(Fr.)

Brit. Barbados

Santo Domingo

Jamaica (Brit.)

Slaves from Africa

Curaçao (Dutch)

(Dutch)

Spanish

BRITISH GUIANA

CARIBBEAN SEA

Spanish

PACIFIC OCEAN

Colonization of North America and the Caribbean

for themselves. For the newcomers were set on bending nature to their will, while the "lazy" Indians had apparently ignored this divine commandment. With the growth of British America and thereafter the United States continuing apace, their fate was sealed, right up to the bitter end in the nineteenth century. A series of conflicts, such as the Indian wars in Virginia in 1622 and 1644, in Massachusetts under Chief Metacomet ("King Philip") in 1675–1676,[335] shortly after in an alliance with the French, and finally the War of 1812, in which the British were pitted against the fledgling United States, may well have cost hundreds or even thousands of whites their lives; in the end, they did nothing to change the outcome, only hastening the demise of the Indians and contributing to a general decline in the civilized conduct of warfare. By 1763, east of the Mississippi, only 100,000 Indians remained, as against 1.3 million whites and 325,000 black African slaves.[336] If it is true to claim that there was a genocide of the indigenous peoples of the Americas, then it took place here rather than in Latin America. Significantly, the Indians in Canada fared better, since even after the British conquest of the country, the population pressure there was not so intense.

Evangelical missions to the Indians such as that led by the Bible translator John Eliot in New England in 1661–1663 met with even less success than those of the Jesuits in Canada, and even the few successes were fleeting. On the one hand, they lacked the organizational infrastructure of the Catholic orders, while on the other, the requirements in particular that the Puritans placed on conversion were so stringent that even many baptized Europeans could not meet them. In any case, in the late seventeenth and early eighteenth centuries, Calvinism began to fade and was forced to seek theological compromises. By contrast, the Great Awakening movement of the mid-eighteenth century gave a new impetus to missionary work.[337] From its eschatological–millenarian perspective, missions (like those once conducted by the Franciscans in Mexico) were meant to help usher in the thousand-year reign of Christ prior to Judgment Day. "At the end of the period of the world mission and the beginning of the millennium, according to Biblical prophesies, Puritan New England will encompass the whole Earth";[338] this remains to the present day not only the mission statement of the worldwide evangelizing American free churches but also, in secular form, that of American imperialism.

This movement found itself in a tense interactive relationship with the numerous Protestant denominations that had been brought to America by successive waves of immigrants, finding a home above all in Pennsylvania. These confessions ranged from Anabaptists and Baptists through various shades of Reformed Christianity to German Lutherans and Anglicans (the last originally represented only in Virginia). Common to all groups, including the Anglicans, was a strong representation of laypeople within the community—all churches suffered from a shortage of educated and ordained personnel. So confessionalization followed its own course in America and was compelled to place especial emphasis on the education system. Competition between the denominations and enlightened utilitarianism during the time of the Great Awakening therefore accelerated cultural development, for example, through the founding of confessional colleges. Following Yale in 1701, the forerunners of Princeton (1746), Columbia (1754), the University of Pennsylvania (1755), Brown (1764), and Rutgers (1766) also came into being. Yet the South was barely touched by this development.

Jews and Catholics played only a marginal role. The latter were, as always, regarded as the archenemies of the Anglo-Saxon world and were embodied in America by the French, who tellingly made common cause with Satan's Indian offspring. In the mind-set of the colonists, this simplistic view of the wars that raged from 1684 to 1763 between France and Great Britain was not compromised in the slightest by the fact that the most terrifying Indians of all, the Iroquois, traditionally tended to be allies of England. The European conflicts of that period must be seen from an Atlantic and global perspective as a world war contested between Britain and France in order to gain the whip hand in European expansion and European worldwide trade; these wars finally ended only with the defeat of Napoleon in 1815. The American Revolution still called upon French assistance against the British, while Napoleon was also familiar with this perspective, even though the main focus of Anglo-French rivalry was then the Indian subcontinent. And indeed the two countries found themselves at war there as early as the eighteenth century, as they also did in the Caribbean.[339] The designation and duration of the individual phases of this long-running conflict differ according to whether they are seen from a French, an Anglo-American, or a German perspective:

French	English	German
1684–1713	*1689–1697*	*1688–1697*
Guerre des Trente Ans en Amérique	King William's War	Pfälzer Krieg
	1702–1713	*1701–1714*
	Queen Anne's War	Spanischer Erbfolgekrieg
1740–1748	*1739–1742*	*1740–1742*
Guerre de la Succession d'Autriche	War of Jenkins' Ear	1. Schlesischer Krieg
	1744–1748	*1744–1745*
	King George's War	2. Schlesischer Krieg
1754–1763	*1754–1763*	*1756–1763*
Guerre des Sept Ans	French and Indian War	Siebenjähriger Krieg

Despite some impressive feats of arms by the French and their Indian allies, and the temporary loss of Hudson Bay, which was easier for the French to reach from their base in Canada, France was forced to renounce its claims there in 1713, as well as on Newfoundland, where both powers had been present hitherto (though it was able to retain fishing rights). In addition, the French had to cede Acadia to the British, though in practice this meant only the peninsula of Nova Scotia, with the mainland area now occupied by the province of New Brunswick being successfully defended with Indian help. This territory was lost only in the last of the wars, which erupted in the Ohio River valley, where the French had established thriving settlements, two years before it broke out in Europe. Fort Duquesne, later Fort Pitt and now the modern city of Pittsburgh, played a strategic role in this conflict. In 1757, British prime minister William Pitt the Elder's massive deployment of regular British forces turned the tables against the French, who were beginning to show signs of exhaustion. Quebec fell in 1759, followed by Montréal in 1760. France was finally forced to relinquish control of Canada and the areas east of the Mississippi to Britain in 1763, while Louisiana west of the Mississippi was ceded to Spain as recompense for its loss of Florida, which now likewise came under British rule. The North Atlantic had by now become definitively British, while the French Atlantic was henceforth restricted to its islands in the Caribbean.

With the withdrawal of the French from North America, a major threat that had qualified the English colonies' strong urge to self-determination suddenly evaporated. However, the imperial policies of the British mother country now began themselves to restrict this autonomy, through a curtailment of further expansion by setting a firm demarcation line with the Indian lands to the west and the north and through taxation and a tightening of economic controls designed to defray the expense of the wars. The escalation of the clash between vested interests ultimately led to armed conflict and American independence.

Meanwhile, in the colonies, political systems with the same basic organizational template had bedded in; this template largely corresponded to the European ideal of a mixed constitution embracing the monarchy, the nobility, and the democratic will of the people. The central organs of government were the governor, the council, and the assembly. The governor was appointed by the crown (in Pennsylvania and Maryland by the proprietor), while in Connecticut and Rhode Island both the governor and the council were elected by the assembly. The governor was at the same time the king's representative, the head of the executive, and the supreme military commander. The power he exercised over the assembly in enacting the king's directives was more extensive even than that wielded by the king over the House of Commons. But in practice his position was more precarious. The council (generally comprising twelve members) took a hand in important affairs of state, forming with the governor the supreme court and without him the upper chamber of the assembly. Since council seats, like all the important offices, were generally directly appointed by the crown, the governor could not cultivate a following within the colonial elite through patronage in filling these posts. But above all the assembly's sovereignty in levying taxation constituted a counterbalance. Even though the assemblies were created through a charter issued by the crown, the free assent of those subject to taxation to scrutiny of their affairs was deemed essential. In accordance with this, depending on different property qualifications in each colony, some 50–80 percent of the male population had the right to vote. Unlike European states-general, the assemblies in America could not be persuaded to make fixed allocations of funds to the governor but on the contrary attempted to make the approval of taxes contingent on the level of expenditure in the colony. In addition, most governors' salaries were paid by the assemblies.

Transatlantic Trade Boom

Britain's North American colonies enjoyed considerable prosperity and a relatively high standard of living. Their growing populations became not just successful suppliers of agricultural produce to the British, West Indian, and Mediterranean markets—which they transported mostly with their own merchant fleet—but, thanks to their prosperity, they also became avid consumers of European (especially, of course, British) manufactured goods. Between 1768 and 1772, it has been calculated that every resident of the colonies spent £3–£4 out of an average yearly income of £10.7–£12.5 on imported goods.

Ninety percent of the people lived off the land. Land was relatively cheap, whereas labor was relatively expensive. As a result, agriculture remained extensive, and the Agrarian Revolution did not reach America. Even so, farmers grew not just for local markets—for example, supplying their produce to the rapidly expanding towns—but also for export. Rice exports to England made the plantation colony of South Carolina probably the richest of all. Likewise, North Carolina employed slave labor to produce pitch, tar, turpentine, and other important naval stores for other colonies and Britain alike. Meanwhile Virginia and the other plantation colonies midway up the Eastern Seaboard cornered the global market, via Great Britain, in tobacco, while also (in common with Pennsylvania and New York) exporting wheat to the Mediterranean. By contrast, in New England, livestock farming was more important. The vast majority of the beef, pork, and fish exported to the West Indies came from here, along with salt cod for the Mediterranean. Finally, timber and wooden wares (barrels) were sent to the West Indies, Britain, and other countries, while ships were built not just for local use but also for sale abroad. Imported goods included rum, molasses, and sugar from the West Indies and a wide range of commercial manufactured goods from Britain, plus luxury items from other countries, first and foremost tea from China.

In the first half of the eighteenth century, it is estimated that some 40–50 percent of all the ships leaving Boston, New York, and Philadelphia were bound for the West Indies—only in Charleston did this proportion of vessels embarking from the port sail to Britain. In the period 1768–1772, for all their manifold differences, the colonies all had a positive balance of trade with the Mediterranean, trade parity with the West Indies, and a massive deficit vis-à-vis the mother country.

Even so, invisible income would have helped balance the books: for instance, cargo revenue earned by the colonial merchant fleet, which by this stage had grown very large; shipping insurance; and the slave trade—plus, around 1700 at least, piracy, which was conducted on a large scale from New York at that time. Only from the 1750s on, when the export of tobacco was taken over by Scottish and English firms, while at the same time British imports continued to increase, did an overall negative balance of payments ensue in the colonies. This was evident in a sudden outflow of precious metals to England, money shortages in America, and an increase in Americans' debt to British lenders. Restriction in the circulation of paper money in the colonies became another grievance in America against the crown.

Although Britain did not manage to completely prevent the production of manufactured goods in the colonies—for example, there were many workshops that produced and worked iron—the demand for British textile, metalwares, and other goods continued to grow. This once again begs the question of what significance should be ascribed to transatlantic trade in the development of the British economy and the beginnings of the Industrial Revolution, especially if one treats North America and the West Indies as a unit and considers that Caribbean profits did not just directly benefit Britain but also contributed to the growth of North American purchasing power, thereby boosting the demand for British goods. In any event, in 1700 12 percent, in 1753 20 percent, and in 1773 42 percent of British exports were to its Atlantic colonies, an upward trend that was to continue. By 1800, exports to North America and the West Indies had increased more than twentyfold from a century earlier. A random sample taken at the time showed these to be comprised as follows: 55–76 percent increase of iron and copper and 12–79 percent of various textiles, with linen (79 percent), "Spanish cloths" (70 percent), printed cottons and linen goods (59 percent), and silks (57 percent) as the front runners. Given that the cotton and ironworking industries were at the forefront of the Industrial Revolution, the strategic role played by colonial demand seems self-evident.

However, from the standpoint of a more contemporary, supply-side-oriented economic theory, it might be contended that the demand did not stimulate the supply, and hence industrialization, but rather that a supply generated by internal economic factors was the prime mover in creating this demand in the first place. Admittedly, population growth in America is an independent variable that lends plausibility to the idea of an autonomous development of demand. Overall, though, no one seriously questions, nor ever has done, the significance of transatlantic trade, including the slave trade, for the economic development of Britain—albeit less in a direct sense, due to the profits it generated, than indirectly, as a result of the stimuli it gave to the most diverse sectors of industry. Thus far, then, we can see transatlantic trade as a necessary (but by no means the sufficient, that is, the main determining) precondition of this development. Yet if one does not work from aggregated national data but rather examines how industrialization in England actually developed on the ground, and argues not from aggregated values but from increments, then foreign trade can perfectly well be construed as the main determining precondition in the context of a multifactorial model. According to this view, the beginning of English industrialization can be traced back to import substitution, and its continuing expansion to region- and sector-specific increments in foreign trade, procured through reexport substitution. If one takes into account not only trade with Africa and the slave trade but also the largely overlooked fact that plantation commodities from America, primarily sugar and cotton, were also produced by Africans (as, indeed, was all the New World's gold and perhaps around one-quarter of its silver), then it is clear that Africans should be accorded a new key role in the development of Europe and the Atlantic world,[340] and the "black Atlantic" takes on a quite different complexion.[341]

Translated from the German by Peter Lewis

Notes

Introduction

1. Matthias Middell and Ulf Engel, eds., *Theoretiker der Globalisierung* (Leipzig: Universitäts-verlag, 2010); Jerry H. Bentley, ed., *The Oxford Handbook of World History* (Oxford: Oxford University Press, 2011); Jürgen Osterhammel, "World History," in *The Oxford History of Historical Writing*, vol. 5, *Historical Writing since 1945*, ed. Axel Schneider and Daniel Woolf (Oxford: Oxford University Press, 2001), 93–112; Dominic Sachsenmaier, *Global Perspectives on Global History: Theories and Approaches in a Connected World* (Cambridge: Cambridge University Press, 2011).

2. Catherine B. Asher and Cynthia Talbot, *India before Europe* (Cambridge: Cambridge University Press, 2006), 51.

3. Wolfgang Reinhard, *Geschichte der europäischen Expansion,* 4 vols. (Stuttgart: Kohlhammer, 1983–1990).

4. Shmuel N. Eisenstadt, *Die Vielfalt der Moderne* (Weilerswist: Velbrück Wissenschaft, 2000).

5. Markus Völkel, *Geschichtsschreibung: Eine Einführung in globaler Perspektive* (Cologne: Böhlau Verlag, 2006); Daniel Woolf, *A Global History of History* (Cambridge: Cambridge University Press, 2011).

6. Dipesh Chakrabarty, *Provincializing Europe: Postcolonial Thought and Historical Difference* (Princeton, NJ: Princeton University Press, 2000).

7. Jörg Döring and Tristan Thielmann, "Der Spatial Turn und das geheime Wissen der Geographie," in *Spatial Turn: Das Raumparadigma in den Kultur- und Sozialwissenschaften,* ed. Jörg Döring and Tristan Thielmann (Bielefeld: Transcript Verlag, 2008), 7–45; Eric Piltz, "Trägheit des Raumes: Fernand Braudel und die Spatial Stories der Geschichtswissenschaft," in Döring and Thielmann, *Spatial Turn,* 75–102.

8. Fernand Braudel, *La Méditerranée et le monde méditerranéen à l'époque de Philippe II* (Paris: Colin, 1949; 2nd ed. in 2 vols., 1966); *The Mediterranean and the Mediterranean World in the Age of Philip II* (London: Collins, 1973); *Das Mittelmeer und die mediterrane Welt in der Epoche Philipps II.,* 3 vols. (Frankfurt: Suhrkamp, 1998).

9. Asher and Talbot, *India before Europe;* Stephen F. Dale, *The Muslim Empires of the Ottomans, Safavids, and Mughals* (Cambridge: Cambridge University Press, 2010).

10. Jörn Leonhard and Ulrike von Hirschhausen, eds., *Comparing Empires: Encounters and Transfers in the Long Nineteenth Century* (Göttingen: Vandenhoek & Ruprecht, 2011); Herfried Münkler, *Imperien: Die Logik der Weltherrschaft vom Alten Rom bis zu den Vereinigten Staaten* (Berlin: Rowohlt, 2005).

11. Thomas T. Allsen, "Pre-Modern Empires," in Bentley, *Oxford Handbook of World History,* 361–378; here, 361.

12. Jane Burbank and Frederick Cooper, *Empires: Power and the Politics of Difference* (Princeton, NJ: Princeton University Press, 2010), 8.

13. Timothy Parsons, *The Rule of Empires: Those Who Built Them, Those Who Endured Them, and Why They Always Fall* (New York: Oxford University Press, 2010).

14. Niall Ferguson, *Empire: How Britain Made the Modern World* (London: Allan Lane, 2003).

15. Burbank and Cooper, *Empires*.

16. English translation by John Lynch, *Spain under the Habsburgs,* 2nd ed. (Oxford: Blackwell, 1981), 105, of Eulogio Zudaire, "Ideario politico de D. Gaspar de Guzman, Privado de Felipe IV," *Hispania* 25 (1965): 413–425, 421.

17. Wolfgang Reinhard, *Geschichte der Staatsgewalt: Eine vergleichende Verfassungsgeschichte Europas von den Anfängen bis zur Gegenwart,* 3rd ed. (Munich: C. H. Beck, 2002).

18. Ibid., 15.

19. Geoffrey R. Elton, *The Tudor Constitution: Documents and Commentary* (Cambridge: Cambridge University Press, 1960), 344.

20. Asher and Talbot, *India before Europe*, 157–158, 187–191.

21. Peter Thorau, "Von Karl dem Großen zum Frieden von Zsitva Torok: Zum Weltherrschaftsanspruch Sultan Mehmets II. und dem Wiederaufleben des Zweikaiserproblems nach der Eroberung Konstantinopels," *Historische Zeitschrift* 279 (2004): 309–334.

22. Franz Bosbach, *Monarchia universalis: Ein politischer Leitbegriff der Frühen Neuzeit* (Göttingen: Vandenhoek & Ruprecht, 1988).

23. Victor Lieberman, *Strange Parallels: Southeast Asia in Global Context, c. 1800–1830,* vol. 1, *Integration on the Mainland* (Cambridge: Cambridge University Press, 2003), 2, 79.

24. Johannes Burkhardt, *Der Dreißigjährige Krieg,* 6th ed. (Frankfurt: Suhrkamp, 2003).

25. Bhawan Ruangsilp, *Dutch East India Company Merchants at the Court of Ayutthaya: Dutch Perceptions of the Thai Kingdom c. 1604–1765* (Leiden: Brill, 2007), 11.

26. Leonhard Harding, *Das Königreich Benin: Geschichte—Kultur—Wirtschaft* (Munich: Oldenbourg, 2010), 111–114.

27. Ibid., 115–122.

28. Richard von Glahn, *Fountain of Fortune: Money and Monetary Policy in China, 1000–1700* (Berkeley: University of California Press, 1996).

29. Marshall G. S. Hodgson, *The Venture of Islam: Conscience and History in a World Civilization,* vol. 3, *The Gunpowder Empires and Modern Times* (Chicago: University of Chicago Press, 1974), 30, 100–102.

30. William H. McNeill, *The Age of Gunpowder Empires, 1450–1800* (Washington, DC: American Historical Association, 1989).

31. Harry Turtledove, *Gunpowder Empire* (New York: Tor Books, 2003).

32. Dale, *Muslim Empires;* André Wink, *Akbar* (Oxford: Oneworld, 2009), 66–68; Jos Gommans, *Mughal Warfare: Indian Frontiers and High Roads to Empire, 1500–1700* (London: Routledge, 2002), 82–85, 133–136; Pál Fodar, "Ottoman Warfare, 1071–1473," in *The Cambridge History of Turkey,* vol. 1, *Byzantium to Turkey, 1071–1453,* ed. Kate Fleet (Cambridge: Cambridge University Press, 2009), 192–226; Virginia Aksan, "War and Peace," in *The Cambridge History of*

Turkey, vol. 3, *The Later Ottoman Empire, 1603–1839,* ed. Suraya Faroqhi (Cambridge: Cambridge University Press, 2006), 81–117.

33. Carlo Cipolla, *Segel und Kanonen: Die europäische Expansion zur See* (Berlin: Wagenbach, 1999), 24–27, 48–52, 79–82, 164.

34. Gommans, *Mughal Warfare,* 114–117, 133–136, 144–162.

35. Joseph Needham, *Science and Civilization in China,* vol. 5, *Chemistry and Chemical Technology,* pt. 6, section 30/2 (Cambridge: Cambridge University Press, 1986), 276–341, 365–414, 429–446; Cipolla, *Segel und Kanonen,* 127–130.

36. Noel Perrin, *Japans Weg zurück zum Schwert von 1543 bis 1879* (Frankfurt: Athenäum, 1989).

37. David Ayalon, *Gunpowder and Firearms in the Mameluk Kingdom,* 2nd ed. (Abingdon, UK: Frank Cass, 1978), 4, 92.

38. Perrin, *Japans Weg zurück zum Schwert,* 39.

39. Gommans, *Mughal Warfare,* 202–203.

40. Cipolla, *Segel und Kanonen,* 138, 142.

41. John Guy, *Woven Cargoes: Indian Textiles in the East* (London: Thames and Hudson, 1998), illustration 93.

42. Bao Leshi, "Ruling out Change: Institutional Impediments to Transfer of Technology in Ship Building and Design in the Far East," *Itinerario* 19, no. 3 (1995): 142–152, 143.

43. Joseph Needham, *Science and Civilization in China,* vol. 4, *Physics and Physical Technology,* pt. 3, section 29 (Cambridge: Cambridge University Press, 1971), 385, 396–402, 480–481, 588–617, 696–697.

44. Cipolla, *Segel und Kanonen,* 82–90.

45. Döring and Thielmann, *Spatial Turn;* Braudel, *La Méditerranée.*

46. David Kirby and Merja-Liisa Hinkkanen, *The Baltic and the North Seas* (London: Routledge, 2000); Donald B. Freeman, *The Pacific* (London: Routledge, 2010); Michael Pearson, *The Indian Ocean* (London: Routledge, 2011).

47. Kirti N. Chaudhuri, *Trade and Civilization in the Indian Ocean: An Economic History from the Rise of Islam to 1750* (Cambridge: Cambridge University Press, 1985); Kirti N. Chaudhuri, *Asia before Europe: Economy and Civilization of the Indian Ocean* (Cambridge: Cambridge University Press, 1990); Stephan Conermann, ed., *Der Indische Ozean in historischer Perspektive* (Hamburg: EB-Verlag, 1998); Jos Gommans and Jacques Leider, eds., *The Maritime Frontier of Burma: Exploring Political, Cultural and Commercial Interaction in the Indian Ocean World, 1200–1800* (Amsterdam: Koninklijke Nederlands Akademie van Wetenschappen, 2002); Kenneth McPherson, *The Indian Ocean: A History of the People and the Sea* (Delhi: Oxford University Press, 1993); Michael N. Pearson, *Port Cities and Intruders: The Swahili Coast, India, and Portugal in the Early Modern Period* (Baltimore: Johns Hopkins University Press, 1998); Dietmar Rothermund and Susanne Weigelin-Schwiedrzik, eds., *Der Indische Ozean: Das afro-asiatische Mittelmeer als Kultur- und Wirtschaftsraum* (Vienna: Promedia-Verlag, 2004); Auguste Toussaint, *Histoire de l'Océan Indien* (Paris: PUF, 1961); Rene J. Barendse, *The Arabian Seas: The Indian Ocean World of the Seventeenth Century* (Armonk, NY: M. E. Sharpe, 2002).

48. See by way of comparison the most recent publication on this topic: Nicholas Canny and Philip Morgan, eds., *The Oxford Handbook of the Atlantic World, 1450–1850* (Oxford: Oxford University Press, 2011).

49. Despite Freeman, *The Pacific.*

50. Gabriele Metzler and Michael Wildt, eds., *Über Grenzen: 84. Deutscher Historikertag in Berlin 2010: Berichtsband* (Göttingen: Vandenhoeck & Ruprecht, 2012), 77.

51. Klaus Herbers and Nikolas Jaspert, eds., *Grenzräume und Grenzüberschreitungen im Vergleich: Der Osten und der Westen des mittelalterlichen Lateineuropa* (Berlin: Akademie Verlag, 2007).

52. http://www.absborderlands.org; Hastings Donnan and Thomas M. Wilson, *Borders: Frontiers of Identity, Nation and State* (Oxford: Berg, 1999); Michael Rösler and Tobias Wendl, eds., *Frontiers and Borderlands: Anthropological Perspectives* (Frankfurt: Peter Lang, 1999).

53. Matthias Waechter, *Die Erfindung des amerikanischen Westens: Die Geschichte der Frontier-Debatte* (Freiburg: Rombach Verlag, 1996).

54. Dietrich Gerhard, "The Frontier in Comparative View," *Comparative Studies in Society and History* 1 (1959): 205–229; Howard Lamar and Leonard Thompson, eds., *The Frontier in History: North America and Southern Africa Compared* (New Haven, CT: Yale University Press, 1981); Robert Bartlett and Angus MacKay, eds., *Medieval Frontier Societies* (Oxford: Clarendon Press, 1989); Daniel Power and Naomi Standen, eds., *Frontiers in Question: Eurasian Borderlands, 700–1700* (Basingstoke, UK: Macmillan, 1999); Christoph Marx, "Grenzfälle: Zu Geschichte und Potential des Frontierbegriffs," *Saeculum* 54 (2003): 123–143; Jürgen Osterhammel, *Die Verwandlung der Welt: Eine Geschichte des 19. Jahrhunderts* (Munich: C. H. Beck, 2009), 465–564.

55. Silvio R. Duncan Baretta and John Markoff, "Civilization and Barbarism: Cattle Frontiers in Latin America," in *States of Violence,* ed. Fernando Coronil and Julie Skurski (Ann Arbor: University of Michigan Press, 2006), 33–82.

56. Alistair Hennessy, *The Frontier in Latin American History* (London: Edward Arnold, 1978), esp. 54–109.

57. Christoph Marx, "Die Grenze und die koloniale Herrschaft: Die 'Frontier' in der Kapkolonie im 18. Jahrhundert," in *Grenzen und Grenzüberschreitungen: Bilanz und Perspektiven der Frühneuzeitforschung,* ed. Christine Roll, Frank Pohle, and Matthias Myrczek (Cologne: Böhlau Verlag, 2010), 475–482.

58. Owen Lattimore, *Studies in Frontier History: Collected Papers, 1928–1958* (Paris: Mouton, 1962).

59. Michael Khodarkovsky, *Russia's Steppe Frontier: The Making of a Colonial Empire* (Bloomington: Indiana University Press, 2002).

60. Bartlett and MacKay, *Medieval Frontier Societies;* Power and Standen, *Frontiers in Question.*

61. Richard White, *The Middle Ground: Indians, Empires, and Republics in the Great Lakes Region, 1650–1815* (Cambridge: Cambridge University Press, 1991).

62. Ibid.

63. Colin Heywood, "The Frontier in Ottoman History: Old Ideas and New Myths," in Power and Standen, *Frontiers in Question,* 228–250.

64. Ann Williams, "Crusaders as Frontiersmen: The Case of the Order of St John in the Mediterranean," in Power and Standen, *Frontiers in Question,* 209–227.

65. Roderich Ptak, *Die maritime Seidenstraße: Küstenräume, Seefahrt und Handel in vorkolonialer Zeit* (Munich: C. H. Beck, 2007).

66. Wolfgang Reinhard, *Kleine Geschichte des Kolonialismus,* 2nd ed. (Stuttgart: Kroener, 2008); Reinhard, *A Short History of Colonialism* (Manchester, UK: Manchester University Press, 2011).

67. David Harvey, *The Conditions of Postmodernity: An Enquiry into the Conditions of Cultural Change* (Oxford: Blackwell, 1989), 240–307.

68. Canny and Morgan, *Oxford Handbook of the Atlantic World,* 318; Dirk Hoerder, *Cultures in Contact: World Migrations in the Second Millennium* (Durham, NC: Duke University Press, 2002).

69. Wolfgang Reinhard, "Gelenkter Kulturwandel im 17. Jahrhundert: Akkulturation in den Jesuitenmissionen als universalhistorisches Problem [1976]," in *Ausgewählte Abhandlungen,* ed. Wolfgang Reinhard (Berlin: Duncker & Humblot, 1997), 347–399.

70. Mark Häberlein, "Kulturelle Vermittler in der atlantischen Welt der Frühen Neuzeit," in *Sprachgrenzen—Kulturkontakte—Kulturelle Vermittler: Kommunikation zwischen Europäern und Außereuropäern (16.–20. Jahrhundert),* ed. Mark Häberlein and Alexander Keese (Stuttgart: Franz Steiner Verlag, 2010), 177–201.

71. Monika Übelhör, "Hsü Kuang-ch'i (1562–1633) und seine Einstellung zum Christentum," *Oriens extremus* 15 (1968): 191–257; 16 (1969): 41–74; Dominic Sachsenmaier, *Die Aufnahme europäischer Inhalte in die chinesische Kultur durch Zhu Zong yuan (ca. 1616–1660)* (Nettetal: Steyler Verlag, 2001).

72. Wolfgang Reinhard, "Sprachbeherrschung und Weltherrschaft. Sprache und Sprachwissenschaft in der europäischen Expansion (1987)," in Reinhard, *Ausgewählte Abhandlungen,* 401–433.

73. Häberlein and Keese, *Sprachgrenzen—Sprachkontakte—Kulturelle Vermittler.*

74. John Robert McNeill, "Biological Exchanges in World History," in Bentley, *Oxford Handbook of World History* (Oxford: Oxford University Press, 2011), 325–342.

75. John Robert McNeill, "The Ecological Atlantic," in Canny and Morgan, *Oxford Handbook of the Atlantic World,* 289–304.

76. Tilman Nagel, *Timur der Eroberer und die islamische Welt des späten Mittelalters* (Munich: C. H. Beck, 1993), 162, 179–180, 334.

77. Dale, *Muslim Empires,* 97.

78. Peter Linebaugh and Marcus Rediker, *Die vielköpfige Hydra: Die verborgene Geschichte des revolutionären Atlantik* (Berlin: Assoziation A, 2008), 134.

79. Jean Gelman Taylor, *The Social World of Batavia: European and Eurasian in Dutch Asia* (Madison: University of Wisconsin Press, 1983), 7–8, 12–13, 14–17.

80. Linebaugh and Rediker, *Die vielköpfige Hydra,* 5.

81. David Abulafia, *The Great Sea: A Human History of the Mediterranean* (London: Allen Lane, 2011), 425–426.

82. Jaap R. Bruijn, Femme S. Gaastra, and Ivo Schöffer, *Dutch Asiatic Shipping in the 17th and 18th Centuries,* vol. 1 (The Hague: Nijhoff, 1987), 153.

83. Charles R. Boxer, *Dutch Merchants and Mariners in Asia, 1602–1795* (London: Ashgate, 1988), 99.

84. Linebaugh and Rediker, *Die vielköpfige Hydra;* Robert Bohn, *Die Piraten* (Munich: C. H. Beck, 2003).

85. R. N. Anderson, "The Quilombo of Palmares: A New Overview of a Maroon State in Seventeenth- Century Brazil," *Journal of Latin American Studies* 28 (1996): 545–566.

86. This concept derives from Mariano Delgado, *Abschied vom erobernden Gott: Studien zur Geschichte und Gegenwart des Christentums in Lateinamerika* (Immensee: Neue Zeitschrift für Missionswissenschaft, 1996).

1. Empires and Frontiers in Continental Eurasia

1. See the Selected Bibliography for general survey histories.

2. John Darwin, *After Tamerlane: The Global History of Empire since 1405* (New York: Bloomsbury Press, 2008); Victor B. Lieberman, *Strange Parallels: Southeast Asia in Global Context, c. 800–1830,* vol. 1, *Integration on the Mainland* (Cambridge: Cambridge University Press, 2003); Victor B. Lieberman, *Strange Parallels: Southeast Asia in Global Context c. 800–1830,* vol. 2, *Mainland Mirrors: Europe, Japan, China, South Asia, and the Islands* (Cambridge: Cambridge University Press, 2009); John F. Richards, *The Unending Frontier: An Environmental History of the Early Modern World* (Berkeley: University of California Press, 2003); Peter C. Perdue, *China Marches West: The Qing Conquest of Central Eurasia* (Cambridge, MA: Belknap Press of Harvard University Press, 2005). This chapter also draws on material from Philippa Levine and John Marriott, eds., *Ashgate Research Companion to Modern Imperial Histories* (Burlington, VT: Ashgate, 2012); and John Coatsworth et al., *Global Connections: A World History: Politics, Exchange, and Social Life in World History* (Cambridge: Cambridge University Press, 2015).

3. Darwin, *After Tamerlane,* 4–6.

4. Biography in L. C. Goodrich and Chaoying Fang, *Dictionary of Ming Biography, 1368–1644,* 2 vols. (New York: Columbia University Press, 1976), 1:381–392.

5. Edward L. Farmer, *Zhu Yuanzhang and Early Ming Legislation: The Reordering of Chinese Society Following the Era of Mongol Rule* (New York: E. J. Brill, 1995).

6. Henry Serruys, *Sino-Mongol Relations during the Ming,* 3 vols. (Brussels: Institut belge des hautes études chinoises, 1967).

7. Biography in Goodrich and Fang, *Dictionary,* 1:355–365; Shih-shan Henry Tsai, *Perpetual Happiness: The Ming Emperor Yongle* (Seattle: University of Washington Press, 2001).

8. J. Duyvendak, *China's Discovery of Africa; Lectures Given at the University of London on January 22 and 23, 1947* (London: A. Probsthain, 1949); Louise Levathes, *When China Ruled the Seas: The Treasure Fleet of the Dragon Throne, 1405–33* (Oxford: Oxford University Press, 1994); Geoff Wade, "The Zheng He Voyages: A Reassessment," *Journal of the Malaysian Branch of the Royal Asiatic Society* 78, no. 1 (2005): 37–58.

9. Joseph Needham, *Science and Civilisation in China,* 7 vols. vol. 4.3, *Civil Engineering and Nautics* (Cambridge: Cambridge University Press, 1971), 487.

10. Ibid., 479.

11. Edward L. Farmer, *Early Ming Government: The Evolution of Dual Capitals* (Cambridge, MA: Harvard University Press, 1968).

12. Alexander Woodside, "Early Ming Expansionism," *Papers on China* 17 (1963): 1–37.

13. Goodrich and Fang, *Dictionary,* 1:418; Frederick Mote, "The Tu-Mu Incident of 1449," in *Chinese Ways in Warfare,* ed. Frank A. Kierman Jr. and John K. Fairbank (Cambridge, MA: Harvard University Press, 1974), 243–272; Morris Rossabi, "Notes on Esen's Pride and Ming China's Prejudice," *Mongolia Society Bulletin* 17 (1970): 31–39.

14. Yang Bin, *Between Winds and Clouds: The Making of Yunnan (Second Century BCE to Twentieth Century CE),* e-book ed. (New York: Columbia University Press, 2008), chapter 4.

15. John E. Herman, *Amid the Clouds and Mist: China's Colonization of Guizhou, 1200–1700* (Cambridge, MA: Harvard University Asia Center, 2007).

16. For a succinct summary of Ming administration, see Charles O. Hucker, *The Traditional Chinese State in Ming Times (1368–1644)* (Tucson: University of Arizona Press, 1961). Extensive details can be found in Frederick Mote and Denis Twitchett, eds., *The Cambridge History of China,* vol. 7, *The Ming Dynasty, 1368–1644, Part 1* (Cambridge: Cambridge University Press, 1988); Frederick Mote and Denis Twitchett, eds., *The Cambridge History of China,* vol. 8, *The Ming Dynasty, 1368–1644, Part 2* (Cambridge: Cambridge University Press, 1998). An outstanding recent survey of the Ming is Timothy Brook, *The Troubled Empire: China in the Yuan and Ming Dynasties* (Cambridge, MA: Belknap Press of Harvard University Press, 2010).

17. G. William Skinner, "Presidential Address: The Structure of Chinese History," *Journal of Asian Studies* 44, no. 2 (1985): 271–292; G. William Skinner, ed., *The City in Late Imperial China* (Stanford, CA: Stanford University Press, 1977).

18. Charles O. Hucker, *The Censorial System of Ming China* (Stanford, CA: Stanford University Press, 1966).

19. Ichisada Miyazaki, *China's Examination Hell: The Civil Service Examinations of Imperial China* (New York: Weatherhill, 1976); Ping-ti Ho, *The Ladder of Success in Imperial China: Aspects of Social Mobility, 1368–1911* (New York: Columbia University Press, 1962); Benjamin Elman, *A Cultural History of Civil Examinations in Late Imperial China* (Berkeley: University of California Press, 2000).

20. Ray Huang, *Taxation and Governmental Finance in Sixteenth-Century Ming China* (Cambridge: Cambridge University Press, 1974); Fang-chung Liang, *The Single-Whip Method of Taxation in China* (Cambridge, MA: Harvard University Press, 1970).

21. Frederick Mote, "The Growth of Chinese Despotism: A Critique of Wittfogel's Theory of Oriental Despotism as Applied to China," *Oriens Extremus* 8, no. 1 (1961): 1–41; Timothy Brook, *The Chinese State in Ming Society* (New York: Routledge Curzon, 2005), 182–185.

22. Ray Huang, *1587: A Year of No Significance* (New Haven, CT: Yale University Press, 1981).

23. John R. Watt, *The District Magistrate in Late Imperial China* (New York: Columbia University Press, 1972); Ch'u T'ung-tsu, *Local Government in China under the Ch'ing* (Cambridge, MA: Harvard University Press, 1962).

24. David Faure, *Emperor and Ancestor: State and Lineage in South China* (Stanford, CA: Stanford University Press, 2007).

25. Michael Szonyi, *Practicing Kinship: Lineage and Descent in Late Imperial China* (Stanford, CA: Stanford University Press, 2002).

26. Timothy Brook, *Praying for Power: Buddhism and the Formation of Gentry Society in Late-Ming China* (Cambridge, MA: Harvard University Press, 1993).

27. Goodrich and Fang, *Dictionary*, 2:1408–1416; Wei-ming Tu, *Neo-Confucian Thought in Action: Wang Yangming's Youth (1472–1509)* (Berkeley: University of California Press, 1976); Wm. Theodore de Bary, ed., *Self and Society in Ming Thought* (New York: Columbia University Press, 1970).

28. Tu, *Neo-Confucian Thought in Action*, 7.

29. Bodo Wiethoff, *Die Chinesische Seeverbotspolitik und der Private Uberseehandel von 1368 Bis 1567* (Hamburg: Gesellschaft für Natur- und Völkerkunde Ostasiens, 1963); Kwan-wai So, *Japanese Piracy in Ming China during the Sixteenth Century* (East Lansing: Michigan State University Press, 1975); Roland Higgins, "Piracy and Coastal Defense in the Ming Period: Governmental Response to Coastal Disturbances, 1523–1549" (PhD diss., University of Michigan, 1981); Peter C. Perdue, "1557: A Year of Some Significance," in *Asia Inside Out*, vol. 1, *Changing Times*, ed. Eric Tagliacozzo, Helen Siu, and Peter C. Perdue (Cambridge, MA: Harvard University Press, 2014), 90–111.

30. Goodrich and Fang, *Dictionary*, 1:6; Peter C. Perdue, "Commerce and Coercion on Two Chinese Frontiers," in *Military Culture in China*, ed. Nicola Di Cosmo (Cambridge, MA: Harvard University Press, 2009), 317–338; Arthur Waldron, *The Great Wall of China: From History to Myth* (Cambridge: Cambridge University Press, 1990); Sechin Jagchid and Van Jay Symons, *Peace, War, and Trade along the Great Wall: Nomadic-Chinese Interaction through Two Millennia* (Bloomington: Indiana University Press, 1989).

31. Peter C. Perdue, "From Turfan to Taiwan: Trade and War on Two Chinese Frontiers," in *Untaming the Frontier: Interdisciplinary Perspectives on Frontier Studies*, ed. Bradley J. Parker and Lars Rodseth (Tucson: University of Arizona Press, 2005), 27–51.

32. Huang, *1587*, 156–188.

33. Kenneth Pomeranz and Steven Topik, *The World That Trade Created* (Armonk, NY: M. E. Sharpe, 1999), 3–21; Philip A. Kuhn, *Chinese among Others: Emigration in Modern Times* (Lanham, MD: Rowman & Littlefield, 2008).

34. Evelyn S. Rawski, *Agricultural Change and the Peasant Economy of South China* (Cambridge, MA: Harvard University Press, 1972).

35. Timothy Brook, *The Confusions of Pleasure: Commerce and Culture in Ming China* (Berkeley: University of California Press, 1998).

36. Craig Clunas, *Superfluous Things: Material Culture and Social Status in Early Modern China* (Urbana: University of Illinois Press, 1991).

37. Zhang Han (1511–1593), in Brook, *Confusions of Pleasure*, frontispiece.

38. Francesca Bray, *Technology and Gender: Fabrics of Power in Late Imperial China* (Berkeley: University of California Press, 1997).

39. Timothy Brook, "Guides for Vexed Travelers: Route Books in the Ming and Qing," *Ch'ing-Shih Wen-T'i* 4 (1981): pt. 5, 32–76; pt. 6, 130–140; pt. 8, 95–109.

40. Hoshi Ayao, *The Ming Tribute Grain System*, trans. Mark Elvin (Ann Arbor: University of Michigan Press, 1969); Mark Elvin, *The Pattern of the Chinese Past* (Stanford, CA: Stanford University Press, 1973), 91–110.

41. Goodrich and Fang, *Dictionary*, 1:807–818; Jean François Billeter, *Li Zhi, Philosophe Maudit (1527–1602): Contribution à une Sociologie du Mandarinat Chinois de la Fin des Ming* (Geneva: Droz, 1979); Huang, *1587*, 189–221.

42. William Theodore de Bary et al., eds., *Sources of Chinese Tradition*, 2nd ed. (New York: Columbia University Press, 1999), 867–868.

43. Brook, *Praying for Power;* Jonathan D. Spence, *Return to Dragon Mountain: Memories of a Late Ming Man* (New York: Viking, 2007).

44. Brook, *Praying for Power,* 40.

45. One of the most famous Chan (Zen) monasteries in the country, the King Asoka monastery was founded in the fifth century and named after the great Indian patron of Buddhism. It was believed to hold a genuine relic of the Buddha. Ibid., 261.

46. Cynthia Joanne Brokaw, *Commerce in Culture: The Sibao Book Trade in the Qing and Republican Periods* (Cambridge, MA: Harvard University Asia Center, 2007); Sakai Tadao, "Confucianism and Popular Educational Works," in de Bary, *Self and Society,* 331–362.

47. Cynthia Joanne Brokaw, *The Ledgers of Merit and Demerit: Social Change and Moral Order in Late Imperial China* (Princeton, NJ: Princeton University Press, 1991).

48. Joanna F. Handlin Smith, *The Art of Doing Good: Charity in Late Ming China* (Berkeley: University of California Press, 2009).

49. Luo Guanzhong, *Three Kingdoms,* trans. Moss Roberts (New York: Pantheon, 1976); Xiaoxiaosheng and F. Clement C. Egerton, *The Golden Lotus; a Translation, from the Chinese Original, of the Novel Chin P'ing Mei,* 4 vols. (London: Routledge, 1972); Wu Cheng'en, *The Journey to the West,* trans. Anthony C. Yu (Chicago: University of Chicago Press, 1977).

50. Huang, *1587,* 1–41; Ray Huang, "The Lung-ch'ing and Wan-li Reigns, 1567–1620," in Mote and Twitchett, *The Cambridge History of China,* 7:511–584; Goodrich and Fang, *Dictionary,* 1:324–338.

51. Huang, *1587,* 53–61.

52. Tanaka Masatoshi, "Popular Uprisings, Rent Resistance, and Bondservant Rebellions in the Late Ming," in *State and Society in China: Japanese Perspectives on Ming-Qing Social and Economic History,* ed. Linda Grove and Christian Daniels (Tokyo: Tokyo University Press, 1984), 165–214.

53. Fuma Susumu, "Minmatsu No Toshi Kaikaku to Kôshû Minpen [Urban reform in late Ming and the Hangzhou uprising]," *Toho Gakuho* 49, no. 1 (1977): 215–262.

54. Helen Dunstan, "The Late Ming Epidemics: A Preliminary Study," *Ch'ing-Shih Wen-T'i* 3, no. 3 (1975): 1–59.

55. Arthur W. Hummel, *Eminent Chinese of the Ch'ing Period, 1644–1912* (Washington, DC: US Government Printing Office, 1943–1944), 594–599; Frederic Wakeman Jr., *The Great Enterprise: The Manchu Reconstruction of Imperial Order* (Berkeley: University of California Press, 1985).

56. Hummel, *Eminent Chinese,* 1–3 (Hung Taiji is mistakenly called "Abahai" here). Mark C. Elliott, *The Manchu Way: The Eight Banners and Ethnic Identity in Late Imperial China* (Stanford, CA: Stanford University Press, 2001).

57. Gertraude Roth, "The Manchu-Chinese Relationship, 1618–36," in *From Ming to Ch'ing: Conquest, Region and Continuity in Seventeenth-Century China,* ed. Jonathan D. Spence and John E. Wills (New Haven, CT: Yale University Press, 1979), 1–38.

58. Bernd-Michael Linke, *Zur Entwicklung des Mandjurischen Khanats Zum Beamtenstaat: Sinisierung und Burokratisierung der Mandjuren Während der Eroberungszeit* (Wiesbaden: Steiner, 1982).

59. Pamela Kyle Crossley, "Thinking about Ethnicity in Early Modern China," *Late Imperial China* 11 (1990): 1–35; Pamela Kyle Crossley, *A Translucent Mirror: History and Identity in Qing Imperial Ideology* (Berkeley: University of California Press, 1999).

60. Hummel, *Eminent Chinese,* 877–880.

61. Pei-kai Cheng, Michael Lestz, and Jonathan D. Spence, *The Search for Modern China: A Documentary Collection* (New York: W. W. Norton, 1999), 21–26.

62. William T. de Bary, ed., *The Unfolding of Neo-Confucianism* (New York: Columbia University Press, 1975).

63. Hummel, *Eminent Chinese,* 351–354; William de Bary, *Waiting for the Dawn: A Plan for the Prince: Huang Tsung-Hsi's Ming-I Tai-Fang Lu* (New York: Columbia University Press, 1993).

64. Hummel, *Eminent Chinese,* 421–427.

65. Ibid., 817–819; Fa-ti Fan, "Nature and Nation in Chinese Political Thought: The National Essence Circle in Early Twentieth-Century China," in *The Moral Authority of Nature,* ed. Lorraine Daston and Fernando Vidal (Chicago: University of Chicago Press, 2004), 409–437; Peter C. Perdue, "Nature and Nurture on Imperial China's Frontiers," *Modern Asian Studies* 43 (January 2009): 245–267.

66. Lynn A. Struve, ed., *The Qing Formation in World-Historical Time* (Cambridge, MA: Harvard University Asia Center, 2004); Lynn A. Struve, *Time, Temporality, and Imperial Transition: East Asia from Ming to Qing* (Honolulu: Association for Asian Studies and University of Hawai'i Press, 2005).

67. William S. Atwell, "Volcanism and Short-Term Climatic Change in East Asian and World History, c. 1200–1699," *Journal of World History* 12, no. 1 (2001): 29–98; William S. Atwell, "International Bullion Flows and the Chinese Economy," *Past and Present* 95 (1982): 68–90.

68. Hummel, *Eminent Chinese,* 327–331; Lawrence D. Kessler, *K'ang-Hsi and the Consolidation of Ch'ing Rule, 1661–1684* (Chicago: University of Chicago Press, 1976); Robert B. Oxnam, *Ruling from Horseback: Manchu Politics in the Oboi Regency, 1661–69* (Chicago: University of Chicago Press, 1975); Jonathan Spence, *Emperor of China: A Portrait of K'ang-Hsi* (New York: Vintage, 1988).

69. On Taiwan's history, see Murray A. Rubinstein, *Taiwan: A New History* (Armonk, NY: M. E. Sharpe, 1999); John Robert Shepherd, *Statecraft and Political Economy on the Taiwan Frontier, 1600–1800* (Stanford, CA: Stanford University Press, 1993); Emma J. Teng, *Taiwan's Imagined Geography: Chinese Colonial Travel Writing and Pictures, 1683–1895* (Cambridge, MA: Harvard University Asia Center, 2004); Tonio Andrade, *How Taiwan Became Chinese: Dutch, Spanish, and Han Colonization in the Seventeenth Century* (New York: Columbia University Press, 2008).

70. Perdue, *China Marches West,* 133–208.

71. James A. Millward, *Beyond the Pass: Economy, Ethnicity, and Empire in Qing Central Asia, 1759–1864* (Stanford, CA: Stanford University Press, 1998).

72. Jonathan Spence, *Ts'ao Yin and the K'ang Hsi Emperor: Bondservant and Master* (New Haven, CT: Yale University Press, 1966).

73. Beatrice S. Bartlett, *Monarchs and Ministers: The Grand Council in Mid-Ch'ing China, 1723–1820* (Berkeley: University of California Press, 1991).

74. Madeleine Zelin, *The Magistrate's Tael: Rationalizing Fiscal Reform in Eighteenth-Century Ch'ing China* (Berkeley: University of California Press, 1984).

75. Pierre-Étienne Will and R. Bin Wong, *Nourish the People: The State Civilian Granary System in China, 1650–1850* (Ann Arbor: University of Michigan Press, 1991).

76. Pierre-Étienne Will, *Bureaucracy and Famine in Eighteenth-Century China,* trans. Elborg Forster (Stanford, CA: Stanford University Press, 1990); R. Bin Wong and Peter C. Perdue, "Famine's Foes in Ch'ing China: Review of Pierre-Étienne Will, Bureaucratie et famine en Chine au 18e siècle," *Harvard Journal of Asiatic Studies* 43, no. 1 (1983): 291–332.

77. Helen Dunstan, *State or Merchant? Political Economy and Political Process in 1740s China* (Cambridge, MA: Harvard University Press, 2006).

78. Nicola Di Cosmo, "Qing Colonial Administration in the Inner Asian Dependencies," *International History Review* 20, no. 2 (1998): 287–309; Chia Ning, "The Lifanyuan and the Inner Asian Rituals in the Early Qing," *Late Imperial China* 14, no. 1 (1991): 60–92.

79. Mark Mancall, *Russia and China: Their Diplomatic Relations to 1728* (Cambridge, MA: Harvard University Press, 1971); Peter C. Perdue, "Boundaries and Trade in the Early Modern World: Negotiations at Nerchinsk and Beijing," *Eighteenth Century Studies* 43, no. 3 (2010): 341–356.

80. Clifford M. Foust, *Muscovite and Mandarin: Russia's Trade with China and Its Setting, 1727–1805* (Chapel Hill: University of North Carolina Press, 1969); Eric Widmer, *The Russian Ecclesiastical Mission in Peking during the Eighteenth Century* (Cambridge, MA: East Asian Research Center, 1976). Primary sources translated in Fu Lo-shu, *A Documentary Chronicle of Sino-Western Relations (1644–1820),* 2 vols. (Tucson: University of Arizona Press, 1966).

81. On frontier settlement globally, including the Qing, see Richards, *The Unending Frontier.*

82. Keith Schoppa, *Xiang Lake: Nine Centuries of Chinese Life* (New Haven, CT: Yale University Press, 1989).

83. Robert B. Marks, *Tigers, Rice, Silk, and Silt: Environment and Economy in Late Imperial South China* (Cambridge: Cambridge University Press, 1998).

84. Peng Ermi, "Ballad of Shuixi," in Mark Elvin, *The Retreat of the Elephants: An Environmental History of China* (New Haven, CT: Yale University Press, 2004), 231–232.

85. Peter C. Perdue, *Exhausting the Earth: State and Peasant in Hunan, 1500–1850* (Cambridge, MA: Council on East Asian Studies, 1987), 166.

86. Kenneth Pomeranz, *The Great Divergence: China, Europe, and the Making of the Modern World Economy* (Princeton, NJ: Princeton University Press, 2000). Mark Elvin, by contrast, cites foreign observers who perceived severe pressure on the land: Elvin, *Retreat,* 454–471.

87. Jonathan Spence, *Treason by the Book* (New York: Viking, 2001); Crossley, *A Translucent Mirror,* 253–260; Perdue, *China Marches West,* 470–471.

88. R. Kent Guy, *The Emperor's Four Treasuries: Scholars and the State in the Late Ch'ien-Lung Era* (Cambridge, MA: Harvard University Press, 1987).

89. Benjamin Elman, *From Philosophy to Philology: Intellectual and Social Aspects of Change in Late Imperial China* (Cambridge, MA: Harvard University Press, 1984).

90. William T. Rowe, *Saving the World: Chen Hongmou and Elite Consciousness in Eighteenth-Century China* (Stanford, CA: Stanford University Press, 2001).

91. Susan Mann, *Precious Records: Women in China's Long Eighteenth Century* (Stanford, CA: Stanford University Press, 1997); Susan Mann, *The Talented Women of the Zhang Family* (Berkeley: University of California Press, 2007); Dorothy Ko, *Teachers of the Inner Chambers: Women and Culture in Seventeenth-Century China* (Stanford, CA: Stanford University Press, 1994).

92. Matthew Harvey Sommer, *Sex, Law, and Society in Late Imperial China* (Stanford, CA: Stanford University Press, 2000); Janet M. Theiss, *Disgraceful Matters: The Politics of Chastity in Eighteenth-Century China* (Berkeley: University of California Press, 2004).

93. Philip A. Kuhn, *Soulstealers: The Chinese Sorcery Scare of 1768* (Cambridge, MA: Harvard University Press, 1990).

94. General works include Nicholas Riasanovsky, *A History of Russia* (Oxford: Oxford University Press, 1993); George Vernadsky, *Kievan Russia* (New Haven, CT: Yale University Press, 1948); Janet Martin, *Medieval Russia, 980–1584* (Cambridge: Cambridge University Press, 1995); Joseph L. Wieczynski, ed., *The Modern Encyclopedia of Russian and Soviet History,* 60 vols. (Gulf Breeze, FL: Academic International Press, 1976–1994); Lieberman, *Strange Parallels,* 2:123–313; Paul Bushkovitch, *A Concise History of Russia* (Cambridge: Cambridge University Press, 2011).

95. Donald Ostrowski, *Muscovy and the Mongols: Cross-Cultural Influences on the Steppe Frontier, 1304–1589* (Cambridge: Cambridge University Press, 1998); Charles Halperin, *Russia and the Golden Horde: The Mongol Impact on Medieval Russia* (Bloomington: Indiana University Press, 1985).

96. Robert O. Crummey, *The Formation of Muscovy, 1304–1613* (London: Longman, 1987).

97. Martin, *Medieval Russia,* 260.

98. Ibid., 264.

99. Paul Bushkovitch, "The Formation of a National Consciousness in Early Modern Russia," *Harvard Ukrainian Studies* 10 (1986): 355–376.

100. Edward Keenan, "Muscovy and Kazan, 1445–1552: A Study in Steppe Politics" (PhD diss., Harvard University, 1965); Edward Keenan, "Muscovy and Kazan, 1445–1552: Some Introductory Remarks on Steppe Diplomacy," *Slavic Review* 26, no. 4 (1967): 548–558; Jaroslaw Pelenski, *Russia and Kazan: Conquest and Imperial Ideology* (Paris: Mouton, 1974).

101. Paul Bushkovitch, *Religion and Society in Russia: The Sixteenth and Seventeenth Centuries* (New York: Oxford University Press, 1992).

102. Mark Bassin, "Expansion and Colonialism on the Eastern Frontier: Views of Siberia and the Far East in Pre-Petrine Russia," *Journal of Historical Geography* 14, no. 1 (1988): 3–21; Mark Bassin, "Russia between Europe and Asia: The Ideological Construction of Geographical Space," *Slavic Review* 50, no. 1 (1991): 1–17; George V. Lantzeff and Richard Pierce, *Eastward to Empire: Exploration and Conquest on the Russian Open Frontier to 1750* (Montreal: McGill-Queen's University Press, 1973).

103. Giles Fletcher, *Of the Russe Commonwealth* (1591; Cambridge, MA: Harvard University Press, 1966), preface.

104. Chester S. L. Dunning, *Russia's First Civil War: The Time of Troubles and the Founding of the Romanov Dynasty* (University Park: Pennsylvania State University Press, 2001).

105. Edward L. Keenan, "Muscovite Political Folkways," *Russian Review* 45 (1986): 115–181.

106. Nancy Shields Kollmann, *By Honor Bound: State and Society in Early Modern Russia* (Ithaca, NY: Cornell University Press, 1999).

107. S. H. Baron, ed., *The Travels of Olearius in Seventeenth-Century Russia* (Stanford, CA: Stanford University Press, 1967), 61–62.

108. Paul Bushkovitch, *The Merchants of Moscow, 1580–1650* (Cambridge: Cambridge University Press, 1980).

109. Valerie A. Kivelson, "The Devil Stole His Mind: The Tsar and the 1648 Moscow Uprising," *American Historical Review* 98, no. 3 (1993): 733–756; Valerie Kivelson, "Merciful Father, Impersonal State: Russian Autocracy in Comparative Perspective," *Modern Asian Studies* 3 (1997): 635–663; Valerie A. Kivelson, *Autocracy in the Provinces: The Muscovite Gentry and Political Culture in the Seventeenth Century* (Stanford, CA: Stanford University Press, 1996); Victor B. Lieberman, ed., *Beyond Binary Histories: Re-Imagining Eurasia to ca. 1830* (Ann Arbor: University of Michigan Press, 1999).

110. Richard Hellie, *Enserfment and Military Change in Muscovy* (Chicago: University of Chicago Press, 1971); Carol B. Stevens, *Soldiers on the Steppe: Army Reform and Social Change in Early Modern Russia* (DeKalb: Northern Illinois University Press, 1995).

111. V. O. Klyuchevsky, *Peter the Great* (New York: Vintage, 1958); Paul Bushkovitch, *Peter the Great: The Struggle for Power, 1671–1725* (Cambridge: Cambridge University Press, 2001); Paul Bushkovitch, *Peter the Great* (Lanham, MD: Rowman & Littlefield, 2001); James Cracraft, *The Petrine Revolution in Russian Culture* (Cambridge, MA: Harvard University Press, 2004).

112. Evgenii V. Anisimov, *The Reforms of Peter the Great* (Armonk, NY: M. E. Sharpe, 1993), 94.

113. Loren Graham, *Science in Russia and the Soviet Union* (Cambridge: Cambridge University Press, 1993).

114. Klyuchevsky, *Peter the Great*, 155.

115. Anisimov, *The Reforms of Peter the Great*, 239.

116. Arcadius Kahan and Richard Hellie, *The Plow, the Hammer, and the Knout: An Economic History of Eighteenth-Century Russia* (Chicago: University of Chicago Press, 1985).

117. Orlando Figes, *Natasha's Dance: A Cultural History of Russia* (New York: Metropolitan Books, 2002).

118. Michael Khodarkovsky, *Russia's Steppe Frontier: The Making of a Colonial Empire, 1500–1800* (Bloomington: Indiana University Press, 2002); Willard Sunderland, *Taming the Wild Field: Colonization and Empire on the Russian Steppe* (Ithaca, NY: Cornell University Press, 2004).

119. Valerie A. Kivelson, *Cartographies of Tsardom: The Land and Its Meanings in Seventeenth-Century Russia* (Ithaca, NY: Cornell University Press, 2006), 148.

120. Michael Khodarkovsky, *Where Two Worlds Met: The Russian State and the Kalmyk Nomads, 1600–1771* (Ithaca, NY: Cornell University Press, 1992); Peter C. Perdue, *China Marches West: The Qing Conquest of Central Eurasia* (Cambridge, MA: Harvard University Press, 2005).

121. Rene Grousset, *The Empire of the Steppes* (New Brunswick, NJ: Rutgers University Press, 1970); Svat Soucek, *A History of Inner Asia* (Cambridge: Cambridge University Press, 2000); Nicola Di Cosmo, Allen J. Frank, and Peter B. Golden, *The Cambridge History of Inner Asia: The Chinggisid Age* (Cambridge: Cambridge University Press, 2009).

122. Joseph F. Fletcher, "China and Central Asia, 1368–1884," in *The Chinese World Order: Traditional China's Foreign Relations,* ed. John K. Fairbank (Cambridge, MA: Harvard University Press, 1968).

123. Thomas J. Barfield, *The Perilous Frontier: Nomadic Empires and China* (Cambridge, MA: Basil Blackwell, 1989), 229–266.

124. Audrey Burton, *The Bukharans: A Dynastic, Diplomatic, and Commercial History, 1550–1702* (Richmond, UK: Curzon, 1997).

125. Babur, *The Baburnama* (Oxford: Oxford University Press, 1996).

126. James A. Millward, *Eurasian Crossroads: A History of Xinjiang* (New York: Columbia University Press, 2007); James Millward, "Eastern Central Asia (Xinjiang): 1300–1800," in Di Cosmo, Frank, and Golden, *The Cambridge History of Inner Asia,* 260–276.

127. Mīrzā Ḥaydar and W. M. Thackston, *Mirza Haydar Dughlat's Tarikh-I Rashidi: A History of the Khans of Moghulistan* (Cambridge, MA: Harvard University, Department of Near Eastern Languages and Civilizations, 1996).

128. I. Ia. Zlatkin, *Istoriia Dzhungarskogo Khanstvo (1635–1758)* [History of the Zunghar khanate (1635–1758)] (Moscow: Nauka, 1964); Miyawaki Junko, *Saigo No Yûboku Teikoku: Jungaru Bu No Kôbô* [The last nomadic empire: The rise and fall of the Zunghars] (Tokyo: Kodansha, 1995); Perdue, *China Marches West.*

129. Goodrich and Fang, *Dictionary,* 1:416–420.

130. Scott Levi, "India, Russia and the Eighteenth-Century Transformation of the Central Asian Caravan Trade," *Journal of the Economic and Social History of the Orient* 42 (1999): 519–548.

131. Burton, *Bukharans.*

132. Surveys of Japan in this period include the following: William Wayne Farris, *Japan's Medieval Population: Famine, Fertility, and Warfare in a Transformative Age* (Honolulu: University of Hawai'i Press, 2006); George Sansom, *A History of Japan* (Stanford, CA: Stanford University Press, 1963); Pierre Souyri, *The World Turned Upside Down: Medieval Japanese Society* (New York: Columbia University Press, 2001); Conrad D. Totman, *Early Modern Japan* (Berkeley: University of California Press, 1993); *A History of Japan,* 2nd ed. (Malden, MA: Blackwell, 2005), *Japan before Perry: A Short History* (Berkeley: University of California Press, 1981), *Politics in the Tokugawa Bakufu* (Berkeley: University of California Press, 1988), *Pre-Industrial Korea and Japan in Environmental Perspective* (Leiden: Brill, 2004); and the *Cambridge History of Japan,* vol. 4.

133. Totman, *Pre-Industrial Korea and Japan in Environmental Perspective.*

134. Sansom, *A History of Japan;* Kozo Yamamura, *The Cambridge History of Japan,* vol. 3, *Medieval Japan* (Cambridge: Cambridge University Press, 2008); Souyri, *World Turned Upside Down;* John Whitney Hall, *Government and Local Power in Japan, 500 to 1700: A Study Based on Bizen Province* (Princeton, NJ: Princeton University Press, 1966); John Whitney Hall, Takeshi Toyoda,

and H. Paul Varley, *Japan in the Muromachi Age* (Ithaca, NY: East Asia Program, Cornell University, 2001); Lieberman, *Strange Parallels,* 2:371–494.

135. Sansom, *A History of Japan,* 323.

136. Andrew Edmund Goble, *Kenmu: Go-Daigo's Revolution* (Cambridge, MA: Council on East Asian Studies, 1996).

137. Souyri, *World Turned Upside Down,* 107.

138. Ibid., 114.

139. Yamamura, *The Cambridge History of Japan,* 285.

140. Jeffrey P. Mass and William Hauser, eds., *The Bakufu in Japanese History* (Stanford, CA: Stanford University Press, 1985); Jeffrey P. Mass, ed., *The Origins of Japan's Medieval World: Courtiers, Clerics, Warriors, and Peasants in the Fourteenth Century* (Stanford, CA: Stanford University Press, 1997).

141. Ikegami Eiko, *The Taming of the Samurai: Honorific Individualism and the Making of Modern Japan* (Cambridge, MA: Harvard University Press, 1995), 121–134.

142. H. Paul Varley, *The Ōnin War: History of Its Origins and Background with a Selective Translation of the Chronicle of Ōnin* (New York: Columbia University Press, 1967).

143. Mary Elizabeth Berry, *The Culture of Civil War in Kyoto* (Berkeley: University of California Press, 1994), 13–14.

144. Souyri, *World Turned Upside Down,* 198–200; Berry, *The Culture of Civil War in Kyoto,* 153–170.

145. Martin Collcutt, *Five Mountains: The Rinzai Zen Monastic Institution in Medieval Japan* (Cambridge, MA: Council on East Asian Studies, 1981).

146. John Whitney Hall, ed., *The Cambridge History of Japan,* vol. 4, *Early Modern Japan* (Cambridge: Cambridge University Press, 1991); Totman, *Early Modern Japan;* Totman, *A History of Japan.*

147. Souyri, *World Turned Upside Down,* 181–217.

148. Farris, *Japan's Medieval Population,* 263.

149. Mary Elizabeth Berry, *Hideyoshi* (Cambridge, MA: Harvard University Press, 1982), 102.

150. Totman, *A History of Japan,* 211.

151. Berry, *Hideyoshi,* 208, 213.

152. Samuel Jay Hawley, *The Imjin War: Japan's Sixteenth-Century Invasion of Korea and Attempt to Conquer China* (Berkeley: Institute of East Asian Studies, University of California, 2005).

153. Lieberman, *Strange Parallels,* 2:418.

154. John W. Hall and Marius Jansen, eds., *Studies in the Institutional History of Early Modern Japan* (Princeton, NJ: Princeton University Press, 1968); Harold Bolitho, *Treasures among Men: The Fudai Daimyo in Tokugawa Japan* (New Haven, CT: Yale University Press, 1974); Totman, *Politics in the Tokugawa Bakufu.*

155. Totman, *Politics in the Tokugawa Bakufu,* 264–268.

156. Herbert Bix, *Peasant Protest in Japan, 1590–1884* (New Haven, CT: Yale University Press, 1986); Anne Walthall, *Social Protest and Popular Culture in Eighteenth-Century Japan* (Tucson: University of Arizona Press, 1986); Stephen Vlastos, *Peasant Protest and Uprisings in Tokugawa Japan* (Berkeley: University of California Press, 1986); E. H. Norman, "Ando Shoeki and the Anatomy of Japanese Feudalism," *Transactions of the Asiatic Society of Japan,* 3rd ser., vol. 2, no. 1 (1949).

157. Totman, *Japan before Perry*, 133.

158. Herman Ooms, *Tokugawa Ideology: Early Constructs, 1570–1680* (Princeton, NJ: Princeton University Press, 1985); Benjamin A. Elman, John B. Duncan, and Herman Ooms, *Rethinking Confucianism: Past and Present in China, Japan, Korea, and Vietnam* (Los Angeles: UCLA Asian Pacific Monograph Series, 2002); Susan L. Burns, *Before the Nation: Kokugaku and the Imagining of Community in Early Modern Japan* (Durham, NC: Duke University Press, 2003); Tsunoda Ryusaku and Wm. Theodore de Bary, eds., *Sources of Japanese Tradition* (New York: Columbia University Press, 1958).

159. Eiko Ikegami, *Bonds of Civility: Aesthetic Networks and the Political Origins of Japanese Culture* (Cambridge: Cambridge University Press, 2005).

160. Kozo Yamamura and Susan B. Hanley, *Economic and Demographic Change in Pre-Industrial Japan, 1600–1868* (Princeton, NJ: Princeton University Press, 1977).

161. Fabian Drixler, *Mabiki: Infanticide and Fertility in Eastern Japan, 1650–1950* (Berkeley: University of California Press, 2013).

162. David L. Howell, *Geographies of Identity in Nineteenth-Century Japan* (Berkeley: University of California Press, 2005); Brett L. Walker, *The Conquest of Ainu Lands: Ecology and Culture in Japanese Expansion, 1590–1800* (Berkeley: University of California Press, 2001).

163. Mary Elizabeth Berry, *Japan in Print: Information and Nation in the Early Modern Period* (Berkeley: University of California Press, 2006).

164. Ikegami, *Bonds of Civility*.

165. Ronald P. Dore, *Education in Tokugawa Japan* (Berkeley: University of California Press, 1965).

166. Basic surveys of this period include John K. Fairbank and Edwin O. Reischauer, *East Asia: The Great Tradition* (Boston: Houghton Mifflin, 1960), 1:394–449; Patricia Buckley Ebrey, Anne Walthall, and James B. Palais, *East Asia: A Cultural, Social, and Political History* (Boston: Houghton Mifflin, 2006), 290–306, 348–364; Takashi Hatada, *A History of Korea* (Santa Barbara, CA: ABC-Clio, 1969), 61–89; William E. Henthorn, *A History of Korea* (New York: Free Press, 1971), 136–226; Ki-baik Lee, *A New History of Korea* (Cambridge, MA: Harvard University Press, 1984), 155–246; Mark Peterson and Phillip Margulies, *A Brief History of Korea* (New York: Facts on File, 2010), 74–140.

167. Fairbank and Reischauer, *East Asia,* 431.

168. Lee, *A New History of Korea,* 186–187.

169. Ibid., 192.

170. C. Dallet, *Histoire de l'église de Corée,* cited in Henthorn, *A History of Korea,* 195.

171. Henthorn, *A History of Korea,* 185.

172. V. D. Roeper et al., *Hamel's World: A Dutch-Korean Encounter in the Seventeenth Century* (Amsterdam: SUN, 2003); Hendrik Hamel, *Hamel's Journal and a Description of the Kingdom of Korea, 1653–1666* (Seoul: Royal Asiatic Society, Korea Branch, 1994).

173. Ki-joo Park and Yang Donghyu, "Standard of Living in the Choson Dynasty Korea in the 17th to 19th Centuries," *Seoul Journal of Economics* 20 (2007): 297–332.

174. Milan Hejtmanek, "Sŏwŏn in Chosŏn Korea, 1543–1741" (PhD diss., Harvard University, 1994).

175. Dieter Eikemeier, *Elemente im Politischen Denken des Yon'am Pak Chiwon (1737–1805)* (Leiden: Brill, 1970); Tu-ki Min, "The Jehol Diary and the Character of Ch'ing Rule," in *National Polity and Local Power: The Transformation of Late Imperial China,* ed. Philip A. Kuhn and Timothy Brook (Cambridge, MA: Harvard University Press, 1989), 2–19.

176. Ssi Hyegyŏnggung Hong and JaHyun Kim Haboush, *The Memoirs of Lady Hyegyong: The Autobiographical Writings of a Crown Princess of Eighteenth-Century Korea* (Berkeley: University of California Press, 1996), 282.

177. Basic studies of this period include Nicholas Tarling, ed., *The Cambridge History of Southeast Asia* (Cambridge: Cambridge University Press, 1992), 1:137–153; Lieberman, *Strange Parallels,* 1:338–456; William J. Duiker, *Historical Dictionary of Vietnam,* 2nd ed. (Lanham, MD: Scarecrow Press, 1998); David Steinberg et al., eds., *In Search of Southeast Asia* (Honolulu: University of Hawai'i Press, 1987), 69–76.

178. Pierre Gourou, *Les Paysans du Delta Tonkinois; Étude de Géographie Humaine* (Paris: Les Éditions d'art et d'histoire, 1936), 8, cited in Lieberman, *Strange Parallels,* 1:343.

179. Nguyen Ngoc Huy et al., *The Lê Code: Law in Traditional Vietnam: A Comparative Sino-Vietnamese Legal Study with Historical-Juridical Analysis and Annotations* (Athens: Ohio University Press, 1987), 1:14.

180. Lieberman, *Strange Parallels,* 1:368.

181. O. W. Wolters, *Two Essays on Dai Viet in the Fourteenth Century* (New Haven, CT: Council on Southeast Asia Studies, 1988), 16–18, 57.

182. John K. Whitmore, *Vietnam, Ho Quý Ly, and the Ming (1371–1421)* (New Haven, CT: Council on Southeast Asia Studies, 1985).

183. Keith W. Taylor, "Surface Orientations in Vietnam: Beyond Histories of Nation and Region," *Journal of Asian Studies* 57 (1998): 949–978.

184. Sanh Thông Huynh, *The Heritage of Vietnamese Poetry* (New Haven, CT: Yale University Press, 1979), 8–9.

185. Sanh Thông Huynh, *An Anthology of Vietnamese Poems: From the Eleventh through the Twentieth Centuries* (New Haven, CT: Yale University Press, 1996), 38.

186. Paul Schneider and Trãi Nguyen, *Nguyên Trai et Son Recueil de Poèmes en Langue Nationale* (Paris: Presses du CNRS Diffusion, 1987).

187. John K. Whitmore, "Foreign Influences and the Vietnamese Cultural Core: A Discussion of the Premodern Period," in *Borrowings and Adaptations in Vietnamese Culture,* ed. Truong Buu Lam (Honolulu: Center for Asian and Pacific Studies, University of Hawai'i at Manoa, 1987), 10.

188. Tana Li, *Nguyen Cochinchina: Southern Vietnam in the Seventeenth and Eighteenth Centuries* (Ithaca, NY: Southeast Asia Program Publications, 1998), 159–172.

189. Alexander Woodside, "Medieval Vietnam and Cambodia: A Comparative Comment," *Journal of Southeast Asian Studies* 15 (1984): 315–319.

190. Nola Cooke, "Nineteenth-Century Vietnamese Confucianization in Historical Perspective: Evidence from the Palace Examinations, 1463–1883," *Journal of Southeast Asian Studies* 25 (1994): 270–312.

191. Tana Li, *Nguyen Cochinchina,* 159–163; Kathlene Baldanza, "The Ambiguous Border: Early Modern Sino-Viet Relations" (PhD diss., University of Pennsylvania, 2010).

192. Cooke, "Nineteenth-Century Vietnamese Confucianization"; Alain Forest and Georges Condominas, *Les Missionnaires Français au Tonkin et au Siam, Xviie–Xviiie Siècles: Analyse Comparée d'un Relatif Succès et d'un Total Échec,* 3 vols. (Paris: L'Harmattan, 1998).

193. Brantly Womack, *China and Vietnam: The Politics of Asymmetry* (Cambridge: Cambridge University Press, 2006); Liam C. Kelley, *Beyond the Bronze Pillars: Envoy Poetry and the Sino-Vietnamese Relationship* (Honolulu: University of Hawai'i Press, 2005).

194. Tana Li, "An Alternative Vietnam? The Nguyen Kingdom in the Seventeenth and Eighteenth Centuries," *Journal of Southeast Asian Studies* 29 (1998): 111–121.

195. Nola Cooke, "Regionalism and the Nature of Nguyen Rule in Seventeenth-Century Dang Trong (Cochinchina)," *Journal of Southeast Asian Studies* 29 (1998): 122–161.

196. Alexander B. Woodside, *Vietnam and the Chinese Model: A Comparative Study of Nguyên and Ch'ing Civil Government in the First Half of the Nineteenth Century* (Cambridge, MA: Harvard University Press, 1971), 115–118.

197. Charles J. Wheeler, "Cross-Cultural Trade and Trans-Regional Networks in the Port of Hoi An: Maritime Vietnam in the Early Modern Era" (PhD diss., Yale University, 2001).

198. Thomas Engelbert, *Die Chinesische Minderheit im Süden Vietnams (Hoa) als Paradigma der Kolonialen und Nationalistischen Nationalitätenpolitik* (Frankfurt am Main: Peter Lang, 2002).

199. Alexander Woodside, "Central Vietnam's Trading World in the Eighteenth Century as Seen in Lê Quý Dôn's 'Frontier Chronicles,'" in *Essays into Vietnamese Pasts,* ed. Keith Weller Taylor and John K. Whitmore (Ithaca, NY: Southeast Asia Program, Cornell University, 1995), 157–172.

200. Le Quy Don, *Phu Bien Tap Luc* [Frontier chronicles] (Hanoi, 1977); Le Quy Don, *Bac Su Thong Luc* [Diary of travel to Beijing], 1760.

201. Huynh, *The Heritage of Vietnamese Poetry,* 15; Goodrich and Fang, *Dictionary,* 1:361, 793–797.

202. Ho Xuân Huong, *Spring Essence: The Poetry of Ho Xuân Huong,* trans. John Balaban (Port Townsend, WA: Copper Canyon Press, 2000); Ho Xuân Huong and Maurice M. Durand, *L'oeuvre de la Poétesse Vietnamienne Ho-Xuân-Huong* (Paris: Ecole française d'Extrême-Orient, 1968).

203. Ho Xuân Huong, *Spring Essence,* 35.

204. Nguyen Du, *The Tale of Kieu: Bilingual Edition* [Truyen Kieu], trans. Sanh Thông Huynh (New Haven, CT: Yale University Press, 1983).

205. George Edson Dutton, *The Tay Son Uprising: Society and Rebellion in Eighteenth-Century Vietnam* (Honolulu: University of Hawai'i Press, 2006); Alexander B. Woodside, "The Tayson Revolution in Southeast Asian History" (unpublished manuscript, Cornell University library, Ithaca, NY, 1976).

206. Peter C. Perdue, "Embracing Victory, Effacing Defeat: Rewriting the Qing Frontier Campaigns," in *The Chinese State at the Borders,* ed. Diana Lary (Vancouver: University of British Columbia Press, 2007).

207. Dutton, *The Tay Son Uprising,* 158.

208. Woodside, *Vietnam and the Chinese Model*. Cooke, "Nineteenth-Century Vietnamese Confucianization," however, argues that the degree of Confucian influence through the examination system was greater in the fifteenth century than in the early nineteenth century.

209. Marks, *Tigers, Rice, Silk, and Silt*, 196, 491; Richards, *The Unending Frontier*, 58–85.

210. Jack A. Goldstone, *Revolution and Rebellion in the Early Modern World* (Berkeley: University of California Press, 1991).

211. Colin McEvedy and Richard Jones, *Atlas of World Population History* (New York: Penguin Press, 1978).

212. Stephen Frederic Dale, *Indian Merchants and Eurasian Trade, 1600–1750* (Cambridge: Cambridge University Press, 1994); Scott Levi, "India, Russia and the Eighteenth-Century Transformation of the Central Asian Caravan Trade," *Journal of the Economic and Social History of the Orient* 42, no. 4 (1999): 519–548.

213. Richards, *The Unending Frontier*, 617.

214. James C. Scott, *The Art of Not Being Governed: An Anarchist History of Upland Southeast Asia* (New Haven, CT: Yale University Press, 2009).

215. Mann, *The Talented Women of the Zhang Family*.

216. Gail Lee Bernstein, ed., *Recreating Japanese Women, 1600–1945* (Berkeley: University of California Press, 1991).

217. David Christian, "Inner Eurasia as a Unit of World History," *Journal of World History* 5, no. 2 (1994): 173–213.

218. Perdue, *China Marches West*, 532–536; Nicola Di Cosmo, "State Formation and Periodization in Inner Asian History," *Journal of World History* 10, no. 1 (1999): 1–40; Owen Lattimore, *Studies in Frontier History: Collected Papers, 1928–1958* (Oxford: Oxford University Press, 1962).

219. Alexander B. Woodside, *Lost Modernities: China, Vietnam, Korea, and the Hazards of World History* (Cambridge, MA: Harvard University Press, 2006).

2. The Ottoman Empire and the Islamic World

This work could not have been written without the generous help of friends and colleagues. Christine Noelle Karimi (Vienna) and Heidi Walcher (London/Munich) patiently read through and commented on my first draft and saved me (as a non-Persianist) from committing countless errors. Yavuz Köse (Munich) and Sinan Çetin (Istanbul) were extremely helpful in obtaining books and ensuring that even occasional computer crashes did not faze me. Christoph Knüttel (Munich) standardized the notes and bibliography with his customary care and attention. And if M. Erdem Kabadayı (Istanbul) had not taken on so much administrative work, I would scarcely have had a moment's peace to write during semesters. My warmest thanks are due to all of them; it goes without saying that these helpful colleagues are in no way responsible for any mistakes or misunderstandings. To quote Eskandar Beg Monshi: "it is also my hope that my readers will correct any slips and errors which they come across, and not censure me for them." *History of Shah Abbas the Great (Tārīk-i Ālam ārā-yiʿAbbāsī)*, trans. Roger Savory (Boulder, CO: Westview Press 1978–1986), 3:1326.

On transcription: For all personal and place-names, as well as technical terms, Turkish Latin script has been used. For Iranian words, the system employed in the *Encyclopaedia of Islam,* new ed., 12 vols. (Leiden: E. J. Brill, 1960–2004) has been adopted, with the modifications that Beatrice F. Manz proposes in her standard work *The Rise and Rule of Tamerlane* (Cambridge: Cambridge University Press, 1989), and which are frequently applied in other works. The names of people and places that have several different variants are mostly given in the form in which they appear in the *Encyclopaedia of Islam* (new ed.) and in Hugh Kennedy, *An Historical Atlas of Islam/Atlas historique de l'Islam* (Leiden: E. J. Brill, 2002).

1. For an excellent discussion of early Ottoman history, see Cemal Kafadar, *Between Two Worlds: The Construction of the Ottoman State* (Berkeley: University of California Press, 1995).

2. Virginia Aksan, *Ottoman Wars: An Empire Besieged, 1700–1870* (Harlow, UK: Longman Pearson, 2007), 154–160.

3. Mehmet Genç, "L'Économie ottomane et la guerre au XVIIIe siècle," *Turcica* 27 (1995): 177–196; Edhem Eldem, *French Trade in Istanbul in the Eighteenth Century* (Leiden: E. J. Brill, 1999); Eugen Wirth, "Aleppo im 19. Jahrhundert—ein Beispiel für die Stabilität und Dynamik spätosmanischer Wirtschaft," in *Osmanistische Studien zur Wirtschafts- und Sozialgeschichte: In Memoriam Vančo Boškov,* ed. Hans Georg Majer (Wiesbaden: Harrassowitz, 1986), 186–206.

4. Ariel Salzmann, "An Ancien Régime Revisited: 'Privatization' and Political Economy in the Eighteenth-Century Ottoman Empire," *Politics and Society* 21, no. 4 (1993): 393–423; Dina Rizk Khoury, *State and Provincial Society in the Ottoman Empire: Mosul, 1540–1834* (Cambridge: Cambridge University Press, 1997), 214.

5. Boğaç Ergene, *Local Court, Provincial Society and Justice in the Ottoman Empire: Legal Practice and Dispute Resolution in Çankırı and Kastamonu (1652–1744)* (Leiden: E. J. Brill, 2003), 99–108.

6. Gabriel Piterberg, "The Alleged Rebellion of Abaza Mehmed Paşa: Historiography and the Ottoman State in the Seventeenth Century," *International Journal of Turkish Studies* 8, nos. 1–2 (2002): 13–24; Baki Tezcan, "The 1622 Military Rebellion in Istanbul: A Historiographical Journey," *International Journal of Turkish Studies* 8, nos. 1–2 (2002): 25–44; Y. Hakan Erdem, *Tarih-Lenk: Kusursuz Yazarlar, Kâğıttan Metinler* (Istanbul: Doğan Kitap, 2008), 235–334.

7. Richard Bulliet, *The Camel and the Wheel* (reprint; New York: Columbia University Press, 1990), 234; Evliya Çelebi b. Derviş Mehemmed Zıllı, *Evliya Çelebi Seyahatnâmesi: Topkapı Sarayı Kütüphanesi Bağdat 304 Numaralı Yazmaların Mukayeseli Transkripsyonu—Dizini,* vol. 2, ed. Yücel Dağlı, Seyit Ali Kahraman, and Zekerya Kurşun (Istanbul: Yapı Kredi Yayınları, 1999), 109.

8. Evliya Çelebi b. Derviş Mehemmed Zıllı, *Evliya Çelebi Seyahatnâmesi: Topkapı Sarayı Kütüphanesi Bağdat 306, Süleymaniye Kütüphanesi Pertev Paşa 462, Süleymaniye Kütüphanesi Hacı Beşir Ağa 452 Numaralı Yazmaların Mukayeseli Transkripsyonu—Dizini,* vol. 9, ed. Yücel Dağlı, Seyit Ali Kahraman, and Robert Dankoff (Istanbul: Yapı Kredi Yayınları, 2005), 286–430.

9. Xavier de Planhol, *L'eau de neige, le tiède et le frais: Histoire de géographie des boissons fraîches* (Paris: Fayard, 1995); Wolf Dieter Hütteroth, "Ecology of the Ottoman Lands," in *The Cambridge History of Turkey,* vol. 3, *The Later Ottoman Empire,* ed. Suraiya Faroqhi (Cambridge: Cambridge University Press, 2006), 18–43.

10. Evliya Çelebi, *Evliya Çelebi Seyahatnâmesi,* 2:54.

11. Bruce McGowan, "The Middle Danube Cul-de-Sac," in *The Ottoman Empire and the World Economy,* ed. Huri İslamoğlu-İnan (Cambridge: Cambridge University Press, 1987), 170–177; Cengiz Orhonlu, "Dicle ve Fırat Nehirlerinde Nakliyat," in *Osmanlı İmparatorluğunda Şehircilik ve Ulaşım,* ed. Salih Özbaran (Izmir: Ege Üniversitesi Edebiyat Fakültesi, 1984), 116–139; Patrick Boulanger, *Marseille, marché international de l'huile d'olive: Un produit et des hommes de 1725 à 1825* (Marseille: Institut Historique de Provence, 1996), 41–60.

12. Augerius Gislenius Busbequius, *Legationis turcicae epistolae quatuor,* ed. Zweder von Martels, translated into Dutch by Michel Goldsteen (Hilversum: Verloren, 1994), 304–305; Halil İnalcık, "Rice Cultivation and the *Çeltükci-re'âyâ* System in the Ottoman Empire," *Turcica* 14 (1982): 69–141.

13. Peter I. Kuniholm, "Archaeological Evidence and Non-Evidence for Climatic Change," *Philosophical Transactions of the Royal Society Series A* 330 (1990): 645–655.

14. Lütfi Güçer, "XVIII, Yüzyıl Ortalarında İstanbul'un İaşesi için Lüzumlu Hububatın Temini Meselesi," *İstanbul Üniversitesi İktisat Fakültesi Mecmuası* 11, nos. 1–4 (1949–1950): 397–416; ibid., "Osmanlı İmparatorluğu dahilinde Hububat Ticaretinin Tabi Olduğu Kayıtlar," *İstanbul Üniversitesi İktisat Fakültesi Mecmuası* 13, nos. 1–4 (1951–1952): 79–98; Salih Aynural, *İstanbul Değirmenleri ve Fırınları: Zahire Ticareti 1740–1830* (Istanbul: Tarih Vakfı Yurt Yayınları, 2001), 34–38.

15. Robert Mantran, *Istanbul dans la seconde moitié du XVIIe siècle: Essai d'histoire institutionelle, économique et sociale* (Istanbul: Institut Français d'Archéologie d'Istanbul, 1962), 428–430; Özer Ergenç, "1600–1615 Yılları Arasında Ankara İktisadi Tarihine Ait Araştırmalar," in *Türkiye İktisat Tarihi Semineri: Metinler-Tartışmalar, 8–10 haziran 1973,* ed. Osman Okyar and Ünal Nalbantoğlu (Ankara: Mars Matbaası, 1975), 145–168.

16. Klára Hegyi and Vera Zimányi, *Muslime und Christen: Das Osmanische Reich in Europa* (Budapest: Corvina, 1988), 131.

17. Orhonlu, "Dicle ve Fırat," 128–130.

18. Martin Hinds and Victor L. Ménage, *Qasr Ibrim in the Ottoman Period: Turkish and Further Arabic Documents* (London: Egypt Exploration Society, 1991); Terence Walz, *Trade between Egypt and Bilad al-Sudan* (Cairo: Institut Français d'Archéologie Orientale, 1978), 32; Alan Mikhail, *Nature and Empire in Ottoman Egypt: An Environmental History* (Cambridge: Cambridge University Press, 2011).

19. Cengiz Orhonlu, *Osmanlı İmparatorluğunun Güney Siyaseti: Habeş Eyaleti* (Istanbul: İstanbul Üniversitesi Edebiyat Fakültesi, 1974); Bradford G. Martin, "Kanem, Bornu, and the Fazzān: Notes on the Political History of a Trade Route," *Journal of African History* 10, no. 1 (1969): 15–27.

20. Hanna Sohrweide, "Der Sieg der Safaviden in Persien und seine Rückwirkungen auf die Schiiten Anatoliens im 16. Jahrhundert," *Der Islam* 41 (1965): 95–223.

21. Nasuhü's-silâhi (Matrâkçı), *Beyan-ı Menazil-i Sefer-i'Irakeyn-i Sultân Suleymân Han,* ed. Hüseyin G. Yurdaydın (Ankara: Türk Tarih Kurumu, 1976).

22. Nicolas Oikonomides, "From Soldiers of Fortune to Gazi Warriors: The Tzympe Affair," in *Studies in Ottoman History in Honour of Professor V. L. Ménage,* ed. Colin Heywood and Colin Imber (Istanbul: Isis Press, 1994), 239–248; Donald Nicol, *The Reluctant Emperor: A Biography of John Cantacuzene, Byzantine Emperor and Monk, c. 1295–1383* (Cambridge: Cambridge University Press, 1996), 76–77.

23. Heath Lowry, *Fifteenth Century Ottoman Realities: Christian Peasant Life on the Aegean Island of Lemnos* (Istanbul: Eren, 2002), especially 29; Halil İnalcık, "Stefan Duşan'dan Osmanlı İmparatorluğuna. XV Asırda Hıristyan Sipahiler ve Menşeleri," in *60. doğum yılı münasebetiyle Fuad Köprülü armağanı / Mélanges Fuad Köprülü* (Istanbul: Osman Yalçın Matbaası, 1953), 207–248.

24. Murat Çizakça, *A Comparative Evolution of Business Partnerships: The Islamic World and Europe, with Specific Reference to the Ottoman Archives* (Leiden: E. J. Brill, 1996), 147–148, 165; Matthew Elliot, "Dress Codes in the Ottoman Empire: The Case of the Franks," in *Ottoman Costumes: From Textile to Identity,* ed. Suraiya Faroqhi and Christoph K. Neumann (Istanbul: Eren, 2004), 103–123; Rossitsa Gradeva, "Apostasy in Rumeli in the Middle of the Sixteenth Century," in *Rumeli under the Ottomans, 15th to 18th Centuries: Institutions and Communities,* ed. Rossitsa Gradeva (Istanbul: Isis Press, 2004), 267–287.

25. Minna Rozen and Benjamin Arbel, "Great Fire in the Metropolis: The Case of the Istanbul Conflagration of 1569 and Its Description by Marcantonio Barbaro," in *Mamluks and Ottomans: Studies in Honour of Michael Winter,* ed. David Wasserstein and Ami Ayalon (London: Routledge, 2006), 134–165, see 147; Lucienne Thys Şenocak, *Ottoman Women Builders: The Architectural Patronage of Hadice Turhan Sultan* (Aldershot, UK: Ashgate, 2006), 189.

26. Antonina Zheljazkova, "Islamization in the Balkans as a Historiographical Problem: The Southeast-European Perspective," in *The Ottomans and the Balkans: A Discussion of Historiography,* ed. Fikret Adanır and Suraiya Faroqhi (Leiden: E. J. Brill, 2002), 233–266.

27. Carter Vaughn Findley, "The Tanzimat," in *The Cambridge History of Turkey,* vol. 4, *Turkey in the Modern World,* ed. Reşat Kasaba (Cambridge: Cambridge University Press, 2008), 11–37, see 18; Ömer Lütfi Barkan, "Edirne Askeri Kassam'ına ait Tereke Defterleri (1545–1659)," in *Belgeler* 3, nos. 5–6 (1966): 1–479; Nelly Hanna, *Making Big Money in 1600: The Life and Times of Isma'il Abu Taqiyya, Egyptian Merchant* (Syracuse, NY: Syracuse University Press, 1998).

28. Cornell H. Fleischer, *Bureaucrat and Intellectual in the Ottoman Empire: The Historian Mustafâ Âli (1541–1600)* (Princeton, NJ: Princeton University Press, 1986), 153–159.

29. Halil Inalcik, "The Socio-Political Effects of the Diffusion of Fire-Arms in the Middle East," in *War, Technology and Society in the Middle East,* ed. Bela Király (London: Oxford University Press, 1974), 195–217; Halil Inalcik, "Military and Fiscal Transformation in the Ottoman Empire, 1600–1700," *Archivum Ottomanicum* 6 (1980): 283–337.

30. Gülru Necipoğlu, *The Age of Sinan: Architectural Culture in the Ottoman Empire* (London: Reaktion Books, 2005), 129; Mantran, *Istanbul,* 390–393; Suraiya Faroqhi, *Towns and Townsmen of Ottoman Anatolia: Trade, Crafts, and Food Production in an Urban Setting* (Cambridge: Cam-

bridge University Press, 1984), 57; André Raymond, *Artisans et commerçants au Caire, au XVIIIᵉ siècle,* 2 vols. (Damascus: Institut Français de Damas, 1973–1974); Charles Wilkins, *Forging Urban Solidarities: Ottoman Aleppo, 1640–1700* (Leiden: E. J. Brill, 2010).

31. Mustafa Akdağ, *Celâlî İsyanları 1550–1603* (Ankara: Ankara Üniversitesi Dil ve Tarih-Coğrafya Fakültesi, 1963); Karen Barkey, *Bandits and Bureaucrats: The Ottoman Route to State Centralization* (Ithaca, NY: Cornell University Press, 1994), 189–228.

32. Metin Kunt, *The Sultan's Servants: The Transformation of Ottoman Provincial Government, 1550–1650* (New York: Columbia University Press, 1983); Jane Hathaway, *The Politics of Households in Ottoman Egypt: The Rise of the Qazdağlıs* (Cambridge: Cambridge University Press, 1997); David Ayalon, "Studies in al-Jabartī. I. Notes on the Transformation of Mamluk Society in Egypt under the Ottomans," *Journal of the Economic and Social History of the Orient* 3, nos. 2–3 (1960): 148–174 and 275–325; see 288–304.

33. Klaus Röhrborn, *Untersuchungen zur osmanischen Verwaltungsgeschichte* (Berlin: De Gruyter, 1973).

34. Mehmed's father, Murad II, retired in 1444 but had to take over again in 1446 when Mehmed was not able to handle a major crisis. Murad died in 1451.

35. Klaus Kreiser, *Der osmanische Staat 1300–1922* (Munich: Oldenbourg, 2001), 24–27; Nicolas Vatin and Gilles Veinstein, *Le sérail ébranlé: Essai sur les morts, dépositions et avènements des sultans ottomans XIVᵉ–XIXᵉ siècle* (Paris: Fayard, 2003), 83–84, 150; Halil Inalcik, *The Ottoman Empire: The Classical Age, 1300–1600* (London: Weidenfeld & Nicolson, 1973), 59.

36. Nicolas Vatin and Gilles Veinstein, "Les obsèques des sultans ottomans de Mehmed II à Ahmed Ier," in *Les ottomans et la mort: Permanences et mutations,* ed. Gilles Veinstein (Leiden: E. J. Brill, 1996), 208–244.

37. Inalcik, *The Ottoman Empire,* 60; Leslie Peirce, *The Imperial Harem: Women and Sovereignty in the Ottoman Empire* (New York: Oxford University Press, 1993), 97–99; Cemal Kafadar, "Eyüp'te Kılıç Kuşanma Törenleri," in *Eyüp: Dün/ Bugün, 11–12 Aralık 1993,* ed. Tülay Artan (Istanbul: Tarih Vakfı Yurt Yayınları, 1994), 50–61; Nicolas Vatin, "Aux origines du pèlerinage à Eyüp des sultans ottomans," *Turcica* 27 (1995): 91–100.

38. Rhoads Murphey, *Ottoman Warfare, 1500–1700* (London: UCL Press, 1999), 116.

39. Fleischer, *Bureaucrat and Intellectual,* especially 214–226; Rifa'at A. Abou-El-Haj, *Formation of the Ottoman State: The Ottoman Empire Sixteenth to Eighteenth Centuries* (Syracuse, NY: Syracuse University Press, 2005), 20, 23.

40. Busbequius, *Legationis turcicae epistolae quatuor,* 102–103.

41. For an interpretation of this situation, see Baki Tezcan, *The Second Empire: The Political and Social Transformation in the Early Modern World* (Cambridge: Cambridge University Press, 2010).

42. Klaus Peter Matschke, "Research Problems Concerning the Transition to Tourkokratia: The Byzantinist Standpoint," in *The Ottomans and the Balkans: A Discussion of Historiography,* ed. Fikret Adanır and Suraiya Faroqhi (Leiden: E. J. Brill, 2002), 79–113; see 102–106; Şevket Pamuk, *A Monetary History of the Ottoman Empire* (Cambridge: Cambridge University Press, 2000), 74–76.

43. Lütfi Güçer, "XV.–XVII. Asırlarda Osmanlı İmparatorluğunda Tuz İnhisarı ve Tuzların İşletme Nizamı," *İstanbul Üniversitesi İktisat Fakültesi Mecmuası* 23, nos. 1–2 (1962–1963):

97–143; Suraiya Faroqhi, "Alum Production and Alum Trade in the Ottoman Empire (about 1560–1830)," *Wiener Zeitschrift für die Kunde des Morgenlandes* 71 (1979): 153–175.

44. Mehmet Genç, "Osmanlı Maliyesinde Malikâne Sistemi," in *Türkiye İktisat Tarihi Semineri: Metinler-Tartışmalar, 8–10 haziran 1973,* ed. Osman Okyar and Ünal Nalbantoğlu (Ankara: Mars Matbaası, 1975), 231–296.

45. Yüksel Duman, "Notables, Textiles and Copper in Ottoman Tokat 1750–1840" (PhD diss., University of Binghamton/SUNY, 1998).

46. Albert Hourani, "Ottoman Reform and the Politics of Notables," in *Beginnings of Modernization in the Middle East: The Nineteenth Century,* ed. William R. Polk and Richard L. Chambers (Chicago: Chicago University Press, 1968), 41–65; Salzmann, "An Ancien Régime Revisited"; Khoury, *State and Provincial Society,* 214.

47. Heath W. Lowry, *The Shaping of the Ottoman Balkans, 1350–1550: The Conquest, Settlement and Infrastructural Development of Northern Greece* (Istanbul: Bahçeşehir University Publications, 2008), 15–64.

48. Gülru Necipoğlu, *Architecture, Ceremonial, and Power: The Topkapı Palace in the Fifteenth and Sixteenth Centuries* (New York: Architectural History Foundation, 1991), 51, 212–213, 244.

49. Stéphane Yérasimos, *La Fondation de Constantinople et de Sainte-Sophie dans les traditions turques* (Istanbul: Institut Français d'Études Anatoliennes, 1990), 60, 92–96, 207–210; Caroline Campbell and Alan Chong, eds., *Bellini and the East* (New Haven, CT: Yale University Press, 2006); Barbara Flemming, "Sahib-kıran und Mahdi: Türkische Endzeiterwartungen im ersten Jahrzehnt der Regierung Süleymans," in *Between the Danube and the Caucasus: A Collection of Papers Concerning Oriental Sources on the History of the Peoples of Central and South-Eastern Europe,* ed. Györgi Kara (Budapest: Verlag der Akademie der Wissenschaften, 1987), 43–62; Gülru Necipoğlu, "Süleyman the Magnificent and the Representation of Power in the Context of Ottoman-Habsburg-Papal Rivalry," *Art Bulletin* 71, no. 3 (1989): 401–427; Jürgen Rapp, "Der Pergamentriss zu Süleymans Vierkronenhelm und weitere venezianische Goldschmiedeentwürfe für den türkischen Hof aus dem sogenannten Schmuckinventar Herzog Albrechts von Bayern," *Münchner Jahrbuch der bildenden Kunst* 3rd ser., 54 (2003): 105–149.

50. Rifa'at A. Abou-El-Haj, *The 1703 Rebellion and the Structure of Ottoman Politics* (Istanbul: Nederlands Historisch-Archeologisch Instituut, 1984), 86.

51. Tülay Artan, "Noble Women Who Changed the Face of the Bosphorus and the Palaces of the Sultanas," in *Istanbul: Biannual, 1992 Selections* (Istanbul: Tarih Vakfı, 1993), 87–97.

52. Seyyidî'Alî Re'îs, *Le miroir des pays: Une anabase ottomane à travers l'Inde et l'Asie centrale,* trans. and with commentary by Jean-Louis Bacqué-Grammont (Aix-en-Provence: Sindbad-Actes Sud, 1999), 115–117.

53. Abdülbaki Gölpınarlı, *Mevlânâ'dan sonra Mevlevîlik* (Istanbul: İnkilap Kitabevi, 1953), 128–150.

54. Ömer Lütfi Barkan and Ekrem Hakkı Ayverdi, eds., *İstanbul Vakıfları Tahrîr Defteri, 953 (1546) Tarîhli* (Istanbul: Istanbul Fetih Cemiyeti, 1970); Mehmet Canatar, ed., *İstanbul Vakıfları Tahrîr Defteri, 1009 (1600) Tarîhli* (Istanbul: Istanbul Fetih Cemiyeti, 2004).

55. Lowry, *Shaping of the Ottoman Balkans,* 157–167.

56. Ömer Lütfi Barkan, "Şehirlerin Teşekkül ve İnkişafı Tarihi Bakımından: Osmanlı İmparatorluğunda İmaret Sitelerinin Kuruluş ve İşleyiş Tarzına ait Araştırmalar," *İstanbul Üniversitesi İktisat Fakültesi Mecmuası* 23, nos. 1–2 (1962–1963): 239–296; Amy Singer, *Constructing Ottoman Beneficence: An Imperial Soup Kitchen in Jerusalem* (Albany: State University of New York Press, 2002), 63; Halil Inalcik, "The Hub of the City: The Bedestan of Istanbul," *International Journal of Turkish Studies* 1, no. 1 (1979–1980): 1–17.

57. Kâzım Çeçen, *İstanbul'da Osmanlı Devrindeki Su Tesisleri* (Istanbul: İstanbul Teknik Üniversitesi, 1984); John Michael Rogers, *Sinan* (London: I. B. Tauris, 2006); Necipoğlu, *Age of Sinan*, 151.

58. Neşet Çağatay, "Osmanlı İmparatorluğunda Para Vakıfları Rıba Faiz Konusu ve Bankacılık," *Vakıflar Dergisi* 9 (1971): 39–56; Jon Mandaville, "Usurious Piety: The Cash Waqf Controversy in the Ottoman Empire," *International Journal of Middle East Studies* 10, no. 3 (1979): 289–308.

59. See by way of comparison the anonymously published travel guide *Holy Monastery of Great Meteoron . . . Byzantine Painting Icons and Frescoes,* 2 vols. (Kalabaka: Holy Monastery of Great Meteoron, 2007); John Alexander (Alexandropoulos), "The Lord Giveth and the Lord Taketh Away: Athos and the Confiscation Affair of 1568–1569," *Athonika Symmeikta* 4 (1997): 149–200; Rossitsa Gradeva, "Ottoman Policy towards Christian Church Buildings," in Gradeva, *Rumeli under the Ottomans, 15th–18th Centuries*, 339–368; Minna Rozen, *A History of the Jewish Community in Istanbul: The Formative Years, 1453–1566* (Leiden: E. J. Brill, 2002), 11.

60. Necipoğlu, *Age of Sinan*, 58–59.

61. This section is based on an unpublished manuscript by Başak Tuğ, "Politics of Honor: The Institutional and Social Frontiers of 'Illicit' Sex in Mid-Eighteenth-Century Ottoman Anatolia" (PhD diss., New York University, 2009). My thanks are due to the author for her friendly assistance.

62. One of the earliest surviving registers is Halil İnalcık, *Hicri 835 tarihli Sûret-i defter-i sancak-i Arvanid* (Ankara: Türk Tarih Kurumu, 1954) (the date Hicri 835 corresponds to 1431–1432; this volume covers part of Albania). For a discussion of the problems involved in interpreting the information in this register, see Ömer Lütfi Barkan, "Research on the Ottoman Fiscal Surveys," in *Studies in the Economic History of the Middle East from the Rise of Islam to the Present Day,* ed. Michael A. Cook (Oxford: Oxford University Press, 1970), 163–171; Leila Erder, "The Measurement of Preindustrial Population Changes: The Ottoman Empire from the 15th to the 17th Century," *Middle Eastern Studies* 11, no. 3 (1975): 284–301; Heath Lowry, "The Ottoman *Tahrir Defterleri* as a Source for Social and Economic History: Pitfalls and Limitations," in *Studies in Defterology: Ottoman Society in the Fifteenth and Sixteenth Centuries,* ed. Heath Lowry (Istanbul: Isis Press 1992), 3–18.

63. For example, see *438 Numaralı Muhasebe-i vilayet-i Anadolu (937/1530),* 2 vols. (Ankara: Başbakanlık Arşivleri Genel Müdürlüğü, 1993); Ömer Lütfi Barkan, "Tarihi Demografi Araştırmaları ve Osmanlı Tarihi," *Türkiyat Mecmuası* 10 (1951): 1–26; Cem Behar, *Osmanlı İmparatorluğu'nun ve Türkiye'nin Nüfusu 1500–1927 / The Population of the Ottoman Empire and Turkey (with a Summary in English)* (Ankara: Başbakanlık Devlet İstatistik Enstitüsü, 1996), 4.

64. Bruce McGowan, *Economic Life in Ottoman Europe: Taxation, Trade, and the Struggle for Land, 1600–1800* (Cambridge: Cambridge University Press, 1981), 114.

65. Barkan, "Ottoman Fiscal Surveys," 170.

66. Ibn Battuta, *Voyages d'Ibn Battuta,* ed. and trans. Charles Defrémery and Beniamino Raffa-
    ello Sanguinetti (Paris: Anthropos, 1968; reprint of the 1854 edition), 2:324; Peirce, *Imperial
    Harem,* 40–41.

67. Abdülbaki Gölpınarlı, *Mevlânâ' dan sonra Mevlevîlik* (reprint; Istanbul: İnkilap Kitabevi, 1983),
    132–133.

68. Bartholomé Bennassar and Lucile Bennassar, *Les chrétiens d'Allah: L'histoire extraordinaire
    des renégats, XVe–XVIIe siècles* (Paris: Perrin, 2006); Raoul Motika, Bezüglich des Buches von
    Lucile, and Bartholomé Bennassar, "Les chrétiens d'Allah: L'histoire extraordinaire des renégats,"
    Turcica 25 (1993): 189–204.

69. Metin Kunt, "Ethnic-Regional (*Cins*) Solidarity in the Seventeenth-Century Ottoman Estab-
    lishment," *International Journal of Middle East Studies* 5 (1974): 233–239.

70. Maria Pia Pedani Fabris, "Safiye's Household and Venetian Diplomacy," *Turcica* 32 (2000): 9–32.

71. One exception is Leslie Peirce, *Morality Tales: Law and Gender in the Ottoman Court of Aintab*
    (Berkeley: University of California Press, 2003).

72. Abraham Marcus, *The Middle East on the Eve of Modernity: Aleppo in the Eighteenth Century*
    (New York: Columbia University Press, 1989), 230–231; Margaret L. Meriwether, *The Kin Who
    Count: Family and Society in Ottoman Aleppo, 1770–1840* (Austin: University of Texas Press,
    1999).

73. Haim Gerber, "Social and Economic Position of Women in an Ottoman City: Bursa, 1600–
    1700," *International Journal of Middle East Studies* 12 (1980): 231–244.

74. Halil Inalcik, "The Policy of Mehmed II toward the Greek Population of Istanbul and the By-
    zantine Buildings of the City," *Dumbarton Oaks Papers* 23 (1970): 213–249.

75. Murat Çizakça, "Ottomans and the Mediterranean: An Analysis of the Ottoman Shipbuilding
    Industry as Reflected in the Arsenal Registers of Istanbul 1529–1650," in *Le gente del mare Med-
    iterraneo,* ed. Rosalba Ragosta (Naples: Pironti, 1981), 2:773–787; Eric Dursteler, *Venetians in
    Constantinople: Nation, Identity, and Coexistence in the Early Modern Mediterranean* (Balti-
    more: Johns Hopkins University Press, 2006), 81.

76. Vera Costantini, "Destini di guerra: L'inventario ottomano dei prigionieri di Nicosia (settembre
    1570)," *Studi Veneziani* n.s. 45 (2003): 229–241; Şenol Çelik, "Türk Fethi sonrasında Kıbrıs
    Adasına Yönelik İskân Çalışmaları," in *Kaf Dağının Ötesine Varmak: Festschrift in Honor of
    Günay Kut. Essays Presented by Her Colleagues and Students,* ed. Zehra Toska (Cambridge, MA:
    Department of Near Eastern Languages and Literatures, Harvard University, 2003), 1:263–304.

77. McGowan, *Economic Life in Ottoman Europe,* 51–55.

78. Ömer Lütfi Barkan, "XVI. Asrın Başında Rumeli'de Nüfusun Yayılış Tarzını Gösterir Harita,"
    İstanbul Üniversitesi İktisat Fakültesi Mecmuası 111 (1949–1950): pasted-in insert, with no
    pagination.

79. Hütteroth, "Ecology of the Ottoman Lands," 32–35; Cengiz Orhonlu, *Osmanlı İmparatorluğunda
    Aşiretleri İskân Teşebbüsü (1691–1696)* (Istanbul: İstanbul Üniversitesi Edebiyat Fakültesi, 1963).

80. Antoine Abdel Nour, *Introduction à l'histoire urbaine de la Syrie ottomane (XVIᵉ–XVIIIᵉ siècle)*
    (Beirut: Université Libanaise, 1982), 61.

81. Christopher A. Bayly, *Rulers, Townsmen, and Bazaars: North Indian Society in the Age of British
    Expansion, 1770–1870* (Cambridge: Cambridge University Press, 1983), 63; Mübahat Kütükoğlu,

ed., *Osmanlılarda Narh Müessesesi ve 1640 Tarihli Narh Defteri* (Istanbul: Enderun Kitabevi, 1983); Abou-l-Hasan Ali ben Mohammed Et-Tamgrouti [Al-Tamghrûtî], *En-nafhat el-miskiya fi-s-sifarat et-Tourkiya: Relation d'une ambassade marocaine en Turquie 1589–1591*, trans. and with a commentary by Henry de Castries (Paris: Paul Geuthner, 1929), 47–61.

82. Mehmet Genç, "Ottoman Industry in the Eighteenth Century: General Framework, Characteristics, and Main Trends," in *Manufacturing in the Ottoman Empire and Turkey, 1500–1950,* ed. Donald Quataert (Albany: State University of New York Press, 1994), 60; Zeki Arıkan, "Osmanlı İmparatorluğunda İhracı Yasak Mallar (Memnu Meta)," in *Professor Dr. Bekir Kütükoğlu'na Armağan* (Istanbul: İstanbul Üniversitesi Edebiyat Fakültesi, 1991), 279–307.

83. Ömer Lütfi Barkan, "Bazı Büyük Şehirlerde Eşya ve Yiyecek Fiyatlarının Tesbit ve Teftişi Hususlarını Tanzim Eden Kanunlar," *Tarih Vesikaları* 1, no. 5 (1942): 326–340; 2, no. 7 (1942): 15–40; 2, no. 9 (1942): 168–177.

84. Halil Inalcik, "Capital Formation in the Ottoman Empire," *Journal of Economic History* 29, no. 1 (1969): 97–140.

85. Catherine Wendy Bracewell, *The Uskoks of Senj: Piracy, Banditry, and Holy War in the Sixteenth-Century Adriatic* (Ithaca, NY: Cornell University Press, 1992), 281–303.

86. Oded Peri, *Christianity under Islam in Jerusalem: The Question of the Holy Sites in Early Ottoman Times* (Leiden: E. J. Brill, 2001); Bruce Masters, *Christians and Jews in the Arab World: The Roots of Sectarianism* (Cambridge: Cambridge University Press, 2001).

87. [Papa Synadinos of Serres], *Conseils et mémoires de Synadinos prêtre de Serrès en Macédoine (XVIIᵉ siècle),* ed., trans., and with a commentary by Paolo Odorico (Paris: Association "Pierre Belon," 1996), 40; Rozen, *History of the Jewish Community in Istanbul,* 82–90.

88. Gershom Sholem, *Sabbatai Sevi: The Mystical Messiah*, trans. Raphael Jehuda Zwi Werblowsky (Princeton, NJ: Princeton University Press, 1973); Cornell H. Fleischer, "The Lawgiver as Messiah: The Making of the Imperial Image in the Reign of Süleymân," in *Soliman le magnifique et son temps: Actes du colloque de Paris, Galeries Nationales du Grand Palais, 7–10 mars 1990,* ed. Gilles Veinstein (Paris: La Documentation Française, 1992), 159–178.

89. Morris Goodblatt, *Jewish Life in Turkey in the Sixteenth Century as Reflected in the Legal Writings of Samuel de Medina* (New York: Jewish Theological Seminary of America, 1952), 161–162; Rozen, *History of the Jewish Community in Istanbul,* document 7, 326–328.

90. Minna Rozen, "Public Space and Private Space among the Jews of Istanbul in the Sixteenth-Seventeenth Centuries," *Turcica* 30 (1998): 331–346, 340.

91. Mantran, *Istanbul,* 360–367; Raymond, *Artisans et commerçants,* 2:541; on the peculiar case of Sarajevo, see Ines Aščerić Todd, "Dervishes and Islam in Bosnia" (PhD diss., Oxford University, n.d.); Suraiya Faroqhi, *Artisans of Empire: Crafts and Craftspeople under the Ottomans* (London: I. B. Tauris, 2009), 27–34.

92. Halil Inalcik, "The Appointment Procedure of a Guild Warden (Kethudâ)," *Wiener Zeitschrift für die Kunde des Morgenlandes* 76 (1986): 135–142.

93. Amnon Cohen, *The Guilds of Ottoman Jerusalem* (Leiden: E. J. Brill, 2000).

94. Ibid.; Halil Sahillioğlu, "Slaves in the Social and Economic Life of Bursa in the Late 15th and Early 16th Centuries," *Turcica* 27 (1985): 43–112.

95. Murat Çizakça, "Price History and the Bursa Silk Industry: A Study in Ottoman Industrial Decline, 1550–1650," in *The Ottoman Empire and the World Economy,* ed. Huri Islamoğlu-Inan (Cambridge: Cambridge University Press, 1987), 247–261; Haim Gerber, *Economy and Society in an Ottoman City: Bursa, 1600–1700* (Jerusalem: Hebrew University, 1988), 63–68, 81–88.

96. Mehmet Genç, "A Study of the Feasibility of Using Eighteenth-Century Ottoman Financial Records as an Indicator of Economic Activity," in Islamoğlu-Inan, *The Ottoman Empire and the World Economy,* 345–373, 358; Özer Ergenç, "1600–1615 Yılları Arasında Ankara İktisadi Tarihine Ait Araştırmalar"; Gerber, *Economy and Society,* 82–83; Abdel Nour, *Introduction,* 296.

97. Halil İnalcık, *The Ottoman Empire: The Classical Age, 1300–1600* (reprint; London: Phoenix, 1995), 110; Suraiya Faroqhi, "Land Transfer, Land Disputes and *Askeri* Holdings in Ankara (1592–1600)," in *Mémorial Ömer Lütfi Barkan,* ed. Robert Mantran (Paris: Maisonneuve, 1980), 87–99, 97.

98. McGowan, *Economic Life in Ottoman Europe,* 67–79.

99. The work of Nicholas Michel, which is still in preparation, will provide a definitive treatment of this topic; for the time being, see Nicholas Michel, "Les 'services communaux' dans les campagnes égyptiennes au début de l'époque ottomane," in *Sociétés rurales ottomanes/Ottoman Rural Societies,* ed. Muhammed Afifi, Rachida Chih, Brigitte Marino, Nicolas Michel, and Işık Tamdoğan (Cairo: Institut Français d'Archéologie Orientale, 2005), 19–46; Hanna, *Making Big Money in 1600,* 83–84.

100. Salih Özbaran, *The Ottoman Response to European Expansion: Studies on Ottoman-Portuguese Relations in the Indian Ocean and Ottoman Administration in the Arab Lands during the Sixteenth Century* (Istanbul: Isis Press, 1994); Andrew Hess, *The Forgotten Frontier: A History of the Sixteenth-Century Ibero-African Frontier* (Chicago: University of Chicago Press, 1978); Soumaya Louhichi, *Das Verhältnis zwischen der osmanischen Zentralgewalt und der Provinz Tunesien: Versuch einer zusammenhängenden Deutung der osmanischen Herrschaft in Tunesien während des 16. und 17. Jahrhunderts* (Saarbrücken: VDM Verlag Dr. Müller, 2008); Barbara von Palombini, *Bündniswerben abendländischer Mächte um Persien 1453–1600* (Wiesbaden: Franz Steiner, 1998).

101. Ildikó Béller-Hann, "Ottoman Perception of China," in *Comité International d'Études Préottomanes et Ottomanes: VIth Symposium, Cambridge, 1st–4th July 1984,* ed. Jean-Louis Bacqué-Grammont and Emeri van Donzel (Istanbul: IFEA, 1987), 55–64. On East Asia, see Giancarlo Casale, "His Majesty's Servant Lutfi," *Turcica* 37 (2005): 43–81, which details the career of a previously unknown sixteenth-century Ottoman envoy to Sumatra based on an account of his travels from the Topkapı Palace archives. Casale, *The Ottoman Age of Exploration* (Oxford: Oxford University Press, 2010).

102. Carl F. Petry, "The Military Institution and Innovation in the Late Mamluk Period," in *The Cambridge History of Egypt,* vol. 1, *Islamic Egypt, 614–1517,* ed. Carl F. Petry (Cambridge: Cambridge University Press, 1998), 462–489; Palmira Brummett, "Competition and Coincidence: Venetian Trading Interests and Ottoman Expansion in the Early Sixteenth Century Levant," *New Perspectives on Turkey* 5–6 (1991): 29–52; Palmira Brummett, *Ottoman Seapower and Levantine Diplomacy in the Age of Discovery* (Albany: State University of New York Press, 1994), 143–145.

103. The term "gunpowder empires" for the realms of Ottoman, Safavid, and Mughal rulers was coined in Marshall G. S. Hodgson, *The Venture of Islam: Conscience and History in a World Civilization* (Chicago: University of Chicago Press, 1974), vol. 3; Petry, "The Military Institution," 479–480.

104. Yakub Mughul, "Portekizlerle Kızıldeniz'de Mücadele ve Hicaz'da Osmanlı Hâkimiyetinin Yerleşmesi hakkında bir Vesika," *Belgeler* 2, nos. 3–4 (1965): 37–48; Refet Yinanç, *Dulkadir Beyliği* (Ankara: Türk Tarih Kurumu, 1989); Shai Har-El, *Struggle for Domination in the Middle East: The Ottoman-Mamluk War, 1485–1491* (Leiden: E. J. Brill 1995), 73, 138.

105. Abdul-Rahim Abu-Husayn, *Provincial Leaderships in Syria, 1575–1650* (Beirut: American University of Beirut, 1985); Jane Hathaway, *The Arab Lands under Ottoman Rule, 1516–1800* (Harlow, UK: Longman Pearson, 2008), 81–99; Salih Özbaran, "The Ottomans in Confrontation with the Portuguese in the Red Sea after the Conquest of Egypt in 1517," in Özbaran, *Ottoman Response to European Expansion,* 89–98; Seyyidî'Alî Re'îs, *Le miroir des pays.*

106. Casale, "His Majesty's Servant Lutfi."

107. İsmail Hakkı Uzunçarşılı, *Mekke-i Mükerreme Emirleri* (Ankara: Türk Tarih Kurumu, 1972), 19–21.

108. Suraiya Faroqhi, *Pilgrims and Sultans* (London: I. B. Tauris, 1994), 67, 75, 81; Stanford J. Shaw, *The Financial and Administrative Development of Ottoman Egypt, 1517–1798* (Princeton, NJ: Princeton University Press, 1962), 5.

109. Abdul Karem Rafeq, *The Province of Damascus, 1723–1783* (Beirut: Khayats, 1966), 213–215; Karl Barbir, *Ottoman Rule in Damascus, 1708–1758* (Princeton, NJ: Princeton University Press, 1980), 178; Faroqhi, *Pilgrims and Sultans,* 110–112.

110. Ahmet Yaşar Ocak, *Bektaşî Menâkıbnâmelerinde İslam Öncesi İnanç Motifleri* (Istanbul: Enderun Kitabevi, 1983), 27–33; Gülru Necipoğlu-Kafadar, "The Süleymaniye Complex in Istanbul: An Interpretation," *Muqarnas* 3 (1986): 92–117.

111. Sohrweide, "Der Sieg der Safaviden," 146–156; Colin Imber, "The Persecution of the Ottoman Shiites according to the Mühimme Defterleri, 1565–1585," *Der Islam* 56 (1979): 245–273.

112. Hodgson, *The Venture of Islam,* 1:222; Ertuğrul Düzdağ, *Şeyhülislam Ebusuud Efendi Fetvaları Işığında 16: Asır Türk Hayatı* (Istanbul: Enderun, 1972), 109; Irène Mélikoff, "Le problème kızılbaş," *Turcica* 6 (1975): 49–67; Abdülbaki Gölpınarlı, ed., *Alevi-Bektaşi Nefesleri* (Istanbul: Remzi, 1963), 94–103.

113. [Ca'fer Efendi], *Risāle-i mi'māriyye: An Early Seventeenth-Century Ottoman Treatise on Architecture,* ed. Howard Crane (Leiden: E. J. Brill, 1987), 67. Sunni Islam recognizes four schools of law, which diverge from one another in particular details but which are all regarded as orthodox. Ottoman sultans were adherents of the Hanafi school, which is also preeminent in modern Turkey. For a more detailed discussion of the Ottoman–Safavid clash, see the following section on Iran.

114. İsmet Parmaksızoğlu, "Kuzey Irak'ta Osmanlı Hâkimiyetinin Kuruluşu ve Memun Beyin Hatıraları," *Belleten* 37, no. 146 (1973): 191–230; Rhoads Murphey, ed., *Kanûn-nâme-i Sultânî li'Azîz Efendi/Aziz Efendi's Book of Sultanic Laws and Regulations: An Agenda for Reform by a Seventeenth-Century Ottoman Statesman* (Cambridge, MA: Harvard University Press, 1985), 12–17.

115. On the establishment of Ottoman rule in North Africa, see Louhichi, *Das Verhältnis;* Mohamed Hédi Chérif, *Pouvoir et société dans la Tunisie de H'usayn BinʿAlī (1705–1740)* (Tunis: Université de Tunis, 1984), 1:74–75; Daniel Panzac, *Barbary Corsairs: The End of a Legend,* trans. Victoria Hobson and John E. Hawkes (Leiden: E. J. Brill, 2005), 20.

116. Bennassar and Bennassar, *Les chrétiens d'Allah,* 312–315, 376–389, 446–473.

117. Lucette Valensi, "Islam et capitalisme: Production et commerce des chéchias en Tunisie et en France aux XVIIIe et XIXe siècles," *Revue d'histoire moderne et contemporaine* 16 (1969): 376–400.

118. Boubaker Sadok, *La Régence de Tunis au XVIIe siècle: Ses relations commerciales avec les ports de l'Europe méditerranéenne, Marseille et Livourne* (Zaghouan: CEROMDI, 1987), 116–117; Chérif, *Pouvoir et société,* 1:194–195.

119. Yücel Öztürk, *Osmanlı Hakimiyetinde Kefe 1474–1600* (Ankara: T. C. Kültür Bakanlığı, 2000); Carl Max Kortepeter, *Ottoman Imperialism during the Reformation: Europe and the Caucasus* (London: University of London Press, 1972).

120. Evliya Çelebi b. Derviş Mehemmed Zıllı, *Evliya Çelebi Seyahatnâmesi: Topkapı Sarayı Revan 1457 Numaralı Yazmasının Transkripsyonu—Dizini,* vol. 6, ed. Yücel Dağlı and Seyit Ali Kahraman (Istanbul: Yapı Kredi Yayınları, 2002), 223.

121. Halil İnalcık, "Osmanlı-Rus Rekabetinin Menşei ve Don-Volga-Kanalı Teşebbüsü, 1569," *Belleten* 12 (1948): 349–402; Akdes Nimet Kurat, *Türkler ve İdil boyu (1569 Astarhan seferi, Ten-İdil kanalı ve XVI.–XVII. yüzyıl Osmanlı-Rus münasebetleri)* (Ankara: Ankara Üniversitesi Dil ve Tarih-Coğrafya Fakültesi, 1966).

122. Dariusz Kołodziejczyk, *Ottoman–Polish Diplomatic Relations (15th–18th Century): An Annotated Edition of ʿAhdnames and Other Documents* (Leiden: E. J. Brill, 2000), 129–130.

123. Faroqhi, *Towns and Townsmen,* 90; Peirce, *The Imperial Harem,* 58–59.

124. Dimitris Kastritsis, *The Sons of Bayezid: Empire Building and Representation in the Ottoman Civil War of 1402–1413* (Leiden: E. J. Brill, 2007); Franz Babinger, "Beiträge zur Geschichte der Malqoč-Oghlus," in *Aufsätze und Abhandlungen zur Geschichte Südosteuropas und der Levante,* ed. Franz Babinger (Munich: Südosteuropa Verlagsgesellschaft, 1962), 1:355–169; Lowry, *Shaping of the Ottoman Balkans,* 15–64.

125. On the border question, see Andrew C. S. Peacock, ed., *The Frontiers of the Ottoman World* (Oxford: Oxford University Press, 2009); Markus Koller, *Eine Gesellschaft im Wandel: Die osmanische Herrschaft in Ungarn im 17. Jahrhundert (1606–1683)* (Stuttgart: Steiner, 2010).

126. Kafadar, *Between Two Worlds,* 62–71. The extensive Ottoman archives of the Monastery of St. John on Patmos are currently being reorganized. See also Anthony Bryer and Heath Lowry, eds., *Continuity and Change in Late Byzantine and Early Ottoman Society* (Birmingham: University of Birmingham Press, 1980); Bernard Geyer and Jacques Lefort, eds., *La Bithynie au Moyen Âge* (Paris: Lethielleux, 2003).

127. Elisabeth Zachariadou, "The Worrisome Wealth of Čelnik Radić," in Heywood and Imber, *Studies in Ottoman History,* 383–397; Machiel Kiel, "Mevlana Neşrī and the Towns of Medieval Bulgaria. Historical and Topographical Notes," in Heywood and Imber, *Studies in Ottoman History,* 165–188.

128. John Haldon, *The Palgrave Atlas of Byzantine History* (Basingstoke, UK: Palgrave Macmillan, 2005); Melek Delilbaşı, "Selânik'in Venedik İdaresine Geçmesi ve Osmanlı-Venedik Savaşı," *Belleten* 40, no. 160 (1976): 575–588; [Johannes Anagnostis], "Johannis Anagnostis: Diigisis peri tis telefteas aloseos tis Thessalonikis," translated into Turkish by Melek Delilbaşı, *Tarih Araştırmaları Dergisi* 8–12, nos. 14–23 (1970–1974): 23–50.

129. Steven Runciman, *The Fall of Constantinople* (Cambridge: Cambridge University Press, 1965), 80–85; Halil Inalcik, "Ottoman Galata, 1453–1553," in *Première Rencontre Internationale sur l'Empire Ottoman et la Turquie Moderne: Institut National des Langues et Civilisations Orientales, Maison des Sciences de l'Homme, 18–22 janvier 1985,* ed. Edhem Eldem (Istanbul: Éditions Isis, 1991), 17–116, 22.

130. Theoharis Stavrides, *The Sultan of Vezirs: The Life and Times of the Ottoman Grand Vezir Mahmud Pasha Angelović (1453–1474)* (Leiden: E. J. Brill, 2001), 75–100.

131. Gustav Bayerle, "The Compromise at Zsitvatorok," *Archivum Ottomanicum* 6 (1980): 5–53, 28; Karl Nehring, *Adam Freiherrn von Herbersteins Gesandtschaftsreise nach Konstantinopel: Ein Beitrag zum Frieden von Zsitvatorok (1606)* (Munich: Oldenbourg, 1983), 61; Jan Paul Niederkorn, *Die europäischen Mächte und der "Lange Türkenkrieg" Kaiser Rudolfs II. (1593–1606)* (Vienna: Verlag der Österreichischen Akademie der Wissenschaften, 1993), 200.

132. Gaston Zeller, "Une légende qui a la vie dure: Les capitulations de 1535," *Revue d'Histoire Moderne et Contemporaine* 2 (1955): 127–132; Gilles Veinstein, "Les capitulations franco-ottomanes de 1536 sont-elles encore controversables?," in *Living in the Ottoman Ecumenical Community: Essays in Honor of Suraiya Faroqhi,* ed. Vera Costantini and Markus Koller (Leiden: E. J. Brill, 2008), 71–88.

133. Géraud Poumarède, "Justifier l'injustifiable' L'alliance turque au miroir de la chrétienté (XVIe–XVIIe siècles)," *Revue d'histoire diplomatique* 111, no. 3 (1997): 217–246; Géraud Poumarède, "Négocier près de la Sublime Porte: Jalons pour une nouvelle histoire des capitulations franco-ottomanes," in *L'invention de la diplomatie: Moyen Âge—Temps modernes,* ed. Lucien Bély (Paris: Presses Universitaires de France, 1998), 71–85; Géraud Poumarède, *Pour en finir avec la croisade: Mythes et réalités de la lutte contre les Turcs aux XVIe et XVIIe siècles* (Paris: Presses Universitaires de France, 2004).

134. Jean-Louis Dusson, Marquis de Bonnac, *Mémoire historique sur l'Ambassade de France à Constantinople,* ed. Charles Schefer (Paris: Ernest Leroux, 1894), 27, 51; Heinz Duchhardt, *Balance of Power und Pentarchie, 1700–1785* (Paderborn: Ferdinand Schöningh, 1997), 127.

135. Georges I. Bratianu, *La mer Noire: Des origines à la conquête ottomane* (Munich: Societas Academica Dacoromana, 1969), 307–328; Kate Fleet, *European and Islamic Trade in the Early Ottoman State* (Cambridge: Cambridge University Press, 1999), 37, 136–137; Philip Argenti, *The Occupation of Chios by the Genoese, 1346–1566,* 3 vols. (Cambridge: Cambridge University Press, 1958).

136. Nicolaas H. Biegman, "Ragusan Spying for the Ottoman Empire," *Belleten* 27, no. 106 (1963): 237–255; Nicolaas H. Biegman, *The Turco-Ragusan Relationship, according to the Firmans of Murad III (1575–1595) Extant in the State Archives of Dubrovnik* (The Hague: Mouton, 1967).

137. Francis W. Carter, *Dubrovnik (Ragusa): A Classic City-State* (London: Seminar Press, 1972), 325–404.

138. Elizabeth Zachariadou, *Trade and Crusade* (Venice: Institute for Byzantine and Post-Byzantine Studies, 1984), 5–20; Ersin Gülsoy, *Girit'in Fethi ve Osmanlı İdaresinin Kurulması* (Istanbul: Tarih ve Tabiat Vakfı, 2004).

139. Elias Kolovos, "A Town for the Besiegers: Social Life and Marriage in Ottoman Candia outside Candia," in *The Eastern Mediterranean under Ottoman Rule: Crete, 1645–1840,* ed. Antonis Anastasopoulos (Rethymnon: University of Crete Press, 2008), 103–175; Fariba Zarinebaf, *A Historical and Economic Geography of Ottoman Greece: The Southwestern Morea in the 18th Century* (Athens: American School of Classical Studies at Athens, 2005).

140. Palmira Brummett, "Competition and Coincidence: Venetian Trading Interests and Ottoman Expansion in the Early Sixteenth Century Levant," *New Perspectives on Turkey* 5–6 (1991): 29–52; Julian Raby, *Venice, Dürer and the Oriental Mode* (London: Islamic Art Publications, 1982); Fernand Braudel, *La Méditerranée et le monde méditerranéen à l'époque de Philippe II,* 2nd ed. (Paris: Librairie Armand Colin, 1966), 1:495–516.

141. Raymond, *Artisans et commerçants,* 1:69–72; Domenico Sella, "The Rise and Fall of the Venetian Woollen Industry," in *Crisis and Change in the Venetian Economy in the Sixteenth and Seventeenth Centuries,* ed. Brian Pullan (London: Methuen, 1968), 106–126.

142. Şerafettin Turan, "Venedik'te Türk Ticaret Merkezi," *Belleten* 32, no. 126 (1968): 247–283; Ennio Concina, *Fondaci: Architettura, arte e mercatura tra Levante, Venezia e Alemagna* (Venice: Marsilio Editori, 1997), 219–246; Maria Pia Pedani Fabris, "Between Diplomacy and Trade: Ottoman Merchants in Venice," in *Merchants in the Ottoman Empire,* ed. Suraiya Faroqhi and Gilles Veinstein (Leuven: Peeters, 2008), 3–22, 6.

143. Frederic C. Lane, *Venice: A Maritime Republic* (Baltimore: Johns Hopkins University Press, 1973), 246; Braudel, *La Méditerranée,* 2:324–325; Niccoló Capponi, *Victory of the West: The Story of the Battle of Lepanto* (London: Macmillan, 2006).

144. Daniel Panzac, *La marine ottomane, de l'apogée à la chute de l'empire (1572–1923)* (Paris: CNRS Éditions, 2009); Iain Fenlon, *The Ceremonial City* (New Haven, CT: Yale University Press, 2007); Braudel, *La Méditerranée,* 2:467–469. Still a seminal text on this subject is Hess, *The Forgotten Frontier.*

145. Jean Delumeau, *Le mystère Campanella* (Paris: Fayard, 2008), 82–101.

146. Gerald MacLean, *Looking East* (Basingstoke, UK: Macmillan, 2007), 46–47, 52, 65; Susan Skilliter, *William Harborne and the Trade with Turkey, 1578–1582* (London: British Academy, 1977), 232–239; Halil Inalcik, "Imtiyāzāt. ii.–The Ottoman Empire," in *Encyclopaedia of Islam,* 2nd ed. (Leiden: E. J. Brill, 1971), 3:1179–1189, 1184; Geoffrey Parker, *Spain and the Netherlands, 1559–1659: Ten Studies,* 2nd ed. (London: Fontana Press, 1990).

147. Daniel Goffman, *Britons in the Ottoman Empire, 1642–1660* (Seattle: University of Washington Press, 1998), 69; Nabil Matar, *Turks, Moors, and Englishmen in the Age of Discovery* (New York: Colombia University Press, 1999); Gerald MacLean, *The Rise of Oriental Travel: English Visitors to the Ottoman Empire, 1580–1720* (Basingstoke, UK: Palgrave-Macmillan, 2004); MacLean, *Looking East,* 20–23.

148. Ralph Davis, *Aleppo and Devonshire Square: English Traders in the Levant in the Eighteenth Century* (London: Macmillan, 1967); Paul Masson, *Histoire du commerce français dans le Levant au XVIIIe siècle* (Paris: Librairie Hachette, 1911), 139–184.

149. Niels Steensgaard, "Consuls and Nations in the Levant from 1570 to 1650," *Scandinavian Economic History Review* 1, no. 2 (1967): 13–54; Marie-Carmen Smyrnelis, *Une société hors de soi: Identités et relations sociales à Smyrne aux XVIIIème et XIXème siècles* (Paris: Peeters, 2005); Oliver Jens Schmitt, *Levantiner: Lebenswelten und Identitäten einer ethnokonfessionellen Gruppe im osmanischen Reich im "langen 19. Jahrhundert"* (Munich: Oldenbourg, 2005).

150. Masson, *Histoire*, 1–32; Claude Marquié, *L'industrie textile carcassonnaise au XVIIIe siècle: Étude d'un groupe social: Les marchands-fabricants* (Carcassonne: Société d'Études Scientifiques de l'Aude, 1993).

151. Alexander H. de Groot, *The Ottoman Empire and the Dutch Republic: A History of the Earliest Diplomatic Relations, 1610–1630* (Leiden: Nederlands Historisch-Archaeologisch Instituut, 1978), 88–105; Parker, *Spain and the Netherlands*, 28–34.

152. A key work on this subject is İsmail Hakkı Kadı, *Ottoman and Dutch Merchants in the Eighteenth Century* (Leiden: Brill, 2012); see also Jonathan Israel, *Dutch Primacy in World Trade, 1585–1740* (Oxford: Clarendon Press, 1989), 262–263.

153. These observations refute the argument put forward by Niels Steensgaard, *The Asian Trade Revolution of the Seventeenth Century: The East India Companies and the Decline of the Caravan Trade* (Chicago: University of Chicago Press, 1973). One exponent of the "comprador" thesis is Ali İhsan Bağış, *Osmanlı Ticaretinde Gayri Müslimler, Kapitülasyonlar, Beratlı Tüccarlar ve Hayriye Tüccarları (1750–1839)* (Ankara: Turhan Kitabevi, 1983). For an excellent all-round discussion of this topic, see Ismail Hakkı Kadı, "Natives and Interlopers: Competition between Ottoman and Dutch Merchants in the 18th Century" (PhD diss., Leiden, 2008); this work forms the starting point for the outline given here.

154. Vassiliki Seirinidou, "Grocers and Wholesalers, Ottomans and Habsburgs, Foreigners and 'Our Own': The Greek Trade Diasporas in Central Europe, Seventeenth to Nineteenth Centuries," in Faroqhi and Veinstein, *Merchants in the Ottoman Empire*, 81–95; Katerina Papakostantinou, "The Pondikas Merchant Family from Thessaloniki, ca. 1750–1800," in Faroqhi and Veinstein, *Merchants in the Ottoman Empire*, 133–149; and Olga Katsiardi Hering, "The Allure of Red Cotton Yarn, and How It Came to Vienna: Associations of Greek Artisans and Merchants Operating between the Ottoman and Habsburg Empires," in Faroqhi and Veinstein, *Merchants in the Ottoman Empire*, 97–131; Traian Stoianovich, "The Conquering Balkan Orthodox Merchant," *Journal of Economic History* 20 (1960): 234–313.

155. Fernand Braudel, *Civilisation matérielle, économie et capitalisme* (Paris: Armand Colin, 1979), 2:133; Zdzisław Zygulski, "The Impact of the Orient on the Culture of Old Poland," in *Land of the Winged Horseman: Art in Poland, 1572–1764,* ed. Jan Ostrowski et al. (Alexandria, VA: Art Service International, 1999), 69–80.

156. Caroline Finkel, *The Administration of Warfare: The Ottoman Military Campaigns in Hungary, 1593–1606* (Vienna: VWGÖ, 1988), 1:15.

157. [Evliya Çelebi], *Im Reiche des Goldenen Apfels: Des türkischen Weltenbummlers Evliya Çelebi denkwürdige Reise in das Giaurenland und in die Stadt und Festung Wien anno 1665,* 2nd ed., trans. Richard F. Kreutel, Erich Prokosch, and Karl Teply (Vienna: Verlag Styria, 1987).

158. Caroline Finkel, *Osman's Dream: The Story of the Ottoman Empire, 1300–1923* (London: John Murray, 2005), 283–287; John Stoye, *The Siege of Vienna: The Last Great Trial between Cross*

and Crescent (New York: Pegasus Books, 2006), 43–45; Thomas Barker, *Double Eagle and Crescent: Vienna's Second Turkish Siege and Its Historical Setting* (Albany: State University of New York Press, 1967), 157–160.

159. Abou-El-Haj, *The 1703 Rebellion*, 60–63; Ferenc Szakály, *Hungaria eliberata: Die Rückeroberung von Buda im Jahr 1686 und Ungarns Befreiung von der Osmanenherrschaft (1683–1718)* (Budapest: Corvina, 1986).

160. Kołodziejczyk, *Ottoman–Polish Diplomatic Relations*, 99–100, 118–119; Kemal Beydilli, *Die polnischen Königswahlen und Interregnen von 1572 und 1576 im Lichte osmanischer Archivalien: Ein Beitrag zur Geschichte der osmanischen Machtpolitik* (Munich: Dr. Rudolf Trofenik, 1974), 16–17; Mehmet İnbaşı, *Ukrayna'da Osmanlılar: Kamaniçe Seferi ve Organizasyon (1672)* (Istanbul: Yeditepe, 2003); Halime Doğru, *Lehistan'da bir Osmanlı Sultanı: IV. Mehmed'in Kamaniçe-Hotin Seferleri ve bir Masraf Defteri* (Istanbul: Kitap Yayınevi, 2005); Dariusz Kołodziejczyk, *Defter-i Mufassal-i Eyalet-i Kamanice: The Ottoman Survey Register of Podolia (ca. 1681): Text, Translation, and Commentary* (Cambridge, MA: Harvard University Press, 2004), 1:51.

161. Ferenc Tóth, *La guerre russo-turque (1768–1774) et la défense des Dardanelles: L'extraordinaire mission du baron de Tott* (Paris: Economica, 2008), 37–41; Finkel, *Osman's Dream*, 334–336; [Şehdî Osman], "Şehdî Osman Efendi Sefaretnamesi," ed. Faik Reşat Unat, *Tarih Vesikaları* 1, no. 1 (1941–1942): 66–80; 1, no. 2: 156–159; 1, no. 3: 232–240; 1, no. 4: 303–320; 1, no. 5: 390–400.

162. Yuzo Nagata, *Muhsin-zâde Mehmed Paşa ve Ayânlık Müessesesi* (Tokyo: Institute for the Study of Languages and Cultures of Asia and Africa, 1982), 63–66.

163. The expression "a tenacious defense" was coined by Frederic C. Lane, *Venice: A Maritime Republic* (Baltimore: Johns Hopkins University Press, 1973), 390. Aksan, *Ottoman Wars*, 94; Virginia Aksan, *An Ottoman Statesman in War and Peace: Ahmed Resmi Efendi, 1700–1783* (Leiden: E. J. Brill, 1995), 166–169; for the quotation, see Lane, *Venice*, 392.

164. Bonnac, *Mémoire historique*, 139.

165. Another reason for my choosing this line of inquiry is that it enables me to incorporate my own field of research, namely, Ottoman history. Unfortunately, because I cannot read or speak Farsi, my research has been confined to secondary literature in Turkish and Western European languages. On the background to the Safavids, see Stephen F. Dale, *The Muslim Empires of the Ottomans, Safavids, and Mughals* (Cambridge: Cambridge University Press, 2010); Willem Floor and Edmund Herzig, eds., *Iran and the World in the Safavid Age* (London: I. B. Tauris, 2012). I have used the name "Timur" throughout here because of its familiarity, although "Temür" is the correct form.

166. Muzaffar Alam and Sanjay Subrahmanyam, *Indo-Persian Travels in the Age of Discoveries, 1400–1800* (Cambridge: Cambridge University Press, 2007); Eva Orthmann, *Abd or-Rahim Han-e Hanan (964–1036/1556–1627): Staatsmann und Mäzen* (Berlin: Klaus Schwarz Verlag, 1996).

167. Robert D. McChesney, "Barrier of Heterodoxy? Rethinking the Ties between Iran and Central Asia in the Seventeenth Century," in *Safavid Persia: The History and Politics of an Islamic Society*, ed. Charles Melville (London: I. B. Tauris, 1996), 231–268.

168. Sussan Babaie, Kathryn Babayan, Ina Baghdiantz McCabe, and Massume Farhad, *Slaves of the Shah: New Elites of Safavid Iran* (London: I. B. Tauris, 2004), 1; Andrew Newman, *Safavid Iran: The Rebirth of a Persian Empire* (London: I. B. Tauris, 2005), 87–90.

169. Sholeh A. Quinn, "The Historiography of Safavid Prefaces," in Melville , *Safavid Persia*, 1–26; Iskandar Beg Munshi, *History of Shah Abbas the Great (Tārīkh-e'Ālam ārā-ye'Abbāsī)*, 3 vols., trans. Roger Savory (Boulder, CO: Westview Press, 1978–1986).

170. Newman, *Safavid Iran*, 142, 232; Christoph Marcinkowski, *Mirza Rafi'a's Dastur al-Muluk: A Manual of Later Safavid Administration: Annotated English Translation, Comments on the Offices and Services, and Facsimile of the Unique Persian Manuscript* (Kuala Lumpur: ISTAC, 2002); *Tadhkirat al-Mulūk*, trans. and with a commentary by Vladimir Minorsky (Cambridge: Gibb Memorial Trust, 1943); Monika Gronke, *Derwische im Vorhof der Macht: Sozial- und Wirtschaftsgeschichte Nordwestirans im 13. und 14. Jahrhundert* (Stuttgart: Franz Steiner Verlag, 1993).

171. Bekir Kütükoğlu, *Osmanlı-İran Siyasi Münasebetleri (1578–1612)*, 2nd ed. (Istanbul: İstanbul Fetih Cemiyeti, 1993); Fariba Zarinebaf-Shahr, "Tabriz under Ottoman Rule (1725–1730)" (PhD diss., University of Chicago, 1991); Michele Membré, *Mission to the Lord Sophy of Persia (1539–1542)*, trans. Alexander H. Morton (Warminster, UK: Gibb Memorial Trust, 1993).

172. Dirk Van der Cruysse, *Chardin le Persan* (Paris: Fayard, 1998).

173. Evliya Çelebi b. Derviş Mehemmed Zılli, *Evliya Çelebi Seyahatnâmesi: Topkapı Sarayı Kütüphanesi 304 Numaralı Yazmanın Transkripsyonu—Dizini*, vol. 2, ed. Zekerya Kurşun, Yücel Dağlı, and Seyit Ali Kahraman (Istanbul: Yapı Kredi Yayınları, 1999); Evliya Çelebi b. Derviş Mehemmed Zılli, *Evliya Çelebi Seyahatnâmesi: Topkapı Sarayı Bağdat 305 Yazmasının Transkripsyonu—Dizini*, vol. 4, ed. Yücel Dağlı and Seyit Ali Kahraman (Istanbul: Yapı Kredi Yayınları, 2001); embassy report by Ahmed Dürri Efendi, "Takrir-i Elçi-i Müşarünleyh," inserted into Mehmed Raşid, *Tarih-i Raşid* (Istanbul: Matba'a-yı amire, 1282/1865–1866), 5:372–398.

174. John Woods, *The Aqquyunlu: Clan, Confederation, Empire*, 2nd rev. ed. (Salt Lake City: University of Utah Press, 1999), 215.

175. Evliya Çelebi, *Evliya Çelebi Seyahatnâmesi*, 2:132–133; Nasuhü's-silahī (Matrākçı), *Beyan-ı Menazil-i Sefer-i'Irakeyn-i Sultān Suleymān Han*, ed. Hüseyin G. Yurdaydın (Ankara: Türk Tarih Kurumu, 1976).

176. Hans Robert Roemer, "The Jalayirids, Muzaffarids, and Sarbadārs," in *The Cambridge History of Iran*, vol. 6, *The Timurid and Safavid Periods*, ed. Peter Jackson and Lawrence Lockhart (Cambridge: Cambridge University Press, 1986), 1–41, 5–9; Beatrice Forbes Manz, *The Rise and Rule of Tamerlane* (Cambridge: Cambridge University Press, 1999), 66–73, 228–231.

177. Manz, *The Rise and Rule of Tamerlane*, 16–17; Woods, *The Aqquyunlu*, 16, refers only to the Aq-Qoyunlu, but the works of Manz and Quiring-Zoche demonstrate that his statement is more generally applicable: Beatrice Forbes Manz, *Power, Politics, and Religion in Timurid Iran* (Cambridge: Cambridge University Press, 2007); Rosemarie Quiring-Zoche, *Isfahan im 15. und 16. Jahrhundert: Ein Beitrag zur persischen Stadtgeschichte* (Freiburg im Breisgau: Klaus Schwarz Verlag, 1980).

178. Manz, *The Rise and Rule of Tamerlane*, 7, 13–48, 96–100, 120.

179. Ibid., 114, 129, 150–151.

180. Manz, *Power, Politics, and Religion*, 79–110, 86–87, 94.

181. Ibid., 113, 117–123.

182. Quiring-Zoche, *Isfahan im 15. und 16. Jahrhundert*, 17–85.

183. Ralph Kauz, *Politik und Handel zwischen Ming und Timuriden: China, Iran und Zentralasien im Spätmittelalter* (Wiesbaden: Ludwig Reichert, 2005).

184. Hans Robert Roemer, "The Successors of Timur," in Jackson and Lockhart, *Cambridge History of Iran,* 6:89–146.

185. Woods, *The Aqquyunlu,* 41–59, 96–110, 137, 260.

186. Monika Gronke, *Derwische im Vorhof der Macht,* 241–358.

187. Fariba Zarinebaf-Shahr, "Economic Activities of Safavid Women in the Shrine-City of Ardabīl," *Iranian Studies* 31, no. 2 (1998): 247–261; Bert Fragner, "Ardabīl zwischen Sultan und Schah: Zehn Urkunden Schah Tahmasps II," *Turcica* 6 (1975): 177–225.

188. Tom Sinclair, "The Ottoman Arrangements for the Tribal Principalities of the Lake Van Region of the Sixteenth Century," in *Ottoman Borderlands: Issues, Personalities, and Political Changes,* ed. Kemal Karpat and Robert W. Zens (Madison: University of Wisconsin Press, 2003), 119–144; Tom Sinclair, "Administration and Fortification in the Van Region under Ottoman Rule in the Sixteenth Century," in *The Frontiers of the Ottoman World,* ed. Andrew C. S. Peacock (Oxford: Oxford University Press, 2009), 211–224.

189. Evliya Çelebi, *Evliya Çelebi Seyahatnâmesi,* 2:171; this passage should be taken with a pinch of salt, as the author knew little about non-Muslims.

190. Rudi Matthee, "The Safavid-Ottoman Frontier: Iraq-i Arab as Seen by the Safavids," in Karpat and Zens, *Ottoman Borderlands,* 157–174.

191. Rudi Matthee, "Unwalled Cities and Restless Nomads: Firearms and Artillery in Safavid Iran," in Melville, *Safavid Persia,* 389–416; Giorgio Rota, "The Horses of the Shah: Some Remarks on the Organization of the Safavid Royal Stables, Mainly Based on Three Persian Handbooks of Administrative Practice," in *Pferde in Asien: Geschichte, Handel und Kultur/Horses in Asia: History, Trade and Culture,* ed. Bert G. Fragner, Ralph Kauz, Roderich Ptak, and Angela Schottenhammer (Vienna: Verlag der Österreichischen Akademie der Wissenschaften, 2009), 33–42.

192. Jean Calmard, "Shii Rituals and Power: II. The Consolidation of Safavid Shi'ism: Folklore and Popular Religion," in Melville, *Safavid Persia,* 139–190; Evliya Çelebi, *Evliya Çelebi Seyahatnâmesi,* 2:129; for a description of another ceremony of this kind, see 4:214–215.

193. Rula Jurdi Abisaab, "History and Self-Image: The'Amili Ulema in Syria and Iran (Fourteenth to Sixteenth Centuries)," in *Distant Relations: Iran and Lebanon in the Last 500 Years,* ed. Houchang E. Chehabi and Rula Jurdi Abisaab (London: Center for Lebanese Studies, 2006), 62–95; Evliya Çelebi, *Evliya Çelebi Seyahatnâmesi,* 4:180, 184; in 2:124 this traveler explains that the caliph Umar was particularly reviled.

194. Wherever possible, Friday prayers should be held only in mosques that have a minaret and a minbar. Mosques without these are only suitable for the people to observe *salat,* the personal obligation to pray five times a day, but not for communal prayers on Friday; Sussan Babaie, *Isfahan and Its Palaces: Statecraft, Shi'ism, and the Architecture of Conviviality in Early Modern Iran* (Edinburgh: Edinburgh University Press, 2008), 83–84.

195. Evliya Çelebi, *Evliya Çelebi Seyahatnâmesi,* 4:188; Kathryn Babayan, *Mystics, Monarchs, and Messiahs: Cultural Landscapes of Early Modern Iran* (Cambridge, MA: Harvard University Press, 2002), 349–402; Stefan Winter, *The Shiites of Lebanon under Ottoman Rule, 1516–1788* (Cam-

bridge: Cambridge University Press, 2010), 20–26; Rula Jurdi Abisaab, *Converting Persia: Religion and Power in the Safavid Empire* (London: I. B. Tauris, 2004), 7–30.

196. Babaie, *Isfahan and Its Palaces*, 96; Sholeh A. Quinn, *Historical Writing during the Reign of Shah 'Abbas: Ideology, Imitation, and Legitimacy in Safavid Chronicles* (Salt Lake City: University of Utah Press, 2000), 84–85; Babayan, *Mystics, Monarchs, and Messiahs*, 245–262; Newman, *Safavid Iran*, 84.

197. Colin Imber, "The Persecution of the Ottoman Shiites according to the Mühimme Defterleri, 1565–1585," *Der Islam* 56 (1979): 245–273.

198. Winter, *The Shiites*, 26–27; Faroqhi, *Pilgrims and Sultans*, 134–139; Alam and Subrahmanyam, *Indo-Persian Travels*, 24–42; Said A. Arjomand, *The Shadow of God and the Hidden Imam: Religion, Political Order, and Societal Change in Shi'ite Iran from the Beginnings to 1890* (Chicago: University of Chicago Press, 1984); Sohrweide, "Der Sieg der Safaviden," 95–223; Abdülbaki Gölpınarlı, *Alevî-Bektaşî nefesleri* (Istanbul: Remzi, 1963), 97–103; Ertuğrul Düzdağ, *Şeyhülislam Ebusuud Efendi Fetvaları Işığında 16. Asır Türk Hayatı* (Istanbul: Enderun, 1972), 109–112.

199. Cornell H. Fleischer, *Bureaucrat and Intellectual in the Ottoman Empire: The Historian Mustafâ Âli (1541–1600)* (Princeton, NJ: Princeton University Press, 1986), 154–159.

200. Maria Szuppe, "Kinship Ties between the Safavids and the Qizilbash Amirs in Late Sixteenth-Century Iran: A Case Study of the Political Career of Members of the Sharaf al-Din Ogli Tekelu Family," in Melville, *Safavid Persia*, 79–104; Leslie Peirce, *The Imperial Harem. Women and Sovereignty in the Ottoman Empire* (New York: Oxford University Press, 1993), 39–42.

201. Eskandar Beg Monshi, *History of Shah Abbas*, 2:911.

202. Newman, *Safavid Iran*, puts the successes of the ghulam into perspective; meanwhile, Kathryn Babayan, in Babaie, Babayan, Baghdiantz McCabe, and Farhad, *Slaves of the Shah*, 34–36, stresses the prominent role played by slaves of the shah in the seventeenth century; Newman, *Safavid Iran*, 26–27, 41–47, 50–51.

203. Alexander H. Morton, "The Early Years of Shah Ismā'īl in the *Afzal al-tavārīkh* and Elsewhere," in Melville, *Safavid Persia*, 27–52; see in particular 32 and 39–40. This princess appears under various names in different chronicles, including "Martha."

204. Peirce, *The Imperial Harem*, 31; Maria Szuppe, "The 'Jewels of Wonder': Learned Ladies and Princess Politicians in the Provinces of Early Safavid Iran," in *Women in the Medieval Islamic World,* ed. Gavin Hambly (New York: St Martin's Press, 1998), 325–347.

205. Shohreh Golsorkhi, "Pari Khan Khanum: A Masterful Safavid Princess," *Iranian Studies* 28, nos. 3–4 (1995): 143–156; Kathryn Babayan, "The 'Aqā'id al-Nisā': A Glimpse at Safavid Women in Local Isfahanī Culture," in Hambly, *Women in the Medieval Islamic World*, 349–381; see 353.

206. Faroqhi, *Pilgrims and Sultans*, 29–32.

207. Babaie, Babayan, Baghdiantz McCabe, and Farhad, *Slaves of the Shah*, 32–33; this section also stresses the similarities to the Ottoman position, likewise 23–40.

208. Sheila R. Canby, *Shah 'Abbas and the Treasures of Imperial Iran* (London: British Museum Press, 2009), 3.

209. Babaie, *Isfahan and Its Palaces*.

210. Roger M. Savory, "The Safavid Administrative System," in Jackson and Lockhart, *Cambridge History of Iran*, 6:351–372.

211. Quiring-Zoche, *Isfahan im 15. und 16. Jahrhundert*, 175–183.

212. Christoph Werner, *An Iranian Town in Transition: A Social and Economic History of the Elites of Tabriz, 1747–1848* (Wiesbaden: Harassowitz Verlag, 2000).

213. Babayan, *Mystics, Monarchs, and Messiahs*, 375–382; Newman, *Safavid Iran*, 110.

214. Babayan, *Mystics, Monarchs, and Messiahs*, 366 and 382; Hamid Algar, "Shi'ism and Iran in the Eighteenth Century," in *Studies in Eighteenth Century Islamic History*, ed. Thomas Naff (Carbondale: Southern Illinois University Press, 1977), 288–302.

215. Klaus Röhrborn, *Provinzen und Zentralgewalt Persiens im 16. und 17. Jahrhundert* (Berlin: De Gruyter, 1966); Cornell H. Fleischer, "Alqās Mīrzā," in *Encyclopaedia Iranica* (London: Routledge, 1985), 1:907–909.

216. This translation comes from Quiring-Zoche, *Isfahan im 15. und 16. Jahrhundert*, 139, 148.

217. For an example, see Manz, *Power, Politics, and Religion in Timurid Iran*, 32; Bert Fragner, "Social and Internal Economic Affairs," in Jackson and Lockhart, *Cambridge History of Iran*, 6:491–567.

218. Fragner, "Social and Internal Economic Affairs," 513 and 547; Quiring-Zoche, *Isfahan im 15. und 16. Jahrhundert*, 169–175; Evliya Çelebi, *Evliya Çelebi Seyahatnâmesi*, 2:126–134.

219. For a facsimile of the first page of the register of the master craftsmen and artists newly arrived from Tabriz, see the exhibition catalog *Onbin Yıllık İran Medeniyeti: Onbin Yıllık Ortak Miras* (Istanbul: National Museum of Iran, 2009), 199; for what became of them in the years that followed, see İsmail Hakkı Uzunçarşılı, "Osmanlı Sarayında Ehl-i Hiref (Sanatkârlar) Defteri," *Belgeler* 11 (1981–86): 23–76.

220. Ehsan Echraqi, "Le Dār al-Saltana de Qazvin, deuxième capitale des Safavides," in Melville, *Safavid Persia*, 105–116; Evliya Çelebi, *Evliya Çelebi Seyahatnâmesi*, 4:218.

221. For the estimates of European visitors in the seventeenth and early eighteenth centuries, including Jean Chardin, see Newman, *Safavid Iran*, 242; Quiring-Zoche, *Isfahan im 15. und 16. Jahrhundert*, 268.

222. Sheila R. Canby, *Shah 'Abbas: The Remaking of Iran* (London: British Museum Press, 2009), 116–123, 190, 220–223; Charles Melville, "Shah 'Abbas and the pilgrimage to Mashhad," in Melville, *Safavid Persia*, 191–230; Wolfram Kleiss, "Safavid Palaces," *Ars Orientalis* 23 (1993): 269–280.

223. Newman, *Safavid Iran*, 106–116; Algar, "Shi'ism and Iran in the Eighteenth Century," 288–302; Dürri Ahmed Efendi, "Takrir-i Elçi-i Müşarünleyh," 396–397.

224. Hans Robert Roemer, "The Safavid Period," in Jackson and Lockhart, *Cambridge History of Iran*, 6:189–350; see especially 310–331, 324–331. By contrast, Edmund Herzig has estimated that European demand for silk at least remained constant throughout the seventeenth century and may even have seen a big surge: Edmund M. Herzig, "The Volume of Iranian Raw Silk Exports in the Safavid Period," *Iranian Studies* 25, nos. 1–2 (1992): 61–79.

225. Ernest S. Tucker, *Nader Shah's Quest for Legitimacy in Post-Safavid Iran* (Gainesville: University Press of Florida, 2006).

226. Peter Avery, "Nader Shah and the Afsharid Legacy," in *The Cambridge History of Iran*, vol. 7, *From Nader Shah to the Islamic Republic*, ed. Peter Avery, Gavin Hambly, and Charles Melville (Cambridge: Cambridge University Press, 1991), 3–62; see p. 20.

227. Tucker, *Nader Shah*, pp. xi–xiv, 72–75.

228. Algar, "Shiʿism and Iran in the Eighteenth Century," 290.

229. Ann K. S. Lambton, *Landlord and Peasant in Persia* (London: I. B. Tauris, 1991), xxxii–lxvi, 105–128; Gene Garthwaite, *Khans and Shahs: A History of the Bakhtiyari Tribe in Iran* (London: I. B. Tauris, 2009); Xavier de Planhol, *Les fondements géographiques de l'histoire de l'Islam* (Paris: Flammarion, 1968), 197–251; Willem Floor, *The Economy of Safavid Persia* (Wiesbaden: Ludwig Reichert Verlag, 2000), 247–302.

230. Halil İnalcık, "Osmanlılarda Raiyyet Rüsûmu," *Belleten* 23 (1959): 575–610.

231. Heinz Gaube and Eugen Wirth, *Der Basar von Isfahan* (Wiesbaden: Ludwig Reichert Verlag, 1978); Mohamed Scharabi, *Der Bazar: Das traditionelle Stadtzentrum im Nahen Osten und seine Handelseinrichtungen* (Tübingen: Ernst Wasmuth, 1985); Quiring-Zoche, *Isfahan im 15. und 16. Jahrhundert*, 91, 272.

232. Evliya Çelebi, *Evliya Çelebi Seyahatnâmesi*, 2:127, 4:185 (relating to Urmiya), 209.

233. Rudolph P. Matthee, *The Politics of Trade in Safavid Iran: Silk for Silver, 1600–1730* (Cambridge: Cambridge University Press, 1999), 163; Evliya Çelebi, *Evliya Çelebi Seyahatnâmesi*, 2:132 (in reference to Tabriz).

234. Fahri Dalsar, *Türk Sanayi ve Ticaret Tarihinde Bursa'da İpekçilik* (Istanbul: İstanbul Üniversitesi İktisat Fakültesi, 1960), 131–137; Jean-Louis Bacqué-Grammont, "Notes sur une saisie de soies d'Iran en 1518," *Turcica* 8, no. 2 (1976): 237–253; Jean-Louis Bacqué-Grammont, *Les Ottomans, les Safavides et leurs voisins* (Istanbul: Nederlands Historisch-Archaeologisch Instituut, 1987).

235. Halil Inalcık, "Ḥarīr," in *Encyclopaedia of Islam*, 2nd ed., vol. 3 (Leiden: E. J. Brill, 1971), 209–221, here 213.

236. Çizakça, "Price History and the Bursa Silk Industry," 247–261.

237. Matthee, *Politics of Trade*, 74, 76–82; but see also the conflicting account by Herzig, "Volume of Iranian Raw Silk Exports."

238. Neşe Erim, "Trade, Traders, and the State in Eighteenth Century Erzurum," *New Perspectives on Turkey* 5–6 (1991): 123–150; Ralph Davis, *Aleppo and Devonshire Square: English Traders in the Levant in the Eighteenth Century* (London: Macmillan, 1967); Ina Baghdiantz McCabe, *The Shah's Silk for Europe's Silver: The Eurasian Trade of the Julfa Armenians in Safavid Iran and India (1530–1750)* (Atlanta, GA: Scholars Press, 1999), 124 (partial translation of the relevant edict); see also 141–170. The manual of adminstration discussed there is the *Tadhkirat al-Mulūk*, translated by Minorsky.

239. Newman, *Safavid Iran*, 6–7; Baghdiantz McCabe, *The Shah's Silk*, 141; Willem Floor, *The Persian Textile Industry in Historical Perspective* (Paris: L'Harmattan, 1999), 1–92; Mehdi Keyvani, *Artisans and Guild Life in the Later Safavid Period: Contributions to the Social-Economic History of Persia* (Berlin: Klaus Schwarz Verlag, 1982).

240. For some images of well-preserved examples of silk fabrics from the Timurid period, see *Onbin Yıllık İran Medeniyeti*, 172–173; Floor, *Persian Textile Industry*, 41; on the basis of mainly European sources, the same information is also in Evliya Çelebi, *Evliya Çelebi Seyahatnâmesi*, 2:128.

241. Evliya Çelebi, *Evliya Çelebi Seyahatnâmesi*, 4:180; Floor, *Persian Textile Industry*, 203.

242. Floor, *Persian Textile Industry*, 277–289, 296–354.

243. Jenny Housego, "Carpets," in *The Arts of Persia*, ed. Ronald Ferrier (New Haven, CT: Yale University Press, 1989), 118–156; Jon Thompson, "Early Safavid Carpets and Textiles," in *Hunt for*

Paradise: Court Arts of Safavid Iran, ed. Jon Thompson and Sheila Canby (Mailand: Skira, 2003), 271–317, 284–308; see also the entries by various authors such as Roger Savory, Jasleen Dhamija, and Walter Denny in "Carpets," in *Encyclopaedia Iranica,* vol. 4 (London: Routledge and Kegan Paul, 1990), 834–896, and vol. 5 (Costa Mesa, CA: Mazda Publishers, 1992), 1–9 (I am obliged to Christoph Knüttel in Munich for this reference).

244. Images of these rugs are found in *Onbin Yıllık İran Medeniyeti,* 238–239.

245. Ernst Grube and Eleanor Sims, "Persian Painting," in Ferrier, *The Arts of Persia,* 200–224.

246. For a courtly scene from the realm of the Ilkhans (1314) depicting this ruler, see *Onbin Yıllık İran Medeniyeti,* 57.

247. Robert Hillenbrand, "The Iconography of the Shāh-nāma-yi Shāhī," in Melville, *Safavid Persia,* 53–78; Grube and Sims, "Persian Painting," 212; Christine Woodhead, *Ta'līkī-zāde's şehnāme-i hümayūn: A History of the Ottoman Campaign into Hungary, 1593–94* (Berlin: Klaus Schwarz Verlag, 1983); on the questionable quality of some verses of the *shehnamecis,* see Fleischer, *Bureaucrat and Intellectual,* 249.

248. Lale Uluç, *Turkman Governors, Shiraz Artisans, and Ottoman Collectors: Sixteenth-Century Shiraz Manuscripts* (Istanbul: İş Bankası Yayınları, 2007).

249. Grube and Sims, "Persian Painting," 212–213, 216; Gül İrepoğlu, *Levni: Painting, Poetry, Colour* (Ankara: Republic of Turkey, Ministry of Culture, 1999), 158–160.

250. Grube and Sims, "Persian Painting," 212–213; David Roxburgh, *The Persian Album: From Dispersal to Collection* (New Haven, CT: Yale University Press, 2005).

251. Yolande Crowe, "Safavid Ceramics and Tiles," in *3 Capitals of Islamic Art: Istanbul, Isfahan, Delhi: Masterpieces from the Louvre Collection,* ed. Nazan Ölçer et al. (Istanbul: Sakip Sabancı Museum, 2008), 75–79; Canby, *Shah 'Abbas,* 84; Babaie, Babayan, Baghdiantz McCabe, and Farhad, *Slaves of the Shah,* 124–127.

252. "To the wise man, nothing is new," after Yolande Crowe, "Safavid Blue and White Bowls and the Chinese Connection," *Iran* 40 (2002): 257–263.

253. Annemarie Schimmel, "Ḥāfiẓ and His Contemporaries," in Jackson and Lockhart, *Cambridge History of Iran,* 6:929–947.

254. Zabihollah Safa, "Persian Literature in the Timurid and Türkmen Periods," in Jackson and Lockhart, *Cambridge History of Iran,* 6:913–928.

255. Orthmann, *Abd or-Rahim Han-e Hanan;* Halil İnalcık, *Şair ve Patron: Patrimonyal Devlet ve Sanat Üzerinde Sosyolojik bir İnceleme* (Istanbul: DoğuBatı, 2005), 54–71.

256. Evliya Çelebi, *Evliya Çelebi Seyahatnâmesi,* 4:214.

257. Barbara Flemming, "Sahib-kıran und Mahdi: Türkische Endzeiterwartungen im ersten Jahrzehnt der Regierung Süleymans," in *Between the Danube and the Caucasus: A Collection of Papers Concerning Oriental Sources on the History of the Peoples of Central and South-Eastern Europe,* ed. Györgi Kara (Budapest: Verlag der Akademie der Wissenschaften, 1987), 43–62; Cornell Fleischer, "The Lawgiver as Messiah: The Making of the Imperial Image in the Reign of Süleyman," in *Soliman le Magnifique et son temps. Actes du Colloque de Paris, Galeries Nationales du Grand Palais, 7–10 mars 1990,* ed. Gilles Veinstein (Paris: La Documentation Française, 1992), 159–178; Kaya Şahin, "Constantinople and the Endtime: The Ottoman Conquest as a Portent of the Last Hour," *Journal of Early Modern History* 14 (2010): 317–354.

3. South Asia and the Indian Ocean

I would like to extend my warmest thanks to Verena Ricken and Sarah Dusend for their invaluable support in the preparation of this chapter.

1. See Leslie Ronald Marchant, *The Papal Line of Demarcation and Its Impact in the Eastern Hemisphere on the Political Division of Australia, 1479–1829* (Greenwood: Woodside Valley Foundation, 2008).

2. For background reading on this topic, see Robert Bartlett, *The Making of Europe: Conquest, Colonization, and Cultural Change, 950–1350* (Princeton, NJ: Princeton University Press, 1993).

3. John Darwin, *After Tamerlane: The Global History of Empire* (London: Allen Lane, 2007).

4. On the following, see Markus P. M. Vink, "Indian Ocean Studies and the 'New Thalassology,'" *Journal of Global History,* no. 2 (2007): 41–62, which provides an excellent overview of the current state of research also John E. Wills, "Maritime Asia, 1500–1800: The Interactive Emergence of European Domination: A Review Article," *American Historical Review* 98, no. 1 (1993): 83–105; Sinnappah Arasaratnam, "Recent Trends in the Historiography of the Indian Ocean, 1500 to 1800," *Journal of World History* 1 (1990): 225–248.

5. See, for example, Peter Feldbauer and Gottfried Liedl, "1250–1620: 'Archaische' Globalisierung?," in *Rhythmen der Globalisierung: Expansion und Kontraktion zwischen dem 13. und 20. Jahrhundert,* ed. Peter Feldbauer, Gerald Hödl, and Jean-Paul Lehners (Vienna: Mandelbaum, 2009), 17–54.

6. K. N. Chaudhuri, *Trade and Civilization in the Indian Ocean: An Economic History from the Rise of Islam to 1750* (Cambridge: Cambridge University Press, 1985); ibid., *Asia before Europe: Economy and Civilization of the Indian Ocean from the Rise of Islam to 1750* (Cambridge: Cambridge University Press, 1990).

7. Fernand Braudel, *Civilization and Capitalism,* 3 vols. (New York: Harper & Row, 1981–1984); Braundel, *The Mediterranean and the Mediterranean World in the Age of Philip II,* 2nd ed. (London: Collins, 1972).

8. Michael N. Pearson, *The Indian Ocean* (London: Routledge, 2003).

9. See Kenneth McPherson, *The Indian Ocean: A History of People and the Sea* (Delhi: Oxford University Press, 2000).

10. See Pierre Chaunu, *European Expansion in the Later Middle Ages* (Amsterdam: North Holland Publications, 1979).

11. See Niels Steensgard, *The Asian Trade Revolution of the Seventeenth Century: The East India Companies and the Decline of the Caravan Trade* (Chicago: University of Chicago Press, 1973).

12. Andre Gunder Frank and Barry Gills, eds., *The World System: Five Hundred Years or Five Thousand?* (London: Routledge, 1989); Samuel Adshead, *Central Asia in World History* (London: Macmillan, 1993); Janet Abu-Lughod, *Before European Hegemony: The World System AD 1250–1350* (New York: Oxford University Press, 1989); and Andre Gunder Frank, *ReOrient: Global Economy in the Asian Age* (Berkeley: University of California Press, 1998).

13. In the main, it is scholars from the so-called Aligarh School who have adopted this position. They include, among others, Irfan Habib, Satish Chandra, M. Athar Ali, Norman Siddiqi, S. Nurul Hasan, Iqtidar Alam Khan, and Shireen Moosvi.

14. Paul Bairoch, "International Industrialization Levels from 1750–1980," *Journal of European Economic History* 11, no. 2 (1982): 269–333.

15. On the individual titles, see Vink, "Indian Ocean Studies."

16. An excellent overview of the Indian Ocean and a possible way of dividing the period into distinct eras is provided by Ravi Ahuja, "Indischer Ozean," in *Enzyklopädie der Neuzeit,* ed. Friedrich Jaeger (Stuttgart: Metzler, 2007), 5:857–890. The following section owes many of its insights and arguments to this essay. However, see also the attempts at a global historical perspective by Dietmar Rothermund, "Von der Krise des 17. Jahrhunderts zum Triumph der Industriellen Revolution," in Feldbauer, Hödl, and Lehners, *Rhythmen der Globalisierung,* 55–84; and Peter Feldbauer and Andrea Komlosy, "Globalgeschichte 1450–1820: Von der Expansions- zur Interaktionsgeschichte," in *"Die Welt quer denken": Festschrift für Hans-Heinrich Nolte zum 65. Geburtstag,* ed. Carl-Hans Hauptmeyer et al. (Frankfurt am Main: Lang, 2003), 60–93.

17. The background to the Genizah documents is recounted in Adina Hoffmann and Peter Cole, *Sacred Trash: The Lost and Found World of the Cairo Geniza* (New York: Nextbook, 2011) (with suggestions for further reading).

18. See, for example, Anthony Reid, *Southeast Asia in the Age of Commerce, 1450–1680,* 2 vols. (New Haven, CT: Yale University Press, 1988–1993); or McPherson, *The Indian Ocean.*

19. Jürgen Osterhammel, *The Transformation of the World: A Global History of the Nineteenth Century* (Princeton, NJ: Princeton University Press, 2014), xx.

20. See Jürgen Osterhammel, *Die Entzauberung Asiens: Europa und die asiatischen Reiche im 18. Jahrhundert,* 2nd ed. (Munich: Beck, 2010), 31–37.

21. On the Delhi sultanate, see Khaliq A. Nizami, *Some Aspects of Religion and Politics in India during the Thirteenth Century* (New Delhi: Idarah-I Adabiyat-I Delhi, 1971); Khaliq A. Nizami and Irfan Habib, eds., *The Delhi Sultanate,* vol. 4 of *A Comprehensive History of India* (New Delhi: People's Publishers House, 1970); Simon Digby, *War-Horse and Elephant in the Delhi Sultanate: A Study of Military Supplies* (Karachi: Orient Monographs, 1971); Bruce B. Lawrence, *Sufi Literature in the Sultanate Period* (Patna: Khuda Bakhsh Oriental Public Library, 1979); Peter Jackson, *The Delhi Sultanate: A Political and Military History* (Cambridge: Cambridge University Press, 1999); André Wink, *Indo-Islamic Society: 14th–15th Centuries,* vol. 3 of *The Making of the Indo-Islamic World* (Leiden: Brill, 2004); Satish Chandra, *Delhi Sultanat (1206–1526),* part 1 of *Medieval India: From the Sultanat to the Mughals,* 4th rev. ed. (New Delhi: Har-Anand Publications, 2009); see also the essays in Tapan Raychaudhuri and Irfan Habib, eds., *C. 1200–c. 1750,* vol. 1 of *The Cambridge Economic History of India* (Cambridge: Cambridge University Press, 1982), 45–161. An insightful work on the first phase of the sultanate is Sunil Kumar, *The Emergence of the Delhi Sultanate, 1192–1286* (New Delhi: Permanent Black, 2007); and on the Tughluq dynasty, see Mohammad Husain, *The Tughluq Dynasty* (Calcutta: Thacker Spink, 1963). On the subsequent history, see Stephan Conermann, *Die Beschreibung Indiens in der "Rihla" des Ibn Battuta: Eine herrschaftssoziologische Einordnung des Delhisultanates unter Muhammad Ibn Tuġluq* (Berlin: Schwarz, 1993).

22. "Hindu" and "Hinduistic" are modern collective terms for very different religious traditions. For this reason, the terms have been placed in quotation marks throughout this chapter. See,

for example, Axel Michaels, *Der Hinduismus: Geschichte und Gegenwart* (Munich: C. H. Beck, 1998).

23. Sh. Abdur Rashid, "Dastur-ul-Albab fi ilm-il-Hisab," *Medieval India Quarterly* 1 (1954): 59–99, here, 80.

24. No substantial new studies have been written on the individual sultanates. Researchers are therefore still reliant on the sections relating to them in Ramesh Chandra Majumdar, ed., *The Delhi Sultanate*, vol. 6 of *The History and Culture of the Indian People* (Bombay: Bharatiya Vidya Bhavan, 1960).

25. Two highly informative studies are available on the Sayyids and the Lodis: Khaliq A. Nizami, "The Saiyids (1414–51)" and "The Lodis (1451–1526)" in Nizami and Habib, *The Delhi Sultanate* (630–663 and 664–709, respectively), together with Kishori S. Lal, *Twilight of the Sultanate*, 2nd rev. ed. (New Delhi: Munshiram Manoharlal, 1980).

26. On the history of Vijayanagara, see Anna L. Dallapiccola and Stephanie Zingel-Avé Lallement, eds., *Vijayanagara: City and Empire: New Currents of Research* (Wiesbaden: Steiner, 1985); Noboru Karashima, *Towards a New Formation: South Indian Society under Vijayanagara Rule* (New Delhi: Oxford University Press, 1992); George Michell, *The Vijayanagara Courtly Style: Incorporation and Synthesis in the Royal Architecture of Southern India, 15th–17th Centuries* (New Delhi: Manohar, 1992); Burton Stein, *Vijayanagara* (Cambridge: Cambridge University Press, 1994); John M. Fritz and George Michell, eds., *City of Victory: Vijayanagara, the Medieval Hindu Capital of Southern India* (New York: Aperture, 1991); Catherine B. Asher and Cynthia Talbot, eds., *India before Europe* (Cambridge: Cambridge University Press, 2006), 53–84.

27. Specifically on Hampi, see John M. Fritz and George Michell, eds., *New Light on Hampi: Recent Research at Vijayanagara* (Mumbai: Marg Publications, 2001); Anila Verghese, *Hampi* (New Delhi: Oxford University Press, 2002).

28. This passage is based on Stephan Conermann, "Unterwegs im Auftrag des Šāhs: 'Abd ar-Razzāq as-Samarqandīs (d. AH 887/1482), Indische Mission," in *Studia Eurasiatica: Kieler Festschrift für Hermann Kulke zum 65. Geburtstag*, ed. Stephan Conermann and Jan Kusber (Schenefeld: EB-Verlag, 2003), 51–70. However, see also Muzaffar Alam and Sanjay Subrahmanyam, "From Timur to the Bahmanids: Fifteenth-Century Views," in *Indo-Persian Travels in the Age of Discoveries, 1400–1800* (Cambridge: Cambridge University Press, 2007), 45–92.

29. See Stein, *Vijayanagara*, 29–30 and 70–71.

30. See Philip B. Wagoner, *Tidings of the King: A Translation and Ethnohistorical Analysis of the Rayavacakamu* (Honolulu: University of Hawai'i Press, 1993); ibid., "'Sultan among Hindu Kings': Dress, Titels, and the Islamicisation of Hindu Culture at Vijyanagara," *Journal of Asian Studies* 55 (1996): 851–880; ibid., "Harihara, Bukka and the Sultan: The Delhi Sultanate in the Political Imagination of Vijayanagara," in *Beyond Turk and Hindu: Rethinking Religious Identities in Islamicate South Asia*, ed. David Gilmartin and Bruce B. Lawrence (Gainesville: University of Florida Press, 2000), 300–326.

31. A seminal monograph on Babur has now been produced: Stephen F. Dale, *The Garden of the Eight Paradises: Babur and the Culture of Empire in Central Asia, Afghanistan and India (1483–1530)* (London: Brill, 2004). See also Mohibbul Hasan, *Babur: Founder of the Mughal Empire in India* (Delhi: Manohar, 1985); Satish Chandra, *Mughal Empire (1526–1748)*, part 2 of

Medieval India: From Sultanate to the Mughals (New Delhi: Har-Anand Publications, 1999), 21–46. On the establishment of Mughal rule in northern India, see Douglas E. Streusand, *The Formation of the Mughal Empire* (Delhi: Oxford University Press, 1989).

32. The following are key studies on the Mughal Empire: John F. Richards, *The Mughal Empire* (Cambridge: Cambridge University Press, 1996); Stephan Conermann, *Das Mogulreich: Geschichte und Kultur des muslimischen Indien* (Munich: Beck, 2006); Stephen F. Dale, *The Muslim Empires of the Ottomans, Safavids, and Mughals* (Cambridge: Cambridge University Press, 2009); Chandra, *Mughal Empire;* in addition to the essays in Raychaudhuri, *The Cambridge Economic History,* 1:163–478. Also of use is Muzaffar Alam and Sanjay Subrahmanyam, "Introduction," in *The Mughal State, 1526–1750,* ed. Muzaffar Alam and Sanjay Subrahmanyam (Delhi: Oxford University Press, 1998), 1–71.

33. On Humayun, in addition to Chandra, *Mughal Empire,* 47–69, see Nader Purnaqcheband, *Strategien der Kontingenzbewältigung: Der Mogulherrscher Humayun (r. 1530–1540 und 1555–1556) dargestellt in der "Tazkirat al-Waqi'at" seines Leibdieners Jauhar Aftabci* (Schenefeld: EB-Verlag, 2007).

34. The following sections are largely based on the excellent essays in the compendium volume compiled by Muzaffar Alam und Sanjay Subrahmanyam under the title *The Mughal State, 1526–1750.* The first section draws on Dirk H. A. Kolff, "A Warlord's Fresh Attempt at Empire," in *Naukar, Rajput, and Sepoy: The Ethnohistory of the Military Labour Market of Hindustan, 1450–1850* (Cambridge: Cambridge University Press, 1990), 32–70. See also Basheer Ahmad Khan Matta, *Sher Shah Suri: A Fresh Perspective* (Karachi: Oxford University Press, 2005); Chandra, *Mughal Empire,* 70–90.

35. On the following section, see Ram Prasad Tripathi, "Turko-Mongol Theory of Kingship," in *Some Aspects of Muslim Administration* (Allahabad: Indian Press, 1936), 105–121. A very good and more recent study reaches the same conclusions: A. Azfar Moin, *The Millennial Sovereign: Sacred Kingship and Sainthood in Islam* (New York: Columbia University Press, 2012). But see also Lisa Balabanlilar, *Imperial Identity in the Mughal Empire: Memory and Dynastic Politics in Early Modern South and Central Asia* (London: Tauris, 2012); Corinne Lefèvre, "In the Name of the Fathers: Mughal Genealogical Strategies from Babur to Shah Jahan," in *Genealogy and History in South Asia,* ed. Simon Brodbeck and James Hegarty (London: Equinox, 2011), 409–442.

36. This section is based on John F. Richards, "The Formulation of Imperial Authority under Akbar and Jahangir," in *Kingship and Authority in South Asia,* ed. John F. Richards (Madison: University of Wisconsin Press, 1978), 285–326.

37. A good biography of Akbar is now available: André Wink, *Akbar* (Oxford: Oneworld, 2009). See also Heike Franke, *Akbar und Gahangir: Untersuchungen zur politischen und religiösen Legitimation in Wort und Bild* (Hamburg: EB-Verlag, 2007); Chandra, *Mughal Empire,* 91–185.

38. See also Anna Kollatz, "Der Kaiser als Kitt der Gesellschaft—Kontingenzbewältigung durch Herrscher-Apotheose in der frühen Regierungszeit Ğāhangīrs (r. 1605–27)," in *Strategien zur Bewältigung von Kontingenz: (Be-)Gründung von Herrschaft: Eine interdisziplinäre Annäherung,* ed. Mathias Becher and Stephan Conermann (Berlin: de Gruyter, 2014).

39. On the hagiographic portrayal of Jahangir, see Anna Kollatz, "The Creation of a Saint Emperor: Retracing Narrative Strategies of Mughal Legitimation and Representation in *Majālis-i Jahāngīrī* by ʿAbd al-Sattār b. Qāsim Lāhōrī (ca. 1608–11)," in *Narrative Pattern and Genre in Hagiographic Life Writing,* ed. S. Conermann and J. Rheingans (Berlin: EB-Verlag, 2014), 227–266.

40. On Sufism in India, see Richard M. Eaton, *Sufis of Bijapur, 1300–1700: Social Roles of Sufis in Medieval India* (Princeton, NJ: Princeton University Press, 1977); Carl Ernst, *Eternal Garden: Mysticism, History, and Politics in a South Asian Sufi Center* (Albany: State University of New York Press, 1992); Nile Green, *Indian Sufism since the Seventeenth Century: Saints, Books and Empires in the Muslim Deccan* (London: Routledge, 2006); ibid., *Making Space: Sufis and Settlers in Early Modern India* (New Delhi: Oxford University Press, 2012).

41. On this and on Jahangir in general, see Sajida, "Religion and State during the Reign of Mughal Emperor Jahangir (1605–27): Non-Juristical Perspectives," *Studia Islamica* 69 (1989): 95–119; Franke, *Akbar und Ğahāngīr;* Chandra, *Mughal Empire,* 231–256; Corinne Levèvre, "Recovering a Missing Voice from Mughal India: The Imperial Discourse of Jahāngīr (r. 1605–1627) in His Memoirs," *Journal of the Economic and Social History of the Orient* 50, no. 4 (2007): 452–489; Munis D. Faruqui, *Princes of the Mughal Empire, 1504–1719* (Cambridge: Cambridge University Press, 2012); also Moin, *Millennial Sovereign.* Corinne Lefèvre in particular has written about Jahangir and his time in a series of groundbreaking articles: "Une autobiographie à la mode moghole: Les Mémoires de l'empereur Jahāngīr (r. 1605–1627)," in *Les Autobiographies souveraines,* ed. Pierre Monnet and Jean-Claude Schmitt (Paris: Publications de la Sorbonne, 2012), 119–158; ibid., "Comment un 'conquérant du monde' devint l'esclave d'une femme: L'historiographie de l'empereur moghol Jahāngīr (r. 1605–1627)," in *Mémoires partagées, mémoires disputées: Écriture et réécriture de l'histoire,* ed. Stéphane Benoist et al. (Metz: Centre régional universitaire lorrain d'histoire, 2010), 93–118; ibid., "Recovering a Missing Voice from Mughal India: The Imperial Discourse of Jahāngīr (r. 1605–1627) in His Memoirs," *Journal of the Economic and Social History of the Orient* 50, no. 4 (2007): 452–489; ibid., "Pouvoir et noblesse dans l'Empire moghol: Perspectives du règne de Jahāngīr (1605–1627)," *Annales: Histoire, Sciences Sociales* 62, no. 6 (2007): 1287–1312.

42. The basis for the following observations is provided by Norman P. Ziegler, "Some Notes on Rajput Loyalties during the Mughal Period," in Richards, *Kingship and Authority in South Asia,* 215–251. On this topic, also see Satish Chandra, *Mughal Religious Policies, the Rajputs and the Deccan* (New Delhi: Vikas Publishing House, 1993). See Allison Busch, "Portrait of a Raja in a Badshah's World: Amrit Rai's Biography of Man Singh (1585)," *Journal of the Economic and Social History of the Orient* 55, nos. 2–3 (2012): 287–328; Cynthia Talbot, "Justifying Defeat: A Rajput Perspective on the Age of Akbar," *Journal of the Economic and Social History of the Orient* 55, nos. 2–3 (2012): 329–368.

43. This subsection draws extensively on Chetan Singh, "Conformity and Conflict: Tribes in the 'Agrarian System' of Mughal India," *Indian Economic and Social History Review* 23, no. 3 (1988): 319–340.

44. See William H. Moreland, "Rank (*mansab*) in the Mogul State Service," *Journal of the Royal Asiatic Society of Great Britain and Ireland,* 1936, 641–665. More recent studies on the bureaucracy of the Mughal period include John F. Richards, *The Mughal Administration in Golkonda*

(Oxford: Clarendon Press, 1975); and M. Athar Ali, *The Apparatus of Empire: Awads of Ranks, Offices, and Titles to the Mughal Nobility, 1573–1658* (Delhi: Oxford University Press, 1985). Other important studies are Irfan Habib, "Mansab System, 1595–1637," *Proceedings of the Indian History Congress* 29 (1967): 221–242; and Shireen Moosvi, "Evolution of Mansab System under Akbar until 1596–7," *Journal of the Royal Asiatic Society* 2 (1981): 175–813.

45. To date, no serious academic study of Shah Jahan and his age has been written.

46. On the following paragraph, see Norman Ahmad Siddiqui, "The Faujdar and Faujdari under the Mughals," *Medieval India Quarterly* 4 (1961): 22–35. A history of individual offices and posts in the Mughal Empire is urgently required. But see also Mohammed Z. Siddiqi, "The Muhtasib under Aurangzeb," *Medieval Indian Quarterly* 5 (1963): 113–119; and especially M. P. Singh, *Town, Market, Mint and Port in the Mughal Empire, 1556–1707: An Administrative-Cum-Economic Study* (Delhi: Adam Publishers, 1985).

47. This paragraph is based on A. Jan Qaisar, "Distribution of Revenue Resources of the Mughal Empire among the Nobility," *Proceedings of the Indian History Congress 1965,* 237–242. Other important treatments of this topic are Tapan Raychaudhuri, "The State and the Economy: 1. The Mughal Empire," and Irfan Habib, "Agrarian Relations and Land Revenue: 1. North India," both in Raychaudhuri and Habib, *Cambridge Economic History,* 1:172–191 and 1:235–248, respectively.

48. Sher Shah had already introduced the silver rupee with a weight of 11.5 grams; under Akbar this coin finally became widely accepted silver currency throughout the Mughal Empire. A rupee was subdivided into 40 copper dam.

49. For this section, see Tapan Raychaudhuri, "The Agrarian System of Mughal India: A Review Essay," *Enquiry* 2, no. 1 (1965): 92–121. In general here, see also Tapan Raychaudhuri, *Bengal under Akbar and Jahangir: An Introductory Study in Social History,* 2nd ed. (Delhi: Munshiram Manoharlar, 1966); and Ahsan Raza Khan, *Chieftains in the Mughal Empire during the Reign of Akbar* (Shimla: Indian Institute for Advanced Study, 1977).

50. Raychaudhuri alludes here to Nurul Hasan, "The Position of the *Zamindars* in the Mughal Empire," *Indian Economic and Social History Review* 1, no. 4 (1964): 107–119; and B. R. Grover, "Nature of Land-Rights in Mughal India," *Indian Economic and Social History Review* 1, no. 1 (1964): 1–23.

51. Raychaudhuri cites Irfan Habib, *The Agrarian System of Mughal India (1556–1707)* (London: Asia Publishing House 1963), 136–137.

52. The following observations are based on S. Nurul Hasan, "Zamindar under the Mughals," in *Land Control and Social Structure in Indian History,* ed. Robert E. Frykenberg (Madison: University of Wisconsin, 1969), 17–31.

53. See the following articles by Chandra Jnan, "Aurangzēb and Hindu Temples," *Journal of Pakistan Historical Society* 5 (1957): 247–254; "Ālamgīr's Grant to Hindu Pujārīs," *Journal of Pakistan Historical Society* 6 (1958): 55–65; "Freedom of Worship for the Hindus under ʿĀlamgīr," *Journal of Pakistan Historical Society* 6 (1958): 24–125; "ʿĀlamgīr's Patronage of Hindū Temples," *Journal of Pakistan Historical Society* 6 (1958): 208–213; "ʿĀlamgīr's Attitude towards Non-Muslim Institutions," *Journal of Pakistan Historical Society* 7 (1959): 36–39; and "ʿĀlamgīr's Grant to a Brahmin," *Journal of Pakistan Historical Society* 7 (1959): 99–100. See also Katherine B. Brown,

"Did Aurangzeb Ban Music? Questions for the Historiography of His Reign," *Modern Asian Studies* 41, no. 1 (2007): 77–120; Richard Eaton, "Temple Desecration and Indo-Muslim States," *Journal of Islamic Studies* 11, no. 3 (2000): 283–319; Muzaffar Alam, *The Languages of Political Islam* (London: Hurst, 2004); Manohar Lal Bhatia, *The Ulama, Islamic Ethics and Courts under the Mughals: Aurangzīb Revisited* (New Delhi: Mank Publications, 2006); Munis Faruqi, *The Princes of the Mughal Empire, 1504–1719* (New York: Cambridge University Press, 2012).

54. The following account here is based on Conermann, *Das Mogulreich,* 105–112. See also Chandra, *Mughal Empire,* 267–357.

55. There are a number of good introductions to the Marathas: Stewart Gordon, *The Marathas, 1600–1818* (Cambridge: Cambridge University Press, 1993); André Wink, *Land and Sovereignty in India: Agrarian Society and Politics under the Eighteenth-Century Maratha Svarajya* (Cambridge: Cambridge University Press, 1986).

56. Satish Chandras's chapter, "Review of the Crisis of the Jagirdaran System," in *Medieval India: Society, the Jagirdaran Crisis and the Village* (Delhi: Macmillan, 1982), 61–75, provides the basis for this section.

57. On this rupture zone, see Gautam Bhadra, "Two Frontier Uprisings in Mughal India" in *Subaltern Studies,* vol. 2, ed. Ranajit Guha (Delhi: Oxford University Press, 1982), 43–59.

58. This line of argument follows Muzaffar Alam, "Aspects of Agrarian Uprisings in North India in the Early Eighteenth Century," in *Situating Indian History for Sarvepalli Gopal,* ed. Sabyasachi Bhattacharya and Romila Thapar (Delhi: Oxford University Press, 1986), 146–170.

59. On the following, see Karen Leonard, "The 'Great Firm' Theory of the Decline of the Mughal Empire," *Comparative Studies in Society and History* 21, no. 2 (1979): 151–167. See also the discussion in Alam and Subrahmanyam, "Introduction," 55–68.

60. Ashin Das Gupta provides the rationale for the following paragraphs in "Trade and Politics in Eighteenth Century India," in *Islam and the Trade of Asia,* ed. Donald S. Richards (Philadelphia: University of Pennsylvania Press, 1970), 181–214.

61. On Gujarat, see Michael N. Pearson, *Merchants and Rulers in Gujarat: The Response to the Portuguese in the Sixteenth Century* (Berkeley: University of California Press, 1976).

62. On Masulipatnam, see Sinnappah Arasaratnam and Aniruddha Ray, *Masulipatnam and Cambay: A History of Two Port-Towns, 1500–1800* (New Delhi: Munshiram Manoharlar, 1994).

63. See also Janet Abu-Lughod, "The World System in the Thirteenth Century: Dead-End or Precursor?" in *Islamic and European Expansion: The Forging of a Global Order,* ed. Michael Adas (Philadelphia: Temple University Press, 1993), 75–102.

64. On this topic, see Morris Rossabi, "Ming China's Relations with Hami and Central Asia, 1414–1513: A Reexamination of Traditional Chinese Foreign Policy" (PhD diss., Columbia University, 1970); ibid., "Ming China and Turfan, 1406–1517," *Central Asiatic Journal* 16 (1972): 206–222; and ibid., "The Ming and Inner China," in *The Ming Dynasty, 1368–1644,* vol. 8, part 2 of *The Cambridge History of China,* ed. Frederick W. Mote and Denis Twitchett (Cambridge: Cambridge University Press, 1998), 221–271.

65. A good introduction is provided by Klaus Bergdolt, *Der schwarze Tod in Europa,* 3rd ed. (Munich: Beck, 2011). See also Neithard Bulst, "Der schwarze Tod: Demographische, wirtschafts-

und kulturgeschichtliche Aspekte der Pestkatastrophe von 1347–1352. Bilanz der neueren Forschung," *Saeculum* 30 (1979): 45–67. On the Near East, see Michael W. Dols, *The Black Death in the Middle East* (Princeton, NJ: Princeton University Press, 1976); Stuart J. Borsch, *The Black Death in Egypt and England: A Comparative Study* (Austin: University of Texas Press, 2005).

66. See Chaudhuri, *Trade and Civilization,* 34–63.

67. H. Neville Chittick, "The East Coast, Madagascar, and the Indian Ocean," in *From c. 1050 to c. 1600,* vol. 3 of *The Cambridge History of Africa,* ed. Roland Oliver (Cambridge: Cambridge University Press, 1977), 183–231. See also John Henrik Clark, "East Africa and the Orient: Ports and Trade before the Arrival of the Portuguese," and Michel Mollat, "Historical Contacts of Africa and Madagascar with South and South-East Asia: The Role of the Indian Ocean," both in *Historical Relations across the Indian Ocean: Reports and Papers of the Meeting of Experts Organized by Unesco at Port Louis, Mauritius, from 15 to 19 July 1974* (Paris: Unesco, 1980), 13–22 and 45–60, respectively; H. Neville Chittick, "East African Trade with the Orient," in *Islam and the Trade of Asia: A Colloquium,* ed. Donald S. Richards (Oxford: Cassirer, 1970), 97–104.

68. On the following, see Rita Rose Di Meglio, "Arab Trade with Indonesia and the Malay Peninsula from the 8th to the 16th Century," in Richards, *Islam and the Trade,* 105–136; Marie A. P. Meilink-Roelofsz, "Trade and Islam in the Malay-Indonesian Archipelago Prior to the Arrival of the Europeans," in Richards, *Islam and the Trade,* 137–158; Luis F. Thomasz, "Malaka et ses communautés marchandes au tournant du 16ème siècle," in *Marchands et hommes d'affaires asiatiques dans l'Ocean Indien et la Mer de Chine 13–20 siecles,* ed. Jean Aubin and Denys Lombard (Paris: Editions de l'école des études en sciences sociales, 1988), 31–48; Stefan Dietrich, "Islam, Handel und neue Reiche im 13.–17. Jahrhundert," in *Versunkene Königreiche Indonesiens,* ed. Arne Eggebrecht and Eve Eggebrecht (Mainz: Zabern, 1995), 112–125.

69. Varvara P. Adrianova-Peretc et al., eds. and trans., *Choženie za tri morja Afanasija Nikitina, 1466–1472 gg.,* 2nd rev. ed. (Moscow: Izdat. Akad. Nauk SSSR, 1958), 80.

70. On this model, see Chaudhuri, *Trade and Civilization,* 98–118; but also Archibald Lewis, "Maritime Skills in the Indian Ocean, 1368–1500," *Journal of the Economic and Social History of the Orient* 16 (1973): 238–264, here 241–247.

71. This section is a somewhat abridged version of Stephan Conermann, "Vertraute Zeichen—Fremde Zeichen: Zur Frage der möglichen Exilerfahrung in der mittelalterlichen islamischen Welt," in *Vermischte Schriften: Koran, Šāh-nāme, Exil und Viktor Klemperer,* ed. Werner Schmucker and Stephan Conermann (Schenefeld: EB-Verlag, 2007), 37–46. On this topic, see also Patricia Risso, *Merchants & Faith: Muslim Commerce and Culture in the Indian Ocean* (Boulder, CO: Westview Press, 1995).

72. See Ulrich Haarmann, "Glaubensvolk und Nation im islamischen und lateinischen Mittelalter," *Berlin-Brandenburgische Akademie der Wissenschaften: Berichte und Abhandlungen* 2 (1996): 161–199.

73. Regarding this work, see Hillary Kilpatrick, "A 10th Century Anthology of Exile and Homesickness," *Azure: Review of Arab Literature, Arts and Culture* 5 (1980): 23–27.

74. On Ibn Battuta, see, for example, Conermann, *Die Beschreibung Indiens in der "Rihla" des Ibn Battuta.*

75. An introduction to Ibn Sina is provided by the excellent overview: "Avicenna," in *Ataš-Bayhaqi*, vol. 3 of *Encyclopaedia Iranica* (London: Routledge, 1989), col. 66a–110a.

76. On the following, see Roland Posner, "Kultursemiotik," in *Konzepte der Kulturwissenschaften*, ed. Ansgar Nünning and Vera Nünning (Stuttgart: Metzler, 2003), 39–72.

77. An outstanding introduction to Islamic law can be found in Bernard G. Weiss, *The Spirit of Islamic Law* (Athens: University of Georgia Press, 1998). Another useful source is Gotthelf Bergsträsser, *Grundzüge des islamischen Rechtes,* ed. Joseph Schacht (Berlin: W. de Gruyter, 1935).

78. This subsection is a shortened version of Stephan Conermann, "Muslimische Seefahrt auf dem Indischen Ozean vom 14. bis zum 16. Jahrhundert," in *Der Indische Ozean in historischer Perspektive,* ed. Stephan Conermann (Hamburg: EB-Verlag, 1998), 143–180.

79. Marco Polo, *The Description of the World,* trans. Arthur-Christopher Moule and Paul Pelliot (London: Routledge, 1938). Josaphat Barbaro's work is published under the title *Travels to Tana and Persia by Yosafa Barbaro and Ambrogio Contarini* (London: Hakluyt Society, 1873). For Nicolò Conti, see "The Travels of Nicolò de'Conti in the East," in *The Most Noble and Famous Travels of Marco Polo together with the Travels of Nicolo de'Conti,* ed. and trans. John Frampton (London: Argonaut Press, 1929), 123–149 and 259–260. On Girolamo da Santo Stefano, see Mario Longhena, ed., *Viaggi in Persia, India e Giava di Nicolo di Conti, Girolamo Adorno e Girolamo da Santo Stefano* [The travels of Nicolo di Conti, Girolamo Adorno and Girolamo da Santo Stefano in Persia, India and on Java] (Milan: Edizioni "Alpes," 1929). On Ludovico di Varthema, see Ludovico de Varthema, *Reisen im Orient,* trans. Folker Reichert (Sigmaringen: Thorbecke, 1996); Richard Carnac, trans., *The Itinerary of Ludovico di Varthema of Bologna from 1502–1508* (London: Argonaut Press, 1928). On Duarte Barbosa, see *The Book of Duarte Barbosa: An Account of the Countries Bordering on the Indian Ocean and Their Inhabitants, Written by Duarte Barbosa, and Completed about the Year 1518 AD,* 2 vols. (London: Hakluyt Society, 1918–1921). For Tomé Pires, see Armando Cortesao, trans., *The Suma Oriental of Tomé Pires: An Account of the East, from the Red Sea to Japan, Written in Malacca and India in 1512–1515* (London: Hakluyt Society, 1944; reprint, Wiesbaden: Kraus, 1967).

80. Descriptions of various different ship types are given in Robert B. Serjeant, *The Portuguese off the South Arabian Coast: Hadrami Chronicles, with Yemeni and European Accounts of Dutch Pirates off Mocha in the Seventeenth Century* (Oxford: Clarendon Press, 1963), 134–136; and especially in Hans Kindermann, *Schiff im Arabischen* (Zwickau: n.p., 1934). See also William H. Moreland, "The Ship of the Arabian Sea about AD 1500," *Journal of the Royal Asiatic Society* 1939, 63–74 and 173–192. On Ottoman ship types, see Svat Soucek, "Certain Types of Ships in Ottoman Turkish Terminology," *Turcica* 7 (1975): 233–249. A great deal of information is available regarding the following period: A. Jan Qaisar, "Shipbuilding in India during the Seventeenth Century," *Indian Economic and Social History Review* 5 (1940–1941): 142–164; A. Jan Qaisar, "Merchant Shipping in India during the Seventeenth Century," in *Medieval India: A Miscellany,* ed. Aligarh Muslim University, Centre of Advanced Studies, Department of History (London: Asia Publishing House, 1970), 2:195–220; Atul C. Roy, *A History of Mughal Navy and Naval Warfares* (Calcutta: World Press, 1972); Colin H. Imber, "The Navy of Süleyman the Magnificent," *Archivum Ottomanicum* 6 (1980): 211–282.

81. Ibn Battuta, *Rihla,* 565–566, as cited in Stephan Conermann, *Die Beschreibung Indiens in der 'Rihla' des Ibn Battūta. Eine herrschaftssoziologische Einordnung des Delhisultanates unter Muhammad Ibn Tuġluq* (Berlin: Schwarz, 1993).

82. Mahmud Shah, "Code maritime du royaume de Malaca," ed. and trans. Édouard Dulaurier, in *Collection de lois maritimes antèrieures au XVIII siècle,* ed. Jean Marie Pardessus (Paris: L'imprimerie royale, 1845), 6:389–440, here 391.

83. Abul Fazl Allami, *Ain-i Akbari,* ed. Henry Blochmann (Calcutta: Asiatic Society, 1867), 1:202–203.

84. Ibn Majid, *K. Fawa'id fi usul ilm al-bahr wa'l-qawa'id,* ed. Gabriel Ferrand et al. *Instructions nautiques et routiers arabes et portugais des XVe et XVIe siècles* (Paris: Paul Geuthner, 1921), 1:1b–88b, here 51b–5Sa.

85. Shah, "Code maritime du royaume de Malaca," 405–406.

86. Sulayman al-Mahri, *Tuhfat al-fulul fi tamhid al-usul,* ed. von Ferrand, *Instructions nautiques,* 2: 4a–10a, here 2:9b–10a.

87. Forming the basis of the following observations and at the same time the best introductions to Arab seafaring in this period are the following studies by Gerald R. Tibbetts, *The Navigational Theory of the Arabs in the Fifteenth and Sixteenth Centuries* (Lisbon: Royal Asiatic Society, 1969); "The Navigators and Their Works," "Navigational Theory," and "The Topography of the Navigational Texts," all in *Arab Navigation in the Indian Ocean before the Coming of the Portuguese* (London: Royal Asiatic Society, 1971), 1–64, 269–392, and 393–504, respectively; "Stellar Navigation in the Medieval Indian Ocean," *Journal of the Institute of Navigation* 19 (1972): 139–144; and "Milaha: In the Indian Ocean," in *Encyclopaedia of Islam,* new edition (Leiden: E. J. Brill, 1993), 7:50–53. See also Theodor A. Šumovskij, "Issledovanie," in *Tri neizvestnye locii Achmada ibn Madžida, arabskogo locmana Vasko da Gamy* [Three unknown maritime handbooks by Ahmad ibn Majid, the pilot of Vasco da Gama] (Moscow: Izdat. Akad. Nauk SSSR, 1957), 63–105; and Šumovskij, *Arabskie locii kak istoriko-literatunrye pamjatniki novogo kačestva* [Arab maritime manuals as curious literary-historical remains] (Moscow: Izdat. Akad. Nauk SSSR, 1960). Other important studies are the following by Henri Grosset-Grange: "La navigation dans l'Océan Indien au temps de Vasco da Gama," *Tilas* 12 (1972): 28–36; "Les traités arabes de navigation: De certaines difficultés particulières à leur étude," *Arabica* 19 (1972): 240–254; "Les marins arabes du moyen âge: De certaines étoiles observées en Océan Indien," *Arabica* 24 (1977): 42–57; "Les manuscrits nautiques anciens (Océan Indien): Considérations relatives à certains termes particuliers," *Arabica* 26 (1979): 90–99; and "Les procédés arabes de navigation Océan Indien au moment des Grandes Découvertes," in *Sociétés et companies de commerce en Orient et dans l'océan Indien,* ed. Michel Mollat (Paris: S.E.V.P.E.N., 1970), 227–246. See also Alfred Clark, "Medieval Arab Navigation on the Indian Ocean: Latitude Determinations," *Journal of the American Oriental Society* 113 (1993): 360–373.

88. See Tibbetts, *Arab Navigation,* 354–360.

89. See Sidi Ali Re'is, *Muhit*—Ms. of the National Library in Vienna (=Flügel 1277), fol. 96a–96b.

90. On the Mamluk period, see Carl F. Petry, ed., *Islamic Egypt, 640–1517,* vol. 1 of *The Cambridge History of Egypt* (Cambridge: Cambridge University Press, 1998), 242–498. A brief overview is given by Ulrich Haarmann, "Der arabische Osten im späten Mittelalter," in *Geschichte der*

arabischen Welt, 5th. ed., ed. Heinz Halm and Ulrich Haarmann (Munich: Beck, 2004), 217–263. On the more recent state of research in this field, see Stephan Conermann and Anja Pistor-Hatam, eds., *Die Mamluken: Studien zu ihrer Geschichte und Kultur: Zum Gedenken an Ulrich Haarmann (1942–1999)* (Schenefeld: EB-Verlag, 2003); Doris Behrens-Abouseif, ed., *The Arts of the Mamluk in Egypt and Syria—Evolution and Impact* (Göttingen: V&R Unipress, 2012); and Stephan Conermann, ed., *Ubi sumus? Quo vademus? Mamluk Studies—State of the Art* (Göttingen: V&R Unipress, 2013).

91. See Stephan Conermann, "Das Mittelmeer zur Zeit der Mamlukenherrschaft in Ägypten und Syrien (1250–1517): Vorstudien zu einer globalgeschichtlichen Perspektive," in *Randgänge der Mediävistik,* ed. Michael Stolz (Bern: Stämpfli, 2013), 21–61. The following are important studies on the trade links of the Mamluk Empire: Subhi Labib, *Handelsgeschichte Ägyptens im Spätmittelalter, 1171–1517* (Wiesbaden: Steiner, 1965); Damien Coulon, *Barcelone et le grand commerce d'Orient au Moyen Âge: Un siècle de relations avec l'Egypte et la Syrie-Palestrine (ca. 1330–ca. 1430)* (Madrid: Casa de Velázques, 2004); Javier Appelániz Ruiz de Galarretain, *Pouvoir et finance en Méditerranée pré-moderne: Le deuxième etat mamlouk et le commerce de épices (1382–1517)* (Barcelona: CSIC, 2009); and Georg Christ, *Trading Conflicts: Venetian Merchants and Mamluk Officials in Late Medieval Alexandria* (Leiden: Brill, 2012).

92. See Walter J. Fischel, "Über die Gruppe der Karimi-Kaufleute: Ein Beitrag zur Geschichte des Orienthandels Ägyptens unter den Mamluken," *Studia Arabica* 1 (1937): 65–82; Fischel, "The Spice Trade in Mamluk Egypt: A Contribution to the Economic History of the Medieval Islam," *Journal of the Social and Economic History of the Orient* 1 (1958): 157–174; Gaston Wiet, *Les merchands d'épices sous les sultans mamlouks* (Cairo: Editions des Cahiers d'histoire égyptienne, 1955); Eliyahu Ashtor, "The Karimi Merchants," *Journal of the Royal Asiatic Society* 1956, 45–56. D. Goitein, "The Beginnings of the Karim Merchants and the Character of Their Organization," in *Studies in Islamic History and Institutions* (Leiden: Brill, 1968), 351–360; Subhi Labib, "Les merchands Karimis en Orient et sur l'océan Indien," in Mollat, *Sociétés et companies,* 209–214; and Lucian Reinfandt, "Kārimī-Kaufleute als Stifter," in *Studia Eurasiatica. Kieler Festschrift für Hermann Kulke zum 65. Geburtstag,* ed. Stephan Conermann and Jan Kusber (Schenefeld: EB-Verlag, 2003), 369–382.

93. Evidently, the Karimi merchants also included Jews and Christians. See Ashtor, "Karimi Merchants," 55.

94. On Alexandria as an entrepôt for spices, see Éric Vallet Eric, "Le marché des épices d'Alexandrie et les mutations du grand commerce de la mer Rouge (XIVe–XVe siècle)," *Alexandrie Médiévale* 4 (2011): 213–228. On medieval Alexandria in general, see the four studies in the series *Alexandrie médiévale* published by the Institut français d'archéologie orientale du Caire (IFAO) in 1998, 2002, 2008, and 2011.

95. Barbosa, *Book of Duarte Barbosa,* 1:42–43.

96. John L. Meloy, *Imperial Power and Maritime Trade: Mecca and Cairo in the Later Middle Ages* (Chicago: Middle East Documentation Center, 2010).

97. Ibid., 5.

98. The standard work on the Rasulids is Éric Vallet, *L'Arabie marchande: État et commerce sous les sultans Rasūlides du Yémen (626–858 / 1229–1454)* (Paris: Publications de la Sorbonne, 2010).

99. Barbosa, *Book of Duarte Barbosa,* 1:53–55.

100. On the flow of commodities between Egypt and Aden, see Éric Vallet, "Entre deux 'mondes': Les produits du commerce égyptien à Aden (XIIIe–XVe siècle)," in *La configuration des réseaux,* vol. 1 of *Espaces et réseaux en Méditerranée VIe–XVIe siècle,* ed. Damien Coulon, Christophe Picard, and Dominique Valérian (Paris: Éditions Bouchène, 2007), 204–236.

101. See also Éric Vallet, "1424—Les navires de Calicut se détournent d'Aden au profit de Djedda, L'avènement d'une nouvelle route des épices," in *Histoire du monde au XVe siècle,* ed. Patrick Boucheron et al. (Paris: Fayard, 2009), 325–328.

102. The following observations are based on the study by Éric Vallet, "Les sultans rasûlides du Yémen, protecteurs des communautés musulmanes de l'Inde (VIIe–VIIIe / XIIe–XIVe siècle)," *Annales Islamologiques* 41 (2007): 149–176.

103. A French translation is given in Vallet, "Les sultans rasûlides," 165–169.

104. See Alka Patel, *Building Communities in Gujarat: Architecture and Society during the Twelfth through Fourteenth Centuries* (Leiden: Brill, 2004).

105. See Vallet, "Les sultans rasûlides," 153–154.

106. Ibid., 155.

107. Ibid., 156–157.

108. A French translation of this text appears in ibid., 169–171.

109. Ibid., 157–158.

110. Ibid., 159–161.

111. Ibid., 161–163.

112. Ibid., 163–164.

113. Ibid., 164.

114. The collection of articles by the Indian economic historian Ashin Das Gupta, in *The World of the Indian Ocean Merchant, 1500–1800* (New Delhi: Oxford University Press, 2001), provided the foundation for the following section.

115. On the traders and their networks, see especially Denys Lombard and Jean Aubin, eds., *Marchands et hommes d'affaires asiatiques dans l'Océan Indien et la Mer Chine 13e–20e siècles* (Paris: Éditions de l'Ecole des hautes études en sciences sociales, 1988); Ashin Das Gupta, *Merchants of Maritime India, 1500–1800* (Aldershot, UK: Variorum, 1994); Sinnappah Arasaratnam, *Maritime India in the Seventeenth Century* (New Delhi: Oxford University Press, 1994), 173–219; and R. J. Barendse, *The Arabian Seas: The Indian Ocean World of the Seventeenth Century* (New York: M. E. Sharpe, 2002), 152–196.

116. On the trade between South and Southeast Asia and the Far East, which has not been within the remit of this chapter, see, for instance, the anthology by Roderich Ptak and Dietmar Rothermund, eds., *Emporia, Commodities and Entrepreneurs in Asian Maritime Trade (1400–1700)* (Wiesbaden: Steiner, 1991).

117. The commercial ports on the Indian Ocean have been the focus of research for some time now: Barendse, *Arabian Seas,* 13–86; Frank Broeze, ed., *Brides of the Sea: Port Cities of Asia from the 16th to the 20th Centuries* (Kensington, Australia: New South Wales University Press, 1989); Indu Banga, ed., *Ports and Their Hinterlands in India, 1700–1950* (New Delhi: Manohar, 1992); Arasaratnam, *Maritime India,* 1–32; Frank Broeze, ed., *Gateways of Asia: Port Cities of Asia*

from the 13th to the 20th Centuries (London: Keegan Paul International, 1997); and Michael N. Pearson, *Port Cities and Intruders: The Swahili Coast, India, and Portugal in the Early Modern Era* (Baltimore: Johns Hopkins University Press, 1998).

118. Trade along the East African Swahili Coast is sketched in John Middleton, *The World of the Swahili: An African Mercantile Civilization* (New Haven, CT: Yale University Press, 1992).

119. On Cambay, see Arasaratnam and Ray, *Masulipatnam and Cambay*.

120. See also Holden Furber, *Rival Empires of Trade in the Orient, 1600–1800* (Minneapolis: University of Minnesota Press, 1976), 230–263.

121. On pilgrimage from an Indian Muslim perspective, see Michael N. Pearson, *Pilgrimage to Mecca: The India Experience* (Princeton, NJ: Princeton University Press, 1996).

122. Piracy in the Indian Ocean has not been a well-researched area of study so far. For a general introduction to the subject, see Robert Bohn, *Die Piraten* (Munich: Beck, 2003). A vivid case study in piracy is given by Arne Bialuschewski, *Piratenleben: Die abenteuerlichen Fahrten des Seeräubers Richards Sievers* (Berlin: Ullstein, 1999).

123. See Ashin Das Gupta, *Indian Merchants and the Decline of Surat, c. 1700–1750* (Wiesbaden: Steiner, 1979).

124. The following sections are based on Tapan Raychaudhuri, "Inland Trade," in Raychaudhuri and Habib, *Cambridge Economic History,* 325–359.

125. See Arasaratnam, *Maritime India,* 54–89.

126. On trade in Bengal and Malabar, see ibid., 90–116 and 149–172.

127. The standard work on this topic is Giancarlo Casale, *The Ottoman Age of Exploration* (Oxford: Oxford University Press, 2010). Just as important are studies by Salih Özbaran: "The Ottoman Turks and the Portuguese in the Persian Gulf, 1534–1581," *Journal of Asian History* 6, no. 1 (Spring 1972): 45–88; *The Ottoman Response to European Expansion: Studies on Ottoman-Portuguese Relations in the Indian Ocean and Ottoman Administration in the Arab Lands during the Sixteenth Century* (Istanbul: Isis Press, 1994); *Portuguese Encounters with the World in the Age of the Discoveries: The Near and Middle East* (London: Ashgate, 2008); and *Ottoman Expansion towards the Indian Ocean in the 16th Century* (Istanbul: Istanbul Bilgi University Press, 2009).

128. Many studies are available on the Portuguese presence in the Indian Ocean. The following serve admirably as introductions: Vitorino Magalhães-Godinho, *L'économie de l'empire portugais aux XVe et XVIe siècles: Ports—routes—trafic* (Paris: S.E.V.P.E.N., 1969); Roderich Ptak, ed., *Portuguese Asia: Aspects in History and Economic History, Sixteenth and Seventeenth Centuries* (Wiesbaden: Steiner, 1987); Michael N. Pearson, *The Portuguese in India* (Cambridge: Cambridge University Press, 1987); Sanjay Subrahmanyam, *The Portuguese Empire in Asia, 1500–1700: A Political and Economic History* (London: Longman, 1993); Rudi Matthee and Jorge Flores, eds., *Portugal, the Persian Gulf and Safavid Persia* (Leuven: Peeters, 2011).

129. See Cengiz Orhonlu, "Hint Kaptanlığı ve Piri Reis" [The Indian Captain and Piri Reis], *Belleten* 34 (1967): 235–254; Andrew Hess, "Piri Reis and the Ottoman Response to the Voyages of Discovery," *Terrae Incognitae* 6 (1974): 19–37; Svat Soucek, *Piri Reis and Turkish Map Making after Columbus* (Oxford: Oxford University Press, 1996); and Svat Soucek, "Piri Reis and the Ottoman Discovery of the Great Discoveries," *Studia Islamica* 79 (1994): 121–142.

130. There is a very good article on Selman Reis by İdris Bostan in *Türkiye Diyanet Vakfı İslâm Ansiklopedisi*, vol. 36, *Sakal-Sevm* (Istanbul: Türkiye Diyanet Vakfı, 2009), cols. 444a–446b.

131. See Ebru Turan, "The Sultan's Favorite: Ibrahim Paşa and the Making of the Ottoman Universal Sovereignty in the Reign of Sultan Süleyman, 1516–1526" (PhD diss., University of Chicago, 2007).

132. See Faisal Alkanderei, "Selman Reis and His Report of 931/1525," *Arab Historical Review for Ottoman Studies* 7–8 (1993): 103–126.

133. On this phase, see Casale, *Ottoman Age of Exploration,* 117–151.

134. This is described at length in Giancarlo Casale, "Global Politics in the 1580s: A Canal, Twenty Thousand Cannibals, and an Ottoman Plot to Rule the World," *Journal of World History* 18, no. 3 (2007): 267–296.

135. On the Battle of Lepanto, see Andrew Hess, "The Battle of Lepanto and Its Place in Mediterranean History," *Past and Present* 57 (1972): 53–73; and also the monographs by Angus Konstam, *Lepanto 1571: The Greatest Naval Battle of the Renaissance* (Oxford: Osprey, 2003); Hugh Bicheno, *Crescent and Cross: The Battle of Lepanto, 1571* (London: Phoenix, 2004); and Niccolò Capponi, *Victory of the West: The Story of the Battle of Lepanto* (London: Macmillan, 2006).

136. Among the many biographies of Philip II, the following is worthy of mention: Friedrich Edelmayer, *Philipp II: Biographie eines Weltherrschers* (Stuttgart: Kohlhammer, 2009).

137. On this period of transformation, see Suraiya Faroqhi, "Crisis and Change, 1590–1699," in *Economic and Social History of the Ottoman Empire, 1300–1914,* ed. Halil Inalcik and Donald Quataert (Cambridge: Cambridge University Press, 1995), 2:411–623.

138. The following observations are based on Rudi Matthee, *The Politics of Trade in Safavid Iran: Silk for Silver, 1600–1730* (Cambridge: Cambridge University Press, 1999). Matthee points to Marshal Hodgson, *The Venture of Islam* (Chicago: University of Chicago Press, 1974), here 2:330–335. On Safavid trade, also see Willem Floor, *The Persian Textile Industry in Historical Perspective, 1500–1925* (Paris: Harmattan, 1999).

139. For introductions to the Safavid period, see Roger Savory, *Iran under the Safavids* (Cambridge: Cambridge University Press, 1980); and Andrew J. Newman, *Safavid Iran: Rebirth of a Persian Empire* (London: Tauris, 2006). See also the relevant sections in Hans-Robert Roemer, *Persien auf dem Weg in die Neuzeit: Iranische Geschichte von 1350–1750* (Stuttgart: Steiner, 1989); and David Morgan, *Medieval Persia* (London: Longman, 1988).

140. See Jean-Louis Bacqué-Grammont, *Les Ottomans, les Safavides et leur voisins: Contributions à l'histoire des relations internationales dans l'Orient islamique des 1514 à 1524* (Leiden: Brill, 1987); and more generally Stephen F. Dale, *The Muslim Empires of the Ottomans, Safavids, and Mughals* (Cambridge: Cambridge University Press, 2010).

141. On Bursa as a trade hub, see Halil Inalcik, "Bursa and the Commerce of the Levant," *Journal of the Economic and Social History of the Orient* 3 (1960): 131–147.

142. On the trade network of the Armenians, see Edmund Herzig, "The Armenian Merchants of New Julfa, Isfahan: A Study in Pre-Modern Asian Trade" (PhD diss., Oxford University, 1991); and Ina Baghdiantz, "The Armenian Merchants of New Julfa: Some Aspects of Their International Trade in the Late Seventeenth Century" (PhD diss., Columbia University, 1993); Sebouh David Aslanian, *From the Indian Ocean to the Mediterranean: The Global Trade*

Networks of Armenian Merchants from New Julfa (Berkeley: University of California Press, 2011).

143. On trade in the Levant, see Eliyahu Ashtor, *Levant Trade in the Later Middle Ages* (Princeton, NJ: Princeton University Press, 1983).

144. Artur Attman, *The Russian and Polish Markets in International Trade, 1500–1650* (Göteborg: Institute of Economic History of Gothenburg University, 1973) remains a seminal work on this subject. See likewise Paul Buscovitch, *The Merchants of Moscow, 1580–1650* (Cambridge: Cambridge University Press, 1980); Rudi Matthee, "Anti-Ottoman Politics and Transit Rights: The Seventeenth-Century Trade in Silk between Safavid Iran and Muscovy," *Cahiers du Mond Russe (et Soviétique)* 35 (1994): 739–762.

145. On Hormuz as a trade hub, see Jean Aubin, "Le royaume d'Ormuz au début du XVIe siècle," *Mare Luso Indicum* 2 (1973): 77–179.

146. For a comprehensive bibliography on Portuguese–Safavid relations, see Willem Floor and Farhad Hakimzadeh, *The Hispano-Portuguese Empire and Its Contacts with Safavid Persia, the Kingdom of Hormuz and Yarubid Oman from 1489 to 1720: A Bibliography of Printed Publications* (Leuven: Peeters, 2007). See also Jorge M. Flores and Rudi Matthee, eds., *Portugal, the Persian Gulf and Safavid Persia* (Leuven: Peeters, 2011).

147. See Rudi Matthee, "Caravan Trade in Safavid Iran (First Half of the 17th Century)," in *Études safavides*, ed. Jean Calmard (Paris: Institut français de recherche en Iran, 1993), 305–318.

148. See the subsection that follows.

149. See, for example, Marie A. P. Meilink-Roelofsz, "The Dutch and the Persian Silk Trade," in *Safavid Persia: The History and Politics of an Islamic Society*, ed. Charles Melville (London: Tauris, 1996), 323–368; Ronald W. Ferrier, "The Terms and Conditions under Which English Trade Was Transacted with Safavid Persia," *Bulletin of the School of Oriental and African Studies* 49 (1986): 48–66.

150. Matthee, *Politics of Trade*, 91–119, discusses this topic.

151. On Shah Sulayman's policies toward the Ottomans, see Rudi Matthee, "Iran's Ottoman Policy under Shah Sulayman (1666/1076–1695/1105)," in *Iran and Iranian Studies: Papers in Honor of Iraj Afshar*, ed. Kambiz Eslami (Princeton, NJ: Zagrois, 1998), 148–177.

152. See Rudi Matthee, "Administrative Stability and Change in Late 17th-Century Iran: The Case of Shaykh 'Ali Khan Zanganah (1669–1689)," *International Journal of Middle East Studies* 26 (1994): 77–98.

153. Matthee, *Politics of Trade*, 235–237.

154. The following works are good general overviews of Portuguese Asia: Charles R. Boxer, *The Portuguese Seaborne Empire, 1415–1825* (London: Hutchinson, 1969); ibid., *Portuguese Conquest and Commerce in Southern Asia, 1500–1750* (London: Variorum Reprints, 1985); Michael N. Pearson, *The Portuguese in India* (Cambridge: Cambridge University Press, 1987); Sanjay Subrahmanyam, *The Portuguese Empire in Asia, 1500–1700: A Political and Economic History* (London: Longman, 1993); James C. Boyajjan, *Portuguese Trade in Asia under the Habsburgs, 1580–1640* (Baltimore: Johns Hopkins University Press, 1993); Barendse, *Arabian Seas*, 299–380; and Anthony R. Disney, *The Portuguese Empire* (Cambridge: Cambridge University Press, 2009). For a wide-ranging study of European encroachment in Asia, see Wolfgang Reinhard,

Die Alte Welt bis 1818, vol. 1 of *Geschichte der europäischen Expansion* (Stuttgart: Kohlhammer, 1983). Also of interest here is Kenneth McPherson and Sanjay Subrahmanyam, eds., *From Biography to History: Essays in the History of Portuguese Asia (1500–1800)* (New Delhi: Transbooks, 2005).

155. See Kallor M. Mathew, *History of the Portuguese Navigation in India, 1497–1600* (Delhi: Mittal Publications, 1988).

156. On Goa, see Catarina M. Santos, *Goa é a chave de toda a Índia: Perfil político da capital do Estado da Índia, 1505–1570* [Goa is the key to the whole of India: The political profile of the Estado da Índia, 1505–1570] (Lisbon: Comissão Nacional para as Comemorações des dos Descobrimentos Portugueses, 1999).

157. See Kuzhippalli Skaria Mathew, *Portuguese and the Sultanate of Gujarat, 1500–1573* (New Delhi: Mittal Publications, 1986), 25–35.

158. This system is described by Kuzhippalli Skaria Mathew, "Trade in the Indian Ocean and the Portuguese System of Cartazes," in *The First Portuguese Colonial Empire,* ed. Malyn Newitt (Exeter, UK: University of Exeter Press, 1986), 69–83.

159. See Geneviève Bouchon, "Glimpses of the Beginning of the *Carreira Da India (1500–1518),*" in *Indo-Portuguese History: Old Issues—New Questions,* ed. Teotonio R. de Souza (New Delhi: Concept, 1985), 40–55; Glenn J. Ames, "The Carreira da India, 1668–1682," *Journal of European Economic History* 20 (1991): 7–28.

160. See Reinhard, *Geschichte der europäischen Expansion,* 1:90.

161. Ibid., 1:103. The financing of the Estado da India is presented in exhaustive detail in two works by Vitorino Magalhães-Godinho: *L'économie de l'empire portugais aux XVe et XVIe siècles* (Paris: S.E.V.P.E.N., 1969) and *Les finances de l'État portugais des Indes orientales 1517–1635: Materiaux por une étude structurale et conjuncturelle* (Paris: Fundação Calouste Gulbenkian—Centro Cultural Purtuguês, 1982). Graphs showing the flow of precious metals and money appear in Reinhard, *Geschichte der europäischen Expansion,* 1:101.

162. See George Winius, "The 'Shadow Empire' of Goa: The Bay of Bengal," *Itinerario* 7, no. 2 (1983): 83–101.

163. Reinhard, *Geschichte der europäischen Expansion,* 1:106. See Anthony R. Disney, *Twilight of the Pepper Empire: Portuguese Trade in Southwest India in the Early Seventeenth Century* (Cambridge, MA: Harvard University Press, 1978).

164. On the incorporation of the East African trading area, see Malyn D. Newitt, "East Africa and Indian Ocean Trade, 1500–1800," in *India and the Indian Ocean, 1500–1800,* ed. Ashin Das Gupta and Michael N. Pearson (Calcutta: Oxford University Press, 1987), 201–223.

165. See Kuzhippalli Skaria Mathew, *Portuguese Trade with India in the Sixteenth Century* (New Delhi: Manohar, 1983). On Cochin, see Jean Aubin, "L'apprentissage de l'Inde: Cochin, 1503–1515," *Moyen Orient & Océan Indien, XVIe–XIXe s.* 4 (1987): 1–96; plus the extensive monograph by Pius Malekandathil, *Portuguese Cochin and the Maritime Trade of India, 1500–1663* (New Delhi: Manohar, 2001).

166. On the connections to Vijayanagara, see Maria Augusta Lima Cruz, "Notes on Portuguese Relations with Vijyanagara, 1500–1565," in *Sinners and Saints: The Successors of Vasco da Gama,* ed. Sanjay Subrahmanyam (Oxford: Oxford University Press, 1995), 13–39.

167. See Jorge M. Flores, *Os Portugueses e o Mar de Ceilão, Trato, diplomacia e guerra, 1498–1543* [The Portuguese and the Sea of Ceylon: Commerce, diplomacy and war, 1498–1543] (Lisbon: Edições Cosmos, 1998).

168. See Reinhard, *Geschichte der europäischen Expansion*, 1:60.

169. These statistics are taken from the new edition of Reinhard, *Geschichte der europäischen Expansion,* which is due to appear in 2015. Wolfgang Reinhard kindly allowed me to consult part of his manuscript.

170. Good general overviews of the activities of the European trading companies are given in Niels Steensgaard, *The Asian Trade Revolution of the Seventeenth Century: The East India Companies and the Decline of the Caravan Trade* (Chicago: University of Chicago Press, 1974); Furber, *Rival Empires;* Leonard Blussé and Femme S. Gaastra, eds., *Companies and Trade: Essays in Overseas Trading Compagnies during the Ancient Régime* (Leiden: Leiden University Press, 1981); Ashin Das Gupta and Michael N. Pearson, *India and the Indian Ocean, 1500–1800* (Calcutta: Oxford University Press, 1987); Om Prakash, *European Commercial Enterprise in Pre-Colonial India* (Aldershot, UK: Variorum, 1998); Jürgen G. Nagel, *Abenteuer Fernhandel: Die Ostindienkompanien* (Darmstadt: Wissenschaftliche Buchgesellschaft, 2007); Om Prakash, ed., *European Commercial Expansion in Early Modern Asia* (Aldershot, UK: Variorum, 1997).

171. On trade on the Coromandel Coast, see Sinnappah Arasaratnam, *Merchants, Companies and Commerce on the Coromandel Coast, 1650–1740* (New Delhi: Oxford University Press, 1986).

172. See Nagel, *Abenteuer Fernhandel,* 110–111.

173. Research on the VOC is complex and diffuse. Among the many general studies of the company's activities, the following are to be recommended: Charles R. Boxer, *The Dutch Seaborne Empire: 1600–1800* (London: Hutchinson, 1965); Femme S. Gaastra, *The Dutch East India Company: Expansion and Decline* (Zutphen: Walburg, 2003); Om Prakash, *Precious Metals and Commerce: The Dutch East India Company in the Indian Ocean Trade* (Aldershot, UK: Variorum, 1994); Els M. Jacobs, *De Vereenigde Oost-Indische Compagnie* (Utrecht: Teleac, 1997); Jan de Vries and A. van der Woude, *The First Modern Economy: Success, Failure, and Perseverance of the Dutch Economy, 1500–1815* (Cambridge: Cambridge University Press, 1997); Harms Stevens, *Dutch Enterprise and the VOC, 1602–1799* (Zutphen: Walburg, 1998); Barendse, *Arabian Seas,* 381–422; Menno Witteveen, *Een onderneming van landsbelang: De oprichting van de Vereenigde Oost-Indische Compagnie in 1602* [An undertaking of national importance: The founding of the Vereenigde Oost-Indische Compagnie] (Amsterdam: Amsterdam University Press Salomé, 2002). The principal work on the economic history of the VOC is still Kristof Glamann, *Dutch Asiatic Trade, 1620–1740* (Copenhagen: Danish Science Press, 1958).

174. See especially Hugo s'Jacob, *The Rajas of Cochin, 1663–1720: Kings, Chiefs, and the Dutch East India Company* (New Delhi: Munshiram Manoharlar, 2000).

175. Many studies are available on the history of the East India Company. The following can be recommended: Philip Lawson, *The East India Company: A History* (London: Longman, 1987); K. N. Chaudhuri, *The English East India Company: The Study of an Early Joint-Stock Company, 1600–1640* (London: Cass, 1965); Sudipta Sen, *Empire of Free Trade: The East India Company and the Making of the Colonial Marketplace* (Philadelphia: University of Philadelphia Press,

1998); H. V. Bowen, Margaret Lincoln, and Nigel Rigby, eds., *The Worlds of the East India Company* (Woodbridge: Boydell, 2002). See also Barendse, *Arabian Seas,* 424–459.

176. See Michael Strachan, *Sir Thomas Roe, 1581–1644: A Life* (Salisbury, UK: M. Russell, 1989).

177. See Nagel, *Abenteuer Fernhandel,* 76.

178. On the role of Bengal in the history of the East India Company, see Sukumar Battacharya, *The East India Company and the Economy of Bengal from 1704 to 1740* (Calcutta: Mukhopadhyay, 1969); Susil Chaudhuri, *Trade and Commercial Organisation in Bengal, 1650–1720* (New Delhi: Manohar, 1975); and P. J. Marshall, *Bengal, the British Bridgehead: Eastern India, 1740–1828* (Cambridge: Cambridge University Press, 1987). An overview can be found in Sanjay Subrahmanyam, *Improvising Empire: Portuguese Trade and Settlement in the Bay of Bengal, 1500–1700* (New Delhi: Oxford University Press, 1990).

179. See Nagel, *Abenteuer Fernhandel,* 103–104.

180. Ibid., 80.

181. The standard work on the French involvement in South Asia remains Philippe Haudrère, *La compagnie française des Indes au XVIIIe siècle (1719–1795),* 4 vols. (Paris: Librairie de l'Inde, 1989). On Danish mercantile activity in India, see Ole Feldbeak, *India Trade under the Danish Flag, 1772–1808: European Enterprise and Anglo-Indian Remittance and Trade* (Lund: Studentlitteratur, 1969); Martin Krieger, *Kaufleute, Seeräuber und Diplomaten: Der dänische Handel auf dem Indischen Ozean (1620–1868)* (Cologne: Böhlau, 1989); Stephan Diller, *Die Dänen in Indien, Südostasien und China, 1620–1845* (Wiesbaden: Harrassowitz, 1999).

182. See Artur Attman, *The Bullion Flow between Europe and the East, 1000–1750* (Göteborg: Kungl. Vetenskap—och Vitterhets-Samhället, 1981) John F. Richards, ed., *Precious Metals in the Later Medieval and Early Modern World* (Durham, NC: Carolina Academic Press, 1983), 397–495.

183. See Hameeda Hossain, *The Company Weavers of Bengal: The East India Company and the Organisation of the Textile Production in Bengal, 1750–1813* (New Delhi: Oxford University Press, 1968); Sergio Aiolfi, *Calicos und gedrucktes Zeug: Die Entwicklung der englischen Textilveredlung und der Tuchhandel der East India Company, 1650–1750* (Stuttgart: Steiner, 1987); Prasannan Parthasarathi, *The Transition to a Colonial Economy: Weavers, Merchants, and Kings in South India, 1720–1800* (Cambridge: Cambridge University Press, 2001); Giorgio Riello and Prasannan Parthasarathi, eds., *The Spinning World: A Global History of Cotton Textiles, 1200–1850* (Oxford: Oxford University Press, 2009); Giorgio Riello and Tirthankar Roy, eds., *How India Clothed the World: The World of South Asian Textiles, 1500–1850* (Leiden: Brill, 2009).

184. Reinhard Schulze, "Das Warten auf die Moderne: Die Islamische Welt," in *Die Welt im 18. Jahrhundert,* ed. Bernd Hausberger and Jean-Paul Lehners (Vienna: Mandelbaum, 2011), 243–272, at 244. Schulze in fact made this observation on the Near East and Africa, but it applies equally to South Asia.

185. Michael Mann, "Ein langes Jahrhundert. Südasien," in Hausberger and Lehners, *Die Welt im 18. Jahrhunder,* 274–301, here 276.

186. This is the conclusion reached by Stephen Blake, "The Patrimonial-Bureaucratic Empire of the Mughals," *Journal of Asian Studies* 39 (1979): 77–94.

187. See Michael Mann, *Geschichte Indiens: Vom 18. bis zum 21. Jahrhundert* (Paderborn: Schöningh, 2005), 37–38.

188. On Nadir Shah, see Ernest Tucker, "Art: Nader Shah," in *Encyclopaedia Iranica,* http://www.iranicaonline.org/articles/nader-shah.

189. Though old, the study by Lawrence Lockhart, *Nader Shah: A Critical Study Based Mainly upon Contemporary Sources* (London: Luzac, 1938), is nevertheless still useful.

190. See Gordon, *The Marathas, 1600–1818,* 114–159. At greater length, see Stewart Gordon, *Marathas, Marauders, and State Formation in Eighteenth-Century India* (New Delhi: Oxford University Press, 1994).

191. A short but very good introduction to the Sikhs is Eleanor Nesbitt, *Sikhism: A Very Short Introduction* (Oxford: Oxford University Press, 2005). An extensive treatment of the period under consideration here is given in Hari Ram Gupta, *Evolution of Sikh Confederacies (1708–1769),* vol. 2 of *History of the Sikhs,* 4th ed. (Delhi: Munshiram Manoharlar, 1992).

192. See Richard B. Barnett, *North India between Empires: Awadh, the Mughals, and the British, 1720–1801* (New Delhi: Manohar, 1987); Muzaffar Alam, *The Crisis of Empire in Mughal North India: Awadh and the Punjab, 1707–48* (New Delhi: Oxford University Press, 1986); Michael H. Fisher, *A Clash of Cultures: Awadh, the British, and the Mughals* (Delhi: Manohar, 1987); Surendra Mohan, *Awadh under the Nawabs: Politics, Culture and Communal Relations, 1722–1856* (Delhi: Manohar, 1997).

193. On the development of Bengal in the first half of the eighteenth century, see Richard M. Eaton, *The Rise of Islam and the Bengal Frontier, 1204–1760* (Berkeley: University of California Press, 1993); Marshall, *Bengal;* John R. McLane, *Land and Local Kingship in Eighteenth-Century Bengal* (Cambridge: Cambridge University Press, 1993). For the subsequent period, see Michael Mann, *Bengalen im Umbruch: Die Herausbildung des britischen Kolonialstaates, 1754–1793* (Stuttgart: Steiner, 2000).

194. On the Battle of Plassey, see Sushil Chaudhury, *The Prelude to Empire: Plassey Revolution of 1757* (New Delhi: Manohar, 2000).

195. See M. A. Nayeem, *Mughal Administration of Deccan under Nizamul Mulk Asaf Jah (1720–1748 AD)* (Bombay: Jaico Publishing House, 1985); Munis D. Faruqui, "At Empire's End: The Nizam, Hyderabad and Eighteenth-Century India," *Modern Asian Studies* 43 (2009): 5–43.

196. See Adapa Satyanarayana, *History of the Wodeyars of Mysore (1610–1748)* (Mysore: Directorate of Archeology and Museums, 1996).

197. See, for example, Joachim Radkau, *Nature and Power: A Global History of the Environment* (Cambridge: Cambridge University Press, 2008); John F. Richards, *The Unending Frontier: An Environmental History of the Early Modern World* (Berkeley: University of California Press, 2003); Sylvia Hahn and Reinhold Reith, eds., *Umwelt-Geschichte: Arbeitsfelder, Forschungsansätze, Perspektiven* (Munich: Oldenbourg, 2001).

198. See Gudrun-Axeli Knapp, "Traveling Theories: Anmerkungen zur neueren Diskussion über 'Race, Class, and Gender,'" *Österreichische Zeitschrift für Geschichtswissenschaften* 16, no. 1 (2005): 88–110; Mieke Bal, *Travelling Concepts in the Humanities: A Rough Guide* (Toronto: University of Toronto Press, 2002); Ute Frietsch, "Travelling Concepts," in *Über die Praxis des kulturwissenschaftlichen Arbeitens: Ein Handwörterbuch,* ed. Ute Frietsch and Jörg Rogge (Bielefeld: Transcript, 2013), 393–398; Birgit Neumann and Ansgar Nünning, eds., *Travelling Concepts for the Study of Culture* (Berlin: de Gruyter, 2012).

199. The two following sections derive from Stephan Conermann, "Unter dem Einfluss des Monsuns: Der Handel zwischen Arabien und Südasien," in *Damals: Das aktuelle Magazin für Geschichte und Kultur, Fernhandel in Antike und Mittelalter* (Darmstadt: Wissenschaftliche Buchgesellschaft, 2008), 61–80.

200. R. J. Barendse, "Trade and State in the Arabian Seas: A Survey from the Fifteenth to the Eighteenth Century," *Journal of World History* 11, no. 2 (2000): 273–275.

4. Southeast Asia and Oceania

1. See Harald Uhlig, *Südostasien* (Frankfurt am Main: Fischer, 1988); and Hanns J. Buchholz, *Australien—Neuseeland—Südpazifik* (Frankfurt am Main: Fischer, 1984).

2. Peter Boomgaard, *Southeast Asia: An Environmental History* (Santa Barbara: ABC-CLIO, 2007), 20.

3. Michaela Appel, *Ozeanien: Weltbilder der Südsee* (Munich: Staatliches Museum für Völkerkunde, 2005), 14.

4. Johannes Voigt, *Geschichte Australiens* (Stuttgart: Kröner, 1988), 3–6.

5. Boomgaard, *Southeast Asia,* 18–20.

6. Anthony Reid, *Expansion and Crisis*, vol. 2 of *Southeast Asia in the Age of Commerce, 1450–1680* (New Haven, CT: Yale University Press, 1993), 291–298; Victor Lieberman, *Integration on the Mainland,* vol. 1 of *Strange Parallels: Southeast Asia in Global Context, c. 800–1830* (Cambridge: Cambridge University Press, 2003), 1:49; Boomgaard, *Southeast Asia,* 91–105.

7. Boomgaard, *Southeast Asia,* 19–20, 77.

8. Ibid., 3, 6, 76.

9. See Frank M. LeBar, Gerald C. Hickey, and John K. Musgrave, *Ethnic Groups of Mainland Southeast Asia* (New Haven, CT: Human Relations Area Files Press, 1964); Frank M. LeBar, *Ethnic Groups of Insular Southeast Asia,* 2 vols. (New Haven, CT: Human Relations Area Files Press, 1972–1975); Donald Denoon, Philippa Mein-Smith, and Marivic Wyndham, *A History of Australia, New Zealand, and the Pacific* (Oxford: Blackwell, 2000).

10. R. L. Heathcote, *Australia* (Essex, UK: Longman, 1994), 56–60.

11. Hans-Dieter Kubitschek, *Südostasien: Völker und Kulturen* (Berlin: Akademie, 1984), 94.

12. A key text on rice growing in Southeast Asia is Lucien M. Hanks, *Rice and Man: Agricultural Ecology in Southeast Asia* (Chicago: Aldine, 1972); a more general text on the significance of rice in the region is Francesca Bray, *The Rice Economies: Technology and Development in Asian Societies* (Berkeley: University of California Press, 1994).

13. Thomas Beck, "Monopol und Genozid: Die Muskatnußproduktion auf den Banda-Inseln," in *Gewürze: Produktion, Handel und Konsum in der Frühen Neuzeit,* ed. Markus A. Denzel (St. Katharinen: Scripta Mercaturae, 1999), 71–90; Gerrit J. Knaap, *Kruidnagelen en christenen: De Verenigde Oostindische Compangnie en de bevolking van Ambon 1656–1696* (Dordrecht: Foris, 1987), 228–259.

14. Anthony Reid, *The Lands below the Winds,* vol. 1 of *Southeast Asia in the Age of Commerce, 1450–1680* (New Haven, CT: Yale University Press, 1988), 14; by 2000, the figure was 580 million.

15. Antonio de Morga, *Sucesos de las Islas Filipinas (México 1609),* trans. and ed. J. P. P. Cummins (Cambridge: Cambridge University Press, 1971), 271–274.

16. John N. Miksic, "Die frühe Stadtentwicklung Indonesiens und ihre Auswirkung auf Gesellschaft, Technologie und Kunstschaffen," in *Versunkene Königreiche Indonesiens,* ed. Arne Eggebrecht and Eva Eggebrecht (Mainz: von Zabern, 1995), 93–111.

17. Jürgen G. Nagel, "Kota, Kampung und fließende Grenze: Einige Überlegungen zur frühneuzeitlichen Stadtgeschichte Indonesiens," in *Das Wichtigste ist der Mensch": Festschrift für Klaus Gerteis zum 60. Geburtstag,* ed. Angela Giebmeyer and Helga Schnabel-Schüle (Mainz: von Zabern, 2000), 153–180.

18. Reid, *Southeast Asia in the Age of Commerce,* 2:62–131; statistical data are to be found on 2:69 and 2:71–72.

19. Jürgen G. Nagel, *Der Schlüssel zu den Molukken: Makassar und die Handelsstrukturen des Malaiischen Archipels im 17. und 18. Jahrhundert—Eine exemplarische Studie* (Hamburg: Kovač, 2003), 296–297.

20. Reid, *Southeast Asia in the Age of Commerce,* 2:90.

21. Dietmar Rothermund, "Asian Emporia and European Bridgeheads," in *Emporia, Commodities and Entrepreneurs in Asian Maritime Trade, c. 1400–1750,* ed. Roderich Ptak and Dietmar Rothermund (Stuttgart: Steiner, 1991), 3–8.

22. The concept of the "city-state," well established in the historical city geography of Southeast Asia, denotes a combination of a bureaucratic core of highly centralized institutional authority with a more or less informally controlled surrounding region; see Peter J. M. Nas, "The Early Indonesian Town: Rise and Decline of the City-State and Its Capital," in *The Indonesian City: Studies in Urban Development and Planning,* ed. Peter J. M. Nas (Dordrecht: Foris, 1986), 18–36.

23. For a fundamental treatment of the taxonomy of diaspora groups, see Robin Cohen, *Global Diasporas: An Introduction* (London: UCL Press, 1997).

24. James N. Anderson and Walter T. Vorster, "In Search of Melaka's Hinterland: Beyond the Entrepôt," in *The Rise and Growth of the Colonial Port City in Asia,* ed. Dilip K. Basu (Lanham, MD: University Press of America, 1985), 1–6.

25. Nas, "Early Indonesian Town."

26. D. R. Sar Desai, "The Portuguese Administration of Malacca, 1511–1641," *Journal of Southeast Asian Studies* 10 (1969): 501–512; Malcolm Dunn, *Kampf um Melaka: Eine wirtschaftsgeschichtliche Studie über den portugiesischen und niederländischen Kolonialismus in Südostasien* (Wiesbaden: Steiner, 1984).

27. On Batavian society, see Pauline Milone, " 'Indische' Culture and Its Relationship to Urban Life," *Comparative Studies in Society and History* 9 (1966–1967): 407–426; and Jean G. Taylor, *The Social World of Batavia: European and Eurasian in Dutch Asia* (Madison: University of Wisconsin Press, 1983).

28. David E. Sopher, *The Sea Nomads: A Study of the Maritime Boat People of Southeast Asia* (Singapore: National Museum, 1965); Clifford Sather, *The Bajau Laut: Adaption, History, and Fate in a Maritime Fishing Society of South-Eastern Sabah* (Kuala Lumpur: Oxford University Press, 1997); Christian Pelras, "Notes sur quelques populations aquatiques de l'Archipel nusantarien," *Archipel* 3 (1972): 133–168.

29. J. N. Voesmaer, "Korte Beschrijving van het Zuid-oosteleijk Schiereiland van Celebes," *Verhandelingen van het Bataviaasch Genootschap van Kunsten en Wetenschapen* 17 (1839): 63–184, here 109.

30. For a detailed overview, see Gerd Koch, ed., *Boote aus aller Welt* (Berlin: Fröhlich & Kaufmann, 1984); and Mochtar Lubis, *Indonesia: Land under the Rainbow* (Singapore: Oxford University Press, 1987), 27–125.

31. G. Adrian Horridge: *The Prahu: Traditional Sailing Boat of Indonesia* (Singapore: Oxford University Press, 1985).

32. R. H. Barnes, "Educated Fishermen: Social Consequences of Development in an Indonesian Whaling Community," *Bulletin de l'Ecole Française d'Extrême-Orient* 75 (1986): 295–314.

33. Roderich Ptak, *Die maritime Seidenstraße: Küstenräume, Seefahrt und Handel in vorkolonialer Zeit* (Munich: C. H. Beck, 2007).

34. Richard Winstedt and P. E. Josselin de Jong, eds., "The Maritime Laws of Melaka," *Journal of the Malayan Branch of the Royal Asiatic Society* 29 (1956): 22–59; Philip O. L. Tobing, "The Navigation and Commercial Law of Amanna Gappa: A Philological-Cultural Study: Abbrievated Version," in *Hukum Pelayaran dan Perdaganan Ammana Gappa: Pembahasan philologis-kulturil dengan edisi yang diperpendek dalam bahasa inggris* (Makassar: Jajasan Kebudajaan Sulawesi Selatan dan Tenggara, 1961), 149–203.

35. J. V. Mills, "Arab and Chinese Navigators in Malaysian Waters about AD 1500," *Journal of the Malayan Branch of the Royal Asiatic Society* 47 (1974): 1–82.

36. Donald A. Wise, "Primitive Cartography in the Marshall Islands," *Cartographica* 13 (1976): 11–20.

37. Lieberman, *Integration on the Mainland*, 377–383.

38. Reid, *Southeast Asia in the Age of Commerce*, 2:192–201.

39. Hermann Kulke, "Srivijaya—Ein Großreich oder die Hanse des Ostens?," in *Versunkene Königreiche Indonesiens,* ed. Arne Eggebrecht and Eva Eggebrecht (Mainz: von Zabern, 1995), 46–76.

40. On the history of Pohnpei, see David L. Hanlon, *Upon a Stone Altar: A History of the Island of Pohnpei to 1890* (Honolulu: University of Hawai'i Press, 1988).

41. Johannes T. Vermeulen, *De Chineezen te Batavia en de troebelen van 1740* (Leiden: Ijdo, 1938); Willem Remmelink, *The Chinese War and the Collapse of the Javanese State, 1725–1743* (Leiden: KITLV Press, 1994).

42. Edmund R. Leach, *Political Systems of Highland Burma: A Study of Kachin Social Structure* (London: London School of Economics and Political Science, 1954).

43. On Oceania, see Denoon, Mein-Smith, and Wyndham, *History of Australia,* 43, 46.

44. Lieberman, *Integration on the Mainland,* 14.

45. For a general overview, see Maud Girard-Geslan, *Südostasien: Kunst und Kultur* (Freiburg: Herder, 1995); and Anthony J. P. Meyer and Olaf Wipperfürth, *Ozeanische Kunst* (Cologne: Könemann, 1995).

46. Ulrich Menter, *Ozeanien—Kult und Visionen: Verborgene Schätze aus deutschen Völkerkundemuseen* (Munich: Prestel, 2003), 14.

47. Hilke Thode-Arora, *Tapa und Tiki: Die Polynesien-Sammlung des Rautenstrauch-Joest-Museums* (Cologne: Rautenstrauch-Joest-Museum für Völkerkunde, 2001), 27.

48. Denoon, Mein-Smith, and Wyndham, *History of Australia,* 38.

49. For general background on the art of textiles in Southeast Asia, see Heide Leigh-Theisen and R. Mittersak-Schmöller, *Lebensmuster: Textilien in Indonesien* (Vienna: Museum für Völkerkunde, 1995); Michaela Appel, "Textilien in Südostasien," in *Ostasiatische Kunst,* ed. Gabriele Fahr-Becker and Michaela Appel (Cologne: Könemann, 1998), 2:110–159.

50. Appel, *Ozeanien,* 155–157; Meyer and Wipperfürth, *Ozeanische Kunst,* 468.

51. Appel, *Ozeanien,* 130, 161, 162; Jutta Frings, ed., *James Cook und die Entdeckung der Südsee* (Munich: Hirmer, 2009), 252–254.

52. For a general overview of architecture in the region, see Daigoro Chihara, *Hindu-Buddhist Architecture in Southeast Asia* (Leiden: Brill, 1996).

53. Winand Klassen, *Architecture in the Philippines: Filipino Building in a Cross-Cultural Context* (Cebu City: University of San Carlos, 1986), 82–102, 119–124.

54. Meyer and Wipperfürth, *Ozeanische Kunst,* 478, 486, 514, 568, 619.

55. See Roxana Waterson, *The Living House: An Anthropology of Architecture in South-East Asia* (Singapore: Oxford University Press, 1990).

56. Meyer and Wipperfürth, *Ozeanische Kunst,* 69.

57. de Morga, *Sucesos,* 270

58. Klassen, *Architecture,* 45–47, 57–58.

59. See David Smyth, ed., *The Literary Canon in South-East Asia: Literatures of Burma, Cambodia, Indonesia, Laos, Malaysia, Philippines, Thailand and Vietnam* (London: Trans Academic Studies, 1999).

60. Teofilo del Castillo y Tuazon and Buenaventura S. Medina, *Philippine Literature from Ancient Times to the Present* (Manila: Del Castillo, 1966), 107–122; Reinhard Wendt, " 'Talking' and " 'Writing' during the Spanish Colonial Era," in *Old Ties and New Solidarities: Studies on Philippine Communities,* ed. Guillermo Pesigan and Charles Macdonald (Manila: Ateneo de Manila University Press, 2000), 208–218; Ricardo Trimillos, "Pasyon: Lenten Observance of the Philippines as Southeast Asian Theater," in *Essays on Southeast Asian Performing Arts: Local Manifestations and Cross-Cultural Implications,* ed. Susan Foley (Berkeley: International and Area Studies, University of California, 1992), 5–22.

61. U Tet Htoot, "The Nature of the Burmese Chronicles," in *Historians of South East Asia,* ed. D. G. E. Hall (London: Oxford University Press, 1961), 50–62.

62. Charnvit Kasetisiri, "Thai Historiography from Ancient Times to the Modern Period," in *Perceptions of the Past in Southeast Asia,* ed. Anthony Reid and David Marr (Singapore: Heinemann, 1979), 156–170, here 156–160; David G. Wyatt, "Chronicle Tradition in Thai Historiography," in *Southeast Asian History and Historiography: Essays Presented to D. G. E. Hall,* ed. C. D. Cowan and O. W. Wolters (Ithaca, NY: Cornell University Press, 1976), 107–122.

63. Fritz Schulze, "Die traditionelle malaiische Geschichtsschreibung," *Periplus* 4 (1994): 137–155; A. H. Johns, "The Turning Image: Myth and Reality in Malay Perceptions of the Past," in Reid and Marr, *Perceptions of the Past,* 43–67; J. C. Bottoms, "Some Malay Historical Sources:

A Bibliographical Note," in *An Introduction to Indonesian Historiography,* ed. Soedjatmoko et al. (Ithaca, NY: Cornell University Press, 1965), 156–193.

64. Thérèse de Vet, "Context and the Emerging Story: Improvised Performance in Oral and Literate Societies," *Oral Tradition* 23 (2008): 159–179, here 162–165.

65. Donald F. Lach, *Asia in the Making of Europe,* vol. 2, *Century of Wonder,* book 2, *The Literary Arts* (Chicago: University of Chicago Press, 1977), especially 117–160, and vol. 3, *A Century of Advance,* book 3, *Southeast Asia* (Chicago: University of Chicago Press, 1993).

66. A representative selection of such works is Pedro Chirino S. J., *Relación de las Islas Filipinapp: The Philippines in 1600,* trans. Ramón Echeverría (Original 1600) (Manila: Bookmark, 1969); Francisco Colín, *Labor evangélica, ministerios apostólicos de los obreros de la Compañía de Jesús, fundación y progresos de su provincial en las Islas Filipinas,* 3 vols. (Original 1663) (Barcelona: Henrich y Compañía en comandita, 1904); and Gaspar de San Agustín, *Conquistas de las Islas Philipinias: La temporal por las armas del Señor Don Phelipe Segundo el Prudente, y la espíritual por los Religiosos del Orden de Nuestro Padre San Agustín: Fundacion y progressos de su provincial del Santissimo Nombre de Jesús* (Madrid: Ruiz de Murga, 1698).

67. de Morga, *Sucesos.*

68. A particularly seminal and influential example of this is George Coedès, *The Indianized States of Southeast Asia* (Honolulu: East-West Center Press, 1968).

69. Reid, *Southeast Asia in the Age of Commerce,* vol. 2.

70. André Gunder Frank, *ReOrient: Global Economy in the Asian Age* (Berkeley: University of California Press, 1998).

71. Kirti N. Chaudhuri, *Asia before Europe: Economy and Civilization in the Indian Ocean from the Rise of Islam to 1750* (Cambridge: Cambridge University Press, 1990).

72. J. D. Freeman, "The Tradition of Sanalala: Some Notes on Samoan Folk-Lore," *Journal of the Polynesian Society* 56 (1947): 295–317.

73. Bernhard Dahm and Roderich Ptak, "Vorwort," in *Südostasienhandbuch: Geschichte, Gesellschaft, Politik, Wirtschaft, Kultur* (Munich: C. H. Beck, 1999), 9–19, here 9.

74. Denoon, Mein-Smith, and Wyndham, *History of Australia,* 30.

75. Ibid., 30, 43.

76. Andreas Lommel, *Motiv und Variation in der Kunst des zirkumpazifischen Raumes* (Munich: Museum für Völkerkunde, 1962).

77. Boomgaard, *Southeast Asia,* 17.

78. Lieberman, *Integration on the Mainland,* 460.

79. Reid, *Southeast Asia in the Age of Commerce,* 1:3–10.

80. Bernhard Dahm, "Kulturelle Identität und Modernisierung in Südostasien," in *Kulturbegriff und Methode: Der stille Paradigmenwechsel in den Geisteswissenschaften,* ed. Klaus P. Hansen (Tübingen: Narr, 1993), 27–39, here 31.

81. Trimillos, "Pasyon."

82. Ptak, *Die maritime Seidenstraße;* Michel Jacq-Hergoualc'h, *The Malay Peninsula: Crossroads of the Maritime Silk Road* (Leiden: Brill, 2002).

83. Janet Abu-Lughod, *Before European Hegemony: The World System, AD 1250–1350* (Oxford: Oxford University Press, 1989).

84. For general information on Southeast Asia's relations with its neighboring regions, see Leonard Y. Andaya, "Interactions with the Outside World and Adaption in Southeast Asian Society," in *From Early Times to c. 1800,* vol. 1 of *Cambridge History of Southeast Asia,* ed. Nicholas Tarling (Cambridge: Cambridge University Press, 1992), 345–401; on Asian merchants, see Denys Lombard and Jean Aubin, eds., *Asian Merchants and Business Men in the Indian Ocean and the China Sea* (Delhi: Oxford University Press, 2000).

85. Gavin Menzies, *1421: The Year China Discovered the World* (London: Bantam Press, 2002).

86. Jos Gommans and Jacques Leider, eds., *The Maritime Frontier of Burma* (Amsterdam: Koninklijke Nederlandse Akademie van Wetenschapen, 2002).

87. Anthony Reid, "The Islamization of Southeast Asia," in *Charting the Shape of Early Modern Southeast Asia,* ed. Anthony Reid (Chiang Mai: Silkworm Books, 1999), 15–39.

88. Peter Feldbauer, *Der Estado da India: Die Portugiesen in Asien 1498–1620* (Vienna: Mandelbaum, 2003); Sanjay Subrahmanyam, *The Portuguese Empire in Asia, 1500–1700: A Political and Economic History* (New York: Longman, 1993).

89. Reinhard Wendt, *Vom Kolonialismus zur Globalisierung: Europa und die Welt seit 1500* (Paderborn: Schöningh, 2007), 50, 62–63, 76.

90. Geoffrey C. Gunn, *First Globalization: The Eurasian Exchange, 1500–1800* (Lanham, MD: Rowman & Littlefield, 2003).

91. Reinhard Wendt, "'Dinner for One' und die versteckte Präsenz des Fremden im Kulinarischen," in *Grenzgänge: Festschrift zu Ehren von Wilfried Wagner,* ed. Dietmar Rothermund (Hamburg: Abera, 2004), 225–246.

92. Campbell C. Macknight, *The Voyage to Marege': Macassan Trepangers in Northern Australia* (Carlton, Victoria: Melbourne University Press, 1976).

93. Bronislaw Malinowski, *Argonauts of the Western Pacific: An Account of Native Enterprise and Adventure in the Archipelagoes of Melanesian New Guinea* (London: Routledge & Kegan Paul, 1922).

94. Job C. van Leur, *Indonesian Trade and Society: Essays in Asian Social and Economic History* (The Hague: Van Hoeve, 1955); Niels Steensgaard, *The Asian Trade Revolution of the Seventeenth Century: The East India Companies and the Decline of the Caravan Trade* (Chicago: University of Chicago Press, 1974).

95. Luis Felipe Ferreira Reis Thomasz, "The Indian Merchant Communities in Malacca under the Portuguese Rule," in *Indo-Portuguese History: Old Issues, New Questions,* ed. Teotónio de Souza (New Delhi: Concept Publishers, 1985), 56–72.

96. Kenneth R. Hall, "The Textile Industry in Southeast Asia, 1400–1800," *Journal of the Economic and Social History of the Orient* 39 (1996): 87–135; Robyn Maxwell, *Textiles of Southeast Asia: Tradition, Trade, and Transformation* (Melbourne: Oxford University Press, 1990).

97. John S. Guy, *Oriental Trade Ceramics in Southeast Asia, 9th to 16th Century: With a Catalogue of Chinese, Vietnamese and Thai Wares in Australian Collections* (Singapore: Oxford University Press, 1990).

98. Jürgen G. Nagel, "Makassar und der Molukkenhandel: Städte und Handelsrouten im indonesischen Gewürzhandel des 16. und 17. Jahrhunderts," in Denzel, *Gewürze,* 93–121.

99. On the reconstruction of figures relating to quantities and prices of commodities in early Southeast Asian trade, see David Bulbeck et al., eds., *Southeast Asian Exports since the 14th Century: Cloves, Pepper, Coffee, and Sugar* (Leiden: KITLV Press, 1998).

100. Reid, *Southeast Asia in the Age of Commerce,* 2:1–61.

101. Anthony Reid, "The Seventeenth Century Crisis in Southeast Asia," *Modern Asian Studies* 24 (1990): 639–660. For further information on this, see also Niels Steensgaard, "The Seventeenth Century Crisis and the Unity of Eurasian History," *Modern Asian Studies* 24 (1990): 683–698.

102. Tilman Frasch, "Eine Region in der Krise? Südostasien," in *Die Welt im 17. Jahrhundert,* ed. Bernd Hausberger (Vienna: Mandelbaum, 2008), 247–274, here 269–271.

103. Clara B. Wilpert, *Südsee: Inseln, Völker und Kulturen* (Hamburg: Christians, 1987), 136.

104. Hermann Kulke, "Maritimer Kulturtransfer im Indischen Ozean" Theorien zur 'Indisierung' Südostasiens im 1. Jahrtausend n.Chr.," *Saeculum* 56 (2005): 173–197.

105. For a general overview of religion on Bali, see I Gusti Putu Phalgunadi, *Evolution of Hindu Culture in Bali: From the Earliest Period to the Present Time* (Delhi: Sundeep Prakashan, 1991); see also Willard A. Hanna, *Bali Profile: People, Events, Circumstances (1001–1976)* (New York: American University Field Staff, 1976); James A. Boone, *The Anthropological Romance of Bali, 1597–1972: Dynamic Perspectives in Marriage and Caste, Politics and Religion* (Cambridge: Cambridge University Press, 1977).

106. Reid, *Southeast Asia in the Age of Commerce,* 2:140–142.

107. Jürgen G. Nagel, "Predikanten und Ziekentrooster: Der Protestantismus in der Welt der Verenigden Oostindischen Compagnie," in *Europäische Aufklärung und protestantische Mission in Indien,* ed. Michael Mann (Heidelberg: Draupadi, 2006), 101–121. On the relationship between the VOC, the Protestant church, and missionary activity, also see the individual chapters in Gerrit J. Schutte, ed., *Het Indische Sion: De Gereformeerde kerk onder de Verenigde Oost-Indische Compagnie* (Hilversum: Verloren, 2002).

108. Boomgaard, *Southeast Asia,* 77.

109. Appel, *Ozeanien,* 20.

110. Ibid., 18, 153–154.

111. Nico de Jonge and Toos van Dijk, *Forgotten Islands of Indonesia: The Art and Culture of the Southeast Moluccas* (Singapore: Periplus Editions, 1995), 33–46.

112. Pierre-Yves Manguin, "Shipshape Societies: Boat Symbolism and Political Systems in Insular Southeast Asia," in *Southeast Asia in the 9th to the 14th Centuries,* ed. David G. Marr and A. C. Milner (Singapore: Institute of Southeast Asian Studies, 1986), 187–207, here 188–191, 195–196, 201.

113. For an overview, see Stephen A. Wurm and Shirô Hattori, eds., *Language Atlas of the Pacific Area,* 2 vols. (Canberra: Linguistic Circle of Canberra, 1981).

114. Cf. Stephen A. Wurm, *Papuan Languages of Oceania* (Tübingen: Narr, 1982).

115. Mary-Anne Gale, *Dhanum Djorra 'Wuy Dhäwu: A History of Writing in Aboriginal Languages* (Underdale: Aboriginal Research Institute, University of South Australia, 1997), 1.

116. Wendt, " 'Talking' and 'Writing.' "

117. Bernard Comrie, *The Major Languages of East and South-East Asia* (London: Routledge, 1987).

118. Hilke Thode-Arora, *Tapa und Tiki. Die Polynesien-Sammlung des Rautenstrauch-Joest-Museums* (Cologne: Rautenstrauch-Joest.Museum für Völkerkunde, 2001), 9.

119. Lommel, *Motiv und Variation,* 22.

120. Harald Haarmann, *Geschichte der Schrift* (Munich: C. H. Beck, 2007), 98.

121. Ismail Hamid, "Kitab Jawi: Intellectualizing Literary Tradition," in *Islamic Civilization in the Malay World,* ed. Mohamed Taib Osman (Kuala Lumpur: Dewan Bahasa dan Pustaka, 1997), 197–243, here 201, 203, 224; Yusof Ahmad Talib, "Jawa Script: Its Significance and Contribution to the Malay World," in *Proceedings of the International Seminar on Islamic Civilisation in the Malay World,* ed. Taufik Abdullah (Istanbul: IRCICA, 1999), 151–156.

122. Samuel K. Tan, *Surat Maguindanaon: Jawi Documentary Series,* vol. 1 (Quezon City: University of the Philippines Press, 1996).

123. Wendt, "'Talking' and 'Writing,'" 210–211.

124. Jörg Fisch, *Hollands Ruhm in Asien, François Valentyns Vision des niederländischen Imperiums im 18. Jahrhundert* (Stuttgart: Steiner, 1986), 115–117.

125. See the following general sources on the history of Southeast Asia and the formation of early empires there: Lorraine Gesick, ed., *Centers, Symbols, and Hierarchies: Essays on the Classical States of Southeast Asia* (New Haven, CT: Yale University Southeast Asian Studies, 1983); Renée Hagesteijn, *Circles of Kings: Political Dynamics in Early Continental Southeast Asia* (Dordrecht: Foris, 1989); D. G. E. Hall, *A History of Southeast Asia* (London: Macmillan, 1981); David G. Marr and A. C. Milner, eds., *Southeast Asia in the 9th to the 14th Centuries* (Singapore: Institute of Southeast Asian Studies, 1986); Nicholas Tarling, ed., *From Early Times to c. 1500,* vol. 1 of *The Cambridge History of Southeast Asia* (Cambridge: Cambridge University Press, 1999); John Villiers, *Südostasien vor der Kolonialzeit* (Frankfurt am Main: Fischer, 1965).

126. Boomgaard, *Southeast Asia,* 57, 67, 70–76; Jonathan Rigg, ed., *The Gift of Water: Water Management, Cosmology and the State in South East Asia* (London: School of Oriental and African Studies, 1992).

127. Oliver William Wolters, *History, Culture, and Region in Southeast Asian Perspectives* (Singapore: Institute of Southeast Asia Studies, 1982), 17–33.

128. Hermann Kulke, "The Early and the Imperial Kingdom in Southeast Asian History," in Marr and Milner, *Southeast Asia,* 1–22.

129. Lieberman, *Integration on the Mainland,* 2.

130. Tilman Frasch, *Pagan: Stadt und Staat* (Stuttgart: Steiner, 1996).

131. For a detailed overview of Cambodia, see David Chandler, *A History of Cambodia* (Boulder, CO: Westview Press, 2007).

132. Roland Fletcher, "Seeing Angkor: New Views on an Old City," *Journal of the Oriental Society of Australia* 32–33 (2000–2001): 1–25.

133. Kulke, "Early and the Imperial Kingdom," 8, 15.

134. For general information on the history of Thailand, see David K. Wyatt, *Thailand: A Short History* (Chiang Mai: Silkworm Books 1991); Helmut Fessen and Hans Dieter Kubitschek, *Geschichte Thailands* (Münster: Lit, 1994); Chris Baker and Pasuk Phongpaichit, *A History of Thailand* (Cambridge: Cambridge University Press, 2005).

135. Sarassawadee Ongsakul, *History of Lan Na* (Chiang Mai: Silkworm Books, 2005).

136. Chris Baker, "Ayutthaya Rising: From Land or Sea?," *Journal of Southeast Asian Studies* 34 (2000): 41–62.

137. Martin Stuart-Fox, *The Lao Kingdom of Lan Xang: Rise and Decline* (Bangkok: White Lotus, 1998).

138. For an overview of the history of Laos, see Martin Stuart-Fox, *A History of Laos* (Cambridge: Cambridge University Press, 1997); and Grant Evans, *A Short History of Laos: The Land in Between* (Chiang Mai: Silkworm Books, 2002).

139. Kulke, "Early and the Imperial Kingdom," 8.

140. Li Tana, *Nguyen Cochinchina: Southern Vietnam in the 17th and 18th Centuries* (Ithaca, NY: Southeast Asia Program, Cornell University, 1998).

141. Willem van Schendel, "Geographies of Knowing, Geographies of Ignorance: Jumping Scale in Southeast Asia," in *Locating Southeast Asia: Geographies of Knowledge and Politics of Space,* ed. Paul Krotoska, Remco Raben, and Henk Schulte Nordholt (Singapore: Singapore University Press, 2001), 275–307.

142. James Scott, *The Art of Not Being Governed: An Anarchist History of Upland Southeast Asia* (New Haven, CT: Yale University Press, 2009).

143. On the Chinese in Vietnam, see Thomas Engelbert, *Die chinesische Minderheit im Süden Vietnams (Hoa) der kolonialen und nationalistischen Nationalitätenpolitik* (Frankfurt am Main: Lang, 2002).

144. On the VOC in mainland Southeast Asia, see Wilhelmina O. Dijk, *Seventeenth-Century Burma and the Dutch East India Company* (Singapore: Singapore University Press, 2006).

145. Jurrien van Goor, "Merchant in Royal Service: Constantin Phaulkon as Phraklang in Ayutthaya, 1683–1688," in *Emporia, Commodities and Entrepreneurs in Asian Maritime Trade, c. 1400–1750,* ed. Dietmar Rothermund and Roderich Ptak (Wiesbaden: Steiner, 1991), 445–465.

146. Bhawan Ruangslip, *Dutch East India Company Merchants at the Court of Ayutthaya* (Leiden: Brill, 2007).

147. See Dirk van der Cruysse, *Siam and the West, 1500–1700* (Chiang Mai: Silkworm Books, 2002).

148. See Alfred W. Crosby, *The Columbian Exchange: Biological and Cultural Consequences of 1492* (Westport, CT: Greenwood Press, 1972).

149. R. B. Slametmuljana, *A Story of Majapahit* (Singapore: Singapore University Press, 1976).

150. For an overview of Bali, see Hanna, *Bali Profile.*

151. Hans Hägerdal, *Hindu Rulers, Muslim Subjects: Lombok and Bali in the Seventeenth and Eighteenth Centuries* (Bangkok: White Lotus, 2001).

152. John Anderson, *Acheen and the Ports of the North and East Coast of Sumatra* (Kuala Lumpur: Oxford University Press, 1971).

153. Luis Felipe Ferreira Reis Thomaz, "The Malay Sultanate of Melaka," in *Southeast Asia in the Early Modern Era,* ed. Anthony Reid (Ithaca, NY: Cornell University Press, 1993), 69–90; Marcus Scott-Ross, *A Short History of Malacca* (Singapore: Chopmen, 1971).

154. Robert W. McRoberts, "A Study of Growth" An Economic History of Melaka, 1400–1510," *Journal of the Malayan Branch of the Royal Asiatic Society* 64 (1991): 47–78.

155. Kenneth R. Hall, "The Opening of the Malay World to European Trade in the Sixteenth Century," *Journal of the Malayan Branch of the Royal Asiatic Society* 58 (1985): 85–106; Robert

W. McRoberts, "An Examination of the Fall of Malacca in 1511," *Journal of the Malayan Branch of the Royal Asiatic Society* 57 (1984): 26–39; Sanjay Subrahmanyam, "Commerce and Conflict: Two Views of Portuguese Melaka in the 1620s," *Journal of Southeast Asian Studies* 19 (1988): 62–79.

156. Denys Lombard, *Le Sultanate d'Atjéh au temps d'Iskandar Muda, 1607–1636* (Paris: École française d'Extrême-Orient, 1967); L. F. Brakel, "State and Statecraft in 17th-Century Aceh," in *Pre-Colonial State Systems in Southeast Asia: The Malay Peninsula, Sumatra, Bali-Lombok, Celebes,* ed. Anthony Reid and Lance Castles (Kuala Lumpur: Perchetakan Mas Sdn., 1975), 56–66.

157. Charles R. Boxer, *Francisco Vieira: A Portuguese Merchant Adventurer in South East Asia, 1624–1667* (The Hague: Nijhoff, 1967).

158. Leonard Y. Andaya, *The Heritage of Arung Palakka: A History of South Sulawesi (Celebes) in the Seventeenth Century* (The Hague: Nijhoff, 1981).

159. Jeyamalar Kathirithamby-Wells, "Banten: A West Indonesian Port and Polity during the Sixteenth and Seventeenth Centuries," in *The Southeast Asian Port and Polity: Rise and Demise,* ed. Jeyamalar Kathirithamby-Wells and John Villiers (Singapore: Singapore University Press, 1990), 107–125.

160. Willem Remmelink, *Chinese War and the Collapse of the Javanese State, 1725–1743* (Leiden: KITLV Press, 1994).

161. Merle C. Ricklefs, *Mystic Synthesis in Java: A History of Islamization from the Fourteenth to the Early Nineteenth Centuries* (Norwalk, CT: EastBridge, 2006).

162. Leonard Y. Andaya, *The World of Maluku: Eastern Indonesia in the Early Modern Period* (Honolulu: University of Hawai'i Press, 1993).

163. Om Prakash, "Restrictive Trade Regimes: VOC and Asian Spice Trade in the Seventeenth Century," in Ptak and Rothermund, *Emporia,* 107–126.

164. For key background reading on the Sulu Archipelago, see James F. Warren, *The Sulu Zone, 1768–1898: The Dynamics of Trade, Slavery and Ethnicity in the Transformation of a Southeast Asian Maritime State* (Singapore: Singapore University Press, 1981); James F. Warren, *The Global Economy and the Sulu Zone: Connections, Commodities, and Culture* (Quezon City: New Day Publishers, 2000).

165. Luís Felipe Thomaz, "The Indian Merchant Communities in Malacca under Portuguese Rule," in de Souza, *Indo-Portuguese History,* 56–72; D. R. Sar Desai, "The Portuguese Administration in Malacca, 1511–1641," *Journal of Southeast Asian History* 10 (1969): 501–512.

166. K. S. Mathew, "Trade in the Indian Ocean and the Portuguese System of Cartazes," in *The First Portuguese Colonial Empire,* ed. Malyn D. D. Newitt (Exeter, UK: University of Exeter, 1986), 69–83.

167. The following is key reading on the continuing Portuguese presence in Southeast Asia: Sanjay Subrahmanyam, *The Portuguese Empire in Asia, 1500–1700* (London: Longman, 2001); George B. Souza, *The Survival of Empire: Portuguese Trade and Society in China and the South China Sea, 1630–1754* (Cambridge: Cambridge University Press, 1986).

168. Thomas Beck, "Monopol und Genozid" Die Muskatproduktion auf den Banda-Inseln im 17. Jahrhundert," in Denzel, *Gewürze,* 71–90.

169. Jürgen G. Nagel, "Usurpatoren und Pragmatiker: Einige typologische Überlegungen zur Strategie der niederländischen Ostindienkompanie (1602–1799)," in *Praktiken des Handels: Geschäfte und soziale Beziehungen europäischer Kaufleute in Mittelalter und früher Neuzeit,* ed. Mark Häberlein and Christoph Jeggle (Konstanz: UVK, 2010), 71–98.

170. Leonard Blussé, "Batavia, 1619–1740: The Rise and Fall of a Chinese Colonial Town," *Journal of Southeast Asian Studies* 12 (1981): 159–178; Milone, " 'Indische' Culture."

171. For background information on the Spanish conquest of the Philippines, see John L. Phelan, *The Hispanization of the Philippines: Spanish Aims and Filipino Responses, 1565–1700* (Madison: University of Wisconsin Press, 1967).

172. William L. Schurz, *The Manila Galleon* (New York: Dutton, 1959).

173. Robert R. Reed, *Colonial Manila: The Context of Hispanic Urbanism and Process of Morphogenesis* (Berkeley: University of California Press, 1978), 33.

174. For background information on the economic history of the Philippines, see Onofre D. Corpuz, *An Economic History of the Philippines* (Quezon City: University of the Philippines Press, 1997).

175. Edgar Wickberg, "The Chinese Mestizo in Philippine History," *Journal of Southeast Asian History* 5 (1964): 62–100.

176. For an introduction to the Christianization of the Philippines, see Reinhard Wendt, "Das Christentum," in Dahm and Ptak, *Südostasienhandbuch,* 454–469. On the processes of cultural exchange and transformation, see Reinhard Wendt, *Fiesta Filipina: Koloniale Kultur zwischen Imperialismus und neuer Identität* (Freiburg im Breisgau: Rombach, 1997).

177. Roderich Ptak, "The Northern Trade Route to the Spice Islands: South China Sea—Sulu Zone—North Moluccas (14th to 16th Century)," *Archipel* 43 (1992): 27–56. For a thorough overview of foreign trade, see the contributions in ibid., *China's Seaborne Trade with South and Southeast Asia (1200–1750)* (Aldershot, UK: Ashgate, 1999).

178. Kathirithamby-Wells, "Banten."

179. On the Chinese character of Batavia, see Blussé, "Batavia."

180. Christine Dobbin, "From Middlemen Minorities to Industrial Entrepreneurs: The Chinese in Java and the Parsis in Western India, 1619–1939," in *India and Indonesia: General Perspectices* (Leiden: Brill, 1989), 109–132, here 111–118.

181. Nagel, *Schlüssel zu den Molukken,* 392–394.

182. Gerrit J. Knaap, *Shallow Waters, Rising Tide: Shipping and Trade in Java around 1775* (Leiden: KITLV Press, 1996).

183. For key background information on the Chinese in the Philippines, see, among others, Teresita Ang See, ed., *The Story of the Chinese in Philippine Life* (Manila: Kaisa Para Sa Kaunlaran, 2005); Jacques Amyot, *The Manila Chinese in the Philippine Environment* (Quezon City: Institute of Philippine Culture, 1973); Reinhard Wendt, "Der Achte Mond: Religiöse Feste in der chinesischen Diaspora auf den spanischen Philippinen," *Periplus* 14 (2004): 89–116.

184. Jacobus Noorduyn, "Arung Singkang (1700–1765): How the 'Victory of Wadjo' Began," *Indonesia* 13 (1972): 61–68.

185. Richard Z. Lairissa, "The Bugis-Makassarese in the Port Towns: Ambon and Ternate through the Nineteenth Century," *Bijdragen tot de Taal-, Land- en Volkenkunde* 156 (2000): 619–633.

186. Fort a concrete example of such a fall in currency value, see Nagel, *Schlüssel zu den Molukken,* 211–212.

187. See, for example, Gerrit J. Knaap, "Coffee for Cash: The Dutch East India Company and the Expansion of Coffee Cultivation in Java, Ambon and Ceylon, 1700–1730," in *Trading Companies in Asia, 1600–1830,* ed. Jurrien van Goor (Utrecht: HES Uitgevers, 1986), 33–49.

188. Nagel, *Schlüssel zu den Molukken,* 767–799.

189. J. A. Bakkers, "De eilanden Bonerate en Kalao," *Tijschrift van hat Bataviaasch Genootschap* 11 (1861): 215–264.

190. Leonard Y. Andaya, "The Trans-Sumatra Trade and the Ethnicization of the 'Batak,'" *Bijdragen tot de Taal-, Land- en Volkenkunde* 158 (2002): 367–409.

191. Albert Schrauwers, "Houses, Hierarchy, Headhunting and Exchange: Rethinking Political Relations in the Southeast Asian Realm of Luwu," *Bijdragen tot de Taal-, Land- en Volkenkunde* 153 (1997): 356–380.

192. For general information on this island group, see Josef Kreiner, ed., *Ryukyu in World History* (Bonn: Bier'sche Verlags-Anstalt, 2001).

193. Josef Kreiner, "Okinawa und Ainu," in *Grundriß der Japanologie,* ed. Klaus Kracht and Markus Rüttermann (Wiesbaden: Harrassowitz, 2001), 433–474, here 435–436.

194. Angela Schottenhammer, "China und die Ryukyu-Inseln während der späten Ming- und der Qing-Dynastie: Einige Beispiele zum Produkte- und Ideenaustausch im Bereich der Medizin," in *Mirabilia Asiatica: Seltene Waren im Seehandel,* ed. Jorge M. dos Santos Alves, Claude Guillot, and Roderich Ptak (Wiesbaden: Harrassowitz, 2003), 85–119, here 86–87, 89–90.

195. Kreiner, "Okinawa und Ainu," 435–436.

196. Reinhard Zöllner, *Geschichte Japans: Von 1800 bis zur Gegenwart* (Paderborn: Schöningh, 2006), 49–50; Reinhard Zöllner, "Verschlossen wider Wissen—Was Japan von Kaempfer über sich lernte," in *Engelbert Kaempfer (1651–1716) und die kulturelle Begegnung zwischen Europa und Asien,* ed. Sabine Klocke-Daffa, Jürgen Scheffler, and Gisela Wilbertz (Lemgo: Institut für Lippische Landeskunde, 2003), 185–209, here 197.

197. On Ming dynasty China's relationship to Southeast Asia, see the excellent and detailed overview by Geoff Wade, "Engaging the South: Ming China and Southeast Asia in the Fifteenth Century," *Journal of the Economic and Social History of the Orient* 51 (2008): 578–638.

198. Roderich Ptak, *Die chinesische maritime Expansion im 14. und 15. Jahrhundert* (Bamberg: Forschungsstiftung für europäische Überseegeschichte, 1992), 9–16.

199. Ptak, *Maritime Seidenstraße,* 234–249.

200. Kenneth R. Hall, "Multi-Dimensional Networking: Fifteenth-Century Indian Ocean Maritime Diaspora in Southeast Asian Perspective," *Journal of the Economic and Social History of the Orient* 49 (2006): 454–481. See also Craig A. Lockard, "'The Sea Common to All': Maritime Frontiers, Port Cities, and Chinese Traders in the Southeast Asian Age of Commerce," *Journal of World History* 21 (2010): 219–247.

201. Ng Chin Keong, "Chinese Trade with Southeast Asia in the 17th and 18th Centuries," in *Kapal dan Harta Karam: Ships and Sunken Treasures,* ed. Mohammad Yusoff Hashim (Kuala Lumpur: United Selangor Press, 1986), 88–106.

202. Ng Chin Keong, *Trade and Society: The Amoy Network on the China Coast, 1683–1735* (Singapore: Singapore University Press, 1983), 167–177.

203. Roderich Ptak, "Zwischen zwei 'Mittelmeeren': Taiwan als Barriere und Brücke," in *Eroberungen aus dem Archiv: Festschrift für Lutz Bieg,* ed. Birgit Häse (Wiesbaden: Harassowitz, 2009), 169.

204. Ibid., 149–170.

205. Thomas O. Höllmann, "Statusbestimmung und Entscheidungsfindung bei den autochthonen Bevölkerungsgruppen Taiwans nach Schriftzeugnissen des 17. und 18. Jahrhunderts," *Saeculum* 55 (2004): 323–332.

206. Tonio Andrade, "The Rise and Fall of Dutch Taiwan, 1624–1662: Cooperative Colonization and the Statist Model of European Expansion," *Journal of World History* 17 (2006): 429–450.

207. Wolfgang Reinhard, "Gelenkter Kulturwandel im 17. Jahrhundert: Akkulturation in den Jesuitenmissionen als universalhistorisches Problem," *Historische Zeitschrift* 223 (1976): 529–590.

208. The entire region is discussed in Douglas L. Oliver, *Oceania: The Native Cultures of Australia and the Pacific Islands,* 2 vols. (Honolulu: University of Hawai'i Press, 1989). Overviews can be found in Kerry Howe, *Where the Waves Fall: A New South Sea Islands History from First Settlement to Colonial Rule* (Sydney: Allen & Unwin, 1984); Donald Denoon, ed., *Cambridge History of the Pacific Islanders* (Cambridge: Cambridge University Press, 1997).

209. Rose Schubert, Ernst Feist, and Caroline Zelz, "Zur frühen Seefahrt in der Südsee: Schiffahrt und Navigation in Polynesien und Mikronesien," in *Kolumbus oder wer entdeckte Amerika?,* ed. Wolfgang Stein (Munich: Hirmer, 1992), 90–99, here 90.

210. Wilpert, *Südsee,* 28–30.

211. Denoon, Mein-Smith, and Wyndham, *History of Australia,* 40–41, 44.

212. B. Finney, "Colonizing an Island World," in *Prehistoric Settlement of the Pacific,* ed. Ward H. Goodenough (Philadelphia: American Philosophical Society, 1996), 71–116; Peter Bellwood, "The Austronesian Dispersal," in *Arts of the South Seas: Island South East Asia, Melanesia, Polynesia, Micronesia,* ed. Douglas Newton (Munich: Prestel, 1999), 8–17; Ingrid Heermann, *Mythos Tahiti: Südsee—Traum und Realität* (Berlin: Reimer, 1987).

213. Meyer and Wipperfürth, *Ozeanische Kunst,* 18, 275.

214. Menter, *Ozeanien,* 20

215. Thoda-Arora, *Tapa und Tiki,* 9, 382.

216. Heermann, *Mythos Tahiti.*

217. Frings, *James Cook,* 58.

218. Meyer and Wipperfürth, *Ozeanische Kunst,* 582, 585.

219. For a general overview, see Maurice P. K. Sorrenson, *Maori Origins and Migrations: The Genesis of Some Pakeha Myths and Legends* (Auckland: Auckland University Press, 1979); William H. Oliver and B. R. Williams, eds., *The Oxford History of New Zealand* (Wellington: Oxford University Press, 1981); Janet M. Davidson, *The Prehistory of New Zealand* (Auckland: Longman Paul, 1992); James Belich, *Making Peoples: A History of the New Zealanders from Polynesian Settlement to the End of the Nineteenth Century* (Rosedale: Penguin, 1996), 13–116; Philippa Mein-Smith, *A Concise History of New Zealand* (Cambridge: Cambridge University Press, 2005), 5–20.

220. Denoon, Mein-Smith, and Wyndham, *History of Australia,* 39, 41–42.

221. John Rickard, *Australia: A Cultural History* (London: Longman, 1988).

222. Voigt, *Geschichte Australiens,* 9–10.

223. Tim Flannery, *The Future Eaters: An Ecological History of the Australasian Lands and People* (Chatswood: Reed, 1994); Voigt, *Geschichte Australiens,* 6.

224. Derek J. Mulvaney, *Encounters in Place: Outsiders and Aboriginal Australians, 1606–1985* (St. Lucia: University of Queensland Press, 1989).

225. For the history of European exploration of Oceania, see Urs Bitterli, *Asien, Australien, Pazifik,* vol. 2 of *Die Entdeckung und Eroberung der Welt: Dokumente und Berichte* (Munich: C. H. Beck, 1981); Heinrich Lamping, ed., *Australia: Studies on the History of Discovery and Exploration* (Frankfurt am Main: Institut für Sozialgeographie der Johann-Wolfgang-Goethe-Universität, 1994); Günter Schilder, *Australia Unveiled: The Share of Dutch Navigators in the Discovery of Australia* (Amsterdam: Theatrum Orbis Terrarum, 1976); Eberhard Schmitt, *Dokumente zur Geschichte der europäischen Expansion,* vol. 2 (Munich: C. H. Beck, 1984), 522–536; Oskar Hermann Khristian Spate, *The Pacific since Magellan,* 3 vols. (Canberra: Australian National University Press, 1977–1988).

226. *Spanish Lake* is the title of the first volume of Spate's history, *Pacific since Magellan.*

227. Schurz, *Manila Galleon.*

228. Reinhard Wendt, "The Spanisch–Dutch War, Japanese Trade and World Politics," in *The Road to Japan: Social and Economic Aspects of Early European–Japanese Contacts,* ed. Josef Kreiner (Bonn: Bier, 2005), 43–62, here 52–57.

229. Hugh Edwards, *Islands of Angry Ghosts* (Sydney: Hodder & Stoughton, 1966).

230. Heermann, *Mythos Tahiti;* Joachim Meißner, *Mythos Südsee: Das Bild von der Südsee im Europa des 18. Jahrhunderts* (Hildesheim: Olms, 2006); Bernard Smith, *European Vision and the South Pacific* (New Haven, CT: Yale University Press, 1985).

231. Mulvaney, *Encounters.*

232. Maria Nugent, *Captain Cook Was Here* (Port Melbourne: Cambridge University Press, 2009).

5. Europe and the Atlantic World

1. Bernard Bailyn, *Atlantic History: Concept and Contours* (Cambridge, MA: Harvard University Press, 2005); Nicholas Canny and Philip Morgan, eds., *The Oxford Handbook of the Atlantic World, 1450–1850* (Oxford: Oxford University Press, 2011).

2. Jan-Georg Deutsch and Albert Wirz, eds., *Geschichte in Afrika: Einführung in Probleme und Debatten* (Berlin: Verlag das Arabische Buch, 1997), 12; Horst Pietschmann, "Lateinamerikanische Geschichte und deren wissenschaftliche Grundlagen," in *Handbuch der Geschichte Lateinamerikas,* ed. Horst Pietschmann (Stuttgart: Klett Cotta, 1994), 1:1–22; George G. Iggers, Q. Edward Wang, and Supriya Mukherjee, *A Global History of Modern Historiography* (Harlow, UK: Pearson, 2008), 290–300; Markus Völkel, *Geschichtsschreibung: Eine Einführung in globaler Perspektive* (Cologne: Böhlau, 2006), 360–372; another study that remains highly informative is Hanna Vollrath, "Das Mittelalter in der Typik oraler Gesellschaften," *Historische Zeitschrift* 233 (1981): 571–594.

3. Key texts on Atlantic Africa are Roland Oliver, ed., *Africa from c. 1050 to c. 1600*, vol. 3 of *The Cambridge History of Africa* (Cambridge: Cambridge University Press, 1977); Richard Gray, ed., *Africa from c. 1600 to c. 1790*, vol. 4 of *The Cambridge History of Africa* (Cambridge: Cambridge University Press, 1975); Djibril Tamsir Niane, ed., *Africa from the 12th to the 16th Century*, vol. 4 of *General History of Africa* (Oxford: James Currey, 1984); Bethwell A. Ogot, ed., *Africa from the 16th to the 18th Century*, vol. 5 of *General History of Africa*, 2nd ed. (Oxford: James Currey, 1999); John Iliffe, *Africans: The History of a Continent* (Cambridge: Cambridge University Press, 1995); Roland Oliver and Anthony Atmore, *Medieval Africa, 1250–1800* (Cambridge: Cambridge University Press, 2001); Ulrike Schuerkens, *Geschichte Afrikas: Eine Einführung* (Cologne: Böhlau, 2009).

4. Joseph O. Vogel, ed., *Encyclopedia of Precolonial Africa: Archeology, History, Languages, Cultures, and Environments* (Walnut Creek, CA: Alta Mira, 1997), 247–288.

5. Kwame A. Appiah, ed., *Africana: The Encyclopedia of the African and African American Experience* (New York: Basic Civitas Books, 1999), 51.

6. James Giblin, "Trypanosomiasis Control in African History: An Evaded Issue?," *Journal of African History* 31 (1990): 59–80; Willie F. Page, ed., *Encyclopedia of African History and Culture* (New York: Facts on File, 2001), 1:6; Vogel, *Encyclopedia*, 33, 217, 222.

7. Al-Omari on the Kingdom of Mali, cited in Rudolf Fischer, *Gold, Salz und Sklaven: Die Geschichte der großen Sudanreiche Gana, Mali, Songhai*, 2nd ed. (Oberdorf: Edition Piscator, 1991), 108.

8. Eugenia W. Herbert, *Red Gold of Africa: Copper in Precolonial History and Culture* (Madison: University of Wisconsin Press, 1984); Iliffe, *Africans*, 83–84.

9. John K. Thornton, *Africa and Africans in the Making of the Atlantic World, 1400–1680* (Cambridge: Cambridge University Press, 1992), 7.

10. Robin C. C. Law, *The Horse in West African History: The Role of the Horse in the Societies of Precolonial West Africa* (Oxford: Oxford University Press for the International African Institute, 1980), 6–7, 9–13, 89, 119, 122.

11. Catherine Cocquery-Vidrovitch, *Histoire des villes d'Afrique noire des origins à la colonisation* (Paris: Albin Michel, 1993); Graham Connah, *African Civilization: An Archeological Perspective*, 2nd ed. (Cambridge: Cambridge University Press, 2001), 144–180.

12. Frieda-Nela Williams, *Precolonial Communities of Southwestern Africa: A History of Ovambo Kingdoms, 1600–1920* (Windhoek: National Archives of Namibia, 1991), 99.

13. David Birmingham in Gray, *Cambridge History of Africa*, 4:369–377; Edna G. Bay, "Belief, Legitimacy and the Kpojito: An Institutional History of the 'Queen Mother' in Precolonial Dahomey," *Journal of African History* 36 (1995): 1–27; Suzanne Preston Blier, "The Path of the Leopard: Motherhood and Majesty in Early Dahomé," *Journal of African History* 36 (1995): 391–417.

14. Anne Hilton, *The Kingdom of Kongo* (Oxford: Clarendon Press, 1985), 102.

15. John P. Mbiti et al., after Samuel A. Floyd, *The Power of Black Music: Interpreting Its History from Africa to the United States* (New York: Oxford University Press, 1995), 14–27; Iliffe, *Africans*, 85–90.

16. Hilton, *Kingdom of Kongo*, 8–34, 48–53, 91–92.

17. Christopher Ehret, *The Civilizations of Africa: A History to 1800* (Oxford: James Currey, 2002), 37–55.

18. Emile Boonzaier et al., *The Cape Herders: A History of the Khoikhoi of Southern Africa* (Cape Town: Philip, 1996).

19. Nehemia Levtzion, ed., *Corpus of Early Arabic Sources for West African History* (Fontes Historiae Africanae, Series Arabica, 4) (Cambridge: Cambridge University Press, 1981); John O. Hunwick, ed., *Timbuktu and the Songhay Empire: Al–Saidi's Ta'rikh al-Sudan down to 1613 and Other Contemporary Documents* (Leiden: Brill, 1999).

20. Robin C. C. Law, "Constructing the Precolonial History of West Africa: Reflections on the Methodology of Oral and Written History" (unpublished manuscript, Leiden, 1993); an exemplary text on this subject is Hilton, *Kingdom of Kongo;* cf. Adam Jones, ed., *Brandenburg Sources for West African History, 1680–1700* (Stuttgart: Steiner, 1985).

21. John D. Fage, *A History of Africa,* 3rd ed. (New York: Routledge, 1995), 79; John O. Hunwick, "Secular Power and Religious Authority in Muslim Society: The Case of Songhay," *Journal of African History* 37 (1996): 175–194.

22. However, Iliffe, *Africans,* 144, claims that they arose as a reaction to the Atlantic slave trade.

23. Basic texts on this topic include the following: *Lexikon des Mittelalters,* 10 vols. (Stuttgart: Metzler, 1980–1999); *Enzyklopädie der Neuzeit,* 16 vols. (Stuttgart: Metzler, 2005–2012); Ulf Dirlmeier, Gerhard Fouquet, and Bernd Fuhrmann, *Europa im Spätmittelalter 1215–1378* (Oldenbourg Grundriss der Geschichte 8) (Munich: Oldenbourg, 2003); Erich Meuthen and Claudia Märtl, *Das 15. Jahrhundert* (Oldenbourg Grundriss der Geschichte 9), 4th ed. (Munich: Oldenbourg, 2006); Günter Vogler, *Europas Aufbruch in die Neuzeit 1500–1650* (Handbuch der Geschichte Europas 5) (Stuttgart: Ulmer, 2003); Heinz Duchhardt, *Europa am Vorabend der Moderne 1650–1800* (Handbuch der Geschichte Europas 6) (Stuttgart: Ulmer, 2003); Thomas A. Brady Jr., Heiko A. Oberman, and James D. Tracy, eds., *Handbook of European History, 1400–1600,* 2 vols. (Leiden: Brill, 1994–1995); Heinz Schilling, *Die neue Zeit: Vom Christenheitseuropa zum Europa der Staaten 1250–1750* (Berlin: Siedler, 1999); Michael Jones, ed., *C. 1300–c. 1415,* vol. 6 of *The New Cambridge Medieval History* (Cambridge: Cambridge University Press, 2000); Christopher T. Allmand, ed., *C. 1415–c. 1500,* vol. 7 of *The New Cambridge Medieval History* (Cambridge: Cambridge University Press, 1998); Robert Fossier, *Le moyen âge,* 3 vols. (Paris: Colin, 1982–1983); Ferdinand Seibt and Winfried Eberhard, eds., *Europa 1400: Die Krise des Spätmittelalters* (Stuttgart: Klett Cotta, 1984); Ferdinand Seibt and Winfried Eberhard, eds., *Europa 1500: Integrationsprozesse im Widerstreit: Staaten, Regionen, Personenverbände, Christenheit* (Stuttgart: Klett Cotta, 1987); Johan Huizinga, *Herbst des Mittelalters: Studien über Lebens- und Geistesformen des 14. und 15. Jahrhunderts in Frankreich und in den Niederlanden,* 2nd ed. (Munich: Drei-Masken-Verlag, 1928; Dutch ed., 1919).

24. Wolfgang Reinhard, *Die Alte Welt bis 1818,* vol. 1 of *Geschichte der europäischen Expansion* (Stuttgart: Kohlhammer, 1983), 153; ibid., *Die Neue Welt,* vol. 2 of *Geschichte der europäischen Expansion* (Stuttgart: Kohlhammer, 1985), 134; Otto Heinz Mattiesen, *Die Kolonial- und Überseepolitik der kurländischen Herzöge im 17. und 18. Jahrhundert* (Stuttgart: Kohlhammer, 1940).

25. Basic texts include Wolfgang Reinhard, *Lebensformen Europas: Eine historische Kulturanthropologie,* 2nd ed. (Munich: C. H. Beck, 2006); Michael Mitterauer, *Warum Europa? Mittelalterliche Grundlagen eines Sonderwegs* (Munich: C. H. Beck, 2003); Philippe Ariès and Georges Duby, eds., *Vom Feudalzeitalter zur Renaissance,* vol. 2 of *Geschichte des privaten Lebens,* 2nd ed. (Frankfurt am Main: P. Fischer, 1991); Philippe Ariès and Roger Chartier, eds., *Von der Renaissance zur Aufklärung,* vol. 3 of *Geschichte des privaten Lebens* (Frankfurt am Main: P. Fischer, 1991); Fernand Braudel, *La Méditerranée et le monde méditerranéen à l'époque de Philippe II* (Paris: Colin, 1949; English ed.: London: Fontana, 1949; English ed.: London: Fontana, 1972–1973; German: Frankfurt am Main: Suhrkamp, 1990); *Kolloquien der Kommission der Göttinger Akademie der Wissenschaften zur Erforschung der Kultur des Spätmittelalters* Bericht über Kolloquien 1975–77 bis Bericht über Kolloquien 1999–2002, 7 vols. (Göttingen: Vandenhoeck und Ruprecht, 1980–2003); Rudolf Suntrup et al., eds., *Medieval to Early Modern Culture—Kultureller Wandel vom Mittelalter zur Frühen Neuzeit,* 5 vols. (Frankfurt am Main: Peter Lang, 2001–2005).

26. Pierre Alexandre, *Le climat en Europe au Moyen Âge: Contribution à l'histoire des variations climatiques de 1000 à 1425, d'après les sources narratives de l'Europe occidentale* (Paris: Editions de l'École des Hautes Études en Sciences Sociales, 1987); Rüdiger Glaser, *Klimageschichte Mitteleuropas: 1200 Jahre Wetter, Klima, Katastrophen,* 2nd ed. (Darmstadt: Wissenschaftliche Buchgesellschaft, 2008); Hubert H. Lamb, *Klima und Kulturgeschichte: Der Einfluß des Wetters auf den Gang der Geschichte* (Reinbek: Rowohlt, 1989); Christian Pfister, *Bevölkerungsgeschichte und historische Demographie 1500–1800* (Munich: Oldenbourg, 1994).

27. Kenneth. F. Kiple, ed., *The Cambridge World History of Human Disease* (Cambridge: Cambridge University Press, 1993), 247–293, 642–649, 807–811, 855–862, 987–988, 1008–1014; Jean–Noël Biraben, *Les hommes et la peste en France et dans les pays européens et méditerranéens,* 2 vols. (Paris: Mouton, 1975–1976); Klaus Bergdolt, *Der Schwarze Tod in Europa: Die Große Pest und das Ende des Mittelalters* (Munich: C. H. Beck, 1994); Ole Benedictow, *The Black Death, 1346–1353: The Complete History* (Woodbridge, UK: Boydell Press, 2004). Manfred Vasold, *Die Pest: Das Ende eines Mythos* (Stuttgart: Theiss, 2003), demonstrates that central European cities suffered only small population losses.

28. Dirlmeier, Fouquet, and Fuhrmann, *Europa im Spätmittelalter,* 18, 166; Meuthen and Märtl, *Das 15. Jahrhundert,* 3, 123; Vogler, *Europas Aufbruch,* 263; Duchhardt, *Europa am Vorabend der Moderne,* 83; cf. Carlo M. Cipolla and Knut Borchardt, eds., *Bevölkerungsgeschichte Europas* (Munich: Piper, 1971); Jean-Pierre Bardet and Jacques Dupáquier, eds., *Histoire des populations de l'Europe,* vol. 1 (Paris: Fayard, 1997).

29. John Hajnal, "European Marriage Patterns in Perspective," in *Population in History,* ed. David V. Glass and David E. Eversley (London: Arnold, 1965), 101–143.

30. Alberto Tenenti, *La vie et la mort à travers l'art du XVe siècle,* 2nd ed. (Paris: Fleury, 1983).

31. André Burguière, Christiane Klapisch-Zuber, Martine Segalen, Françoise Zonabend, eds., *Geschichte der Familie,* vols. 2–3 (Frankfurt am Main: Campus, 1996–1998); Andreas Gestrich, Jens-Uwe Krause, and Michael Mitterauer, eds., *Geschichte der Familie* (Stuttgart: Kröner, 2003).

32. Teresa A. Meade and Merry E. Wiesner–Hanks, eds., *A Companion to Gender History* (Malden, MA: Blackwell, 2004); Anne Echols and Marty Williams, eds., *An Annotated Index of Medieval Women* (New York: Wiener, 1992); Georges Duby and Michelle Perrot, *Geschichte der Frauen*, vols. 2–3 (Frankfurt am Main: Campus Verlag, 1991–1993); Margaret L. King, *Frauen in der Renaissance* (Munich: C. H. Beck, 1993); Olwen Hufton, *Frauenleben: Eine europäische Geschichte 1500–1800,* 2nd ed. (Frankfurt am Main: Fischer, 1998); Ute Gerhard, ed., *Frauen in der Geschichte des Rechts: Von der Frühen Neuzeit bis zur Gegenwart* (Munich: C. H. Beck, 1997); Peter J. P. Goldberg, *Women, Work, and Life Cycle in a Medieval Economy: Women in York and Yorkshire, c. 1300–1520* (Oxford: Clarendon, 1992).

33. Johann A. Steiger et al., eds., *Passion, Affekt und Leidenschaft in der Frühen Neuzeit* (Wolfenbütteler Arbeiten zur Barockforschung 43), 2 vols. (Wiesbaden: Harrassowitz, 2005).

34. Barbara Stollberg-Rilinger, *Europa im Jahrhundert der Aufklärung* (Stuttgart: Reclam, 2000), 151–160, quoted on 158.

35. Winfried Schulze, ed., *Ständische Gesellschaft und soziale Mobilität* (Munich: Oldenbourg, 1988); Klaus Schreiner and Gerd Schwerhoff, eds., *Verletzte Ehre: Ehrkonflikte in Gesellschaften des Mittelalters und der Frühen Neuzeit* (Cologne: Böhlau, 1995).

36. Georges Dumézil, *L'idéologie tripartie des Indo-européens* (Brussels: Latomus, 1958); Georges Duby, *Les trois ordres ou l'imaginaire du féodalisme* (Paris: Gallimard, 1978); Otto G. Oexle, "Tria genera hominum: Zur Geschichte eines Deutungsschemas der sozialen Wirklichkeit in Antike und Mittelalter," in *Institutionen, Kultur und Gesellschaft im Mittelalter: Festschrift für Josef Fleckenstein zu seinem 65. Geburtstag,* ed. Lutz Fenske (Sigmaringen: Thorbecke, 1984), 483–500.

37. Hans Erich Feine, *Kirchliche Rechtsgeschichte: Die katholische Kirche,* 4th ed. (Cologne: Böhlau, 1964).

38. Erwin Gatz, ed., *Die Bischöfe des Heiligen Römischen Reiches: Ein biographisches Lexikon,* 2 vols. (Berlin: Duncker & Humblot, 1990–1996).

39. Luise Schorn–Schütte, *Evangelische Geistlichkeit in der Frühneuzeit* (Gütersloh: Gütersloher Verlagshaus, 1996).

40. Marc Bloch, *Die Feudalgesellschaft* (Frankfurt am Main: Propylaeen, 1982); Maurice Keen, *Das Rittertum* (Munich: Artemis, 1987; U.S. ed., 1984); Otto G. Oexle and Werner Paravicini, eds., *Nobilitas: Funktion und Repräsentation des Adels in Alteuropa* (Göttingen: Vandenhoeck und Ruprecht, 1997); Hamish M. Scott, ed., *The European Nobilities in the 17th and 18th Centuries,* 2 vols., 2nd ed. (Houndmills, UK: Palgrave Macmillan, 2007–2008); Ronald G. Asch, ed., *Der europäische Adel im Ancien Regime: Von der Krise der ständischen Monarchien bis zur Revolution (ca. 1600–1789)* (Cologne: Böhlau, 2001).

41. Marie-Thérèse Caron, *Noblesse et pouvoir royale en France, XIIIe–XVIe siècle* (Paris: Colin, 1994); Marie-Claude Gerbet, *Les noblesses espagnoles au Moyen Âge, XIe–XVe siècle* (Paris: Colin, 1994); Kenneth B. McFarlane, *The Nobility of Later Medieval England* (Oxford: Clarendon, 1973); Chris Given-Wilson, *The English Nobility in the Late Middle Ages: The Fourteenth-Century Political Community* (London: Routledge & Kegan Paul, 1987); Michael Jones, ed., *Gentry and Lesser Nobility in Late Medieval Europe* (Gloucester, UK: Sutton, 1986).

42. John Edwards, *The Jews in Christian Europe, 1400–1700* (London: Routledge, 1988); Friedrich Battenberg, *Von den Anfängen bis 1650*, vol. 1 of *Das europäische Zeitalter der Juden: Zur Entwicklung einer Minderheit in der nichtjüdischen Umwelt Europas* (Darmstadt: Wissenschaftliche Buchgesellschaft, 1990); Michael Toch, *Die Juden im mittelalterlichen Reich* (Munich: Oldenbourg, 1998); Frantisek Graus, *Pest—Geißler—Judenmorde: Das 14. Jahrhundert als Krisenzeit*, 3rd ed. (Göttingen: Vandenhoeck und Ruprecht, 1994).

43. Bronislaw Geremek, *Les marginaux parisiens aux XIVe et XVe siècles* (Paris: Flammarion, 1976); Bernd–Ulrich Hergemöller, ed., *Randgruppen der spätmittelalterlichen Gesellschaft,* 3rd ed. (Warendorf: Fahlbusch, 2001); Frank Rexroth, *Das Milieu der Nacht: Obrigkeit und Randgruppen im spätmittelalterlichen London* (Göttingen: Vandenhoeck und Ruprecht, 1999); Ernst Schubert, *Fahrendes Volk im Mittelalter* (Bielefeld: Verlag für Regionalgeschichte, 1995); Kathy Stuart, *Defiled Trades and Social Outcasts: Honor and Ritual Pollution in Early Modern Germany* (Cambridge: Cambridge University Press, 1999).

44. Michel Mollat, *Die Armen im Mittelalter,* 2nd ed. (Munich: C. H. Beck, 1987); Thomas Fischer, *Städtische Armut und Armenfürsorge im 15. und 16. Jahrhundert: Sozialgeschichtliche Untersuchungen am Beispiel der Städte Basel, Freiburg i. Br. und Straßburg* (Göttingen: Schwartz, 1979); Robert Jütte, *Arme, Bettler, Beutelschneider: Eine Sozialgeschichte der Armut in der Frühen Neuzeit* (Cologne: Böhlau, 2000).

45. Otto G. Oexle, ed., *Memoria als Kultur* (Göttingen: Vandenhoeck & Ruprecht, 1995).

46. *Die Anfänge der Landgemeinde und ihr Wesen,* 2 vols. (Vorträge und Forschungen 7–8) (Konstanz: Thorbecke, 1986); Léopold Génicot, *Rural Communities in the Medieval West* (Baltimore: Johns Hopkins University Press, 1990); Heide Wunder, *Die bäuerliche Gemeinde in Deutschland* (Göttingen: Vandenhoeck und Ruprecht, 1986).

47. Karl Siegfried Bader, *Studien zur Rechtsgeschichte des mittelalterlichen Dorfes,* 3 vols. (Weimar: Böhlau, 1957–1974).

48. Hans Patze, ed., *Die Grundherrschaft im späten Mittelalter,* 2 vols. (Vorträge und Forschungen 27) (Sigmaringen: Thorbecke, 1983).

49. Jan Peters and Axel Lubinski, eds., *Gutsherrschaftsgesellschaften im europäischen Vergleich* (Berlin: Akademie Verlag, 1997); Eduard Maur, *Gutsherrschaft und "zweite Leibeigenschaft" in Böhmen* (Munich: Oldenbourg, 2001); Peter Blickle, *Von der Leibeigenschaft zu den Menschenrechten: Eine Geschichte der Freiheit in Deutschland* (Munich: C. H. Beck, 2003).

50. Irene Erfen, ed., *Fremdheit und Reisen im Mittelalter* (Stuttgart: Steiner, 1997); Hermann Bausinger, Klaus Beyrer, and Gottfried Korff, eds., *Reisekultur: Von der Pilgerfahrt zum modernen Tourismus* (Munich: C. H. Beck, 1991); Holger Thomas Gräf and Ralf Pröve, *Wege ins Ungewisse: Reisen in der Frühen Neuzeit 1500–1800* (Frankfurt am Main: P. Fischer, 1997).

51. Christopher Hibbert, *The Grand Tour* (London: Methuen, 1987).

52. Karl-Heinz Spiess, "Zur Landflucht im Mittelalter," in Patze, *Grundherrschaft,* 1:157–204; Fernand Braudel, ed., *Villages désertés et histoire économique, XIe–XVIIIe siècle* (Paris: S.E.V.P.E.N., 1965).

53. Charles Higounet, Jean-Bernard Marquette, and Philippe Wolff, eds., *Atlas historique des villes de France,* 46 vols. (Paris: CNRS, 1982–2000); Mary D. Lobel, ed., *The Atlas of Historic Towns,* 3 vols. (Baltimore: Johns Hopkins University Press, 1972–1991); Heinz Stoob and Wilfried

Ehrbrecht, eds., *Deutscher Städteatlas,* 6 vols. (Dortmund: Grösschen, 1973–2000); Leonardo Benevolo, *Die Stadt in der europäischen Geschichte,* 2nd ed. (Munich: C. H. Beck, 1998); P. Feldbauer, ed., *Die vormoderne Stadt: Asien und Europa im Vergleich* (Munich: Oldenbourg, 2002); Edith Ennen, *Die europäische Stadt des Mittelalters,* 4th ed. (Göttingen: Vandenhoeck & Ruprecht, 1987); Hartmut Boockmann, *Die Stadt im späten Mittelalter,* 3rd ed. (Munich: C. H. Beck, 1994); Peter Clark, ed., *Small Towns in Early Modern Europe* (Cambridge: Cambridge University Press, 1995); Evamaria Engel, *Die deutsche Stadt im Mittelalter* (Munich: C. H. Beck, 1993); Eberhard Isenmann, *Die deutsche Stadt im Spätmittelalter, 1250–1500: Stadtgestalt, Recht, Stadtregiment, Kirche, Gesellschaft, Wirtschaft* (Stuttgart: Ulmer, 1988); Georges Duby, ed., *Histoire de la France urbaine,* vols. 2–3 (Paris: Editions du Seuil, 1980–1981); Rodney H. Hilton, *English and French Towns in Feudal Society: A Comparative Study* (Cambridge: Cambridge University Press, 1992); Charles Tilly and Wim P. Blockmans, eds., *Cities and the Rise of States in Europe, 1000–1800* (Boulder, CO: Westview Press, 1994).

54. Albrecht Jockenhövel, ed., *Bergbau, Verhüttung und Waldnutzung im Mittelalter: Auswirkungen auf Mensch und Umwelt* (Stuttgart: Steiner, 1996).

55. Ernst Schubert and Bernd Herrmann, eds., *Von der Angst zur Ausbeutung: Umwelterfahrung zwischen Mittelalter und Neuzeit* (Frankfurt am Main: Fischer Taschenbuch Verlag, 1994); Albert Zimmermann and Andreas Speer, eds., *Mensch und Natur im Mittelalter,* 2 vols. (Berlin: de Gruyter, 1991–1992); Roland Bechmann, *Trees and Man: The Forest in the Middle Ages* (New York: Paragon House, 1990).

56. Mitterauer, *Warum Europa?,* 184–186, 289–292; Arnold Angenendt, *Geschichte der Religiosität im Mittelalter,* 2nd ed. (Darmstadt: Wissenschaftliche Buchgesellschaft, 2000); Marek Derwich and Martial Staub, eds., *Die "Neue Frömmigkeit" in Europa im Spätmittelalter* (Göttingen: Vandenhoeck und Ruprecht, 2004); Peter Dinzelbacher and Dieter R. Bauer, eds., *Volksreligion im hohen und späten Mittelalter* (Paderborn: Schöningh, 1990); Berndt Hamm, "Theologie und Frömmigkeit im ausgehenden Mittelalter," in *Handbuch der Geschichte der evangelischen Kirche in Bayern,* ed. Gerhard Müller et al. (St. Ottilien: EOS-Verlag, 2002), 159–211.

57. Jean Delumeau, *Angst im Abendland: Die Geschichte kollektiver Ängste im Europa des 14. bis 18. Jahrhunderts* (Reinbek: Rowohlt, 1985); Thilo Esser, *Pest, Heilsangst und Frömmigkeit: Studien zur religiösen Bewältigung der Pest am Ausgang des Mittelalters* (Altenberge: Oros-Verlag, 1999).

58. Sönke Lorenz, Jürgen Michael Schmidt, and Stefan Kötz, eds., *Wider alle Hexerei und Teufelswerk: Die europäische Hexenverfolgung und ihre Auswirkungen auf Südwestdeutschland* (Ostfildern: Thorbecke, 2004); Wolfgang Behringer, *Witches and Witch-Hunts: A Global History* (Cambridge: Polity Press, 2004).

59. Basic texts on this subject include Norman Kretzman, Anthony Kenny, Jan Pinborg, and Eleonore Stump, eds., *From the Rediscovery of Aristotle to the Disintegration of Scholasticism 1100–1600,* vol. 1 of *The Cambridge History of Later Medieval Philosophy* (Cambridge: Cambridge University Press, 1982); Charles B. Schmitt, ed., *The Cambridge History of Renaissance Philosophy* (Cambridge: Cambridge University Press, 1988); Notker Hammerstein, ed., *Handbuch der deutschen Bildungsgeschichte,* vols. 1–2 (Munich: Beck, 1996–2005).

60. Michel Mollat du Jourdin and Bernhard Schimmelpfennig, eds., *Die Zeit der Zerreißproben (1274–1449),* vol. 6 of *Die Geschichte des Christentums* (Freiburg im Breisgau: Herder, 1991); Marc Venard and Heribert Smolinsky, eds., *Von der Reform zur Reformation (1450–1530),* vol. 7 of *Die Geschichte des Christentums* (Freiburg im Breisgau: Herder, 1995); Marc Venard and Heribert Smolinsky, eds., *Die Zeit der Konfessionen (1530–1620/30),* vol. 8 of *Die Geschichte des Christentums* (Freiburg im Breisgau: Herder, 1992); Marc Venard and Albert Boesten-Stengel, eds., *Das Zeitalter der Vernunft (1620/30–1750),* vol. 9 of *Die Geschichte des Christentums* (Freiburg im Breisgau: Herder, 1998); Miri Rubin and Walter Simons, eds., *Christianity in Western Europe, c. 1100–c. 1500,* vol. 4 of *The Cambridge History of Christianity* (Cambridge: Cambridge University Press, 2009); Ronnie Po-Chia Hsia, ed., *Reform and Expansion, 1500–1660,* vol. 6 of *The Cambridge History of Christianity* (Cambridge: Cambridge University Press, 2007); Stewart J. Brown and Timothy Tackett, eds., *Enlightenment, Reawakening, and Revolution, 1660–1815,* vol. 7 of *The Cambridge History of Christianity* (Cambridge: Cambridge University Press, 2006).

61. Walter Rüegg and Asa Briggs, eds., *Mittelalter,* vol. 1, and *Von der Reformation zur Französischen Revolution,* vol. 2 of *Geschichte der Universität in Europa* (Munich: C. H. Beck, 1993–1996), especially 1:66–67, 104–108, 234–263; 2:181–182; English ed.: *A History of the University in Europe,* vols. 1–2 (Cambridge: Cambridge University Press, 1992–1996).

62. Myron P. Gilmore, *Humanists and Jurists: Six Studies in the Renaissance* (Cambridge, MA: Harvard University Press, 1963); Albert Rabil, ed., *Renaissance Humanism: Foundations, Form, and Legacy,* 3 vols. (Philadelphia: University of Pennsylvania Press, 1988).

63. James H. Overfield, *Humanism and Scholasticism in Late Medieval Germany* (Princeton, NJ: Princeton University Press, 1984); see also Johannes Helmrath, "'Humanismus und Scholastik' und die deutschen Universitäten um 1500," *Zeitschrift für Historische Forschung* 15 (1988): 187–203.

64. Hans Baron, *The Crisis of the Early Italian Renaissance: Civic Humanism and Republican Liberty in an Age of Classicism and Tyranny,* 2nd ed. (Princeton, NJ: Princeton University Press, 1966).

65. Quentin Skinner, *Machiavelli zur Einführung,* 3rd ed. (Hamburg: Junius, 2001).

66. Paul Oscar Kristeller, *Il pensiero filosofico di Marsilio Ficino,* 2nd ed. (Florence: Sansoni, 1988).

67. Jean-Claude Margolin, *L'humanisme en Europe au temps de la Rénaissance* (Paris: PUF, 1981); Heiko A. Oberman and Thomas A. Brady Jr., eds., *Itinerarium Italicum: The Profile of the Italian Renaissance in the Mirror of Its European Transformations* (Leiden: Brill, 1975).

68. Cornelis Augustijn, *Erasmus von Rotterdam: Leben—Werk—Wirkung* (Munich: C. H. Beck, 1986).

69. Eugenio Garin, ed., *Der Mensch der Renaissance* (Frankfurt am Main: Campus, 1988); John J. Martin, *Myths of Renaissance Individualism* (Basingstoke, UK: Palgrave Macmillan, 2004).

70. Fernand Roulier, *Jean Pic de la Mirandola (1463–1494): Humaniste, philosophe et théologien* (Geneva: Slatkine, 1989).

71. Ludwig H. Heydenreich, André Chastel, and Günter Passavant, *Italienische Renaissance,* 4 vols. (Munich: C. H. Beck, 1965–1975).

72. Anthony Grafton, *Leon Battista Alberti: Baumeister der Renaissance* (Berlin: Berlin–Verlag, 2002).

73. Martin Kemp, *Leonardo* (Munich: C. H. Beck, 2005; English ed.: Oxford: Oxford University Press, 2004).

74. Dirlmeier, Fouquet, and Fuhrmann, *Europa im Spätmittelalter,* 91; Uta Lindgren, ed., *Europäische Technik im Mittelalter 800–1400: Tradition und Innovation: Ein Handbuch,* 2nd ed. (Berlin: Gebr. Mann, 1997).

75. Meuthen and Märtl, *Das 15. Jahrhundert,* 105.

76. Jacob Burckhardt, *Die Kultur der Renaissance in Italien: Ein Versuch* (Basel: Schweighauser, 1860); August Buck, ed., *Zu Begriff und Problem der Renaissance* (Darmstadt: Wissenschaftliche Buchgesellschaft, 1969); André Chastel, *Der Mythos der Renaissance, 1420–1520* (Genf: Skira, 1969); Wallace K. Ferguson, *The Renaissance in Historical Thought: Five Centuries of Interpretation* (Boston: Mifflin, 1948); Peter Burke, *Die Renaissance in Italien: Sozialgeschichte einer Kultur zwischen Tradition und Erfindung* (Berlin: Wagenbach, 1984); Peter Burke, *Die Renaissance* (Berlin: Wagenbach, 1990); Georg Kaufmann, ed., *Die Renaissance im Blick der Nationen Europas* (Wiesbaden: Harrassowitz, 1991).

77. Donald K. McKim, ed., *The Cambridge Companion to Martin Luther* (Cambridge: Cambridge University Press, 2003); Martin Brecht, *Martin Luther,* 3 vols. (Stuttgart: Calwer Verlag, 1981–1987).

78. Donald K. McKim, ed., *The Cambridge Companion to John Calvin* (Cambridge: Cambridge University Press, 2004); William Stanford Reid, ed., *John Calvin: His Influence in the Western World* (Grand Rapids, MI: Zondervan Publishing House, 1982).

79. Steven Ozment, ed., *Reformation Europe: A Guide to Research* (St. Louis, MO: Center for Reformation Research, 1982).

80. Alastair Duke, Gillian Lewis, and Andrew Pettegree, eds., *Calvinism in Europe, 1540–1610: A Collection of Documents* (Manchester, UK: Manchester University Press, 1992); Andrew Pettegree, ed., *Calvinism in Europe, 1540–1620* (Cambridge: Cambridge University Press, 1994); Philip Benedict, *Christ's Churches Purely Reformed: A Social History of Calvinism* (New Haven, CT: Yale University Press, 2002).

81. Hubert Jedin, *Geschichte des Konzils von Trient,* 4 vols. in 5 parts (Freiburg im Breisgau: Herder, 1949–1975); Paolo Prodi and Wolfgang Reinhard, eds., *Das Konzil von Trient und die Moderne* (Berlin: Duncker und Humblot, 2001).

82. Wolfgang Reinhard, "Konfession und Konfessionalisierung in Europa" [1981], in *Ausgewählte Abhandlungen* (Berlin: Duncker und Humblot, 1997), 103–125; Heinz Schilling, ed., *Die reformierte Konfessionalisierung in Deutschland* (Gütersloh: Gütersloher Verlagshaus, 1986); Hans-Christoph Rublack, ed., *Die lutherische Konfessionalisierung in Deutschland* (Gütersloh: Gütersloher Verlagshaus, 1992); Wolfgang Reinhard and Heinz Schilling, eds., *Die katholische Konfessionalisierung* (Gütersloh: Gütersloher Verlagshaus, 1995); Robert Bireley, *The Refashioning of Catholicism: A Reassessment of the Counter Reformation, 1450–1700* (Houndmills, UK: Palgrave Macmillan, 1999).

83. Mitterauer, *Warum Europa?,* 257–273; Guglielmo Cavallo and Roger Chartier, eds., *A History of Reading in the West* (Oxford: Polity Press, 1999); Johannes Burkhardt, *Das Reformation-*

sjahrhundert: Deutsche Geschichte zwischen Medienrevolution und Institutionenbildung 1517–1617 (Stuttgart: Kohlhammer, 2002).

84. Johannes Wallmann, *Der Pietismus,* 2nd ed. (Göttingen: Vandenhoeck & Ruprecht, 2005); Martin Brecht, ed., *Geschichte des Pietismus,* 5 vols. (Göttingen: Vandenhoeck & Ruprecht, 1993–2005).

85. Rupert E. Davies, ed., *A History of the Methodist Church in Great Britain,* 4 vols. (London: Epworth Press, 1965–1988).

86. Stanley Sadie and Alison Latham, eds., *Das Cambridge Buch der Musik* (Frankfurt am Main: Zweitausendeins, 1994).

87. Michael Hunter, *Establishing the New Science: The Experience of the Early Royal Society* (Woodbridge, UK: Boydell Press, 1989); Roger Hahn, *The Anatomy of a Scientific Institution: The Paris Academy of Sciences, 1666–1803* (Berkeley: University of California Press, 1971); James E. McClellan, *Science Reorganized: Scientific Societies in the Eighteenth Century* (New York: Columbia University Press, 1985); Klaus Garber and Heinz Wismann, eds., *Europäische Sozietätsbewegung und demokratische Tradition: Die europäischen Akademien der Frühen Neuzeit zwischen Frührenaissance und Spätaufklärung,* 2 vols. (Tübingen: Niemeyer, 1996).

88. Nicholas Jolley, *Leibniz* (London: Routledge, 2005).

89. David Goodman and Colin A. Russell, *The Rise of Scientific Europe, 1500–1800* (Sevenoaks, UK: Hodder and Stoughton, 1991); Steven Shapin, *Die wissenschaftliche Revolution* (Frankfurt am Main: Fischer Taschenbuchverlag, 1998; English ed., 1996); Roy Porter, *Eighteenth-Century Science* (Cambridge History of Science 4) (Cambridge: Cambridge University Press, 2003).

90. Peter Machamer, *The Cambridge Companion to Galileo* (Cambridge: Cambridge University Press, 1998).

91. Werner Schneiders, ed., *Christian Wolff (1679–1754): Interpretationen zu seiner Philosophie und deren Wirkung: Mit einer Bibliographie der Wolff-Literatur,* 2nd ed. (Hamburg: Meiners, 1986).

92. Karl Otmar von Aretin, ed., *Der Aufgeklärte Absolutismus* (Cologne: Kiepenheuer und Witsch, 1974); Marc Raeff, *The Well-Ordered Police State: Social and Institutional Change through Law in the Germanies and Russia, 1600–1800* (New Haven, CT: Yale University Press, 1983); Hamish M. Scott, ed., *Enlightened Absolutism: Reform and Reformers in Later Eighteenth-Century Europe* (Houndmills, UK: Macmillan, 1990); Hans Erich Bödeker and Etienne François, eds., *Aufklärung/Lumières und Politik: Zur politischen Kultur der deutschen und französischen Aufklärung* (Leipzig: Leipziger Universitätsverlag, 1996).

93. Paul Hazard, *Die Krise des europäischen Geistes (1680–1715)* (Hamburg: Hoffmann und Campe, 1939); ibid., *Die Herrschaft der Vernunft: Das europäische Denken im 18. Jahrhundert* (Hamburg: Hoffmann und Campe, 1949); Peter Gay, *The Enlightenment: An Interpretation,* 2 vols. (New York: Knopf, 1967–1969); Roy Porter, *Kleine Geschichte der Aufklärung,* 2nd ed. (Berlin: Wagenbach, 1995); Timothy C. W. Blanning, *The Culture of Power and the Power of Culture: Old Regime Europe, 1660–1789* (Oxford: Oxford University Press, 2002); Roy Porter and Mikuláš Teich, eds., *The Enlightenment in National Context* (Cambridge: Cambridge University Press, 1981); John Brewer, *The Pleasures of the Imagination: English Culture in the Eigh-*

teenth Century (London: HarperCollins, 1997); John Lynch, *Bourbon Spain, 1700–1808* (Oxford: Oxford University Press, 1989); Daniel Roche, *La France des lumières* (Paris: Fayard, 1993); Franco Venturi, *Italy and the Enlightenment: Studies in a Cosmopolitan Century* (London: Longman, 1972).

94. John Dunn, *Locke* (Oxford: Oxford University Press, 1984).

95. Stollberg-Rilinger, *Europa im Jahrhundert der Aufklärung*, 280–281.

96. Hubert Bost, ed., *Critique, savoir et erudition à la veille des Lumières: Le Dictionnaire historique et critique de Pierre Bayle (1647–1706)* (Amsterdam: APA Holland University Press, 1998).

97. Theodore Besterman, *Voltaire* (Munich: Winkler, 1971).

98. Hippolyte Rigault, *Histoire de la querelle des anciens et des modernes* (Paris: Hachette, 1856; New York: Franklin, 1963).

99. Robert Shackleton, *Montesquieu: A Critical Biography* (London: Oxford University Press, 1961).

100. Pierre Lepape, *Denis Diderot: Eine Biographie* (Frankfurt am Main: Campus, 1994).

101. Robert Darnton, *Glänzende Geschäfte: Die Verbreitung von Diderots Encyclopédie oder: Wie verkauft man Wissen mit Gewinn?* (Berlin: Wagenbach, 1993).

102. Monika Fick, *Lessing-Handbuch: Leben, Werk, Wirkung* (Stuttgart: Metzler, 2004).

103. Nicholas J. H. Dent, *Rousseau* (London: Routledge, 2005); Raymond Trousson, *Jean-Jacques Rousseau* (Paris: Tallandier, 2003).

104. Helmut Reinalter, ed., *Aufklärung und Geheimgesellschaften: Freimaurer, Illuminaten, Rosenkreuzer: Ideologie, Struktur und Wirkungen* (Bayreuth: Selbstverlag der freimaurerischen Forschungsgesellschaft, 1992).

105. Peter Burke, *Vico* (Oxford: Oxford University Press, 1985).

106. Wolfgang Schmale and Nan L. Dodde, eds., *Revolution des Wissens? Europa und seine Schulen im Zeichen der Aufklärung 1750–1825* (Bochum: Winkler, 1991).

107. Jürgen Habermas, *Strukturwandel der Öffentlichkeit: Untersuchungen zu einer Kategorie der bürgerlichen Gesellschaft* (Neuwied: Luchterhand, 1962); Christoph Heyl, *A Passion for Privacy: Untersuchungen zur Genese der bürgerlichen Privatsphäre in London 1660–1800* (Munich: Oldenbourg, 2004); Holger Böning, *Die Genese der Volksaufklärung und ihre Entwicklung bis 1780* (Stuttgart: Frommann-Holzboog, 1990); Benoît Garnot, *Le peuple au siècle des lumières: Échec d'un dressage culturel* (Paris: Editions Imago, 1990).

108. Ulrich Im Hof, *Das gesellige Jahrhundert. Gesellschaft und Gesellschaften im Zeitalter der Aufklärung* (Munich: C. H. Beck, 1982); Daniel Roche, *Le siècle des lumières en province: Académies et académiciens provinciaux 1680–1789* (Paris: Éditions de l'École des Hautes Études en Sciences Sociales, 1978).

109. Basic texts: Wim Blockmans and Jean-Pilippe Genet, eds., *The Origins of the Modern State in Europe: 13th–18th Centuries,* 7 vols. (Oxford: Clarendon Press, 1995–2000); Wolfgang Reinhard, *Geschichte der Staatsgewalt: Eine vergleichende Verfassungsgeschichte Europas von den Anfängen bis zur Gegenwart*, 3rd ed. (Munich: C. H. Beck, 2002); Ferdinand Seibt, ed., *Europa im Hoch- und Spätmittelalter*, vol. 2 of *Handbuch der europäischen Geschichte* (Stuttgart: Klett Cotta, 1987); Josef Engel, ed., *Die Entstehung des neuzeitlichen Europa*, vol. 3 of *Handbuch der europäischen Geschichte* (Stuttgart: Union Verlag, 1971); Fritz Wagner, ed., *Europa im Zeitalter des Absolutismus und der Aufklärung*, vol. 4 of *Handbuch der europäischen*

Geschichte (Stuttgart: Union Verlag, 1968); Richard Bonney, *The European Dynastic States, 1494–1660*, 3rd ed. (Oxford: Oxford University Press, 1991); William Doyle, *The Old European Order, 1660–1800*, 2nd ed. (Oxford: Oxford University Press, 1992); Alfred Kohler, *Expansion und Hegemonie 1450–1559*, vol. 1 of *Handbuch der Geschichte der Internationalen Beziehungen*, ed. Heinz Duchhardt and Franz Knipping (Paderborn: Schöningh, 2008); Heinz Schilling, *Konfessionalisierung und Staatsinteressen 1559–1660*, vol. 2 of *Handbuch der Geschichte der Internationalen Beziehungen*, ed. Duchhardt and Knipping (Paderborn: Schöningh, 2007); Heinz Duchhardt, *Balance of Power und Pentarchie*, vol. 4 of *Handbuch der Geschichte der Internationalen Beziehungen*, ed. Duchhardt and Knipping (Paderborn: Schöningh, 1997); Jean-Michel Sallmann, *Géopolitique du XVIe siècle 1490–1618*, vol. 1 of *Nouvelle histoire des relations internationales* (Paris: Seuil, 2003); Claire Gantet, *Guerre, paix et construction des Etats 1618–1714*, vol. 2 of *Nouvelle histoire des relations internationales* (Paris: Seuil, 2003); Jean-Pierre Bois, *De la paix des rois à l'ordre des empereurs 1714–1815*, vol. 3 of *Nouvelle histoire des relations internationales* (Paris: Seuil, 2003); John Watts, *The Making of Polities: Europe, 1300–1500* (Cambridge: Cambridge University Press, 2009).

110. Mitterauer, *Warum Europa?*, 54–151; Peter Blickle, *Kommunalismus*, 2 vols. (Munich: Oldenbourg, 2000); John H. Elliott, "A Europe of Composite Monarchies," *Past and Present* 137 (1992): 48–71; Thomas Fröschl, ed., *Föderationsmodelle und Unionsstrukturen* (Vienna: Verlag für Geschichte und Politik, 1994).

111. W. Gordon East, *An Historical Geography of Europe*, 5th ed. (London: Methuen, 1966); Guy P. Marchal, ed., *Grenzen und Raumvorstellungen (11.–20. Jahrhundert)* (Zurich: Chronos, 1996); Peter Sahlins, *Boundaries: The Making of France and Spain in the Pyrenées* (Berkeley: University of California Press, 1989); Tom Scott, *Regional Identity and Economic Change: The Upper Rhine, 1450–1600* (Oxford: Clarendon Press, 1997).

112. Thomas Eichenberger, *Patria: Studien zur Bedeutung des Wortes im Mittelalter* (Sigmaringen: Thorbecke, 1991).

113. Walter Ullmann, *Kurze Geschichte des Papsttums im Mittelalter* (Berlin: de Gruyter, 1978; English ed., 1972); Harald Zimmermann, *Das Papsttum im Mittelalter: Eine Papstgeschichte im Spiegel der Historiographie* (Stuttgart: Ulmer, 1981); Bernhard Schimmelpfennig, *Das Papsttum von der Antike bis zur Renaissance*, 4th ed. (Darmstadt: Wissenschaftliche Buchgesellschaft, 1996).

114. Peter G. Stein, *Römisches Recht und Europa: Die Geschichte einer Rechtskultur* (Frankfurt am Main: Fischer Taschenbuchverlag, 1996); Harold J. Berman, *Recht und Revolution: Die Bildung der westlichen Rechtstradition* (Frankfurt am Main: Suhrkamp, 1991; US ed., 1983).

115. Hans Hattenhauer, *Europäische Rechtsgeschichte*, 4th ed. (Heidelberg: Müller, 2004).

116. Vincenzo Lavenia, *L'infamia e il perdono: Tributi, pene e confessione nella teologia morale della prima età moderna* (Bologna: il Mulino, 2004).

117. Roman Schnur, ed., *Die Rolle der Juristen bei der Entstehung des modernen Staates* (Berlin: Duncker und Humblot, 1986); Günther Schulz, ed., *Sozialer Aufstieg: Funktionseliten im Spätmittelalter und in der frühen Neuzeit* (Munich: Boldt im Oldenbourg Verlag, 2002); John Bartier, *Légistes et gens de finances au XVe Siècle: Les conseillers des ducs de Bourgogne Philippe le Bon et Charles le Téméraire*, 2 vols. (Brussels: Palais des Académies, 1955–1957).

118. Hugo Rahner, *Kirche und Staat im frühen Christentum: Dokumente aus acht Jahrhunderten und ihre Deutung,* 2nd ed. (Munich: Kösel, 1961); Robert Grant, Peter Moraw, Volker Press, and Hanns Kerner, "Kirche und Staat," in *Theologische Realenzyklopädie,* vol. 18 (Berlin: de Gruyter, 1988), 354–397.

119. Hans Fenske, Dieter Mertens, Wolfgang Reinhard, and Klaus Rosen, *Geschichte der politischen Ideen,* 5th ed. (Frankfurt am Main: Fischer Taschenbuchverlag, 2000); Iring Fetscher and Herwig Münkler, eds., *Pipers Handbuch der politischen Ideen,* vols. 2–3 (Munich: Piper, 1985–1993); Anthony Black, *Political Thought in Europe, 1250–1450* (Cambridge: Cambridge University Press, 1992); James H. Burns, ed., *The Cambridge History of Political Thought, 1450–1700* (Cambridge: Cambridge University Press, 1991).

120. Michael Roberts, "Die militärische Revolution 1560–1660" [1967], in *Absolutismus,* ed. Ernst Hinrichs (Frankfurt am Main: Suhrkamp, 1986), 273–309; Jeremy Black, ed., *A Military Revolution? Military Change and European Society, 1550–1800* (Basingstoke, UK: Macmillan, 1991); Geoffrey Parker, *Die militärische Revolution: Die Kriegskunst und der Aufstieg des Westens 1500–1800* (Frankfurt am Main: Campus, 1990; English ed., 1988).

121. Samuel Finer in Charles Tilly, ed., *The Formation of National States in Western Europe* (Princeton, NJ: Princeton University Press, 1975).

122. Peter Blickle, ed., *Resistance, Representation, and Community* (Origins of the Modern State in Europe) (Oxford: Clarendon Press, 1997); Rodney H. Hilton and Trevor H. Aston, eds., *The English Rising of 1381* (Cambridge: Cambridge University Press, 1984); Michel Mollat and Philippe Wolff, *Ongles bleus, Jacques et Ciompi: Les révolutions populaires en Europe aux XIVe et XVe siècles* (Paris: Calmann-Lévy, 1970); Horst Buszello, Peter Blickle, and Rudolf Endres, eds., *Der deutsche Bauernkrieg,* 3rd ed. (Paderborn: Schöningh, 1995); Yves-Marie Bercé, *Revoltes et révolutions dans l'Europe moderne (XVIe–XVIIIe siècle)* (Paris: PUF, 1980); Winfried Schulze, ed., *Europäische Bauernrevolten der Frühen Neuzeit* (Frankfurt am Main: Suhrkamp, 1982); Perez Zagorin, *Rebels and Rulers, 1500–1660,* 2 vols. (Cambridge: Cambridge University Press, 1982); Samuel K. Cohn, *Lust for Liberty: The Politics of Social Revolt in Medieval Europe, 1200–1425* (Cambridge, MA: Harvard University Press, 2006).

123. Wim P. Blockmans, "A Typology of Representative Institutions in Late Medieval Europe," *Journal of Medieval History* 4 (1978): 189–215; *Las Cortes de Castilla y León en la Edad Media,* 2 vols. (Valladolid: Cortes de Castilla y León, 1988); Jack R. Lander, *The Limitations of the English Monarchy in the Later Middle Ages* (Toronto: University of Toronto Press, 1989); John Smith Roskell et al., eds., *The History of Parliament: The House of Commons, 1386–1421,* 4 vols. (Stroud, UK: Sutton, 1992–1993); Robert Wellens, *Les États Généraux des Pays-Bas, des origines à la fin du règne de Philippe le Beau, 1464–1506,* vol. 1 (Kortrijk-Heule: UGA, 1974); Dietrich Gerhard, ed., *Ständische Vertretungen in Europa im 17. und 18. Jahrhundert* (Göttingen: Vandenhoeck & Ruprecht, 1969); Thomas Ertman, *Birth of the Leviathan: Building States and Regimes in Medieval and Early Modern Europe* (Cambridge: Cambridge University Press, 1997); J. Russell Major, *From Renaissance Monarchy to Absolute Monarchy: French Kings, Nobles, and Estates* (Baltimore: Johns Hopkins University Press, 1994); Peter Moraw, "Hoftag und Reichstag von den Anfängen im Mittelalter bis 1806," in *Parlamentsrecht und Parlamentspraxis,* ed. Hans-Peter Schneider and Wolfgang Zeh (Berlin: de Gruyter, 1989), 3–47;

Francis L. Carsten, *Princes and Parliaments in Germany from the 15th to the 18th Century* (Oxford: Clarendon Press, 1959).

124. Kersten Krüger, "Absolutismus in Dänemark—Ein Modell für Begriffsbildung und Typologie," *Zeitschrift der Gesellschaft für Schleswig-Holsteinische Geschichte* 104 (1979): 171–206; Peter Brandt, "Von der Adelsmonarchie zur königlichen 'Eingewalt': Der Umbau der Ständegesellschaft in der Vorbereitungs- Und Frühphase des dänischen Absolutismus," *Historische Zeitschrift* 250 (1990): 33–72.

125. Jonathan I. Israel, ed., *The Anglo-Dutch Moment: Essays on the Glorious Revolution and Its World Impact* (Cambridge: Cambridge University Press, 1991); Eveline Cruickshanks, *The Glorious Revolution* (London: St. Martin's Press, 2000).

126. Douglas Biggs, Sharon D. Michalove, and Albert C. Reeves, *Traditions and Transformations in Late Medieval England* (Leiden: Brill, 2002); Alfred L. Brown, *The Governance of Late Medieval England, 1272–1461* (London: Edward Arnold, 1989); Anthony Goodman, *The Wars of the Roses: Military Activity and English Society, 1452–1497* (London: Routledge & Kegan Paul, 1981; reprint, 1991); Anthony Goodman, *The New Monarchy: England, 1471–1534* (Oxford: Blackwell, 1988).

127. Bernard Guillemain, *La cour pontificale d'Avignon (1309–1376): Étude d'une société,* 2nd ed. (Paris: Boccard, 1966); Guillaume Mollat, *Les papes d'Avignon,* 9th ed. (Paris: Letouzey et Ané, 1949; English ed., 1965); Yves Renouard, *La papauté à Avignon,* 3rd ed. (Paris: PUF, 1969).

128. Jean Favier, *Frankreich im Zeitalter der Lehensherrschaft 1000–1515,* vol. 2 of *Geschichte Frankreichs* (Stuttgart: Deutsche Verlagsanstalt, 1989); Christopher T. Allmand, *The Hundred Years' War: England and France at War c. 1300–c. 1450* (Cambridge: Cambridge University Press, 1988; reprint, 1991); Philippe Contamine, *La guerre de cent ans,* 8th ed. (Paris: PUF, 2002).

129. Werner Paravicini, *Karl der Kühne: Das Ende des Hauses Burgund* (Göttingen: Muster-Schmidt, 1976); Walter Prevenier and Wim P. Blockmans, *Die burgundischen Niederlande* (Weinheim: VCH, 1986); Bertrand Schnerb, *L'état bourgignon (1363–1477)* (Paris: Perrin, 1999); Richard Vaughan, *Philip the Bold: The Formation of the Burgundian State,* 2nd ed. (London: Longman, 1979); Richard Vaughan, *John the Fearless: The Growth of Burgundian Power* (London: Longman, 1966); ibid., *Philip the Good: The Apogee of Burgundy* (London: Longman, 1970; reprint, 2002); ibid., *Charles the Bold: The Last Valois Duke of Burgundy* (London: Longman, 1973; reprint, 2002); ibid., *Valois Burgundy* (London: Lane, 1975).

130. Hartmut Boockmann and Heinrich Dormeier, *Konzilien, Kirchen- und Reichsreform 1410–1495,* vol. 8 of Gebhardt, *Handbuch der deutschen Geschichte* (Stuttgart: Klett Cotta, 2005); Peter Moraw, *Von offener Verfassung zu gestalteter Verdichtung: Das Reich im späten Mittelalter 1250 bis 1490,* 2nd ed. (Berlin: Ullstein, 1989); Karl-Friedrich Krieger, *König, Reich und Reichsreform im Spätmittelalter,* vol. 14 of *Enzyklopädie deutscher Geschichte* (Munich: Oldenbourg, 1992); Heinz Stoob, *Kaiser Karl IV. und seine Zeit* (Graz: Styria, 1990); Heinrich Koller, *Kaiser Friedrich III* (Darmstadt: Wissenschaftliche Buchgesellschaft, 2005); Hermann Wiesflecker, *Kaiser Maximilian I. Das Reich, Österreich und Europa an der Wende zur Neuzeit,* 5 vols. (Munich: Oldenbourg, 1971–1986); Heinz Angermeier, "Der Wormser Reichstag 1495—Ein europäisches Ereignis," *Historische Zeitschrift* 261 (1995): 739–768; Claudia Helm, ed.,

1495—Kaiser, Reich, Reformen: Der Reichstag zu Worms (Koblenz: Landesarchivverwaltung Rheinland-Pfalz, 1995).

131. *Handbuch der Schweizer Geschichte,* vol. 1, 2nd ed. (Zurich: Berichthaus, 1980); Hans Conrad Peyer, *Verfassungsgeschichte der alten Schweiz* (Zurich: Schulthess Polygraphischer Verlag, 1978).

132. Frederic C. Lane, *Seerepublik Venedig* (Munich: Prestel, 1980; US ed., 1973).

133. Werner Goez, *Grundzüge der Geschichte Italiens in Mittelalter und Renaissance* (Darmstadt: Wissenschaftliche Buchgesellschaft, 1975); *Storia d'Italia,* vols. 4, 5, 7:1–2, 15:1 (Turin: UTET, 1992–1999); Giorgio Chittolini, Anthony Molho, and Pierangelo Schiera, eds., *Origini dello Stato: Processi di formazione statale in Italia fra medioevo ed età moderna* (Bologna: il Mulino, 1994); Lauro Martines, *Power and Imagination: City-States in Renaissance Italy* (New York: Knopf, 1979).

134. *Historia general de España y América,* 19 vols. in 25 parts (Madrid: RIALP, 1981–1992); Jocelyn N. Hillgarth, *The Spanish Kingdoms, 1250–1516,* 2 vols. (Oxford: Clarendon Press, 1976–1978); Joseph Pérez, *Ferdinand und Isabella, Spanien zur Zeit der katholischen Könige* (Munich: Callwey, 1989); Henry Kamen, *Spain, 1469–1714: A Society of Conflict,* 3rd ed. (Harlow, UK: Pearson Longman, 2005); John Lynch, *Spain, 1516–1598: From Nation State to World Empire* (Oxford: Blackwell, 1991); John Lynch, *The Hispanic World in Crisis and Change, 1598–1700* (Oxford: Blackwell, 1992); José Mattoso, ed., *Historia de Portugal,* 8 vols. (Lisbon: Estampa, 1993–1994); Antonio Henrique de Oliveira Marques, *Portugal na crise dos séculos XIV e XV,* vol. 4 of *Nova Historia de Portugal* (Lisbon: Editora Presença, 1987).

135. Detlef Kattinger et al., eds., *"Huruthet war talet j kalmarn"—Union und Zusammenarbeit in der nordischen Geschichte: 600 Jahre Kalmarer Union 1397–1997* (Hamburg: Kova, 1997); Michael Roberts, *The Early Vasas: A History of Sweden, 1523–1611* (Cambridge: Cambridge University Press, 1968).

136. Norman Davies, *God's Playground: A History of Poland,* vol. 1 (Oxford: Clarendon Press, 1982).

137. Hartmut Boockmann, *Der Deutsche Orden: Zwölf Kapitel aus seiner Geschichte,* 4th ed. (Munich: C. H. Beck, 1994).

138. András Kubinyi, *Matthias Corvinus: Die Regierung eines Königsreichs in Ostmitteleuropa 1458–1490* (Herne: Schäfer, 1999).

139. *Genèse et débuts du Grand Schisme d'occident* (Paris: Éditions du CNRS, 1980).

140. Remigius Bäumer, ed., *Die Entwicklung des Konziliarismus* (Darmstadt: Wissenschaftliche Buchgesellschaft, 1976); Walter Brandmüller, *Das Konzil von Konstanz,* 2 vols. (Paderborn: Schöningh, 1991–1999); Phillip H. Stump, *The Reforms of the Council of Constance (1414–1418)* (Leiden: Brill, 1994).

141. Johannes Helmrath, *Das Basler Konzil 1431–1449: Forschungsstand und Probleme* (Cologne: Böhlau, 1987); Joseph Gill, *The Council of Florence* (Cambridge: Cambridge University Press, 1959; reprint, 1979); Stefan Sudman, *Das Basler Konzil: Synodale Praxis zwischen Routine und Revolution* (Frankfurt am Main: Peter Lang, 2005).

142. Reinhard, *Geschichte der Staatsgewalt,* 163–166; Roberto Bizzocchi, *Chiesa e potere nella Toscana del Quattrocento* (Bologna: il Mulino, 1987); Giorgio Chittolini, ed., *Gli Sforza, la Chiesa*

lombarda, la corte di Roma: Strutture e pratiche beneficiarie nel ducato di Milano (1450–1535) (Naples: Liguori, 1989); Helmut Rankl, *Das vorreformatorische landesherrliche Kirchenregiment in Bayern 1378–1526* (Munich: Wölfle, 1971); Manfred Schulze, *Fürsten und Reformation: Geistliche Reformpolitik weltlicher Fürsten vor der Reformation* (Tübingen: Mohr, 1991); Dieter Stievermann, *Landesherrschaft und Klosterwesen im spätmittelalterlichen Württemberg* (Sigmaringen: Thorbecke, 1989); Götz-Rüdiger Tewes, *Die römische Kurie und die europäischen Länder am Vorabend der Reformation* (Tübingen: Niemeyer, 2001); John A. F. Thomson, *Popes and Princes, 1417–1517: Politics and Polity in the Late Medieval Church* (London: Allen and Unwin, 1980).

143. Gerhard Oestreich, "Strukturprobleme des europäischen Absolutismus," in *Geist und Gestalt des frühmodernen Staates* (Berlin: Duncker und Humblot, 1969), 179–197.

144. Michael Stolleis, ed., *Policey im Europa der Frühen Neuzeit*, vol. 83 of *Studien zur europäischen Rechtsgeschichte* (Frankfurt am Main: Klostermann, 1996); Karl Härter, ed., *Policey und frühneuzeitliche Gesellschaft*, vol. 129 of *Studien zur europäischen Rechtsgeschichte* (Frankfurt am Main: Klostermann, 2000); Karl Härter, *Policey und Strafjustiz in Kurmainz: Gesetzgebung, Normdurchsetzung und Sozialkontrolle im frühneuzeitlichen Territorialstaat*, vol. 190, 1–2 of *Studien zur europäischen Rechtsgeschichte* (Frankfurt am Main: Klostermann, 2005).

145. Johannes Burkhardt, "Die Friedlosigkeit der Frühen Neuzeit: Grundlegung einer Theorie der Bellizität Europas," *Zeitschrift für Historische Forschung* 24 (1997): 509–574.

146. Wolfgang Reinhard, *Probleme deutscher Geschichte 1495–1806: Reichsreform und Reformation 1495–1555*, vol. 9 of Gebhardt, *Handbuch der deutschen Geschichte*, 10th ed. (Stuttgart: Klett Cotta, 2001); Horst Rabe, *Deutsche Geschichte 1500–1600: Das Jahrhundert der Glaubenspaltung* (Munich: C. H. Beck, 1991); Alfred Kohler, *Karl V. 1550–1558: Eine Biographie* (Munich: C. H. Beck, 1999).

147. *Storia d'Italia*, vols. 9, 11, 12, 13 (Turin: UTET, 1976–1992); Eric Cochrane, *Italy, 1530–1630* (London: Longman, 1988); Domenico Sella, *Italy in the Seventeenth Century* (London: Longman, 1997).

148. Maximilian Lanzinner, *Konfessionelles Zeitalter 1555–1618*, vol. 10 of Gebhardt, *Handbuch der deutschen Geschichte*, 10th ed. (Stuttgart: Klett Cotta, 2001); Axel Gotthard, *Der Augsburger Religionsfrieden* (Münster: Aschendoff, 2004).

149. Johannes Burkhardt, *Der Dreißigjährige Krieg* (Frankfurt am Main: Suhrkamp, 1992); Burkhardt, *Vollendung und Neuorientierung des frühmodernen Reiches 1648–1763*, vol. 11 of Gebhardt, *Handbuch der deutschen Geschichte*, 10th ed. (Stuttgart: Klett Cotta, 2006); Walter Demel, *Reich, Reformen und sozialer Wandel 1763–1806*, vol. 12 of Gebhardt, *Handbuch der deutschen Geschichte*, 10th ed. (Stuttgart: Klett Cotta, 2005); Ronald G. Asch, *The Thirty Years' War: The Holy Roman Empire and Europe, 1618–1648* (Basingstoke, UK: Macmillan, 1997).

150. Charles W. Ingrao, *The Habsburg Monarchy, 1618–1815* (Cambridge: Cambridge University Press, 1994); Harm Klueting, *Das Reich und Österreich 1648–1740* (Münster: LIT, 1999); Jean Bérenger, *Histoire de l'empire des Habsbourg 1273–1918* (Paris: Fayard, 1990); Peter G. M. Dickson, *Finance and Government under Maria Theresia, 1740–1780*, 2 vols. (Oxford: Clarendon Press, 1987).

151. Philip G. Dwyer, ed., *The Rise of Prussia, 1700–1830* (Harlow, UK: Longman, 2000); Wolfgang Neugebauer, *Die Hohenzollern*, vol. 1 (Stuttgart: Kohlhammer, 1996); Johannes Kunisch, *Friedrich der Große: Der König und seine Zeit* (Munich: C. H. Beck, 2004).

152. Heinz Duchhardt, *Balance of Power und Pentarchie: Internationale Beziehungen 1700–1785*, vol. 4 of *Handbuch der Geschichte der internationalen Beziehungen* (Paderborn: Schöningh, 1997).

153. John Lynch, *Bourbon Spain, 1700–1808* (Oxford: Blackwell, 1989); William N. Hargreaves-Mawdsley, *Eighteenth-Century Spain, 1700–1788: A Political, Diplomatic and Institutional History* (Basingstoke, UK: Macmillan, 1979).

154. Jean Meyer, *Frankreich im Zeitalter des Absolutismus 1515–1789*, vol. 3 of *Geschichte Frankreichs* (Stuttgart: Deutsche Verlagsanstalt, 1990); Richard Bonney, *The Limits of Absolutism in Ancien Régime France* (Aldershot, UK: Variorum, 1995).

155. Michel Pernot, *Les guerres de religion en France 1559–1598* (Paris: Sedes, 1987).

156. Richard Bonney, *Society and Government in France under Richelieu and Mazarin, 1624–1661* (Basingstoke, UK: Macmillan, 1988); Klaus Malettke, *Ludwig XIV. von Frankreich: Leben, Politik und Leistung* (Göttingen: Muster-Schmidt, 1994); David J. Sturdy, *Louis XIV* (Basingstoke, UK: Macmillan, 1998).

157. John Robertson, ed., *A Union for Empire: Political Thought and the British Union of 1707* (Cambridge: Cambridge University Press, 1995).

158. Christopher Haigh, *English Reformations: Religion, Politics, and Society under the Tudors* (Oxford: Clarendon, 1993); ibid., *Elizabeth I* (London: Longman, 1988); David M. Loades, *Politics and Nation: England, 1450–1660*, 5th ed. (Oxford: Blackwell, 1999).

159. Art Cosgrove, ed., *Medieval Ireland, 1169–1534*, vol. 2 of *A New History of Ireland* (Oxford: Clarendon Press, 1987); Theodore W. Moody, ed., *Early Modern Ireland, 1534–1691*, vol. 3 of *A New History of Ireland* (Oxford: Clarendon Press, 1991); Sean J. Connolly, *Religion, Law, and Power: The Making of Protestant Ireland, 1660–1760* (Oxford: Clarendon Press, 1992).

160. David L. Smith, *A History of the Modern British Isles, 1603–1707: The Double Crown* (Oxford: Blackwell, 1998); Ronald G. Asch, *Jakob I. (1566–1625), König von England und Schottland, Herrscher des Friedens im Zeitalter der Religionskriege* (Stuttgart: Kohlhammer, 2005); ibid., *Der Hof Karls I. von England: Politik, Provinz und Patronage 1625–1640* (Cologne: Böhlau, 1993).

161. Kevin Sharpe, *The Personal Rule of Charles I* (New Haven, CT: Yale University Press, 1992).

162. John P. Kenyon and Jane H. Ohlmeyer, eds., *The Civil Wars: A Military History of England, Scotland, and Ireland, 1638–1660* (Oxford: Oxford University Press, 1998).

163. Gerald E. Aylmer, *The Levellers in the English Revolution* (Ithaca, NY: Cornell University Press, 1975); Christopher Hill, *The World Turned Upside Down: Radical Ideas during the English Revolution* (London: Temple Smith, 1972).

164. John P. Morrill, ed., *Oliver Cromwell and the English Revolution* (London: Longman, 1990); Peter Gaunt, *Oliver Cromwell* (Oxford: Blackwell, 1997).

165. John Brewer, *The Sinews of Power: War, Money, and the English State, 1688–1783* (Cambridge, MA: Harvard University Press, 1988); Linda Colley, *Britons: Forging the Nation, 1707–1837*

(New Haven, CT: Yale University Press, 1992); Geoffrey Holmes, *The Making of a Great Power: Late Stuart and Early Georgian Britain, 1660–1722* (London: Longman, 1993); Michael Braddick, *State Formation in Early Modern England, ca. 1550–1700* (Cambridge: Cambridge University Press, 2000).

166. Jakob Rosenberg, *Rembrandt: Life and Letters,* 2 vols. (Cambridge, MA: Harvard University Press, 1948).

167. James D. Tracy, *Holland under Habsburg Rule, 1506–1566: The Formation of a Body Politic* (Berkeley: University of California Press, 1990); Simon Schama, *Überfluss und schöner Schein: Zur Kultur der Niederlande im Goldenen Zeitalter* (Munich: Kindler, 1988); English ed., *The Embarrassment of Riches: An Interpretation of Dutch Culture in the Golden Age* (London: Collins, 1987); Jonathan Israel, *The Dutch Republic: Its Rise, Greatness, and Fall, 1477–1806* (Oxford: Clarendon Press, 1995).

168. Jan K. Fedorowicz et al., eds., *A Republic of Nobles: Studies in Polish History to 1864* (Cambridge: Cambridge University Press, 1982); Józef A. Gierowski, *The Polish–Lithuanian Commonwealth in the 18th Century* (Krakow: Polska Akad. Umiejętności, 1996); Jerzy Lukowski, *The Partitions of Poland, 1772, 1793, 1795* (London: Longman, 1999).

169. Michael Roberts, *Gustavus Adolphus and Rise of Sweden,* 2nd ed. (London: Longman, 1992); Michael F. Metcalf, ed., *The Riksdag: A History of the Swedish Parliament* (New York: St. Martin's Press, 1987); Michael Roberts, *The Age of Liberty: Sweden, 1719–1772* (Cambridge: Cambridge University Press, 1986).

170. Gerald Mattingly, *Renaissance Diplomacy* (London: Cape, 1955; reprint, 1973); Matthew P. Anderson, *The Rise of Modern Diplomacy, 1450–1919* (London: Longman, 1993); Lucien Bély, ed., *L'invention de la diplomatie: Moyen Âge—Temps modernes* (Paris: PUF, 1998).

171. Fundamental background reading includes the following: Jan A. van Houtte, ed., *Europäische Wirtschafts- und Sozialgeschichte im Mittelalter,* vol. 2 of *Handbuch der europäischen Wirtschafts- und Sozialgeschichte* (Stuttgart: Klett Cotta, 1980); Hermann Kellenbenz, ed., *Europäische Wirtschafts- Und Sozialgeschichte vom ausgehenden Mittelalter bis zur Mitte des 17. Jahrhunderts,* vol. 3 of *Handbuch der europäischen Wirtschafts- und Sozialgeschichte* (Stuttgart: Klett Cotta, 1986); Ilja Mieck, ed., *Europäische Wirtschafts- und Sozialgeschichte von der Mitte des 17. Jahrhunderts bis zu Mitte des 19. Jahrhunderts,* vol. 4 of *Handbuch der europäischen Wirtschafts- und Sozialgeschichte* (Stuttgart: Klett Cotta, 1993); Fernand Braudel, *Civilisation matérielle, économie et capitalisme, XVe–XVIIIe siècle,* 3 vols. (Paris: Colin, 1979); English ed., *Civilization and Capitalism,* 3 vols. (London: Fontana, 1981–1982); German ed., *Sozialgeschichte des 15.–18. Jahrhunderts,* 3 vols. (Munich: Kindler, 1990); John Landers, *The Field and the Forge: Population, Production, and Power in the Pre-Industrial West* (Oxford: Oxford University Press, 2003); Hermann Aubin and Wolfgang Zorn, eds., *Von der Frühzeit bis zum Ende des 18. Jahrhunderts,* vol. 1 of *Handbuch der deutschen Wirtschafts- und Sozialgeschichte* (Stuttgart: Union Verlag, 1971; reprint, 1978); Friedrich-Wilhelm Henning, *Deutsche Wirtschafts- und Sozialgeschichte im Mittelalter und in der frühen Neuzeit,* vol. 1 of *Handbuch der Wirtschafts- und Sozialgeschichte Deutschlands* (Paderborn: Schöningh, 1991); James L. Bolton, *The Medieval English Economy, 1150–1500,* 3rd ed. (London: Dent, 1988); Michael M. Postan, *The Medieval Economy and Society: An Economic History of Britain in the*

Middle Ages, 2nd ed. (Harmondsworth, UK: Penguin, 1975); Roderick Floud, ed., *The Cambridge Economic History of Modern Britain,* 3 vols. (Cambridge: Cambridge University Press, 2004–2009); Fernand Braudel and Ernest Labrousse, eds., *Histoire économique et sociale de la France,* vols. 1 and 2 (Paris: PUF, 1970–1977); Philip J. Jones, *Economia e società nell'Italia medievale* (Turin: Einaudi, 1980); Jaime Vicens Vives, *An Economic History of Spain* (Princeton, NJ: Princeton University Press, 1969); Braudel, *Mittelmeer;* Mitterauer, *Warum Europa?* A somewhat conventional interpretation is available in Hubert Kiesewetter, *Das einzigartige Europa: Wie ein Kontinent reich wurde,* 2nd ed. (Stuttgart: Steiner, 2006).

172. Georges Duby, *L'économie rurale et la vie des campagnes dans l'occident médiéval (France, Angleterre, Empire), IXe–XVe siècles,* 2 vols. (Paris: Aubier, 1962; English ed., 1968); W. Bernard H. Slicher van Bath, *The Agrarian History of Western Europe, AD 500–1850* (London: Arnold, 1963); Werner Rösener, *Die Bauern in der europäischen Geschichte* (Munich: C. H. Beck, 1993); Wilhelm Abel, *Geschichte der deutschen Landwirtschaft vom frühen Mittelalter bis zum 19. Jahrhundert,* vol. 2 of *Deutsche Agrargeschichte,* 3rd ed. (Stuttgart: Ulmer, 1978); Friedrich Lütge, *Geschichte der deutschen Agrarverfassung vom frühen Mittelalter bis zum 19. Jahrhundert,* vol. 3 of *Deutsche Agrargeschichte,* 2nd ed. (Stuttgart: Ulmer, 1967); Günther Franz, *Geschichte des deutschen Bauernstandes vom frühen Mittelalter bis zum 19. Jahrhundert,* vol. 4 of *Deutsche Agrargeschichte,* 2nd ed. (Stuttgart: Ulmer, 1976); Friedrich-Wilhelm Henning, *Deutsche Agrargeschichte des Mittelalters. 9. bis 15. Jahrhundert* (Stuttgart: Ulmer, 1994); Edward Miller, ed., *1348–1500,* vol. 3 of *The Agrarian History of England and Wales* (Cambridge: Cambridge University Press, 1991); Joan Thirsk, ed., *1500–1640,* vol. 4 of *The Agrarian History of England and Wales* (Cambridge: Cambridge University Press, 1967); Joan Thirsk, ed., *1640–1750,* vol. 5, parts 1–2 of *The Agrarian History of England and Wales* (Cambridge: Cambridge University Press, 1984–1985); Hugues Neveux et al., eds., *L'âge classique des paysans de 1340 à 1789,* vol. 2 of *Histoire de la France rurale,* ed. Georges Duby and Armand Wallon (Paris: Seuil, 1975).

173. Dirlmeier, Fouquet, and Fuhrmann, *Europa im Spätmittelalter,* 34–35; Meuthen and Märtl, *Das 15. Jahrhundert,* 15; James A. Galloway, ed., *Trade, Urban Hinterlands and Market Integration, c. 1300–1600* (London: Centre for Metropolitan History, Institute of Historical Research, 2000); Rolf Kiessling, *Die Stadt und ihr Land. Umlandpolitik, Bürgerbesitz und Wirtschaftsgefüge in Ostschwaben vom 14. Bis ins 16. Jahrhundert* (Cologne: Böhlau, 1989); Ulrich Köpf, "Stadt und Land im Deutschen Reich des Spätmittelalters und der Reformationszeit," in *Relationen: Studien zum Übergang vom Spätmittelalter zur Reformation: Festschrift zu Ehren von Prof. Dr. Karl-Heinz zur Mühlen,* ed. Athina Lexut and Wolfgang Matz (Münster: LIT, 2000), 94–110.

174. Marcel Lachiver, *Vins, vignes et vignobles: Histoire du vignoble français* (Paris: Fayard, 1988); Otto Volk, "Weinbau und Weinabsatz im späten Mittelalter: Forschungsstand und Forschungsprobleme," in *Weinbau, Weinhandel und Weinkultur,* ed. Alois Gerlich (Stuttgart: Steiner, 1993), 49–163.

175. Julius Klein, *The Mesta: A Study in Spanish Economic History, 1273–1836* (Cambridge, MA: Harvard University Press, 1920); Pedro García Martín, *La Mesta* (Madrid: Historia 16, 1990); Braudel, *Mittelmeer.*

176. Maurice Beresford, ed., *Deserted Medieval Villages,* 2nd ed. (London: Lutterworth, 1972); Fernand Braudel, ed., *Villages désertés et histoire économique (XIe–XVIIIe siècle)* (Paris: S.E.V.P.E.N., 1965).

177. Knut Schulz, ed., *Handwerk in Europa: Vom Spätmittelalter bis zur Frühen Neuzeit* (Munich: Oldenbourg, 1999).

178. Steven A. Epstein, *Wage Labor and Guilds in Medieval Europe* (Chapel Hill: University of North Carolina Press, 1991); Pascale Lambrechts and Jean-Pierre Sosson, eds., *Les métiers au moyen âge: Aspects économiques et sociaux* (Louvain-la-Neuve: Collège Erasme, 1994); Knut Schulz, *Handwerksgesellen und Lohnarbeiter: Untersuchungen zur oberrheinischen und oberdeutschen Stadtgeschichte des 14. bis 17. Jahrhunderts* (Sigmaringen: Thorbecke, 1985).

179. Ulf Dirlmeier, Gerhard Fouquet, Bernd Fuhrmann, and Rainer P. Elkar, eds., *Öffentliches Bauen in Mittelalter und früher Neuzeit* (St. Katherinen: Scripta Mercaturae-Verlag, 1991); Gerhard Fouquet, *Bauen für die Stadt: Finanzen, Organisation und Arbeit in kommunalen Baubetrieben des Spätmittelalters: Eine vergleichende Studie vornehmlich zwischen den Städten Basel und Marburg* (Cologne: Böhlau, 1999).

180. Dominique Cardon, *La draperie au moyen âge: Essor d'une grande industrie européenne* (Paris: CNRS, 1999); Hironobu Sakuma, *Die Nürnberger Tuchmacher, Weber, Färber und Bereiter vom 14. bis 17. Jahrhundert* (Nuremberg: Stadtarchiv, 1993); Claus-Peter Clasen, *Textilherstellung in Augsburg in der Frühen Neuzeit,* 2 vols. (Augsburg: Wißner, 1995).

181. Wolfgang Stromer von Reichenbach, "Gewerbereviere und Protoindustrien in Spätmittelalter und Frühneuzeit," in *Gewerbe- und Industrielandschaften vom Spätmittelalter bis ins 20. Jahrhundert,* ed. Hans Pohl (Stuttgart: Steiner, 1986), 39–111; Herman van der Wee, ed., *The Rise and Decline of Urban Industries in Italy and the Low Countries (Late Middle Ages–Early Modern Times)* (Leuven: Leuven University Press, 1988); Sheilagh C. Ogilvie and Markus Cerman, eds., *European Proto-Industrialization* (Cambridge: Cambridge University Press, 1996).

182. Jean-François Bergier, *Die Geschichte vom Salz* (Frankfurt am Main: Campus, 1989).

183. Hanno-Walter Kruft, *Städte in Utopia: Die Idealstadt vom 15. bis 18. Jahrhundert zwischen Staatsutopie und Wirklichkeit* (Munich: C. H. Beck, 1989).

184. Mitterauer, *Warum Europa?,* 279–284; Adolf Laube, *Studien über den erzgebirgischen Silberbergbau von 1470 bis 1546* (Berlin: Akademie Verlag, 1974); Helmut Wilsdorf and Werner Quellmalz, *Bergwerke und Hüttenanlagen der Agricola-Zeit* (Berlin: Deutscher Verlag der Wissenschaften, 1971).

185. Michel Mollat, *Der königliche Kaufmann Jacques Coeur oder der Geist des Unternehmertums* (Munich: C. H. Beck, 1991); Iris Origo, *"Im Namen Gottes und des Geschäfts": Lebensbild eines toskanischen Kaufmanns der Frührenaissance: Francesco di Marco Datini 1335–1410,* 2nd ed. (Munich: C. H. Beck, 1986).

186. Peter Johanek and Heinz Stoob, eds., *Europäische Messen und Märktesysteme in Mittelalter und Neuzeit* (Cologne: Böhlau, 1995).

187. Raymond de Roover, *The Rise and Decline of the Medici Bank, 1397–1494* (Cambridge, MA: Harvard University Press, 1963); Mark Häberlein, *Die Fugger: Geschichte einer Augsburger Familie (1367–1650)* (Stuttgart: Kohlhammer, 2006).

188. Philippe Dollinger, *Die Hanse,* 5th ed. (Stuttgart: Kröner, 1998); Heinz Stoob, *Die Hanse* (Graz: Styria, 1995); Rolf Hammel-Kiesow, *Die Hanse,* 4th ed. (Munich: C. H. Beck, 2008).

189. Jean-François Bergier, "Le trafic à travers les Alpes et les liaisons transalpines du haut moyen âge au 17e siècle," in *Le Alpi e l'Europa* (Bari: Laterza, 1975), 3:1–72.

190. Herman van der Wee, *The Growth of the Antwerp Market and the European Economy (14th– 16th Centuries),* 3 vols. (The Hague: Nijhoff, 1963).

191. Federigo Melis, *Le fonti,* vol. 1 of *Origini e sviluppo delle assicurazioni in Italia (secoli XIV–XVI)* (Rome: Istituto Nazionale delle Assicurazioni, 1975).

192. *Banchi pubblici, banchi privati e monti di pietà nell'Europa preindustriale,* 2 vols. (Genoa: Società Ligure di Storia Patria, 1990); Markus A. Denzel, *"La Pratica della Cambiatura": Europäischer Zahlungsverkehr vom 14. bis zum 17. Jahrhundert* (Stuttgart: Steiner, 1994); Raymond de Roover, *L'évolution de la lettre de change (XIVe–XVIIIe siècles)* (Paris: Colin, 1953).

193. Dirlmeier, Fouquet, and Fuhrmann, *Europa im Spätmittelalter,* 50–51.

194. Meuthen and Märtl, *Das 15. Jahrhundert,* 18.

195. M. A. Denzel, *Kurialer Zahlungsverkehr im 13. und 14. Jahrhundert* (Stuttgart: Steiner, 1991); Clemens Bauer, "Die Epochen der Papstfinanz," *Historische Zeitschrift* 138 (1927): 457–503.

196. Bryce Lyon and Adriaan Verhulst, *Medieval Finance: A Comparison of Financial Institutions in Northwestern Europe* (Brugge: De Tempel, 1967); Michael North, *Kommunikation, Handel, Geld und Banken in der Frühen Neuzeit* (Munich: Oldenbourg, 2000).

197. Hans Pohl, *Europäische Bankengeschichte* (Frankfurt am Main: Knapp, 1993).

198. Geoffrey Parker and Leslie M. Smith, eds., *The General Crisis of the Seventeenth Century* (London: Routledge & Kegan Paul, 1978).

199. Till Wahnbaeck, *Luxury and Public Happiness: Political Economy in the Italian Enlightenment* (Oxford: Clarendon Press, 2004).

200. Neil MacKendrick, John Brewer, and John H. Plumb, eds., *The Birth of a Consumer Society: The Commercialization of Eighteenth-Century England* (London: Europa Publications, 1982).

201. Jan de Vries, "The Industrial Revolution and the Industrious Revolution," *Journal of Economic History* 54 (1994): 249–270; Gregory Clark and Ysbrand van der Werf, "Work in Progress? The Industrious Revolution," *Journal of Economic History* 58 (1998): 830–843.

202. Basic background reading includes Reinhard, *Die Neue Welt;* James D. Tracy, ed., *The Rise of Merchant Empires: Long Distance Trade in the Early Modern World, 1350–1750* (Minneapolis: University of Minnesota Press, 1987; Cambridge: Cambridge University, Press, 1990); ibid., ed., *The Political Economy of Merchant Empires: State Power and World Trade, 1350–1750* (Minneapolis: University of Minnesota Press, 1987); Anthony J. R. Russell-Wood, ed., *An Expanding World: The European Impact on World History, 1450–1800,* 31 volumes in 34 parts (Aldershot, UK: Ashgate Variorum, 1995–2004); Caroline A. Williams, ed., *Bridging the Early Modern Atlantic World: People, Products, and Practices on the Move* (Farnham, UK: Ashgate, 2009); Canny and Morgan, *Handbook of the Atlantic World.*

203. *The Cambridge History of the Native Peoples of the Americas,* 3 vols. in 6 parts (Cambridge: Cambridge University Press, 1997–2000).

204. Eugene R. Fingerhut, *Who First Discovered America? A Critique of Pre-Columbian Voyages* (Claremont, CA: Regina Books, 1984).

205. Kirsten A. Seaver, *The Frozen Echo: Greenland and the Exploration of North America, c. AD 1000–1500* (Stanford, CA: Stanford University Press, 1996).

206. Holger Afflerbach, *Das entfesselte Meer: Die Geschichte des Atlantik* (Munich: Piper, 2001); Paul Butel, *Histoire de l'Atlantique* (Paris: Perrin, 1997).

207. David Armitage, "Three Concepts of Atlantic History," in *The British Atlantic World, 1500–1800,* ed. David Armitage and Michael Braddick (New York: Palgrave Macmillan, 2002), 11–27.

208. John B. Hattendorf, *The Boundless Deep: The European Conquest of the Oceans, 1450–1840* (Providence, RI: John Carter Brown Library, 2003); Bernhard Klein and Gesa Mackenthun, eds., *Sea Changes: Historicizing the Ocean* (London: Routledge, 2004).

209. Dietmar Henze, *Enzyklopädie der Entdecker und Erforscher der Erde,* 5 vols. (Graz: Akademische Druck-und Verlagsanstalt, 1978–2004); Angus Konstam, *Historical Atlas of Exploration* (New York: Checkmark Books, 2000); Simonetta Conti, *Bibliografia Colombiana 1793–1990* (Genoa: Cassa di risparmio di Genova e Imperia, 1991); Titus Heydenreich, ed., *Columbus zwischen zwei Welten: Historische und literarische Wertungen aus fünf Jahrhunderten,* 2 vols. (Frankfurt am Main: Vervuert, 1992); Ramón Ezquerra Abadía, "Medio siglo de estudios colombinos," *Anuario de estudiosamericanos* 38 (1981): 1–24; Horst Pietschmann, "Christoph Columbus im deutschsprachigen Schrifttum," *Historisches Jahrbuch* 112 (1992): 157–179; Ulrich Knefelkamp, "500 Jahre Entdeckung Amerikas: Ein Literaturbericht zu den Fahrten des Kolumbus und ihren Folgen," *Historische Zeitschrift* 258 (1994): 697–712; Paolo Emilio Taviani, *I viaggi di Colombo: La grande scoperta,* 2 vols. (Novara: Istituto geografico de Agostini, 1990); Antonio Ballesteros y Beretta, *Cristóbal Colón y el descubrimiento de América,* 2 vols. (Barcelona: Salvat, 1945); Samuel E. Morison, *Admiral of the Ocean Sea: A Life of Christopher Columbus,* 2 vols. (Boston: Little, Brown, 1942).

210. Reinhard, *Die Alte Welt,* 28–49; Horst Pietschmann, ed., *Mittel-, Südamerika und die Karibik bis 1760,* vol. 1 of *Handbuch der Geschichte Lateinamerikas* (Stuttgart: Klett Cotta, 1994), 207–273, here 211–227.

211. Pietschmann, *Handbuch der Geschichte Lateinamerikas,* 227–228; Felipe F. R. Fernandez-Armesto, *The Canary Islands after the Conquest: The Making of a Colonial Society in the Early Sixteenth Century* (Oxford: Clarendon Press, 1976); Klaus Herbers, "Die Eroberung der Kanarischen Inseln—Ein Modell für die spätere Expansion Portugals und Spaniens nach Afrika und Amerika?," in *Afrika: Entdeckung und Erforschung eines Kontinents,* ed. Heinz Duchhardt (Cologne: Böhlau, 1989), 51–95.

212. Hans-Christian Freiesleben, *Geschichte der Navigation,* 2nd ed. (Stuttgart: Steiner, 1978).

213. Luís Adão de Fonseca and José M. Ruiz Asencio, eds., *Corpus documental del tratado de Tordesillas* (Valladolid: Sociedad V Centenario del Tratado de Tordesillas, 1995).

214. James Lockhart, *The Men of Cajamarca: A Social and Biographical Study of the First Conquerors of Peru* (Austin: University of Texas Press, 1972).

215. Francisco Morales Padrón, *Historia del descubrimiento y conquista de América,* 5th ed. (Madrid: Gredos, 1990).

216. José Luis Martinez, *Hernán Cortés* (Mexico City: Universidad Nacional Autónoma, 1993).

217. Rafael Varón Gabai, *Francisco Pizarro and His Brothers: The Illusion of Power in Sixteenth-Century Peru* (Norman: University of Oklahoma Press, 1997); Manuel Ballesteros Gaibrois, *Descubrimiento y conquista del Perú* (Barcelona: Salvat, 1963).

218. Grant D. Jones in *Cambridge History of the Native Peoples of the Americas,* vol. 2/2, 352–353; ibid., *The Conquest of the Last Maya Kingdom* (Cambridge: Cambridge University Press, 1999).

219. Georg Thomas in Pietschmann, *Handbuch der Geschichte Lateinamerikas,* 301–307; Frank Lestringant, *L'atelier du cosmographe ou l'image du monde à la Renaissance* (Paris: Michel, 1991).

220. Alfred W. Crosby, *The Columbian Exchange: Biological and Cultural Consequences of 1492* (Westport, CT: Greenwood Press, 1972); cf. ibid., *Ecological Imperialism: The Biological Expansion of Europe, 900–1900,* 2nd ed. (Cambridge: Cambridge University Press, 2004).

221. Juan Ginés de Sepúlveda, *Democrates secundus De iustis belli causis,* ed. Angel Losada (Madrid: Consejo Superior de Investigaciones Científicas, Instituto Francisco de Vitoria, 1951), 79. I am indebted to Michael Sievernich, Frankfurt, for this reference.

222. On this topic, see Wolfgang Reinhard, *Parasit oder Partner? Europäische Wirtschaft und Neue Welt 1500–1800* (Münster: LIT, 1997), 157–175.

223. Jennifer A. Woolfe, *Sweet Potato: An Untapped Food Resource* (Cambridge: Cambridge University Press, 1992).

224. Geoffrey C. Gunn, *First Globalization: The Eurasian Exchange, 1500–1800* (Lanham, MD: Rowman & Littlefield, 2003), 68–69.

225. James McCann, *Maize and Grace: Africa's Encounter with a New World Crop, 1500–2000* (Cambridge, MA: Harvard University Press, 2005).

226. David Birmingham in Gray, *Cambridge History of Africa,* 4:368–369.

227. Giuseppe Michele Ravagnan, *Sunflower in Africa* (Florence: Istituto agronomico per l'oltremare, 1993).

228. Reinhard Wendt, "Dinner for One und die versteckte Präsenz im Kulinarischen," in Dietmar Rothermund, ed., *Grenzgänge* (Hamburg: Abera, 2004), 235–238; Redcliffe N. Salaman, *The History and Social Influence of the Potato* (Cambridge: Cambridge University Press, 1949; new ed., 1970).

229. Chris and Tilde Stuart, *Africa: A Natural History* (Shrewsbury, UK: Swan Hill, 1995), 123–125.

230. John W. Verano and Douglas H. Ubelaker, eds., *Disease and Demography in the Americas* (Washington, DC: Smithsonian Institution Press, 1992).

231. Noble David Cook in Kenneth F. Kiple and Stephen V. Beck, eds., *Biological Consequences of the European Expansion, 1450–1800* (Aldershot, UK: Ashgate Variorum, 1997), 37–69, here 42–43; Renate Pieper in Pietschmann, *Handbuch der Geschichte Lateinamerikas,* 318; David P. Jones, *Rationalizing Epidemics: Meanings and Uses of American Indian Mortality since 1600* (Cambridge, MA: Harvard University Press, 2004).

232. Cf. Brenda B. Baker and George J. Armelagos in Kiple and Beck, *Biological Consequences,* 1–35 (including a discussion of the findings).

233. John Duffy in Kiple and Beck, *Biological Consequences,* 233–250, here 249.

234. Background reading includes Reinhard, *Die Neue Welt,* 58–114; Reinhard, *Parasit oder Partner,* 39–76; Pietschmann, *Handbuch der Geschichte Lateinamerikas,* 205–596, 751–788; Victor

Bulmer–Thomas, John H. Coatsworth, and Roberto Cortés Conde, eds., *The Colonial Era and the Short Nineteenth Century,* vol. 1 of *The Cambridge Economic History of Latin America* (Cambridge: Cambridge University Press, 2006); Matthew Restall, *Seven Myths of the Spanish Conquest* (New York: Oxford University Press, 2003); Kenneth Mills and William B. Taylor, *Colonial Spanish America: A Documentary History* (Wilmington, DE: Scholarly Resources, 1998); James Lockhart and Stuart B. Schwartz, *Early Latin America: A History of Colonial Spanish America and Brazil* (Cambridge: Cambridge University Press, 1997); David A. Brading, *The First America: The Spanish Monarchy, Creole Patriots, and the Liberal State, 1492–1867* (Cambridge: Cambridge University Press, 1991); Manuel José de Ayala, *Diccionario de gobierno e legislación de Indias,* 10 vols., ed. Marta Milagros del Vas Mingo (Madrid: Cultura Hispánica, 1991–1998); Leslie Bethell, ed., *The Cambridge History of Latin America,* vols. 1–2 (Cambridge: Cambridge University Press, 1984); vol. 11, 1995; *Historia general de España y América,* vols. 7, 9, 11, part 2 (Madrid: Rialp, 1982–1990); Lyle N. McAlister, *Spain and Portugal in the New World, 1492–1700* (New York: Oxford University Press, 1984); Peter Gerhard, *A Guide to the Historical Geography of New Spain,* 2nd ed. (Cambridge: Cambridge University Press, 1994).

235. Huguette et Pierre Chaunu, *Séville et l'Atlantique (1504–1650),* 8 vols. in 12 parts (Paris: Colin, 1957–1960); Eufemio Lorenzo Sanz, *Comercio de España con América en la época de Felipe II,* 2 vols. (Valladolid: Servicio de Publicaciones de la Diputacion Provincial, 1979–1980); Lutgardo Garcia Fuentes, *El comercio español con América (1650–1700)* (Seville: Escuela de Estudios Hispanoamericanos, 1980); Antonio Garcia–Baquero Gonzalez, *Cadiz y el Atlantico (1717–1778),* 2 vols. (Seville: Escuela de Estudios Hispanoamericanos, 1976); Antonio-Miguel Bernal, *La financiación de la carrera de Indias 1492–1824: Dinero y crédito en el comercio colonial español con América* (Seville: Fundación El Monte, 1993); Klaus-Peter Starke, *Der spanisch-amerikanische Kolonialhandel: Die Entwicklung der neueren Historiographie und künftige Forschungsperspektiven* (Münster: LIT, 1995).

236. Adriano Prosperi, "America e apocalisse: Note sulla *conquista spirituale* del Nuovo Mondo," in *America e apocalisse e altri saggi* (Pisa: Istituti editoriali e poligrafici internazionali, 1999), 15–63; Robert Ricard, *La conquête spirituelle du Mexique: Essai sur l'apostolat et les méthodes missionaires des orders mendiants en Nouvelle Espagne de 1523 à 1572* (Paris: Institut d'ethnologie, 1933).

237. Mariano Delgado, *Abschied vom erobernden Gott. Studien zu Geschichte und Gegenwart des Christentums in Lateinamerika* (Immensee: Neue Zeitschrift für Missionswissenschaft, 1996).

238. Carlos Sempat Assadourian, "La renta de la encomienda en la década de 1550: Piedad cristiana y desconstrucción," *Revista de Indias* 48 (1988): 109–146; Robert Himmerich y Valencia, *The Encomenderos of New Spain, 1521–1555* (Austin: University of Texas Press, 1991); Javier Ortiz de la Tabla Ducasse, *Los encomenderos de Quito, 1534–1660: Origen y evolución de una elite colonial* (Seville: Escuela de Estudios Hispanoamericanos, 1993).

239. W. George Lovell in *Cambridge History of the Native Peoples of the Americas,* vol. 2, part 2, 405–407.

240. Guillermo Lohmann Villena, "Las Cortes en las Indias," in *Las Cortes de Castilla y León 1188–1988* (Valladolid: Cortes de Castilla y León, 1990), 1:589–623.

241. Antonio García-Abásolo, "Mujeres andaluzas en la América colonial (1550–1650)," *Revista de Indias* 49 (1989): 91–110; Auke Pieter Jacobs, *Los movimientos migratorios entre Castilla e Hispanoamérica durante el reinado de Felipe III, 1598–1621* (Amsterdam: Rodopi, 1995); Maria del Carmen Martínez Martínez, *La emigración castellana y leonesa al Nuevo Mundo 1571–1700*, 2 vols. (Valladolid: Junta de Castilla y León, 1993); Enrique Otte, ed., *Cartas privadas de emigrantes a Indias 1540–1616* (Mexico City: Fondo de Cultura Económica, 1993).

242. Dora P. Crouch, Daniel J. Garr, and Axel I. Mundigo, *Spanish City Planning in North America* (Cambridge, MA: MIT Press, 1982); Inge Wolff-Buisson, *Regierung und Verwaltung der kolonialspanischen Städte in Hochperu 1538–1650,* (Cologne: Böhlau, 1970).

243. *Cambridge History of the Native Peoples of the Americas,* vols. 2, part 2 and 3, part 2; Thomas M. Stephens, *Dictionary of Latin American Racial and Ethnic Terminology* (Gainesville: University of Florida Press, 1989).

244. Felix Becker, *Die politische Machtstellung der Jesuiten in Südamerika im 18. Jahrhundert: Zur Kontroverse um den Jesuitenkönig Nikolaus I. von Paraguay* (Cologne: Böhlau, 1980); James P. Saeger in *Cambridge History of the Native Peoples of the Americas,* vol. 3, part 2, 274–283; Barbara Ganson, *The Guarani under Spanish Rule in the Rio de la Plata* (Stanford: Stanford University Press, 2003).

245. Lutgero García Fuentes, *Los peruleros y el comercio de Sevilla con las Indias, 1580–1630* (Seville: Escuela de Estudios Hispanoamericanos, 1997).

246. Enrique Tandeter, *Coercion and Market: Silver Mining in Colonial Potosí, 1692–1826* (Albuquerque: University of New Mexico Press, 1993); Teresa Cañedo-Argüelles Fábrega, *Potosí: La versión aymara de un mito europeo: La mineria y sus efectos en las sociedades andinas del siglo XVII* (Madrid: Edicion Catriel, 1993).

247. Herbert P. Klein, *The American Finances of the Spanish Empire: Royal Income and Expenditures in Colonial Mexico, Peru, and Bolivia, 1680–1809* (Albuquerque: University of New Mexico Press, 1998).

248. Michel Morineau, *Incroyables gazettes et fabuleux métaux: Les retours des trésors américains d'après les gazettes hollandaises* (Cambridge: Cambridge University Press, 1985).

249. Murdo J. MacLeod, Susan M. Deeds, Susan Deans-Smith, Maria de los Angeles Romero Frizzi, and Grant D. Jones in *Cambridge History of the Native Peoples of the Americas,* vol. 2, part 2, 20–21, 59, 287, 316–317, 373; Luis Miguel Glave in *Cambridge History of the Native Peoples of the Americas,* vol. 3, part 2, 502–557.

250. Reinhard, *Die Neue Welt,* 116–152; Reinhard, *Parasit oder Partner,* 77–116; Georg Thomas in Pietschmann, *Handbuch der Geschichte Lateinamerikas,* 597–659, 789–806; Frédéric Mauro in Pietschmann, *Handbuch der Geschichte Lateinamerikas,* 676–691; Leslie Bethell, ed., *Colonial Brazil* (Cambridge: Cambridge University Press, 1987); Inês C. Inácio and Tania Regina de Luca, eds., *Documentos do Brasil colonial* (São Paulo: Atica, 1993); Frédéric Mauro, *Le Brésil du XVe siècle à la fin du XVIIIe siècle* (Paris: Société d'édition d'enseignement supérieur, 1977).

251. Georg Thomas in Pietschmann, *Handbuch der Geschichte Lateinamerikas,* 624–625; Noël Deerr, *The History of Sugar,* 2 vols. (London: Chapman and Hall, 1949–1950); Stuart B. Schwartz, *Sugar Plantations in the Formation of Brazilian Society: Bahia, 1550–1835* (Cambridge: Cambridge University Press, 1998).

252. Stuart B. Schwartz in *Cambridge History of Latin America*, 2:434.

253. Wim Klooster in Johannes Postma and Victor Enthoven, eds., *Riches from Atlantic Commerce: Dutch Transatlantic Trade and Shipping, 1585–1817* (Leiden: Brill, 2003), 369, 382; Victor Enthoven in ibid., 445; Christopher Ebert in ibid., 49–75, gives a much more conservative estimate.

254. Ruud Spruit, *Zout en slaven: De geschiedenis van de Westindische Compagnie* (Houten: de Haan, 1988).

255. Charles R. Boxer, *The Dutch in Brazil, 1624–54* (Oxford: Clarendon Press, 1957; reprint, Hamden, CT: Archon, 1973).

256. Evaldo Cabral de Mello, *Olinda restaurada: Guerra e açúcar no Nordeste 1630–1654* (Rio de Janeiro: Topbooks, 1998).

257. Oliver A. Rink, *Holland on the Hudson: An Economic and Social History of Dutch New York* (Ithaca, NY: Cornell University Press, 1986).

258. Peter Stuyvesant, *Correspondence, 1647–1653*, ed. Charles T. Gehring (Syracuse: Syracuse University Press, 1998).

259. Robert Louis Paquette and Stanley L. Engerman, eds., *The Lesser Antilles in the Age of Expansion* (Gainesville: University of Florida Press, 1996); Kenneth R. Andrews, *The Spanish Caribbean: Trade and Plunder, 1530–1630* (New Haven, CT: Yale University Press, 1978).

260. Carl and Roberta Bridenbaugh, *No Peace beyond the Line: The English in the Caribbean, 1624–1690* (New York: Oxford University Press, 1972).

261. Michel Devèze, *Antilles, Guyanes, la Mer des Caraïbes de 1492 à 1789* (Paris: Société d'Edition d'Enseignement Supérieur, 1977), 131–152.

262. Cornelis C. Goslinga, *The Dutch in the Caribbean and on the Wild Coast, 1580–1680* (Assen: van Gorcum, 1971); ibid., *The Dutch in the Caribbean and in the Guianas, 1680–1791* (Assen: van Gorcum, 1985).

263. Robert Bohn, *Die Piraten* (Munich: C. H. Beck, 2003); Kris E. Lane, *Pillaging the Empire: Piracy in the Americas, 1500–1750* (Armonk, NY: M. E. Sharpe, 1998); Robert C. Ritchie, *Captain Kidd and the War against the Pirates* (Cambridge, MA: Harvard University Press, 1986).

264. Reinhard, *Parasit oder Partner*, 95; Richard P. Dunn, *Sugar and Slaves: The Rise of the Planter Class in the English West Indies, 1624–1713* (London: Cape, 1972; reprint, 2000).

265. Nikolaus Böttcher, *Aufstieg und Fall eines atlantischen Handelsimperiums: Portugiesische Kaufleute und Sklavenhändler in Cartagena de Indias von 1580 bis zur Mitte des 17. Jahrhunderts* (Frankfurt am Main: Vervuert, 1995), 22.

266. Reinhard, *Die Neue Welt*, 124, but the number of Jews follows Günter Böhm, *Los sefardíes en los dominios olandeses de America del Sur y del Caribe, 1630–1750* (Frankfurt am Main: Vervuert, 1992), 69.

267. Claudia Schnurmann, *Atlantische Welten: Engländer und Niederländer im amerikanisch-atlantischen Raum 1648–1713* (Cologne: Böhlau, 1998), 173, 191, 218–219, 229–252, 279–280, 294, 365; Wim Klooster in Postma and Enthoven, *Riches from Atlantic Commerce*, 205.

268. Peer Schmidt in Pietschmann, *Atlantic History*, 87–88; Henry L. Feingold, ed., *The Jewish People in America*, 2nd ed., 5 vols. (Baltimore: Johns Hopkins University Press, 1992); Natalie

Zacek, "'A People Too Subtle': Sephardic Jewish Pioneers of the English West Indies," in Williams, *Bridging the Early Modern Atlantic World*, 97–112.

269. Synesio Sampaio Goes, *Navegantes, bandeirantes, diplomatas: Aspectos da descoberto do continente, da penetração do territorio brasileiro extra–Tordesilhas e do establecimento das fronteiras da Amazônia* (Brasília: IPRI, 1991).

270. Charles R. Boxer, *The Golden Age of Brazil, 1695–1750* (Berkeley: University of California Press, 1962; reprint, Manchester: Carcanet, 1995).

271. Virgilio Noya Pinto, *O ouro brasileiro e o comércio anglo-portugûes* (Sâo Paulo: Editora Nacional, 1979), 114.

272. Morineau, *Incroyables gazetteset fabuleux métaux*. If Noya Pinto's figures are not taken, as is usually the case, as five-yearly totals, but rather as annual averages and then multiplied by five, the result is the identical figure of 852 tons.

273. Reinhard, *Parasit oder Partner*, 77–116; Iliffe, *Africans*, 127–158; Klein, *Slave Trade*. The Transatlantic Slave Trade database (www.slavevoyages.org), maintained at Emory University, currently contains information on more than 35,000 voyages between 1514 and 1866. David Eltis and David Richardson, *Atlas of the Transatlantic Slave Trade* (New Haven, CT: Yale University Press, 2010); Stanley L. Engerman, Seymour Drescher, and Robert Louis Paquette, eds., *Slavery* (New York: Oxford University Press, 2001); Norbert Finzsch, James Oliver Horton, and Lois E. Horton, *Von Benin nach Baltimore: Die Geschichte der African Americans* (Hamburg: Hamburger Edition, 1999); Patrick Manning, ed., *Slave Trades, 1500–1800: Globalization of Forced Labour* (Aldershot, UK: Ashgate Variorum, 1997); Elizabeth Donnan, ed., *Documents Illustrative of the History of the Slave Trade*, 4 vols. (Washington, DC: Carnegie Institution, 1930–1935; reprint, 1965).

274. Herbert P. Klein, *The Atlantic Slave Trade* (Cambridge: Cambridge University Press, 1999), 211; following: Phillip D. Curtin, *The Atlantic Slave Trade: A Census* (Madison: University of Wisconsin Press, 1969).

275. Reinhard, *Parasit oder Partner*, 98–101, after Curtin, *Atlantic Slave Trade;* and Paul E. Lovejoy, "The Volume of the Atlantic Slave Trade: A Synthesis," *Journal of African History* 23–24 (1982): 473–501, whose figures (following Herbert P. Klein in Pietschmann, *Atlantic History*, 301–320, here 319) have been revised according to Eltis and Richardson, *Atlas*.

276. David K. O'Rourke, *How America's First Settlers Invented Chattel Slavery: Dehumanizing Native Americans and Africans with Language, Laws, Guns, and Religion* (New York: Peter Lang, 2005); Edmund P. Morgan, *American Slavery—American Freedom: The Ordeal of Colonial Virginia* (New York: Norton, 1975).

277. Imanuel Geiss, *Geschichte des Rassismus* (Frankfurt am Main: Suhrkamp, 1988); Robert Miles, *Rassismus: Einführung in die Theorie und Geschichte eines Begriffs* (Hamburg: Argument-Verlag, 1992).

278. Klein, *Slave Trade*, 21; David W. Galenson, "The Rise and Fall of Indentured Servitude in the Americas: An Economic Analysis," *Journal of Economic History* 44 (1984): 1–26.

279. Martin A. Klein, "The Slave Trade and Decentralized Societies," *Journal of African History* 42 (2001): 49–65.

280. Boubacar Barry, *Senegambia and the Atlantic Slave Trade* (Cambridge: Cambridge University Press, 1998); George E. Brooks, *Eurafricans in Western Africa: Commerce, Social Status, Gender, and Religious Observance from the 16th to the 18th Century* (Athens; Ohio University Press, 2003).

281. Oliver and Atmore, *Medieval Africa*, 93; Randy J. Sparks, *The Two Princes of Calabar: An Eighteenth-Century Atlantic Odyssey* (Cambridge, MA: Harvard University Press, 2004; German ed., Berlin: Rogner u. Bernhard, 2004).

282. Hilton, *Kingdom of Kongo*, 66–90, 104–133.

283. Reinhard, *Parasit oder Partner*, 100; James Walvin, *Black Ivory: Slavery in the British Empire*, 2nd ed. (Oxford: Blackwell, 2001); Betty Wood, *The Origins of American Slavery: Freedom and Bondage in the English Colonies, a Critical Issue* (New York: Hill and Wang, 1997); Robert Louis Stein, *The French Slave Trade in the Eighteenth Century: An Old Regime Business* (Madison: University of Wisconsin Press, 1979); Johannes Postma in Postma and Enthoven, *Riches from Atlantic Commerce*, 136–137.; Willie F. Page, *The Dutch Triangle: The Netherlands and the Atlantic Slave Trade, 1621–1664* (New York: Garland, 1997); Christian Degn, *Die Schimmelmanns im atlantischen Dreieckshandel: Gewinn und Gewissen* (Neumünster: Wachholtz, 1974).

284. Eric Williams, *Capitalism and Slavery* (Chapel Hill: University of North Carolina Press, 1944; reprint, London: Deutsch, 1964). According to Kenneth Morgan, *Slavery, Atlantic Trade, and the British Economy, 1660–1800* (Cambridge: Cambridge University Press, 2000), 29–35, Williams developed this theory based on a master's thesis by an unknown author of the university he was then attending while preparing his book for publication. Cf. Heather Cateau and Selwyn H. H. Carrington, eds., *Capitalism and Slavery Fifty Years Later: Eric Eustace Williams—A Reassessment of the Man and His Work* (New York: Peter Lang, 2000).

285. David Eltis and Stanley L. Engerman, "The Importance of Slavery and the Slave Trade to Industrializing Britain," *Journal of Economic History* 60 (2000): 123–144.

286. Gilberto Freyre, *Herrenhaus und Sklavenhütte* (Stuttgart: Klett Cotta, 1982); Brazilian ed., *Casa-grande e senzala* (1933).

287. Klein, *Slave Trade*, 167–173; Franklin W. Knight, ed., *The Slave Societies of the Caribbean*, vol. 3 of *General History of the Caribbean* (Paris: UNESCO, 1997); Gwendolyn M. Hall, *Social Control in Slave Plantation Societies: A Comparison of Saint-Domingue and Cuba* (Baltimore: Johns Hopkins University Press, 1971); Arthur L. Stinchcombe, *Sugar Island Slavery in the Age of Enlightenment: The Political Economy of the Caribbean World* (Princeton, NJ: Princeton University Press, 1995).

288. Jerome P. Handler et al. in Kenneth F. Kiple, ed., *The African Exchange: Toward a Biological History of Black People* (Durham, NC: Duke University Press, 1988), 140–166.

289. Kenneth F. Kiple, *The Caribbean Slave: A Biological History* (Cambridge: Cambridge University Press, 1984), 76; Kenneth F. Kiple in Kiple, *African Exchange*, 7–34.

290. Stuart B. Schwartz and Frank Salomon in *Cambridge History of the Native Peoples of the Americas*, vol. 3, part 2, 467–471.

291. James Walvin, *Making the Black Atlantic: Britain and the African Diaspora* (London: Cassell, 2000), 75–77; Klein, *Slave Trade*, 177.

292. Rainer Flasche, *Geschichte und Typologie afrikanischer Religiosität in Brasilien* (Marburg: Universität, 1973); Horst H. Figge, *Geisterkult, Besessenheit und Magie in der Umbanda-Religion Brasiliens* (Freiburg im Breisgau: Alber, 1973); Pierre Verger, *Orisha: Les dieux Yoruba en Afrique et au Nouveau Monde* (Paris: Mtailié, 1982); Ralph M. Becker, *Trance und Geistbesessenheit in Candomblé von Bahia* (Münster: LIT, 1995); Angelina Pollak-Eltz, *Trommel und Trance: Die afroamerikanischen Religionen* (Freiburg im Breisgau: Herder, 1995); Rómulo Lachatañeré, *Afro-Cuban Myths: Yemanyá and Other Orishas* (Princeton, NJ: Wiener, 2006); Frances Henry, *Reclaiming African Religions in Trinidad: The Socio-Political Legitimation of the Orisha and Spiritual Baptist Faith* (Kingston, Jamaica: University of the West Indies Press, 2003); James H. Sweet, "Slaves, Convicts, and Exiles: African Travellers in the Portuguese Atlantic World, 1720–1750," in Williams, *Bridging the Early Modern Atlantic World*, 191–202.

293. Hilton, *Kingdom of Kongo*, 90–103.

294. John K. Thornton, *The Kongolese Saint Anthony: Dona Beatriz Kimpa Vita and the Antonine Movement, 1684–1706* (Cambridge: Cambridge University Press, 1998); Hilton, *Kingdom of Kongo*, 208–210.

295. Cf. Herbert P. Klein, Leonhard Harding, and Andreas Eckert in Pietschmann, *Atlantic History*, 301–220, 322–323, 337–348; Patrick Manning, *Slavery and African Life: Occidental, Oriental, and African Slave Trades* (Cambridge: Cambridge University Press, 1990); Joseph Inikori in Ogot, *General History of Africa*, 5:108–109; Klein, *Slave Trade*, 127.

296. David Northrup, *Africa's Discovery of Europe, 1450–1850* (New York: Oxford University Press, 2002), 186; Thornton, *Africa and Africans*, 7; Kenneth G. Kelly, "Controlling Traders. Slave Coast Strategies at Savi and Ouidah," in Williams, *Bridging the Early Modern Atlantic World*, 151–171.

297. Bruce Trigger and William R. Swagerty in *Cambridge History of the Native Peoples of the Americas*, vol. 1, part 1, 343–361; Martin J. Daunton and Rick Halpern, eds., *Empire and Others, British Encounters with Indigenous Peoples, 1600–1850* (London: UCL Press, 1998).

298. Key background reading includes Robert D. Mitchell, ed., *North America: The Historical Geography of a Changing Continent* (Lanham, MD: Rowman & Littlefield, 1990); John J. McCusker and Kenneth Morgan, eds., *The Early Modern Atlantic Economy* (Cambridge: Cambridge University Press, 2000); Hermann Wellenreuther, *Niedergang und Aufstieg: Geschichte Nordamerikas vom Beginn der Besiedlung bis zum Ausgang des 17. Jahrhunderts* (Münster: LIT, 2000); ibid., *Ausbildung und Neubildung: Die Geschichte Nordamerikas vom Ausgang des 17. Jahrhunderts bis zum Ausbruch der amerikanischen Revolution* (Münster: LIT, 2001); David B. Quinn, *North America from Earliest Discovery to the First Settlements: The Norse Voyages to 1612* (New York: Harper & Row, 1977); David B. Quinn, ed., *New American World: A Documentary History of North America to 1612*, 5 vols. (London: Macmillan, 1979); Andrew N. Porter, *Atlas of British Overseas Expansion* (London: Routledge, 1994); ibid., ed., *Bibliography of Imperial, Colonial, and Commonwealth History since 1600* (Oxford: Oxford University Press, 2002); Benedikt Stuchtey, "Nation und Expansion: Das Britische Empire in der neuesten Forschung," *Historische Zeitschrift* 274 (2002): 87–118; Merrill Jensen, ed., *American Colonial Documents*, vol. 9 of *English Historical Documents* (London: Eyre and Spottiswoode, 1955); Nicholas P. Canny, ed., *The Origins of Empire. British Overseas Enterprise to the Close of*

the 17th Century, vol. 1 of *The Oxford History of the British Empire,* ed. William Roger Louis (Oxford: Oxford University Press, 1998); Peter J. Marshall, ed., *The Eighteenth Century,* vol. 2 of *The Oxford History of the British Empire,* ed. William Roger Louis (Oxford: Oxford University Press, 1998); David B. Quinn and A. N. Ryan, *England's Sea Empire, 1550–1642* (London: Allen and Unwin, 1983); Claudia Schnurmann, *Vom Inselreich zur Weltmacht: Die Entwicklung des englischen Weltreichs vom Mittelalter bis ins 20. Jahrhundert* (Stuttgart: Kohlhammer, 2001); Charles M. Andrews, *The Colonial Period of American History,* 4 vols. (New Haven, CT: Yale University Press, 1934–1938); Richard C. Simmons, *The American Colonies from Settlement to Independence* (London: Longman, 1976); Richard Middleton, *Colonial America: A History, 1607–1760* (Oxford: Blackwell, 1992); Stanley L. Engerman and Robert E. Gallman, *The Colonial Era,* vol. 1 of *The Cambridge Economic History of the United States* (Cambridge: Cambridge University Press, 1997); Pierre Pluchon, *Histoire de la colonisation française,* vol. 1 (Paris: Fayard, 1991); Jean Meyer, Jean Tarrade, and Annie Rey-Goldzeiguer, *Des origines à 1914,* vol. 1 of *Histoire de la France coloniale* (Paris: Colin, 1991); Gilles Havard and Cécile Vidal, *Histoire de l'Amérique française,* 2nd ed. (Paris: Flammarion, 2006); Laurier Turgeon, "Codfish, Consumption, and Colonization: The Creation of the French Atlantic World during the Sixteenth Century," in Williams, *Bridging the Early Modern Atlantic World,* 33–56.

299. Marcel Trudel, *The Beginnings of New France, 1524–1663* (Toronto: McClelland and Stewart, 1973).

300. Bruce G. Trigger, *The Children of Aataentsic: A History of the Huron People to 1660,* 2 vols. (Montreal: McGill–Queen's University Press, 1976).

301. Trudel, *Beginnings of New France,* 218; Dean R. Snow, *The Iroquois* (Oxford: Blackwell, 1994); William Engelbrecht, *Iroquoia: The Development of a Native World* (Syracuse, NY: Syracuse University Press, 2003).

302. Marcel Trudel, *Débuts du regime seigneurial au Canada* (Montreal: Fides, 1974); Louise Dechêne, *Habitants and Merchants in Seventeenth-Century Montreal* (Montreal: McGill–Queen's University Press, 1992; French ed., 1974).

303. Marcel Trudel, *Montréal: La formation d'une société 1642–1663* (Montreal: Fides, 1976), 39.

304. Klaus-Dieter Ertler, ed., *Von Schwarzröcken und Hexenmeistern: Jesuitenberichte aus Neu–Frankreich (1616–1649)* (Berlin: Reimer, 1997); Franz-Josef Post, *Schamanen und Missionare: Katholische Mission und indigene Spiritualität in Nouvelle-France* (Münster: LIT, 1997).

305. Marcel Trudel, *La population du Canada en 1666: Recensement reconstitué* (Sillery: Septentrion, 1995), 47–48, 58.

306. Karen Anderson, *Chain Her by One Foot: The Subjugation of Native Women in Seventeenth-Century New France* (New York: Routledge, 1993).

307. Cornelius J. Jaenen, *Friend and Foe, Aspects of French–Amerindian Cultural Contact in the Sixteenth and Seventeenth Centuries* (New York: Columbia University Press, 1976), 110–116; Mark Edward Lender and J. K. Martin, *Drinking in America: A History* (New York: Free Press, 1982), 1–40; Peter C. Mancall, *Deadly Medicine: Indians and Alcohol in Early America* (Ithaca, NY: Cornell University Press, 1997); Sven Kuttner, *Handel, Religion und Herrschaft:*

Kulturkontakt und Ureinwohnerpolitik in Neufrankreich im frühen 17. Jahrhundert (Frankfurt am Main: Peter Lang, 1998).

308. Kenneth R. Andrews, Nicholas P. Canny, and Paul E. H. Hair, eds., *The Westward Enterprise: English Activities in Ireland, the Atlantic, and America, 1480–1650* (Liverpool: Liverpool University Press, 1978); Nicholas P. Canny, "The Ideology of English Colonization: From Ireland to America," *William and Mary Quarterly* 30 (1973): 575–598.

309. David Armitage, *The Ideological Origins of the British Empire* (Cambridge: Cambridge University Press, 2000).

310. Philip L. Barbour, ed., *The Jamestown Voyages under the First Charter, 1606–1609*, Hakluyt Society, 2nd ser., 2 vols., 136–137 (Cambridge, 1969; reprint, Nendeln: Kraus Reprint, 1976).

311. George F. Willison, *Saints and Strangers* (New York: Raynal and Hitchcock, 1945).

312. Virginia D. Anderson, *New England's Generation: The Great Migration and the Formation of Society and Culture in the Seventeenth Century* (Cambridge: Cambridge University Press, 1991).

313. Wellenreuther, *Niedergang und Aufstieg,* 321–324, 338–339, 343; Reinhard, *Die Neue Welt,* 198; Bernard Bailyn, *The New England Merchants in the Seventeenth Century* (Cambridge, MA: Harvard University Press, 1955).

314. Nathaniel B. Shurtleff, ed., *Records of the Governor and Company of Massachusetts Bay in New England,* 5 vols. in 6 parts (Boston: White, 1853–1854; reprint, New York: AMS Press, 1968).

315. Perry Miller, *The New England Mind,* 2 vols. (Cambridge, MA: Harvard University Press, 1953–1954); Reinhard, *Die Neue Welt,* 189–190; Wellenreuther, *Niedergang und Aufstieg,* 340, 342–343, 363; David D. Hall, ed., *Puritans in the New World: A Critical Anthology* (Princeton, NJ: Princeton University Press, 2004); ibid., *The Faithful Shepherd: A History of the New England Ministry in the Seventeenth Century* (Cambridge, MA: Harvard University Press, 2005).

316. Robert M. Bliss, *Revolution and Empire: English Politics and the American Colonies in the Seventeenth Century* (Manchester, UK: Manchester University Press, 1990); Carla G. Pestana, *The English Atlantic in an Age of Revolution, 1640–1661* (Cambridge, MA: Harvard University Press, 2004).

317. Edmund P. Morgan, *Roger Williams; the Church and the State* (New York: Harcourt, Brace & World, 1967); Edwin P. Gaustad, *Liberty of Conscience: Roger Williams in America* (Grand Rapids, MI: W. B. Eerdmans, 1991).

318. Mary J. A. Jones, *Congregational Commonwealth: Connecticut, 1636–1662* (Middleton, CT: Wesleyan University Press, 1968).

319. Isabel M. Calder, *The New Haven Colony* (New Haven, CT: Yale University Press, 1934).

320. David E. van Deventer, *The Emergence of Provincial New Hampshire, 1623–1741* (Baltimore: Johns Hopkins University Press, 1976).

321. John D. Krugler, "Lord Baltimore, Roman Catholics, and Toleration: Religious Policy in Maryland during the Early Catholic Years, 1634–1649," *Catholic Historical Review* 65 (1979): 49–75; David B. Quinn, ed., *Maryland in a Wider World* (Detroit: Wayne State University Press, 1982); Wellenreuther, *Niedergang und Aufstieg,* 282–297.

322. Rink, *Holland on the Hudson;* Van Cleaf Bachman, *Peltries or Plantations: The Economic Policy of the Dutch West India Company in New Netherland, 1623–39* (Baltimore: Johns Hopkins

University Press, 1969); Donna Merwick, *Possessing Albany, 1630–1710: The Dutch and English Experiences* (Cambridge: Cambridge University Press, 1990).

323. William J. Eccles, *Canada under Louis XIV, 1663–1701* (Toronto: McClelland and Stewart, 1969).

324. Dirk Hoerder, *Cultures in Contact: World Migrations in the Second Millennium* (Durham, NC: Duke University Press, 2002), 221–222; Yves Landry and Jacques Légaré, "The Life Course of Seventeenth-Century Immigrants to Canada," *Journal of Family History* 12 (1987): 201–212; Peter N. Moogk, "Reluctant Exiles: The Problems of Colonization in French North America: Emigrants from France in Canada before 1760," *William and Mary Quarterly* 46 (1989): 463–505.

325. Wellenreuther, *Niedergang und Aufstieg,* 458; Morris Altman, "Economic Growth in Canada, 1695–1739: Estimates and Analysis," *William and Mary Quarterly* 45 (1988): 684–711.

326. Peter H. Wood, "La Salle: Discovery of a Lost Explorer," *American Historical Review* 89 (1984): 294–323; Marcel Giraud, *Histoire de la Louisiane française,* 4 vols. (Paris: PUF, 1953–1974).

327. Richard P. Dunn, ed., *The World of William Penn* (Philadelphia: University of Pennsylvania Press, 1986); Mary K. Geiter, *William Penn* (London: Longman, 2000).

328. Richard R. Johnson, *Adjustment to Empire: The New England Colonies, 1675–1715* (Leicester, UK: Leicester University Press, 1981); Jack M. Sosin, *English America and the Revolution of 1688: Royal Administration and the Structure of Provincial Government* (Lincoln: University of Nebraska Press, 1982); Michael Hall, Lawrence Leder, and Michael Kammen, eds., *The Glorious Revolution in America: Documents on the Colonial Crisis of 1689* (New York: Norton, 1972).

329. Kenneth Coleman, *Colonial Georgia: A History* (New York: Scribner, 1976).

330. Alison Games, "Migration," in Armitage and Braddick, *British Atlantic World,* 31–50, here 41; ibid., *Migration and the Origins of the English Atlantic World* (Cambridge, MA: Harvard University Press, 1999); Bernard Bailyn, *Voyagers to the West: Emigration from Britain to America on the Eve of the Revolution* (London: Tauris, 1987); David Cressy, *Coming Over: Migrations and Communication between England and New England in the Seventeenth Century* (Cambridge: Cambridge University Press, 1987); Georg Fertig, *Lokales Leben, atlantische Welt: Die Entscheidung zur Auswanderung vom Rhein nach Nordamerika im 18. Jahrhundert* (Osnabrück: Universitätsverlag Rasch, 2000); Mark Häberlein, *Vom Oberrhein zum Susquehanna: Studien zur badischen Auswanderung nach Pennsylvania im 18. Jahrhundert* (Stuttgart: Kohlhammer, 1993).

331. Hoerder, *Cultures in Contact,* 222–223; Patrick Griffin, *The People with No Name: Ireland's Ulster Scots, America's Scots Irish, and the Creation of a British Atlantic World, 1689–1764* (Princeton, NJ: Princeton University Press, 2001).

332. Hoerder, *Cultures in Contact,* 220; Wellenreuther, *Ausbildung und Neubildung,* 99, cites some rather anomalous figures; David W. Galenson, *White Servitude in Colonial America: An Economic Analysis* (Cambridge: Cambridge University Press, 1981).

333. A. Roger Ekirch, *Bound for America: The Transportation of British Convicts to the Colonies, 1718–1775* (Oxford: Clarendon Press, 1987).

334. David W. Galenson, *Traders, Planters, and Slaves: Market Behavior in Early English America* (Cambridge: Cambridge University Press, 1986); Oscar Reiss, *Blacks in Colonial America* (Jefferson, NC: McFarland, 2006).

335. James D. Drake, *King Philip's War: Civil War in New England, 1675–1676* (Amherst: University of Massachusetts Press, 2000).

336. Wellenreuther, *Ausbildung und Neubildung,* 351–382, here 373; Reinhard, *Die Neue Welt,* 199; Stuart Banner, *How the Indians Lost Their Land: Law and Power on the Frontier* (Cambridge, MA: Belknap Press, 2005), 1–190.

337. Wellenreuther, *Ausbildung und Neubildung,* 133–137, 314–339; Nathan O. Hatch and Harry P. Stout, eds., *Jonathan Edwards and the American Experience* (New York: Oxford University Press, 1988).

338. Erich Beyreuther, *Die Erweckungsbewegung,* vol. 4 of *Die Kirche in ihrer Geschichte* (Göttingen: Vandenhoeck & Ruprecht, 1963), chap. R 1, 11.

339. Juan M. Zapatero, *La guerra del Caribe en el siglo XVIII* (San Juan, Puerto Rico: Istituto de Cultura Puertorriqueña, 1964); Joseph L. Rutledge, *Century of Conflict: The Struggle between the French and British in Colonial America* (Garden City, NY: Doubleday, 1956); George F. G. Stanley, *New France: The Last Phase, 1744–1760* (Toronto: McClelland and Stewart, 1968); William. R. Nester, *The Great Frontier War: Britain, France, and the Imperial Struggle for North America, 1607–1755* (Westport, CT: Praeger, 2000); ibid., *The First Global War: Britain, France, and the Fate of North America, 1756–1775* (Westport, CT: Praeger, 2000); John Grenier, *The First Way of War: American War Making on the Frontier, 1607–1814* (Cambridge: Cambridge University Press, 2005).

340. J. E. Inikori, *Africans and the Industrial Revolution in England: A Study in International Trade and Economic Development* (Cambridge: Cambridge University Press, 2002).

341. Paul Gilroy, *The Black Atlantic: Modernity and Double Consciousness* (Cambridge, MA: Harvard University Press, 1993).

Selected Bibliography

Introduction

Abulafia, David. *The Great Sea: A Human History of the Mediterranean*. London: Allen Lane, 2011.

Allsen, Thomas T. "Pre-Modern Empires." In *Oxford Handbook of World History,* ed. Jerry H. Bentley. Oxford: Oxford University Press, 2011.

Asher, Catherine B., and Cynthia Talbot. *India before Europe*. Cambridge: Cambridge University Press, 2006.

Ayalon, David. *Gunpowder and Firearms in the Mamluk Kingdom*. 2nd ed. London: Frank Cass, 1978.

Barendse, René J. *Arabian Seas, 1700–1763*. 4 vols. Leiden: Brill, 2009.

———. *The Arabian Seas: The Indian Ocean World of the Seventeenth Century*. Armonk, NY: M. E. Sharpe, 2002.

Bartlett, Robert, and Angus MacKay, eds. *Medieval Frontier Societies*. Oxford: Clarendon Press, 1989.

Bentley, Jerry H., ed. *The Oxford Handbook of World History*. Oxford: Oxford University Press, 2011.

Bosbach, Franz. *Monarchia universalis: Ein politischer Leitbegriff der Frühen Neuzeit*. Göttingen: Vandenhoek & Ruprecht, 1988.

Boxer, Charles R. *Dutch Merchants and Mariners in Asia, 1602–1795*. London: Variorum, 1988.

Braudel, Fernand. *The Mediterranean and the Mediterranean World in the Age of Philip II*. 2 vols. London: Collins, 1972.

Bruijn, Jaap R., Femme S. Gaastra, and Ivo Schöffer. *Dutch-Asiatic Shipping in the 17th and 18th Centuries*. 3 vols. The Hague: Nijhoff, 1979–1987.

Burbank, Jane, and Frederick Cooper. *Empires in World History: Power and the Politics of Difference*. Princeton, NJ: Princeton University Press, 2010.

Burkhardt, Johannes. *Der Dreißigjährige Krieg*. 6th ed. Frankfurt am Main: Suhrkamp, 2003.

Canny, Nicholas, and Philip Morgan, eds. *The Oxford Handbook of the Atlantic World, 1450–1850*. Oxford: Oxford University Press, 2011.

Chakrabarty, Dipesh. *Provincializing Europe: Postcolonial Thought and Historical Difference*. Princeton, NJ: Princeton University Press, 2007.

Chaudhuri, Kirti N. *Asia before Europe: Economy and Civilisation of the Indian Ocean*. Cambridge: Cambridge University Press, 1990.

———. *Trade and Civilisation in the Indian Ocean: An Economic History from the Rise of Islam to 1750.* Cambridge: Cambridge University Press, 1985.

Cipolla, Carlo. *Vele e cannoni.* Bologna: Mulino, 1983.

Conermann, Stephan, ed. *Der Indische Ozean in historischer Perspektive.* Hamburg: EB-Verlag, 1998.

Dale, Stephen F. *The Muslim Empires of the Ottomans, Safavids, and Mughals.* Cambridge: Cambridge University Press, 2010.

Delgado, Mariano. *Abschied vom erobernden Gott: Studien zur Geschichte und Gegenwart des Christentums in Lateinamerika.* Immensee: Neue Zeitschrift für Missionswissenschaft, 1996.

Donnan, Hastings, and Thomas M. Wilson. *Borders: Frontiers of Identity, Nation, and State.* New York: Berg, 1999.

Döring, Jörg, and Tristan Thielmann, eds. *Spatial Turn: Das Raumparadigma in den Kultur- und Sozialwissenschaften.* Bielefeld: Transcript Verlag, 2008.

Duncan Baretta, Silvio R., and John Markoff. "Civilization and Barbarism: Cattle Frontiers in Latin America." In *States of Violence,* ed. Fernando Coronil and Julie Skurski. Ann Arbor: University of Michigan Press, 2006.

Eisenstadt, S. N. *Die Vielfalt der Moderne.* Weilerswist: Velbrück Wissenschaft, 2000.

Ferguson, Niall. *Empire: How Britain Made the Modern World.* London: Allen Lane, 2003.

Freeman, Donald B. *The Pacific.* New York: Routledge, 2010.

Gerhard, Dietrich. "The Frontier in Comparative View." *Comparative Studies in Society and History* 1, no. 3 (1959): 205–229.

Gommans, Jos. *Mughal Warfare: Indian Frontiers and High Roads to Empire, 1500–1700.* New York: Routledge, 2002.

Gommans, Jos, and Jacques Leider, eds. *The Maritime Frontier of Burma: Exploring Political, Cultural and Commercial, Interaction in the Indian Ocean World, 1200–1800.* Amsterdam: Koninklijke Nederlands Akademie van Wetenschappen, 2002.

Guy, John. *Woven Cargoes: Indian Textiles in the East.* London: Thames and Hudson, 1998.

Häberlein, Mark. "Kulturelle Vermittler in der atlantischen Welt der Frühen Neuzeit." In *Sprachgrenzen—Sprachkontakte—Kulturelle Vermittler: Kommunikation zwischen Europäern und Außereuropäern (16.–20. Jahrhundert),* ed. Mark Häberlein and Alexander Keese. Stuttgart: Steiner, 2010.

Harding, Leonhard. *Das Königreich Benin: Geschichte—Kultur—Wirtschaft.* Munich: Oldenbourg, 2010.

Harvey, David. *The Condition of Postmodernity: An Enquiry into the Origins of Cultural Change.* Oxford: Blackwell, 1989.

Hennessy, Alistair. *The Frontier in Latin American History.* London: Arnold, 1978.

Herbers, Klaus, and Nikolas Jaspert, eds. *Grenzräume und Grenzüberschreitungen im Vergleich: Der Osten und der Westen des mittelalterlichen Lateineuropa.* Berlin: Akademie, 2007.

Heywood, Colin. "The Frontier in Ottoman History: Old Ideas and New Myths." In *Frontiers in Question: Eurasian Borderlands, 700–1700,* ed. Daniel Power and Naomi Standen. Basingstoke, UK: Macmillan, 1999.

Hodgson, Marshall G. S. *The Gunpowder Empires and Modern Times.* Vol. 3 of *The Venture of Islam: Conscience and History in a World Civilization.* Chicago: University of Chicago Press, 1974.

Hoerder, Dirk. *Cultures in Contact: World Migrations in the Second Millennium.* Durham, NC: Duke University Press, 2002.

Khodarkovsky, Michael. *Russia's Steppe Frontier: The Making of a Colonial Empire, 1500–1800.* Bloomington: Indiana University Press, 2002.

Kirby, David, and Merja-Liisa Hinkkanen. *The Baltic and the North Seas.* New York: Routledge, 2000.

Lamar, Howard, and Leonard Thompson, eds. *The Frontier in History: North America and Southern Africa Compared.* New Haven, CT: Yale University Press, 1981.

Lattimore, Owen. *Studies in Frontier History: Collected Papers, 1928–1958.* Paris: Mouton, 1962.

Leonhard, Jörn, and Ulrike von Hirschhausen, eds. *Comparing Empires: Encounters and Transfers in the Long Nineteenth Century.* Göttingen: Vandenhoeck & Ruprecht, 2011.

Lieberman, Victor. *Integration on the Mainland.* Vol. 1 of *Strange Parallels: Southeast Asia in Global Context, c. 800–1830.* Cambridge: Cambridge University Press, 2003.

Linebaugh, Peter, and Marcus Rediker. *Die vielköpfige Hydra: Die verborgene Geschichte des revolutionären Atlantiks.* Berlin: Assoziation, 2008.

Marx, Christoph. "Grenzfälle: Zu Geschichte und Potential des Frontierbegriffs." *Saeculum* 54, no. 1 (2003): 123–143.

McNeill, John R. "Biological Exchanges in World History." In *Oxford Handbook of World History,* ed. Jerry H. Bentley. Oxford: Oxford University Press, 2011.

———. "The Ecological Atlantic." In *Oxford Handbook of the Atlantic World 1450–1850,* ed. Nicholas Canny and Philip Morgan. Oxford: Oxford University Press, 2011.

McNeill, William H. *The Age of Gunpowder Empires, 1450–1800.* Washington, DC: American Historical Association, 1989.

McPherson, Kenneth. *The Indian Ocean: A History of the People and the Sea.* Delhi: Oxford University Press, 1993.

Metzler, Gabriele, and Michael Wildt, eds. *Über Grenzen: 84. Deutscher Historikertag in Berlin 2010. Berichtsband.* Göttingen: Vandenhoeck & Ruprecht, 2012.

Middell, Matthias, and Ulf Engel, eds. *Theoretiker der Globalisierung.* Leipzig: Universitätsverlag, 2010.

Münkler, Herfried. *Imperien: Die Logik der Weltherrschaft—Vom Alten Rom bis zu den Vereinigten Staaten.* Berlin: Rowohlt, 2005.

Nagel, Tilman. *Timur der Eroberer und die islamische Welt des späten Mittelalters.* Munich: Beck, 1993.

Needham, Joseph, et al. *Science and Civilization in China.* 7 vols. 13 parts. Cambridge: Cambridge University Press, 1954–2004.

Osterhammel, Jürgen. *The Transformation of the World: A Global History of the Nineteenth Century.* Translated by Patrick Camiller. Princeton, NJ: Princeton University Press, 2014.

———. "World History." In *Historical Writing since 1945.* Vol. 5 of *The Oxford History of Historical Writing.* Edited by Axel Schneider and Daniel Woolf. Oxford: Oxford University Press, 2011.

Parsons, Timothy H. *The Rule of Empires: Those Who Built Them, Those Who Endured Them, and Why They Always Fall.* New York: Oxford University Press, 2010.

Pearson, Michael N. *The Indian Ocean.* New York: Routledge 2003.

———. *Port Cities and Intruders: The Swahili Coast, India, and Portugal in the Early Modern Era.* Baltimore: Johns Hopkins University Press, 1998.

Perrin, Noel. *Giving up the Gun: Japan's Reversion to the Sword, 1543–1879.* Boston: Godine, 1979.

Piltz, Eric. "'Trägheit des Raums': Fernand Braudel und die Spatial Stories der Geschichtswissenschaft." In *Spatial Turn: Das Raumparadigma in den Kultur- und Sozialwissenschaften,* ed. Jörg Döring and Tristan Thielmann. Bielefeld: Transcript Verlag, 2008.

Power, Daniel, and Naomi Standen, eds. *Frontiers in Question: Eurasian Borderlands, 700–1700.* Basingstoke, UK: Macmillan, 1999.

Ptak, Roderich. *Die maritime Seidenstraße: Küstenräume, Seefahrt und Handel in vorkolonialer Zeit.* Munich: Beck, 2007.

Reinhard, Wolfgang. "Gelenkter Kulturwandel im 17. Jahrhundert: Akkulturation in den Jesuitenmissionen als universalhistorisches Problem" [1976]. In *Ausgewählte Abhandlungen.* Berlin: Duncker & Humblot, 1997.

———. *Geschichte der europäischen Expansion.* 4 vols. Stuttgart: Kohlhammer, 1983–1990. New edition, 2015.

———. *Geschichte der Staatsgewalt: Eine vergleichende Verfassungsgeschichte Europas von den Anfängen bis zur Gegenwart.* 3rd ed. Munich: Beck, 2002.

———. *Kleine Geschichte des Kolonialismus.* 2nd ed. Stuttgart: Kröner, 2008.

———. "Sprachbeherrschung und Weltherrschaft: Sprache und Sprachwissenschaft in der europäischen Expansion" [1987]. In *Ausgewählte Abhandlungen.* Berlin: Duncker & Humblot, 1997.

Rösler, Michael, and Tobias Wendl, eds. *Frontiers and Borderlands: Anthropological Perspectives.* Frankfurt am Main: Peter Lang, 1999.

Rothermund, Dietmar, and Susanne Weigelin-Schwiedrzik, eds. *Der Indische Ozean: Das afroasiatische Mittelmeer als Kultur- und Wirtschaftsraum.* Vienna: Promedia, 2004.

Sachsenmaier, Dominic. *Global Perspectives on Global History: Theories and Approaches in a Connected World.* Cambridge: Cambridge University Press, 2011.

Taylor, Jean Gelman. *The Social World of Batavia: European and Eurasian in Dutch Asia*. Madison: University of Wisconsin Press, 1983.

Toussaint, Auguste. *Histoire de l'Ocean Indien*. Paris: PUF, 1961.

Turtledove, Harry. *Gunpowder Empire*. New York: Tor Books, 2003.

Völkel, Markus. *Geschichtsschreibung: Eine Einführung in globaler Perspektive*. Cologne: Böhlau, 2006.

Waechter, Matthias. *Die Erfindung des amerikanischen Westens: Die Geschichte der Frontier-Debatte*. Freiburg im Breisgau: Rombach, 1996.

White, Richard. *The Middle Ground: Indians, Empires, and Republics in the Great Lakes Region, 1650–1815*. Cambridge: Cambridge University Press, 1991.

Wink, André. *Akbar*. Oxford: Oneworld, 2009.

Woolf, Daniel. *A Global History of History*. Cambridge: Cambridge University Press, 2011.

Empires and Frontiers in Continental Eurasia

Andrade, Tonio. *How Taiwan Became Chinese: Dutch, Spanish, and Han Colonization in the Seventeenth Century*. New York: Columbia University Press, 2008.

Atwell, William S. "International Bullion Flows and the Chinese Economy." *Past and Present* 95, no. 1 (1982): 68–90.

———. "Volcanism and Short-Term Climatic Change in East Asian and World History, c. 1200–1699." *Journal of World History* 12, no. 1 (2001): 29–98.

Babur. *The Baburnama*. Translated by Wheeler Thackston. Oxford: Oxford University Press, 1996.

Baldanza, Kathlene. "The Ambiguous Border: Early Modern Sino-Viet Relations." PhD diss., University of Pennsylvania, 2010.

Barfield, Thomas J. *The Perilous Frontier: Nomadic Empires and China*. Cambridge, MA: Basil Blackwell, 1989.

Bartlett, Beatrice S. *Monarchs and Ministers: The Grand Council in Mid-Ch'ing China, 1723–1820*. Berkeley: University of California Press, 1991.

Bassin, Mark. "Expansion and Colonialism on the Eastern Frontier: Views of Siberia and the Far East in Pre-Petrine Russia." *Journal of Historical Geography* 14, no. 1 (1988): 3–21.

———. "Russia between Europe and Asia: The Ideological Construction of Geographical Space." *Slavic Review* 50, no.1 (1991): 1–17.

Beckwith, Christopher I. *Empires of the Silk Road: A History of Central Eurasia from the Bronze Age to the Present*. Princeton, NJ: Princeton University Press, 2009.

Bernstein, Gail Lee, ed. *Recreating Japanese Women, 1600–1945*. Berkeley: University of California Press, 1991.

Berry, Mary Elizabeth. *The Culture of Civil War in Kyoto*. Berkeley: University of California Press, 1994.

———. *Japan in Print Information and Nation in the Early Modern Period*. Berkeley: University of California Press, 2006.

Bix, Herbert P. *Peasant Protest in Japan, 1590–1884*. New Haven, CT: Yale University Press, 1986.

Bolitho, Harold. *Treasures among Men: The Fudai Daimyo in Tokugawa Japan*. New Haven, CT: Yale University Press, 1974.

Bray, Francesca. *Technology and Gender: Fabrics of Power in Late Imperial China*. Berkeley: University of California Press, 1997.

Brokaw, Cynthia Joanne. *Commerce in Culture: The Sibao Book Trade in the Qing and Republican Periods*. Cambridge, MA: Harvard University Asia Center, 2007.

———. *The Ledgers of Merit and Demerit: Social Change and Moral Order in Late Imperial China*. Princeton, NJ: Princeton University Press, 1991.

Brook, Timothy. *The Chinese State in Ming Society*. New York: Routledge Curzon, 2005.

———. *The Confusions of Pleasure: Commerce and Culture in Ming China*. Berkeley: University of California Press, 1998.

———. *Praying for Power: Buddhism and the Formation of Gentry Society in Late-Ming China*. Cambridge, MA: Council of East Asian Studies, 1993.

———. *The Troubled Empire: China in the Yuan and Ming Dynasties*. Cambridge, MA: Belknap Press of Harvard University Press, 2010.

Burns, Susan L. *Before the Nation: Kokugaku and the Imagining of Community in Early Modern Japan*. Durham, NC: Duke University Press, 2003.

Burton, Audrey. *The Bukharans: A Dynastic, Diplomatic, and Commercial History, 1550–1702*. Richmond, UK: Curzon, 1997.

Bushkovitch, Paul. "The Formation of a National Consciousness in Early Modern Russia." *Harvard Ukrainian Studies* 10 (1986): 355–376.

———. *The Merchants of Moscow, 1580–1650*. Cambridge: Cambridge University Press, 1980.

———. *Peter the Great*. Lanham, MD: Rowman & Littlefield, 2001.

———. *Peter the Great: The Struggle for Power, 1671–1725*. Cambridge: Cambridge University Press, 2001.

———. *Religion and Society in Russia: The Sixteenth and Seventeenth Centuries*. New York: Oxford University Press, 1992.

Cheng, Pei-kai, Michael Lestz, and Jonathan D. Spence. *The Search for Modern China: A Documentary Collection*. New York: W. W. Norton, 1999.

Christian, David. "Inner Eurasia as a Unit of World History." *Journal of World History* 5, no. 2 (1994): 173–211.

Ch'ü T'ung-tsu. *Local Government in China under the Ch'ing*. Cambridge, MA: Harvard University Press, 1962.

Clunas, Craig. *Superfluous Things: Material Culture and Social Status in Early Modern China*. Urbana: University of Illinois Press, 1991.

Coatsworth, John, Juan Cole, Michael Hanagan, Charles Tilly, Louise Tilly, and Peter C. Perdue. *Global Connections: A World History*. Cambridge: Cambridge University Press, forthcoming.

Collcutt, Martin. *Five Mountains: The Rinzai Zen Monastic Institution in Medieval Japan*. Cambridge, MA: Harvard University Press, Council on East Asian Studies, 1981.

Cooke, Nola. "Regionalism and the Nature of Nguyen Rule in Seventeenth-Century Dang Trong (Cochinchina)." *Journal of Southeast Asian Studies* 29, no. 1 (1998): 122–161.

Cracraft, James. *The Petrine Revolution in Russian Culture*. Cambridge, MA: Belknap Press of Harvard University Press, 2004.

Crossley, Pamela Kyle. "Thinking about Ethnicity in Early Modern China." *Late Imperial China* 11 (1990): 1–35.

———. *A Translucent Mirror: History and Identity in Qing Imperial Ideology*. Berkeley: University of California Press, 1999.

Crummey, Robert O. *The Formation of Muscovy, 1304–1613*. London: Longman, 1987.

Dale, Stephen Frederic. *Indian Merchants and Eurasian Trade, 1600–1750*. Cambridge: Cambridge University Press, 1994.

Darwin, John. *After Tamerlane: The Global History of Empire since 1405*. New York: Bloomsbury Press, 2008.

De Bary, William Theodore, ed. *Self and Society in Ming Thought*. New York: Columbia University Press, 1970.

———, ed. *The Unfolding of Neo-Confucianism*. New York: Columbia University Press, 1975.

De Bary, William Theodore, Irene Bloom, and Richard John Lufrano. *Sources of Chinese Tradition*. 2nd ed. New York: Columbia University Press, 2000.

Di Cosmo, Nicola. "Qing Colonial Administration in the Inner Asian Dependencies." *The International History Review* 20, no. 2 (1998): 287–309.

———. "State Formation and Periodization in Inner Asian History." *Journal of World History* 10, no. 1 (1999): 1–40.

Di Cosmo, Nicola, Allen J. Frank, and Peter B. Golden, eds. *The Cambridge History of Inner Asia: The Chinggisid Age*. Cambridge: Cambridge University Press, 2009.

Dore, Ronald P. *Education in Tokugawa Japan*. Berkeley: University of California Press, 1965.

Dower, John W., ed. *Origins of the Modern Japanese State: Selected Writings of E. H. Norman*. New York: Pantheon, 1975.

Drixler, Fabian. *Mabiki: Infanticide and Fertility in Eastern Japan, 1650–1950*. Berkeley: University of California Press, 2013.

Duiker, William J. *Historical Dictionary of Vietnam*. 2nd ed. Lanham, MD: Scarecrow Press, 1998.

Dunning, Chester S. L. *Russia's First Civil War: The Time of Troubles and the Founding of the Romanov Dynasty*. University Park: Pennsylvania State University Press, 2001.

Dunstan, Helen. *State or Merchant? Political Economy and Political Process in 1740s China*. Cambridge, MA: Harvard University Press, 2006.

Dutton, George. *The Tây Son Uprising: Society and Rebellion in Eighteenth-Century Vietnam*. Honolulu: University of Hawai'i Press, 2006.

Duyvendak, Jan J. *China's Discovery of Africa; Lectures Given at the University of London on January 22 and 23, 1947*. London: Probsthain, 1949.

Ebrey, Patricia Buckley, Anne Walthall, and James B. Palais. *East Asia: A Cultural, Social, and Political History*. Boston: Houghton Mifflin, 2006.

Eikemeier, Dieter. *Elemente im politischen Denken des Yon'am Pak Chiwon (1737–1805)*. Leiden: Brill, 1970.

Elliott, Mark C. *The Manchu Way: The Eight Banners and Ethnic Identity in Late Imperial China*. Stanford, CA: Stanford University Press, 2001.

Elman, Benjamin. *A Cultural History of Civil Examinations in Late Imperial China*. Berkeley: University of California Press, 2000.

———. *From Philosophy to Philology: Intellectual and Social Aspects of Change in Late Imperial China*. Cambridge, MA: Harvard University Press, 1984.

Elman, Benjamin A., John B. Duncan, and Herman Ooms. *Rethinking Confucianism: Past and Present in China, Japan, Korea, and Vietnam*. Los Angeles: UCLA Asian Pacific Monograph Series, 2002.

Elvin, Mark. *The Pattern of the Chinese Past*. Stanford, CA: Stanford University Press, 1973.

Engelbert, Thomas. *Die Chinesische Minderheit im Süden Vietnams (Hoa) als Paradigma der kolonialen und nationalistischen Nationalitätenpolitik*. Frankfurt am Main: Peter Lang, 2002.

Fairbank, John K., and Edwin O. Reischauer. *East Asia: The Great Tradition. Vol. 1*. Boston: Houghton Mifflin, 1960.

Farmer, Edward L. *Early Ming Government: The Evolution of Dual Capitals*. Cambridge, MA: Harvard University Press, 1976.

———. *Zhu Yuanzhang and Early Ming Legislation: The Reordering of Chinese Society Following the Era of Mongol Rule*. New York: E. J. Brill, 1995.

Farris, William Wayne. *Japan's Medieval Population: Famine, Fertility, and Warfare in a Transformative Age*. Honolulu: University of Hawai'i Press, 2006.

Faure, David. *Emperor and Ancestor: State and Lineage in South China*. Stanford, CA: Stanford University Press, 2007.

Figes, Orlando. *Natasha's Dance: A Cultural History of Russia*. New York: Metropolitan Books, 2002.

Fletcher, Joseph F. "China and Central Asia, 1368–1884." In *The Chinese World Order: Traditional China's Foreign Relations,* ed. John K. Fairbank. Cambridge, MA: Harvard University Press, 1968.

Forest, Alain, and Georges Condominas. *Les Missionnaires français au Tonkin et au Siam, XVIIème–XVIIIème siècles: Analyse comparée d'un relatif succès et d'un total échec.* 3 vols. Paris: L'Harmattan, 1998.

Foust, Clifford M. *Muscovite and Mandarin: Russia's Trade with China and Its Setting, 1727–1805.* Chapel Hill: University of North Carolina Press, 1969.

Fu, Lo-shu. *A Documentary Chronicle of Sino-Western Relations (1644–1820).* 2 vols. Tucson: University of Arizona Press, 1966.

Fuma Susumu. "Minmatsu No Toshi Kaikaku to Kôshû Minpen [Urban reform in late Ming and the Hangzhou Uprising]." *Toho Gakuho* 49, no. 1 (1977): 215–262.

Goble, Andrew Edmund. *Kenmu: Go-Daigo's Revolution.* Cambridge, MA: Harvard University Press, Council on East Asian Studies, 1996.

Goldstone, Jack A. *Revolution and Rebellion in the Early Modern World.* Berkeley: University of California Press, 1991.

Goodrich, L. Carrington, and Chaoying Fang, eds. *Dictionary of Ming Biography, 1368–1644.* 2 vols. New York: Columbia University Press, 1976.

Gourou, Pierre. *Les Paysans du delta Tonkinois: Étude de géographie humaine.* Paris: Les Éditions d'art et d'histoire, 1936.

Graham, Loren R. *Science in Russia and the Soviet Union.* Cambridge: Cambridge University Press, 1993.

Grousset, René. *The Empire of the Steppes.* New Brunswick, NJ: Rutgers, 1970.

Grove, Linda, and Christian Daniels, eds. *State and Society in China: Japanese Perspectives on Ming-Qing Social and Economic History.* Tokyo: Tokyo University Press, 1984.

Hall, John Whitney, ed. *Early Modern Japan.* Vol. 4 of *The Cambridge History of Japan.* Cambridge: Cambridge University Press, 1991.

———. *Government and Local Power in Japan, 500 to 1700: A Study Based on Bizen Province.* Princeton, NJ: Princeton University Press, 1966.

Hall, John Whitney, and Marius B. Jansen, eds. *Studies in the Institutional History of Early Modern Japan.* Princeton, NJ: Princeton University Press, 1968.

Hall, John Whitney, Toyoda Takeshi, and Paul Varley, eds. *Japan in the Muromachi Age* (Original 1977). Ithaca, NY: East Asia Program, Cornell University, 2001.

Halperin, Charles J. *Russia and the Golden Horde: The Mongol Impact on Medieval Russia.* Bloomington: Indiana University Press, 1985.

Hamel, Hendrik. *Hamel's Journal and a Description of the Kingdom of Korea, 1653–1666.* Seoul: Seoul Press, 1994.

Hanley, Susan B., and Kozo Yamamura. *Economic and Demographic Change in Pre-Industrial Japan, 1600–1868.* Princeton, NJ: Princeton University Press, 1977.

Hatada, Takashi. *A History of Korea.* Santa Barbara, CA: ABC-Clio, 1969.

Hawley, Samuel Jay. *The Imjin War: Japan's Sixteenth-Century Invasion of Korea and Attempt to Conquer China.* Seoul: Royal Asiatic Society, Korea Branch, 2005.

Ḥaydar Dughlat, Mīrzā, and Wheeler M. Thackston. *Mirza Haydar Dughlat's Tarikh-I Rashidi: A History of the Khans of Moghulistan*. Cambridge, MA: Harvard University Department of Near Eastern Languages and Civilizations, 1996.

Hejtmanek, Milan. "Sŏwŏn in Chosŏn Korea, 1543–1741." PhD diss., Harvard University Press, 1994.

Hellie, Richard. *Enserfment and Military Change in Muscovy*. Chicago: University of Chicago Press, 1971.

Henthorn, William E. *A History of Korea*. New York: Free Press, 1971.

Herman, John E. *Amid the Clouds and Mist: China's Colonization of Guizhou, 1200–1700*. Cambridge, MA: Harvard University Asia Center, 2007.

Higgins, Roland. *Piracy and Coastal Defense in the Ming Period: Governmental Response to Coastal Disturbances, 1523–1549*. Ann Arbor: University of Michigan Press, 1981.

Ho, Ping-ti. *The Ladder of Success in Imperial China: Aspects of Social Mobility, 1368–1911*. New York: Columbia University Press, 1962.

Hoshi Ayao. *The Ming Tribute Grain System*. Ann Arbor: University of Michigan Press, 1969.

Howell, David L. *Geographies of Identity in Nineteenth-Century Japan*. Berkeley: University of California Press, 2005.

Huang, Ray. *1587: A Year of No Significance*. New Haven, CT: Yale University Press, 1981.

———. *Taxation and Governmental Finance in Sixteenth Century Ming China*. London: Cambridge University Press, 1974.

Hucker, Charles O. *The Censorial System of Ming China*. Stanford, CA: Stanford University Press, 1966.

———. *The Traditional Chinese State in Ming Times (1368–1644)*. Tucson: University of Arizona Press, 1961.

Hummel, Arthur W., ed. *Eminent Chinese of the Ch'ing Period, 1644–1912*. Washington, DC: U.S. Government Printing Office, 1943–1944.

Ikegami, Eiko. *Bonds of Civility: Aesthetic Networks and the Political Origins of Japanese Culture*. Cambridge: Cambridge University Press, 2005.

———. *The Taming of the Samurai: Honorific Individualism and the Making of Modern Japan*. Cambridge, MA: Harvard University Press, 1995.

Jagchid, Sechin, and Van Jay Symons. *Peace, War, and Trade along the Great Wall: Nomadic-Chinese Interaction through Two Millennia*. Bloomington: Indiana University Press, 1989.

Kahan, Arcadius, and Richard Hellie. *The Plow, the Hammer, and the Knout: An Economic History of Eighteenth-Century Russia*. Chicago: University of Chicago Press, 1985.

Keenan, Edward L. "Muscovite Political Folkways." *Russian Review* 45 (1986): 115–181.

———. "Muscovy and Kazan, 1445–1552: A Study in Steppe Politics." PhD diss., Harvard University, 1965.

Kelley, Liam C. *Beyond the Bronze Pillars: Envoy Poetry and the Sino-Vietnamese Relationship*. Honolulu: Association for Asian Studies: University of Hawai'i Press, 2005.

Kessler, Lawrence D. *K'ang-Hsi and the Consolidation of Ch'ing Rule, 1661–1684*. Chicago: University of Chicago Press, 1976.

Khodarkovsky, Michael. *Russia's Steppe Frontier: The Making of a Colonial Empire, 1500–1800*. Bloomington: Indiana University Press, 2002.

———. *Where Two Worlds Met: The Russian State and the Kalmyk Nomads, 1600–1771*. Ithaca, NY: Cornell University Press, 1992.

Kivelson, Valerie A. *Autocracy in the Provinces: The Muscovite Gentry and Political Culture in the Seventeenth Century*. Stanford, CA: Stanford University Press, 1996.

———. *Cartographies of Tsardom: The Land and Its Meanings in Seventeenth-Century Russia*. Ithaca, NY: Cornell University Press, 2006.

———. "Merciful Father, Impersonal State: Russian Autocracy in Comparative Perspective." *Modern Asian Studies* 31, no. 3 (1997): 635–663.

Klyuchevsky, Vasili O. *Peter the Great*. New York: Vintage, 1958.

Ko, Dorothy. *Teachers of the Inner Chambers: Women and Culture in Seventeenth-Century China*. Stanford, CA: Stanford University Press, 1994.

Kollmann, Nancy Shields. *By Honor Bound: State and Society in Early Modern Russia*. Ithaca, NY: Cornell University Press, 1999.

Kuhn, Philip A. *Chinese among Others: Emigration in Modern Times*. Lanham, MD: Rowman & Littlefield, 2008.

———. *Soulstealers: The Chinese Sorcery Scare of 1768*. Cambridge, MA: Harvard University Press, 1990.

Lantzeff, George V., and Richard A. Pierce. *Eastward to Empire: Exploration and Conquest on the Russian Open Frontier to 1750*. Montreal: McGill-Queen's University Press, 1973.

Lattimore, Owen. *Studies in Frontier History: Collected Papers, 1928–1958*. London: Oxford University Press, 1962.

Lee, Ki-baik. *A New History of Korea*. Cambridge, MA: Harvard University Press, 1984.

Levathes, Louise. *When China Ruled the Seas: The Treasure Fleet of the Dragon Throne, 1405–1433*. New York: Simon & Schuster, 1994.

Levi, Scott. "India, Russia and the Eighteenth-Century Transformation of the Central Asian Caravan Trade." *Journal of the Economic and Social History of the Orient* 42, no. 4 (1999): 519–548.

Levine, Philippa, and John Marriott, eds. *The Ashgate Research Companion to Modern Imperial Histories*. Farnham, UK: Ashgate, 2012.

Liang, Fang-chung. *The Single-Whip Method of Taxation in China*. 2nd ed. Cambridge, MA: Harvard University Press, 1970.

Lieberman, Victor B., ed. *Beyond Binary Histories: Re-Imagining Eurasia to c.1830*. Ann Arbor, MI: University of Michigan Press, 1999.

———. *Integration of the Mainland*. Vol. 1 of *Strange Parallels: Southeast Asia in Global Context, c. 800–1830*. Cambridge: Cambridge University Press, 2003.

———. *Mainland Mirrors: Europe, Japan, China, South Asia, and the Islands.* Vol. 2 of *Strange Parallels: Southeast Asia in Global Context, c. 800–1830.* Cambridge: Cambridge University Press, 2009.

Linke, Bernd-Michael. *Zur Entwicklung des Mandjurischen Khanats zum Beamtenstaat: Sinisierung und Bürokratisierung der Mandjuren während der Eroberungszeit.* Wiesbaden: Steiner, 1982.

Li Tana. *Nguyen Cochinchina: Southern Vietnam in the Seventeenth and Eighteenth Centuries.* Ithaca, NY: Southeast Asia Program Publications, 1998.

Mancall, Mark. *Russia and China: Their Diplomatic Relations to 1728.* Cambridge, MA: Harvard University Press, 1971.

Mann, Susan. *Precious Records: Women in China's Long Eighteenth Century.* Stanford, CA: Stanford University Press, 1997.

Marks, Robert B. *Tigers, Rice, Silk, and Silt: Environment and Economy in Late Imperial South China.* Cambridge: Cambridge University Press, 1998.

Martin, Janet. *Medieval Russia, 980–1584.* Cambridge: Cambridge University Press, 1995.

Mass, Jeffrey P., ed. *The Origins of Japan's Medieval World: Courtiers, Clerics, Warriors, and Peasants in the Fourteenth Century.* Stanford, CA: Stanford University Press, 1997.

Mass, Jeffrey P., and William B. Hauser, eds. *The Bakufu in Japanese History.* Stanford, CA: Stanford University Press, 1985.

Millward, James A. *Beyond the Pass: Economy, Ethnicity, and Empire in Qing Central Asia, 1759–1864.* Stanford, CA: Stanford University Press, 1998.

———. *Eurasian Crossroads: A History of Xinjiang.* New York: Columbia University Press, 2007.

Min, Tu-ki. *National Polity and Local Power: The Transformation of Late Imperial China.* Cambridge, MA: Harvard University Press, 1989.

Miyawaki Junko. *Saigo No Yûboku Teikoku: Jungaru Bu No Kôbô* [The last nomadic empire: The rise and fall of the Zunghars]. Tokyo: Kodansha, 1995.

Miyazaki, Ichisada. *China's Examination Hell: The Civil Service Examinations of Imperial China.* New York: Weatherhill, 1976.

Mote, Frederick W. *Imperial China: 900–1800.* Cambridge, MA: Harvard University Press, 1999.

Mote, Frederick, and Denis C. Twitchett, eds. *The Ming Dynasty, 1368–1644.* Vols. 7 and 8 of *The Cambridge History of China.* Cambridge: Cambridge University Press, 1988/1998.

Nguyen Ngoc Huy, Ta Van Tai, and Tran Van Liêm. *The Lê Code: Law in Traditional Vietnam: A Comparative Sino-Vietnamese Legal Study with Historical-Juridical Analysis and Annotations.* 3 vols. Athens: Ohio University Press, 1987.

Ning, Chia. "The Lifanyuan and the Inner Asian Rituals in the Early Qing (1644–1795)." *Late Imperial China* 14, no. 1 (1993): 60–92.

Ooms, Herman. *Tokugawa Ideology: Early Constructs, 1570–1680.* Princeton, NJ: Princeton University Press, 1985.

Ostrowski, Donald. *Muscovy and the Mongols: Cross-Cultural Influences on the Steppe Frontier, 1304–1589.* Cambridge: Cambridge University Press, 1998.

Oxnam, Robert B. *Ruling from Horseback: Manchu Politics in the Oboi Regency, 1661–1669.* Chicago: University of Chicago Press, 1975.

Park, Ki-joo, and Donghyu Yang. "The Standard of Living in the Choson Dynasty Korea in the 17th to the 19th Centuries." *Seoul Journal of Economics* 20, no. 3 (2007): 297–332.

Pelenski, Jaroslaw. *Russia and Kazan: Conquest and Imperial Ideology.* The Hague: Mouton, 1974.

Perdue, Peter C. "Boundaries and Trade in the Early Modern World: Negotiations at Nerchinsk and Beijing." *Eighteenth-Century Studies* 43, no. 3 (2010): 341–356.

———. *China Marches West: The Qing Conquest of Central Eurasia.* Cambridge, MA: Harvard University Press, 2005.

———. "Coercion and Commerce on Two Chinese Frontiers." In *Military Culture in Imperial China,* ed. Nicola Di Cosmo. Cambridge, MA: Harvard University Press, 2009.

———. "Embracing Victory, Effacing Defeat: Rewriting the Qing Frontier Campaigns." In *The Chinese State at the Borders,* ed. Diana Lary. Vancouver: University of British Columbia Press, 2007.

———. *Exhausting the Earth: State and Peasant in Hunan, 1500–1850.* Cambridge, MA: Council on East Asian Studies, 1987.

———. "1557: A Year of Some Significance." Paper presented at Asia Inside Out Conference, Hong Kong Institute for Humanities and Social Sciences, December 2010.

———. "From Turfan to Taiwan: Trade and War on Two Chinese Frontiers." In *Untaming the Frontier in Anthropology, Archeology, and History,* ed. Bradley J. Parker and Lars Rodseth. Tucson: University of Arizona Press, 2005.

———. "Nature and Nurture on Imperial China's Frontiers." *Modern Asian Studies* 43, no. 1 (2009): 245–267.

Peterson, Mark, and Phillip Margulies. *A Brief History of Korea.* New York: Facts on File, 2010.

Peterson, Willard J., ed. *The Ch'ing Empire to 1800.* Vol. 9, Part 1 of *The Cambridge History of China.* Cambridge: Cambridge University Press, 2002.

Pomeranz, Kenneth. *The Great Divergence: China, Europe, and the Making of the Modern World Economy.* Princeton, NJ: Princeton University Press, 2000.

Pomeranz, Kenneth, and Steven Topik. *The World That Trade Created.* Armonk, NY: M. E. Sharpe, 1999.

Rawski, Evelyn S. *Agricultural Change and the Peasant Economy of South China.* Cambridge, MA: Harvard University Press, 1972.

Riasanovsky, Nicholas Valentine. *A History of Russia.* 6th ed. Oxford: Oxford University Press, 2000.

Rossabi, Morris. *China and Inner Asia: From 1368 to the Present Day.* New York: Pica Press, 1975.

Roth, Gertraude. "The Manchu-Chinese Relationship, 1618–36." In *From Ming to Ch'ing: Conquest, Region and Continuity in Seventeenth-Century China,* ed. Jonathan D. Spence and John E. Wills. New Haven, CT: Yale University Press, 1979.

Rowe, William T. *China's Last Empire: The Great Qing.* Cambridge, MA: Belknap Press of Harvard University Press, 2009.

———. *Saving the World: Chen Hongmou and Elite Consciousness in Eighteenth-Century China.* Stanford, CA: Stanford University Press, 2001.

Rubinstein, Murray A. *Taiwan: A New History.* Armonk, NY: M. E. Sharpe, 1999.

Sansom, George Bailey. *A History of Japan.* London: Cresset Press, 1963.

Schoppa, R. Keith. *Xiang Lake: Nine Centuries of Chinese Life.* New Haven, CT: Yale University Press, 1989.

Scott, James C. *The Art of Not Being Governed: An Anarchist History of Upland Southeast Asia.* New Haven, CT: Yale University Press, 2009.

Serruys, Henry. *Sino-Mongol Relations during the Ming.* 3 vols. Brussels: Institut belge des hautes études chinoises, 1967–1975.

Shepherd, John Robert. *Statecraft and Political Economy on the Taiwan Frontier, 1600–1800.* Stanford, CA: Stanford University Press, 1993.

Skinner, G. William, ed. *The City in Late Imperial China.* Stanford, CA: Stanford University Press, 1977.

———. "Presidential Address: The Structure of Chinese History." *Journal of Asian Studies* 44, no. 2 (1985): 271–292.

Slezkine, Yuri. *Arctic Mirrors: Russia and the Small Peoples of the North.* Ithaca, NY: Cornell University Press, 1994.

Smith, Joanna Handlin. *The Art of Doing Good: Charity in Late Ming China.* Berkeley: University of California Press, 2009.

So, Kwan-wai. *Japanese Piracy in Ming China during the Sixteenth Century.* East Lansing: Michigan State University Press, 1975.

Sommer, Matthew Harvey. *Sex, Law, and Society in Late Imperial China,* Stanford, CA: Stanford University Press, 2000.

Soucek, Svat. *A History of Inner Asia.* Cambridge: Cambridge University Press, 2000.

Souyri, Pierre. *The World Turned Upside Down: Medieval Japanese Society.* New York: Columbia University Press, 2001.

Spence, Jonathan D. *Emperor of China: Self-Portrait of K'ang-Hsi.* New York: Vintage, 1988.

———. *Return to Dragon Mountain: Memories of a Late Ming Man.* New York: Viking, 2007.

———. *Treason by the Book.* New York: Viking, 2001.

———. *Ts'ao Yin and the K'ang Hsi Emperor: Bondservant and Master.* New Haven, CT: Yale University Press, 1966.

Steinberg, David J., ed. *In Search of Southeast Asia.* Honolulu: Hawai'i University Press, 1987.

Stevens, Carol B. *Soldiers on the Steppe: Army Reform and Social Change in Early Modern Russia.* DeKalb: Northern Illinois University Press, 1995.

Struve, Lynn A., ed. *The Qing Formation in World-Historical Time.* Cambridge, MA: Harvard University Asia Center, 2004.

———, ed. *Time, Temporality, and Imperial Transition: East Asia from Ming to Qing.* Honolulu: Association for Asian Studies and University of Hawai'i Press, 2005.

Sunderland, Willard. *Taming the Wild Field: Colonization and Empire on the Russian Steppe.* Ithaca, NY: Cornell University Press, 2004.

Tarling, Nicholas. *The Cambridge History of Southeast Asia.* 2 vols. Cambridge: Cambridge University Press, 1992.

Taylor, Keith W. "Surface Orientations in Vietnam: Beyond Histories of Nation and Region." *Journal of Asian Studies* 57, no. 4 (1998): 949–978.

Teng, Emma J. *Taiwan's Imagined Geography: Chinese Colonial Travel Writing and Pictures, 1683–1895.* Cambridge, MA: Harvard University Asia Center, 2004.

Theiss, Janet M. *Disgraceful Matters: The Politics of Chastity in Eighteenth-Century China.* Berkeley: University of California Press, 2004.

Totman, Conrad D. *Early Modern Japan.* Berkeley: University of California Press, 1993.

———. *A History of Japan.* 2nd ed. Malden, MA: Blackwell, 2005.

———. *Japan before Perry: A Short History.* Berkeley: University of California Press, 1981.

———. *Politics in the Tokugawa Bakufu, 1600–1843.* Berkeley: University of California Press, 1988.

———. *Pre-Industrial Korea and Japan in Environmental Perspective.* Leiden: Brill, 2004.

Tsunoda, Ryusaku, and William Theodore de Bary, eds. *Sources of Japanese Tradition*: New York: Columbia University Press, 1958.

Tu, Wei-ming. *Neo-Confucian Thought in Action: Wang Yangming's Youth (1472–1509).* Berkeley: University of California Press, 1976.

Varley, H. Paul. *The Ōnin War: History of Its Origins and Background with a Selective Translation of the Chronicle of Ōnin.* New York: Columbia University Press, 1967.

Vernadsky, George. *Kievan Russia.* New Haven, CT: Yale University Press, 1948.

Vlastos, Stephen. *Peasant Protests and Uprisings in Tokugawa Japan.* Berkeley: University of California Press, 1986.

Wakeman, Frederic, Jr. *The Great Enterprise: The Manchu Reconstruction of Imperial Order in Seventeenth-Century China.* Berkeley: University of California Press, 1985.

Waldron, Arthur. *The Great Wall of China: From History to Myth.* Cambridge: Cambridge University Press, 1990.

Walker, Brett L. *The Conquest of Ainu Lands: Ecology and Culture in Japanese Expansion, 1590–1800.* Berkeley: University of California Press, 2001.

Walthall, Anne. *Social Protest and Popular Culture in Eighteenth-Century Japan.* Tucson: University of Arizona Press, 1986.

Watt, John R. *The District Magistrate in Late Imperial China*. New York: Columbia University Press, 1972.

Wheeler, Charles J. "Cross-Cultural Trade and Trans-Regional Networks in the Port of Hoi An: Maritime Vietnam in the Early Modern Era." PhD diss., Yale University, 2001.

Whitmore, John K. *Vietnam, Hồ Quý Ly, and the Ming (1371–1421)*. New Haven, CT: Council on Southeast Asia Studies, 1985.

Widmer, Eric. *The Russian Ecclesiastical Mission in Peking during the Eighteenth Century*. Cambridge, MA: Harvard University Press, 1976.

Wieczynski, Joseph L., ed. *The Modern Encyclopedia of Russian and Soviet History*. 60 vols. Gulf Breeze, FL: Academic International Press, 1976–1994.

Wiethoff, Bodo. *Die chinesische Seeverbotspolitik und der private Überseehandel von 1368 bis 1567*. Wiesbaden: Harrassowitz, 1963.

Will, Pierre-Étienne. *Bureaucracy and Famine in Eighteenth-Century China*. Translated by Elborg Forster. Stanford, CA: Stanford University Press, 1990.

Will, Pierre-Étienne, and R. Bin Wong. *Nourish the People: The State Civilian Granary System in China, 1650–1850*. Ann Arbor: Center for Chinese Studies, University of Michigan, 1991.

Womack, Brantly. *China and Vietnam: The Politics of Asymmetry*. Cambridge: Cambridge University Press 2006.

Wong, R. Bin, and Peter C. Perdue. "Famine's Foes in Ch'ing China (Review of Pierre-Étienne Will, *Bureaucratie et famine en Chine au 18e siècle*)." *Harvard Journal of Asiatic Studies* 43, no. 1 (1983): 291–332.

Woodside, Alexander B. "Early Ming Expansionism (1406–1427)." *Harvard Papers on China* 17 (1963): 1–37.

———. *Lost Modernities: China, Vietnam, Korea, and the Hazards of World History*. Cambridge, MA: Harvard University Press, 2006.

———. "Medieval Vietnam and Cambodia: A Comparative Comment." *Journal of Southeast Asian Studies* 15, no. 2 (1984): 315–319.

———. "The Tayson Revolution in Southeast Asian History." Unpublished manuscript, Cornell University Library, Ithaca, NY, 1976.

———. *Vietnam and the Chinese Model: A Comparative Study of Nguyễn and Ch'ing Civil Government in the First Half of the Nineteenth Century*. Cambridge, MA: Harvard University Press, 1971.

Wu Cheng'en. *The Journey to the West*. 4 vols. Translated by Anthony C. Yu. Chicago: University of Chicago Press, 1977.

Xiaoxiaosheng, and F. Clement C. Egerton. *The Golden Lotus; a Translation, from the Chinese Original, of the Novel Chin P'ing Mei*. 4 vols. London: Routledge & Kegan Paul, 1972.

Yamamura, Kozo, ed. *Medieval Japan*. Vol. 3 of *The Cambridge History of Japan*. Cambridge: Cambridge University Press, 1990.

Yang Bin. *Between Winds and Clouds: The Making of Yunnan (Second Century BCE to Twentieth Century CE)*. New York: Columbia University Press, 2009.

Zelin, Madeleine. *The Magistrate's Tael: Rationalizing Fiscal Reform in Eighteenth-Century Ch'ing China*. Berkeley: University of California Press, 1984.

Zlatkin, Ilia Jakovlevich. *Istoriia Dzhungarskogo Khanstva (1635–1758)* [History of the Zunghar khanate]. Moscow: Nauka, 1964.

The Ottoman Empire and the Islamic World

Abdel Nour, Antoine. *Introduction à l'histoire urbaine de la Syrie ottomane (XVIe–XVIIIe siècle)*. Beirut: Université Libanaise, 1982.

Abisaab, Rula Jurdi. *Converting Persia: Religion and Power in the Safavid Empire*. London: I. B. Tauris, 2004.

Abou-El-Haj, Rifa'at Ali. *Formation of the Ottoman State: The Ottoman Empire Sixteenth to Eighteenth Centuries*. 2nd ed. Syracuse, NY: Syracuse University Press, 2005.

———. *The 1703 Rebellion and the Structure of Ottoman Politics*. Istanbul: Nederlands Historisch-Archaeologisch Instituut, 1984.

Abu-Husayn, Abdul-Rahim. *Provincial Leaderships in Syria, 1575–1650*. Beirut: American University of Beirut, 1985.

Adanır, Fikret, and Suraiya Faroqhi, eds. *The Ottomans and the Balkans: A Discussion of Historiography*. Leiden: E. J. Brill, 2002.

Akdağ, Mustafa. *Celâlî İsyanları 1550–1603*. Ankara: Ankara Üniversitesi Dil ve Tarih-Coğrafya Fakültesi, 1963.

Aksan, Virginia H. *An Ottoman Statesman in War and Peace: Ahmed Resmi Efendi, 1700–1783*. Leiden: E. J. Brill, 1995.

———. *Ottoman Wars: An Empire Besieged, 1700–1870*. Harlow, UK: Longman Pearson, 2007.

Al-Sayyid Marsot, Afaf Lutfi. *Women and Men in Late Eighteenth-Century Egypt*. Austin: University of Texas Press, 1995.

Alam, Muzaffar, and Sanjay Subrahmanyam. *Indo-Persian Travels in the Age of Discoveries, 1400–1800*. Cambridge: Cambridge University Press, 2007.

And, Metin. *Osmanlı Şenliklerinde Türk Sanatları*. Ankara: Kültür ve Turizm Bakanlığı, 1982.

Arbel, Benjamin. *Trading Nations: Jews and Venetians in the Early Modern Eastern Mediterranean*. Leiden: E. J. Brill, 1995.

Arıkan, Zeki. "Osmanlı İmparatorluğunda İhracı Yasak Mallar (Memnu Meta)." In *Professor Dr. Bekir Kütükoğlu'na Armağan*. Istanbul: İstanbul Üniversitesi Edebiyat Fakültesi, 1991.

Arjomand, Said A. *The Shadow of God and the Hidden Imam: Religion, Political Order, and Societal Change in Shi'ite Iran from the Beginnings to 1890*. Chicago: University of Chicago Press, 1984.

Aščerić Todd, Ines. *Dervishes and Islam in Bosnia.* PhD thesis, University of Oxford, 2004.

Atasoy, Nurhan. *1582 Surname-i hümayun: An Imperial Celebration.* Istanbul: Koçbank, 1997.

Atasoy, Nurhan, and Julian Raby. *Iznik: The Pottery of Ottoman Turkey.* London: Alexandria Press, 1989.

Atıl, Esin. *Levni and the Surnâme: The Story of an Eighteenth-Century Ottoman Festival.* Istanbul: Koçbank, 1999.

Avery, Peter, Gavin Hambly, and Charles Melville, eds. *From Nadir Shah to the Islamic Republic.* Vol. 7 of *The Cambridge History of Iran.* Cambridge: Cambridge University Press, 1991.

Aynural, Salih. *İstanbul Değirmenleri ve Fırınları: Zahire Ticareti 1740–1830.* Istanbul: Tarih Vakfı Yurt Yayınları, 2002.

ʾAzîz Efendi. *Kanûn-nâme-i Sultânî liʾAzîz Efendi / Aziz Efendi's Book of Sultanic Laws and Regulations: An Agenda for Reform by a Seventeenth-Century Ottoman Statesman.* Edited by Rhoads Murphey. Cambridge, MA: Harvard University Press, 1985.

Babaie, Sussan. *Isfahan and Its Palaces: Statecraft, Shiʿism, and the Architecture of Conviviality in Early Modern Iran.* Edinburgh: Edinburgh University Press, 2008.

Babaie, Sussan, Kathryn Babayan, Ina Baghdiantz McCabe, and Massume Farhad. *Slaves of the Shah: New Elites of Safavid Iran.* London: I. B. Tauris, 2004.

Babayan, Kathryn. *Mystics, Monarchs, and Messiahs: Cultural Landscapes of Early Modern Iran.* Cambridge, MA: Harvard University Press, 2002.

Babinger, Franz. *Mehmed der Eroberer und seine Zeit: Weltenstürmer einer Zeitenwende.* Munich: Bruckmann, 1953.

Bacqué-Grammont, Jean-Louis. *Les Ottomans, les Safavides et leurs voisins.* Istanbul: Nederlands Historisch-Archaeologisch Instituut, 1987.

Baer, Marc David. *Honored by the Glory of Islam: Conversion and Conquest in Ottoman Europe.* Oxford: Oxford University Press, 2008.

Baghdiantz McCabe, Ina. *The Shah's Silk for Europe's Silver: The Eurasian Trade of the Julfa Armenians in Safavid Iran and India (1530–1750).* Atlanta, GA: Scholars Press, 1999.

Bağış, Ali İhsan. *Osmanlı Ticaretinde Gayri Müslimler, Kapitülasyonlar, Beratlı Tüccarlar ve Hayriye Tüccarları (1750–1839).* Ankara: Turhan Kitabevi, 1983.

Barbir, Karl K. *Ottoman Rule in Damascus, 1708–1758.* Princeton, NJ: Princeton University Press, 1980.

Barkan, Ömer Lütfi. "Edirne Askeri Kassam'ına ait Tereke Defterleri (1545–1659)." *Belgeler* 3, nos. 5–6 (1966): 1–479.

———. "Şehirlerin Teşekkül ve İnkişafı Tarihi Bakımından: Osmanlı İmparatorluğunda İmaret Sitelerinin Kuruluş ve İşleyiş Tarzına ait Araştırmalar." *İstanbul Üniversitesi İktisat Fakültesi Mecmuası* 23, nos. 1–2 (1962–1963): 239–296.

———. *Süleymaniye Cami ve İmareti İnşaatı.* 2 vols. Ankara: Türk Tarih Kurumu, 1972 and 1979.

———. "Tarihi Demografi Araştırmaları ve Osmanlı Tarihi." *Türkiyat Mecmuası* 10 (1951): 1–26.

Barkan, Ömer Lütfi, and Ekrem Hakkı Ayverdi, eds. *İstanbul Vakıfları Tahrîr Defteri, 953 (1546) Tarîhli*. Istanbul: Istanbul Fetih Cemiyeti, 1970.

Barker, Thomas M. *Double Eagle and Crescent: Vienna's Second Turkish Siege and Its Historical Setting*. Albany: State University of New York Press, 1967.

Barkey, Karen. *Bandits and Bureaucrats: The Ottoman Route to State Centralization*. Ithaca, NY: Cornell University Press, 1994.

Bayly, Christopher A. *Rulers, Townsmen and Bazaars: North Indian Society in the Age of British Expansion, 1770–1870*. Cambridge: Cambridge University Press, 1983.

Behar, Cem. *Osmanlı İmparatorluğu'nun ve Türkiye'nin Nüfusu 1500–1927/The Population of the Ottoman Empire and Turkey (with a Summary in English)*. Ankara: Başbakanlık Devlet İstatistik Enstitüsü, 1996.

Bennassar, Bartolomé, and Lucile Bennassar. *Les chrétiens d'Allah: L'histoire extraordinaire des renégats, XVIe–XVIIe siècles*. New ed. Paris: Perrin, 2006.

Biegman, Nicolaas H. *The Turco-Ragusan Relationship, according to the Firmans of Murad III (1575–1595) Extant in the State Archives of Dubrovnik*. The Hague: Mouton, 1967.

Bonnac, Jean-Louis Dusson, Marquis de. *Mémoire historique sur l'Ambassade de France à Constantinople*. Edited by Charles Schefer. Paris: Ernest Leroux, 1894.

Boulanger, Patrick. *Marseille, marché international de l'huile d'olive: Un produit et des hommes de 1725 à 1825*. Marseille: Institut Historique de Provence, 1996.

Bracewell, Catherine Wendy. *The Uskoks of Senj: Piracy, Banditry and Holy War in the Sixteenth-Century Adriatic*. Ithaca, NY: Cornell University Press, 1992.

Bratianu, Georges I. *La mer Noire: Des origines à la conquête ottomane*. Munich: Societas Academica Romana, 1969.

Braudel, Fernand. *Civilisation matérielle, économie et capitalisme*. 3 vols. Paris: Armand Colin, 1979.

———. *La Méditerranée et le monde méditerranéen à l'époque de Philippe II*. 2 vols. 2nd ed. Paris: Librairie Armand Colin, 1966.

Brummett, Palmira. *Ottoman Seapower and Levantine Diplomacy in the Age of Discovery*. Albany: State University of New York Press, 1994.

Bryer, Anthony, and Heath Lowry, eds. *Continuity and Change in Late Byzantine and Early Ottoman Society*. Birmingham: University of Birmingham Press, 1986.

Bulliet, Richard. *The Camel and the Wheel*. New ed. New York: Columbia University Press, 1990.

Çağatay, Neşet. "Osmanlı İmparatorluğunda Para Vakıfları Rıba Faiz konusu ve Bankacılık." *Vakıflar Dergisi* 9 (1971): 39–56.

Campbell, Caroline, Alan Chong, et al. *Bellini and the East*. New Haven, CT: Yale University Press, 2005.

Canatar, Mehmet, ed. *İstanbul Vakıfları Tahrîr Defteri, 1009 (1600) Tarîhli*. Istanbul: Istanbul Fetih Cemiyeti, 2004.

Canby, Sheila R. *Shah 'Abbas: The Remaking of Iran*. London: British Museum Press, 2009.

———. *Shah 'Abbas and the Treasures of Imperial Iran*. London: British Museum Press, 2009.

Capponi, Niccolò. *Victory of the West: The Story of the Battle of Lepanto*. London: Macmillan, 2006.

Carter, Francis W. *Dubrovnik (Ragusa): A Classic City-State*. London: Seminar Press, 1972.

Casale, Giancarlo. *The Ottoman Age of Exploration*. Oxford: Oxford University Press, 2010.

Çeçen, Kâzım. *İstanbul'da Osmanlı Devrindeki Su Tesisleri*. Istanbul: İstanbul Teknik Üniversitesi, 1984.

Chérif, Mohamed Hédi. *Pouvoir et société dans la Tunisie de H'usayn Bin 'Alī (1705–1740)*. 2 vols. Tunis: Université de Tunis, 1984 and 1986.

Choulia, Susanna. *Das Herrenhaus des Georgios Schwarz in Ambelakia*. Athens: Kasse für Archäologische Mittel und Enteignungen, 2003.

Çizakça, Murat. *A Comparative Evolution of Business Partnerships: The Islamic World and Europe, with Specific Reference to the Ottoman Archives*. Leiden: E. J. Brill, 1996.

Cohen, Amnon. *The Guilds of Ottoman Jerusalem*. Leiden: E. J. Brill, 2001.

Dale, Stephen F. *The Muslim Empires of the Ottomans, Safavids, and Mughals*. Cambridge: Cambridge University Press, 2010.

Dalsar, Fahri. *Türk Sanayi ve Ticaret Tarihinde Bursa'da İpekçilik*. Istanbul: İstanbul Üniversitesi İktisat Fakültesi, 1960.

Davis, Ralph. *Aleppo and Devonshire Square: English Traders in the Levant in the Eighteenth Century*. London: Macmillan, 1967.

De Groot, Alexander H. *The Ottoman Empire and the Dutch Republic: A History of the Earliest Diplomatic Relations, 1610–1630*. Leiden: Nederlands Historisch-Archaeologisch Instituut, 1978.

Delilbaşı, Melek. "Selânik'in Venedik İdaresine Geçmesi ve Osmanlı-Venedik Savaşı." *Belleten* 40, no. 160 (1976): 575–588.

Delumeau, Jean. *Le mystère Campanella*. Paris: Fayard, 2008.

De Planhol, Xavier. *Les fondements géographiques de l'histoire de l'Islam*. Paris: Flammarion, 1968.

Doğru, Halime. *Lehistan'da bir Osmanlı Sultanı: IV. Mehmed'in Kamaniçe-Hotin Seferleri ve bir Masraf Defteri*. Istanbul: Kitap Yayınevi, 2005.

Duchhardt, Heinz. *Balance of Power und Pentarchie, 1700–1785*. Paderborn: Ferdinand Schöningh, 1997.

Dursteler, Eric R. *Venetians in Constantinople: Nation, Identity, and Coexistence in the Early Modern Mediterranean*. Baltimore: Johns Hopkins University Press, 2006.

Düzdağ, Ertuğrul. *Şeyhülislam Ebusuud Efendi Fetvaları Işığında 16. Asır Türk Hayatı*. Istanbul: Enderun, 1972.

Eldem, Edhem. *French Trade in Istanbul in the Eighteenth Century.* Leiden: E. J. Brill, 1999.

Elliot, Matthew. "Dress Codes in the Ottoman Empire: The Case of the Franks." In *Ottoman Costumes. From Textile to Identity,* ed. Suraiya Faroqhi and Christoph K. Neumann. Istanbul: Eren, 2004.

Erdem, Y. Hakan. *Tarih-Lenk: Kusursuz Yazarlar, Kâğıttan Metinler.* Istanbul: Doğan Kitap, 2008.

Ergene, Boğaç A. *Local Court, Provincial Society, and Justice in the Ottoman Empire: Legal Practice and Dispute Resolution in Çankırı and Kastamonu (1652–1744).* Leiden: E. J. Brill, 2003.

Eskandar Beg Monshī. *History of Shah Abbas the Great (Tārīk-e ʾĀlam ārā-ye ʾAbbāsī).* 3 vols. Translated by Roger Savory. Boulder, CO: Westview Press, 1978–1986.

Et-Tamgrouti [Al-Tamghrûtî], Abou-l-Hasan Ali ben Mohammed. *En-nafhat el-miskiya fi-s-sifarat et-Tourkiya: Relation d'une ambassade marocaine en Turquie 1589–1591.* Edited and translated by Henry de Castries. Paris: Paul Geuthner, 1929.

Evliya Çelebi b. Derviş Mehemmed Zıllî. *Evliya Çelebi Seyahatnâmesi.* Vols. 2, 4, 6 and 9. Edited by Yücel Dağlı. Istanbul, 1999–2005.

Faroqhi, Suraiya. *Artisans of Empire: Crafts and Craftspeople under the Ottomans.* London: I. B. Tauris, 2009.

———, ed. *The Later Ottoman Empire.* Vol. 3 of *The Cambridge History of Turkey.* Cambridge: Cambridge University Press, 2006.

———. *Men of Modest Substance: House Owners and House Property in Seventeenth-Century Ankara and Kayseri.* Cambridge: Cambridge University Press, 1987.

———. "Migration into Eighteenth-Century 'Greater Istanbul' as Reflected in the Kadi Registers of Eyüp." *Turcica* 30 (1998): 163–183.

———. "Ottoman Textiles in European Markets," In *The Renaissance and the Ottoman World,* ed. Anna Contadini and Claire Norton. Aldershot, UK: Ashgate, 2013.

———. "The Peasants of Saideli in the Later Sixteenth Century." *Archivum Ottomanicum* 8 (1983): 215–250.

———. "Presenting the Sultans' Power, Glory and Piety: A Comparative Perspective." In *Prof. Dr. Mübahat Kütükoğlu'na Armağan,* ed. Zeynep Tarım Ertuğ. Istanbul: İstanbul Üniversitesi Edebiyat Fakültesi Tarih Bölümü, 2006.

———. "A Prisoner of War Reports: The Camp and Household of Grand Vizier Kara Mustafa Paşa in an Eyewitness Account." In *Another Mirror for Princes: The Public Image of the Ottoman Sultans and Its Reception.* Istanbul: Isis Press, 2008.

———. "Seventeenth Century Agricultural Crisis and the Art of Flute Playing: The Worldly Affairs of the Mevlevi Dervishes (1595–1652)." *Turcica* 20 (1988): 43–70.

———. "Supplying Seventeenth- and Eighteenth-Century Istanbul with Fresh Produce." In *Nourrir les cités de la Méditerranée: Antiquité—Temps modernes,* ed. Brigitte Marin and Catherine Virlouvet. Paris: Maisonneuve & Larose, 2003.

———. *Towns and Townsmen of Ottoman Anatolia: Trade, Crafts, and Food Production in an Urban Setting*. Cambridge: Cambridge University Press, 1984.

Faroqhi, Suraiya, and Gilles Veinstein, eds. *Merchants in the Ottoman Empire*. Paris: Editions Peeters, 2008.

Fenlon, Iain. *The Ceremonial City*. New Haven, CT: Yale University Press 2007.

Finkel, Caroline. *The Administration of Warfare: The Ottoman Military Campaigns in Hungary, 1593–1606*. Vienna: VWGÖ, 1988.

———. *Osman's Dream: The Story of the Ottoman Empire, 1300–1923*. London: John Murray, 2005.

Fleet, Kate. *European and Islamic Trade in the Early Ottoman State*. Cambridge: Cambridge University Press, 1999.

Fleischer, Cornell H. *Bureaucrat and Intellectual in the Ottoman Empire: The Historian Mustafâ Âli (1541–1600)*. Princeton, NJ: Princeton University Press, 1986.

Floor, Willem. *The Economy of Safavid Persia*. Wiesbaden: Ludwig Reichert Verlag, 2000.

———. *The Persian Textile Industry in Historical Perspective*. Paris: L'Harmattan, 1999.

Floor, Willem, and Mohammad H. Faghfoory, eds. *Dastur al-Moluk: A Safavid State Manual, Mohammad Rafi' al-Dīn Ansarî, mostowfi al-mamâlek*. Costa Mesa, CA: Mazda Publishers, 2007.

Floor, Willem, and Edmund Herzig. *Iran and the World in the Safavid Age*. London: I. B. Tauris, 2012.

Garthwaite, Gene. *Khans and Shahs: A History of the Bakhtiyari Tribe in Iran*. London: I. B. Tauris, 2009.

Gaube, Heinz, and Eugen Wirth. *Der Basar von Isfahan*. Wiesbaden: Ludwig Reichert Verlag, 1978.

Genç, Mehmet. "L'Économie ottomane et la guerre au XVIIIe siècle." *Turcica* 27 (1995): 177–196.

Gerber, Haim. *Economy and Society in an Ottoman City: Bursa, 1600–1700*. Jerusalem: Hebrew University, 1988.

Geyer, Bernard, and Jacques Lefort, eds. *La Bithynie au Moyen Âge*. Paris: Lethielleux, 2003.

Gibb, H. R., et al., eds. *The Encyclopaedia of Islam*. New ed. 12 vols. Leiden: Brill, 1960–2004.

Goffman, Daniel. *Britons in the Ottoman Empire, 1642–1660*. Seattle: University of Washington Press, 1998.

Goodblatt, Morris S. *Jewish Life in Turkey in the Sixteenth Century as Reflected in the Legal Writings of Samuel de Medina*. New York: Jewish Theological Seminary of America, 1952.

Gradeva, Rossitsa. *Rumeli under the Ottomans, 15th to 18th Centuries: Institutions and Communities*. Istanbul: Isis Press, 2004.

Griswold, William J. *Anadolu'da Büyük İsyan 1591–1611*. Istanbul: Tarih Vakfı Yurt Yayınları, 2000.

———. *The Great Anatolian Rebellion, 1000–1020/1591–1611*. Berlin: Klaus Schwarz, 1983.

Gronke, Monika. *Derwische im Vorhof der Macht: Sozial- und Wirtschaftsgeschichte Nordwestirans im 13. und 14. Jahrhundert.* Stuttgart: Franz Steiner Verlag, 1993.

Gülsoy, Ersin. *Girit'in Fethi ve Osmanlı İdaresinin Kurulması.* Istanbul: Tarih ve Tabiat Vakfı, 2004.

Haldon, John. *The Palgrave Atlas of Byzantine History.* Basingstoke, UK: Palgrave Macmillan, 2005.

Hanna, Nelly. *Making Big Money in 1600: The Life and Times of Isma'il Abu Taqiyya, Egyptian Merchant.* Syracuse, NY: Syracuse University Press, 1998.

Har-El, Shai. *Struggle for Domination in the Middle East: The Ottoman-Mamluk War, 1485–91.* Leiden: E. J. Brill, 1995.

Hathaway, Jane. *The Arab Lands under Ottoman Rule, 1516–1800.* Harlow, UK: Longman Pearson, 2008.

———. *Beshir Agha: Chief Eunuch of the Ottoman Imperial Harem.* Oxford: Oneworld Publications, 2005.

———. *The Politics of Households in Ottoman Egypt: The Rise of the Qazdağlıs.* Cambridge: Cambridge University Press, 1997.

Hegyi, Klára, and Vera Zimányi. *Muslime und Christen: Das Osmanische Reich in Europa.* Budapest: Corvina, 1988.

Herrmann, Gottfried. *Persische Urkunden der Mongolenzeit.* Wiesbaden: Harrassowitz, 2004.

Hess, Andrew. *The Forgotten Frontier: A History of the Sixteenth-Century Ibero-African Frontier.* Chicago: University of Chicago Press, 1978.

Hinds, Martin, and Victor L. Ménage. *Qasr Ibrim in the Ottoman Period: Turkish and Further Arabic Documents.* London: Egypt Exploration Society, 1991.

Hodgson, Marshall G. S. *The Venture of Islam: Conscience and History in a World Civilization.* 3 vols. Chicago: Chicago University Press, 1974.

Hoensch, Jörg. *Matthias Corvinus: Diplomat, Feldherr und Mäzen.* Graz: Verlag Styria, 1998.

Hoffmann, Birgit. *Persische Geschichte 1694–1835 erlebt, erinnert und erfunden: Das Rustam at-tawārīḫ in deutscher Bearbeitung.* 2 vols. Bamberg: Aku-Verlag, 1986.

Holy Monastery of Great Meteoron Byzantine Painting Icons and Frescoes. 2 vols. Kalabaka: Holy Monastery of Great Meteoron, 2007.

Howard, Deborah. *Venice & the East: The Impact of the Islamic World on Venetian Architecture, 1100–1500.* New Haven, CT: Yale University Press, 2000.

Hütteroth, Wolf-Dieter, and Kamal Abdulfattah. *Historical Geography of Palestine, Transjordan, and Southern Syria in the Late Sixteenth Century.* Erlangen: Fränkische Geographische Gesellschaft, 1977.

Inalcik, Halil. *The Ottoman Empire: The Classical Age, 1300–1600.* New ed. London: Phoenix, 1995.

Israel, Jonathan. *Dutch Primacy in World Trade, 1585–1740.* Oxford: Clarendon Press, 1989.

Jackson, Peter, and Lawrence Lockhart, eds. *The Timurid and Safavid Periods*. Vol. 6 of *The Cambridge History of Iran*. Cambridge: Cambridge University Press, 1986.

Kadı, Ismail Hakkı. "Natives and Interlopers: Competition between Ottoman and Dutch Merchants in the 18th Century." PhD diss., Universiteit Leiden, 2008.

Kafadar, Cemal. *Between Two Worlds: The Construction of the Ottoman State*. Berkeley: University of California Press, 1995.

———. "A Death in Venice (1575): Anatolian Muslim Merchants Trading in the Serenissima." Special issue, *Journal of Turkish Studies* 10 (1986): 191–218.

———. "Eyüp'te Kılıç Kuşanma Törenleri." In *Eyüp. Dün/Bugün, 11–12 Aralık 1993,* ed. Tülay Artan. Istanbul: Tarih Vakfı Yurt Yayınları, 1994.

Kasaba, Reşat, ed. *Turkey in the Modern World*. Vol. 4 of *The Cambridge History of Turkey*. Cambridge: Cambridge University Press, 2008.

Kastritsis, Dimitris J. *The Sons of Bayezid: Empire Building and Representation in the Ottoman Civil War of 1402–1413*. Leiden: E. J. Brill, 2007.

Katsiardi-Hering, Olga. "The Allure of Red Cotton Yarn, and How It Came to Vienna: Associations of Greek Artisans and Merchants Operating between the Ottoman and Habsburg Empires." In *Merchants in the Ottoman Empire,* ed. Suraiya Faroqhi and Gilles Veinstein. Paris: Peeters, 2008.

Kauz, Ralph. *Politik und Handel zwischen Ming und Timuriden: China, Iran und Zentralasien im Spätmittelalter*. Wiesbaden: Ludwig Reichert, 2005.

Keyvani, Mehdi. *Artisans and Guild Life in the Later Safavid Period: Contributions to the Social-Economic History of Persia*. Berlin: Klaus Schwarz Verlag, 1982.

Khoury, Dina Rizk. *State and Provincial Society in the Ottoman Empire: Mosul, 1540–1834*. Cambridge: Cambridge University Press, 1997.

Kırlı, Cengiz. "A Profile of the Labor Force in Early Nineteenth-Century Istanbul." *International Labor and Working-Class History* 60 (2001): 125–140.

Klein, Denise. *Die osmanischen Ulema des 17. Jahrhunderts: Eine geschlossene Gesellschaft?* Berlin: Klaus Schwarz Verlag, 2007.

Koller, Markus. "Wahrnehmung und Erfassung eines Raumes im Zeichen eines gesellschaftlichen Wandels: Die osmanische Herrschaft in Ungarn bis zum Ausbruch des 'Großen Türkenkrieges'" (1683). Unpublished thesis of habilitation.

Kortepeter, Carl Max. *Ottoman Imperialism during the Reformation: Europe and the Caucasus*. New York: New York University Press, 1972.

Kreiser, Klaus. *Der osmanische Staat 1300–1922*. Munich: Oldenbourg, 2001.

———. "Über den 'Kernraum' des Osmanischen Reichs." In *Die Türkei in Europa,* ed. Klaus-Detlev Grothusen. Göttingen: Vandenhoeck & Ruprecht, 1979.

Kunt, Metin I. *The Sultan's Servants: The Transformation of Ottoman Provincial Government, 1550–1650*. New York: Columbia University Press, 1983.

Kurat, Akdes Nimet. *Türkler ve İdil boyu (1569 Astarhan seferi, Ten-İdil kanalı ve XVI.–XVII. yüzyıl Osmanlı-Rus münasebetleri)*. Ankara: Ankara Üniversitesi Dil ve Tarih-Coğrafya Fakültesi, 1966.

Kurz, Otto. "A Gold Helmet Made in Venice for Sulayman the Magnificent." In *The Decorative Arts of Europe and the Islamic East*. New ed. London: Dorian Press, 1977.

Kütükoğlu, Bekir. *Osmanlı-İran Siyasi Münasebetleri (1578–1612)*. 2nd ed. Istanbul: İstanbul Fetih Cemiyeti, 1993.

Kütükoğlu, Mübahat, ed. *Osmanlılarda Narh Müessesesi ve 1640 Tarihli Narh Defteri*. Istanbul: Enderun Kitabevi, 1983.

Lambton, Ann K. S. *Landlord and Peasant in Persia*. New ed. London: I. B. Tauris, 1991.

Lane, Frederic C. *Venice: A Maritime Republic*. Baltimore: Johns Hopkins University Press, 1973.

Lier, Thomas. *Haushalte und Haushaltspolitik in Bagdad 1704–1831*. Würzburg: Ergon Verlag, 2004.

Lowry, Heath W. *Fifteenth-Century Ottoman Realities: Christian Peasant Life on the Aegean Island of Limnos*. Istanbul: Eren, 2002.

———. *The Shaping of the Ottoman Balkans, 1350–1550: The Conquest, Settlement and Infrastructural Development of Northern Greece*. Istanbul: Bahçeşehir University Publications, 2008.

MacLean, Gerald. *Looking East*. Basingstoke, UK: Palgrave Macmillan, 2007.

———. *The Rise of Oriental Travel: English Visitors to the Ottoman Empire, 1580–1720*. Basingstoke, UK: Palgrave Macmillan, 2004.

Malcolm, Noel. *Kosovo: A Short History*. New York: HarperCollins, 1999.

Mantran, Robert. *Istanbul dans la seconde moitié du XVIIe siècle: Essai d'histoire institutionelle, économique et sociale*. Paris: Adrien Maisonneuve, 1962.

Manz, Beatrice Forbes. *Power, Politics, and Religion in Timurid Iran*. Cambridge: Cambridge University Press, 2007.

———. *The Rise and Rule of Tamerlane*. New ed. Cambridge: Cambridge University Press, 1999.

Marcus, Abraham. *The Middle East on the Eve of Modernity: Aleppo in the Eighteenth Century*. New York: Columbia University Press, 1989.

Marquié, Claude. *L'industrie textile carcassonnaise au XVIIIe siècle: Étude d'un groupe social: Les marchands-fabricants*. Carcassonne: Société d'Études Scientifiques de l'Aude, 1993.

Masson, Paul. *Histoire du commerce français dans le Levant au XVIIIe siècle*. Paris: Librairie Hachette, 1911.

Masters, Bruce. *Christians and Jews in the Arab World: The Roots of Sectarianism*. Cambridge: Cambridge University Press, 2001.

Matar, Nabil. *Turks, Moors, and Englishmen in the Age of Discovery.* New York: Colombia University Press, 1999.

Matthee, Rudolph P. *The Politics of Trade in Safavid Iran: Silk for Silver, 1600–1730.* Cambridge: Cambridge University Press, 1999.

McGowan, Bruce. *Economic Life in Ottoman Europe: Taxation, Trade, and the Struggle for Land, 1600–1800.* Cambridge: Cambridge University Press, 1981.

Melville, Charles, ed. *Safavid Persia: The History and Politics of an Islamic Society.* London: I. B. Tauris, 1996.

Meriwether, Margaret L. *The Kin Who Count: Family and Society in Ottoman Aleppo, 1770–1840.* Austin: University of Texas Press, 1999.

Minkov, Anton. *Conversion to Islam in the Balkans: Kisve Bahası Petitions and Ottoman Social Life, 1670–1730.* Leiden: E. J. Brill, 2004.

[Mirzā Sami'ā]. *Tadhkirat al-Mulūk.* Translated by Vladimir Minorsky. London: Luzzac, 1943.

Murphey, Rhoads. *Ottoman Warfare, 1500–1700.* New Brunswick, NJ: Rutgers University Press, 1999.

Nagata, Yuzo. *Muhsin-zâde Mehmed Paşa ve Ayânlık Müessesesi.* Tokyo: Institute for the Study of Languages and Cultures of Asia and Africa, 1982.

Nasuhü's-silāhi (Matrākçı). *Beyan-ı Menazil-i Sefer-i İrakeyn-i Sultān Suleymān Han.* Edited by Hüseyin G. Yurdaydın. Ankara: Türk Tarih Kurumu, 1976.

Nayır, Zeynep. *Osmanlı Mimarlığında Sultan Ahmet Külliyesi ve Sonrası (1609–1690).* Istanbul: İstanbul Teknik Üniversitesi Mimarlık Fakültesi, 1975.

Necipoğlu, Gülru. *The Age of Sinan: Architectural Culture in the Ottoman Empire.* London: Reaktion Books, 2005.

———. *Architecture, Ceremonial, and Power: The Topkapı Palace in the Fifteenth and Sixteenth Centuries.* Cambridge, MA: MIT Press, 1991.

Newman, Andrew J. *Safavid Iran: The Rebirth of a Persian Empire.* London: I. B. Tauris, 2005.

Nicol, Donald. *The Reluctant Emperor: A Biography of John Cantacuzene, Byzantine Emperor and Monk, c. 1295–1383.* Cambridge: Cambridge University Press, 1996.

Niederkorn, Jan Paul. *Die europäischen Mächte und der "Lange Türkenkrieg" Kaiser Rudolfs II. (1593–1606).* Vienna: Verlag der Österreichischen Akademie der Wissenschaften, 1993.

Ocak, Ahmet Yaşar. *Bektaşî Menâkıbnâmelerinde İslam Öncesi İnanç Motifleri.* Istanbul: Enderun Kitabevi, 1983.

Onbin Yıllık İran Medeniyeti: Onbin Yıllık Ortak Miras. Istanbul: National Museum of Iran, 2009.

Orhonlu, Cengiz. "Dicle ve Fırat Nehirlerinde Nakliyat." In *Osmanlı İmparatorluğunda Şehircilik ve Ulaşım,* ed. Salih Özbaran. Izmir: Ege Üniversitesi Edebiyat Fakültesi, 1984.

———. *Osmanlı İmparatorluğunda Aşiretleri İskân Teşebbüsü (1691–1696).* Istanbul: İstanbul Üniversitesi Edebiyat Fakültesi, 1963.

———. *Osmanlı İmparatorluğunun Güney Siyaseti: Habeş Eyaleti*. Istanbul: İstanbul Üniversitesi Edebiyat Fakültesi, 1974.

Orthmann, Eva. *Abd or-Rahim Han-e Hanan (964–1036 /1556–1627): Staatsmann und Mäzen*. Berlin: Klaus Schwarz Verlag, 1996.

Özbaran, Salih. *The Ottoman Response to European Expansion: Studies on Ottoman–Portuguese Relations in the Indian Ocean and Ottoman Administration in the Arab Lands during the Sixteenth Century*. Istanbul: Isis Press, 1994.

Öztürk, Yücel. *Osmanlı Hakimiyetinde Kefe 1474–1600*. Ankara: T. C. Kültür Bakanlığı, 2000.

Palombini, Barbara von. *Bündniswerben abendländischer Mächte um Persien 1453–1600*. Wiesbaden: Franz Steiner, 1968.

Pamuk, Şevket. *A Monetary History of the Ottoman Empire*. Cambridge: Cambridge University Press, 2000.

Panzac, Daniel. *Barbary Corsairs: The End of a Legend*. Translated by Victoria Hobson and John E. Hawkes. Leiden: E. J. Brill, 2005.

———. *La marine ottomane, de l'apogée à la chute de l'empire (1572–1923)*. Paris: CNRS Éditions, 2009.

[Papa Synadinos von Serres]. *Conseils et mémoires de Synadinos prêtre de Serrès en Macédoine (XVIIe siècle)*. Edited and translated by Paolo Odorico, S. Asdrachas, T. Karanastassis, K. Kostis, and S. Petmézas. Paris: Association "Pierre Belon," 1996.

Papakonstantinou, Katerina. "The Pondikas Merchant Family from Thessaloniki, ca. 1750–1800." In *Merchants in the Ottoman Empire,* ed. Suraiya Faroqhi and Gilles Veinstein. Paris: Peeters, 2008.

Parker, Geoffrey. *Spain and the Netherlands, 1559–1659: Ten Studies*. 2nd ed. London: Fontana Press, 1990.

Parmaksızoğlu, İsmet. "Kuzey Irak'ta Osmanlı Hâkimiyetinin Kuruluşu ve Memun Beyin Hatıraları." *Belleten* 37, no. 146 (1973): 191–230.

Peacock, Andrew C. S., ed. *The Frontiers of the Ottoman World*. Oxford: Oxford University Press, 2009.

Pedani Fabris, Maria Pia. "Between Diplomacy and Trade: Ottoman Merchants in Venice." In *Merchants in the Ottoman Empire,* ed. Suraiya Faroqhi and Gilles Veinstein. Paris: Peeters, 2008.

Peirce, Leslie. *The Imperial Harem: Women and Sovereignty in the Ottoman Empire*. Oxford: Oxford University Press, 1993.

———. *Morality Tales: Law and Gender in the Ottoman Court of Aintab*. Berkeley: University of California Press, 2003.

Peri, Oded. *Christianity under Islam in Jerusalem: The Question of the Holy Sites in Early Ottoman Times*. Leiden: E. J. Brill, 2001.

Petry, Carl. F., ed. *Islamic Egypt, 640–1517*. Vol. 1 of *The Cambridge History of Egypt*. Cambridge: Cambridge University Press, 1998.

Poumarède, Géraud. *Pour en finir avec la croisade: Mythes et réalités de la lutte contre les Turcs aux XVIe et XVIIe siècles.* Paris: Presses Universitaires de France, 2004.

Quinn, Sholeh A. *Historical Writing during the Reign of Shah 'Abbas: Ideology, Imitation, and Legitimacy in Safavid Chronicles.* Salt Lake City: University of Utah Press, 2000.

Quiring-Zoche, Rosemarie. *Isfahan im 15. und 16. Jahrhundert: Ein Beitrag zur persischen Stadtgeschichte.* Freiburg im Breisgau: Klaus Schwarz Verlag, 1980.

Raby, Julian. *Venice, Dürer and the Oriental Mode.* London: Islamic Art Publications, 1982.

Rafeq, Abdul Karem. *The Province of Damascus, 1723–1783.* Beirut: Khayats, 1966.

Rambert, Gaston, ed. *Histoire du commerce de Marseille.* Vols. 3, 4, and 5. Paris: Librairie Plon, 1951–1957.

Raymond, André. *Artisans et commerçants au Caire, au XVIIIe siècle.* 2 vols. Damas: Institut Français de Damas, 1973–1974.

Rizvi, Kishwar. "Gendered Patronage: Women and Benevolence during the Early Safavid Empire." In *Women, Patronage, and Self-Representation in Islamic Societies,* ed. D. Fairchild Ruggles. Albany: State University of New York Press, 2000.

Rogers, John Michael. *Sinan.* London: I. B. Tauris, 2006.

Röhrborn, Klaus. *Provinzen und Zentralgewalt Persiens im 16. und 17. Jahrhundert.* Berlin: De Gruyter, 1966.

———. *Untersuchungen zur osmanischen Verwaltungsgeschichte.* Berlin: De Gruyter, 1973.

Roxburgh, David J. *The Persian Album: From Dispersal to Collection.* New Haven, CT: Yale University Press, 2005.

Rozen, Minna. *A History of the Jewish Community in Istanbul: The Formative Years, 1453–1566.* Leiden: E. J. Brill, 2002.

Runciman, Steven. *The Fall of Constantinople.* Cambridge: Cambridge University Press, 1965.

Sadok, Boubaker. *La Régence de Tunis au XVIIe siècle: Ses relations commerciales avec les ports de l'Europe méditerranéenne, Marseille et Livourne.* Zaghouan: CEROMA, 1987.

Scharabi, Mohamed. *Der Bazar: Das traditionelle Stadtzentrum im Nahen Osten und seine Handelseinrichtungen.* Tübingen: Ernst Wasmuth, 1985.

Schmitt, Oliver Jens. *Levantiner: Lebenswelten und Identitäten einer ethnokonfessionellen Gruppe im osmanischen Reich im "langen 19. Jahrhundert."* Munich: Oldenbourg, 2005.

Seng, Yvonne J. "Standing at the Gates of Justice: Women in the Law Courts of Early-Sixteenth-Century Üsküdar, Istanbul." In *Contested States: Law, Hegemony and Resistance,* ed. Susan F. Hirsch and Mindie Lazarus-Black. New York: Routledge, 1994.

Shaw, Stanford J. *The Financial and Administrative Organization and Development of Ottoman Egypt 1517–1798.* Princeton, NJ: Princeton University Press, 1962.

Singer, Amy. *Constructing Ottoman Beneficence: An Imperial Soup Kitchen in Jerusalem.* Albany: State University of New York Press, 2002.

Skilliter, Susan. *William Harborne and the Trade with Turkey, 1578–1582.* London: Oxford University Press, 1977.

Smyrnelis, Marie-Carmen. *Une société hors de soi: Identités et relations sociales à Smyrne aux XVIIIe et XIXe siècles.* Paris: Peeters, 2005.

Stavrides, Theoharis. *The Sultan of Vezirs: The Life and Times of the Ottoman Grand Vezir Mahmud Pasha Angelović (1453–1474).* Leiden: E. J. Brill, 2001.

Steensgaard, Niels. *The Asian Trade Revolution of the Seventeenth Century: The East India Companies and the Decline of the Caravan Trade.* Chicago: Chicago University Press, 1973.

Stoianovich, Traian. "Le maïs dans les Balkans." *Annales ESC* 21 (1966): 1026–1040.

Stoye, John. *The Siege of Vienna.* London: Collins, 1964.

Szakály, Ferenc. *Hungaria eliberata: Die Rückeroberung von Buda im Jahr 1686 und Ungarns Befreiung von der Osmanenherrschaft (1683–1718).* Budapest: Corvina, 1986.

Tayyip Gökbilgin. *Rumeli'de Yürükler, Tatarlar ve Evlâd-ı Fâtihan.* Istanbul: İstanbul Üniversitesi Edebiyat Fakültesi, 1957.

Thompson, Jon, and Sheila Canby, eds. *Hunt for Paradise: Court Arts of Safavid Iran.* Milan: Skira, 2003.

Thys-Şenocak, Lucienne. *Ottoman Women Builders: The Architectural Patronage of Hadice Turhan Sultan.* Aldershot, UK: Ashgate, 2006.

Tóth, Ferenc. *La guerre russo-turque (1768–1774) et la défense des Dardanelles: L'extraordinaire mission du baron de Tott.* Paris: Economica, 2008.

Tucker, Ernest S. *Nadir Shah's Quest for Legitimacy in Post-Safavid Iran.* Gainesville: University Press of Florida, 2006.

Tuğ, Başak. "Politics of Honor: The Institutional and Social Frontiers of 'Illicit' Sex in Mid-Eighteenth-Century Ottoman Anatolia." PhD diss., New York University, 2009.

Uluç, Lale. *Turkman Governors, Shiraz Artisans, and Ottoman Collectors: Sixteenth-Century Shiraz Manuscripts.* Istanbul: İş Bankası Yayınları, 2006.

Uzunçarşılı, İsmail Hakkı. *Mekke-i Mükerreme Emirleri.* Ankara: Türk Tarih Kurumu, 1972.

Van der Cruysse, Dirk. *Chardin le Persan.* Paris: Fayard, 1998.

Vatin, Nicolas, and Gilles Veinstein. *Le sérail ébranlé: Essai sur les morts, dépositions et avènements des sultans ottomans XIVe–XIXe siècle.* Paris: Fayard, 2003.

Walz, Terence. *Trade between Egypt and Bilad al-Sudan.* Cairo: Institut Français d'Archéologie Orientale, 1978.

Werner, Christoph. *An Iranian Town in Transition: A Social and Economic History of the Elites of Tabriz, 1747–1848.* Wiesbaden: Harrassowitz Verlag, 2000.

Wilkins, Charles L. *Forging Urban Solidarities: Ottoman Aleppo, 1640–1700.* Leiden: E. J. Brill, 2010.

Woods, John. *The Aqquyunlu: Clan, Confederation, Empire.* 2nd ed. Salt Lake City: University of Utah Press, 1999.

Yarshater, Ehsan, ed. *Encyclopaedia Iranica.* 15 vols. London: Routledge, 1982–2011.

Yérasimos, Stéphane. *La Fondation de Constantinople et de Sainte-Sophie dans les traditions turques.* Paris: Maisonneuve, 1990.

Yıldız, Hakkı Dursun, ed. *150. Yılında Tanzimat.* Ankara: Türk Tarih Kurumu, 1992.

Yıldız, Sara Nur. "Karamanoğlu Mehmed Bey: Medieval Anatolian Warlord or Kemalist Language Reformer? History, Language, Politics, and the Celebration of the Language Festival in Karaman, Turkey, 1961–2008." In *Religion, Ethnicity, and Contested Nationhood in the Former Ottoman Space,* ed. Jørgen Nielsen. Leiden: E. J. Brill, 2012.

Yinanç, Refet. *Dulkadir Beyliği.* Ankara: Türk Tarih Kurumu, 1989.

Zachariadou, Elisabeth. *Trade and Crusade Venetian Crete and the Emirates of Menteshe and Aydin, 1300–1415.* Venice: Hellenic Institute of Byzantine and Post-Byzantine Studies, 1983.

Zarinebaf-Shahr, Fariba. "Tabriz under Ottoman Rule (1725–1730)." PhD diss., University of Illinois at Chicago, 1991.

Zarinebaf, Fariba, John Bennet, and Jack L. Davis. *A Historical and Economic Geography of Ottoman Greece: The Southwestern Morea in the 18th Century.* Athens: American School of Classical Studies at Athens, 2005.

Zilfi, Madeline. *The Politics of Piety: The Ottoman Ulema in the Postclassical Age, 1600–1800.* Minneapolis: Bibliotheca Islamica, 1988.

South Asia and the Indian Ocean

Abu-Lughod, Janet. *Before European Hegemony: The World System, AD 1250–1350.* New York: Oxford University Press, 1989.

———. "The World System in the Thirteenth Century: Dead-End or Precursor?" In *Islamic and European Expansion: The Forging of a Global Order,* ed. Michael Adas. Philadelphia: Temple University Press, 1993.

Adshead, Samuel A. *Central Asia in World History.* Basingstoke, UK: Macmillan, 1993.

Ahuja, Ravi. "Indischer Ozean." In *Enzyklopädie der Neuzeit,* vol. 5, ed. Friedrich Jaeger. Stuttgart: Metzler, 2007.

Alam, Muzaffar. *The Crisis of Empire in Mughal North India: Awadh and the Punjab, 1707–48.* Delhi: Oxford University Press, 1986.

———. *The Languages of Political Islam.* London: Hurst, 2004.

Alam, Muzaffar, and Sanjay Subrahmanyam, eds. *The Mughal State, 1526–1750.* Delhi: Oxford University Press, 1998.

Ali, M. Athar. *The Apparatus of Empire: Awards of Ranks, Offices, and Titles to the Mughal Nobility, 1574–1658.* Delhi: Oxford University Press, 1985.

Appelániz Ruiz de Galarreta, Francisco Javier. *Pouvoir et finance en Méditerranée prémoderne: Le deuxième Etat mamlouk et le commerce des épices (1382–1517).* Barcelona: CSIC, 2009.

Arasaratnam, Sinnappah. *Maritime India in the Seventeenth Century.* Delhi: Oxford University Press, 1994.

———. *Merchants, Companies, and Commerce on the Coromandel Coast, 1650–1740*. Delhi: Oxford University Press, 1986.

Arasaratnam, Sinnappah, and Aniruddha Ray. *Masulipatnam and Cambay: A History of Two Port-Towns, 1500–1800*. New Delhi: Munshiram Manoharlal, 1994.

Asher, Catherine B., and Cynthia Talbot, eds. *India before Europe*. New York: Cambridge University Press, 2006.

Ashtor, Eliyahu. *Levant Trade in the Later Middle Ages*. Princeton, NJ: Princeton University Press, 1983.

Aslanian, Sebouh David. *From the Indian Ocean to the Mediterranean: The Global Trade Networks of Armenian Merchants from New Julfa*. Berkeley: University of California Press, 2011.

Attman, Artur. *The Bullion Flow between Europe and the East, 1000–1750*. Göteborg: Kungl. Vetenskaps—och Vitterhets-Samhället, 1981.

———. *The Russian and Polish Markets in International Trade, 1500–1650*. Göteborg: Institute of Economic History of Gothenburg University, 1973.

Babur. *The Baburnama: Memoirs of Babur, Prince and Emperor*. Translated, edited, and annotated by Wheeler M. Thackston. Washington, DC: Freer Gallery of Art, 1996.

Bacqué-Grammont, Jean-Louis. *Les Ottomans, les Safavides et leurs voisins: Contributions à l'histoire des relations internationales dans l'Orient islamique de 1514 à 1524*. Istanbul: Nederlands Historisch-Archaeologisch Instituut te Istanbul, 1987.

Bal, Mieke. *Travelling Concepts in the Humanities: A Rough Guide*. Toronto: University of Toronto Press, 2002.

Balabanlilar, Lisa. *Imperial Identity in the Mughal Empire: Memory and Dynastic Politics in Early Modern South and Central Asia*. London: Tauris, 2012.

Banerjee, Jamini M. *History of Firuz Shah Tughluq*. Delhi: Munshiram Manoharlal, 1967.

Banga, Indu, ed. *Ports and Their Hinterlands in India, 1700–1950*. New Delhi: Manohar, 1992.

Barendse, R. J. *The Arabian Seas: The Indian Ocean World of the Seventeenth Century*. Armonk, NY: M. E. Sharpe, 2002.

———. *Arabian Seas, 1700–1763*. 4 vols. Leiden: Brill, 2009.

Bartlett, Robert. *The Making of Europe: Conquest, Colonization, and Cultural Change, 950–1350*. Princeton, NJ: Princeton University Press, 1993.

———. *North India between Empires: Awadh, the Mughals, and the British, 1720–1801*. Berkeley: University of California Press, 1980.

Battacharya, Sukumar. *The East India Company and the Economy of Bengal from 1704 to 1740*. London: Luzac, 1954.

Behrens-Abouseif, Doris, ed. *The Arts of the Mamluks in Egypt and Syria—Evolution and Impact*. Göttingen: V&R Unipress, 2012.

Bergdolt, Klaus. *Der schwarze Tod in Europa*. 3rd ed. Munich: Beck, 2011.

Bhatia, Manohar Lal. *The Ulama, Islamic Ethics and Courts under the Mughals: Aurangzeb Revisited*. New Delhi: Manak, 2006.

Bialuschewski, Arne. *Piratenleben: Die abenteuerlichen Fahrten des Seeräubers Richard Sievers.* Berlin: Ullstein, 1999.

Bicheno, Hugh. *Crescent and Cross: The Battle of Lepanto 1571.* London: Phoenix, 2004.

Blussé, Leonard, and Femme Gaastra, eds. *Companies and Trade: Essays on Overseas Trading Companies during the Ancient Régime.* Leiden: Leiden University Press, 1981.

Borsch, Stuart James. *The Black Death in Egypt and England: A Comparative Study.* Austin: University of Texas Press, 2005.

Bowen, Huw V., Margarette Lincoln, and Nigel Rigby, eds. *The Worlds of the East India Company.* Woodbridge: Boydell, 2002.

Boxer, Charles R. *The Dutch Seaborne Empire: 1600–1800.* London: Hutchinson, 1965.

———. *Portuguese Conquest and Commerce in Southern Asia, 1500–1750.* London: Variorum Reprints, 1985.

———. *The Portuguese Seaborne Empire, 1415–1825.* London: Hutchinson, 1969.

Boyajian, James C. *Portuguese Trade in Asia under the Habsburgs, 1580–1640.* Baltimore: Johns Hopkins University Press, 1993.

Braudel, Fernand. *Civilization and Capitalism.* 3 vols. New York: Harper & Row, 1981–1984.

———. *The Mediterranean and the Mediterranean World in the Age of Philip II.* 2 vols. London: Collins, 1972.

Broeze, Frank, ed. *Brides of the Sea: Port Cities of Asia from the 16th to the 20th Centuries.* Kensington, Australia: New South Wales University Press, 1989.

———. *Gateways of Asia: Port Cities of Asia in the 13th–20th Centuries.* London: Kegan Paul International, 1997.

Brown, Katherine B. "Did Aurangzeb Ban Music? Questions for the Historiography of His Reign." *Modern Asian Studies* 41, no. 1 (2007): 77–120.

Bushkovitch, Paul. *The Merchants of Moscow, 1580–1650.* Cambridge: Cambridge University Press, 1980.

Capponi, Niccolò. *Victory of the West: The Story of the Battle of Lepanto.* London: Macmillan, 2006.

Casale, Giancarlo. *The Ottoman Age of Exploration.* Oxford: Oxford University Press, 2010.

Chandra, Satish. *Medieval India: From Sultanat to the Mughals. Part One: Delhi Sultanat (1206–1526).* 4th ed. New Delhi: Har-Anand Publications, 2009.

———. *Medieval India: From Sultanat to the Mughals. Part Two: Mughal Empire (1526–1748).* New Delhi: Har-Anand Publications, 1999.

———. *Medieval India: Society, the Jagirdari Crisis and the Village.* Delhi: Macmillan, 1982.

———. *Mughal Religious Policies, the Rajputs and the Deccan.* New Delhi: Vikas Publishing House, 1993.

Chaudhuri, Kirti Narayan. *Asia before Europe: Economy and Civilization of the Indian Ocean from the Rise of Islam to 1750.* Cambridge: Cambridge University Press, 1990.

———. *The English East India Company: The Study of an Early Joint-Stock Company, 1600–1640.* London: Cass, 1965.

———. *Trade and Civilization in the Indian Ocean: An Economic History from the Rise of Islam to 1750*. Cambridge: Cambridge University Press, 1985.

Chaudhury, Sushil. *The Prelude to Empire: Plassey Revolution of 1757*. New Delhi: Manohar, 2000.

———. *Trade and Commercial Organization in Bengal, 1650–1720*. Calcutta: Mukhopadhyay, 1975.

Chaunu, Pierre. *European Expansion in the Later Middle Ages*. Amsterdam: North-Holland Publications, 1979.

Chittick, H. Neville. "The East Coast, Madagascar and the Indian Ocean." In *The Cambridge History of Africa*. Vol. 3: *From c. 1050 to c. 1600,* ed. Roland A. Oliver. Cambridge: Cambridge University Press, 1977.

Christ, Georg. *Trading Conflicts: Venetian Merchants and Mamluk Officials in Late Medieval Alexandria*. Leiden: Brill, 2012.

Conermann, Stephan. "Das Mittelmeer zur Zeit der Mamlukenherrschaft in Ägypten und Syrien (1250–1517)—Vorstudien zu einer globalgeschichtlichen Perspektive." In *Randgänge der Mediävistik (Vorträge der Vorlesungsreihe "Das Mittelmeer—Mare nostrum?" des Berner Mittelalterzentrums im Frühjahrssemester 2012),* ed. Michael Stolz. Bern: Stämpfli, 2014.

———. *Das Mogulreich: Geschichte und Kultur des muslimischen Indien*. Munich: Beck, 2006.

———. *Die Beschreibung Indiens in der "Rihla" des Ibn-Battuta: Aspekte einer herrschaftssoziologischen Einordnung des Delhi-Sultanates unter Muhammad Ibn-Tuğluq*. Berlin: Schwarz, 1993.

———. "Muslimische Seefahrt auf dem Indischen Ozean vom 14. bis zum 16. Jahrhundert." In *Der Indische Ozean in historischer Perspektive,* ed. Stephan Conermann. Hamburg: EB-Verlag, 1998.

———, ed. *Ubi sumus? Quo vademus? Mamluk Studies—State of the Art*. Göttingen: V&R Unipress, 2013.

———. "Unter dem Einfluss des Monsuns: Der Handel zwischen Arabien und Südasien." In *Fernhandel in Antike und Mittelalter,* ed. Robert Bohn. Darmstadt: WBG, 2008.

———. "Vertraute Zeichen—Fremde Zeichen: Zur Frage der möglichen Exilerfahrung in der mittelalterlichen islamischen Welt." In *Vermischte Schriften: Koran, Šah-name, Exil und Viktor Klemperer,* ed. Werner Schmucker and Stephan Conermann. Schenefeld: EB-Verlag, 2007.

Conermann, Stephan, and Jan Kusber, eds. *Studia Eurasiatica: Kieler Festschrift für Hermann Kulke zum 65. Geburtstag*. Schenefeld: EB-Verlag, 2003.

Conermann, Stephan, and Anja Pistor-Hatam, eds. *Die Mamluken: Studien zu ihrer Geschichte und Kultur: Zum Gedenken an Ulrich Haarmann (1942–1999)*. Schenefeld: EB-Verlag, 2003.

Conti, Nicolò de. "The Travels of Nicolò de Conti in the East." In *The Most Noble and Famous Travels of Marco Polo together with the Travels of Nicolò de Conti*. Translated and edited by John Frampton. London: Argonaut Press, 1929.

Coulon, Damien. *Barcelone et le grand commerce d'Orient au Moyen Âge: Un siècle de relations avec l'Égypte et la Syrie-Palestrine (ca. 1330–ca. 1430)*. Madrid: Casa de Velázquez, 2004.

Dale, Stephen F. *The Garden of the Eight Paradises: Babur and the Culture of Empire in Central Asia, Afghanistan and India (1483–1530)*. Leiden: Brill 2004.

———. *The Muslim Empires of the Ottomans, Safavids, and Mughals*. Cambridge: Cambridge University Press, 2010.

Dallapiccola, Anna L., and Stephanie Zingel-Avé Lallemant, eds. *Vijayanagara: City and Empire: New Currents of Research*. Stuttgart: Steiner, 1985.

Das Gupta, Ashin. *Indian Merchants and the Decline of Surat, c. 1700–1750*. New Delhi: Manohar, 1994.

———. *Merchants of Maritime India, 1500–1800*. Aldershot, UK: Variorum, 1994.

———. "Trade and Politics in Eighteenth Century India." In *Islam and the Trade of Asia*, ed. Donald S. Richards. Philadelphia: University of Pennsylvania Press, 1970.

———. *The World of the Indian Ocean Merchant, 1500–1800*. Compiled by Uma Das Gupta. New Delhi: Oxford University Press, 2001.

Das Gupta, Ashin, and Michael N. Pearson, eds. *India and the Indian Ocean, 1500–1800*. Calcutta: Oxford University Press, 1987.

De Vries, Jan, and Ad van der Woude. *The First Modern Economy: Success, Failure, and Perseverance of the Dutch Economy, 1500–1815*. Cambridge: Cambridge University Press, 1997.

Digby, Simon. *War-Horse and Elephant in the Delhi Sultanate: A Study of Military Supplies*. Oxford: Orient Monographs, 1971.

Diller, Stephan. *Die Dänen in Indien, Südostasien und China, 1620–1845*. Wiesbaden: Harrassowitz, 1999.

Disney, Anthony R. *The Portuguese Empire*. Vol. 2 of *A History of Portugal and the Portuguese Empire: From Beginnings to 1807*. Cambridge: Cambridge University Press, 2009.

———. *Twilight of the Pepper Empire: Portuguese Trade in Southwest India in the Early Seventeenth Century*. Cambridge, MA: Harvard University Press, 1978.

Dols, Michael W. *The Black Death in the Middle East*. Princeton, NJ: Princeton University Press, 1977.

Eaton, Richard M. *The Rise of Islam and the Bengal Frontier, 1204–1760*. Berkeley: University of California Press, 1993.

———. *Sufis of Bijapur, 1300–1700: Social Roles of Sufis in Medieval India*. Princeton, NJ: Princeton University Press, 1978.

———. "Temple Desecration and Indo-Muslim States." *Journal of Islamic Studies* 11, no. 3 (2000): 283–319.

Ernst, Carl W. *Eternal Garden: Mysticism, History, and Politics in a South Asian Sufi Center*. Albany: State University of New York Press, 1992.

Faroqhi, Suraiya. "Crisis and Change, 1590–1699." In *Economic and Social History of the Ottoman Empire, 1300–1914,* ed. Halil Inalcik and Donald Quataert. Cambridge: Cambridge University Press, 1994.

Faruqui, Munis D. *Princes of the Mughal Empire, 1504–1719.* Cambridge: Cambridge University Press, 2012.

Feldbaek, Ole. *India Trade under the Danish Flag, 1772–1808: European Enterprise and Anglo-Indian Remittance and Trade.* Lund: Studentlitteratur, 1969.

Feldbauer, Peter. *Estado da India: Die Portugiesen in Asien, 1498–1620.* Vienna: Mandelbaum, 2003.

Fisher, Michael H. *A Clash of Cultures: Awadh, the British, and the Mughals.* New Delhi: Manohar, 1987.

Floor, Willem. *The Persian Textile Industry in Historical Perspective, 1500–1925.* Paris: Harmattan, 1999.

Flores, Jorge M. *Os Portugueses e o Mar de Ceilão: Trato, diplomacia e guerra 1498–1543.* Lisbon: Edições Cosmos, 1998.

Flores, Jorge M., and Rudi Matthee, eds. *Portugal, the Persian Gulf and Safavid Persia.* Leuven: Peeters, 2011.

Frank, Andre Gunder. *ReOrient: Global Economy in the Asian Age.* Berkeley: University of California Press, 1998.

Frank, Andre Gunder, and Barry K. Gills, eds. *The World System: Five Hundred Years or Five Thousand?* London: Routledge, 1993.

Franke, Heike. *Akbar und Gahangir: Untersuchungen zur politischen und religiösen Legitimation in Text und Bild.* Schenefeld: EB-Verlag, 2005.

Fritz, John M., and George Michell, eds. *City of Victory: Vijayanagara, the Medieval Hindu Capital of Southern India.* New York: Aperture, 1991.

———. *New Light on Hampi: Recent Research at Vijayanagara.* Mumbai: Marg Publications, 2001.

Furber, Holden. *Rival Empires of Trade in the Orient, 1600–1800.* Minneapolis: University of Minnesota Press, 1976.

Gaastra, Femme S. *The Dutch East India Company: Expansion and Decline.* Translated by Peter Daniels. Zutphen: Walburg Pers, 2003.

Glamann, Kristof. *Dutch Asiatic Trade, 1620–1740.* Copenhagen: Danish Science Press, 1958.

Gommans, Jos J. L. *Mughal Warfare: Indian Frontiers and High Roads to Empire, 1500–1700.* London: Routledge 2002.

———. *The Rise of the Indo-Afghan Empire, c. 1710–1780.* Leiden: Brill, 1995.

Gommans, Jos J. L., Lennart Bes, and Gijs Kruijtzer, eds. *Dutch Sources on South Asia c. 1600–1825: Bibliography and Archival Guide to the National Archives at the Hague (the Netherlands).* New Delhi: Manohar, 2001.

Gordon, Stewart. *Marathas, Marauders, and State Formation in Eighteenth-Century India.* Delhi: Oxford University Press, 1994.

———. *The Marathas, 1600–1818.* Cambridge: Cambridge University Press, 1993.

Green, Nile. *Indian Sufism since the Seventeenth Century: Saints, Books and Empires in the Muslim Deccan.* London: Routledge, 2006.

———. *Making Space: Sufis and Settlers in Early Modern India.* New Delhi: Oxford University Press, 2012.

Gupta, Hari Ram. *Evolution of Sikh Confederacies (1708–1769).* Vol. 2 of *History of the Sikhs.* 4th ed. New Delhi: Munshiram Manoharlal, 1992.

Habib, Irfan. "Mansab System, 1595–1637." *Proceedings of the Indian History Congress* 29 (1967): 221–242.

Hahn, Sylvia, and Reinhold Reith, eds. *Umwelt-Geschichte: Arbeitsfelder, Forschungsansätze, Perspektiven.* Munich: Oldenbourg, 2001.

Hasan, Mohibbul. *Babur: Founder of the Mughal Empire in India.* New Delhi: Manohar, 1985.

Hasan, S. Nurul. "Zamindar under the Mughals." In *Land Control and Social Structure in Indian History,* ed. Robert E. Frykenberg. Madison: University of Wisconsin Press, 1969.

Haudrère, Philippe. *La compagnie française des Indes au XVIIIe siècle (1719–1795).* 4 vols. Paris: Librairie de l'Inde, 1989.

Herzig, Edmund. *The Armenian Merchants of New Julfa, Isfahan: A Study in Pre-Modern Asian Trade.* PhD thesis, Oxford University, 1991.

Hodgson, Marshal. *The Venture of Islam.* 3 vols. Chicago: University of Chicago Press, 1974.

Hoffman, Adina, and Peter Cole. *Sacred Trash: The Lost and Found World of the Cairo Geniza.* New York: Schocken Books, 2011.

Hossain, Hameeda. *The Company Weavers of Bengal: The East India Company and the Organization of Textile Production in Bengal, 1750–1813.* Delhi: Oxford University Press, 1988.

Husain, Mahdī. *The Tughluq Dynasty.* Calcutta: Thacker Spink, 1963.

Jackson, Peter. *The Delhi Sultanate: A Political and Military History.* Cambridge: Cambridge University Press, 1999.

Jacob, Hugo Karl s'. *The Rajas of Cochin, 1663–1720: Kings, Chiefs, and the Dutch East India Company.* New Delhi: Munshiram Manoharlal, 2000.

Jacobs, Els M. *De Vereenigde Oost-Indische Compagnie.* Utrecht: Teleac/NOT, 1997.

Karashima, Noboru. *Towards a New Formation: South Indian Society under Vijayanagar Rule.* Delhi: Oxford University Press, 1992.

Khan, Ahsan Raza. *Chieftains in the Mughal Empire during the Reign of Akbar.* Simla: Indian Institute of Advanced Study, 1977.

Kindermann, Hans. *"Schiff" im Arabischen.* Zwickau: n.p., 1934.

Kollatz, Anna. "The Creation of a Saint Emperor: Retracing Narrative Strategies of Mughal Legitimation and Representation in Majalis-i Jahangiri by Abd al-Sattar b. Qasim Lahori (ca. 1608–11)." In *Narrative Pattern and Genre in Hagiographic Life Writing,* ed. Stephan Conermann and Jim Rheingans. Berlin: EB-Verlag, 2014.

Konstam, Angus. *Lepanto 1571: The Greatest Naval Battle of the Renaissance.* Oxford: Osprey, 2003.

Krieger, Martin. *Kaufleute, Seeräuber und Diplomaten: Der dänische Handel auf dem Indischen Ozean (1620–1868).* Cologne: Böhlau, 1998.

Kulke, Tilmann. "Review of John Darwin: *After Tamerlane: The Global History of Empire,* London: Penguin Books 2007." *sehepunkte* 9, no. 10 (October 15, 2009). www.sehepunkte .de/2009/10/17151.html.

Kumar, Sunil. *The Emergence of the Delhi Sultanate, 1192–1286.* New Delhi: Permanent Black, 2007.

Labib, Subhi. *Handelsgeschichte Ägyptens im Spätmittelalter, 1171–1517.* Wiesbaden: Steiner, 1965.

Lal, Kishori S. *Twilight of the Sultanate.* 2nd ed. New Delhi: Munshiram Manoharlal, 1980.

Lawrence, Bruce B. *An Overview of Sufi Literature in the Sultanate Period.* Patna: Khuda Bakhsh Oriental Public Library, 1979.

Lawson, Philip. *The East India Company: A History.* London: Longman, 1993.

Lefèvre, Corinne. "In the Name of the Fathers: Mughal Genealogical Strategies from Bābur to Shāh Jahān." In *Religions of South Asia 5.* Vols. 1–2: *Genealogy and History in South Asia,* ed. Simon Brodbeck and James M. Hegarty. London: Equinox, 2011.

———. "Pouvoir et noblesse dans l'Empire moghol: Perspectives du règne de Jahāngīr (1605–1627)." *Annales: Histoire, Sciences Sociales* 62, no. 6 (2007): 1287–1312.

Lewis, Archibald. "Maritime Skills in the Indian Ocean, 1368–1500." *Journal of the Economic and Social History of the Orient* 16 (1973): 238–264.

Lockhart, Laurence. *Nadir Shah: A Critical Study Based Mainly upon Contemporary Sources.* London: Luzac, 1938.

Lombard, Denys, and Jean Aubin, eds. *Marchands et hommes d'affaires asiatiques dans l'Océan Indien et la mer de Chine 13e–20e siècles.* Paris: Editions de l'Ecole des hautes études en sciences socials, 1988.

Longhena, Mario, ed. *Viaggi in Persia, India e Giava di Nicolo de Conti, Girolamo Adorno e Girolamo da Santo Stefano.* Mailand: Edizioni "Alpes," 1929.

Magalhães-Godhino, Vitorino. *L'économie de l'empire portugais aux XVe et XVIe siècles: Ports—routes—traffic.* Paris: S.E.V.P.E.N., 1969.

———. *Les finances de l'État portugais des Indes orientales 1517–1635: Matériaux pour une étude structurale et conjuncturelle.* Paris: Fundação Calouste Gulbenkian, 1982.

Majumdar, Ramesh Chandra, ed. *The Delhi Sultanate.* Vol 6 of *The History and Culture of the Indian People.* Bombay: Bharatiya Vidya Bhavan, 1960.

Malekandathil, Pius. *Portuguese Cochin and the Maritime Trade of India, 1500–1663.* New Delhi: Manohar, 2001.

Mann, Michael. *Bengalen im Umbruch: Die Herausbildung des britischen Kolonialstaates, 1754–1793*. Stuttgart: Steiner, 2000.

———. "Ein langes 18. Jahrhundert: Südasien." In *Die Welt im 18. Jahrhundert,* ed. Bernd Hausberger and Jean-Paul Lehners. Vienna: Mandelbaum, 2011.

———. *Geschichte Indiens. Vom 18. bis zum 21. Jahrhundert.* Paderborn: Schöningh, 2005.

Marchant, Leslie Ronald. *The Papal Line of Demarcation and Its Impact in the Eastern Hemisphere on the Political Division of Australia, 1479–1829.* Greenwood: Woodside Valley Foundation, 2008.

Marshall, Peter J., ed. *Bengal: The British Bridgehead: Eastern India, 1740–1828.* Vol. 2, Part 2 of *The New Cambridge History of India.* Cambridge: Cambridge University Press, 1987.

Mathew, Kalloor M. *History of the Portuguese Navigation in India, 1497–1600.* Delhi: Mittal Publications, 1988.

———. *Portuguese and the Sultanate of Gujarat, 1500–1573.* New Delhi: Mittal Publications, 1986.

———. *Portuguese Trade with India in the Sixteenth Century.* New Delhi: Manohar, 1983.

Matta, Basheer Ahmad Khan. *Sher Shah Suri: A Fresh Perspective.* Karachi: Oxford University Press, 2005.

Matthee, Rudi. *The Politics of Trade in Safavid Iran: Silk for Silver, 1600–1730.* Cambridge: Cambridge University Press, 1999.

Matthee, Rudi, and Jorge Flores, eds. *Portugal, the Persian Gulf and Safavid Persia.* Leuven: Peeters, 2011.

McLane, John R. *Land and Local Kingship in Eighteenth-Century Bengal.* Cambridge: Cambridge University Press, 1993.

McPherson, Kenneth. *The Indian Ocean: A History of People and the Sea.* 2nd ed. Delhi: Oxford University Press, 2001.

McPherson, Kenneth, and Sanjay Subrahmanyam, eds. *From Biography to History: Essays in the History of Portuguese Asia (1500–1800).* New Delhi: Transbooks, 2005.

Meloy, John L. *Imperial Power and Maritime Trade: Mecca and Cairo in the Later Middle Ages.* Chicago: Middle East Documentation Center, 2010.

Michaels, Axel. *Hinduism: Past and Present.* Princeton, NJ: Princeton University Press, 2004.

Michell, George. *The Vijayanagara Courtly Style: Incorporation and Synthesis in the Royal Architecture of Southern India, 15th–17th Centuries.* New Delhi: Manohar, 1992.

Middleton, John. *The World of the Swahili: An African Mercantile Civilization.* New Haven, CT: Yale University Press, 1992.

Mohan, Surendra. *Awadh under the Nawabs: Politics, Culture and Communal Relations, 1722–1856.* New Delhi: Manohar, 1997.

Moin, A. Azfar. *The Millennial Sovereign: Sacred Kingship and Sainthood in Islam.* New York: Columbia University Press, 2012.

Morgan, David. *Medieval Persia, 1040–1797*. London: Longman, 1988.

Nagel, Jürgen G. *Abenteuer Fernhandel: Die Ostindienkompanien*. Darmstadt: Wissenschaftliche Buchgesellschaft, 2007.

Nayeem, Muhammad A. *Mughal Administration of Deccan under Nizamul Mulk Asaf Jah (1720–1748 AD)*. Bombay: Jaico Publishing House, 1985.

Nesbitt, Eleanor. *Sikhism: A Very Short Introduction*. Oxford: Oxford University Press, 2005.

Newman, Andrew J. *Safavid Iran: Rebirth of a Persian Empire*. London: Tauris, 2006.

Nizami, Khaliq A. *Some Aspects of Religion and Politics in India during the Thirteenth Century*. New Delhi: Idarah-i Adabiyat-i Delli, 1974.

Nizami, Khaliq A., and Mohammad Habib, eds. *The Delhi Sultanat*. Vol. 5 of *A Comprehensive History of India*. New Delhi: People's Publishers House, 1970.

Osterhammel, Jürgen. *Die Entzauberung Asiens: Europa und die asiatischen Reiche im 18. Jahrhundert*. 2nd ed. Munich: Beck, 2010.

———. *The Transformation of the World: A Global History of the Nineteenth Century*. Translated by Patrick Camiller. Princeton, NJ: Princeton University Press, 2014.

Özbaran, Salih. *Ottoman Expansion towards the Indian Ocean in the 16th Century*. Istanbul: Istanbul Bilgi University Press, 2009.

———. *The Ottoman Response to European Expansion: Studies on Ottoman-Portuguese Relations in the Indian Ocean and Ottoman Administration in the Arab Lands during the Sixteenth Century*. Istanbul: Isis Press, 1994.

———. *Portuguese Encounters with the World in the Age of the Discoveries: The Near and Middle East*. London: Ashgate, 2008.

Parthasarathi, Prasannan. *The Transition to a Colonial Economy: Weavers, Merchants and Kings in South India, 1720–1800*. Cambridge: Cambridge University Press, 2001.

Patel, Alka. *Building Communities in Gujarat: Architecture and Society during the Twelfth through Fourteenth Centuries*. Leiden: Brill, 2004.

Pearson, Michael N. *The Indian Ocean*. London: Routledge, 2003.

———. *Merchants and Rulers in Gujarat: The Response to the Portuguese in the Sixteenth Century*. Berkeley: University of California Press, 1976.

———. *Pilgrimage to Mecca: The Indian Experience*. Princeton, NJ: Wiener, 1996.

———. *Port Cities and Intruders: The Swahili Coast, India, and Portugal in the Early Modern Era*. Baltimore: Johns Hopkins University Press, 1998.

———. *The Portuguese in India*. Cambridge: Cambridge University Press, 1987.

Petry, Carl F., ed. *Islamic Egypt, 640–1517*. Vol. 1 of *The Cambridge History of Egypt*. Cambridge: Cambridge University Press, 1998.

———. *Modern Egypt, from 1517 to the End of the Twentieth Century*. Vol. 2 of *The Cambridge History of Egypt*. Cambridge: Cambridge University Press, 1998.

Polo, Marco. *The Description of the World*. Translated by Arthur-Christopher Moule and Paul Pelliot. London: Routledge, 1938.

Prakash, Om. *European Commercial Enterprise in Pre-Colonial India*. Cambridge: Cambridge University Press, 1998.

———, ed. *European Commercial Expansion in Early Modern Asia*. Aldershot, UK: Variorum, 1997.

———. *Precious Metals and Commerce: The Dutch East India Company in the Indian Ocean Trade*. Aldershot, UK: Variorum, 1994.

Ptak, Roderich, ed. *Portuguese Asia: Aspects in History and Economic History, Sixteenth and Seventeenth Centuries*. Wiesbaden: Steiner, 1987.

Ptak, Roderich, and Dietmar Rothermund, eds. *Emporia, Commodities and Entrepreneurs in Asian Maritime Trade, c. 1400–1700*. Stuttgart: Steiner, 1991.

Purnaqcheband, Nader. *Strategien der Kontingenzbewältigung: Der Mogulherrscher Humayun (r. 1530–1540 und 1555–1556) dargestellt in der "Tazkirat al-Waqi'at" seines Leibdieners Jauhar Aftabci*. Schenefeld: EB-Verlag, 2007.

Radkau, Joachim. *Natur und Macht: Eine Weltgeschichte der Umwelt*. Munich: Beck, 2000.

Raychaudhuri, Tapan. "The Agrarian System of Mughal India: A Review Essay." *Enquiry* 2, no. 1 (1965): 92–121.

———. *Bengal under Akbar and Jahangir: An Introductory Study in Social History*. 2nd ed. Delhi: Munshiram Manoharlal, 1969.

———. "The State and the Economy: 1. The Mughal Empire." In *The Cambridge Economic History of India*. Vol. 1: *c. 1200–c. 1750*, ed. Tapan Raychaudhuri and Irfan Habib. Cambridge: Cambridge University Press, 1982.

Raychaudhuri, Tapan, and Irfan Habib, eds. *C. 1200–c. 1750*. Vol. 1 of *The Cambridge Economic History of India*. Cambridge: Cambridge University Press, 1982.

Reid, Anthony. *Southeast Asia in the Age of Commerce, 1450–1680*. 2 vols. New Haven, CT: Yale University Press, 1988–1993.

Reinhard, Wolfgang. *Die Alte Welt bis 1818*. Vol. 1 of *Geschichte der europäischen Expansion*. Stuttgart: Kohlhammer, 1983.

Richards, John F. *The Mughal Administration in Golconda*. Oxford: Clarendon Press, 1975.

———. *The Mughal Empire*. Cambridge: Cambridge University Press, 1993.

———. *The Unending Frontier: An Environmental History of the Early Modern World*. Berkeley: University of California Press, 2003.

Riello, Giorgio, and Tirthankar Roy, eds. *How India Clothed the World: The World of South Asian Textiles, 1500–1850*. Leiden: Brill, 2009.

Risso, Patricia. *Merchants and Faith: Muslim Commerce and Culture in the Indian Ocean*. Boulder, CO: Westview Press, 1995.

Roemer, Hans Robert. *Persien auf dem Weg in die Neuzeit: Iranische Geschichte von 1350–1750*. Stuttgart: Steiner, 1989.

Roy, Atul C. *A History of Mughal Navy and Naval Warfares*. Calcutta: World Press, 1972.

Santos, Catarina M. *Goa é a chave de toda a Índia: Perfil político da capital do Estado da Índia 1505–1570.* Lisbon: Comissão Nacional para as Comemorações dos Descobrimentos Portugueses, 1999.

Satyanarayana, Adapa. *History of the Wodeyars of Mysore (1610–1748).* Mysore: Directorate of Archaeology and Museums, 1996.

Savory, Roger. *Iran under the Safavids.* Cambridge: Cambridge University Press, 1980.

Schulze, Reinhard. "Das Warten auf die Moderne: Die Islamische Welt." In *Die Welt im 18. Jahrhundert,* ed. Bernd Hausberger and Jean-Paul Lehners. Vienna: Mandelbaum, 2011.

Sen, Sudipta. *Empire of Free Trade: The East India Company and the Making of the Colonial Marketplace.* Philadelphia: University of Pennsylvania Press, 1998.

Serjeant, Robert B. *The Portuguese off the South Arabian Coast: Hadrami Chronicles, with Yemeni and European Accounts of Dutch Pirates off Mocha in the Seventeenth Century.* Oxford: Clarendon Press, 1963.

Singh, Mahendra P. *Town, Market, Mint and Port in the Mughal Empire, 1556–1707: An Administrative-Cum-Economic Study.* New Delhi: Adam Publishers, 1985.

Soucek, Svat. *Piri Reis and Turkish Mapmaking after Columbus.* London: Nor Foundation, 1996.

Steensgaard, Niels. *The Asian Trade Revolution of the Seventeenth Century: The East India Companies and the Decline of the Caravan Trade.* Chicago: University of Chicago Press, 1974.

Stein, Burton. *Vijayanagara.* Cambridge: Cambridge University Press, 1994.

Stevens, Harm. *Dutch Enterprise and the VOC, 1602–1799.* Zutphen: Walburg, 1998.

Strachan, Michael. *Sir Thomas Roe, 1581–1644: A Life.* Salisbury, UK: M. Russell, 1989.

Streusand, Douglas E. *The Formation of the Mughal Empire.* Delhi: Oxford University Press, 1989.

Subrahmanyam, Sanjay. *Improvising Empire: Portuguese Trade and Settlement in the Bay of Bengal, 1500–1700.* Delhi: Oxford University Press, 1990.

———. *The Portuguese Empire in Asia 1500–1700: A Political and Economic History.* London: Longman, 1993.

Šumovskij, Theodor A. *Arabskie locii kak istoriko-literaturnye pamjatniki novogo kačestva.* Moscow: Izdat. Akad. Nauk SSSR, 1960.

———. *Tri neizvestnye locii Achmada ibn Madžida, arabskogo locmana Vasko da Gamy.* Moscow: Izdat. Akad. Nauk SSSR, 1957.

Tibbetts, Gerald R. *Arab Navigation in the Indian Ocean before the Coming of the Portuguese.* London: Royal Asiatic Society, 1971.

———. *The Navigational Theory of the Arabs in the Fifteenth and Sixteenth Centuries.* Coimbra: Junta de Investigações do Ultramar, 1969.

Turan, Ebru. "The Sultan's Favorite: Ibrahim Paşa and the Making of the Ottoman Universal Sovereignty in the Reign of Sultan Süleyman, 1516–1526." PhD diss., University of Chicago, 2007.

Vallet, Éric. *L'Arabie marchande: État et commerce sous les sultans Rasūlides du Yémen (626–858 /1229–1454)*. Paris: Publications de la Sorbonne, 2010.

———. "Les sultans rasûlides du Yémen, protecteurs des communautés musulmanes de l'Inde (VIIe–VIIIe / XIIe–XIVe siècle)." *Annales Islamologiques* 41 (2007): 149–176.

Varthema, Ludovico de. *The Itinerary of Ludovico di Varthema of Bologna from 1502–1508*. Translated and edited by John Winter Jones. London: Argonaut Press, 1928.

———. *The Travels of Ludovico di Varthema in Egypt, Syria, Arabia Deserta and Arabia Felix, in Persia, India, and Ethiopia, AD 1503–1508*. Translated and edited by John Winter Jones. London: Hakluyt Society, 1863.

Verghese, Anila. *Hampi*. New Delhi: Oxford University Press, 2002.

Wagoner, Phillip B. *Tidings of the King: A Translation and Ethnohistorical Analysis of the Rayavacakamu*. Honolulu: University of Hawai'i Press, 1993.

Weiss, Bernard G. *The Spirit of Islamic Law*. Athens: University of Georgia Press, 1998.

Wiet, Gaston. *Les marchands d'épices sous les sultans mamlouks*. Cairo: Editions des Cahiers d'histoire égyptienne, 1955.

Winius, George. "The 'Shadow Empire' of Goa in the Bay of Bengal." *Itinerario* 7, no. 2 (1983): 83–101.

Wink, André. *Akbar*. Oxford: Oneworld, 2009.

———. *Indo-Islamic Society: 14th–15th Centuries*. Vol. 3 of *The Making of the Indo-Islamic World*. Leiden: Brill, 2004.

———. *Land and Sovereignty in India: Agrarian Society and Politics under the Eighteenth-Century Maratha Svarajya*. Cambridge: Cambridge University Press, 1986.

Witteveen, Menno. *Een onderneming van landsbelang: De oprichting van de Verenigde Oost-Indische Compagnie in 1602*. Amsterdam: Amsterdam University Press, 2002.

Ziegler, Norman P. "Some Notes on Rajput Loyalties during the Mughal Period." In *Kingship and Authority in South Asia*. 2nd ed. Edited by John F. Richards. Madison: University of Wisconsin Press, 1981.

Southeast Asia and Oceania

Abu-Lughod, Janet. *Before European Hegemony: The World System, AD 1250–1350*. Oxford: Oxford University Press, 1989.

Ahrndt, Wiebke, and Udo Allerbeck, eds. *Ozeanien: Lebenswelten in der Südsee*. Bremen: Übersee-Museum, 2003.

Alberts, Tara. *Conflict and Conversion: Catholicism in Southeast Asia, 1500–1700*. Oxford: Oxford University Press, 2013.

Amyot, Jacques. *The Manila Chinese: Familism in the Philippine Environment*. Quezon City: Institute of Philippine Culture, 1973.

Andaya, Leonard Y. *The Heritage of Arung Palakka: A History of South Sulawesi (Celebes) in the Seventeenth Century*. The Hague: Nijhoff, 1981.

———. *The World of Maluku: Eastern Indonesia in the Early Modern Period*. Honolulu: University of Hawai'i Press, 1993.

Andrade, Tonio. "The Rise and Fall of Dutch Taiwan, 1624–1662: Cooperative Colonization and the Statist Model of European Expansion." *Journal of World History* 17, no. 4 (2006): 429–450.

Ang See, Teresita, ed. *Tsinoy: The Story of the Chinese in Philippine Life*. Manila: Kaisa Para Sa Kaunlaran, 2005.

Appel, Michaela. *Ozeanien: Weltbilder der Südsee*. Munich: Staatliches Museum für Völkerkunde, 2005.

———. "Textilien in Südostasien." In *Ostasiatische Kunst*. Vol. 2, ed. Gabriele Fahr-Becker. Cologne: Könemann, 1998.

Appel, Michaela, and Rose Schubert. "Schiffahrt und frühe Schiffsdarstellungen in Südostasien." In *Kolumbus oder wer entdeckte Amerika?*, ed. Wolfgang Stein. Munich: Hirmer, 1992.

Baker, Chris. "Ayutthaya Rising: From Land or Sea?" *Journal of Southeast Asian Studies* 34 (2003): 41–62.

Basu, Dilip K., ed. *The Rise and Growth of the Colonial Port Cities in Asia*. Lanham, MD: University Press of America, 1985.

Belich, James. *Making Peoples: A History of the New Zealanders, from Polynesian Settlement to the End of the Nineteenth Century*. Auckland: Lane, 1996.

Bellwood, Peter. "The Austronesian Dispersal." In *Arts of the South Seas: Island Southeast Asia, Melanesia, Polynesia, Micronesia*, ed. Douglas Newton. Munich: Prestel, 1999.

Bitterli, Urs. *Asien, Australien, Pazifik*. Vol. 2 of *Die Entdeckung und Eroberung der Welt: Dokumente und Berichte*. Munich: C. H. Beck, 1981.

Blussé, Leonard. "Batavia 1619–1740: The Rise and Fall of a Chinese Colonial Town." *Journal of Southeast Asian Studies* 12 (1981): 159–178.

Bonn, Gerhard. *Engelbert Kaempfer (1651–1716): Der Reisende und sein Einfluß auf die europäische Bewußtseinsbildung über Asien*. Frankfurt am Main: Peter Lang, 2003.

Boomgaard, Peter. *Southeast Asia: An Environmental History*. Santa Barbara, CA: ABC-Clio, 2007.

Boon, James A. *The Anthropological Romance of Bali, 1597–1972: Dynamic Perspectives in Marriage and Caste, Politics and Religion*. Cambridge: Cambridge University Press, 1977.

Boxer, Charles R. *Francisco Vieira: A Portuguese Merchant Adventurer in South East Asia, 1624–1667*. The Hague: Nijhoff, 1967.

Bray, Francesca. *The Rice Economies: Technology and Development in Asian Societies*. Berkeley: University of California Press, 1994.

Buchholz, Hanns J. *Australien—Neuseeland—Südpazifik*. Frankfurt am Main: Fischer, 1984.

Bulbeck, David, et al., eds. *Southeast Asian Exports since the 14th Century: Cloves, Pepper, Coffee, and Sugar*. Leiden: KITLV Press, 1998.

Byrnes, Giselle, ed. *The New Oxford History of New Zealand*. South Melbourne: Oxford University Press, 2009.

Castillo y Tuazon, Teofilo del, and Buenaventura S. Medina. *Philippine Literature from Ancient Times to the Present*. Manila: Del Castillo, 1966.

Chandler, David. *A History of Cambodia*. 4th ed. Boulder, CO: Westview Press, 2008.

Chaudhuri, Kirti N. *Asia before Europe: Economy and Civilisation of the Indian Ocean from the Rise of Islam to 1750*. Cambridge: Cambridge University Press, 1990.

Chihara, Daigoro. *Hindu-Buddhist Architecture in Southeast Asia*. Leiden: Brill, 1996.

Chirino S. J., Pedro. *Relación de las Islas Filipinas: The Philippines in 1600*. Translated by Ramón Echevarría [1600]. Manila: Bookmark, 1969.

Coedès, George. *The Indianized States of Southeast Asia*. Honolulu: East-West Center Press, 1968.

Cohen, Robin. *Global Diasporas: An Introduction*. London: UCL Press, 1997.

Colín, Francisco. *Labor evangélica, ministerios apostólicos de los obreros de la Compañía de Jesús, fundación y progresos de su provincia en las Islas Filipinas*. 3 vols. [1663]. Barcelona: Henrich y Compañía en comandita, 1904.

Comrie, Bernard. *The Major Languages of East and South-East Asia*. London: Routledge, 1990.

Corpuz, Onofre D. *An Economic History of the Philippines*. Quezon City: University of the Philippines Press, 1997.

Cribb, Robert. *Historical Atlas of Indonesia*. Honolulu: University of Hawai'i Press, 2000.

———. *Historical Dictionary of Indonesia*. Metuchen, NJ: Scarecrow Press, 1992.

Crosby, Alfred W. *The Columbian Exchange: Biological and Cultural Consequences of 1492*. Westport, CT: Greenwood Press, 1972.

Dahm, Bernhard. "Kulturelle Identität und Modernisierung in Südostasien." In *Kulturbegriff und Methode: Der stille Paradigmenwechsel in den Geisteswissenschaften*, ed. Klaus P. Hansen. Tübingen: Narr, 1993.

Dahm, Bernhard, and Roderich Ptak, eds. *Südostasien-Handbuch: Geschichte, Gesellschaft, Politik, Wirtschaft, Kultur*. Munich: C. H. Beck, 1999.

Daus, Ronald. *Portuguese Eurasian Communities in Southeast Asia*. Singapore: Institute for Southeast Asian Studies, 1989.

Davidson, Janet M. *The Prehistory of New Zealand*. 2nd ed. Auckland: Longman Paul, 1992.

Demel, Walter, ed. *Entdeckungen und neue Ordnungen, 1200 bis 1800*. Vol. 4 of *Wissenschaftliche Buchgesellschaft Weltgeschichte [WB Weltgeschichte]*. Darmstadt: Wissenschaftliche Buchgesellschaft, 2010.

———. "Europäische Entdeckungsreisen vor Kolumbus." In *Kolumbus oder wer entdeckte Amerika?*, ed. Wolfgang Stein. Munich: Hirmer, 1992.

Denoon, Donald, ed. *The Cambridge History of the Pacific Islanders.* Cambridge: Cambridge University Press, 1997.

Denoon, Donald, Philippa Mein-Smith, and Marivic Wyndham. *A History of Australia, New Zealand, and the Pacific.* Oxford: Blackwell, 2000.

Dijk, Wil O. *Seventeenth-Century Burma and the Dutch East India Company.* Singapore: Singapore University Press, 2006.

Dunn, Malcolm. *Kampf um Melakka: Eine wirtschaftsgeschichtliche Studie über den portugiesischen und niederländischen Kolonialismus in Südostasien.* Wiesbaden: Steiner, 1984.

Edwards, Hugh. *Islands of Angry Ghosts.* London: Hodder & Stoughton, 1966.

Eggebrecht, Arne, and Eva Eggebrecht, ed. *Versunkene Königreiche Indonesiens.* Mainz: von Zabern, 1995.

Ehrenpreis, Stefan. "Erziehung, Bildung und Wissenschaft." In *Entdeckungen und neue Ordnungen, 1200 bis 1800.* Vol. 4 of *WBG Weltgeschichte,* ed. Walter Demel. Darmstadt: Wissenschaftliche Buchgesellschaft, 2010.

Emmerson, Donald K. "'Southeast Asia': What's in a Name." *Journal of Southeast Asian Studies* 15, no. 1 (1984): 1–21.

Engelbert, Thomas. *Die chinesische Minderheit im Süden Vietnams (Hoa) als Paradigma der kolonialen und nationalistischen Nationalitätenpolitik.* Frankfurt am Main: Lang, 2002.

Ertl, Thomas, and Michael Limberger, eds. *Die Welt 1250–1500.* Vol. 1 of *Globalgeschichte. Die Welt 1000–2000.* Vienna: Mandelbaum, 2009.

Feldbauer, Peter. *Estado da India: Die Portugiesen in Asien 1498–1620.* Vienna: Mandelbaum, 2003.

Feldbauer, Peter, and Jean-Paul Lehners, eds. *Die Welt im 16. Jahrhundert.* Vol. 3 of *Globalgeschichte. Die Welt 1000–2000.* Vienna: Mandelbaum, 2008.

Fessen, Helmut, and Hans Dieter Kubitschek. *Geschichte Thailands.* Münster: Lit, 1994.

Finney, Ben. "Colonizing an Island World." In *Prehistoric Settlement of the Pacific,* ed. Ward H. Goodenough. Philadelphia: American Philosophical Society, 1996.

Fisch, Jörg. *Hollands Ruhm in Asien: François Valentyns Vision des niederländischen Imperiums im 18. Jahrhundert.* Stuttgart: Steiner, 1986.

Flannery, Tim. *The Future Eaters: An Ecological History of the Australasian Lands and People.* Chatswood: Reed, 1994.

Foley, Kathy, ed. *Essays on Southeast Asian Performing Arts: Local Manifestations and Cross-Cultural Implications.* Berkeley: International and Area Studies, University of California, 1992.

Frank, André Gunder. *ReOrient: Global Economy in the Asian Age.* Berkeley: University of California Press, 1998.

Frasch, Tilman. "Eine Region in der Krise? Südostasien." In *Die Welt im 17. Jahrhundert.* Vol. 4 of *Globalgeschichte. Die Welt 1000–2000,* ed. Bernd Hausberger. Vienna: Mandelbaum, 2008.

———. "Muslime und Christen: Gewürze und Kanonen" In *Die Welt im 16. Jahrhundert.* Vol. 3 of *Globalgeschichte. Die Welt 1000–2000,* ed. Peter Feldbauer and Jean-Paul Lehners. Vienna: Mandelbaum, 2008.

———. *Pagan: Stadt und Staat.* Stuttgart: Steiner, 1996.

———. "Partikularismus und Kulturtransfer am Rande der Welt: Südostasien." In *Die Welt 1250–1500.* Vol. 1 of *Globalgeschichte. Die Welt 1000–2000,* ed. Thomas Ertl and Michael Limberger. Vienna: Mandelbaum, 2009.

Frings, Jutta, ed. *James Cook und die Entdeckung der Südsee.* Munich: Hirmer, 2009.

Gale, Mary-Anne. *Dhanum Djorra'Wuy Dhawu: A History of Writing in Aboriginal Languages.* Underdale: Aboriginal Research Institute, University of South Australia, 1997.

Gesick, Lorraine, ed. *Centers, Symbols, and Hierarchies: Essays on the Classical States of Southeast Asia.* New Haven, CT: Yale University Southeast Asian Studies, 1983.

Giesing, Cornelia. "Das vorkolumbische Amerika aus circumpazifischer Sicht." In *Kolumbus oder wer entdeckte Amerika?,* ed. Wolfgang Stein. Munich: Hirmer, 1992.

Girard-Geslan, Maud. *Südostasien: Kunst und Kultur.* Freiburg: Herder, 1995.

Goch, Ulrich. "Das Neue an der Japansicht Engelbert Kaempfers." In *Engelbert Kaempfer (1651–1716): Ein Gelehrtenleben zwischen Tradition und Innovation,* ed. Detlef Haberland. Wiesbaden: Harrassowitz, 2004.

Gommans, Jos, and Jacques Leider, ed. *The Maritime Frontier of Burma.* Amsterdam: Koninklijke Nederlandse Akademie van Wetenschapen, 2002.

Guillot, Claude, Denys Lombard, and Roderich Ptak, eds. *From the Mediterranean to the China Sea.* Wiesbaden: Harrassowitz, 1998.

Gunn, Geoffrey C. *First Globalization: The Eurasian Exchange, 1500–1800.* Lanham, MD: Rowman & Littlefield, 2003.

Guy, John S. *Oriental Trade Ceramics in South-East Asia, 9th to 16th Century: With a Catalogue of Chinese, Vietnamese and Thai Wares in Australian Collections.* Singapore: Oxford University Press, 1990.

Hägerdal, Hans. *Hindu Rulers, Muslim Subjects: Lombok and Bali in the Seventeenth and Eighteenth Centuries.* Bangkok: White Lotus, 2001.

Hagesteijn, Renée. *Circles of Kings: Political Dynamics in Early Continental Southeast Asia.* Dordrecht: Foris, 1989.

Hall, Daniel George Edward, ed. *Historians of South East Asia.* London: Oxford University Press, 1961.

———. *A History of South-East Asia.* 4th ed. London: Macmillan, 1981.

Hall, Kenneth R. "Multi-Dimensional Networking: Fifteenth-Century Indian Ocean Maritime Diaspora in Southeast Asian Perspective." *Journal of the Economic and Social History of the Orient* 49, no. 4 (2006): 454–481.

———. "The Opening of the Malay World to European Trade in the Sixteenth Century." *Journal of the Malaysian Branch of the Royal Asiatic Society* 58, no. 2 (1985): 85–106.

———. "The Textile Industry in Southeast Asia, 1400–1800." *Journal of the Economic and Social History of the Orient* 39, no. 2 (1996): 87–135.

Hanks, Lucien M. *Rice and Man: Agricultural Ecology in Southeast Asia*. Chicago: Aldine, 1972.

Hanlon, David L. *Upon a Stone Altar: A History of the Island of Pohnpei to 1890*. Honolulu: University of Hawai'i Press, 1988.

Hanna, Willard A. *Bali Profile: People, Events, Circumstances (1001–1976)*. New York: American University Field Staff, 1976.

Hausberger, Bernd, ed. *Die Welt im 17. Jahrhundert*. Vol. 4 of *Globalgeschichte. Die Welt 1000–2000*. Vienna: Mandelbaum, 2008.

Heathcote, Ronald L. *Australia*. 2nd ed. Harlow, UK: Longman, 1994.

Heermann, Ingrid. *Mythos Tahiti: Südsee—Traum und Realität*. Berlin: Reimer, 1987.

Höllmann, Thomas O. "Statusbestimmung und Entscheidungsfindung bei den autochthonen Bevölkerungsgruppen Taiwans nach Schriftzeugnissen des 17. und 18. Jahrhunderts." *Saeculum* 55 (2004): 323–332.

Horridge, G. Adrian. *The Prahu: Traditional Sailing Boat of Indonesia*. 2nd ed. Singapore: Oxford University Press, 1985.

Howe, Kerry. *Where the Waves Fall: A New South Sea Islands History from First Settlement to Colonial Rule*. Sydney: Allen & Unwin, 1984.

Ishii, Yoneo. *Sangha, State and Society: Thai Buddhism in History*. Honolulu: University of Hawai'i Press, 1986.

Jacq-Hergoualc'h, Michel. *L'Europe et le Siam du XVIe au XVIIIe Siècle: Apports culturels*. Paris: L'Harmattan, 1993.

———. *The Malay Peninsula: Crossroads of the Maritime Silk Road*. Leiden: Brill, 2002.

Jonge, Nico de, and Toos van Dijk. *Forgotten Islands of Indonesia: The Art and Culture of the Southeast Moluccas*. Singapore: Periplus Editions, 1995.

Kathirithamby-Wells, Jeyamalar, and John Villiers, ed. *The Southeast Asian Port and Polity: Rise and Demise*. Singapore: Singapore University Press, 1990.

King, Victor T. *The Peoples of Borneo*. Oxford: Blackwell, 1993.

Knaap, Gerrit J. *Kruidnagelen en christenen: De Verenigde Oostindische Compangnie en de bevolking van Ambon 1656–1696*. Dordrecht: Foris, 1987.

———. *Shallow Waters, Rising Tide: Shipping and Trade in Java around 1775*. Leiden: KITLV Press, 1996.

Knapen, Han. *Forests of Fortune? The Environmental History of Southeast Borneo, 1600–1880*. Leiden: KITLV Press, 2001.

Kratoska, Paul, Remco Raben, and Henk Schulte Nordholt, eds. *Locating Southeast Asia: Geographies of Knowledge and Politics of Space*. Singapore: Singapore University Press, 2005.

Kreiner, Josef. "Okinawa und Ainu." In *Grundriß der Japanologie,* ed. Klaus Kracht and Markus Rüttermann. Wiesbaden: Harrassowitz, 2001.

———, ed. *The Road to Japan: Social and Economic Aspects of Early European-Japanese Contacts*. Bonn: Bier'sche Verlagsanstalt, 2005.

———. *Ryûkyû in World History*. Bonn: Bier'sche Verlagsanstalt, 2001.

Kubitscheck, Hans-Dieter. *Südostasien: Völker und Kulturen*. Berlin: Akademie-Verlag, 1984.

Kulke, Hermann. "The Early and the Imperial Kingdom in Southeast Asian History." In *Southeast Asia in the 9th to 14th Centuries,* ed. David G. Marr and A. C. Milner. Singapore: Institute of Southeast Asian Studies, 1986.

———. "Maritimer Kulturtransfer im Indischen Ozean. Theorien zur 'Indisierung' Südostasiens im 1. Jahrtausend n.Chr." *Saeculum* 56 (2005): 173–197.

Lach, Donald F. *Asia in the Making of Europe*. Vol. 2: *A Century of Wonder*. Book 2: *The Literary Arts*. Chicago: University of Chicago Press, 1977.

———. *Asia in the Making of Europe*. Vol. 3: *A Century of Advance*. Book 3: *Southeast Asia*. Chicago: University of Chicago Press, 1993.

Lamping, Heinrich, ed. *Australia: Studies on the History of Discovery and Exploration*. Frankfurt am Main: Institut für Sozialgeographie der Johann-Wolfgang-Goethe-Universität, 1994.

Leach, Edmund R. *Political Systems of Highland Burma: A Study of Kachin Social Structure*. London: London School of Economics and Political Science, 1954.

LeBar, Frank M. *Ethnic Groups of Insular Southeast Asia*. 2 vols. New Haven, CT: Human Relations Area Files Press, 1972–1975.

LeBar, Frank M., Gerlad C. Hickey, and John K. Musgrave. *Ethnic Groups of Mainland Southeast Asia*. New Haven, CT: Human Relations Area Files Press, 1964.

Leigh-Theisen, Heide, and Reinhold Mittersakschmöller. *Lebensmuster: Textilien in Indonesien*. Vienna: Museum für Völkerkunde, 1995.

Leur, Jacob C. van. *Indonesian Trade and Society: Essays in Asian Social and Economic History*. The Hague: Van Hoeve, 1955.

Lieberman, Victor. *Integration on the Mainland*. Vol. 1 of *Strange Parallels: Southeast Asia in Global Context, c. 800–1830*. Cambridge: Cambridge University Press, 2003.

Li Tana. *Nguyen Cochinchina: Southern Vietnam in the 17th and 18th Centuries*. Ithaca, NY: Southeast Asia Program, Cornell University, 1998.

Lockard, Craig A. "'The Sea Common to All': Maritime Frontiers, Port Cities, and Chinese Traders in the Southeast Asian Age of Commerce." *Journal of World History* 21 (2010): 219–247.

Lombard, Denys. *Le carrefour javanais: Essai d'histoire globale*. 3 vols. Paris: École des Hautes Études en Sciences Sociales, 1990.

———. *Le Sultanat d'Atjéh au temps d'Iskandar Muda, 1607–1636*. Paris: École français d'Extrême-Orient, 1967.

Lombard, Denys, and Jean Aubin, eds. *Asian Merchants and Businessmen in the Indian Ocean and the China Sea*. New Delhi: Oxford University Press, 2000.

Lommel, Andreas. *Motiv und Variation in der Kunst des zirkumpazifischen Raumes.* Munich: Museum für Völkerkunde, 1962.

Lubis, Mochtar. *Indonesia: Land under the Rainbow.* 2nd ed. Singapore: Oxford University Press, 1991.

Macintyre, Stuart. *A Concise History of Australia.* 3rd ed. Canberra: Cambridge University Press, 2009.

Macknight, Charles Campbell. *The Voyage to Marege': Macassan Trepangers in Northern Australia.* Carlton, Victoria: Melbourne University Press, 1976.

Malinowski, Bronislaw. *Argonauts of the Western Pacific: An Account of Native Enterprise and Adventure in the Archipelagoes of Melanesian New Guinea.* London: Routledge & Kegan Paul, 1922.

Manguin, Pierre-Yves. "Shipshape Societies: Boat Symbolism and Political Systems in Insular Southeast Asia." In *Southeast Asia in the 9th to 14th Centuries,* ed. David G. Marr and A. C. Milner. Singapore: Institute of Southeast Asian Studies, 1986.

Marr, David G., and Anthony C. Milner, eds. *Southeast Asia in the 9th to the 14th Centuries.* Singapore: Institute of Southeast Asian Studies, 1986.

Masashi, Haneda, ed. *Asian Port Cities, 1600–1800: Local and Foreign Cultural Interactions.* Singapore: National University of Singapore Press, 2009.

Matsuda, Matt K. *Pacific Worlds: A History of Seas, Peoples, and Cultures.* Cambridge: Cambridge University Press, 2012.

Maxwell, Robyn. *Textiles of Southeast Asia: Tradition, Trade, and Transformation.* Melbourne: Oxford University Press, 1990.

Mein Smith, Philippa. *A Concise History of New Zealand.* Cambridge: Cambridge University Press, 2005.

Meißner, Joachim. *Mythos Südsee: Das Bild von der Südsee im Europa des 18. Jahrhunderts.* Hildesheim: Olms, 2006.

Menter, Ulrich. *Ozeanien—Kult und Visionen: Verborgene Schätze aus deutschen Völkerkundemuseen.* Munich: Prestel, 2003.

Menzies, Gavin. *1421. The Year China Discovered America.* London: Bantam 2002.

Meyer, Anthony J. P., and Olaf Wipperfürth. *Oceanic Art.* Cologne: Könemann, 1995.

Mills, J. V. "Arab and Chinese Navigators in Malaysian Waters about AD 1500." *Journal of the Malaysian Branch of the Royal Asiatic Society* 47 (1974): 1–82.

Minahan, James. *Ethnic Groups of South Asia and the Pacific: An Encyclopedia.* Santa Barbara, CA: ABC-Clio, 2012.

Morga, Antonio de. *Sucesos de las Islas Filipinas (México 1609).* Translated and edited by J. S. Cummins. Cambridge: Cambridge University Press, 1971.

Mückler, Hermann. *Kolonialismus in Ozeanien.* Vienna: Facultas, 2012.

Mulvaney, Derek J. *Encounters in Place: Outsiders and Aboriginal Australians, 1606–1985.* St. Lucia: University of Queensland Press, 1989.

Nagel, Jürgen G. *Abenteuer Fernhandel: Die Ostindienkompanien.* 2nd ed. Darmstadt: Wissenschaftliche Buchgesellschaft, 2011.

———. "Kota, Kampung und fließende Grenze: Einige Überlegungen zur frühneuzeitlichen Stadtgeschichte Indonesien." In *"Das Wichtigste ist der Mensch": Festschrift für Klaus Gerteis zum 60. Geburtstag,* ed. Angela Giebmeyer and Helga Schnabel-Schüle. Mainz: Von Zabern, 2000.

———. "Makassar und der Molukkenhandel: Städte und Handelsnetze im indonesischen Gewürzhandel des 16. und 17. Jahrhunderts." In *Gewürze: Produktion, Handel und Konsum in der Frühen Neuzeit,* ed. Markus A. Denzel. St. Katharinen: Scripta Mercaturae, 1999.

———. "Predikanten und Ziekentrooster: Der Protestantismus in der Welt der Verenigden Oostindischen Compagnie." In *Europäische Aufklärung und protestantische Mission in Indien,* ed. Michael Mann. Heidelberg: Draupadi, 2006.

———. *Der Schlüssel zu den Molukken: Makassar und die Handelsstrukturen des Malaiischen Archipels im 17. und 18. Jahrhundert—eine exemplarische Studie.* Hamburg: Kovač, 2003.

———. "Usurpatoren und Pragmatiker: Einige typologische Überlegungen zur Strategie der niederländischen Ostindienkompanie (1602–1799)." In *Praktiken des Handels: Geschäfte und soziale Beziehungen europäischer Kaufleute in Mittelalter und früher Neuzeit,* ed. Mark Häberlein and Christof Jeggle. Konstanz: UVK, 2010.

Nas, Peter J. M., ed. *The Indonesian City: Studies in Urban Development and Planning.* Dordrecht: Foris, 1986.

Newitt, Malyn, ed. *The First Portuguese Colonial Empire.* Exeter, UK: University of Exeter, 1986.

Newton, Douglas, ed. *Arts of the South Seas: Island Southeast Asia, Melanesia, Polynesia, Micronesia.* Munich: Prestel, 1999.

Ng Chin Keong. *Trade and Society: The Amoy Network on the China Coast, 1683–1735.* Singapore: Singapore University Press, 1983.

Nugent, Maria. *Captain Cook Was Here.* Cambridge: Cambridge University Press, 2009.

Oliver, Douglas L. *Oceania: The Native Cultures of Australia and the Pacific Islands.* 2 vols. Honolulu: University of Hawai'i Press, 1989.

Oliver, William H., and Bridget R. Williams, eds. *The Oxford History of New Zealand.* Oxford: Clarendon Press, 1981.

Osman, Mohamed Taib, ed. *Islamic Civilization in the Malay World.* Kuala Lumpur: Dewan Bahasa dan Pustaka, 1997.

Owen, Norman G., ed. *Routledge Handbook of Southeast Asian History.* London: Routledge, 2014.

Pan, Lynn, ed. *The Encyclopedia of the Chinese Overseas.* Richmond, UK: Curzon, 1998.

Pelras, Christian. *The Bugis.* Oxford: Blackwell, 1996.

———. "Notes sur quelques populations aquatiques de l'Archipel nusantarien." *Archipel* 3 (1972): 133–168.

Pesigan, Guillermo M., and Charles J.-H. Macdonald, eds. *Old Ties and New Solidarities: Studies on Philippine Communities*. Manila: Ateneo de Manila University Press, 2000.

Phalgunadi, I Gusti Putu. *Evolution of Hindu Culture in Bali: From the Earliest Period to the Present Time*. Delhi: Sundeep Prakashan, 1991.

Phelan, John L. *The Hispanization of the Philippines: Spanish Aims and Filipino Responses, 1565–1700*. Madison: University of Wisconsin Press, 1967.

Pluvier, Jan M. *Historical Atlas of South-East Asia*. Leiden: Brill, 1995.

Prieto, Ana Maria. *El Contacto Hispano-Indígena en Filipinas según la Historiografía de los Siglos XVI y XVII*. Córdoba: Servicio de Publicaciones Universidad de Córdoba, 1993.

Ptak, Roderich. *China's Seaborne Trade with South and Southeast Asia (1200–1750)*. Aldershot, UK: Ashgate, 1999.

———. *Die chinesische maritime Expansion im 14. und 15. Jahrhundert*. Bamberg: Forschungsstiftung für Vergleichende europäische Überseegeschichte, 1992.

———. *Die maritime Seidenstraße: Küstenräume, Seefahrt und Handel in vorkolonialer Zeit*. Munich: C. H. Beck, 2007.

———. "Ming Maritime Trade to Southeast Asia, 1368–1567: Version of a 'System.'" In *From the Mediterranean to the China Sea,* ed. Claude Guillot, Denys Lombard, and Roderich Ptak. Wiesbaden: Harrassowitz, 1998.

Reed, Robert R. *Colonial Manila: The Context of Hispanic Urbanism and Process of Morphogenesis*. Berkeley: University of California Press, 1978.

Reid, Anthony, ed. *Charting the Shape of Early Modern Southeast Asia*. Chiang Mai: Silkworm Books, 2000.

———. *Expansion and Crisis*. Vol. 2 of *Southeast Asia in the Age of Commerce, 1450–1680*. New Haven, CT: Yale University Press, 1993.

———. "The Islamization of Southeast Asia." In *Charting the Shape of Early Modern Southeast Asia,* ed. Anthony Reid. Chiang Mai: Silkworm Books, 2000.

———. *The Lands below the Winds*. Vol. 1 of *Southeast Asia in the Age of Commerce, 1450–1680*. New Haven, CT: Yale University Press, 1988.

———. "The Seventeenth Century Crisis in Southeast Asia." *Modern Asian Studies* 24, no. 3 (1990): 639–659.

———, ed. *Southeast Asia in the Early Modern Era: Trade, Power, and Belief*. Ithaca, NY: Cornell University Press, 1993.

Remmelink, Willem. *The Chinese War and the Collapse of the Javanese State, 1725–1743*. Leiden: KITLV Press, 1994.

Rickard, John. *Australia: A Cultural History*. London: Longman, 1988.

Ricklefs, Merle C. *A History of Modern Indonesia since c. 1200*. 4th ed. Basingstoke, UK: Palgrave Macmillan, 2008.

———. *Mystic Synthesis in Java: A History of Islamization from the Fourteenth to the Early Nineteenth Centuries*. Norwalk, CT: EastBridge, 2006.

Rigg, Jonathan, ed. *The Gift of Water: Water Management, Cosmology and the State in South East Asia*. London: School of Oriental and African Studies, 1992.

Rodao, Florentino. *Españoles en Siam (1540–1939): Una aportación al estudio de la presencia hispana an Asia Oriental*. Madrid: Consejo Superior de Investigaciones Científicas, 1997.

Rothermund, Dietmar, and Roderich Ptak, eds. *Emporia, Commodities and Entrepreneurs in Asian Maritime Trade, c. 1400–1750*. Wiesbaden: Steiner, 1991.

Ruangsilp, Bhawan. *Dutch East India Company Merchants at the Court of Ayutthaya*. Leiden: Brill, 2007.

Salmon, Claudine. "Chinese Merchants in Southeast Asia." In *Asian Merchants and Businessmen in the Indian Ocean and the China Sea,* ed. Denys Lombard and Jean Aubin. New Delhi: Oxford University Press, 2000.

SarDesai, D. R. "The Portuguese Administration in Malacca, 1511–1641." *Journal of Southeast Asian History* 10 (1969): 501–512.

Sather, Clifford. *The Bajau Laut: Adaptation, History, and Fate in a Maritime Fishing Society of South-Eastern Sabah*. Kuala Lumpur: Oxford University Press, 1997.

Schilder, Günter. *Australia Unveiled: The Share of Dutch Navigators in the Discovery of Australia*. Amsterdam: Theatrum Orbis Terrarum, 1976.

Schrauwers, Albert. "Houses, Hierarchy, Headhunting and Exchange: Rethinking Political Relations in the Southeast Asian Realm of Luwu." *Bijdragen tot de Taal-, Land- en Volkenkunde* 153 (1997): 356–380.

Schubert, Rose, Ernst Feist, and Caroline Zelz. "Zur frühen Seefahrt in der Südsee: Schiffahrt und Navigation in Polynesien und Mikronesien." In *Kolumbus oder wer entdeckte Amerika?,* ed. Wolfgang Stein. Munich: Hirmer 1992.

Schultze, Michael. *Die Geschichte von Laos: Von den Anfängen bis zum Beginn der neunziger Jahre*. Hamburg: Institut für Asienkunde, 1994.

Schurz, William L. *The Manila Galleon*. New York: Dutton, 1959.

Scott, James C. *The Art of Not Being Governed: An Anarchist History of Upland Southeast Asia*. New Haven, CT: Yale University Press, 2009.

Scott-Ross, Marcus. *A Short History of Malacca*. Singapore: Chopmen, 1971.

Simms, Peter, and Sanda Simms. *The Kingdoms of Laos: Six Hundred Years of History*. Richmond, UK: Curzon, 1999.

Slametmuljana, R. B. *A Story of Majapahit*. Singapore: Singapore University Press, 1976.

Smith, Bernard. *European Vision and the South Pacific*. 2nd ed. New Haven, CT: Yale University Press, 1985.

Smyth, David, ed. *The Canon in Southeast Asian Literatures: Literatures of Burma, Cambodia, Indonesia, Laos, Malaysia, the Philippines, Thailand and Vietnam*. Richmond, UK: Curzon Press, 2000.

Soedjatmoko et al., eds. *An Introduction to Indonesian Historiography*. Ithaca, NY: Cornell University Press, 1965.

Solano, Francisco de, Florentino Rodao, and Luis E. Togores, eds. *Extremo Oriente Ibérico: Investigaciones Históricas: Metodología y Estado de la Cuestión*. Madrid: Centro de Estudios Históricos, 1989.

Sopher, David E. *The Sea Nomads: A Study Based on the Literature of the Maritime Boat People of Southeast Asia*. Singapore: National Museum, 1965.

Sorrenson, Maurice P. K. *Maori Origins and Migrations: The Genesis of Some Pakeha Myths and Legends*. Auckland: Auckland University Press, 1979.

Souza, George B. *The Survival of Empire: Portuguese Trade and Society in China and the South China Sea, 1630–1754*. Cambridge: Cambridge University Press, 1986.

Souza, Teotonio de, ed. *Indo-Portuguese History: Old Issues, New Questions*. New Delhi: Concept Publishers, 1985.

Spate, Oskar Hermann Khristian. *The Pacific since Magellan*. 3 vols. Canberra: Australian National University Press, 1979–1988.

Steensgaard, Niels. *The Asian Trade Revolution of the Seventeenth Century: The East India Companies and the Decline of the Caravan Trade*. Chicago: University of Chicago Press, 1974.

Stuart-Fox, Martin. *A History of Laos*. Cambridge: Cambridge University Press, 1997.

Suárez, Thomas. *Early Mapping of Southeast Asia*. Singapore: Periplus Editions, 1999.

Subrahmanyam, Sanjay. *The Portuguese Empire in Asia, 1500–1700: A Political and Economic History*. London: Longman, 1993.

Talib, Yusof Ahmad. "Jawa Script: Its Significance and Contribution to the Malay World." In *Proceedings of the International Seminar on Islamic Civilisation in the Malay World,* ed. Taufik Abdullah. Istanbul: IRCICA, 1999.

Tan, Samuel K. *Surat Maguindanaon: Jawi Documentary Series*. Vol. 1. Quezon City: University of the Philippines Press, 1996.

Tarling, Nicholas, ed. *From Early Times to c. 1800*. Vol. 1 of *The Cambridge History of Southeast Asia*. Cambridge: Cambridge University Press, 1992.

———. *Southeast Asia: A Modern History*. Oxford: Oxford University Press, 2001.

Taylor, Jean G. *The Social World of Batavia: European and Eurasian in Dutch Asia*. Madison: University of Wisconsin Press, 1983.

Taylor, Keith W. "Nguyen Hoang and the Beginning of Vietnam's Southward Expansion." In *Southeast Asia in the Early Modern Era: Trade, Power, and Belief,* ed. Anthony Reid. Ithaca, NY: Cornell University Press, 1993.

Thode-Arora, Hilke. *Tapa und Tiki: Die Polynesien-Sammlung des Rautenstrauch-Joest-Museums*. Cologne: Rautenstrauch-Joest-Museum für Völkerkunde, 2001.

Trakulhun, Sven. *Siam und Europa: Das Königreich Ayutthaya in westlichen Berichten 1500–1670*. Hannover-Laatzen: Wehrhahn, 2006.

Uhlig, Harald. *Südostasien*. 2nd ed. Frankfurt am Main: Fischer 1988.

Van Esterik, Penny: *Women of Southeast Asia*. De Kalb: Northern Illinois University, Center for Southeast Asian Studies, 1996.

Van Goor, Jurrien, ed. *Trading Companies in Asia, 1600–1830.* Utrecht: HES Uitgevers, 1986.

Vermeulen, Johannes T. *De Chineezen te Batavia en de troebelen van 1740.* Leiden: Ijdo, 1938.

Villiers, John. *Südostasien vor der Kolonialzeit.* Vol. 18 of *Fischer Weltgeschichte.* Frankfurt am Main: Fischer, 1965.

Voigt, Johannes H. *Geschichte Australiens.* Stuttgart: Kröner, 1988.

Wade, Geoff. "Engaging the South: Ming China and Southeast Asia in the Fifteenth Century." *Journal of the Economic and Social History of the Orient* 51, no. 4 (2008): 578–638.

Wade, Geoff, and Li Tana, eds. *Anthony Reid and the Study of the Southeast Asian Past.* Singapore: Institute of Southeast Asian Studies, 2012.

Warren, James F. *The Global Economy and the Sulu Zone: Connections, Commodities, and Culture.* Quezon City: New Day Publishers, 2000.

———. *The Sulu Zone, 1768–1898: The Dynamics of External Trade, Slavery, and Ethnicity in the Transformation of a Southeast Asian Maritime State.* Singapore: Singapore University Press, 1981.

Waterson, Roxana. *The Living House: An Anthropology of Architecture in South-East Asia.* Singapore: Oxford University Press, 1990.

Watson Andaya, Barbara, ed. *Other Pasts: Women, Gender and History in Early Modern Southeast Asia.* Honolulu: Center for Southeast Asian Studies, 2000.

Wendt, Reinhard. "Der Achte Mond: Religiöse Feste in der chinesischen Diaspora auf den spanischen Philippinen." *Periplus* 14 (2004): 89–116.

———. "'Dinner for One' und die versteckte Präsenz des Fremden im Kulinarischen." In *Grenzgänge: Festschrift zu Ehren von Wilfried Wagner,* ed. Dietmar Rothermund. Hamburg: Abera, 2004.

———. *Fiesta Filipina: Koloniale Kultur zwischen Imperialismus und neuer Identität.* Freiburg im Breisgau: Rombach, 1997.

———. "The Spanish-Dutch War, Japanese Trade and World Politics." In *The Road to Japan: Social and Economic Aspects of Early European-Japanese Contacts,* ed. Josef Kreiner. Bonn: Bier'sche Verlagsanstalt, 2005.

———. "'Talking' and 'Writing' during the Spanish Colonial Era." In *Old Ties and New Solidarities: Studies on Philippine Communities,* ed. Guillermo Pesigan and Charles Macdonald. Quezon City: Ateneo de Manila University Press, 2000.

———. *Vom Kolonialismus zur Globalisierung: Europa und die Welt seit 1500.* Paderborn: Ferdinand Schöningh, 2007.

Wheatley, Paul. *The Golden Khersonese: Studies in the Historical Geography of the Malay Peninsula before AD 1500.* Kuala Lumpur: University of Malaya Press, 1961.

Wickberg, Edgar. "The Chinese Mestizo in Philippine History." *Journal of Southeast Asian History* 5, no. 1 (1964): 62–100.

Wilpert, Clara B. *Südsee: Inseln, Völker und Kulturen.* Hamburg: Christians, 1987.

Wolters, Oliver William. *History, Culture, and Region in Southeast Asian Perspectives.* Singapore: Institute of Southeast Asia Studies, 1982.

Wulf, Annaliese. *Vietnam: Pagoden und Tempel im Reisfeld—Im Fokus indischer und chinesischer Kultur.* 2nd ed. Cologne: DuMont, 1995.

Wurm, Stephen A. *Papuan Languages of Oceania.* Tübingen: Narr, 1982.

Wurm, Stephen A., and Shirô Hattori, eds. *Language Atlas of the Pacific Area.* 2 vols. Canberra: Linguistic Circle of Canberra, 1981.

Wyatt, David K. "Chronicle Traditions in Thai Historiography." In *Southeast Asian History and Historiography: Essays Presented to D. G. E. Hall,* ed. Charles D. Cowan and Oliver William Wolters. Ithaca, NY: Cornell University Press, 1976.

———. *Thailand: A Short History.* Chiang Mai: Silkworm Books, 1984.

Zöllner, Reinhard. *Geschichte Japans: Von 1800 bis zur Gegenwart.* Paderborn: Schöningh, 2006.

Europe and the Atlantic World

Abel, Wilhelm. *Geschichte der deutschen Landwirtschaft vom frühen Mittelalter bis zum 19. Jahrhundert.* Vol. 2 of *Deutsche Agrargeschichte.* 3rd ed. Stuttgart: Ulmer, 1978.

Abulafia, David. *The Discovery of Mankind: Atlantic Encounters in the Age of Columbus.* New Haven, CT: Yale University Press, 2008.

Afflerbach, Holger. *Das entfesselte Meer: Die Geschichte des Atlantik.* Munich: Piper, 2001.

Alexandre, Pierre. *Le climat en Europe au Moyen Âge: Contribution à l'histoire des variations climatiques de 1000 à 1425, d'après les sources narratives de l'Europe occidentale.* Paris: Editions de l'École des Hautes Études en Sciences Sociales, 1987.

Allmand, Christopher T., ed. *C. 1415–c. 1500.* Vol. 7 of *The New Cambridge Medieval History.* Cambridge: Cambridge University Press, 1998.

Anderson, Matthew S. *The Rise of Modern Diplomacy, 1450–1919.* London: Longman 1993.

Andrews, Charles M. *The Colonial Period of American History.* 4 vols. New Haven, CT: Yale University Press, 1934–1938.

Andrews, Kenneth R. *The Spanish Caribbean: Trade and Plunder, 1530–1630.* New Haven, CT: Yale University Press, 1978.

Andrews, Kenneth R., Nicholas P. Canny, and Paul E. H. Hair, eds. *The Westward Enterprise: English Activities in Ireland, the Atlantic, and America, 1480–1650.* Liverpool: Liverpool University Press, 1978.

Angenendt, Arnold. *Geschichte der Religiosität im Mittelalter.* 2nd ed. Darmstadt: Wissenschaftliche Buchgesellschaft, 2000.

Angermeier, Heinz. "Der Wormser Reichstag 1495—Ein europäisches Ereignis." *Historische Zeitschrift* 261 (1995): 739–768.

Appiah, Kwame Anthony, and Henry Louis Gates, eds. *Africana: The Encyclopedia of the African and African American Experience.* New York: Basic Civitas Books, 1999.

Aretin, Karl Otmar von, ed. *Der Aufgeklärte Absolutismus.* Cologne: Kiepenheuer und Witsch, 1974.

Ariès, Philippe, and Georges Duby, eds. *Revelations of the Medieval World.* Vol. 2 of *A History of Private Life.* Cambridge, MA: Belknap Press of Harvard University Press, 1988.

Ariès, Philippe, and Roger Chartier, eds. *Passions of the Renaissance.* Vol. 3 of *A History of Private Life.* Cambridge, MA: Belknap Press of Harvard University Press, 1989.

Armitage, David. "Three Concepts of Atlantic History." In *The British Atlantic World, 1500–1800,* ed. David Armitage and Michael Braddick. New York: Palgrave Macmillan, 2002.

Asch, Ronald G., ed. *Der europäische Adel im Ancien Regime: Von der Krise der ständischen Monarchien bis zur Revolution (ca. 1600–1789).* Cologne: Böhlau, 2001.

———. *The Thirty Years War: The Holy Roman Empire and Europe, 1618–1648.* Basingstoke, UK: Macmillan, 1997.

Aubin, Hermann, and Wolfgang Zorn, eds. *Von der Frühzeit bis zum Ende des 18. Jahrhunderts.* Vol. 1 of *Handbuch der deutschen Wirtschafts- und Sozialgeschichte.* Stuttgart: Union, 1971.

Ayala, Manuel José de. *Diccionario de gobierno e legislación de Indias,* ed. Marta Milagros del Vas Mingo. 10 vols. Madrid: Cultura Hispánica, 1991–1998.

Bader, Karl Siegfried. *Studien zur Rechtsgeschichte des mittelalterlichen Dorfes.* 3 vols. Weimar: Böhlau, 1957–1973.

Bailyn, Bernard. *Atlantic History: Concept and Contours.* Cambridge, MA: Harvard University Press, 2005.

Bakewell, Peter J. *A History of Latin America.* 2nd ed. Malden, MA: Blackwell, 2004.

Bamji, Alexandra, Geert H. Janssen, and Mary Laven, eds. *The Ashgate Research Companion to the Counter-Reformation.* Farnham, UK: Ashgate, 2013.

Banner, Stuart. *How the Indians Lost Their Land: Law and Power on the Frontier.* Cambridge, MA: Belknap Press, 2005.

Bardet, Jean-Pierre, and Jacques Dupâquier, eds. *Des origines aux prémices de la révolution demographique.* Vol. 1 of *Histoire des populations de l'Europe.* Paris: Fayard, 1997.

Barry, Boubacar. *Senegambia and the Atlantic Slave Trade.* Cambridge: Cambridge University Press, 1998.

Battenberg, Friedrich. *Von den Anfängen bis 1650.* Vol. 1 of *Das europäische Zeitalter der Juden: Zur Entwicklung einer Minderheit in der nichtjüdischen Umwelt Europas.* Darmstadt: Wissenschaftliche Buchgesellschaft, 1990.

Bäumer, Remigius, ed. *Die Entwicklung des Konziliarismus.* Darmstadt: Wissenschaftliche Buchgesellschaft, 1976.

Becker, Felix. *Die politische Machtstellung der Jesuiten in Südamerika im 18. Jahrhundert: Zur Kontroverse um den Jesuitenkönig Nikolaus I. von Paraguay.* Cologne: Böhlau, 1980.

Behringer, Wolfgang. *Witches and Witch-Hunts: A Global History.* Cambridge: Polity, 2004.

Bély, Lucien, ed. *L'invention de la diplomatie: Moyen Âge—Temps modernes.* Paris: PUF, 1998.

Benedict, Philip. *Christ's Churches Purely Reformed: A Social History of Calvinism.* New Haven, CT: Yale University Press, 2002.

Benedictow, Ole J. *The Black Death, 1346–1353: The Complete History.* Woodbridge, UK: Boydell Press, 2004.

Benevolo, Leonardo. *The European City.* Oxford: Blakwell 1993.

Bercé, Yves-Marie. *Révoltes et révolutions dans l'Europe moderne (XVIe–XVIIIe siècles).* Paris: PUF, 1980.

Bérenger, Jean. *Histoire de l'empire des Habsbourg 1273–1918.* Paris: Fayard, 1990.

Bergdolt, Klaus. *Der Schwarze Tod in Europa: Die Große Pest und das Ende des Mittelalters.* Munich: C. H. Beck, 1994.

Bethell, Leslie, ed. *Bibliographical Essays.* Vol. 11 of *The Cambridge History of Latin America.* Cambridge: Cambridge University Press, 1995.

———. *Colonial Brazil.* Cambridge: Cambridge University Press, 1987.

———. *Colonial Latin America.* Vols. 1 and 2 of *The Cambridge History of Latin America.* Cambridge: Cambridge University Press, 1984.

Biggs, Douglas, Sharon D. Michalove, and Albert C. Reeves. *Traditions and Transformations in Late Medieval England.* Leiden: Brill, 2002.

Black, Anthony. *Political Thought in Europe, 1250–1450.* Cambridge: Cambridge University Press, 1992.

Black, Jeremy, ed. *A Military Revolution? Military Change and European Society, 1550–1800.* Basingstoke, UK: Macmillan, 1991.

Blanning, Timothy C. W. *The Culture of Power and the Power of Culture: Old Regime Europe, 1660–1789.* Oxford: Oxford University Press, 2002.

Blickle, Peter. *Von der Leibeigenschaft zu den Menschenrechten: Eine Geschichte der Freiheit in Deutschland.* Munich: C. H. Beck, 2003.

Bliss, Robert M. *Revolution and Empire: English Politics and the American Colonies in the Seventeenth Century.* Manchester: Manchester University Press, 1990.

Bloch, Marc. *Feudal Society.* 2 vols. London: Routledge & Kegan Paul, 1971.

Blockmans, Wim P., and Jean-Pilippe Genet, eds. *The Origins of the Modern State in Europe: 13th–18th Centuries.* 7 vols. Oxford: Clarendon Press, 1995–2000.

Bödeker, Hans Erich, and Etienne François, eds. *Aufklärung / Lumières und Politik: Zur politischen Kultur der deutschen und französischen Aufklärung.* Leipzig: Leipziger Universitätsverlag, 1996.

Böning, Holger. *Die Genese der Volksaufklärung und ihre Entwicklung bis 1780.* Stuttgart: Frommann-Holzboog, 1990.

Bonney, Richard. *The European Dynastic States, 1494–1660.* 3rd ed. Oxford: Oxford University Press, 1991.

Boockmann, Hartmut. *Die Stadt im späten Mittelalter.* 3rd ed. Munich: C. H. Beck, 1994.

Boonzaier, Emile et al. *The Cape Herders: A History of the Khoikhoi of Southern Africa.* Cape Town: Philip, 1996.

Böttcher, Nikolaus. *Aufstieg und Fall eines atlantischen Handelsimperiums: Portugiesische Kaufleute und Sklavenhändler in Cartagena de Indias von 1580 bis zur Mitte des 17. Jahrhunderts.* Frankfurt am Main: Vervuert, 1995.

Boucher, Philip P. *France and the American Tropics to 1700.* Baltimore: Johns Hopkins University Press, 2008.

Boxer, Charles R. *The Golden Age of Brazil, 1695–1750.* Berkeley: University of California Press 1962.

Braddick, Michael J. *State Formation in Early Modern England, ca. 1550–1700.* Cambridge: Cambridge University Press, 2000.

Brading, David A. *The First America: The Spanish Monarchy, Creole Patriots and the Liberal State, 1492–1867.* Cambridge: Cambridge University Press, 1991.

Brady, Thomas A., Jr., Heiko A. Oberman, and James D. Tracy, eds. *Handbook of European History, 1400–1600.* 2 vols. Leiden: Brill, 1994–1995.

Brandmüller, Walter. *Das Konzil von Konstanz.* 2 vols. Paderborn: Schöningh, 1991–1999.

Braudel, Fernand. *Civilization and Capitalism.* 3 vols. London: Fontana, 1981–1982.

———. *The Mediterranean and the Mediterranean World in the Age of Philip II.* 2 vols. London: Fontana, 1949.

Brecht, Martin et al. ed. *Geschichte des Pietismus.* 4 vols. Göttingen: Vandenhoeck & Ruprecht, 1993–2004.

Brendecke, Arndt. *Imperium und Empirie: Funktionen des Wissens in der spanischen Kolonialherrschaft.* Cologne: Böhlau, 2009.

Bridenbaugh, Carl, and Roberta Bridenbaugh. *No Peace beyond the Line: The English in the Caribbean, 1624–1690.* Oxford: Oxford University Press, 1972.

Brooks, George E. *Eurafricans in Western Africa: Commerce, Social Status, Gender, and Religious Observance from the 16th to the 18th Century.* Athens: Ohio University Press, 2003.

Brown, Stewart J., and Timothy Tackett, eds. *Enlightenment, Reawakening, and Revolution, 1660–1815.* Vol. 7 of *The Cambridge History of Christianity.* Cambridge: Cambridge University Press, 2006.

Buisson-Wolff, Inge. *Regierung und Verwaltung der kolonialspanischen Städte in Hochperu 1538–1650.* Cologne: Böhlau, 1970.

Bulmer-Thomas, Victor, John H. Coatsworth, and Roberto Cortés Conde, eds. *The Colonial Era and the Short Nineteenth Century.* Vol. 1 of *The Cambridge Economic History of Latin America.* Cambridge: Cambridge University Press, 2006.

Burguière, André, Christiane Klapisch-Zuber, Martine Segalen, and Françoise Zonabend, eds. *A History of the Family*. 2 vols. Cambridge, MA: Belknap Press, 1996.

Burke, Peter. *Culture and Society in Renaissance Italy, 1420–1540*. London: Batsford, 1972.

———. *The Renaissance*. Basingstoke, UK: Macmillan 1994.

Burkhardt, Johannes. *Der Dreißigjährige Krieg*. Frankfurt am Main: Suhrkamp, 1992.

———. "Die Friedlosigkeit der Frühen Neuzeit. Grundlegung einer Theorie der Bellizität Europas." *Zeitschrift für Historische Forschung* 24 (1997): 509–574.

———. *Vollendung und Neuorientierung des frühmodernen Reiches 1648–1763*. Stuttgart: Klett-Cotta, 2006.

Burns, James H., ed. *The Cambridge History of Political Thought, 1450–1700*. Cambridge: Cambridge University Press, 1991.

Buszello, Horst, Peter Blickle, and Rudolf Endres, eds. *Der deutsche Bauernkrieg*. 3rd ed. Paderborn: Schöningh, 1995.

Butel, Paul. *Histoire de l'Atlantique*. Paris: Perrin, 1997.

The Cambridge History of the Native Peoples of the Americas. 3 vols. in 6 parts. Cambridge: Cambridge University Press, 1996–2000.

Canny, Nicholas, P., ed. *The Origins of Empire: British Overseas Enterprise to the Close of the 17th Century*. Vol. 1 of *The Oxford History of the British Empire*. Oxford: Oxford University Press, 1998.

Canny, Nicholas, and Philip Morgan. *The Oxford Handbook of the Atlantic World, 1450–1850*. Oxford: Oxford University Press, 2011.

Carsten, Francis L. *Princes and Parliaments in Germany from the 15th to the 18th Century*. Oxford: Clarendon, 1959.

Cavallo, Guglielmo, and Roger Chartier, eds. *A History of Reading in the West*. Oxford: Polity, 1999.

Chaunu, Huguette et Pierre. *Séville et l'Atlantique (1504–1650)*. 8 vols. in 12 parts. Paris: Colin, 1955–1960.

Chittolini, Giorgio, Anthony Molho, and Pierangelo Schiera, eds. *Origini dello Stato: Processi di formazione statale in Italia fra medioevo ed età moderna*. Bologna: Il Mulino, 1994.

Cipolla, Carlo M., and Knut Borchardt, eds. *Bevölkerungsgeschichte Europas*. Munich: Piper, 1971.

Clark, Peter, ed. *Small Towns in Early Modern Europe*. Cambridge: Cambridge University Press, 1995.

Connah, Graham. *African Civilizations: An Archaeological Perspective*. 2nd ed. Cambridge: Cambridge University Press, 2001.

Contamine, Philippe. *La guerre de cent ans*. 8th ed. Paris: PUF, 2002.

Coquery-Vidrovitch, Catherine. *Histoire des villes d'Afrique noire: Des origines à la colonisation*. Paris: Albin Michel, 1993.

Cressy, David. *Coming Over: Migration and Communication between England and New England in the Seventeenth Century.* Cambridge: Cambridge University Press, 1987.

Crosby, Alfred W. *The Columbian Exchange: Biological and Cultural Consequences of 1492.* Westport, CT: Greenwood Press, 1972.

———. *Ecological Imperialism: The Biological Expansion of Europe, 900–1900.* 2nd ed. Cambridge: Cambridge University Press, 2004.

Crouch, Dora P., Daniel J. Garr, and Axel I. Mundigo. *Spanish City Planning in North America.* Cambridge, MA: MIT Press, 1982.

Curtin, Phillip D. *The Atlantic Slave Trade: A Census.* Madison: University of Wisconsin Press, 1969.

Daunton, Martin, and Rick Halpern, eds. *Empire and Others, British Encounters with Indigenous Peoples, 1600–1850.* Philadelphia: University of Pennsylvania Press, 1999.

Deerr, Noël. *The History of Sugar.* 2 vols. London: Chapman and Hall, 1949–1950.

Delgado, Mariano. *Abschied vom erobernden Gott: Studien zu Geschichte und Gegenwart des Christentums in Lateinamerika.* Immensee: Neue Zeitschrift für Missionswissenschaft, 1996.

Delumeau, Jean. *La peur en occident: XIVe–XVIIIe siècles.* Paris: Hachette, 1978.

Denzel, Markus A. *"La Practica della Cambiatura": Europäischer Zahlungsverkehr vom 14. bis zum 17. Jahrhundert.* Stuttgart: Steiner, 1994.

Derwich, Marek, and Martial Staub, eds. *"Die Neue Frömmigkeit" in Europa im Spätmittelalter.* Göttingen: Vandenhoeck & Ruprecht, 2004.

Devèze, Michel. *Antilles, Guyanes, la mer des Caraïbes de 1492 à 1789.* Paris: Société d'Édition d'Enseignement Supérieur, 1977.

Dinzelbacher, Peter, and Dieter R. Bauer, eds. *Volksreligion im hohen und späten Mittelalter.* Paderborn: Schöningh, 1990.

Dirlmeier, Ulf, Gerhard Fouquet, Bernd Fuhrmann, and Rainer S. Elkar, eds. *Öffentliches Bauen in Mittelalter und früher Neuzeit.* St. Katharinen: Scripta Mercaturae-Verlag, 1991.

Disney, Anthony R. *The Portuguese Empire.* Vol. 2 of *A History of Portugal and the Portuguese Empire.* Cambridge: Cambridge University Press, 2009.

Dollinger, Philippe. *Die Hanse.* 5th ed. Stuttgart: Kröner, 1998.

Donnan, Elizabeth, ed. *Documents Illustrative of the History of the Slave Trade.* 4 vols. Washington, DC: Carnegie Institution, 1930–1935.

Doyle, William. *The Old European Order, 1660–1800.* 2nd ed. Oxford: Oxford University Press, 1992.

Duby, Georges. *Rural Economy and Country Life in the Medieval West.* London: Arnold, 1968.

Duby, Georges, and Michelle Perrot, eds. *A History of Women in the West.* Vols. 2 and 3. Cambridge, MA: Belknap Press of Harvard University Press, 1992–1993.

Duke, Alastair, Gillian Lewis, and Andrew Pettegree, eds. *Calvinism in Europe, 1540–1610: A Collection of Documents.* Manchester: Manchester University Press, 1992.

Dunn, Richard S. *Sugar and Slaves: The Rise of the Planter Class in the English West Indies, 1624–1713*. London: Cape, 1973.

Dwyer, Philip G., ed. *The Rise of Prussia, 1700–1830*. Harlow, UK: Longman, 2000.

East, W. Gordon. *An Historical Geography of Europe*. 5th ed. London: Methuen, 1966.

Edwards, John. *The Jews in Christian Europe, 1400–1700*. London: Routledge, 1988.

Ehret, Christopher. *The Civilizations of Africa: A History to 1800*. Oxford: James Currey, 2002.

Elliott, John H. *Empires of the Atlantic World: Britain and Spain in America, 1492–1830*. New Haven, CT: Yale University Press, 2006.

Eltis, David, and David Richardson. *Atlas of the Transatlantic Slave Trade*. New Haven, CT: Yale University Press, 2010.

Eltis, David et al. *The Trans-Atlantic Slave Trade: A Database*. Atlanta, GA: Emory University: www.slavevoyages.org.

Engelbrecht, William. *Iroquoia: The Development of a Native World*. Syracuse, NY: Syracuse University Press, 2003.

Engerman, Stanley L., Seymour Drescher, and Robert Louis Paquette, eds. *Slavery*. New York: Oxford University Press, 2001.

Engerman, Stanley L., and Robert E. Gallman. *The Colonial Era*. Vol. 1 of *The Cambridge Economic History of the United States*. Cambridge: Cambridge University Press, 1996.

Ertman, Thomas. *Birth of the Leviathan: Building States and Regimes in Medieval and Early Modern Europe*. Cambridge: Cambridge University Press, 1997.

Esser, Thilo. *Pest, Heilsangst und Frömmigkeit: Studien zur religiösen Bewältigung der Pest am Ausgang des Mittelalters*. Altenberge: Oros-Verlag, 1999.

Fage, John D. *A History of Africa*. 3rd ed. New York: Routledge, 1995.

Falola, Toyin, and Kevin D. Roberts, eds. *The Atlantic World, 1450–2000*. Bloomington: Indiana University Press, 2008.

Feldbauer, Peter, ed. *Die vormoderne Stadt: Asien und Europa im Vergleich*. Munich: Oldenbourg, 2002.

Ferguson, Wallace K. *The Renaissance in Historical Thought: Five Centuries of Interpretation*. Boston: Houghton Mifflin, 1948.

Finzsch, Norbert, James Oliver Horton, and Lois E. Horton. *Von Benin nach Baltimore: Die Geschichte der African Americans*. Hamburg: Hamburger Edition, 1999.

Fischer, Rudolf. *Gold, Salz und Sklaven: Die Geschichte der großen Sudanreiche Gana, Mali, Songhai*. 2nd ed. Oberdorf: Edition Piscator, 1991.

Flasche, Rainer. *Geschichte und Typologie afrikanischer Religiosität in Brasilien*. Marburg: Universität Marburg, 1973.

Franz, Günther. *Geschichte des deutschen Bauernstandes vom frühen Mittelalter bis zum 19. Jahrhundert*. Vol. 4 of *Deutsche Agrargeschichte*. 2nd ed. Stuttgart: Ulmer, 1976.

Freiesleben, Hans-Christian. *Geschichte der Navigation*. 2nd ed. Wiesbaden: Steiner, 1978.

Galenson, David W. *Traders, Planters, and Slaves: Market Behavior in Early English America.* Cambridge: Cambridge University Press, 1986.

———. *White Servitude in Colonial America: An Economic Analysis.* Cambridge: Cambridge University Press, 1981.

Galloway, James A., ed. *Trade, Urban Hinterlands and Market Integration, c. 1300–1600.* London: Centre for Metropolitan History, Institute of Historical Research, 2000.

Games, Alison. *Migration and the Origins of the English Atlantic World.* Cambridge, MA: Harvard University Press, 1999.

Gantet, Claire. *Guerre, paix et construction des États 1618–1714.* Vol. 2 of *Nouvelle histoire des relations internationales.* Paris: Seuil, 2003.

Garćia Fuentes, Lutgardo. *El comercio español con América (1650–1700).* Seville: Escuela de Estudios Hispano-Americanos, 1980.

Garin, Eugenio, ed. *Renaissance Characters.* Chicago: University of Chicago Press, 1997.

Garnot, Benoît. *Le peuple au siècle des lumières: Échec d'un dressage culturel.* Paris: Editions Imago, 1990.

Gay, Peter. *The Enlightenment: An Interpretation.* 2 vols. New York: Knopf, 1967–1969.

Gerhard, Peter. *A Guide to the Historical Geography of New Spain.* 2nd ed. Norman: University of Oklahoma Press, 1993.

Gestrich, Andreas, Jens-Uwe Krause, and Michael Mitterauer. *Geschichte der Familie.* Stuttgart: Kröner, 2003.

Gilroy, Paul. *The Black Atlantic: Modernity and Double Consciousness.* Cambridge, MA: Harvard University Press, 1993.

Giraud, Marcel. *Histoire de la Louisiane française.* 4 vols. Paris: PUF, 1953–1974.

Glaser, Rüdiger. *Klimageschichte Mitteleuropas: 1200 Jahre Wetter, Klima, Katastrophen.* 2nd ed. Darmstadt: Wissenschaftliche Buchgesellschaft, 2008.

Goodman, Anthony. *The New Monarchy: England, 1471–1534.* Oxford: Blackwell, 1988.

Goodman, David, and Colin A. Russell, eds. *The Rise of Scientific Europe, 1500–1800.* Sevenoaks: Hodder and Stoughton, 1991.

Goslinga, Cornelis C. *The Dutch in the Caribbean and in the Guianas, 1680–1791.* Assen: Van Gorcum, 1985.

———. *The Dutch in the Caribbean and on the Wild Coast, 1580–1680.* Assen: Van Gorcum, 1971.

Gräf, Holger Thomas, and Ralf Pröve. *Wege ins Ungewisse: Reisen in der Frühen Neuzeit 1500–1800.* Frankfurt am Main: S. Fischer, 1997.

Graus, František. *Pest—Geißler—Judenmorde: Das 14. Jahrhundert als Krisenzeit.* 3rd ed. Göttingen: Vandenhoeck & Ruprecht, 1994.

Gray, Richard, ed. *From c. 1600 to c. 1790.* Vol. 4 of *The Cambridge History of Africa.* Cambridge: Cambridge University Press, 1975.

Greene, Jack P., and Philip D. Morgan, eds. *Atlantic History: A Critical Appraisal.* Oxford: Oxford University Press, 2009.

Grenier, John. *The First Way of War: American War Making on the Frontier, 1607–1814.* Cambridge: Cambridge University Press, 2005.

Gunn, Geoffrey C. *First Globalization: The Eurasian Exchange, 1500–1800.* Lanham, MD: Rowman & Littlefield, 2003.

Häberlein, Mark, and Alexander Keese, eds. *Sprachgrenzen—Sprachkontakte—Kulturelle Vermittler.* Stuttgart: Steiner, 2010.

Habermas, Jürgen. *The Structural Transformation of the Public Sphere.* Cambridge, MA: MIT Press, 1998.

Haigh, Christopher. *English Reformations: Religion, Politics, and Society under the Tudors.* Oxford: Clarendon, 1993.

Hall, David D., ed. *Puritans in the New World: A Critical Anthology.* Princeton, NJ: Princeton University Press, 2004.

Hall, Gwendolyn M. *Social Control in Slave Plantation Societies: A Comparison of St. Domingue and Cuba.* Baltimore: Johns Hopkins University Press, 1971.

Hammel-Kiesow, Rolf. *Die Hanse.* 4th ed. Munich: C. H. Beck, 2008.

Hargreaves-Mawdsley, William N. *Eighteenth-Century Spain, 1700–1788: A Political, Diplomatic and Institutional History.* London: Macmillan, 1979.

Härter, Karl, ed. *Policey und frühneuzeitliche Gesellschaft.* Frankfurt am Main: Klostermann, 2000.

Hassig, Ross. *Mexico and the Spanish Conquest.* 2nd ed. Norman: University of Oklahoma Press, 2006.

Hattendorf, John B. *"The Boundless Deep . . .": The European Conquest of the Oceans, 1450–1840.* Providence, RI: John Carter Brown Library, 2003.

Hattenhauer, Hans. *Europäische Rechtsgeschichte.* 4th ed. Heidelberg: Müller, 2004.

Havard, Gilles, and Cécile Vidal. *Histoire de l'Amérique française.* 2nd ed. Paris: Flammarion, 2008.

Hazard, Paul. *The European Mind (1680–1715).* Cleveland, OH: World Publishing, 1963.

———. *European Thought in the Eighteenth Century from Montesquieu to Lessing.* London: Hollis & Carter, 1954.

Herbert, Eugenia W. *Red Gold of Africa: Copper in Precolonial History and Culture.* Madison: University of Wisconsin Press, 1984.

Hergemöller, Bernd-Ulrich, ed. *Randgruppen der spätmittelalterlichen Gesellschaft.* 3rd ed. Warendorf: Fahlbusch, 2001.

Heydenreich, Ludwig H., André Chastel, and Günter Passavant. *Italienische Renaissance.* 4 vols. Munich: C. H. Beck, 1965–1975.

Hillgarth, Jocelyn N. *The Spanish Kingdoms, 1250–1516.* 2 vols. Oxford: Clarendon, 1976–1978.

Hilton, Anne. *The Kingdom of Kongo.* Oxford: Clarendon Press, 1985.

Hilton, Rodney H. *English and French Towns in Feudal Society: A Comparative Study.* Cambridge: Cambridge University Press, 1992.

Historia general de España y América. 19 vols. in 25 parts. Madrid: RIALP, 1981–1992.

Hoerder, Dirk. *Cultures in Contact: World Migrations in the Second Millennium.* Durham, NC: Duke University Press, 2002.

Holmes, Geoffrey. *The Making of a Great Power: Late Stuart and Early Georgian Britain, 1660–1722.* London: Longman, 1993.

Houtte, Jan A. van, ed. *Europäische Wirtschafts- und Sozialgeschichte im Mittelalter.* Vol. 2 of *Handbuch der europäischen Wirtschafts- und Sozialgeschichte.* Stuttgart: Klett-Cotta, 1980.

Hsia, Ronnie Po-Chia, ed. *Reform and Expansion, 1500–1660.* Vol. 6 of *The Cambridge History of Christianity.* Cambridge: Cambridge University Press, 2007.

Hufton, Olwen. *The Prospect before Her: A History of Women in Western Europe, 1500–1800.* London: HarperCollins 1995.

Iliffe, John. *Africans: The History of a Continent.* Cambridge: Cambridge University Press, 1995.

Im Hof, Ulrich. *Das gesellige Jahrhundert: Gesellschaft und Gesellschaften im Zeitalter der Aufklärung.* Munich: C. H. Beck, 1982.

Inácio, Inês da Conceição, and Tania Regina de Luca, eds. *Documentos do Brasil colonial.* São Paulo: Atica, 1993.

Inikori, Joseph E. *Africans and the Industrial Revolution in England: A Study in International Trade and Economic Development.* Cambridge: Cambridge University Press, 2002.

Isenmann, Eberhard. *Die deutsche Stadt im Spätmittelalter, 1250–1500: Stadtgestalt, Recht, Stadtregiment, Kirche, Gesellschaft, Wirtschaft.* Stuttgart: Ulmer, 1988.

Israel, Jonathan I. *The Dutch Republic: Its Rise, Greatness, and Fall, 1477–1806.* Oxford: Clarendon, 1995.

Jaeger, Friedrich, ed. *Enzyklopädie der Neuzeit.* 16 vols. Stuttgart: Metzler, 2005–2012.

Jaenen, Cornelius J. *Friend and Foe, Aspects of French-Amerindian Cultural Contact in the Sixteenth and Seventeenth Centuries.* New York: Columbia University Press, 1976.

Jedin, Hubert. *Geschichte des Konzils von Trient.* 4 vols. in 5 parts. Freiburg im Breisgau: Herder, 1949–1975.

Jensen, Merrill, ed. *American Colonial Documents to 1776.* Vol. 9 of *English Historical Documents.* London: Eyre and Spottiswoode, 1955.

Jockenhövel, Albrecht, ed. *Bergbau, Verhüttung und Waldnutzung im Mittelalter: Auswirkungen auf Mensch und Umwelt.* Stuttgart: Steiner, 1996.

Johanek, Peter, and Heinz Stoob, eds. *Europäische Messen und Märktesysteme in Mittelalter und Neuzeit.* Cologne: Böhlau, 1996.

Jones, Michael, ed. *C. 1300–c. 1415.* Vol. 6 of *The New Cambridge Medieval History.* Cambridge: Cambridge University Press, 2000.

———. *Gentry and Lesser Nobility in Late Medieval Europe.* Gloucester, UK: Sutton, 1986.

Jones, Philip J. *Economia e società nell'Italia medievale.* Turin: Einaudi, 1980.

Jütte, Robert. *Arme, Bettler, Beutelschneider: Eine Sozialgeschichte der Armut in der Frühen Neuzeit.* Cologne: Böhlau, 2000.

Kamen, Henry. *Spain, 1469–1714: A Society of Conflict*. 3rd ed. Harlow, UK: Pearson, 2005.

Kellenbenz, Hermann, ed. *Europäische Wirtschafts- und Sozialgeschichte vom ausgehenden Mittelalter bis zur Mitte des 17. Jahrhunderts*. Vol. 3 of *Handbuch der europäischen Wirtschafts- und Sozialgeschichte*. Stuttgart: Klett-Cotta, 1986.

Kempe, Michael. *Fluch der Weltmeere: Piraterie, Völkerrecht und international Beziehungen 1500–1900*. Frankfurt am Main: Campus, 2010.

Kiple, Kenneth F., ed. *The African Exchange: Toward a Biological History of Black People*. Durham, NC: Duke University Press, 1988.

———. *The Cambridge World History of Human Disease*. Cambridge: Cambridge University Press, 1993.

———. *The Caribbean Slave: A Biological History*. Cambridge: Cambridge University Press, 1984.

Kiple, Kenneth F., and Stephen V. Beck, eds. *Biological Consequences of the European Expansion, 1450–1800*. Aldershot, UK: Ashgate Variorum, 1997.

Klein, Bernhard, and Gesa Mackenthun, eds. *Sea Changes: Historicizing the Ocean*. London: Routledge, 2004.

Klein, Herbert S. *The Atlantic Slave Trade*. Cambridge: Cambridge University Press, 1999.

Klein, Herbert S., and Francisco V. Luna. *Slavery in Brazil*. Cambridge: Cambridge University Press, 2010.

Klein, Julius. *The Mesta: A Study of Spanish Economic History, 1273–1836*. Cambridge, MA: Harvard University Press, 1920.

Knight, Franklin W., ed. *The Slave Societies of the Caribbean*. Vol. 3 of *General History of the Caribbean*. London: UNESCO, 1997.

Konstam, Angus. *Historical Atlas of Exploration, 1492–1600*. New York: Checkmark Books, 2000.

Kruft, Hanno-Walter. *Städte in Utopia: Die Idealstadt vom 15. bis zum 18. Jahrhundert zwischen Staatsutopie und Wirklichkeit*. Munich: C. H. Beck, 1989.

Kuhn, Gabriel. *Life under the Jolly Roger: Reflections on Golden Age Piracy*. Oakland, CA: PM Press, 2010.

Kuttner, Sven. *Handel, Religion und Herrschaft: Kulturkontakt und Ureinwohnerpolitik in Neufrankreich im frühen 17. Jahrhundert*. Frankfurt am Main: Peter Lang, 1998.

Lachatañeré, Rómulo. *Afro-Cuban Myths: Yemayá and Other Orishas*. Princeton, NJ: Wiener, 2006.

Lamb, Hubert H. *Klima und Kulturgeschichte: Der Einfluß des Wetters auf den Gang der Geschichte*. Reinbek: Rowohlt, 1989.

Lambrechts, Pascale, and Jean-Pierre Sosson, eds. *Les métiers au moyen âge: Aspects économiques et sociaux*. Louvain-la-Neuve: Collège Erasme, 1994.

Landers, John. *The Field and the Forge: Population, Production, and Power in the Pre-Industrial West*. Oxford: Oxford University Press, 2003.

Lane, Kris E. *Pillaging the Empire: Piracy in the Americas, 1500–1750.* Armonk, NY: M. E. Sharpe, 1998.

Lanzinner, Maximilian. *Konfessionelles Zeitalter 1555–1618.* Stuttgart: Klett-Cotta, 2001.

Law, Robin C. C. *Constructing the Pre-Colonial History of West Africa: Reflections on the Methodology of Oral and Written History.* Leiden: Afrika-Studiecentrum, 1993.

Lestringant, Frank. *L'atelier du cosmographe ou l'image du monde à la Renaissance.* Paris: Michel, 1991.

Levtzion, Nehemia, ed. *Corpus of Early Arabic Sources for West African History.* Cambridge: Cambridge University Press, 1981.

Linebaugh, Peter, and Marcus Rediker. *The Many-Headed Hydra: Sailors, Slaves, Commoners, and the Hidden History of the Revolutionary Atlantic.* Boston: Beacon Press, 2000.

Livi Bacchi, Massimo. *Conquest: The Destruction of the American Indios.* Cambridge: Polity Press, 2008.

Lockhart, James. *The Nahuas after the Conquest: A Social and Cultural History of the Indians of Central Mexico, Sixteenth through Eighteenth Centuries.* Stanford, CA: Stanford University Press, 1992.

Lockhart, James, and Stuart B. Schwartz. *Early Latin America: A History of Colonial Spanish America and Brazil.* Cambridge: Cambridge University Press, 1997.

Lyon, Bryce, and Adriaan Verhulst. *Medieval Finance: A Comparison of Financial Institutions in Northwestern Europe.* Brugge: De Tempel, 1967.

Mancall, Peter C. *Deadly Medicine: Indians and Alcohol in Early America.* Ithaca, NY: Cornell University Press, 1997.

Manning, Patrick. *The African Diaspora: A History through Culture.* New York: Columbia University Press, 2009.

———. *Slavery and African Life: Occidental, Oriental, and African Slave Trades.* Cambridge: Cambridge University Press, 1990.

———, ed. *Slave Trades, 1500–1800: Globalization of Forced Labour.* Aldershot, UK: Variorum, 1996.

Marchal, Guy P., ed. *Grenzen und Raumvorstellungen (11.–20. Jahrhundert).* Zurich: Chronos, 1996.

Margolin, Jean-Claude. *L'humanisme en Europe au temps de la Rénaissance.* Paris: PUF, 1981.

Martines, Lauro. *Power and Imagination: City-States in Renaissance Italy.* New York: Knopf, 1979.

Mattoso, José, ed. *Historia de Portugal.* 8 vols. Lisbon: Estampa, 1992–1994.

Mauro, Frédéric. *Le Brésil du XVe siècle à la fin du XVIIIe siècle.* Paris: Société d'édition d'enseignement supérieur, 1977.

McAlister, Lyle N. *Spain and Portugal in the New World, 1492–1700.* Oxford: Oxford University Press, 1984.

McCann, James. *Maize and Grace: Africa's Encounter with a New World Crop, 1500–2000.* Cambridge, MA: Harvard University Press, 2005.

McCusker, John J., and Kenneth Morgan, eds. *The Early Modern Atlantic Economy.* Cambridge: Cambridge University Press, 2000.

McKendrick, Neil, John Brewer, and John H. Plumb, eds. *The Birth of a Consumer Society: The Commercialization of Eighteenth-Century England.* London: Europa Publications, 1982.

McNeill, John R. *Mosquito Empires: Ecology and War in the Greater Caribbean, 1620–1914.* Cambridge: Cambridge University Press, 2010.

Meuthen, Erich, and Claudia Märtl. *Das 15. Jahrhundert.* 5th ed. Munich: Oldenbourg, 2012.

Meyer, Jean, Jean Tarrade, and Annie Rey-Goldzeiguer. *Des origines à 1914.* Vol. 1 of *Histoire de la France coloniale.* Paris: Colin, 1991.

Middleton, Richard. *Colonial America: A History, 1607–1760.* Oxford: Blackwell, 1992.

Mieck, Ilja, ed. *Europäische Wirtschafts- und Sozialgeschichte von der Mitte des 17. Jahrhunderts bis zu Mitte des 19. Jahrhunderts.* Vol. 4 of *Handbuch der europäischen Wirtschafts- und Sozialgeschichte.* Stuttgart: Klett-Cotta, 1993.

Miles, Robert. *Racism.* London: Routledge, 1989.

Miller, Perry. *The New England Mind.* 2 vols. Cambridge, MA: Harvard University Press, 1953–1954.

Mills, Kenneth, and William B. Taylor. *Colonial Spanish America: A Documentary History.* Wilmington, DE: Scholarly Resources, 1998.

Mitchell, Robert D., ed. *North America: the Historical Geography of a Changing Continent.* Lanham, MD: Rowman & Littlefield, 1990.

Mollat du Jourdin, Michel. *The Poor in the Middle Ages.* New Haven, CT: Yale University Press, 1986.

Mollat du Jourdin, Michel, and Bernhard Schimmelpfennig, eds. *Die Zeit der Zerreißproben (1274–1449).* Vol. 6 of *Die Geschichte des Christentums.* Freiburg im Breisgau: Herder, 1991.

Morales Padrón, Francisco. *Historia del descubrimiento y conquista de America.* 5th ed. Madrid: Gredos, 1990.

Moraw, Peter. *Von offener Verfassung zu gestalteter Verdichtung: Das Reich im späten Mittelalter 1250 bis 1490.* 2nd ed. Frankfurt am Main: Ullstein, 1989.

Morgan, Edmund S. *American Slavery—American Freedom: The Ordeal of Colonial Virginia.* New York: Norton, 1975.

Morgan, Kenneth. *Slavery, Atlantic Trade and the British Economy, 1660–1800.* Cambridge, Cambridge University Press, 2000.

Moya, Jose C., ed. *The Oxford Handbook of Latin American History.* Oxford: Oxford University Press, 2011.

Nester, William R. *The First Global War: Britain, France, and the Fate of North America, 1756–1775.* Westport, CT: Praeger, 2000.

———. *The Great Frontier War: Britain, France, and the Imperial Struggle for North America, 1607–1755*. Westport, CT: Praeger, 2000.

Neveux, Hugues, Jean Jacquart, and Emmanuel Le Roi Ladurie, eds. *L'âge classique des paysans de 1340 à 1789*. Vol. 2 of *Histoire de la France rurale*. Paris: Seuil, 1992.

Newitt, Malyn. *The Portuguese in West Africa, 1415–1670: A Documentary History*. Cambridge: Cambridge University Press, 2010.

Niane, Djibril Tamsir, ed. *Africa from the 12th to the 16th Century*. Vol. 4 of *General History of Africa*. London: Heinemann 1984.

North, Michael. *Kommunikation, Handel, Geld und Banken in der Frühen Neuzeit*. Munich: Oldenbourg, 2000.

Northrup, David. *Africa's Discovery of Europe, 1450–1850*. New York: Oxford University Press, 2002.

Oberman, Heiko A., and Thomas A. Brady Jr., eds. *Itinerarium Italicum: The Profile of the Italian Renaissance in the Mirror of its European Transformations*. Leiden: Brill, 1975.

Oestreich, Gerhard. "Strukturprobleme des europäischen Absolutismus." In *Geist und Gestalt des frühmodernen Staates*. Berlin: Duncker und Humblot, 1969.

Oexle, Otto G., and Werner Paravicini, eds. *Nobilitas: Funktion und Repräsentation des Adels in Alteuropa*. Göttingen: Vandenhoeck & Ruprecht, 1997.

Ogilvie, Sheilagh C., and Markus Cerman, eds. *European Proto-Industrialization*. Cambridge: Cambridge University Press, 1996.

Ogot, Bethwell A., ed. *Africa from the 16th to the 18th Century*. Vol. 5 of *General History of Africa*. 2nd ed. Oxford: James Currey, 1999.

Oliver, Roland, ed. *From c. 1050 to c. 1600*. Vol. 3 of *The Cambridge History of Africa*. Cambridge: Cambridge University Press, 1977.

Oliver, Roland, and Anthony Atmore. *Medieval Africa, 1250–1800*. Cambridge: Cambridge University Press, 2001.

Otte, Enrique, ed. *Cartas privadas de emigrantes a Indias 1540–1616*. Mexico City: Fondo de Cultura Económica, 1993.

Page, Willie F. *The Dutch Triangle: The Netherlands and the Atlantic Slave Trade, 1621–1664*. New York: Garland, 1997.

———, ed. *Encyclopedia of African History and Culture*. 3 vols. New York: Facts on File, 2001.

Parker, Geoffrey. *The Military Revolution: Military Innovation and the Rise of the West, 1500–1800*. Cambridge: Cambridge University Press, 1988.

Parker, Geoffrey, and Lesley M. Smith, eds. *The General Crisis of the Seventeenth Century*. London: Routledge & Kegan Paul, 1978.

Pestana, Carla G. *The English Atlantic in an Age of Revolution, 1640–1661*. Cambridge, MA: Harvard University Press, 2004.

Peters, Jan, and Axel Lubinski, eds. *Gutsherrschaftsgesellschaften im europäischen Vergleich*. Berlin: Akademie Verlag, 1997.

Pettegree, Andrew, ed. *Calvinism in Europe, 1540–1620*. Cambridge: Cambridge University Press, 1994.

Pfister, Christian. *Bevölkerungsgeschichte und historische Demographie 1500–1800*. Munich: Oldenbourg, 1994.

Pietschmann, Horst, ed. *Atlantic History: History of the Atlantic System, 1580–1830*. Göttingen: Vandenhoeck & Ruprecht, 2002.

Pollak-Eltz, Angelina. *Trommel und Trance: Die afroamerikanischen Religionen*. Freiburg im Breisgau: Herder, 1995.

Porter, Andrew N. *Atlas of British Overseas Expansion*. London: Routledge, 1994.

———, ed. *Bibliography of Imperial, Colonial, and Commonwealth History since 1600*. Oxford: Oxford University Press, 2002.

Porter, Roy, ed. *Eighteenth-Century Science*, Vol. 4 of *The Cambridge History of Science*. Cambridge: Cambridge University Press, 2003.

———. *The Enlightenment*. London: Macmillan 1990.

Post, Franz-Joseph. *Schamanen und Missionare: Katholische Mission und indigene Spiritualität in Nouvelle-France*. Münster: LIT, 1997.

Postma, Johannes, and Victor Enthoven, eds. *Riches from Atlantic Commerce: Dutch Transatlantic Trade and Shipping, 1585–1817*. Leiden: Brill, 2003.

Powers, Karen V. *Women in the Crucible of Conquest: The Gendered Genesis of Spanish American Society, 1500–1600*. Albuquerque: University of New Mexico Press, 2005.

Prodi, Paolo, and Wolfgang Reinhard, eds. *Das Konzil von Trient und die Moderne*. Berlin: Duncker und Humblot, 2001.

Quinn, David B., ed. *New American World: A Documentary History of North America to 1612*. 5 vols. London: Macmillan, 1979.

———. *North America from Earliest Discovery to First Settlements: The Norse Voyages to 1612*. New York: Harper & Row, 1977.

Quinn, David B., and A. N. Ryan. *England's Sea Empire, 1550–1642*. London: Allen and Unwin, 1983.

Rabil, Albert, ed. *Renaissance Humanism: Foundations, Forms and Legacy*. 3 vols. Philadelphia: University of Pennsylvania Press, 1988.

Ravagnan, Giuseppe Michele. *Sunflower in Africa: The History of a Wonderful Plant That Entered and Developed in Africa from Central America Where It Was Domesticated*. Florence: Istituto agronomico per l'Oltremare, 1993.

Reid, William Stanford, ed. *John Calvin: His Influence in the Western World*. Grand Rapids, MI: Zondervan Publishing House, 1982.

Reinhard, Wolfgang. *Die Alte Welt bis 1818*. Vol. 1 of *Geschichte der europäischen Expansion*. Stuttgart: Kohlhammer, 1983.

———. *Die Neue Welt*. Vol. 2 of *Geschichte der europäischen Expansion*. Stuttgart: Kohlhammer, 1985.

——. *Geschichte der Staatsgewalt: Eine vergleichende Verfassungsgeschichte Europas von den Anfängen bis zur Gegenwart.* 3rd ed. Munich: C. H. Beck, 2002.

——. "Konfession und Konfessionalisierung in Europa" [1981]. In *Ausgewählte Abhandlungen.* Berlin: Duncker und Humblot, 1997.

——. *Lebensformen Europas: Eine historische Kulturanthropologie.* 2nd ed. Munich: C. H. Beck, 2006.

——. *Parasit oder Partner? Europäische Wirtschaft und Neue Welt 1500–1800.* Münster: LIT, 1997.

——. *Probleme deutscher Geschichte 1495–1806: Reichsreform und Reformation 1495–1555.* Stuttgart: Klett-Cotta, 2001.

Reiss, Oscar. *Blacks in Colonial America.* Jefferson, NC: McFarland, 2006.

Ritchie, Robert C. *Captain Kidd and the War against the Pirates.* Cambridge, MA: Harvard University Press, 1986.

Roberts, Michael. *The Age of Liberty: Sweden 1719–1772.* Cambridge: Cambridge University Press, 1986.

——. *The Early Vasas: A History of Sweden, 1523–1611.* Cambridge: Cambridge University Press, 1968.

Roper, Louis H., and Bertrand van Ruymbeke, eds. *Constructing Early Modern Empires: Proprietary Ventures in the Atlantic World, 1500–1750.* Leiden: Brill, 2007.

Rösener, Werner. *Die Bauern in der europäischen Geschichte.* Munich: C. H. Beck, 1993.

Rubin, Miri, and Walter Simons, eds. *Christianity in Western Europe, c. 1100–c. 1500.* Vol. 4 of *The Cambridge History of Christianity.* Cambridge: Cambridge University Press, 2009.

Rüegg, Walter, ed. *Universities in Early Modern Europe (1500–1800).* Vol. 2 of *A History of the University in Europe.* Cambridge: Cambridge University Press, 1996.

——. *Universities in the Middle Ages.* Vol. 1 of *A History of the University in Europe.* Cambridge: Cambridge University Press, 1992.

Russell-Wood, Anthony J. R., ed. *An Expanding World: The European Impact on World History, 1450–1800.* Vols. 1–31. Aldershot, UK: Ashgate Variorum, 1995–2000.

Rutledge, Joseph L. *Century of Conflict: The Struggle between the French and British in Colonial America.* Garden City, NY: Doubleday, 1956.

Salaman, Redcliffe N. *The History and Social Influence of the Potato.* Cambridge: Cambridge University Press, 1949.

Sallmann, Jean-Michel. *Géopolitique du XVIe siècle 1490–1618.* Vol. 1 of *Nouvelle histoire des relations internationales.* Paris: Seuil, 2003.

Schilling, Heinz. *Die neue Zeit: Vom Christenheitseuropa zum Europa der Staaten 1250–1750.* Berlin: Siedler, 1999.

——. *Konfessionalisierung und Staatsinteressen 1559–1660.* Vol. 2 of *Handbuch der Geschichte der internationalen Beziehungen.* Paderborn: Schöningh, 2007.

Schmieder, Ulrike, and Hans-Heinrich Nolte, eds. *Atlantik: Sozial- und Kulturgeschichte in der Neuzeit*. Vienna: Promedia, 2010.

Schmitt, Charles B., ed. *The Cambridge History of Renaissance Philosophy*. Cambridge: Cambridge University Press, 1988.

Schneiders, Werner, ed. *Christian Wolff (1679–1754): Interpretationen zu seiner Philosophie und deren Wirkung: Mit einer Bibliographie der Wolff-Literatur*. 2nd ed. Hamburg: Meiner, 1986.

Schneidmüller, Bernd. *Grenzerfahrung und monarchische Ordnung: Europa 1200–1500*. Munich: C. H. Beck, 2011.

Schnur, Roman, ed. *Die Rolle der Juristen bei der Entstehung des modernen Staates*. Berlin: Duncker und Humblot, 1986.

Schnurmann, Claudia. *Atlantische Welten: Engländer und Niederländer im amerikanisch-atlantischen Raum 1648–1713*. Cologne: Böhlau, 1998.

———. *Vom Inselreich zur Weltmacht: Die Entwicklung des englischen Weltreichs vom Mittelalter bis ins 20. Jahrhundert*. Stuttgart: Kohlhammer, 2001.

Schorn-Schütte, Luise. *Konfessionskriege und europäische Expansion: Europa 1500–1648*. Munich: C. H. Beck, 2010.

Schreiner, Klaus, Gerd Schwerhoff, eds. *Verletzte Ehre: Ehrkonflikte in Gesellschaften des Mittelalters und der Frühen Neuzeit*. Cologne: Böhlau, 1995.

Schubert, Ernst, and Bernd Herrmann, eds. *Von der Angst zur Ausbeutung: Umwelterfahrung zwischen Mittelalter und Neuzeit*. Frankfurt am Main: Fischer Taschenbuch Verlag, 1994.

Schuerkens, Ulrike. *Geschichte Afrikas: Eine Einführung*. Cologne: Böhlau, 2009.

Schulz, Günther, ed. *Sozialer Aufstieg: Funktionseliten im Spätmittelalter und in der frühen Neuzeit*. Munich: Boldt im Oldenbourg Verlag, 2002.

Schulz, Knut, ed. *Handwerk in Europa: Vom Spätmittelalter bis zur Frühen Neuzeit*. Munich: Oldenbourg, 1999.

Schulze, Winfried, ed. *Europäische Bauernrevolten der Frühen Neuzeit*. Frankfurt am Main: Suhrkamp, 1982.

Schwartz, Stuart B. *Sugar Plantations in the Formation of Brazilian Society: Bahia, 1550–1835*. Cambridge: Cambridge University Press, 1985.

Scott, Hamish M., ed. *The European Nobilities in the Seventeenth and Eighteenth Centuries*. 2 vols. 2nd ed. Basingstoke, UK: Palgrave Macmillan, 2007.

Seibt, Ferdinand, ed. *Europa im Hoch- und Spätmittelalter*. Vol. 2 of *Handbuch der europäischen Geschichte*. Stuttgart: Klett-Cotta, 1987.

Seibt, Ferdinand, and Winfried Eberhard, eds. *Europa 1400: Die Krise des Spätmittelalters*. Stuttgart: Klett-Cotta, 1984.

———. *Europa 1500: Integrationsprozesse im Widerstreit. Staaten, Regionen, Personenverbände, Christenheit*. Stuttgart: Klett-Cotta, 1987.

Shapin, Steven. *The Scientific Revolution*. Chicago: University of Chicago Press, 1996.

Simmons, Richard C. *The American Colonies from Settlement to Independence*. London: Longman, 1976.

Slicher van Bath, Bernard H. *The Agrarian History of Western Europe, AD 500–1850*. London: Arnold, 1963.

Spruit, Ruud. *Zout en slaven: De geschiedenis van de Westindische Compagnie*. Houten: Haan, 1988.

Steiger, Johann A. et al., eds. *Passion, Affekt und Leidenschaft in der Frühen Neuzeit*. 2 vols. Wiesbaden: Harrassowitz, 2005.

Stein, Peter G. *Roman Law in European History*. Cambridge: Cambridge University Press, 1999.

Stein, Robert Louis. *The French Slave Trade in the Eighteenth Century: An Old Regime Business*. Madison: University of Wisconsin Press, 1979.

Stenzel, Werner. *Das kortesische Mexiko: Die Eroberung Mexikos und der darauf folgende Kulturwandel*. Frankfurt am Main: Peter Lang, 2006.

Stephens, Thomas M. *Dictionary of Latin American Racial and Ethnic Terminology*. Gainesville: University of Florida Press, 1989.

Stinchcombe, Arthur L. *Sugar Island Slavery in the Age of Enlightenment: The Political Economy of the Caribbean World*. Princeton, NJ: Princeton University Press, 1995.

Stollberg-Rilinger, Barbara. *Des Kaisers alte Kleider: Verfassungsgeschichte und Symbolsprache des Alten Reiches*. 2nd ed. Munich: C. H. Beck, 2013.

———. *Europa im Jahrhundert der Aufklärung*. Stuttgart: Reclam, 2000.

Stolleis, Michael, ed. *Policey im Europa der Frühen Neuzeit*. Frankfurt am Main: Klostermann, 1996.

Stuart, Chris, and Tilde Stuart. *Africa: A Natural History*. Shrewsbury, UK: Swan Hill, 1995.

Suntrup, Rudolf et al., eds. *Medieval to Early Modern Culture—Kultureller Wandel vom Mittelalter zur Frühen Neuzeit*. 5 vols. Frankfurt am Main: Peter Lang, 2001–2005.

Tewes, Götz-Rüdiger. *Die römische Kurie und die europäischen Länder am Vorabend der Reformation*. Tübingen: Niemeyer, 2001.

Thornton, John. *Africa and Africans in the Making of the Atlantic World, 1400–1680*. Cambridge: Cambridge University Press, 1992.

Tilly, Charles, ed. *The Formation of National States in Western Europe*. Princeton, NJ: Princeton University Press, 1975.

Tilly, Charles, and Wim P. Blockmans, eds. *Cities and the Rise of States in Europe, 1000–1800*. Boulder, CO: Westview Press, 1994.

Tracy, James D., ed. *The Political Economy of Merchant Empires: State Power and World Trade, 1350–1750*. Cambridge: Cambridge University Press, 1991.

———. *The Rise of Merchant Empires: Long Distance Trade in the Early Modern World, 1350–1750*. Cambridge: Cambridge University Press, 1990.

Trudel, Marcel. *The Beginnings of New France, 1524–1663.* Toronto: McClelland and Stewart, 1973.

Varela, Consuelo, and Isabel Aguirre. *La caida de Cristobal Colon: El juicio de Bobadilla.* Madrid: Marcial Pons Historia, 2006.

Vasold, Manfred. *Die Pest: Das Ende eines Mythos.* Stuttgart: Theiss, 2003.

Venard, Marc, and Albert Boesten-Stengel, eds. *Das Zeitalter der Vernunft (1620/30–1750).* Vol. 9 of *Die Geschichte des Christentums.* Freiburg im Breisgau: Herder, 1998.

Venard, Marc, and Heribert Smolinsky, eds. *Die Zeit der Konfessionen (1530–1620/30).* Vol. 8 of *Die Geschichte des Christentums.* Freiburg im Breisgau: Herder, 1992.

———. *Von der Reform zur Reformation (1450–1530).* Vol. 7 of *Die Geschichte des Christentums.* Freiburg im Breisgau: Herder, 1995.

Verano, John W., and Douglas H. Ubelaker, eds. *Disease and Demography in the Americas.* Washington, DC: Smithsonian Institution Press, 1992.

Verger, Pierre. *Orisha: Les dieux Yoruba en Afrique et au Nouveau Monde.* Paris: Métailié, 1982.

Vicens Vives, Jaime. *An Economic History of Spain.* Princeton, NJ: Princeton University Press, 1969.

Vogel, Joseph O., ed. *Encyclopedia of Precolonial Africa: Archaeology, History, Languages, Cultures, and Environments.* Walnut Creek, CA: Altamira, 1997.

Vogler, Günter. *Europas Aufbruch in die Neuzeit 1500–1650.* Vol. 5 of *Handbuch der Geschichte Europas.* Stuttgart: Ulmer, 2003.

Wagner, Fritz, ed. *Europa im Zeitalter des Absolutismus und der Aufklärung.* Vol. 4 of *Handbuch der europäischen Geschichte.* Stuttgart: Union Verlag, 1968.

Walvin, James. *Black Ivory: Slavery in the British Empire.* 2nd ed. Oxford: Blackwell, 2001.

———. *Making the Black Atlantic: Britain and the African Diaspora.* London: Cassell, 2000.

Watts, John. *The Making of Polities: Europe, 1300–1500.* Cambridge: Cambridge University Press, 2009.

Wellenreuther, Hermann. *Ausbildung und Neubildung: Die Geschichte Nordamerikas vom Ausgang des 17. Jahrhunderts bis zum Ausbruch der Amerikanischen Revolution.* Münster: LIT, 2001.

———. *Niedergang und Aufstieg: Geschichte Nordamerikas vom Beginn der Besiedlung bis zum Ausgang des 17. Jahrhunderts.* Münster: LIT, 2000.

Williams, Caroline A. *Bridging the Early Modern Atlantic World: People, Products and Practices on the Move.* Farnham, UK: Ashgate, 2009.

Williams, Eric. *Capitalism and Slavery.* Chapel Hill: University of North Carolina Press, 1944.

Williams, Frieda-Nela. *Precolonial Communities of Southwestern Africa: A History of Owambo Kingdoms, 1600–1920.* Windhoek: National Archives of Namibia, 1991.

Woolfe, Jennifer A. *Sweet Potato: An Untapped Food Resource.* Cambridge: Cambridge University Press, 1992.

Zagorin, Perez. *Rebels and Rulers, 1500–1660.* 2 vols. Cambridge: Cambridge University Press, 1982.

Zapatero, Juan M. *La guerra del Caribe en el siglo XVIII.* San Juan, Puerto Rico: Istituto de Cultura Puertorriquéña, 1964.

Zeuske, Michael. *Handbuch der Geschichte der Sklaverei: Eine Globalgeschichte von den Anfängen bis zur Gegenwart.* Berlin: de Gruyter, 2013.

Zimmermann, Albert, and Andreas Speer, eds. *Mensch und Natur im Mittelalter.* 2 vols. Berlin: de Gruyter, 1991–1992.

Contributors

Stephan Conermann is Professor of Islamic Studies at the University of Bonn. Among his special research interests are the history and society of the Mughal Empire and of the Mamluk regime in Egypt and Syria, particularly in relation to questions of narratology, historiography, and cultural studies. His publications include *Das Mogulreich: Geschichte und Kultur des muslimischen Indien* (2006), *Mamlukica—Studien zu Geschichte und Gesellschaft der Mamlukenzeit* (2013), and *Narrative Pattern and Genre in Hagiographic Life Writing: Comparative Perspectives from Asia to Europe* (ed. with Jim Rheingans, 2014).

Suraiya Faroqhi taught at the Middle East Technical University in Ankara and at the University of Munich. Since retiring from her post in Munich, she has been working at Istanbul Bilgi University. Her more recent publications include *The Ottoman Empire and the World around It, 1540s to 1774* (2004), *Artisans of Empire: Crafts and Craftspeople under the Ottomans* (2009), and *Travel and Artisans in the Ottoman Empire: Employment and Mobility in the Early Modern Era* (2014). She is the coeditor, with Kate Fleet and Reşat Kasaba, of the *Cambridge History of Turkey* (4 vols., 2006–2013).

Jürgen G. Nagel is an associate professor in the faculty of modern European and non-European history at the FernUniversität (distance teaching university) in Hagen. His work focuses on the regions of maritime Southeast Asia, the Indian Ocean, and sub-Saharan Africa. His research has treated such topics as the economic history of European expansion, knowledge and science in colonialism, and the history of modern colonial rule, as well as questions of "glocalization" in a global–historical context. Among other works, he is the author of *Der Schlüssel zu den Molukken: Makassar und die Handelsstrukturen des Malaiischen Archipels im 17. und 18. Jahrhundert* (2003) and *Abenteuer Fernhandel: Die Ostindien-Kompanien* (2011).

Peter C. Perdue is Professor of History at Yale University. His first book, *Exhausting the Earth: State and Peasant in Hunan, 1500–1850 AD* (Harvard University Press, 1987), examined long-term agricultural change in one Chinese province. His second book, *China Marches West: The Qing Conquest of Central Eurasia* (Harvard University Press, 2005), discusses environmental change, ethnicity, long-term economic change, and military conquest in an integrated account of the Chinese, Mongolian, and Russian contention over Siberia and Central Eurasia during the seventeenth and eighteenth centuries. He is a coeditor of two books on empires: *Imperial Formations* (SAR Press, 2007) and *Shared Histories of Modernity* (Routledge, 2008). His current research focuses on Chinese frontiers, Chinese environmental history, and the history of tea.

Wolfgang Reinhard is Professor Emeritus of Modern History at the University of Freiburg and corresponding fellow of the Max Weber Kolleg in Erfurt. His special areas of research interest are Europe in the sixteenth and seventeenth centuries, particularly with regard to religious history (*Paul V. Borghese,* 2009), the history of the modern state (*Geschichte der Staatsgewalt,* 1999), historical anthropology (*Lebensformen Europas,* 2003), and, above all, the history of European expansion. He is the author of a four-volume study of this phenomenon from 1415 to 1989 (*Geschichte der europäischen Expansion,* 1983–1990; revised edition, 2015); of a shorter treatment of the topic (*Kleine Geschichte des Kolonialismus,* 2008) that has been translated into English, French, and Italian; and of ten other books and numerous papers on this same theme. He was awarded the Historical College award in 2001.

Reinhard Wendt has since 1998 been the head of the faculty of modern European and non-European history at the FernUniversität (distance teaching university) in Hagen. His research, which focuses primarily on Southeast Asia and Oceania, treats the history of interactions between Western and non-Western cultures, European–overseas relations in the area of conflict between the "allure of the distant" and the "exploitation of the foreign," missionary philology and the writing down of non-Western languages, and emigration and the formation of diasporas among multicultural societies. His key publications include *Fiesta Filipina: Koloniale Kultur zwischen Imperialismus und neuer Identität* (1997) and *Vom Kolonialismus zur Globalisierung: Europa und die Welt seit 1500* (2007).

Index